Fodor's 2010

SPAIN

Where to Stay and Eat for All Budgets

Must-See Sights and Local Secrets

Ratings You Can Trust

Fodor's Travel Publications New York, Toronto, London, Sydney, Auckland

www.fodors.com

FODOR'S SPAIN 2010
Editor: Caroline Trefler

Editorial Contributors: Paul Cannon, Ignacio Gómez, Jared Lubarsky, George Semler, Hannah Semler

Production Editor: Jennifer DePrima
Maps & Illustrations: Mark Stroud, Moon Street Cartography; David Lindroth, Inc., *cartographers*; Bob Blake, Rebecca Baer, *map editors*; William Wu, *information graphics*
Design: Fabrizio La Rocca, *creative director*; Guido Caroti, Siobhan O'Hare, *art directors*; Tina Malaney, Chie Ushio, Ann McBride, Jessica Walsh, *designers*; Melanie Marin, *senior picture editor*
Cover Photo: (Casares, Málaga Province): José Fuste Raga/age fotostock
Production Manager: Amanda Bullock

COPYRIGHT

ISBN 978-1-4000-0864-3

ISSN 0071-6545

SPECIAL SALES

This book is available at special discounts for bulk purchases for sales promotions or premiums. Special editions, including personalized covers, excerpts of existing books, and corporate imprints, can be created in large quantities for special needs. For more information, write to Special Markets/Premium Sales, 1745 Broadway, MD 6-2, New York, New York 10019, or e-mail specialmarkets@randomhouse.com.

AN IMPORTANT TIP & AN INVITATION

Although all prices, opening times, and other details in this book are based on information supplied to us at press time, changes occur all the time in the travel world, and Fodor's cannot accept responsibility for facts that become outdated or for inadvertent errors or omissions. So **always confirm information when it matters,** especially if you're making a detour to visit a specific place. Your experiences—positive and negative—matter to us. If we have missed or misstated something, **please write to us.** We follow up on all suggestions. Contact the Spain editor at editors@fodors.com or c/o Fodor's at 1745 Broadway, New York, NY 10019.

PRINTED IN THE UNITED STATES OF AMERICA

10 9 8 7 6 5 4 3 2 1

Be a Fodor's Correspondent

Your opinion matters. It matters to us. It matters to your fellow Fodor's travelers, too. And we'd like to hear it. In fact, we need to hear it.

When you share your experiences and opinions, you become an active member of the Fodor's community. That means we'll not only use your feedback to make our books better, but we'll publish your names and comments whenever possible. Throughout our guides, look for "Word of Mouth," excerpts of your unvarnished feedback.

Here's how you can help improve Fodor's for all of us.

Tell us when we're right. We rely on local writers to give you an insider's perspective. But our writers and staff editors—who are the best in the business—depend on you. Your positive feedback is a vote to renew our recommendations for the next edition.

Tell us when we're wrong. We're proud that we update most of our guides every year. But we're not perfect. Things change. Hotels cut services. Museums change hours. Charming cafés lose charm. If our writer didn't quite capture the essence of a place, tell us how you'd do it differently. If any of our descriptions are inaccurate or inadequate, we'll incorporate your changes in the next edition and will correct factual errors at fodors.com immediately.

Tell us what to include. You probably have had fantastic travel experiences that aren't yet in Fodor's. Why not share them with a community of like-minded travelers? Maybe you chanced upon a beach or bistro or B&B that you don't want to keep to yourself. Tell us why we should include it. And share your discoveries and experiences with everyone directly at fodors.com. Your input may lead us to add a new listing or highlight a place we cover with a "Highly Recommended" star or with our highest rating, "Fodor's Choice."

Give us your opinion instantly at our feedback center at www.fodors.com/feedback. You may also e-mail editors@fodors.com with the subject line "Spain Editor." Or send your nominations, comments, and complaints by mail to Spain Editor, Fodor's, 1745 Broadway, New York, NY 10019.

You and travelers like you are the heart of the Fodor's community. Make our community richer by sharing your experiences. Be a Fodor's correspondent.

¡Buen Viaje!

Tim Jarrell, Publisher

CONTENTS

Fodor's Features

CONTENTS

MAPS

ABOUT THIS BOOK

Our Ratings

Sometimes you find terrific travel experiences and sometimes they just find you. But usually the burden is on you to select the right combination of experiences. That's where our ratings come in.

As travelers we've all discovered a place so wonderful that its worthiness is obvious. And sometimes that place is so experiential that superlatives don't do it justice: you just have to be there to know. These sights, properties, and experiences get our highest rating, **Fodor's Choice,** indicated by orange stars throughout this book.

Black stars highlight sights and properties we deem **Highly Recommended,** places that our writers, editors, and readers praise again and again for consistency and excellence.

By default, there's another category: any place we include in this book is by definition worth your time, unless we say otherwise. And we will.

Disagree with any of our choices? Care to nominate a place or suggest that we rate one more highly? Visit our feedback center at www.fodors.com/feedback.

Budget Well

Hotel and restaurant price categories from ¢ to $$$$ are defined in the opening pages of each chapter. For attractions, we always give standard adult admission fees; reductions are usually available for children, students, and senior citizens. Want to pay with plastic? **AE, D, DC, MC, V** after restaurant and hotel listings indicate if American Express, Discover, Diners Club, MasterCard, and Visa are accepted.

Restaurants

Unless we state otherwise, restaurants are open for lunch and dinner daily. We mention dress only when there's a specific requirement and reservations only when they're essential or not accepted—it's always best to book ahead.

Hotels

Hotels have private bath, phone, TV, and air-conditioning and operate on the European Plan (aka EP, meaning without meals), unless we specify that they use the Continental Plan (CP, with a Continental breakfast), Breakfast Plan (BP, with a full breakfast), or Modified American Plan (MAP, with breakfast and dinner) or are all-inclusive (including all meals and most activities). We always list facilities but not whether you'll be charged an extra fee to use them, so when pricing accommodations, find out what's included.

Many Listings

- ★ Fodor's Choice
- ★ Highly recommended
- ⊠ Physical address
- ✣ Directions
- Mailing address
- ☎ Telephone
- Fax
- On the Web
- E-mail
- Admission fee
- Open/closed times
- Ⓜ Metro stations
- Credit cards

Hotels & Restaurants

- Hotel
- Number of rooms
- Facilities
- Meal plans
- ✕ Restaurant
- Reservations
- Smoking
- BYOB
- ✕ Hotel with restaurant that warrants a visit

Outdoors

- Golf
- Camping

Other

- Family-friendly
- ⇨ See also
- Branch address
- ☞ Take note

Experience Spain

Consuegra, Toledo province

WORD OF MOUTH

"My wife and I returned from our first trip to Spain . . . A great trip. A wonderful country. EVERYONE was nice, courteous and efficient. We only speak a little Spanish, but it was not a problem."

—nhulberg

www.fodors.com/community

WHAT'S WHERE

The following numbers refer to chapters.

2 Madrid. Its boundless energy makes sights and sounds larger than life. The Prado, Reina Sofía, and Thyssen-Bornemisza museums comprise among them one of the greatest repositories of Western art in the world. The cafés in the Plaza Mayor and the wine bars in the nearby Cava Baja buzz, and nightlife stretches into the wee hours around Plaza Santa Ana. Sunday's crowded flea market in El Rastro is thick with overpriced oddities.

3 Castile-La Mancha and Castile-León. The Spanish heartland—*meseta*—is an arid reach of windy skies and wide vistas. Castille-León is cut with rocky gorges and fringed with gaunt mountains. Salamanca, Segovia, León, and Burgos exude a seriousness marked with religiosity and a hardworking, simple life. Castille-La Mancha is punctuated by Toledo's austerity, Cuenca's quirky natural architecture, and Soria's and Sigüenza's medieval preservation.

4 Galicia and Asturias. On the way to Santiago de Compostela to pay homage to St. James, Christian pilgrims once crossed Europe to a corner of Spain so remote it was called *finis terrae* (end of the earth). Santiago still resonates with mystic importance. In the more mountainous Asturias, towns are among green hills in the highlands, and sandy beaches stretch out along the Atlantic.

5 Bilbao and the Basque Country. Greener and cloudier than the rest of Spain, and stubbornly independent in spirit, the Basque region is a country within a country, proud of its own language and culture as well as its coastline along the Bay of Biscay—one of the peninsula's wildest and toughest shores.

6 The Pyrenees. Cut by some 23 steep north–south valleys on the Spanish side alone, with four independent geographical entities—the valleys of Camprodón, Cerdanya, Aran, and Baztán—the Pyrenees has a wealth of areas to explore, with a dozen highland cultures and languages to match.

7 Barcelona. The Rambla in the heart of the Old City is packed day and night with strollers, artists, street entertainers, vendors, and vamps, all preparing you for Barcelona's startling architectural landmarks. Antoni Gaudí's sinuous Casa Milà and unique Sagrada Família church are masterpieces of the Moderniste oeuvre.

Bay of Biscay
BASQUE COUNTRY
(EUSKADI)
Gijón
Oviedo
Santander
CANTABRIA
TURIAS
San
Sebastián
Bilbao
5
Vitoria
Pamplona
FRANCE
ANDORRA
León
Treviño
NAVARRE
PYRENEES
Burgos
Logroño
LA RIOJA
Huesca
6
Girona
Palencia
CATALONIA
Soria
3
Valladolid
Duero
Zaragoza
Lleida
COSTA
BRAVA
Zamora
CASTILE–LEÓN
ARAGON
7
Tarragona
BARCELONA
Salamanca
Segovia
Tortosa
COSTA
DORADA
MADRID
Ávila
Teruel
2
Balearic
Sea
Castellón
de la Plana
Toledo
Tajo
Aranjuez
Cuenca
COSTA DEL AZAHAR
Mallorca
Trujillo
CASTILE–
LA MANCHA
Requena
Valencia
ADURA
Alcazár
Jucar
BALEARIC
ISLANDS
Guadiana
Mérida
Ciudad
Real
Ibiza
Albacete
Segura
VALENCIA
Formentera
Valdepeñas
COSTA BLANCA
Alicante
MURCIA
Jaén
Murcia
0
100 miles
Córdoba
Cartagena
ANDALUSIA
Lorca
0
150 km
Seville
Antequera
Granada
Jerez
Almería
Mediterranean
Sea
Málaga
Cádiz
COSTA DEL SOL
COSTA DE
ALMERIA
Gibraltar
Ceuta
ALGERIA
Melilla
MOROCCO

WHAT'S WHERE

8 Catalonia and Valencia. A cultural connection with France and Europe defines Catalonia. The citrus-scented, mountain-backed plain of the Levante is dotted with Christian and Moorish landmarks and extensive Roman ruins. Valencia's signature dish, *paella*, fortifies visitors touring the city's medieval masterpieces and exuberant modern architecture.

9 The Balearic Islands. Ibiza is still the famous—infamous—summer playground for all-night clubbers from all over, but even this isle has its quiet coves. Majorca has its built-up and heavily touristed pockets, and long vistas of pristine, rugged mountain beauty. On comparatively serene Minorca, the two cities of Ciutadella and Mahón have remarkably different histories, cultures, and points of view. Formentera, pastoral in comparison, retains a wild beauty.

10 The Southeast. There are party-'til-dawn resort towns like Benidorm as well as small villages where time seems suspended in the last century. The rice paddies and fragrant orange groves of the Costa Blanca lead to the palm-fringed port city of Alicante. In La Manga del Mar Menor, tired travelers go for a saltwater soak.

11 Andalusia. Eight provinces, five of which are coastal (Huelva, Cádiz, Málaga, Granada, and Almería) and three of which are landlocked (Seville, Córdoba, and Jaén), compose this southern autonomous community known for its Moorish influences. High-lights are the romantic Alhambra and seductive Seville.

12 Costa del Sol. With more than 320 days of sunshine a year, the Costa is especially seductive to northern Europeans eager for a break from the cold. As a result, vast holiday resorts sprawl along much of the coast, though there are respites: Marbella, a longtime glitterati favorite, has a pristine Andalusian old quarter, and villages such as Casares seem immune to the goings-on along the water.

13 Extremadura. Remote and rustic defines Spain's far west borderland with Portugal. Highlights include prosperous Cáceres, packed with medieval and Renaissance churches and palaces; Trujillo, lined with mansions of Spain's imperial age; ancient Mérida, Spain's richest trove of Roman remains; and the Jerte Valley, which turns white in late March with the blossoming of its 1 million cherry trees.

Bay of Biscay
BASQUE COUNTRY (EUSKADI)
Santander
San Sebastián
CANTABRIA
Bilbao
FRANCE
Trevino
NAVARRE
ANDORRA
PYRENEES
Burgos
Logroño
LA RIOJA
Huesca
Girona
Palencia
CATALONIA
Soria
Ebro
Valladolid
Duero
Zaragoza
Lleida
COSTA BRAVA
CASTILE–LEÓN
ARAGON
8
Barcelona
Tarragona
Segovia
Tortosa
COSTA DORADA
Tajo
Ávila
MADRID
Teruel
Balearic Sea
Castellón de la Plana
Minorca
Toledo
Aranjuez
Cuenca
Majorca
CASTILE–LA MANCHA
Requena
Jucar
Valencia
COSTA DEL AZAHAR
BALEARIC ISLANDS
Guadiana
Alcazár
VALENCIA
Ciudad Real
Ibiza
9
Albacete
10
Valdepeñas
Formentera
Segura
Alicante
COSTA BLANCA
Córdoba
11
0
100 miles
MURCIA
Jaén
Murcia
0
150 km
Cartagena
Lorca
ANDALUSIA
Mediterranean Sea
Antequera
Granada
Almería
12
Málaga
COSTA DE ALMERIA
COSTA DEL SOL
Ceuta

SPAIN PLANNER

When to Go

Summer in Spain is hot and temperatures frequently hit 100°F (38°C). Although air-conditioning is the norm in hotels and museums, walking and general exploring can be uncomfortable. Winters are mild and rainy along the coasts and bitterly cold elsewhere. Snow is infrequent except in the mountains, where you can ski December through March in the Pyrenees and at resorts near Granada, Madrid, and Burgos.

May and October are optimal for visiting Spain as it's generally warm and dry. May has more hours of daylight; October offers a chance to enjoy the harvest season, which is especially colorful in the wine regions.

April has spectacular fiestas, particularly Valencia's *Las Fallas* and Seville's *Semana Santa* (Holy Week), which is followed by the Feria de Abril (April Fair), showcasing horses, bulls, and flamenco. April in southern Spain is warm but still cool enough to make sightseeing comfortable.

July and August mean crowds and heat. In August, major cities empty, with Spaniards migrating to the beach—expect huge traffic jams August 1 and 31. Many small shops and some restaurants shut down; most museums remain open.

Getting Here

Most flights into Spain go to Madrid or Barcelona, though certain destinations in Andalusia are popular with carriers traveling from England and other European countries. You can also reach Spain via a ferry from the United Kingdom into northern Spain, a ferry or catamaran from Morocco into southern Spain, or on a cruise—Barcelona is Spain's main port-of-call, but other ports-of-call include Málaga, Cádiz, Gibraltar, Valencia, A Coruña, and stops on the Balearic Islands. From France or Portugal you can drive in or take a bus.

Getting Around

Once in Spain, you can travel by bus, car, or train. The bus is usually much faster than the train, and bus fares tend to be lower as well. Service is extensive, though less frequent on weekends. Various bus companies provide local connections; the major national bus line is Alsa-Enatcar (☎ *902/422242*).

For rail travel, the local-route RENFE trains are economical and run on convenient schedules (such as the commuter trains around Madrid and Barcelona). The AVE, Spain's high-speed train, is wonderfully fast—it can go from Madrid to Seville or to Barcelona in under three hours. ■ TIP→ **Rail passes like the Eurailpass must be purchased before you leave for Europe.**

Large chain car rental companies all have branches in Spain, though the online outfit Pepe Car (🌐 *www.pepecar.com*) may have better deals. Its modus operandi is the earlier you book, the less you pay. In Spain, most vehicles have a manual transmission. ■ TIP→ **If you don't want a stick shift, reserve well in advance and specify automatic transmission.**

A few rules of the road: Children under 10 may not ride in the front seat, and seat belts are mandatory for all passengers. ■ TIP→ **Follow speed limits. Rental cars are frequently targeted by police monitoring speeding vehicles.**

For more travel info, ⇨ see the Travel Smart chapter.

Restaurant Basics

Most restaurants in Spain don't serve breakfast (*desayuno*); for coffee and carbs, head to a bar or *cafetería*. Outside major hotels, which serve morning buffets, breakfast in Spain is usually limited to coffee and toast or a roll. Lunch (*comida* or *almuerzo*) traditionally consists of an appetizer, a main course, and dessert, followed by coffee and perhaps a liqueur. Between lunch and dinner the best way to snack is to sample *tapas* (appetizers) at a bar; there is often a variety to choose from. Dinner (*cena*) is somewhat lighter than lunch, with perhaps only one course. In addition to an à la carte menu, most restaurants offer a daily fixed-price menu (*menú del día*), including two courses, wine, and dessert at an attractive price. It's traditionally offered only at lunch but is increasingly offered at dinner in popular tourist destinations.

Hotel Basics

There are many types of lodgings in Spain, from youth hostels (different from a hostal, which is a budget hotel) to boutique hotels and modern high-rises, and various options in between. One of the most popular types of lodgings in Spain is the *parador*—government run, upmarket hotels, many of them in historic buildings or in visit-worthy locations. Rates are reasonable, considering that most *paradores* have four- or five-star amenities, including a restaurant serving regional specialties. (⇨ *See the "A Night with History" In-focus feature for more information.*)

Do I Have to Eat So Late?

Many of the misunderstandings for visitors to Spain concern the dinner table. The Spanish eat no earlier than 1:30 PM for lunch, preferably after 2, and not before 9 PM for dinner. Dining out on the weekend can begin at 10 PM or even later. In areas with heavy tourist traffic, some restaurants open a bit earlier.

Siesta?

Dining is not the only part of Spanish life with a bizarre timetable. Outside of major cities most shops shut in the afternoons from 2 to 5, when shopkeepers go home to eat the main meal of the day, and perhaps snooze for a while. It's best to work this into your plans on an "if you can't beat them, join them" basis, taking a quick siesta after lunch in preparation for a long night out on the town.

Smoking?

One of the major drawbacks of drinking and eating in Spanish bars and restaurants used to be the amount of cigarette smoke. Antismoking laws introduced in 2006, however, now require bars and clubs with 100 square meters of space or more to provide a nonsmoking section; in most of the better restaurants, smoking is not allowed at all.

SPAIN TODAY

Politics

Spain's socialist party, PSOE, led by José Luis Rodriguez Zapatero, continues to hold power after the events of March 11, 2004, dropped the socialists into office against all the odds: with elections looming three days after the train bombings that killed 191 civilians, the Partido Popular (PP) was blamed, and they were voted out despite having been clear favorites to win only days before.

Once in power, the socialists were forced to keep certain pre-electoral promises they never expected to be able to put into place: gay marriage became legal, and the Plan Hidrológico Nacional, a much-debated plan to divert water from the waterlogged north to the parched south of the country, was scrapped almost overnight. The historic cease-fire declared by the Basque Separatists (ETA), on March 22, 2006, looked set to place Zapatero's government firmly in the annals of Spanish history, until the terrorist organization dashed hopes of lasting peace by bombing a car park in Madrid's airport on December 30, 2006, killing two civilians. ETA declared an end to the cease-fire in June 2007, but the level of violence has since been relatively low, and more moderate voices for Basque autonomy continue to gain public support. Batasuna, the political wing of ETA, is banned from participation in regional politics.

The economic crisis of 2009 appeared to give the right-wing PP and its leader Mariano Rajoy new strength, particularly in hard-hit constituencies like Galicia, but corruption scandals cost the party some of the edge it may have had in the March 2009 elections. The PSOE made significant gains in both Catalonia and the Basque region, and Zapatero will continue to govern until 2013, although without an absolute parliamentary majority.

The Economy

The introduction of the euro in January 2002 brought about a major change in Spain's economy, as shopkeepers, hoteliers, restaurateurs, and real estate agents all rounded up prices in an attempt to make the most of the changeover from the old currency, and the country became markedly more expensive. This did little to harm Spain's immense tourism machine, at least until the recession began to take its toll in 2009; visitor spending was essentially flat for most of that year, and in some destinations was off as much as 7%. Even so, a substantially weaker euro has made the country more attractive again to North American and Asian visitors, and Spain remains the biggest tourist destination in Europe—receiving some 60 million visitors a year, who contribute around 12% to the country's GDP.

Immigration is a major factor in Spain's changing economy and demography. With an average influx of half a million immigrants a year, foreigners now constitute almost 11% of the country's population. Moroccans, Ecuadorans and Bolivians, Romanians, and Chinese are among the largest numbers of these new arrivals. One of the most important benefits of this immigration has been an increase in Spain's birthrate, which at the beginning of the millennium had been among the lowest in the world.

Religion

The state-funded Catholic church, closely tied to the right-wing PP, and with the national Cadena Cope radio station as its voice, continues to hold considerable social and political influence in Spain, with members of secretive groups such as

Opus Dei and the Legionarios de Cristo holding key government and industry positions.

Despite the church's influence, at street level, Spain has become a distinctly secular country, as demonstrated by the fact that 70% of Spaniards supported the decidedly un-Catholic 2005 law allowing gay marriage. And although more than 75% of the population claim to be Catholic, less than 20% go to church on a regular basis.

More than 1 million Muslims reside in Spain, making Islam the country's second-largest religion. Meanwhile, Catholic masses have been greatly bolstered over the last decade by strongly Catholic South American and Eastern European immigrants.

The Arts

Spain's devotion to the arts is clearly shown by the attention, both national and international, paid to its annual Principe de Asturias prize, where Prince Felipe hands out accolades to international high achievers such as Woody Allen, and homegrown talent such as the architect/sculptor Santiago Calatrava and filmmaker Pedro Almodóvar. While Calatrava takes the world of architecture by storm (he designed the yet-to-be-completed World Trade Center PATH station at Ground Zero in New York), Almodóvar and his muse Penelope Cruz continue to flourish at home and abroad with movies such as *Volver.* With Spanish household names such as Paz Vega and Javier Bardem also making a splash in Hollywood, film is without doubt at the forefront of the Spanish arts scene.

In contrast, Spanish music continues to be a rather local affair, though the summer festival scene, including the Festival Internacional de Benicàssim, WOMAD (World of Music and Dance), and Summercase in Barcelona and Madrid (a victim of the recession in 2009, but due for a comeback), serves up top names to revelers who come from all over Europe to soak up music in the sun.

While authors such as Miguel Delibes, Rosa Montero, and Maruja Torres flourish in Spain, very few break onto the international scene, with the exception of Arturo Pérez Reverte, whose books include *Captain Alatriste* and *The Fencing Master,* and Carlos Ruiz Zafón, author of the internationally acclaimed *Shadow of the Wind.* Spain's contribution to the fine arts is still dominated by two names: the Majorcan-born artist Miquel Barceló and the Basque sculptor Eduardo Chillida, who died in 2002 and whose work can be seen at the Chillida-Leku museum close to San Sebastián.

Sports

With Real Madrid and FC Barcelona firmly established as international brands, and La Liga recognized as one of the world's most exciting leagues, soccer remains the nation's favorite sport, right up there with motor racing, believe it or not. When Fernando Alonso won the Formula One championship in 2005 and 2006, the Asturian was paraded around his native Oviedo in an open-topped bus. Second only to Alonso in terms of national pride are Dani Pedrosa, the prodigious motorcycling star who triumphed in the 125cc and 250cc Moto GP events, and Majorcan-born tennis player Rafael Nadal, ranked No. 1 on the professional circuit for 2009.

WHAT'S NEW IN SPAIN

Held back for decades by the Franco dictatorship, Spain emerged late in the 20th century with a new sense of freedom and revived passion for life. Culturally, too, Spain has spread its wings. Here's a look at what's new this year . . .

Sand in Your Sandwich

Spain's Ministry of the Environment touched off a storm of protest last spring, when it ruled that the *chiringuitos*—the prefab shacks that go up by the thousands on the nation's beaches as soon the swimming season opens, serving an estimated €900 millon worth of food and drink every year—were a threat to the environment. Invoking a decades-old "Law of the Coasts," the Ministry told the *chiringuitos* to get off the sand and relocate at least to the first line of paved promenade. Decades of tradition and some 300,000 summer jobs were at stake; the owners fought back, with multi-party political support, and the Ministry caved in. The shacks are back.

More Perfect Union

Spain's turn in the Presidency of the European Union Council for the first six months of 2010 should bring the country some unaccustomed diplomatic muscle: the Council proposes and approves a range of legislation binding on the member countries, including taxes and monetary policy—and rules on the qualifications of new candidates for EU admission.

Latin Lovers

Film director/music producer Fernando Trueba last made international headlines with his *Belle Epoque,* which won an Academy Award for Best Foreign Film in 1993. With Barcelona-based graphic designer Javier Mariscal he began work on his first full-length animation film, set for release in 2010: *Chico and Rita and All that Jazz,* a love story inspired by a Compay Segundo song, set in the Havana and New York of the 1940s and '50s. *Buena Vista Social Club* and Afro-Cuban music fans take note: this could be the best Spanish film of the year.

Kicks

In May 2009 FC Barcelona—the beloved *Barça*—became the first team in the country's soccer history to win the Triple Crown: the Spanish *Liga,* the King's Cup, and the European Champions League. With most of last year's team in place, *Barça* is a good bet to be in the finals again—to be played this year in arch-rival Real Madrid's Bernabéu Stadium. Runner-up in the *Liga,* Madrid itself is no unlikely candidate for the European Championship: post-season last year, it acquired boy wonder Cristiano Ronaldo from Manchester United—where *Barça* held him scoreless in the 2009 final—for a US$131 transfer fee. An all-Spanish show-down in 2010? Will it be *Barça* and Real Madrid, *mano a mano* (or foot to foot) on Madrid's home pitch?

Getting Around

In-country connections are better than ever. In the air, with the merger of rival low-cost carriers Vueling and Clickair, and Spanair's code-sharing route expansions with Air Europa, Madrid and Barcelona bristle with connections to more than 20 regional cities—including Alicante, Bilbao, Minorca, Santiago de Compostella, Valencia, and Seville. The Madrid–Barcelona shuttle flights face stiff competition on the ground from the national railway's high-speed AVE trains: pricey, but at two hours and 40 minutes the fastest and most comfortable center-city to center-city connection.

See the Travel Smart chapter for details.

MAKING THE MOST OF YOUR EUROS

Way back when, people would travel to Europe because it was relatively cheap; not so today. A weak dollar and a strong euro are making trips to Europe more and more daunting, but we don't think that should stop you from going—you just need to think more creatively about how to spend your money. Where better to get tips on beating the euro in Spain than from the Fodor's forums at www.fodors.com.

Sightsee, Don't Sight-Spend

"We planned our museum visits to coincide with the free admission days, which was especially easy to do in Madrid since they aren't all on the same day. In Barcelona, we bought the Articket, which more than paid for itself after visiting three of the seven featured attractions." —misty_in_stl

". . . the Prado is free from 6 PM onward every day (Sundays from 5). Strangely enough, it's not really crowded at that time, and you can have a very enjoyable evening." —cova

Travel Wisely

"I agree that travel by bus (rather than train) is a great way to save some money. Yes, it takes a bit longer, but you can use that time to catch up on your sleep, read, etc." —AJMelheim

"Renfe has discounted tickets if bought in advance. WEB fares are 60% off and ESTRELLA fares are 40% off. Good deal if your itinerary is set in stone." —yk

Think with Your Stomach

"Food: avoid touristy places (on Barcelona's Ramblas, for example) and go where locals are. Eat your main meal at lunchtime when 'Menu del Dia' is available: 3 courses with drink starting from 6 to 10 euro. Tapas are a pleasant way to eat but watch what you are ordering. Cost can mount up. Put together a picnic from local market or shops. Instead of often poor-value hotel breakfast, get coffee and toast in a local bar for a few euro." —Alec

"In Barcelona the Boqueria Market is ideal not only for the experience of browsing but for picking up a great picnic lunch. Lots of fresh salads, fresh-pressed juices etc. Walk a few minutes down to the port for a great setting." —grimy

"In cafés, eat/drink at the bar on a stool, which is cheaper than an inside table, which is cheaper than an outdoor terrace table (in most cases) . . . and remember beer costs less than soft drinks many a time!" —lincasanova

Bargains for Lodgings

"I think the best bargain are the paradores, but they're mostly located outside of cities. . . . They are a fantastic experience. One tip I can add is to become an 'amigo,' which can be done on their Web site, and you can get notices for specials. . . . The five-day or seven-day cards are truly terrific bargains. We've done this on our last two trips and all I can say is that I've never stayed in a parador I didn't like!" —artlover

"The single place you can save the most money is by choosing a less expensive place to stay." —suze

TOP SPAIN ATTRACTIONS

La Alhambra, Granada

(A) Nothing can prepare you for the Moorish grandeur of Andalusia's greatest monument. The palace is set around sumptuous courtyards and gardens complete with bubbling fountains and magnificent statues. (⇨ *Chapter 11.*)

Toledo

(B) Castile's crowning glory, Toledo is often cited as being Spain's spiritual capital, and past inhabitants—including Jews, Romans, and Muslims—have all felt its spiritual pull. This open-air museum of a city on a ridge high above the Río Tajo is an architectural tapestry of medieval buildings, churches, mosques, and synagogues threaded by narrow, cobbled streets and squares. (⇨ *Chapter 3.*)

La Sagrada Família, Barcelona

(C) *The* symbol of Barcelona, Gaudí's extraordinary unfinished cathedral should be on everyone's must-see list. The pointed spires, with organic shapes that resemble honeycombed stalagmites, give the whole city a fairy-tale quality. (⇨ *Chapter 7.*)

Guggenheim, Bilbao

(D) All swooping curves and rippling forms, the architecturally innovative museum—one of Frank Gehry's most breathtaking projects—was built on the site of the city's former shipyards and inspired by the shape of a ship's hull. The Guggenheim's cachet is its huge spaces: there's room to stand back and admire works in the permanent collection such as Richard Serra's monumental steel forms; sculpture by Miquel Barceló and Eduardo Chillida; and paintings by Anselm Kiefer, Willem de Kooning, Mark Rothko, and Jim Dine. (⇨ *Chapter 5.*)

Museo del Prado, Madrid

(E) Set in a magnificent Neoclassical building on one of the capital's most elegant boulevards, the Prado is Spain's answer to the Louvre and a regal home to renowned Spanish masterpieces. Much of

the collection dates back to the museum's inauguration in 1819. (⇨ *Chapter 2.*)

Mérida's Roman Ruins

(F) You may be tempted to rub your eyes in disbelief: in the center of a somewhat drab modern town is the largest Roman city on the Iberian Peninsula. Ogle at the fabulously preserved Roman amphitheater with its columns, statues, and tiered seating, or the humbler, yet equally beguiling, 2nd-century house with mosaics and frescoes. (⇨ *Chapter 13.*)

Cuenca's Hanging Houses

(G) The old town of Cuenca is all honey-color buildings, handsome mansions, ancient churches, and earthy local bars. Seek out the famous Casas Colgadas, or "Hanging Houses," with their facades dipping precipitously over a steep ravine. Dating from the 15th century, the balconies appear as an extension of the rock face. (⇨ *Chapter 3.*)

San Lorenzo de El Escorial

(H) Seriously over the top, this giant palace-monastery (with no less than 2,673 windows), built by the megalomaniac Felipe II, makes visitors stop in their tracks. The exterior is austere, but inside, the Bourbon apartments and library are lush with rich, colorful tapestries, ornate frescoes, and paintings by such masters as El Greco, Titian, and José de Ribera. (⇨ *Chapter 2.*)

Mezquita, Córdoba

An extraordinary mosque, the Mezquita is famed for its thicket of red-and-white striped columns resembling a palm grove oasis interspersed with arches and traditional Moorish embellishments. It's a fabulous, massive monument that comprises a whole block in the center of Córdoba's tangle of ancient streets and squares. (⇨*See Chapter 11.*)

SPAIN'S TOP EXPERIENCES

Stroll with Your Sweetheart on Festa de Sant Jordi

Barcelona's Festa de Sant Jordi is like Valentine's Day with a Catalan twist. Celebrating St. George, the patron saint of Barcelona, for his heroism in allegedly saving a princess from a dragon, this day has come to be associated with chivalry and romance. All over the city you'll find couples strolling, smooching, and buying each other tokens of affection—tradition dictates that the men buy their true love a rose, and since the Festa de Sant Jordi shares a date with International Book Day, women reciprocate by buying their beau a book. The result is fragrant, rose-scented streets lined with bookstalls.

Have the Ultimate Food Fight in Buñol

Buñol, a tiny town outside Valencia, may hold the key to the best stress relief without a prescription. Every year on the last Wednesday of August townsfolk hold La Tomatina, a giant tomato-throwing extravaganza. The modest town of 9,000 swells to three times its size, as visiting tomato-chuckers ride the RENFE in to participate. The affair, with unknown origins (some say it began with a tomato thrown at a pedestrian), now literally paints the town red as hundreds of thousands of tomatoes are thrown. It's the tomato version of a snowball fight, in all its bloody glory.

Dance 'til Dawn in Ibiza

If Spain is a country for night owls and 3 AM dance marathons, then Ibiza is its party capital. Unapologetically hedonistic, this little island knows how to get it on. Where else would you find a dance club with a pool? Or a "Discobus" to shuttle tipsy clubbers to the next multifloor nightclub? And where do the models, film stars, and other beautiful people go, when the music stops? To the beaches, of course, to work on their tans.

Surf the Seas

Tarifa, located on the Atlantic Coast in Cadíz Province, has fast become the wind- and kite-surfing capital of Europe, and every year seems to attract more devotees from all over the world. Silhouetted against a bold blue backdrop, the vivid sails flutter in the breeze like tropical butterflies. The most popular beaches for the sport are just northwest of the town along what is known as the Costa de la Luz (Coast of Light)—wide stretches of silvery white sand, washed by magical rollers and flanked by rolling dunes. The winds here are the eastern Levante and the western Poniente, which can be a gusty problem if you are trying to read the paper under a beach umbrella, but they're ideal for surfing the waves. There are plenty of places here where you can enroll in courses and rent gear.

Play Top Chef at the Spanish Market

Markets (*mercados*) are the key to delicious local cuisine and represent an essential part of Spanish life, largely unaffected by competition from supermarkets and hypermarkets. You'll find fabulous produce sold according to whatever is in season: counters neatly piled with shiny purple eggplants, blood-red peppers, brilliant orange cantaloupes and all variety of fruit, including fresh figs, a couple sliced open to show their succulent pink flesh. Some towns have markets on one or two days a week only, while others have daily fruit and vegetable markets from Monday through Saturday. Take the opportunity to get a culinary education. Vendors are authorities and connoisseurs on their offerings and are only too happy to share their secrets.

Hit the Slopes in the Pyrenees

Simply drinking in the view around the Vall d'Aran with a pair of skis clapped to your feet is worth the trip, but then the skiing itself is world famous. Just note all the accents from neighboring countries that come to Spain for peak snow conditions (with a boost from the artificial snow machines).

Dance in the Streets During the Ferias

Throughout Spain and particularly Andalusia, the year revolves around *ferias* (fairs), which are far more than a holiday from work. While city-based ferias are rich and glittering affairs attracting millions of visitors, others, such as the feria of Casares village near the Costa del Sol, is more an exuberant street party. The most famous fair of all is Seville's Feria de Abril (April Fair), when sultry foot-stomping señoritas wear traditional, brilliantly colored flamenco dresses. From 1 to 5 every afternoon, Sevillana society parades around in carriages drawn by glossy high-stepping horses. The atmosphere is electric and infectious and, like all ferias, the charm lies in the universal spontaneity of enjoyment.

Catch the Carnaval

Second only to Rio in terms of revelry and costumes, the annual Carnaval in Spain can reach serious partying proportions. Aside from the Canary Islands (legendary for its full-on fiestas), Cadíz in southern Spain is famous for its annual extravaganza of drinking, dancing, and dressing up—the more outrageous the better. The celebrations typically carry on for 10 days. There are processions of costumed groups, and everyone is dressed up, including a healthy number of drag queens. Book your hotel months in advance, because you're not likely to find a single vacancy in town during the celebration.

Drink Like a Madrileño

To experience Madrid like a local, you have to eat and drink like a local, and in the capital an aperitif is a crucial part of daily life. In fact, there are more bars per square mile here than in any other capital in Europe, so finding a venue poses no great challenge. Go the traditional route and try a *vermut* (vermouth) on tap, typically served with a squirt of soda. Or try a glass of ice-cold *fino* (dry sherry) with its common tapas accompaniment of a couple of *gambas* (prawns). *Cervecerías* are also rife in the capital. These beer houses typically serve several local varieties on tap. In Madrid's Plaza Santa Ana some of the best-loved cervecerías line the pretty central square. Turn to your neighbor and give your best "*¡Salud!*"

Spend a Few Nights in a Parador

A quintessential experience for many visitors to Spain is spending a night, or several, in one of the government-run paradores. The settings are unique—perhaps a castle, a citadel, a monastery, or a historic mansion near the sea or in the mountains, and most are decorated in the style of the region. Each parador has a restaurant that strives to serve local food in traditional recipes. The paradores attract Spanish and international travelers alike and receive almost consistently rave reviews.

QUINTESSENTIAL SPAIN

La Siesta

The unabashed Spanish pursuit of pleasure and the unswerving devotion to establishing a healthy balance between work and play is nowhere more apparent than in the midday shutdown. However, as air-conditioning, fitness clubs, and other distractions gain ascendancy in modern Spain, and Mom-cooked lunches, once a universal ritual, become all but extinct in the two-salary, 21st-century Spanish family, the classic midday snooze—described by novelist Camilo José Cela as "*de padrenuestro y pyjama*" (with a prayer and pajamas)—is rarely practiced these days. The fact remains, however, that most stores and businesses close from about 1:30 to 4:30, whether people are sleeping, feasting, exercising, or canoodling.

El Fútbol and the Tortilla de Patata

The Spanish National Fútbol (soccer) League and the *tortilla de patata* (potato omelet) have been described as the only widely shared phenomena that bind the nation together. In the right chef's hands, the *tortilla* can be elevated to a gourmet delicacy, but even in a hole-in-the-wall tapas bar, you can't go too far wrong. In the case of the soccer league, the tie that binds often resembles tribal warfare, as bitter rivalries centuries old are played out on the field. Some of these, such as the Real Sociedad (San Sebastián)–Athletic de Bilbao feud, are fraternal in nature, brother Basques battling for boasting rights, but others, such as the Madrid–Barcelona standoffs, are as basic to Spanish history as Moros y Cristianos (a reenactment of the battle between the Moors and the Christians). The beauty of the game is best appreciated in the stadiums, but local sports bars, many of them

If you want to get a sense of Spanish culture and indulge in some of its pleasures, start by familiarizing yourself with the rituals of Spanish life. These are a few things you can take part in with relative ease.

official fan clubs of local teams, are where you see *fútbol* passions at their wildest.

El Paseo

One of the most delightful Spanish customs is *el paseo* (the stroll), which traditionally takes place during the early evening and is common throughout the country but particularly in *pueblos* and towns. Given the modern hamster-wheel pace of life, there is something appealingly old-fashioned about families and friends walking around at a leisurely pace with no real destination or purpose. Dress is usually formal or fashionable: elderly señoras with their boxy tweed suits, men with jackets slung, capelike, round the shoulders, teenagers in their latest Zara gear, and younger children in their Sunday best. *El paseo* provides everyone with an opportunity to participate in a lively slice of street theater.

Sunday Lunch

The Spanish love to eat out, especially on Sunday, the traditional day when families will drive to restaurants for long leisurely lunches. Depending on the time of year, this is most likely to be a seaside *chiringuito* or rural *venta*. The latter thrive, particularly in southern Spain, born from bygone days when much of the region's seasonal work was done by itinerant labor. Cheap, hearty meals were much in demand, and some enterprising country housewife saw the opportunity and decided to provide *ventas* (meals for sale); an idea that quickly mushroomed. Ventas are still a wonderfully good value today, not just for the food but also for the atmosphere: long, scrubbed wooden tables, large, noisy Spanish families, and a convivial informality. Sunday can be slow. So relax, and remember that all good things are worth waiting for.

IF YOU LIKE

Art

During the Spanish Golden Age (1580–1680), the empire's wealth flowed to the imperial capital of Madrid, and Spanish monarchs used it not only for defense and civil projects but to finance the arts. Painters from El Greco to Rubens, and writers from Lope de Vega to Cervantes, were drawn to the luminous (and free-spending) royal court. For the first time in Europe, the collecting of art became an important symbol of national wealth and power.

Centro de Arte Reina Sofía, Madrid. The modern collection focuses on Spain's three great modern masters: Pablo Picasso, Salvador Dalí, and Joan Miró. It houses Picasso's *Guernica.*

Museo de Bellas Artes, Seville. Among the fabulous works are those of Murillo, Zurbarán, Valdés Leal, and El Greco, and there are examples of Seville Gothic art, baroque religious sculptures, and Sevillian art from the 19th and 20th centuries.

Museo del Prado, Madrid. One of the world's greatest museums, it holds masterpieces by Italian and Flemish painters but its jewels are the works of Spaniards: Goya, Velázquez, and El Greco.

Museo Thyssen-Bornemisza, Madrid. An ambitious collection of 800 paintings traces the development of Western humanism as no other in the world.

Museo Guggenheim, Bilbao. The world-famous building houses works from the Venetian and the New York Guggenheim collections, but also from the most prominent of the Spanish modern artists.

Beaches

Virtually surrounded by bays, oceans, gulfs, straits, and seas, Spain is a beach-lover's dream as well as an increasingly popular destination for water-sports enthusiasts.

La Manga del Mar Menor, Costa Blanca. Known for its warm-water temperatures and the healing properties of its brine and iodine content, the 26 mi of beach here offer year-round beach fun.

Málaga to Estepona, Costa del Sol. The beaches here are warm enough for swimming year-round, though the overdeveloped high-rise apartments that have replaced fishing villages along this strip are ugly and depressing. The Costa de La Luz, just beyond Algeciras, presents a very different picture, with its white sandy beaches and a refreshing lack of concrete—particularly around Tarifa, which is famous for its water sports.

Matalascañas, at the western end of the Andalusian coast, and La Antilla, west of Huelva, are fine beaches except in late July and August when there's no towel space on the sand. South of Huelva are Cadíz's Atlantic wild and very windy beaches, appreciated by water-sports fans and by locals fleeing from the Mediterranean clamor and crowds.

Spain's **northern coast**, from the French border at Hondarribia to the border with Portugal at the Río Miño, offers a variety of urban beaches and remote strands.

The **Balearic Islands** are better known for their secluded coves and inlets than for the occasional long open stretches of sand; in general, the beaches here are too cold for swimming from November to May.

Food

Spanish cooking has really come into its own over the last 20 years. The Mediterranean diet, with its emphasis on olive oil, fish, vegetables, garlic, onions, and red wine, is now understood to be not only delicious but a healthy way to eat. Innovative chefs, including Ferran Adrià and Pedro Subijana, and such masters as Juan Mari Arzak and Santi Santamaría, are making Spain's regional cuisines famous throughout the world, and newer stars—Martín Berasategui, Sergi Arola, Fermí Puig, and Carme Ruscalleda Puig—are filling the firmament with new aromas and textures. These are some of the best venues:

Arzak, San Sebastián. The father-and-daughter team of Juan Mari and Elena Arzak endow traditional Basque food with an irresistible array of innovative tastes and textures at this extremely popular, internationally renowned restaurant.

El Celler de Can Roca, Girona, Costa Brava. Perhaps for its oddball combinations, the best restaurant in town is also one of Catalonia's top six.

El Racó de Can Fabes, Sant Celoni, near Barcelona. One of Spain's top four restaurants, it's well worth the train ride from Barcelona.

Gastro, Madrid. Celebrity chef Sergi Arola—Ferran Adrià's—most popular disciple—opened a modern bistro where, surrounded by a topnotch team, he offers three sampler menus that showcase some of his classic dishes with nods to his Catalonian roots.

Tragabuches, Ronda. This stylish restaurant, known for its modern Andalusian cuisine, has a superb taster's menu of six courses and two desserts.

Exploring the Outdoors

Crisscrossed with mountain ranges, Spain has areas that are ideal for walking, mountain biking, and backpacking. Mountain streams in the Pyrenees and other ranges throughout Spain offer trout- and salmon-fishing opportunities that can combine nicely with hiking and camping expeditions. Perhaps the best thing about exploring Spain's great outdoors is that it often brings you nearer to some of the finest architecture and cuisine in Iberia.

The **Pyrenees** offer superior hiking and trekking on well-marked trails from the Bay of Biscay to the Mediterranean, among them the 40- to 45-day GR-11 trail that runs from the Atlantic Ocean to the Mediterranean Sea.

The 57,000-acre **Parque Nacional de Ordesa y Monte Perido**, in the Pyrenees, is especially good for hiking: it's Spain's version of the Grand Canyon, with waterfalls, caves, forests, meadows, and more.

The **Sierra de Gredos,** west of Madrid, in Castile and León, bordering Extremadura, is a popular destination for climbing and trekking.

Hiking is excellent in the interior of Spain, in the **Alpujarras** Mountains southeast of Granada and in the **Picos de Europa.**

The **pilgrimage road to Santiago de Compostela** is still in vogue after hundreds of years; it traverses the north of Spain from either Roncesvalles in Navarra or the Aragonese Pyrenees to Galicia.

Doñana National Park, in Andalusia, is one of Europe's last tracts of true wilderness, with wetlands, beaches, sand dunes, marshes, 150 species of rare birds, and countless kinds of wildlife, including the endangered imperial eagle and lynx.

GREAT ITINERARIES

MADRID AND THE SOUTH

Days 1–3: Welcome to Madrid

The elegant Plaza Mayor is the perfect jumping-off point for a tour of the Spanish capital. To the west, see the Plaza de la Villa, Palacio Real (the Royal Palace), Teatro Real (Royal Theater), and the royal convents; to the south wander around the maze of streets of La Latina and the Rastro and indulge yourself in local tapas. Start or end the day with a visit to the Prado, the Museo Thyssen-Bornemisza, or the Centro de Arte Reina Sofía.

On Day 2, visit the sprawling Barrio de las Letras, centered on the Plaza de Santa Ana. This was the favorite neighborhood of writers during the Spanish golden literary age in the 17th century, and it's still crammed with theaters, cafés, and good tapas bars. It borders the Paseo del Prado on the east, allowing you to comfortably walk to any of the art museums in the area. If the weather is pleasant, take an afternoon stroll in the Parque del Buen Retiro.

For your third day in the capital, wander in Chueca and Malasaña, the two neighborhoods most favored by young Madrileños. Fuencarral, a landmark street that serves as the border between the two, is one of the city's trendiest shopping enclaves. From there you can walk to the Parque del Oeste and the Templo de Debod—the best spot from which to see the city's sunset. Among the lesser-known museums, consider visiting the captivating Museo Sorolla, Goya's frescoes and tomb at the Ermita de San Antonio de la Florida, or the Real Academia de Bellas Artes de San Fernando for classic painting. People-watch at any of the terrace bars in either Plaza de Chueca or Plaza 2 de Mayo in Malasaña. ⇨*See Chapter 2 for details on Madrid.*

Logistics: If you're traveling light, the subway (Metro) or the bus will take you from the airport to the city for €1–€1.25. A taxi will do the same for around €25–€30. Once in the center consider either walking or taking the subway rather than driving in gridlock traffic.

Days 4 and 5: Castilian Charmers

There are several excellent options for half- or full-day side trips from Madrid to occupy Days 4 and 5. Toledo and Segovia are two of the oldest Castilian cities—both have delightful old quarters dating back to the Romans. There's also El Escorial, which houses the massive monastery built by Felipe II. Two other nearby towns also worth visiting are Aranjuez and Alcalá de Henares. ⇨*See Chapter 3 for details on these Castilian cities.*

Logistics: In 2007, Toledo and Segovia became stops on the high-speed train line (AVE), so you can get to either of them in a half-hour from Madrid. To reach the old quarters of both cities take a bus or cab from the train station. Or take the bus from Madrid; by bus is also the best way to get to El Escorial. Reach Aranjuez and Alcalá de Henares via the intercity train system.

Day 6: Córdoba and Its Mosque or Extremadura

Córdoba, the capital of both Roman and Moorish Spain, was the center of Western art and culture between the 8th and 11th centuries. The city's sprawling mosque (now a cathedral) and the medieval Jewish Quarter bear witness to the city's brilliant past. From Madrid you could also rent a car and visit the lesser-known cities north of Extremadura, such as Guadalupe, Trujillo, and Cáceres, overnighting

in Cáceres, a UNESCO World Cultural Heritage city, and returning to Madrid the next day. ⇨ *See Chapter 11 for Córdoba and Chapter 13 for Extremadura.*

Logistics: The AVE train will take you to Córdoba from Madrid in under two hours. A good alternative is to sleep over in Toledo, also on the route heading south, and then head to Córdoba the next day. Once in Córdoba, take a taxi for a visit out to the summer palace at Medina Azahara.

Days 7 and 8: Seville

Seville's Giralda tower, cathedral, bullring, and Barrio de Santa Cruz are visual feasts. Forty minutes south you can sip the world-famous sherries of Jerez de la Frontera, then munch jumbo shrimp on the beach at Sanlúcar de Barrameda. *For more on Seville,* ⇨ *see Chapter 11.*

Logistics: From Seville's AVE station, take a taxi to your hotel. After that, walking and hailing the occasional taxi are the best ways to explore the city.

Days 9 and 10: Granada

The hilltop Alhambra palace, Spain's most visited attraction, was conceived by the Moorish caliphs as heaven on earth. Try any of the city's famous tapas bars and tea shops, and make sure to roam the magical, steep streets of the Albayzín, the ancient Moorish quarter. *For more on Andalusia,* ⇨ *see Chapter 11.*

Logistics: The Seville–Granada leg of this trip is best accomplished by renting a car. However, the Seville-to-Granada trains (four daily, just over three hours, costing less than €23) are an alternative. Another idea is to head first from Madrid to Granada, skipping Córdoba, and then from Granada to Seville.

> **TIP**
>
> Spain's modern freeways are as good as any in the world—with the exception of the signs, which have writing that's often too small to decipher while comfortably traveling at the routine speed of 120 km/hr (74 mph).

GREAT ITINERARIES

BARCELONA AND THE NORTH

Days 1–3: Welcome to Barcelona

To get a feel of Barcelona, begin with the Rambla and Boquería market. Then set off for the Gothic Quarter to see the Catedral de la Seu, Plaça del Rei, and the Catalan and Barcelona government palaces in Plaça Sant Jaume. Next, cross Via Laietana to the Ribera-Born (waterfront neighborhood), for the Catalan Gothic Santa Maria del Mar and nearby Museu Picasso.

Make Day 2 a Gaudí day: Visit the Temple Expiatori de la Sagrada Família first thing, then Park Güell. In the afternoon see the Casa Milà and Casa Batlló, part of the Manzana de la Discòrdia on Passeig de Gràcia. Palau Güell, off the lower Rambla, is probably too much Gaudí for one day, but don't miss it. (Learn more about Gaudí and Barcelona's Moderniste architecture in the In-focus feature "Gaudí: Architecture Through the Looking Glass" in Chapter 7.)

On Day 3, climb Montjuïc for the Museu Nacional d'Art de Catalunya, in the hulking Palau Nacional. Investigate the Fundació Miró, Estadi Olímpic, the Mies van de Rohe Pavilion, and Casaramona (aka CaixaForum). At lunchtime, take the cable car across the port for seafood in Barceloneta. ⇨*See Chapter 7 for more on Barcelona.*

Logistics: The bus will take you from the airport to the city for €4.75. A taxi will do the same for around €23. In Barcelona's city center, walking or taking the subway is better than cabbing it.

Days 3 and 4: San Sebastián

San Sebastián is one of Spain's most beautiful—and delicious—cities. Belle Epoque buildings nearly encircle the tiny bay, and tapas bars flourish in the old quarter. Visiting San Sebastián without a look at Pasajes de San Juan is a mistake. Likewise, an excursion to Hondarribia is a must. The cider mills in Astigarraga are another important off–San Sebastián visit. *For more on San Sebastián,* ⇨*see Chapter 5.*

Logistics: Whether you arrive by plane, train, or car, you really need your own vehicle to explore the Basque Country properly. You don't need a car in San Sebastián proper, but visits to cider houses in Astigarraga, Chillida Leku on the outskirts of town, and many of the finest restaurants around San Sebastián are possible only with your own transportation or a taxi (the latter with the perk that you won't get lost.) The freeway west to Bilbao is beautiful and fast, but the coastal road through Orio, Zarautz, Guetaria, and Zumaia is recommended at least as far as Zumaia.

Days 5 and 6: The Basque Coast

The Basque coast between San Sebastián and Bilbao is lined with beaches, rocky cliffs, and picture-perfect fishing ports. The wide beach at Zarautz, the fishermen's village of Getaria, the Zuloaga Museum in Zumaia, Mundaka's famous left-breaking surfing wave, and Bermeo's port and fishing museum should all be near the top of your list. ⇨*See Chapter 5 for information on the Basque country.*

Logistics: To see the Basque coast, forget about time and wind along the coastal roads that twist through places such as Elantxobe, Bakio, Mundaka, and San Juan Gaztelugatxe. From Bilbao there

is a train, the Euskotren, that runs from the Atxuri station through the Urdaibai wetlands and the Ría de Gernika to Mundaka.

Days 7 and 8: Bilbao

Bilbao's Guggenheim Museum is worth a trip for the building itself, and the Museum of Fine Arts has an impressive collection of Basque and Spanish paintings. Restaurants and tapas bars are famously good in Bilbao, and the city's cultural offerings, from opera to jazz to bullfights (in August), have always been first-rate. ⇨*See Chapter 5 for more details on Bilbao.*

Logistics: In Bilbao, use the subway or the Euskotram, which runs up and down the Nervión estuary.

Days 9 and 10: Santander and Cantabria

The elegant beach town of Santander has an excellent summer music festival every August. Nearby, Santillana del Mar is one of Spain's best Renaissance towns, and the museum at the Altamira Caves displays famous early-day cave paintings. Exploring the Picos de Europa will take you through some the peninsula's wildest reaches, and the port towns along the coast provide some of Spain's wildest and purest beaches. ⇨*See Chapter 4 for more on Santander and other Cantabria destinations.*

Logistics: Santander stretches for several miles along its Sardinero beachfront. There is little traffic, except in mid-August, but parking is expensive and scarce, so it's better to make use of the bus service. For explorations into the towns and hills of Cantabria, a car is indispensable.

Days 11–13: Oviedo and Asturias

The coast road through Ribadesella and the cider capital Villaviciosa to Oviedo is a scenic tour punctuated with numerous tempting beaches. Oviedo, its cathedral, and its pre-Romanesque churches are worlds away from Córdoba's Mezquita and Granada's Alhambra. Gijón is a fishing and freight port, summer resort, and university town, and the villages along the coast such as Cudillero and Luarca remain quite unspoiled and serve wonderful fish and seafood. ⇨*See Chapter 4 for details on Asturias.*

Logistics: The A8 coastal freeway gets you quickly and comfortably from points east to Oviedo and just beyond. From there, go west into Galicia via the two-lane N634 or the coastal N632—both are slow but scenic routes to Santiago de Compostela.

Days 14–16: Santiago de Compostela and Galicia

Spain's northwest corner, with Santiago de Compostela at its spiritual and geographic center, is a green land of bagpipes and apple orchards. Lugo, Ourense, A Coruña, and Vigo are the major cities, and the Albariño wine country, along the Río Miño border with Portugal, and the *rías* (estuaries), full of delicious seafood, will keep you steeped in *enxebre*—Gallego for "local specialties and atmosphere." ⇨ *See Chapter 4 for more on Galicia.*

Logistics: Once in Galicia, the four-lane freeways AP9 and A6 whisk you from Lugo and Castro to Santiago de Compostela and down into the Rías Baixas. Cars are the only way to tour Galicia, and the slower the better. The AC552 route around the upper northwest corner and the Rías Altas turns into the AC550 coming back into Santiago.

TIP

Be prepared for bilingual traffic signs and local spellings that do not match your map, which probably adheres to the "traditional" Castilian spelling. Languages across the north of Spain go from Basque, or Euskera, in the eastern Basque Country; to Castilian Spanish in Santander and Cantabria; to Bable, a local dialect, in Asturias; and Gallego, a Portuguese-like Romance language, in Galicia.

FAQ

What are my lodging options in Spain? For a slice of Spanish culture, stay in a parador; to indulge your pastoral fantasies, try a *casa rural* (country house), Spain's version of a bed-and-breakfast. On the other end of the spectrum are luxurious high-rise hotels along the coastline, and chain hotels in the major cities. Traveling with your family? Consider renting an apartment.

Do I need to book hotels beforehand, or can I just improvise once I'm in Spain? In big cities or popular tourist areas it's best to reserve well ahead. In smaller towns and rural areas you can usually find something on the spot, except when local fiestas are on—for those dates you may have to book months in advance.

How can I avoid looking like a tourist in Spain? Ditch the white tennis shoes and shorts for a start, and try to avoid baseball caps. A fanny pack will betray you instantly; a *mochila*—an all-purpose cloth or leather bag with a long shoulder strap, bought locally, will serve you better.

Do shops really close for siesta? In general, shop close from 2 PM to 5 PM, particularly in small towns and villages. The exceptions are supermarkets and large department stores, which tend to be open from 9 AM to 9 PM in the center of Madrid and Barcelona, and at major resorts stores often stay open all day.

How much should I tip at a restaurant? You won't find a service charge on the bill, but the tip is included. For stellar service, leave a small sum in addition to the bill, but not more than 10%. If you're indulging in tapas, just round out the bill to the nearest euro. For cocktails, tip about €0.50 a drink.

If I only have time for one city, should I choose Barcelona or Madrid? It depends on what you're looking for. Madrid will give you world-class art and much more of a sense of a workaday Spanish city, while cosmopolitan Barcelona has Gaudí, Catalan cuisine, and its special Mediterranean atmosphere.

Can I get dinner at 7, or do I really have to wait until the Spanish eat at 9? If you really can't wait, head for the most touristy part of town; there you should be able to find bars and cafés that will serve meals at any time of day. But it won't be nearly as good as the food the Spaniards are eating a couple of hours later. You might be better off just dining on tapas.

How easy is it to cross the border from Spain into neighboring countries? Spain, Portugal, and France are members of the EU, so borders are open. Good trains connect Madrid and Lisbon (about €57), and Madrid and Paris (about €75). U.S. citizens need only a valid passport to enter Morocco; ferries run regularly to Tangier for about €30 one-way.

Can I bring home the famous ibérico ham, Spanish olives, almonds, or baby eels? Products you can legally bring into the United States include olive oil, cheese, olives, almonds, wood-smoked paprika, and saffron. Ibérico ham, even vacuum-sealed, is not legal, so you may not get past customs agents and their canine associates. If caught, you risk confiscation and fines. And don't even think about trying to bring back the *angulas* (eels).

For more help on trip planning, see the Travel Smart chapter.

HISTORY YOU CAN SEE

Ancient Spain

The story of Spain, a romance-tinged tale of counts, caliphs, crusaders, and kings, begins long before written history. The Basques were among the first here, fiercely defending the green mountain valleys of the Pyrenees. Then came the Iberians, apparently crossing the Mediterranean from North Africa around 3000 BC. The Celts arrived from the north about a thousand years later. The seafaring Phoenicians founded Gadir (now Cádiz) and several coastal cities in the south three millennia ago. The parade continued with the Greeks, who settled parts of the east coast, and then the Carthaginians, who founded Cartagena around 225 BC—and who dubbed the then-wild, forested and game-rich country Ispania, after their word for rabbit: *span.*

What to See: Near Barcelona, on the Costa Brava, rocket yourself back almost 3,000 years at **Ullastret,** a settlement occupied by an Iberian people known as the Indiketas. On a tour, actors guide groups through the homes and fortifications of some of the peninsula's earliest inhabitants, the defensive walls attesting to the constant threat of attack and the bits of pottery evidence of the settlement's early ceramic industry. Not far away in **Empúries** are ruins of the Greek colony established in the 6th century BC. At the **Museo de Cádiz** you can view sarcophagi dating back to the 1100 BC founding of the city.

The Roman Epoch

Modern civilization in Iberia began with the Romans, who expelled the Carthaginians and turned the peninsula into three imperial provinces. It took the Romans 200 years to subdue the fiercely resisting Iberians, but their influence is seen today in the fortifications, amphitheaters, aqueducts, and other ruins in cities across Spain, as well as in the country's legal system, and in the Latin base of Spain's Romance languages and dialects.

What to See: Segovia's nearly 3,000-foot-long **Acueducto Romano** is a marvel of Roman engineering. Mérida's Roman ruins are some of Spain's finest, including its **bridge, theater,** and **outdoor amphitheater.** Tarragona was Rome's most important city in Catalonia, as the **walls, circus,** and **amphitheater** bear witness, while Zaragoza boasts a **Roman amphitheater** and a **Roman fluvial port** that dispatched flat-bottomed riverboats loaded with wine and olive oil down the Ebro.

1100 BC	Earliest Phoenician colonies are formed, including Cádiz, Villaricos, Almuñecar, and Málaga. Natives include Basques in the Pyrenees, Iberians in the south, and Celts in the northwest.
237 BC	Carthaginians land in Spain.
206 BC	Romans expel Carthaginians from Spain and gradually conquer peninsula.
AD 74	Roman citizenship extended to all Spaniards.
419	Visigothic kingdom established in northern Spain, with capital at Toledo.
711–12	Visigothic kingdom destroyed by invading Muslims (Moors), who create an emirate, with the capital at Córdoba.
813	Discovery of remains of St. James; the cathedral of Santiago de Compostela is built and becomes a major pilgrimage site.
1085–1270	Main years of the Reconquest.
1478	Spanish Inquisition begins.

The Visigoths and Moors

In the early 5th century, invading tribes crossed the Pyrenees to attack the weakening Roman empire. The Visigoths became the dominant force in northern Spain by 419, establishing their kingdom at Toledo and eventually adopting Christianity. But the Visigoths, too, were to fall before a wave of invaders. The Moors, an Arab-led Berber force, crossed the Strait of Gibraltar in 711 and swept through Spain in an astonishingly short time, launching almost eight centuries of Muslim rule. The Moors brought with them citrus fruits, rice, cotton, sugar, palm trees, glassmaking, and the complex irrigation system still used around Valencia. The influence of Arabic in modern Spanish includes words beginning with "al," such as *albóndiga* (meatball), *alcalde* (mayor), *almohada* (pillow), and *alcázar* (fortress), as well as prominent phonetic characteristics ranging from the fricative "j" to, in all probability, the lisping "c" (before "e" and "i") and "z." The Moorish and Mudejar (Moorish decorative details) architecture found throughout most of Spain tells much about the splendor of the Islamic culture that flourished here.

What to See: Moorish culture is most spectacularly evident in Andalusia, derived from the Arabic name for the Moorish reign on the Iberian Peninsula, al-Andalus, which meant "western lands." The fairytale **Alhambra** palace overlooking Granada captures the refinement of the Moorish aesthetic, while the earlier **9th-century mesquite** (mosque) at Córdoba bears witness to the power of Islam in al-Andalus.

Spain's Golden Age

By 1085, Alfonso VI of Castile had captured Toledo, giving the Christians a firm grip on the north. In the 13th century, Valencia, Seville, and finally Córdoba—the capital of the Muslim caliphate in Spain—fell to Christian forces, leaving only Granada in Moorish hands. Nearly 200 years later, the so-called Catholic Monarchs—Ferdinand of Aragón and Isabella of Castile—were joined in a marriage that would change the world. Finally, on January 2, 1492, 244 years after the fall of Córdoba, Granada surrendered and the Moorish reign was over.

The year 1492 was the beginning of the nation's political golden age: Christian forces conquered Granada and unified all of current-day Spain as a single kingdom; in what was, at the time, viewed

1479 –1504	Isabella and Ferdinand rule jointly.
1492	Granada, the last Moorish outpost, falls. Christopher Columbus, under Isabella's sponsorship discovers America, setting off a wave of Spanish exploration. Ferdinand and Isabella expel Jews and Muslims from Spain.
1516 –22	Ferdinand dies. His grandson Charles I inaugurates the Hapsburg dynasty.
1519	First circumnavigation of the world by Ferdinand Magellan's ships.
ca. 1520 –1700	Spain's Golden Age.
1605	Miguel de Cervantes publishes the first part of Don Quijote de la Mancha.
1618 –1648	Thirty Years' War: a dynastic struggle between Hapsburgs and Bourbons.
1701 –14	War of the Spanish Succession. Claimants to the throne are Louis XIV of France, Holy Roman Emperor Leopold I, and electoral prince Joseph Ferdinand of Bavaria.

as a peacekeeping measure promoting national unity, Jews and Muslims who did not convert to Christianity were expelled from the country. The departure of educated Muslims and Jews was a blow to the nation's agriculture, science, and economy from which it would take nearly 500 years to recover. The Catholic monarchs and their centralizing successors maintained Spain's unity, but they sacrificed the spirit of international free trade that was bringing prosperity to other parts of Europe. Carlos V weakened Spain with his penchant for waging war, and his son, Felipe II (Phillip II), followed in the same expensive path, defeating the Turks in 1571 but losing the "Invincible Spanish Armada" in the English Channel in 1588.

What to See: Celebrate Columbus's voyage to America with **festivities in Seville, Huelva, Granada, Cádiz, and Barcelona,** all of which display venues where "The Discoverer" was either commissioned, confirmed, set out, returned, or buried. Wander through the somber **El Escorial,** a monastery northwest of Madrid whose construction Felipe II oversaw and which is the resting place of Carlos V.

War of the Spanish Succession

The 1700–14 War of the Spanish Succession ended with the fall of Barcelona, which had sided with the Hapsburg Archduke Carlos against the Bourbon Prince Felipe V. El Born market, completed in 1876, covered the buried remains of the Ribera neighborhood where the decisive battle took place. Ribera citizens were required to tear down a thousand houses to clear space for the Ciutadella fortress, from which fields of fire were directed, quite naturally, toward the city the Spanish and French forces had taken a year to subdue. The leveled neighborhood, then about a third of Barcelona, was plowed under and forgotten by the victors, though never by Barcelonins.

What to See: In Barcelona, the **Fossar de les Moreres cemetery,** next to the Santa María del Mar basilica, remains a powerful symbol for Catalan nationalists who gather there every September 11, Catalonia's National Day, to commemorate the fall of the city in 1714.

Spanish Civil War

Spain's early-19th-century War of Independence required five years of bitter guerrilla fighting to rid the peninsula of Napoleonic troops. Later, the Carlist

1756–63	Seven Years' War: Spain and France versus Great Britain.
1808	Napoleon takes Madrid.
1809–14	The Spanish War of Independence: Napoleonic armies thrown out of Spain.
1834–39	First Carlist War: Don Carlos contests the crown; an era of upheaval begins.
1873	First Spanish Republic declared. Three-year Second Carlist War begins.
1898	Spanish-American War: Spain loses Cuba, Puerto Rico, and the Philippines.
1936–39	Spanish civil war; more than 600,000 die. Gen. Francisco Franco wins and rules Spain for the next 36 years.
1977–78	First democratic election in 40 years; new constitution restores civil liberties and freedom of the press.
1992	Olympic Games held in Barcelona.
2000	Juan Carlos celebrates 25 years as Spain's king.
2004	Terrorist bombs on Madrid trains claim almost 200 lives.

wars set the stage for the Spanish civil war (1936–39), in which more than half a million people died. Intellectuals and leftists sympathized with the elected government; the International Brigades, with many American, British, and Canadian volunteers, took part in some of the worst fighting, including the storied defense of Madrid. But General Francisco Franco, backed by the Catholic Church, got far more help from Nazi Germany, whose Condor legions destroyed the Basque town of Gernika (in a horror made infamous by Picasso's monumental painting, *Guernica*), and from Fascist Italy. For three years, European governments stood quietly by as Franco's armies ground their way to victory. After the fall of Barcelona in January 1939, the Republican cause became hopeless, and Franco's Nationalist forces entered Madrid on March 27, 1939.

What to See: Snap a shot of **Madrid's Plaza Dos de Mayo,** in the Malasaña neighborhood; it is the site of the heroic stand of officers Daoiz and Velarde against vastly superior French forces at the start of the popular uprising against Napoleon. The archway in the square is all that remains of the armory Daoiz and Velarde defended to the death. Trace the shrapnel marks on the wall of the **Sant Felip Neri church** in Barcelona, material evidence of the 1938 bombing of the city by Italian warplanes under Franco's orders. East of Zaragoza, the town of **Belchite** was the scene of bloody fighting during the decisive Battle of the Ebro. The town has been left exactly as it appeared on September 7, 1937, the day the battle ended.

HIDDEN MEANINGS

It's interesting to note that what is *not* present in Spain is just as revealing. For example, there are no Roman ruins in Madrid, since it was founded as a Moorish outpost in the late 10th century and was not the capital of Spain until 1560, a recent date in Spanish history. Likewise, Barcelona has no Moorish architecture—the Moors sacked Barcelona but never established themselves there, testifying to Catalonia's medieval past as part of Charlemagne's Frankish empire: Al-Andalus, the 781-year Moorish sojourn on the peninsula, was farther south and west.

LANGUAGES OF SPAIN

Spanish

Often identified as *castellano* or Castilian Spanish, **Spanish** is the main language spoken throughout Spain. A Romance language derived from Latin, Spanish contains considerable Arabic influence as a result of the nearly eight centuries of Moorish presence on the Iberian Pensinsula. The first recorded use of Spanish was the *Roman paladino,* recited by the poet Gonzalo de Berceo in the 13th century at the Monasterio de Suso in La Rioja. Two centuries later, Antonio de Nebrija's famous Spanish grammar book helped spread Spanish throughout Spain's sprawling global empire. Felipe V, in 1714, decreed Spanish the official language of Spain. Spanish is presently spoken by more than 400 million people around the world.

Spain's Other Languages

Spain's other main languages, most of which predate Castilian Spanish, include the Romance languages Catalan and Gallego (or Galician-Portuguese) and the non–Indo-European Basque language, Euskera. A third tier of local dialects include Asturiano (or Bable), Aranés, and the variations of Fabla Aragonesa, the languages of the north-central community of Aragón. In Extremadura the provincial dialect is Extremaduran.

Catalan is spoken in Barcelona and in Spain's northeastern autonomous community of Catalonia, in southern France's Roussillon region, in the city of L'Alguer on the Italian island of Sardinia, and in Andorra (where it is the national language). It is derived from Provençal French and is closer to Langue d'Oc and Occitan than to Spanish, as is clarified by eminent Spanish philologist Ramón Menéndez Pidal (1869–1968) in his *Orígenes del Español.* Both **Valenciano** and **Mallorquín,** spoken respectively in the Valencia region and in the Balearic Islands in the Mediterranean east of Barcelona, are considered dialects of Catalan.

Gallego is spoken in Galicia in Spain's northwestern corner and more closely resembles Portuguese than Spanish.

Euskera, the Basque language, is Spain's greatest linguistic mystery. Links to Japanese, Sanskrit, Finnish, Gaelic, or the language of the lost city of Atlantis have proven to be false leads or pure mythology. The best theory on Euskera, developed by Menéndez Pidal in his *En Torno a la Lengua Vasca* (*On the Basque Language*) suggests that a language similar to Euskera was spoken by the aboriginal inhabitants of the Iberian Peninsula and was best defended in the remote hills of the Basque Country. Euskera is presently spoken by about a million inhabitants of the Spanish and French Basque provinces.

Asturiano (or Bable) is a Romance language (sometimes called a dialect) spoken in Asturias and in parts of León, Zamora, Salamanca, Cantabria, and Extremadura by some 700,000 people.

Aranés (or Occitan), derived from Gascon French, is spoken in Catalonia's westernmost valley, the Vall d'Arán.

Fabla aragonesa is the collective term for all of Aragón's mountain dialects. Aragón has some 15 active dialects, including Patués, Chistabino, Pandicuto, Tensino, and Ribagorzano. All are more closely related to Gascon French and Occitan than to Spanish.

Extremaduran, a Spanish dialect, is spoken in Extremadura.

Gain access to the inner chambers of paradores in Santiago de Compostela (left) and Sigüenza (above).

A NIGHT WITH HISTORY

Spain's nearly 100 paradores all have one thing in common: heritage status. More often than not they also have killer views. Plan a trip with stays at a number of paradores, and you'll have the chance to experience an authentic slice of Spanish culture around the country. Spaniards themselves love the paradores and make up about 70 percent of visitors.

Parador accommodations come in all manner of distinguished settings, including former castles, convents, and Arab fortresses—soon, in Madrid, you'll even be able to check into a former women's prison. Talk about ex-cell-ent sleeping. . . .

Even if you find yourself in a parador that's a (ho-hum) stately historic home, you'll most likely be perched above, or nestled in, some lovely surroundings—from the *pueblos blancos* (whitewashed villages) and verdant golf courses of Andalusia to the rolling fields, mountains, and beaches of northern Spain.

THE PARADOR'S TRUE CHARM: PAY LESS, GET MORE

Why pay top-euro prices when you can get top-notch quality for considerably less? In most cases, the accommodations, interior decoration, and cuisine at paradores are just as good and, in many cases, vastly superior to that of four- and five-star hotels. Just as strong a selling point is that paradores have the luxury of beautiful and peaceful settings. The variety of settings is perhaps what attracts most visitors, from a balcony overlooking the Alhambra or views of snow-peaked mountains to sweeping views of plains in countryside venues.

FROM ROYAL HUNTING LODGE TO FIRST PARADOR

An advocate for Spain tourism in the early 20th century, King Alfonso XIII was eager to develop a countrywide hotel infrastructure that would cater to local and overseas travelers. He directed the Spanish government to set up the Royal Tourist Commission to mull it over, and in 1926, commissioner Marquis de la Vega Inclán came up with the parador ("stopping place") idea and searched for where to build the first such inn. His goal was to find a setting that would reflect both the beauty of Spain and its cultural heritage. He nominated the wild Gredos Mountains, where royalty came to hunt and relax, a few hours west of Madrid.

King Alfonso XIII

By October of 1928, the Parador de Gredos opened at a spot chosen by King Alfonso himself, amid pine groves, rocks, and the clear waters of Avilá. In 1937, this parador is where the fascist Falange party was established, and a few decades later, in 1978, it's where national leaders drafted the Spanish Constitution.

SPAIN'S PARADOR CHAIN

When Alfonso gave his blessing to the establishment of Spain's first parador, he probably didn't realize that he was sitting on a financial, cultural, and historical gold mine. But after it opened, the Board of Paradores and Inns of Spain was formed and focused its energies on harnessing historical, artistic, and cultural monuments with lovely landscapes into a chain—an effort that has continued to this day.

The number of state-run paradores today approaches nearly 100, with the latest two being the Parador La Granja on the grounds of the royal summer home of Carlos III and Isabel de Farnesio in Segovia, and the Parador de Gran Canaria in Cruz in Tejeda in Las Canarias.

Pillow Talk

Grace Kelly

Given that many paradores were once homes and residences to noble families and royalty, it's no surprise that they've continued to attract the rich and famous. Italian actress Sophia Loren stayed at the Parador de Hondarribia, as did distinguished Spanish writer José Cela, and Cardona's castle and fortress was the backdrop for Orson Welles's movie *Falstaff.* Topping the list, though, may be the Parador de Granada: President Johnson, Queen Elizabeth, actress Rita Hayworth, and even Franco himself all stayed here. Additionally, Grace Kelly celebrated some of her honeymoon trip with Prince Rainier of Monaco in these hallowed walls, and many a Spanish intellectual and artist also have gotten cozy in this charming, sophisticated abode.

WHAT TO EXPECT

Walk where famous people have walked in the Parador de Granada's courtyard.

Paradores have been restored to provide modern amenities. Depending on the location, some have swimming pools, while others have fitness rooms and/or saunas. Most paradores have access to cable TV, but if they veer more toward four-star status, English channels may be limited to news services such as CNN and BBC World, though films may be available via a pay-for-view service. Some rooms have DVDs and a rental service. Laundry facilities are available at almost all of the paradores. Internet access is limited.

Lodging at the paradores is generally equivalent to a four-star hotel and occasionally a five-star. The dining is what sets the paradores apart—you'd pay considerably more to eat the quality of food they serve at the same caliber restaurant in town. Another advantage of the paradores is that unlike hotels, the room rates do not vary much in the peak months of June, July, and August.

Cost: Prices at the paradores vary, depending on location and time of year. In general, one-night stays range from €95 to €200, though the Parador de Granada will hit your wallet for at least 60 euros more per night. July through September and Easter Week tend to be the most expensive times.

GREAT FOR DAY VISITS, TOO

While paradores are a great means of accommodation, they also attract huge numbers of day visitors. The reasons for this are two-fold. First, the buildings are often spectacular and historically significant and many contain great views. Secondly, the restaurants are consistently excellent but reasonable priced. Each parador strives to use local produce and reproduce the traditional gastronomy found in its region.

PARADORES WORTH VISITING

With its Spanish plateresque façade, the Parador de León adorns the Plaza de San Marcos.

PARADOR DE CANGAS DE ONIS, *Asturias.* This beautiful former monastery is in the mountains of Picos de Europa.

PARADOR DE GRANADA, *Granada.* Within the walls of Alhambra, this former monastery is Spain's most popular, and most expensive, parador.

PARADOR DE HONDARRIBIA, *Hondarribia.* This 10th-century castle-cum-fortress in the heart of Hondarribia looks severe from the outside but is elegant and lovely inside, with sweeping views of the French coastline.

PARADOR DE LEON, *Castilla y León.* Pure luxury sums up this five-star monastery, with arguably the best restaurant in the parador network.

PARADOR DE PLASENCIA, This Gothic convent lies in the heart of Plasencia's beautiful old quarters.

PARADOR DE SANTILLANA GIL BLAS, *Cantabria.* Santillana de Mar may be one of the most beautiful villages in Spain; this parador in the mountains is perfect if you're looking for peace and quiet.

PARADOR DE SIGÜENZA, *Castilla–La Mancha.* This sprawling 12th-century Moorish citadel is arguably the finest architectural example of all the parador castles.

SANTO DOMINGO DE LA CALZADA, *La Rioja.* This 12th-century hospital is popular for its restaurant and its wines.

■ TIP→ If you plan to spend at least five nights in the paradors, the "five-night card" offers excellent savings. You can purchase and use the card at any parador but in most, discounted nights aren't available in June, July, and August, and are offered only Sunday through Thursday in spring. Note that the card does not guarantee a room; you must make reservations in advance.

PARADOR INFORMATION

For more information about paradores, consult the official parador Web site, www.paradores.es/english, e-mail reservas@parador.es, or call 34 902/547979.

Madrid

Parque del Retiro

WORD OF MOUTH

"In Madrid there are the world-class museums but also a great night time ambience in the summer when everyone goes out to the cafes and bars until late at night when the weather cools off. And flamenco!"

—Nikki

WELCOME TO MADRID

TOP REASONS TO GO

★ **Hitting the Centro Histórico:** The Plaza Mayor on any late night when it's almost empty is the place that best evokes the glory of Spain's golden age.

★ **Strolling Down Museum Row:** Find a pleasant mix of art and architecture in the Prado, the Reina Sofía, and the Thyssen, all of which display extensive and impressive collections.

★ **Nibbling tapas into the night:** Indulge in a *madrileño* way of socializing. Learn about the art of tapas and sample local wines while wandering among the bars of Cava Baja.

★ **Relaxing in the Retiro Gardens:** Visit on a Sunday morning, when it's at its most boisterous, to unwind and take in the sun and merrymaking.

★ **Burning the Midnight Oil:** When other cities turn off their lights, *madrileños* swarm to the bars of the liveliest neighborhoods—Malasaña, Chueca, Lavapiés, and more—and stretch the party out until dawn.

1 Old Madrid. This area comprises the three present-day neighborhoods of Sol, Palacio, and La Latina. The latter two have the city's highest concentration of aristocratic buildings and elegant yet affordable bars and restaurants. And Sol has some of the city's busiest streets and oldest shops.

2 Barrio de las Letras. This area, home to the city's first open-air theaters in the late 16th century, is where all the major Spanish writers eventually settled. There's still a bohemian spirit here, good nightlife, and some of the city's trendiest hotels.

GETTING ORIENTED

Sitting in the center of Spain's heartland, Madrid dates back to the 9th century, but its perimeter wasn't enlarged by much until the mid-19th century, when an urban planner knocked down the wall built in 1625 and penciled new neighborhoods in what were formerly the outskirts. This means that even though there are now more than 3.12 million people living in a sprawling metropolitan area, the almond-shaped historic center is a concentrated area that can pleasantly be covered on foot. The newer neighborhoods (Chamberí, Salamanca, Argüelles, Embajadores) are easily pinpointed on a map by their clean-cut layout, a complete contrast with the chaotic maze of streets left behind by the Hapsburg monarchs.

3 Chueca and Malasaña. These neighborhoods offer eclectic, hip restaurants, shops run by young proprietors selling a unique variety of goods, and landmark cafés where young people sip cappuccinos, read books, and surf the Web.

4 Rastro and Lavapiés. Tracing back to the 16th century, these two areas are full of winding streets. The Rastro thrives every Sunday with the flea market; Lavapiés is the city's multicultural beacon, with plenty of low-budget African and Asian restaurants.

5 Salamanca and Retiro. Salamanca has long been the upper-middle class's favorite enclave and has great designer shops and sophisticated and expensive restaurants. Retiro, so called for its proximity to the park of the same name, holds some of the city's most expensive buildings.

2

MADRID PLANNER

When to Go

Madrid is hot and dry in summer—with temperatures reaching 95°F to 105°F in July and August—and chilly in winter, with minimum temperatures in the low 30s or slightly below in January and February, though snow in the city is rare. **The most pleasant time to visit the city is spring, especially May,** when the city honors its patron saint and bullfighting season begins. June is also a good month, as are the last four months of the year—in September and October it's likely you can still wear a T-shirt.

If you can, avoid traveling to Madrid in July and August—especially August, even though fares are better and there are plenty of concerts and open-air activities. Many locals flee to the coast or to the mountains, and as a result several restaurants, bars, and shops are closed for vacation.

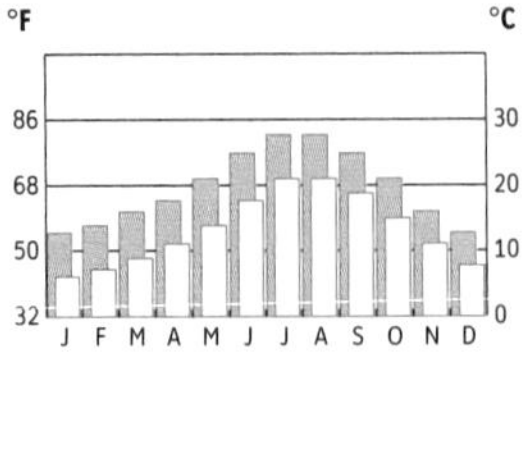

Tours

The **Plaza Mayor tourist office** (✉ *Plaza Mayor 27, Centro* ☎ *91/588–2906*) runs popular bus tours, cycling tours (there's a €6 bicycle rental fee), and usually crowded walking tours put together by the *ayuntamiento* (city hall) under the rubric "Descubre Madrid/Discover Madrid." There are three tours in English every weekday (the first one at 10 AM, and the other two usually at noon and 4 in the afternoon) and more on the weekends, with departure points depending on the tour selected. Tickets run from €3.90 for walking tours to €12.95 if a bus is needed. You can reserve tickets by phone or show up a few minutes before departure (weekday tours only).

The **Madrid Visión** (☎ *91/765–1016* 🌐 *www.madridvision.es*) tourist buses make two different 1½-hour circuits of the city (Historic Madrid and Modern Madrid) with recorded commentary in English. No reservation is needed; just show up at Puerta del Sol 5, Puerta de Alcalá (Plaza de la Independencia 3), Plaza de Cibeles (Paseo de Recoletos 2), or in front of the Prado Museum. Buses depart every 20 minutes, starting at 10 AM (9:30 in summer). The one-day and two-day passes, which allow you to get on and off at various attractions, cost €17 and €21, and you get better deals if you buy and print the tickets through their Web site.

Contact the **Asociación Profesional de Guías de Turismo** (✉ *Ferraz 82, Moncloa* ☎ *91/542–1214* 🌐 *www.apit.es*) for tailor-made history and art walks.

The not-so-mainstream **Carpetania Madrid** (✉ *Jesús del Valle 11, Malasaña* ☎ *91/531–1418, 658/233545* 🌐 *www.carpetaniamadrid.com*) offers literary walks (€100 for up to eight people) in English on the works and life of some of Spain's most reputed classical and contemporary authors.

For half-day and one-day trips to sites outside Madrid, including Toledo, El Escorial, and Segovia, contact **Julià Tours** (✉ *Gran Vía 68, Centro* ☎ *91/559–9605* 🌐 *www.juliatours.es*).

Planning Your Time

Madrid's most valuable art treasures are all on display within a few blocks of Paseo del Prado. This area is home to the Prado Museum, with its astounding selection of masterworks from Velázquez, Goya, El Greco, and others; the Centro de Arte Reina Sofía, with an excellent collection of contemporary art; and the Thyssen Museum, with a singular collection that stretches from the Renaissance to the 21st century. Each can take a number of hours to explore, so it's best to alternate museum visits with less overwhelming attractions. If you're running short on time and want to pack everything in, replenish your energy at any of the tapas bars or restaurants in the Barrio de las Letras (behind the Paseo del Prado, across from the Prado Museum).

Any visit to Madrid should include a walk in the old area between Puerta del Sol and the Royal Palace. Leave the map in your back pocket as you come across the Plaza Mayor, the Plaza de la Villa, and the Plaza de Oriente, and let the streets guide you to some of the oldest churches and convents standing. End or begin the day visiting the Royal Palace, built some centuries later than many of the churches but nonetheless quite staggering—it makes an easy start/end point.

WHAT IT COSTS IN EUROS

	¢	$	$$	$$$	$$$$
Restaurants	under €10	€10–€15	€16–€22	€23–€29	over €29
Hotels	under €75	€75–€124	€125–€174	€175–€225	over €225

Restaurant prices are per person for a main course at dinner. Hotel prices are for two people in a standard double room in high season, excluding tax.

Discounts and Deals

For €45, €58, or €72 for one, two, or three days, respectively, you can get the **Madrid Card,** which gives you entry to 40 museums and monuments, a tourist bus called Madrid Visión, all the guided visits in the Discover Madrid program (🌐 *www.esmadrid.com*), and admission to the Faunia biological park and the zoo. Purchase it at tourist offices (Plaza Mayor and Colón), on Madrid Visión buses, and at its kiosk next to the Prado Museum on Felipe IV, at Viajes Brújula at Atocha and Chamartín train stations. It's also available at 🌐 *www.madridcard.com.*

The **Abono Turístico** (Tourist Pass) allows unlimited use of public buses and the subway for a period of one (€5) to seven (€23.50) days. Purchase it at tourist offices, subway stations, or select newsstands.

GETTING HERE AND AROUND

By Air

Madrid's Barajas Airport (12 km [7 mi] east of the city) is Europe's fourth-largest airport. The massive Terminal 4 (T-4) handles flights from 32 carriers, including American Airlines, British Airways, and Iberia. All other American and British airlines use Terminal 1.

Airport terminals are connected by a bus service and also to a subway (line 8, *Línea 8*) that reaches both Terminal 2 (T-2) and the more remote Terminal 4 (T-4) and takes you to the city center in 30 to 45 minutes for €2 (€1 plus a €1 airport supplement). The metro runs every few minutes between Nuevos Ministerios (where you can check your luggage) and Barajas Airport. For €1 there's also a convenient bus to Avenida de América, where you can catch the subway or a taxi to your hotel.

In bad traffic, the 20-minute taxi ride to Madrid can take the better part of an hour, but it makes sense if you have a lot of luggage; expect to pay up to €30, more in heavy traffic (and more from Terminal 4, which is farther out), including a surcharge that goes up each year (it was €5.50 in 2009).

By Bus

Buses are generally less popular than trains (though they're sometimes faster). Madrid has no central bus station. Most of southern and eastern Spain (including Toledo) is served by the Estación del Sur. Estación de Avenida de América and Estación del Sur have subway stops (Avenida de América and Méndez Álvaro) that leave you right at the station. La Sepulvedana bus company serves Segovia, Ávila, and La Granja. Herranz goes to El Escorial (it leaves from the Intercambiador de Moncloa; that is, the Moncloa bus station) and from there to the Valle de los Caídos. La Veloz has service to Chinchón, and Aisa goes to Aranjuez and from there to Chinchón.

Red city buses run from about 6 AM to 11:30 PM and cost €1 per ride. After midnight, buses called *búhos* ("night owls") run out to the suburbs from Plaza de Cibeles for the same price. Drivers will generally make change for anything up to a €10 note. If you've bought a 10-ride ticket, step just behind the driver and insert it in the ticket-punching machine until the mechanism rings.

Bus Stations Estación del Avenida de América (✉ *Av. de América, 9, Salamanca* Ⓜ *Av. de América*). **Estación del Sur** (✉ *Méndez Álvaro s/n, Atocha* 🌐 *www.estaciondeautobuses.com* Ⓜ *Méndez Álvaro*). **Intercambiador de Moncloa** (✉ *Princesa 89, Moncloa* Ⓜ *Moncloa*).

By Taxi

Taxis work under three different tariff schemes. Tariff 1 is for the city center from 6 AM to 10 PM; meters start at €2.05. Supplemental charges include €5.50 to or from the airport and €2.95 from bus and train stations. Tariff 2 is from 10 PM to 6 AM in the city center (and 6 AM to 10 PM in the suburbs); the meter runs faster and charges more per kilometer. Tariff 3 runs at night beyond the city limits. All tariffs are listed on taxi windows.

Taxi Services **Radio Taxi Gremial** (☎ *91/447–5180*). **Radioteléfono Taxi** (☎ *91/547–8200*). **Tele-Taxi** (☎ *91/371–2131*).

By Subway

You can buy a €1 single ticket or the cheaper 10-ride Metrobus ticket, or a daily ticket that costs €7.40 and can also be used on buses as well. You might consider buying the Abono Turístico (Tourist Pass) if you intend to hop on and off the metro for a few days *(see Discounts and Deals on the Planner page)*. The metro is open from 6 AM to 1:30 AM, though a few entrances close earlier. ⇨ *See the inside front cover of this book for a map of the Madrid subway.*

Metro Madrid (☎ *902/444403* 🌐 *www.metromadrid.es*).

By Train

Madrid is in the geographical center of Spain and all the major train lines depart from one of its two main train stations (Chamartín and Atocha) or at least pass through Madrid (the third train station, Norte, is primarily for commuter trains). Although train travel is comfortable, for some destinations buses run more frequently and make fewer stops; this is true for Segovia and Toledo, unless you choose to take the more expensive high-speed train.

Commuter trains to El Escorial, Aranjuez, and Alcalá de Henares, run frequently. The best way to get a ticket for such trains is to use one of the automated reservation terminals at the station (they're in the *cercanías* area), but you can buy tickets online for the high-speed AVE regional lines. You can reach Segovia from the Atocha station in a half hour, the same time it takes you to get to Toledo. If you return within the same day, the ticket will cost you less than €16. The AVE stations in Toledo and Segovia are located outside the city, meaning once there you'll have to either take a bus or a taxi to get to their old quarters.

The AVE line can get you to Barcelona in less than three hours. If you buy the ticket more than two weeks ahead and are lucky enough to find a Web fare, you'll pay less that €50 each way. Otherwise expect to pay between €110 and €130 each way—the more expensive being the AVE +, which is nonstop. ⇨ *For more information about buying train tickets, see the Travel Smart chapter.*

Train Information Estación de Atocha (✉ *Glorieta del Emperador Carlos V, Atocha* ☎ *91/528–4630* Ⓜ *Atocha*). **Estación Chamartín** (✉ *Calle Agustín de Foxá s/n, Chamartín* ☎ *91/315–9976* Ⓜ *Chamartín*). **Estación de Príncipe Pío (Norte)** (✉ *Paseo de la Florida s/n, Moncloa* ☎ *902/240202 RENFE* Ⓜ *Príncipe Pío*).

By Car

Many of the nation's highways radiate from Madrid, inlcuding the A6 (Segovia, Salamanca, Galicia); A1 (Burgos and the Basque Country); the A2 (Guadalajara, Barcelona, France); the A3 (Cuenca, Valencia, the Mediterranean coast); the A4 (Aranjuez, La Mancha, Granada, Seville); the A42 (Toledo); and the A5 (Talavera de la Reina, Portugal). The city is surrounded by ring roads (M30, M40, and M50), from which most of these highways are easily picked up. There are also radial toll highways (marked R1, R2, R3, R4, and R5) that bypass the major highways, as well as the A41, a toll highway connecting Madrid and Toledo. These options are worth considering, especially if you're driving on a summer weekend or holiday.

Driving in Madrid is best avoided: parking is a nightmare and traffic is almost always heavy except in August when most madrileños are on vacation.

By Ignacio Gómez

Swashbuckling Madrid celebrates itself and life in general around the clock. A vibrant crossroads, Madrid—the Spanish capital since 1561—has an infectious appetite for art, music, and epicurean pleasure, and it's turned into a cosmopolitan, modern urban center while fiercely preserving its traditions.

The modern city spreads eastward into the 19th-century grid of the Barrio de Salamanca and sprawls northward through the neighborhoods of Chamberí and Chamartín. But the Madrid you should explore thoroughly on foot is right in the center, in Madrid's oldest quarters, between the Royal Palace and the midtown forest, the Parque del Buen Retiro. Wandering around the sprawling conglomeration of residential buildings with ancient red-tile rooftops punctuated by redbrick Mudejar churches and grand buildings with gray-slate roofs and spires left by the Hapsburg monarchs, you're more likely to grasp what is probably the city's major highlight: the buzzing bustle of people who are elated when they're outdoors.

And then there are the paintings, the artistic legacy of one of the greatest global empires ever assembled. King Carlos I (1500–58), who later became Emperor Carlos V, made sure the early masters of all European schools found their way to Spain's palaces. The collection was eventually placed in the Prado Museum. Among the Prado, the contemporary Reina Sofía museum, the eclectic Thyssen-Bornemisza collection, and Madrid's smaller artistic repositories—the Real Academia de Bellas Artes de San Fernando, the Convento de las Descalzas Reales, the Sorolla Museum, the Lázaro Galdiano Museum, and the CaixaForum—there are more paintings than anyone can admire in a lifetime.

But the attractions go beyond the well-known baroque landmarks. Now in the middle of an expansion plan, Madrid has made sure some of the world's best architects leave their imprint on the city. This is the case with Jacques Herzog and Pierre de Meuron, both of whom are responsible for a new arts center, CaixaForum, opened in 2008 across from the Botanical Garden. Major renovations of the Museo del Prado and the Centro Reina Sofía are by Rafael Moneo and Jean Nouvel, respectively. Looming towers by Norman Foster and César Pelli have changed the city's northern landscape. Other projects include the daring renovation project of the whole area of Paseo del Prado that's been entrusted to Portuguese architect Alvaro Siza.

EXPLORING MADRID

The real Madrid is not to be found along major arteries like the Gran Vía and the Paseo de la Castellana. To find the quiet, intimate streets and squares that give the city its true character, duck into the warren of villagelike byways in the downtown area that extends 2 km (1 mi) from the Royal Palace to the Parque del Buen Retiro and from Plaza de Lavapiés to the Glorieta de Bilbao. Broad *avenidas,* twisting medieval alleys, grand museums, stately gardens, and tiny, tile taverns are all jumbled together, creating an urban texture so rich that walking is really the only way to soak it in.

Madrid is composed of 21 districts, each broken down into several neighborhoods. The most central district is called just that, Centro. It stretches from Recoletos and Paseo del Prado in the east to behind the Royal Palace in the west, and from Sagasta and Alberto Aguilera in the north to Ronda de Valencia and Ronda de Segovia in the south. Within this district you'll find all of Madrid's oldest neighborhoods: Palacio, Sol, La Latina, Lavapiés, Barrio de las Letras, Malasaña, and Chueca. Other well-known districts, which we'll call neighborhoods in this chapter for the sake of convenience, are Salamanca, Retiro, Chamberí (north of Centro), Moncloa (east of Chamberí), and Chamartín. ■ TIP→ **Petty street crime is a serious problem in Madrid, and tourists are frequent targets. Be on your guard, and try to blend in by keeping cameras concealed, avoiding obvious map reading, and securing bags and purses, especially on buses and subway and outside restaurants.**

Numbers in the text correspond to numbers in the margin and on chapter maps.

OLD MADRID

The narrow streets of the Madrid's old section, which includes the Palacio, La Latina, and Sol neighborhoods—part of Madrid's greater Centro district—wind back through the city's history to its beginnings as an Arab fortress. As elsewhere in Madrid, there is a mix of old buildings and new ones: the neighborhoods here might not be as uniformly ancient as the neighborhoods in the nearby cities of Toledo and Segovia (or as grand), but the quiet alleys make for wonderful exploring.

Beyond the most central neighborhoods, Madrid also has several other sites of interest scattered around the city. Moncloa and Casa de Campo are the neighborhoods to the north and east of Palacio—that is, you can easily walk to the Templo de Debod or visit Goya's tomb if you're in the vicinity of the Royal Palace.

TOP ATTRACTIONS

21 **Basílica de San Francisco el Grande.** In 1760 Carlos III built this impressive basilica on the site of a Franciscan convent, allegedly founded by St. Francis of Assisi in 1217. The dome, 108 feet in diameter, is the largest in Spain, even larger than that of St. Paul's in London. The seven main doors were carved of American walnut by Casa Juan Guas. Three chapels adjoin the circular church, the most famous being that of **San Bernardino de Siena,** which contains a Goya masterpiece depicting a preaching San Bernardino. The figure standing on the right, not looking up, is a self-portrait of Goya. The 16th-century Gothic choir stalls came from La Cartuja del Paular, in rural Segovia Province. ✉ *Pl. de San Francisco, La Latina* ☎ *91/365–3800* 💶 *€3 guided tour* ⏲ *Oct.–May, Tues.–Fri. 11–12:30 and 4–6:30, Sat. 11–noon; June–Sept., Tues.–Fri. 11–12:30 and 5–7:30, Sat. 11–noon.*

28 **Monasterio de las Descalzas Reales** *(Monastery of the Royal Discalced, or Barefoot, Nuns).* This 16th-century building was restricted for 200 years to women of royal blood. Its plain, brick-and-stone facade hides paintings by Zurbarán, Titian, and Brueghel the Elder—all part of the dowry the novices had to provide when they joined the monastery—as well as a hall of sumptuous tapestries crafted from drawings by Peter Paul Rubens. The convent was founded in 1559 by Juana of Austria, one of Felipe II's sisters, who ruled Spain while he was in England and the Netherlands. It houses 33 different chapels—the age of Christ when he died and the maximum number of nuns allowed to live at the monastery at the same time—and more than 100 sculptures of Jesus as a baby. About 30 nuns (not necessarily of royal blood) still live here, cultivating their own vegetables in the convent's garden. TIP→ **You must take a tour in order to visit the convent; it's conducted in Spanish only.** ✉ *Plaza de las Descalzas Reales 3, Palacio* ☎ *91/454–8800* *€5, €6 combined ticket with Convento de la Encarnación* ⏲ *Tues.–Thurs. and Sat. 10:30–12:45 and 4–5:45, Fri. 10:30–12:45, Sun. 11–1:30.*

RAINY DAY TREAT

Despite what ads say, Madrid is not always sunny. If you hit a rainy or a chilly day, walk along the western side of the Convento de las Descalzas Reales until you see on your left the Chocolatería Valor (✉ ***Calle Postigo de San Martín 7, Centro*****); there you'll find the thick Spanish version of hot chocolate, perfect for dipping crispy churros.**

17 Fodor's Choice ★

Palacio Real. The Palace was commissioned in the early 18th century by the first of Spain's Bourbon rulers, Felipe V. Outside, you can see the classical French architecture on the graceful **Patio de Armas:** King Felipe was obviously inspired by his childhood days at Versailles with his grandfather Louis XIV. Look for the stone statues of Inca prince Atahualpa and Aztec king Montezuma, perhaps the only tributes in Spain to these pre-Columbian American rulers. Notice how the steep bluff drops westward to the Manzanares River—on a clear day, this vantage point commands a view of the mountain passes leading into Madrid from Old Castile; it's easy to see why the Moors picked this spot for a fortress.

Inside, 2,800 rooms compete with each other for over-the-top opulence. A two-hour guided tour in English winds a mile-long path through the palace; highlights include the **Salón de Gasparini,** King Carlos III's private apartments, with swirling, inlaid floors and curlicued, stucco wall and ceiling decoration, all glistening in the light of a 2-ton crystal chandelier; the **Salón del Trono,** a grand throne room with the royal seats of King Juan Carlos and Queen Sofía; and the **banquet hall,** the palace's largest room, which seats up to 140 people for state dinners. No monarch has lived here since 1931, when Alfonso XIII was deposed after a republican electoral victory. The current king and queen live in the far simpler Zarzuela Palace on the outskirts of Madrid; this palace is used only for official occasions.

Also worth visiting are the **Museo de Música** (Music Museum), where five stringed instruments by Stradivarius form the world's largest such collection; the **Painting Gallery,** which displays works by Spanish,

Flemish, and Italian artists from the 15th century onward; the **Armería Real** (Royal Armory), with historic suits of armor and frightening medieval torture implements; and the **Real Oficina de Farmacía** (Royal Pharmacy), with vials and flasks used to mix the king's medicines. ✉ *Calle Bailén s/n, Palacio* ☎ *91/454–8800* 💳 *€8, guided tour €10; Royal Armory only €3.40; Painting Gallery only €2* ⏲ *Apr.–Sept., Mon.–Sat. 9–6, Sun. 9–3; Oct.–Mar., Mon.–Sat. 9:30–5, Sun. 9–2.*

23 **Plaza de la Paja.** At the top of the hill, on Costanilla San Andrés, the Plaza de la Paja was the most important square in medieval Madrid. The plaza's jewel is the **Capilla del Obispo** (Bishop's Chapel), built between 1520 and 1530; this was where peasants deposited their tithes, called *diezmas*—literally, one-tenth of their crop. The stacks of wheat on the chapel's ceramic tiles refer to this tradition. Architecturally, the chapel marks a transition from the blockish Gothic period, which gave the structure its basic shape, to the Renaissance, the source of the decorations. It houses an intricately carved polychrome altarpiece by Francisco Giralta, with scenes from the life of Christ. The chapel has been under renovations for more than 11 years and at this writing is expected to reopen sometime in 2009. It's part of the complex of the domed church of **San Andrés,** one of Madrid's oldest, which for centuries held the remains of Madrid's male patron saint, San Isidro Labrador (they are now with his wife's remains, at the Real Colegiata de San Isidro, on nearby Calle Toledo). The church was severely damaged during the civil war. St. Isidore the Laborer was a peasant who worked fields belonging to the Vargas family. The 16th-century **Vargas Palace** forms the eastern side of the Plaza de la Paja. According to legend, St. Isidro worked little but had the best-tended fields thanks to many hours of prayer. When Señor Vargas came out to investigate the phenomenon, Isidro made a spring of sweet water spurt from the ground to quench his master's thirst. A hermitage (Ermita de San Isidro), now on Paseo de la Ermita del Santo, west of the Manzanares River, was built next to the spring in 1528. Every May 15 there's a procession followed by festivities in the meadow next to the hermitage. (In olden days, his remains were traditionally paraded through the city in times of drought.) ✉ *Plaza de la Paja, La Latina.*

26 **Plaza de Oriente.** The stately plaza in front of the Royal Palace is surrounded by massive stone statues of Spanish monarchs. These sculptures were meant to be mounted on the railing on top of the palace, but Queen Isabel of Farnesio, one of the first royals to live in the palace, had them removed because she was afraid their enormous weight would bring the roof down. (Well, that's the *official* reason; according to palace insiders, the queen wanted the statues removed because her own likeness had not been placed front and center.) A Velázquez painting of King Felipe IV is the inspiration for the statue in the plaza's center. It's the first equestrian bronze ever cast with a rearing horse. The sculptor, Italian artist Pietro de Tacca, enlisted Galileo's help in configuring the statue's weight so it wouldn't tip over. For most madrileños, the Plaza de Oriente is forever linked with Francisco Franco. The *generalísimo* liked to speak from the roof of the Royal Palace to his followers as they crammed into the plaza below. Each year in November, on the

anniversary of Franco's death, the plaza draws a decreasing number of old-timers. ✉*Plaza de Oriente, Palacio.*

29 **Plaza Mayor.** Austere, grand, and often surprisingly quiet compared with the rest of Madrid, this 360-foot-by-300-foot public square—finished in 1620 under Felipe III, whose equestrian statue stands in the center—is one of the largest in Europe. It's seen it all: autos-de-fé (trials of faith, i.e., public burnings of heretics); the canonization of saints; criminal executions; royal marriages, such as that of Princess María and the King of Hungary in 1629; bullfights (until 1847); masked balls; and all manner of other events. Special events still take place here.

This space was once occupied by a city market, and many of the surrounding streets retain the charming names of the trades and foods once headquartered there. Nearby are Calle de Cuchilleros (Knifemakers' Street), Calle de Lechuga (Lettuce Street), Calle de Fresa (Strawberry Street), and Calle de Botoneros (Buttonmakers' Street). The plaza's oldest building is the one with the brightly painted murals and the gray spires, called Casa de la Panadería (Bakery House) in honor of the bread shop over which it was built; it is now the tourist office. Opposite is the Casa de la Carnicería (Butcher Shop), now a police station.

The plaza is closed to motorized traffic, making it a pleasant place to sit at one of the sidewalk cafés, watching alfresco artists, street musicians, and madrileños from all walks of life. Sunday morning brings a stamp and coin market. Around Christmas the plaza fills with stalls selling trees, ornaments, and nativity scenes. ✉*Plaza Mayor, Sol.*

31 **Real Academia de Bellas Artes de San Fernando** *(St. Ferdinand Royal Academy of Fine Arts).* Designed by Churriguera in the waning baroque years of the early 18th century, this museum showcases 500 years of Spanish painting, from Ribera and Murillo to Sorolla and Zuloaga. The tapestries along the stairways are stunning. Because of a lack of personnel, only the first floor is now open, displaying paintings up to the 18th century, including Goya. The same building houses the **Instituto de Calcografía** (Prints Institute), which sells limited-edition prints from original plates engraved by Spanish artists, including Goya. Check listings for classical and contemporary concerts in the small upstairs hall. ✉*Alcalá 13, Sol* ☎*91/524–0864* *€3, free Wed.* ⏲*Tues.–Fri. 9–7, Sat. 9–2:30 and 4–7, Sun.–Mon. 9–2:30; free guided tour Wed. 5–7.*

WORTH NOTING

20 **Arab Wall.** The remains of the Moorish military outpost that became the city of Madrid are visible on Calle Cuesta de la Vega. The sections of wall here protected a fortress built in the 9th century by Emir Mohammed I. In addition to being an excellent defensive position, the site had plentiful water and was called *Mayrit,* Arabic for "source of life" (this is the likely origin of the city's name). All that remains of the *medina*—the old Arab city that formed within the walls of the fortress—is the neighborhood's crazy quilt of streets and plazas, which probably follow the same layout they followed more than 1,100 years ago. The park **Emir Mohammed I,** alongside the wall, is the site of concerts and plays in summer. ✉*Cuesta de la Vega, Palacio.*

22 ★ **Cava Baja.** The epicenter of the fashionable and historic La Latina neighborhood—a maze of narrow streets that extend south of Plaza Mayor and across Calle Segovia—Cava Baja is a diagonal street crowded with excellent tapas bars and traditional restaurants. Its lively atmosphere spills over into nearby streets and squares, including Almendro, Cava Alta, Plaza del Humilladero, and Plaza de la Paja. ✉ *Cava Baja, La Latina.*

18 **Campo del Moro** *(Moors' Field).* Below the Sabatini Gardens, but accessible only by an entrance on the far side, is the Campo del Moro. Enjoy the clusters of shady trees, winding paths, and lawn leading up to the Royal Palace. Inside the gardens is a **Museo de Carruajes** (Carriage Museum), displaying royal carriages and equestrian paraphernalia from the 16th through 20th century. ✉ *Paseo Virgen del Puerto s/n, Palacio.*

19 **Catedral de la Almudena.** The first stone of the cathedral (which adjoins the Royal Palace) was laid in 1883 by King Alfonso XII, and the result was consecrated by Pope John Paul II in 1993. Built on the site where the old church of Santa María de la Almudena stood (thought to be the city's main mosque during Arab rule), the new cathedral was intended to be Gothic in style, with needles and spires; funds ran low, so the design was simplified into the existing, more austere classical form. The cathedral has a wooden statue of Madrid's female patron saint, the Virgin of Almudena, reportedly discovered after the 1085 Christian Reconquest of Madrid. Legend has it that when the Arabs invaded Spain, the local Christian population hid the statue of the Virgin in a vault carved in the old Roman wall that encircled the city. When Christians reconquered Madrid in 1085, they looked for it, and after nine days of intensive praying—others say it was after a procession honoring the Virgin—the wall opened up to show the statue framed by two lighted candles. Its name is derived from the place where it was found: the wall of the old citadel (in Arabic, *almudeyna*). ✉ *Bailén 10, Palacio* ☎ *91/542–2200* 🎫 *Free* ⏲ *Daily 9–9.*

16 **Monasterio de la Encarnación** *(Monastery of the Incarnation).* Once connected to the Royal Palace by an underground passageway, this Augustinian convent now houses less than a dozen nuns. Founded in 1611 by the wife of Felipe III, it has several artistic treasures, including a reliquary where a vial with the dried blood of St. Pantaleón is said to liquefy every July 27. The ornate church has superb acoustics for medieval and Renaissance choral concerts. ✉ *Plaza de la Encarnación 1, Palacio* ☎ *91/454–8800 tourist information office* 🎫 *€3.60, €6 combined ticket with Convento de las Descalzas Reales* ⏲ *Tues.–Thurs. and Sat. 10:30–12:45 and 4–5:45, Fri. 10:30–12:45, Sun. 11–1:45.*

14 **Ermita de San Antonio de la Florida (Goya's tomb).** Built from 1792 to 1798 by the Italian architect Francisco Fontana, this neoclassical church was financed by King Carlos IV, who also commissioned Goya to paint the vaults and the main dome: he took 120 days to complete his assignment, painting alone, with only the help of a little boy who would stir the pigments for him. This gave him absolute freedom to depict events of the 13th century (Saint Anthony of Padua resurrecting a dead man) as if they had happened five centuries later, and using naturalistic images

never used before to paint religious scenes. Opposite the image of the frightening dead man on the main dome, Goya painted himself as a man covered with a black cloak. The frescoes' third-restoration phase ended in 2005, and visitors can now admire them in their full splendor. Goya, who died in Bordeaux in 1828, is buried here (without his head, since it was stolen in France), under an unadorned gravestone. ✉ *Glorieta de San Antonio de la Florida 5, Príncipe Pío* ☎ *91/542–0722* 🎫 *Free* ⏲ *Tues.–Fri. 9:30–8, Sun. 10–2.*

15 **Jardines Sabatini** *(Sabatini Gardens).* The formal gardens to the north of the Royal Palace are crawling with stray cats—but are still a pleasant place to rest or watch the sun set. ✉ *Bailén s/n, Palacio.*

10 **Museo del Traje** *(Costume Museum).* This museum traces the evolution of dress in Spain from the old burial garments worn by kings and nobles (very few pieces of which have withstood the erosion of time) and the introduction of French fashion by Phillip V to the 20th-century creations of couturiers such as Balenciaga and Pertegaz. The 18th century claims the largest number of pieces. Explanatory notes are in English and the museum has a superb restaurant. To get here, from Moncloa take Bus 46 or walk along the northeastern edge of Parque del Oeste. ✉ *Av. Juan de Herrera 2, Ciudad Universitaria* ☎ *91/549–7150* 🌐 *museodeltraje.mcu.es* 🎫 *€3, free Sat. after 2:30 and Sun.* ⏲ *Tues.–Sat. 9:30–7, Sun. 10–3.*

24 **Plaza de la Villa.** Madrid's town council used to meet in this medieval-looking complex starting in the Middle Ages, though in the second quarter of 2009 they moved to the new city hall headquarters in the post office building at Plaza Cibeles. The oldest building is the **Casa de los Lujanes,** on the east side—it's the one with the Mudejar tower. Built as a private home in the late 15th century, the house carries the Lujanes crest over the main doorway. Also on the plaza's east end is the brick-and-stone **Casa de la Villa,** built in 1629, a classic example of Madrid design with clean lines and spire-topped corner towers. Connected by an overhead walkway, the **Casa de Cisneros** was commissioned in 1537 by the nephew of Cardinal Cisneros. It's one of Madrid's rare examples of the flamboyant plateresque style, which has been likened to splashed water. ✉ *Mayor, Palacio* ⏲ *Closed to public except for free guided tour in Spanish Mon. at 5.*

30 **Puerta del Sol.** Crowded with people and exhaust—and now made even more chaotic by the construction of a massive underground station that has been delayed several times due to the discovery of archaeological remains—Sol is the nerve center of Madrid's traffic. The city's main subway interchange is below, and buses fan out from here. A brass plaque in the sidewalk on the south side of the plaza marks Kilometer 0, the spot from which all distances in Spain are measured. The restored 1756 French-neoclassical building near the marker now houses the offices of the regional government, but during Franco's reign it was the headquarters of his secret police, and it's still known folklorically as the Casa de los Gritos (House of Screams). Across the square are a bronze statue of Madrid's official symbol, a bear with a *madroño*

(strawberry tree), and a statue of King-Mayor Carlos III on horseback. ✉ *Puerta del Sol, Sol.*

25 **San Nicolás de los Servitas** *(Church of St. Nicholas of the Servitas).* This church tower is one of the oldest buildings in Madrid. There's some debate over whether it once formed part of an Arab mosque. It was more likely built after the Christian Reconquest of Madrid in 1085, but the brickwork and the horseshoe arches are evidence that it was crafted by either Mudejars (Moorish workers) or Spaniards well versed in the style. Inside, exhibits detail the Islamic history of early Madrid. *Plaza de San Nicolás, La Latina* ☎ *91/559–4064* *Donation suggested* *Tues.–Sat. 8:30 AM–9:30 AM and 6:30–9 PM, Sun. and Mon. 8:30–2 and 6–9; groups by appointment.*

27 **Teatro Real** *(Royal Theater).* Built in 1850, this neoclassical theater was long a cultural center for madrileño society. A major restoration project has left it filled with golden balconies, plush seats, and state-of-the-art stage equipment for operas and ballets. ✉ *Plaza de Isabel II, Palacio* ☎ *91/516–0660* *www.teatro-real.com.*

11 **Teleférico.** Kids love this cable car, which takes you from the Rosaleda gardens in the Parque del Oeste to the center of Casa de Campo in about 10 minutes—note though, that this is not the best way to get to the zoo if you're with children because the walk from where the cable car drops you off to the zoo and theme park is at least 2 km (1 mi), and you'll probably have to ask for directions. You're better off just taking the bus to the zoo and saving yourself the walk, or ride the Teleferico out, and back, then bus it to the zoo. ✉ *Estación Terminal Teleférico, Paseo de Pintor Rosales, at C. Marques de Urquijo, Moncloa* ☎ *91/541–7450* *€3.50 one-way, €5.10 round-trip* *Apr.–Sept., daily noon–dusk; Oct.–Mar., weekends noon–dusk.*

12 **Templo de Debod.** This 4th-century BC Egyptian temple was donated to Spain in thanks for its technical assistance with the construction of the Aswan Dam. The western side of the small park around the temple is the best place to watch Madrid's outstanding sunsets. ✉ *Pintor Rosales, Moncloa* ☎ *91/765–1008* *Free* *Oct.–Mar., Tues.–Fri. 9:45–1:45 and 4:15–6:15, weekends 10–2; Apr.–Sept., Tues.–Fri. 10–2 and 6–8, weekends 10–2; free guided tour Sat. at 11:30 and 12:30.*

13 **Zoo-Aquarium.** One of the most comprehensive zoological parks in Europe, Madrid's zoo houses a large variety of animals (including rarities such as an albino tiger) that are grouped according to their geographical origin. It also has a dolphinarium and a wild bird reservoir that hold entertaining exhibitions twice a day on weekdays and several more times on weekends. To get a good seat, arrive a few minutes before the show begins. The zoo is in the Casa de Campo, a large park right outside the western part of the city. It's best reached via subway to Príncipe Pío and then Bus 33. ✉ *Casa de Campo s/n Moncloa* ☎ *91/512–3770* *www.zoomadrid.com* *€18.50* *Feb.–Mar., weekdays 11–6, weekends 10:30–7; Apr.–June, weekdays 10:30–7, weekends 10:30–9; July–Aug., weekdays 10:30–7:30, weekends 10:30–9; Sept.–Oct., weekdays 11–6:30, weekends 10:30–7:30; Nov.–Dec., weekdays 11–6, weekends 10:30–6.*

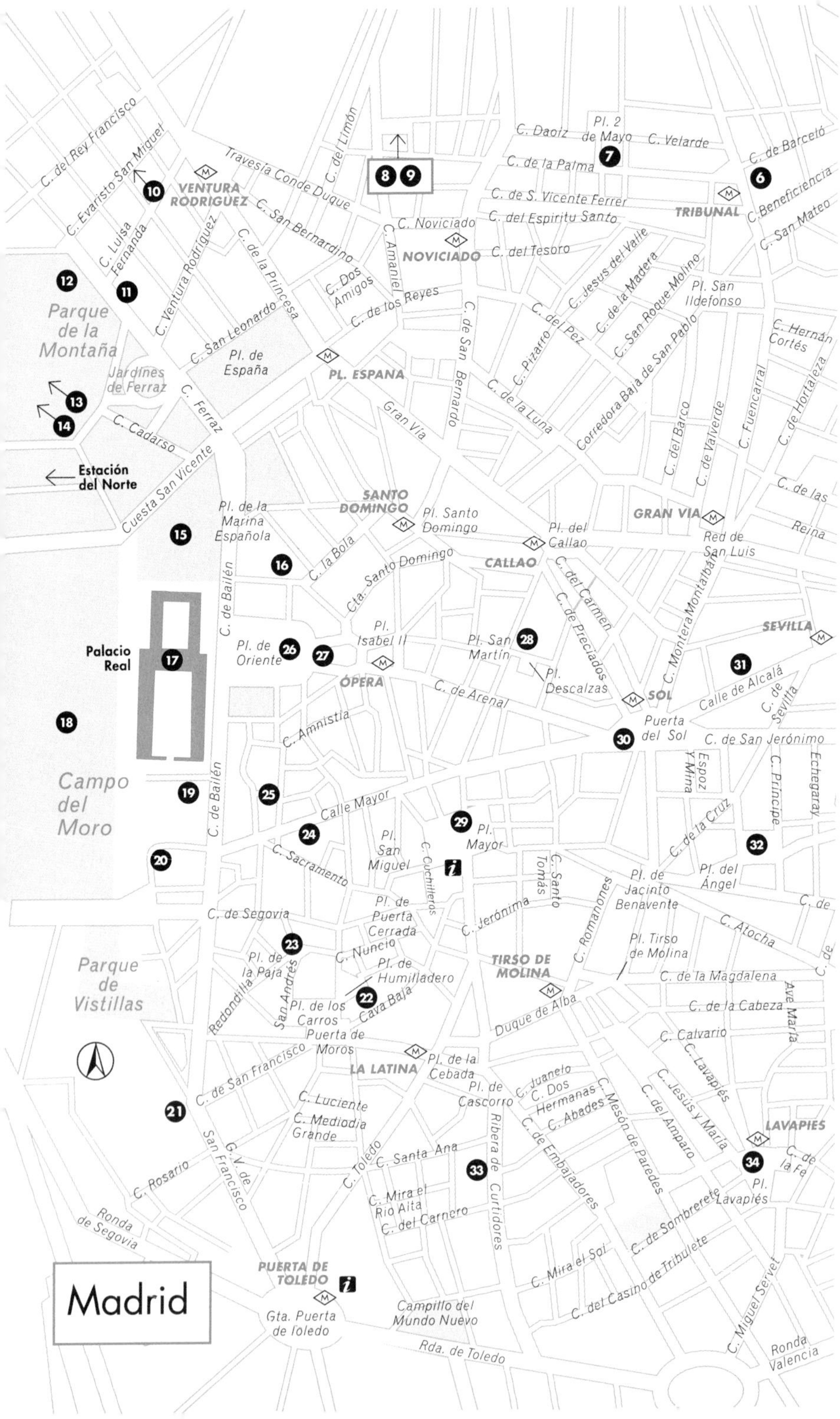
Madrid
C. del Rey Francisco
C. Evaristo San Miguel
C. Luisa Fernanda
Travesía Conde Duque
VENTURA RODRIGUEZ
C. San Bernardino
C. Ventura Rodríguez
C. de la Princesa
C. del Limón
C. Noviciado
C. Amaniel
NOVICIADO
C. Dos Amigos
C. de los Reyes
C. Daoiz
Pl. 2 de Mayo
C. Velarde
C. de la Palma
C. de S. Vicente Ferrer
C. del Espíritu Santo
C. del Tesoro
TRIBUNAL
C. de Barceló
C. Beneficiencia
C. San Mateo
C. Jesús del Valle
C. de la Madera
C. San Roque Molino
Pl. San Ildefonso
C. del Pez
C. Pizarro
C. Hernán Cortés
C. de San Bernardo
C. de la Luna
Corredora Baja de San Pablo
C. del Barco
C. de Valverde
C. Fuencarral
C. de Hortaleza
Parque de la Montaña
Jardines de Ferraz
C. San Leonardo
Pl. de España
PL. ESPANA
C. Ferraz
Gran Vía
C. Cadarso
Estación del Norte
Cuesta San Vicente
Pl. de la Marina Española
SANTO DOMINGO
Pl. Santo Domingo
Pl. del Callao
CALLAO
GRAN VIA
C. de las Reina
Red de San Luis
C. la Bola
Cta. Santo Domingo
C. de Bailén
C. del Carmen
C. de Preciados
C. Montera
Montalbán
SEVILLA
Palacio Real
Pl. de Oriente
Pl. Isabel II
Pl. San Martín
Pl. Descalzas
ÓPERA
C. de Arenal
SOL
Calle de Alcalá
C. de Sevilla
Puerta del Sol
C. de San Jerónimo
C. Amnistía
Espoz y Mina
C. Príncipe
Echegaray
Campo del Moro
Calle Mayor
C. de la Cruz
Pl. Mayor
Pl. San Miguel
C. Cuchilleros
C. Sacramento
C. Santo Tomás
Pl. de Jacinto Benavente
Pl. del Ángel
C. de
C. de Segovia
Pl. de Puerta Cerrada
C. Jerónima
C. Romanones
C. Atocha
Pl. Tirso de Molina
C. Nuncio
Pl. de la Paja
Pl. de Humilladero
TIRSO DE MOLINA
C. de la Magdalena
Parque de Vistillas
Redondilla
San Andrés
Pl. de los Carros
Cava Baja
Duque de Alba
C. de la Cabeza
Ave María
Puerta de Moros
C. Calvario
C. Lavapiés
LA LATINA
Pl. de la Cebada
C. de San Francisco
Pl. de Cascorro
C. Juanelo
C. Dos Hermanas
C. Abades
C. Mesón de Paredes
C. Jesús y María
C. del Amparo
C. Luciente
C. Mediodía Grande
C. de Embajadores
Ribera de Curtidores
LAVAPIES
C. de la Fe
G. V. de San Francisco
C. Rosario
C. Toledo
C. Santa Ana
C. Mira el Río Alta
C. del Carnero
Pl. Lavapiés
C. de Sombrerete
Ronda de Segovia
C. Mira el Sol
C. del Casino de Tribulete
PUERTA DE TOLEDO
Gta. Puerta de Toledo
Campillo del Mundo Nuevo
C. del Miguel Servet
Rda. de Toledo
Ronda Valencia
6
7
8
9
10
11
12
13
14
15
16
17
18
19
20
21
22
23
24
25
26
27
28
29
30
31
32
33
34

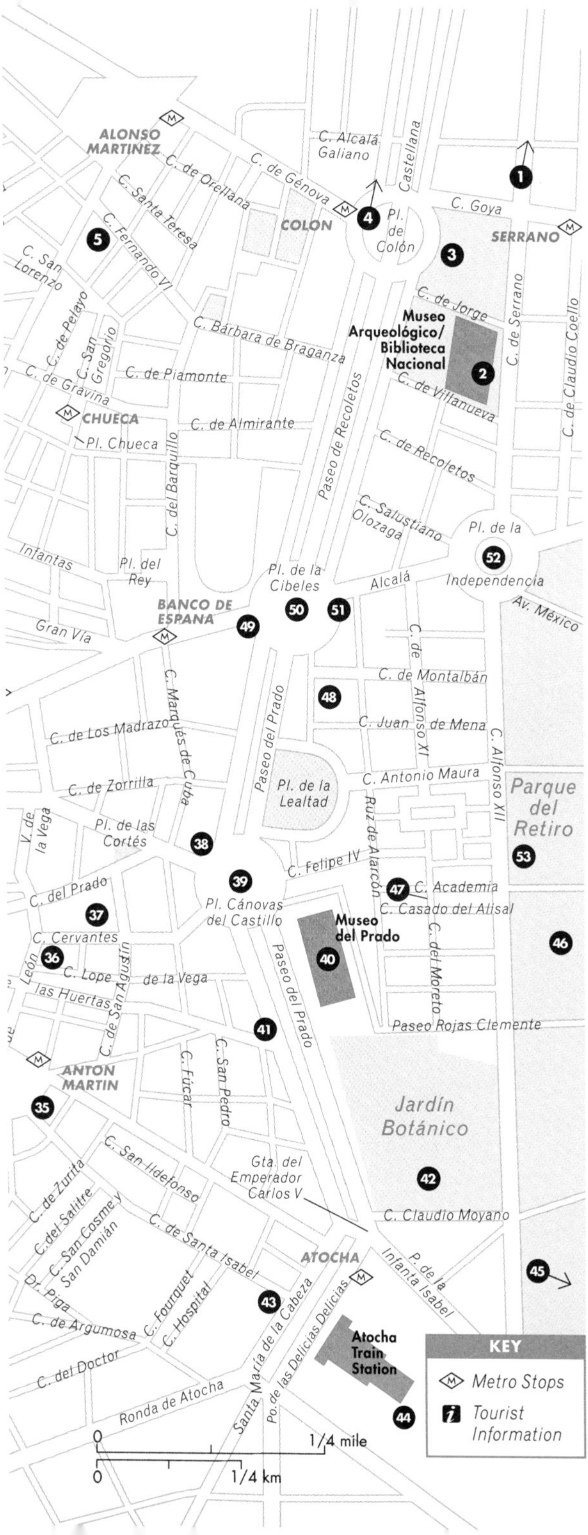

Arab Wall 20
Banco de España 49
Basílica de San Francisco el Grande . 21
CaixaForum 41
Campo del Moro (Moors' Field) 18
Casa de Cervantes 36
Casa de Lope de Vega 37
Casa Longoria 5
Casón del Buen Retiro 53
Catedral de la Almudena 19
Cava Baja 22
Centro de Arte Reina Sofía 43
Centro de Conde Duque 9
Cine Doré 35
El Rastro 33
Ermita de San Antonio de la Florida (Goya's tomb) 14
Estación de Atocha 44
Fuente de Neptuno 39
Jardín Botánico 42
Jardines Sabatini 15
Monasterio de las Descalzas Reales . 28
Monasterio de la Encarnación 16
Museo Arqueológico 2
Museo del Prado 40
Museo del Traje 10
Museo Lázaro Galdiano 1
Museo Municipal 6
Museo Municipal de Arte Contemporáneo 8
Museo Naval 48
Museo Sorolla 4
Museo Thyssen-Bornemisza 38
Palacio de Comunicaciones 51
Palacio Real 17
Parque del Buen Retiro 46
Plaza del 2 de Mayo 7
Plaza de la Cibeles 50
Plaza Colón 3
Plaza de Oriente 26
Plaza de la Paja 23
Plaza de la Villa 24
Plaza Lavapiés 34
Plaza Mayor 29
Plaza Santa Ana 32
Puerta de Alcalá 52
Puerta del Sol 30
Real Academia de Bellas Artes de San Fernando 31
Real Fábrica de Tapices 45
San Jerónimo el Real 47
San Nicolás de los Servitas 25
Teatro Real 27
Teleférico 11
Templo de Debod 12
Zoo-Aquarium 13

BARRIO DE LAS LETRAS

The Barrio de las Letras, long favored by tourists for its clean-cut looks and its fun places to hang out, was named for the many writers and playwrights from the Spanish golden age (16th and 17th centuries) who historically set up house within a few blocks of Plaza Santa Ana. Once a shelter to the *los madrileños castizos*—the word *castizo* means "authentic"—it is fast becoming one of the favored living areas of Spanish and foreign professionals affluent enough to pay the soaring real estate prices and willing to withstand the chaos of living within these lively and creative enclaves. Calle de las Huertas (full of bars and clubs), is pedestrian only, making the neighborhood even more attractive for walking around and socializing.

TOP ATTRACTIONS

41 **CaixaForum.** Swiss architects Jacques Herzog and Pierre de Meuron—who transformed a factory into London's Tate Modern—took this early-20th-century power station turned into a stunning arts complex fit to be considered the fourth point in Madrid's former triangle of great art institutions—the Prado, the Reina Sofía, and the Thyssen-Bornemisza museums. The Caixa belongs to one of the country's wealthiest foundations (La Caixa), and seems to float on a newly created sloped public plaza, with a tall vertical living garden designed by French botanist Patrick Blanc on its northern side contrasting with a geometic rust-colored roof. Inside, the huge exhibition halls display ancient as well as contemporary art, including a sample of La Caixa's own collection. There's a cafeteria on the fourth floor that has good views. ✉*Paseo del Prado 36, Cortes* ☎*91/330–7300* 🌐*obrasocial.lacaixa.es/centros/caixaforummadrid_es.html* 🎫*Free* 🕒*Daily 10–8.*

43 **Centro de Arte Reina Sofía** *(Queen Sofía Art Center).* Madrid's museum of modern art was once a hospital, the classical granite austerity of the space is somewhat relieved (or ruined, depending on your point of view) by the playful pair of glass elevator shafts on its facade. Three separate buildings joined by a common vault were added to the original complex in a renovation that was completed at the end of 2005. The first contains an art bookshop and a public library, the second a center for contemporary exhibitions, and the third an auditorium and restaurant/cafeteria managed by Sergi Arola of Gastro. The latter, although expensive, makes an excellent stop for a refreshment, be it a cup of tea or coffee, a snack, or even a cocktail.

The permanent artwork collection was reorganized in mid-2009. It now features 1,000 works on four different floors (the second and fourth floor of the Sabatini building and the ground and first floor of the Nouvel annex), and despite concentrating on painting, puts a much higher emphasis on other artistic manifestations such as photography and cinema. The new collection breaks apart from the traditional habit of grouping works around major artistic movements and individual artists. Instead the current director has chosen to contextualize the works of the great modern masters—Pablo Picasso, Joan Miró, and Salvador Dalí—and of other big local names, such as Juan Gris, Jorge Oteiza, Pablo Gargallo, Julio Gonzalez, Eduardo Chillida, and Antoni

A GOOD WALK: BARRIO DE LAS LETRAS

Allow between one and a half and two hours for this tour, assuming you'll spend some time visiting Lope de Vega's house.

Begin in the Barrio de las Letras, at the **Plaza Santa Ana** 32, hub of the theater district in the 17th century and now a center of nocturnal activity. The plaza's notable buildings include, at the lower end, the Teatro Español. Walk up to the sunny Plaza del Ángel (next to the ME Reina Victoria hotel) and turn down Calle de Las Huertas, past the ancient olive tree and plant nursery behind the San Sebastián church—once the church cemetery. This was the final resting place of Lope de Vega, whose sepulchre is inside the church. Walk down Huertas to No. 18, Casa Alberto, an ancient (though excellent) bar and restaurant as well as the house where Miguel de Cervantes was living when he finished the second part of *Don Quijote.* Continue to Calle León, named for a lion kept here long ago by a resident Moor. A short walk to your left brings you to the corner of Calle Cervantes. As the plaque on the wall overhead attests, *Don Quijote's* author died on April 23, 1616, in what is now called the **Casa de Cervantes** 36. Down the street, at No. 11, is the **Casa de Lope de Vega** 37, where the "Spanish Shakespeare," Fray Lope Félix de la Vega Carpio, lived and worked.

A right from Calle Cervantes onto Calle Quevedo takes you past the Basque *sidrería* (cider house) Zerain down to the corner across from the convent and church of the Trinitarias Descalzas (Discalced, or Barefoot, Trinitarians, a cloistered order of nuns). Just before the corner, on the wall to your left, is a plaque honoring Quevedo, the 17th-century poet who gives the street its name, and who lived in a building that was once on this site. (Credited with having the best command of the Spanish language ever, Quevedo acquired the building and ousted a tenant who couldn't pay his bills because of his gambling debts. This tenant just happened to be another famous poet, Góngora, with whom Quevedo sustained a poetry rivalry that had lasted for decades.)

Miguel de Cervantes was buried inside the Trinitarias Descalzas. His remains were misplaced at the end of the 17th century and haven't been found since.

Tàpies, into broader narratives that attempt to better explain the evolution of modern art. This means, for instance, that in the first room of the collection (201), you'll find a selection of Goya's "Disasters of War" engravings (the proto-romantic and proto-surrealist great master serving as a precursor of the rupturist movements of the 20th century) next to one of the first movies ever recorded, "Employees leaving the Lumière family," by the Lumière brothers, and that you won't find the Picassos or Dalís all displayed together in a single room, but scattered around the 38 rooms of the permanent collection.

The museum's showpiece is Picasso's *Guernica,* in room 206 on the second floor. The huge black-and-white canvas—now displayed in better lighting and without distracting barriers—depicts the horror of the Nazi Condor Legion's bombing of the ancient Basque town of

Gernika in 1937, during the Spanish civil war. The work, something of a national shrine, was commissioned from Picasso by the Republican government for the Spanish pavilion at the 1937 World's Fair in an attempt to gather sympathy for the Republican side during the civil war—the museum rooms adjacent to the *Guernica*'s now reconstruct the artistic significance of the Spanish participation in the World's Fair, with works from other artists such as Miró, Josep María Sert, and Alexander Calder. *Guernica* did not reach Madrid until 1981, as Picasso had stipulated in his will that the painting return to Spain only after democracy was restored.

The fourth floor in the Sabatini building is devoted to art after the Second World War, and those in the Nouvel annex display paintings, sculptures, photos, videos, and installations of the last quarter of the 20th century. ✉ *Santa Isabel 52, Atocha* ☎ *91/467–5062* 🌐 *museoreinasofia.mcu.es* 🎫 *€6, free Sat. after 2:30 and all day Sun.; €14.40 combined Paseo del Arte (Art Walk) ticket for the Prado, Reina Sofia, and Thyssen-Bornemisza* ⏲ *Mon. and Wed.–Sat. 10–9, Sun. 10–2:30.*

See "The Art Walk" box on page 66 for how to include the Centro de Arte Reina Sofía as part of an art-theme Paseo del Arte excursion.

38 **Museo Thyssen-Bornemisza.** The newest of Madrid's "big three" art centers (not including CaixaForum), the Thyssen opened in 1992 and occupies spacious galleries filled with natural light in the late-18th-century Villahermosa Palace, finished in 1771. This ambitious collection of almost 1,000 paintings traces the history of Western art with examples from every important movement, from the 13th-century Italian Gothic through 20th-century American pop art. The works were gathered from the 1920s to the 1980s by Swiss industrialist Baron Hans Heinrich Thyssen-Bornemisza and his father. At the urging of his wife, the baron donated the entire collection to Spain in 1993. A renovation in 2004 increased the number of paintings on display to include the baron's wife's personal collection (considered of lesser quality). Critics have described the museum's paintings as the minor works of major artists and the major works of minor artists, but, be that as it may, the collection traces the development of Western humanism as no other in the world.

Fodor's Choice ★

One of the high points here is Hans Holbein's *Portrait of Henry VIII* (purchased from the late Princess Diana's grandfather, who used the money to buy a Bugatti sports car). American artists are also well represented; look for the Gilbert Stuart portrait of George Washington's cook, and note how closely the composition and rendering resemble the artist's famous painting of the Founding Father. Two halls are devoted to the impressionists and postimpressionists, including many works by Pissarro and a few each by Renoir, Monet, Degas, Van Gogh, and Cézanne. Find Pissarro's *Saint-Honoré Street in the Afternoon, Effect of Rain* for a jolt of mortality, or Renoir's *Woman with a Parasol in a Garden* for a sense of bucolic beauty lost.

Within 20th-century art, the collection is strong on dynamic German expressionism, with some works by Georgia O'Keeffe and Andrew Wyeth along with Hoppers, Bacons, Rauschenbergs, and Lichtensteins.

The temporary exhibits can be fascinating, and in summer, are sometimes open until 11 PM. A rooftop restaurant serving tapas and drinks is open in the summer until past midnight. Note that you can buy tickets in advance online. ✉ *Paseo del Prado 8, Cortes* ☎ *91/369–0151* 🌐 *www.museothyssen.org* 💳 *Permanent collection €6, temporary exhibition €5, combined €9; €14.40 combined Paseo del Arte (Art Walk) ticket for the Prado, Reina Sofía, and Thyssen-Bornemisza* ⏲ *Tues.–Sun. 10–7.*

See "The Art Walk" box on page 66 for how to include the Museo Thyssen-Bornemisza as part of an art-theme Paseo del Arte excursion.

2

32 **Plaza Santa Ana.** This plaza was the heart of the theater district in the 17th century—the Golden Age of Spanish literature—and is now the center of Madrid's thumping nightlife. A statue of 17th-century playwright Pedro Calderón de la Barca faces the **Teatro Español,** where playwrights such as Lope de Vega, Tirso de Molina, Calderón de la Barca, and Valle Inclán released some of their plays. (Opposite the theater and off to the side of a hotel is the diminutive **Plaza del Ángel,** with one of Madrid's best jazz clubs, the Café Central.) One of Madrid's most famous cafés, the former Ernest Hemingway hangout **Cervecería Alemana,** is on Plaza Santa Ana and is still catnip to writers and poets. ✉ *Plaza Santa Ana s/n, Barrio de las Letras.*

WORTH NOTING

49 **Banco de España.** This massive 1884 building, Spain's central bank, takes up an entire block. It's said that part of the nation's gold reserves are held in vaults that stretch under the Plaza de la Cibeles traffic circle all the way to the fountain. (Some reserves are also stored in Fort Knox, in the United States.) The bank is not open to visitors, but the architecture is worth viewing. If you can dodge traffic well enough to reach the median strip in front of it, the fountain and palaces with the Puerta de Alcalá arch in the background make a lovely photo. ✉ *Paseo del Prado s/n, at Plaza de la Cibeles, Cortes.*

36 **Casa de Cervantes.** A plaque marks the private home where Miguel de Cervantes Saavedra, author of *Don Quijote de la Mancha,* committed his final words to paper: "*Puesto ya el pie en el estribo, con ansias de la muerte...*" ("One foot already in the stirrup and yearning for death..."). The Western world's first runaway best seller, and still one of the most widely translated and read books in the world, Cervantes' spoof of a knightly novel playfully but profoundly satirized Spain's rise and decline while portraying man's dual nature in the pragmatic Sancho Panza and the idealistic Don Quijote, ever in search of wrongs to right. ✉ *C. Cervantes and C. León, Barrio de las Letras.*

37 **Casa de Lope de Vega.** Considered the Shakespeare of Spanish literature, Fray Lope Félix de la Vega Carpio (1562–1635) is best known as Lope de Vega. A contemporary and adversary of Cervantes, he wrote some 1,800 plays and enjoyed great success during his lifetime. His former home is now a museum with an intimate look into a bygone era: everything from the whale-oil lamps and candles to the well in the tiny garden and the pans used to warm the bedsheets brings you closer to the great dramatist. The space was enlarged in 2008 and now accommodates

THE ART WALK

With a visit to the Prado—at least two or three hours—and a short stroll in Parque del Buen Retiro, you can do this walk in about five hours. Set aside a morning or an afternoon each to return to the Reina Sofía and Thyssen-Bornemisza.

■ TIP→The *Paseo del Arte* (Art Walk) pass allows you to visit the three museums for €14.40. You can buy it at any of the three museums, and you don't have to visit all of them on the same day.

Madrid's three major art museums are all within walking distance of one another via the Paseo del Prado. The Paseo was designed by Carlos III as a leafy nature walk with glorious fountains and a botanical garden for respite in scorching summers.

Start on Plaza de las Cortés, down Calle San Jerónimo, right next to the **Plaza Santa Ana** ㉜ tapas area. The granite building on the left, its stairs guarded by bronze lions, is the Congreso, lower house of Las Cortes, Spain's parliament. Walk past the landmark Westin Palace on the right to the **Fuente de Neptuno** ㊴, in the Plaza Cánovas del Castillo, on the wide Paseo del Prado. The **Museo del Prado** ㊵ is across the boulevard to the right. On your left is the **Museo Thyssen-Bornemisza** ㊳, and across the plaza on the left is the elegant Ritz hotel, alongside the obelisk dedicated to all those who have died for Spain. Tackle one or both of these museums now, or continue strolling.

Turning right and walking south on Paseo del Prado, you'll bump into a sloping plaza leading up to the **CaixaForum** ㊶, a free and impressive exhibition arts center. Across the street from it you'll find the **Jardín Botánico** ㊷ and **Estación de Atocha** ㊹, a railway station on the southern edge of the Glorieta (roundabout) del Emperador Carlos V resembling the overturned hull of a ship. The **Centro de Arte Reina Sofía** ㊸, site of Picasso's *Guernica*, is across the street in the building with the exterior glass elevators, best accessed by walking up Calle Atocha from the station and taking the first left.

A block after the Ministry of Agriculture (back at the big roundabout noted by the immense pile of painted tiles and winged statues), make a left on Calle Alfonso XII, which puts the Anthropology Museum on your left. Calle Alfonso XII runs along the west side of the vast **Parque del Buen Retiro** ㊻ (most just call it Parque del Retiro). If you walk down Felipe IV you can get back to the Plaza Cánovas del Castillo and the Fuente de Neptuno.

Back at the fountain, turn right and walk up the right side of Paseo del Prado (or, even better, the central promenade). Cross Calle Montalbán. Finally, you'll reach the **Plaza de la Cibeles** ㊿. Turn right at Cibeles, walk up Calle Alcalá, toward Madrid's unofficial symbol, the Puerta de Alcalá, and, again, the Parque del Buen Retiro.Continue north for the **Museo Arqueológico** ❷, which adjoins the National Library, and the **Plaza Colón** ❸.

Consider also visiting the **Museo Sorolla** ❹, on Calle Martínez Campos in Chamberí, or **Museo Lázaro Galdiano** ❶, on Calle Serrano in Salamanca.

poetry readings and workshops. It offers a 45-minute guided tour in English starting every half hour that runs through the playwright's professional and personal life (covering his intense love life), but also touching on the XVII century's traditions. Don't miss the Latin inscription over the door: PARVA PROPIA MAGNA / MAGNA ALIENA PARVA (small but mine big / big but someone else's small). ✉ *C. Cervantes 11, Santa Ana* ☎ *91/429–9216* *Free* ⏲ *Mon.–Sun. 10–3.*

5 **Casa Longoria.** A moderniste palace commissioned in 1902 by the businessman and politician Javier González Longoria, the Casa Longoria was built by José Grases Riera, a Catalan architect who was also a disciple of Gaudí. The winding shapes, the plant motifs, and the wrought-iron balconies are reminiscent of Gaudí's works in Barcelona. The building's jewel is its main iron, bronze, and marble staircase; unfortunately this is off-limits to tourists, because the building is now in private hands. ✉ *Fernando VI 4, Chueca.*

39 **Fuente de Neptuno** *(Neptune's Fountain).* At Plaza Cánovas del Castillo, midway between the Palace and Ritz hotels and the Prado and Thyssen-Bornemisza museums, this fountain is at the hub of Madrid's Paseo del Arte. It is a rallying point for Atlético de Madrid soccer triumphs (counterpoint to Real Madrid's celebrations at the Fuente de la Cibeles up the street). ✉ *Plaza Cánovas del Castillo, Cortes.*

CHUECA AND MALASAÑA

Once known primarily for thumping nightlife and dodgy streets, these are two Madrid neighborhoods that have changed significantly in the past decade. Money from City Hall and from private investors was used to renovate buildings and public zones, thereby drawing prosperous businesses and many professional and young inhabitants. Chueca, especially, has been completely transformed by the gay community. Noisy bars and overcrowding nightclubs are still trademarks of both areas, but they now also make for pleasant daytime walks and have many inexpensive restaurants, some of the hippest shops, a great cultural life, and inviting summer terraces.

Chamberí is a large area to the north of Chueca and Malasaña. It's mostly residential, but has a few lively spots, especially the streets around Plaza de Olavide.

TOP ATTRACTIONS

9 **Centro de Conde Duque.** Built by Pedro de Ribera in 1717–30 to accommodate the Regiment of the Royal Guard, this imposing building has gigantic proportions (its facade is 250 yards long) and was used as a military academy and an astronomical observatory in the 19th century. A fire damaged the upper floors in 1869, and after some decay it was partially renovated and turned into a cultural and arts center. The center features temporary art exhibitions in some of its spaces, including the public and historical libraries. In summer, outdoor concerts are held in the main plaza. ✉ *Conde Duque 9 and 11, Malasaña* ⏲ *Tues.–Sat. 10–2 and 6–9, Sun. 10:30–2 exhibitions only.*

NEED A BREAK?

Walking past the **Cisne Azul** ✉ *Gravina 19, Chueca* ☎ *900/521–3799* You may wonder why such a bland-looking bar is crowded with locals in a neighborhood that's obsessed with style. The reason is simple: wild mushrooms. In Spain there are more than 2,000 different species, and here they bring the best from the province of León, grill them on the spot with a pinch of olive oil and serve them in a variety of ways: with a fried egg yoke, scallops, *foie*, etc. We suggest: you elbow yourself up to the bar and get the popular *mezcla de setas* (mushroom sampler) with fried egg yoke. You'll discover that there's more to mushrooms than what's offered at your local supermarket.

WORTH NOTING

6 **Museo Municipal.** Founded in 1929 on what was formerly a hospice from the 17th century, this museum displays paintings, drawings, pictures, ceramics, furniture, and other objects explaining Madrid history. There is a good exhibition on Madrid that will be best enjoyed by those who speak Spanish and already know a bit about the city's history; but the ornamented facade—a baroque jewel by Pedro de Ribera—and the painstakingly precise, nearly 18-foot model of Madrid, a project coordinated by León Gil de Palacio in 1830, are two exhibits anyone can appreciate. As of the time of writing, the museum is temporarily closed for some major renovations, scheduled to reopen sometime in late 2010. ✉ *Fuencarral 78, Malasaña* ☎ *91/532–6499* *Free* *Tues.–Fri. 9:30–8, weekends 10–2.*

NEED A BREAK?

If you find yourself out on a pleasant day and want to eat or dine out for just a few euros, stop at **La vita e'bella** (✉ *Calle Espíritu Santo XX* or *Plaza de San Ildefonso 5, Malasaña 91/521–4108*), grab any of their savory takeaway dishes (strombolis, calzones, pizzas, arancinis, or pastas), and enjoy it with other young madrileños while sitting on a bench at the nearby and bustling Plaza de San Ildefonso or Plaza de Juan Pujol.

8 **Museo Municipal de Arte Contemporáneo.** To reach this museum inside the Centro de Conde Duque, take the door to your right after the entrance and walk up the stairs. Founded in 2001, the museum displays 200 modern artworks acquired by City Hall since 1980. The paintings, graphic artwork, sculpture, and photography are mostly by local artists. ✉ *Conde Duque 9 and 11, Malasaña* ☎ *91/588–5928* *Free* *Tues.–Sat. 10–2 and 5:30–9, Sun. 10:30–2:30.*

7 **Plaza del 2 de Mayo.** On this unassuming square stood the Monteleón Artillery barracks, where some brave Spanish soldiers and citizens fought Napoléon's invading troops on May 2, 1808. The arch that now stands in the middle of the plaza was once at the entrance of the old barracks, and the sculpture under the arch represents captains Daoiz and Velarde. All the surrounding streets carry the names of that day's heroes. The plaza, now filled with spring and summer terraces, makes a good place to stop for a drink. One of the most popular cafés, Pepe Botella, carries the demeaning nickname the people of Madrid gave to Joseph Bonaparte, Napoléon's brother, who ruled Spain from 1808 to

CLOSE UP

The Events of May 2nd

In 1808 Spain was ruled by Carlos IV, a king more interested in hunting than in the duties attached to government. The king delegated power to his wife, María Luisa, and she to the chief minister, Godoy, one of the country's most despised statesmen of all time. Godoy succeeded in tripling the country's debt in 20 years, and signed the secret Convention of Fontainebleau with Napoléon, which allowed the French troops to freely cross Spain on their way to Portugal. Napoléon's plans were different—he intended to use the convention as an excuse to annex Spain to his vast domains. While the French troops entered Spain, the Spanish people, tired of the inept king and the greedy Godoy, revolted against the French in Aranjuez on March 17, 1808, hoping Napoléon would hand the throne over to the king's elder son, Prince Ferdinand. In the following days Carlos IV abdicated, and his son was proclaimed the new king, Fernando VII. Napoléon had already chosen a person for that job, though—one of his brothers, José Bonaparte. The shrewd French emperor managed to attract the Spanish royal family to France and had Carlos IV, his wife, and Ferdinand VII imprisoned in Bayona, France, and his brother placed on the Spanish throne.

When French General Murat arrived in Madrid a few days later, on March 23, 1808, with 10,000 men (leaving 20,000 more camped outside the city) following Napoléon's orders, Madrid's Captain General Francisco Javier Negrete ordered the Spanish troops to remain in their military quarters, arguing that resistance was futile. On the morning of May 2, a raging group of civilians revolted in front of the Palacio Real, fearing the French troops intended to send Francisco de Paula, King Carlos IV's youngest son, to Bayona with his brother and father. Gunfire ensued, and word of the events spread all over the city. People rose up, fighting the mightier French troops with whatever they could use as weapons. Two captains, Daoiz and Velarde, and a lieutenant, Ruiz, disobeyed Negrete's orders and quartered at the Monteleón Artillery barracks, which stretched from what is now Plaza de 2 de mayo to Calle Carranza. Helped by a small group of soldiers and some brave citizens who had marched to the barracks from the Royal Palace, the group resisted the French for three hours, doing so with very little ammunition, since they couldn't access the armory.

Daoiz and Velarde died in the bloody fight. Ruiz managed to escape, only to die from his wounds later. Murat's forces executed soldiers and civilians throughout the city, including in the Casa de Campo and what's now the Parque del Oeste, captured by Goya in one of his two famous paintings of the executions—both restored in 2008 to celebrate the bicentennial of the events. The events marked the beginning of the five-year War of Independence against the French. The remains of the three military heroes, together with those who were executed at Paseo del Prado, are now held in an obelisk-mausoleum at Plaza de la Lealtad.

Paradoxically, José Bonaparte proved to be a good ruler, implementing some wise renovations in the then quite congested and unhygienic city. He built new squares, enlarged key streets, and moved some of the cemeteries outside the city.

1813: Botella ("bottle" in English) is a reference to his alleged—but false—fondness for drink. ✉ *Plaza del 2 de Mayo, Malasaña.*

4 **Museo Sorolla.** See the world through the exceptional eye of Spain's most famous Impressionist painter, Joaquín Sorolla (1863–1923), who lived and worked most of his life at the home and garden he designed. Entering this diminutive but cozy domain is a little like stepping into a Sorolla painting, because it's filled with the artist's best-known works, most of which shimmer with the bright Mediterranean light and color of his native Valencia. ✉ *General Martinez Campos 37, Chamberí* ☎ *91/310–1584* 🌐 *museosorolla.mcu.es* 🎫 *€2.40, free Sun.* 🕐 *Tues.–Sat. 9:30–8, Sun. 10–3.*

RASTRO AND LAVAPIÉS

Bordering the old city wall (torn down by the mid-19th century) to the south, Rastro and Lavapiés were Madrid's industrial areas in the 17th and 18th centuries. The old slaughterhouses in the Rastro area (and all of the other businesses related to that trade) are the origins of today's flea market, which spreads all over the neighborhood on Sundays. Lavapiés has the highest concentration of immigrants—mostly Chinese, Indian, and North African—in Madrid, and as a result, the area has plenty of ethnic markets and inexpensive restaurants as well as bustling crowds, especially at the Plaza de Lavapíes. Purse snatching and petty crime are not uncommon in these two areas, so be alert.

TOP ATTRACTIONS

33 **El Rastro.** Named for the *arrastre* (dragging) of animals in and out of the slaughterhouse that once stood here and, specifically, the *rastro* (blood trail) left behind, this site explodes into a rollicking flea market every Sunday from 10 to 2, with dozens and dozens of street vendors with truly bizarre bric-a-brac ranging from stolen earrings to sent postcards to thrown-out love letters. There are also more formal shops where it's easy to turn up treasures such as old iron grillwork, a marble tabletop, or a gilt picture frame. The shops (not the vendors) are also opened during the week, allowing for quieter and more serious bargaining. Even so, people-watching on Sundays is the best part. For serious browsing and bargaining, any *other* morning is a better time to turn up treasures. ✉ *Ribera de los Curtidores s/n, Rastro.*

WORTH NOTING

35 **Cine Doré.** A rare example of Art Nouveau architecture in Madrid, the hip Cine Doré shows movies from the Spanish National Film Archives and eclectic foreign films for €2.50 per session. Showtimes are listed in newspapers under "*Filmoteca.*" The pink neon-trimmed lobby has a sleek café-bar and a bookshop. ✉ *Santa Isabel 3, Lavapiés* ☎ *91/369–1125* 🕐 *Tues.–Sun.; 4–5 shows daily, starting at 5:30* PM.

34 **Plaza Lavapiés.** The heart of the historic Jewish barrio, this plaza remains a neighborhood hub. To the east is the Calle de la Fe (Street of Faith), which was called Calle Sinagoga until the expulsion of the Jews in 1492. The church of **San Lorenzo** at the end was built on the site of the razed synagogue. Legend says Jews and Moors who chose baptism over exile

had to walk up this street barefoot to the ceremony to demonstrate their new faith. ✉ *Top of Calle de la Fe, Lavapiés.*

2

SALAMANCA AND RETIRO

By the mid-19th century, city officials decided to expand Madrid beyond the 1625 wall erected by Phillip IV. The result was a handful of new, well-laid-out neighborhoods. Salamanca became a home to the working classes, though today it draws a more mixed crowd, along with most of the city's expensive restaurants and shops. The Retiro holds the city's best-known park. The area between the western side of the park and the Paseo del Prado showcases some of the city's most exclusive, expensive, and sought-after real estate.

TOP ATTRACTIONS

2 **Museo Arqueológico** *(Museum of Archaeology).* The biggest attraction here is a replica of the early cave paintings in Altamira. (Access to the real thing, in Cantabria Province, is highly restricted.) Also here, look for *La Dama de Elche,* a bust of a wealthy, 5th-century BC Iberian woman, and notice that her headgear is a rough precursor to the mantillas and hair combs still associated with traditional Spanish dress. The ancient Visigothic votive crowns are another highlight; discovered in 1859 near Toledo, they are believed to date back to the 8th century. The museum—now under renovation—shares its neoclassical building with the **Biblioteca Nacional** (National Library). ✉ *Calle Serrano 13, Salamanca* ☎ *91/577–7912, 91/580–7823 library* 🌐 *man.mcu.es* 🎟 *Free (while the renovations last)* 🕑 *Museum Tues.–Sat. 9:30–8, Sun. 9:30–3. Library (now closed for renovations) weekdays 9–9, Sat. 9–2.*

40 ★ **Museo del Prado** *(Prado Museum). See the In-focus feature "El Prado: Madrid's Brush with Greatness."* See "The Art Walk" box on page 66 for how to include the Centro de Arte Reina Sofía as part of an art-theme Paseo del Arte excursion. A combined ticket for the Prado, Reina Sofia, and Thyssen-Bornemisza costs €14.40.

NEED A BREAK?

La Dolores (✉ *Plaza de Jesús 4, Barrio de las Letras* ☎ *91/429–2243*) is an atmospheric ceramic-tile bar that's the perfect place for a beer or glass of wine and a plate of olives. It's a great alternative to the Prado's basement cafeteria and is just across the Paseo, and one block up on Calle Lope de Vega.

46 **Parque del Buen Retiro** *(The Retreat).* Once the private playground of royalty, Madrid's crowning park is a vast expanse of green encompassing formal gardens, fountains, lakes, exhibition halls, children's play areas, outdoor cafés, and a **Puppet Theater** featuring free slapstick routines that even non–Spanish speakers will enjoy. Shows take place on Saturday at 1 and on Sunday at 1, 6, and 7. The park is especially lively on weekends, when it fills with street musicians, jugglers, clowns, gypsy fortune-tellers, and sidewalk painters, along with hundreds of Spanish families out for a walk. The park holds a book fair in May and occasional flamenco concerts in summer. From the entrance at the Puerta de Alcalá, head straight toward the center and you can find the **Estanque**

Continued on page 79

EL PRADO: MADRID'S BRUSH WITH GREATNESS

Don't let the Prado's immense size intimidate you. You can't see it all in a day. But if you zero in on some of the museum's undisputed masterpieces, then you can have a rich art experience without collapsing.

Let's face it: While the Prado has sculptures, drawings, and other treasures spanning centuries, it's "why-go"—it's "*must*-go"—is its paintings.

Most of the attention, all of it deserved, goes to the Prado's perennial headliners: Diego Velázquez, El Greco, and Francisco Goya. The museum's most famous canvas is Velázquez's *Las Meninas* (*The Maids of Honor*), which combines a self-portrait of the artist at work with a mirror reflection of the King Philip IV and Queen Doña Mariana of Austria in a revolutionary interplay of space and perspectives. Picasso was so taken with this work that he painted several copies of it in his own abstract style (most of these are on display in the Picasso Museum in Barcelona). If you find fellow visitors taken with the painting and need to wait a bit before studying it, you can while away some time with the 46 other Velázquez works in the collection; the Prado owns all but a handful of the paintings ever created by the artist.

Likewise, of the Prado's 42 El Grecos, the two that stir up the most interest are his passionately spiritual *The Resurrection* and *The Adoration of the Shepherds*. And Goya fans will have 119 oil-on-canvas paintings for their delectation, including one of his more scandalous works, *The Naked Maja*.

CONTACT INFORMATION

✉ Paseo del Prado s/n, 28014 Madrid
☎ (+34) 91 330 2800.

HOURS OF OPERATION

9AM to 8PM, Tues. to Sat., 9AM to 7PM Sun., except 9AM to 9PM on Christmas Eve, New Year's Eve, and Three Kings Day (January 6). Closed Monday, New Year's Day, Good Friday, Fiesta del Trabajo (May 1), and Christmas.

ADMISSION

€6. Free Mon. to Sat. 6AM–8PM, Sun. 5AM–8PM. To avoid lines, buy tickets in advance online.

GETTING HERE

Ⓜ Atocha (line 1); by bus, take line 9, 10, 14, 19, 27, 34, 37, or 45.

The Trinity by El Greco, 1577. Oil on canvas.

A MUCH-NEEDED FACE LIFT

A collective "it's about time" rang forth during the Prado's long-awaited facelift. Although the Prado is the most-visited tourist destination in Spain, its patrons were frequently stymied by erratic opening hours and especially frustrated by the lack of amenities that they take for granted in other museums of the Prado's stature. The Madrid museum, one of Europe's best, had languished comfortably, but maddeningly, in the status quo of the 19th century. A gleaming new addition by Spanish architect Rafael Moneo, which opened in June 2007, brought an end to all that.

(top) A Velázquez statue graces the museum's old entrance. (bottom) Visitors now enter via a new $202 million wing, designed by Rafael Moneo.

Like I. M. Pei's pyramid at Paris's Louvre, Moneo's new steel-and-glass wedge has thrust the Prado dynamically into the 21st century. With the expansion, the Prado has doubled its exhibition space to a total of 16,000 square meters (52,800 square feet). Visitors now enter into a reception hall in the new wing and walk through a corridor to the green space of the Retiro Park, where the building connects with the formerly sleepy cloister of the Jerónimos Church beyond. In between is a 400-seat auditorium, temporary exhibitions, a library, studios for art conservation, and expanded shops and eateries.

The best part of the expansion is that the museum now showcases thousands more of its collection. Previously, more than three-quarters of the 9,000 paintings of art in Prado's world-class collection remained in storage, with only 2,000 of the most intriguing pieces on display in the elegant 1819-vintage galleries. A re-hang is underway, as curators fit in some of these previously hidden works.

El Prado

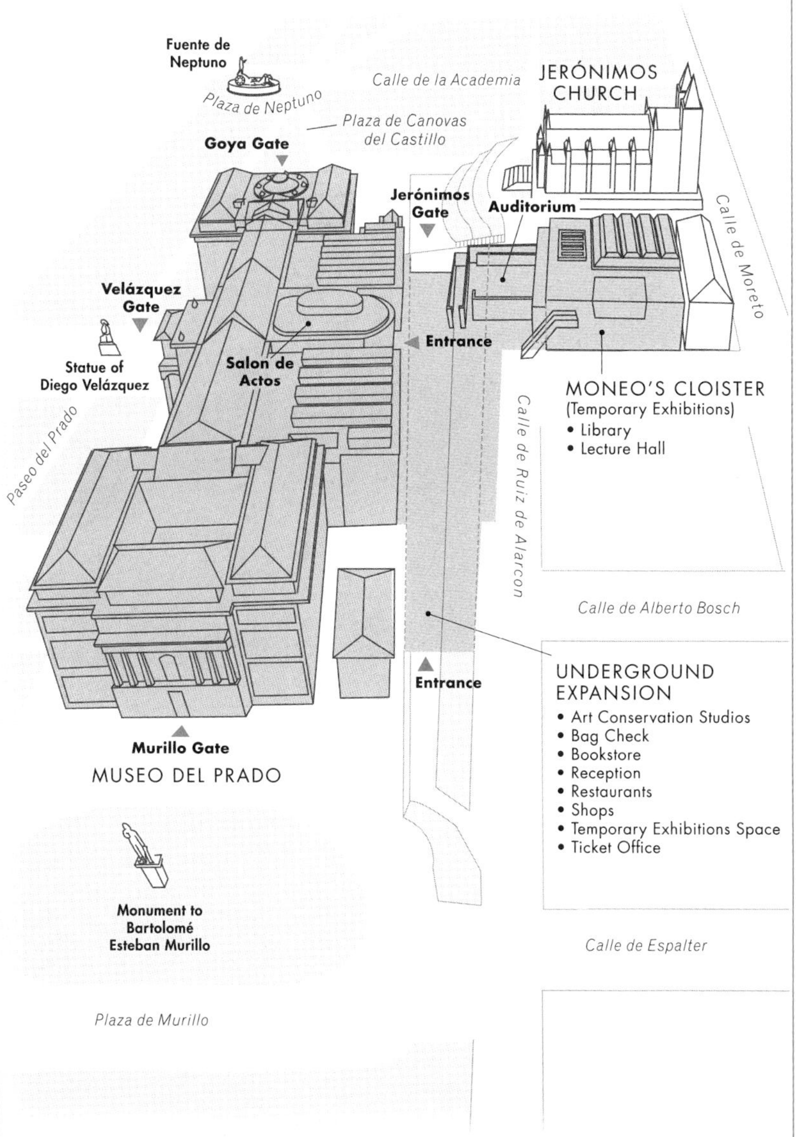
Fuente de Neptuno
Plaza de Neptuno
Calle de la Academia
JERÓNIMOS CHURCH
Plaza de Canovas del Castillo
Goya Gate
Jerónimos Gate
Auditorium
Calle de Moreto
Velázquez Gate
Statue of Diego Velázquez
Salon de Actos
Entrance
Paseo del Prado
MONEO'S CLOISTER
(Temporary Exhibitions)
• Library
• Lecture Hall
Calle de Ruiz de Alarcon
Calle de Alberto Bosch
UNDERGROUND EXPANSION
• Art Conservation Studios
• Bag Check
• Bookstore
• Reception
• Restaurants
• Shops
• Temporary Exhibitions Space
• Ticket Office
Entrance
Murillo Gate
MUSEO DEL PRADO
Monument to Bartolomé Esteban Murillo
Calle de Espalter
Plaza de Murillo

THREE GREAT MASTERS

FRANCISCO DE GOYA 1746–1828

Goya's work spans a staggering range of tone, from bucolic to horrific, his idyllic paintings of Spaniards at play and portraits of the family of King Carlos IV contrasting with his dark, disturbing "black paintings." Goya's attraction to the macabre assured him a place in posterity, an ironic statement at the end of a long career in which he served as the official court painter to a succession of Spanish kings, bringing the art of royal portraiture to unknown heights.

Francisco de Goya

Goya found fame in his day as a portraitist, but he is admired by modern audiences for his depictions of the bizarre and the morbid. Beginning as a painter of decorative Rococo figures, he evolved into an artist of great depth in the employ of King Charles IV. The push-pull between Goya's love for his country and his disdain for the enemies of Spain yielded such masterpieces as *Third of May 1808,* painted after the French occupation ended. In the early 19th century, Goya's scandalous *The Naked Maja* brought him before the Spanish Inquisition, whose judgment was to end his tenure as a court painter.

DIEGO VELÁZQUEZ 1599–1660

A native of Seville, Velázquez gained fame at age 24 as court painter to King Philip IV. He developed a lifelike approach to religious art in which both saints and sinners were specific people rather than generic types. The supple brushwork of his ambitious history paintings and portraits was unsurpassed. Several visits to Rome, and his friendship with Rubens, made him the quintessential baroque painter with an international purview.

Diego Velázquez

DOMENIKOS THEOTOKOPOULOS (AKA "EL GRECO") 1541–1614

El Greco's art was one of rapture and devotion, but beyond that his style is almost impossible to categorize. "The Greek" found his way from his native Crete to Spain through Venice; he spent most of his life in Toledo. His twisted, elongated figures imbue both his religious subjects and portraits with a sense of otherworldliness. While his palette and brushstrokes were inspired by Italian Mannerism, his approach to painting was uniquely his own. His inimitable style left few followers.

Domenikos Theotokopoulos

SIX PAINTINGS TO SEE

SATURN DEVOURING ONE OF HIS SONS (1819)

FRANCISCO DE GOYA Y LUCIENTES

In one of fourteen nightmarish "Black Paintings" executed by Goya to decorate the walls of his home in the later years of his life, the mythological God Kronos, or Saturn, cannibalizes one of his children in order to derail a prophecy that one of them would take over his throne. *Mural transferred to canvas.*

Saturn Devouring One of His Sons

THE GARDEN OF DELIGHTS OR LA PINTURA DEL MADROÑO (1500)

HIËRONYMUS BOSCH

Very little about the small-town environment of the Low Countries where the Roman Catholic Bosch lived in the late Middle Ages can explain his thought-provoking, and downright bizarre, paintings. His depictions of mankind's sins and virtues, and the heavenly rewards or demonic punishments that await us all, have fascinated many generations of viewers, who have called the devout painter a "heretic," and most recently compared him to Salvador Dalí for his disturbingly twisted renderings. In this three-panel painting, Adam and Eve are created, mankind celebrates its humanity, and hell awaits the wicked, all within a journey of 152 inches! *Wooden Triptych.*

The Garden of Delights

LAS MENINAS (THE MAIDS OF HONOR) (1656-57)

DIEGO VELÁZQUEZ DE SILVA

Velázquez's masterpiece of spatial perspective occupies pride-of-place in the center of the Spanish baroque galleries. In this complex visual game, *you* are the king and queen of Spain, reflected in a distant hazy mirror as the court painter (Velázquez) pauses in front of his easel to observe your features. The actual subject is the Princess Margarita, heir to the throne in 1656. *Oil on canvas.*

Las Meninas

STILL LIFE (17th Century; no date)

FRANCISCO DE ZURBARÁN

Best known as a painter of contemplative saints, Zurbarán, a native of Extremadura who found success working with Velázquez in Seville, was a peerless observer of beauty in the everyday. His rendering of the surfaces of these homely objects elevates them to the stature of holy relics, urging the viewer to touch them. But the overriding mood is one of serenity and order. *Oil on canvas.*

Still Life

DAVID VICTORIOUS OVER GOLIATH (1599)
MICHELANGELO MERISI (CARAVAGGIO)

Caravaggio used intense contrasts between his dark and light passages (called *chiaroscuro* in Italian) to create drama in his bold baroque paintings. Here, a surprisingly childlike David calmly ties up the severed head of the giant Philistine Goliath, gruesomely featured in the foreground plane of the picture. The astonishing realism of the Italian painter, who was as well known for his tempestuous personal life as for his deftness with a paint brush, had a profound influence on 17th century Spanish art. *Oil on canvas.*

David Victorious over Goliath

THE TRINITY (1577)
DOMENIKOS THEOTOKOPOULOS (EL GRECO)

Soon after arriving in Spain, Domenikos Theotokopoulos created this view of Christ ascending into heaven supported by angels, God the Father, and the Holy Spirit. It was commissioned for the altar of a convent in Toledo. The acid colors recall the Mannerist paintings of Venice, where El Greco was trained, and the distortions of the upward-floating bodies show more gracefulness than the anatomical contortions that characterize his later works. *Oil on canvas.*

The Trinity

PICASSO AND THE PRADO

The Prado contains no modern art, but one of the greatest artists of the 20th century had an important history with the museum. **Pablo Picasso** (1891–1973) served as the director of the Prado during the Spanish civil war, from 1936 to 1939. The Prado was a "phantom museum" in that period, Picasso once noted, since it was closed for most of the war and its collections hidden elsewhere for safety.

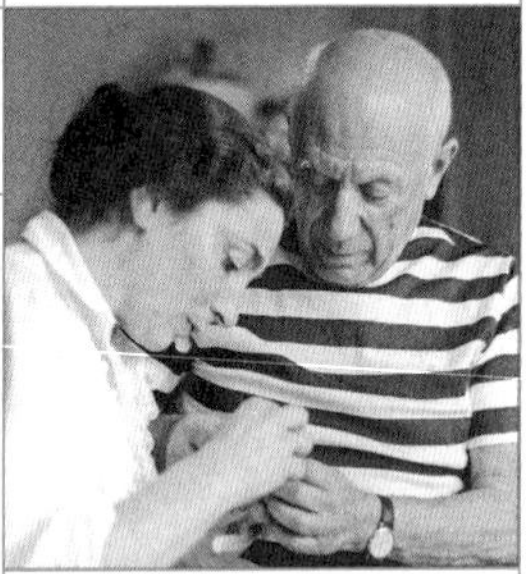
Picasso with his wife Jacqueline Roque

Later that century, the abstract artist's enormous *El Guernica* hung briefly on the Prado's walls, returning to Spain from the Museum of Modern Art in 1981. Picasso had stipulated that MoMA give up his anti-war masterpiece after the death of fascist dictator Francisco Franco, and it was displayed at the Prado and the Casón del Buen Retiro until the nearby Reina Sofia was built to house it in 1992.

Picasso in his atelier

(lake), presided over by a grandiose equestrian statue of King Alfonso XII, erected by his mother. Just behind the lake, north of the statue, is one of the best of the park's many cafés.

The 19th-century **Palacio de Cristal** (Crystal Palace), southeast of the Estanque, was built to house exotic plants from the Philippines, a Spanish possession at the time. This airy marvel of steel and glass sits on a base of decorative tile. Next door is a small lake with ducks and swans. Along the Paseo del Uruguay at the park's south end is the **Rosaleda** (Rose Garden), bursting with color and heavy with floral scents for most of the summer. West of the Rosaleda, look for a statue called the **Ángel Caído** (Fallen Angel), which madrileños claim is the only one in the world depicting the prince of darkness before (during, actually) his fall from grace. ✉*Puerta de Alcalá, Retiro* 🎫*Free.*

WORTH NOTING

53 A five-minute walk from the museum is the **Casón del Buen Retiro.** This annex, once a ballroom, and the formal gardens in the Retiro are all that remain of Madrid's second royal complex—at one time it filled the entire neighborhood. A 10-year, regal restoration of the complex, completed by the beginning of 2008, rejuvenated the original splendor of the fresco paintings in the main vault by the baroque artist Luca Giordano. After a short exhibition with some of the other Napolitan artist's works, this building reopened in late 2008 as the Prado's official study center, but you need to be a researcher to access the library. ✉*Alfonso XII s/n, Retiro* ☎*91/330–2800* 🌐*www.museodelprado.es/.*

44 **Estación de Atocha.** A steel-and-glass hangar, Madrid's main railroad station was built in the late 19th century by Alberto Palacio Elissague, the architect who became famous for his work with Ricardo Velázquez in the creation of the Palacio de Cristal (Crystal Palace) in Madrid's Retiro Park. Closed for years, and nearly torn down, Atocha was restored and refurbished by Spain's internationally acclaimed architect Rafael Moneo. ✉*Paseo de Atocha s/n, Retiro* ☎*91/420–9875.*

42 **Jardín Botánico** *(Botanical Garden).* Just south of the Prado, the gardens provide a pleasant place to stroll or sit under the trees. True to the wishes of King Carlos III, they hold many plants, flowers, and cacti from around the world. ✉*Plaza de Murillo 2, Retiro* ☎*91/420–3017* 🌐*www.rjb.csic.es* 🎫*€2* ⏲*Nov.–Feb., daily 10–6; Mar. and Oct., daily 10–7; Apr. and Sept., daily 10–8; May–Aug., daily 10–9.*

1 **Museo Lázaro Galdiano.** This stately mansion of writer and editor José Lázaro Galdiano (1862–1947), located just a 10-minute walk across the Castellana from the Museo Sorolla, has decorative items and paintings by Bosch, El Greco, Murillo, and Goya, among others. The remarkable collection comprises five centuries of Spanish, Flemish, English, and Italian art. Bosch's *St. John the Baptist* and the many Goyas are the stars of the show, with El Greco's *San Francisco de Assisi* and Zurbarán's *San Diego de Alcalá* close behind. ✉*Calle Serrano 122, Salamanca* ☎*91/561–6084* 🌐*www.flg.es* 🎫*€4, free Sun.* ⏲*Wed.–Mon. 10–4:30.*

48 **Museo Naval.** Anyone interested in Patrick O'Brian's painstakingly detailed naval novels or in old vessels and war ships will be bouncing off

the walls experiencing the 500 years of Spanish naval history displayed in this museum. The collection, which includes documents, maps, weaponry, paintings, and hundreds of ship models of different sizes, is best enjoyed by those who speak some Spanish. Beginning with Queen Isabella and King Ferdinand's reign and the expeditions led by Christopher Columbus and the conquistadors, exhibits also reveal how Spain built a naval empire that battled Turkish, Algerian, French, Portuguese, and English armies and commanded the oceans and the shipping routes for a century and a half. Moving to the present day, the museum covers Spain's more recent shipyard and naval construction accomplishments. ✉*Paseo del Prado 5, Retiro* ☎*91/523–8789* 🌐*www.museonavalmadrid.com* 🎫*Free* ⏲*Tues.–Sun. 10–2. Guided tour, in Spanish only, weekends at 11:30.*

51 **Palacio de Comunicaciones.** This ornate building on the southeast side of Plaza de la Cibeles, built at the start of the 20th century, is a massive stone compound of French, Viennese, and traditional Spanish influences. It now houses the office of the mayor of Madrid and still functions as the main post office. ✉*Plaza de Cibeles, Retiro* ☎*902/197197* ⏲*Weekdays 8:30 AM–9:30 PM, Sat. 8:30–2.*

50 **Plaza de la Cibeles.** A tree-lined walkway runs down the center of Paseo del Prado to the grand Plaza de la Cibeles, where the famous Fuente de la Cibeles (Fountain of Cybele) depicts the nature goddess driving a chariot drawn by lions. Even more than the officially designated bear and arbutus tree of Madrid's coat of arms, this monument, beautifully lighted at night, has come to symbolize Madrid—so much so that during the civil war, patriotic madrileños risked life and limb to sandbag it as Nationalist aircraft bombed the city. ✉*Plaza de la Cibeles, Cortes.*

3 **Plaza Colón.** Named for Christopher Columbus, this plaza has a statue of the explorer (identical to the one in Barcelona's port) looking west from a high tower in the middle of the square. Beneath the plaza is the **Teatro Fernán-Gómez** (☎*91/480–0300*), a performing-arts facility. Behind Plaza Colón is **Calle Serrano,** the city's premier shopping street (think Gucci, Prada, and Loewe). Stroll in either direction on Serrano for some window-shopping. ✉*Plaza Colón, Salamanca.*

52 **Puerta de Alcalá.** This triumphal arch was built by Carlos III in 1778 to mark the site of one of the ancient city gates. You can still see the bomb damage inflicted on it during the civil war. ✉*C. de Alcalá s/n, Retiro.*

45 **Real Fábrica de Tapices.** Tired of the previous monarchs' dependency on the Belgium and Flemish thread mills and craftsmen, King Philip V decided to establish the Royal Tapestry factory in Madrid in 1721. It was originally housed near Alonso Martínez, and moved to its current location in 1889. From early on some of Europe's best artists collaborated in the factory's tapestry designs. The most famous was Goya, who produced 63 cartoons (rough plans), some of which can be seen at the Prado. It's said that he put so much detail into them that the craftsmen complained he'd made their work miserable. The factory, still in operation, applies traditional weaving techniques from the 18th and 19th centuries to modern and classic designs—including Goya's. Carpets are available for sale (you can suggest your own

design), at skyrocketing prices (€1,000 a square meter [10¾ square feet] for carpets, €9,000–€12,000 a square meter for tapestries). The factory also runs a training center that teaches traditional weaving techniques to unemployed teenagers, who later become craftspeople. ✉*Fuenterrabía 2, Atocha* ☎*91/434–0550* 🌐*www.realfabricadetapices.com* 🎟*€4* ⏲*Weekdays 10–2; guided tour every 30 min starting at 10.*

47 **San Jerónimo el Real.** Ferdinand and Isabella used this church and cloister as a *retiro,* or place of meditation—hence the name of the nearby park. The building was devastated in the Napoleonic Wars, then rebuilt in the late 19th century. ✉*Moreto 4, behind Prado Museum, Retiro* ☎*91/420–3578* ⏲*Daily 10–1 and 5–8:30.*

TAPAS BARS AND CAFÉS

Use the coordinate (✥B2) at the end of each listing to locate a site on the corresponding map.

The best tapas areas in Madrid are in the La Latina, Chueca, Sol, Santa Ana, Salamanca, and Lavapiés neighborhoods. Trendy La Latina's has a concentration of good tapas bars in Plaza de la Paja and on Cava Baja, Cava Alta, and Almendro streets. Chueca is colorful and lively, and the tapas bars there reflect this casual and cheerful spirit in the food and decor. The bars around Sol are quite traditional (many haven't changed in decades), but the constant foot traffic guarantees customers (and means they don't always have to strive for better food and service). In touristy Santa Ana, avoid the crowded and usually pricey tapas bars in the main plaza and go instead to the ones on the side streets. The tapas bars in the Salamanca neighborhood are more sober and traditional, but the food is often excellent. In Lavapiés, the neighborhood with the highest concentration of immigrants, there are plenty of tapas bars serving Moroccan, African, and Asian-inspired food.

Most of the commendable cafés you'll find in Madrid can be classified into two main groups. The ones that have been around for many years (Café Gijóon, Café del Círculo, Café de Oriente), where writers, singers, poets, and discussion groups still meet and where conversations are usually more important than the coffee itself; and the new ones (Faborit, Diurno, Delic, Anglona), which are tailored to hip and hurried urbanites and tend to have a wider product selection, modern decor, and Wi-Fi access.

TAPAS BARS

CHUECA

El Bocaíto. This spot has three dining areas and more than 130 tapas on the menu, including 15 to 20 types of *tostas* (toast topped with prawns, egg and garlic, pâté with caviar, cockles, and so on), and surely the best *pescaito frito* (deep-fried whitebait) in the city. ✉*Libertad 6, Chueca* ☎*91/532–1219* ⏲*Closed Sun. and Aug.* ✥*F3.*

La Bardemcilla. Candid photos of Javier Bardem on the wall will tip you off to the fact that this homey bar belongs to Bardem's family. There are plenty of tables, and a good selection of wines and tapas.

Highlights include the grilled vegetables, *huevos estrellados* (fried eggs with potatoes and sausage), and the *croquetas* (béchamel and meat—usually chicken or ham—with a fried bread-crumb crust). There's a fixed-price lunch for less than €10. ✉ *Augusto Figueroa 47, Chueca* ☎ *91/521–4256* ⊗ *Closed Sun. No lunch Sat.* ✣ *F2.*

LA LATINA

Casa Lucas. Some of the favorites at this small, cozy bar with a short but creative selection of homemade tapas include the *Carinena* (grilled pork sirloin with caramelized onion), *Madrid* (scrambled eggs with onion, *morcilla,* or blood pudding, and pine nuts in a tomato base), and *huevos a la Macarena* (puff pastry with mushrooms, fried artichokes, fried ham, béchamel, and pine nuts). ✉ *Cava Baja 30, La Latina* ☎ *91/365–0804* ⊗ *No lunch Wed.* ✣ *C5.*

El Almendro. Getting a weekend seat in this rustic old favorite is quite a feat, but drop by any other time and you'll be served great *roscas* (round hot bread filled with various types of cured meats), *huevos rotos* (fried eggs with potatoes), *pistos* (sautéed vegetables with a tomato base), or *revueltos* (a favorite is the *habanero,* scrambled eggs with fava beans and blood pudding). Note that drinks and food need to be ordered separately (a bell rings when your food is ready). ✉ *Almendro 13, La Latina* ☎ *91/365–4252* ✣ *C5.*

Juana la Loca. This tempting spot serves sophisticated and unusual tapas that can be as pricey as they are delightful (don't miss the *tortilla de patatas*—Spanish omelet; it's made with caramelized onions and is sweeter and juicier than the ones you might find elsewhere). If you drop by the bar during the weekend, go early, when the tapas are freshest. On weekdays, order from the menu. ✉ *Plaza Puerta de Moros 4, La Latina* ☎ *91/364–0525* ⊗ *Closed Mon.* ✣ *B5.*

Matritum. This is one of those places where the wine list is three times the length of the menu; it's also quieter and cozier than most of the tapas spots in this bar-filled neighborhood. Some of the stars include *patatas a los cinco quesos* (five-cheese potatoes), *vieiras gratinadas* (grilled grated scallops), and *delicias de berenjena* (eggplant in three textures with sun-dried tomatoes and goat cheese). ✉ *Cava Alta 17, La Latina* ☎ *91/365–8237* ⊗ *No lunch weekdays* ✣ *C5.*

Txirimiri. It's easy to spot this Basque tapas place by the people that gather at its door. The crush of humanity may make it uncomfortable at times, but the food is worth being jostled a bit. Among the highlights, try the Unai hamburger (fried in tempura with foie) or the Spanish omelet, one of the city's best. Show up early and you may be lucky enough to get one of the tables in the back. ✉ *Humilladero 6, La Latina* ☎ *91/364–1196* ⊗ *No lunch Mon, and Tues.* ✣ *C5.*

LAVAPIÉS

La Bodega de Lete. The laid-back spirit of the neighborhood is represented here in bold colors and unassuming decor, but it's the simple yet superb *raciones* (large portions for sharing) that keep the six tables here in high demand. Split an *entraña* (a cut of grilled beef), the *patatas chimichurri* (potatoes with a garlic, oregano, and parsley sauce), or the Atlantic salad—all with the young house Rioja. Your smile won't fade when the tab comes. ✉*Buenavista 42, Lavapiés* ☎*91/530–0259* ⌚*Closed Mon. No dinner Sun. No lunch Tues.–Sat.* ✥*E6.*

MALASAÑA

Bodega de la Ardosa. Big wooden barrels serve as tables at this charming tavern with more than 100 years of history. There's great vermouth and draft beer, along with specialties such as *salmorejo* (a thick, cold tomato soup similar to gazpacho), a very juicy *tortilla de patatas* (Spanish omelet) made by the owner's mother, and *croquetas,* including varieties with béchamel and prawns (*carabineros*) as well as aromatic cheese (*Cabrales*). Expect to hear a good selection of jazz. ✉*Colón 13, Malasaña* ☎*91/521–4979* ✥*E2.*

PALACIO

Taberneros. This museumlike wine bar has wine racks and decanters exhibited all over the tavern, and a menu that includes both local specialties (*croquetas,* grilled mussels, duck sirloin, fresh liver) and Asian-inspired ones (tuna burger, sirloin in soy sauce). A tapas sampler and a weekly lunch menu are also available. Show up early or prepare to wait awhile. ✉*Santiago 9, Palacio* ☎*91/542–2460* ⌚*No lunch Mon.* ✥*C4.*

RETIRO

Laredo. The nine tables here are some of the most sought after in the city—you need to reserve two or three days in advance—but you can also walk in and order at the bar. Variety and quality walk hand in hand here: Laredo serves fresh and simple food (asparagus, prawns, and clams), as well as more scrumptious and elaborate dishes, such as the superb mushroom risotto with duck liver, rice with chicken, small rabbit chops, and mushroom *croquetas.* If the exhaustive menu overwhelms you, go ahead and just follow the waiters' advice). ✉*Menorca 14, Retiro* ☎*91/573–3061* ⌚*Closed Sun and Aug.* ✥*H3.*

SALAMANCA

Estay. A two-story bar and restaurant with functional furnishings, this place has quickly become a landmark among the city's posh crowd for outstanding food. The tapas menu is plentiful and diverse. Specialties include the *tortilla española con atún y lechuga* (Spanish omelet with tuna fish and lettuce), and the *rabas* (fried calamari). There is a dish of the day for €12, and a few tapas samplers. ✉*Hermosilla 46, Salamanca* ☎*91/578–0470* ⌚*Closed Sun.* ✥*H1.*

Jurucha. If you're shopping in the Serrano area, this is the place to go for a quick bite. There's a long bar with all the food on display; tapas highlights include the *gambas con allioli* (prawns with a garlic-mayo sauce), fried *empanadillas* (small empanadas), and Spanish omelets. A small seating space has wooden stools, and there are tables at the back. ✉*Ayala 19, Salamanca* ☎*91/575–0098* ⌚*Closed Sun and Aug.* ✥*H1.*

BARRIO DE LAS LETRAS

Estado Puro. At this hyper-sleek dining space (with a great summer terrace) cooking wizard Paco Roncero reinvents popular dishes such as the *patatas bravas* or the *pepito de ternera* (a beef sandwich which resembles a kebab). Don't skip out on dessert; try his version of the almond-based Tarta de Santiago. ✉ *Plaza Cánovas del Castillo 4, Barrio de las Letras* ☎ *91/330–2400* ⊙ *No dinner Sun.* ⊕ *1:F4.*

El Cervantes. Clean, elegant and very popular among locals (be prepared to elbow up to the bar on the weekends), this spot serves plenty of hot and cold tapas and one of best and most refreshing draught beers in the city. Good choices are the *pulpo a la gallega* (octopus with potatoes, olive oil, and paprika), any of the *tostas* (toast topped with mushroom, shrimp, etc.), or the tapas sampler. ✉ *Plaza de Jesús 7, Barrio de las Letrasa* ☎ *91/429–6093* ⊕ *F4.*

La Dolores. Usually crowded and noisy, this bar serves one of the best draft beers in Madrid. It also has a decent, though pricey, selection of tapas, which you can enjoy at one of the few tables in the back. ✉ *Plaza de Jesús 4, Barrio de las Letras* ☎ *91/429–2243* ⊕ *F5.*

La Parpusa de Moratín. This bohemian spot shares the bustling spirit of traditional taverns but in a modern setting. A tranquil dining area at the back and hearty food options like *ropa vieja* (shredded beef in a tomato base) and *rabo de toro* (bull's tail in red wine) bring it closer to a restaurant. ✉ *Moratín 19, Antón Martín* ☎ *91/360–0943* ⊙ *Closed Sun. No dinner Mon.* ⊕ *F5.*

CAFÉS

CHAMBERÍ

Cacao Sampaka. Heaven on earth for any chocolate lover, this café–shop sells cute little paninis, tantalizing blends of fresh juices, a great selection of pastries, and, of course, chocolate in just about every form and flavor imaginable. (They also have a top-notch selection of English-language magazines.) ✉ *Orellana 4, Chamberí* ☎ *91/319–5840* ⊙ *Closed Sun. except 1st Sun. of month* ⊕ *F1.*

SOL

Café del Círculo *(La Pecera).* Spacious and elegant, with large velvet curtains, marble columns, hardwood floors, painted ceilings, and sculptures scattered throughout, this eatery inside the famous art center Círculo de Bellas Artes feels more like a private club than a café. Expect a bustling, intellectual crowd. ✉ *Marqués de Casa Riera 2, Sol* ☎ *91/522–5092* ⊕ *F3.*

Chocolatería San Ginés. Gastronomical historians suggest that the practice of dipping explains Spaniards' lasting fondness for superthick hot chocolate. Only a few of the old places where this hot drink was served exclusively (with crispy churros), such as this *chocolatería,* remain standing. Open from 6 PM to 7 AM, it also has the privilege of being the last stop for many a bleary-eyed soul after a night out. ✉ *Pasadizo de San Ginés, enter by Arenal 11, Sol* ☎ *91/365–6546* ⊙ *Closed Mon.* ⊕ *C4.*

Faborit. A chain spot bold enough to open next door to Starbucks had better serve some great coffee, and for less money; Faborit does, and offers a warm, high-tech environment to boot. Whether your feet hurt and the sun is blazing, or it's chilly out and you're tired of shivering, indulge in the mug of cappuccino with cream or the chai cappuccino—you'll still be able to splurge later. Their first café is two blocks away from the Puerta del Sol, but since then they've also opened up branches on Paseo del Prado, near the CaixaForum, across from the Palace Hotel, and on San Bernardo, just a block off Gran Vía. ✉*Alcalá 21, Sol* ☎*91/521–8616* ⊕*E3.*

PALACIO

Café de Oriente. This landmark spot has a magnificent view of the Royal Palace and its front yard. Inside, the café is divided into two sections—the left one serves tapas and raciones; the right serves more elaborate food. The café also has a splendid terrace that's open when the sun is out. ✉*Plaza de Oriente 2, Palacio* ☎*91/547–1564* ⊕*B3.*

MALASAÑA

El Jardín Secreto. The romantic and exotic setting, with eclectic furniture and lamps (all for sale), savory chocolates, and a generous selection of tasty pastries makes this "secret garden" a perfect place to sip and unwind. ✉*Conde Duque 2, Malasaña* ☎*91/364–5450* ⊕*D1.*

Lolina Café. Diverging in its spirit and decor (think vintage furniture and pop art wallpaper) from the classier baroque cafés of the neighborhood, this hectic spot attracts the young and techno-savvy with its free Wi-Fi and its good assortment of teas, chocolates, cakes, and drinks. ✉*Espíritu Santo 9, Malasaña* ☎*667/201–169* ⊕*D1.*

CHUECA

Café Gijón. Madrid's most famous literary café has hosted highbrow *tertulias* (discussion groups that meet regularly to hash out the political and artistic issues of the day) since the 19th century. ✉*Paseo de Recoletos 21, Chueca* ☎*91/521–5425* ⊕*G2.*

Diurno. A Chueca landmark, this café, DVD rental stop, and takeout spot is spacious, with large windows facing the street, sleek white chairs and couches, and lots of plants. Diurno serves healthful snacks and sandwiches along with some indulgent desserts. ✉*San Marcos 37, Chueca* ☎*91/522–0009* ⊕*F3.*

Maison Blanche. Here's multitasking at its best: In front you can shop for wine, pricey bottled waters, and Champagne; in back eat at the restaurant-café serving international dishes such as crepes, couscous, pastas, soups salads. If you have a sweet tooth, don't miss the tiramisu or chocolate cake. ✉*C. Piamonte 10, Chueca* ☎*91/522–8217* ⊙*Closed Sun. nights after 5* PM ⊕*F2.*

LA LATINA

Anglona. A good option for those dining in La Latina neighborhood, this small café serves a variety of hot chocolates (with cognac, caramel, mint, and more) and imported teas, as well as some sweets, including chocolate cake, carrot cake, and custard crème mille-feuille. At night, sip *mojitos* or *caipirinhas* and take in the scene-setting jazz or bossanova. ✉*Príncipe de Anglona 3, La Latina* ☎*91/365–0587* ⊙*Closed Mon.* ⊕*B5.*

Delic. This warm, inviting café is a hangout for Madrid's trendy crowd. Besides the *patatitas con mousse de parmesano* (potatoes with a Parmesan-cheese mousse) and zucchini cake, homesick travelers will find carrot cake, brownies, and pumpkin pie among the offerings. ✉*Costanilla de San Andrés 14, Plaza de la Paja, La Latina* ☎*91/364–5450* ⊙*Closed Mon. and Aug. 1–15* ⊕*B5.*

Giangrossi. Madrid's tastiest, most fashionable, and priciest ice cream parlor chain started off with this spot on the northern border of Malasaña and has been expanding ever since. Creative flavors include *dulce de leche*, mascarpone, and *turrón* (a type of candy eaten at Christmas, usually with dried fruit in it), as well as pink grapefruit, pineapple, and melon sorbets. What's with the funny-looking, triangular scoops? That's the way they serve a cone in Argentina. (✉*Cava Baja 40, La Latina* ☎*900/555009* ✉*Alberto Aguilera 1, Malasaña* ☎*900/555–009*) ✣*C5.*

LAVAPIÉS

Gaudeamus Café. Along with the theater on the neighborhood's main plaza, the reconstruction of the Escuelas Pías—an 18th-century religious school burnt down during the Spanish civil war and now turned into a university center—is one of Lavapiés's modern highlights. The rooftop has a hidden café: the large terrace is open all year round and has great views for enjoying the wide selection of tea and coffee. It opens at 3:30 PM on weekdays and at 8 PM on Saturday. ✉*Tribulete 14, 4th floor, Lavapiés* ☎*91/528–2594* ⏲*Closed Sun.* ✣*D6.*

WHERE TO EAT

Spain in general has become a popular foodie pilgrimage and Madrid showcases its strengths with a cornucopia of cuisine, cutting-edge decor, and celebrated chefs that put the city on par with Europe's celebrated dining capitals.

Top Spanish chefs, who often team up with hotels, fearlessly borrow from other cuisines and reinvent traditional dishes. The younger crowd, as well as movie stars and artists, flock to the casual Malasaña, Chueca, and La Latina neighborhoods for the affordable restaurants and the tapas bars with truly scintillating small creations. When modern cuisine gets tiresome, seek out such local enclaves as Casa Ciriaco, Casa Botín, and Casa Paco for unpretentious and hearty home cooking.

THE CUISINE

Madrid's traditional cuisine is based on the roasts and stews of Castile, Spain's high central *meseta* (plain). Roast suckling pig and lamb are standard Madrid feasts, as are baby goat and chunks of beef from Ávila and the Sierra de Guadarrama. *Cocido madrileño* and *callos a la madrileña* are local specialties. *Cocido* is a hearty winter meal of broth, garbanzo beans, vegetables, potatoes, sausages, pork, and hen. The best *cocidos* are simmered in earthenware crocks over coals and served in three courses: broth, chickpeas, then meat. *Cocido* anchors the midday winter menu in the most elegant restaurants as well as the humblest holes-in-the-wall. *Callos* are simpler concoctions of veal tripe stewed with tomatoes, onions, hot paprika, and garlic. *Jamón serrano* (serrano ham)—a specialty from the livestock lands of Teruel, Extremadura, and Andalusia—has become a Madrid staple; wanderers are likely to come

BEST BETS FOR MADRID DINING

Need a cheat sheet for Madrid's restaurants? Fodor's writers have selected their favorites by price, cuisine, and experience. Details are in the full reviews. ¡Buen provecho!

Fodor's Choice ★

Asiana, $$$$, p. 89
Casa Paco, $$–$$$, p. 93
Gastro, $$$$, p. 97
Goizeko Wellington, $$$, p. 97
Mercado de la Reina, $–$$, p. 92
La Terraza—Casino, $$$$, p. 100
Las Tortillas de Gabino, $–$$, p. 98
Santceloni, $$$$, p. 99
Zalacaín, $$$$, p. 99

By Price

¢

Arabia, p. 89
Bazaar, p. 89
Casa Mingo, p. 95
Nueva Galicia, p. 101

$

Casa Ciriaco, p. 93
Home Burger, p. 89
La Musa, p. 89
Las Tortillas de Gabino, p. 98
Mercado de la Reina, p. 92
Puerto Lagasca, p. 98
Pulcinella, p. 92
Taberna Bilbao, p. 93

$$

Boccondivino, p. 96
Champagnería Gala, p. 94
La Gamella, p. 96
La Gastroteca de Santiago, p. 96
Le Petit Bistrot, p. 95
Paulino de Quevedo, p. 99
Sacha, p. 88

$$$

Dassa Bassa, p. 97
Espacio Alboroque, p. 94
Goizeko Wellington, p. 97
Viridiana, p. 96

$$$$

DiverXo, p. 88
La Terraza—Casino, p. 100

By Cuisine

CONTEMPORARY SPANISH

Dassa Bassa, $$$, p. 97
Espacio Alboroque, $$$, p. 94
Estado Puro*, p. 83
Goizeko Wellington, $$$, p. 97
La Gastroteca de Santiago, $$, p. 96
Sacha, $$, p. 88
Zalacaín, $$$$, p. 99

PAELLA-RICE

Casa Benigno, $$, p. 88
Champagnería Gala, $$, p. 94

SEAFOOD

Goizeko Wellington, $$$, p. 97
La Trainera, $$$, p. 98

STEAK HOUSE

Asador Frontón I, $$$, p. 94
Casa Paco, $$–$$$, p. 93
Julián de Tolosa, $$$, p. 93

TAPAS

El Bocaíto*, p. 81
Estay*, p. 83
Juana la Loca*, p. 82
Laredo*, p. 83
La Parpusa de Moratín*, p. 84
Taberna Bilbao, $, p. 93
Taberneros*, p. 83
Txirimiri*, p. 82

TRADITIONAL SPANISH

Casa Botín, $$$, p. 92
Casa Ciriaco, $–$$, p. 93
El Landó, $$$, p. 93
La Bola, $$, p. 95
La Trucha, $, p. 101
Las Tortillas de Gabino, $$$, p. 98
Mercado de la Reina, $, p. 92
Paulino de Quevedo, $$, p. 98
Puerto Lagasca, $, p. 98
Taberna Bilbao, $, p. 93

Tapas bars are marked with *

across bars and restaurants where legs of the dried delicacy dangle in the window.

The house wine in basic Madrid restaurants is often a sturdy, uncomplicated Valdepeñas from La Mancha. Serious dining is normally accompanied by a Rioja or a more powerful, complex Ribera de Duero, the latter from northern Castile. Ask your waiter's advice; a smooth Rioja, for example, may not be up to the task of accompanying a *cocido* or roast suckling pig. After dinner, try the anise-flavor liqueur (*anís*) produced outside the nearby village of Chinchón.

MEALTIMES

Madrileños tend to eat their meals even later than people in other parts of Spain, and that's saying something. Restaurants open for lunch at 1:30 and fill up by 3. Dinnertime begins at 9, but reservations for 11 are common, and meals can be lengthy—up to three hours. If you face hunger meltdown several hours before Madrid dinner, make the most of the early-evening tapas hour.

Use the coordinate (✢B2) at the end of each listing to locate a site on the corresponding map.

CHAMARTÍN AND TETUÁN

$$ SPANISH **Casa Benigno.** Owner Don Norberto takes gracious care in what he does, providing a carefully chosen menu and painstakingly selected wines to devoted customers. Evidence of craftsmanship is alive in every corner of the casual and understated hideaway from the best rice in the city (cooked with extra-flat paella pans made especially for the restaurant) to the ceramic plates from Talavera. But the star attraction is the chef and his astounding knowledge of food (check out his own brand of tuna, olive oil, and vinegar). He generously talks (and often sings) to his guests. ✉ *Benigno Soto 9, Chamartín* ☎ *91/416–9357* *Reservations essential* ▭ *AE, DC, MC, V* ⊗ *No dinner Sun. and Mon. Closed Christmas and Easter wks* ✢ *H1.*

$$$$ ECLECTIC **DiverXo.** With so much working against it (poor location and a low starting budget clearly reflected in the decor), this small restaurant has nonetheless become a shrine for those with an adventurous palate. The reason is David Muñoz, a young Spanish chef who worked for years at London's Nobu and Hakkasan, and his uncanny ability to mix traditions without transgressing them—witness his Spanish tortilla: a dough ball filled with potato and caramelized onions with a side of bean purée and Mexican chili sauce, reminiscent of both the Spanish omelet and Chinese dim sum. The restaurant serves only three sampler menus—the most challenging is a 15-dish proposal, for €70. ✉ *Francisco Medrano 5, Tetuán* ☎ *91/570–0766* *Reservations essential* ▭ *DC, MC, V* ⊗ *Closed Sun. and Mon.* ✢ *F1.*

$$ SPANISH **Sacha.** Playful sketches decorate the walls of this French bistrolike restaurant filled with oversize antique furniture. The cuisine is provincial Spanish—with a touch of imagination. The *lasaña de erizo de mar* (sea urchin lasagna), *arroz con setas y perdiz* (rice with mushrooms and partridge), and the *Villagodio* (a thick, grilled cut of beef) are just some of the house specialties. Its small terrace, secluded and sheltered by trees, is a popular culinary retreat in the summer. ✉ *Juan Hurtado*

de Mendoza 11, Chamartín ☎ *91/345–5952* ✍ *Reservations essential* ▭ *AE, DC, MC, V* ⊙ *Closed Sun., Easter, and Aug.* ✣ *G1.*

CHUECA AND MALASAÑA

¢ MOROCCAN ✕ **Arabia.** Pass through the heavy wool rug hanging at the entrance and you may feel as if you've entered Aladdin's cave, decorated as it is with adobe, wood, brass, whitewashed walls, and lavish palms. Full of young, boisterous madrileños, it's a great place to try elaborate Moroccan dishes like stewed lamb with honey and dry fruits or vegetarian favorites such as couscous with milk and pumpkin. To start, order the best falafel anywhere outside of Morocco or the yogurt cucumber salad. Make reservations if you want to eat here on the weekend. ✉ *Piamonte 12, Chueca* ☎ *91/532–5321* ⊙ *Closed Mon. No lunch Tues.–Fri.* ✣ *F2.*

$$$$ ECLECTIC Fodor's Choice ★ ✕ **Asiana.** Young chef Renedo surprises even the most jaded palates in this unique setting—hiss mother's Asian antiques furniture store, which used to be a ham-drying shed Renedo brings to his job a contagious enthusiasm for cooking and experimentation as well as painstaking attention to detail. Sit among a Vietnamese bed, a life-size Buddha, and other merchandise for sale while enjoying an eclectic 10-dish fixed menu, which perfectly balances the Spanish, East Asian, and Peruvian cooking traditions. The sommelier is also Japanese, and one of the best in the city. If you're willing to forfeit exclusiveness but want to indulge in a milder version of the chef's creations, try the adjacent and much more affordable Asiana Next Door. ✉ *Travesía de San Mateo 4, Chueca* ☎ *91/310–4020 or 91/310–0965* ✍ *Reservations essential* ▭ *AE, MC, V* ⊙ *Closed Sun., Mon., and Aug. No lunch* ✣ *E1.*

¢ MEDITERRANEAN ✕ **Bazaar.** The owners of La Finca de Susana opened this Chueca restaurant, which resembles an old-fashioned convenience store. Done in tones of white, Bazaar serves low-priced, creative Mediterranean food of reasonable quality in a trendy environment. The square-shaped upper floor has big windows facing the street, high ceilings, and hardwood floors; the downstairs is larger though less interesting. Standout dishes include the tuna *rosbif* (roasted and sliced thinly, like beef) with mango chutney and the tender ox with Parmesan and arugula. For dessert, a popular choice is the *chocolatísimo* (chocolate soufflé). To get a table, arrive by 1 for lunch and by 8:30 for dinner. ✉ *C. Libertad 21, Chueca* ☎ *91/523–3905* ✍ *Reservations not accepted* ▭ *MC, V* ✣ *F2.*

$ AMERICAN ✕ **Home Burger.** If you're getting nostalgic after days of traveling across Spain, don't miss out on this mishmash of two deeply ingrained American concepts—the hamburger and the diner—with a European twist. The result is a very affordable menu, favored by Chueca and Malasaña hipsters, that includes your traditional beef hamburgers but also plenty of unusual offerings, such the Tandoori burger; the Mexican—with chicken, avocado, and a salsa made with red chiles; the *Caprichosa*, with Brie and onion jam; or the vegetarian options with falafel or Indian pakoras. It's usually packed, so try to reserve in advance. ✉ *San Marcos 26, Chueca* ☎ *91/522–9728* ✉ *Espíritu Santo 12, Malasaña* ☎ *91/521–8531* ✍ *Reservations essential* ▭ *MC, V* ✣ *D1, E2.*

$ MEDITERRANEAN ✕ **La Musa.** The trendy, elegant vibe and creative menu of unique salads and tapas (try the *bomba,* a potato filled with meat or vegetables in a

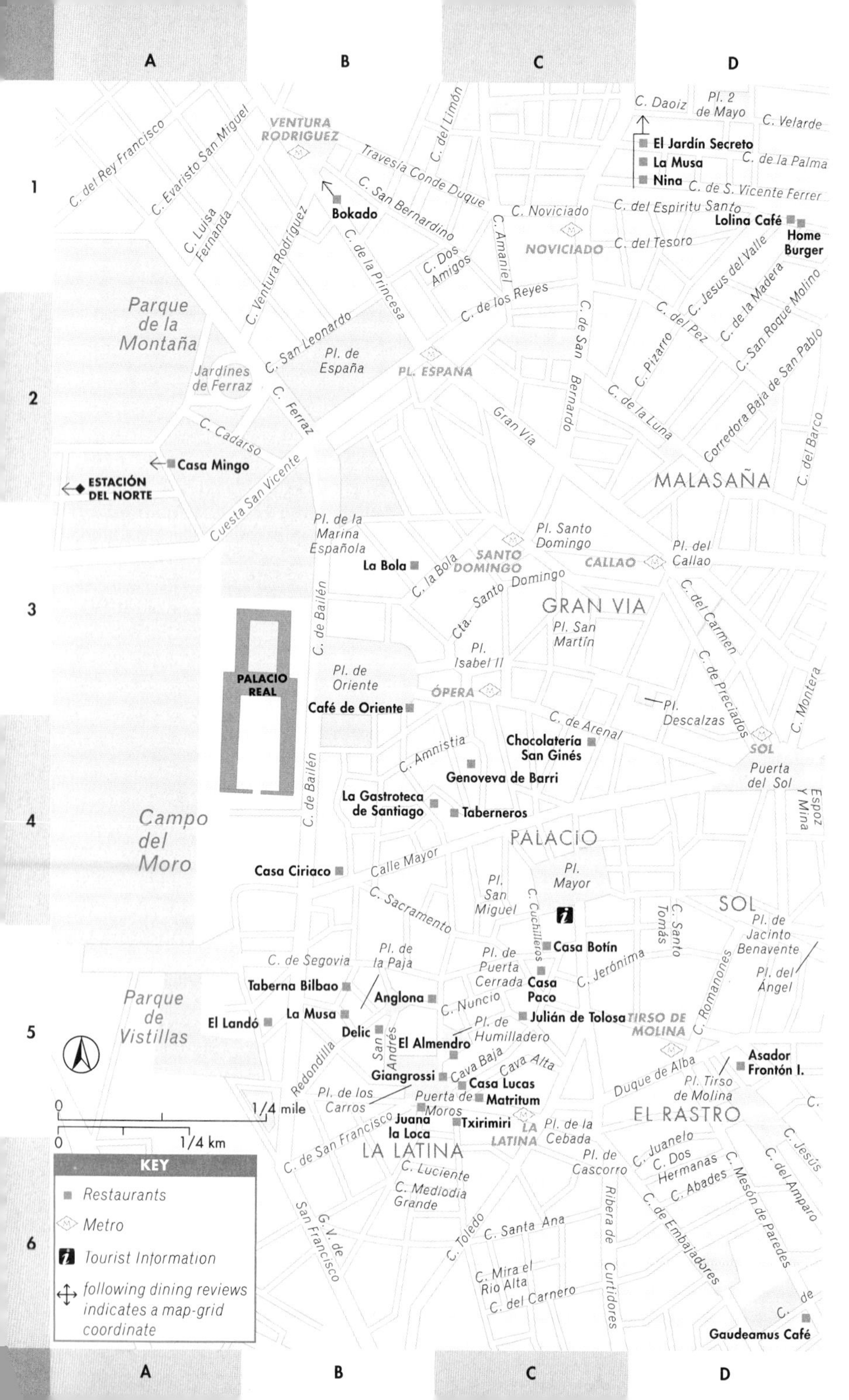
A
B
C
D
1
2
3
4
5
6
VENTURA RODRIGUEZ
C. del Rey Francisco
C. Evaristo San Miguel
C. Luisa Fernanda
C. Ventura Rodriguez
Travesía Conde Duque
C. San Bernardino
C. del Limón
Bokado
C. de la Princesa
C. Dos Amigos
C. Amaniel
C. Noviciado
NOVICIADO
C. Daoiz
Pl. 2 de Mayo
C. Velarde
El Jardín Secreto
La Musa
Nina
C. de la Palma
C. de S. Vicente Ferrer
C. del Espiritu Santo
Lolina Café
Home Burger
C. del Tesoro
C. Jesus del Valle
C. de la Madera
C. San Roque Molino
C. del Pez
C. Pizarro
C. San Pablo
Corredora Baja de San Pablo
C. de la Luna
C. de San Bernardo
C. de los Reyes
Parque de la Montaña
Jardines de Ferraz
C. San Leonardo
Pl. de España
PL. ESPAÑA
C. Ferraz
C. Cadarso
Gran Vía
Casa Mingo
ESTACIÓN DEL NORTE
Cuesta San Vicente
MALASAÑA
C. del Barco
Pl. de la Marina Española
La Bola
C. la Bola
SANTO DOMINGO
Pl. Santo Domingo
CALLAO
Pl. del Callao
Cta. Santo Domingo
GRAN VIA
C. del Carmen
Pl. San Martín
C. de Bailén
PALACIO REAL
Pl. Isabel II
Pl. de Oriente
ÓPERA
Café de Oriente
Pl. Descalzas
C. de Preciados
C. Montera
SOL
C. de Arenal
Chocolatería San Ginés
C. Amnistia
Genoveva de Barri
Puerta del Sol
Espoz Y Mina
La Gastroteca de Santiago
Taberneros
Campo del Moro
PALACIO
Casa Ciriaco
Calle Mayor
Pl. Mayor
Pl. San Miguel
C. Sacramento
C. Cuchilleros
C. Santo Tomás
SOL
Pl. de Jacinto Benavente
Casa Botín
Pl. de la Paja
C. de Segovia
Pl. de Puerta Cerrada
Casa Paco
C. Jerónima
Pl. del Ángel
Taberna Bilbao
Anglona
C. Romanones
Parque de Vistillas
El Landó
La Musa
C. Nuncio
Julián de Tolosa
TIRSO DE MOLINA
Delic
San Andrés
El Almendro
Pl. de Humilladero
Redondilla
Cava Baja
Cava Alta
Asador Frontón I.
Giangrossi
Casa Lucas
Duque de Alba
Pl. Tirso de Molina
Pl. de los Carros
Puerta de Moros
Matritum
0
1/4 mile
1/4 km
C. de San Francisco
Juana la Loca
Txirimiri
LA LATINA
Pl. de la Cebada
EL RASTRO
C. Juanelo
C. Dos Hermanas
C. Jesús
LA LATINA
C. Luciente
Pl. de Cascorro
C. Abades
C. Mesón de Paredes
C. del Amparo
C. Mediodia Grande
C. de Embajadores
G.V. de San Francisco
C. Toledo
C. Santa Ana
Ribera de Curtidores
C. Mira el Rio Alta
C. del Carnero
C. de
Gaudeamus Café
KEY
Restaurants
Metro
Tourist Information
following dining reviews indicates a map-grid coordinate

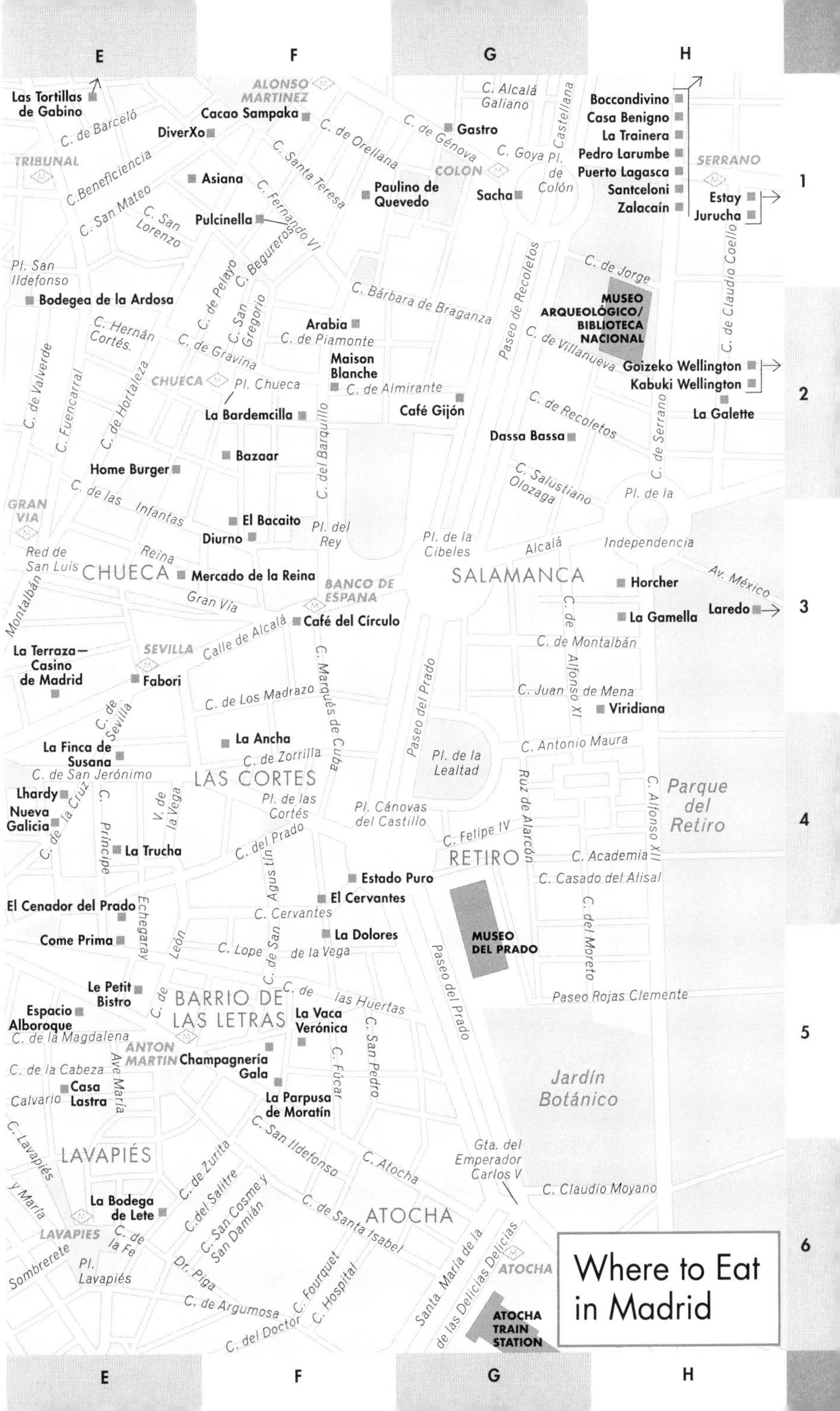

Where to Eat in Madrid
E
F
G
H
1
2
3
4
5
6
Las Tortillas de Gabino
Cacao Sampaka
DiverXo
Asiana
Pulcinella
Paulino de Quevedo
Gastro
Sacha
Boccondivino
Casa Benigno
La Trainera
Pedro Larumbe
Puerto Lagasca
Santceloni
Zalacaín
Estay
Jurucha
Bodegea de la Ardosa
Arabia
Maison Blanche
La Bardemcilla
Café Gijón
Goizeko Wellington
Kabuki Wellington
La Galette
Dassa Bassa
Bazaar
Home Burger
El Bacaito
Diurno
Mercado de la Reina
Horcher
La Gamella
Laredo
Café del Círculo
La Terraza—Casino de Madrid
Fabori
Viridiana
La Ancha
La Finca de Susana
Lhardy
Nueva Galicia
La Trucha
Estado Puro
El Cervantes
El Cenador del Prado
Come Prima
La Dolores
Le Petit Bistro
Espacio Alboroque
La Vaca Verónica
Champagnería Gala
Casa Lastra
La Parpusa de Moratín
La Bodega de Lete
MUSEO ARQUEOLÓGICO/ BIBLIOTECA NACIONAL
MUSEO DEL PRADO
ATOCHA TRAIN STATION
CHUECA
SALAMANCA
LAS CORTES
RETIRO
BARRIO DE LAS LETRAS
LAVAPIÉS
ATOCHA
Parque del Retiro
Jardín Botánico
ALONSO MARTINEZ
TRIBUNAL
COLON
SERRANO
CHUECA
GRAN VIA
BANCO DE ESPANA
SEVILLA
ANTON MARTIN
LAVAPIES
ATOCHA
C. de Barceló
C. Beneficiencia
C. San Mateo
C. San Lorenzo
Pl. San Ildefonso
C. Fernando VI
C. Santa Teresa
C. de Orellana
C. de Génova
C. Alcalá Galiano
C. Goya
Pl. de Colón
Castellana
C. de Jorge
C. de Claudio Coello
C. Bárbara de Braganza
Paseo de Recoletos
C. de Villanueva
C. de Pelayo
C. Beguerero
C. San Gregorio
C. Hernán Cortés.
C. de Gravina
C. de Piamonte
C. de Almirante
Pl. Chueca
C. de Valverde
C. Fuencarral
C. de Hortaleza
C. del Barquillo
C. de Recoletos
C. de Serrano
C. Salustiano Olozaga
Pl. de la Independencia
C. de las Infantas
Pl. del Rey
Pl. de la Cibeles
Alcalá
Av. México
Red de San Luis
Reina
Montalbán
Gran Vía
Calle de Alcalá
C. de Alfonso XI
C. de Montalbán
C. Marqués de Cuba
Paseo del Prado
C. Juan de Mena
C. de Los Madrazo
C. de Sevilla
C. Antonio Maura
C. de Zorrilla
C. de San Jerónimo
Pl. de la Lealtad
Ruz de Alarcón
C. Alfonso XII
Pl. de las Cortés
Pl. Cánovas del Castillo
C. Felipe IV
C. de la Cruz
C. Príncipe
V. de la Vega
C. del Prado
C. Academia
C. Casado del Alisal
C. de San Agustín
C. Cervantes
C. del Moreto
Echegaray
León
C. Lope de la Vega
C. de las Huertas
Paseo Rojas Clemente
C. de la Magdalena
C. San Pedro
C. Fúcar
C. de la Cabeza
Ave María
Calvario
C. San Ildefonso
C. Atocha
Gta. del Emperador Carlos V
C. Claudio Moyano
C. Lavapiés
y María
C. de Zurita
C. del Salitre
C. San Cosme y San Damián
C. de Santa Isabel
C. de la Fe
Sombrerete
Pl. Lavapiés
Dr. Piga
C. de Argumosa
C. Fourquet
C. Hospital
C. del Doctor
Santa María de la
de las Delicias Delicias

spinach sauce, or the huge marinated venison brochette) draw a stylish young crowd. Breakfast is served during the week and there's a good fixed-price lunch menu. The second, bigger La Musa in Plaza de la Paja in La Latina neighborhood has a larger menu and has an even trendier and more expensive restaurant in the basement: Junk Club, with vintage decor and sophisticated dishes that reinvent staples like chocolate with churros ("chocolate" is a cup with mascarpone topped with *foie* and a layer of chocolate sprinkled with spices, and churros on the side) or the fried calamari sandwich. Show up early whichever one you go to, or expect to wait. ✉ *Manuela Malasaña 18, Malasaña* ☎ *91/448–7558* ✍ *Reservations not accepted* ✉ *Costanilla de San Andrés 12, Plaza de la Paja, La Latina* ☎ *91/354–0255* ▭ *DC, MC, V* ✥ *D1, B5.*

$ SPANISH Fodor's Choice ★ ✕ **Mercado de la Reina.** Plentiful and inexpensive tapas and succulent larger portions—scrambled eggs with a variety of meats and vegetables, tasty local cheeses, and salads—make this large and tastefully decorated bar-restaurant a handy stop for people who want to replenish themselves without having to sit through a long meal. And where else can you sip a beer standing next to an olive tree? There's also a more formal dining area with long tables where groups can share some of the more elaborate meat and fish options; a lounge downstairs—with an extensive gin menu—accommodates those who want to keep the night rolling. ✉ *Gran Vía 12, Chueca* ☎ *91/521–3198* ▭ *AE, MC, V* ✥ *E3.*

$ MEDITERRANEAN ✕ **Nina.** One of the first restaurants to bring sophistication and refinement to a neighborhood best known for its wild and unrestricted spirit, Nina has an airy loftlike interior with high ceilings, exposed brick-and-alabaster walls, and dark hardwood floors. Waiters dressed in black serve the creative Mediterranean cuisine with an Eastern touch to a mostly young, hip crowd. Highlights include goat cheese *milhojas* (pastry puffs), glazed codfish with honey sauce, and venison and mango in a mushroom sauce. There is a good weekday fixed-price lunch menu, and brunch is served on weekends. ✉ *Manuela Malasaña 10, Malasaña* ☎ *91/591–0046* ▭ *AE, DC, MC, V* ✥ *D1.*

$ ITALIAN ✕ **Pulcinella.** Tired of not being able to find a true Italian restaurant in the city, owner Enrico opened this homey trattoria filled with memorabilia of Italian artists. Always bustling and frequented by families and young couples, it seems like a direct transplant from Naples. Superb fresh pastas, the best pizzas and focaccias in the city, cooked in a brick oven, and the homemade tiramisu are the standout dishes. The branch across from it, Cantina di Pulcinella, serves the same food but permits smoking. ✉ *Regueros 7, Chueca* ☎ *91/319–7363* ✍ *Reservations essential* ▭ *AE, DC, MC, V* ✥ *F1.*

LA LATINA

$$$ SPANISH ✕ **Casa Botín.** The *Guinness Book of Records* calls this the world's oldest restaurant (est. 1725), and Hemingway called it the best. The latter claim may be a bit over the top, but the restaurant *is* excellent and extremely charming (and so successful that the owners opened a "branch" in Miami, Florida). There are four floors of tile and wood-beam dining rooms, and, if you're seated upstairs, you'll pass ovens dating back centuries. Musical groups called *tunas* (mostly made up of students dressed in old costumes) often drop in. Specialties are *cochinillo*

(roast pig) and *cordero* (roast lamb). It's rumored Goya washed dishes here before he made it as a painter. ✉ *Cuchilleros 17, off Plaza Mayor, La Latina* ☎ *91/366–4217* ▭ *AE, DC, MC, V* ✥ *C5.*

$–$$ SPANISH ✕ **Casa Ciriaco.** One of Madrid's most traditional restaurants—host to a long list of Spain's who's who, from royalty to philosophers, painters, and bullfighters—serves up simple home cooking in an unpretentious environment. You can get a carafe of Valdepeñas or a split of a Rioja reserve to accompany the *perdiz con judiones* (partridge with broad beans). The *pepitoria de gallina* (hen in an almond sauce) is another favorite. ✉ *C. Mayor 84, La Latina* ☎ *91/559–5066* ▭ *DC, MC, V* ⊗ *Closed Wed. and Aug.* ✥ *B4.*

$$–$$$ STEAK Fodor's Choice ★ ✕ **Casa Paco.** This Castilian tavern wouldn't have looked out of place two or three centuries ago, and today you can still squeeze past the old, zinc-top bar, crowded with madrileños downing Valdepeñas red wine, and into the tiled dining rooms. Feast on thick slabs of red meat, sizzling on plates so hot the meat continues to cook at your table. The Spanish consider overcooking a sin, so expect looks of dismay if you ask for your meat well done (*bien hecho*). You order by weight, so remember that a *medio kilo* is more than a pound. To start, try the *pisto manchego* (La Mancha version of ratatouille) or the Castilian *sopa de ajo* (garlic soup). ✉ *Puerta Cerrada 11, La Latina* ☎ *91/366–3166* ✍ *Reservations essential* ▭ *DC, MC, V* ⊗ *Closed Sun. and Aug.* ✥ *C5.*

$$$ SPANISH ✕ **El Landó.** This *castizo* (authentic or highly traditional) restaurant with dark wood-panel walls and lined with bottles of wine, serves classic Spanish food. Specialties of the house are *huevos estrellados* (fried eggs with potatoes and sausage), grilled meats, a good selection of fish (sea bass, haddock, grouper) with many different sauces, and steak tartare. As you sit down for your meal, you'll immediately be served a plate of bread with tomato, a salad, and Spanish ham. Check out the pictures of famous celebrities who've eaten at this typically noisy landmark; they line the staircase that leads to the main dining area. ✉ *Plaza Gabriel Miró 8, La Latina* ☎ *91/366–7681* ✍ *Reservations essential* ▭ *AE, DC, MC, V* ⊗ *Closed Sun., Easter, and Aug.* ✥ *B5.*

$$$ SPANISH ✕ **Julián de Tolosa.** This rustic, designer-decorated spot is famous for *alubias rojas* (red kidney beans) from the Basque town of Tolosa, but the *ibérico* (acorn-fed) ham here is finely sliced and juicy, and the two-person *chuletón* (T-bone steak) is also excellent. The *pimientos de piquillo* (roasted sweet red peppers) come to the table sizzling and wonderful. Try a Basque *txakolí* (tart, young white wine) with your first course and a Ribera de Duero later, then let maître d' and owner Angela talk you into a small flask of *pacharán,* the famous Basque sloe-berry liqueur, served after coffee. ✉ *Cava Baja 18, La Latina* ☎ *91/365–8210* ✍ *Reservations essential* ▭ *DC, MC, V* ⊗ *No dinner Sun.* ✥ *C5.*

$ SPANISH ✕ **Taberna Bilbao.** Run by a couple, this popular tavern—highly praised by locals—is somewhere between a tapas bar and a restaurant. It has three small dining areas, floor and walls of red Italian marble, plain wooden furniture, and a menu that is representative of Basque cuisine. Try any of the fish or mushroom *revueltos* (scrambled eggs), the *habas* (fava beans), or the *bacalao* (cod), and order a glass of *txakolí* (tart, young Basque white wine). ✉ *Costanilla de San Andrés 8, Plaza de la*

Paja, La Latina ☎91/365–6125 ▭DC, MC, V ⏲Closed 2 wks in Feb. No lunch Mon. ✥B5.

LAVAPIÉS AND ANTÓN MARTÍN

$$$ SPANISH ✕**Asador Frontón I.** Uptown's Asador Frontón II is swankier, but this downtown original is more charming, and fine meat and fish are the headliners on the menu. Appetizers include *anchoas frescas* (fresh grilled anchovies) and *pimientos rellenos con bacalao* (peppers stuffed with cod). The huge *chuletón* (T-bone steak), seared over charcoal and sprinkled with sea salt, is for two or more; order *cogollo de lechuga* (lettuce hearts) as an accompaniment. The *cogotes de merluza* (hake jowls) are light and aromatic. *✉Tirso de Molina 7, entrance on Jesus y Maria 1, Lavapiés ☎91/369–1617 ✍Reservations essential ▭AE, DC, MC, V ⏲Closed 1 wk in Aug. and Easter week. No dinner Sun. ✥D5.*

$$ SPANISH ✕**Casa Lastra.** Established in 1926, this Asturian tavern is popular with Lavapiés locals. The rustic, half-tile walls are strung with relics from the Asturian countryside, including wooden clogs, cow bells, sausages, and garlic. Specialties include *fabada* (Asturian white beans stewed with sausage), *fabes con almejas* (white beans with clams), and *queso de cabrales,* aromatic cheese made in the Picos de Europa. Great hunks of crisp bread and hard Asturian cider complement a hearty meal; desserts include tangy baked apples. There's an inexpensive fixed-price lunch menu on weekdays. *✉Olivar 3, Lavapiés ☎91/369–0837 ▭MC, V ⏲Closed Wed. and July. No dinner Sun. ✥E5.*

$$ MEDITERRANEAN ✕**Champagnería Gala.** Hidden on a back street not far from Calle Atocha and the Reina Sofía museum, this cheerful Mediterranean restaurant is usually packed, thanks to the choice of paellas, *fideuás* (paellas with noodles instead of rice), risottos, and hearty bean and chickpea stews—all served with salad, dessert, and a wine jar. The same type of rice must be ordered for tables of four and fewer. The front dining area is modern and festive; the back room incorporates trees and plants in a glassed-in patio. *✉Moratín 22, Antón Martín ☎91/429–2562 ✍Reservations essential ▭No credit cards ⏲Closed Mon. ✥F5.*

$$$ MEDITERRANEAN ✕**Espacio Alboroque.** Chef Andrés Madrigal unleashes his creativity in this rehabilitated 19th-century mansion that has two dining floors filled with contemporary artwork. The young chef delivers two different sampler menus (€55 and €75), as well as a short array of choices from a menu that changes every two to three weeks. He and his team subtly reinvent such traditional dishes as sole *meunière,* royal hare (a traditional French dish made with stuffed, marinated hare and simmered for many more hours than the average), and Andalusian shrimp omelet. The restaurant has an astounding wine cellar, and there's a courtyard for summer dining. *✉Calle Atocha 34, Antón Martín ☎91/389–6570 ▭AE, DC, MC, V ⏲Closed Sun. No lunch Sat. ✥E5.*

$$ MEDITERRANEAN ✕**La Vaca Verónica.** In the golden-age literary quarter, this romantic little hideaway resembling a Parisian bistro with yellow painted walls and antique furniture has built a following for its Argentinian grilled meats (the *bandeja de vaca* or beef tray, their heartiest offering, also comes with pork sausage, blood pudding, sweetbreads, and potatoes), *pescado a la sal* (fish cooked in a shell of salt), homemade pastas with various seafood dressings, and terrific salads. The pasta *a los carabineros*

(with scarlet shrimp) is a seductive choice. ✉ *Moratín 38, Antón Martín* ☎ *91/429–7827* ▭ *AE, DC, MC, V* ⏲ *No lunch Sat.* ✣ *F5.*

$$ FRENCH ✕ **Le Petit Bistrot.** Carlos and his wife, Frederique, took on a challenge converting what was once a bullfighting-themed tavern into a Parisian bistro. Though some elements, such as the long brass copper bar, hint at its *castizo* ("authentic," as in old and traditional) origins, there's much that's truly French here, including the service, the wine, and the cocktails. Specialties include Brie *croquetas* (in a bread-crumb crust and deep fried), the *escargots*, the assortment of oysters, and the chateaubriand steak with butter, tarragon, and vinegar. ✉ *Plaza de Matute 5, Barrio de las Letras* ☎ *91/429–6265* ▭ *AE, MC, V* ⏲ *Closed Sun. and Mon.* ✣ *E5.*

MONCLOA

$$$$ BASQUE ✕ **Bokado.** Chefs Mikel and Jesús Santamaría, best known for breaking ground in the world of tapas in both Navarra and the Basque Country, have brought their talent to Madrid. Away from the bustling city center and five minutes from Moncloa, the restaurant, a spacious, elegant, and design-rich setting, is part of the Museo del Traje's building. The menu includes sophisticated combinations such as oysters, monkfish, haddock, stews, mushroom delicacies, and savory game dishes. Its terrace is one of the city's best choices for summer dining. If you're not feeling whimsical, try their more affordable tapas menu in the adjacent cafeteria. ✉ *Av. Juan de Herrera 2, Moncloa* ☎ *91/549–0041* ▭ *AE, MC, V* ⏲ *Closed Sun. and Mon.* ✣ *B1.*

¢ SPANISH ✕ **Casa Mingo.** This bustling place, built into a stonewall beneath the Estación del Norte (across the street from the hermitage of San Antonio de la Florida), resembles an Asturian cider tavern. The only items on the menu are succulent roast chicken, cheese, salad, and sausages, all to be taken with *sidra* (hard cider). Expect to share long tables with other diners, though small tables are set up on the sidewalk in summer. If you don't come early (1 for lunch, 8:30 for dinner), you may have to wait. ✉ *Paseo de la Florida 34, Moncloa* ☎ *91/547–7918* ✍ *Reservations not accepted* ▭ *No credit cards* ✣ *A2.*

PALACIO

$$ MEDITERRANEAN ✕ **Genoveva de Barri.** A few blocks from Palacio Real, this charming restaurant is on a *callejuela* (small street) that's easy to miss. The diminutive space is the playground of young chef and sommelier Gonzalo Lara, who broke away from his father (owner and chef of the acclaimed Laray) to experiment on his own. Inside, a handful of tables are accented with a few baroque touches: white-and-gold wallpaper, fringed mirrors, and a hanging crystal lamp. The short menu is full of surprises: ox tartare; scrambled eggs with lobster, asparagus, and mushrooms; and an unconventional, although expert, selection of wines. ✉ *Espejo 10, Ópera* ☎ *91/547–8014* ✍ *Reservations essential* ▭ *AE, V* ⏲ *Closed Sun. No lunch Sat. and Mon.* ✣ *C4.*

$$ SPANISH ✕ **La Bola.** First opened as a *botellería* (wine shop) in 1802, La Bola developed slowly into a tapas bar and then a full-fledged restaurant. The traditional setting is the draw: the bar is original, and the dining nooks, decorated with polished wood, Spanish tile, and lace curtains, are charming. Amazingly, the restaurant belongs to the same

founding family, with the seventh generation currently in training. Try the house specialty: *cocido a la madrileña* (a hearty meal of broth, garbanzo beans, vegetables, potatoes, and pork). ✉ *Bola 5, Ópera* ☎ *91/547–6930* ▭ *No credit cards* ⏲ *No dinner Sun. Closed Sun. in Aug. No dinner Sat. in Aug.* ✣ *B3.*

$$ MEDITERRANEAN ✕ **La Gastroteca de Santiago.** Among the trendy new restaurants with talented chefs, this one offers the best value, with a short and creative menu (barely a dozen dishes) that changes monthly and expert wine advice. It's an excellent place to see where contemporary creative Spanish cuisine is heading without having to guess what's on your plate. The restaurant seats only 16—the open kitchen is as big as the dining area. If you feel adventurous, ask for the €60 sampler menu (€20 more if you get the wine to partner), or show up for their Sunday-only special meat and rice dishes. ✉ *Plaza de Santiago 1, Ópera* ☎ *91/548–0707* ✍ *Reservations essential* ▭ *AE, MC, V* ⏲ *Closed Sun. No lunch Mon.* ✣ *B4.*

RETIRO

$$$$ GERMAN ✕ **Horcher.** The faithful continue to fill this traditional shrine to fine dining, once considered Madrid's best restaurant and still worth seeking out. Wild boar, venison, hare, partridge, wild duck, as well as unique hamburgers (ostrich and turkey, monkfish, and swordfish) are standard fare. Fish and meat Stroganoff, pork chops with sauerkraut, and *baumkuchen* (a chocolate-covered fruit-and-cake dessert) reflect the restaurant's Germanic roots. The dining room is decorated with brocade and antique Austrian porcelain; an ample selection of French and German wines rounds out the menu. ✉ *Alfonso XII 6, Retiro* ☎ *91/522–0731* ✍ *Reservations essential. Jacket and tie* ▭ *AE, DC, MC, V* ⏲ *Closed Sun., Easter Week, and Aug. No lunch Sat.* ✣ *H3.*

$$ MEDITERRANEAN ✕ **La Gamella.** Some of the classic American dishes—Caesar salad, hamburger, steak tartare—are still highly regarded staples of the reasonably priced menu at this perennially popular dinner spot. New selections are a fusion of Mediterranean and American dishes. The sophisticated rust-red dining room, batik tablecloths, oversize plates, and attentive service remain the same. The lunchtime *menú del día* (fixed menu) is a great value. ✉ *Alfonso XII 4, Retiro* ☎ *91/532–4509* ▭ *AE, DC, MC, V* ⏲ *Closed Sat. No dinner Sun.* ✣ *H3.*

$$$ ECLECTIC ✕ **Viridiana.** This place has a relaxed, somewhat cramped bistro feel, its black-and-white scheme punctuated by prints from Luis Buñuel's classic anticlerical film, the restaurant's namesake. Iconoclast chef Abraham Garcia says "market-based" is too narrow a description for his creative menu, which changes every two weeks: standards include *foie de pato con chutney de frutas* (duck *foie* with fruit chutney) and *huevos sobre mousse de hongos* (eggs on a mushroom mousse). Or try the superb duck pâté drizzled with sherry and served with Sauternes or Tokay wine. ✉ *Juan de Mena 14, Retiro* ☎ *91/531–1039* ✍ *Reservations essential* ▭ *AE, MC, V* ⏲ *Closed Sun. and Easter* ✣ *H3.*

SALAMANCA AND CHAMBERÍ

$$ ITALIAN ✕ **Boccondivino.** After years of low-quality Italian restaurants, madrileños are witnessing the resurrection of transalpine gastronomy, thanks to a handful of star-studded newcomers. At the top of most lists is this Sardinian restaurant whose menu is a feast for the eye—extensive,

with many dishes not usually found in Italian restaurants—and the stomach. Dinner options include *malloreddus* (small shell-shaped wheat pasta) either with sheep's-milk cheese and black truffle or eggplant and curd cheese, Carnaroli rice risottos, and dishes made with spicy Italian pork sausages. Along with the painstakingly selected homemade cheeses, everything here feels more authentic than what Madrid is used to. There's also a good selection of savory and fruity wines from Sardinia and sweet delicacies such as *seada,* a pastry filled with milk-based curd and honey made with truffles. ✉ *C. Castelló 81, Salamanca* ☎ *91/575–7947* ▭ *AE, DC, MC, V* ⊙ *Closed Mon. and Aug. No dinner Sun.* ✥ *H1.*

$$$ ECLECTIC

Dassa Bassa. What look like stairs leading you into a disco actually open up into an old underground coal bunker, now a trendy restaurant. Young chef Darrio Barrio combines conventional recipes with more adventuresome creations inspired by his stints with some of Spain's most reputed chefs (such as Adrià, Larumbe, and Subijana), and his menu changes according to what's available at the market. Recent highlights include sardines marinated in Moroccan tea, St. Peter's fish with pumpkin roasted in cardamom and coconut, and oxtail with a wine and chocolate sauce. ✉ *C. Villalar 7, Salamanca* ☎ *91/576–7397* ✍ *Reservations essential* ▭ *AE, DC, MC, V* ⊙ *Closed Sun. and Mon., Easter wk, and Aug.* ✥ *G2.*

$$$$ LA NUEVA COCINA Fodor's Choice ★

Gastro. At the end of 2007, celebrity chef Sergi Arola—Ferran Adrià's most popular disciple—left La Broche, the restaurant where he vaulted to the top of the Madrid dining scene, to go solo. The result is a smaller, less minimalist though equally modern bistro space crafted to enhance the dining experience, just 30 customers at a time. At the height of his career and surrounded by an impeccable team—which now also includes a talented and talkative bartender in the lounge—Arola offers only three sampler menus (a short one, a long one, and one entirely made up of cheeses), which include some of his classic surf-and-turf dishes (such as the rabbit filled with giant scarlet shrimp), nods to its Catalonian roots (the sautéed broad beans and peas with blood sausage), and more than 600 different wines mostly from small producers, all available by the glass. ✉ *Zurbano 31, Chamberí* ☎ *91/310–2169* ✍ *Reservations essential* ▭ *AE, DC, MC, V* ✥ *G1.*

$$$ SPANISH Fodor's Choice ★

Goizeko Wellington. Aware of the more sophisticated palate of Spain's new generation of diners, the owners of the madrileño traditional dreamland that is Goizeko Kabi have opened a new restaurant that shares the virtues of its kin but none of its stuffiness. The menu delivers the same quality Northern white fishes, house staples such as the *kokotxas de merluza* (hake jowls), and the *chipirones en su tinta* (line-caught calamari cooked in its own ink), and also includes pastas, risottos, and hearty bean stews. The interior is warm and modern with citrus-yellow walls, lattices, and screens. ✉ *Villanueva 34, in the Hotel Wellington, Salamanca* ☎ *91/577–6026* ✍ *Reservations essential* ▭ *AE, DC, MC, V* ⊙ *Closed Sun. No lunch Sat. in July and Aug.* ✥ *H2.*

$$$–$$$$ JAPANESE

Kabuki Wellington. Atypical and elegant, this Japanese dining spot serves the kind of superbly fresh sushi and sashimi you'll find in other parts of the world. But where it excels most is in chef Ricardo Sanz's

Spanish-based combinations, such as the raw calamari carpaccio (*usuzukuri)* with tempura crumbs, a tribute to a national Spanish staple, the fried calamari sandwich; the beef marrow-bone nigiri sushi (honoring another classic, the *madrileño cocido*); or the oxtail with teriyaki sauce. For dessert, don't miss the reinvented hot chocolate with crispy *churros*. ✉ *Velázquez 6, in the Hotel Wellington Salamanca* ☎ *91/575–4400* 💳 *AE, DC, MC, V* ⊙ *Closed Sun. No lunch Sat.* ✣ *H2.*

$–$$ VEGETARIAN ✕ **La Galette.** This quaint restaurant will satisfy vegetarians and nonvegetarians alike. In the evening it's candlelit, and baroque music plays in the background, setting the stage for the food. Specialties include apple *croquetas* (béchamel and apple mixed in a bread-crumb crust and then deep-fried), spinach with tofu, onion soup, and zucchini soup. There are meat dishes, too. It also has a tearoom open from 5 to 9 PM serving, among other things, scrumptious apple and raspberry tarts. ✉ *C. Conde de Aranda 11, Salamanca* ☎ *91/576–0641* 💳 *AE, DC, MC, V* ⊙ *No dinner Sun.* ✣ *H2.*

$$$ SEAFOOD ✕ **La Trainera.** With its nautical theme and maze of little dining rooms, this informal restaurant is all about fresh seafood—the best that money can buy. Crab, lobster, shrimp, mussels, and a dozen other types of shellfish are served by weight in *raciones* (large portions)—many Spanish diners share several plates of these shellfish as their entire meal, but the grilled hake, sole, or turbot makes an unbeatable second course. To accompany the legendary *carabineros* (giant scarlet shrimp), skip the listless house wine and go for a bottle of Albariño, from the southern Galician coast. ✉ *Lagasca 60, Salamanca* ☎ *91/576–8035* 💳 *AE, DC, MC, V* ⊙ *Closed Sun. and Aug.* ✣ *H1.*

$–$$ SPANISH Fodor's Choice ★ ✕ **Las Tortillas de Gabino.** Few national dishes raise more intense debates among Spaniards than the *tortilla de patata* (Spanish omelet). Deceivingly simple, some like it soft with the eggs runny, others spongy yet evenly cooked. At this lively restaurant, decked out with subdued light wooden fixtures, you'll find heaps of Spaniards gobbling up one of the city's finest, as well as some other unconventional tortilla creations like potatoes with octopus, potato chips with *salmorejo* (a gazpacho-like soup), with garlic soup, with codfish and leek stew, with truffles (when available) and a potato mousse, etc., that are best enjoyed when shared by everyone at the table. They also have plenty of equally succulent non-egg choices and a green-apple sorbet that shouldn't be missed. ✉ *Rafael Calvo 20, Chamberí* ☎ *91/3197505* 💳 *MC, V* ⊙ *Closed Sun. No lunch Sat.* ✣ *E1.*

$ SPANISH ✕ **Puerto Lagasca.** Although the old tapas bars with prawn tails and cigarette butts on the floor are still a majority of what you'll find in the city, there's a new breed of locales that compete with more upscale restaurants with menus that don't leave you gasping for air when the check arrives. This is one of the best in its league, with a menu based on availability of the market that allows diners to share traditional appetizers—*salmorejo*, roasted peppers, fresh anchovies, a tomato and melva tuna salad, as well as a good assortment of meat and fish options—among the latter, a good pick is the fried-fish sampler. Note that they also serve half portions. ✉ *Lagasca 81, Salamanca* ☎ *91/5764111* 💳 *MC, V* ⏲ *No dinner Sun.* ✥ *H1.*

$$ SPANISH ✕ **Paulino de Quevedo.** What appears to be a completely refurbished barn serves as the dining room for the eponymous big-name chef in traditional Spanish cooking; de Quevedo opened this second restaurant (the first is simply called Paulino) to cater to a more sophisticated crowd. The menu takes traditional dishes on a detour, creating winning combinations such as the grilled haddock with *calcots* (a type of tender scallion from Cataluña), or the fresh *foie* with figs and glazed apples. Some of the best tapas in Madrid (main courses in miniature plus original creations) are served in the front casual dining area. ✉ *C. Jordán 7, Chamberí* ☎ *91/591–3929* ✍ *Reservations essential* 💳 *AE, DC, MC, V* ⏲ *Closed Sun. and Aug.* ✥ *F1.*

$$–$$$ SPANISH ✕ **Pedro Larumbe.** This restaurant is literally the pinnacle of the ABC shopping center between Paseo de la Castellana and Calle Serrano. Dining quarters include a summer roof terrace (it turns into a lively bar after dinner) and an Andalusian patio. For more than a decade chef-owner Pedro Larumbe has built a reputation for market food that respectfully breaks away from tradition, and his menu features such contemporary dishes as veal meatballs with truffle and king prawns, and roasted sea bass with bacon and tomato. The dessert buffet is an art exhibit, and a good wine list complements the fare. ✉ *Serrano 61, Salamanca* ☎ *91/575–1112* 💳 *AE, DC, MC, V* ⏲ *Closed Sun., Holy Week and 2 wks in Aug. No dinner Mon.* ✥ *H1.*

$$$$ MEDITERRANEAN Fodor's Choice ★ ✕ **Santceloni.** Santi Santamaría's Madrid branch of his Racó de Can Fabes (near Barcelona) has proved an immediate and major success in the Spanish capital. One of the reigning troika of chief Spanish chefs, Santamaría works in a sophisticated environment, where the service is as impeccable as the food: exquisite combinations of Mediterranean ingredients accompanied by a comprehensive and daring wine list. Go with an appetite and lots of time (a minimum of three hours) because a meal here is ceremonious. If you're a meat lover, don't leave without trying the *jarrete* (veal shank). And if you love cheese you'll be bewitched by the cheese sampler offered before dessert. ✉ *Paseo de la Castellana 57, Chamberí* ☎ *91/210–8840* ✍ *Reservations essential* 💳 *AE, DC, MC, V* ⏲ *Closed Sun., Easter wk, and Aug. No lunch Sat.* ✥ *H1.*

$$$$ SPANISH Fodor's Choice ★ ✕ **Zalacaín.** This restaurant introduced nouvelle Basque cuisine to Spain in the 1970s and has since become a Madrid classic. It's particularly known for using the best and freshest seasonal products available, as well as for having the best service in town. From the variety of fungi and game meat to hard-to-find seafood, the cuisine here tends to be unusual—you won't find many of these sorts of ingredients, or dishes, elsewhere. The dining room's deep-apricot color scheme is made more dramatic by dark wood and gleaming silver, giving off a villa vibe. ✉ *Alvarez de Baena 4, Salamanca* ☎ *91/561–4840* ✍ *Reservations essential. Jacket and tie* 💳 *AE, DC, V* ⏲ *Closed Sun., Aug., and Holy Week. No lunch Sat.* ✥ *H1.*

2

SOL, SANTA ANA, AND BARRIO DE LAS LETRAS

$$–$$$ ITALIAN **Come Prima.** There are fancier and surely more expensive Italian restaurants in the city but none as warm or authentic as this one. Decorated with black-and-white photos of Italian actors and movie scenes, the interior is divided into three nooks; the bistrolike front, with the green-and-white checkered tablecloths, is the most charming. The portions are large, eye-catching, and tastefully presented; diners love risottos, such as the Milanesa with lobster and the risotto porcini. The menu also offers fresh pasta dishes and surprises such as liver- or pumpkin-filled ravioli, and the timbale *come prima* (a molded pasta cake filled with vegetables). *C. Echegaray 27, Barrio de las Letras 91/420–3042 Reservations essential MC, V No lunch Sun. and Mon. E5.*

$$ MEDITERRANEAN **El Cenador del Prado.** The name means "The Prado Dining Room," and the space includes a boldly painted dining room as well as a plant-filled conservatory, also for dining. There is a separate baroque salon, too: a sitting area, mainly occupied by large groups. Its innovative menu has French and Asian touches, as well as exotic Spanish dishes. The house specialty is *patatas a la importancia* (sliced potatoes fried in a sauce of garlic, parsley, and clams); other options include black rice with baby squid and prawns, and sirloin on a pear pastry puff. For dessert try the *bartolillos* (custard-filled pastries). *C. del Prado 4, Retiro 91/429–1561 DC, V Closed 1 wk in Aug. No dinner Sun. E4.*

$$ SPANISH **La Ancha.** The traditional Spanish menu here includes some of the best lentils, meat cutlets, and croquettes in Madrid, as well as more elaborate dishes, such as the juicy *tortilla con almejas* (Spanish omelet with clams). Both locations of the restaurant belong to the same family and are unpretentious inside and outstanding in quality. The original Príncipe de Vergara location has a tented patio for the summer; the newer one behind the Congress is often filled with politicians. *Príncipe de Vergara 204, Chamartín 91/563–8977 Zorrilla 7, Centro 91/429–8186 AE, DC, MC, V Closed Sun. and 1 wk in Aug.; Zorrilla branch closed 3 wks in Aug. F4.*

¢–$ MEDITERRANEAN **La Finca de Susana.** A huge, diverse crowd comes here in search of grilled vegetables, oven-cooked *bacalao* (salt cod) with spinach, and caramelized duck with plums and couscous. Not irrelevant is the fact that this is also one of the best bargains in the city. The loftlike interior has hardwood floors, and it's decorated with warm tones; one end of the dining room has a huge bookcase lined with wine bottles. Arrive by 1 for lunch and 8:30 for dinner or be prepared to wait. *C. Arlabán 4, Centro 91/369–3557 Reservations not accepted MC, V E4.*

$$$$ LA NUEVA COCINA Fodor's Choice ★ **La Terraza—Casino de Madrid.** This rooftop terrace just off Puerta del Sol is in one of Madrid's oldest, most exclusive clubs (the *casino* is a club for gentlemen, not gamblers; the club is for members only, but the restaurant is open to everybody). When it premiered the food was inspired and overseen by the celebrity chef Ferran Adrià, but as the years have gone by, chef Francisco Roncero has departed from Adrià's influence and built a reputation of his own. Try any of the light and tasty mousses,

foams, and liquid jellies, or indulge in the unique tapas—experiments of flavor, texture, and temperature, such as the *ventresca* salmon in miso with radish ice cream, or the spherified sea urchin. There's also a sampler menu. ✉ *Alcalá 15, Sol* ☎ *91/521–8700* ✍ *Reservations essential* ▭ *AE, DC, MC, V* ⊙ *Closed Sun. and Aug. No lunch Sat.* ✥ *E3.*

$ SPANISH ✕ **La Trucha.** This Andalusian deep-fry specialist, decorated with hanging hams, ceramic plates, and garlic, is one of the happiest places in Madrid. The staff is jovial, and the house specialty, *trucha a la truchana* (trout stuffed with ham and garlic), is a work of art. Other star entrées are *chopitos* (baby squid), *pollo al ajillo* (chunks of chicken in crisped garlic), and *espárragos trigueros* (wild asparagus). *Jarras* (pitchers) of chilled Valdepeñas act like laughing gas on the merry guests. The Nuñez de Arce branch, near the Hotel Reina Victoria, is usually less crowded. ✉ *Manuel Fernandez y Gonzalez 3, Barrio de las Letras* ☎ *91/429–5833* ✉ *Nuñez de Arce 6, Santa Ana* ☎ *91/532–0890* ▭ *AE, MC, V* ⊙ *Nuñez de Arce branch closed Sun., Mon., and Aug.* ✥ *E4.*

$$$$ SPANISH ✕ **Lhardy.** Serving Madrid specialties for more than 150 years, Lhardy looks about the same as it must have on day one, with dark-wood paneling, brass chandeliers, and red-velvet chairs. Most people come for the traditional *cocido a la madrileña* (a hearty meal of broth, meat, and garbanzo beans) and *callos a la madrileña* (veal tripe stewed with onions and tomatoes), but game, sea bass, and a good fish soup are also available. Dining rooms are upstairs; the ground-floor entry doubles as a delicatessen and stand-up coffee bar. ✉ *Carrera de San Jerónimo 8, Sol* ☎ *91/522–2207* ▭ *AE, DC, MC, V* ⊙ *Closed Aug. No dinner Sun.* ✥ *E4.*

¢ SPANISH ✕ **Nueva Galicia.** This small family-run bar and restaurant has long been one of the best values in the center of Madrid—it's two blocks from the Puerta del Sol—and you can eat inside or, during summer, at tables on the pedestrian-only side street. It is usually noisy and serves simple food, yet a starter, main course, dessert, and a full bottle of wine can be consumed for a ridiculously low €8.50, or you can choose to share some of the larger portions (*raciones*) of octopus, cuttlefish, *lacón* (cooked ham with Galician potatoes), or *pisto* (a Spanish ratatouille). If you're heading out, get a sandwich to go. ✉ *Cruz 6, Sol* ☎ *91/522–5289* ▭ *No credit cards* ⊙ *Closed Sun. and Aug.* ✥ *E4.*

WHERE TO STAY

Madrid kicked off the new millennium with a hotel boom, adding more than 17,000 new hotel rooms—meaning that in the last nine years the city has increased the number of hotel rooms by about 50%—and more are becoming available every year, though now at a slower rate.

BEST BETS FOR MADRID LODGING

Having trouble deciding where to stay in Madrid? Fodor's writers have selected some of their favorites in the lists below. Details are in the full reviews.

Fodor's Choice ★

AC Palacio del Retiro, $$$$, p. 110

De las Letras, $$$–$$$$, p. 113

Hostal Adriano, ¢, p. 114

Hotel Intur Palacio San Martín, $$$–$$$$, p. 114

Hotel Urban, $$$$, p. 105

Hospes Madrid, $$$$, p. 111

Hotel Urban, $$$$, p. 105

ME Reina Victoria, $$$$, p. 108

Orfila, $$$$, p. 111

Silken Puerta de América, $$$$, p. 112

Vincci Soma, $$$$, p. 112

Westin Palace, $$$$, p. 109

By Price

¢

Hostal Adriano, ¢, p. 114

Hostal Villar, ¢, p. 104

$

Abalú, $, p. 113

Inglés, $, p. 105

$$

Hotel Catalonia Las Cortes, $$–$$$, p. 104

$$$

Hotel NH Paseo del Prado, $$$–$$$$, p. 105

$$$$

AC Santo Mauro, $$$$, p. 110

By Experience

MOST CHARMING

Abalú, $, p. 113

AC Santo Mauro, $$$$, p. 110

Hospes Madrid, $$$$, p. 111

Hostal Adriano, ¢, p. 114

Hotel Intur Palacio San Martín, $$$–$$$$, p. 114

Orfila, $$$$, p. 111

Quo Puerta del Sol, $$–$$$, p. 108

Room Mate Alicia, $$, p. 108

Room Mate Laura, $, p. 112

MOST HISTORIC

Hotel Intur Palacio San Martín, $$$–$$$$, p. 114

Ritz, $$$$, p. 111

Tryp Ambassador, $$$–$$$$, p. 115

Westin Palace, $$$$, p. 109

BEST DESIGN

Abalú, $, p. 113

De las Letras, $$$–$$$$, p. 113

Hotel Urban, $$$$, p. 105

ME Reina Victoria, $$$$, p. 108

Room Mate Alicia, $$, p. 108

Room Mate Laura, $, p. 112

Room Mate Óscar, $, p. 113

Silken Puerta de America, $$$$, p. 112

Vincci Soho, $$$–$$$$, p. 109

Vincci Soma, $$$$, p. 112

BEST FOR FAMILIES

Chic and Basic Colors (Apartments), $, p. 104

Jardín de Recoletos, $$$, p. 111

Suite Prado, $$, p. 109

MOST CENTRAL

Hotel Urban, $$$$, p. 105

Hotel Intur Palacio San Martín, $$$–$$$$, p. 114

Ritz, $$$$, p. 111

Room Mate Alicia, $$, p. 108

Room Mate Laura, $, p. 112

Westin Palace, $$$$, p. 109

BEST FOR HIPSTERS

Abalú, $, p. 113

Chic and Basic Colors, $, p. 104

De las Letras, $$$–$$$$, p. 113

Hostal Adriano, ¢, p. 114

Hotel Urban, $$$$, p. 105

ME Reina Victoria, $$$$, p. 108

Room Mate Laura, $, p. 112

Room Mate Óscar, $, p. 113

WHERE SHOULD I STAY?

	Neighborhood Vibe	Pros	Cons
Barrio de las Letras (including Carrera de San Jerónimo and Paseo del Prado)	A magnet for tourists, this classic literary nest has gone up a few notches with the pedestrianization of some streets. It features the most exciting recent hotel openings.	Renovated Plaza Santa Ana and Plaza del Ángel; the emergence of posh hotels and restaurants; conveniently located between the oldest part of the city and all the major art museums.	Noisy, especially around Plaza Santa Ana; some bars and restaurants overpriced due to the tourists.
Chamberí, Retiro, and Salamanca	Swanky, posh, and quite safe, these are the neighborhoods many high-end hotels and restaurants call home.	Quiet at day's end; plenty of good restaurants; the city's major upscale shopping (Salamanca) and residential (Salamanca and the Eastern side of Retiro) areas.	Blander and with less character (except for the expensive area of Retiro, which is also less lively) than other districts; expensive.
Chueca and Malasaña	Vibrant and bustling, this is where you want to be if you're past your twenties but still don't want to be in bed before midnight.	These barrios burst with a bit of everything: busy nightlife, alternative shops, charming cafés, and fancy and inexpensive local and international restaurants.	Extremely loud, especially on the weekends; dirtier than most other neighborhoods.
Gran Vía and Callao	This big commercial area has some of the city's most crowded streets—especially on weekends.	Easy access to museums, shops, and sightseeing; has a good feel of Madrid hustle and bustle and nightlife energy.	When the shops close it loses some of its charm. At night you'll find characters of all sorts roaming the streets.
Sol and the Royal Palace	Anchored by the locally flavored Plaza Mayor, this historic quarter is full of narrow streets and taverns.	Has the most traditional feel of Madrid neighborhoods; lodging and dining of all sorts, including many inexpensive (though usually indistinctive) hostals and old-flavor taverns.	Can be tough to navigate; many tourist traps.

Plenty of the new arrivals are medium-price chain hotels that try to combine striking design with affordable prices. One step higher is the handful of new hotels that lure the hip crowd with top-notch design and superb food and nightlife. These have caused quite a stir in the five-star range and forced some of the more traditional hotels—long favored by dignitaries, star athletes, and artists—to enhance their food and service. Meanwhile, *hostals* and small hotels have shown that low prices can walk hand in hand with good taste and friendly service.

DEALS AND DISCOUNTS

Most hotels offer special weekend plans and discount prices during the month of August. Prices fluctuate, even with hotels of the same category belonging to the same chain, so it's best to shop around. *Hostal* rooms found on the upper floors of apartment buildings often go for €50 or less. These cheap lodgings are frequently full, especially on the weekends, and sometimes don't take reservations, so you simply have to try your luck door-to-door. Many are in the old city, in the trapezoid between the Puerta del Sol, the Atocha Station, the Basílica de San Francisco on Calle Bailén, and the Royal Palace; start your quest around Plaza Santa Ana or on the streets that are behind Puerta de Sol, near Plaza Mayor and Calle Atocha.

Use the coordinate (↔B2) at the end of each listing to locate a site on the corresponding map.

BARRIO DE LAS LETRAS

$$–$$$ **Catalonia Moratín.** A regal corridor leading to the reception desk, the atrium (where the walls are partly made of original granite blocks), and the magnificent main wooden staircase, presided over by a lion statue—these are the elements that best reveal this building's 18th-century origins. The other common areas, including the restaurant and a reading room with a small library, have less character. Guest rooms are comfortable, with functional wooden furniture and striped curtains and bedspreads. Bathrooms have cream-color tiles and green marble sinks. **Pros:** grand, quiet building; spacious rooms. **Cons:** the street looks a bit scruffy. ✉*Calle Atocha 23, Sol* ☎*91/369–7171* 🌐*www.hotelescatalonia.es* *63 rooms* *In-room: safe, Wi-Fi. In-hotel: restaurant, bar, public Wi-Fi* ▭*AE, DC, MC, V* ↔*E5.*

$ **Chic and Basic Colors.** Primarily but not exclusively catering to gay travelers, this is the perfect place for those who love playful design but don't plan on spending too much time in their rooms. Based on the concept of color therapy, each room is decorated in a specific color with integrated bathrooms; you can play with the intensity of light to suit your mood. The yellow, red, and orange rooms have balconies and face the street. Get more space with the double superior room for a little extra. The rectangular black table at the entrance serves as a meeting and breakfast room. In late 2008, Chic and Basic began offering five apartments above the hotel. Tastefully decorated and reasonably priced, two of them fit up to four people, and the remaining two are catered to couples. Reserve rooms and apartments in advance. **Pros:** unusual decor, gay-friendly, great location. **Cons:** more expensive on the weekends, hotel rooms not for the claustrophobic, no elevator. ✉*Huertas 14, 2nd exterior left, Santa Ana* ☎*91/429–6935* 🌐*www.chicandbasic.com/* *10 rooms* *In-hotel: public Internet* ▭*AE, DC, MC, V* *CP* ↔*E5.*

¢ **Hostal Villar.** Rooms here go from single to quadruple, with or without bathrooms (those facing the busy Calle Príncipe are among the ones without baths), and are reasonably large, clean, and comfortably decorated with matching bedspreads and curtains. The bathrooms, however, are rather small. Service is friendly and attentive. **Pros:** good value and location. **Cons:** worn-out rooms and public areas. ✉*Príncipe 18, Santa Ana* ☎*91/531–6600* 🌐*www.villar.es* *40 rooms, 27 with bath* *In-room: no TV (some), a/c (some)* ▭*MC, V* ↔*E4.*

$$–$$$ **Hotel Catalonia Las Cortes.** A late 18th-century palace formerly owned by the Duke of Noblejas, this hotel retains a good part of its aristocratic

past: a gorgeous wooden staircase, some of the old moldings, and stained windows. It has a classic feel without being ostentatious or overwhelming. Rooms are elegant and wallpapered in tones of gray, whereas bathrooms—with blander decor—are quite decent in size for the city's standards. Better still, it's just a few yards from Plaza Santa Ana. **Pros:** tasteful room decor, big walk-in shower, has triple rooms, great location. **Cons:** common areas are rather dull. ✉ *Prado 6, Santa Ana* ☎ *91/389–6051* 🌐 *www.hoteles-catalonia.com* *65 rooms, 8 junior suites, 2 suites* *In-room: safe, Wi-Fi. In-hotel: restaurant, bar, laundry facilities, public Wi-Fi, parking (fee)* *AE, DC, MC, V* ✥ *E4.*

$$$–$$$$ **Hotel NH Paseo del Prado.** Once the residence of a count, this fully restored hotel, a block from the Prado, is a reasonable yet luxurious alternative to the five-star hotels that populate the area. In the common areas feature odd combinations, like period chairs around a brown leather couch, but guest rooms are spacious and more stylish, with hand-painted Canarian motifs, bold-colored carpets from the Royal Factory of Tapestries, and wooden furniture. The tapas bar, open to the public, is overseen by one of the city's best chefs and a magnet for peckish passersby. **Pros:** sizable and elegant bathrooms, close to some of the city's best tapas bars. **Cons:** you'll have to upgrade if you want good views. ✉ *Plaza Cánovas del Castillo 4, Retiro* ☎ *91/330–2400* 🌐 *www.nh-hoteles.es* *114 rooms, 5 suites* *In-room: safe, Wi-Fi. In-hotel: restaurant, public Wi-Fi, parking (fee)* *AE, DC, MC, V* ✥ *F4.*

$$$$ Fodor's Choice ★ **Hotel Urban.** With a stylish mix of the ancient (New Guinean carvings in the lobby, a small Egyptian museum, and antique Chinese or Burmese statues in every room, all belonging to the owner, a renowned art collector) and daring sophistication (the tall alabaster column that majestically stands in the lobby's atrium, the tiled and gold inlaid wall on the main staircase, and the sleek cocktail bar), this is the hotel that best conveys Madrid's new cosmopolitan spirit. Rooms, done in dark hues, are less flamboyant, and some are small. There's a great restaurant here and an ultrachic bar on the roof, where the glamorous gather on summer nights to enjoy the views and sip Champagne cocktails. **Pros:** ultrachic, superb restaurant and bars; rooftop swimming pool. **Cons:** smallish rooms. ✉ *Carrera de San Jerónimo 34, Barrio de las Letras* ☎ *91/787–7770* 🌐 *www.derbyhotels.com* *96 rooms, 3 junior suites, 4 suites* *In-room: safe, Wi-Fi. In-hotel: 2 restaurants, bar, pool, gym, parking (fee)* *AE, DC, MC, V* ✥ *E4.*

$ **Inglés.** Virginia Woolf was among the first luminaries to discover this hotel in the middle of the old city's bar-and-restaurant district. Since then, the Inglés has attracted more than its share of less-celebrated artists and writers. Half of the rooms were tiled and painted in 2005, and new bathrooms were installed, but the decor still resembles the ornate and outdated lobby. Suites, which are double rooms with a salon, are nonetheless a bargain. You get twice the space for what you'd pay for a standard double elsewhere. Also, if your room faces Calle Echegaray, you can get an unusual aerial view of the medieval quarter, which is all red tiles and ramshackle gables. **Pros:** huge rooms by local standards, centrally located. **Cons:** outdated decor, noisy street. ✉ *Echegaray 8,*

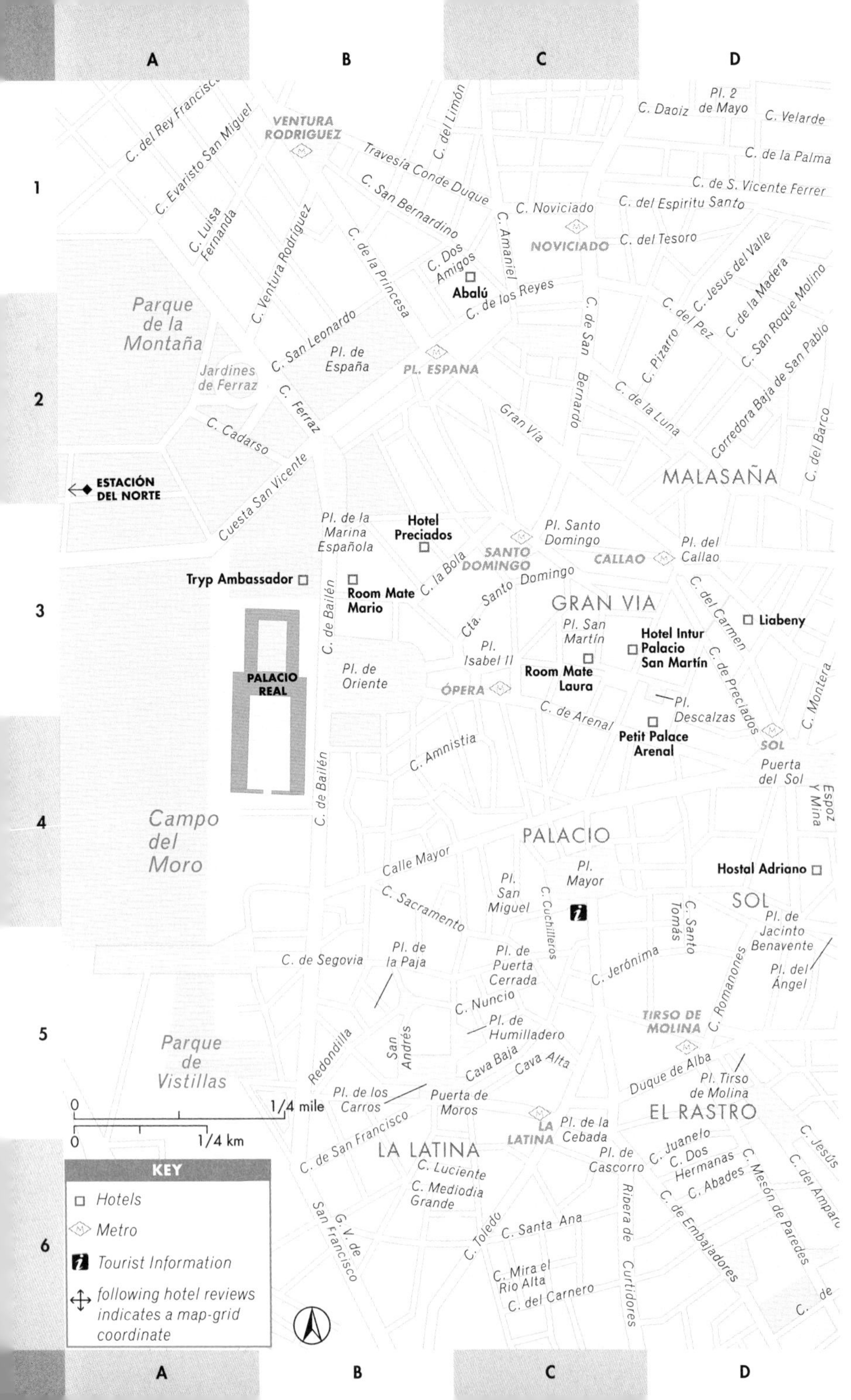

A
B
C
D
1
2
3
4
5
6
C. del Rey Francisco
C. Evaristo San Miguel
VENTURA RODRIGUEZ
C. del Limón
Travesía Conde Duque
C. San Bernardino
C. Daoiz
Pl. 2 de Mayo
C. Velarde
C. de la Palma
C. de S. Vicente Ferrer
C. del Espiritu Santo
C. Noviciado
NOVICIADO
C. del Tesoro
C. Amaniel
C. Luisa Fernanda
C. Ventura Rodríguez
C. de la Princesa
C. Dos Amigos
Abalú
C. de los Reyes
C. de San Bernardo
C. Jesus del Valle
C. de la Madera
C. San Roque Molino
C. del Pez
C. Pizarro
C. San Pablo
Corredora Baja de San Pablo
C. de la Luna
C. del Barco
Parque de la Montaña
Jardines de Ferraz
C. San Leonardo
Pl. de España
PL. ESPANA
C. Ferraz
Gran Vía
C. Cadarso
MALASAÑA
ESTACIÓN DEL NORTE
Cuesta San Vicente
Pl. de la Marina Española
Hotel Preciados
SANTO DOMINGO
Pl. Santo Domingo
CALLAO
Pl. del Callao
Tryp Ambassador
Room Mate Mario
C. la Bola
Cta. Santo Domingo
GRAN VIA
C. del Carmen
Liabeny
C. de Bailén
PALACIO REAL
Pl. de Oriente
Pl. Isabel II
Pl. San Martín
Hotel Intur Palacio San Martín
Room Mate Laura
ÓPERA
Pl. Descalzas
C. de Preciados
C. Montera
C. de Arenal
Petit Palace Arenal
SOL
Puerta del Sol
C. Amnistia
Espoz Y Mina
Campo del Moro
PALACIO
Calle Mayor
Pl. Mayor
Hostal Adriano
C. Sacramento
Pl. San Miguel
C. Cuchilleros
C. Santo Tomás
SOL
Pl. de Jacinto Benavente
Pl. del Ángel
C. de Segovia
Pl. de la Paja
Pl. de Puerta Cerrada
C. Jerónima
C. Romanones
C. Nuncio
Pl. de Humilladero
TIRSO DE MOLINA
Parque de Vistillas
Redondilla
San Andrés
Cava Baja
Cava Alta
Duque de Alba
Pl. Tirso de Molina
0
1/4 mile
0
1/4 km
Pl. de los Carros
Puerta de Moros
C. de San Francisco
LA LATINA
Pl. de la Cebada
EL RASTRO
LA LATINA
C. Luciente
C. Mediodia Grande
Pl. de Cascorro
C. Juanelo
C. Dos Hermanas
C. Abades
C. Mesón de Paredes
C. Jesús
C. del Amparo
G. V. de San Francisco
C. Toledo
C. Santa Ana
Ribera de Curtidores
C. de Embajadores
C. Mira el Rio Alta
C. del Carnero
C. de
KEY
Hotels
Metro
Tourist Information
following hotel reviews indicates a map-grid coordinate

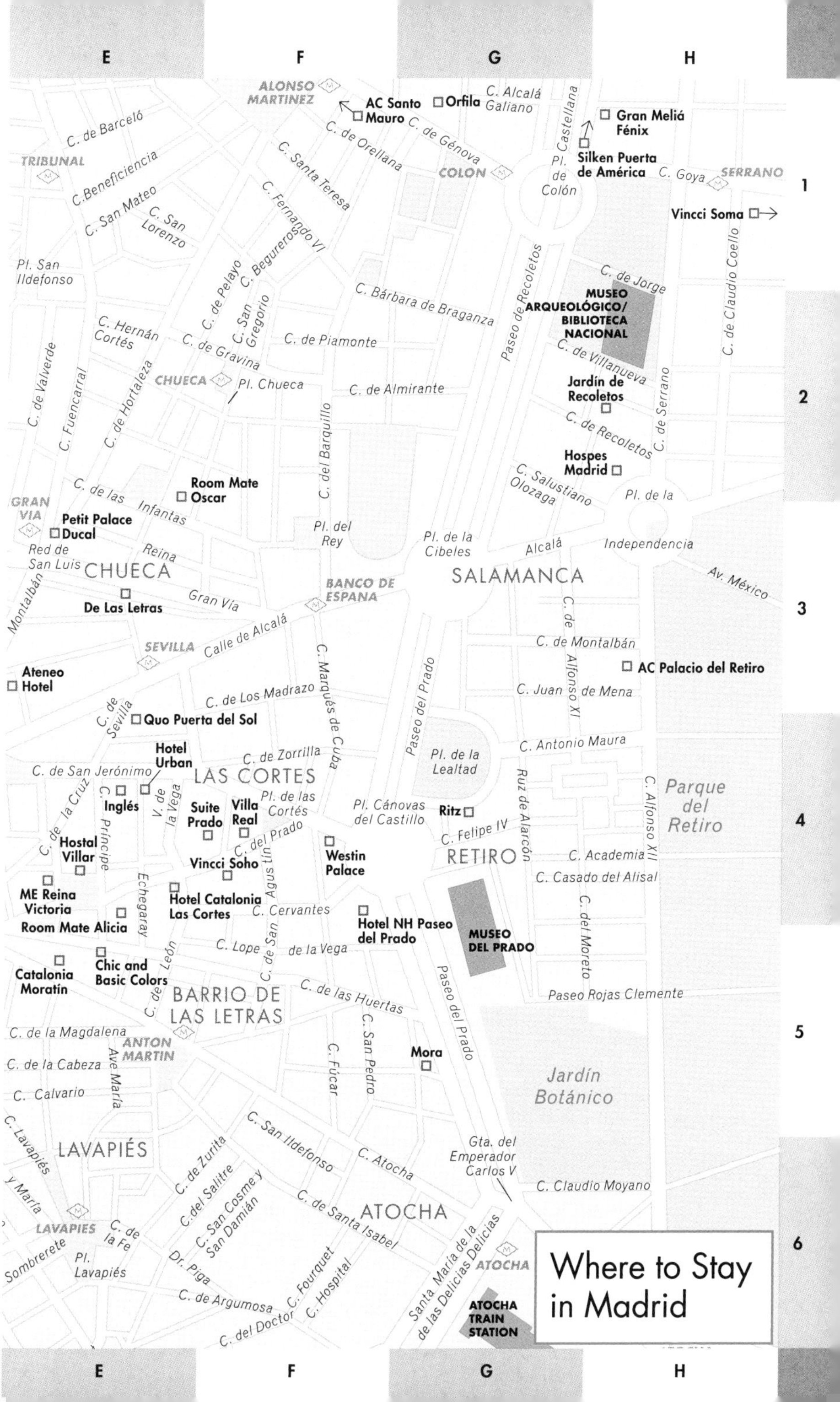
E
F
G
H
1
2
3
4
5
6
Where to Stay in Madrid
AC Santo Mauro
Orfila
Gran Meliá Fénix
Silken Puerta de América
Vincci Soma
Jardín de Recoletos
Hospes Madrid
Room Mate Oscar
Petit Palace Ducal
De Las Letras
AC Palacio del Retiro
Ateneo Hotel
Quo Puerta del Sol
Hotel Urban
Inglés
Suite Prado
Villa Real
Ritz
Hostal Villar
Vincci Soho
Westin Palace
ME Reina Victoria
Room Mate Alicia
Hotel Catalonia Las Cortes
Hotel NH Paseo del Prado
Catalonia Moratín
Chic and Basic Colors
Mora
MUSEO ARQUEOLÓGICO/ BIBLIOTECA NACIONAL
MUSEO DEL PRADO
ATOCHA TRAIN STATION
CHUECA
SALAMANCA
LAS CORTES
RETIRO
BARRIO DE LAS LETRAS
LAVAPIÉS
ATOCHA
Parque del Retiro
Jardín Botánico
ALONSO MARTINEZ
TRIBUNAL
COLON
SERRANO
CHUECA
GRAN VIA
BANCO DE ESPANA
SEVILLA
ANTON MARTIN
LAVAPIES
ATOCHA
C. Alcalá Galiano
C. Castellana
C. de Barceló
C. de Orellana
C. de Génova
C. Goya
C. Beneficiencia
C. Santa Teresa
Pl. de Colón
C. San Mateo
C. San Lorenzo
C. Fernando VI
Pl. San Ildefonso
C. Beguerero
C. de Pelayo
C. San Gregorio
C. Bárbara de Braganza
Paseo de Recoletos
C. de Jorge
C. de Claudio Coello
C. Hernán Cortés
C. de Gravina
C. de Piamonte
C. de Villanueva
C. de Valverde
C. Fuencarral
C. de Hortaleza
Pl. Chueca
C. de Almirante
C. de Serrano
C. de Recoletos
C. del Barquillo
C. Salustiano Olozaga
C. de las Infantas
Pl. de la Independencia
Pl. del Rey
Pl. de la Cibeles
Alcalá
Red de San Luis
Reina
Av. México
Montalbán
Gran Vía
C. de Alfonso XI
Calle de Alcalá
C. de Montalbán
C. Marqués de Cuba
Paseo del Prado
C. de Los Madrazo
C. Juan de Mena
C. de Sevilla
C. Antonio Maura
C. de Zorrilla
Pl. de la Lealtad
C. de San Jerónimo
Ruz de Alarcón
C. Alfonso XII
C. de la Cruz
C. Príncipe
V. de la Vega
Pl. de las Cortés
Pl. Cánovas del Castillo
C. Felipe IV
C. del Prado
C. de San Agustín
C. Academia
C. Casado del Alisal
Echegaray
C. Cervantes
C. del Moreto
C. Lope de la Vega
C. de León
C. de las Huertas
Paseo Rojas Clemente
C. de la Magdalena
C. San Pedro
C. de la Cabeza
Ave María
C. Fúcar
C. Calvario
C. Lavapiés
C. San Ildefonso
Gta. del Emperador Carlos V
C. Atocha
C. de Zurita
C. del Salitre
C. San Cosme y San Damián
C. de Santa Isabel
C. Claudio Moyano
y María
C. de la Fe
Sombrerete
Pl. Lavapiés
Dr. Piga
C. de Argumosa
C. Fourquet
C. Hospital
Santa María de la Cabeza
de las Delicias
Delicias
C. del Doctor

Santa Ana ☎*91/429–6551* *58 rooms* *In-room: no a/c (some). In-hotel: restaurant, bar, gym, parking (fee)* *AE, DC, MC, V* ✣*E4.*

$$$$ **ME Reina Victoria.** A few bulls' heads hanging in the lounge and some abstract pictures of bullfighting scattered around this ultramodern hotel are all that remain to remind visitors that this was once the place where bullfighters convened before heading off toward Las Ventas. The old flair has been superseded by cutting-edge services in the rooms: a USB port for recharging iPods, MP3 players, and the like; a large flat-screen TV with surround sound; an advanced latex memory-foam mattress; and a minibar that's double the usual size. Common areas have round-the-clock entertainment; it has a good restaurant; and two of the city's fanciest and busiest bars are here, including one rooftop establishment with a 360-degree panoramic view of the city. **Pros:** unbeatable location, modern vibe, trendy bars and restaurant. **Cons:** rooms are a bit small. ✉*Plaza Santa Ana 14, Santa Ana* ☎*91/531–4500* *www.solmelia.com* *182 rooms, 9 suites* *In-room: safe, DVD, Wi-Fi. In-hotel: restaurant, bars, laundry facilities, public Wi-Fi, some pets allowed, parking (fee)* *AE, DC, MC, V* ✣*E4.*

ROOM MATES

The Room Mate chain has hit on a winning combination: great design and limited services at a low price. They all have free Wi-Fi, and their breakfast is served until noon. Room Mate Mario was the first one and has since been joined by Laura, Alicia, and the chain's flagship, Oscar. Full reviews are in the neighborhoods. *www.room-matehoteles.com*

$ **Mora.** This cheery hotel with a sparkling, faux-marble lobby and bright, carpeted hallways is within steps of the CaixaForum and across from the Botanical Garden. Guest rooms are modestly decorated (those on the third and fourth floors were renovated in 2008) but are large and comfortable; those facing the street have great views of the gardens and the Prado, and double-pane windows keep them fairly quiet. For breakfast and lunch, the café is excellent, affordable, and popular with locals. **Pros:** close to all major museums, has triple rooms. **Cons:** busy and touristy street, uninspiring decor. ✉*Paseo del Prado 32, Centro* ☎*91/420–1569* *www.hotelmora.com* *62 rooms* *In-hotel: restaurant* *AE, DC, MC, V* ✣*G5.*

$$–$$$ **Quo Puerta del Sol.** Between Santa Ana and Sol, this modern, design-oriented boutique hotel has rooms with views of the city center that are equipped with cutting-edge technology, dark hardwood floors, and modern touches such as the stainless-steel-and-glass sinks in the bathrooms. Common areas may not be ample in size but are charming, trendy, and full of character. **Pros:** good design, centrally located. **Cons:** small lobby, no restaurant. ✉*C. Sevilla 4, Centro* ☎*91/532–9049* *www.hotelesquo.com* *61 rooms, 1 junior suite* *In-room: Wi-Fi. In-hotel: Wi-Fi, parking (fee)* *AE, DC, MC, V* ✣*E4.*

$$ **Room Mate Alicia.** The all-white lobby with curvaceous walls, ceiling, and lamps set the mood for the mostly young urbanite visitors of this former trench coat factory. Carpeted rooms, although not large, are very modern; the black-slate bathrooms, all with showers (no tubs), are in

the bedroom separated only by a glass door. For just a few more euros you can upgrade to an executive room with a terrace or a minisuite with large windows overlooking Plaza Santa Ana. **Pros:** great value, chic design, laid-back atmosphere, and unbeatable location. **Cons:** standard rooms are small, some might not like that bathrooms are not in a separate space. ✉ *Prado 2, Santa Ana* ☎ *91/389–6095* 🌐 *wwww.room-matehoteles.com* *34 rooms, 3 suites* *In-room: Wi-Fi. In-hotel: bar, Wi-Fi, parking (fee)* ▭ *AE, DC, MC, V* ✥ *E4.*

$$ **Suite Prado.** Popular with Americans, this stylish apartment hotel is near the Prado, the Thyssen-Bornemisza, and the Plaza Santa Ana tapas area. The attractive attic studios on the fourth floor have sloped ceilings with wood beams; there are larger suites downstairs. All apartments are brightly decorated and have marble baths and basic kitchens. They have an agreement with the nearby Hotel Prado for breakfast, which can also be ordered as room service. Triples and quadruples are a great deal. **Pros:** large rooms, great for families and longer stays. **Cons:** a bit noisy; kitchens not always available for use. ✉ *Manuel Fernández y González 10, Santa Ana* ☎ *91/420–2318* 🌐 *www.suiteprado.com* *18 suites* *In-room: kitchen, Wi-Fi. In-hotel: parking (fee)* ▭ *AE, DC, MC, V* ✥ *F4.*

$$$$ **Villa Real.** For a medium-size hotel that combines elegance, modern amenities, friendly service, and a great location, look no further: the Villa Real faces Spain's parliament and is convenient to almost everything, particularly the Prado and Thyssen-Bornemisza museums. The simulated 19th-century facade gives way to an intimate lobby with modern furnishings. Many rooms are split level, with a small sitting area. Some suites have whirlpool baths. Rooms are spacious with a very clean contemporary look in lush earthy tones with marble bathrooms. **Pros:** great location, very helpful service. **Cons:** expensive Wi-Fi, few facilities. ✉ *Plaza de las Cortés 10, Retiro* ☎ *91/420–3767* 🌐 *www.derbyhotels.es* *94 rooms, 20 suites* *In-room: Wi-Fi. In-hotel: restaurant, bar, public Wi-Fi, parking (fee)* ▭ *AE, DC, MC, V* ✥ *F4.*

$$$–$$$$ **Vincci Soho.** Faithful to its surname, this hotel seems as if it had been transplanted from London or New York into one of Madrid's busiest neighborhoods. Everything on its ground floor—the lamps, the mustard color circular divan that sits in front of the reception desk, the meeting lounges with velvet armchairs and silk screens, the steel butterfly cutouts on the restaurant walls—highlights urban elegance and imagination. No two rooms are alike in shape—the hotel is made of five old private houses—but they're all comfortable and bright—even the interior ones, thanks to a large open courtyard that keeps the street noise out and lets the sun in. **Pros:** very stylish, central location, great breakfast buffet. **Cons:** some rooms are noisy. ✉ *Prado 18, Santa Ana* ☎ *91/141–4100* 🌐 *www.vinccihoteles.com* *167 rooms* *In-room: safe, Wi-Fi. In-hotel: restaurant, bar, public Wi-Fi, parking (fee)* ▭ *AE, DC, MC, V* ✥ *F4.*

$$$$ **Westin Palace.** Built in 1912, Madrid's most famous grand hotel is a Belle Epoque creation of Alfonso XIII and has hosted the likes of Salvador Dalí, Marlon Brando, Rita Hayworth, and Madonna. Guest rooms are high-tech and generally impeccable; banquet halls and lobbies have

been beautified, and the facade has been restored. The Art Nouveau stained-glass dome over the lounge remains exquisitely original, and guest-room windows are double-glazed against street noise. The hotel also houses the popular Asia Gallery restaurant. **Pros:** grand hotel with tons of history, weekend brunch with opera performances. **Cons:** fourth floor has not been renovated yet, standard rooms face a back street. *☒Plaza de las Cortés 7, Retiro ☎91/360–8000 ⊕www.palacemadrid.com ⇨465 rooms, 45 suites ♿In-room: Internet, Wi-Fi. In-hotel: 2 restaurants, bar, gym, public Wi-Fi, parking (fee) ▭AE, DC, MC, V ✣F4.*

CHAMBERÍ, RETIRO, AND SALAMANCA

$$$$ Fodor's Choice ★ **AC Palacio del Retiro.** An early-20th-century restored palatial building owned by a noble family with extravagant habits (the elevator carried the horses up and down from the exercise ring on the roof), this spectacular hotel closely follows the path of the first AC Santo Mauro with its tasteful, modern decor in a historical building. Palacio preserves even more of its grandiose past: baseboards and fountains covered with ceramics from Talavera, original Parisian stained-glass windows, marble floors and columns, and original moldings. All rooms have superb views of the nearby Retiro Park. Bathroom doors in the double superior rooms are full-size Lichtenstein silk-screen prints. **Pros:** spacious, stylish rooms; within walking distance of the Prado; bathrooms stocked with all sorts of complimentary products. **Cons:** pricey, lower rooms facing the park can get noisy. *☒Alfonso XII 14, Retiro ☎91/523–7460 ⊕www.ac-hotels.com ⇨50 rooms, 8 suites ♿In-room: safe, DVD, Wi-Fi. In-hotel: restaurant, bar, gym, spa, public Wi-Fi, parking (fee) ▭AE, DC, MC, V ✣H3.*

$$$$ **AC Santo Mauro.** Once the Canadian embassy, this turn-of-the-20th-century mansion is now an intimate luxury hotel, an oasis of calm a short walk from the city center. The neoclassical architecture is accented by contemporary furniture in white, gray, eggplant, and black hues. Some of the rooms in the main building still maintain the original details and fixtures. The top-notch restaurant is in what used to be the mansion's library. Views vary; request a room with a terrace overlooking the gardens. **Pros:** quite private, sizable rooms with comfortable beds; good restaurant. **Cons:** pricey, not in the historic center. *☒Zurbano 36, Chamberí ☎91/319–6900 ⊕www.ac-hotels.com ⇨51 rooms ♿In-room: DVD, Wi-Fi. In-hotel: restaurant, bar, pool, gym, public Wi-Fi, parking (fee) ▭AE, DC, MC, V ✣F1.*

$$$$ **Gran Meliá Fénix.** An impressive lobby with marble floors, antique furniture, and a stained-glass dome ceiling define the style of this refurbished Madrid institution. Overlooking Plaza de Colón on the Castellana, the hotel is a mere hop from the posh shops of Calle Serrano. Spacious rooms are decorated in reds and golds and are amply furnished; flowers abound. Ask for a room facing the Plaza de Colón; otherwise, the view is rather dreary. **Pros:** close to shopping, great breakfast buffet. **Cons:** rather small bathrooms, below-average restaurant. *☒Hermosilla 2, Salamanca ☎91/431–6700 ⊕www.solmelia.com ⇨214 rooms, 11 suites ♿In-room: Internet. In-hotel: 2 restaurants, bar, gym, spa, sauna, Wi Fi, parking (fee) ▭AE, DC, MC, V ✣H1.*

2

$$$$ **Hospes Madrid.** The newest five-star addition to the city center, the Hospes has all the right ingredients to meet the demands of today's discerning travelers: a historic 19th-century building facing Retiro Park; stylish design that isn't overwhelming or uncomfortable and is enhanced by elegant details such as iron columns, original moldings, and a restored main staircase; an interior patio turned into a deck; a good restaurant with an emerging and innovative young chef; and a spa with a two-page service list. **Pros:** intimate and quiet, right next to Madrid's version of Central Park. **Cons:** some rooms have a shower but no bathtub; standard rooms don't face the park. ✉ *Plaza de la Independencia 3, Retiro* ☎ *91/432–2911* 🌐 *www.hospes.com* *41 rooms, 6 suites* *In-room: DVD, Internet, Wi-Fi. In-hotel: 2 restaurants, gym, spa* *AE, DC, MC, V* ✣ *H2.*

$$$ **Jardín de Recoletos.** This apartment hotel offers great value on a quiet street close to Plaza Colón and upmarket Calle Serrano. The large lobby has marble floors and a stained-glass ceiling and adjoins a café, restaurant, and the hotel's restful private garden. The large rooms, with light wood trim and beige-and-yellow furnishings, include sitting and dining areas. "Superior" rooms and suites have hydromassage baths and large terraces. Book well in advance. **Pros:** spacious rooms with kitchens, good for families. **Cons:** bland decor. ✉ *Gil de Santivañes 6, Salamanca* ☎ *91/781–1640* 🌐 *www.vphoteles.com* *36 rooms, 7 suites* *In-room: kitchen, VCR, Internet, Wi-Fi. In-hotel: restaurant, room service, public Wi-Fi, parking (fee)* *AE, DC, MC, V* ✣ *H2.*

$$$$ **Orfila.** This elegant 1886 town house, hidden away on a leafy little residential street not far from Plaza Colón, has every comfort of a larger hotel, but in more intimate, personalized surroundings. Originally the in-town residence of the literary and aristocratic Gomez-Acebo family, Orfila 6 was an address famous for theater performances in the late 19th and early 20th centuries. The restaurant, garden (superb for summer dining), and tearoom have period furniture; guest rooms are draped with striped and floral silks. **Pros:** quiet street, refined decor, really attentive service. **Cons:** no gym (though the Orfila has an agreement with one nearby, for guests to use for a fee), pricey breakfast. ✉ *Orfila 6, Chamberí* ☎ *91/702–7770* 🌐 *www.hotelorfila.com* *20 rooms, 12 suites* *In-room: Internet, Wi-Fi. In-hotel: restaurant, bar, public Wi-Fi, parking (fee)* *AE, DC, MC, V* ✣ *G1.*

$$$$ **Ritz.** Alfonso XIII, about to marry Queen Victoria's granddaughter, encouraged the construction of this hotel, the most exclusive in Spain, for his royal guests. Opened in 1910 by the king himself (who personally supervised construction), the Ritz is a monument to the Belle Epoque, its salons furnished with rare antiques, hand-embroidered linens, and handwoven carpets. All rooms (which are slowly being revamped for its centennial) have canopy beds; some have views of the Prado. The famous and pricey restaurant, Goya, serves a Sunday brunch feast that's accompanied by the soothing strains of harp music; from February to May, you'll enjoy chamber music during weekend tea and supper. **Pros:** old-world flair, the tearoom and the summer terrace, excellent location. **Cons:** what's classic for some may feel stuffy and outdated to others. ✉ *Plaza de la Lealtad 5, Retiro* ☎ *91/701–6767* 🌐 *www.ritzmadrid.*

com 167 *rooms* *In-room: Internet, Wi-Fi. In-hotel: restaurant, bar, gym, spa, public Wi-Fi, parking (fee)* AE, DC, MC, V G4.

$ **Room Mate Laura.** On Plaza de las Descalzas, this branch is in an old apartment building refurbished following the company's mantra of good design, distinctiveness (all rooms, many duplex, have different layouts), and friendly service—without burning a hole in the customer's pocket. **Pros:** kitchenettes for long stays, rooms are large enough to fit three people comfortably. **Cons:** only the best rooms have views of the convent, no restaurant, some bathrooms need to be revamped. *Travesía de Trujillos 3, Palacio* 91/701–1670 *www.room-matehotels.com* 36 *rooms* *In-room: Wi-Fi, kitchenette, DVD. In-hotel: restaurant, Wi-Fi* AE, DC, MC, V C3.

$ **Room Mate Mario.** In the city center, just steps from the major sights and nightlife, Mario is small and limited in services, but its bold modern style—original silk-printed headboards and combinations of white, gray, and black tones—and friendly service are a welcome alternative to Madrid's traditional hotel options. There's a great breakfast, but no restaurant. **Pros:** unusual decor, centrally located, great breakfast, convivial staff, it's the cheapest of the chain. **Cons:** no restaurant, its rooms are slightly smaller and offer less external views than the other Room Mate hotels. *Campomanes 4, Palacio* 91/548–8548 *www.room-matehoteles.com* 54 *rooms, 3 suites* *In-room: Wi-Fi. In-hotel: Wi-Fi, laundry facilities* AE, DC, MC, V CP B3.

$$$$ **Silken Puerta de América.** Inspired by Paul Eluard's *La Liberté* (whose verses are written across the facade), the owners of this hotel granted an unlimited budget to 19 of the world's top architects and designers. The result: 12 hotels in one, with floors by Zaha Hadid, Norman Foster, Jean Nouvel, David Chipperfield, and more. You can pick the floor of your choice online; most popular are the futuristic all-white layout by Hadid, the elegant black wood and white leather proposal by Foster, and the imaginative re-creation of space by Ron Arad. There's also a reputed restaurant and two bars (one on the rooftop), which are all just as impressive in design. The only snag: you'll need a taxi or the subway to get to the city center. **Pros:** an architect's dreamland, top-notch restaurant and bars. **Cons:** less than convenient location. *Av. de América 41, Prosperidad* 91/744–5400 *www.hotelpuertamerica.com* 282 *rooms, 21 junior suites, 12 suites* *In-room: safe, Wi-Fi. In-hotel: 2 restaurants, bars, pool, gym, public Wi-Fi, parking (fee)* AE, DC, MC, V G1.

$$$$ **Vincci Soma.** Balancing modern style with elegance, this hotel has dark wood floors, stereos in every room, and details, such as the environmentally friendly motorized bikes for guests, that make it a good alternative to the higher-end hotels. Each room has functional yet distinctive furniture, original artwork, and colorful bedspreads. The restaurant serves Mediterranean-fusion food and has great views of one of Madrid's great shopping streets, Calle Goya. **Pros:** close to all top name-brand stores, charming reading room, tasteful decor. **Cons:** noisy street, small rooms. *Calle Goya 79, Salamanca* 91/435–7545 *www.vinccihoteles.com* 167 *rooms, 3 suites, 7 apartments* *In-room: Internet, Wi-Fi.*

In-hotel: restaurant, bar, gym, public Wi-Fi, parking (fee) ▭*AE, DC, MC, V* ✣*H1.*

CHUECA AND MALASAÑA

$ **Abalú.** Each of the 16 rooms of this hotel at the heart of one of the city's youngest and liveliest neighborhoods is a small oasis of singular design. Designer Luis Delgado's mission is to make each room special, with a hodgepodge of one-of-a-kind accents, such as the black stenciled butterflies scattered along the walls of the White Room. If you're interested in feeling Malasaña's vibe and are not easily daunted by noise, ask for one of the three rooms facing the street, or for a little more, one of the junior suites with a Jacuzzi. **Pros:** unique room decor, very charming cafeteria. **Cons:** rooms smaller than average, the scruffy neighborhood may turn some people off. ✉*Pez 19, Centro* ☎*91/531–4744* ⊕*www.hotelabalu.com* *15 rooms, 2 suites* *In-room: safe, DVD, Wi-Fi* ▭*AE, MC, V* *CP* ✣*C1.*

$$$ **Petit Palace Ducal.** At the core of Madrid's most youthful shopping district, this former hostel is now a modern high-tech hotel that preserves some of the original elements (such as the wrought-iron elevator and staircase). The rooms have dark wood floors and headboards, track lighting, hidromassage showers, and laptops; some have bunk beds and can house up to five people. The café has large windows that face the street. **Pros:** very central location, friendly staff, unusual services such as the bikes for guests and strollers for babies, most rooms have external views. **Cons:** small public areas, some of the rooms look a bit worn out. ✉*Hortaleza 3, Chueca* ☎*91/521–1043* ⊕*www.hthoteles.com* *58 rooms* *In-room: safe, Wi-Fi, laptop. In-hotel: cafeteria, Wi-Fi, public Internet* ▭*AE, DC, MC, V* ✣*E3.*

$ **Room Mate Óscar.** Bold, bright, and modern, the flagship Room Mate is undeniably hip and glamorous. It has sizable rooms decorated with graffiti art, a lively restaurant, a trendy bar with a mostly gay crowd that stays opens late every night, and a summer terrace that's the envy of the city. The location, just off the Gran Vía, bustles but is excellent for getting around. **Pros:** friendly staff, hip clientele, and fashionable facilities. **Cons:** noisy street, it may be *too* happening to some. ✉*Pza. Vázquez de Mella, 12, Centro* ☎*91/701–1173* ⊕*www.room-matehoteles.com* *69 rooms, 6 suites* *In-room: Wi-Fi. In-hotel: restaurant, bar, Wi-Fi, laundry facilities, pool* ▭*AE, DC, MC, V* *CP* ✣*E2.*

GRAN VÍA AND CALLAO

$$$–$$$$ Fodor's Choice ★ **De Las Letras.** This hotel inspired by great literature (it even has a book catalog in every room) is a seamless mix of modern-pop interior design that respects and accents the original details of the 1917 structure (glazed tiles, canopies, original wood-and-iron elevator, wooden staircase, stone carvings). Rooms are painted in tones of ocher, orange, or burgundy, and have high ceilings, wooden floors, indirect lighting, and over-the-top modern bathrooms; each junior suite has a terrace with a whirlpool bath. The hotel has a charming rooftop terrace bar open to everyone. Enjoying a meal or a cocktail in the restaurant-lounge on the street level, you would never think you're around the corner from the bustling Gran Vía. **Pros:** young vibe, charming spa, very happening rooftop bar. **Cons:** small gym. ✉*Gran Vía 11, Centro* ☎*91/523–7980*

www.hoteldelasletras.com 103 rooms, 1 suite, 6 junior suites In-room: DVD, Wi-Fi. In-hotel: restaurant, bar, spa, gym, public Wi-Fi, parking (fee) AE, DC, MC, V E3.

$$–$$$ **Hotel Preciados.** In a 19th-century building on the quieter edge of one of Madrid's main shopping areas, this hotel is both charming and convenient. Rooms are modern and sophisticated, with hardwood floors and opaque glass closets. Some of the "double superiors" (slightly more expensive) have skylights in the bathrooms. **Pros:** conveniently located, good-size bathrooms, free Wi-Fi. **Cons:** expensive breakfast, bustling area. *C. Preciados 37, Centro 91/454–4400 www.preciadoshotel.com 74 rooms, 6 suites In-room: Wi-Fi. In-hotel: restaurant, bar, gym, public Wi-Fi, parking (fee) AE, DC, MC, V B3.*

SOL AND THE ROYAL PALACE

$ **Ateneo Hotel.** This hotel is in the restored 18th-century building that once housed the Ateneo, a club founded in 1835 to promote freedom of thought. The spacious rooms are done in cream and light wood tones with parquet flooring and red-and-gold-striped bedspreads. Exterior rooms have balconies overlooking the crowded street, except those on the fourth floor, which have sloped ceilings and skylights above the beds. **Pros:** large rooms, free Internet. **Cons:** though now pedestrianized and safe thanks to the police station, the street still attracts some sketchy characters. *Montera 22, Sol 91/521–2012 www.hotel-ateneo.com 38 rooms, 6 junior suites In-room: Internet AE, DC, MC, V BP E3.*

¢ Fodor's Choice ★ **Hostal Adriano.** Tucked away on a street with dozens of bland competitors, and a couple of blocks from Sol, this hotel stands out for its price and quality. The rooms, though not especially big, are charming and far from the standard *hostal* fare. They're thoughtfully decorated with the brightly colored walls and bedspreads, and by the furniture and accessories collected over the years by the two friendly Argentine owners. The best of the lot has been wallpapered with some old María Callas pictures and the musical score from *Tosca*. In case it's fully booked, note that the owners opened another small (10 rooms, 1 quadruple) and equally welcoming *hostal* but with no elevator (Adria Santa Ana) on nearby Nuñez de Arce 15. **Pros:** friendly service, great value, charming touches. **Cons:** short on facilities. *De la Cruz 26, 4th fl., Sol 91/521–1339 www.hostaladriano.com 22 rooms In-room: safe. In-hotel: Wi-Fi MC, V D4.*

$$$–$$$$ Fodor's Choice ★ **Hotel Intur Palacio San Martín.** In an unbeatable location across from one of Madrid's most celebrated monuments (the Convent of Descalzas), this hotel, once the old U.S. embassy and later a luxurious residential building crowded with noblemen, still exudes a kind of glory. The entrance leads to a glass-dome atrium that serves as a tranquil sitting area. There's an antique elevator, and many of the ceilings are carved and ornate. Rooms are spacious and carpeted; the five at street level have a much more modern decor, with stenciled headboards and ceramic floors; request one facing the big plaza. **Pros:** charming location, spacious rooms. **Cons:** no restaurant. *Plaza de San Martín 5, Palacio 91/701–5000 www.intur.com 94 rooms, 8 suites In-*

room: safe, Wi-Fi. In-hotel: gym, public Wi-Fi, parking (fee) ▭*AE, DC, MC, V* ✣*C3.*

$$ **Liabeny.** Although unassuming in style and a bit outdated, this 1960s hotel near a plaza (and several department stores) between Gran Vía and Puerta del Sol has large, comfortable carpeted rooms with striped fabrics and big windows. Interior and top-floor rooms are the quietest. **Pros:** centrally located, near Princesa's shopping area. **Cons:** small rooms and bathrooms, crowded and noisy neighborhood. ✉*Salud 3, Sol* ☎*91/531–9000* 🌐*www.liabeny.es* *220 rooms* *In-room: Internet, Wi-Fi. In-hotel: restaurant, bar, gym, sauna, public Wi-Fi, parking (fee)* ▭*AE, DC, MC, V* ✣*D3.*

$$$–$$$$ **Petit Palace Arenal.** Near the bustling tourist area Sol, this fairly new and popular hotel maintains some of the location's original characteristics, including a wooden staircase, some wooden beams, and the vaulted exposed-brick walls in the meeting and breakfast rooms downstairs. The rooms, tastefully done with deep-purple ceilings and outfitted with modern light fixtures and tempered-glass sinks, already show some wear and tear. This chain boutique hotel has two nearby locations with similar features: the Petit Palace Puerta del Sol on the same street but closer to Sol, and the Posada del Peine at C. Postas 17. **Pros:** modern-looking design, it has triple and quadruple rooms. **Cons:** no restaurant, very busy and noisy street, cheap room materials. ✉*Arenal 16, Sol* ☎*91/564–4355* 🌐*www.hthoteles.com* *64 rooms* *In-room: safe, Internet. In-hotel: breakfast room, public Internet* ▭*AE, DC, MC, V* ✣*D4.*

$$$–$$$$ **Tryp Ambassador.** On an old street between Gran Vía and the Royal Palace, the Ambassador occupies the renovated 19th-century palace of the Dukes of Granada. The facade (restored in 2007), a magnificent front door, and a graceful three-story staircase recall the building's aristocratic past. The rest has been transformed into the elegant, though somewhat soulless type of lodgings favored by executives. Large guest rooms have sitting areas, wooden floors, and mahogany furnishings. The greenhouse restaurant, filled with plants and songbirds, is especially pleasant on cold days. **Pros:** grand building, central location, the better rooms have big balconies with good views. **Cons:** some worn out rooms need to be revamped. ✉*Cuesta Santo Domingo 5 and 7, Palacio* ☎*91/541–6700* 🌐*www.solmelia.com* *183 rooms, 25 suites* *In-room: Wi-Fi. In-hotel: restaurant, bar, airport shuttle, public Wi-Fi, parking (fee)* ▭*AE, DC, MC, V* ✣*B3.*

NIGHTLIFE AND THE ARTS

THE ARTS

As Madrid's reputation as a vibrant, contemporary arts center has grown, artists and performers have been arriving in droves. Consult the weekly *Guía del Ocio* (published Friday) or the daily listings and Friday supplements in any of the leading newspapers—*El País, El Mundo,* or *ABC,* all of which are fairly easy to understand even if you don't read much Spanish. The Festival de Otoño (Autumn Festival), from late September to late November, blankets the city with pop concerts, poetry readings, flamenco, and ballet and theater from world-renowned companies. Other annual events include outstanding bonanzas of film, contemporary art, and jazz, salsa, rock, and African music, all at reasonable prices. Seats for the classical performing arts can usually be purchased through your hotel concierge, on the Internet, or at the hall itself. **El Corte Inglés** (☎*902/400222* 🌐*www.elcorteingles.es/entradas*) sells tickets for major concerts. **FNAC** (✉*Preciados 28, Sol* ☎*91/595–6100* 🌐*www.fnac.es*), a large retail media store, also sells tickets to musical events. Ticket brokers to try are **Tel-Entrada** (☎*902/101212* 🌐*www.telentrada.com*) and **Entradas.com** (☎*902/221622*).

DANCE AND MUSIC PERFORMANCES

In addition to concert halls listed below, the Convento de la Encarnación and the Real Academia de Bellas Artes de San Fernando museum (⇨*Exploring Madrid*) hold concerts. The modern **Auditorio Nacional de Música** (✉*Príncipe de Vergara 146, Salamanca* ☎*91/337–0100* 🌐*www.auditorionacional.mcu.es*) is Madrid's main concert hall, with spaces for both symphonic and chamber music. The resplendent **Teatro Real** (✉*Plaza de Isabel II, Ópera* ☎*91/516–0660* 🌐*www.teatro-real.com*) is the site of opera and dance performances.

The **Matadero Madrid** (✉*Paseo de la Chopera 14, Legazpi* ☎*91/517–7309*) is the city's newest and the biggest arts center. It sits in the city's old slaughterhouse—a massive early-20th-century *neomudejar* compound of 13 buildings. It has a theater, multiple exhibition spaces, workshops, and a lively bar. It's so large, it won't be completely finished until 2011, but some of the exhibition spaces and the theater are now open.

The **Círculo de Bellas Artes** (✉*Marqués de Casa Riera 2, Centro* ☎*902/422442* 🌐*www.circulobellasartes.com*) has concerts, theater, dance performances, art exhibitions, and other arts events. The **Centro de Conde Duque** (✉*Conde Duque 11, Centro* ☎*91/588–5834*) is best known for its summer live-music concerts (flamenco, jazz, pop), but it also has free and often interesting exhibitions. **La Casa Encendida** (✉*Ronda de Valencia 2, Lavapiés* ☎*91/506–3875* 🌐*www.lacasaencendida.com*) is an exhibition space with movie festivals, art shows, dance performances, and weekend events for children.

FILM

Of Madrid's 60 movie theaters, only 12 show foreign films, generally in English, with original soundtracks and Spanish subtitles. These are listed in newspapers and in the *Guía de Ocio* under "v.o."—*versión original,* that is, undubbed. Your best bet for catching a new release is the **Ideal Yelmo Cineplex** (✉*Doctor Cortezo 6, Centro* ☎*902/220922*). The excellent, classic v.o. films at the **Filmoteca Cine Doré** (✉*Santa Isabel 3, Lavapiés* ☎*91/369–1125*) change daily.

FLAMENCO

Although the best place in Spain to find flamenco is Andalusia, there are a few possibilities in Madrid. Note that *tablaos* (flamenco venues) charge around €30–€40 for the show only (with a complimentary drink included), so save money by dining elsewhere. If you want to dine at the *tablaos* anyway, note that three of them, Carboneras, Corral de la

Moreriá, and Café de Chinitas, also offer a show and fixed-menu option that's worth considering.

Café de Chinitas. It's expensive, but the flamenco is the best in Madrid. Reserve in advance; shows often sell out. The restaurant opens at 8:00 PM and there are performances at 8:30 PM and 10:15 PM Monday through Saturday. ✉ *Torija 7, Ópera* ☎ *91/559–5135.*

Casa Patas. Along with tapas, this well-known space offers good, relatively authentic (according to the performers) flamenco. Prices are more reasonable than elsewhere. Shows are at 10:30 PM Monday through Thursday, and at 9 PM and midnight on Friday and Saturday. ✉ *Cañizares 10, Lavapiés* ☎ *91/369–0496.*

Corral de la Morería. Dinner à la carte and well-known visiting flamenco stars accompany the resident dance troupe here. Since Morería opened its doors in 1956, celebrities such as Frank Sinatra and Ava Gardner have left their autographed photos for the walls. Shows are nightly at 10 PM and midnight. ✉ *Morería 17, on C. Bailén; cross bridge over C. Segovia and turn right, Centro* ☎ *91/365–8446.*

Las Carboneras. A prime flamenco showcase, this venue rivals Casa Patas as the best option in terms of quality and price. Performers here are both the young, less commercial artists and the more established stars on tour. The nightly show is staged at 10:30 Monday through Thursday and at 8:30 and 11 Friday and Saturday. ✉ *Plaza del Conde de Miranda 1, Centro* ☎ *91/542–8677.*

THEATER

English-language plays are rare, and when they do come to town, they're staged at any of a dozen venues. One theater you won't need Spanish for is the **Teatro de la Zarzuela** (✉ *Jovellanos 4, Centro* ☎ *91/524–5400*), which specializes in the traditional Spanish operetta known as *zarzuela,* a kind of bawdy comedy.

NIGHTLIFE

Nightlife—or *la marcha*—reaches legendary heights in Madrid. It's been said that madrileños rarely sleep, largely because they spend so much time in bars socializing in the easy, sophisticated way that's unique to this city. This is true of young and old alike, and it's not uncommon for children to play on the sidewalks past midnight while multigenerational families and friends convene over coffee or cocktails at an outdoor café. For those in their thirties, forties, and up who don't plan on staying out until sunrise, the best options are the bars along the Cava Alta and Cava Baja, Calle Huertas near Plaza Santa Ana, and Moratín near Antón Martín. Younger people have more options: Calle Príncipe and Calle De la Cruz—also in Santa Ana—and the Plaza de Anton Martín, especially the scruffier streets that lead onto Plaza Lavapiés. The biggest night scene—with a mixed crowd—happens in Malasaña, which has plenty of trendy hangouts on both sides of Calle San Vicente Ferrer, on Calle La Palma, and on the streets that come out onto Plaza 2 de Mayo. Also big is nearby Chueca, where tattoo parlors and street-chic boutiques break up the endless alleys of gay and lesbian bars, techno discos, and after-hours clubs.

Continued on page 124

THE ART OF BULLFIGHTING

Whether you attend is your choice, but love it or hate it, you can't ignore it. Bullfighting in Spain is big. For all the animal-rights protests, attempted local bans, failed European parliamentary censures, and general worldwide antipathy, you'd be hard pressed to find a higher volume of fans than you would around Spain's bullrings between March and October.

Its opponents call it a blood sport, its admirers—Hemingway, Picasso, and Goya among them—an art form. The latter win when it comes to media placement: you won't find tales of a star matador's latest conquest on a newspaper's jump page with car racing stories; you'll spy bullfighting news alongside theater and film reviews. This is perhaps the secret to understanding bullfighting's powerful cultural significance and why its popularity has risen over the past decade.

Bullfighting is making certain people very, very rich, via million-dollar TV rights, fight broadcasts, and the 300-plus bull-breeding farms. The owners of these farms comprise a powerful lobby that receives subsidies from the EU and exemption from a 1998 amendment to the Treaty of Rome that covers animal welfare. The Spanish Ministry of Culture also provides considerable money to support bullfighting, as do local and regional governments.

The Spanish media thrive on it, too. The matador is perhaps Spain's last remaining stereotypical *macho hombre*, whose popularity outside the ring in the celebrity press is often dramatically disproportionate to what he achieves inside it.

How bullfighting came to Spain is an unsettled issue. It may have been introduced by the Moors in the 11th century or via ancient Rome, where human vs. animal events were held as a warm-up for the gladiators.

Historically speaking, the bull was fought from horseback with a javelin and was used by the noble classes as a substitute and preparation for war, like hunting and jousting. Religious festivities and royal weddings were celebrated by fights in the local plaza, where noblemen would ride competing for royal favor, with the populace enjoying the excitement. In the 18th century, the Spanish introduced the practice of fighting on foot. As bullfighting developed, men on foot started using capes to aid the horsemen in positioning the bulls. This type of fighting drew more attention from the crowds, thus the modern *corrida*, or fight, started to take form.

THE CASE AGAINST BULLFIGHTING

Animal welfare activists aggressively protest bullfighting for the cruelity it afflicts on both bulls and horses. The argue that the bulls die a cruel (usually slow and painful) death; in fact, activists argue, the bull is essentially butchered alive and bleeds to death. The horses involved are knocked around and sometimes die or are injured as they're used as shields for the picadors riding atop them.

Activists have had little success in banning the bullfight on a national level. However, while the sport is as popular as ever in the south of Spain and Madrid, it has been halted in several Catalonian towns, and in 2003, the Catalan regional parliament became the first in Spain to ban children under 14 from attending bullfights. Then, in 2004, the Barcelona City Council banned bullfighting altogether, a historic first in Spain. The decision still needs to be ratified by the regional government.

SUITING UP

Matadors are easily distinguished by their spectacular and quite costly *traje de luces* (suit of lights), inspired by 18th-century Andalusian clothing. This ensemble can run several thousand dollars, and a good matador uses at least six of them each season. The Matador's team covers the cost.

OTHER BULLFIGHTING TERMS

Alguacilillo—the title given to the two men in the arena who represent the presiding dignitary and apply his orders.

Banderilleros—the torero's team members who place a set of banderillas (barbed sticks mounted on colored shafts) into the bull's neck.

Corrida de toros—bullfight (literally, running of the bulls); sometimes just referred to as *corrida.*

Cuadrilla—the matador's team of three *banderilleros* and two *picadors.*

Matador or Torero—matador literally means "killer."

Paseíllo—the parade that the participants make when they enter the bullring.

Picador—lancers mounted on horseback.

Presidente—the presiding dignitary.

Varas—lances.

MATADOR LEGENDS, PAST AND PRESENT

YESTERDAY'S HEROES

Modern-day Spanish bullfighting's most famous son is **Juan Belmonte.** He's credited for the daring and revolutionary style that kept him and the bull always within inches of one another. **Manuel Rodríguez Sánchez** (Manolete), comes a close second. After hundreds of performances, and in Manolete's final year before retirement, he was mortally wounded in a *corrida* in Linares, Spain, resulting in a national mourning. **Jose Tomas,** who retired in 2002 at the peak of his career without explanation, returned to the ring in 2007 but was badly gored by not one but *two* bulls during a bullfight in June 2008. Only time will tell if he's going to come back for more.

Manuel Rodríguez Sánchez

TODAY'S HOT MATADORS

WHAT YOU'LL SEE

Modern-day bullfights in Spain follow a very strict ritual that's played out in 3 stages ("*tercios*" or "thirds").

1ST STAGE: TERCIO DE VARAS

After the procession of the matador and his *cuadrilla* (entourage), the bull is released into the arena. A trumpet sounds and the *picadors* (lancers on horseback) encourage the bull to attack the heavily padded horse. They use the lances to pierce the bull's back and neck muscles.

2ND STAGE: TERCIO DE BANDERILLAS

Three *banderilleros* (hit squad) on foot each attempt to plant barbed sticks mounted on colored shafts into the bull's neck and back. These further weaken the enormous ridges of the bull's neck and shoulder in order to make it lower its head. Rather than use capes, the banderilleros use their bodies to attract the bull.

3RD STAGE: TERCIO DE MUERTE (DEATH)

The torero reenters with his red cape and, if he so chooses, dedicates the bull to an individual, or to the audience. The *faena* (work), which is the entire performance with the *muleta* (cape), ends with a series of passes in which the matador attempts to maneuver the bull into a position so he can drive his sword between the shoulder blades and through the heart.

Lancers astride heavily padded horses parade around the bullring near the beginning of a fight.

HOW TO BEHAVE

The consummate bullfighting fan is both passionate and knowledgeable. Audiences are in fact part of the spectacle, and their responses during the event is often an indicator of the quality of the *corrida*. For instance, during the *tercio de varas*, or first third of the fight, when the matador performs with art and courage, he will be rewarded with an ovation. If a picador is over-zealous in stabbing the bull and leaves it too weak to fight, the crowd will boo him.

Similarly, the *estocada*, the act of thrusting the sword by the matador, can generate boos from the crowd if it's done clumsily and doesn't achieve a quick and clean death. A *trofeo* (trophy) is the usual indicator of a job well done. When the records of bullfights are kept, *trofeos* earned by the matador are always mentioned. If the crowd demands, the matador is allowed to take a lap of victory around the ring. If more than or about half the spectators petition the *presidente* by waving handkerchiefs, the presidente is obliged to award the matador with one ear of the bull. The best trofeo is the two ears and the tail of a single bull, awarded only on memorable days. When this happens the bullfighter is usually carried out on someone's shoulder through the main entrance gate *(puertagrande)* in celebration of a spectacular fight.

TIP→ Many bullrings have eight or more entrances. It is always advisable to specify whether you want a seat in the sun *(sol)* or shade *(sombra)* or a mix of sun and shade as time passes *(sol y sombra)* as the bullfighting season coincides with the hot summer months. It's also recommended to take a cushion or rent one for €1 so you're not sitting on the hard concrete. Seats at the top rows in the sun can be as little as €5, whereas shaded bottom row seats can cost as much as €120. If you want tickets for a major bullfight, buy them well in advance—call 902/150025 or go online to www.taquillatoros.com.

STARGAZING

It's not uncommon for local Spanish celebrities to attend bullfights, and during the most prestigious summer carnival, the San Isidro in Madrid, King Juan Carlos often makes an appearance.

BARS AND NIGHTCLUBS

Jazz, rock, classical, and flamenco music are all popular in Madrid's many small clubs.

Bar Cock. Resembling a room at some very exclusive club (with all the waiters in suits), this bar with a dark wood interior, cathedral-like ceilings, and large leather chairs at every table serves about 20 different cocktails (hence the name). It caters to an older, more classic crowd. ✉*Reina 16, Chueca* ☎*91/532–2826.*

Café Belén. The handful of tables here are rarely empty on weekends, thanks to the candlelight and cozy atmosphere—it attracts a young, mixed, postdinner crowd. Weekdays are mellower. ✉*Belen 5, Chueca* ☎*91/308–2747.*

Café Central. Madrid's best-known jazz venue is chic, and the musicians are often internationally known. Performances are usually from 10 PM to midnight. ✉*Plaza de Ángel 10, Santa Ana* ☎*91/369–4143.*

Café la Palma. There are four different spaces here: a bar in front, a music venue for intimate concerts, a chill-out room in the back, and a café in the center room. Don't miss it if you're in the Malasaña neighborhood. ✉*La Palma 62, Malasaña* ☎*91/522–5031.*

Coquette. Come here to check out the most authentic blues bar in the city, with live music Tuesday to Thurday at 11 PM, smoke-filled air, barmen with jeans and leather jackets, and bohemian executives who've left the suit at home and parked their Harley-Davidson at the door. ✉*Torrecilla del Leal 18, Lavapiés* ☎*91/530–8095*

Costello. A multispace that combines a café and a lounge, Costello caters to a relaxed and conversational crowd; the bottom floor is suited to partygoers, with the latest in live and club music. On weekdays, it also features theater and stand-up comedy. ✉*Caballero de Gracia 10, Sol* ☎*91/522–1815.*

Del Diego. Arguably Madrid's trendiest cocktail bar, this place is frequented by a variety of crowds from movie directors to moviegoers. ✉*Calle de la Reina 12, Centro* ☎*91/523–3106* ⏲*Closed Sun.*

El Clandestino. This bar-café is a hidden hot spot with a local following. Jam sessions on the bottom floor (open Thursday through Saturday) alternate mellow jazz with house and ambient music. ✉*Barquillo 34, Centro* ☎*91/521–5563* ⏲*Closed Sun.*

El Junco. Owners turned what was just another bar into a happening jazz venue, but while the live music is a plus, what really gets the crowd going (and coming back for more) are the DJs that mix late into the night. ✉*Plaza Santa Bárbara 10, Alonso Martínez* ☎*91/319–2081* 🌐*www.eljunco.com* ⏲*Closed Sun. and Mon.*

El Viajero. This establishment serves food but is best known for the madrileños who swarm around La Latina on the weekends for its middle-floor bar, which is usually filled by those looking for a drink between lunch and dinner. Its irresistible terrace is usually packed. ✉*Plaza de la Cebada 11, La Latina* ☎*91/366–9064* ⏲*Closed Sun. night and Mon.*

La Piola. With a truly bohemian spirit and a shabby-chic decor—a second-hand couch, just a handful of tables, and a brass bar—this small place, which serves a great Spanish omelet during the day and cocktails at night, is a magnet for people who want to get away from the bustle of the Santa Ana area. ✉*León 9, Barrio de las Letras* ☎*679744898* ⏲*Closed Sun.*

Maluca Reasonable prices and soft jazz and soul music draw a forty-ish crowd to this cocktail bar/lounge. Besides the well-known mojitos, martinis, and negronis, you'll find other creative concoctions such as the wasabi daiquiri and the sweet mustard *kaipiroska.* ✉*Calatrava 13, La Latina* ☎*91/365–0996* ⏲*Closed Mon.*

BEST BETS FOR ENTERTAINMENT

- **Best flamenco: Café de Chinitas**
- **Best jazz venue: Café Central**
- **Best salsa: Azúcar.**

Marula Café. Popular for its quiet summer terrace under the Puente de Segovia arches, its unbeatable electro-funk mixes, and for staying open into the wee hours, this is a cleverly designed narrow space with lots of illuminated wall art. ✉*C. Caños Viejos 3, Palacio* ☎*91/366–1596.*

Midnight Rose and the Penthouse. This is two different spaces connected by an elevator that could easily be confused for a dance floor. The bottom lounge takes up most of the ground floor of the chic ME Reina Victoria, including the reception area; the rooftop terrace in the same hotel offers an unbeatable view of the city. ✉*Covarrubias 24, Chamberí* ☎*91/445–6886.*

Museo Chicote. Recently refurbished and regaining popularity, this landmark cocktail bar–lounge is said to have been one of Hemingway's haunts. ✉*Gran Vía 12, Centro* ☎*91/532–6737* ⏲*Closed Sun.*

Ramsés A multispace venue across from Retiro Park designed by Philippe Starck with two restaurants, a club in the basement, and a bar at street level, this spot is perfect for an early yet expensive cocktail, before or after dinner, and preferably on the weekdays. Order a Ramsés (black vodka, absinthe, and cranberry juice) and enjoy the parade of the glamorous see-and-be-seen set. ✉*Plaza de la Independencia 4, Retiro* ☎*91/435–1666*

Why not? Long and narrow and always packed with a very local (mostly gay) crowd from the neighborhood, this is a great place to hear '70s and '80s Spanish and American pop music. When it closes, the throng of people moves over to the even wilder Polana, on C. Barbieri, which has the same owner. ✉*San Bartolomé 6, Chueca* ☎*91/523–0581.*

CABARET

Berlin Cabaret (✉*Costanilla de San Pedro 11, Centro* ☎*91/366–2034* ⏲*Closed Sun.*) professes to provide cabaret as it was performed in Berlin in the '30s. The concept might not be Spanish, but the performers are—and with the combination of magic, chorus girls, and ribaldry, it's a good time. The crowd is eccentric and on Friday and Saturday the fun often lasts until daybreak.

DISCOS

Five minutes away from Plaza de Castilla, **69 Pétalos** (✉*C. Alberto Alcocer, 32, Chamartín* ☎*No phone* ⏲*Closed Sun.–Wed.*) is a popular disco among people in their thirties; there's an eclectic music vibe—pop, hip-hop, swing, electronic—and on-stage performances by actors, go-go dancers, and musicians. Salsa has become a fixture in Madrid; check out the most spectacular moves at **Azúcar** (✉*Paseo Reina Cristina 7, Atocha* ☎*91/501–6107*). A few blocks away from the Royal Palace **Charada** (✉*Calle de la Bola 13, Palacio* ☎*91/541–9291* ⊙*Closed Mon.–Thurs.*) is one of the sleekest clubs in the city, with a huge LED screen on the ceiling, professional barmen serving cocktails until six in the morning, lots of house and funk music, and a crowd mostly in their late thirties. **Clamores** (✉*Albuquerque 14, Chamberí* ☎*91/445–7938* ⊙*Closes at 11 PM Sun.*) usually plays live music until 2:30 AM. An indie and hip crowd flocks to **Elástico** (✉*Montera 25 [entrance on Plaza del Carmen], Sol* ☎*91/531–6378*), the Saturday-night pop session at Wind club. It has two different spaces and a new DJ every week. Madrid's oldest disco, and one of the hippest clubs for all-night dancing to an international music mix, is **El Sol** (✉*Jardines 3, Centro* ☎*91/532–6490*), open until 5:30 AM. There's live music starting at around midnight, Thursday through Saturday. **Fortuny** (✉*Fortuny 34, Chamberí* ☎*91/319–0588*) attracts a celebrity crowd, especially in summer when the lush outdoor patio opens. Put on your best dancing duds: the door is ultraselective. **Golden Boite** (✉*Duque de Sesto 54, Retiro* ☎*91/573–8775*) is always hot from midnight on. **Joy Eslava** (✉*Arenal 11, Sol* ☎*91/366–3733*), a downtown disco in a converted theater, is an old standby. **Pachá** (✉*Barceló 11, Centro* ☎*91/447–0128* ⊙*Closed Mon.–Wed.*) is always energetic. **Palacio de Gaviria** (✉*Arenal 9, Sol* ☎*91/526–6069*), a maze of rooms turned into a disco, caters mainly to foreigners. Magical and chameleonlike thanks to the use of LED lighting and the undulating shapes of the columns and walls, **Reina Bruja** (✉*Jacometrezo 6, Palacio* ☎*91/445–6886* ⊙*Closed Sun.–Wed.*) is the place to go if you want a late-night drink—it opens at 11 and closes at 5:30 AM—without the thunder of a full-blown disco. For funky rhythms, try **Stella** (✉*Arlabán 7, Centro* ☎*91/531–6378* ⊙*Closed Sun.–Wed.*). On Thursdays and Fridays it houses the famous Mondo session (electronic, house, and Afro music). Show up late.

SPORTS AND THE OUTDOORS

HIKING

The region north of Madrid is lined by a mountain range, the Sierra de Guadarrama. Also running into some parts of Ávila and Segovia, the range is on its way to becoming Spain's 14th national park. Long favored by naturalists, writers (including John Dos Passos), painters, poets, and historians, it also attracts sporty madrileños looking to get away from the chaos of the capital. The Sierra's eastern border lies at Puerto de Somosierra, west of the A1 highway heading to Burgos; the little town of Robledo de Chavela, southwest of El Escorial, marks the park's western edge. Near the middle of this long stretch sprouts another branch to the northeast, giving the Sierra de Guadarrama the shape of a fork, with the Valle de Lozoya in between the fork's tines. Hiking options are nearly limitless, but two destinations stand out because of their geological importance: the Parque de la Pedriza, a massive, orangish, fancifully shaped granite landscape in the Cuenca Alta del Manzanares, and the Peñalara's alpine cirques (basins) and lakes.

CLOSE UP

Summer Terraces

Madrid is blazing hot in the late spring and summer, and madrileños seem to have a nearly relentless yearning for nightlife. As a result, the city allows nearly 2,000 bars and restaurants to create outdoor spaces for enjoying the cooler, dry summer nighttime air while sipping a beer. For formal summer dining, we recommend some of the lovely hotel restaurants, most of which have private and peaceful gardens or roof terraces that avoid the street noise. Possibilities include the Ritz hotel, La Biblioteca del Santo Mauro (at Hotel Santo Mauro), El Jardín de Orfila (at Hotel Orfila), and La Terraza del Casino. Three mid-range restaurants with good terraces are Sacha, Bokado, and Pedro Larumbe—the latter's rooftop restaurant turns into one of Madrid's most fashionable terraces at night. If you just want to grab a bite or an early-evening drink, drop by La Latina neighborhood, especially Plaza de la Paja or Plaza de San Andrés, across from the Church of San Andrés, or sit on any of the terraces at Plaza de Olavide, an enclave favored mostly by locals, near Malasaña and the Bilbao subway stop. Plaza Santa Ana is a pricier, more touristy alternative. Plaza Chueca, in the neighborhood of the same name, along with the Mercado de Fuencarral (halfway between Gran Vía and Tribunal), the Plaza de 2 de Mayo, and the Plaza de las Comendadoras in the Malasaña neighborhood are always bustling and crowded with younger people. The best nightlife is along the terraces on Castellana, at Terraza Atenas on Calle Segovia, and at the hotel rooftop bars that have spread out in the last few years: Hotel Urban, ME Reina Victoria, Silken Puerta de América, De las Letras, and Room Mate Óscar.

The **Arawak Viajes Madrid** (✉*Peñuelas 12, Atocha* ☎*91/474–2524* 🌐*www.arawakviajes.com*) travel agency offers three or four different one-day trips every weekend to different spots in the Madrid Sierra (and to Guadalajara or Sierra de Gredos), plus a weekend trek every month. Prices to the Sierra de Guadarrama are usually around €20–€25. You must reserve in advance and pay within one day of making the reservation. Buses depart from Estación de Autobuses Ruiz on Ronda de Atocha 12.

RUNNING

Madrid's best running spots are the Parque del Buen Retiro, where the main path circles the park and others weave under trees and through gardens, and the Parque del Oeste, with more uneven terrain but fewer people. The Casa de Campo is crisscrossed by numerous, sunnier trails.

SOCCER

Fútbol is Spain's number-one sport, and Madrid has four teams, Real Madrid, Atlético Madrid, Rayo Vallecano, and Getafe. The two major teams are Real Madrid and Atlético Madrid. For tickets, either call a week in advance to reserve and pick them up at the stadium or stand in line at the stadium of your choice. The **Estadio Santiago Bernabeu** (✉*Paseo de la Castellana 140, Chamartín* ☎*91/398–4300* 🌐*www.realmadrid.es*), which seats 75,000, is home to Real Madrid, winner of a staggering nine European Champion's Cups. Atlético Madrid plays at the **Estadio Vicente Calderón** (✉ *Virgen del Puerto 67, Arganzuela* ☎ *91/366–4707 or 91/364–0888* 🌐 *www.clubatleticodemadrid.com*), on the edge of the Manzanares River south of town.

SHOPPING

Spain has become one of the world's design centers. You'll have no trouble finding traditional crafts, such as ceramics, guitars, and leather goods, albeit not at countryside prices (think Rodeo Drive, not outlet mall). Known for contemporary furniture and decorative items as well as chic clothing, shoes, and jewelry, Spain's capital has become stiff competition for Barcelona. Keep in mind that many shops, especially those that are small and family run, close during lunch hours, on Sunday, and on Saturday afternoon. Shops generally accept most major credit cards.

DEPARTMENT STORES

El Corte Inglés. Spain's largest department store carries the best selection of everything, from auto parts to groceries, electronics, lingerie, and designer fashions. They also sell tickets for major sports and arts events and have their own travel agency, a restaurant (usually the building's top floor), and a great gourmet store. Madrid's biggest branch is the one on the corner of Calle Raimundo Fernández Villaverde and Castellana, which is not a central location. Try instead the one at Sol-Callao (split into three separate buildings), or the ones at Serrano or Goya (these are also in two independent buildings). ✉ *Preciados 1, 2, and 3, Sol* ☎ *91/379–8000, 901/122122 general information, 902/400222 ticket sales* 🌐 *www.elcorteingles.es* ✉ *Callao 2, Centro* ☎ *91/379–8000* ✉ *Calle Goya 76 and 85, Salamanca* ☎ *91/432–9300* ✉ *Princesa 41, 47, and 56, Centro* ☎ *91/454–6000* ✉ *Calle Serrano 47 and 52, Salamanca* ☎ *91/432–5490* ✉ *Raimundo Fernández Villaverde 79, Chamartín* ☎ *91/418–8800.*

SHOPPING DISTRICTS

Madrid has three main shopping areas. The first, the area that stretches from Callao to Puerta del Sol (Calle Preciados, Gran Vía on both sides of Callao, and the streets around the Puerta del Sol), includes the major department stores (El Corte Inglés and the French music-and-book chain FNAC) and popular brands such as H&M and Zara.

The second area, far more elegant and expensive, is in the eastern Salamanca district, bounded roughly by Serrano, Juan Bravo, Jorge Juan (and its blind alleys), and Velázquez; the shops on Goya extend as far as Alcalá. The streets just off the Plaza de Colón, particularly Calle Serrano and Calle Ortega y Gasset, have the widest selection of designer fashions—think Prada, Loewe, Armani, or Louis Vuitton—as well as other mainstream and popular local designers (Purificación García, Pedro del Hierro, Adolfo Domínguez, or Roberto Verino). Hidden within Calle Jorge Juan, Calle Lagasca, and Calle Claudio Coello is the widest selection of smart boutiques from renowned young Spanish designers, such as Sybilla, Josep Font, Amaya Arzuaga, and Victorio & Lucchino.

Finally, for hipper clothes, Chueca, Malasaña, and what's now called the Triball (the triangle formed by Fuencarral, Gran Vía, and Corredera Baja, with Calle Ballesta in the middle) are your best bets. Calle Fuencarral, from Gran Vía to Tribunal, is the street with the most shops in this area. On Fuencarral you can find name brands such as Diesel, Gas, and Billabong, but also local brands such as Homeless, Adolfo Domínguez U (selling the Galician designer's younger collection), and Custo, as well as some makeup stores (Madame B and M.A.C). Less mainstream and sometimes more exciting is the selection you can find on nearby calles Hortaleza, Almirante, Piamonte, and in the Triball area.

FLEA MARKET

On Sunday morning, Calle de Ribera de Curtidores is closed to traffic and jammed with outdoor booths selling everything under the sun—this is its weekly transformation into the **El Rastro** flea market. Crowds get so thick that it takes awhile just to advance a few feet amid the hawkers and gawkers. Be careful: pickpockets abound here, so hang on to your purse and wallet, and be especially careful if you choose to bring a camera. The flea market sprawls into most of the surrounding streets, with certain areas specializing in particular products. Many of the goods are wildly overpriced. But what goods! The Rastro has everything from antique furniture to exotic parrots and cuddly puppies; from pirated cassette tapes of flamenco music to key chains emblazoned with symbols of the CNT, Spain's old anarchist trade union. Practice your Spanish by bargaining with the vendors over paintings, colorful Gypsy oxen yokes, heraldic iron gates, new and used clothes, and even hashish pipes. They may not lower their prices, but sometimes they'll throw in a handmade bracelet or a stack of postcards to sweeten the deal. Plaza General Vara del Rey has some of the Rastro's best antiques, and the streets beyond—Calles Mira el Río Alta and Mira el Río Baja—have some truly magnificent junk and bric-a-brac. The market shuts down shortly after 2 PM, in time for a street party to start in the area known as La Latina, centered on the bar El Viajero in Plaza Humilladero. Off the Ribera are two *galerías*, courtyards with higher-quality, higher-price antiques shops. All the shops (except for the street vendors) are open during the week.

SPECIALTY STORES

BOOKS

Casa del Libro (⊠*Maestro Victoria 3, Centro* ☎*91/521–4898*), not far from the Puerta del Sol, has an impressive collection of English-language books, including translated Spanish classics. It's also a good source for maps. Its discount store around the corner, on Calle Salud 17, sells English classics. **Booksellers** (⊠*Plaza de Olavide 10, Chamberí* ☎*91/702–7944*), just off the upper Castellana near the Hotel Miguel

Ángel, has a large selection of books in English. **J&J** (✉*Espíritu Santo 47, Centro* ☎*91/521–8576*), a block off San Bernardo, is a charming café and bookstore run by a woman from Alabama and her Spanish husband. The store stocks a good selection of used books in English. Established in 1950, **La Tienda Verde** (✉*Maudes 23 and 38, Chamberí* ☎*91/535–3810*) is perfect for outdoor enthusiasts planning hikes, mountain-climbing expeditions, spelunking trips, and so forth; they have detailed maps and Spanish-language guidebooks.

BOUTIQUES AND FASHION

The trapezoidal neighborhood that's roughly contained by calles Génova and Sagasta to the north, Fuencarral on the west, Gran Vía and Alcalá to the south, and Paseo de Recoletos to the east can provide a satisfying and usually more affordable (than Salamanca) shopping experience.

Chueca shelters some local name brands (Hoss, Adolfo Domínguez, and Mango) on Calle Fuencarral, and also has a multifloor and multistore market (Mercado de Fuencarral) selling modern outfits for younger crowds at No. 45 on the same street.

CHUECA AND MALASAÑA

Brothers Custodio and David Dalmau are the creative force behind the success of **Custo** (✉*Mayor 37, Sol* ☎*91/354–0099* ✉*Fuencarral 29, Chueca* ☎*91/360–4636* ✉*Gran Vía 26, Chueca* ☎*91/521–4895*), whose eye-catching T-shirts can be found in the closets of such stars as Madonna and Julia Roberts. They have expanded their collection to incorporate pants, dresses, and accessories, never relinquishing the traits that have made them famous: bold colors and striking graphic designs.

Chueca's trademark are its multibrand boutiques and small multibrand fashion shops, often managed by eccentric and outspoken characters. A good example of this is **H.A.N.D.** (✉*Hortaleza 26, Chueca* ☎*91/521–5152*), a cozy, tasteful store owned by two Frenchmen: Stephan and Thierry. They specialize in feminine, colorful, and young French prêt-à-porter designers (Stella Forest, La Petite, Tara Jarmon). Prominent designer **Jesús del Pozo** (✉*Almirante 9, Chueca* ☎*91/531–3646*) has clothes for both sexes. It's an excellent, if pricey, place to try on some classic Spanish style. **L'Habilleur** (✉*Plaza de Chueca 8, Chueca* ☎*91/531–3222*) is a fancy outlet selling samples and end-of-season designer clothes at a large discount.

Mango. The Turkish brothers Isaac and Nahman Andic opened their first store in Barcelona in 1984. Two decades later Mango has stores all over the world, and the brand rivals Zara as Spain's most successful fashion venture. Mango's target customer is the young, modern, and urban woman. In comparison with Zara, Mango has fewer formal options and favors bohemian sundresses, sandals, and embellished T-shirts. ✉*Fuencarral 70, Malasaña* ☎*91/523–0412* 🌐*www.mango.com* ✉*Fuencarral 140, Bilbao* ☎*91/445–7811* ✉*Calle Goya 83, Salamanca* ☎*91/435–3958* ✉*Hermosilla 22, Salamanca* ☎*91/576–8303*.

A favorite among fashion magazine editors, **Pez** (✉*Regueros 15, Chueca* ☎*91/308–6677*), on the corner of Calle Fernando VI, features a very chic and seductive European collection—especially Parisian and Scandinavian. The highly energetic owner of **Próxima Parada** (✉*Piamonte 25, Chueca* ☎*91/310–3421*) enthusiastically digs into racks looking for daring garments from Spanish designers in her quest to quickly redefine and modernize her customers' look. The store also sells some original clothespins made by art school students. **Uno de 50** (✉*Fuencarral 25, Malasaña* ☎*91/523–9975* ✉*Jorge Juan 17, Salamanca* ☎*91/308–2953*) carries original, youngish, and inexpensive (all pieces less than €200) costume jewelry (mostly made in leather and a silver-plated tin alloy) and accessories by Spanish designer Concha Díaz del Río.

SALAMANCA

Salamanca is the area with the most concentrated local fashion offering, especially on Calles Claudio Coello, Lagasca, and the first few blocks of Serrano. You'll find a good mix of mainstream designers, small-scale exclusive boutiques, and multibrand stores. Most mainstream designer stores are located on Calle Serrano.

The top stores for non-Spanish fashions are mostly scattered along Ortega y Gasset, between Nuñez de Balboa and Serrano, but if you want the more exclusive of the local brands, head to the smaller designer shops unfolding along Calles Claudio Coello, Jorge Juan, and Lagasca. Start on Calle Jorge Juan and its alleys, and then move northward along Claudio Coello and Lagasca toward the core of the Salamanca district.

A quemarropa (✉*Lagasca 58, Salamanca* ☎*91/435–7264*) sells very informal clothes for young and modern women from French and Italian designers such as Patrizia Pepe or Et-Vous, and from some Spanish ones such as Masscob. **Adolfo Domínguez** (✉*Calle Serrano 18 and 96, Salamanca* ☎*91/576–7053*) is a Galician designer with simple, sober, and elegant lines for both men and women. Of his eight other locations in the city, the one at Calle Fuencarral 5, a block away from Gran Vía, is geared toward a younger crowd, with more affordable and colorful clothes. **Alma Aguilar** (✉*Jorge Juan 12, Salamanca* ☎*91/577–6698*) is known for using natural and luxe fabrics (silks, cashmere, wool, crepe), and for her sundresses and romantic and feminine coats. Drapes, lines, ribbons, and polka dots are some of the trademarks of **Amaya Arzuaga** (✉*Lagasca 50, Salamanca* ☎*91/426–2815*) and its highly elaborate—yet simple-looking—glamorous party dresses. A men's collection is downstairs. For shoes to excite even the most jaded shopper, drop by the small **Columela** (✉*Columela 6, Salamanca* ☎*91/435–1925*). You won't find Jimmy Choos or Manolo Blahniks, but rather a more personal selection: Italy's Trans-parents and Costume National, France's L'Autre Chose, America's Marc Jacobs, local brands such as Juan Antonio López, and shoes made in Italy expressly for the store.

The three young female designers working for **Hoss** (✉*Calle Serrano 16, Salamanca* ☎*91/781–0612* ✉*Fuencarral 16, Chueca* ☎*91/524–1728*) and their hip and fashionable clothes are gaining a growing acceptance with younger crowds. Next to Sybilla is **Jocomomola** (✉*Jorge Juan 12, Salamanca* ☎*91/575–0005*), Sybilla's younger and more affordable second brand. Here you'll find plenty of informal and provocative, colorful pieces, as well as some accessories. Young and highly praised Catalonian designer **Josep Font** (✉*Don Ramón de la Cruz 51, Salamanca* ☎*91/575–9716*) sells his seductive clothes a few blocks from the customary shopping route in the Salamanca neighborhood. Worth the detour, his clothes are distinctive and colorful, with original shapes and small, subtle touches such as ribbons or flounces that act as the designer's signature. If you're on a tight schedule, dropping by some of the multibrand fashion shops in the neighborhood may save you from a headache. **Nac** (✉ *Génova 17, Chamberí* ☎ *91/310–6050* ✉ *Conde de Aranda 6, Salamanca* ☎ *91/431–2515*) has a good selection of Spanish designer brands (Antonio Miró, Hoss, Josep Font, Jocomomola, and Ailanto). The store on Calle Génova is the biggest among their four in Madrid. Also popular is the madrileño designer **Pedro del Hierro** (✉ *Calle Serrano 24 and 63, Salamanca* ☎ *91/575–6906*), who has built himself a good reputation for his sophisticated but uncomplicated clothes for both sexes. **Purificación García** (✉ *Calle Serrano 28 and 92, Salamanca* ☎ *91/435–8013*) is a good choice for women searching for contemporary all-day wear. **Roberto Torretta** (✉ *Jorge Juan 12, at end of one of two cul-de-sacs, Salamanca* ☎ *91/435–7989*) is another designer with a celebrity following and elegant, sophisticated clothes for the urban woman.

Sybilla (✉ *Jorge Juan 12, at the end of one of two cul-de-sacs, Salamanca* ☎ *91/578–1322*) is the studio of Spain's best-known female designer. Her fluid dresses and hand-knit sweaters have made her a favorite with Danish former supermodel and now editor and designer Helena Christensen.

At **Victorio & Lucchino** (✉ *Lagasca 75, Salamanca* ☎ *91/431–8786*) you can find sophisticated party dresses (many with characteristic Spanish features) in materials such as gauze, silk, and velvet, as well as more casual wear and a popular line of jewelry and accessories. Young professionals who want the latest look without the sticker shock hit **Zara** for hip clothes that won't last more than a season or two. The store's minimalist window displays are hard to miss; inside you'll find the latest looks for men, women, and children. Zara is self-made entrepreneur Amancio Ortega's textile empire flagship, which you will find all over the city. Its clothes are considerably cheaper in Spain than in the United States or the United Kingdom. There are also two outlet stores in Madrid—in the Gran Vía store and in Calle Carretas; both are called Lefties. If you choose to try your luck at the outlets, keep in mind that Monday and Thursday are when new deliveries arrive—and therefore the days when you have the best chance of finding the good stuff. ✉ *Centro Comercial ABC, Calle Serrano 61, Salamanca* ☎ *91/575–6334* ✉ *Gran Vía 34, Centro* ☎ *91/521–1283* ✉ *Velázquez 49, Salamanca* ☎ *91/575–1476* ✉ *Carretas 6, Sol* ☎ *91/522–6945* ✉ *Princesa 63, Centro* ☎ *91/543–2415* ✉ *Conde de Peñalver 4, Salamanca* ☎ *91/435–4135.*

SOL The area around Sol is more mainstream, with big names such as Zara and H&M, and retail media and department stores (i.e., FNAC, El Corte Inglés). However, there are some interesting isolated stops such as **Seseña** (✉ *De la Cruz 23, Sol* ☎ *91/531–6840*), which since the turn of the 20th century has outfitted international celebrities in wool and velvet capes, some lined with red satin.

CERAMICS

Antigua Casa Talavera (✉*Isabel la Católica 2, Centro* ☎*91/547–3417*) is the best of Madrid's many ceramics shops. Despite the name, the finest wares sold here are from Manises, near Valencia, but the blue-and-yellow Talavera ceramics are also excellent. **Cántaro** (✉*Flor Baja 8, Centro* ☎*91/547–9514*) sells traditional handmade ceramics and pottery. **Cerámica El Alfar** (✉*Claudio Coello 112, Salamanca* ☎*91/411–3587*) has pottery from around Spain. **Sagardelos** (✉*Zurbano 46, Chamberí* ☎*91/310–4830*), specializing in modern Spanish ceramics from Galicia, has breakfast sets, coffeepots, and objets d'art.

FOOD AND WINE

SALAMANCA **Lavinia** (✉*José Ortega y Gasset 16, Salamanca* ☎*91/426–0604*) claims to be the largest wine store in Europe. It has a large selection of bottles, books, and bar accessories, and even a restaurant where you can sample its products. In the middle of Salamanca's shopping area is **Mantequerías Bravo** (✉*Ayala 24, Salamanca* ☎*91/576–7641*), which sells Spanish wines, olive oils, cheeses, and hams. You can find more than 120 different cheeses from all over Spain as well as almost 300 others from nearby countries such as France, Portugal, Italy, and Holland at **Poncelet** (✉*Argensola 27, Alonso Martínez* ☎*91/308–0221*). Marmalades, wines, and items to help you savor your cheese are also available.

SANTA ANA Just across from Los Gabrieles, behind Plaza Santa Ana, **Mariano Aguado** (✉*Echegaray 19, Barrio de las Letras* ☎*91/429–6088*) is a charming 150-year-old wine store with a broad range of wines and fine spirits. The traditional food store **González** (✉*León 12, Barrio de las Letras* ☎*91/429–5618*) has a secret in back—a cozy and well-hidden bar where you can sample most of the fare they sell: canned asparagus; olive oil; honey; cold cuts; smoked anchovies, salmon, and other fish; and a good selection of Spanish cheeses and local wines. They also serve good, inexpensive breakfasts. Named after the current owner, the liquor store **David Cabello** (✉*Cervantes 6, Barrio de las Letras* ☎*91/429–5230*) has been in the family for more than 100 years. It's rustic and a bit dusty, and looks like a warehouse rather than a shop, but David knows what he's selling. Head here for a good selection of Rioja wines (some dating as far back as 1920) and local liqueurs, including anisettes and *pacharan*, a fruity liquor made with sloes (wild European plums).

LEATHER GOODS

The owners of **Boxcalf** (✉*Jorge Juan 34, Salamanca* ☎*91/531–5343*), on the corner of one of Calle Jorge Juan's alleys, sell exclusive suede, napa, and leather coats for women, as well as accessories, made in Majorca. On a street full of bargain shoe stores, or *muestrarios*, **Caligae** (✉*Augusto Figueroa 18, 20, and 31, Chueca* ☎*91/531–5343*) is probably the best of the bunch. Posh **Loewe** (✉*Calle Serrano 26 and 34, Salamanca* ☎*91/577–6056* ✉*Gran Vía 8, Centro* ☎*91/532–7024*) carries high-quality designer purses, accessories, and clothing made of butter-soft leather in dyed, jewel-like colors. The store on Serrano 26 displays the women's collection; items for men are a block away, on Serrano 34. Prices can hit the stratosphere.

MUSIC

José Ramírez (✉*Calle de la Paz 8, Centro* ☎*91/531–4229*) has provided Spain and the rest of the world with guitars since 1882, and his store includes a museum of antique instruments. Prices for new ones range from €120 to €225 for children and €150 to €2,200 for adults, though some of the top concert models easily break the €10,000 mark. **Percusión Campos** (✉*Olivar 36, Lavapiés* ☎*91/539–2178*) is an easy-to-miss percussion shop-workshop where the young Canarian Pedro Navarro crafts his own *cajones flamencos,* or flamenco box drums, that are greatly appreciated among professionals. Prices range between €120 and €250 and vary according to the quality of woods used. **Musical Ópera** (✉*Carlos III 1, Centro* ☎*91/540–1672*), around the corner from the Teatro Real, is a music lover's dream, with books, CDs, sheet music, memorabilia, guitars, and a knowledgeable staff.

SIDE TRIPS FROM MADRID

EL ESCORIAL

50 km (31 mi) northwest of Madrid.

Felipe II was one of history's most deeply religious and forbidding monarchs—not to mention one of its most powerful—and the great granite monastery that he had constructed in a remarkable 21 years (1563–84) is an enduring testament to his character. Outside Madrid in the foothills of the Sierra de Guadarrama, the **Real Monasterio de San Lorenzo de El Escorial** *(Royal Monastery of St. Lawrence of Escorial)* is severe, rectilinear, and unforgiving—one of the most gigantic yet simple architectural monuments on the Iberian Peninsula.

Felipe built the monastery in the village of San Lorenzo de El Escorial to commemorate Spain's crushing victory over the French at Saint-Quentin on August 10, 1557, and as a final resting place for his all-powerful father, the Holy Roman Emperor Carlos V. He filled the place with treasures as he ruled the largest empire the world had ever seen, knowing all the while that a marble coffin awaited him in the pantheon deep below. The building's vast rectangle, encompassing 16 courts, is modeled on the red-hot grille upon which St. Lawrence was martyred—appropriate enough, since August 10 was that saint's day. (It's also said that Felipe's troops accidentally destroyed a church dedicated to St. Lawrence during the battle and sought to make amends.)

The building and its adjuncts—a palace, museum, church, and more—can take hours or even days to tour. Easter Sunday's candlelight midnight Mass draws crowds, as does the summer tourist season.

GETTING HERE AND AROUND

El Escorial is easily reached by car, train, bus, or organized tour from Madrid. If you plan on taking public transportation, the bus is probably the best alternative. Herranz's Lines 661 (through Galapagar) and 664 (through Guadarrama) depart a few times every hour (they run less frequently on the weekends) from bay number 30 at the *Intercambiador* (station) at Moncloa. The 50-minute ride leaves you within a

El Escorial

Apartments of Philip II **14**
Basilica **4**
Biblioteca (Library) **9**
Choir **3**
Colegio **11**
Convent........ **10**
Main Entrance **1**
Museum **13**
Patio de los Evangelistas (Court of the Evangelists) **7**
Patio de los Reyes (Court of the Kings) **2**
Royal Palace **12**
Sacristy **6**
Salas Capitulares (Chapter Houses) **8**
Stairway to Panteón de los Reyes (Royal Pantheon) **5**
Tour Entrance **15**

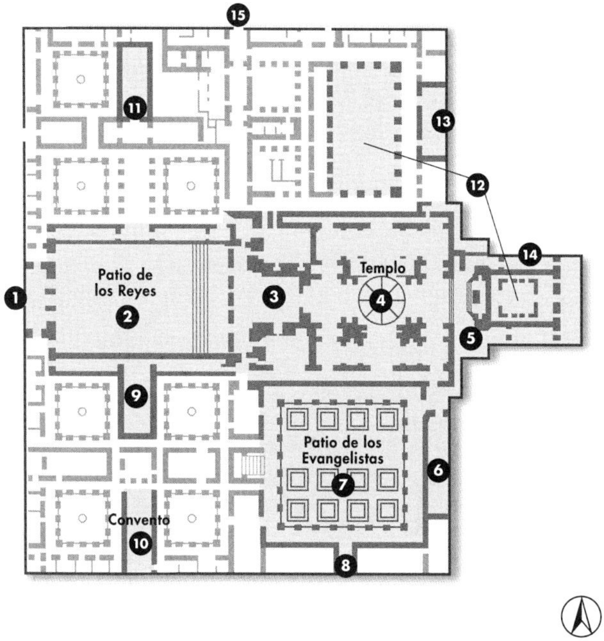

five-minute walk of the monastery. You can also take the *cercanías C-8a* (commuter train C-8a) from either Atocha or Chamartín. However, trains run less frequently than the buses and stop at the town of El Escorial, from where you must either take Bus L-4 (also run by Herranz) to San Lorenzo de El Escorial (where the monastery is) or take a strenuous, long walk uphill. To get to the **local tourist office** (✉ *Calle Grimaldi 4* ☎ *91/890–5313*), cross the arch that's across from the visitors' entrance to the monastery.

The monastery was begun by Juan Bautista de Toledo but finished in 1584 by Juan de Herrera, who would eventually give his name to a major Spanish architectural school. It was completed just in time for Felipe to die here, gangrenous and tortured by the gout that had plagued him for years, in the tiny, sparsely furnished bedroom that resembled a monk's cell more than the resting place of a great monarch. It's in this bedroom—which looks out, through a private entrance, into the royal chapel—that you most appreciate the man's spartan nature. Spain's later Bourbon kings, such as Carlos III and Carlos IV, had clearly different tastes, and their apartments, connected to Felipe's by the Hall of Battles, and which can be visited only with an appointment, are far more luxurious.

Perhaps the most interesting part of the entire Escorial is the **Panteón de los Reyes** (Royal Pantheon), a baroque construction room from the 17th century that contains the body of every king since Carlos I except three—Felipe V (buried at La Granja), Ferdinand VI (in Madrid), and Amadeus of Savoy (in Italy). The body of Alfonso XIII, who died in Rome in 1941, was brought to El Escorial in January 1980. The rulers' bodies lie in 26 sumptuous marble-and-bronze sarcophagi that line the walls (three of which are empty, awaiting future rulers). Only those queens who bore sons later crowned lie in the same crypt; the others, along with royal sons and daughters who never ruled, lie nearby, in the **Panteón de los Infantes** built during the reign of Elizabeth II in the third quarter of the 19th century. Many of the royal children are in a single circular tomb made of Carrara marble.

Another highlight is the monastery's surprisingly lavish and colorful **library,** with ceiling paintings by Michelangelo disciple Pellegrino Tibaldi (1527–96). The imposing austerity of El Escorial's facades makes this chromatic explosion especially powerful; try to save it for last. The library houses 50,000 rare manuscripts, codices, and ancient books, including the diary of St. Teresa of Ávila and the gold-lettered, illuminated Codex Aureus. Tapestries woven from cartoons by Goya, Rubens, and El Greco cover almost every inch of wall space in huge sections of the building, and extraordinary canvases by Velázquez, El Greco, David, Ribera, Tintoretto, Rubens, and other masters, collected from around the monastery, are displayed in the **Museos Nuevos** (New Museums). In the **basilica,** don't miss the fresco above the choir, depicting heaven, or Titian's fresco *The Martyrdom of St. Lawrence,* which shows the saint being roasted alive. ✉ *San Lorenzo de El Escorial* ☎ *91/890–5904 or 91/890–5905* 🎫 *General admission €8; without Panteón €7; with guided tour €10* ⏲ *Apr.–Sept., Tues.–Sun. 10–6; Oct.–Mar., Tues.–Sun. 10–5.*

WHERE TO EAT

$$$–$$$$ SPANISH ✕ **Charolés.** Some go to El Escorial for the monastery and others go for Charolés. It's a landmark that attracts a crowd of its own for its noble bearing, with thick stone walls and vaulted ceilings, wooden beams and floors, and stuffy service; its summer terrace a block from the monastery; and its succulent dishes, such as the heavy beans with clams or mushrooms, and the game meats served grilled or in stews. The four-course mammoth *cocido* (broth, chickpeas, meats, and in this case, also a salad) on Wednesday and Friday tests the endurance of even those with the heartiest appetites. ✉ *Calle Floridablanca 24* ☎ *91/890–5975* 💳 *DC, MC, V.*

$$ SPANISH ✕ **La Cañada Real.** After visiting the massive monastery, this little restaurant with sketches of bullfighters on the walls is welcoming and cozy. It has fewer than 10 tables and a laid-back crowd. The menu includes a good selection of wines, grilled meats, salads, and hearty stews. The apple tart is a must for rounding off any meal. ✉ *Calle Floridablanca 30* ☎ *91/890–2703* 💳 *MC, V* ⏲ *No dinner Sun. and Mon.*

$$ SPANISH ✕ **La Horizontal.** Away from town and surrounded by trees in what used to be a mountain cabin, this family-oriented restaurant is coveted by madrileños, who come here to enjoy the terrace in summer and the cozy

bar area with a fireplace in winter. It has a good selection of fish and rice dishes, but the meats and seasonal plates are what draw the large following. Take Paseo Juan de Borbón, which surrounds the monastery, exit through the arches and pass the *casita del infante* (Prince's Quarters) on your way up to the Monte Abantos, or get a cab at the taxi station on Calle Floridablanca. ✉*C. Horizontal s/n* ☎*91/890–3811* 💳*AE, MC, V* ⊙*No dinner Mon.–Wed. Nov.–Mar.*

VALLE DE LOS CAÍDOS

13 km (8 mi) north of El Escorial on M600.

Ranked as a not-to-be-missed visit until the death of Generalísimo Francisco Franco in 1975, this massive monument to fascism's victory over democracy (religion's victory over communism to some) in the 1936–39 Spanish civil war has become something of an anachronism in modern democratic Spain. It's now relegated to a rallying point for the extreme right on key dates, such as the July 18 commemoration of the military uprising of 1936 or the November 20 death of Franco. The Valley of the Fallen is just a few minutes north of El Escorial. A lovely pine forest leads up to a massive basilica carved out of a solid granite mountain. Topped with a cross nearly 500 feet high (accessible by elevator and through a trail starting from the monastery behind the basilica; as of the time of writing both are closed due to maintenance work on the sculptures of the cross), the basilica holds the tombs of both General Franco and José Antonio Primo de Rivera, founder of the fascist Spanish Falange, but also the bodies of nearly 34,000 Spaniards (of both sides) who died during the civil war, and whose remains were removed from communal graves and buried here between 1959 and 1983.

The monument was built with the forced labor of postwar Republican prisoners and dedicated, rather disingenuously, to all who died in the three-year conflict. Tapestries of the Apocalypse add to the terrifying air inside as every footstep resounds off the polished marble floors and stone walls. An eerie midnight Mass is held here on Easter Sunday, the granite peak lit by candlelight.

GETTING HERE AND AROUND

To get here by public transportation, take the 3:15 PM bus from the Herranz station at San Lorenzo de El Escorial. The bus makes a return drive at 5:30 (the bus plus the visit is €8.30). If you go by car, note that the adjacent Benedictine monastery has a *hospedería* (guesthouse) and a restaurant serving good, inexpensive food. ☎*91/890–5611* 🎫*Basilica €5; combined with guided tour of El Escorial €11; combined with unguided tour of El Escorial €10* ⊙*Apr.–Sept., Tues.–Sun. 10–6; Oct.–Mar., Tues.–Sun. 10–5.*

CHINCHÓN

54 km (33 mi) southeast of Madrid, A3 to M832 to M311.

A true Castilian town, the village of Chinchón seems a good four centuries removed. It makes an ideal day trip, especially if you save time for lunch at one of its many rustic restaurants; the only problem is that

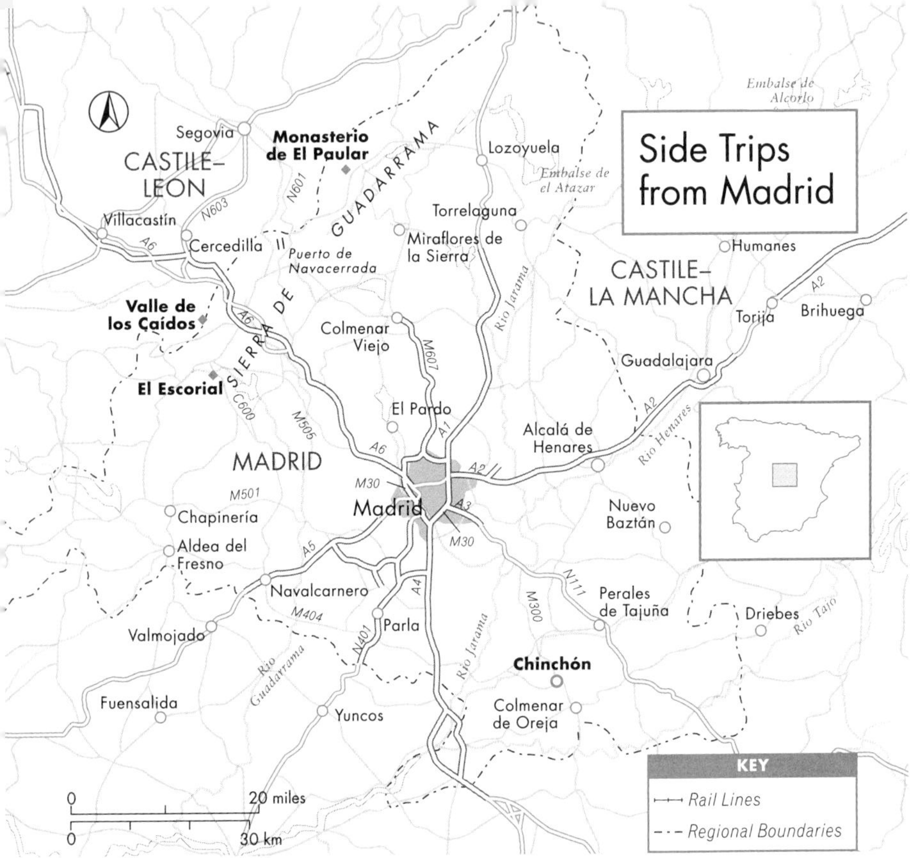

swarms of madrileños have the same idea, so it's often hard to get a table at lunchtime on weekends.

The high point of Chinchón is its charming **Plaza Mayor,** an uneven circle of ancient three- and four-story houses embellished with wooden balconies resting on granite columns. Restored in 2006–07, it's something like an open-air Elizabethan theater but with a Spanish flavor.

East of the M311 runs the Río Jarama. The stretch known as **Valle del Jarama** between the A3 and Ciempozuelos was the scene of one of the bloodiest battles of the Spanish civil war. American volunteers in the Abraham Lincoln Battalion, part of the 15th International Brigade (comprised of volunteers from 26 nations), which fought with the democratically elected Spanish Republican government against Franco's military insurgency, were mauled here in a baptism of fire. Between 15,000 to 20,000 soldiers from both sides lost their lives on the river banks in a 20-day battle. The trenches are still visible, and bits of rusty military hardware can still be found in the fields.

WHERE TO EAT

$$–$$$ ✕ **Mesón de las Cuevas del Vino.** A rambling tavern with roaring fireplaces, a giant olive press in the main room, and immense antique wine and olive oil amphorae—signed by illustrious guests—this is arguably the town's best-known restaurant. Madrileños swarm here for the suckling

pig and the roasted lamb. For starters, try the hearty beans, the *asadillo* (roasted peppers), or the blood pudding. Wine tastings are held in the carved caves here, which can be visited only on weekends. ✉ *Calle Benito Hortelano 13* ☎ *91/894–0285* ✍ *Reservations essential* ▭ *MC, V* ⊗ *Closed Tues. and Aug. No dinner Sun.*

$$$ ✕ **Parador de Chinchón (El Convento).** In the village's best hotel, this restaurant compensates for its rustic decor with a varied menu that includes many fish courses, vegetables such as broad beans with clams and vegetables, suckling pig filled with mushroom, and the hearty *migas* (a traditional dish made with pieces of bread fried in olive oil, paprika, and garlic, and served with a variety of meats and a fried egg on top). There is also has a daily prix-fixe menu for €32. ✉ *Calle Los Huertos 1* ☎ *91/894–0836* ▭ *AE, DC, MC, V.*

2

MONASTERIO DE EL PAULAR AND LOZOYA VALLEY

100 km (62 mi) north of Madrid.

Rising from Spain's great central *meseta* (plain), the Sierra de Guadarrama looms northwest of Madrid like a dark, jagged shield separating Old and New Castile. Snowcapped for much of the year, the mountains are indeed rough hewn in many spots, particularly on their northern face, but there is a dramatic exception—the Lozoya Valley.

About 100 km (62 mi) north of the capital, this valley of pines, poplars, and babbling brooks is a cool, green retreat from the often searing heat of the plain. Madrileños come here for a picnic or a simple drive, rarely sharing the space with foreign travelers, to whom the area is virtually unknown.

GETTING HERE AND AROUND

You need a car to make this trip, and the drive is a pleasant one. Take the A6 northwest from Madrid and exit at signs for the Navacerrada Pass on the N601. As you climb toward the 6,100-foot mountain pass, you come to a road bearing to the left toward Cercedilla. (This little village, a popular base for hikes, is also accessible by train.) Just above Cercedilla, an old Roman road leads up to the ridge of the Guadarrama, where an ancient fountain, known as Fuenfría, for a long time produced the spring water that fed the Roman aqueduct of Segovia. The path traced by this cobblestone road is very close to the route Hemingway has his hero Robert Jordan take in *For Whom the Bell Tolls* and eventually takes you near the bridge that Jordan blows up in the novel. On the right is the exit for Navacerrada, a mountain village with a nice main plaza whose terraces get crowded during summer weekends with locals sipping beer and having tapas.

EXPLORING

If you continue past the Cercedilla road, you come to a ski resort at the highest point of the Navacerrada Pass. Take a right here on M604 and follow the ridge of the mountains for a few miles before descending into the **Lozoya Valley.** The valley is filled with picnic spots along the Lozoya River. The monastery is on your left as you approach the floor of the Lozoya Valley.

Before visiting the monastery, stop across the road at the **Centro de Educación Ambiental Puente del Perdón** (☎*91/869–1757* ⏲*Daily 10–6*), which provides information on the area, including some lodging and eating options in Rascafría and nearby villages, and suggestions for interesting treks—one of the most beautiful is a route that takes you to La Cascada del Purgatorio (Purgatory Falls). Next to the center is El Arboreto Giner de los Ríos, an arboretum worth visiting.

The highlight of this excursion is the **Monasterio de El Paular** (☎*91/869–1425*), built by King Juan I in 1390 and the first Carthusian monastery in Castile. It was plundered five centuries later with the Disentailment of 1836, when the religious organization's art treasures were taken by the state and its land and buildings auctioned. The state repurchased the monastery (at a much higher price) in two phases, one in 1874 and the other one in 1936, right before the beginning of the civil war. The winner of this last conflict, Francisco Franco, himself a devout Catholic, decided in 1948 to have a Benedictine monastery in Madrid, and nine years later (and 119 years after the last Carthusian left the building) the first monks arrived in El Paular. Nowadays fewer than a dozen Benedictine monks still live here, living and praying exactly as their predecessors did centuries ago. Tours (in Spanish only and conducted by one of the monks) are given Monday–Saturday at noon, 1, and 5 (on Thursday there's no 5 PM tour); Sunday tours are at 1, 4, and 5, October to April, and at 1, 5, and 6, May to September. If you're here on a Sunday, don't miss the noon Mass. You'll have the privilege of listening to the monks' Gregorian chants.

Attached to the monastery, the **Sheraton Santa María de El Paular** (☎*91/869–1011* 🌐*www.hotelsantamariapaular.com*) is a cozy mountain hotel with two good restaurants: Dom Lope, open daily and specializing in traditional Spanish food, and Trastámara, open weekends at lunch for great roasted lamb and suckling pig. Oteruelo del Valle, 1½ mi from Rascafría, also has some good eateries.

To get back to Madrid, from M604 in Rascafría turn right on a smaller and scenic road marked as Miraflores de la Sierra (M611). In that town turn right again, following signs for Colmenar Viejo, and then pick up a short expressway back to Madrid.

Castile–León and Castile–La Mancha

3

Magaña, Soria province

WORD OF MOUTH

"Our day in Toledo was just magical. The cathedral there is indeed stunning and awe-inspiring and the buildings which used to be synagogues are worth the visit as well. Take the fast train from Atocha and it takes less than half an hour, i.e. 25 minutes. If you are a lover of marzipan (or *mazapan* as it is called there) DO NOT MISS the Santo Tome store. It is right on the main Plaza Zocodover and you cannot miss it. Toledo is known for it."

—Flame123

www.fodors.com/community

WELCOME TO CASTILE–LEÓN AND CASTILE–LA MANCHA

TOP REASONS TO GO

★ **Defying Gravity:** Check out the astounding Casas Colgadas (Hanging Houses) from Cuenca's vertiginous San Pablo Bridge.

★ **Searching for Pancho:** Ruminate along the windmilled route in Consuegra's wide-open horizon, absorbing Don Quixote's inspirational views.

★ **Toledo's Maze:** Enjoy getting lost in Toledo's labyrinthine streets.

★ **Soria's Serenity:** Stroll along the Duero River, where Antonio Machado used to write poetry.

★ **Royal Snacking:** Aranjuez is known for its strawberries, and in spring and summer vendors sell them, with whipped cream, at the market and along the river by the Royal Palace of La Granja's San Ildefonso, whose opulent gardens rival those at Versailles.

★ **Roman Splendor:** Segovia's dazzling 2,000-year-old aqueduct in the late afternoon sun is a never-to-be-forgotten sight.

1 Castile–León. In Castile–León, you'll find the spectacular peaks of the Sierra de Gredos, the walled city of Ávila, and medieval Segovia, with its famed Roman aqueduct and Alcázar palace. Farther north is Salamanca, dominated by luminescent sandstone buildings, and the ancient capitals of Burgos and León: Burgos, an early outpost of Christianity, brims with medieval architecture, and you'll see a multitude of nuns roaming its streets; León is a fun university town with some of its Roman walls still in place.

2 Castile–La Mancha. The tourist hub of Castile–La Mancha is Toledo, once home to Spain's famous artist El Greco. Other highlights of the area include Consuegra, with its windmills that inspired Cervantes's masterpiece; lovely Cuenca with its "hanging houses" architecture; and Alcalá de Henares, a bustling university town where Cervantes was born, now renowned for its tapas.

Remains of the Convent of the Rosal in Cuenca.

Typical ceramics from Toledo.

GETTING ORIENTED

Castile–La Mancha and Castile–León are like parentheses around Madrid, one north and one south, split by the Guadarrama mountains just north of the capital. The name Castilla refers to the great east–west line of castles and fortified towns built in the 12th century between Salamanca and Soria. Segovia's Alcázar, Ávila's fully intact city walls, and other bastions are among Castile's greatest monuments. Many have been converted into splendid hotels.

Segovia province's Castle of Cuéllar.

CASTILE–LEÓN AND CASTILE–LA MANCHA PLANNER

When to Go

July and August can be brutally hot; November through February can get bitterly cold, especially in the Sierra de Guadarrama. May and October, when the weather is sunny but relatively cool, are the two best months to visit central Spain.

Cuenca's Easter celebration and Toledo's Corpus Christi draw people from all over Spain. During the pre-Lenten carnival, León and nearby La Bañeza are popular party centers. Expect crowds and book accommodations months in advance if going during these times.

Tours

In summer the tourist offices of Segovia, Toledo, and Aranjuez organize Trénes Turísticos (miniature tourist trains) that glide past all the major sights; contact the local tourist office for schedules, or call 925/142274 for information. Equiberia leads horseback tours ranging from 1 to 10 days, a unique way to experience the gorges, fields, and forests of the Sierra de Guadarrama.

Tour Operators **Equiberia** (☎ *920/348338* ⊕ *www.equiberia.com*).

Planning Your Time

Madrid is the natural starting point for trips to Castilian destinations, most of which can be visited as either one- or several-day trips.

If you have three or four days for La Mancha, try this possible itinerary: visit sight-brimming Toledo for a day and night, then stop off to see Quixote's windmills in Consuegra. Next, swing northeast to Cuenca to enjoy its architecturally intriguing old town, with its hanging houses. Complete the journey with a day and night in serene Sigüenza or Soria.

For Castile–León, an ideal three- or four-day trip might include Segovia, famous for its aqueduct as well as its pretty old quarter and the gardens of the Palacio Real de la Granja, and Ávila, once home to St. Teresa. En route between Segovia and Ávila, stop by the medieval Castillo de Coca. You'll also want to visit Salamanca, both for its architecture and for its lively student-led nightlife. Farther north, Burgos's monasteries at Santo Domingo de Silos and San Pedro de Cardeñá are both well worth visiting—spending a night at one of the two is highly recommended.

WHAT IT COSTS (IN EUROS)

	¢	$	$$	$$$	$$$$
Restaurants	under €8	€8–€12	€13–€17	€18–€22	over €22
Hotels	under €60	€60–€90	€91–€125	€126–€180	over €180

Prices are per person for a main course at dinner, and for two people in a standard double room in high season, excluding tax.

GETTING HERE AND AROUND

By Bus

Bus connections between Madrid and Castile are excellent. There are several stations and stops in Madrid; buses to **Toledo** (1 hour) leave every half hour from the Estación del Sur, and buses to **Segovia** (1½ hours) leave every hour from La Sepulvedana's headquarters, which are near Príncipe Pío. Larrea sends buses to **Ávila** from the Méndez Alvaro Metro stop. Alsa and Movelia have service to **León** (4½ hours), and Alsa also travels to **Valladolid** (2¼ hours). Auto Res serves **Cuenca** (2¾ hours) and **Salamanca** (3 hours). Buses to **Soria** (3 hours), **El Burgo de Osma** (2½ hours), and **Burgos** (3½ hours) are run by Continental Auto.

From Burgos, buses head north to the Basque Country; from León, you can press on to Asturias. Service between towns is not as frequent as it is to and from Madrid, so you may find it quicker to return to Madrid and make your way from there. Reservations are rarely necessary.

TIP→ **Note that it's best to avoid taking the bus at rush hour, as journeys can be delayed by more than an hour.**

By Car

Major divided highways—the A1 through A6—radiate out from Madrid, making Spain's farthest corners no more than five- to six-hour drives. The capital's outlying towns are only minutes away. If possible, avoid returning to Madrid on major highways at the end of a weekend or a holiday. The beginning and end of August are notorious for traffic jams, as is Easter week, which starts on Palm Sunday and ends on Easter Sunday. Side roads vary in quality but provide one of the great pleasures of driving around the Castilian countryside—surprise encounters with architectural monuments and wild and spectacular vistas. The Travel Smart chapter has contact info for major car rental agencies. Madrid is the natural starting point for trips to Castilian destinations, most of which can be visited as either one- or several-day trips. If you're traveling by car, it's very possible to visit two nearby places in one day (e.g., Sigüenza and Mendinaceli).

By Air

The only international airport in Castile is Madrid's Barajas; Salamanca, León, and Valladolid have domestic airports.

By Train

Though it's often faster and more comfortable to travel by bus, all the main towns in Castile–León and Castile–La Mancha are accessible by train from Madrid. Several make feasible day trips: there are commuter trains from Madrid to Segovia (2 hours), Alcalá de Henares (45 minutes), Guadalajara (1 hour), and Toledo (1½ hours). Trains to Toledo depart from Madrid's Atocha station; trains to Salamanca, Burgos, and León depart from Chamartín; and both stations serve Ávila, Segovia, El Escorial, and Sigüenza, though Chamartín may have more frequent service. The one important town that's accessible only by train (and not bus) is Sigüenza. Trains from Segovia go only to Madrid, but you can change at Villalba for Ávila and Salamanca.

Updated by Hannah Semmler

For all the variety in the towns and countryside around Madrid, there's an underlying unity in Castile—the high, wide meseta (plain) of gray, bronze, and (briefly) green. This central Spanish steppe is divided into what was historically known as Old and New Castile, the former north of Madrid, the latter south (known as "New" because it was captured from the Moors a bit later). No Spaniard refers to either as "Old" or "New" anymore, preferring instead Castilla y León or Castile–León for the area north of Madrid, and Castilla y La Mancha or Castile–La Mancha for the area to the south.

Stone, a dominant element in the Castilian countryside, gives the region much of its character. Gaunt mountain ranges frame the horizons; gorges and rocky outcrops break up flat expanses; and the fields around Ávila and Segovia are littered with giant boulders. Castilian villages are built predominantly of granite, and their solid, formidable look contrasts markedly with the whitewashed walls of most of southern Spain. Over the centuries, poets—most notably Antonio Machado, whose experiences at Soria in the early 20th century inspired his haunting *Campos de Castilla* (Fields of Castile)—and others have characterized Castile as austere and melancholy. There is a distinct, chilly beauty in the stark lines and soothing colors of these breezy expanses.

EXPLORING CASTILE

ABOUT THE RESTAURANTS

Castilian food is hearty. Classic dishes are *cordero* (lamb) and *cochinillo* (suckling pig) roasted in a wood oven, while prized entrées include *perdiz en escabeche,* the marinated partridge of Soria, and *perdiz estofada a la Toledana,* the stewed partridge of Toledo. The mountainous districts of Salamanca, particularly the villages of Guijuelo and Candelario, are renowned for their hams and sausages—as the Spanish saying goes, "*Del cerdo, hasta los andares*" (literally "From the pig, even the way it walks," meaning all parts of the pig can be used). A typical dish in the El Bierzo area, near León, is *botillo*—pig's tail, ribs, and cheeks stuffed into pig's stomach. Bean dishes are specialties of the villages El Barco (Ávila) and La Granja (Segovia), and *trucha* (trout) and *cangrejos de río* (river crab) are common in Guadalajara. Castile's most complex and exotic cuisine is perhaps that of Cuenca; here a Moorish influence appears in such dishes as *gazpacho pastor,* a hot terrine made with a mix of game, topped with grapes.

Among the region's sweets are the *yemas* (sugared egg yolks) of Ávila, *almendras garrapiñadas* (candied almonds) of Alcalá de Henares, *mazapán* (marzipan) of Toledo, and *ponche Segovia* (Segovian egg toddy). *Manchego* cheeses (from La Mancha) are staples throughout Spain, and Aranjuez is known for both its strawberries and asparagus.

ABOUT THE HOTELS

The majority of the oldest and most attractive *paradores* in Castile are in quieter towns such as Almagro, Ávila, Chinchón, Cuenca, León, and Sigüenza. Those in Toledo, Segovia, Salamanca, and Soria are modern buildings with magnificent views and, in the case of Segovia, have wonderful indoor and outdoor swimming pools. There are plenty of pleasant alternatives to paradores, too, such as Segovia's Infanta Isabel, Salamanca's Rector, and Cuenca's Posada San José, a 16th-century convent.

CASTILE–LA MANCHA

TOLEDO

Fodor's Choice ★

71 km (44 mi) southwest of Madrid.

Long the spiritual capital of Spain, Toledo perches atop a rocky mount with steep ocher hills rising on either side, bound on three sides by the Río Tajo (Tagus River). When the Romans came in 192 BC, they fortified the highest point of the rock, where you now see the Alcázar. This stronghold was later remodeled by the Visigoths. In the 8th century, the Moors arrived.

The Moors strengthened Toledo's reputation as a center of religion and learning. Unusual tolerance was extended to those who practiced Christianity (the Mozarabs), as well as to the town's exceptionally large Jewish population. Today, the Moorish legacy is evident in Toledo's strong crafts tradition, the mazelike arrangement of the streets, and the predominance of brick rather than stone. For the Moors, beauty was a quality to be savored within rather than displayed on the surface, and it's significant that even Toledo's cathedral—one of the most richly endowed in Spain—is hard to see from the outside, largely obscured by the warren of houses around it.

Alfonso VI, aided by El Cid ("Lord Conqueror"), captured the city in 1085 and styled himself emperor of Toledo. Under the Christians, the town's strong intellectual life was maintained, and Toledo became famous for its school of translators, who spread knowledge of Arab medicine, law, culture, and philosophy. Religious tolerance continued, and during the rule of Peter the Cruel (so named because he allegedly had members of his own family murdered to advance himself), a Jewish banker, Samuel Levi, became the royal treasurer and one of the wealthiest men in town. By the early 1600s, however, hostility toward Jews and Arabs had grown as Toledo developed into a bastion of the Catholic Church.

As Florence had the Medici and Rome the papacy, so Toledo had its long line of cardinals, most notably Mendoza, Tavera, and Cisneros. Under these patrons of the arts, Renaissance Toledo emerged as a center of humanism. Economically and politically, however, Toledo began to decline in the 16th century. The expulsion of the Jews from Spain in 1492, as part of the Spanish Inquisition, had serious economic consequences for Toledo. When Madrid became the permanent center of the Spanish court in 1561, Toledo's political importance eroded, and the expulsion from Spain of the converted Arabs (Moriscos) in 1601 led to the departure of most of Toledo's artisan community. The years the painter El Greco spent in Toledo—from 1572 to his death in 1614—were those of the town's decline. Its transformation into a major tourist center began in the late 19th century, when the works of El Greco came to be widely appreciated after years of neglect. Today, Toledo is conservative, prosperous, and expensive.

Toledo's winding streets and steep hills can be exasperating, especially when you're looking for a specific sight. Take the entire day to absorb the town's medieval trappings, and expect to get a little lost.

GETTING HERE AND AROUND

The best way to get to Toledo from Madrid is the high-speed AVE train. The AVE leaves from Madrid eight times daily from Atocha station and gets you there in 30 minutes (the normal train takes 1½ hours). Buses leave every half hour from Méndez Alvaro/Estación del Sur and take 1¼ hours.

If you're with children, check out the **Zocotren Imperial** (*925/220300 €4.20 Daily 11–11*), a tourist train that chugs past many of the sights. It departs from the Plaza de Zocodover.

ESSENTIALS

Visitor Information Toledo (*Puerta de Bisagra s/n 925/220843*).

EXPLORING

5 **Alcázar.** Expected to reopen in late 2009 after years of renovations, the Alcázar ("fortress" in Arabic) was originally a Moorish citadel that stood here from the 10th century to the Reconquest. A tour around the exterior reveals the south facade, the building's most severe—the work of Juan de Herrera, of El Escorial fame. The east facade incorporates a large section of battlements. The finest facade is the northern, one of many Toledan works by Alonso de Covarrubias, who did more than any other architect to introduce the Renaissance style here. When the renovations are finished, the Alcázar will be the new site for the Museo del Ejército (Military Museum), formerly in Madrid. The Alcázar's architectural highlight is Covarrubias's Italianate courtyard, which, like most other parts of the building, was largely rebuilt after the civil war, when the Alcázar was besieged by the Republicans. Though the Nationalists' ranks were depleted, they held on to the building. Franco later turned the Alcázar into a monument to Nationalist bravery. More cheerful is a ground-floor room full of beautifully crafted swords, a Toledo specialty introduced by Moorish silversmiths. At the top of the grand staircase are rooms displaying a vast collection of toy soldiers. *Calle Cuesta Carlos V 2 925/238800 €5 Tues.–Sun. 9:30–2:30.*

3

A GOOD WALK

The eastern end of the Tagus gorge, along Calle de Circunvalación, is a good place to park your car and look down over most of historic Toledo. For quicker access to your car, park by the Alcázar. Remember that the streets in Toledo are steep and windy, and it can be hard to find sights. To avoid frustration, you might prefer to choose only some of these sights, or spread your tour over several days.

A complete tour starts at the **Puente de Alcántara** ❶. If you skirt the city walls traveling northwest, a long walk past the Puerta de Bisagra on Calle Cardenal Tavera brings you to the **Hospital de Tavera** ❷. If you enter the city wall, walk west and pass the **Museo de la Santa Cruz** ❸ to emerge in the **Plaza de Zocodover** ❹. Due south, on Calle Cuesta de Carlos V, is the **Alcázar** ❺; a short walk northwest on Calle Nueva brings you to the **Mezquita del Cristo de la Luz** ❻. From the southwestern corner of the Alcázar, a series of alleys descends to the **cathedral** ❼. Make your way around the southern side of the building, passing the mid-15th-century Puerta de los Leones. Emerging into the small square in front of the cathedral's west facade, you'll see the stately *ayuntamiento* (town hall) to your right.

Near the Museo de los Concilios, on Calle de San Clemente, take in the richly sculpted portal by Covarrubias on the Convento de San Clemente; across the street is the church of **San Román** ❽. Almost every wall in this part of town belongs to a convent, and the empty streets make for contemplative walks. This was a district loved by the Romantic poet Gustavo Adolfo Bécquer, author of *Rimas* (*Rhymes*), the most popular collection of Spanish verse before García Lorca's *Romancero Gitano.* Bécquer's favorite corner was the tiny square in front of the 16th-century convent church of **Santo Domingo** ❾, a few minutes' walk north of San Román, below the Plazuela de Padilla.

Backtrack, following Calle de San Clemente through Plaza de Valdecaleros to Calle de Santo Tomé, to get to the church of **Santo Tomé** ❿. Downhill from Santo Tomé, off Calle de San Juan de Díos, is the **Casa y Museo de El Greco** ⓫ (follow the signs, as it's a bit of a labyrinth). Next to the Casa de El Greco is the 14th-century **Sinagoga del Tránsito** ⓬, financed by Samuel Levi, and the accompanying Museo Sefardí. From the synagogue, turn right up Calle de Reyes Católicos. A few steps past the town's other synagogue, **Santa María la Blanca** ⓭, is the late-15th-century church of **San Juan de los Reyes** ⓮. The town's western extremity is the **Puente de San Martín** ⓯.

⓫ **Casa y Museo del Greco** *(El Greco House and Museum)*. Still undergoing renovations, this house on the property that belonged to Peter the Cruel's treasurer, Samuel Levi, is said to have been El Greco's home. Although he once lived in a house owned by Levi, this version of the story is pure conjecture. The interior, decorated in the late 19th century to resemble a "typical" house of El Greco's time, is a fake, albeit a pleasant one. The museum next door has a few of El Greco's paintings,

Alcázar 5
Casa y Museo del Greco 11
Cathedral 7
Hospital de Tavera 2
Mezquita del Cristo de la Luz 6
Museo de la Santa Cruz 3
Plaza de Zocodover 4
Puente de Alcántara 1
Puente de San Martín 15
San Juan de los Reyes 14
San Román 8
Santa María la Blanca 13
Santo Domingo 9
Santo Tomé 10
Sinagoga del Tránsito 12

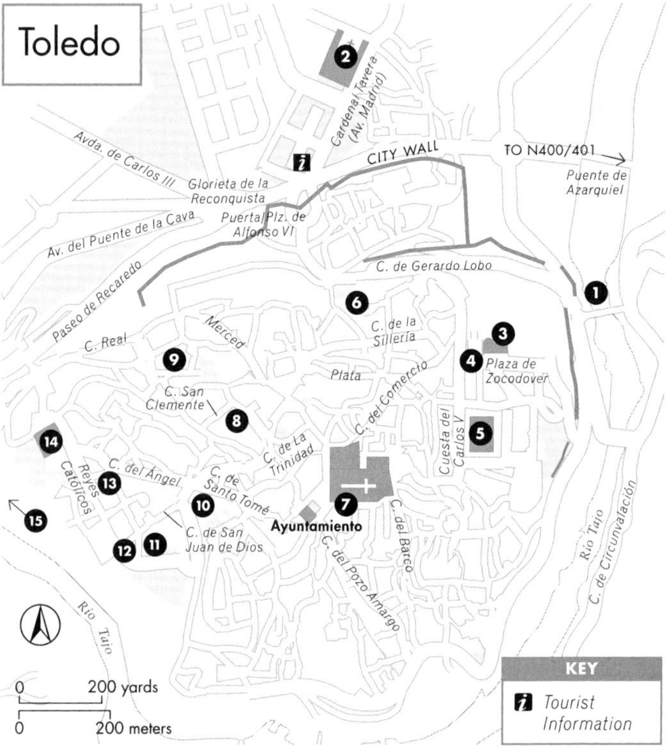

including a panorama of Toledo with the Hospital of Tavera in the foreground. ✉ *Calle Samuel Levi s/n* ☎ *925/224046* *€2.50, free Sat. afternoon and Sun. morning* ⏲ *Tues.–Sat. 10–2 and 4–9, Sun. 10–2.*

7 **Cathedral.** Jorge Manuel Theotokópoulos was responsible for the cathedral's Mozarabic chapel, the elongated dome of which crowns the right-hand side of the west facade. The rest of this facade is mainly early 15th century and has a depiction of Mary presenting her robe to Toledo's patron saint, the Visigothic Ildefonsus. Enter the cathedral from the 14th-century cloisters to the left of the west facade. The primarily 13th-century architecture was inspired by Chartres and other Gothic cathedrals in France, but the squat proportions give it a Spanish feel, as do the wealth and weight of the furnishings and the location of the elaborate choir in the center of the nave. Immediately to your right as you enter the building is a beautifully carved plateresque doorway by Covarrubias, marking the entrance to the Treasury. The latter houses a small Crucifixion by the Italian painter Cimabue and an extraordinarily intricate late-15th-century monstrance by Juan del Arfe, a silversmith of German descent; the ceiling is an excellent example of Mudejar (11th- to 16th-century Moorish-influenced) workmanship.

From here, walk around to the ambulatory; off to the right side is a chapter house with a strange and quintessentially Spanish mixture of

Italianate frescoes by Juan de Borgoña. In the middle of the ambulatory is an example of baroque illusionism by Narciso Tomé known as the *Transparente,* a blend of painting, stucco, and sculpture. Finally, off the northern end of the ambulatory, you'll come to the sacristy and several El Grecos, including one version of *El Espolio* (Christ Being Stripped of His Raiment). This painting is considered to be the first recorded instance of the painter in Spain. Before leaving the sacristy, look up at the colorful and spirited late-baroque ceiling painting by the Italian Luca Giordano. ✉*Arco Palacio s/n* ☎*925/222241* *€7* *Mon.–Sat. 10–6:30, Sun. 2–6:30.*

10 **Santo Tomé.** Topped with a Mudejar tower, this chapel was specially built to house El Greco's most famous painting, *The Burial of Count Orgaz,* and remains devoted to that purpose. The painting portrays the benefactor of the church being buried with the posthumous assistance of St. Augustine and St. Stephen, who have miraculously appeared at the funeral to thank him for all the money he gave to religious institutions named after them. Though the count's burial took place in the 14th century, El Greco painted the onlookers in contemporary costumes and included people he knew; the boy in the foreground is one of El Greco's sons, and the sixth figure on the left is said to be the artist himself. To avoid crowds in summer, come as soon as the building opens. ✉*Pl. del Conde 1* ☎*925/256098* *www.santotome.org* *€2.30* *Mar.–mid-Oct., daily 10–6:45; mid-Oct.–Feb., daily 10–5:45.*

2 **Hospital de Tavera.** You can find this hospital, architect Alonso de Covarrubias's last work, outside the walls beyond Toledo's main northern gate, Covarrubias's imposing Puerta de Bisagra. Unlike the former Hospital of Santa Cruz, this complex is unfinished and slightly dilapidated, but it is nonetheless full of character and has the evocatively ramshackle **Museo de Duque de Lema** in its southern wing. The most important work in the museum's miscellaneous collection is a painting by the 17th-century artist José Ribera. The hospital's monumental chapel holds El Greco's *Baptism of Christ* and the exquisitely carved marble tomb of Cardinal Tavera, the last work of Alonso de Berruguete. Descend into the crypt to experience some bizarre acoustical effects. ✉*Calle Duque de Lerma 2* ☎*925/220451* *€4.50* *Daily 10–1:30 and 3:30–5:30.*

6 **Mezquita del Cristo de la Luz** *(Mosque of Christ of the Light).* A gardener will show you around this mosque-chapel, in a park above the ramparts; if he's not around, ask at the house opposite. Originally a tiny Visigothic church, the chapel was transformed into a mosque during the Moorish occupation; the Islamic arches and vaulting survived, making this the most important relic of Moorish Toledo. The chapel got its name when the horse of Alfonso VI, riding into Toledo in triumph in 1085, fell to its knees out front (a white stone marks the spot); it was then discovered that a candle had burned continuously behind the masonry the whole time the Muslims had been in power. Allegedly, the first Mass of the Reconquest was held here, and later a Mudejar apse was added. ✉*Calle Cuesta de los Carmelitas Descalzas 10* ☎*925/254191* *€2.30* *Oct. 1–Mar. 1, daily 10–5:45; Mar. 2–Sept. 30, daily 10–6:45.*

CLOSE UP

El Greco: the Titan of Toledo

"Crete gave him his life, and brushes; Toledo, a better land, where he begins with Death to attain Eternity." With these words, the Toledan poet Fray Hortensio Paravicino paid homage to his friend El Greco—and to the symbiotic connection between El Greco and his adopted city of Toledo. El Greco's intensely individual and expressionist style—elongated and sometimes distorted figures, charged colors, and a haunting mysticism—was seen as strange and disturbing, and his work remained largely neglected until the late 19th century, when he found wide acclaim and joined the ranks of Velazquez and Goya as one of the old masters of Spanish painting.

Born Domenikos Theotokópoulos on the island of Crete, El Greco ("The Greek") received his artistic education and training in Italy, then moved to Spain around 1577, lured in part by the prospect of painting frescoes for the royal monastery of El Escorial. King Felipe II, however, rejected El Greco's work for being too unusual. It was in Toledo that El Greco came into his own, creating many of his greatest works and honing his singular style and unique vision. He remained here until his death in 1614.

The master painter immortalized the city and its citizens. In his masterpiece *The Burial of Count Orgaz,* which hangs in Toledo's Chapel of Santo Tomé, El Greco pays tribute to Toledan society. The burial onlookers, beneath a vibrant heaven full of angels, include many of El Greco's distinguished contemporaries, their white 16th-century ruff collars framing their angular, ascetic faces. Perhaps the most famous rendering of Toledo is El Greco's dramatic *View of Toledo,* in which the cityscape crackles with a sinister energy underneath a stormy sky.

❸ **Museo de Santa Cruz.** This museum is in a beautiful Renaissance hospital with a stunning classical-plateresque facade; unlike Toledo's other sights, it's open all day without a break. The light and elegant interior has changed little since the 16th century, the main difference being that works of art have replaced the hospital beds; among the displays is El Greco's *Assumption* of 1613, the artist's last known work. A small **Museo de Arqueología** (Museum of Archaeology) is in and around the hospital's delightful cloister. ✉ *Calle Cervantes 3* ☎ *925/221036* 🎫 *Free* ⏲ *Mon.–Sat. 10–6:30, Sun. 10–2.*

❹ **Plaza de Zocodover.** Toledo's main square was built in the early 17th century as part of an unsuccessful attempt to impose a rigid geometry on the chaotic Moorish ground plan. This teeny plaza is also home to the largest and oldest marzipan store in town, Santo Tomé—and Toledo's only McDonald's. You can catch inner-city buses here, and the tourist office is just around the corner. Nearby, you can find **Calle del Comercio,** the town's narrow and lively pedestrian thoroughfare, lined with bars and shops and shaded in summer by awnings.

❶ **Puente de Alcántara.** Roman in origin, this is the town's oldest bridge. Next to it is a heavily restored castle built after the Christian capture of 1085 and, above this, a vast and depressingly severe military academy, a typical example of fascist architecture under Franco.

15 **Puente de San Martín.** This pedestrian bridge on the western edge of the town dates from 1203 and has splendid horseshoe arches.

14 **San Juan de los Reyes.** This convent church in western Toledo was erected by Ferdinand and Isabella to commemorate their victory at the Battle of Toro in 1476 and was intended to be their burial place. (The tomb of the Catholic Monarchs is in Granada's Capilla Real). The building is largely the work of architect Juan Guas, who considered it his masterpiece and asked to be buried here himself. In true plateresque fashion, the white interior is covered with inscriptions and heraldic motifs. ✉ *Calle de Reyes Católicos 17* ☎ *925/223802* 🎫 *€2.30* ⏲ *Oct. 1–Mar. 1, daily 10–5:45; Mar. 2–Sept. 30, daily 10–7.*

8 **San Román.** A virtually unspoiled part of Toledo hides this early-13th-century Mudejar church with extensive remains of frescoes inside. It has been deconsecrated and is now the **Museo de los Concilios y de la Cultura Visigótica,** and has statuary, manuscript illustrations, and jewelry. ✉ *San Clemente 4* ☎ *925/227872* 🎫 *Free* ⏲ *Tues.–Sat. 10–2 and 4–6:30, Sun. 10–2.*

NEED A BREAK?

If the convolutions of Toledo's maze exhaust you, unwind at Palacio Sancara (✉ *Alfonso X El Sabio 6*). Around the corner from the church of San Román, off Plaza Juan de Mariana, this Arabian café-bar has plush couches, low tables, soothing classical music, and colorful tapestries.

13 **Santa María la Blanca.** Founded in 1203, Toledo's second synagogue is nearly two centuries older than the more elaborate Tránsito. The white interior has a forest of columns supporting capitals of enchanting filigree workmanship. ✉ *Calle de Reyes Católicos 21* ☎ *925/227257* 🎫 *€2.30* ⏲ *Apr.–Sept., daily 10–7; Oct.–Mar., daily 10–6.*

9 **Santo Domingo.** A few minutes' walk north of San Román is this 16th-century convent church, where you'll find the earliest of El Greco's Toledo paintings as well as the crypt where the artist is believed to be buried. The friendly nuns at the convent will show you around an odd little museum that includes documents bearing El Greco's signature. ✉ *Pl. Santo Domingo el Antiguo s/n* ☎ *925/222930* 🎫 *€2* ⏲ *Mon.–Sat. 11–1:30 and 4–7, Sun. 4–7.*

12 **Sinagoga del Tránsito.** Financed by Samuel Levi, this 14th-century rectangular synagogue is plain on the outside, but the inside walls are covered with intricate Mudejar decoration, as well as Hebraic inscriptions glorifying God, Peter the Cruel, and Levi himself. It's said that Levi imported cedars from Lebanon for the building's construction, à la Solomon when he built the First Temple in Jerusalem. Adjoining the main hall is the **Museo Sefardí,** a small museum of Jewish culture in Spain. ✉ *Samuel Levi s/n* ☎ *925/223665* 🎫 *€3, free Sat. afternoon and Sun.* ⏲ *Mar.–Nov., Tues.–Sat. 10–9, Sun. 10–2; Dec.–Feb., Tues.–Sat. 10–2 and 4–9, Sun. 10–2.*

WHERE TO EAT AND STAY

$$–$$$ SPANISH ✕ **Asador Adolfo.** Steps from the cathedral but discreetly hidden away, this restaurant has an intimate interior with a coffered ceiling painted in the 14th century. From the entryway you can see the game, fresh produce, and traditional Toledan recipes being prepared in the kitchen,

combining local tastes with tendencies from la Nueva Cocina. The *tempura de flor de calabacín* (tempura battered zucchini blossoms in a saffron sauce) makes for a tasty starter; King Juan Carlos I has declared Adolfo's partridge stew the best in Spain. Finish with a Toledan specialty, *delicias de mazapán* (marzipan sweets). ✉ *Calle de La Granada 6, corner of Calle Hombre de Palo* ☎ *925/227321* 🌐 *www.adolforestaurante.com* *Reservations essential* ▭ *AE, DC, MC, V* ⊙ *Closed Mon. No dinner Sun.*

¢–$$ SPANISH **Bar Ludeña.** Down a couple steps from the square, locals and visitors come together at this bar to have a beer and share the typical Toledan *caramusas,* a kind of meat stew with peas and tomatoes served in a hot dish. ✉ *Plaza de la Madalena 13* ☎ *925/223384* ▭ *AE, DC, MC, V.*

$$–$$$$ SPANISH **Casón de los López de Toledo.** A vaulted foyer leads to a patio with marble statues, twittering caged birds, a fountain, and abstract religious paintings; in the dining room, carved wood abounds. The menu outlines an appetizer list for two, a fresh market entrée selection, and a variety of fish and meat specialties, and includes ravioli filled with truffle and bull tail, venison done in a truffled dried-fruit oil, braised rabbit with sesame sauce and mashed potatoes, or cod with manchego cheese. Try the *mazapán* cake topped with cream cheese. ✉ *Calle Sillería 3* ☎ *902/198344* 🌐 *www.casontoledo.com* *Reservations essential* ▭ *AE, DC, MC, V* ⊙ *No dinner Sun.*

$–$$ ★ **Hostal del Cardenal.** Built in the 18th century (restored in 1972) as a summer palace for Cardinal Lorenzana, this quiet and beautiful hotel is fully outfitted with antique furniture. Some rooms overlook the hotel's enchanting wooded garden, which lies at the foot of the town's walls. The restaurant, popular with tourists, has a long-standing reputation; dishes are mainly local, and in season you can find delicious asparagus and strawberries from Aranjuez. **TIP→ If you have a car, reserve a parking spot when you book your room, or you may not be guaranteed a space.** **Pros:** lovely courtyard, convenient parking. **Cons:** restaurant often full and somewhat pricey. ✉ *Paseo de Recaredo 24* ☎ *925/224900* 🌐 *www.hostaldelcardenal.com* *27 rooms* *In-hotel: restaurant, no elevator, laundry service, public Wi-Fi (some), parking (no fee), some pets allowed* ▭ *AE, DC, MC, V.*

$$–$$$ **Hotel Pintor El Greco Sercotel.** Next door to the painter's house, this friendly hotel occupies what was once a 17th-century bakery. Restored to a chic contemporary look punctuated with ancient stones, the modern interior is warm and elegant, with tawny colors and antique touches. An exposed-brick vaulting pulls your imagination back to El Greco's time. **Pros:** parking garage adjacent. **Cons:** street noise in most rooms, the elevator goes to the second floor only. ✉ *Alamillos del Tránsito 13* ☎ *925/285191* 🌐 *www.hotel-pintorelgreco.com* *33 rooms* *In-hotel: laundry service, public Wi-Fi, parking (fee)* ▭ *AE, DC, MC, V.*

$$–$$$ **Parador de Toledo.** This modern building with Mudéjar-style touches on Toledo's outskirts has an unbeatable panorama of the town from the rooms' terraces where you can sit and watch the sunset. Architecture and furnishings nod to traditional style, emphasizing brick and wood. The restaurant ($$$–$$$$) is stately and traditional, with top-quality regional wines and products. **Pros:** outdoor swimming pool.

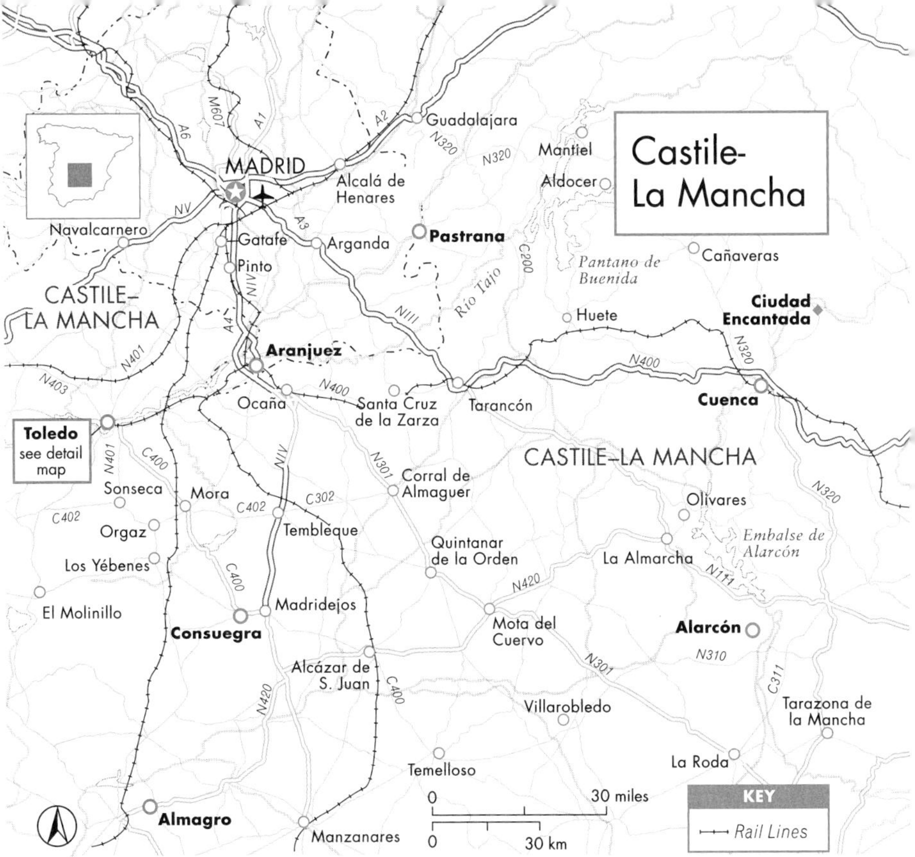

Cons: austere setting can be dark. ✉*Calle Cerro del Emperador s/n* ☏*925/221850* 🌐*www.parador.es* *80 rooms* *In-room: Wi-Fi* *In-hotel: restaurant, pool* 💳*AE, DC, MC, V.*

SHOPPING

The Moors established silver work, damascene (metalwork inlaid with gold or silver), pottery, embroidery, and marzipan traditions here, and next to San Juan de los Reyes a turn-of-the-20th-century art school keeps these crafts alive. For inexpensive pottery, stop at the large emporia on the outskirts of town, on the main road to Madrid. Most of the region's pottery is made in Talavera la Reina, 76 km (47 mi) west of Toledo. At **Museo Ruiz de Luna** (✉*Pl. de San Augustín* ☏*925/800149* *Museum €0.60, weekends free* ⏲*Tues.–Sat. 10–2 and 4–6:30, Sun. 10–2*) watch artisans throw local clay, then you can trace the development of Talavera's world-famous ceramics—chronicled through 1,500 tiles, bowls, vases, and plates dating back to the 15th century.

ARANJUEZ

47 km (29 mi) south of Madrid, 35 km (22 mi) northwest of Toledo.

Founded where the Tagus and Jarama rivers meet, Aranjuez was for centuries the spring quarters of the Hapsburg and Bourbon kings. Felipe

V, the first of the Bourbon line, decided to transform the impressive Royal Palace, first built by Hapsburg's Felipe II in 1561, to meet the French aesthetic requirements of his time and gave a boost to the construction of the impressive gardens and parks that surround the palace. Prohibiting people from settling near his lands (a prohibition perpetuated by other monarchs), Felipe II helped make Aranjuez a privileged green royal oasis praised by travelers visiting the court.

The Aranjuez of today is a medium-size town that still retains the splendor of its palace, gardens, and *sotos*—magnificent avenues in the northern part of the city with groves of trees—elms, ash, poplars, linden, and oaks. Try to visit Aranjuez in the spring or fall, when nature is showing off its brightest colors. To see the quiet town liven up, visit in May or June, when the first of two local festivals celebrates ancient music with an array of concerts in the royal gardens. All concerts are performed from their respective periods with the original instruments used to create each style of music. In spring and summer you can find street vendors selling strawberries with whipped cream by the riverbank near the palace—you can also get them at the city's food market, a restored building across from city hall.

GETTING HERE AND AROUND

By commuter train (*tren de cercanías*), the ride from Madrid to Aranjuez is 50 minutes. Trains leave often from Madrid's Atocha Station. Another option is the **Tren de la Fresa** *(Strawberry Train)*. From April to mid-June, it departs on Saturday and Sunday from Atocha at 10:05 AM. After a 90-minute trip, you reach Aranjuez, where you get a guided tour of the city. On the way, train staff serve you strawberries, one of the region's best-known products. Round-trip fare is €25 for adults.

ESSENTIALS

Visitor Information Aranjuez (✉ *Pl. San Antonio 9* ☎ *91/891–0427*).

EXPLORING

A 10-minute walk along the narrow avenue of Palacio Real will lead you onto the southeastern corner of the **Royal Palace.** The palace dates back to the year 1561, when Felipe II entrusted its design and construction to architect Juan Bautista de Toledo. The work was continued by Bautista's disciple, Juan de Herrera, but it was the Bourbon kings and architects (especially Giacomo Bonavia, who also built the facade) who decided to part with the austerity of the former dynasty, enlarging the palace to adapt it to the ostentatious baroque period and to the increasing number of members of the court. The interior reflects the taste of the last monarch who inhabited it (Elizabeth II, in the mid-1800s). East and north of the palace extend two gardens: the Parterre, designed during the Bourbon period, and the Island, originally designed by Herrera and mixing Spanish, Flemish, and Italian elements. A tourist train departs from the palace, making an hour tour of the city. ✉ *Av. del Palacio s/n* ☎ *918/910740* *Guided tour €5, special tour with access to royal family's rooms €7* ⏲ *Oct.–Mar., Tues.–Sun. 10–5:15; Apr.–Sept., Tues.–Sun. 10–6:15.*

The city's most impressive garden is the **Jardín del Príncipe** (✉ *Calle de La Reina s/n* *Free* ⏲ *Oct.–Apr., 8 AM–6:30 PM, Mar.–Sept., 8*

AM–*8:30* PM), which spreads between the Tagus course and Calle de la Reina. Designed at the end of the 18th century, it's divided into a dozen distinctive sections. In the northwestern corner of the garden is the old royal jetty and the **Museo de Falúas** (Felucca Museum ✉ *Calle de La Reina s/n* ☎ *918/912453* 🎫 *€2 visit, €3 guided tour* ⊙ *Oct.–Mar., daily 10–5:15, Apr.–Sept., Tues.–Sun. 10–6:15*), home to seven impressive gondolas used by Spanish royalty for festive outings on the Tagus and other Spanish rivers. In the eighth garden to the east of Jardín del Príncipe is **La Casita del Labrador** (*Royal Laborer's House* ☎ *918/910305*) displaying a unique neo-classic style, built by Carlos IV as a rustic escape from palace activity. During its construction, however, the king got carried away, creating an ostentatious small palace with all the sumptuous decorative arts of the period on display. The house can be visited only via a guided tour (🎫 *€5*), conducted in Spanish, and must be reserved in advance (maximum 10 people). When you've finished your tour, the best way to get back to town is to walk the path parallel to the Calle de la Reina, inside the park.

NEED A BREAK?

The city's most renowned restaurant is Casa Pablo (✉ *Calle Almíbar 42* ☎ *918/911451*), decorated with an array of carefully placed bullfighting paraphernalia, over a predominantly wooden space, with an elegant combination of white and red tablescapes. The menu offers a delicious fish soup, barnacles, and duck pâté, among other varied choices. It's a fun spot to get a bite to eat and catch a glimpse of a bullfighter, or maybe even members of the Royal Family.

CONSUEGRA

78 km (48 mi) south of Aranjuez (Km 119 on A4).

This small, historic town is dominated by a spectacular hilltop castle and 11 white windmills.

ESSENTIALS

Visitor Information Consuegra (✉ *Calle Molino de Viento/Bolero Windmill* ☎ *925/475731*).

EXPLORING

★ You can drive straight up to the first windmill, **El Bolero** (restored to house the local tourist office), and walk upstairs to see the intricate 16th-century machinery. In October, the fields all around Consuegra are purple with **saffron crocuses.** These flowers appear overnight, and the three threads of the female stigmas and styles must be handpicked from each one immediately. The threads are then dried over braziers in private homes to become the "red gold" worth €1,800 per kilogram. The process, which requires 4,000 crocuses to make 2 grams of saffron, has been used for 700 years. Consuegra's **Fiesta de la Rosa del Azafrán** (Saffron Festival), complete with competitions and saffron-based foods, is held here the last week of October.

Moors and Christians once did battle for the 10th-century **Castillo de Consuegra,** and during the second week in August the town reenacts their medieval conflict twice a day. In the 12th century the castle housed the Knights of St. John of Jerusalem, and you can imagine that most notorious knight of all, Don Quixote, tilting at the windmills. The ramparts have romantic views of the La Mancha plains and saffron fields. ✉ *Calle del Acueducto s/n* ☎ *925/475731 tourist office and castle* 🌐 *www.consuegra.es* 🎫 *€2* ⏲ *Mid-Sept.–mid-May, weekdays 9–2 and 3:30–6, weekends 10:30–2 and 3:30–6; mid-May–mid-Sept., weekdays 9–2 and 4:30–7, Sat. 10–2 and 3:30–6, Sun. 10:30–2 and 3:30–6.*

ALMAGRO

65 km (40 mi) south of Consuegra.

The center of this noble town contains the only preserved medieval theater in Europe, which stands beside the ancient Plaza Mayor, where 85 Roman columns form two facing colonnades supporting green-frame 16th-century buildings. Near the plaza are granite mansions embellished with the heraldic shields of their former owners and a splendid parador in a restored 17th-century convent.

ESSENTIALS

Visitor Information Almagro (✉ *Plaza Mayor 1* ☎ *926/860717* 🌐 *www.ciudad-almagro.com*).

EXPLORING

★ The **Corral de Comedias** theater stands almost as it did in the 16th century, when it was built, with wooden balconies on four sides and the stage at one end of the open patio. During the golden age of Spanish theater—the time of playwrights Calderón de la Barca, Cervantes, and Lope de Vega—touring actors came to Almagro, which prospered from mercury mines and lace making. The Corral is the site of an international theater festival each July. Festival tickets may be purchased with a credit card through Tele-Entrada (☎ *926/882458*) or with cash (after mid-May only) at Palacio de los Medrano on San Agustín 7. ✉ *Pl. Mayor 18* ☎ *926/861539* 🎫 *Audio Tour €2.50 individuals, €2 for group members; Dramatized Tour: €3 individuals, €3 for group members* ⏲ *Daily Apr.–June and Aug.–Sept. 10–2 and 5–8, July 10–2 and 6–9, Oct.–Mar. 10–2 and 4–7.*

The **Museo Nacional del Teatro** displays models of the Roman amphitheaters in Mérida (Extremadura) and Sagunto (near Valencia), both still in use, as well as costumes, pictures, and documents relating to the history of Spanish theater. ✉ *Calle Gran Maestre 2* ☎ *926/261014* 🌐 *museoteatro.mcu.es* 🎫 *€3 individuals, €1.50 groups* ⏲ *Tues.–Fri. 10–2 and 4–7 (6–9 July), Sat. 11–2 and 4–6 (6–8 July), Sun. 11–2.*

WHERE TO EAT AND STAY

$–$$ SPANISH ✕ **El Corregidor.** Several old houses stuffed with antiques make up this fine restaurant and tapas bar. You can enjoy your meal alfresco in the garden or terrace, or take refuge in the air-conditioned dining room. The menu centers on rich local fare, including game, fish, and spicy Almagro eggplant, a local delicacy. The €50 *menú de degustación* (house menu) yields seven savory tapas (courses), and the €30 *menu Manchego gastronómico,* a three-course meal of more traditional, regional specialties, including *pisto manchego,* a La Mancha–style vegetable ratatouille, and *ravioli de cordero* (lamb-stuffed ravioli). ✉*Jerónimo Ceballos 2* ☎*926/860648* 🌐*www.elcorregidor.com* 💳*AE, DC, MC, V* ⏲*Closed Mon. Aug.–June.*

$$–$$$ ★ **Parador de Almagro.** Only five minutes from the Plaza Mayor of Almagro, this parador is a finely restored 17th-century Franciscan convent with cells, cloisters, and patios. Indeed, some rooms still resemble monks' cells, albeit with lots of modern conveniences, and the patios inspire a meditative tranquility. **Pros:** pretty indoor courtyards, has its own parking. **Cons:** old bathroom fixtures throughout. ✉*Ronda San Francisco 31* ☎*926/860100* 🌐*www.parador.es* *54 rooms* *In-hotel: restaurant, bar, pool, laundry service* 💳*AE, DC, MC, V.*

CUENCA

★ *167 km (104 mi) southeast of Madrid and 150 km (93 mi) northwest of Valencia.*

Though somewhat isolated, Cuenca makes a good overnight stop if you're traveling between Madrid and Valencia. The delightful old town is one of the strangest in Spain: it's built on a sloping, curling finger of rock whose precipitous sides plunge down to the gorges of the Huécar and Júcar rivers. Because the town ran out of room to expand, some medieval houses hang right over the abyss and are now a unique architectural attraction: the Casas Colgadas (Hanging Houses). The old town's dramatic setting grants spectacular gorge views, and its cobblestone streets, cathedral, churches, bars, and taverns contrast starkly with the modern town, which sprawls beyond the river gorges.

GETTING HERE AND AROUND

From Madrid, buses leave for Cuenca about every two hours from Conde de Casal. From Valencia, four buses leave every four to six hours, starting at 8:30 AM. Trains stop in Cuenca from either Madrid or Valencia twice a day, but this is not recommended as the train is bumpy, makes many stops, and is much slower than the bus.

ESSENTIALS

Visitor Information Cuenca (✉*C. Alfonso VIII 2* ☎*969/241050*).

EXPLORING

Cuenca has 14 churches and two cathedrals—unfortunately, visitors are allowed inside only about half of them. The best views of the city are from the square in front of a small palace at the very top of Cuenca, where the town tapers out to the narrowest of ledges. Here, gorges are on either side of you, and old houses sweep down toward a distant plateau in front. The lower half of the old town is a maze of tiny streets, any of which will take you up to the Plaza del Carmen. From here the town narrows and a single street, Calle Alfonso VIII, continues the ascent to the Plaza Mayor, which you reach after passing under the arch of the town hall. Calle San Pedro shoots off from the northern side of Plaza Mayor; just off Calle San Pedro, clinging to the western edge of Cuenca, is the tiny **Plaza San Nicolás,** a pleasingly dilapidated square.

Nearby, the unpaved Ronda del Júcar hovers over the Júcar gorge and commands remarkable views of the mountainous landscape.

Santa María de Gracia Cathedral looms large and casts an enormous shadow in the evening throughout the adjacent Plaza Mayor. Built during the Gothic era in the 12th century, the cathedral's massive tryptic facade has lost all its Gothic origins thanks to the Renaissance. Inside are the tombs of the cathedral's founding bishops, an impressive portico of the Apostles, and a Byzantine reliquary. ✉ *Pl. Mayor s/n* ☎ *969/224626* 🎫 *€2.80* 🕓 *Daily 10:30–1:30 and 4–6 (4–7 Aug.–Sept.).*

The **Museo Diocesano de Arte Sacro** *(Diocesan Museum of Sacred Art)* is in what were once the cellars of the Bishop's Palace. The beautifully clear display includes a jewel-encrusted, Byzantine diptych of the 13th century; a Crucifixion by the 15th-century Flemish artist Gerard David; and two small El Grecos. From the Plaza Mayor, take Calle Obispo Valero and follow signs toward the Casas Colgadas. ✉ *Calle Obispo Valero 3* ☎ *969/224210* 🎫 *€2* 🕓 *Oct.–May, Tues.–Sat. 11–2 and 4–6, Sun. 11–2; June–Sept., Tues.–Sat. 11–2 and 5–8, Sun. 11–2.*

Fodor's Choice ★ As if Cuenca's famous **Casas Colgadas** *(Hanging Houses)* suspended impossibly over the cliffs below were not already eye-popping and miraculous enough, they also house one of Spain's finest and most curious museums, the **Museo de Arte Abstracto Español** (Museum of Spanish Abstract Art)—not to be confused with the Museo Municipal de Arte Moderno, which is next to the Casas Colgadas. Projecting over the town's eastern precipice, these houses originally formed a 15th-century palace, which later served as a town hall before falling into disrepair in the 19th century. In 1927 the cantilevered balconies that had once hung over the gorge were rebuilt, and finally, in 1966, the painter Fernando Zóbel decided to create (inside the houses) the world's first museum devoted exclusively to abstract art. The works he gathered are almost all by the remarkable generation of Spanish artists who grew up in the 1950s and were essentially forced to live abroad during the Franco regime: the major names include Carlos Saura, Eduardo Chillida, Lucio Muñoz, Manuel Millares, Antoni Tàpies, and Zóbel himself. ✉ *Calle Obispo Valero* ☎ *969/212983* 🌐 *www.march.es/arte/cuenca/index.asp* 🎫 *€3* 🕓 *Tues.–Fri. 11–2 and 4–6, Sat. 11–2 and 4–8, Sun. 11–2:30.*

★ The **Puente de San Pablo,** an iron footbridge over the Huécar gorge, was built in 1903 for the convenience of the Dominican monks of San Pablo, who live on the other side. If you don't have a fear of heights, cross the narrow bridge to take in the vertiginous view of the river below and the equally thrilling panorama of the Casas Colgadas; it's by far the best view of the city. A path from the bridge descends to the bottom of the gorge, landing you by the bridge that you crossed to enter the old town.

WHERE TO EAT AND STAY

Much of Cuenca's cuisine is based around wild game: partridge, lamb, rabbit, and hen. Given the river's adjacency, trout is the fish of choice and is seen in many main courses and soups. Found in almost every town restaurant is Cuenca's pâté, *morterualo,* a mixture of wild boar, rabbit, partridge, hen, liver, pork loin, and spices, as well as *galianos,*

Step into 14th-century Spain at Majorca's Bellver Castle.

(top left) Wine makers roll barrels of sherry in Cádiz, (top right) an Asturian house is tucked away in the region's verdant countryside, and (bottom) whimsical, scaly creatures adorn Gaudí's Casa Batllló.

(top) Valencia's City of Arts & Sciences complex abuts the Turia River. (bottom) Alcazaba is the original fortress of Granada's Moorish marvel, Alhambra.

(top left) Viura grapes are harvested for white wine in the Rueda region, (top right) candles reflect pilgrims' devotion at Montserrat's monastery, (bottom) and a Moroccan Barbary Ape sits atop a cannon in Gilbraltar.

An architectural triumph of titanium, the Guggenheim Museum is Bilbao's top attraction.

(top left) Galicia's Celtic roots pop up near Torre de Hercules in its modern port city of A Coruña, (top right) Tapas entice in Jerez de la Frontera. (bottom) In Olite, the parador originated as a French-style castle.

(top) Guernica at the Queen Sofía Art Center is one of Picasso's works not to be missed in Madrid. (bottom) Men dressed with cow bells try to scare off evil spirits during La Endiablada in Cuenca.

(top) Horses carry festive pilgrims in El Rocío to the Virgin of the Dew site. (bottom) Yachts in Marina Bay transport vacationers around the Rock.

a thick stew served on wheat cake. For dessert, there are almond-based confections called *alajú,* which are enriched with honey, nuts, and lemon, and delicious *torrijas,* made of bread dipped in milk, fried, and decorated with confectioner's sugar.

$$–$$$ SPANISH Fodor's Choice ★ **El Figón de Huécar.** Replacing Pedro Torres Pacheco's famous Figón de Pedro, this restaurant is currently run by his daughter Mercedes Torres Ortega, who is continuing the legacy of one of Spain's most celebrated restaurateurs. Having done much to promote the excellence of Cuenca's cuisine, the original Figón was famous for having hosted Cuenca's celebrated *Semana de la Tapa* (Tapa Week) year after year. Try some of their specialty dishes: "*pichón*" (dove) stuffed with a basket of quail eggs; old wine veal with potatoes "*al montón*"; Huecar cold vegetable mousse; or fish "melodies" with potato comfit and vegetables. ✉ *Julián Romero 6* ☎ *969/240062* 🌐 *www.figondelhuecar.com* 💳 *AE, DC, MC, V* ⏲ *Closed Mon. No dinner Sun.*

$–$$ SPANISH **La Ponderosa.** Famous all over Spain for Cuenca's finest tapas and *raciones*, this popular place on the town's liveliest tippling and tapeo street is always filled and buzzing. *Chuletillas de lechal* (suckling lamb chops), *huevos fritos con pócima secreta* (fried eggs with a secret potion), *setas* (wild mushrooms), *mollejas* (sweetbreads), and a carefully selected list of wines all add up to a superior tapas experience. The one drawback here is that the only place to sit down is on the terrace. ✉ *Calle de San Francisco 20* ☎ *969/213214* 💳 *DC, MC, V* ⏲ *Closed Sun. in June and July.*

$–$$$ SPANISH **Las Brasas.** Meats and vegetables cooked over wood coals and hearty bean concoctions are the top draw here. You can spy on the kitchen from the bar of this cozy, oak-floored enclave near the San Felipe Neri church. The owners also use vegetables from their garden to make a delicious *puchero ete* (white-bean soup). Rustic decor, with wood beams, stone floors, and exposed brick walls, adds to charm of this classic Castilian tavern well known for its warmth and good value. ✉ *Alfonso VIII 105* ☎ *969/213821* 💳 *DC, MC, V* ⏲ *Closed Wed. and July.*

$–$$$$ SPANISH **Mesón Casas Colgadas.** Run by the former owners of the famous El Figón de Pedro (currently closed), this place offers much the same local produce, fish, and a variety of game during hunting season, albeit with a more upscale vibe. The sleek and modern white dining room is next to the Museum of Abstract Art in one of the iconic, gravity-defying Casas Colgadas. There are fantastic views of the hanging houses and the plunging gorge below—not for the acrophobic! ✉ *Canónigos s/n* ☎ *969/223509* ✍ *Reservations essential* 💳 *AE, DC, MC, V* ⏲ *No dinner Mon.*

¢ **Hostal Cánovas.** Near Plaza España, in the heart of the new town, this is one of Cuenca's best bargains. The lobby's not impressive, but the inviting rooms more than compensate with hardwood floors, gold-trim burgundy fabrics, and decorative white moldings. Brothers Edilio and Paulino, the owners, spent more than two years restoring the run-down 1878 building when they opened the hostal in 1998. **Pros:** low prices even during the high season. **Cons:** can be noisy, old bulky furniture makes rooms feel cramped. ✉ *Calle Fray Luis de León 38* ☎ *969/213973* 🌐 *www.hostalcanovas.com* 🛏 *17 rooms* 💳 *AE, MC, V.*

$$–$$$ **Parador de Cuenca.** In the gorge next to the Huécar river beneath the Casas Colgadas, this parador is the exquisitely restored 16th-century convent of San Pablo. The coffered ceilings and ceramic tile murals are justly famous, while the glassed-in cloister and the classic Castilian furniture complete the noble decor. Rooms are furnished in a lighter and more luxurious style than is usually the norm for Castilian houses of this vintage. **Pros:** great views of the hanging houses and gorge. **Cons:** restaurant is hit or miss, expensive (€17) breakfasts. ✉ *Subida a San Pablo s/n* ☎ *969/232320* 🌐 *www.parador.es* *63 rooms* *In-hotel: restaurant, bar, tennis court, pool, no-smoking rooms* 💳 *AE, DC, MC, V.*

¢–$$$ ★ **Posada San José.** In a 17th- to 18th-century convent, formerly the San José choir school, this posada (inn) clings to the top of the Huécar gorge in Cuenca's old town. Intimate and personal touches, like a leafy garden and cozy nooks and crannies distributed around the public spaces, give the inn its charm. Most rooms have balconies or terraces over the river. Furnishings are traditional, but the mood is informal and friendly. Of the 31 rooms, 22 have their own bathrooms. **Pros:** cozy rooms, views of gorge. **Cons:** difficult to reach by car, not recommendable for anyone with vertigo. ✉ *Calle Julián Romero 4* ☎ *969/211300* 🌐 *www.posadasanjose.com* *31 rooms* *In-room: no a/c, no TV (some). In-hotel: restaurant, bar* 💳 *AE, DC, MC, V.*

OFF THE BEATEN PATH

Ciudad Encantada *(Enchanted City)*. Not really a city at all, the Ciudad Encantada (35 km [22 mi] north of Cuenca) is a series of large and fantastic mushroomlike rock formations erupting in a landscape of pines. This commanding spectacle, deemed a "site of national interest," was formed over thousands of years by the forces of water and wind on limestone rocks. Of the ones with names, the most notable are *Cara* (Face), *Puente* (Bridge), *Amantes* (Lovers), and *Olas en el Mar* (Waves in the Sea). You can stroll through this enchanted city in under two hours.

ALARCÓN

69 km (43 mi) south of Cuenca.

This fortified village on the edge of the great plains of La Mancha stands on a high spur of land encircled almost entirely by a bend of the Júcar River.

ESSENTIALS

Visitor Information Alarcón (✉ *Posada 6* ☎ *969/330301*).

EXPLORING

Alarcón's **castle** (✉ *Av. Amigos de los Castillos 316214*) dates from the 8th century, and in the 14th century it came into the hands of the *infante* (child prince) Don Juan Manuel, who wrote a collection of classic moral tales. Today the castle is one of Spain's finest paradors. If you're not driving, a bus to Motilla will leave you a short taxi ride away (call ☎ *969/331797* for a cab).

WHERE TO EAT AND STAY

$$$$ **Parador de Alarcón.** This 8th- to 12th-century gorge-top castle is in a fairytale setting: a fortress of Moorish origin decorated in a military motif. The turret room is the best and biggest; the rooms in the corner towers have arrow-slit windows, and others have window niches where women did needlework. Dinner ($$$–$$$$) is served in an arched baronial hall complete with shields, armor, and a gigantic fireplace. **Pros:** worth the price, ambience to spare, good for a romantic getaway from Madrid. **Cons:** after 11 PM, room service prices jump 25%. ✉ *Av. Amigos de los Castillos 3* ☎ *969/330315* 🌐 *www.parador.es* *14 rooms* *In-hotel: restaurant, bar, laundry service* 💳 *AE, DC, MC, V.*

3

OFF THE BEATEN PATH

Guadalajara, about 40 km (25 mi) northeast of Madrid, was severely damaged in the civil war, but its **Palacio del Infantado** *(Palace of the Prince's Territory)* still stands and is one of the most important Spanish palaces of its period. Built between 1461 and 1492 by Juan Guas, the palace is a bizarre and potent mixture of Gothic, classical, and Mudejar influences. The main facade is rich; the lower floors are studded with diamond shapes; and the whole is crowned by a complex Gothic gallery supported on a frieze pitted with intricate Moorish cellular work (the honeycomb motif). Inside is a fanciful and exciting courtyard. The ground floor holds the Museo de Bellas Artes, a modest provincial art gallery. ✉ *Pl. de los Caídos 13* ☎ *949/213301* *Free* ⏲ *Museum, Sala Azul y del Duque Tues.–Sat. 10–2 and Sun. 10–2; Patio de los Leones y Jardines, weekdays 9–9:30, Sat. 9–2:30 and 4–7:30, Sun. 10–2:30 and 5–7:30.*

PASTRANA

46 km (28 mi) south of Guadalajara via N320 and the CM 2006 fork, 101 km (61 mi) southeast of Madrid.

This pretty village was once the capital of a small duchy.

ESSENTIALS

Visitor Information **Pastrana** (✉ *Plaza de la Hora 1* ☎ *949/370672*).

EXPLORING

The town's top attractions, **Museo de Recuerdos de Santa Teresa de Ávila y de San Juan de la Cruz** *(Museum of Santa Teresa de Ávila and San Juan de la Cruz)* and **Museo de Ciencias Naturales** *(Museum of Natural Sciences)* share the same Convento del Carmen's 16th- to 17th-century building. A unique combination of mysticism, science, and art set in a stunning structure, the museums' treasures include medieval wood carvings, paintings by masters Luca Giordano and Sebastiano Ricci, memorabilia from the lives and works of Santa Teresa and St. John of the Cross, and a display of shells, woods, and birds from the Philippines brought back by missionary monks. ✉ *C. Extramuros s/n* ☎ *949/370057* *€2.40* ⏲ *Sept.–June, Tues.–Sun. 11–1:30 and 3–6:30; July–Aug., Tues.–Sun. 4–6.*

CASTILE–LEÓN

SIGÜENZA

86 km (53 mi) northeast of Guadalajara.

Sigüenza has splendid architecture and one of the most beautifully preserved cathedrals in Castile.

ESSENTIALS

Visitor Information Sigüenza (✉ *Serrano Sanz 9* ☎ *949/347007*).

EXPLORING

An enchanting **castle**, overlooking wild, hilly countryside from above Sigüenza, is now a parador. Founded by the Romans but rebuilt at various later periods, most of the structure went up in the 14th century, when it became a residence for the queen of Castile, Doña Blanca de Borbón, who was banished here by her husband, Peter the Cruel.

Begun around 1150 and not completed until the early 16th century, Sigüenza's remarkable **cathedral** combines aspects of Spanish architecture from the Romanesque period to the Renaissance. The sturdy western front is forbidding but hides a wealth of ornamental and artistic masterpieces. Go directly to the sacristan (the sacristy is at the north end of the ambulatory) for a guided tour, which is obligatory when visiting the cathedral. The late-Gothic cloister leads to a room lined with 17th-century Flemish tapestries. In the north transept is the late-15th-century plateresque sepulchre of Dom Fadrique of Portugal. The Chapel of the Doncel (to the right of the sanctuary) contains the tomb of Don Martín Vázquez de Arca, commissioned by Queen Isabella, to whom Don Martín served as *doncel* (page) before dying young (at 25) at the gates of Granada in 1486. ✉ *Pl. Mayor* 🎫 *€3* ⏲ *Tues.–Sun. 9:30–1:30 and 4:30–7. Guided tours Tues.–Sat. at 11, noon, 4:30, and 5:30, and Sun. at noon and 5:30.*

In a refurbished early-19th-century house next to the cathedral's west facade, the **Museo Diocesano de Arte Sacro** *(Diocesan Museum of Sacred Art)* contains a prehistoric section and much religious art from the 12th to 18th centuries. ✉ *Pl. Mayor* ☎ *949/391023* 🎫 *€3* ⏲ *Tues.–Sun. 11–2 and 4–7.*

WHERE TO EAT AND STAY

$$$ ★ **Parador de Sigüenza.** This mighty 12th-century fortress has hosted royalty for centuries, from Ferdinand and Isabella right up to Spain's present king, Juan Carlos. Some rooms have four-poster beds and balconies overlooking the wild landscape. The excellent dining room ($$$–$$$$) makes for a leisurely lunch, an essential part of the experience here; your choices might include roast goat, pheasant, or cod with truffles and cheese. **Pros:** excellent breakfast buffet. **Cons:** much of this fantastical medieval castle, though still beautiful, is a neo-medieval replica. ✉ *Pl. del Castillo s/n* ☎ *949/390100* 🌐 *www.parador.es* *81 rooms* *In-hotel: restaurant, parking (fee)* 💳 *AE, DC, MC, V.*

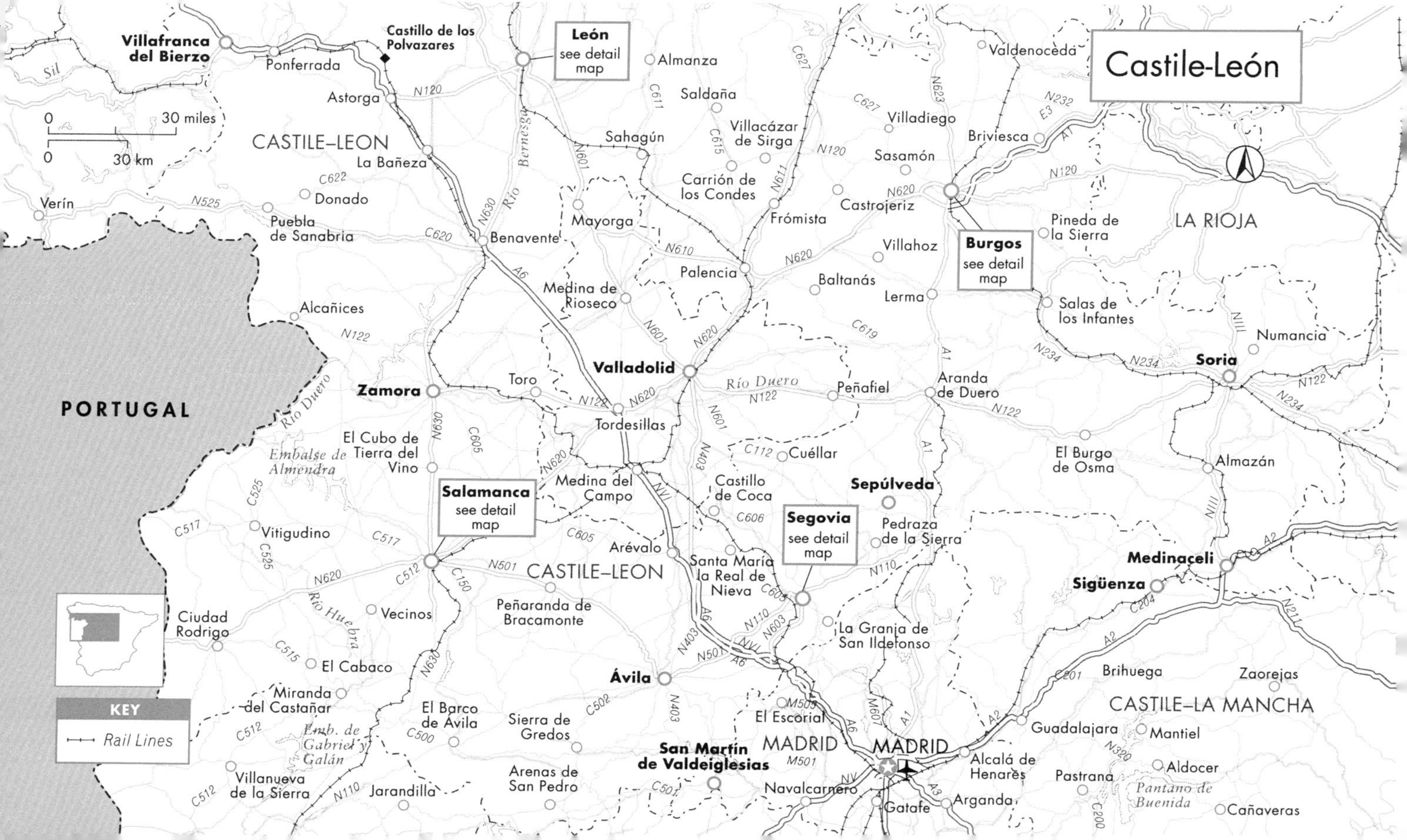

Castile-León
Villafranca del Bierzo
Ponferrada
Castillo de los Polvazares
León see detail map
Almanza
Saldaña
Villacázar de Sirga
Villadiego
Valdenoceda
Brivíesca
Astorga
La Bañeza
CASTILE-LEON
0 30 miles
0 30 km
Sahagún
Carrión de los Condes
Sasamón
Castrojeriz
Frómista
Verín
Donado
Puebla de Sanabria
Benavente
Mayorga
Palencia
Villahoz
Burgos see detail map
Pineda de la Sierra
LA RIOJA
Baltanás
Lerma
Salas de los Infantes
Medina de Rioseco
Alcañices
Numancia
Soria
Valladolid
Zamora
Toro
Peñafiel
Aranda de Duero
PORTUGAL
Río Duero
Tordesillas
El Cubo de Tierra del Vino
Embalse de Almendra
Cuéllar
El Burgo de Osma
Almazán
Medina del Campo
Castillo de Coca
Sepúlveda
Salamanca see detail map
Segovia see detail map
Pedraza de la Sierra
Vitigudino
Arévalo
Santa María la Real de Nieva
Medinaceli
Sigüenza
CASTILE-LEON
Ciudad Rodrigo
Peñaranda de Bracamonte
Vecinos
Río Huebra
La Granja de San Ildefonso
El Cabaco
Ávila
Brihuega
Zaorejas
Miranda del Castañar
El Barco de Ávila
Sierra de Gredos
El Escorial
CASTILE-LA MANCHA
Emb. de Gabriel y Galán
San Martín de Valdeiglesias
MADRID
MADRID
Guadalajara
Mantiel
Villanueva de la Sierra
Arenas de San Pedro
Alcalá de Henares
Aldocer
Jarandilla
Navalcarnero
Pastrana
Pantano de Buenida
Gatafe
Arganda
Cañaveras
KEY
Rail Lines
Sil
Bernesga
Río
N120
N525
C622
N630
C620
N601
C611
C615
N611
C627
N623
E3
N232
A1
N610
N620
A6
N122
N601
C619
N234
NIII
N122
N234
N630
C605
N403
C112
N620
C525
C517
C606
NVI
C605
N501
C512
C150
N110
C603
A2
N211
C204
N603
N110
A6
N403
N501
C515
N630
C502
C512
C500
M505
M607
A1
N110
C512
M501
C501
NV
A3
C201
N320
C200

MEDINACELI

32 km (20 mi) northeast of Sigüenza.

The preserved village of Medinaceli—literally "city in the sky"—commands exhilarating views from the top of a long, steep ridge. Dominating the skyline is a Roman triumphal arch from the 2nd or 3rd century AD, the only surviving triple archway of this period in Spain (the arch's silhouette is featured on road signs to national monuments throughout the country). The surrounding village, once the seat of one of Spain's most powerful dukes, was virtually abandoned by the end of the 19th century, and if you come here during the week, you can find yourself in a near ghost town. Madrileños have weekend houses here, as do some Americans. The town is archaic and beautiful, with houses overgrown by shrubs and trees, and unpaved lanes into wild countryside.

ESSENTIALS

Tourist Information Medinaceli (✉ *Calle Campo de San Nicolás* ☎ *975/343911*).

EN ROUTE

If you're driving to Soria, this stop is approximately 56 km (35 mi) west of Soria along the way. **El Burgo de Osma** is an enticing medieval and Renaissance town dominated by a Gothic cathedral and a baroque bell tower. There are also many historic buildings that have been elegantly restored.

WHERE TO EAT AND STAY

$$–$$$ SPANISH ★ **Virrey Palafox.** The white walls, wood-beam ceiling, and furnishings in this family-run establishment are traditional Castilian design, setting the tone for the food to come. This restaurant, which has long attracted demanding diners from miles around, specializes in fresh and seasonal produce. Vegetables are homegrown, and excellent local game, from wild boar stew to venison fillet, is served year-round. The house specialty is fish, in particular *merluza Virrey* (hake stuffed with eels and salmon). Saturdays and Sundays, from the last weekend in January through March, a pig is slaughtered and a feast ensues (reservations required). ✉ *Calle Universidad 7* ☎ *975/340222* ▭ *AE, DC, MC, V* ⊙ *Closed Mon. No dinner Sun.*

$$ **Il Virrey.** Under the same management as the popular Virrey Palafox restaurant, this pleasant hotel in the town's iconic Plaza Mayor is just 150 meters from the Gothic cathedral and occupies part of what was once the 16th-century Convent of San Agustín. Constructed with traditional materials, its rooms overlook the plaza and have polished marble floors, stone walls, bronze 19th-century beds, walnut antique furniture, and an elegant flourish. **Pros:** large rooms with state-of-the-art bathrooms and equipment, quiet surroundings. **Cons:** antique furniture sometimes in need of repair, slim pickings at the somewhat expensive (€12) breakfast. ✉ *C. Mayor 2* ☎ *975/341311* 🌐 *www.virreypalafox.com* *52 rooms* *In-room: safe. In-hotel: restaurant, concierge, laundry service, parking (fee)* ▭ *AE, DC, MC, V.*

SORIA

74 km (46 mi) north of Medinaceli via NIII.

Prosperous as a sheep farming center during the 15th-century European wool monopoly that laid the groundwork for Spain's golden age, this provincial capital has been marred to some degree by modern development. Still, the Duero River valley is splendid, as are the Romanesque monuments throughout the town and its hilly environs.

Soria is a comfortable base for exploring the surrounding countryside, which offers bountiful options for hiking and cycling through pine forests and along Roman roadways, plus rugged climbs with soaring vistas. Inquire at the Office of Tourism on Caballeros 17 for maps.

GETTING HERE AND AROUND

Urbano de Soria (🌐*www.urbanodesoria.com*) runs buses throughout the city. A special line connects the center of town with the Museo Numantino on Paseo del Espolón. Line No. 4 connects the center of town with the Catedral de San Pedro. There are no buses between the Parador de Soria and the center of town.

ESSENTIALS

Visitor Information Soria (✉*Calle Medinaceli 2* ☎*975212052*).

EXPLORING

Nearly all roads to Soria converge onto the wide, modern promenade El Espolón, the location of the **Museo Numantino** *(Museum of Numancia)*. Founded in 1919, the museum contains archaeological finds rich in both prehistoric and Iberian items. One section on the top floor is dedicated to the important Iberian settlement at nearby Numancia that became famous in Spanish legend for its heroic resistance to invading Roman forces in 133 BC. As historical evidence has confirmed, Numancia resisted a lengthy siege, and its few survivors chose to take their own lives rather than fall into Roman hands. Even today, an ultradefensive soccer or political strategy is invariably described as *una defensa numantina* (a Numancian defense). ✉*Paseo del Espolón 8* ☎*975/221397* 🎫*€1.20, free weekends* ⏲*July–Sept., Tues.–Sat. 10–2 and 5–8, Sun. 10–2; Oct.–June, Tues.–Sat. 10–2 and 4–7, Sun. 10–2.*

The late-12th-century church of **Santo Domingo** (✉*C. Aduana Vieja*) has a richly carved, Romanesque west facade. The imposing 16th-century **Palacio de los Condes de Gomara** (*Palace of the Counts of Gomara* ✉*C. Estudios*) is now a courthouse.

Dominating the hill just south of the Duero River is Soria's **Parador Antonio Machado** (✉*Parque del Castillo s/n* ☎*975/240800*), which shares the Parque Municipal de El Castillo with the ruins of the town's castle. Calle de Santiago, leading to the parador, passes the church and cemetery of El Espino, where Machado's wife, Leonor, is buried.

Across the Duero River from Soria is the Monastery of **San Juan de Duero** (also known as Los Arcos), once the property of the Knights Hospitalers, a monastic military order of the Crusades. Outside the church are the curious ruins of a Romanesque cloister, displaying a stunning example of interlaced arching with Moorish echoes. The church itself, now maintained by the Museo Numantino, is a small museum of Romanesque art and architecture. ✉*Piso de las Ánimas s/n* ☎*975/230218 (run by the Museo Numantino)* *€0.60, free on weekends* ⏲*Oct.–June, Tues.–Sat. 10–2 and 4–7, Sun. 10–2; July–Sept., Tues.–Sat. 10–2 and 5–8, Sun. 10–2.*

The poet Machado wrote fondly of strolling along the Duero River from the Monastery of San Polo to the **Ermita de San Saturio,** a unique 18th-century chapel built into the steep rocky hillside. You'll follow a poplar-lined path from a parking and picnic area for about 1 km (½ mi) to a little chapel perched above the cave where the Anchorite St. Saturio fasted and prayed. You can climb up to San Saturio through the cave. ✉*Paseo San Saturio s/n* ☎*975/180703* *Free* ⏲*Tues.–Sat. 10:30–2 and 4:30–6:30 (4:30–7:30 Jan.–Mar. and Nov.–Dec., 4:30–8:30 July–Aug.), Sun. 10:30–2.*

WHERE TO EAT AND STAY

$$$$ SPANISH ✕**Mesón Castellano.** The most traditional restaurant in town, this cozy, rustic Castilian establishment uses a large open fire for roasting succulent *chuletón de ternera* (veal chops), *chuletillas de cordero* (lamb chops), and a varied list of vegetables. Another house specialty is *migas pastoriles* (soaked bread crumbs fried with peppers and bacon). For all the meat-roasting enthusiasm here, fish and seafood are also well represented, with everything from roast *besugo* (sea bream) to *bacalao* (cod) and rodaballo (turbot), usually fresh from Spain's northern coast. ✉*Pl. Mayor 2* ☎*975/213045* *AE, DC, MC, V.*

$$–$$$$ SPANISH ✕**Restaurante Iruña.** Offering an innovative menu of tapas and entrées, this traditional Castilian space attracts Soria's gourmets and bon vivants with good food and a lively vibe. This is a fashionable choice for a drink or meal off the lively Plaza San Clemente. Sample classical Castilian cuisine in miniature with creative touches such as *ensalada templada de bacalao* (warm codfish salad), *solomillo de ciervo al vino tinto* (venison fillet cooked in red wine), *revuelto de boletus edulis* (eggs scrambled with wild mushrooms), or *carpaccio de hongos* (thinly sliced laminas of wild mushrooms) accompanied by an admirable wine list with a strong selection of wines from La Ribera del Duero, Soria's home river. ✉*Pl. San Clemente 2* ☎*975/226831* *AE, DC, MC, V.*

$$$ **Parador de Soria.** On a hilltop surrounded by trees and parkland offering panoramic views of the Duero Valley, this modern parador resembles a luxurious alpine ski lodge. It's easy to see why poet Antonio Machado came often to this site for inspiration, especially before the parador was built in the 1960s. A chance to contemplate that same panorama is reason enough to spend a night or two here. Rooms are comfortable and furnished efficiently in subdued tones but lack the romanticism of the surroundings. The restaurant specializes in Castilian fare, from roasts of pig and lamb to *migas de pastor.* **Pros:** spacious rooms, most staff speaks English. **Cons:** modern architecture lacking typical parador romanticism, expensive breakfasts (€17) and restaurant. ✉*Parque del Castillo s/n* ☎*975/240800* 🌐*www.parador.es* *67 rooms* *In-hotel: restaurant, bar, parking, public Internet, laundry service* *AE, DC, MC, V.*

SEGOVIA

Fodor'sChoice ★ *87 km (54 mi) north of Madrid.*

Breathtaking Segovia—on a ridge in the middle of a gorgeously stark, undulating plain—is defined by its Roman and medieval monuments, its excellent cuisine, its embroideries and textiles, and its sense of well-being. An important military town in Roman times, Segovia was later established by the Moors as a major textile center. Captured by the Christians in 1085, it was enriched by a royal residence, and in 1474 the half-sister of Henry IV, Isabella the Catholic (married to Ferdinand of Aragón), was crowned queen of Castile here. By that time Segovia was a bustling city of about 60,000 (there are 53,000 today), but its importance soon diminished as a result of its taking the (losing) side of the Comuneros in the popular revolt against the emperor Carlos V. Though the construction of a royal palace in nearby La Granja in the 18th century revived the town's fortunes somewhat, it never recovered its former vitality. Early in the 20th century, Segovia's sleepy charm came to be appreciated by artists and writers, among them painter Ignacio Zuloaga and poet Antonio Machado. Today the streets swarm with tourists from Madrid—if you can, visit sometime other than in summer.

If you approach Segovia on N603, the first building you see is the cathedral, which seems to rise directly from the fields. Between you and Segovia lies, in fact, a steep and narrow valley, which shields the old town from view. Only when you descend into the valley do you begin to see the old town's spectacular position, rising on top of a narrow rock ledge shaped like a ship. As soon as you reach the modern outskirts, turn left onto the Paseo E. González and follow the road marked **Ruta Panorámica**—you'll soon descend on the narrow and winding Cuesta de los Hoyos, which takes you to the bottom of the wooded valley that dips to the south of the old town. Above, you can see the Romanesque church of San Martín to the right, the cathedral in the middle, and on the far left, where the rock ledge tapers, the turrets, spires, and battlements of Segovia's castle, known as the Alcázar.

Tourists on a day trip from Madrid generally hit the triumvirate of basic sights: the aqueduct, Alcázar, and the cathedral.

ESSENTIALS

Visitor Information Segovia (✉ *Plaza Mayor 9* ☎ *921/466070*).

EXPLORING

❷ Fodor'sChoice ★ **Acueducto Romano.** Segovia's Roman aqueduct ranks with the Pont du Gard in France as one of the greatest surviving examples of Roman engineering, and this is the city's main event, sightseeing-wise. If you take the AVE in from Madrid on a day trip, the inner-city bus drops you right there. Spanning the dip that stretches from the walls of the old town to the lower slopes of the Sierra de Guadarrama, it's about 2,952 feet long and rises in two tiers—above what is now the Plaza del Azoguejo, whose name means "highest point"—to a height of 115 feet. The raised section of stonework in the center originally carried an inscription, of which only the holes for the bronze letters remain. The massive granite blocks are held together by neither mortar nor clamps,

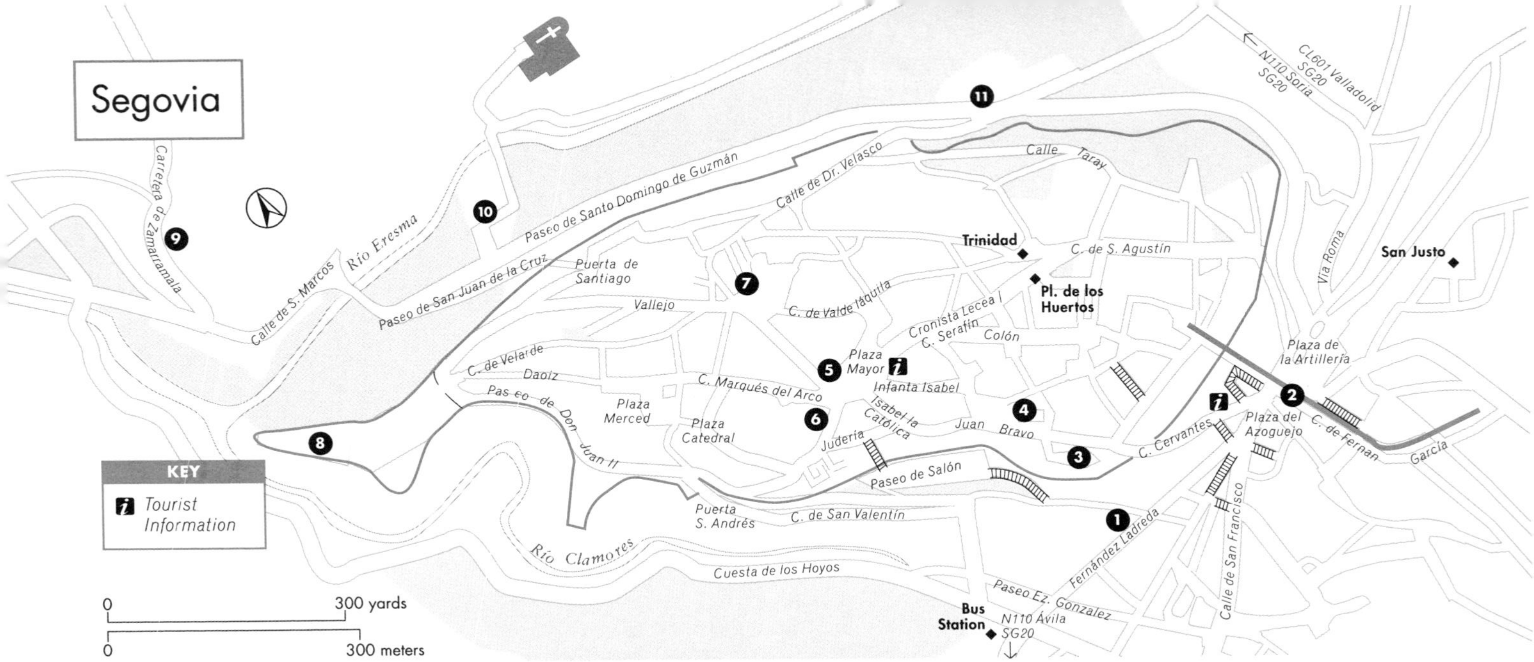

Acueducto Romano 2
Alcázar 8
Ayuntamiento 5
Casa de la Moneda 10
Cathedral 6
Monasterio de la Santa Cruz 11
Palacio de Aspiroz/ Palacio de los Condes de Alpuente 3
San Estéban 7
San Martín 4
San Millán 1
Vera Cruz 9

but the aqueduct has been standing since the end of the 1st century AD. The only damage it has suffered is the demolition of 35 of its arches by the Moors, and these were later replaced on the orders of Ferdinand and Isabella. Steps at the side of the aqueduct lead up to the walls of the old town. Because pollution from the freeway that passes through the aqueduct has weakened the structure, the road underneath has been closed to traffic. ✉ *Pl. del Azoguejo.*

8 **Alcázar.** Possibly dating from Roman times, this castle was considerably expanded in the 14th century, remodeled in the 15th, altered again toward the end of the 16th, and completely redone after being gutted by a fire in 1862, when it was used as an artillery school. The exterior, especially when seen from the Ruta Panorámica, is certainly imposing, and striking murals and stained-glass windows pepper the interior. Crowned by crenellated towers that seem to have been carved out of icing (it's widely believed that the Walt Disney logo is modeled after this castle's silhouette), the rampart can be climbed for superb views; the claustrophobia-inducing winding tower is worth the knee-wobbling climb and small extra fee, though the views of the green hillside from inside are excellent as well. ✉ *Pl. de la Reina Victoria s/n* ☎ *921/460759* 🌐 *www.alcazardesegovia.com* 🎟 *€4 individual entrance fee, €2 to climb the tower, €1 to see the Segovianos, €1 for a guided tour* 🕑 *Apr.–Sept., daily 10–7; Oct.–Mar., Mon.–Thurs. 10–6, Fri.–Sun. 10–7.*

5 **Ayuntamiento.** The 17th-century town hall stands on the active **Plaza Mayor.** It's closed to the public, but it's a great place to sit and watch the world go by. ✉ *Pl. Mayor.*

10 **Casa de la Moneda** *(Mint).* All Spanish coinage was struck here from 1455 to 1730. The mint, scheduled for reconstruction work, offers tours every first and third Saturday of the month, with English-language guides available by prior arrangement. Call or e-mail (✍ *info@segoviamint.org*) to reserve a tour. ✉ *C. de la Moneda, just south of Eresma River* ☎ *921/420921* 🌐 *www.segoviamint.org* 🎟 *Free.*

6 **Cathedral.** Begun in 1525 and completed 65 years later, Segovia's cathedral was intended to replace an earlier one near the Alcázar, destroyed during the revolt of the Comuneros against Carlos V. It's one of the country's last great examples of the Gothic style. The designs were drawn up by the leading late-Gothicist Juan Gil de Hontañón but executed by his son Rodrigo, in whose work can be seen a transition from the Gothic to the Renaissance. The interior, illuminated by 16th-century Flemish windows, is light and uncluttered, the one distracting detail being the wooden, neoclassical choir. Enter through the north transept, which is marked MUSEO; turn right, and the first chapel on your right has a lamentation group (carved figures who are lamenting) in wood by the baroque sculptor Gregorio Fernández. Across from the entrance, on the southern transept, is a door opening into the late-Gothic cloister—this and the elaborate door leading into it were transported from the old cathedral and are the work of architect Juan Guas. Under the pavement immediately inside the cloisters are the tombs of Juan and Rodrigo Gil de Hontañón; that these two lie in a space designed by Guas is appropriate, for the three men together dominated the last phase of

the Gothic style in Spain. Off the cloister, a small museum of religious art, installed partly in the first-floor chapter house, has a white-and-gold 17th-century ceiling, a late example of Mudejar *artesonado* work. At night the cathedral is lit up with lovely amber lights. ■ TIP→ **Watch your purse as you enter: there are usually at least half a dozen beggars at the door of the church.** ✉*Pl. Mayor s/n* ☎*921/462205* 🎟*Cathedral cloister and museum €2* ⏲*Apr.–Oct., Mon.–Sat. 9–6:30, Sun. 9–2:30; Nov.–Mar., Mon.–Sat. 9–5:30, Sun. 9–2:30.*

11 **Monasterio de la Santa Cruz.** Built in the 13th century, this church was established by St. Dominick of Guzmán, founder of the Dominican order, and rebuilt in the 15th century by Ferdinand and Isabella. Now it's a private university, La Universidad Sec, and during the academic year, you can see the Gothic interior with plateresque and Renaissance touches. ✉*Calle Cardenal Zúñiga s/n* ☎*921/471997.*

3 **Palacio de Aspiroz/Palacio de los Condes de Alpuente** *(Palace of the Counts of Alpuente).* This late-Gothic palace is covered with a type of plasterwork known as *esgrafiado* (sgraffito), incised with regular patterns; the style was most likely introduced by the Moors and is characteristic of Segovian architecture. The building, now used for city administrative offices, is not open to the public. ✉*Pl. del Platero Oquendo.*

7 **San Estéban.** Though the interior has a baroque facing, the exterior has kept some splendid capitals, as well as an exceptionally tall tower. Due east of the church square is the **Capilla de San Juan de Dios,** next to which is the former pension where the poet Antonio Machado spent his last years in Spain. The family who looked after Machado still owns the building and will show you the poet's room on request, with its kerosene stove, iron bed, and round table. The church is open for Mass only. ✉*Pl. de San Estéban* ⏲*Mass daily at 8* AM *and 7* PM.

4 **San Martín.** This elevated Romanesque church is on the main street between the aqueduct and cathedral, in a small plaza of the same name. It's not the most impressive of churches, but it's hard to miss in the middle of the city. It's open for Mass only. ✉*Pl. San Martín* ☎*921/443402* ⏲*Mass daily at 8* AM *and 7* PM.

1 **San Millán.** A perfect example of the Segovian Romanesque, this 12th-century church is perhaps the finest in town apart from the cathedral. The exterior is notable for its arcaded porch, where church meetings were once held. The virtually untouched Romanesque interior is dominated by massive columns, whose capitals carry such carved scenes as the Flight into Egypt and the Adoration of the Magi. The vaulting on the crossing shows the Moorish influence on Spanish medieval architecture. It's open for Mass only. ✉*Av. Fernández Ladreda 26, 5-min walk outside town walls* ⏲*Mass daily at 8* AM *and 7* PM.

9 **Vera Cruz.** Made of the local warm-orange stone, this isolated Romanesque church was built in 1208 for the Knights Templar. Like other buildings associated with this order, it has 12 sides, inspired by the Church of the Holy Sepulchre in Jerusalem. The trek out here pays off in full when you climb the bell tower and see all of Segovia profiled against the Sierra de Guadarrama. ✉*Ctra. de Zamarramia s/n, on northern outskirts of town, off Cuesta de los Hoyos* ☎*921/431475*

€1.50 *May–Sept., Tues.–Sun. 10:30–1:30 and 3:30–7; Oct. and Dec.–Apr., Tues.–Sun. 10:30–1:30 and 3:30–6:30; closed Nov.*

WHERE TO EAT AND STAY

$$–$$$$ SPANISH **Casa Duque.** Founded in 1895 and still run by the same family, this restaurant, the oldest in Segovia, has an intimate interior, with handsome wood beams and a plethora of fascinating bric-a-brac from wood carvings to coats of armor stashed in every nook and cranny. Roasts and meats are the main specialty here, but the *judiones de La Granja Duque*—enormous white beans from the family farm stewed with sausages or partridge—are also excellent. The local Ribera de Duero wines hold up well with roasts, while *setas* (wild mushrooms) from the Sierra de Guadarrama add a forest fragrance. Be prepared for wedding parties; but if you're lucky, you might get included. *Calle Cervantes 12 921/462487 www.restauranteduque.es Reservations essential AE, DC, MC, V.*

$$–$$$$ SPANISH ★ **Mesón de Cándido.** Cándido began life as an inn near the end of the 18th century and was declared a national monument in 1941. Tucked beside the aqueduct, it has a medley of small, irregular dining rooms decorated with memorabilia. Amid the dark-wood beams and Castilian knickknacks hang photos of celebrities who have dined here, from Ernest Hemingway to Princess Grace. Cándido's son now runs the place. If it's your first time here, the *cochinillo* (piglet), roasted in a wood-fire oven, is a great choice, while the partridge stew and roast lamb are also memorable, especially on cold winter afternoons with sunlight illuminating the ocher aqueduct just a few feet away. *Pl. de Azoguejo 540001 921/428103 Reservations essential AE, DC, MC, V.*

$$$–$$$$ SPANISH Fodor's Choice ★ **Mesón de José María.** With a lively and boisterous bar setting the tone and decibel level, this *mesón* (traditional tavern-restaurant) is hospitable, and the owner is devoted to maintaining traditional Castilian specialties while concocting innovations of his own, changing dishes with the seasons. The large, old-style, brightly lighted dining room is often packed, and the waiters are uncommonly friendly. Although it's a bit touristy, it's equally popular with locals, and the *cochinillo*, roasted piglet, is delicious in any company. *Calle Cronista Lecea 11 921/461111 www.rtejosemaria.com AE, DC, MC, V.*

$–$$$ **Infanta Isabel.** You'll get great views of the cathedral from this 19th-century town house perched on the corner of Plaza Mayor—with an entrance on a charming, if congested, pedestrian shopping street. Rooms are true to the name "Princess Isabel," with light and feminine furnishings like wrought-iron beds and little round tables; those on the plaza have floor-length shutters and small verandas. **Pros:** boutiquey in design, central location, some rooms have balconies overlooking the plaza. **Cons:** some rooms are oddly shaped and small. *Pl. Mayor 12 921/461300 www.hotelinfantaisabel.com 37 rooms In-hotel: restaurant, meeting rooms, parking (fee) AE, DC, MC, V.*

$ **Las Sirenas.** If you stay here, not only will you be just steps from the Plaza Mayor, above Segovia's nicest shops, but you'll have the benefit of a prime downtown location, a pillared marble lobby, and, from the best rooms, splendid balcony views of the church of San Millán.

Sensuous and classical accents include statues of mermaids at the foot of a curving staircase and Greek vases on antique bedside tables. **Pros:** excellent location, great quality for the price. **Cons:** tiny showers, slightly faded furnishings, some noise from hallways. ✉ *C. Juan Bravo 30* ☎ *921/462663* 🌐 *www.hotelsirenas.com* *39 rooms* *In-room: no a/c. In-hotel: bar* *AE, DC, MC, V.*

$$$ **Parador de Segovia.** Architecturally one of the most interesting of Spain's modern paradores (if you like naked concrete), this low building is set on a hill overlooking the city; it's a very long walk to the city center. The rooms are cold in appearance, but from the large windows the panorama of Segovia and its aqueduct are spectacular. (The ground floors have views of hedges, so request a room with a view if you want one.) The restaurant ($$$$) serves Segovian and international dishes, such as *lomo de merluza al aroma de estragón* (hake fillet with tarragon and shrimp). **Pros:** beautiful views of the city. **Cons:** need a car to get here, rooms not as elegant as in some other paradores. ✉ *Ctra. de Valladolid s/n, 2 km (1 mi) from Segovia* ☎ *921/443737* 🌐 *www.parador.es* *113 rooms* *In-hotel: restaurant, pools, gym, parking (fee)* *AE, DC, MC, V.*

OFF THE BEATEN PATH

Fodor's Choice ★ While in the Segovia area, don't miss the **Palacio Real de La Granja (Royal Palace of La Granja)** in the town of La Granja de San Ildefonso, about 11 km (7 mi) southeast of Segovia (on N601) on the northern slopes of the Sierra de Guadarrama. The palace site was once occupied by a hunting lodge and a shrine to San Ildefonso, administered by Hieronymite monks from the Segovian monastery of El Parral. Commissioned by the Bourbon king Felipe V in 1719, the palace has been described as the first great building of the Spanish Bourbon dynasty. The Italian architects Juvarra and Sachetti, who finished it in 1739, were responsible for the imposing garden facade, a late-baroque masterpiece anchored throughout its length by a giant order of columns. The interior has been badly gutted by fire; the highlight is the collection of 15th- to 8th-century tapestries kept in a special museum. Even if you don't go into the palace, walking through the gardens is magnificent: terraces, ornamental ponds, lakes, classical statuary, woods, and baroque fountains dot the mountainside. On Wednesday, Saturday, and Sunday evenings in the summer (May–September, 6–7 PM), the fountains are turned on, one by one, creating an effect to rival that of Versailles. The starting time has been known to change on a whim, so call ahead. ☎ *921/470020* 🌐 *www.patrimonionacional.es* *Palace €5, gardens free* *Palace Oct.–Mar., Tues.–Sat. 10–1:30 and 3–5, Sun. 10–2; Apr.–Sept., Tues.–Sun. 10–6. Gardens daily 10–sunset.*

SHOPPING

After Toledo, the province of Segovia is Castile's most important for crafts. Glass and crystal are specialties of La Granja, and ironwork, lace, and embroidery are famous in Segovia itself. You can buy good lace from the Gypsies in Segovia's Plaza del Alcázar, but be prepared for some strenuous bargaining, and never offer more than half the opening price. For genuine crafts, go to **San Martín 4** (✉ *Pl. San Martín 4*), an excellent antiques shop. **Calle Daiza,** leading to the Alcázar, overflows with touristy ceramic, textile, and gift shops.

OFF THE BEATEN PATH

Tucked away amid the tourist ceramics shops in Segovia is a witchcraft museum, **El Antiguo Museo de Brujería.** The eight-room creep show of spells, artifacts, and jarred curiosities features standouts like the shrunken head of vampire Oktavius von Bergengruen, as well as torture instruments from the Inquisition. ✉ *Calle Daoiz 9* ☎ *921/460443* 🌐 *www.seamp.net/museobrujeriasegovia.htm* 🎟 *€4.*

SEPÚLVEDA

60 km (37 mi) northeast of Segovia.

ESSENTIALS

Visitor Information **Sepúlveda** (✉ *Plaza del Trigo 6* ☎ *921/540237*).

EXPLORING

A walled village with a commanding position, Sepúlveda has a charming main square, but its main attraction is the 11th-century **El Salvador,** the oldest Romanesque church in Segovia's province. It has a crude but amusing example of the porches found in later Segovian buildings: the carvings on its capitals, probably by a Moorish convert, are quite fantastical. ✉ *Cerro de Somosierra.*

OFF THE BEATEN PATH

Perhaps the most famous medieval sight near Segovia—worth a detour between Segovia and Ávila or Valladolid—is the **Castillo de Coca,** 52 km (32 mi) northwest of the city. Built in the 15th century for Archbishop Alonso de Fonseca I, the castle is a turreted structure of plaster and red brick, surrounded by a deep moat. It looks like a stage set for a fairy tale, and, indeed, it was intended not as a defense but as a place for the notoriously pleasure-loving Archbishop Fonseca to hold riotous parties. The interior, now occupied by a forestry school, has been modernized, with only fragments of the original decoration preserved. Note that opening hours are erratic; call ahead if possible. ☎ *921/586622* 🎟 *€2.50* ⏲ *May–Aug., weekdays 10:30–1 and 4:30–7, weekends 11–1 and 4–6; Sept.–Apr., weekdays 10:30–1 and 4:30–6, weekends 11–1 and 4–6. Closed 1st Tues. of every month.*

ÁVILA

107 km (66 mi) northwest of Madrid.

In the middle of a windy plateau littered with giant boulders, Ávila can look wild and sinister, especially with the Sierra de Gredos in the background. Modern development on its outskirts partially obscures Ávila's surrounding **walls,** which, restored in parts, look as they did in the Middle Ages. Begun in 1090, shortly after the town was reclaimed from the Moors, the walls were completed in only nine years—accomplished by the daily employment of an estimated 1,900 men. With nine gates and 88 cylindrical towers bunched together, they are unique to Spain in form, unlike the Moorish defense architecture that the Christians adapted elsewhere. They're most striking when seen from outside town; for the best view on foot, cross the Adaja River, turn right on the Carretera de Salamanca, and walk uphill about 250 yards to a monument of four pilasters surrounding a cross.

3

The walls reflect Ávila's importance during the Middle Ages. Populated by Alfonso VI mainly with Christians from Asturias, the town came to be known as Ávila of the Knights because of its many nobles. Decline set in at the beginning of the 15th century, with the gradual departure of the nobility to the court of Carlos V in Toledo. Ávila's fame later on was largely because of St. Teresa. Born here in 1515 to a noble family of Jewish origin, Teresa spent much of her life in Ávila, leaving a legacy of convents and the ubiquitous *yemas* (candied egg yolks), originally distributed free to the poor but now sold for high prices to tourists. Ávila is well preserved, but the mood is slightly sad, austere, and desolate. The quietude is dispelled during Fiestas de la Santa Teresa, beginning October 8. The weeklong celebration includes lighted decorations, parades, singing in the streets, and religious observances.

GETTING HERE AND AROUND

Avilabus (🌐*www.avilabus.com*) serves the city of Ávila and surrounding villages, though the city itself is easily manageable on foot.

ESSENTIALS

Visitor Information **Ávila** (✉ *Pl. Pedro Dávila 4* ☎ *920/211387*).

EXPLORING

Cathedral. Its battlement apse forms the most impressive part of Ávila's walls. Entering the town gate to the right of the apse, you can reach the sculpted north portal (originally the west portal, until it was moved in 1455 by the architect Juan Guas) by turning left and walking a few steps. The present west portal, flanked by 18th-century towers, is notable for the crude carvings of hairy male figures on each side; known as "wild men," these figures appear in many Castilian palaces of this period. The Transitional Gothic interior, with its granite nave, is heavy and severe. The Lisbon earthquake of 1755 deprived the building of its Flemish stained glass, so the main note of color appears in the beautiful mottled stone in the apse, tinted yellow and red. Elaborate, plateresque choir stalls built in 1547 complement the powerful high altar of circa 1504 by painters Juan de Borgoña and Pedro Berruguete. On the wall of the ambulatory, look for the early-16th-century marble sepulchre of Bishop Alonso de Madrigal, a remarkably lifelike representation of the bishop seated at his writing table. Known as "El Tostado" (the Toasted One) for his swarthy complexion, the bishop was a tiny man of enormous intellect, the author of 54 books. When on one occasion Pope Eugenius IV ordered him to stand—mistakenly thinking him to still be on his knees—the bishop indicated the space between his eyebrows and hairline, retorting, "A man's stature is to be measured from here to here!" ✉ *Pl. de la Catedral 8* ☎ *920/211641* 🎫 *€4* ⏲ *June–Aug., weekdays 10–7, Sat. 10–6:30, Sun. noon–6; Sept.–May, weekdays 10–5, Sat. 10–6, Sun. noon–6.*

The 15th-century **Mansión de los Deanes** *(Deans' Mansion)* houses the cheerful **Museo Provincial de Ávila,** a provincial museum full of local archaeology and folklore; it's adjacent to the old romanesc temple of San Tomé el Viejo, a few minutes' walk east of the cathedral apse. ✉ *Pl. de Nalvillos 3* ☎ *920/211003* 🎫 *€1.20, weekends free* ⏲ *July–Sept.,*

Tues.–Sat. 10–2 and 5–8, Sun. 10–2; Oct.–June, Tues.–Sat. 10–2 and 4–7, Sun. 10–2.

In the **Convento de San José** *(de Las Madres)*, four blocks east of the cathedral on Calle Duque de Alba, is the **Museo Teresiano,** with musical instruments used by St. Teresa and her nuns (Teresa specialized in percussion). ✉*Plaza delas Madres 4* ☎*920/222127* *€1* *Apr.–Oct., daily 10–1:30 and 4–7; Nov.–Mar., daily 10–1:30 and 3–6.*

North of Ávila's cathedral, on Plaza de San Vincente, is the much-venerated Romanesque **Basílica de San Vicente** *(Basilica of St. Vincent)*, founded on the supposed site where St. Vincent was martyred in 303 with his sisters Sts. Sabina and Cristeta. The west front, shielded by a vestibule, has damaged but expressive Romanesque carvings depicting the death of Lazarus and the parable of the rich man's table. The sarcophagus of St. Vincent forms the centerpiece of the basilica's Romanesque interior; the extraordinary, Asian-looking canopy above the sarcophagus is a 15th-century addition. ✉*Pl. de San Vicente 1* ☎*920/255230* *www.basilicasanvicente.com* *€1.40* *Daily 10–1:30 and 4–6:30.*

The elegant chapel of **Mosen Rubi** (circa 1516) is illuminated by Renaissance stained glass by Nicolás de Holanda. Try to persuade the nuns in the adjoining convent to let you inside. ✉*C. de Lopez Nuñez.*

At the west end of the town walls, next to the river in a farmyard nearly hidden by poplars, is the small Romanesque **Ermita de San Segundo** *(Hermitage of St. Secundus)*. Founded on the site where the remains of St. Secundus (a follower of St. Peter) were reputedly discovered, the hermitage has a realistic marble monument to the saint, carved by Juan de Juni. You may have to ask for the key in the adjoining house. ✉*Plaza de San Segundo s/n* ☎*920/353900* *€0.60* *July–Sept., daily 10–1 and 3:30–6; Oct.–June, daily 11–1 and 4–5.*

Inside the south wall on the corner of Calle Dama and Plaza de la Santa, the **Convento de Santa Teresa** was founded in the 17th century on the site of the saint's birthplace. Teresa's famous written account of an ecstatic vision in which an angel pierced her heart influenced many baroque artists, most famously the Italian sculptor Giovanni Bernini. The convent has a small museum with relics—including one of Teresa's fingers; you can also see the small and rather gloomy garden where she played as a child. The restaurant is closed Monday from October through Easter. ✉*Pl. de la Santa s/n* ☎*920/211030* *Museum €2* *Museum May–Sept., weekdays 10–1:30 and 3:30–5:30, Sat. 10–1 and 4–6; Apr.–Oct., weekdays 10–2 and 4–7, Sat. 10–1 and 4–6.*

On the south side of the city is the **Convento de Nuestra Señora de Gracia,** built over the Ermita de los Santos Justo y Pastor in 1509 and currently a small church. The surrounding gardens are lovely, with benches, fountains, and statues, and a good view of the city. Inside is a taxidermy crocodile brought back from the Americas by a Spanish explorer. Prime Minister José Luis Rodríguez Zapatero was married here—his wife is from Ávila. There is a very pleasant restaurant on the property, the Posada de Nuestra Señora de Sonsoles, featuring traditional Spanish fare such as roasted meats, fish, and paella. It's sometimes in use for wedding receptions but is also available for lunch and dinner reservations.

✉*Cuesta de Gracias s/n* ☎*920/223367* *Free* ⏲*Restaurant closed Tues. Nov.–Mar.*

The **Museo del Convento de la Encarnación** is the convent where St. Teresa first took orders and was then based for almost 40 years. Its Museo Teresiano has an interesting drawing of the Crucifixion by her teacher St. John of the Cross, as well as a reconstruction of the cell she used when she was a prioress here. The convent is outside the walls in the northern part of town. ✉*Paseo de la Encarnación s/n* ☎*920/211212* *€1.05* ⏲*May–Oct., weekdays 9:30–1 and 4–7, weekends 10–1 and 4–6; Nov.–Apr., weekdays 9:30–1:30 and 3:30–6, weekends 10–1 and 4–6.*

The most interesting architectural monument on Ávila's outskirts is the **Monasterio de Santo Tomás.** A good 10-minute walk from the walls among housing projects, it's not where you would expect to find one of the most important religious institutions in Castile. The monastery was founded by Ferdinand and Isabella with the financial assistance of the notorious Inquisitor-General Tomás de Torquemada, who is buried in the sacristy. Further funds were provided by the confiscated property of converted Jews who ran afoul of the Inquisition. Three decorated cloisters lead to the church; inside, a masterly high altar (circa 1506) by Pedro Berruguete overlooks a serene marble tomb by the Italian artist Domenico Fancelli. One of the earliest examples of the Italian Renaissance style in Spain, this influential work was built for Prince Juan, the only son of Ferdinand and Isabella, who died at 19 while a student at the University of Salamanca. After Juan's burial here, his heartbroken parents found themselves unable to return; in happier times they had often attended Mass here, seated in the upper choir behind a balustrade exquisitely carved with their coats of arms. ✉*Pl. de Granada 1* ☎*920/220400* 🌐*www.monasteriosantotomas.com* *€3* ⏲*Tues.–Sun. 10–1 and 4–8.*

WHERE TO EAT AND STAY

$$–$$$ SPANISH ★ ✕ **El Molino de la Losa.** Sitting at the edge of the serenely flowing Adaja River, with one of the best views of the town walls, Molino is in a 15th-century mill, the working mechanism of which has been well preserved and provides much distraction for those seated in the animated bar. Lamb is roasted in a medieval wood oven, and the beans from nearby El Barco (*judías de El Barco*) are famous. The garden has a small playground for children. ✉*Bajada de la Losa 12* ☎*920/211101 or 920/211102* 🌐*www.elmolinodelalosa.com* *AE, MC, V* ⏲*Closed Mon.*

$–$$$ SPANISH ✕ **Las Cancelas.** Locals flock to this little tavern for the ample selection of tapas, but you can also push your way through the loud bar area to the dining room, where wooden tables are heaped with combination platters of roast chicken, french fries, sunny-side-up eggs, and chunks of home-baked bread. The classic T-bone steak, *chuletón de Ávila,* is enormous and offers good value at €20. The succulent *cochinillo*, roast pig, bursts with flavor. There are 14 hotel rooms available, too; simple, slightly ramshackle arrangements at moderate prices. ✉*Cruz Vieja 6* ☎*920/212249* *AE, DC, MC, V* ⏲*Closed Jan. 7–Feb. 3.*

$$–$$$ SPANISH ✕ **Mesón del Rastro.** In the former stables of the medieval Palacio de los Dávila Abrantes, this restaurant has a bucolic rustic Castilian interior

with exposed stone walls and beams, low lighting, and dark wood furniture, perfectly setting the tone for the traditional dishes. Try the lamb or the *tostón asado* (roast suckling pig), or any dish made with the famous beans from El Barco de Ávila. Equally hearty and filled with flavor is the stick-to-your-ribs *caldereta de cabrito* (goat stew). The place has one dining room for 145 and occasionally suffers somewhat from its popularity with tour buses, making service sometimes slow and impersonal. Try for the smaller dining room for 30. ✉*Pl. Rastro 1* ☎*920/211218* 💳*AE, DC, MC, V.*

3

$$–$$$$ ★ **Palacio de los Velada.** Ávila's top hotel occupies a beautifully restored 16th-century palace in the heart of the city next to the cathedral. (It's ideal if you like to relax between sightseeing jaunts.) Upscale locals like to gather in the bar and the lovely interior patio at Ávila's vortex. Rooms are elegantly decorated, modern, and comfortable. **Pros:** gorgeous glass-covered patio, quality service that alone is worth the price. **Cons:** some rooms don't have views because the windows are placed too high on the walls. ✉*Pl. de la Catedral 10* ☎*920/255100* 🌐*www.veladahoteles.com* *145 rooms* *In-hotel: restaurant, bar* 💳*AE, DC, MC, V.*

$$ **Parador de Ávila.** A largely rebuilt 16th-century medieval castle attached to the massive town walls, Ávila's parador has the advantage of a lush garden. The interior is unusually warm, done mostly in tawny tones, and the common rooms, elegantly decorated, if somewhat formal, are convivial places to meet for a beverage. Guest rooms have terra-cotta tile floors and clubby leather chairs. **Pros:** central location. **Cons:** staff isn't overly friendly, limited parking, run-down here and there with a few well-worn carpets. ✉*Calle Marqués de Canales de Chozas 2* ☎*920/211340* 🌐*www.parador.es* *61 rooms* *In-hotel: restaurant, bar* 💳*AE, DC, MC, V.*

SAN MARTÍN DE VALDEIGLESIAS

73 km (45 mi) west of Madrid.

ESSENTIALS

Visitor Information San Martín de Valdeiglesias (✉*Plaza Real 1* ☎*91/861–1308*).

EXPLORING

Just 6 km (4 mi) before San Martín, on the right side of the road, is a stone inscription in front of a hedge; this marks the site where, in 1468, Isabella the Catholic was acknowledged by the assembled Castilian nobility as rightful successor to Henry IV. The **Toros de Guisando,** or stone bulls, dating from the 6th century BC, are thought to have been used as territorial border markers for a Celtiberian tribe. Just three of many such bulls once scattered around the Castilian countryside (they take their name from the nearby Cerro Guisando, or Guisando Hill), they're now a symbol of the Spanish Tourist Board. To see these taurine effigies, head back east from Arenas on the C501; it's a pleasant drive through countryside bordered to the north by the Gredos range. ✉*Near Cerro Guisando, 6 km (4 mi) before San Martín, on right side of road, on other side of hedge with stone inscription.*

SALAMANCA

Fodor'sChoice ★ *205 km (127 mi) northwest of Madrid.*

Salamanca's radiant sandstone buildings, immense Plaza Mayor, and hilltop riverside perch make it one of the most attractive and beloved cities in Spain. Today, as it did centuries ago, the university predominates, providing an intellectual flavor, a stimulating arts scene, and nightlife—best experienced on the weekend—to match.

If you approach from Madrid or Ávila, you'll first see Salamanca rising on the northern banks of the wide and winding River Tormes. In the foreground is its sturdy, 15-arch Roman bridge, above which soars the combined bulk of the old and new cathedrals. Piercing the skyline to the right is the Renaissance monastery and church of San Estéban. Behind San Estéban and the cathedrals, and largely out of sight from the river, extends a stunning series of palaces, convents, and university buildings that culminates in the Plaza Mayor. Despite considerable damage over the centuries, Salamanca remains one of Spain's greatest cities architecturally, a showpiece of the Spanish Renaissance. It is the warmth of golden sandstone, which seems to glow throughout the city, that you will remember above all things.

GETTING HERE AND AROUND

Salamanca de Transportes (☎ *923/190545*) runs 64 municipal buses equipped with lifts for disabled passengers throughout the city of Salamanca. The main destinations requiring bus travel are the train and bus stations located on the outskirts of the city.

ESSENTIALS

Two tourist offices are located in town.

Visitor Information Salamanca–Municipal Tourist Office (✉ *Pl. Mayor 32* ☎ *923/218342*). **Salamanca–Casa de las Conchas** (✉ *Calle Rua Mayor s/n* ☎ *923/268571*).

EXPLORING

3 Fodor'sChoice ★ For a complete exterior tour of the old and new **Cathedrals,** take a 10-minute walk around the complex, circling counterclockwise. Nearest the river stands the **Catedral Vieja** (Old Cathedral), built in the late 12th century, one of the most interesting examples of the Spanish Romanesque. Because the dome of the crossing tower has strange, plumelike ribbing, it's known as the Torre del Gallo (Rooster's Tower). The much larger **Catedral Nueva** (New Cathedral) dates mainly from the 16th century, though some parts, including the dome over the crossing and the bell tower attached to the west facade, had to be rebuilt after the Lisbon earthquake of 1755. Work began in 1513 under the direction of the distinguished late-Gothic architect Juan Gil de Hontañón, and as at Segovia's cathedral, Juan's son Rodrigo took over the work after his father's death in 1526. The New Cathedral's north facade (which contains the main entrance) is ornamental enough, but the west facade is dazzling in its sculptural complexity. Try to visit in late afternoon, when the sun shines on it.

The interior of the New Cathedral is as light and harmonious as that of Segovia's cathedral but larger. It's a triumphant baroque effusion

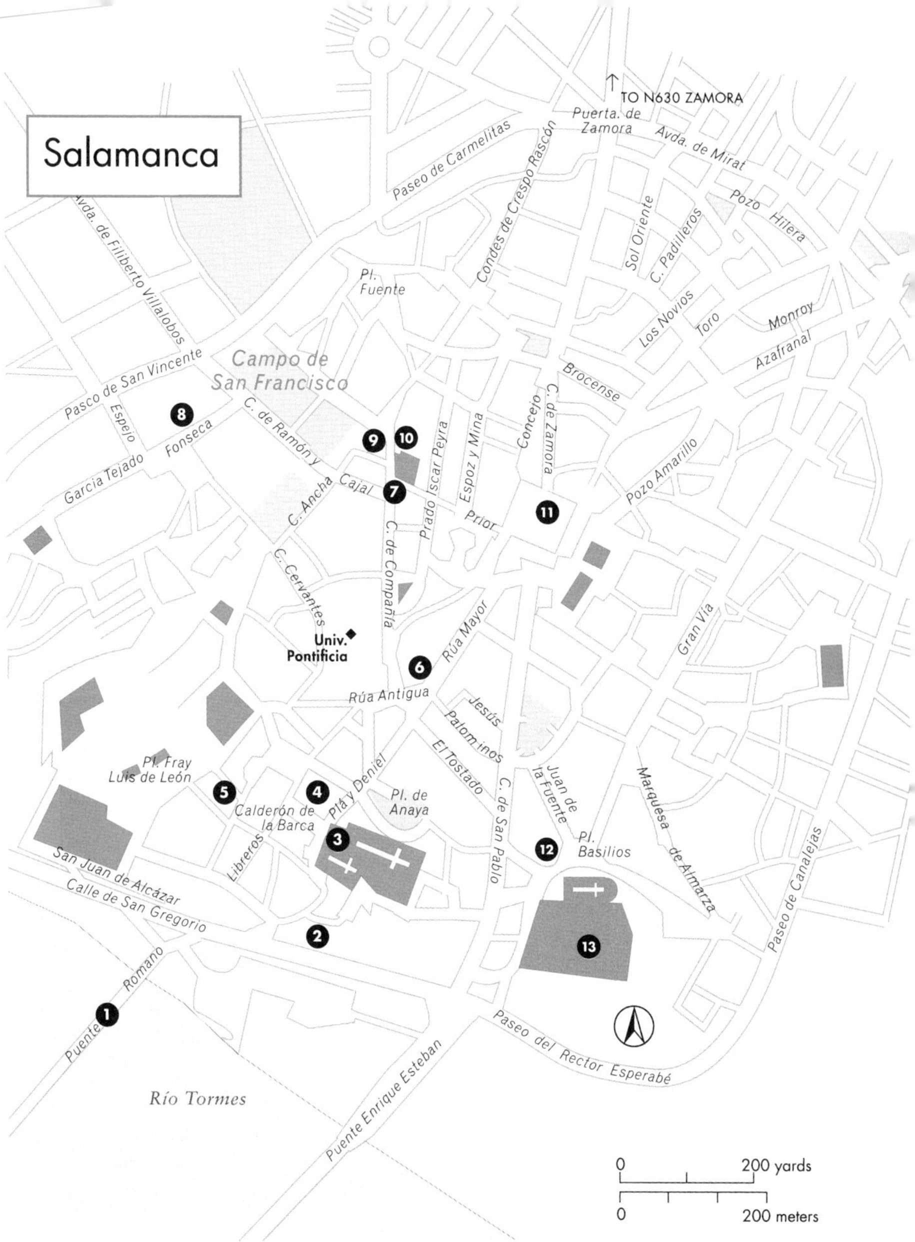

Casa de Las Conchas **6**
Casa de Las Muertes **10**
Cathedrals **3**
Colegio Mayor Arzobispo Fonseca/ Colegio de Los Irlandeses **8**
Convento de Las Dueñas **12**
Convento de Las Ursulas **9**
Convento de San Estéban **13**
Museo Art Nouveau y Art Deco **2**
Museo de Salamanca **5**
Palacio de Monterrey.................. **7**
Plaza Mayor **11**
Puente Romano **1**
Universidad **4**

designed by the Churrigueras. The wooden choir seems almost alive with active cherubim and saints. From a door in the south aisle, steps descend into the Old Cathedral, where boldly carved capitals supporting the vaulting are accented by foliage, strange animals, and touches of pure fantasy. Then comes the dome, which seems to owe much to Byzantine architecture; it's a remarkably light structure raised on two tiers of arcaded openings. Not the least of the Old Cathedral's attractions are its furnishings, including sepulchres from the 12th and 13th centuries and a curved high altar comprising 53 colorful and delicate scenes by the mid-15th-century artist Nicolás Florentino. In the apse above, Florentino painted an astonishingly fresh Last Judgment fresco.

From the south transept of the Old Cathedral, a door leads into the cloister, begun in 1177. From about 1230 until the construction of the main university building in the early 15th century, the chapels around the cloister served as classrooms for the university students. In the Chapel of St. Barbara, on the eastern side, theology students answered the grueling questions meted out by their doctoral examiners. The chair in which they sat is still there, in front of a recumbent effigy of Bishop Juan Lucero, on whose head the students would place their feet for inspiration. Also attached to the cloister is a small cathedral museum with a 15th-century triptych of St. Catherine by Salamanca's greatest native artist, Fernando Gallego. ✉ *Calle Cardenal Plá y Deniel s/n* ☎ *923/217476* 🌐 *www.catedralsalamanca.org* 🎟 *New Cathedral free. Old Cathedral €4.50, free Tues. 10–12* ⏲ *New Cathedral, Apr.–Sept., daily 10–8; Oct.–Mar., daily 9–1 and 4–6; Old Cathedral, Apr.–Sept., daily 10–7:30; Oct.–Mar., daily 10–12:30 and 4–5:30. Nov.–Feb., both cathedrals close on Sunday afternoons.*

12 **Convento de Las Dueñas** *(Convent of the Dames).* Founded in 1419, this convent hides a 16th-century cloister that is the most fantastically decorated in Salamanca, if not in the whole of Spain. The capitals of its two superimposed Salmantine arcades are crowded with a baffling profusion of grotesques that can absorb you for hours. As you're wandering through, take a moment to look down. The interlocking diamond pattern on the ground floor of the cloister is decorated with the knobby vertebrae of goats and sheep. It's an eerie yet perfect accompaniment to all the grinning, disfigured heads sprouting from the capitals looming above you. There's another reason to come here: the nuns make and sell excellent sweets. ✉ *Calle de Juan de la Fuente* ☎ *923/215442* 🎟 *€1.50* ⏲ *Apr.–Oct., Mon.–Sat. 10:30–1 and 4:30–6, Sun. 11–12:45 and 4:30–6:45; Nov.–Mar., Mon.–Sat. 10:30–1 and 4:30–5:45, Sun. 11–12:45 and 4:30–5:45.*

11 **Plaza Mayor.** Built in the 1730s by Alberto and Nicolás Churriguera, Salamanca's Plaza Mayor is one of the largest squares in Spain, and many find it the most beautiful. Its northern side is dominated by the lavishly elegant, pinkish **ayuntamiento** (city hall). The square and its arcades are popular gathering spots for most of Salmantino society, and the many surrounding cafés make this the perfect spot for a coffee break. At night, the plaza swarms with students meeting "under the clock" on the plaza's north side. *Tunas* (strolling musicians in tradi-

Fodor's Choice ★

tional garb) often meander among the cafés and crowds, playing for smiles and applause rather than tips.

4 **Universidad.** Parts of the university's walls, like those of the cathedral and other structures in Salamanca, are covered with large, ocher lettering recording the names of famous university graduates. The earliest names are said to have been written in the blood of the bulls killed to celebrate the successful completion of a doctorate. The **Escuelas Mayores** (Major Schools) dates to 1415, but it was not until more than 100 years later that an unknown architect provided the building with its elaborate facade. Above the main door is the famous double portrait of Isabella and Ferdinand, surrounded by ornamentation that plays on the yoke-and-arrow heraldic motifs of the two monarchs. The double-eagle crest of Carlos V, flanked by portraits of the emperor and empress in classical guise, dominates the middle layer of the frontispiece. Perhaps the most famous rite of passage for new students is to find the carved frog that squats atop a skull at the very top left-hand corner. Legend has it that if you spot the frog on your first try, you'll pass all your exams and have a successful university career; for this reason, it's affectionately called *la rana de la suerte* (the lucky frog). It can be hard to pin down the elusive amphibian but the ticket booth has posted a detail of the frontispiece for precisely this purpose. You can then see the beloved frog all over town, on sweatshirts, magnets, pins, jewelry, and postcards.

The interior of the Escuelas Mayores, drastically restored in parts, comes as a slight disappointment after the splendor of the facade. But the *aula* (lecture hall) of Fray Luis de León, where Cervantes, Calderón de la Barca, and numerous other luminaries of Spain's golden age once sat, is of particular interest. Cervantes carved his name on one of the wooden pews up front. After five years' imprisonment for having translated the *Song of Songs* into Spanish, Fray Luis returned to this hall and began his lecture, "As I was saying yesterday . . ."

Your ticket to the Escuelas Mayores also admits you to the nearby Colegio Mayor Arzobisbo Fonseca, built in the early 16th century as a secondary school preparing candidates for the university proper. Passing through a gate crowned with the double-eagle crest of Charles V, you'll come to a green, on the other side of which is a modern building with a fascinating ceiling fresco of the zodiac, originally in the library of the Escuelas Mayores. A fragment of a much larger whole, this painting is generally attributed to Fernando Gallego. ✉ *Calle Fonseca, 4* ☎ *923/294550 or 923/294400* 🌐 *www.usal.es* 🎫 *€4, free Mon. 9–2* ⏲ *Weekdays 9–2 and 4–7, Sat. 9–2 and 4–6:30, Sun. 10–1.*

NEED A BREAK?

Unwind at La Regenta (✉ ***Calle Espoz y Mina 19–20*** ☎ ***923/123230*** 🌐 ***www.cafelaregenta.com*****), a warm, plush, baroque-style café-bar that shines like a beacon of light (the flickering candle kind) in the thronged heart of town. Heavy green-and-gold curtains block most of the street noise, making the Plaza Mayor, a half a block off, a distant memory. Try a *café al caramelo* (coffee with caramel). In the evening you can order potent cocktails with names like "Kiss Me Boy" and "Sangre de Toro" (Bull's Blood).**

6 **Casa de Las Conchas** *(House of Shells)*. This house was built around 1500 for Dr. Rodrigo Maldonado de Talavera, a professor of medicine at the university and a doctor at the court of Isabella. The scallop motif was a reference to Talavera's status as chancellor of the Order of St. James (Santiago), whose symbol is the shell. Among the playful plateresque details are the lions over the main entrance, engaged in a fearful tug-of-war with the Talavera crest. The interior has been converted into a public library. Duck into the charming courtyard, which has an upper balustrade carved with virtuoso intricacy in imitation of basketwork. ✉ *Calle de Meléndez Compañía 2* ☎ *923/269317* 🎫 *Free* ⏲ *Weekdays 9–9, Sat. 9–2 and 4–7, Sun. 10–2 and 4–7.*

10 **Casa de Las Muertes** *(House of the Dead)*. Built in about 1513 for the majordomo of Alonso de Fonseca II, the house takes its name from the four tiny skulls that adorn its top two windows. Alonso de Fonseca II commissioned them to commemorate his deceased uncle, the licentious archbishop who lies in the Convento de Las Ursulas, across the street. For the same reason, the facade also bears the archbishop's portrait. The small square in front of the house was a favorite haunt of the poet, philosopher, and university rector Miguel de Unamuno, whose statue stands here. Unamuno supported the Nationalists under Franco at the outbreak of the civil war, but he later turned against them. Placed under virtual house arrest, Unamuno died in the house next door in 1938. During the Franco period, students often daubed his statue red to suggest that his heart still bled for Spain. ✉ *Cuesta del Carmen.*

8 **Colegio Mayor Arzobispo Fonseca/Colegio de Los Irlandeses** *(Irish College)*. Also known as *Escuelas Menores*, or the Minor Schools, this small college was founded by Alonso de Fonseca II in 1521 to train young Irish priests. It's now a residence hall for guest lecturers at the university. This part of town was the most severely damaged during the Peninsular War of the early 19th century and still has a slightly derelict character. The interior, however, is a treat. To the right immediately inside is a late-Gothic chapel, and beyond it lies one of the most classical and genuinely Italianate of Salamanca's many courtyards. ✉ *Paseo de San Vicente* ☎ *923/294570* 🎫 *Free* ⏲ *Daily 10–2 and 4–7.*

9 **Convento de Las Ursulas** *(Convent of the Ursulines)*. Archbishop Alonso de Fonseca I lies here, in a splendid marble tomb created by Diego de Siloe during the early 1500s. ✉ *Calle Las Ursulas 2* ☎ *923/219877* 🎫 *€2* ⏲ *Daily 11–1 and 4:30–6. Closed last Sun. of every month.*

13 **Convento de San Estéban** *(Convent of St. Stephen)*. The convent's monks, among the most enlightened teachers at the university, were the first to take Columbus's ideas seriously and helped him gain his introduction to Isabella (hence his statue in the nearby Plaza de Colón, back toward Calle de San Pablo). The complex was designed by one of San Estéban's monks, Juan de Alava. The door to the right of the west facade leads you into a gloomy cloister with Gothic arcading, interrupted by tall, spindly columns adorned with classical motifs. From the cloister, you enter the church at its eastern end. The interior is unified and uncluttered but also dark and severe. The one note of color is provided by the ornate and gilded high altar of 1692, a baroque masterpiece by José

Churriguera. The most exciting part of San Estéban, though, is the massive west facade, a thrilling plateresque work in which sculpted figures and ornamentation are piled up to a height of more than 98 feet. ✉ *Pl. Concilio de Trento* ☎ *923/215000* 🎫 *€2* ⏲ *Apr.–Sept., daily 10–2 and 4–8; Oct.–Mar., daily 10–2 and 4–7.*

2 **Museo Art Nouveau y Art Deco.** The museum is in the Casa Lis, a modernist building from the end of the 19th century. On display are 19th-century paintings and glass, as well as French and German china dolls, Viennese bronze statues, furniture, jewelry, enamels, and jars. ✉ *Calle Gibraltar 14* ☎ *923/121425* 🌐 *www.museocasalis.org* 🎫 *€2.50* ⏲ *Apr.–Oct., Tues.–Fri. 11–2 and 5–9, weekends and holidays 11–9, closed Mon. (open Mon. in Aug and Bank Holidays). Oct.–Mar., Tues.–Fri. 11–2 and 4–7, weekends and holidays 11–8, closed Mon.*

3

5 **Museum of Salamanca** *(Museo de Bellas Artes).* Consisting mainly of minor 17th- and 18th-century paintings, this museum, also known as the Museo de Bellas Artes (Museum of Fine Arts), is interesting for its 15th-century building, which belonged to Isabella's physician, Alvárez Abarca. ✉ *Calle del Patio de Escuelas Menores 2* ☎ *923/212235* 🎫 *€1.20, free weekends* ⏲ *Oct.–June, Tues.–Sat. 10–2 and 4–7, Sun. 10–2; July–Sept., Tues.–Sat. 10–2 and 5–8, Sun. 10–2.*

7 **Palacio de Monterrey.** Built after 1538 by Rodrigo Gil de Hontañón, the Monterrey Palace was meant for an illegitimate son of Alonso de Fonseca I. As in Rodrigo's other local palaces, the building is flanked by towers and has an open arcaded gallery running the length of the upper level. Such galleries—which in Italy you would expect to see on the ground floor—are common in Spanish Renaissance palaces and were intended to provide privacy for the women of the house and cool the floor below during the summer. Privately owned, the palace is not open to visitors, but you can stroll its grounds. ✉ *Plaza de las Agustinas.*

1 **Puente Romano** *(Roman Bridge).* Next to the bridge is an Iberian stone bull, and opposite the bull is a statue commemorating Lazarillo de Tormes, the young hero of the eponymous (but anonymous) 16th-century work that is one of the masterpieces of Spanish literature.

WHERE TO EAT AND STAY

¢–$$ SPANISH ✕ **Bambú.** At peak times, it's standing room only at this jovial basement tapas bar catering to students. The floor may be littered with napkins, and you might have to shout to be heard, but it's the generous tapas and big sloppy *bocadillos* (sandwiches) that draw the crowds. Although paella is usually the exclusive domain of pricey paella restaurants, here (during lunch) you can enjoy a *ración* of paella, ladled out from a large *caldero* (shallow pan). Another bonus: even if you just order a drink, you'll be served a liberal helping of the "tapa of the day." ✉ *C. Prior 4* ☎ *923/260092* 💳 *MC, V.*

$$$$ CONTINENTAL ✕ **Chez Víctor.** Try this chic restaurant for a break from traditional Castilian food. Chef-owner Victoriano Salvador learned his trade in France and adapts French cuisine to Spanish taste, with whimsical touches all his own. Sample the traditional *carrillada de buey braseada con jengibre* (cheek of beef braised in ginger) or the more Continental *hojaldre de verduras y foie con salsa de trufas* (puff pastry filled with leeks, foie, and

julienned carrots in a truffle sauce). Desserts are outstanding, especially the chocolate ones. ✉ *Espoz y Mina 26* ☎ *923/213123* ▭ *AE, DC, MC, V* ⏲ *Closed Mon. and Aug. No dinner Sun.*

$$–$$$$ SPANISH ✕ **El Candil Viejo.** Beloved by locals for its superb, no-nonsense Castilian fare, this tavern is an old favorite with professors in pinstripes and students on dates. Aside from a simple salad, the menu consists of meat, meat, and more meat, including pork, lamb, kid, sausage, and fantastic *marucha* (short ribs). The homemade pork sausages are especially good. For tapas, try the *farinato* sausage, made from pork, onion, eggs, and bread crumbs, or the *picadillo,* similar but spicier with pepper, garlic, and tomato. ✉ *Calle Ventura Ruiz Aguilera 14–16* ☎ *923/217239* ▭ *AE, DC, MC, V* ⏲ *Closed 3 wks in Jan.*

$–$$ VEGETARIAN ✕ **El Grillo Azul.** A vegetarian restaurant is a rare sight in Spain, and this, the only one in Salamanca, has an adventurous menu of heaping dishes that easily trump any of the limp salads and veggie options you'll find elsewhere in town. Dig into the *arroz basmati con calabacín, zanahorias, y piñones* (basmati rice topped with zucchini, carrots, and pine nuts) or an omelet stuffed with almonds and mushrooms. There's a lot to choose from and the portions are quite hearty. ✉ *C. El Grillo 1* ☎ *923/219233* ▭ *AE, DC, MC, V* ⏲ *Closed Mon. No dinner Sun.*

$$–$$$$ SPANISH ✕ **La Hoja 21.** Just off the Plaza Mayor, this restaurant has a glass facade, high ceilings, butter-yellow walls, and minimalist art—signs of a different-from-the-usual Castilian dining experience. Young chef-owner Alberto López Oliva prepares an innovative menu of traditional fare with a twist. *Manitas, manzana, y langostinas al aroma de Módena* are pig trotters with prawns and apple slices, all in Módena vinegar; *perdiz al chocolate con berza* is partridge cooked in chocolate, served with cabbage. ✉ *Calle San Pablo 21* ☎ *923/264028* ▭ *AE, MC, V* ⏲ *Closed Mon. and last 2 wks of Feb. and Aug. No dinner Sun.*

$$–$$$ **AC Palacio de San Estéban.** Near the cathedrals, this upscale hotel is in a former part of the 17th-century Convento de San Estéban. The rooms are comfortable and contemporary, finished in cream and white with dark-wood trim. The hotel's dining room is a sleek modern space with massive stone arches overhead that serves creditable local cuisine. **Pros:** top-notch service, elegant traditional architecture with chic contemporary facilities. **Cons:** bathrooms have tacky plastic tiles, restaurant overpriced. ✉ *Calle Arroyo de Santo Domingo 3* ☎ *923/262296* 🌐 *www.ac-hoteles.com* *51 rooms* *In-hotel: restaurant, bar, gym, laundry service, parking (fee), no-smoking rooms* ▭ *AE, DC, MC, V.*

$ **Hostal Plaza Mayor.** You can't beat the location of this great little *hostal,* just steps from the Plaza Mayor. Rooms are small but modern; the only drawback is the noise level on weekends (bring earplugs), when student *tunas* (musicians or bands) sing ballads at the plaza's crowded cafés until the wee hours. Reservations are advisable, as rooms fill up fast. **Pros:** good value, views of the plaza, international and polyglot staff. **Cons:** occasional noise on the street side; with porters few and far between and no elevator, hauling bags upstairs can be grueling. ✉ *Pl. del Corrillo 20* ☎ *923/262020* 📠 *923/217548* 🌐 *www.hostalplazamayor.es* *19 rooms* *In-hotel: restaurant, no elevator* ▭ *MC, V.*

$$–$$$ ★ **Rector.** From the stately entrance to the high-ceiling guest rooms, this lovely hotel is a true European experience. Rooms offer everything from twice-daily maid service to complimentary Internet hookups, while double-glazed windows eliminate virtually all street noise. Mahogany antique furniture pieces and marble bathrooms add to the elegance. The sitting areas, hallways, and breakfast room are all spotless, spacious, warm, and quiet. Owners and staff are very helpful and can tell you all about Salamanca. **Pros:** terrific, personal service; good location. **Cons:** breakfast is an additional cost (€12 per person), no balconies. ✉ *Paseo Rector Esperabé 10* ☎ *923/218482* 🌐 *www.hotelrector.com* *14 rooms* *In-hotel: bar* *AE, DC, MC, V.*

$ **San Polo.** Built on the foundations of the old Romanesque church by the same name—the ruins of which you can see through windows in the foyer and hall—this hotel is near the city center and offers an interesting architectural study of combining old and new construction. The modern facade is in striking contrast with the 11th-century ruins inside. The smallish but comfortable rooms are decorated in ocher tones, with white curtains. **Pros:** modern yet charming, friendly staff. **Cons:** noise from street, no parking available. ✉ *Arroyo de Santo Domingo 2* ☎ *923/211177* 🌐 *www.hotelsanpolo.com* *37 rooms, 1 suite* *In-room: no a/c. In-hotel: restaurant, bar* *AE, DC, MC, V.*

NIGHTLIFE

Particularly in summer, Salamanca sees the greatest influx of foreign students of any city in Spain—by day they study Spanish, and by night they fill Salamanca's bars and clubs to capacity. **Mesón Cervantes** (✉ *Entrance on southeast corner of Pl. Mayor*), an upstairs tapas bar, draws crowds to its balcony for a drink and the unparalleled views of the action below. Bask in the romantic glow emanating from stained-glass lamps in the baroque-style **Posada de las Almas** (✉ *Pl. San Boal s/n*), the preferred cocktail-and-conversation nightspot for stylish students. Wrought-iron chandeliers hang from the high wood-beam ceilings, harp-strumming angels top elegant pillars, and one entire wall of shelves showcases colorful dollhouses. After 11, a well-dressed twenty- and thirtysomething crowd comes to dance at **Camelot** (✉ *Rua Bordadores 3*), an ancient stone-wall warehouse in one corner of the 16th-century Convento de Las Ursulas. For good wine, heaping portions of tapas, and live music, try the **Café Principal** (✉ *Rua Mayor 9*). After-hours types end (if not spend) the night at **Café Moderno** (✉ *Gran Vía 75*), tucking into *chocolate con churros* at daybreak.

SHOPPING

On Sunday, the **Rastro** flea market is held on Avenida de Aldehuela. Buses leave from Plaza de España. The husband-and-wife team in tiny **Artesanía Duende** (✉ *C. San Pablo 29–31* ☎ *923/213622*) have been creating and selling unique wooden crafts for decades. Their music boxes, thimbles, photo frames, and other items are beautifully carved or stenciled with local themes, from the *bailes charros*, Salamanca's regional dance, to the floral designs embroidered on the hems of provincial dresses.

ZAMORA

248 km (154 mi) northwest of Madrid.

On the rocky bluff overlooking the gleaming surface of the Duero River, Zamora's two dozen 12th- and 13th-century Romanesque churches, more than any other European city, constitute a virtual museum of Romanesque art. An evening stroll around this ancient town, through narrow medieval alleyways and past noble facades, is a hauntingly peaceful respite from the pace of modern metropolitan life.

GETTING HERE AND AROUND

Zamora's historic center is nearly completely pedestrianized and easily manageable without resorting to public transport. The municipal bus company AURZA (*980/515010 www.ayto-zamora.org/Transporte*) connects the city outskirts with the center.

ESSENTIALS

Visitor Information Zamora (*Príncipe de Asturias 1 980/531845*).

EXPLORING

Zamora is famous for its Holy Week celebrations. The **Museo de Semana Santa** *(Holy Week Museum)* houses the sculptures paraded around the streets in processions during that time. Of relatively recent vintage, these works have an appealing provincial quality—for instance, a Crucifixion group filled with what appears to be the contents of a hardware store, including bales of rope, a saw, a spade, and numerous nails. The museum is in an unsightly modern building next to the church of Santa María. *Pl. de Santa María la Nueva 980/532295 €3 Tues.–Sat. 10–2 and 5–8, Sun. 10–2.*

Zamora's **cathedral** is in a hauntingly beautiful square at the highest and westernmost point of the old town. Most of the building is Romanesque, but it's most remarkable for its dome, which is flanked by turrets, articulated by spiny ribs, and covered in overlapping stones. The interior is notable for its early-16th-century carved choir stalls. The austere, late-16th-century cloister has a small museum, with an intricate *custodia* (monstrance, or receptacle for the Host) by Juan de Arce and some badly displayed but intriguing Flemish tapestries from the 15th and 16th centuries. *Pl. Catedral 980/530644 Cathedral free, museum €3 Mar.–Sept., Tues.–Sun. 10–2 and 5–8; Oct.–Feb., Tues.–Sun. 10–2 and 4:30–6:30.*

Surrounding Zamora's cathedral to the north is a sizable park incorporating the heavily restored **castle,** begun in the 11th century. Now a municipal school, it's open to visitors only when classes are in session. Calle Trascastillo, descending south from the cathedral to the river, allows for views of the fertile countryside to the south and the town's old **Roman bridge.** *Calle Trascastillo s/n.*

WHERE TO EAT AND STAY

$$$–$$$$ SPANISH **El Rincón de Antonio.** Zamora's finest *cocina de autor* (signature cuisine) comes off the burners behind this stone facade, served in a dining room decorated in sleek contemporary lines. Local upland ingredients and seafood dishes from the nearby Atlantic and Cantabrican coasts balance a constantly changing menu rich in creativity. Look for celebrations of

Continued on page 196

Sherry wine at the *Feria del Caballo* of Jerez de la Frontera, Cádiz.

THE WINES OF SPAIN

Copitas (traditional sherry wine glasses) and casks at González Byass winery.

After years of being in the shadows of other European wines, Spanish wines are finally gunning for the spotlight—and what has taken place is nothing short of a revolution. The wines of Spain, like its cuisine, are currently experiencing a firecracker explosion of both quality and variety that has brought a new level of interest, awareness, and recognition throughout the world, propelling them to superstar status. A generation of young, hot-to-trot winemakers has jolted dormant areas awake, rediscovered long-forgotten local grapes, and introduced top international varieties. Even the most established regions submitted to makeovers in order to keep up with these dramatic changes and compete in the global market.

THE ROAD TO GREAT WINE

(top) Vineyard in Navarra. (below) Men with *cunachos* (grape baskets) near Málaga.

In the beginning, it wasn't so rosy. Spanish wine has a long and agitated history dating back to the time when the Phoenicians introduced viticulture over 3,000 years ago. Some wines achieved fame in Roman times, and the Visigoths enacted wine laws, but in the regions under Muslim rule, winemaking slowed down for centuries. Starting in the 16th century, wine trade expanded along with the Spanish Empire, and by the 18th and 19th centuries the Sherry region *bodegas* (wineries) were already established.

In the middle of the 19th century, seeds of change blossomed throughout the Spanish wine industry. In 1846 the estate that was to become Vega Sicilia, Spain's most revered winery, was set up in Castile. Three years later the famous Tío Pepe brand was established to produce the excellent dry fino wines. Marqués de Murrieta and the Marqués de Riscal wineries opened in the 1860s creating the modern Rioja region and clearing the way for many centenary wineries. *Cava*—Spain's white or pink sparkling wine—was created the following decade in Catalunya.

After this flurry of activity, Spanish wines languished for almost a century. Vines were hit hard by phylloxera, and then a civil war and a long dictatorship left the country stagnant and isolated. Just 30 short years ago, Spain's wines were somehow split between the same dominant trio of Sherry, Rioja, and Cava, and loads of cheap, watered-down wines made by local cooperatives with little gumption to improve and even less expertise.

Starting in the 1970s, however, a wave of innovation crashed through Rioja and emergent regions like Ribera del Duero and Penedés. In the 1990s, it turned into a revolution that spread all over the landscape—and is still going strong. Today, Spain is the third largest wine producer in the world and makes enticing wines at all price ranges, in never before seen levels of quality and variety. As a result, in 2006 Spain became the second largest wine exporting country by volume, beating out France and trailing just behind Italy.

TYPE OF WINES BY AGING

A unique feature of Spanish wines is their indication of aging. DO wines (see "A *Vino* Primer" on following page) show this on mandatory back labels. They apply to white, rosé, and sparkling wines, but are much more prevalent among reds, whose requirements are the following:

Joven or Cosecha

A young wine with less than the legal *crianza* barrel-aging period. This is the basic category. But quality-oriented winemakers have begun to shun the traditional aging regulations and have produced new, cutting-edge wines in this category. To distinguish the ambitious new reds from the charming-easy-drinking *jovenés*, check the price.

Crianza

A wine aged for at least 24 months, six of which are in barrels (12 in Rioja, Ribera del Duero, and Navarra). A great bargain in top vintages from the most reliable wineries and regions.

Reserva

A wine aged for a minimum of 36 months, at least 12 of which are in oak.

Gran Reserva

Traditionally the top of the Spanish wine hierarchy, and the pride of the centenary Rioja wineries. A red wine aged for at least 24 months in oak, followed by at least an additional 36 in the bottle before release.

READING LABELS LIKE A PRO

A *VINO* PRIMER

Spain offers a daunting assortment of wine styles, regions, and varietals. But don't worry: a few pointers will help you understand unfamiliar names and terms. Most of Spain's quality wines come from designated regions called *Denominaciones de Origen* (Appelations of Origin) often abbreviated as DO. Spain has more than 60 of these areas, which are tightly regulated to protect the integrity and characteristics of the wines produced there.

Beyond international grape varieties like Cabernet Sauvignon and Chardonnay, Spain is home to several additional, high-quality varietals. Reds include Tempranillo, an early-ripening grape (the name comes from Spanish *temprano*, which means early) that blends and ages well. Garnacha is the Spanish name for France's Grenache, producing spicy, full-bodied red wines. The most common white grape is Albariño, which produces light, crisp, aromatic wines. Of growing importance is Malvasia, which makes full-bodied white wines.

1 The green and more humid areas of the Northwest deliver crisp, floral white albariños in Galicia's Rias Biaxas. In the Bierzo DO, the Mencía grape distills the essence of the schist slopes, where it grows into minerally infused red wines.

2 Moving east, in the iron-rich riverbanks of the Duero, Tempranillo grapes, here called "Tinto Fino," produce complex and age-worthy Ribera del Duero reds and hefty Toro wines. Close by, the Rueda DO adds aromatic and grassy whites from local Verdejo and adopted Sauvignon Blanc.

3 The Rioja region is a winemaker's paradise. Here a mild, nearly perfect vine-growing climate marries limestone and clay soils with Tempranillo, Spain's most noble grape, to deliver wines that possess the two main features of every great region: personality and quality. Tempranillo-based Riojas evolve from a young cherry color and aromas of strawberries and red fruits, to a brick hue, infused with scents of tobacco and leather. Whether medium or full-bodied, tannic or velvety, these reds are some of the most versatile and food-friendly wines, and have set the standard for the country for over a century.

Nearby, Navarra and three small DO's in Aragón deliver great wines made with the local Garnacha, Tempranillo, and international grape varieties.

4 Southwest of Barcelona is the region of Catalunya, which encompasses the areas of Penedés and Priorat. Catalunya is best known as the heartland of *cava*, the typically dry, sparkling wine made from three indigenous Spanish varietals: Parellada, Xarel-lo,

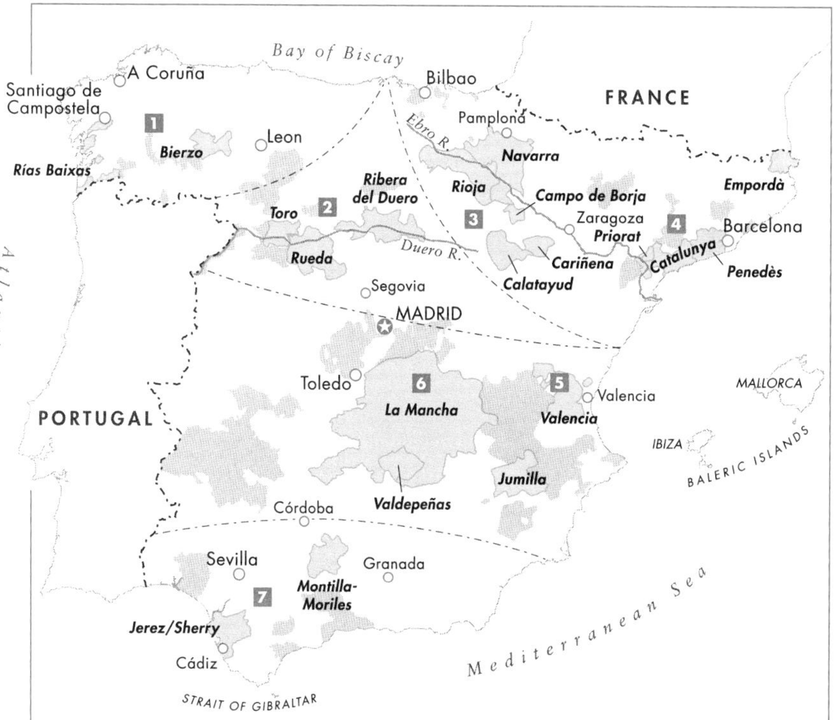

and Macabeo. The climactically varied Penedés—just an hour south of Barcelona—produces full-bodied reds like Garnacha on coastal plains, and cool-climate varietals like Riesling and Sauvignon Blanc in the mountains. Priorat is a region that has emerged into the international spotlight during the past decade, as innovative winemakers have transformed winemaking practices there. Now, traditional grapes like Garnacha and Cariñena are blended with Cabernet Sauvignon and Syrah to produce rich, concentrated reds with powerful tannins.

5 The region of Valencia is south of Catalunya on the Mediterranean coast. The wines of this area have improved markedly in recent years, with red wines from Jumilla and other appellations finding their way onto the international market. Tempranillo and Monastrell (France's Mourvèdre) are the most common reds. A local specialty of the area is Moscatel de Valencia, a highly aromatic sweet white wine.

6 In the central plateau south of Madrid, rapid investment, modernization, and replanting is resulting in medium bodied, easy drinking, and fairly priced wines made with Tempranillo (here called "Cencíbel"), Cabernet, Syrah, and even Petit Verdot, that are opening the doors to more ambitious endeavors.

7 In sun-drenched Andalusia, where the white albariza limestone soils reflect the powerful sunlight while trapping the scant humidity, the fortified Jerez (Sherry) and Montilla emerge. In all their different incarnations, from dry finos, Manzanillas, amontillados, palo cortados, and olorosos, to sweet creams and Pedro Ximénez, they are the most original wines of Spain.

JUST OFF THE VINE

Beyond Tempranillo: The current wine revolution has recovered many native varieties. Albariño, Godello, and Verdejo among the white, and Callet, Cariñena, Garnacha, Graciano, Mandó, Manto Negro, Mencía, and Monastrell among the red are currently gaining momentum and will become more popular over the years.

Cult Wines: For most of the past century, Vega Sicilia Unico was the only true cult wine from Spain. The current explosion has greatly expanded the roster: L'Ermita, Pingus, Clos Erasmus, Artadi, Cirsion, Terreus, and Termanthia are the leading names in a list that grows every year.

Vinos de Pagos: *Pago*, a word meaning plot or vineyard, is the new legal term chosen to create Spain's equivalent of a *Grand Cru* hierarchy, by protecting quality oriented wine producers that make wine from their own estates.

V.O.S. and V.O.R.S: Sherry's most dramatic change in over a century is the creation of the "Very Old Sherry" designation for wines over 20 years of age, and the addition of "Rare" for those over 30, to easier distinguish their best, oldest, and most complex wines.

Petit Verdot: Winemakers in Spain are discovering that Petit Verdot, the "little green" grape of Bordeaux, ripens much easier in warmer climates than in its birthplace. This is leading to a dramatic increase in the presence of Petit Verdot in blends, and even to the production of varietals.

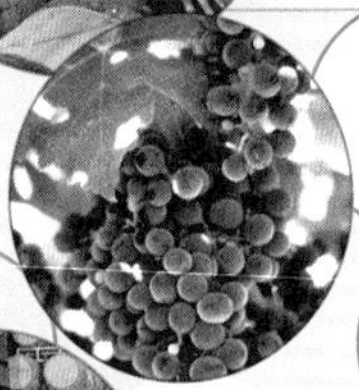

Innovative New Blends: A few wine regions have strict regulations concerning the varieties used in their wines, but most allow for experimentation. All over the country, *bodegas* are crafting wines with unsuspecting blends that involve local varieties, Tempranillo, and famous international grapes.

Andalusia's New Wines: For centuries, scorching southern Andalusia has offered world-class Sherry and Montilla wines. Now trailblazing winemakers are making serious inroads in the production of quality white, red, and new dessert wines, something deemed impossible a few years back.

Island Wines: In both the Balearic and Canary Islands the strong tourist industry helped to revive local winemaking. Although hard to find, the best Callet and Manto Negro based red wines of Majorca, and the sweet *malvasías* of Lanzarote will reward the adventurous drinker.

SUPERSTAR WINEMAKERS

Mariano García

Peter Sisseck

Alvaro Palacios

Josep Lluís Pérez

The current wine revolution has made superstars out of a group of dynamic, innovative, and visionary winemakers. Here are some of the top names:

Mariano García. His 30 years as winemaker of Vega Sicilia made him a legend. Now García displays his deft touch in the Duero and Bierzo through his four family projects: Mauro, Aalto, San Román, and Paixar.

Peter Sisseck. A Dane educated in Bordeaux, Sisseck found his calling in the old Ribera de Duero vineyards, where he crafted Pingus, Spain's quintessential new cult wine.

Alvaro Palacios. Palacios is the engine behind the current renaissance of Bierzo, and previously of Priorat, where he created L'Ermita, which is, along with Pingus, Spain's ultimate collector item.

Josep Lluís Pérez. From his base in Priorat and through his work as a winemaker, researcher, teacher, and consultant, Pérez (along with his daughter Sara Pérez) has become the main driving force in shaping the modern Mediterranean wines of Spain.

MATCHMAKING KNOW-HOW

A pairing of wine with *jamon* and Spanish olives.

Spain has a great array of regional products and cuisines, and its avant-garde chefs are culinary world leaders. As a general rule, you should match local food with local wines—but Spanish wines can be matched very well with some of the most unexpected dishes.

Albariños and the white wines of Galicia are ideal partners for seafood and fish. Dry sherries complement Serrano and Iberico hams, *lomo, chorizo,* and *salchichón* (white dry saugage), as well as olives and nuts. Pale, light, and dry finos and Manzanillas are the perfect aperitif wines, and the ideal companion for fried fish. Fuller bodied amontillados, *palo cortados,* and *olorosos* go well with hearty soups. Ribera del Duero reds are the perfect match for the outstanding local lamb. Try Priorat and other Mediterranean reds with strong cheeses and barbecue meats. Traditional Rioja harmonizes well with fowl and game. But also take an adventure off the beaten path: manzanilla and fino are great with sushi and sashimi; Rioja *reserva* fit tuna steaks; and cream sherry will not be out of place with chocolate. ¡Salud!

products from Zamora and beyond such as the *garbanzos de Fuentesauco al ajoarriero y setas de temporada* (chickpeas from Fuentesauco cooked in garlic and wild mushrooms) or, for dessert, *cañas zamoranas rellenas de haba de tonka* (crust of toast stuffed with a Venezuelan licorice-cinnamon bean). ✉ *Rúa de los Francos 6* ☎ *980/535370* ▭ *AE, DC, MC, V* ⊙ *No dinner Sun.*

$$$ **Parador de Zamora.** This restored 15th-century palace is central yet quiet, with a distinctive Renaissance patio courtyard adorned with coats of arms and classical medallions of historical and mythological figures. The views are excellent, and the staff is friendly and resourceful. Rooms are comfortable, and an elegant Castilian restaurant serves polished regional fare. **Pros:** high ceilings, good location in the old part of town near chic shops and restaurants. **Cons:** ancient and somewhat weary furnishings, the annex is an architectural eyesore, expensive (€15) breakfast. ✉ *Pl. de Viriato 5* ☎ *980/514497* ⊕ *www.parador.es* *52 rooms* *In-hotel: restaurant, bar, pool* ▭ *AE, DC, MC, V.*

VALLADOLID

96 km (60 mi) east of Zamora, 193 km (120 mi) northwest of Madrid.

Modern Valladolid, capital of Castile–León, is a sprawling industrial center in the middle of a flat stretch of Castilian terrain. The surrounding countryside has a desolate, wintry sort of beauty, its vast, brittle fields unfolding grandly toward the horizon, punctuated here and there with swaths of green. The city has an important place in Spain's history: Ferdinand and Isabella were married here, Felipe II was born and baptized here, and Felipe III made Valladolid the capital of Spain for six years. Though not an especially scenic town, Valladolid has the National Museum of Sculpture and plenty of interesting history.

GETTING HERE AND AROUND

Valladolid's Bus Turístico (€5) departs from the Acera de Recoletos at 5, 6, and 7 PM, Fri.–Sun., and at noon and 1 PM on Saturday and Sunday. AUVASA (⊕ *www.auvasa.es*) is the municipal bus company serving the outskirts and suburbs of the city.

ESSENTIALS

Visitor Information Valladolid (✉ *Acera de Recoletos [Pabellón de Cristal Campo Grande]* ☎ *983/219310*).

EXPLORING

Fodor's Choice ★ At the northernmost point of the old town is the late-15th-century Colegio de San Gregorio building where the **Museo Nacional de Escultura** *(National Museum of Sculpture)* is housed. The structure is a masterpiece itself, with playful, naturalistic detail. The facade is especially fantastic, with ribs in the form of cut-back trees, sprouting branches, and—to complete the forest motif—a row of wild men bearing mighty clubs. Across the walkway from the main museum is a Renaissance palace that houses temporary exhibitions. The main museum is arranged in rooms off an elaborate, arcaded courtyard. Its collections do for Spanish sculpture what those in the Prado do for Spanish painting—the only difference is that most people have heard of Velázquez, El Greco, and

Goya, but fewer are familiar with Alonso de Berruguete, Juan de Juni, and Gregorio Fernández, the three artists represented here.

Attendants and directional cues encourage you to tour the museum in chronological order. Begin on the ground floor, with Alonso de Berruguete's remarkable sculptures from the dismantled high altar in Valladolid's church of San Benito (1532). Berruguete, who trained in Italy under Michelangelo, is the most widely appreciated of Spain's post-medieval sculptors. He strove for pathos rather than realism, and his works have an extraordinarily expressive quality. The San Benito altar was the most important commission of his life, and the fragments here allow you to scrutinize his powerfully emotional art. In the museum's elegant chapel (which you normally see at the end of the tour) is a Berruguete retable from 1526, his first known work; on either side kneel gilded bronze figures by the Italian-born Pompeo Leoni.

Many critics of Spanish sculpture think that decline set in with the late-16th-century artist Juan de Juni, who used glass for eyes and pearls for tears. Juni's many admirers, however, find his works intensely exciting, and these pieces are, in any case, the highlights of the museum's upper floor. Dominating Castilian sculpture of the 17th century was Galician-born Gregorio Fernández, in whose works the dividing line between sculpture and theater becomes tenuous. Respect for Fernández has been diminished by the number of vulgar imitators his work has spawned, but at Valladolid you can see his art at its best. The enormous, dramatic, and moving sculptural groups assembled in the last series of rooms form a suitably spectacular climax to this fine collection. ✉ *Calle Cadenas de San Gregorio 1–2* ☎ *983/250375* 🌐 *museoescultura.mcu.es* 🎟 *€3, free Sun. 10–2* ⏲ *Sept. 21–Mar. 20, Tues.–Sat. 10–2 and 4–6; Mar. 21–Sept. 20, Tues.–Sat. 10–2 and 4–9, Sun. 10–2.*

San Pablo (✉ *Pl. de San Pablo*), a late-15th-century church, has an overwhelmingly elaborate facade.

Though the foundations of Valladolid's **cathedral** were laid in late-Gothic times, the building owes much of its appearance to designs executed in the late 16th century by Juan de Herrera, the architect of the Escorial. Further work was carried out by Alberto de Churriguera in the early 18th century. The Juni altarpiece is the one bit of color in an otherwise visually chilly place. ✉ *Calle del Cardenal Clos* ☎ *983/304362* 🎟 *www.catedral-valladolid.com* 🎟 *Cathedral free, museum €2.50* ⏲ *Tues.–Fri. 10–1:30 and 4:30–7, weekends 10–2.*

The old **university building** (✉ *Pl. Santa Cruz*) sits opposite the garden just south of the cathedral. Now housing Valladolid's University Law School, it remains an exuberant and dynamic late-baroque frontispiece by Narciso Tomé, creator of the remarkable *Transparente* in Toledo's cathedral. Valladolid's Calle Librería leads south from the main building to the magnificent **Colegio de Santa Cruz** (✉ *Pl. Colegio de Santa Cruz*), a large university college begun in 1487 in the Gothic style and completed in 1491 by Lorenzo Vázquez in a tentative, pioneering Renaissance mode. Inside is a courtyard.

WHO WAS HERE?

Three important Spanish men have integral roots in Valladolid.

An interesting remnant of Spain's golden age is the tiny house where the writer Miguel de Cervantes lived from 1603 to 1606. A haven of peace set back from a noisy thoroughfare, **Casa de Cervantes** *(Cervantes's House)* is best reached by taxi. It was furnished in the early 20th century in a pseudo-Renaissance style by the Marquis of Valle-Inclan—the creator of the El Greco Museum in Toledo. ✉ *Calle del Rastro 7* ☎ *983/308810* 🌐 *museocasacervantes.mcu.es* 🎫 *€2.40, free Sun.* ⏲ *Tues.–Sat. 9:30–3, Sun. 10–3.*

The house where Christopher Columbus died is now the **Museo de Colón** *(Columbus Museum)* with a well-arranged collection of objects and explanatory panels illuminating the explorer's life. ✉ *Plaza de Colón s/n* ☎ *983/291353* 🎫 *Free* ⏲ *Tues.–Sat. 10–2 and 5–7, Sun. 10–2.*

The Palacio de Pimentel, birthplace of Felipe II (✉ *Corner of Calle Angustias*) is a private brick home not open to the public.

WHERE TO EAT AND STAY

$$–$$$ **Olid Meliá.** This hotel, which passes for the city's best, sits on a modern block amid one of Valladolid's oldest and most attractive districts. The building was erected in the early 1970s, and the lobby and first two floors have a pristine, marble hotel-elegant feel. Rooms have blond wood furniture. For a splurge, book a room with a sauna or hot tub. **Pros:** all the comforts of a mid-to-upscale chain hotel, PCs available to rent. **Cons:** service is polite but doesn't go the extra mile. ✉ *Pl. de San Miguel 10* ☎ *983/357200* 🌐 *www.solmelia.com* *211 rooms* *In-hotel: restaurant, bar, laundry service* 💳 *AE, DC, MC, V.*

NIGHTLIFE

Valladolid is a university town with a dynamic nightlife. The cafés on the Plaza Mayor are the best places to people-watch as evening falls. Tapas are good in the Zona Santa María la Antigua and on the adjacent Calle Marqués and Calle Paraíso. The modern Zona Paco Suárez is popular with students. More fashionable and less rowdy are the Zona Cantarranas and hidden hot spots around the Plaza del Salvador. Make for the boisterous, standing-room-only **Bar El Corcho** (✉ *Calle Correos 2* ☎ *983/330861*), just off the Plaza Mayor, for Castilian tapas—the house specialty is *tostada de gambas,* toasted French bread heaped with shrimp and drizzled with olive oil. A hopping dance spot is **Disco Bagur** (✉ *C. de la Pasión 13*), off Plaza Mayor.

BURGOS

240 km (149 mi) north of Madrid on A1.

On the banks of the Arlanzón River is this small city with some of Spain's most outstanding medieval architecture. The first signs of Burgos, if you approach on the A1 from Madrid, are the spiky twin spires of its cathedral, rising above the main bridge. Burgos's second glory is its heritage as the city of El Cid, the part-historical, part-mythical hero of the Christian Reconquest of Spain. The city has been known for centuries as a center of both militarism and religion, and even today you can see more nuns on its streets than almost anywhere else in Spain. Burgos was born as a military camp in 884—a fortress built on the orders of the Christian king Alfonso III, who was having a hard time defending the upper reaches of Old Castile from the constant forays of the Arabs. It quickly became vital in the defense of Christian Spain, and its identity as an early outpost of Christianity was sealed with the founding of the Royal Convent of Las Huelgas, in 1187. Burgos also became a place of rest and sustenance for Christian pilgrims on the Camino de Santiago.

GETTING HERE AND AROUND

Burgos municipal buses cover 45 routes throughout the city, many of then originating in Plaza de España.

ESSENTIALS

Visitor Information Burgos (✉ *Plaza Alonso Martinez 7* ☎ *947/203125*).

EXPLORING

❷ ★ Start your tour of the city with the **cathedral,** the city's high point, which contains such a wealth of art and other treasures that the local burghers actually lynched their civil governor in 1869 for trying to take an inventory of it. The proud Burgalese apparently feared that the man was angling to remove riches. Most of the outside of the cathedral is sculpted in the Flamboyant Gothic style. The cornerstone was laid in 1221, and the two 275-foot towers were completed by the middle of the 14th century, though the final chapel was not finished until 1731. There are 13 chapels, the most elaborate of which is the hexagonal Condestable Chapel. You'll find the **tomb of El Cid** (1026–99) and his wife, Ximena, under the transept. El Cid (whose real name was Rodrigo Díaz de Vivar) was a feudal warlord revered for his victories over the Moors; the medieval *Song of My Cid* transformed him into a Spanish national hero.

At the other end of the cathedral, high above the West Door, is the **Reloj de Papamoscas** (Flycatcher Clock), so named for the sculptured bird that opens its mouth as the mechanism marks each hour. The grilles around the choir have some of the finest wrought-iron work in central Spain, and the choir itself has 103 delicately carved walnut stalls, no two alike. The 13th-century stained-glass windows that once shed a beautiful, filtered light were destroyed in 1813, one of many cultural casualties of Napoléon's retreating troops. ✉ *Between Pl. del Rey San Fernando and Pl. de Santa María* ☎ *947/204712* 🌐 *www.catedraldeburgos.es* 🎫 *Museum and cloister €4* ⏲ *Mar. 19–June and Oct., daily 9:30–1:15 and 4–7; July–Sept., daily 9:30–7:15; Nov.–Mar. 18, daily 10–1:15 and 4–6:45.*

❸ Across the Plaza del Rey San Fernando from the cathedral is the city's main gate, the **Arco de Santa María**; walk through toward the river and look above the arch at the 16th-century statues of the first Castilian judges; El Cid; Spain's patron saint James; and King Carlos I.

Arco de Santa María **3**

Cartuja de Miraflores **6**

Casa del Cordón **5**

Cathedral **2**

Espolón **4**

Monasterio de las Huelgas Reales **1**

4 The Arco de Santa María fronts the city's loveliest promenade, the **Espolón.** Shaded with black poplars, it follows the riverbank.

5 The **Casa del Cordón,** a 15th-century palace, is where the Catholic Monarchs received Columbus after his second voyage to the New World. It's now a bank. ✉ *Pl. de la Libertad.*

6 Founded in 1441, the **Cartuja de Miraflores** is an old Gothic monastery, the outside of which is rather sober. Inside, however, is a mass of rich decoration. The Isabelline church has an altarpiece by Gil de Siloe that is said to be gilded with the first gold brought back from the Americas. To get there, follow signs from the city's main gate. ✉ *Carretera de la Cartuja, 3 km (2 mi) east of Burgos, at end of a poplar- and elm-lined road* 🌐 *www.cartuja.org* *Free* *Church open for Mass, Mon.–Sat. at 9* AM, *Sun. at 7:30 and 10:15* AM; *main building Mon.–Sat. 10:15–3 and 4–6, Sun. 11–3 and 4–6.*

7 On the western edge of town—a mile-long walk from the town center—is the **Monasterio de Santa María La Real de Las Huelgas,** still run by nuns. Founded in 1187 by King Alfonso VIII, the convent has a royal mausoleum. All but one of the royal coffins were desecrated by Napoléon's soldiers; the one that survived contained clothes that form the basis of the convent's textile museum. Visitors are not allowed inside the Monastery, only into the museum. ✉ *Avenida Ramon y Cajal s/n, 1½ km (1 mi) southwest of town, along Paseo de la Isla and left across Malatos Bridge* ☎ *983/291395* 🌐 *www3.planalfa.es/lashuelgas* *€5, Wed. free for EU citizens* *Tues.–Sat. 10–1 and 3:45–5:30, Sun. 10:30–2.*

WHERE TO EAT AND STAY

$$–$$$$ SPANISH ★ **Casa Ojeda.** Across from the Casa del Cordón, this popular restaurant, a Castilian classic, is known for inspired Burgos standards, especially roast suckling pig and lamb straight from the 200-year-old wood oven, which looks as if it might have cooked a piglet or two for El Cid Campeador himself. Other hard-to-resist opportunities, in case you aren't feeling the roast-suckling-pig, are the *alubias rojas ibeas con chorizo, morcilla, y tocino* (red beans with chorizo sausage, blood sausage, and bacon) or the *corazones de solomillo con foie al vinagre de frambuesa* (hearts of beef fillet with duck liver and raspberry vinegar). ✉ *C. Vitoria 5* ☎ *947/209052* 🌐 *www.restauranteojeda.com* *AE, DC, MC, V* *Closed Sun.*

$$$ **Mesón del Cid.** Once a 15th-century printing press, this family-run hotel and restaurant ($$$$) has been hosting travelers and serving Burgalese food for four generations. Guest rooms face the cathedral and are done in traditional Castilian style. The dining rooms have hand-hewn beams and views of the cathedral. The *pimientos rellenos* (stuffed peppers) are excellent, as is the *sopa de Doña Jimena* (garlic soup with bread and egg). **Pros:** English-speaking staff, comfy beds, central location. **Cons:** older plumbing and door handles might break, but the staff is good about remedying the situation. ✉ *Pl. Santa María 8* ☎ *947/208715* 🌐 *www.mesondelcid.es* *56 rooms* *In-hotel: restaurant, bar, laundry service, public Wi-Fi, parking (no fee), some pets allowed* *AE, DC, MC, V.*

NIGHTLIFE

Due to its university students, Burgos has a lively *vida nocturna* (nightlife). House wines and *cañas* (small glasses of beer) flow freely at the crowded tapas bars along Calles Laín Calvo and San Juan, near the Plaza Mayor. Calle Puebla, a small, dark street off Calle San Juan, also gets constant revelers, who pop into Café Principal, La Rebotica, and Spils Cervecería for a quick drink and morsel before moving on. When you order a drink at any Burgos bar, the bartender plunks down a free *pinchito* (small tapa)—a long-standing tradition. The late-night bar scene centers on **Las Llanas,** near the cathedral.

SHOPPING

A good buy is a few bottles of local Ribera de Duero *tinto* wines, now strong rivals to those of Rioja-Alta. Burgos is also known for its cheeses. **Casa Quintanilla** (✉ *C. Paloma 17*) is a good spot to pick up some *queso de Burgos*, a fresh, ricotta-like cheese.

> **EL CAMINO**
>
> West of Burgos, the N120 to León crosses the ancient Way of St. James, occasionally revealing lovely old churches, tiny hermitages, ruined monasteries, and medieval villages in rolling fields. West of León, you can actually follow the well-worn Camino as it approaches Galicia and the very last stops on a pilgrimage route that began all the way back in France or Portugal. Making its way toward the giant cathedral in Santiago de Compostela, this Castilian leg of the Camino passes through medieval towns and quiet valleys as the terrain gets greener, wetter, and hillier. ⇨ *See Chapter 4 for more on El Camino.*

LEÓN

333 km (207 mi) northwest of Madrid, 216 km (134 mi) west of Burgos.

The ancient capital of Castile–León sits on the banks of the Bernesga River in the high plains of Old Castile. Historians say that the name of the city, which was founded as a permanent camp for the Roman legions in AD 70, has nothing to do with the proud lion that has been its emblem for centuries but is instead a corruption of the Roman word *legio* (legion). The capital of Christian Spain was moved to León from Oviedo in 914 as the Reconquest spread southward, launching the city's richest era. Walls went up around the old Roman town, and you can still see parts of the 6-foot-thick ramparts in the middle of the modern city. Today, León is a wealthy provincial capital and prestigious university town. The wide avenues of western León are lined with boutiques, and the twisting alleys of the half-timbered old town hide the bars, bookstores, and *chocolaterías* most popular with students. As you're wandering the old town, look down occasionally and you just might notice small brass scallop shells set into the street. The scallop is the symbol of St. James; the shells were installed by the town government to mark the path for modern-day pilgrims.

GETTING HERE AND AROUND

The municipal bus company Alsa (*www.alsa.es*) runs 14 lines around León, but visitors to the city will rarely need them as the historic center is composed of pedestrian-only streets. A Tren Turístico originating in front of Gaudí's Casa de Botines in Plaza San Marcelo operates during July and August.

ESSENTIALS

Visitor Information León (*Plaza de la Regla 3 987/237082*).

EXPLORING

4 ★ The pride of León is its soaring Gothic **cathedral**, on the Plaza de Regla. Its upper reaches are built with more windows than stone. Flanked by two aggressively square towers, the facade has three arched, weather-worn doorways, the middle one adorned with slender statues of the apostles. Begun in 1205, the cathedral has 125 long, slender stained-glass windows, dozens of decorative small ones, and three giant, spectacular rose windows. On sunny days, the glass casts bejeweled shafts of light on the beautifully spare, pale sandstone interior; the windows themselves depict abstract floral patterns as well as various biblical and medieval scenes. A glass door to the choir gives an unobstructed view of nave windows and the painted altarpiece, framed with gold leaf. The cathedral also contains the sculpted tomb of King Ordoño II, who moved the capital of Christian Spain to León. The **museum** has giant medieval hymnals, textiles, sculptures, wood carvings, and paintings. Look for the carved-wood Mudejar archive, with a letter of the alphabet above each door: it's one of the world's oldest file cabinets. The partial museum visit excludes the museum's best and earliest works: the Romanesque, Gothic, Renaissance, ivory carvings, and silversmithery. The full museum ticket is recommended. *Pl. de Regla 987/875770 www.catedraldeleon.org Cathedral free (€1.70 with guide), full museum €4, partial museum €2, cloister only €1 Cathedral Oct.–May, Mon.–Fri. 9:30–1:30 and 4–7, Sat. 9:30–1:30, closed Sundays; July–Sept., Mon.–Sat. 8:30–1:30 and 4–8, Sun. 8:30–2:30 and 5–8. Museum Oct.–May, weekdays 9:30–1:30 and 4–7, Sat. 9:30–1:30; June–Sept., weekdays 9:30–2 and 4–7:30, Sat. 9:30–2 and 4–7.*

6 Hidden away just north of the cathedral is the **Fundación Vela Zanetti**, a contemporary art museum made of minimalist wood beams and glass panels inside a 15th-century mansion. Zanetti was a 20th-century Castilian artist with a fondness for warm tones and a special interest in human rights. Some of his portraits recall El Greco. Art lovers will find this widely unknown museum a pleasant surprise. *C. Pablo Flórez s/n 987/244121 Free Tues.–Fri. 10–1:30 and 5–8, weekends 5–8.*

3 The **Plaza Mayor**, in the heart of the old town, is surrounded by simple half-timber houses. On Wednesday and Saturday, the arcaded plaza bustles with farmers selling produce and cheeses. Many farmers still wear wooden shoes called *madreñas,* which are raised on three heels, two in front and one in back. They were designed to walk on mud in this usually wet part of Spain.

Antiguo Convento de San Marcos **8**

Casa de Botines **5**

Cathedral **4**

Fundación Vela Zanetti **6**

MUSAC **9**

Museo de León **10**

Plaza Mayor **3**

Plaza San Martín **2**

Plaza de Santa María del Camino **1**

San Isidoro el Real **7**

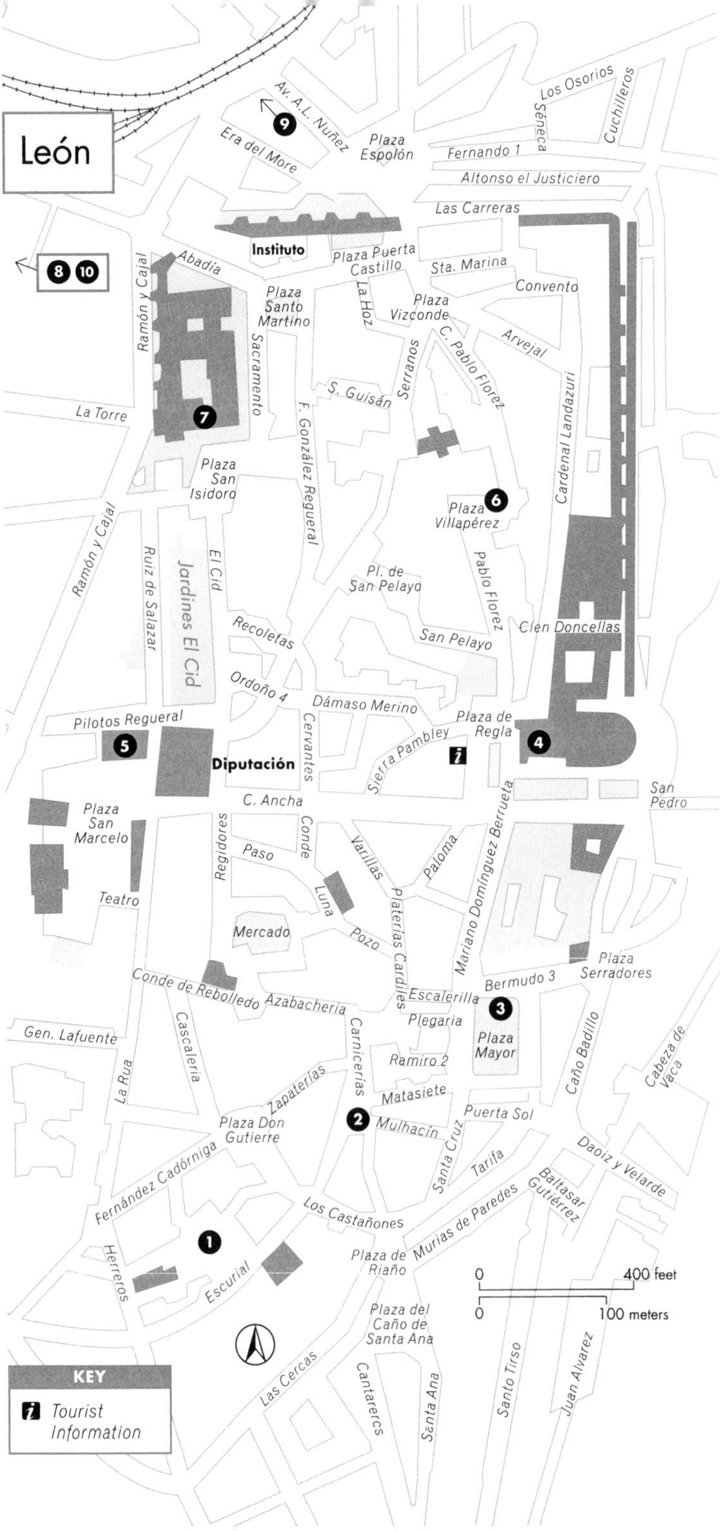

2 Most of León's tapas bars are in the 12th-century **Plaza San Martín.** This area is called the Barrio Húmedo, or Wet Neighborhood, so-called because of the large amount of wine spilled here late at night.

1 Southwest of the Plaza San Martín is the **Plaza de Santa María del Camino,** which, as the plaque here points out, used to be called Plaza del Grano (Grain Square) and hosted the local corn and bread market. Also here is the church of **Santa María del Camino,** where pilgrims stop on their way west to Santiago de Compostela. The strange allegorical fountain in the middle depicts two chubby angels clutching a pillar, symbolizing León's two rivers and the capital.

3

7 ★ The sandstone basilica of **San Isidoro el Real,** on Calle Cid, was built into the side of the city wall in 1063 and rebuilt in the 12th century. The **Panteón de los Reyes** (Royal Pantheon), adjoining the basilica, has been called the Sistine Chapel of Romanesque art for the vibrant 12th-century frescoes on its pillars and ceiling. The pantheon was the first building in Spain to be decorated with scenes from the New Testament. Look for the agricultural calendar painted on one archway, showing which farming task should be performed each month. Twenty-three kings and queens were once buried here, but their tombs were destroyed by French troops during the Napoleonic Wars. Treasures in the adjacent **Museo de San Isidoro** include a jewel-encrusted agate chalice, a richly illustrated, handwritten Bible, and many polychrome wood statues of the Virgin Mary. ☒*Pl. de San Isidoro 4* ☎*987/876161* 🌐*www.sanisidorodeleon.net* 🎫*Basilica free, Royal Pantheon and museum €4* ⏲*July and Aug., Mon.–Sat. 9–8, Sun. 9–2; Sept.–June, Mon.–Sat. 10–1:30 and 4–6:30, Sun. 10–1:30.*

5 Just south of the old town is the **Casa de Botines,** a multigabled, turreted, granite behemoth designed in the late 1800s by that controversial Catalan Antoni Gaudí. It now houses a bank. ☒*Plaza de Obispo Marcelo, 5* ☎*987/292500.*

8 Fronted by a large, airy pedestrian plaza, the sumptuous **Antiguo Convento de San Marcos** is now a luxury hotel, the Parador Hostal San Marcos. Originally a home for knights of the Order of St. James, who patrolled the Camino de Santiago, and a pit stop for weary pilgrims, the monastery you see today was begun in 1513 by the head of the order, King Ferdinand, who thought that knights deserved something better. Finished at the height of the Renaissance, the plateresque facade is a majestic swath of small sculptures (many depicting knights and lords) and intricate ornamentation. Inside are an elegant staircase and a cloister full of medieval statues. Have a drink in the bar—its tiny windows are the original defensive arrow slits. As the Anexo Monumental del Museo de León, the convent also displays historic paintings and artifacts. ☒*Pl. de San Marcos s/n* ☎*987/245061* 🎫*Museum inside the parador €0.60* ⏲*Museum, Mon. 10–2, Tues.–Sat. 10–2 and 5–8:30.*

9 **MUSAC (Museo de Arte Contemparáneo de Castilla y León)** *(Museum of Modern Art of Castillo y León)* reflects the modern León while paying homage to its history with its own cluster of buildings whose exteriors are cascaded with rectangular stained glass, like its cathedral. This "Museum of the Present" brings art to the people by offering varied

workshops and activities for children amid exhibiting modern creations from all over the globe. Films and concerts are also put on throughout the year. ✉*Av. de Los Reyes Leoneses 24* ☎*987/090000* 🌐*www.musac.org.es* 🎫*Free* ⏲*Tues.–Sun. 10–3 and 4–9.*

10 **Museo de León** displays a comprehensive history of the city and region from prehistoric to contemporary times. Pride of place belongs to the Cristo Carrizo (Carrizo Crucifix), a small 11th-century Romanesque ivory carving distinguished by its lifelike expression and powerful presence. Notable are the figure's carefully coiffed hair and beard and the loincloth arranged in sumptuous Byzantine detail. ✉*Pl. de Santo Domingo 8* ☎*987/236405* 🌐*www.museodeleon.com* 🎫*€1.20* ⏲*Tues.–Sun. 10–3 and 4–7.*

WHERE TO EAT AND STAY

¢–$$ SPANISH ✕ **Casa Pozo.** This longtime favorite, a León fixture since 1936, is across from City Hall and next to Antoni Gaudí's Palacio Botines on the historic Plaza de San Marcelo. Past the small bar, the bright dining rooms are furnished with heavy Castilian furniture. Owner Gabriel del Pozo Álvarez—also known as Pin—supervises the busy kitchen, while his son, also called Pin, is maître d'. Specialties include *asado de lechal* (roast lamb), *cangrejo de río con almejas* (river crab with clams), *bacalao con pimientos* (cod with pimiento), and *merluza rebozada* (breaded deep-fried hake). ✉*Pl. de San Marcelo 15* ☎*987/223039* 💳*AE, DC, MC, V* ⏲*No dinner Sun.*

$$–$$$$ SPANISH ✕ **Nuevo Racimo de Oro.** Upstairs from a ramshackle 12th-century tavern in the heart of the old town, this rustic restaurant, once a hostel and hospital for weary pilgrims, now specializes in roast lamb cooked in a wood-burning clay oven. The spicy *sopa de ajo leonesa* (garlic soup) is a classic, whereas the *solomillo Racimo con micuit de foie al aceite de trufa* (veal fillet with duck liver and truffle oil) is criminally good. It's worth saving some room for the *Tarta de San Marcos,* a lemon cake served with whipped cream. ✉*Pl. San Martín 8* ☎*987/214767* 🌐*www.racimodeoro.com* 💳*AE, DC, MC, V* ⏲*Closed Sun. June–Sept. No dinner Tues. Closed Wed. Oct.–May.*

$ 🏨 **Hotel Paris.** This modest but elegant establishment managed by a group of brothers and sisters is both comfortable and conveniently located. The classic basement *mesón* (student tavern and restaurant) snuggles up against the 2,000-year-old stones of a Roman wall. The hotel is on the modern thoroughfare heading east from Plaza Santo Domingo, halfway between the cathedral and the new town. Rooms are classically designed and equipped with traditional furniture. **Pros:** great location, in-house spa. **Cons:** street noise, few staff members speak English. ✉*Calle Ancha 18* ☎*987/238600* 🌐*www.hotelparisleon.com* *61 rooms* *In-hotel: restaurant, bar* 💳*AE, DC, MC, V.*

$$–$$$ Fodor's Choice ★ 🏨 **Parador Hostal San Marcos.** This magnificent parador occupies a restored 16th-century monastery and jail built by King Ferdinand to shelter pilgrims walking the Camino de Santiago. Its plateresque facade also fronts a church and museum of archaeology. Hallways and guest rooms have antiques and high-quality reproductions paired with contemporary art. The modern wing has 175 standard rooms, whereas the original section of the hotel has all the luxury suites and superior

rooms. The elegant dining room ($$$–$$$$) offers regional fare. **Pros:** among the most beautiful paradores in Spain, great restaurant. **Cons:** large disparity in quality between the most and least expensive rooms (this is the place to splurge for the good ones). ✉ *Pl. de San Marcos 7* ☎ *987/237300* 🌐 *www.parador.es* *186 rooms, 16 suites* *In-hotel: 2 restaurants, bar, pool, parking (fee)* ▭ *AE, DC, MC, V.*

NIGHTLIFE

Most of León's liveliest hangouts are clustered in Plaza Mayor and Plaza San Martín, with the former drawing couples and families and the latter a university crowd. The streets around these plazas (Calles Escalerilla, Plegaria, Ramiro 2, Matasiete, and Mulhacén) are packed with tapas bars. In the Plaza Mayor, you might want to start at **Universal, Mesón de Don Quixote, Casa Benito,** or **Bar La Plaza Mayor**. In the Plaza San Martín, the **Latino Bar at No. 10** serves a glass of house wine and your choice of one of four generous tapas.

SHOPPING

Tasty regional treats include roasted red peppers, potent brandy-soaked cherries, and candied chestnuts. You can buy these in food shops all over the city. **Cuesta Castañón** (✉ *Calle Castoñones 2* ☎ *987/260750*), near Plaza San Martín, has a great selection of wines, cured meats, cookies, preserves, and bottled delicacies, not to mention books on related topics. Friendly owner José María González lets you sample the stock. At **Hojaldres Alonso** (✉ *Calle Ancha 7*), near the cathedral, you can browse through the shelves of local goodies (candied nuts, preserves), all produced at their factory in nearby Astorga, and then head to the café in the back. The focus here is on the baked goods, particularly the *hojaldres* (puff pastries) and *torrijas,* a Castilian version of French toast. The café is a favorite among locals who come for their early evening *merienda* (usually between 6 and 8), Spain's answer to the afternoon tea. You can shop while having tapas at **Prada a Tope** (✉ *Calle Alfonso IX 9* ☎ *987/257 221*), where they're packaged by the house. For fine, funky gifts, visit **Tricosis** outside of town (✉ *Carretera León-collanzo 54* ☎ *987/283574*), a gallery opened by art students from the universities of León and Gijón. Colorful papier-mâché and experimental media form outstanding lamps, candleholders, vases, and frames.

VILLAFRANCA DEL BIERZO

135 km (84 mi) west of León.

After crossing León's grape-growing region, where the complex and full-bodied Bierzo wines are produced, you'll arrive in this medieval village, dominated by a massive and still-inhabited feudal fortress. Villafranca was a destination in itself for some of Santiago's pilgrims: visit the Romanesque church of Santiago to see the Puerta del Perdón (Door of Pardon), a sort of spiritual consolation prize for exhausted worshippers who couldn't make it over the mountains. Stroll the streets and seek out the onetime home of the infamous Grand Inquisitor Torquemada. On the way out, you can buy wine at any of three local bodegas.

ESSENTIALS

Visitor Information Villafranca del Bierzo (✉ *Av. Bernardo Díaz Ovelar 10* ☎ *987/540028*).

WHERE TO STAY

$$–$$$ **Parador de Villafranca del Bierzo.** This modern, two-story hotel overlooks the Bierzo valley. Rooms have heavy wood furniture, shuttered windows, and large baths. At the parador's restaurant ($$$$) you can dine on fresh Bierzo trout, *surtido de verduras naturales* (mixed fresh vegetables), or *tournedo con higos agridulces y setas* (a plump, juicy steak wrapped in bacon and served with marinated figs and wild mushrooms). Try the local Bierzo wine, made primarily from the Mencia grape. **Pros:** comfortable beds, quiet surroundings. **Cons:** pricey restaurant, not much to do near hotel, elevator goes only to the first floor. ✉ *Av. de Calvo Sotelo 28* ☎ *987/540175* 🌐 *www.parador.es* *38 rooms, 1 suite* *In-hotel: restaurant, bar* 💳 *AE, DC, MC, V.*

Galicia and Asturias

WITH CANTABRIA

Picos de Europa, Asturias

WORD OF MOUTH

"In the north of Spain there are some beautiful areas that are very peaceful and incredibly scenic, for instance Santander which is not far from San Sebastian. The countryside is lush and green and hilly unlike the barren moonscape of some of the south. Two beautiful villages there are Santillana and Comillas. In the northwest corner of Spain there is Galicia, which is famous not only for its capital, Santiago de Compostela, but also for its countryside and the beautiful ancient stone fishing villages that dot the coast."

—4kidsinEurope

www.fodors.com/community

WELCOME TO GALICIA AND ASTURIAS

Òista del Arenal statue, by Francisco Leiro in Vigo.

TOP REASONS TO GO

★ **Experience Gourmet Heaven:** Santiago de Compostela is said to contain more restaurants and bars per square mile than any other city in Spain. It's beautiful, too.

★ **Sleep in a Luxurious Parador:** El Parador de Baiona is arguably Spain's most elegant parador.

★ **Rugged Hikes and Exploring:** Spend days in the spectacular Picos de Europa range getting lost in forgotten mountain villages.

★ **Getting in on the Grapevine:** The Ribeira region yields Spain's—if not Europe's—finest white wines.

★ **Enjoy the Waterfront Activity:** Watch the oyster hawkers at work while dining on a fresh catch on Vigo's Rúa Pescadería.

★ **Discover Santander:** With its intoxicating schedule of live music, opera, and theater perfomances on the beach and in gardens and monasteries, the city's August festival of music and dance is the perfect backdrop for exploring this vibrant city.

1 Santiago de Compostela and Eastern Galicia. Books and movies have been written about it and millions have walked it, but you don't have to be a pilgrim to enjoy the journey of Camino de Santiago. At the end of the path is Santiago itself, a vibrant university town embedded in hills around the soaring spires of one of Spain's most emblematic cathedrals.

2 The Costa da Morte and Rías Baixas. From Fisterra ("world's end") down to Vigo and the Portuguese border, this area takes in the peaceful seaside towns of Cambados and Baiona, the exquisite beaches of Las Islas Cìes, and the beautifully preserved medieval streets of Pontevedra.

3 A Coruña and Rías Altas. Galicia has more coastline and unspoiled and untouristed beaches than anywhere else in the country. You can opt for vast expanses of sand facing the Atlantic Ocean or tiny, tucked-away coves, but take note: the water is colder than the Mediterranean and the region's weather is more unreliable.

4 Western Asturias. Also known as the Costa Sendera (Coastal Way), this partly paved nature route between Pendueles and Llanes takes in some of Asturias's most spectacular coastal scenery, including noisy *bufones* (large water spouts created naturally by the erosion of the sea) and the Playa de Ballota.

5 Picos de Europa. One of Spain's best-kept secrets, the Peaks of Europe lie across Asturias, Cantabria, and León. In addition to 2,700-meter (8,910-foot) peaks, the area has deep caves, excellent mountain refuges, and interesting wildlife. This region is also known for its fine cheeses.

6 Cantabria. Santander's wide beaches and summer music and dance festival are highlights of this mountain and maritime community. The Picos de Europa are the wildest heights on the Iberian Peninsula. The Liébana valley, the Renaissance town at Santillana del Mar, and ports and beaches such as San Vicente de la Barquera all rank among northern Spain's finest treasures.

The lively town of Santiago de Compostela.

GETTING ORIENTED

The bewitching provinces of Galicia and Asturias lie in Spain's northwest; these rugged Atlantic regions hide a corner of Spain so remote it was once called finis *terrae* (the end of the earth). Galicia is famous for Santiago de Compostela, to which Christian pilgrims travel many miles to pay homage to St. James. Asturias attracts with its verdant hills, sandy beaches, and the massive Picos de Europa mountain range. To the east, Cantabria borders the Bay of Biscay.

GALICIA AND ASTURIAS PLANNER

When to Go

Galicia can get very hot (over 30°C/90°F) between June and September, though summer is the best time for swimming and water sports and for Celtic music festivals—the **Ortigueira Festival** (*www.festivaldeortigueira.com*) in early July attracts leading Celtic musicians worldwide.

Due to its mountainous villages, Asturias is considerably cooler than Galicia, though Galicia can be rainy to the point of saturation—not for nothing is this region called Green Spain. Avoid traveling in the area in winter: the rain, wind, and freezing temperatures make driving an arduous experience.

TIP→ **Spring and fall may be the ideal time to explore, as the weather is reasonable and crowds are few.**

Festivals

Semana Santa (Holy Week) is observed in Viveiro with a barefoot procession of flagellants illuminated by hundreds of candles. On June 14, during the feast of **Corpus Christi,** Pontevedra celebrates flowers and the harvest.

The **Rapa das Bestas** (Taming of the Beasts—the breaking of wild horses) takes place the first weekend of July in various locales, including Sabuceda, near Pontevedra, and Monte Buyo, near Viveiro. **El Día de Santiago** (St. James's Day), July 25, is celebrated in Santiago with processions, fireworks, and the appearance of the dramatic *botafumeiro* (incense burner) at mass in the cathedral. On the first Sunday in August, the **Festa do Vino Albariño** (Albariño Wine Festival) enlivens Cambados with the fruit of the vine. In Gijón, during the last two weeks of August, the **Fiesta de Muestras** (Exposition) transforms Gijón into a street party with bullfights, sports, crafts, concerts, and all-night parties. On August 15, sailors and fishermen in Luarca celebrate **Nuestra Señora del Rosario** (Our Lady of the Rosary) by parading their boats through the harbor. The late September **Procesión de las Mortajas** (Procession of the Shrouded), in A Coruña, dating from the 15th century, carries survivors of illness, bad luck, or bad love around town in open coffins. At O Grove's **Festa do Marisco** (Seafood Festival), the second Sunday in October, crowds feast on lobster, mussels, clams, *percebes* (gooseneck barnacles), crabs, shrimp, and other delicacies from the sea.

In Cantabria, Santander's big event is the Festival Internacional Santander (www.festivalsantander.com), which attracts top international music and dance artists throughout August.

Discounts and Deals

Compostela 48 Horas is a €15 visitor's card providing discounts or free entry to key Santiago sites. (*www.santiagoturismo.com*).

If You Like Beaches

Galician and Asturian beaches include urban strands with big-city amenities steps from the sand, as well as remote expanses that rarely become as crowded as the beaches of the Mediterranean. When the sun comes out, you can relax on the sand on the Asturian beaches of (from east to west) Llanes, Ribadesella, Cudillero, Santa Ana (by Cadavedo), Luarca, and Tapia de Casariego, among others. In Galicia, the beaches of Muros, Noya, O Grove, the Islas Cíes, Boa, and Testal are the top destinations. For surfers, Galicia's Montalvo, Foxos, and Canelas beaches, near Pontevedra, are tops. Others with good waves are Nerga and Punto de Couso, near Cangas, and, farther south, El Vilar, Balieros, Rio Sieira, and Os Castros. Santander has excellent sandy beaches, and the beach at Laredo, between Santander and Bilbao, is one of Spain's best and relatively undiscovered.

Galician Gastronomy

Ask anybody who's spent time in Galicia and he'll tell you that one of the highlights is the food. To get to know the cuisine here is akin to understanding the Galicians, so a visit to this region will surely be enhanced with good chunks of time spent in tapas bars and restaurants. Seafood in particular is a delight. It's cooked simply, with lots of respect, and served generously. The delicious *pulpo a Gallego* (tender octopus) and the second-to-none scallops are famed, and Asturian meat and dairy products are widely considered the best in Spain. Over in Cantabria, Santander offers nonpareil seafood riches.

WHAT IT COSTS (IN EUROS)

	¢	$	$$	$$$	$$$$
Restaurants	under €6	€6–€9	€10–€15	€16–€20	over €20
Hotels	under €40	€40–€59	€60–€100	€101–€180	over €180

Prices are per person for a main course at dinner, and for two people in a standard double room in high season, excluding tax.

Planning Your Time

Santiago de Compostela is a good option for flying into and can be covered easily in a few days. From there you may want to drive down the C550 to Cambados, stopping on the way at fishing villages along the Ría de Arousa. If you stick with the coast road to Pontevedra, you can spend time there exploring the medieval streets and tapas bars, then drive down to Vigo for a lunch of oysters on Rúa Pescadería. Continue south and arrive before dark at the Baiona parador. The more adventurous will want to explore the Camino villages of Samos, Sarria, Portomarín, and Vilar de Donas—they embody all that is spiritual about Galicia.

Alternatively, travel to A Coruña, and from there head north to some of Spain's loveliest beaches and Viveiro. From here cross into Asturias and spend time in Luarca or Gijón. Another attractive option is getting lost in a small village in the Picos de Europa, spending some days there to walk, rest, and eat the local produce.

Heading farther east, Santillana del Mar's Renaissance architecture, the Altamira Caves, and the Sardinero Beach at Santander are top spots, while the fishing villages and beaches between Santander and the French border have charming ports and inlets.

GETTING HERE AND AROUND

By Air

The region's domestic airports are in Santander, A Coruña, Vigo, and near San Estéban de Pravia, 47 km (29 mi) north of Oviedo. Airport shuttles usually take the form of ALSA buses from the city bus station. Iberia sometimes runs a private shuttle from its office to the airport; inquire when you book your ticket.

By Bus

ALSA runs daily buses from Madrid to Galicia and Asturias. Once here there is good bus service between the larger destinations in the area, like Santiago, Vigo, Pontevedra, Lugo, La Coruña, Gijón, and Oviedo, though train travel is generally smoother, faster, and easier.

Getting to the smaller towns by bus can be difficult, especially those that are inland.

By Train

RENFE runs several trains a day from Madrid to Santander (4.5 hours), Oviedo (7 hours), and Gijón (8 hours), and a separate line serves Santiago (11 hours). Local RENFE trains connect the region's major cities with most of the surrounding small towns, but be prepared for dozens of stops. In addition to the RENFE trains to the area, there are narrow-gauge FEVE trains, which clatter slowly across northern Spain, connecting Galicia and Asturias with Santander, Bilbao, and Irún, on the French border. FEVE's Transcantábrico narrow-gauge train tour (🌐 *www.transcantabrico.feve.es*) is an eight-day, 1,000-km (600-mi) journey through the Basque country, Asturias, and Galicia. English-speaking guides narrate, and a private bus takes the group from train stations to artistic and natural attractions. Passengers sleep on the train in suites and dine on local specialties. Trains run May–October; the all-inclusive cost is €4,400 for two people in a suite.

By Car

A car is the recommended way to get around here. The four-lane A6 expressway links the area with central Spain; it takes about five hours (650 km [403 mi]) to get from Madrid to Santiago, and from Madrid, it's 240 km (149 mi) on the N1 or the A1 toll road to Burgos, after which you can take the N623 to complete the 390 km (242 mi) to Santander.

The expressway north from León to Oviedo and Gijón is the fastest way to cross the Cantabrian mountains. The AP9 north–south Galician ("Atlantic") expressway links A Coruña, Santiago, Pontevedra, and Vigo, and the A8 in Asturias links Santander to Ribadeo. Local roads along the coast or through the hills are more scenic but two to three times as slow.

Updated by
Paul Cannon

Spain's most Atlantic region is en route to nowhere, an end in itself. Though Galicia and Asturias are off the beaten track for many foreigners, they are not undiscovered. These magical, remote regions are sure to pull at your heartstrings, so be prepared to fall in love. In Gallego they call the feeling *morriña,* a powerful longing for a person or place you've left behind.

Stretching northwest from the lonesome Castilian plains to the rocky seacoast, Asturias and Galicia incorporate lush hills and vineyards, gorgeous *rías* (estuaries), and the country's wildest mountains, the Picos de Europa. Santander and the entire Cantabrian region are cool summer refuges with sandy beaches, high sierra (including part of the Picos de Europa Mountains), and tiny highland towns. Santander, once the main seaport for Old Castile on the Bay of Biscay, is in a mountainous zone wedged between the Basque Country and, to the west, Asturias.

Northwestern Spain is a series of rainy landscapes, stretching from your feet to the horizon. Ancient granite buildings wear a blanket of moss, and even the stone *horreos* (granaries) are built on stilts above the damp ground. Swirling fog and heavy mist help keep local folktales of the supernatural alive. Rather than a guitar, you'll hear the *gaita* (bagpipe), legacy of the Celts' settlements here in the 5th and 6th centuries BC.

Spanish families flock to these cool northern beaches and mountains each summer, and Santiago de Compostela, where a cathedral holds the remains of the apostle James, has drawn pilgrims for 900 years, leaving churches, shrines, and former hospitals in their path. Asturias, north of the main pilgrim trail, has always maintained a separate identity, isolated by the rocky Picos de Europa. This and the Basque Country are the only parts of Spain never conquered by the Moors, so Asturian architecture shows little Moorish influence. It was from a mountain base at Covadonga that the Christians won their first decisive battle against the Moors and launched the Reconquest of Spain.

EXPLORING GALICIA AND ASTURIAS

Santiago de Compostela holds center stage in Spain's northwest corner, the final destination of the Camino de Santiago. To the south are the Rías Baixas, to the west the beaches along the Atlantic coast. Farther north is the thriving port of A Coruña; the Bay of Biscay lies east, along the coast of Asturias. Oviedo is just inland, backed by the Picos de Europa, with Cantabria to the east.

ABOUT THE RESTAURANTS

Galicia and Asturias are famous for their seafood, and the quality of the fish is so high that chefs frown on drowning inherent flavors in heavy sauces or pungent seasonings; expect simplicity rather than spice. Fish specialties are *merluza a la gallega,* steamed hake with sweet paprika sauce (Galicia), and *merluza a la sidra,* steamed hake in a tangy Asturian cider sauce (Asturias). Salmon and trout from Asturian rivers are additional treats. The scallop, a symbol of the pilgrimage to Santiago, is popular in Galicia, where you can also find bars serving nothing but wine and *pulpo a feira* (boiled and broiled octopus) or *berberechos* (cockles). Cheeses are delicious all over northwestern Spain: try the tangy *queso Cabrales* (Asturian blue cheese) and the Galician *queixo tetilla* (a semisoft cheese in the form of a woman's breast), a delicious dessert when served with *membrillo* (quince jelly). Valdeón cheese, from the Picos de Europa village of the same name, is one of the world's finest blue cheeses, made from cow's milk and fat, then perfumed with herbs. In Asturias, try *fabada* (bean-and-sausage stew), and in Galicia *caldo gallego* (white beans, turnip greens, chickpeas, cabbage, and potatoes). Those savory fish or meat pies called *empanadas* are native to Galicia, as is the famous *lacón con grelos* (cured ham with turnips and chorizo sausage). Asturians enjoy *entrecôte con queso Cabrales,* steak topped with a sauce made of the local blue cheese. Cantabria's cooking is part mountain fare, such as roast kid and lamb or *cocidos* (bean stews) in the highlands, and part seafood on the coast. *Soropotun* is Santander's stew of bonito, potatoes, and vegetables.

The best Galician wine is the fruity, full-bodied, white Albariño, perfect with seafood. The acidic Ribeiro wine is often served in a ceramic bowl. Brandy buffs should try Galicia's *queimada* (which superstitious locals claim is a witches' brew), made of potent, grappalike *orujo* mixed with lemon peel, coffee beans, and sugar in an earthenware bowl, then set aflame and stirred until the desired amount of alcohol is burned off. Asturias is known for its *sidra* (hard cider), served carbonated or still. Traditionally, cider is poured from overhead and drunk immediately for full enjoyment of its effervescent flavor.

SANTIAGO DE COMPOSTELA AND EASTERN GALICIA

Entering Galicia from the Castile-León area puts travelers into the zone of Spain's famous pilgrimage, the Camino de Santiago. The main pilgrimage route, the *camino francés,* crosses the Pyrenees from France and heads west across northern Spain. If you drive into Galicia on the A6 expressway from Castile-León, you enter the homestretch. Many fly into Santiago de Compostela, however, and start exploring from here.

SANTIAGO DE COMPOSTELA

★ *650 km (403 mi) northwest of Madrid.*

A large, lively university makes Santiago one of the most exciting cities in Spain, and its cathedral makes it one of the most impressive. The building is opulent and awesome, yet its towers create a sense of harmony as a benign St. James, dressed in pilgrim's costume, looks down from his perch. Santiago de Compostela welcomes more than 4.5

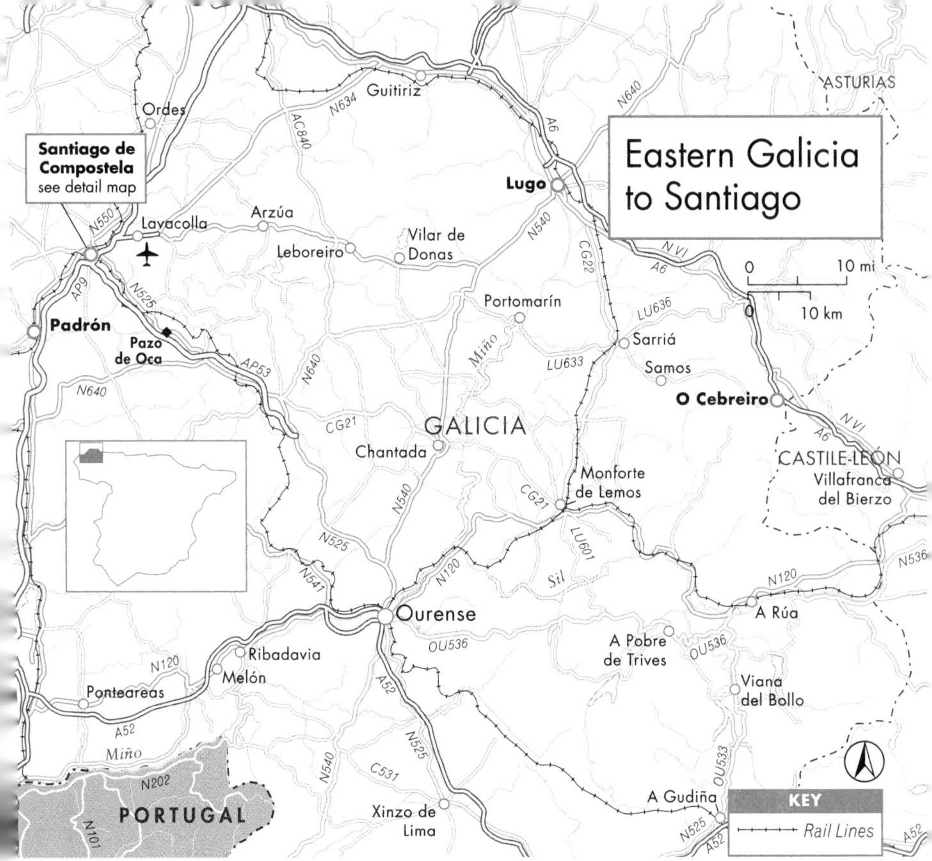

million visitors a year, with an extra million during Holy Years (the next is in 2010), when St. James's Day, July 25, falls on a Sunday.

GETTING HERE AND AROUND

Santiago is connected to Pontevedra (61 km [38 mi]) and A Coruña (57 km [35 mi]) via the AP9 tollway. The N550 is free, but slower. Parking anywhere in the city center can be difficult unless you use one of the numerous car parks around its edges.

Bus service out of Santiago's Castromil Station is plentiful, with eight daily buses to Madrid (seven to nine hours) and hourly buses to A Coruña.

The fast train Talgo service to Madrid takes seven hours; there is daily service to Irún, on the French border, via León and Santander; trains depart every hour for Galicia's other major towns.

Santiago's center is very pedestrian-friendly, and the distances between attractions are relatively short, so walking is the best, often the only, way around town.

ESSENTIALS

Bus Station Santiago (✉ *Rúa de San Caetano s/n* ☎ *981/542416*).

Bike Rentals Bici Total (✉ *Av. de Lugo 221, Santiago de Compostela* ☎ *981/564562*).

Visitor Information Santiago de Compostela (✉ *Rúa do Vilar 30–32* ☎ *981/555129*).

EXPLORING

For excellent views of the city, join a tour across the granite steps of the **cathedral roofs.** Pilgrims made the same 100-foot climb in medieval times to burn their travel-worn clothes below the *Cruz dos Farrapos* (Cross of Rags). ✉ *Pazo de Xelmírez, Praza do Obradoiro* ☎ *981/552985* *€10* *Tues.–Sun. 10–2 and 4–8.*

Santiago de Compostela's streets hold many old *pazos* (manor houses), convents, and churches that in most towns would receive headline attention. The best way to spend your time here is simply to walk around the **casco antiguo** *(old town)*, losing yourself in its maze of stone-paved narrow streets and little plazas. The most beautiful pedestrian thoroughfares are Rúa do Vilar, Rúa do Franco, and Rúa Nova—portions of which are covered by arcaded walkways called *soportales,* designed to keep walkers out of the rain.

3 From the Praza do Obradoiro, climb the two flights of stairs to the main entrance of Santiago's **cathedral.** Although the facade is baroque, the interior holds one of the finest Romanesque sculptures in the world, the **Pórtico de la Gloria.** Completed in 1188 by Maestro Mateo, this is the cathedral's original entrance, its three arches carved with figures from the Apocalypse, the Last Judgment, and Purgatory. Below Jesus is a serene St. James, poised on a carved column. Look carefully and you can see five smooth grooves, formed by the millions of pilgrims who have placed their hands here over the centuries. On the back of the pillar, people, especially students preparing for exams, lean forward to touch foreheads with the likeness of Maestro Mateo in the hope that his genius can be shared. In his bejeweled cloak, St. James presides over the **high altar.** The stairs behind it are the cathedral's focal point, surrounded by dazzling baroque decoration, sculpture, and drapery. Here, as the grand finale of their spiritual journey, pilgrims embrace St. James and kiss his cloak. In the crypt beneath the altar lie the remains of St. James and his disciples, St. Theodore and St. Athenasius.

A pilgrims' mass is celebrated every day at noon. On special, somewhat unpredictable occasions, the *botafumeiro* (huge incense burner) is attached to the thick ropes hanging from the ceiling and prepared for a ritual at the end of the pilgrims' mass: as small flames burn inside, eight strong laymen move the ropes to swing the vessel in a massive semicircle across the apse. In earlier centuries, this rite served as an air freshener—by the time pilgrims reached Santiago, they smelled a bit . . . well, you can imagine. A *botafumeiro* and other cathedral treasures are on display in the **museums** downstairs and next door. On the right (south) side of the nave is the **Porta das Praterías** (Silversmiths' Door), the only purely Romanesque part of the cathedral's facade. The statues on the portal were cobbled together from parts of the cathedral. The double doorway opens onto the **Praza das Praterías,** named for the silversmiths' shops that used to line it. ✉ *Praza do Obradoiro* ☎ *981/560527 museum, 981/583548 cathedral* *Cathedral free, combined museum ticket €5* *Cathedral daily 7 AM–9 PM; museums June–Oct., Mon.–Sat. 10–2* *and 4–8, Sun. 10–2; Nov.–May, Mon.–Sat. 10–1:30 and 4–6:30, Sun. 10–1:30.*

6 On the north side of town, off the Porta do Camino, the **Centro Galego de Arte Contemporánea** *(Galician Center for Contemporary Art)* is a stark but elegant modern building that contrasts Santiago's ancient feel. Portuguese designer Álvaro Siza built the museum of smooth, angled granite, which mirrors the medieval convent of San Domingos de Bonaval next door. Inside, a gleaming lobby of white Italian marble gives way to white-walled, high-ceiling exhibition halls flooded with light from massive windows and skylights. The museum has a good permanent collection and even better changing exhibits. ✉ *Rúa de Valle Inclán s/n* ☎ *981/546619* 🌐 *www.cgac.org* 🎫 *Free* 🕐 *Tues.–Sun. 11–8.*

1 The **Hostal dos Reis Católicos** *(Hostel of the Catholic Monarchs)*, facing the cathedral from the left, was built in 1499 by Ferdinand and Isabella to house the pilgrims who slept on Santiago's streets every night. Having lodged and revived travelers for nearly 500 years, it's the oldest refuge in the world and was converted from a hospital to a parador in 1953. The facade bears a Castilian coat of arms along with Adam, Eve, and various saints; inside, the four arcaded patios have gargoyle rainspouts said to be caricatures of 16th-century townsfolk. There's a small art gallery behind the lobby. Walk-in spectators without room keys risk being asked to leave, but for a negotiable cost, as part of a city tour, you can visit in the company of an official guide from the tourist office. ✉ *Praza do Obradoiro 1* ☎ *981/582200 hostel, 981/555129 tourist office* 🌐 *www.parador.es* 🕐 *Daily 10–1 and 4–6.*

2 Step into the rich 12th-century **Pazo de Xelmírez** *(Palace of Archbishop Xelmírez)*, an unusual example of Romanesque civic architecture with a cool, clean, vaulted dining hall. The little figures carved on the corbels (supports) in this graceful, 100-foot-long space are lifelike, partaking of food, drink, and music with great medieval gusto. Each is different, so stroll around for a tableau of mealtime merriment. ✉ *Praza do Obradoiro* 🎫 *Combined ticket for Pazo and cathedral €5* 🕐 *Tues.–Sun. 10–2 and 4–8.*

4 The wide **Praza da Quintana,** behind the Santiago cathedral, is the haunt of young travelers and folk musicians in summer.

5 North of Azabachería (follow Ruela de Xerusalén) is the **Museo de las Peregrinaciones** *(Pilgrimage Museum)*, with Camino de Santiago iconography from sculptures and carvings to *azabache* (compact black coal, or jet) items. For an overview of the history of the pilgrimage and the Camino's role in the development of the city itself, this is a key visit. ✉ *Rúa de San Miguel 4* ☎ *981/581558* 🎫 *€2.50* 🕐 *Tues.–Fri. 10–8, Sat. 10:30–1:30 and 5–8, Sun. 10:30–1:30.*

7 Next door to the Center for Contemporary Art is the **Museo do Pobo Galego** *(Galician Folk Museum)*, in the medieval convent of Santo Domingo de Bonaval. Photos, farm implements, and other displays illustrate aspects of traditional Galician life. The star attraction is the 13th-century self-supporting spiral granite staircase that still connects three floors. ✉ *Rúa de Bonaval* ☎ *981/583620* 🌐 *www.museodopobo.es* 🎫 *Free* 🕐 *Tues.–Sat. 10–2 and 4–8, Sun. 11–2.*

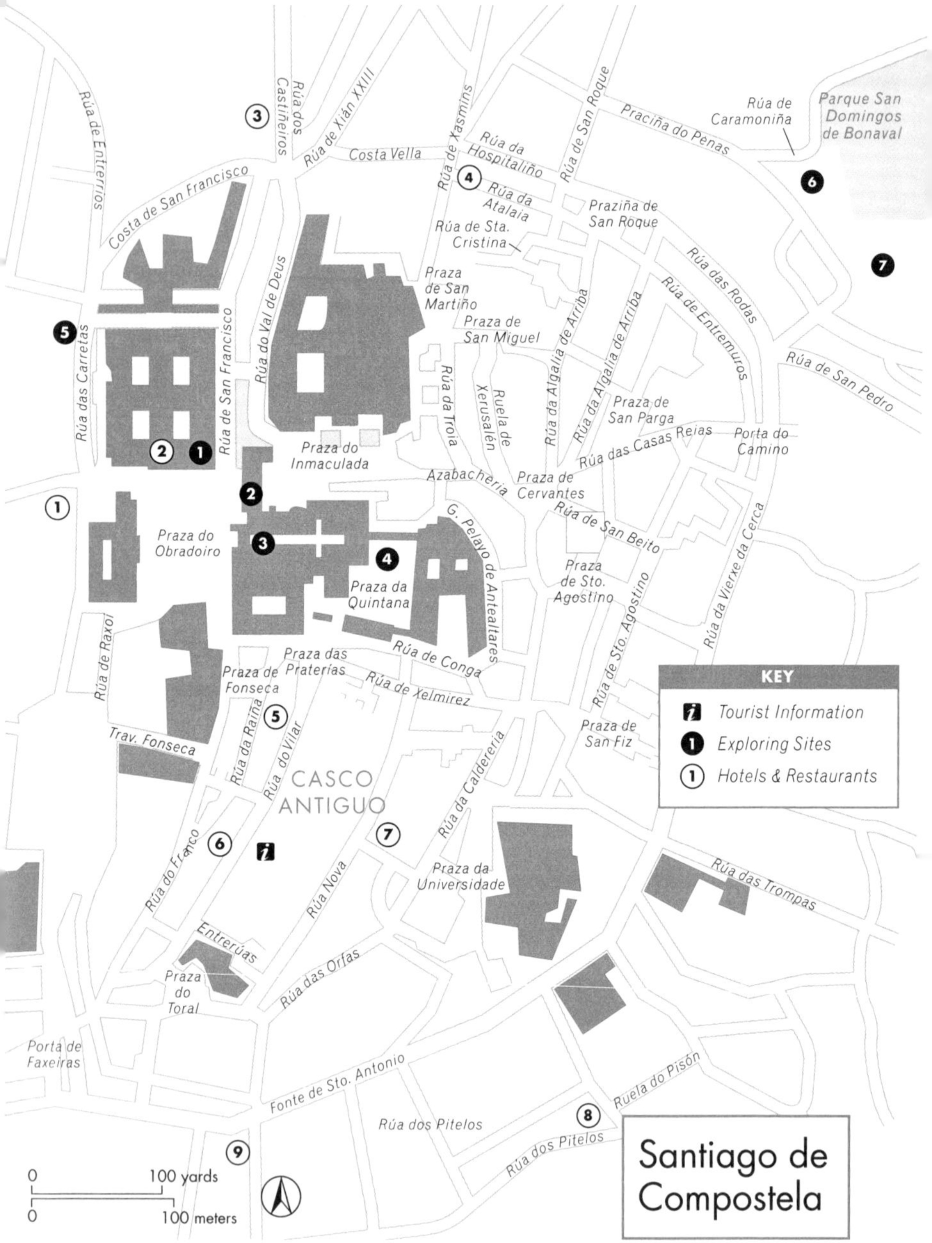

Exploring Sites

Cathedral 3
Centro Galego de Arte Contemporánea 6
Hostal de los Reyes Católicos 1
Museo de las Peregrinaciones 5
Museo do Pobo Galego 7
Pazo de Xelmírez 2
Praza da Quintana 4

Hotels & Restaurants

A Barrola 6
Carretas 5
Casa Marcelo 1
Don Gaiferos 7
Hotel-Residencia Costa Vella 4
Hotel Monumento San Francisco 3
Moncho Vilas 9
Parador de Santiago de Compostela: Hostal dos Reis Católicos 2
Pazo Cibrán 10

WHERE TO EAT AND STAY

$$–$$$$ SPANISH **A Barrola.** Now one of a chain of four restaurants in the area, A Barrola has polished wooden floors, a lively terrace, and is a favorite with the university faculty. The house salads, mussels with *santiaguiños* (crabmeat), *arroz con bogavante* (rice with lobster), and seafood empanadas are superb. If options overwhelm and you can't decide, you might opt for the *parillada de pescados* (mixed seafood grill). Sister restaurants Casa Elisa, Xantares, and A Barrola II are all equally popular and within a stone's throw on the Rúa do Franco. ✉*Rúa do Franco 29* ☎*981/577999* ▭*AE, MC, V* ⊙*Closed Mon. and Jan.–Mar.*

$$–$$$$ SEAFOOD **Carretas.** This casual spot for fresh Galician seafood is around the corner from the Hostal dos Reis Católicos. Fish dishes abound, but the specialty here is shellfish. For the full experience, order the labor-intensive *variado de mariscos,* a comprehensive platter of langostinos, king prawns, crab, and "goose" barnacles, a white or grey crustacean found in deep waters that resembles a goose's neck and head. *Salpicón de mariscos* presents the same creatures preshelled. For dessert, there's the tastier-than-it-sounds fried milk pudding. ✉*Rúa de Carretas 21* ☎*981/563111* ▭*AE, DC, MC, V* ⊙*Closed Sun.*

$$$$ SPANISH **Casa Marcelo.** When it's open, this eruption into Santiago's culinary field is a find. Leek-and-potato soup with clams, scallops in cream of seaweed, tuna carpaccio with tomato jelly, and other refined dishes based on local ingredients are the rule. The €60 prix-fixe meal (there is no à la carte) consists of a selection of six main dishes and two desserts. For wine, try the Pedralonga, a white Albariño from the Rías Baixas, whose presence in restaurants is something of a rarity. ✉*Rúa Hortas 1* ☎*981/558580* ▭*AE, MC, V* ⊙*Closed Sun.–Tues. and Feb.*

$$–$$$$ SEAFOOD **Don Gaiferos.** Tucked away behind the Rúa Nova's columned porticos is one of Santiago's most distinguished restaurants, equally popular with tourists and locals. The exposed stone walls and tile floors lend it a certain medieval charm, while the food is decidedly up to date: jumbo prawns stuffed with smoked salmon, exquisite baked scallops, and white Ribeiro and Albariño wines are among its many delights. The spicy fish stew is enough for two, and should you still have room for dessert, the *tarta de almendra* (almond tart) and the bilberry cheesecake are irresistible. ✉*Rúa Nova 23* ☎*981/583894* ▭*AE, DC, MC, V* ⊙*Closed Sun. and Dec. 24–31.*

$$$ SPANISH ★ **Moncho Vilas.** The unassuming facade of this rustic tavern belies a formidable culinary reputation; indeed, the owner of the eponymous restaurant reached a zenith when he prepared a banquet for the late Pope John Paul II (the pontiff visited Santiago in 1989). Word on the streets says Moncho is in mild decline, but with specialties including salmon with clams and *merluza a la gallega* (hake with paprika sauce) or *a la vasca* (in a green sauce), it's still a Santiago classic. ✉*Av. Villagarcia 21* ☎*981/598637* ▭*AE, DC, MC, V* ⊙*No dinner Sun. Closed Mon.*

$$$ ★ **Hotel Monumento San Francisco.** Contemporary stained-glass windows add a touch of pizzazz to the solemn interior of this converted 13th-century convent. Guest rooms are pious in nature, with Franciscan dark browns, wooden beams, and stone walls but are enlivened by views of the cathedral or gardens. Adjoining the church of the same name, the

4

San Francisco is run with monastic efficiency. **Pros:** superb location in tranquil corner of Santiago's old town; clean and tidy; easily accessible by car. **Cons:** cell-like rooms; a bit too quiet at times. ✉ *Campillo San Francisco 3* ☎ *981/581634* 🌐 *www.sanfranciscohm.com* *76 rooms* *In-hotel: restaurant, bar, pool, parking* 💳 *AE, DC, MC, V.*

$$ **Hotel-Residencia Costa Vella.** A classically Galician inn, the cheerful interior of this property is awash in smooth blond wood and natural light from floor-to-ceiling windows—the better to behold the perfect little garden, red-tile rooftops, the baroque convent of San Francisco, and the green hills beyond (ask for a garden view). Enjoy nice vistas from the airy breakfast room and reading area. Owner José also offers rooms around the corner in the sleek and spotless Hotel Altair. **Pros:** charming views; ideal location; accommodating staff. **Cons:** creaky floors; no elevator. ✉ *Rúa Porta da Pena 17* ☎ *981/569530* 🌐 *www.costavella.com* *14 rooms* *In-hotel: bar, public Wi-Fi* 💳 *AE, DC, MC, V.*

$$$$ Fodor's Choice ★ **Parador de Santiago de Compostela: Hostal dos Reis Católicos.** One of the parador chain's most highly regarded hotels, this 15th-century masterpiece was originally built as a royal hospital for sick pilgrims. A mammoth baroque doorway gives way to austere courtyards of box hedge and simple fountains, and to rooms furnished with antiques, some with canopy beds. Libredón, the restaurant ($$$–$$$$) in the grand, vaulted dining room, serves top-notch regional fare, including *lonchas de pulpo* (octopus with paprika and potato), foie gras, and *filloas de manzana y crema caramelizadas* (apple-and-caramel-cream pancakes). The tapas bar, Enxebre, is lively and informal. **Pros:** views of Obradoiro square; excellent cuisine; fascinating collection of antiques and paintings. **Cons:** confusing corridors; often filled with people on guided tours. ✉ *Praza do Obradoiro 1* ☎ *981/582200* 🌐 *www.parador.es* *137 rooms* *In-hotel: 2 restaurants, bar, parking (fee)* 💳 *AE, DC, MC, V.*

$$ **Pazo Cibrán.** This 18th-century Galician farm mansion is 7 km (4 mi) from Santiago de Compostela. Owner Mayka Iglesias maintains six rooms in the main house and five large rooms in the old stable. The antique-packed living room overlooks gardens with camellias, magnolias, palms, vines, and a bamboo walk. Breakfast is served in the *pazo* itself, with lunch and dinner available in the nearby Casa Roberto. To get here, take the N525 toward Ourense from Santiago and turn right at Km 11, after the gas station. **Pros:** personal hospitality; authentic character of a stately country home; delightful gardens. **Cons:** inaccessible without a car; poor local dining options. ✉ *Rua San Xulián de Sales* ☎ *981/511515* 🌐 *www.pazocibran.com* *11 rooms* *In-room: no a/c. In-hotel: no elevator* 💳 *AE, DC, MC, V.*

TAPAS BARS

A five-minute walk behind the Colegio San Jerónimo, **Adega Abrigadoiro** (✉ *Carreira do Conde 5* ☎ *981/563163*) serves one of the best selections of Galician delicacies in town. Behind the cathedral, **Bierzo Enxebre** (✉ *Rua La Troia 10* ☎ *981/581909*) specializes in products from El Bierzo, either at the bar or in one of the dining rooms. **La Bodeguilla de San Roque**(✉ *Rua San Roque 13* ☎ *981/564379*), one of Santiago's favorite spots for *tapeo* (tapas grazing) and *chiquiteo* (wine sampling), this tavern is a five-minute walk from the cathedral. . Specialists in small servings of great products, **O Dezaseis** (✉*Rúa de San Pedro 16* ☎*981/564880*), near the town's center, is a must on any tapas crawl.

IT'S GALLEGO TO ME

In the Gallego language, the Castilian Spanish plaza (town square) is praza and the Castilian playa (beach) is praia. Closer to Portuguese than to Castilian Spanish, Gallego is the language of choice for nearly all road signs in Galicia.

CAFÉS

Santiago is a great city for European-style coffee nursing. Popular with students, **A Caldereria** (✉*Rua Caldereria 26* ☎*981/572045*) juxtaposes contemporary and traditional aesthetics. Try the Clip Nougat: ice cream with pistachios and toasted almonds. Once a gathering place for Galician poets, the **Cafe Bar Derby** (✉*Rúa das Orfas 29* ☎*981/586417*) remains a serene place for coffee and pastries. Cozy **Iacobus** (✉*Rua Azibechería 5* ☎*981/582804* ✉*Rua Caldereria 42* ☎*981/583415*) blends stone walls with contemporary wood trim and light fixtures; there's a glass cache of coffee beans in the floor.

NIGHTLIFE AND THE ARTS

Santiago's nightlife peaks on Thursday night because many students spend weekends at home with their families. For up-to-date info on concerts, films, and clubs, pick up the *Compostelan* magazine at newsstands or check the monthly *Compostela,* available at the main tourist office on Rúa do Vilar. Bars and seafood-theme tapas joints line the old streets south of the cathedral, particularly **Rúa do Franco, Rúa da Raiña,** and **Rúa do Vilar**. A great first stop, especially if you haven't eaten dinner, is **Rúa de San Clemente**, off the Praza do Obradoiro, where several bars offer two or three plates of tapas free with each drink.

Drink to Galicia's Celtic roots with live music at **Casa das Crechas** (✉*Vía Sacra 3* ☎*981/560751*), where Celtic wood carvings hang from thick stone walls and dolls of playful Galician witches ride their brooms above the bar. Galicia's oldest pub is also one of its most unusual: **Modus Vivendi** (✉*Praza Feixóo 1*) is in a former stable. The old stone feeding trough is now a low table, and instead of stairs you walk on ridged stone inclines designed for the former occupants—horses and cattle. On weekends the bar hosts live music (jazz, ethnic, Celtic) and sometimes storytelling. **O Beiro** (✉*Rúa da Raiña 3* ☎*981/581370*) is a rustic wine bar with a laid-back professional crowd. **Retablo Concerto** (✉*Rúa Nova 13* ☎*981/564851*) is cozy and has live music on weekends.

SHOPPING

Galicia is known throughout Spain for its distinctive blue-and-white ceramics with bold modern designs, made in Sargadelos and O Castro. There is a wide selection at **Sargadelos** (✉*Rúa Nova 16* ☎*981/581905*)

SIDE TRIP FROM SANTIAGO: PADRÓN

20 km (12 mi) south of Santiago.

Padrón grew up beside the Roman port of Iría Flavia and is where the body of St. James is believed to have washed ashore after its miraculous maritime journey. The town is known for its *pimientos de Padrón,* tiny green peppers fried and sprinkled with sea salt. The fun in eating these is that one in five or so is spicy-hot. Galicia's biggest **food market** is held here every Sunday.

Padrón was the birthplace of one of Galicia's heroines, the 19th-century poet Rosalía de Castro. The lovely **Casa-Museo Rosalía de Castro,** where she lived with her husband, a historian, now displays family memorabilia. ✉ *Ctra. de Herbón* ☎ *981/811204* 🌐 *www.rosaliadecastro.org* *€1.50* ⏲ *May–Sept., Tues.–Sat. 10–2 and 4–8, Sun. 10–1:30; Oct.–Apr., Tues.–Sat. 10–1:30 and 4–7, Sun. 10–1:30.*

WHERE TO STAY

$$ ★ **A Casa Antiga do Monte.** This graceful manor house combines modern comfort with vintage furniture and Asturian architecture. The crackling fire in the dining room and the 18th-century *horreo* (granary) in the yard add up to perfect rustic comfort, and there's a swimming pool for hot days. Meals ($) include local delights such as *fabada* (bean-and-sausage stew) and *chorizo a la sidra* (chorizo sausage soaked in cider). **Pros:** authentic rustic feel; genuine hospitality; very clean. **Cons:** bit of a walk from Padrón itself. ✉ *Boca do Monte-Lestrove, 1½ km (1 mi) southwest of Padrón* ☎ *981/812400* 🌐 *www.susavilaocio.es* *16 rooms* *In-room: no a/c, Wi-Fi (some). In-hotel: restaurant, bar, pool, gym, parking (fee)* *AE, DC, MC, V.*

LUGO

27 km (17 mi) northeast of Vilar de Donas; 35 km (22 mi) east of Santiago.

ESSENTIALS

Bus Station Lugo (✉ *Pl. de la Constitución s/n* ☎ *982/223985*).

Visitor Information Lugo (✉ *Praza Maior 27, Galerías* ☎ *982/231361*).

EXPLORING

Just off the A6 freeway, Galicia's oldest provincial capital is most notable for its 2½-km (1½-mi) **Roman wall.** These beautifully preserved ramparts completely surround the hidden granite streets of the old town. The walkway on top has good views. The baroque *ayuntamiento* (city hall) has a magnificent rococo facade overlooking the tree-lined **Praza Maior** (Plaza Mayor). There's a good view of the Río Miño valley from the **Parque Rosalía de Castro,** outside the Roman walls near the cathedral. Lugo's **cathedral,** is a mixture of the Romanesque, Gothic, baroque, and neoclassical styles.

WHERE TO EAT AND STAY

$$–$$$$ SPANISH **Mesón de Alberto.** A hundred meters from the cathedral, this cozy venue has excellent Galician fare and professional service. The bar and adjoining bodega (winery) serve plenty of cheap *raciónes* (appetizers). The *surtido de quesos Gallegos* provides generous servings of four local cheeses; ask for some *membrillo* (quince jelly) to go with them and the brown, crusty corn bread. For dessert, try the *filloas flameadas con fresas* (flambéed pancakes with strawberries). The dining room upstairs

has an inexpensive set menu. ✉ *Rúa da Cruz 4* ☎ *982/228310* 💳 *AE, DC, MC, V* ⏲ *Closed Sun.*

$$ **Gran Hotel Lugo.** In a garden near the Praza Maior but outside the city walls, this spacious modern hotel has comfortable rooms done in shades of yellows and browns. Rooms overlook the garden swimming pool or a broad street. There's a spa, too, to soothe a weary travelers' limbs. **Pros:** very close to central monuments; spacious rooms; extensive spa facilities. **Cons:** the spa is costly and can get crowded; pricey parking. ✉ *Av. Ramón Ferreiro 21* ☎ *982/224152* 🌐 *www.gh-hoteles.com* *156 rooms, 11 suites* *In-hotel: restaurant, pool, spa, Wi-Fi, parking (fee)* 💳 *AE, DC, MC, V.*

O CEBREIRO

334 km (209 mi) southeast of Santiago; 72 km (45 mi) southeast of Lugo.

Deserted and haunting when it's not high season (and often fogged in or snowy to boot), O Cebreiro is a stark mountaintop hamlet built around a 9th-century church. Known for its round, thatched-roof stone huts called *pallozas*, the village has been perfectly preserved and is now an open-air museum showing what life was like in these mountains in the Middle Ages—indeed, up until a few decades ago. One hut is now a museum of the region's Celtic heritage. Higher up, at 3,648 feet, you can visit a rustic 9th-century sanctuary.

WHERE TO STAY

$ **Hostal San Giraldo de Aurillac.** This rural lodging surrounded by the distinctive, local, thatched *palloza* huts has been a fixture for weary pilgrims walking the Camino de Santiago since the 19th century. It's a good budget base for discovering the surrounding mountains, the kitchen turns out hearty home cooking, and there are lovely views of the mountains. The Santuario do Cebreiro next door is run by the same establishment. **Pros:** good food; cheap and cheerful; well located. **Cons:** spartan interior; only six rooms available; no elevator. ✉ *Calle O Cebreiro, O Cebreiro* ☎ *982/367125* 🖷 *982/367115* *6 rooms* *In-room: no a/c. In-hotel: restaurant, bar* 💳 *MC, V.*

THE COSTA DA MORTE AND RÍAS BAIXAS

West of Santiago, scenic C543 leads to the coast. Straight west, the shore is windy, rocky, and treacherous—hence its name, the "Coast of Death." The series of wide, quiet estuaries south of here is called the Rías Baixas (Low Estuaries). The hilly drive takes you through a green countryside dappled with vineyards, tiny farms, and Galicia's trademark *horreos* (granaries), most with a cross at one or both ends.

MUROS

65 km (40 mi) southwest of Santiago.

Muros is a popular summer resort with lovely, arcaded streets framed by Gothic arches. The quiet back alleys of the old town reveal some well-

SPORTS AND THE OUTDOORS

With so much rugged wilderness, Spain's northwest has become the country's main outdoor-adventure region. The Picos de Europa and the green hills of Galicia beg to be hiked, trekked, climbed, or simply walked. Ribadesella is Spain's white-water capital, with an international kayak race held in August on the Sella River from Arriondas to Ribadesella.

BALLOONING

Stable weather conditions and outstanding mountain landscapes make the Picos de Europa ideal for year-round ballooning. Flights cost from €150 for a 30-minute introduction to €545 for a three-hour trip (per person).

Contacts Globoastur (✉ *Gijón, Asturias* ☎ *985/355818* 🌐 *www.globoastur.com*).

GOLF

Asturias has golf courses in Gijón, Siero, and just outside of Llanes, atop a plateau 300 feet above sea level, where nine holes have views of the Asturian coastline, and the other nine facing the towering Picos de Europa.

Galician courses include Monte la Zapateira, near A Coruña; Domaio, in Pontevedra province; La Toja, on the island of the same name near O Grove; and Padrón. Santiago's links are near the airport, at Labacolla. Call a day in advance to reserve equipment.

Contacts Campo de Golf del Aero Club Lavacolla (✉ *General Pardiñas, 34, Lugar de Mourena* ☎ *981/888276*). **Campo Municipal de Golf de las Caldas** (✉ *Av. La Premaña s/n, Las Caldas, Oviedo* ☎ *985/798132*). **Campo Municipal la Llorea** (✉ *N632, Km 62, La Llorea, Gijón* ☎ *985/181030*). **Club de Golf de Castiello** (✉ *N632, 5 km [3 mi] from Gijón toward Santander* ☎ *985/366313*). **Club de Golf La Cuesta** (✉ *Ctra. N634, Km 298, Llanes 3 km [2 mi] east of Llanes, near Cué* ☎ *985/403–319* 🌐 *www.golflacuesta.com*). **Domaio** (✉ *San Lorenzo* ☎ *986/327051*). **La Barganiza** (✉ *San Martí de Anes-Siero, 12 km [7 mi] from Oviedo and 14 km [9 mi] from Gijón* 📬 *La Barganiza 33192–Carretera Siero-Asturias* ☎ *985/742468*). **La Toja** (✉ *El Grove* ☎ *986/730158*). **Monte la Zapateira** (✉ *C. Zapateira s/n, A Coruña* ☎ *981/285200*). **Padrón** (☎ *981/453910*).

HIKING

The tourist offices in Oviedo and Cangas de Onís can help you organize a Picos de Europa trek. The Picos visitor center in Cangas has general information, route maps, and a useful scale model of the range. In summer, another reception center opens between Lakes Enol and Ercina, on the mountain road from Covadonga. The Centro de Aventuro Monteverde can organize canoeing, canyon rappelling, spelunking, horseback riding, and jeep trips. Turismo y Aventura Viesca offers rafting, canoeing, jet skiing, climbing, trekking, bungee jumping, and archery. In A Coruña, Nortrek is a one-stop source for information and equipment pertaining to hiking, rock climbing, and skiing.

Contacts **Centro de Aventura Monteverde** (✉ *Calle Sargento Provisional 5, Cangas de Onís* ☎ *985/848079*) is closed November to March. **Nortrek** (✉ *Calle Inés de Castro 7, bajo, A Coruña* ☎ *981/151674*). **Picos de Europa visitor center** (✉ *Casa Dago, Av. Covadonga 43, Cangas de Onís* ☎ *985/848614*). **Turismo y Aventura Viesca** (✉ *Av. del Puente Romano 1, Cangas de Onís* ☎ *985/357369* 🌐 *www.aventuraviesca.com*).

HORSEBACK RIDING

Trastur leads wilderness trips on horseback through the remote valleys of western Asturias. The five- to 10-day outings are designed for both beginners and experienced cowboys; mountain cabins provide shelter along the trail. Tours begin and end in Oviedo and cost about €108 a day, all-inclusive. The Centro Hípico de Turismo Ecuestre y de Aventuras / "Granjo O Castelo" conducts horseback rides along the pilgrimage routes to Santiago from O Cebreiro and Braga (Portugal). Federación Hípica Gallega has a list of all riding facilities in Galicia.

Contacts **Centro Hípico de Turismo Ecuestre y de Aventuras / "Granja O Castelo"** (✉ *Rúa Urzáiz 91–5D, Vigo* ☎ *986/425937* 🌐 *www.galicianet.com/castelo*). **Federación Hípica Gallega** (✉ *Fotografo Luis Ksado 17, Edificio Federaciones Deportivas, Vigo* ☎ *986/213800* 📠 *986/201461* 🌐 *www.fhgallega.com*). **Trastur** (✉ *Muñalen-Cal Teso, Tineo* ☎ *985/806036 or 985/806310*).

SKIING

The region's three small ski areas cater mostly to local families. The largest is San Isidro, in the Cantabrian Mountains, with four chairlifts, eight drag lifts, and more than 22½ km (14 mi) of slopes. East of here is Valgrande Pajares, with two chairlifts, eight slopes, and cross-country trails. West of Ourense, in Galicia, Mazaneda has two chairlifts, 17 slopes, and one cross-country trail.

Contacts **Mazaneda** (✉ *A Pobra de Trives* ☎ *988/309080*). **San Isidro** (✉ *Puerto San Isidro* ☎ *987/731115*). **Valgrande Pajares** (✉ *Brañillín* ☎ *985/496123 or 985/957123*).

WATER SPORTS

In Santiago, contact diving experts Turisnorte for information on scuba lessons, equipment rental, guided dives, windsurfing, and parasailing. Courageous and experienced sailors might find yachting a spectacular way to discover hidden coastal sights; Yatesport Coruña (also in Santiago) rents private yachts and can arrange sailing lessons.

Contacts **Turisnorte** (✉ *Raxoeira 14, Milladoiro, A Coruña* ☎ *981/530009 or 902/162172*). **Yatesport Coruña** (✉ *Puerto Deportivo, Marina Sada, Sada, A Coruña* ☎ *981/620624*).

preserved Galician granite houses, but the real action takes place when fishing boats return to dock from the mussel-breeding platforms that dot the bay. At around 6 PM a siren signals the start of the *lonja* (fish auction), and anyone is welcome, though you need a special license to buy. Good nearby beaches include Praia de San Francisco and Praia de Area.

ESSENTIALS

Visitor Information Muros (☎ *981/826050*).

NOIA

30 km (19 mi) east of Muros; 36 km (22 mi) west of Santiago.

Deep within the Ría de Muros y Noia, the compact medieval town of Noia nuzzles up to the foot of the Barbanza mountain range. The Gothic church of **San Martín** rises over the old town's Praza do Tapal, facing resolutely out to sea. In the town center, **La Alameda** is a lovely sculpted park that gives way to a tiled pedestrian street lined with palm trees and wrought-iron and stone benches. You can catch glimpses of the *ría* through the trees; in the summer, the street fills with terrace cafés. Near Noia are Testal and Boa beaches.

PONTEVEDRA

55 km (34 mi) southeast of Noia; 59 km (37 mi) south of Santiago.

At the head of its *ría,* Pontevedra is approached through prefab suburbs, but the old quarter is well preserved and largely undiscovered. Speckled with bars, it can get very lively on weekends.

ESSENTIALS

Bus Station Pontevedra (✉ *Calvo Sotelo s/n* ☎ *986/852408*).

Visitor Information Pontevedra (✉ *Pl. de España* ☎ *986/850814* ✉ *La Herreria* ⏲ *July–Sept., outdoor kiosks*).

The 16th-century seafarers' basilica of **Santa María Mayor,** with a 1541 facade, has lovely, sinuous vaulting and, at the back of the nave, a Romanesque portal. At the end of the right nave is an 18th-century Christ by the Galician sculptor Ferreiro. ✉ *Av. de Santa María s/n* ☎ *986/862* *Free* ⏲ *Daily 11–1 and 6–8.*

★ Pontevedra's **Museo Provincial** is in two 18th-century mansions connected by a stone bridge. Displays include exquisite Celtic jewelry, silver from all over the world, and several large model ships. The original kitchen, with stone fireplace, is intact; nearby, descend steep wooden stairs to the reconstructed captain's chamber on the battleship *Numancia,* which limped back to Spain after the Dos de Mayo battle with Peru in 1866. Complete the loop by going upstairs in the first building, where there are Spanish and Italian paintings and some inlay work. ✉ *Praza de Leña* ☎ *986/851455* *Free* ⏲ *Tues.–Sat. 10–2 and 4–7, Sun. 11–2.*

WHERE TO EAT AND STAY

$$$–$$$$ SPANISH ★ ✕ **Casa Solla.** Pepe Solla brings Galicia's bounty to his terrace garden restaurant, 2 km (1 mi) outside of town toward O Grove. Try the *menu degustación* (tasting menu) to sample a selection of regional favorites,

Continued on page 236

Cathedral of Santiago de Compostela

EL CAMINO DE SANTIAGO

Traversing meadows, mountains, and villages across Spain, some 50,000 travelers embark each year on a pilgrimage to Galicia's Santiago de Compostela, the sacred city of St. James. Following one of seven main routes to this remote corner of Spain, the pilgrims log about 19 miles a day in a nearly 500-mile journey. Along the way, they encounter incredible hospitality by the Spaniards and trade stories with fellow adventurers. It is all part of a ritual that has been going on for centuries.

A SPIRITUAL JOURNEY

Puente La Reina, a town heavily influenced by the Pilgrim's Road to Santiago de Compostela, owes its foundation to the bridge that Queen Doña Mayor built over the Arga River.

The surge of spiritual seekers heading to Spain's northwest coast began as early as the 9th century, when news spread that the Apostle James's remains were there. By the middle of the 12th century, about 1 million pilgrims were arriving in Santiago each year. An entire industry of food hawkers, hoteliers, and trinket sellers awaited their arrival. They even had the world's first travel guide, the Codex Calixtinus (published in the 1130s), to help them on their way.

Some made the journey in response to their conscience, to do penance for their sins against God, while others were sentenced by law to make the long walk as payment for crimes against the state.

Legend claims that St. James's body was transported secretly to the area by boat after his martyrdom in Jerusalem in AD 44. The idea picked up steam in 814, when a hermit claimed to see miraculous lights in the sky, accompanied by the sound of angels singing, on a wooded hillside near Padrón. Human bones were quickly discovered at the site, and immediately—and perhaps somewhat conveniently—declared to be those of the apostle (the bones may actually have belonged to Priscillian, the leader of a 4th-century Christian sect).

Word of this important find quickly spread across a relic-hungry Europe. Within a couple of centuries, the road to Santiago had become as popular as the other two major medieval pilgrimages, to Rome and Jerusalem.

After the 12th century, pilgrim numbers began to gradually decline, due to the dangers of robbery along the route, a growing scepticism about the genuineness of St. James's remains, and the popular rise of science in place of religion. It was only in 1993, when the Galician government launched the *Xacobeo* initiative to increase the number of visitors to the region, that the pilgrimage's popularity experienced a massive resurgence. In holy years—years when July 25th, the feast of St. James Day, falls on a Sunday (the next is in 2010)—the annual number of people making the journey to Santiago doubles to 100,000. The determined bunch is composed of spiritual seekers as well as nature lovers—scenery along the route is wild and stunning, ranging from untouched beech forests in the Pyrenees to wildflower-covered plains in central Spain and verdant forests and empty peaks in Galicia.

SCALLOP SHELLS

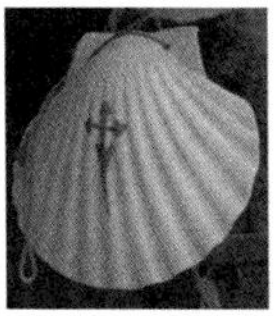

The scallop shell can be bought at most *albergues* along the route. After carrying it on the Camino, pilgrims take it home with them as a keepsake.

WHO WAS ST. JAMES?

After his martyrdom, the apostle James was revered even more by some and made a saint.

St. James the Great, brother of St. John the Evangelist (author of the Gospel of John and Revelation), was one of Jesus's first apostles. Sent by Jesus to preach that the kingdom of heaven had come, he crossed Europe and ended up in Spain. Along the way, he saved a knight from drowning in the sea. As legend goes, the knight resurfaced, covered in scallop shells. This is why Camino pilgrims carry this same type of seashell with them on their journey.

Beheaded by King Herod Agrippa on his return to Judea in AD 44, St. James, says the legend, was rescued by angels and transported in a rudderless boat to Spain, where his lifeless body was encased in stone. James is said to have resurfaced to aid the Christians in the Reconquista Battle of Clavijo, gaining him the title of Matamoros, or Moor Killer.

When the body of St. James (Santiago) was found, people came in droves to see his remains. The notion that their sins would be cleansed was developed to provide a kind of reward for walking so far, an idea no doubt subscribed to and encouraged by the church at the time.

THE PILGRIMAGE EXPERIENCE

A key Camino stop in La Rioja is the Romanesque-Gothic cathedral Santo Domingo de la Calzada, named for an 11th-century saint who had roads and bridges built along the route.

Not everyone does the route in one trip. Some split it into manageable chunks and take years to complete the whole course. Most, however, will walk an average of 19 miles (30 kilometers) a day to arrive in Santiago after a month-long trek. Though not as obvious as Dorothy's yellow-brick road to Oz, the Camino pathway, which sometimes follows a mountain trail or road and other times goes through a village or across a field, is generally so well marked that most travelers claim not to need a map (bringing one is highly recommended, however). Travelers simply follow the path's golden route markers—gold clamshell designs on blue backgrounds posted on buildings or painted on rocks and trail posts.

Walking is not the only option. Bicycles are common along the Camino and will cut the time needed to complete the pilgrimage in half. Arriving in Santiago on horseback is another option, as is walking with a donkey in tow, carrying the bags.

Your chosen mode of transport will have an effect on where you get to sleep for the night. Every town along the route has an official Camino *albergue*, or hostel, often housed in an ancient monastery or original pilgrim's hospice. (To learn where they are, ask each local tourist office.) They generally accommodate between 40 and 80 people. You can bunk down for free—though a token donation is expected—in the company of fellow walkers, but may only stay one night, unless severe Camino injuries prevent you from moving on at once. Beware that these places can fill up fast. Walkers get first priority, followed by cyclists and those on horseback, with organized walking groups at the bottom of the pecking order. Leave early every morning to ensure yourself a place for the night. (Sometimes you need to wait until after lunch for them to open.) If there is no room at the official albergues, there are plenty of paid hostels along the route. Wherever you stay, be sure to get your Pilgrims' Passport, or *credencial*, stamped, as it will provide proof along the way of just how far you've walked.

A typical day on the Camino involves setting off around 8 o'clock, walking hard through the morning—about 19 miles (30 kilometers)—then pressing on to the next village in the hope that you arrive in time to get a free bed. The afternoon is a time for catching up with fellow pilgrims, having a look around town, and doing a bit of washing. The Spanish people you meet along the way and the camaraderie with fellow pilgrims is a highlight of the trip for many.

Some albergues serve a communal evening meal, but there is always a bar in town that offers a lively atmosphere and a cheap (8–10 euros) Pilgrim's set menu (quality and fare varies; it consists of three courses plus bread and beverage). Sore feet are compared, local wine is consumed, and new walking partners are found for the following day's stage. Just make sure you get back to the albergue before curfew time around 10 or 11, or you may find a locked door awaits you at the end of the night!

On the Camino, all roads lead to the cathedral at Santiago de Compostela.

THE END OF THE LINE

Arriving at the end of the Camino de Santiago is an emotional experience. It is common to see small groups of pilgrims, hands clasped tightly together, tearfully approaching the moss- and lichen-covered cathedral in Santiago's Plaza del Obradoiro. After entering the building through the Pilgrim's Door and hugging the statue of St. James, a special mass awaits them at midday, the highlight of which is seeing the *Botafumeiro*, a giant incense-filled censer, swinging from the ceiling.

Those that have covered more than 62 miles (100 kilometers) on foot, or twice that distance on a bicycle—as evidenced by the stamped passport—can then collect their *Compostela* certificate from the Pilgrim's office (near the cathedral, at Rúa do Vilar 1). Each day, the first 10 pilgrims to request it are entitled to free meals for three days at the Hostal de los Reyes Catolicos, once a pilgrims' hospice, and now a five-star parador hotel next to the cathedral. Travelers who want to experience more scenery and gain the achievement of going to the "ends of the Earth" continue on to Finisterre at the western tip of Galicia's Atlantic coast, once thought to be the end of the world.

THE CAMINO FRANCÉS (FRENCH WAY)

The most popular of the seven main routes of the Camino de Santiago is the 497-mile (800-kilometer) Camino Francés (French Way), which starts in Spain, in Roncesvalles or Jaca, or in France, in St. Jean de Pied de Port, and

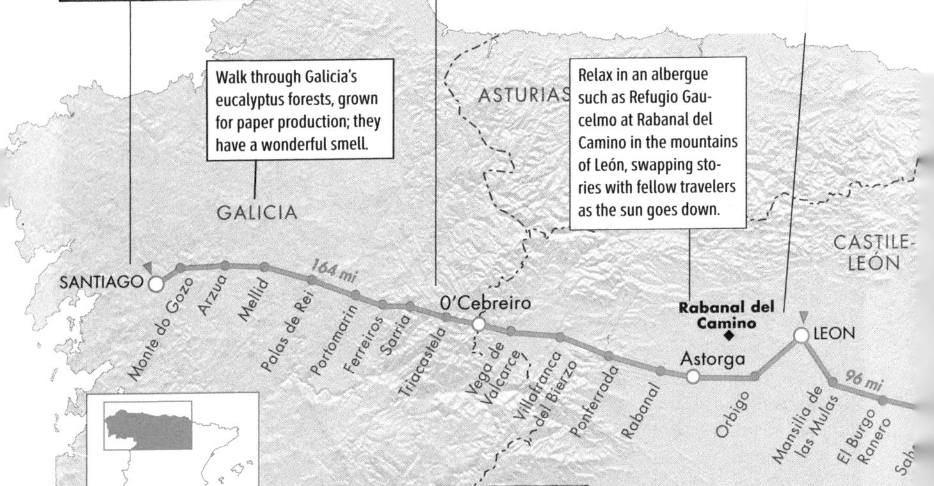

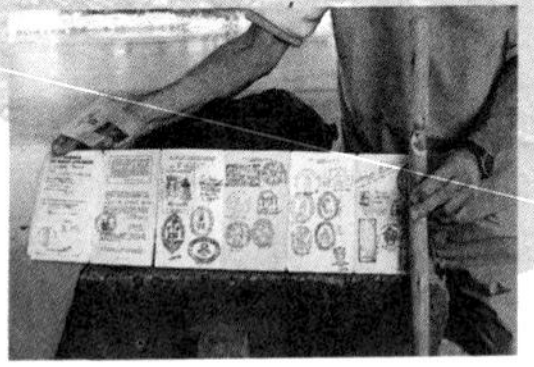

Take home a record of your trip.

IF YOU DO IT

The busiest time on the Camino is in the summer months, from June to September, when many of the Spanish make the most of their summer holidays to join the route. That means crowded paths and problems finding a room at night, particularly if you start the Camino on the first few days of any month. This time of year is also very hot. To avoid the intense heat and crowds, many pilgrims choose to start the Camino in April, May, or September. Some even make the journey in winter, but this is not at all advised, as Galicia and central Spain can get very cold at that time of year. The month of September is ideal because the heat has abated somewhat but the sun still rises early and stays out late.

You will need to be fully prepared for tough walking conditions before you set out. The single most important part of your equipment is your boot, which should be as professional as your budget allows and well worn in before you hit the trail. Other essentials include a good-quality—and crosses the high Mesata plains into Galicia. The Camino Norte (Northern Way), which runs through the woodlands of Spain's rugged north coast, is also gaining in popularity.

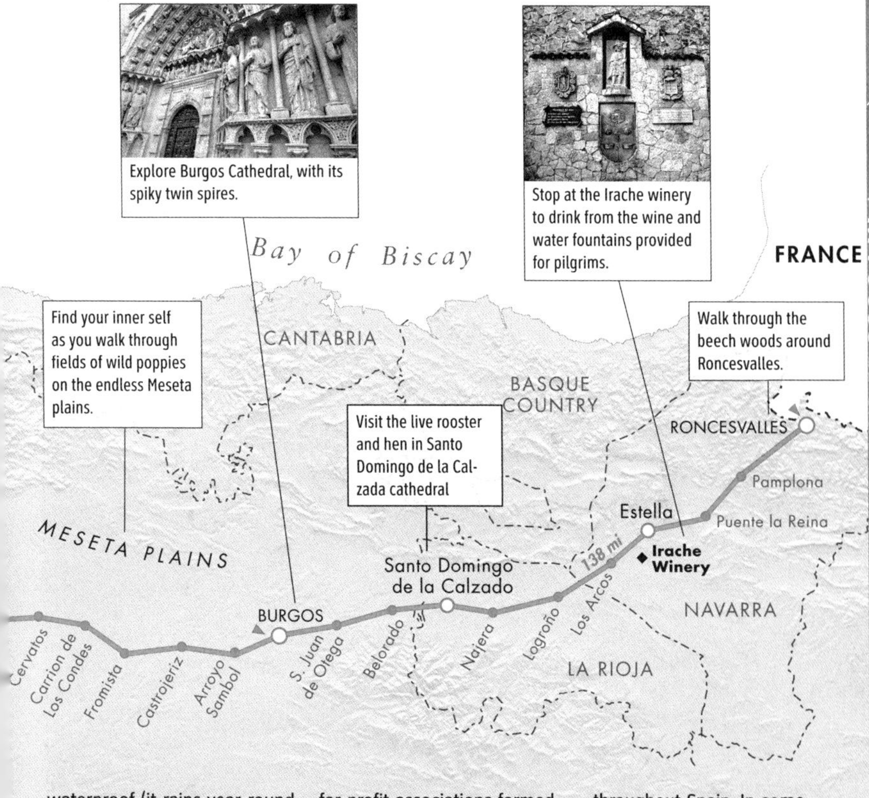

waterproof (it rains year-round in Galicia)—backpack, sleeping bag, sun cream, and a medical kit, including Vaseline and blister remedies for sore feet. Don't forget a set of earplugs as well, to keep out the sound of other pilgrims' snores and dawn departures.

To get hold of your *credencial*, or pilgrim's passport, contact one of the Camino confraternity groups. These are not-for-profit associations formed by previous pilgrims to help those in their own country who are thinking about doing the Camino (see *www.csj.org.uk/other-websites.htm* for a list of groups). You can also pick up a passport at many of the common starting points, such as the abbey in Roncesvalles, the cathedral in Le Puy, and local churches and Amigos del Camino de Santiago in villages throughout Spain. In some cases, even police stations and city halls have them.

Many albergues throughout Spain also can provide you with a valid *credencial* for a small fee.

HELPFUL WEB SITES

www.santiago-today.com
www.csj.org.uk
www.caminodesantiago.me.uk

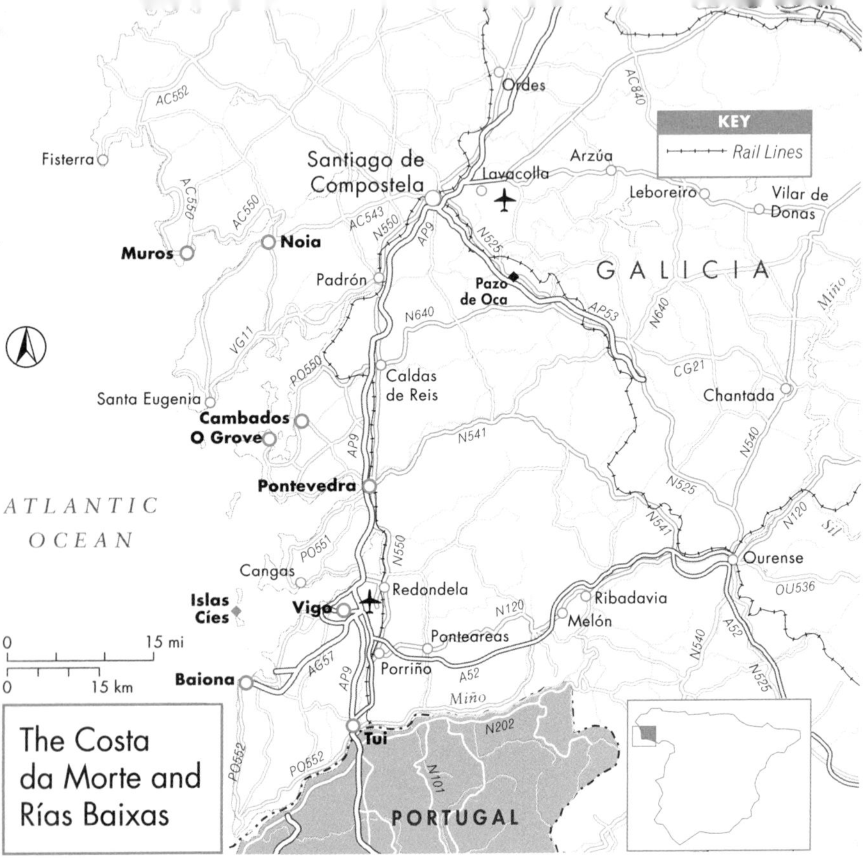

The Costa da Morte and Rías Baixas

such as *lomo de caballa* (grilled mackerel), *caldo gallego de chorizo* (Galician chorizo sausage soup), *merluza con acelga* (cod with chard), or *jarrete de cordero* (sliced lamb shank). Finish off with *fresas con espuma de coco* (strawberries with coconut foam) or *tarta de manzana* (apple tart). ✉ *Av. Sineiro 7, Ctra. de La Toja, Km 2, San Salvador de Poio* ☎ *986/872884* ▭ *AE, DC, MC, V* ⏲ *Closed Mon. and late Dec.–early Jan. No dinner Thurs. or Sun.*

$$$ **Casa del Barón.** A 16th-century manor house built on the foundations of a Roman villa in the heart of the old quarter, the fairly dark Parador de Pontevedra has a baronial stone stairway winding up from the front lobby. Guest rooms have recessed windows with lace curtains and large wooden shutters; some face a small rose garden. The restaurant ($$–$$$$), which serves fine Galician food, is full of antique mirrors, candelabras, and portraits. **Pros:** interesting collection of bric-a-brac; tranquil yet central location. **Cons:** moody staff; pokey corridors, gloomy rooms—a bit haunted house-ish. ✉ *Barón 19* ☎ *986/855800* 🌐 *www.parador.es* *47 rooms* *In-room: Wi-Fi. In-hotel: restaurant, bar, no elevator* ▭ *AE, DC, MC, V.*

TAPAS BARS

Jaqueyui. This cozy, convenient bar has a lively atmosphere and serves one of the most impressive slices of tortilla in Spain, ideally washed down with a glass of the fine house Rioja. ✉ *Rúa de Doña Tareixa 1* ☎ *986/861820.*

EN ROUTE

Driving west on the C550, you pass **the vineyards of Albariño.** As you wind your way through the small towns around here, you may come across the occasional donkey hauling wagons heaped with grapes.

O GROVE

31 km (19 mi) northwest of Pontevedra; 75 km (47 mi) south of Santiago.

4

ESSENTIALS

Visitor Information O Grove (✉ *Pl. de O Corgo 1* ☎ *986/731415*).

EXPLORING

O Grove throws an illustrious shellfish festival the second week of October, but you can enjoy the day's catch in taverns and restaurants year-round. From O Grove, you can cross a bridge to the island of **A Toxa** (La Toja), famous for its spas—the waters are said to have healing properties. Legend has it that a man abandoned an ailing donkey here and found it up on all fours, fully rejuvenated, upon his return. The island's south side has a palm-filled garden anchored on one side by the **Capilla de San Sebastián,** a tiny church covered in cockleshells.

Nearby Reboredo is the home of **Acquarium/Galicia,** one of Spain's finest aquariums, showcasing Galician marine life in an original and interactive manner. ✉ *Punta Moreiras s/n* ☎ *986/731515* 🌐 *www.acquariumgalicia.com* 🎟 *€9* ⏲ *Mon. and Thurs. 10–5, Tues., Wed., and Fri.–Sun. 10–8.*

WHERE TO EAT AND STAY

$$–$$$$ SEAFOOD

El Crisol. Photos of famous diners greet you as you enter this secluded spot, which has been serving lobster, shrimp, spider crabs, scallops, and freshly caught fish from Pontevedra's *ría* for more than 68 years. If you can't make up your mind, the house *sopa de pescados mixtos* (mixed-fish soup) combines most of the above and is an appropriate dish, given the establishment's name: El Crisol means "the melting pot." Save room for the *torta de queso,* a rich cheesecake dessert. ✉ *Hospital 10* ☎ *986/730029* 💳 *AE, DC, MC, V* ⏲ *Closed Mon. Sept.–June. No lunch Mon. July and Aug.*

$$$$

Gran Hotel Hesperia La Toja. Extravagant and exorbitant (for the region), this classic spa hotel is on the breezy island of La Toja, just across the bridge from O Grove. Surrounded by pine trees and spilling out onto a delightful golf course, the hotel has simple guest rooms, their charm slightly faded compared with the grandiose formality of the foyers and salons. Try to book a room with a sea view. **Pros:** glittering sea views; golf course; excellent services. **Cons:** expensive; rather noisy rooms. ✉ *Isla de la Toja* ☎ *986/730025* 🌐 *www.hesperia.com* *197 rooms* *In-room: Wi-Fi. In-hotel: restaurant, bar, golf course, tennis court, pool, gym, spa, beachfront* 💳 *AE, DC, MC, V.*

CAMBADOS

34 km (21 mi) north of Pontevedra; 61 km (37 mi) southwest of Santiago.

This breezy seaside town has a charming, almost entirely residential old quarter. The impressive main square, **Praza de Fefiñanes,** is bordered on almost two sides by an imposing Albariño bodega.

WHERE TO EAT AND STAY

$$–$$$$ SEAFOOD ★ **María José.** From its privileged first-floor spot across from the parador, the Ribadomar family produces inventive dishes—salads of scallops or large prawns with bacon. Specialties are *arroz de marisco caldoso* (shellfish, stock, and rice) and *mariscada* (fresh seafood). ✉ *San Gregorio 2* ☎ *986/542281* ▭ *MC, V* ⊗ *Closed last wk in Dec. and 1st wk in Jan.; no dinner Sun. Oct.–June; closed Mon. Oct.–June.*

$$$ **Parador de Cambados (El Albariño).** The bar of this airy mansion is large and inviting, with natural light and wooden booths. Rooms are warmly furnished with wrought-iron lamps, area rugs, and full-length wood shutters over small-pane windows. The kitchen's ($$–$$$$) *lenguado al vino albariño* (sole in Albariño wine sauce) is divine, and be sure to order some Albariño wine to go with it. **Pros:** easily accessible; comfortable rooms; excellent dining. **Cons:** it's almost perfect, but still a bit pricey. ✉ *Paseo de Cervantes s/n* ☎ *986/542250* ⊕ *www.parador.es* *58 rooms* *In-room: Wi-Fi. In-hotel: restaurant, tennis court, pool* ▭ *AE, DC, MC, V.*

SHOPPING

Cambados is the hub for Albariño, one of Spain's best white wines—full bodied and fruity, yet fresh. **A Casa do Albariño** (✉ *Rúa Principe 3* ☎ *986/542236*) is a tiny, tasteful emporium of Galician wines and cheeses. Head to **Cucadas** (✉ *Praza de Fefiñanes* ☎ *986/542511*) for a particularly large selection of baskets, copper items, and lace.

VIGO

31 km (19 mi) south of Pontevedra, 90 km (56 mi) south of Santiago.

Vigo's formidable port is choked with trawlers and fishing boats and lined with clanging shipbuilding yards. Its sights (or lack thereof) fall far short of its commercial swagger. The city's casual appeal lies a few blocks inland where the port commotion gives way to the narrow, dilapidated streets of the old town.

ESSENTIALS

Bus Station Vigo (✉ *Av. de Madrid 57* ☎ *986/373411*).

Visitor Information Vigo (✉ *C. Cánovas del Castillo 22* ☎ *986/430577*).

EXPLORING

From 8:30 to 3:30 daily, on **Rúa Pescadería** in the barrio called La Piedra, Vigo's famed *ostreras*—a group of rubber-glove fisherwomen who have been peddling fresh oysters to passersby for more than 50 years—shuck the bushels of oysters hauled into port that morning. Healthy rivalry has made them expert hawkers who cheerfully badger all who walk by. You buy a dozen (for about €6), the women plate them and plunk a lemon on top, and you can then take your catch into any nearby restaurant and turn it into a meal. A short stroll southwest of the old town brings you to the fishermen's barrio of **El Berbés** with its pungent and cacophonous *lonja* (fish market), where fishermen sell their morning catch to vendors and restaurants. **Ribera del Berbés,** facing the port, has several seafood restaurants, most with outdoor tables in summer. South of Vigo's old town is the hilltop **Parque del Castro** (✉*Between Praza de España and Praza do Rei, beside Av. Marqués de Alcedo*), a quiet, stately park with sandy paths, palm trees, mossy embankments, and stone benches. Atop a series of steps are the remains of an old fort and a *mirador* (lookout) with fetching views of Vigo's coastline and the Islas Cíes.

4

Islas Cies. The Cíes Islands, 35 km (21 mi) west of Vigo, are a nature reserve and one of the last unspoiled refuges on the Spanish coast. From July to September, about eight boats a day leave Vigo's harbor, returning later in the day, for the round-trip fare of €12. The 45-minute ride brings you to white-sand beaches. Birds abound, and the only land transportation is your own two feet: it takes about an hour to cross the main island.

WHERE TO EAT

$–$$$ SPANISH ✕ **Bar Cocedero La Piedra.** This jovial tapas bar is perfectly located to relieve the Rúa Pescadería fisherwomen of their freshest catch, and it does a roaring lunch trade with Vigo locals. The chefs serve heaping plates of *mariscos* (shellfish) and scallops with roe at market prices. Fresh and fruity Albariño wines are the beverages of choice; the chummy, elbow-to-elbow crowd sits at round tables covered with paper, although on a nice day you might want to grab a seat on the terrace to enjoy your oysters and watch the old town bustle. ✉*Rúa Pescadería 3* ☎*986/413204* ▭*AE, DC, MC, V.*

$$–$$$$ SPANISH ✕ **El Mosquito.** Signed photos from the likes of King Juan Carlos and Julio Iglesias cover the walls of this elegant rose- and stone-wall restaurant, open since 1928. The brother-and-sister team of Manolo and Carmiña have been at the helm for the last few decades, and their specialties include *lenguado a la plancha* (grilled sole) and *navajas* (razor clams). The *tocinillos,* a sugary, caramel flan, is also definitely worth trying. The restaurant's name refers to an era when wine arrived in wooden barrels: if mosquitoes gathered at the barrel's mouth, it held good wine. ✉*Praza da Pedra 4* ☎*986/224441* ▭*AE, DC, MC, V* ⊙*Closed Sun. and Aug.*

$–$$ SPANISH ✕ **Tapas Areal.** This ample and lively bar flanked by ancient stone and exposed redbrick walls is a good spot for tapas and beer or Albariños and Ribeiros. ✉*México 36* ☎*986/418643* ▭*MC, V.*

BAIONA

12 km (8 mi) southwest of Vigo.

At the southern end of the AP9 freeway and the Ría de Vigo, Baiona (Bayona in Castilian) is a summer haunt of affluent Gallegos. When Columbus's *Pinta* landed here in 1492, Baiona became the first town to receive the news of the discovery of the New World. Once a castle,

Monte Real is one of Spain's most popular paradores; walk around the battlements for superb views. Inland from Baiona's waterfront, Paseo Marítima, a jumble of streets, has seafood restaurants and lively cafés and bars. Calle Ventura Misa is one of the main drags. On your way into or out of town, check out Baiona's **Roman bridge.** The best nearby beach is Praia de América, north of town toward Vigo.

WHERE TO EAT AND STAY

$$$$ Fodor'sChoice ★ **Parador de Baiona.** This baronial parador was built inside the walls of a medieval castle on a hilltop. Rooms are plush, and some have balconies with ocean views toward the Islas Cíes. The restaurant serves fine seafood; try a sampler of *entremeses variados* (mixed appetizers) or a *parillada de pescados* (grilled swordfish, salmon, and cod). **Pros:** stupendous medieval architecture; views of the *ría*; luxurious bathrooms. **Cons:** especially pricey for rooms with sea views (almost double the cost of a room with a patio view); occasional problems with plumbing. ✉ *Ctra. de Baiona at Monterreal* ☎ *986/355000* 🌐 *www.parador.es* 🛏 *122 rooms* *In-room: Wi-Fi. In-hotel: restaurant, bar, tennis court, pool, gym, beachfront* 💳 *AE, DC, MC, V.*

TUI

14 km (9 mi) southeast of Baiona, 26 km (16 mi) south of Vigo.

From Vigo, take the scenic coastal route PO552, which goes up the banks of the Miño River along the Portuguese border, or, if time is short, jump on the inland A55; both routes lead to Tui, where steep, narrow streets rich with emblazoned mansions suggest the town's past as one of the seven capitals of the Galician kingdom. Today it's an important border town; the mountains of Portugal are visible from the cathedral. Across the river in Portugal, the old fortress town of Valença contains reasonable shops, bars, restaurants, and a hotel with splendid views of Tui.

WHERE TO EAT AND STAY

$$$ **Parador de Tui.** This stately granite-and-chestnut hotel on the bluffs overlooking the Miño is filled with art by local artists. Guest rooms are furnished with antiques and light-colored fabrics. Views of the woods surround the dining room ($$–$$$$), where specialties from the river Miño include Atlantic salmon, lamprey eel, sea trout, and river trout. For dessert, try the *pececitos,* almond-flavor pastries made by local convent nuns. **Pros:** enticing gardens; varied services; fine fish cuisine. **Cons:** a bit of a walk from Tui proper; not inexpensive. ✉ *Av. del Portugal s/n* ☎ *986/600300* 🌐 *www.parador.es* 🛏 *32 rooms* *In-room: Wi-Fi. In-hotel: restaurant, bar, tennis court, pool, parking (no fee)* 💳 *AE, DC, MC, V.*

A CORUÑA AND RÍAS ALTAS

Galicia's gusty and rainy northern coast has inspired poets to wax lyrical about raindrops falling continuously on one's head. The sun does shine between bouts of rain, though, suffusing town and country with

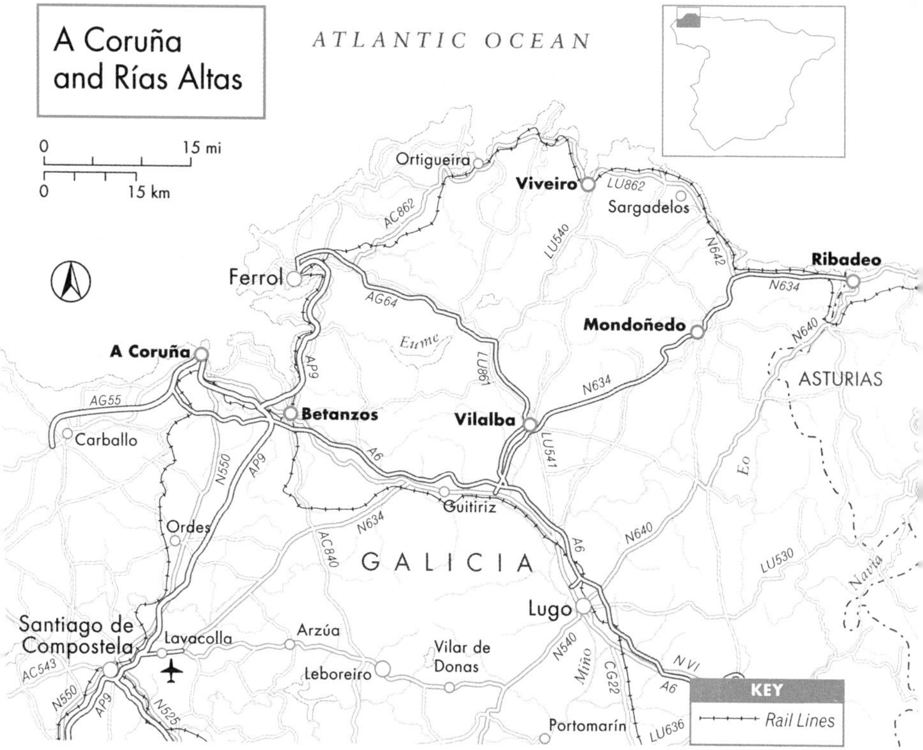

a golden glow. North of A Coruña, the Rías Altas (Upper Estuaries) notch the coast as you head east toward the Cantabrian Sea.

A CORUÑA

57 km (35 mi) north of Santiago.

One of Spain's busiest ports, A Coruña (La Coruña in Castilian) prides itself on being the most progressive city in the region. The weather can be fierce, wet, and windy—hence the glass-enclosed, white-pane galleries on the houses lining the harbor.

GETTING HERE AND AROUND

The A9 motorway provides excellent access to and from Santiago de Compostela, Pontevedra, Vigo, and Portugal, while Spain's north coast and France are accessible along the N634.

There are buses every hour from A Coruña to Santiago. Trains also operate on an hourly basis to Santiago and Pontevedra from the city's San Cristóbal rail station; Madrid can be reached in eight hours on the fast track Talgo service.

Outside the old town, the city's network of local buses shuttle back and forth between the Darsena de la Marina seafront and relatively far-flung attractions such as the Domus science museum and Torre de Hercules lighthouse.

ESSENTIALS

Bus Station A Coruña (✉ *Caballeros 21* ☎ *981/184335*).

Train Station San Cristóbal station (✉ *C. Joaquín Planells*).

Visitor Information A Coruña (✉ *Edificio Sol, Rúa Sol s/n* ☎ *981/184344*).

EXPLORING

To see why sailors once nicknamed A Coruña *la ciudad de cristal* (the glass city), stroll **Dársena de la Marina,** said to be the longest seaside promenade in Europe. Although the congregation of boats is charming, the real sight is across the street: a long, gracefully curved row of houses. Built by fishermen in the 18th century, the houses face *away* from the sea—at the end of a long day, these men were tired of looking at the water. Nets were hung from the porches to dry, and fish was sold on the street below. When Galicia's first glass factory opened nearby, someone thought to enclose these porches in glass, like the latticed stern galleries of oceangoing galleons, to keep wind and rain at bay. The resulting **glass galleries** ultimately spread across the harbor and eventually throughout Galicia.

Plaza de María Pita is the focal point of the *ciudad vieja* (old town). Its north side is given over to the neoclassical **Palacio Municipal,** or city hall, built 1908–12 with three Italianate domes. The **monument** in the center, built in 1998, depicts the heroine, Maior (María) Pita. When England's Sir Francis Drake arrived to sack A Coruña in 1589, the locals were only half finished building the defensive Castillo de San Antón, and a 13-day battle ensued. When María Pita's husband died, she took up his lance, slew the Briton who tried to plant the Union Jack here, and revived the exhausted Coruñesos, inspiring other women to join the battle.

The 12th-century church of **Santiago** (✉ *Pl. de la Constitución s/n*), the oldest church in A Coruña, was the first stop on the *camino inglés* (English route) toward Santiago de Compostela. Originally Romanesque, it's now a hodgepodge of Gothic arches, a baroque altarpiece, and two 18th-century rose windows.

The **Colegiata de Santa María** (✉ *Pl. de Santa María*) is a Romanesque beauty from the mid-13th century, often called Santa María del Campo (St. Mary of the Field) because it was once outside the city walls. The facade depicts the Adoration of the Magi; the celestial figures include St. Peter, holding the keys to heaven. Because of an architectural miscalculation the roof is too heavy for its supports, so the columns inside lean outward and the buttresses outside have been thickened.

At the northeastern tip of the old town is the **Castillo de San Antón** *(St. Anthony's Castle)*, a 16th-century fort. Inside is A Coruña's **Museum of Archaeology,** with remnants of the prehistoric Celtic culture that once thrived in these parts. The collection includes silver artifacts as well as pieces of the Celtic stone forts called *castros.* ☎ *981/189850* 💶 *€2* ⏲ *July and Aug., Tues.–Sat. 10–8:30, Sun. 10–2:30; Sept.–June, Tues.–Sat. 10–7, Sun. 10–2.*

Across town, on a hill, is the **Casa de las Ciencias** *(Science Museum)*, a hands-on museum where children can learn the principles of physics and technology. *Parque de Santa Margarita 981/189844 www.casaciencias.org Museum €2, planetarium €1 Sept.–June, daily 10–7; July and Aug., daily 11–9.*

Much of A Coruña sits on a peninsula, on the tip of which is the **Torre de Hercules**—the oldest still-functioning lighthouse in the world. Originally built during the reign of Trajan, the Roman emperor born in Spain in AD 98, the lighthouse was rebuilt in the 18th century and looks strikingly modern; all that remains from Roman times are inscribed foundation stones. Scale the 245 steps for superb views of the city and coastline—if you're here on a summer weekend, the tower opens for views of city lights along the Atlantic. Lining the approach to the lighthouse are sculptures depicting figures from Galician and Celtic legends. *Ctra. de la Torre s/n 981/223730 €2 Sept.–June, daily 10–6; July and Aug., Sun.–Thurs. 10–6, Fri. and Sat. 10 AM–11:45 PM.*

Designed in the shape of a ship's sail by Japanese architect Arata Isozaki, the **Domus/Casa del Hombre** *(Museum of Mankind)* is dedicated to the study of the human being, particularly the human body. Many exhibits are interactive. An IMAX film shows a human birth. *C. Santa Teresa 1 981/189840 www.casaciencias.org Museum €2, IMAX €1 July and Aug., daily 11–9; Sept.–June, daily 10–7.*

WHERE TO EAT AND STAY

$$–$$$$ SPANISH ★ **Adega o Bebedeiro.** Steps from the ultramodern Domus, this tiny restaurant is beloved by locals for its authentic food and low prices. It feels like an old farmhouse, with stone walls and floors, a fireplace, pine tables and stools, dusty wine bottles (*adega* means "wine cellar"). Appetizers such as *setas rellenas de marisco y salsa holandesa* (wild mushrooms with seafood and hollandaise sauce) are followed by fresh fish at market prices and an ever-changing array of delicious desserts. *C. Ángel Rebollo 34 981/210609 AE, DC, MC, V Closed Mon., no dinner Sun.; closed last 2 wks in June and last 2 wks in Dec.*

$$$–$$$$ SPANISH **Casa Pardo.** Near the port, this chic, double-decker dining room has soft ocher tones, with perfectly matched wood furniture. Try the *zamburiñas rebazadas* (battered mini scallops) and then the *rape a la cazuela* (bay leaf–scented monkfish and potatoes sprinkled with paprika, baked in a clay casserole) to find out why this establishment was the first in A Coruña to be awarded a Michelin star. For dessert, there's flaky pastry with banana cream or chocolate soufflé. *Novoa Santos 15 981/280021 AE, DC, MC, V Closed Sun.*

$$–$$$$ SEAFOOD **El Coral.** The window is an altar of shellfish, with varieties of mollusks and crustaceans you've probably never seen before. Inside, wood-panel walls, crystal chandeliers, and 12 white-clad tables help create an elegant yet casual experience. Specialties include *turbante de mariscos* (a platter—literally, a "turban"—of steamed and boiled shellfish). *Callejón de la Estacada 9, at Av. Marina 981/200569 Reservations essential AE, DC, MC, V Closed Sun.*

$$–$$$ SEAFOOD ★ **La Penela.** Try at least a few crabs or mussels with béchamel, for which this restaurant is locally famous. If shellfish isn't your speed, the roast veal is also popular. Enjoy the smart, contemporary, bottle-green

dining room while feasting on fresh fish and sipping some Albariño. The restaurant occupies a modernist building on a corner of the lively Praza María Pita. Some tables have views of the harbor, or you can eat in a glassed-in terrace on the square itself. ✉*Praza María Pita 12* ☎*981/209200* ▭*AE, DC, MC, V* ⊗*Closed Sun. and Jan. 10–25.*

$$$$ **Hesperia Finisterre.** This grande dame, where the old town joins the bay, is the oldest and busiest of A Coruña's top hotels. A favorite with business folk and families, it has large rooms with modern wood furnishings and bright upholstery. Ask for a room overlooking the bay. **Pros:** port and city views; helpful staff; good leisure activities. **Cons:** inconvenient outdoor parking; unimpressive breakfast. ✉*Paseo del Parrote 2* ☎*981/205400* ⊕*www.hesperia-finisterre.com* *92 rooms* *In-room: Wi-Fi. In-hotel: restaurant, bar, tennis courts, pools, gym* ▭*AE, DC, MC, V.*

NIGHTLIFE

Begin your evening in the **Plaza de María Pita**—cafés and tapas bars proliferate off the plaza's western corners and inland. **Calles Franja, Riego de Agua, Barrera,** and **Galera** and the **Plaza del Humor** have many bars, some of which serve Ribeiro wine in bowls. Night owls head for the posh and pricey clubs around **Praia del Orzán** (Orzán Beach), particularly along Calle Juan Canalejo. For lower-key entertainment, the old town has cozy taverns. Try **A Roda 2** (✉*Capitán Troncoso 8* ☎*981/228671*) for tapas (such as octopus in its own ink and garlic garbanzo beans) and a lively evening crowd.

SHOPPING

Calle Real has boutiques with contemporary fashions. A stroll down **Calle San Andrés,** two blocks inland from Calle Real, or **Avenida Juan Flórez,** leading into the newer town, may yield some sartorial treasures. Galicia has spawned some of Spain's top designers, notably **Adolfo Dominguez** (✉*Av. Finisterre 3* ☎*981/252539*). For hats and Galician folk clothing, stop into **Sastrería Iglesias** (✉*Rúa Rego do Auga 14* ☎*981/221634*)—founded in 1864—where artisan José Luis Iglesias Rodrígues sells his textiles. Authentic Galician *zuecos* (hand-painted wooden clogs) are still worn in some villages to navigate mud; the cobbler **José López Rama** (✉*Rúa do Muiño 7* ☎*981/701068*) has a workshop 15 minutes south of A Coruña in the village of Carballo. **Alfares de Buño** (✉*Plazuela de los Angeles 6* ☎*No phone*) sells glazed terra-cotta ceramics from Bunho, 40 km (25 mi) west of A Coruña on C552. These crafts are prized by aficionados—to see where they're made, drive out to Bunho itself, where potters work in private studios all over town. Stop in to **Alfarería y Cerámica de Buño** (✉*C. Barreiros s/n, Bunho* ☎*981/721658*) to see the results. A wide selection of classic blue-and-white pottery is sold at **Cerámicas del Castro** (✉*O Castro s/n, Sada* ☎*981/620200*), north of Coruña in Sada.

BETANZOS

★ *25 km (15 mi) east of A Coruña, 65 km (40 mi) northeast of Santiago.*

The charming, slightly ramshackle medieval town of Betanzos is still surrounded by parts of its old city wall. It was an important Galician port in the 13th century but is now silted up.

ESSENTIALS

Visitor Information Betanzos (✉ *Pr. Irmáns García Naveira s/n* ☎ *981/776666*).

EXPLORING

The 1292 monastery of **San Francisco** was converted into a church in 1387 by the nobleman Fernán Perez de Andrade, whose magnificent sepulchre, to the left of the west door, has him lying on the backs of a stone bear and boar, with hunting dogs at his feet and an angel receiving his soul by his head. The 15th-century church of **Santa María de Azougue** has 15th-century statues that were stolen in 1981 but subsequently recovered. It's a few steps uphill from the church of San Francisco. The tailors' guild put up the Gothic-style church of **Santiago,** which includes a Door of Glory inspired by the one in Santiago's cathedral. Above the door is a carving of St. James as the Slayer of the Moors.

4

VILALBA

87 km (52 mi) east of A Coruña.

Known as *Terra Cha* (Flat Land) or the Galician Mesopotamia, Vilalba is the source of several rivers, most notably the Miño, which flows down into Portugal. Hills and knolls add texture to the plain.

WHERE TO EAT AND STAY

$$$ **Parador Condes de Vilalba.** Part of the inn is in a massive 15th-century tower that was once a fortress. A drawbridge leads to the two-story lobby, hung with tapestries. The three large octagonal chambers in the tower have beamed ceilings, wood floors, hand-carved Spanish furniture, and chandeliers. The restaurant ($$–$$$) offers empanada *de Rax,* made of beef loin, and empanada *de atún* (with tuna); for dessert, order the *San Simón,* a cone-shaped, birch-smoked cheese served with apples or pears. **Pros:** the historic tower itself; elegant guest rooms; spa facilities. **Cons:** the uninspiring new building across the drawbridge. ✉ *Valeriano Valdesuso s/n* ☎ *982/510011* 🌐 *www.parador.es* *48 rooms* *In-hotel: restaurant, bar, gym* *AE, DC, MC, V.*

MONDOÑEDO

34 km (20 mi) northeast of Vilalba.

Founded in 1156, this town was one of the seven capitals of the kingdom of Galicia from the 16th to early 19th century. The **cathedral,** consecrated in 1248, has a museum, a bishop's tomb with inlaid stone, and medieval murals showing the Slaying of the Innocents and St. Peter. The cathedral dominates the ancient **Plaza Mayor,** where a medieval pageant and market are held the first Sunday in August. The quiet streets and squares are filled with old buildings, monasteries, and churches, and include a medieval Jewish quarter.

The shop **El Rey de las Tartas** (✉ *Obispo Sarmiento 2* ☎ *982/521178*) is known for its dessert pies, or *tartas,* made with pastry, sponge cake, *cabello de ángel* ("angel's hair," a filling of fine strands of pumpkin and syrup), and almonds.

VIVEIRO

★ *81 km (50 mi) northeast of Vilalba.*

The once-turreted city walls of this popular summer resort are still partially intact. Two festivals are noteworthy here: the **Semana Santa** processions, when penitents follow religious processions on their knees, and the **Rapa das Bestas**, a colorful roundup of wild horses the first Sunday in July (on nearby Monte Buyo).

ESSENTIALS

Visitor Information Viveiro (✉ *Avda. Ramón Canosa s/n* ☎ *982/560879*).

WHERE TO EAT AND STAY

$$$ **Hotel Ego.** The view of the *ría* from this hilltop hotel outside Viveiro is unbeatable and every room has a view. The glassed-in breakfast room also faces the *ría,* as well as a cascade of trees; on a rainy day, you'd much rather be cooped up here than in town. Adjoining the hotel is the elegant Nito restaurant ($$–$$$$), which serves excellent Galician cuisine, such as *percebes* (gooseneck barnacles), spider crab, and lobster. **Pros:** hilltop views; relaxing public areas and spa. **Cons:** lacks distinctive character; airport terminal facade. ✉ *Playa de Area, off N642* ☎ *982/560987* *29 rooms* *In-room: Wi-Fi. In-hotel: restaurant, bar* *AE, MC, V.*

OFF THE BEATEN PATH

Distinctive blue-and-white-glazed contemporary ceramics are made at **Cerámica de Sargadelos** (✉ *Ctra. Paraño s/n, Cervo* ☎ *982/557841*), 21 km (13 mi) east of Viveiro. Watch artisans work weekdays 8:30–12:30 and 2:30–5:30. Shop hours are 11–2 and 4–7 on weekends and holidays.

RIBADEO

50 km (31 mi) southeast of Viveiro.

Perched on the broad *ría* of the same name, Ribadeo is the last coastal town before Asturias. The views up and across the estuary are marvelous—depending on the wind, the waves appear to roll *across* the ría rather than straight inland. Salmon and trout fishermen congregate upriver.

ESSENTIALS

Visitor Information Ribadeo (✉ *Pl. de España* ☎ *982/128689*).

WHERE TO EAT AND STAY

$$$ **Parador de Ribadeo.** Most rooms have glassed-in sitting areas with views (Room 208 has the best) across the *ría* to Asturias. Parquet floors and harvest-yellow walls are accented by watercolors of the area. In the dining room ($$–$$$$) a cornucopia of shellfish is served, much of it swimming around in a holding tank. Try the *sopa de mariscos,* seafood soup with a pastry top, and the ice cream flavored with Tetilla cheese and drizzled with honey. Fishing, horseback riding, and boating can be arranged. **Pros:** balconies in rooms, *ría* views, tasty seafood. **Cons:** rooms are smallish, restaurant opens at 9 PM. ✉ *Amador Fernández 7* ☎ *982/128825* 🌐 *www.parador.es* *46 rooms, 1 suite* *In-hotel: restaurant, bar* 💳 *AE, DC, MC, V.*

WESTERN ASTURIAS

As you cross into the Principality of Asturias, the intensely green countryside continues, belying the fact that this is a major mining region once exploited by the Romans for its iron- and gold-rich earth. Asturias is bordered to the southeast by the imposing Picos de Europa.

LUARCA

75 km (47 mi) east of Ribadeo, 92 km (57 mi) northeast of Oviedo.

The village of Luarca is tucked into a cove at the end of a final twist of the Río Negro, with a fishing port and, to the west, a sparkling bay. The town is a maze of cobblestone streets, stone stairways, and whitewashed houses, with a harborside decorated with painted flowerpots.

ESSENTIALS

Visitor Information Luarca (✉ *Calle Caleros 11* ☎ *985/640083*).

WHERE TO EAT AND STAY

$$–$$$$ SPANISH ★ **Casa Consuelo.** Four miles west of Luarca in Otur, which has a delightful beach, Casa Consuelo is one of the most popular spots on Spain's northern coast. It first opened in 1935 and is famed for *merluza* (hake) served with the northern Spanish delicacy *angulas* (baby eels) and blue cheese (about €55 for two, depending on market prices). This dish and the busy restaurant itself, whose name means "house of comfort," are not to be missed; portions are generous. ✉ *Ctra. N634, Km 511, 6 km (4 mi) west of Luarca, Otur* ☎ *985/641809* *Reservations essential* 💳 *AE, DC, MC, V* ⏲ *Closed Mon.*

$–$$$ SEAFOOD **El Barómetro.** In a 19th-century building decorated with an ornate barometer to gauge the famously unpredictable local weather, this small, family-run seafood eatery in the middle of the harbor front has an inexpensive *menú del día* (daily menu) and a good choice of local fresh fish, including *calamares* (squid) and *espárragos rellenos de erizo de mar* (asparagus stuffed with sea urchins). For a bit more money, you can dig into *bogavante,* a large-claw lobster. For dessert, the cheesecake is highly rated. ✉ *Paseo del Muelle 4* ☎ *985/470662* 💳 *MC, V* ⏲ *Closed late Sept.–late Oct. No dinner Wed.*

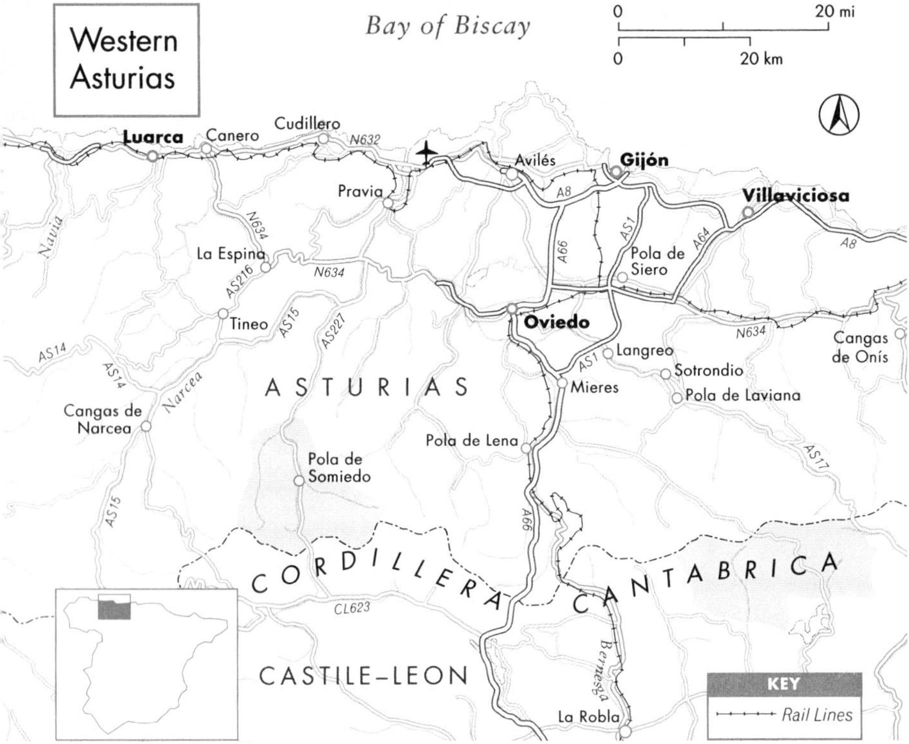

$$ **Hotel Villa La Argentina.** This charming Asturian mansion on the hill above Luarca was built in 1899 by a wealthy "Indiano" (the term for a Spaniard who made his fortune in South America). On-site is a small antiques museum and an old coach house, surrounded by palm trees and imported shrubs. You can choose between the newly constructed apartments in the garden or the Belle Epoque suites in the main building, one of which has a pleasant glassed-in reading room. **Pros:** friendly staff, lovely gardens, peace and quiet. **Cons:** a short walk from town, no restaurant. ✉ *Villar de Luarca s/n* ☎ *985/640102* 🌐 *www.villalaargentina.com* *9 rooms, 3 suites* *In-room: Wi-Fi. In-hotel: restaurant, bar, tennis court, pool.* 💳 *DC, MC, V* ⊙ *Closed early Jan.–mid-Mar.*

OVIEDO

92 km (57 mi) southeast of Luarca, 50 km (31 mi) southeast of Cudillero, 30 km (19 mi) south of Gijón.

Inland, the Asturian countryside starts to look more prosperous. Wooden, thatch-roof horreos (granaries) strung with golden bundles of drying corn replace the stark granite sheds of Galicia. A drive through the hills and valleys brings you to the capital city, Oviedo. Though primarily industrial, Oviedo has three of the most famous pre-Romanesque churches in Spain and a large university, giving it both ancient charm and youthful zest. Start your explorations with the two exquisite 9th-century chapels outside the city, on the slopes of Monte Naranco.

GETTING HERE AND AROUND

Oviedo is served by the A66 tollway, which links to Gijón and Avilés, where you can get on the A8 west to A Coruña or east toward Santander. Madrid is reached on the N630 south.

There are several buses per day to Gijón (30 minutes) and to Santiago and A Coruña (5½ hours). Madrid is 5½ hours away by rail from Oviedo's RENFE station, situated on Calle Uría. The FEVE service operates across the north coast, with Gijón easily reached in half an hour and Bilbao just under eight hours away.

Local buses operate along the main arteries of Oviedo, between the rail station and shopping areas, but skirt around the rim of the historical center, where Oviedo's oldest buildings are clustered in the labyrinth of streets around the Plaza Alfonso. Considering the short distances, walking is the best option, though taxis are inexpensive.

ESSENTIALS

Bus Station (✉ *Cl. Pepe Cosmen s/n* ☎ *901/499949*).

Train Station (✉ *Cl. Pepe Cosmen s/n* ☎ *901/499949*).

Visitor Information (✉ *Calle Uría*).

EXPLORING

★ The church of **Santa María del Naranco,** with superb views, and its plainer sister, **San Miguel de Lillo** 275 meters uphill, are the jewels of an early architectural style called Asturian pre-Romanesque, a more primitive, hulking, defensive line that preceded Romanesque architecture by nearly three centuries. Commissioned as part of a summer palace by King Ramiro I when Oviedo was the capital of Christian Spain, these masterpieces have survived for more than 1,000 years. The **Reception Center** (☎ *985/114901* ⏲ *Wed.–Mon. 11–1:30 and 4–6*) near the site provides videos that explain Asturian pre-Romanesque architecture. ✉ *Ctra. de los Monumentos, 2 km (1 mi) north of Oviedo* ☎ *676/032087* 🎫 *€2.20 (includes guided tour), free Mon. (without guided tour)* ⏲ *Apr.–Sept., Mon.–Sat. 9:30–1 and 3:30–7, Sun. 9:30–1; Oct.–Mar., Mon.–Sat. 10–12:30 and 3–4:30, Sun. 10–12:30.*

Oviedo's Gothic **cathedral** was built between the 14th- and the 16th centuries around the city's most cherished monument, the **Cámara Santa** (Holy Chamber). King Ramiro's predecessor, Alfonso the Chaste (792–842), built this chamber to hide the treasures of Christian Spain during the struggle with the Moors. Damaged during the Spanish civil war, it has since been rebuilt. Inside is the gold-leaf **Cross of the Angels,** commissioned by Alfonso the Chaste in 808 and encrusted with pearls and jewels. On the left is the more elegant **Victory Cross,** actually a jeweled sheath crafted in 908 to cover the oak cross used by Pelayo in the battle of Covadonga. ✉ *Pl. Alfonso II El Casto* ☎ *985/221033* 🎫 *Cathedral free, Cámara Santa €1.25, museum €3* ⏲ *Sept.–Aug., Mon.–Sat. 10–1 and 4–7 (until 8 July and Aug.), Sun. for mass only, at 10* AM *and 11* AM.

Across the Plaza Alfonso is the still-inhabited 15th-century **Palacio de la Rúa,** the oldest palace in town.On Calle San Francisco, is the 16th-century **Antigua Universidad de Oviedo.** Behind the cathedral, the **Museo Arqueológico,** housed in the splendid Monastery of San Vicente, contains fragments of pre-Romanesque buildings. ✉ *San Vicente 3* ☎ *985/215405* 🎫 *Free* ⏲ *Tues.–Sat. 10–1:30 and 4–6, Sun. 11–1.*

WHERE TO EAT AND STAY

$$$–$$$$ SPANISH ★ ✕ **Casa Fermín.** Skylights, plants, and an air of modernity belie the age of this sophisticated pink-and-granite restaurant, which opened in 1924. Founder Luis Gil introduced traditional Asturian cuisine at seminars around the world. Specialties include *fabada* (bean-and-sausage stew), *mero con costra de pistachios y su jugo tostado* (grouper roasted in a pistachio crust with its own juices), and wild game in season. If you're feeling adventurous, wash it all down with a Bloody Mary *con berberechos,* with cockles. ✉ *Calle San Francisco 8* ☎ *985/216452* 💳 *AE, DC, MC, V* ⏲ *Closed Sun.*

$$ SPANISH ★ ✕ **La Máquina.** For the best *fabada* (bean-and-sausage stew) in Asturias, head 6 km (4 mi) outside Oviedo toward Avilés and stop at the farmhouse with the miniature locomotive out front. The creamy fava beans of the signature dish are heaped with delicious hunks of morcilla sausage, chorizo, and Tocino ham. To leave without trying the *arroz con leche* (rice pudding), though, would be imponderable. The simple, whitewashed dining room has attracted diners from across Spain for decades, some of whom think nothing of making a weekend trip just to eat here. ✉ *Av. Conde de Santa Bárbara 59, Lugones* ☎ *985/263636* 💳 *DC, MC, V* ⏲ *Closed Sun. and mid-June–mid-July. No dinner.*

$$$ 🏨 **Barceló Oviedo Cervantes.** A playful revamp of this town house in the city center has seen a Neo-Moorish–style portico added to the original latticed facade, while public areas have a quirky, informal feel. Delicious seafood from the Bay of Biscay is served in the restaurant. To really soak up the luxury, ask for a room with an in-bath home entertainment system. **Pros:** helpful and amiable staff; playful art and design features; central location close to rail station. **Cons:** uninteresting views; confusing light switches. ✉ *Cervantes 13* ☎ *985/255000* 🌐 *www.barcelo.com* 🛏 *72 rooms* 👍 *In-hotel: restaurant, bar, public Wi-Fi, parking* 💳 *AE, DC, MC, V.*

$$$$ Fodor's Choice ★ 🏨 **Hotel de la Reconquista.** An 18th-century hospice emblazoned with a huge stone coat of arms, the ultraluxurious Reconquista costs almost twice as much as any other hotel in Asturias and is by far the most distinguished hotel in Oviedo. The wide lobby, encircled by Doric pillars and an oak-wood balcony, is decked out with velvet upholstery and 18th-century paintings. Guest rooms are large and modern, with comfortable beds and large armchairs. **Pros:** enormous rooms; palatial public areas; historic feel. **Cons:** expensive; poorly lit rooms; ambience can be rather haughty. ✉ *Calle Gil de Jaz 16* ☎ *985/241100* 🌐 *www.hoteldelareconquista.com* 🛏 *132 rooms, 10 suites* 👍 *In-room: Wi-Fi. In-hotel: restaurant, bar* 💳 *AE, DC, MC, V.*

NIGHTLIFE AND THE ARTS

The old town's main strip of dance clubs is on **Calle Canóniga.** A rather rowdy town after dark, Oviedo has plenty in the way of loud live music. **Calle Carta Puebla** is packed with pubs, many of which are Irish, owing to the region's Celtic heritage.

SHOPPING

Some antiques shops are clustered together for a few blocks on **Calle de Mon.** On Thursday and Sunday mornings a colorful outdoor market, **El Rastrillo,** is held in El Fontan. Shops throughout the city carry **azabache jewelry** made of jet. For handcrafted leather bags and belts, check out **Artesania Escanda** (☒*Jovellanos 5* ☎*985/210467*). Vacuum-packed *fabada* is sold at **Casa Veneranda** (☒*Melquíades Álvarez 23* ☎*985/212454*).

GIJÓN

30 km (19 mi) north of Oviedo.

Gijón is part fishing port, part summer resort, and part university town, packed with cafés.

ESSENTIALS

Visitor Information Gijón (☒*Calle Rodriguez San Pedro s/n* ☎*985/341771*).

EXPLORING

The promenade along **Praia San Lorenzo** extends from one end of town to the other. Across the narrow peninsula and the Plaza Mayor is the harbor, where the fishing fleet comes in with the day's catch. The steep peninsula is the old fishermen's quarter, **Cimadevilla,** now the hub of Gijón's nightlife. From the park at the highest point on the headland, beside Basque sculptor Eduardo Chillida's massive sculpture *Elogio del Horizonte* (In Praise of the Horizon), there's a panoramic view of the coast and city.

Termas Romanas (*Roman baths*), dating to the time of Augustus, are under the plaza at the end of the beach. ☒*Campo Valdés* ☎*985/345147* *€2.40* *Tues.–Sat. 10–1 and 5–8, Sun. 11–2 and 5–7.*

The **Museo de la Gaita** (*Bagpipe Museum*) is across the river on the eastern edge of town, past Parque Isabel la Católica. A collection of bagpipes from all over the world is augmented by workshops where you can see the instruments crafted. ☒*Paseo del Doctor Fleming 877, La Güelga s/n* ☎*985/182960* *€2.35* *Sept.–June, Tues.–Sat. 10–1 and 5–8, Sun. 11–2 and 5–7; July and Aug., Tues.–Sat. 10–1:30 and 5–9, Sun. 11–2 and 5–8.*

WHERE TO EAT AND STAY

$$$–$$$$ SPANISH ✕ **El Puerto.** This glass-enclosed dining room overlooks the harbor and serves fine, imaginative shellfish, seafood, and meats. Locals claim that the best meals in Gijón are to be had here, and the *merluza con bogavante en salsa verde* (hake and lobster with a parsley sauce) is a house specialty, though if you're really hungry, try the four-plate menu or *parillada de mariscos* (mixed grilled shellfish); El Puerto prides itself on its Cantabrian catch. Game is also served in season, and the wine list is

substantial. ✉*Calle Claudio Alvargonzález* ☎*985/349096* ✍*Reservations essential* ▭*AE, DC, MC, V* ⊙*No dinner Sun.*

$$$ **Parador de Gijón.** In an old water mill in a park not far from the San Lorenzo Beach, this parador is one of the simplest and friendliest in Spain. Rooms in the newer wing are small, with wood floors and pine shutters, but most have wonderful views over the lake or the park. In the restaurant ($–$$$), try the *tigres* (spicy stuffed mussels), *pimientos de piquillo rellenos* (green peppers stuffed with squid, mushrooms, and rice), or *oricios* (sea urchins), served raw or steamed with lemon juice or a spicy sauce. For dessert, try fresh figs (in season) with Cabrales cheese. **Pros:** park views; friendly staff; great food. **Cons:** austere guest rooms; badly thought-out bathrooms; difficult to find. ✉*Calle Torcuato Fernández Miranda 15* ☎*985/370511* 🌐*www.parador.es* *40 rooms* *In-room: Wi-Fi. In-hotel: restaurant* ▭*AE, DC, MC, V.*

CIDER HOUSE RULES

In order to aerate the cider, cider houses generally insist that either you or your waiter pour cider correctly—that is, from overhead to a glass held at knee level. This process is called the *escancio* (pouring), a much-valued skill around which entire tournaments are held. Give it a try. Spilling is allowed. The region's main cider center is in Villaviciosa.

EN ROUTE

East of Gijón is apple-orchard country, source of the famous hard cider of Asturias. Rolling green hills, grazing cows, and white chalets make a remarkably Alpine landscape.

VILLAVICIOSA

32 km (20 mi) east of Gijón, 45 km (28 mi) northeast of Oviedo.

Cider-capital Villaviciosa has a large dairy and several bottling plants as well as an attractive old quarter. The Hapsburg Emperor Charles V first set foot in Spain just down the road from here. The town's annual five-day Fiesta de la Manzana (Apple Festival) begins the first Friday after September 8.

ESSENTIALS

Visitor Information Villaviciosa (✉*Parque Vallina* ☎*985/891759*).

EXPLORING

To taste the regional hard cider, stop into **El Congreso** (✉*Pl. Generalísimo 25* ☎*No phone*), a popular *sidrería* (cider house) that also serves tasty tapas and shellfish straight from the tank.

WHERE TO STAY

$ **Carlos I.** Right in the *pedestrian* heart of the *casco antiguo* (old town), this late-17th-century mansion is loaded with character. From the crests emblazoned on the facade, to the wood floors, antique furniture, plants, and oil paintings not to mention the cozy, tile-floored bar-cafeteria, the Carlos I is a local classic, and relatively cheap as well. Guest rooms are spotless and comparatively large. **Pros:** great location; oozes historical character; clean and tidy. **Cons:** old bath facilities; noisy in morning. ✉*Pl. Carlos I 4* ☎*985/890121* 📠*985/890051* *16 rooms* *In-hotel: bar* ▭*MC, V.*

THE PICOS DE EUROPA

With craggy peaks soaring up to the 8,688-foot Torre Cerredo, the northern skyline of the Picos de Europa has helped seafarers and fishermen navigate the Bay of Biscay for ages. To the south, pilgrims on their way to Santiago enjoy distant but inspiring views of the snowcapped range from the plains of Castile between Burgos and León. Over the years, regular, very heavy rain and snow have created canyons plunging 3,000 feet, natural arches, caves, and sinkholes (one of which is 5,213 feet deep).

The Picos de Europa National Park, covering 646.6 square km (250 square mi), is perfect for climbers and trekkers: you can explore the main trails, hang glide, ride horses, cycle, or canoe. There are two adventure-sports centers in Cangas de Onís, near the Roman Bridge.

RIBADESELLA

67 km (40 mi) east of Gijón, 84 km (50 mi) northeast of Oviedo.

The N632 twists around green hills dappled with eucalyptus groves, allowing glimpses of the sea and sandy beaches below and the snowcapped Picos de Europa looming inland. This fishing village and beach resort is famous for its seafood, its cave, and the canoe races held on the Sella River the first Saturday of August.

ESSENTIALS

Visitor Information Ribadesella (✉ *C. Marqueses de Argüelles s/n* ☎ *985/860038* ⏲ *Closed Mon.*).

EXPLORING

Discovered in 1968 by Señor Bustillo, the **Cueva Tito Bustillo** (Tito Bustillo Cave) has 20,000-year-old paintings on par with those in Lascaux, France, and Altamira. Giant horses and deer prance about the walls. To protect the paintings, no more than 375 visitors are allowed inside each day. The guided tour is in Spanish. There's also a museum of Asturian cave finds open year-round. ☎ *985/861120* 🌐 *www.titobustillo.com* 🎫 *€4* ⏲ *Museum and cave Apr.–Sept., Wed.–Sun. 10–5.*

LLANES

40 km (25 mi) east of Ribadesella.

This sprightly beach town is on a pristine stretch of the Costa Verde. The shores in both directions outside town have vistas of cliffs looming over white-sand beaches and isolated caves.

ESSENTIALS

Visitor Information Llanes (✉ *Calle La Torre, Alfonso IX s/n* ☎ *985/400164*).

EXPLORING

The peaceful, well-conserved **Plaza Cristo Rey** marks the center of the old town, partially surrounded by the remains of its medieval walls. The 13th-century church of **Santa María** rises over the square. Nearby, off Calle Alfonso IX, a medieval tower houses the tourist office. A long canal, connected to a small harbor, cuts through the heart of Llanes, and along its banks rise colorful houses with glass galleries against a backdrop of the Picos de Europa. At the daily portside fish market, usually held around 1 PM, vendors display heaping mounds of freshly caught seafood. Steps from the old town is **Playa del Sablón,** a little swath of sand that gets crowded on summer weekends. On the eastern edge of town is the larger **Playa de Toró.** Just 1 km (½ mi) east of Llanes is one of the area's most secluded beaches, the immaculate **Playa Ballota,** with private coves for picnicking and one of the few stretches of nudist sand in Asturias. West of Llanes, the most pleasant beaches lie between the towns of Barro and Celorio.

Dotting the Asturian coast east and west of Llanes are *bufones* (blowholes), cave-like cavities that expel water when waves are sucked in. Active blowholes shoot streams of water as high as 100 feet into the air; unfortunately, it's hard to predict when this will happen, as it depends on the tide and the size of the surf. They are clearly marked so you can find them, and there are barriers to protect you when they expel water. There's a blowhole east of Playa Ballota; try to watch it in action from the **Mirador Panorámico La Boriza,** near the entrance to the golf course. If you miss it, the view is still worth a stop—on a clear day you can see the coastline all the way east to Santander.

WHERE TO EAT AND STAY

$–$$$ SEAFOOD ✕ **Mirentxu.** Minutes from the fish market, near the small harbor bobbing with colorful fishing boats, this friendly Basque-influenced spot serves a fusion of sea and farm produce, including heaping portions of *congrio con arbejos* (conger eel with peas), *habas con almejas* (broad beans with shellfish), and *lechazo al horno* (roasted lamb), all at reasonable prices. Also worth trying are the delicious homemade desserts, including *buñuelos* (sugar-coated fritters), *hojaldre* (puff pastry), and *arroz con leche* (rice pudding). ✉ *Calle Marinero 14* ☎ *985/402236* 💳 *DC, MC, V* ⏲ *Closed Oct.–June.*

$$$ **La Posada de Babel.** This exquisite family-run inn just outside Llanes stands among oak, chestnut, and birch trees on the edge of the Sierra de Cuera. With some unusual architecture, including a granary converted into a guestroom but you can still expect plenty of personal attention and roaring fires in the public rooms. **Pros:** extremely amiable staff, comfy base for hiking. **Cons:** slippery stairs to certain rooms, closed in winter. ✉ *La Pereda s/n* ☎ *985/402525* 🌐 *www.laposadadebabel.com* *13 rooms* *In-hotel: restaurant, bar, bicycles* 💳 *DC, MC, V* ⏲ *Closed Nov.–Feb.*

CANGAS DE ONÍS

25 km (16 mi) south of Ribadesella, 70 km (43 mi) east of Oviedo.

The first capital of Christian Spain, Cangas de Onís is also the unofficial capital of the Picos de Europa National Park. Partly in the narrow valley carved by the Sella River, it has the feel of a mountain village.

ESSENTIALS

Visitor Information Cangas de Onís (✉ *Calle Camila Beceña 1* ☎ *985/848005*).

A GOOD TOUR: THE PICOS DE EUROPA

The best-known road trip in the Picos connects **Cangas de Onís** and **Riaño** along the twisting Sella River Gorge. Part of this trip is along the **Ruta de los Beyos** through the Beyo canyon, on the N625 road, a two-hour drive up to the pass at **Puerto del Pontón** (Pontón Pass; 4,232 feet). Just beyond the pass, turn left (northeast) and drive up to the **Puerto de Panderruedas** (4,757 feet) for a panoramic view of the peaks, especially in the early evening sun. From here you can descend northeast to the town of Posada de Valdeón and continue to Caín for a look at the famous Ruta del Cares.

For the **Ruta del Cares,** drive east on the AS114 from **Cangas de Onís** toward **Panes,** stopping just before **Arenas de Cabrales**: here the road descends a wide valley and reaches a *mirador* (lookout) onto the **Naranjo de Bulnes,** a huge tooth of rock way up in the peaks. The mountain was named for its occasional tendency to glow orange, *naranja,* at sunrise and sunset. Turn south in **Arenas de Cabrales** into the AS264 road to reach **Poncebos**, and leave the car near here for the four-hour Ruta de Cares walk to **Caín** through the **Garganta de Cares** gorge. The canyon presents itself fairly soon, so you can turn back without pangs if you don't want to make the full hike. This route is popular, so arrive in Poncebos early in the day to avoid parking problems.

If you have another day, leave **Cangas** and drive via **Panes** and **Potes** around the entire park. Consider relocating to the southern side and staying at the **Parador de Fuente Dé.** South of Panes, turn right at **Urdón**'s hydroelectric power station to **Tresviso** for unforgettable views and a chance to buy some local cheese. South of **La Hermida** on the N621 the **Garganta de La Hermida** cuts through sheer 600-foot limestone cliffs up to **Potes**.

West of **Potes** off the CA185 is the left turn for the **Monasterio de Santo Toribio de Liébana,** with a 13th-century Gothic church and 17th-century cloisters. The CA185 ends at **Fuente Dé**, where a cable car can whisk you to the top of the Picos. South of **Potes** the N621 continues south to Riaño, a two-hour drive. About halfway there, **Puerta de San Glorio** is the jumping-off point for the 2.2-km (1.3-mi) walk up to the Monumento al Oso, where a white stone bear marks another splendid view.

EXPLORING

A high, humpback **medieval bridge** (also known as the Puente Romano, or Roman Bridge, because of its style) spans the Sella River gorge with a reproduction of Pelayo's Victory Cross, or La Cruz de la Victoria, dangling underneath. To help plan your rambles, consult the scale model of the park outside the **Picos de Europa visitor center** (✉ *Casa Dago, Av. Covadonga 43* ☎ *985/848614*). The store opposite (at No. 22), El Llagar, sells maps and guidebooks, a few in English.

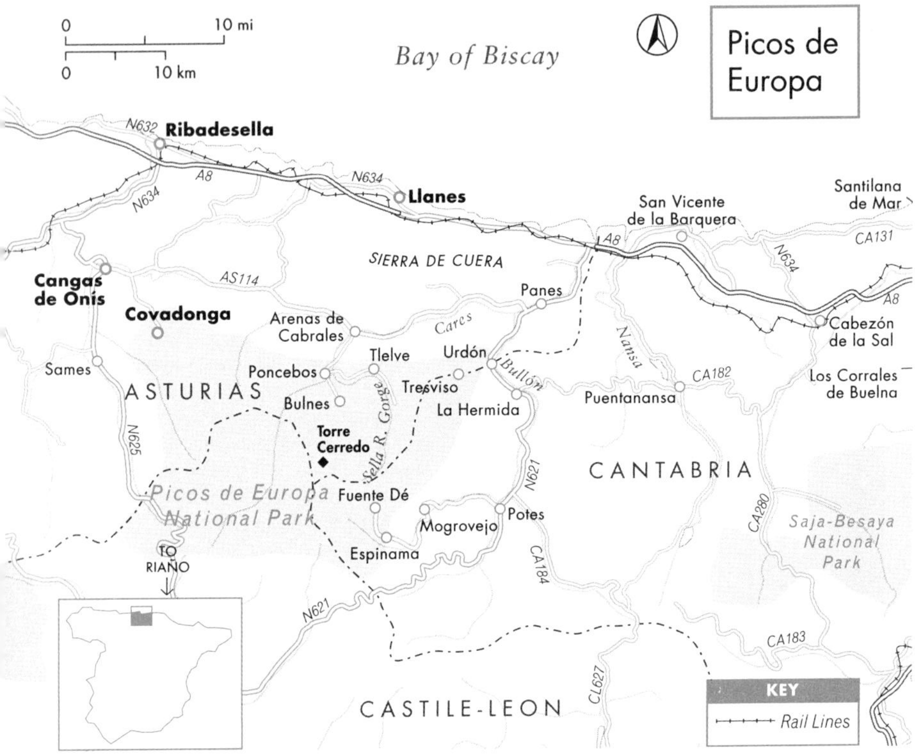

WHERE TO EAT AND STAY

$–$$$ SPANISH ✕ **Sidrería Los Arcos.** This busy tavern on one of the town's main squares has lots of polished wood and serves local cider, fine Spanish wines, and sizzling T-bone steaks. The mouth-watering selection of *tapas* includes *revuelto de morcilla* (scrambled eggs with blood sausage), which is served on *torto de maíz* (a corn pastry base). Or there's always the customary Asturian *fabada* (bean-and-sausage stew). ✉ *Pl. del Ayuntamiento, enter on Av. Covadonga* ☎ *985/849277* ▭ *AE, MC, V* ⏲ *Closed Feb.*

$$ **Aultre Naray.** This 19th-century mansion overlooking the Escapa mountain range is a rare find. It's perfectly placed for hiking, camping, canoeing, and swimming (which the staff can help organize). Despite the wooden beams and many original features, it's not rustic—guest rooms have modern furniture, plenty of light, and, in some cases, pleasant sitting rooms. The hotel is 15 km (9 mi) east of town. **Pros:** fine base for outdoor activities; great views. **Cons:** a bit of a hike from Cangas. ✉ *N634, Km 335, Peruyes* ☎ *985/840808* ⊕ *www.aultrenaray.com* *10 rooms* *In-hotel: restaurant, bar, public Wi-Fi, no elevator* ▭ *DC, MC, V.*

$ **Hospedería del Peregrino.** The name means "pilgrim's guest house," and this simple but adequate hotel looks out at a magnificent nearby church on the main road between Cangas de Onís and Covadonga.

Rooms are small but cozy and decorated with abundant wood furnishings and checked curtains. The restaurant does suitably hearty local dishes, including every Camino de Santiago pilgrim's cherished *fabada* (bean-and-sausage stew). **Pros:** church views; easily accessed; neat and tidy. **Cons:** uninspiring roadside location; small rooms. *✉AS 262 s/n, Covadonga ☎985/846047 ⊕www.picosdeuropa.net/peregrino 7 rooms In-room: no a/c. In-hotel: restaurant, bar, no elevator ▭AE, DC, MC, V ⏲Closed Dec.–Feb.*

¢ **La Naturaleza.** The name means "nature," and this hotel, poised among ancient chestnuts at the foot of the Ruta del Cares and enjoying views of Arenas de Cabrales and the Sella River, is surrounded by its namesake, in glorious abundance. The location, at one of the main gateways into the Picos de Europa, is ideal, and the six bright, comfy rooms all have large, clean bathrooms. There's a welcoming cozy fireplace in the lounge. **Pros:** nice vistas, pleasant wooden balconies, comfortable and cozy throughout. **Cons:** only six rooms, doesn't accept credit cards. *✉Calle La Segada ☎985/846487 ☎985/846101 6 rooms In-room: no a/c. In-hotel: restaurant, bar, no elevator ▭No credit cards ⏲Closed Dec. and Jan.*

$$$ ★ **Parador de Cangas de Onís.** On the banks of the Sella River just west of Cangas, this friendly parador is part 8th-century Benedictine monastery and part modern wing: the older building has 11 period-style rooms. Excellent local dishes ($$–$$$), such as *merluza del Cantabrica a la sidra* (hake cooked in cider) garnished with asparagus, are served in the dining room. **Pros:** helpful staff, gorgeous riverside location with mountain views, oodles of history. **Cons:** limited menu, chilly corridors. *✉Monasterio de San Pedro de Villanueva, Ctra. N624, from N634, take right turn for Villanueva ☎985/849402 ⊕www.parador.es 64 rooms In-hotel: restaurant, bar ▭AE, DC, MC, V.*

COVADONGA

14 km (9 mi) southeast of Cangas de Onís.

To see high alpine meadowland, some rare Spanish lakes, and views over the peaks and out to sea (if the mist ever disperses), take the narrow road up past Covadonga to **Lake Enol,** stopping for the view en route. Starting to the right of the lake, a three-hour walk takes in views from the **Mirador del Rey,** where you can find the grave of pioneering climber Pedro Pidal. Farther up the road from Lake Enol are a summer-only tourist office and **Lake Ercina,** where Pope John Paul II picnicked during his 1989 tour of Asturias and Galicia.

ESSENTIALS

Visitor Information Covadonga (*✉Av. Covadonga s/n, Pl. del Ayuntamiento ☎985/846035*).

EXPLORING

NEED A BREAK?

Near Lake Enol is the Restaurante el Casín (*✉Ctra. Santander–Oviedo s/n, Ribadesella ☎985/860231*), with a small terrace bar overlooking the mountains and the lake. The set menu is €9; à la carte options include roasts and restorative *fabada* stews. It's closed January and February.

4

★ Covadonga's **shrine** is considered the birthplace of Spain. Here, in 718, a handful of sturdy Asturian Christians led by Don Pelayo took refuge in the Cave of St. Mary, about halfway up a cliff, where they prayed to the Virgin Mary to give them strength to turn back the Moors. Pelayo and his followers resisted the superior Moorish forces and set up a Christian kingdom that eventually led to the Reconquest. The cave has an 18th-century statue of the Virgin and Don Pelayo's grave. Covadonga itself has a **basilica,** and the **museum** has the treasures donated to the Virgin of the Cave, including a crown studded with more than a thousand diamonds. ☎*985/846096* 🎫*€3* ⏲*Daily 10:30–2 and 4–7:30.*

CANTABRIA

Historically part of Old Castile, the province of Cantabria was called Santander until 1984, when it became an autonomous community. The most scenic route from Madrid via Burgos to Santander is the slow but spectacular N62, past the Ebro reservoir. Faster and safer is the N627 from Burgos to Aguilar de Campóo connecting to the A67 freeway down to Santander. But for a truly memorable glimpse of Cantabria's section of the Picos de Europa Mountains—Potes and Fuente Dé—drive farther west through La Liébana valley via Potes, reaching the coast at San Vicente de la Barquera.

POTES

51 km (31 mi) southwest of San Vicente de la Barquera, 115 km (69 mi) southwest of Santander, 173 km (104 mi) north of Palencia.

Known for its fine cheeses made of milk from cows, goats, and sheep, the region of La Liébana is a highland domain well worth exploring. Potes, the area's main city, is named for and sprinkled with ancient bridges and surrounded with the stunning 9th-century **monasteries** of Santo Toribio de Liébana, Lebeña, and Piasca. The gorges of the Desfiladero de la Hermida pass are 3 km (2 mi) north, and the rustic town of Mogrovejo is on the way to the vertiginous cable car at Fuente Dé, 25 km (15 mi) west of Potes.

ESSENTIALS

Visitor Information Potes (✉*Independencia 30* ☎*942/730787*).

EXPLORING

As you approach the parador of **Fuente Dé**, at the head of the valley northwest of the hamlet of Espinama you'll see a wall of gray stone rising 6,560 feet straight into the air. Visible at the top is the tiniest of huts: El Mirador del cable (the cable car lookout point). Get there via a 2,625-foot funicular (€14 round-trip). At the top, you're hiking along the Ávila Mountain pasturelands, rich in wildlife, between the central and eastern massifs of the Picos. There's an official entrance to Picos de Europa National Park here.

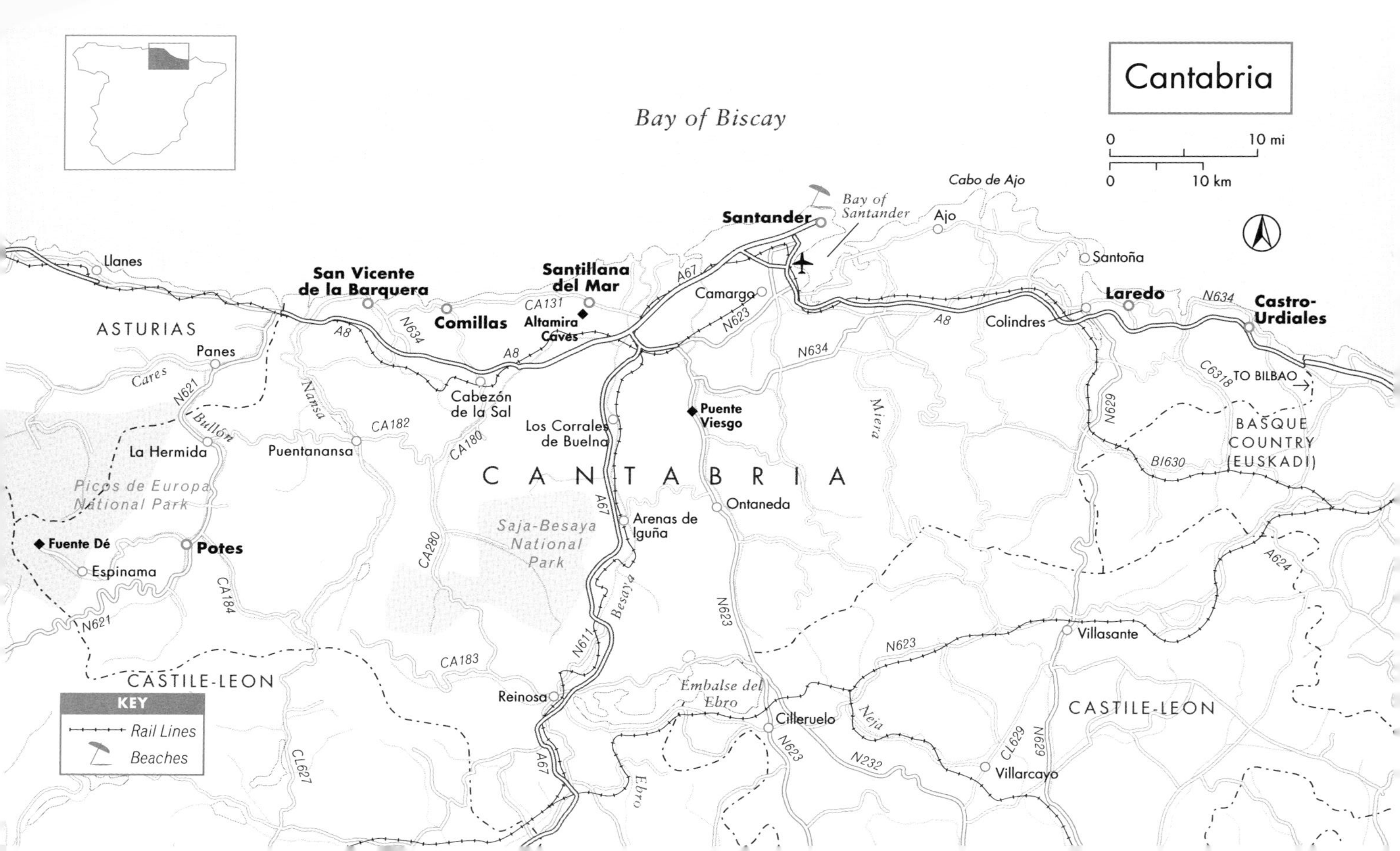

Cantabria
Bay of Biscay
0
10 mi
0
10 km
Cabo de Ajo
Bay of Santander
Santander
Ajo
Santoña
Llanes
San Vicente de la Barquera
Santillana del Mar
Comillas
CA131
Altamira Caves
A67
Camargo
N623
Laredo
N634
Castro-Urdiales
ASTURIAS
Panes
A8
N634
A8
Colindres
Cares
N621
Nansa
Cabezón de la Sal
Puente Viesgo
C6318
TO BILBAO
N629
Bullón
CA182
Los Corrales de Buelna
Miera
BASQUE COUNTRY (EUSKADI)
La Hermida
Puentanansa
CA180
BI630
CANTABRIA
Picos de Europa National Park
A67
Ontaneda
Arenas de Iguña
Saja-Besaya National Park
Fuente Dé
Potes
CA280
A624
Espinama
CA184
Besaya
N623
N621
N611
Villasante
N623
CA183
CASTILE-LEON
Embalse del Ebro
Reinosa
KEY
Rail Lines
Beaches
Cilleruelo
Neja
CASTILE-LEON
N623
CL629
N629
CL627
A67
Ebro
N232
Villarcayo

WHERE TO EAT AND STAY

$–$$$ SPANISH ✕ **El Bodegón.** A simple, friendly, cozy, and surprisingly contemporary space awaits behind the ancient stone facade. Part of the house is original, but much has been renovated, providing an attractive combination of traditional mountain design and modern construction. The menu focuses on standard highland comfort food, such as a delicious *cocido montañes* (mountain stew of sausage, garbanzo beans, and vegetables) at a rock-bottom price. The €9 lunch menu is one of the best values for miles around. ✉ *San Roque 4* ☎ *942/730247* 💳 *AE, DC, MC, V* ⏲ *Closed Mon.*

$$$ **Parador de Fuente Dé.** This modern parador is in a valley beside the cable car that ascends a soaring rock face to 2,705 feet in about four minutes. Somewhat spartan, it's a fine no-frills base for serious climbers and walkers and has a good restaurant ($$–$$$) with *cocido lebaniego* (a sturdy local stew) and steaks topped with Cabrales, local blue cheese. The parador is east of the Cantabrian border, 23 km (14 mi) west of Potes. **Pros:** mountainside location, next to cable car, cheap for a parador. **Cons:** simply furnished, limited access in winter snow. ✉ *Fuente Dé* ☎ *942/736651* 🌐 *www.parador.es* *78 rooms* *In-room: Wi-Fi. In-hotel: restaurant, bar* 💳 *AE, DC, MC, V* ⏲ *Closed Dec.–Feb.*

$$ **Valdecoro.** You literally can't miss this family-run mountain house, which faces the main road through town. Rooms with modern appointments and an efficient staff make for a pleasant stay. The restaurant ($–$$$) is a town favorite for simple and authentic highland products and recipes prepared with care and wisdom. In winter, try the *cocido lebaniego,* a powerful mountain soup made of broth, beans, pork, chard, and chicken. **Pros:** cozy mountain feel, fine rustic restaurant. **Cons:** on the main road through town, rooms efficient but lackluster. ✉ *Roscabado 5* ☎ *942/730025* 📠 *942/730315* *41 rooms* *In-hotel: restaurant, parking (no fee)* 💳 *AE, DC, MC, V.*

SANTANDER

★ *390 km (242 mi) north of Madrid, 154 km (96 mi) north of Burgos, 116 km (72 mi) west of Bilbao.*

One of the great ports on the Bay of Biscay, Santander is surrounded by beaches that are by no means isolated, yet it lacks the package-tour feel of so many Mediterranean resorts. A fire destroyed most of the old town in 1941, so the rebuilt city looks relatively modern, and although it has traditionally been a conservative stronghold loyal to the Spanish state (in contrast to its Basque neighbors), Santander is especially lively in summer, when its summer-university community and music-and-dance festival fill the city with students and performers.

Portus Victoriae, as Santander was then called, was a major port in the 1st- to 4th-century Roman Hispania Ulterior (and even earlier under the aboriginal Cántabros). Commercial life accelerated between the 13th and 16th centuries, but the waning of Spain's naval power and a series of plagues during the reign of Felipe II caused Santander's fortunes to plummet in the late 16th century. Its economy revived after 1778, when Seville's monopoly on trade with the Americas was revoked and

Santander entered fully into commerce with the New World. In 1910 the Palacio de la Magdalena was built by popular subscription as a gift to Alfonso XIII and his queen, Victoria Eugenia, lending Santander prestige as one of Spain's royal watering spots.

Santander benefits from promenades and gardens, most of which face the bay. Walk east along the Paseo de Pereda, the main boulevard, to the Puerto Chico, a small yacht harbor. Past the Puerto Chico, follow Avenida Reina Victoria and you'll find the tree-lined park paths above the first of the city's beaches, Playa de la Magdalena. Walk onto the Península de la Magdalena to the Palacio de la Magdalena, today the summer seat of the University of Menéndez y Pelayo. Beyond the Magdalena Peninsula, wealthy locals have built mansions facing the long stretch of shoreline known as El Sardinero, Santander's best beach.

GETTING HERE AND AROUND

Santander itself is easily navigated on foot, but if you're looking to get to El Sardinero beach take the bus from the central urban transport hub at Jardines de Pereda.

ESSENTIALS

Bus Station Santander (✉ *C. Navas de Tolosa s/n* ☎ *942/211995*).

Train Station Santander (✉ *Estación de Santander, C. Rodríguez s/n* ☎ *942/210211*).

Visitor Information Santander (✉ *Jardines de Pereda* ☎ *942/216120* ✉ *Plaza de Velarde 5* ☎ *942/310708*).

EXPLORING

The blockish **Catedral de Santander** marks the transition between Romanesque and Gothic. Though largely rebuilt in the neo-Gothic style after serious damage in the 1941 fire, the cathedral retained its 12th-century crypt. The chief attraction here is the tomb of Marcelino Menéndez y Pelayo (1856–1912), Santander's most famous literary figure. The cathedral is across Avenida de Calvo Sotelo from the Plaza Porticada. ✉ *Somorrostro s/n* ☎ *942/226024* *Free* *Weekdays 10–1 and 4–7:30, weekends 8–2 and 4:30–8.*

The **Museo Municipal de Bellas Artes** *(Municipal Museum of Fine Arts)* has works by Flemish, Italian, and Spanish artists. Goya's portrait of absolutist king Fernando VII is worth seeking out; the smirking face of the lion at the king's feet clues you in to Goya's feelings toward his patron. The same building holds the **Biblioteca Menéndez y Pelayo** (☎ *942/203120*), a library with some 50,000 volumes, and the writer's study, kept as it was in his day. ✉ *C. Rubio s/n* ☎ *942/203123* *Free* *Museum Tues.–Fri. 10–1 and 5–8, Sat. 10–1. Library weekdays 9–2 and 4–9:30, Sat. 9–1:30.*

In the old city, the center of life is the **Plaza Porticada,** officially called the Plaza Velarde. In August this unassuming little square is the seat of Santander's star event, the outdoor International Festival of Music and Dance.

WHERE TO EAT AND STAY

$$–$$$ SPANISH ✕ **Bodega del Riojano.** The paintings on wine-barrel ends that decorate this classic restaurant have given it the nickname Museo Redondo (Round Museum). The building dates back to the 16th century, when it was a wine cellar, and this incarnation lives on in the heavy wooden beams overhead and the rough and rustic tables. With culinary specialties from La Rioja and fresh seafood from the Bay of Biscay, there is much to choose from. The menu changes daily and seasonally, but the fish of the day is a sure bet. ✉ *Río de la Pila 5* ☎ *942/216750* ▭ *AE, DC, MC, V* ⊙ *Closed Mon. No dinner Sun. Oct.–May.*

$$–$$$$ SPANISH ✕ **Zacarías.** Whether you're looking for a brief tapas interlude or a full dinner, try this popular rustic and refined interior patio ringed with a lovely upstairs balcony. Zacarías is an institution in Santander and justly famous for northern Spanish seafood and upland dishes of all kinds. Owner and chef Zacarías Puente Herboso is also a legendary and well-respected food writer and an authority on Cantabrian recipes. Sample the *maganos encebollados* (calamari and caramelized onion) or the *alubias rojas estofadas* (red beans stewed with sausage). ✉ *General Mola 41* ☎ *942/212333* ▭ *AE, DC, MC, V.*

$$–$$$$ ★ **Bahía.** Classical decor combined with state-of-the-art technology and contemporary furnishings make this Santander's finest hotel, a grand and comfortable perch overlooking the water. Rooms are spacious and filled with gauzy drapes and noble pieces of oak and mahogany furniture, while the public spaces are ample and elegant, recalling Santander's regal past as a summer watering spot for the Spanish Royal family during the late 19th and early 20th centuries. **Pros:** at the nerve center of town, great for watching maritime traffic. **Cons:** nearby cathedral bells can be noisy if you're not on the sea side of the hotel, not right on the beach. ✉ *Av. Alfonso XIII-6* ☎ *942/205000* ⊕ *www.hotelbahia.com* *188 rooms* *In-room: Wi-Fi. In-hotel: restaurant, bar, public Wi-Fi, parking (fee)* ▭ *AE, DC, MC, V.*

$$–$$$ **Las Brisas.** Jesús García and his wife, Teresa, run this 80-year-old mansion as an upscale, cottage-style hotel by the sea. Each room or apartment is different, from dollhouselike alcoves to an odd but attractive family duplex apartment. The basement bar and the breakfast room are especially cozy. The hotel is a short walk from the beach, and many of the rooms have fine views out to sea. **Pros:** proximity to the shore, fresh and briny Atlantic air, traditional decor and furnishings. **Cons:** some rooms are a bit cramped. ✉ *C. la Braña 14* ☎ *942/270991 or 942/275011* ⊕ *www.hotellasbrisas.net* *13 rooms, 12 apartments* *In-hotel: bar* ▭ *AE, DC, MC, V.*

SHOPPING

Santander's ceramics emporium **La Muralla** (✉ *Calle Arrabal 17* ☎ *942/160301*) is known as the best in town. For fashions in a designer setting **Del Rosa al Amarillo** (✉ *Calle Hernán Cortés 37* ☎ *942/261361*) carries a full range of hot items. For footwear, **Loocky** (✉ *Lealtad 6* ☎ *942/211368*) is tops. Fine foods, including the Santanderino specialty *dulces pasiegos* (light and sugary cakes), can be sampled and purchased at **Mantequerías Cántabras** (✉ *Plaza de Italia s/n* ☎ *942/272899*).

SANTILLANA DEL MAR

Fodor's Choice ★ *29 km (18 mi) west of Santander.*

ESSENTIALS

Visitor Information Santillana del Mar (✉*Jesús Otero 20* ☎*942/818812*).

EXPLORING

This stunning ensemble of 15th- to 17th-century stone houses is one of Spain's greatest troves of medieval and Renaissance architecture.The town is built around the **Colegiata,** Cantabria's finest Romanesque structure, with a 17th-century altarpiece, the tomb of local martyr Santa Juliana, and sculpted capitals depicting biblical scenes. The adjoining Regina Coeli convent has a **Museo Diocesano** (☎*942/840317*) with liturgical art. ✉*Av. Le Dorat 2* ☎*942/818004* 🌐*www.santillanamuseodiocesano.com* *€3* *Daily 10–1 and 4–7; closed Mon. Oct.–May.*

The world-famous **Altamira Caves,** 3 km (2 mi) southwest of Santillana del Mar, have been called the Sistine Chapel of Prehistoric Art for the beauty of their drawings, believed to be some 20,000 years old. First uncovered in 1875, the caves are a testament to early man's admiration of aesthetic beauty and his surprising technical skill in representing it—especially in the use of rock forms to accentuate perspective. The caves are closed to visitors, but the reproduction in the **museum** is open to all. ✉*Museo de Altamira, Santillana del Mar, Cantabria* ☎*942/818005* 🌐*www.museodealtamira.mcu.es* *€3* *Daily 10–1 and 4–7; closed Mon. Oct.–May.*

WHERE TO STAY

$$ **Casa del Organista.** A cozy 18th-century house with comfortable and tastefully appointed whitewashed rooms, this is a handy alternative to the pricier and more famous national paradores nearby. A typical *casona montañesa* (noble mountain town house) with painstakingly crafted stone and wood details, this intimate hideaway offers a countrified but elegant base camp for exploring one of Spain's finest Renaissance towns. **Pros:** personal and friendly service, lovely warm decor. **Cons:** limited availability and difficult to book in high season, some rooms are very small. ✉*Los Hornos 4* ☎*942/840352* 🌐*www.casadelorganista.com* *14 rooms* *In-room: Wi-Fi. In hotel: no elevator* *AE, DC, MC, V* *Closed Dec. 15–Jan. 15.*

$$$ Fodor's Choice ★ **Parador de Santillana Gil Blas.** Built in the 16th century, this lovely stone palace occupies what used to be the summer home of the Barreda-Bracho family. Rooms are baronial, with heavy wood beams overhead and splendid antique furnishings. The spacious dining hall ($$–$$$$) has a medieval feel about it and specializes in local cuisine as well as roasts and hearty stews and soups in the Castilian tradition. **Pros:** storybook surroundings, elegant and attentive service. **Cons:** a little breezy and chilly in winter. ✉*Pl. Ramón Pelayo 11* ☎*942/028028* 🌐*www.parador.es* *27 rooms* *In-room: Wi-Fi. In-hotel: restaurant, bar, public Wi-Fi, parking (fee)* *AE, DC, MC, V.*

OFF THE BEATEN PATH

Puente Viesgo. In 1903 this 16th-century hamlet in the Pas Valley excavated four caves under the 1,150-foot peak of Monte del Castillo, two of which—Cueva del Castillo and Cueva de las Monedas—are open to the public. Bison, deer, bulls, and even humanoid stick figures are depicted; the oldest designs are thought to be 35,000 years old. Most arresting are the paintings of 44 hands (curiously, 35 of them left), reaching out through time. The painters are thought to have blown red pigment around their hands through a hollow bone, leaving the negative image. Advance reservations are advised. ✉*N623, Km 28, from Santander* ☎*942/598425* 🌐*www.culturadecantabria.es* 🎫*€4 per cave* ⏲*May–Sept., daily 10–2, 4–7; Oct.–Apr., Wed.–Sun. 9:30–4.*

COMILLAS

49 km (30 mi) west of Santander.

This astounding pocket of Catalan Art Nouveau architecture in the green hills of Cantabria will make you rub your eyes in disbelief. The Marqués de Comillas, a Catalan named Antonio López y López (1817–83), whose daughter Isabel married Gaudí's patron Eusebi Güell, was the wealthiest and most influential shipping magnate of his time, and a fervent patron of the arts, and he encouraged the great Moderniste architects to use his native village as a laboratory. Antonio Gaudí's 1883–89 green-and-yellow-tile villa, El Capricho (a direct cousin of his Casa Vicens in Barcelona), is the town's main Moderniste attraction. The town cemetery is filled with Art Nouveau markers and monuments, most notably an immense angel by eminent Catalan sculptor Josep Llimona.

ESSENTIALS

Visitor Information Comillas (✉*Aldea 639520* ☎*942/720768*).

EXPLORING

Palacio Sobrellano, built in the late 19th century by Catalan architect Joan Martorell for the Marqués de Comillas, is an exuberant neo-Gothic mansion with surprising collections of everything from sculpture and painting to archaeology and ethnographical material. The chapel has benches and kneeling stalls that were designed by Gaudí. ☎*942/720339* 🌐*www.culturadecantabria.es* 🎫*€4 palace, €6 palace and chapel* ⏲*Sept.–May, Wed.–Sun. 10:30–2 and 4–7:30; June–Sept., daily 10–9.*

WHERE TO EAT

$$$–$$$$ SPANISH ✕**El Capricho de Gaudí.** Dining in a Gaudí creation is an opportunity not to be taken lightly, especially if the visual rush is accompanied by fresh turbot with young garlic or roast lamb from the verdant hills of Cantabria. This unique spot may be somewhat overpriced, but even for a cup of coffee or a bowl of soup it's an unforgettable and unique chance to break bread in the same space where the great Moderniste took some of his first steps as a young architect. ✉*Barrio de Sobrellano* ☎*942/720365* 💳*AE, DC, MC, V* ⏲*Closed Jan. 15–Feb. 15 and Mon. Oct.–May. No dinner Sun.*

SAN VICENTE DE LA BARQUERA

64 km (40 mi) west of Santander, 15 km (9 mi) west of Comillas.

Important as a Roman port long before many other larger, modern shipping centers (such as Santander) were, San Vicente de la Barquera is one of the oldest and most beautiful maritime settlements in northern Spain. The 28 arches of the ancient bridge **Puente de la Maza,** which spans the *ría* (fjord), welcome you to town.

ESSENTIALS

Visitor Information San Vicente de la Barquera (✉ *Av. Generalísimo 20* ☎ *942/710797*).

EXPLORING

Thanks to its exceptional Romanesque portals, the 15th-century church of **Nuestra Señora de los Angeles** *(Our Lady of the Angels)* is among San Vicente's most memorable sights. Make sure you check out the arcaded porticoes of the **Plaza Mayor** and the view over the town from the Unquera road (N634) just inland. San Vicente celebrates **La Folía** in late April (the name translates roughly as "folly," and the exact date depends not only on Easter but on the high tide) with a magnificent maritime procession: the town's colorful fishing fleet accompanies the figure of La Virgen de la Barquera as she is transported (in part) by boat from her sanctuary outside town to the village church. There she's honored with folk dances and songs before being returned to her hermitage.

4

LAREDO

49 km (30 mi) southeast of Santander, via N635 southeast and N634 east.

You'd hardly know it today, but Laredo was a home port of the Spanish Armada and remained Spain's chief northern harbor until the French sacked it in the 18th century and Santander became the regional capital. Thus this little town was visited by Spanish royals, including Queen Isabella (Isabela la Católica) and Charles I, better known as Holy Roman Emperor Carlos V, founder of Spain's 16th-century global empire.

ESSENTIALS

Visitor Information Laredo (✉ *Alameda de Miramar* ☎ *942/611096*).

EXPLORING

Carlos V's brass choir desks are on display in the parish church of **La Asunción**, in the center of the town's tiny old quarter, which you may want to walk through to see mansions with heraldic coats of arms.

WHERE TO STAY

$$–$$$ **El Risco.** *Risco* is Spanish for "cliff," which is appropriate for a hotel built on the edge of the craggy slope overlooking Laredo. The food at the restaurant ($$) combines creative interpretations of classical and contemporary Cantabrian fare; try the *pimientos rellenos de cangrejo* (red bell peppers stuffed with crabmeat). Every room has a spectacular view of the town and cove below. Hotel reservations are essential in summer. **Pros:** bird's-eye views of the coast, excellent restaurant. **Cons:** no Internet, no elevator, room decor undistinguished. ✉ *La Arenosa 2*

☎942/605030 🌐www.hotelrisco.com ⇆25 rooms ♨In-room: Wi-Fi. In-hotel: restaurant, bar, no elevator ▭AE, DC, MC, V.

CASTRO-URDIALES

34 km (21 mi) northwest of Bilbao.

Behind Laredo, the N634 winds up into the hills, with views of the Bay of Santoña over your shoulder. A short drive, parts of it within sight of the coast, takes you into the fishing village of Castro-Urdiales, believed to be the oldest settlement on the Cantabrian coast. Castro-Urdiales (*castro* was the Celtiberian word for a fortified village) was the region's leading whaling port in the 13th and 14th centuries, when it had almost three times today's 13,000 residents. Today, the village is known mainly for its seafood.

ESSENTIALS

Visitor Information Castro-Urdiales (*✉Paseo Marítimo 1 [bis] ☎942/871512*).

EXPLORING

Overlooking the town is the mammoth rose-color jumble of roofs and buttresses of the Gothic **Santa María** church. Behind the Santa María church is the medieval **castle,** to which a modern lighthouse has been appended.

The only other things to see here are the arcaded **Plaza del Ayuntamiento** and the narrow streets of its **old quarter** (much of which burned on May 11, 1813) and the harbor-front promenade flanked by a row of glass-gallery houses.

WHERE TO EAT

$$–$$$$ SEAFOOD ✕**Mesón Marinero.** Local fishermen and seafarers rub elbows with visitors of all stripes at this tavern and restaurant. The ample and excellent variety of tapas will tempt you to forgo the main meal, but you won't want to miss dinner in the cozy second-floor dining room overlooking Castro's weathered fishing port. *Besugo* (sea bream) is a delicacy along this rugged coast, while Cantabrian favorites such as *tronco de merluza* (hake) or *rodaballo* (turbot) are both fine northern staples. *✉La Correría 23 ☎942/860005 ▭AE, DC, MC, V.*

EN ROUTE

The 45-minute drive on the N634 from Castro-Urdiales to Bilbao takes you through some of the sprawling industrial development that mars much of Vizcaya (Bizkaia, in Euskera, the Basque language), the westernmost of the three Basque provinces. The A8 freeway also takes you from Castro-Urdiales to Bilbao but bypasses the industrial development. A tempting stop is **Santurtzi,** where El **Hogar del Pescador** in the port is a legendary spot for sardines.

Bilbao and the Basque Country

WITH CANTABRIA, NAVARRA, AND LA RIOJA

Hondarribia's fishing port

WORD OF MOUTH

"They do occasionally have some interesting special exhibitions at the Guggenheim, but the architecture itself is worth the visit, besides, the restaurant is also world class and one of the best in the city and the pintxos bar isn't too bad."

—Robert2533

www.fodors.com/community

WELCOME TO BILBAO AND THE BASQUE COUNTRY

TOP REASONS TO GO

★ **The Basque Coast:** From colorful fishing villages to tawny beaches to Europe's longest surfing wave, the Basque Coast always delights the eye.

★ **Tapas in San Sebastián:** Nothing matches San Sebastián's Parte Vieja (old quarter), booming with the laughter of tavern hoppers tippling and grazing through counters heaped with colorful morsels.

★ **Art and Architecture in Bilbao:** The titanium Guggenheim and the Museo de Bellas Artes (Fine Arts Museum) shimmer where steel mills and shipyards once stood, while verdant pastures loom above and beyond.

★ **Running with the Bulls in Pamplona:** Running with a pack of wild animals (and people) will certainly get the adrenaline pumping, but you might prefer to be a spectator.

★ **Rioja's Wine Country:** Spain's premier wine-growing region in La Rioja Alta and La Rioja Alavesa is filled with wine-tasting opportunities—and fine cuisine.

1 Bilbao and the Basque Country. The contrast between Bilbao and the rest of the Basque Country makes each half of the equation better: a city famous for steel and shipbuilding turned shimmering art and architecture hub, surrounded by sylvan hillsides, tiny fishing ports, and beautiful beaches.

2 San Sebastián to Hondarribia/Fuenterrabía. San Sebastián lures travelers with its sophistication and wide beach. Nearby Hondarribia is a fishing port on the Bidasoa river estuary border with France.

3 Navarra and Pamplona. This region offers much beyond Pamplona's running-with-the-bulls blowout. The green Pyrenean hills to the north contrast with the lunar Bárdenas Reales to the southeast, while the wine country south of Pamplona leads to lovely Camino de Santiago way stations Puente la Reina and Estella. Medieval Vitoria is the capital of the Alava and the whole Basque Country, and is relatively undiscovered by tourists.

Cantabria's countryside.

Bilbao's tramway.

4 La Rioja. Spain's wine country is dedicated to tastes of all kinds. The Sierra de la Demanda mountain range offers culinary destinations such as Francis Paniego's Echaurren or Viniegra de Abajo's Venta de Goyo, while the towns of Logroño, Haro, and Laguardia are well endowed with superb architecture and gastronomy.

GETTING ORIENTED

Bordering the coastline of the Bay of Biscay, Basque Country and, farther inland, Navarra and La Rioja is a Spain apart—a land of moist green foothills, lush vineyards, and rolling meadowlands. A fertile slot between the Picos de Europa and the Pyrenees mountain ranges that stretch from the Mediterranean Cap de Creus all the way to Finisterre (Land's End) on the Atlantic in northwestern Galicia, this northern Arcadia is an often rainy but frequently comforting reprieve from the bright, hot Spanish *meseta* (high plain or tableland) to the south.

La Concha Beach, Donostia, San Sebastián.

BILBAO AND THE BASQUE COUNTRY PLANNER

When to Go

Mid-April through June, and September and October are the best times to enjoy the temperate climate and both the coastal and upland landscapes of this wet and grassy corner of Spain—though any time of year except August, when Europeans are on vacation, is nearly as good.

Pamplona in July is bedlam, though for party animals it's heaven.

The Basque Country is rainy in winter, but the wet Atlantic weather is always invigorating and, as if anyone needed it in this culinary paradise, appetite-enhancing. Much of the classically powerful Basque cuisine evolved with the northern maritime climate in mind.

The September film festival in San Sebastián coincides with the spectacular whaleboat regattas, while the beaches are still ideal and largely uncrowded.

Festivals

Glitterati descend on San Sebastián for its international film festival in the second half of September. Exact dates vary; ask the tourist office on Calle Fueros (☎ *943/426282*). The same goes for the late-July jazz festival, which draws many of the world's top performers. Saint's day is celebrated here January 19 to 20 with **La Tamborrada,** when 100-odd platoons of chefs and Napoleonic soldiers parade hilariously through the streets.

Pamplona's feast of **San Fermín** (July 6–14) was made famous by Ernest Hemingway in *The Sun Also Rises* and remains best known for its running of the bulls. Bilbao's **Semana Grande** (Grand Week), in early August, is notorious for the largest bulls of the season and a fine series of street concerts.

The coastal town of Lequeitio, east of Bilbao, is famous for its unusual **Fiestas de San Antolín** (September 5), in which men dangle from the necks of dead geese strung on a cable over the inlet. Closer to San Sebastián, in the first week of August, the fishing village of **Getaria** celebrates Juan Sebastián Elkano's completion of Magellan's voyage around the world every other year. The fiestas include a solemn procession up from the port of the weather-beaten, starving survivors and a week of feasts, dances, and street parties.

Vitoria's weeklong **Fiesta de la Virgen Blanca** (Festival of the White Virgin) celebrates the city's patron saint with bullfights and more August 4–9.

If You Like Beaches

Lequeitio beach, between Bilbao and San Sebastián, is particularly beautiful, and the smaller beaches at Zumaia, Getaria, and Zarautz are usually quiet. San Sebastián's best beach, La Concha, which curves around the bay along with the city itself, is scenic and clean, but packed in summer; Ondarreta, at the western end of La Concha, is often less crowded. Surfers gather at Zurriola on the northern side of the Urumea River. Hondarribia, the last stop before the French border, has a vast expanse of fine sand along the Bidasoa estuary.

Eat, Drink, and Be Merry . . .

The concentration of celebrated chefs around San Sebastián is so dazzling that food is a natural rallying point here. Beyond the famous names such as Juan Mari Arzak, Martín Berasategui, Pedro Subijana (Akelaŕe), Hilario Arbelaitz (Zuberoa), and Andoni Luis Aduriz (Mugaritz), there are dozens of other rising stars in and around the Basque Country, from Bilbao to Hondarribia. Meanwhile, the everyday excellence of ordinary food prepared with no gourmet pretensions beyond happy dining is everywhere.

. . . And Hike Off Some of Those Calories

Maintaining an appetite (and some semblance of a waistline) can become a problem on a food safari—and hiking is the answer: walking the well-marked hiking trails of the Basque Country, Navarra, and La Rioja is the best way to succeed in wolfing down a significant portion of the terrific cuisine and surviving to tell the tale. Bring good walking shoes and check with local tourist offices for classic hikes such as the full-day walk over the Pyrenees from St-Jean-Pied-de-Port to upper Navarra's Roncesvalles, a unique way to get a never-to-be-forgotten feel for the Pyrenean portal. The network of trails and ancient cobblestone Roman roads up the Basque coast from Zumaia to Getaria, and Zarautz and on to San Sebastián, and all the way to France will offer a look at corners of the Basque Country not seen from the freeways. From San Sebastián, the red and white GR (Gran Recorrido) markings at the end of the Zurriola beach will start you on a gorgeous three-hour hike to Pasajes de San Pedro, where a two-minute boat ride will whisk you across the Rentería shipping passage to Pasajes de San Juan (Pasaia Donibane in Euskera) and the town's several first-rate dining opportunities.

WHAT IT COSTS (IN EUROS)

	¢	$	$$	$$$	$$$$
Restaurants	under €8	€8–€12	€13–€17	€18–€22	over €22
Hotels	under €60	€60–€90	€91–€125	€126–€180	over €180

Prices are per person for a main course at dinner, and for two people in a standard double room in high season, excluding tax.

Planning Your Time

A road trip through the entire region including Basque Country, Navarra, and La Rioja would require at least a week. But a glimpse, however brief, of Bilbao and its Guggenheim, San Sebastián and La Concha Beach, the Baztán Valley, Pamplona, Laguardia, and La Rioja's wine capital at Haro are the top must-see elements in a classic whirlwind tour.

If you doubled the time and spent two days in each of these destinations, the next tier of unmissable spots might include Mundaka and the Vizcayan Coast west of Bilbao, Getaria, Pasajes de San Juan, and Hondarribia in and around San Sebastián, and Logroño in La Rioja.

Even better, if you found a few weeks to wander in a relaxed fashion, you could make it up as you go along, counting on off-season space available in most hotels and *paradores,* while crisscrossing the France–Spain border. La Rioja's Sierra de la Demanda also has some of the finest landscapes in Spain (not to mention culinary pilgrimages to Echaurren in Ezcaray or Venta de Goyo in Viniegra de Abajo).

GETTING HERE AND AROUND

By Air

Bilbao's airport serves much of this area, and there are smaller airports at Hondarribia (serving San Sebastián), Vitoria, Logroño, and Pamplona.

By Boat and Ferry

A 24-hour, twice-weekly ferry between Bilbao and Portsmouth is operated by Ferries Golfo de Vizcaya.

Boat and Ferry Information **Ferries Golfo de Vizcaya** (*Bilbao* ☎ *94/423–4477*).

By Bus

Daily bus service connects the major cities to Madrid, Zaragoza, and Barcelona (and with a layover or transfer to Spain's other destinations). From Madrid, call the bus company Continental Auto for details, or go to the station at Calle Alenza 20. Even better, reserve online at *www.alsa.es*. Bus service between cities and smaller towns is comprehensive, but few have central bus stations; most have numerous bus lines leaving from various points in town.

By Car

Even the remotest points are an easy one-day drive from Madrid, and northern Spain is superbly covered by freeways.

The drive from Madrid to Bilbao is 397 km (247 mi); follow the A1 past Burgos to Miranda del Ebro, where you pick up the AP68. Car rentals are available in the major cities: Bilbao, Pamplona, San Sebastián, and Vitoria. Cars can also be rented at Hondarribia (Fuenterrabía), the San Sebastián (Donostia) airport.

By Taxi

Taxis normally can be hailed on the street, though from more remote spots, such as Pedro Subijana's Akelaŕe restaurant on Igueldo above San Sebastián, the maître d' will need to call a taxi for you.

By Train

Direct trains from Madrid run to Bilbao, San Sebastián, Pamplona, Vitoria, and Logroño. Trains are not the ideal way to travel locally here, but many cities are connected by RENFE trains. Also, the regional company FEVE runs a delightful narrow-gauge train that winds through stunning landscapes. From San Sebastián, lines west to Bilbao and east to Hendaye depart from Estación de Amara; most long-distance trains use Estación del Norte.

Railway Companies **Euskotren** (✉ *Estación de Atxuri, north of Mercado de la Ribera, Bilbao* ☎ *94/433–8007*).

By George Semler

Northern Spain is a misty land of green hills, low russet rooflines, and colorful fishing villages; it's also home to the formerly industrial city of Bilbao, reborn as a center of art and architecture. The semiautonomous Basque Country, with its steady drizzle (onomatopoetically called the *sirimiri*), damp verdant landscape, and rugged coastline, is a distinct national and cultural entity within the Spanish state.

Navarra is considered Basque in the Pyrenees and merely Navarran in its southern reaches, along the Ebro River. La Rioja, tucked between the Sierra de la Demanda (a small-to-midsize mountain range that separates La Rioja from the central Castilian steppe) and the Ebro River, is Spain's premier wine country.

5

Called the País Vasco in Castilian Spanish, and Euskadi in the linguistically mysterious, non-Indo-European Basque language called Euskera, the Basque region is more a country within a country, or a nation within a state (the semantics are much debated). The Basques are known to love competition—it has been said that they will bet on anything that has numbers on it and moves (horses, dogs, runners, weight lifters—anything). Such traditional rural sports as chopping mammoth tree trunks, lifting boulders, and scything grass reflect the Basques' attachment to the land and to farm life as well as an ingrained enthusiasm for feats of strength and endurance. Even poetry and gastronomy become contests in Euskadi, as *bertsolaris* (amateur poets) improvise duels of sharp-witted verse, and male-only gastronomic societies compete in cooking contests to see who can make the best *sopa de ajo* (garlic soup) or *marmitako* (tuna stew).

The much-reported Basque separatist movement is made up of a small but radical sector of the political spectrum. The terrorist organization known as ETA, or Euskadi Ta Askatasuna (Basque Homeland and Liberty), has killed nearly 900 people in more than 35 years of violence. Conflict has waxed and waned over the years, though it has never affected travelers. When ETA declared a "permanent cease-fire" in April 2006, hope flared for an end to Basque terrorism until a late-December bomb at Madrid's Barajas airport killed two and brought progress to a halt. In early 2009 Basque Lehendakari (President) Juan José Ibarretxe and the PNV (Basque Nationalist Party) lost, albeit narrowly, the Basque presidency in favor of Patxi López of the PSOE (Spanish Socialist Party) in coalition with the PP (the right wing Partido Popular), reflecting voter weariness with the nationalist cause.

EXPLORING THE REGIONS

Northern Spain's Bay of Biscay area, at the western end of the Pyrenees along the border with France, is where the Cantabrian Cordillera and the Pyrenees nearly meet. The green foothills of Basque Country gently fill this space between the otherwise unbroken chain of mountains that rises from the Iberian Peninsula's easternmost point at northern Catalonia's Cap de Creus and ends at western Galicia's Fisterra, or Finisterre, land's end. Navarra—part Basque and part Castilian-speaking Navarrese—lies just southeast and inland of the Basque Country, with the backdrop of the Pyrenees rising up to the north. La Rioja, below Navarra, nestles in the Ebro River valley under the Sierra de la Demanda to the south, and stretches east and downriver to Calahorra and the edge of Spain's central *meseta* (plains).

ABOUT THE RESTAURANTS

Basque cuisine in and around San Sebastián and Bilbao combines the fish of the Atlantic with a love of sauces that's rare south of the Pyrenees—a result, no doubt, of Euskadi's proximity to France. The now 30-year-old *nueva cocina vasca* (new Basque cooking), originally inspired by the Basque Country's neighbors to the north, invented light, streamlined versions of classic Basque dishes such as *marmitako* (tuna and potato stew). Traditional San Sebastián specialties include *chuleta de buey* (garlicky beefsteak grilled over coals), and firm, flaky *besugo a la parrilla* (grilled sea bream) covered with crisped garlic. Around Bilbao, *bacalao al pil-pil* is ubiquitous—cod-flank fillets cooked in a boiled emulsion of garlic and gelatin from the cod itself so that the oil makes a popping noise ("pil-pil") and a white sauce is created. Other favorites are *kokotxas* (nuggets of cod jaw) and *pimientos de piquillo* (sweet red peppers stuffed with tuna or cod).

Navarra is famous for beef, lamb, and vegetable dishes, including *menestra de verduras* (a stew of artichokes, green beans, peas, lettuce, potatoes, onion, and chunks of cured ham). La Rioja has meaty stews and roasts in the mountains and vegetable dishes in the Ebro River basin.

The local Basque wine, *txakolí,* is young and white, made from tart green grapes. It is a refreshing accompaniment to both seafood and meats. La Rioja, south of the Basque Country, produces many of the finest wines in Spain; purists insisting on Basque wine with their Basque cuisine could choose a Rioja Alavesa, from the north side of the Ebro. Navarra also produces some fine vintages, especially rosés and reds—and in such quantity that some churches in Allo, Peralta, and other towns were actually built with a mortar mixed with wine instead of water.

Don't miss any chance to go to a *sidrería,* a cider house (in Astigarraga, near San Sebastián, there are no fewer than 17), where *tortilla de bacalao* (cod omelet) and *chuletas de buey* (garlicky beefsteak grilled over coals) provide traditional ballast for copious drinks of hard apple cider.

ABOUT THE HOTELS

The largely industrial and well-to-do north is an expensive part of Spain, and this is reflected in room rates. San Sebastián is particularly pricey, and Pamplona rates double or triple during San Fermín in July. Reserve ahead for Bilbao, where the Guggenheim is filling hotels, and nearly everywhere else in summer. Another lodging option is the Agroturismo lodging network, which often offers rooms in Basque *caseríos* (farmhouses). Check with local tourist offices for details.

BILBAO AND THE BASQUE COAST TO GETARIA (GUETARIA)

Starring Frank Gehry's titanium brainchild—the Museo Guggenheim Bilbao—Bilbao has established itself as one of Spain's 21st-century darlings. The loop around the coast of Vizcaya and east into neighboring Guipúzcoa province to Getaria and San Sebastián is a succession of colorful ports, ocher beaches, and green hills.

BILBAO

34 km (21 mi) southeast of Castro-Urdiales, 116 km (72 mi) east of Santander, 397 km (247 mi) north of Madrid.

Fodor's Choice ★ Time in Bilbao (Bilbo, in Euskera) may be recorded as BG or AG (Before Guggenheim, After Guggenheim). Never has a single monument of art and architecture so radically changed a city—or, for that matter, a nation, and in this case two: Spain and Euskadi. Frank Gehry's stunning museum, Norman Foster's sleek subway system, the glass Santiago Calatrava footbridge, and the leafy park and commercial complex in Abandoibarra have all helped foster a cultural revolution in the commercial capital of the Basque Country.

Greater Bilbao encompasses almost 1 million inhabitants, nearly half the total population of the Basque Country. Founded in 1300 by Vizcayan noble Diego López de Haro, Bilbao became an industrial center in the mid-19th century, largely because of the abundance of minerals in the surrounding hills. An affluent industrial class grew up here, as did the working-class suburbs that line the Margen Izquierda (Left Bank) of the Nervión estuary.

Bilbao's new attractions get more press, but the city's old treasures still quietly line the banks of the rust-color Nervión River. The Casco Viejo (Old Quarter)—also known as Siete Calles (Seven Streets)—is a charming jumble of shops, bars, and restaurants on the river's Right Bank, near the Puente del Arenal bridge. Throughout the old quarter are ancient mansions emblazoned with family coats of arms, noble wooden doors, and fine ironwork balconies. Carefully restored after devastating floods in August 1983, this is an upscale shopping district replete with excellent taverns, restaurants, and nightlife. The most interesting square is the 64-arch Plaza Nueva, where an outdoor market is pitched every Sunday morning. On the Left Bank, the wide, late-19th-century boulevards of the Ensanche neighborhood, such as Gran Vía (the main shopping artery) and Alameda Mazarredo, are the city's more formal face. Bilbao's cultural institutions include, along with the Guggenheim, a major museum of fine arts (the Museo de Bellas Artes) and an opera society (ABAO: Asociación Bilbaína de Amigos de la Ópera) with 7,000 members from all over Spain and parts of southern France. In addition, epicureans have long ranked Bilbao's culinary offerings among the best in Spain. Don't miss a chance to ride the speedy and quiet trolley line, the Euskotram, for a trip along the river from Atxuri Station to Basurto's San Mamés soccer stadium, reverently dubbed "La Catedral del Fútbol" (the Cathedral of Football).

GETTING HERE AND AROUND

Bilbao's subway is the pride and joy of the transport system, with 39 stations on both sides of the Ría de Bilbao, some of which were designed by British architect Sir Norman Foster. The fare is €1.30, and the underground train will also get you out to the beach at Getxo or Plentzia.

Bilbao's Euskotram, running up and down the Ría de Bilbao (aka River Nervión) past the Guggenheim to the Mercado de la Ribera, is an attraction in its own right: silent, swift, and panoramic as it glides up and down its grassy runway. The Euskotren leaving from Atxuri Station north of the Mercado de la Ribera runs along a spectacular route through Gernika and the Urdaibai Nature Preserve to Mundaka, probably the best way short of a boat to see this lovely wetlands preserve.

Bilbao Paso a Paso conducts fine tours of Bilbao for a small charge.

ESSENTIALS

Bus Station Bilbao (✉ *Gurtubay 1* ☎ *94/439–5077*).

Subway Information Subway (🌐 *www.metrobilbao.com*).

Tour Operators Bilbao Paso a Paso (✉ *Mitxel Labegerie Kalea 1, Ofic. 5* ☎ *94/415–3892* 🌐 *www.bilbaopasoapaso.com*).

Train Station Bilbao (✉ *Estación de Abando, C. Hurtado de Amezaga* ☎ *94/423–8623 or 94/423–8636*).

Visitor Information Bilbao (✉ *Av. Abandoibarra 2* ☎ *94/479–5760* ✉ *Plaza del Ensanche 11* ☎ *94/479–5760*).

EXPLORING

6 Near the Ayuntamiento Bridge is the riverside **ayuntamiento** *(city hall)*, built in 1892. Ⓜ *Casco Viejo.*

7 Stop at Calle Esperanza 6 and take the elevator to Bilbao's iconic **Basílica de Begoña** overlooking the city. The church's three-nave Gothic hulk was begun in 1511 on a spot where the Virgin Mary had supposedly appeared long before. Partly destroyed in the First Carlist War of 1835, the facade, tower, and sacristy were rebuilt in the early 20th century. The 24-bell carillon, the largest of which weighs one ton, plays a series of hymns and traditional Basque melodies that change according to the season. On the occasion of the winter and summer solstices, the carillon serenades Bilbao with a short concert that might include anything from Bach to local composer Juan Crisóstomo de Arriaga (1806–26), known as Spain's Mozart. ✉ *C. Virgen de Begoña 38* ☎ *94/412–7091* 🌐 *www.basilicadebegona.com* Ⓜ *Casco Viejo.*

11 The **Casco Viejo** *(Old Quarter)* is folded into an elbow of the Nervión River, behind Bilbao's grand, elaborately restored theater. Inaugurated in 1890, **Teatro Arriaga** was a symbol of Bilbao's industrial might and cultural vibrancy by the time it burned nearly to the ground in 1914. Styled after the Paris Opéra, the theater defies easy classification: although its symmetry suggests neoclassicism, its ornamentation defines the belle epoque style. Walk around to see the stained-glass windows in the back. While exploring, don't miss the colossal food market **El Mercado de la Ribera** at the edge of the river, the Renaissance town house **Palacio Yohn** at the corner of Sant Maria and Perro, and the library and

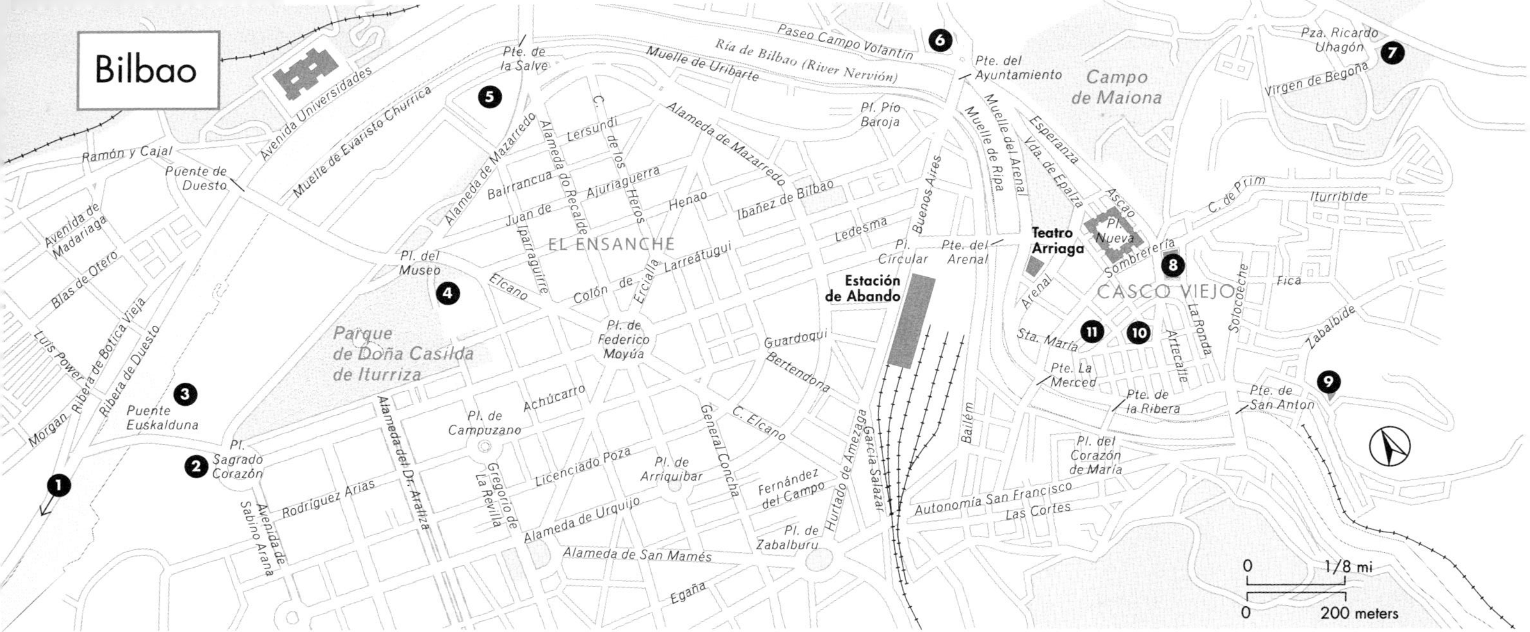

Ayuntamiento 6
Basílica de La Begoña 7
Casco Viejo 11
Catedral de Santiago 10
Museo Arqueológico Etnográfico e Histórico Vasco 8
Museo Diocesano de Arte Sacro 9
Museo de Bellas Artes 4
Museo Guggenheim Bilbao 5
Museo Marítimo de Bilbao 2
Palacio de Euskalduna 3
Puente de Vizcaya (Puente Colgante) 1

cultural center **Biblioteca Municipal Bidebarrieta** at Calle Bidebarrieta 4. ✉*Plaza Arriaga 1* ☎*94/479–2036* Ⓜ*Casco Viejo.*

10 **Catedral de Santiago** *(St. James's Cathedral).* Bilbao's earliest church, this was a pilgrimage stop on the coastal route to Santiago de Compostela. Work on the structure began in 1379, but fire destroyed most of it in 1571; it has a notable outdoor arcade. ✉*Plaza de Santiago* Ⓜ*Casco Viejo.*

8 The **Museo Arqueológico, Etnográfico e Histórico Vasco** *(Museum of Basque Archaeology, Ethnology, and History)* is in a lovely 16th-century convent—its baroque elegance and lush arcaded cloister more than justifies the visit. The collection centers on Basque fishing, crafts, and agriculture. ✉*Pl. Miguel de Unamuno 4* ☎*94/415–5423* 🌐*www.euskal-museoa.org* *€3.50, free Thurs.* ⏲*Tues.–Sat. 10:30–1:30 and 4–7, Sun. 10:30–1* Ⓜ*Casco Viejo.*

NEED A BREAK?

El Kiosko del Arenal (✉***Paseo del Arenal s/n, under the bandstand in Paseo del Arenal*** Ⓜ***Casco Viejo***) **is an excellent stop for coffee, beer, or tapas. Terrace tables offer views of the river in summer, and its spot underneath the bandstand is clean and well-lit in winter.**

4 Fodor's Choice ★ Don't let the Guggenheim eclipse the **Museo de Bellas Artes** *(Museum of Fine Arts).* Depending on your tastes, you may find the art here more satisfying. The museum's fine collection of Flemish, French, Italian, and Spanish paintings includes works by El Greco, Goya, Velázquez, Zurbarán, Ribera, and Gauguin. One large and excellent section traces developments in 20th-century Spanish and Basque art alongside those of their better-known European contemporaries, such as Léger and Bacon. The building sits on the rim of the pretty Doña Casilda Park, about a 30-minute walk from the Old Quarter. ✉*Plaza del Museo 2* ☎*94/439–6060* 🌐*www.museobilbao.com* *€5.50, free Wed., combined ticket with Guggenheim (valid 1 yr) €13* ⏲*Tues.–Sat. 10–1:30 and 4–7:30, Sun. 10–2* Ⓜ*Moyúa.*

9 The **Museo Diocesano de Arte Sacro** *(Diocesan Museum of Sacred Art)* occupies a carefully restored 16th-century cloister. The inner patio alone, ancient and intimate, is worth the visit. On display are religious silver works, liturgical garments, sculptures, and paintings dating back to the 12th century. ✉*Pl. de la Encarnación 9* ☎*94/432–0125* *€2* Ⓜ*Casco Viejo.*

5 Fodor's Choice ★ Covered with a dazzling 30,000 sheets of titanium, the **Museo Guggenheim Bilbao** opened in October 1997 and overnight became Bilbao's main attraction. The shimmering effect of this finned and fluted titanium whale next to the rusty waters of the Nervión is difficult to overdescribe. An enormous atrium, more than 150 feet high, is connected to the 19 galleries by a system of suspended metal walkways and glass elevators. The ground floor is dedicated to large permanent installations. The permanent collection and the excellent audioguide that accompanies it offer an entertaining and instructive survey of 20th-century art. ✉*Avenida Abandoibarra 2* ☎*94/435–9080* 🌐*www.guggenheim-bilbao.es* *€8; combined ticket with Museo de Bellas Artes (valid*

1 yr) €13 ⏲July and Aug., daily 10–8; Sept.–June, Tues.–Sun. 10–8 Ⓜ Moyúa.

2 **Museo Marítimo de Bilbao** *(Maritime Museum of Bilbao)*. This interesting nautical museum on the left bank of the Ría de Bilbao reconstructs the history of the Bilbao waterfront and shipbuilding industry, beginning with medieval times. Temporary exhibits range from visits by extraordinary seacraft such as tall ships or traditional fishing vessels to thematic displays on 17th- and 18th-century clipper ships or the sinking of the *Titanic*. *✉Muelle Ramón de la Sota ☎902/131000 🌐www.museomaritimobilbao.org 🎫€4 ⏲Tues.–Sun. 10–8 Ⓜ San Mamés.*

BILBAO BLUE

The Guggenheim museum's offices, to the right of Jeff Koons's Puppy, are bright blue. Frank Gehry discovered the rich azure while working on his titanium opus and fell in love with it. Known locally as "Bilbao blue," the color comes from the vivid blue sky traditionally visible over Bilbao on the rare days when the persistent Atlantic drizzle lets up. Curiously, as a result of either the reflected light of the Guggenheim, the absence of industrial smog, or climate change, Bilbao's blue skies are thought to be less intensely blue (and less infrequent) than they used to be.

1 Dubbed Bilbao's Eiffel Tower (albeit a horizontal version) the **Puente de Vizcaya** is commonly called the Puente Colgante (Hanging Bridge). Spanning the Nervión, this transporter hung from cables unites two distinct worlds: exclusive, quiet Las Arenas and Portugalete, a much older, working-class town that spawned Dolores Ibarruri, the famous Republican orator of the Spanish civil war, known as La Pasionaria for her ardor. Portugalete is a 15-minute walk from Santurce, where the quayside Hogar del Pescador serves simple and ample fish specialties. *Besugo* (sea bream) is the traditional choice, but the fresh grilled sardines are hard to pass up. To reach the bridge, take the subway to Areeta, or drive across the Puente de Deusto, turn left on Avenida Lehendakari Aguirre, and follow signs for Las Arenas. *☎94/480–1012 🌐www.puente-colgante.org 🎫€0.30 to cross on foot, €1.20 by car (plus €0.30 per person); €5 to visit the observation deck Ⓜ Areeta.*

3 **Palacio de Euskalduna.** In homage to the Astilleros Euskalduna (Basque Country shipbuilders) who operated shipyards here beside the Euskalduna Bridge into the mid-1980s, this music venue and convention hall resembles a rusting ship. Designed by Federico Soriano, Euskalduna opened in 1999 and is Bilbao's main opera venue and home of the Bilbao Symphony Orchestra. *✉Abandoibarra 4, El Ensanche ☎94/403–5000 🌐www.euskalduna.net 🎫Tour €3 ⏲Office weekdays 9–2 and 4–7; box office Mon.–Sat. noon–2 and 5–8:30, Sun. noon–2; guided tours Sat. at noon or by fax appointment Ⓜ San Mamés.*

EN ROUTE

Just outside of Bilbao, 13 km (8 mi), northwest of town, is Getxo, an early watering spot for the elite Bilbao industrial classes. There are rambling mansions, five beaches, and an ancient fishing port. Restaurants and hotels along the beaches here make good hideaways—only a 20-minute ride from the center of Bilbao on the subway line.

CLOSE UP

Glitzy Guggenheim

Bilbao's Guggenheim, an eruption of light and titanium—described by the late Spanish novelist Manuel Vazquez Montalban as a "meteorite"—has completely reinvented Bilbao, a city that used to be perceived as a polluted steel and shipbuilding center—the *barrio industrial* (industrial quarter) in contrast to San Sebastián's *barrio jardín* (garden quarter). The Guggenheim changed all that.

Frank Gehry's gleaming brainchild, hailed as "the greatest building of our time" (architect Philip Johnson), "the best building of the 20th century" (Spain's King Juan Carlos), and "a miracle" (Herbert Muschamp, *New York Times*), has sparked a renaissance in the Basque Country: in its first year, the museum attracted 1.4 million visitors, three times the number expected and more than what the Guggenheim museum in New York received in the same period. Revenue in the first year alone exceeded the original investment, and that was over a decade ago. The Guggenheim holds the Spanish record for single-day visits to a museum (9,300), and the crowds, though abating somewhat, have remained numerous since the museum opened.

The museum itself is as superlative as the hoopla suggests. The smoothly rounded, asymmetrical, ship's-prow-like amalgam of limestone, glass, and titanium ingeniously recalls Bilbao's shipbuilding and steel-manufacturing past while using transparency and reflective materials to create a shimmering, futuristic luminosity. The final section of the Nervión's La Salve Bridge is almost part of the structure, rendering the Guggenheim the virtual doorway to Bilbao.

The collection, described by director Thomas Krens as "a daring history of the art of the 20th century," consists of 242 works, 186 from New York's Guggenheim and 50 acquired by the Basque government. Artists whose names are synonymous with the 20th century (Kandinsky, Picasso, Ernst, Braque, Miró, Calder, Malevich) and particularly artists of the '50s and '60s (Pollock, Rothko, De Kooning, Chillida, Tàpies, Iglesias) are joined by contemporary figures (Nauman, Muñoz, Schnabel, Badiola, Barceló, Basquiat). The huge ground-floor gallery is one of the largest in the world.

WHERE TO EAT

$$$–$$$$ CONTEMPORARY BASQUE **Aizian.** Euskera for "in the wind," the Sheraton Bilbao restaurant—under the direction of chef José Miguel Olazabalaga—has in record time become one of the city's most respected dining establishments. Typically Bilbaíno culinary classicism doesn't keep Mr. Olazabalaga from creating surprising reductions and contemporary interpretations of traditional dishes such as *la marmita de chipirón,* a stew of sautéed cuttlefish with a topping of whipped potatoes covering the sauce of squid ink. ⊠*C. Lehendakari Leizaola 29, El Ensanche* ☎*94/428–0035* ▭*AE, DC, MC, V* ⊙*Closed Sun. and Aug. 1–15* Ⓜ*San Mamés.*

$–$$ CONTEMPORARY BASQUE **Arriaga.** The cider-house experience is a must in the Basque Country. Cider *al txotx* (straight from the barrel), sausage stewed in apple cider, codfish omelets, *txuletón de buey* (beef chops), and *Idiazabal* cheese with quince jelly are the classic fare. Reserving a table here is a good idea, especially on weekends. ⊠*Santa Maria 13, Casco Viejo* ☎*94/416–5670* ▭*AE, DC, MC, V* ⊙*No dinner Sun.* Ⓜ*Casco Viejo.*

5

$$–$$$ CONTEMPORARY BASQUE **Berton.** Dinner is served until 11:30 in this sleek, contemporary bistro in the Casco Viejo. Wood tables with a green-tint polyethylene finish and exposed ventilation pipes give the dining room a designer look, and the classic cuisine ranges from ibérico ham to smoked salmon, foie gras, cod, beef, and lamb. ⊠*Jardines 11, Casco Viejo* ☎*94/416–7035* ▭*AE, DC, MC, V* ⊙*No dinner Sun. and holidays* Ⓜ*Casco Viejo.*

$$$–$$$$ SPANISH Fodor's Choice ★ **El Perro Chico.** Named for the toll once charged here for crossing the footbridge below Bilbao's Mercado de la Ribera (a *perro chico* was the colloquial name for an ancient coin), this restaurant became a Frank Gehry favorite during his time in Bilbao supervising the construction of the Guggenheim. From owner Santiago Diez Ponzoa to chef Rafael García Rossi, everyone here genuinely enjoys preparing innovative and thoughtful cuisine without pretense. Try the *pato a la naranja* (duck à l'orange) or the *bacalao con berenjena* (salt cod with eggplant). ⊠*Aretxaga 2, Casco Viejo* ☎*94/415–0519* ▭*AE, DC, MC, V* ⊙*Closed Sun. No lunch Mon.* Ⓜ*Casco Viejo.*

$$$–$$$$ CONTEMPORARY BASQUE **Etxanobe.** Fernando Canales creates sleek, contemporary cuisine here on a par with the Basque Country's finest, with seasonal offerings ranging from truffles in cream of potato and egg in winter to a superb crab salad in summer. This luminous corner of the Euskalduna palace overlooks the Nervión River, the hills of Artxanda above, and the city of Bilbao. The panoramic elevator up to the restaurant is guaranteed to jump-start appetite-enhancing adrenaline. ⊠*Av. de Abandoibarra 4, El Ensanche* ☎*94/442–1071* ▭*AE, DC, MC, V* ⊙*Closed Sun., Easter wk, and Aug. 1–20* Ⓜ*San Mamés.*

$$–$$$$ SPANISH **Guggenheim Bilbao.** The museum's restaurant-in-residence has a lot to live up to but easily succeeds. Famous for his eponymous restaurant outside San Sebastián, Martín Berasategui (or his staff) will install you at a table overlooking the Nervión and the green heights of Artxanda, then feed you such exciting creations as *pichón de Bresse* (wild pigeon) and *ensalada de bogavante* (lobster salad). ⊠*Av. Abandoibarra 2, El Ensanche* ☎*94/423–9333* ✍*Reservations essential* ▭*AE, DC, MC, V* ⊙*Closed Mon. and Jan. 1–19. No dinner Sun. or Tues.* Ⓜ*Moyúa.*

$$–$$$$ CONTEMPORARY BASQUE ★ ✕ **Guria.** The late, great Genaro Pildain was the hands-down leader of Bilbao chefs, a genius of charm and simplicity. Having learned the art of cooking from his mother, Don Genaro presided over one of Bilbao's finest tables for two decades. His business partner Carlos del Rey and chef Tomás Razquin carry on Don Genaro's tradition of generosity and hospitality. Everything's impeccable here, from the *crema de puerros con patatas* (cream of potato-and-leek soup) to the *perretxikos de Orduña* (small, wild spring mushrooms). ✉ *Gran Vía 66, El Ensanche* ☎ *94/441–5780* ▭ *AE, DC, MC, V* ⊙ *No dinner Sun.* Ⓜ *San Mamés.*

$$$–$$$$ SPANISH Fodor'sChoice ★ ✕ **Jolastoki.** Housed in a graceful mansion, this fine restaurant is 20 minutes from downtown on the city's pride-and-joy Norman Foster subway (and then a seven-minute walk). Wild salmon from the River Cares; dark, red Bresse pigeon roasted in balsamic vinegar; *lubina al vapor* (steamed sea bass) as light as a soufflé; and encyclopedic salads are done to perfection. The red fruit dessert includes 11 varieties with sorbet in raspberry coulis. ✉ *Los Chopos 24, Getxo* ☎ *94/491–2031* ✍ *Reservations essential* ▭ *AE, DC, MC, V* ⊙ *Closed Mon. No dinner Sun. or Tues.* Ⓜ *Getxo.*

$–$$ CONTEMPORARY BASQUE Fodor'sChoice ★ ✕ **Kiskia.** A modern version of the traditional cider house, this rambling tavern near the San Mamés soccer stadium serves the classical *sidrería* menu of chorizo sausage cooked in cider, codfish omelet, *txuleta de buey* (beef chops), *Idiazabal* cheese with quince jelly and nuts, and as much cider as you can drink, all for €28, though you can also order à la carte. Actors, sculptors, writers, soccer stars, and Bilbao's who's who (and Spain's who's who) frequent this boisterous marvel. ✉ *Pérez Galdós 51, San Mamés* ☎ *94/442–0032* ▭ *AE, DC, MC, V* ⊙ *No dinner Sun.–Tues.* Ⓜ *San Mamés.*

$–$$$ CONTEMPORARY BASQUE ✕ **La Deliciosa.** For carefully prepared fare at friendly prices, this unassuming and simple but cozy dining room continues to be one of the best values in the Casco Viejo. The *crema de puerros* (cream of leeks) is as good as any in town, and the *dorada al horno* (roast gilthead bream) is fresh from the nearby La Ribera Market. ✉ *Jardines 1, Casco Viejo* ☎ *94/415–0944* ▭ *AE, DC, MC, V* Ⓜ *Casco Viejo.*

$–$$ SPANISH ✕ **Victor Montes.** A hot spot for the daily *tapeo* (tapas tour), this place is always crowded with congenial grazers. The well-stocked counter might offer anything from wild mushrooms to *txistorra* (spicy sausages) to *Idiazabal* (Basque smoked cheese) or, for the adventurous, *huevas de merluza* (hake roe), all taken with splashes of Rioja, *txakolí*, or cider. ✉ *Pl. Nueva 8, Casco Viejo* ☎ *94/415–7067* ✍ *Reservations essential* ⊙ *Closed Sun. and Aug. 1–15* Ⓜ *Casco Viejo.*

¢–$ SPANISH ✕ **Xukela.** Amid bright lighting and a vivid palette of green and crimson decor—the morsels of ham and bell peppers that line the bar—chef Santiago Ruíz Bombin creates some of the tastiest and most interesting and varied *pinchos* (miniature cuisine presented on toothpicks) in all of tapas-dom. The tavern has the general feel of a small library: lined with books, magazines, paintings, and little reading nooks. Drinks range from beer to the acidic Basque *txakolí* to a handsome selection of red and white wines from all over Spain. ✉ *El Perro 2, Casco Viejo* ☎ *94/415–9772* ▭ *AE, DC, MC, V* Ⓜ *Casco Viejo.*

Continued on page 287

BASQUE SPOKEN HERE

While the Basque Country's future as an independent nation-state has yet to be determined, the quirky, fascinating culture of the Basque people is not restricted by any borders. Experience it for yourself in the food, history, and sport.

Basque solar cross

The cultural footprints of this tiny corner of Europe, which straddle the Atlantic end of the border between France and Spain, have already touched down all over the globe. The sport of jai-alai has come to America. International magazines give an ecstatic thumbs-up to Basque cooking. Historians are pointing to Basque fishermen as the true discoverers of North America. And bestsellers, not without irony, proclaim *The Basque History of the World*. As in the ancient 4 + 3 = 1 graffiti equation, the three French (Labourd, Basse Navarre, and Soule) and the four Spanish (Guipúzcoa, Vizcaya, Alava, and Navarra) Basque provinces add up to a single people with a shared history. Although nationless, Basques have been Basques since Paleolithic times.

Stretching across the Pyrénées from Bayonne in France to Bilbao in Spain, the New Hampshire-sized Basque region retains a distinct culture, neither expressly French nor Spanish, fiercely guarded by its three million inhabitants. Fables stubbornly connect them with Adam and Eve, Noah's Ark, and the lost city of Atlantis, but a leading genealogical theory points to common bloodlines with the Celts. The most tenable theory is that the Basques are descended from aboriginal Iberian peoples who successfully defended their unique cultural identity from the influences of Roman and Moorish domination.

It was only in 1876 that Sabino Arana—a virulent anti-Spanish fanatic—proposed the ideal of a "pure" Basque independent state. That dream was crushed by Franco's dictatorial reign (1939–75, during which many Spanish Basques emigrated to France) and was immortalized in Pablo Picasso's *Guernica*. This famous painting, which depicts the catastrophic Nazi bombing of the Basque town of Guernika stands not only as a searing indictment of all wars but as a reminder of history's brutal assault upon Basque identity.

"THE BEST FOOD YOU'VE NEVER HEARD OF"

So said *Food & Wine* magazine. It's time to get filled in.

An old saying has it that every soccer team needs a Basque goaltender and every restaurant a Basque chef. Traditional Basque cuisine combines the fresh fish of the Atlantic and upland vegetables, beef, and lamb with a love of sauces that is rare south of the Pyrénées. Today, the *nueva cocina vasca* (new Basque cooking) movement has made Basque food less rustic and much more nouvelle. And now that pintxos (the Basque equivalent of tapas) have become the rage from Barcelona to New York City, Basque cuisine is being championed by foodies everywhere. Even superchef Michel Guérard up in Eugénie-les-Bains has, though not himself a Basque, has influenced and been influenced by the master cookery of the Pays Basque.

WHO'S THE BEST CHEF?

Basques are so naturally competitive that meals often turn into comparative rants over who is better: Basque chefs based in France or in Spain. Some vote for Bayonne's Jean-Claude Tellechea (his L'Auberge du Cheval Blanc is famed for groundbreaking surf-and-turf dishes like hake roasted in onions with essence of poultry) or St-Jean-Pied-de-Port's Firmin Arrambide (based at his elegant Les Pyrénées inn). Others prefer the postmodern lobster salads found over the border in San Sebastián and Bilbao, created by master chefs Juan Mark Arzak, Pedro Subijana, and Martin Berasategui, with wunderkind Andoni Aduriz and the Arbelaitz family nipping at their culinary heels.

SIX GREAT DISHES

Angulas. Baby eels, cooked in olive oil and garlic with a few slices of guindilla pepper.

Bacalao al pil-pil. Cod cooked at a low temperature in an emulsion of olive oil and fish juices, which makes a unique pinging sound as it sizzles.

Besugo. Sea bream, or besugo, is so revered that it is a traditional Christmas dish. Enjoy it with sagardo, the signature Basque apple cider.

Marmitako. This tuna stew with potatoes and pimientos is a satisfying winter favorite.

Ttoro. Typical of Labourd fishing villages such as St-Jean-de-Luz, this peppery Basque bouillabaisse is known as *sopa de pescado* (fish soup) south of the French border.

Txuleta de buey. The signature Basque meat is ox steaks marinated in parsley and garlic and cooked over coals.

BASQUE SPORTS: JAI-ALAI TO OXCART-LIFTING

Sports are core to Basque society, and virtually none are immune from the Basque passion for competing, betting, and playing.

Over the centuries, the rugged physical environment of the Basque hills and the rough Cantabrian sea traditionally made physical prowess and bravery valued attributes. Since Basque mythology often involved feats of strength, it's easy to see why today's Basques are such rabid sports fans.

PELOTA

A Basque village without a frontón (pelota court) is as unimaginable as an American town without a baseball diamond. "The fastest game in the world," pelota is called *jai-alai* in Basque (and translated officially as "merry festival"). With rubber balls flung from hooked wicker gloves at speeds up to 150 mph—the impact of the ball is like a machine-gun bullet— jai-alai is mesmerizing. It is played on a three-walled court 175 feet long and 56 feet wide with 40-foot side walls.

Whether singles or doubles, the object is to angle the ball along or off of the side wall so that it cannot be returned. Betting is very much part of pelota and courtside wagers are brokered by bet makers as play proceeds. While pelota is the word for "ball," it also refers to the game. There was even a recent movie in Spain entitled *La Pelota Vasca*, used metaphorically to refer to the greater "ball game" of life and death.

HERRIKIROLAK

Herrikirolak (rural sports) are based on farming and seafaring. Stone lifters (*harrijasotzaileak* in Euskera) heft weights up to 700 pounds. *Aizkolari* (axe men) chop wood in various contests, *Gizon proba* (man trial) pits three-man teams moving weighted sleds; while *estropadak* are whaleboat rowers who compete in spectacular regattas (culminating in the September competition off La Concha beach in San Sebastián). *Sokatira* is tug of war, and *segalariak* is a scything competition. Other events include oxcart-lifting, milk-can carrying, and ram fights.

SOCCER

When it comes to soccer, Basque goaltenders have developed special fame in Spain, where Bilbao's Athletic Club and San Sebastián's Real Sociedad have won national championships with budgets far inferior to those of Real Madrid or FC Barcelona. Across the border, Bayonne's rugby team is a force in the French national competition; the French Basque capital is also home to the annual French pelota championship.

HABLA EUSKERA?

Although the Basque people speak French north of the border and Spanish south of the border, they consider Euskera their first language and identify themselves as the *Euskaldunak* (the "Basque speakers"). Euskera remains one of the great enigmas of linguistic scholarship. Theories connect it with everything from Sanskrit to Japanese to Finnish.

What is certain is where Euskera did not come from, namely the Indo-European family of languages that includes the Germanic, Italic, and Hellenic language groups. Currently used by about a million people in northern Spain and southwestern France, Euskera sounds like a consonant-ridden version of Spanish, with its five pure vowels, rolled "r," and palatal "n" and "l." Basque has survived two millennia of cultural and political pressure and is the only remaining language of those spoken in southwestern Europe before the Roman conquest.

The Euskaldunak celebrate their heritage during a Basque folk dancing festival.

A BASQUE GLOSSARY

Aurresku: The high-kicking *espata danza* or sword dance typically performed on the day of Corpus Christi in the Spanish Basque Country.

Akelarre: A gathering of witches that provoked witch trials in the Pyrénées. Even today it is believed that *jentilak* (magic elves) inhabit the woods and the Olentzaro (the evil Basque Santa Claus) comes down chimneys to wreak havoc—a fire is kept burning to keep him out.

Boina: The Basque beret or *txapela*, thought to have developed as the perfect protection from the siri-miri, the perennial "Scotch mist" that soaks the moist Basque Country.

Eguzki: The sun worship was at the center of the pagan religion that, in the Basque Country, gave way only slowly to Christianity. The Basque solar cross is typically carved into the east-facing facades of ancient *caserios* or farmhouses.

Espadrilles: Rope-soled canvas Basque shoes, also claimed by the Catalans, developed in the Pyrénées and traditionally attached by laces or ribbons wrapped up the ankle.

Etxekoandre: The woman who commands all matters spiritual, culinary, and practical in a traditional Basque farmhouse. Basque matriarchal inheritance laws remain key.

Fueros: Special Basque rights and laws (including exemption from serving in the army except to defend the Basque Country) originally conceded by the ancient Romans and abolished at the end of the Carlist Wars in 1876 after centuries of Castilian kings had sworn to protect Basque rights at the Tree of Guernika.

Ikurriña: The Basque flag, designed by the founder of Basque nationalism, Sabino Arana, composed of green and white crosses over a red background and said to have been based on the British Union Jack.

Lauburu: Resembling a four-leaf clover, lau (four) buru (head) is the Basque symbol.

Twenty: Basques favor counting in units of twenty (*veinte duros*—20 nickels—is a common way of saying a hundred pesetas, for example).

Txakolí: A slightly fizzy young wine made from grapes grown around the Bay of Biscay, this fresh, acidic brew happily accompanies tapas and fish.

WHERE TO STAY

Your main choices for where to stay in Bilbao are between the old city (Casco Viejo) or the relatively newer El Ensanche (late 19th and early 20th), where you'll also find the hotels near the Guggenheim. The old part of town is more resonant; the newer has proximity to the museum, but also heavier traffic.

$$$–$$$$ ★ **Carlton.** Luminaries who have trod the halls of this grande dame include Orson Welles, Ava Gardner, Ernest Hemingway, Lauren Bacall, and most of Spain's great bullfighters. During the civil war it was the seat of the Republican Basque government; later it housed a number of Nationalist generals. It remains high-ceilinged and elegant, with creaky wooden floorboards and floor-to-ceiling windows swathed in heavy drapes. **Pros:** historic location, famous ghosts, a sense of history. **Cons:** surrounded by noisy streets, antique infrastructure and equipment. ✉ *Pl. Federico Moyúa 2, El Ensanche* ☎ *94/416–2200* 🌐 *www.aranzazu-hoteles.com* *137 rooms, 7 suites* *In-room: Wi-Fi. In-hotel: restaurant, bar, parking (fee)* 💳 *AE, DC, MC, V* Ⓜ *Moyúa.*

$$$–$$$$ ★ **Gran Hotel Domine Bilbao.** Half design festival, half hotel, this member of the Silken chain, directly across the street from the Guggenheim, showcases the conceptual wit of Javier Mariscal, creator of Barcelona's 1992 Olympic mascot Cobi, and the structural know-how of Bilbao architect Iñaki Aurreroextea. With adjustable windowpanes reflecting Gehry's titanium leviathan and every lamp and piece of furniture reflecting Mariscal's playful whimsy, this is a bright star in Bilbao's design constellation. Comprehensively equipped and comfortable, it's the next best thing to moving into the Guggenheim. **Pros:** exciting design and decor, professional service. **Cons:** slightly self-conscious runway vibe, noisy streets require closed windows. ✉ *Alameda de Mazarredo 61, El Ensanche* ☎ *94/425–3300* 🌐 *www.granhoteldominebilbao.com* *139 rooms, 6 suites* *In-room: Wi-Fi. In-hotel: restaurant, bar, parking (fee)* 💳 *AE, DC, MC, V* Ⓜ *Moyúa.*

$$–$$$$ **Hotel Ercilla.** This modern hotel fills with the bullfight crowd during Bilbao's Semana Grande in early August because it's near the bullring and because it's the place to see and be seen—not exactly the spot for a quiet getaway. In winter it's *the* business, press, and politico hotel. Impeccable rooms, amenities, and service underscore its reputation. **Pros:** business and politics buzz here, Bilbao nerve center. **Cons:** too much of a business and politics vibe for some, more like a beehive than a pleasure palace. ✉ *C. Ercilla 37, El Ensanche* ☎ *94/470–5700* 🌐 *www.hotelercilla.es* *335 rooms, 10 suites* *In-room: Wi-Fi. In-hotel: restaurant, bar, parking (fee)* 💳 *AE, DC, MC, V* Ⓜ *Moyúa.*

$ **Iturrienea Ostatua.** Euskera (Basque) for "Hostel of the Fountain," this traditional Basque town house in Bilbao's old quarter has overhead wooden beams, stone floors, and ethnographical and historical objects adorning the walls. Management and staff are invariably smart, polite, and helpful. The only caveat is nocturnal noise on the front side, especially in summer. Try for a room in the back, or bring earplugs. **Pros:** top value, smart and helpful staff. **Cons:** rooms not spacious, street noise and summer heat in some rooms. ✉ *Santa María Kalea 14, Casco Viejo* ☎ *94/416–1500* 🌐 *www.iturrieneaostatua.com* *21*

5

rooms *In-room: no a/c, Wi-Fi. In-hotel: no elevator* *AE, DC, MC, V* *Casco Viejo.*

$$$–$$$$ ★ **Lopez de Haro.** Because it's just five minutes from the Guggenheim, Bilbao's traditional top hotel has become quite a scene. The converted 19th-century building has an English feel and all the comforts your heart desires. Club Náutico ($$$–$$$$), a handy place for dinner on one of Bilbao's many rainy evenings, serves modern and classical Basque dishes, ranging from a simple *besugo* (sea bream) or one of the city's famous *bacalao* (codfish) preparations to sleek, contemporary interpretations of traditional favorites. **Pros:** quintessential Bilbao style and comfort, small enough to be clubby. **Cons:** a little too quiet, not a young vibe if that's what you're looking for. *Obispo Orueta 2, El Ensanche* *94/423–5500* *www.hotellopezdeharo.com* *49 rooms, 4 suites* *In-room: Wi-Fi. In-hotel: restaurant, bar, parking (fee)* *AE, DC, MC, V* *Moyúa.*

$$–$$$ Fodor's Choice ★ **Miró Hotel.** Across from the Guggenheim, this boutique hotel designed by Barcelona fashion and interior designer Antonio Miró is exciting, comfortable, and innovative. Rooms are spacious and contemporary, with lots of high-tech design. Expect excellent service and a lavish breakfast with fresh-squeezed orange juice, bacon, eggs, and more. There's a CD and DVD library and plenty of books too borrow, too. **Pros:** all the Guggenheim eyeful you could ever ask for, sexy clientele and staff. **Cons:** overdesigned, certain practicalities such as bedside tables and closet space seem to have been overlooked. *Alameda de Mazarredo 77, El Ensanche* *94/661–1880* *www.mirohotelbilbao.com* *45 rooms, 5 suites* *In-room: Wi-Fi. In-hotel: restaurant, room service, bar, gym, spa, laundry service, airport shuttle, parking (fee)* *AE, DC, MC, V* *Moyúa.*

$$–$$$$ **Sheraton Bilbao Hotel.** This colossus, built over what was once the nerve center of Bilbao's shipbuilding industry, feels like a futuristic ocean liner. Designed by architect Ricardo Legorreta and inspired by the work of Basque sculptor Eduardo Chillida (1920–2002), the hotel is filled with contemporary art and models of Spanish ships. Rooms are high, wide, and handsome, with glass, steel, stone, and wood trimmings. The comforts and the views from upper floors are superb. The Chillida café and the restaurant, Aizian, are both excellent. **Pros:** views over the river and the Guggenheim, polished service. **Cons:** chilly decor, not quite part of the city. *C. Lehendakari Leizaola 29, El Ensanche* *94/428–0000* *www.sheraton-bilbao.com* *199 rooms, 12 suites* *In-room: Wi-Fi. In-hotel: 2 restaurants, bar, gym, parking (fee)* *AE, DC, MC, V* *San Mamés.*

CAFÉS

Bar los Fueros (*C. de los Fueros 4, Casco Viejo*) is one of Bilbao's most authentic enclaves, perfect for a coffee, an *aperitivo* (aperitif), or a nightcap. The **Café Bulevard** (*C. Arenal 3, Casco Viejo*) dates back to 1871. **Café El Tilo** (*C. Arenal 1, Casco Viejo*) may be the best café in Bilbao, with wooden tables and original frescoes by Basque painter Juan de Aranoa (1901–73). It's open weekdays only. The enormous **Café Iruña** (*C. Berástegui 4, Jardines de Albia, El Ensanche*), a turn-of-the-20th-century classic, is a good place to refuel. Founded in 1926, **Café La**

Granja (✉ *Pl. Circular 3, El Ensanche*), near the Puente del Arenal, is a Bilbao classic for coffee, beer, and *tortilla de patata* (potato omelet).

NIGHTLIFE AND THE ARTS

Bilbao holds a music festival in August; inquire at the main tourist office on Paseo de Arenal (☎ *94/479–5770*), as venues change. The city's abundant nightlife breaks neatly down into ages and zones. Students and the under-thirtyish amass on and around Calle Licenciado Poza (known as Pozas, two blocks east of Gran Vía) and the Casco Viejo, where serious *poteo* (tippling) continues until late. Barring holidays, the first half of the week is quieter. **Flash** (✉ *C. Telesforo Aranzadi 4, near Hotel Carlton, El Ensanche*) has dinner, dancing, and cocktails. The bright **Palacio Euskalduna** (✉ *Abandoibarra 4, El Ensanche* ☎ *944/308372*), home of the Orquesta Sinfónica de Bilbao, has all but replaced the Arriaga as Bilbao's prime performing-arts venue. All ages meet for drinks at designer Javier Mariscal's playful **Splash and Crash** (✉ *Alameda Mazarredo 61, El Ensanche*) cocktail lounge and pub in the Hotel Gran Domine. The historic **Teatro Arriaga** (✉ *Pl. Arriaga s/n, Casco Viejo* ☎ *94/416–3244*) still draws the world's top performers in ballet, theater, concerts, opera, and *zarzuela* (comic opera).

5

SHOPPING

Basque *txapelas* (berets) make charming gifts. Best when waterproof, these berets keep you remarkably warm in the rain and mist of Basque Country.

Basandere (✉ *C. Iparaguirre 4, El Ensanche* ☎ *94/423–6386*), near the Guggenheim, has artisanal Basque crafts and foods. Look for Elosegui, the best-known brand of txapelas, in the old quarter's **Sombreros Gorostiaga** (✉ *C. Victor 9, Casco Viejo* ☎ *94/416–1276*).

EN ROUTE

From Bilbao, drive northwest down the Nervión to Neguri and Getxo and follow the coast road around through Baquio, Bermeo, and Mundaka to Gernika before proceeding east—this is the scenic route, but well worth the extra time. Depending on stops for lunch or sprawling on a breezy beach, this can be a two- to six-hour drive, all of it spectacularly scenic. The other choice is to pick up the A8 toll road east toward San Sebastián and France, exiting for Gernika and the BI635 coast road through Vizcaya's hills.

SAN JUAN DE GAZTELUGATXE

12 km (7 mi) west of Bermeo.

★ This tiny, gemlike hermitage clinging to its rocky promontory over the Bay of Biscay is exactly 231 steps up along a narrow corridor built into the top of a rocky ledge connecting what would otherwise be an island to the mainland. A favorite pilgrimage for Bilbaínos on holidays, the Romanesque chapel is said to have been used as a fortress by the Templars in the 14th century.

WHERE TO STAY

¢–$ **Ostatua Gaztelubegi.** In Euskera, the Basque language, *gaztelu* means castle and *begi* is the word for eye, so "Gaztelubegi" adds up to eye-castle, or lookout point, and the views from this diminutive hotel and restaurant ($–$$) overlooking the hermitage of San Juan de Gaztelugatxe are some of the most vertiginous of the Basque coast. The bar is always booming and the food is simple Basque cooking, from *alubias* to *besugo* (white beans to sea bream). **Pros:** simple lodging with panoramas in all directions; friendly service. **Cons:** roadside can be noisy; no Internet; no frills such as hair dryers. ✉*Ctra. BI–3101, Km 3, from Bakio* ☎*94/619–4924* 🌐*www.bakio.com* *7 rooms* *In-room: no a/c. In-hotel: restaurant, bar, no elevator, parking (no fee)* ▭*AE, DC, MC, V.*

> **A HEAVENLY STROLL**
>
> A walk around San Juan de Gaztelugatxe's chapel bell tower is said to cure nightmares and insomnia, as well as to make wishes come true.

BERMEO

34 km (20 mi) north of Bilbao, 3 km (2 mi) west of Mundaka.

The charm of Bermeo is easy to miss if you don't park and walk through the old part of town to the port. With the largest fishing fleet in Spain—some 60 long-distance tuna freezer ships of more than 150 tons, and nearly 100 smaller craft that specialize in hake, sea bream, gilthead, and other local species—Bermeo was long famous as a whaling port. In the 16th century, local whalers reportedly were obliged to donate the tongue of every whale to raise money for the church. Bermeo has one of only two wooden-boat shipyards on the northern coast, and the boats in its harbor make a colorful picture. Drive to the top of the windswept hill, where a cemetery overlooks the crashing waves below.

Bermeo's **Museo del Pescador** is the only museum in the world dedicated to the craft and history of fishermen and the fishing industry, from whales to anchovies. The tower was built by native son Alonso de Ercilla y Zuñiga (1533–94), poet and eminent soldier. Ercilla's "La Araucana," an account of the conquest of Arauco (Chile), is considered one of the best Spanish epic poems. ✉*Torre de Ercilla* ☎*94/688–1171* *Free* *Tues.–Sat. 10–1:30 and 4–7:30, Sun. 10–1:30.*

WHERE TO EAT

$$–$$$$ SEAFOOD ✕**Jokin.** You'll almost certainly have a good view of the *puerto viejo* (old port) from this cheerful, strategically located restaurant, perfectly placed to watch the day's catch being unloaded from the boats in the harbor below. The bar near the front entry serves excellent tapas—good as appetizers or full meals. Try the *rape Jokin* (monkfish in a clam and crayfish sauce) or *chipirones en su tinta* (squid in its ink) and, for dessert, the *tarta de naranja* (orange cake). ✉*Eupeme Deuna 13* ☎*94/688–4089* ▭*AE, DC, MC, V* *No dinner Sun.*

MUNDAKA

37 km (22 mi) northeast of Bilbao.

Tiny Mundaka, famous with surfers all over the world for its left-breaking roller at the mouth of the Ría de Guernica, has much to offer nonsurfers as well. The town's elegant summer homes and stately

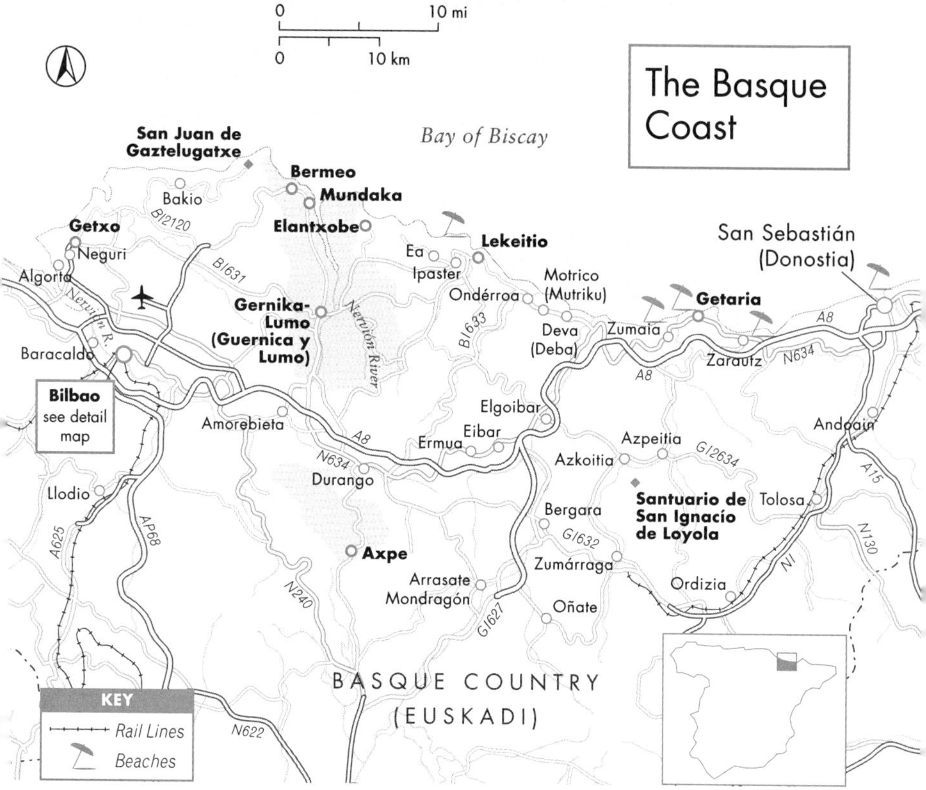

houses bearing family coats of arms compete for pride of place with the hermitage on the Santa Catalina peninsula and the parish church's Renaissance doorway.

ESSENTIALS

Visitor Information Mundaka (✉ *Txorrokopunta 248360* ☎ *946/177201*).

WHERE TO EAT AND STAY

$$–$$$ SEAFOOD ✕ **Casino José Mari.** Built in 1818 as a fish auction house for the local fishermen's guild, this building, with wonderful views of Mundaka's beach, is now a fine restaurant and a well-known and respected eating club. The public is welcome, though, and the Casino is a favorite place for lunches and sunset dinners in summer, when you can sit in the glassed-in, upper-floor porch. Very much a semi-secret local haunt, the club serves excellent fish caught, more often than not, by the members themselves. ✉ *Parque Atalaya, center of town* ☎ *94/687–6005* ▭ *AE, MC, V.*

$–$$$ SEAFOOD ✕ **Portuondo.** Spectacular terraces outside a traditional caserío (Basque farmhouse) overlooking the Laida beach, the aromas of beef and fish cooking over coals, and a comfortable country dining room upstairs, and an easy 15-minute walk outside of Mundaka all make this a good stop for lunch or (in summer) dinner. Offerings are balanced between meat and seafood, the wine list covers an interesting selection

Continued on page 296

MINIATURE FOOD, MAXIMUM FLAVOR

An Introduction to TAPAS

Virtually every day, coworkers head to a tapas bar after work for a *caña* (a 4–6 oz beer) that's almost always paired with a tapa or two. On weeknights, families crowd around tables with drinks and tapas, filling up on several *raciones* or small *cazuelas*. In the evenings, couples out on the town do "tapas crawls," the Spanish version of a pub crawl where *croquetas*

Defining tapas as merely a snack is, for a Spaniard, like defining air as an occasional breathable treat. If that sounds a little dramatic, consider how this bite-sized food influences daily life across all regions and classes throughout Spain.

THE HISTORY OF SHRINKING PORTIONS

The origin of tapas is the stuff of heated tapas bar debates. Various reports cloud the history of when and how it started. Some credit Alfonso X's diet for his delicate stomach. However, the most commonly accepted explanation is that a flat object (be it a slice of bread or a flat card with some nuts or sunflower seeds) was used to cover the rim of wine glasses and keep dive-bombing fruit flies out. (To cover something up is "tapar" in Spanish.)

balance out rich wine. And sometimes the spread for a *pica-pica* (a nibbling marathon) with *tortilla de patata, aceitunas, chorizo,* and *jamon* will cause Spaniards to replace their lunch or dinner outright with tapas. These tiny dishes are such a way of life that a verb had to be created for them: *tapear* (to eat tapas) or "*ir a tapeo*" (to go eat tapas). The staff of life in Spain isn't bread. It's finger food.

TAPAS ACROSS SPAIN

MADRID

It is often difficult to qualify what is authentically from Madrid and what has been gastronomically cribbed from other regions thanks to Madrid's melting-pot status for people and customs all over Spain. While *croquetas, tortilla de patata,* and even *paella* can be served as tapas, *patatas bravas* and *calamares* can be found in almost any restaurant in Madrid. The popular *patatas* are a very simple mixture of fried or roasted potatoes with a "Brava" sauce. The sauce is slightly spicy, which is surprising given a country-wide aversion for dishes with the slightest kick. The *calamares,* fried in olive oil, can be served alone or with alioli sauce, mayonnaise, or—and you're reading correctly—in a sandwich. A slice of lemon usually accompanies your serving.

ANDALUSIA

Known for the warmth of its climate and its people, Andalusian bars tend to be very generous with their tapas—maybe in spite of the fact that they aren't exactly celebrated for their culinary inventiveness. But tapas here are traditional and among the best. Many times ordering a drink will bring you a sandwich large enough to make a meal, or a bowl of gazpacho that you could swim in. Seafood is also extremely popular in Andalusia, and you will find tapas ranging from sizzling prawns to small anchovies soaked in vinegar or olive oil.

Pescado frito (fried fish) and *albondigas* (meatballs) are two common tapas in the region, and it's worth grazing multiple bars to try the different preparations. The fish usually includes squid, anchovies, and other tiny fish, deep fried and served as is. Since the bones are very small, they are not removed and considered fine for digestion. If this idea bothers you, sip some more wine. The saffron-almond sauce (*salsa de almendras* y *azafrán*) that accompanies the meatballs might very well make your eyes roll to the back of your head. And since saffron is not as expensive in Spain as it is in the United States, the meatballs are liberally drenched in it.

Not incidentally, Spain's biggest export, olives, grows in Andalusia, so you can expect many varieties among the tapas served with your drinks.

Tortilla de patata

Calamares

Fried anchovy fish

Albondigas

BASQUE COUNTRY

More than any other community in Spain, the Basque Country is known for its culinary originality. The tapas, like the region itself, tend to be more expensive and inventive. And since the Basques insist on doing things their way, they call their unbelievable bites *pintxos* (or *pinchos* in Spanish) rather than tapas. *Gildas*, probably the most ordered *pintxo* in the Basque Country, is a simple toothpick skewer composed of a special green pepper (called *guindilla vasca*), an anchovy, and a pitted olive. All the ingredients must be of the highest quality, especially the anchovy, which should be marinated in the best olive oil and not be too salty. *Pimientos rellenos de bacalao* (roasted red peppers with cod) is also popular, given the Basque Country's adjacency to the ocean. The festive color of the red peppers and the savoriness of the fish make it a bite-sized Basque delicacy.

Red and green peppers *pintxos*

A spread of tapas selections

GET YOUR TAPAS ON

Madrid

El Bocaíto. Here you'll find the best *pescaito frito* (deep-fried whitebait) and a huge assortment of *tostas* (toast points with different toppings). ✉ *Libertad 6, Chueca.* ☎ *91/532–1219.*

Estay. You'll find delicious *tortilla Espanola con atun y lechuga* (Spanish omelet with tuna and lettuce) and excellent *rabas* (fried calamari). ✉ *Hermosilla 46, Salamanca* ☎ *91/578–0470.*

Andalusia

El Churrasco. With a name like this, you would expect the meats to be delicious, and they are. But don't miss the *berenjenas crujientes con salmorejo* (crispy fried eggplant slices with thick gazpacho). ✉ *Romero 16, Judería, Córdoba* ☎ *95/729–0819.*

El Rinconcillo. It's great for the view of the Iglesia de Santa Catalina and a *caldereta de venado* (venison stew). ✉ *C. Gerona 40, Barrio de la Macarena, Seville* ☎ *95/422–3183.*

The Basque Country

Aloña Berri Bar. The repeat winner of tapas championships, its *contraste de pato* (duck à l'orange) and *bastela de pichón* (pigeon pie) makes foodies swoon. ✉ *C. Bermingham 24, Gros, San Sebastián* ☎ *94/329–0818.*

Bernardo Etxea. Straight up, freshly prepared classics like fried peppers, octopus, and pimientos with anchovies are served here. ✉ *C. Puerto 7, Parte Vieja* ☎ *94/342–2055.*

Bite-sized food and drink

A wine pairing

of wines from all over Spain, and the tapas area downstairs crackles with life on weekends and during the summer. ✉ *Portuondo Auzoa 1* ☎ *94/687–6050* ⊙ *Closed Dec. 9–Jan. 15, No dinner Sun.–Thurs. Jan.–June* ▭ *AE, MC, V.*

$$ ★ **Atalaya.** Tastefully converted from a private house, this 1911 landmark 37 km (22 mi) from Bilbao has become a big favorite for quick railroad-getaway overnights from Bilbao and the Guggenheim. (The train ride out is spectacular.) Guest rooms are charming and comfortable; those upstairs have balconies with marvelous views. Room No. 12 is the best in the house. The breakfast room is cheerful and light. **Pros:** intimate retreat from Bilbao's sprawl and bustle, friendly family service. **Cons:** tight quarters in some rooms. ✉ *Paseo de Txorrokopunta 2* ☎ *94/617–7000* ⊕ *www.hotel-atalaya-mundaka.com* *13 rooms* *In-room: Wi-Fi. In-hotel: restaurant, bar* ▭ *AE, DC, MC, V.*

EN ROUTE

From Mundaka, follow signs for Gernika, stopping at the Mirador de Portuondo—a roadside lookout on the left a kilometer outside of Mundaka (BI635, Km 43)—for an excellent view of the estuary. The Portuondo restaurant (⇨ *see Mundaka*) serves excellent tapas and Basque cooking on a terrace overlooking the Laida beach and the estuary.

GERNIKA-LUMO (GUERNICA Y LUMO)

15 km (9 mi) east of Bilbao, 8 km (5 mi) south of Mundaka.

On Monday, April 26, 1937—market day—Gernika suffered history's second terror bombing against a civilian population. (The first, much less famous, was against neighboring Durango, about a month earlier.) The planes of the Nazi Luftwaffe were sent with the blessings of General Francisco Franco to experiment with saturation bombing of civilian targets and to decimate the traditional seat of Basque autonomy. Since the Middle Ages, Spanish sovereigns had sworn under the ancient **oak tree of Gernika** to respect Basque *fueros* (special local rights—the kind of local autonomy that was anathema to the *generalísimo*'s Madrid-centered "National Movement," which promoted Spanish unity over local identity). More than 1,000 people were killed in the bombing, and today Gernika remains a symbol of independence in the heart of every Basque, known to the world through Picasso's famous canvas *Guernica* (now in Madrid's Centro de Arte Reina Sofía). The city was destroyed—though the oak tree miraculously emerged unscathed—and has been rebuilt as a modern, architecturally uninteresting town. The **Museo de la Paz** offers a closer look at the bombing heard around the world (thanks largely to the Picasso painting), and the **Museo de Euskalerria** provides insights into Basque culture, history, and ethnology. The stump of the sacred oak, which at last died several decades ago, can be found in the courtyard of the **Casa de Juntas** (a new oak has been planted alongside the old one)—the object of many a pilgrimage. Nearby is the Balcón de Vizcaya overlooking the estuary of the **Ría de Gernika,** a stone's throw from some of the area's most colorful fishing towns.

ESSENTIALS

Visitor Information Gernika (✉ *Artekale 5* ☎ *946/255892*).

CLOSE UP

Embattled Gernika

When Spain's Second Republic commissioned Picasso to create a work for the Paris 1937 International Exposition, little did he imagine that his grim canvas protesting the bombing of a Basque village would become one of the most famous paintings in history.

The rural market town of Gernika has been one of the keys to the Basque identity since the 14th century. General Francisco Franco knew the strike would be a blow to Basque nationalism. When the Tuesday, April 26 raid ended, more than 1,000 civilians lay dead or dying in the ruins. Not until the 60th anniversary of the event did Germany officially apologize for the bombing.

Picasso's painting had its own struggle. The Spanish Pavilion in the 1937 International Exposition in Paris nearly substituted a more upbeat work, using *Guernica* as a backdrop. In 1939, Picasso ceded *Guernica* to New York's Museum of Modern Art on behalf of the democratically elected government of Spain—stipulating that the painting should return only to a democratic Spain. Over the next 30 years, as Picasso's fame grew, so did *Guernica*'s—as a work of art and symbol of Spain's captivity.

When Franco died in 1975, two years after Picasso, negotiations with Picasso's heirs for the painting's return to Spain were already under way. Now on display at Madrid's Centro de Arte Reina Sofía, *Guernica* is home for good.

5

WHERE TO EAT AND STAY

$$–$$$$ SPANISH ✕ **Baserri Maitea.** In the village of Forua, 1 km (½ mi) northwest of Gernika, Basseri Maitea is in a stunning 18th-century Basque *caserío* (farmhouse). Strings of red peppers and garlic hang from wooden beams in the cathedral-like interior. Entrées include the *pescado del día* (fish of the day) and *cordero de leche asado al horno de leña* (milk-fed lamb roasted in a wood-burning oven). ✉*BI635 to Bermeo, Km 2* ☎*94/625–3408* ▭*AE, DC, MC, V* ⊗*No dinner Sun.–Thurs. Oct.–May.*

¢–$ **Boliña.** Just a few steps from the famous oak tree in downtown Gernika, where a dozen centuries of Basque leaders swore allegiance to the Spanish crown in exchange for certain specific and unalienable rights, the Boliña is a pleasant and modern base camp for exploring the Vizcayan coast. Rooms are small but comfy. **Pros:** comfortable and efficient, central location, good value. **Cons:** small rooms, restaurant seats 100 and is a local favorite for wedding receptions and gatherings. ✉*Barrenkale 3* ☎*94/625–0300* ⊕*www.hotelbolina.net* *16 rooms* *In-room: Wi-Fi. In-hotel: restaurant, bar, no elevator* ▭*AE, DC, MC, V.*

OFF THE BEATEN PATH

Cuevas de Santimamiñe. On the road to Kortezubi, 5 km (3 mi) from Gernika, the Cuevas de Santimamiñe, also known as Santimamiñe Caverns, have important prehistoric cave paintings. Guided visits are offered weekdays at 10:30, noon, 4, and 5:30, except holidays. On your way out, look for signs for the nearby **Bosque Pintado (Painted**

Forest), rows of trees vividly painted by Basque artist Agustín Ibarrola, a striking and successful marriage of art and nature. ✉ *Barrio Basondo, Kortezubi* ☎ *94/625–2975.*

EN ROUTE For the Santimamiñe Caves, continue northeast from Gernika toward Kortezubi on the BI638. For Elanchove (Elantxobe, in Euskera), turn left at Arteaga and follow the BI3237 around the east side of the Ría de Gernika and the Urdaibai natural preserve. From there, the coast road through Ea and Ipaster leads to Lekeitio, one of the prettiest ports on the Basque coast. But if you long for a taste of lush green highlands 30 minutes inland, drive up to Axpe and see Amboto, Vizcaya's mythical limestone mountain.

AXPE

47 km (28 mi) southeast of Bilbao, 46 km (27 mi) south of Gernika.

The village of Axpe, in the valley of Atxondo, nestles under the limestone heights of 4,777-foot Amboto—one of the highest peaks in the Basque Country outside of the Pyrenees. Home of the legendary Basque mother of nature, Mari Urrika or Mari Anbotokodama (María, Our Lady of Amboto), Amboto, with its spectral gray rock face, is a sharp contrast to the soft green meadows running up to the very foot of the mountain. According to Basque scholar and ethnologist José María de Barandiarán in his *Mitología Vasca* (Basque Mythology), Mari was "a beautiful woman, well constructed in all ways except for one foot, which was like that of a goat."

To reach Axpe from Bilbao, drive east on the A8/E70 freeway toward San Sebastián. From Gernika, drive south on the BI635 to the A6/E70 freeway and turn east for San Sebastián. Get off at the Durango exit 40 km (24 mi) from Bilbao and take the BI632 toward Elorrio. At Apatamonasterio turn right onto the BI3313 and continue to Axpe.

WHERE TO EAT AND STAY

$$–$$$$ SPANISH Fodor's Choice ★ **Etxebarri.** Bittor Etxebarri and his development of innovative techniques for cooking over coals has been hot news around the Iberian Peninsula for a decade now, with woods and coals being tailored for different ingredients and new equipment such as the pan to char-grill *angulas* (baby eels) being improvised one after another. Everything from clams and fish to meats and even the rice with langoustines is healthful, flavorful, and exciting as prepared and served in this blocky stone house in the center of this tiny mountain town. ✉ *Plaza San Juan 1* ☎ *94/658–3042* ▭ *AE, DC, MC, V* ⊙ *Closed Mon. No dinner Sun.*

$$ Fodor's Choice ★ **Mendigoikoa.** This handsome group of hillside farmhouses is among the province of Vizcaya's most exquisite hideaways. The lower farmhouse, Mendibekoa ("lower mountain" in Euskera), has stunning rooms, an elegant breakfast room, and a glassed-in terrace overlooking the valley. At the restaurant Mendigoikoa ("upper mountain"; $$–$$$$), heavy beams loom overhead and a fire usually crackles in the far corner. The *pichón de Navaz a la parrilla* (Navaz wood pigeon cooked over coals) or the *txuleta de buey* (beef steaks) are memorable. **Pros:** gorgeous setting, smart and attentive service. **Cons:** beds not always entirely comfortable, rooms poorly lit. ✉ *Barrio San Juan 33*

☎94/682–0833 ⊕www.mendigoikoa.com 11 rooms In-room: Wi-Fi. In-hotel: restaurant, no elevator ▭AE, DC, MC, V ⊙Closed Dec. 22–Jan. 17. Restaurant closed Mon. No dinner Sun.

ELANTXOBE

27 km (17 mi) from Bermeo.

The tiny fishing village of Elantxobe (Elanchove, in Spanish) is surrounded by huge, steep cliffs, with a small breakwater that protects its fleet from the storms of the Bay of Biscay. The view of the port from the upper village is breathtaking. The lower fork in the road leads to the port.

WHERE TO STAY

¢–$ **Casa Rural Arboliz.** On a bluff overlooking the Bay of Biscay about 2 km (1 mi) outside of Elantxobe on the road to Lekeitio, this rustic inn is removed from the harborside bustle, offering a breath of the country life on the Basque coast. The modern rooms are simple and have balconies overlooking the sea. The restaurant ($–$$) serves simple Basque specialties with an emphasis on fresh seafood. The *besugo a la donostiarra* (sea bream covered in a garlic, oil, and vinegar sauce) is exceptional. **Pros:** bucolic setting; good Basque cooking. **Cons:** almost too isolated and quiet; small rooms. *⊠Arboliz 12, Ibarranguelua ☎94/627–6283 ⊕www.euskalnet.net/arboliz 6 rooms In-room: Wi-Fi. In-hotel: restaurant, no elevator ▭AE, DC, MC, V.*

¢ **Itsasmin Ostatua.** At the foot of Monte Ogoño in the upper part of the charming and colorful fishing and seafaring village of Elantxobe, this cozy place rents simple, cheery rooms and serves home-cooked Basque cuisine in its diminutive dining room ($–$$). Rooms with wood beams overhead look directly down into the deepwater harbor below. A family enterprise, the staff is unfailingly cheerful and helpful. **Pros:** part of the hustle and bustle of village life; simple and comfortable. **Cons:** tight quarters in some rooms; street-side rooms can be noisy on weekends. *⊠Nagusia 32 ☎94/627–6174 ⊕ www.itsasmin.com 12 rooms In-hotel: restaurant, no elevator ▭AE, DC, MC, V ⊙Closed Dec. 15–Jan. 15.*

LEKEITIO

59 km (37 mi) east of Bilbao, 61 km (38 mi) west of San Sebastián.

This bright little town is similar to Bermeo but has two wide, sandy beaches right by its harbor. Soaring over the Gothic church of Santa María (open for mass only) is a graceful set of flying buttresses. Lekeitio is famous for its fiestas (September 1–18), which include a gruesome event in which men dangle for as long as they can from the necks of dead geese tied to a cable over the inlet while the cable is whipped in and out of the water by crowds of burly men at either end.

SANTUARIO DE SAN IGNACIO DE LOYOLA

Cestona is 34 km (21 mi) southwest of San Sebastián.

The Sanctuary of St. Ignatius of Loyola, in Cestona, is an exuberant baroque structure erected in honor of Iñigo Lopez de Oñaz y Loyola (1491–1556) after he was sainted as Ignacio de Loyola in 1622 for his defense of the Catholic Church against the tides of Martin Luther's Reformation. Almost two centuries later, Roman architect Carlos Fontana designed the basilica that would memorialize the saint. The ornate construction contrasts with the austere ways of Saint Ignatius himself, who took vows of poverty and chastity after his conversion. Polychrome marble, flamboyant altar work, and a huge but delicate dome decorate the interior. The fortresslike tower house has the room where Ignatius (Iñigo, in Euskera) experienced conversion while recovering from his wound in an intra-Basque battle. Back on the coastal road is **Zumaia,** a cozy little port and summer resort with the estuary of the Urola River flowing (back and forth, according to the tide) through town. The **Museo Zuloaga** (☎*943/862341* 🌐*www.ignaciozuloaga.com*), on N634 at the eastern edge of town, has an extraordinary collection of paintings by Goya, El Greco, Zurbarán, and others, in addition to works by the Basque impressionist Ignacio Zuloaga himself. The museum is open Easter–September 15, Wednesday–Sunday 4–8 PM. The rest of the year it's open by prior arrangement only. Admission is €6 (€8 September–April).

ESSENTIALS

Visitor Information Zumaia (✉*Playa de Itzurun s/n* ☎*943/143396*).

WHERE TO EAT AND STAY

$–$$ ✕**Bedua.** Local Zumaia natives like to access this rustic hideaway by boat when the tide is right, though you can also drive. A specialist in *tortilla de patatas con pimientos verdes de la huerta* (potato omelet with homegrown green peppers), Bedua is also known for *tortilla de bacalao* (codfish omelet), *txuleta de buey* (beefsteak), and fish of all kinds, especially the classic *besugo* (sea bream) cooked *a la donostiarra* (roasted and covered with a sauce of garlic and vinegar). Txakolí from nearby Getaria is the beverage of choice. ✉*Cestona, Barrio Bedua, 3 km (2 mi) up Urola from Zumaia* ☎*943/860551* 💳*MC, V.*

$ 🏨**Landarte.** For a taste of life in a Basque *caserío* (farmhouse), spend a night or two in this lovely restored 16th-century country manor house an hour's walk from Getaria. The walk down to town will prime you for the pleasures of Basque dining, while the hike back up will prepare you for still more. Stone walls, hand-hewn beams, sea views, and happy and helpful hosts make this a top choice. **Pros:** great location; cheery family. **Cons:** excessively rustic; cramped bathrooms. ✉*Crtra. de Artadi 1, Zumaia* ☎*943/865358* 🌐*www.landarte.net* *6 rooms* *In-room: Wi-Fi, no a/c. In-hotel: no elevator, parking (no fee)* 💳*AE, DC, MC, V.*

GETARIA (GUETARIA)

22 km (14 mi) west of San Sebastián.

From Zumaia, the coast road and several good footpaths lead to Getaria (Guetaria, in Spanish), known as *la cocina de Guipúzcoa,* the kitchen of Guipúzcoa province, for its many restaurants and taverns. Getaria was the birthplace of Juan Sebastián Elcano (1460–1526), the first circumnavigator of the globe and Spain's most emblematic naval hero. Elcano took over and completed Magellan's voyage after he was killed in the Philippines in 1521. The town's galleonlike **church** has sloping wooden floors resembling a ship's deck. **Zarautz,** the next town, has a wide beach and many taverns and cafés.

ESSENTIALS

Visitor Information Getaria (☒ *Parque Aldamar 2* ☎ *943/140957*).

WHERE TO EAT AND STAY

$$$–$$$$ SPANISH ★ ✕ **Kaia Kaipe.** Suspended over Getaria's colorful and busy fishing port and with panoramas looking up the coast past Zarautz and San Sebastián all the way to Biarritz, this spectacular place puts together exquisite fish soups and serves fresh fish right off the boats—you can watch them being unloaded below. The town is the home of Txomin Etxaniz, the premier *txakolí* (tart young Basque white wine), and this is the ideal place to drink it. ☒ *General Arnao 4* ☎ *943/140500* ▭ *AE, DC, MC, V* ⊙ *Closed Mar. 1–15 and Oct. 15–31.*

¢ **Iribar.** The Iribar family has been grilling fish and beef over coals here for more than half a century. Just uphill from Getaria's singular church, the restaurant stands out for value, family-friendliness, and delicious fish and beef ($–$$$). The five rooms are impeccable, inexpensive, and one of the only berths available in the heart of this schooner-like historic village. **Pros:** sleeping in an historic monument; sweet family; excellent dining opportunity. **Cons:** tiny rooms; hard to get a car close to the hotel. ☒ *Kale Nagusia 34* ☎ *943/140406* 🖷 *943/140953* *4 rooms* *In-hotel: restaurant, bar, no elevator* ▭ *AE, DC, MC, V* ⊙ *Closed Thurs. and Oct. 1–15, Apr. 1–15. No dinner Wed.*

$–$$$ **Saiaz Getaria.** For panoramic views over the Bay of Biscay, this 15th-century house on Getaria's uppermost street is a perfect refuge in this little village on a peninsula. Aromas of fish and meat cooking over coals waft up, while the long surfing wave crashing into the beach down below provides perfect water music for sleeping. Rooms on the street side have heavy stone walls, but the plainer rooms on the sea side have the spectacular views. **Pros:** the opportunity to stay in a noble house in a unique fishing village. **Cons:** rooms on the sea side are small and undistinguished except for the views. ☒ *Roke Deuna 25* ☎ *943/140143* 🌐 *www.saiazgetaria.com* *17 rooms* *In-room: Wi-Fi. In-hotel: restaurant, bar* ▭ *AE, DC, MC, V* ⊙ *Closed Dec. 20–Jan. 6.*

OFF THE BEATEN PATH

For a look at an authentic Basque farmhouse, or *caserío,* where the Urdapilleta family farms pigs, sheep, cattle, goats, chickens, and ducks, take a detour up to the village of Bidegoian (8 km [5 mi] short of Tolosa on the Azpeitia–Tolosa road). **Pello Urdapilleta** (which means "pile of pigs" in Euskera) sells artisanal cheeses and sausages and will show you how upland Basques have traditionally lived and farmed. ✉ *Elola Azpikoa Baserria, Bidegoian* ☎ *943/681006.*

SAN SEBASTIÁN TO HONDARRIBIA

Graceful, chic San Sebastián invites you to slow down: you can stroll the beach here, or wander the streets. East of the city is Pasajes, where Lafayette set off to help the colonial forces in the American Revolution, and where Victor Hugo spent a winter writing. Just shy of the French border, you'll hit Hondarribia, a brightly painted, flower-festooned port town.

SAN SEBASTIÁN

Fodor's Choice ★

100 km (62 mi) northeast of Bilbao.

San Sebastián (Donostia, in Euskera) is a sophisticated city arched around one of the finest urban beaches in the world, **La Concha** (the Shell), so named for its resemblance to the shape of a scallop shell, with Ondarreta and Zurriola beaches at the southwestern and northeastern ends. The promontories of Monte Urgull and Monte Igueldo serve as bookends for La Concha, while Zurriola has its own Monte Ulía rising over its far end. The best way to see San Sebastián is to walk around: promenades and pathways lead up the hills that surround the city. The first records of San Sebastián date from the 11th century. A backwater for centuries, the city had the good fortune in 1845 to attract Queen Isabella II, who was seeking relief from a skin ailment in the icy Atlantic waters. Isabella was followed by much of the aristocracy of the time, and San Sebastián became a favored summer retreat for Madrid's well-to-do.

San Sebastián is divided by the **Urumea River,** which is crossed by three bridges inspired by late-19th-century French architecture. At the mouth of the Urumea, the incoming surf smashes the rocks with such force that white foam erupts, and the noise is wild and Wagnerian. The city is laid out with wide streets on a grid pattern, thanks mainly to the 12 different times it has been all but destroyed by fire. The last conflagration came after the French were expelled in 1813; English and Portuguese forces occupied the city, abused the population, and torched the place. Today, San Sebastián is a seaside resort on a par with Nice and Monte Carlo. It becomes one of Spain's most expensive cities in the summer, when French vacationers descend in droves. It is also, like Bilbao, a center of Basque nationalism.

San Sebastián's neighborhoods include La Parte Vieja, tucked under Monte Urgull north of the mouth of the Urumea River; Gros (so named for a corpulent Napoleonic general) across the Urumea to the north; Centro, the main city nucleus around the cathedral; Amara, farther east toward the Anoeta sports complex; La Concha at stage center around the beach; and El Antiguo at the western end of La Concha. Igueldo is the high promontory over the city at the southwestern side of the bay. Alto de Miracruz is the high ground to the northeast toward France;

Errenteria is inland east of Pasaia; Oiartzun is a village farther north; Astigarraga is in apple cider country to the east of Anoeta.

GETTING HERE AND AROUND

San Sebastián is a very walkable city, though local buses (€1.30) are also convenient. Buses for Pasajes, Errenteria, Astigarraga, and Oiartzun originate in Calle Okendo, one block west of the Urumea River behind the Hotel Maria Cristina. Bus A-1 goes to Astigarraga; A-2 is the bus to Pasajes (Pasaia in Euskera).

The Euskotren, the city train, is popularly known as "El Topo" (the mole) for the amount of time it spends underground, and originates at the Amara Viejo station in Paseo Easo and tunnels its way to Hendaye, France, hourly in 45 minutes. Euskotren also serves Zarautz (€1.50) in 40 minutes.

For the funicular up to Monte Igueldo *(☎943/000200 🌐www.dbus.es 🎫€2)* the station is just behind Ondarreta beach at the western end of La Concha.

ESSENTIALS

Bus Information Local info (*☎943/000200 🌐www.dbus.es*). **Bus station** (*✉C. Sancho el Sabio 33 ☎943/463974*).

Car Rental Europcar (*✉Aeropuerto de San Sebastián (Hondarribia [Fuenterrabía], San Sebastián ☎943/668530*).

Train Information Euskotren (*☎93/013500 🌐www.euskotren.es 🎫€1.50*). **San Sebastián train station** (*✉Estación de Amara, Plaza Easo 9 ☎943/450131 or 943/471852 ✉Estación del Norte, Av. de Francia ☎943/283089 or 943/283599*).

Visitor Information San Sebastián-Donostia (*✉Erregina Erregentearen 3 ☎943/481166.*

EXPLORING

Every corner of Spain champions its culinary identity, but San Sebastián's refined fare is in a league of its own. Many of the city's restaurants and tapas spots are in the **Parte Vieja** (Old Quarter), on the east end of the bay beyond the elegant **Casa Consistorial** (City Hall) and formal **Alderdi Eder** gardens. The city hall began as a casino in 1887: after gambling was outlawed early in the 20th century, the town council moved here from the Plaza de la Constitución, the Old Quarter's main square.

The tiny **Isla de Santa Clara,** right in the entrance to the bay, protects the city from Bay of Biscay storms; this makes La Concha one of the calmest beaches on Spain's entire northern coast. A large hill dramatically dominates each side of the entrance to the bay, too.

A visit to **Monte Igueldo,** on the western side of the bay, is a must. (You can drive up for a toll of €1.70 per person or take the funicular—it runs 10–8 in summer, 11–6 in winter, with departures every 15 minutes.) From the top, you get the remarkable panorama for which San Sebastián is famous: gardens, parks, wide tree-lined boulevards, Belle Epoque buildings, and, of course, the bay itself.

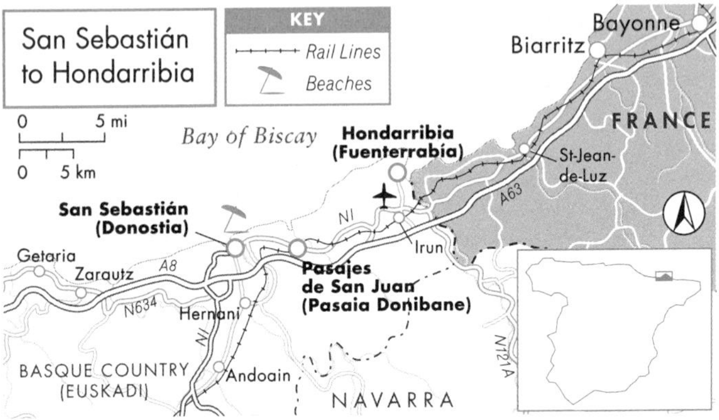

Designed by the world-renowned Spanish architect Rafael Moneo, and situated at the mouth of the Urumea River, the **Kursaal** is San Sebastián's postmodern concert hall, film society, and convention center. The gleaming cubes of glass that make up this bright, rationalist complex were conceived as a perpetuation of the site's natural geography, an attempt to "underline the harmony between the natural and the artificial" and to create a visual stepping-stone between the heights of Monte Urgull and Monte Ulía. It has two auditoriums, a gargantuan banquet hall, meeting rooms, exhibition space, and a sibling set of terraces overlooking the estuary. Martín Berasategui, director of his own restaurant in nearby Lasarte, is the creative force (and financier) behind the Kursaal dining room. ✉*Av. de la Zurriola, Gros* ☎*943/003000* 🌐*www.kursaal.org* 🎫€2 ⏲*Guided tours daily at 1:30. For guided tours in English make arrangements in advance.*

Just in from the harbor, in the shadow of Monte Urgull, is the baroque church of **Santa María,** with a stunning carved facade of an arrow-riddled Saint Sebastian. The interior is strikingly restful; note the ship above Saint Sebastian, high on the altar.

Looking straight south from the front of Santa María, you can see the facade and spires of the **Catedral Buen Pastor** *(Cathedral of the Good Shepherd)* across town.

NEED A BREAK?

Steps from the facade of Santa María, in the heart of the old quarter, have a *chocolate con nata*—thick, dark hot chocolate with whipped cream—at the tiny café Kantoi (✉*C. Mayor 10, Parte Vieja*).

The **Museo de San Telmo** is in a 16th-century monastery behind the Parte Vieja, to the right of the church of Santa María. The former chapel, now a lecture hall, was painted by José María Sert (1876–1945), creator of notable works in Barcelona's city hall, London's Tate Gallery, and New York's Waldorf-Astoria hotel. Here, Sert's characteristic tones of gray, gold, violet, and earthy russets enhance the sculptural power of his work, which portrays events from Basque history. The museum displays Basque ethnographic items, such as prehistoric steles once used as grave markers and paintings by Zuloaga, Ribera, and El Greco. ✉*Pl. de*

Ignacio Zuloaga s/n, Parte Vieja ☎943/424970 Free ⏲Tues.–Sat. 10:30–1:30 and 4–8, Sun. 10:30–2.

OFF THE BEATEN PATH

Chillida Leku. In the Jáuregui section of Hernani, 10 minutes south of San Sebastián (suggestively close to both Martín Bersategui's restaurant in nearby Lasarte *and* the cider houses of the Astigarraga neighbhorhood, like Sidrería Petritegui), the Eduardo Chillida Sculpture Garden and Museum, in a 16th-century farmhouse, is a treat for anyone interested in contemporary art. ✉*Caserío Zabalaga, Barrio Jáuregui 66, Lasarte ☎943/336006 🌐www.museochillidaleku.com €9 ⏲Closed Tues. except July and Aug. and during wk before Easter.*

TAPAS BARS

★ **Aloña Berri Bar.** Perennial winner of tapas championships, this spot across the Urumea River in Gros is well worth the walk. José Ramon Elizondo's miniature creations, from *contraste de pato* (duck à l'orange) to his Moorish-based *bastela de pichón* (pigeon pie), are excellent. Make sure to try the excellent crisp asparagus coated with burnt garlic. ✉*C. Bermingham 24, Gros ☎943/290818.*

★ **Astelena.** On the northeast corner of Plaza de la Constitución, this *bar de toda la vida* (lifetime local favorite bar) is famous for its *pastel de pescado* (fish paste). ✉*C. Iñigo 1, Parte Vieja ☎943/425245.*

Bar Ganbara. Near Plaza de la Constitución, the morsels here range from shrimp and asparagus to ibérico acorn-fed ham on croissants to anchovies, sea urchins, and wild mushrooms in season. ✉*C. San Jerónimo 21, Parte Vieja ☎943/422575.*

★ **Bar Gorriti.** Next to the open-air La Brecha Market, this traditional little *pinchos* bar is a classic, filled with good cheer and delicious tapas. ✉*C. San Juan 3, Parte Vieja ☎943/428353.*

Bar Ormazabal. You may not have *thought* you were starving, but when you catch a glimpse of the multicolor display that goes up on the Ormazabal bar at midday, hunger pangs will really kick in. ✉*C. 31 de Agosto 22, Parte Vieja ☎943/429907.*

Bergara Bar. Winner of many a miniature cuisine award, this rustic tavern just down the street from Aloñ Berri Bar, on the corner of Arteche and Bermingham, also serves roasts along with tapas and *pinchos.* ✉*Arteche 8, Gros ☎943/275026.*

Casa Vergara. This cozy bar, in front of the Santa María del Coro church, is always filled with reverent tapas devotees—and the counter is always piled high with delicious morsels. ✉*C. Mayor 21, Parte Vieja ☎943/431073.*

★ **La Cepa.** This booming and boisterous tavern is one of the all-time standards. Everything from the ibérico ham to the little olive, pepper, and anchovy combos called "penalties" will whet your appetite. ✉*C. 31 de Agosto 7, Parte Vieja ☎943/426394.*

WHERE TO EAT

$$$$ SPANISH

✕ **Akelaŕe.** On the far side of Monte Igueldo (and the far side of culinary tradition, as well) presides Chef Pedro Subijana, one of the most respected and creative chefs in the Basque Country. Prepare for tastes of all kinds, from Pop Rocks in blood sausage to mustard ice cream on tangerine peels. At the same time, Subijana's "straight" or classical dishes are monuments to traditional cookery and impeccable: try the venison with apple and smoked chestnuts or the *lubina* (sea bass) with *percebes* (goose barnacles). ✉ *Barrio de Igueldo, Igueldo* ☎ *943/212052 or 943/214086* ✍ *Reservations essential* ▭ *AE, DC, MC, V* ⊙ *Closed Feb., Oct. 1–15, Tues. Jan.–June, and Mon. except holidays and evenings preceding holidays. No dinner Sun.*

$$$$ SPANISH Fodor's Choice ★ ✕ **Arzak.** Renowned chef Juan Mari Arzak's little house at the crest of Alto de Miracruz on the eastern outskirts of San Sebastián is internationally famous, so reserve well in advance. Here, traditional Basque products and preparations are enhanced to bring out the best in the natural materials. The ongoing culinary dialogue between Juan Mari and his daughter Elena is one of the most endearing attractions here. They disagree often, but it's all in the family, and the food just gets better and better. The sauces are perfect and every dish looks beautiful, but the prices (even of appetizers) are astronomical. ✉ *Alto de Miracruz 21, Alto de Miracruz* ☎ *943/278465* 🖷 *943/272753* ✍ *Reservations essential* ▭ *AE, DC, MC, V* ⊙ *Closed Mon., last 2 wks in June, and Nov. 5–29. No dinner Sun.*

$$$–$$$$ SPANISH ✕ **Kursaal.** This bright, minimalist space, part of Rafael Moneo's dazzling Palacio de Congresos between the Urumea River and the Zurriola beach, serves a lighter, less complex version of traditional Basque dishes, along with original creations by chef Mikel Gallo. Martín Berasategui is the owner and culinary force behind this establishment (as he is in Bilbao's Guggenheim restaurant). Day or night, the corner table over the crashing surf is a fine spot for inventive creations such as a postmodern interpretation of *marmitako* (tuna stew) featuring tiger prawns in a pipérade of ricotta, shallots, zucchini, Iberian bacon bits, and chicken broth. The dark *pichón de Bresse* (Bresse pigeon) is superb, as is the chestnut soup. ✉ *Zurriola Pasealekua 1, Gros* ☎ *943/003162* ▭ *AE, DC, MC, V* ⊙ *Closed Mon. and Dec. 20–Jan. 10. No dinner Sun.*

$$$$ SPANISH Fodor's Choice ★ ✕ **Martín Berasategui.** One of the top four restaurants in San Sebastián (along with Akelaŕe, Arzak, and Mugaritz), the sure bet here is the *lubina asada con jugo de habas, vainas, cebolletas y tallarines de chipirón* (roast sea bass with juice of fava beans, green beans, baby onions, and cuttlefish shavings), but go with whatever Martín suggests, especially if it's woodcock, *pichón de Bresse* (Bresse wood pigeon), or any other kind of game. Lasarte, also the site of San Sebastián's lush green racetrack, is 8 km (5 mi) south of San Sebastián. ✉ *Loidi Kalea 4, Lasarte* ☎ *943/366471* ▭ *AE, DC, MC, V* ⊙ *Closed Mon., Tues., and mid-Dec.–mid-Jan. No lunch Sat. No dinner Sun.*

$$$$ SPANISH Fodor's Choice ★ ✕ **Mugaritz.** This farmhouse in the hills above Errenteria 8 km (5 mi) northeast of San Sebastián is surrounded by spices and herbs tended by boy-genius chef Andoni Luis Aduriz and his crew. In a rustic setting with a modern, open feeling, Aduriz demonstrates his mastery over vegetables, foie, and combining seafood with products of the nearby fields and forest. If you can resist the tasting menu and order carefully à la carte, Aduriz's inventive, contemporary cuisine is within reach of the nontycoon budget at about €65 a head. ✉ *Aldura Aldea 20, Otzazulueta Baserria, Errenteria* ☎ *943/518343* ▭ *AE, DC, MC, V*

Closed Mon., wk before Easter, and Dec. 15–Jan. 15. No dinner Sun. No lunch Tues.

$$–$$$ SPANISH **Sidrería Petritegui.** For hearty dining and a certain amount of carousing and splashing around in hard cider, make this short excursion east of San Sebastián to the town of Astigarraga. Gigantic wooden barrels line the walls, and *sidra al txotx* (cider drawn straight from the barrel) is classically accompanied by ciderhouse specialties such as *tortilla de bacalao* (codfish omelet), *txuleta de buey* (beef chops), the smoky local sheep's-milk cheese from the town of Idiazabal, and, for dessert, walnuts and *membrillo* (quince jelly). *Ctra. San Sebastián–Hernani, Km 7, Astigarraga 943/457188 No credit cards No lunch weekdays.*

TESTOSTERONE ASYLUM

The Basque Country's men-only eating societies may seem another example of Spain's stereotypical machismo, but ethnologists and sociologists have long defined Basque society as a powerful matriarchy wherein the authority of the *etxekoandre*, the female house honcho, was so absolute that men became kitchen exiles. Eating societies were initially drinking clubs for men. Food came later, and, with the Basque passion for competition, cooking contests and the pursuit of culinary excellence followed. Today, there are also coed and all-women eating clubs.

$$$$ SPANISH ★ **Urepel.** Too many cooks may spoil the broth, but not in this family enterprise. Peru Almandoz is the head chef, but the whole family works as a team. The cuisine balances classic and contemporary elements with typical Urepel inventions such as *chicharro al escama dorada* (a skinned, deboned mackerel served under a layer of golden-brown, sliced potatoes) or the unusual foie gras wrapped with veal. The appetizer of finely caramelized scallops with caviar is also excellent. *Paseo de Salamanca 3, Parte Vieja 943/424040 AE, DC, MC, V Closed Sun., Tues., Christmas and Easter wks, and 3 wks in July.*

$$$$ SPANISH Fodor's Choice ★ **Zuberoa.** Working in a 15th-century Basque farmhouse 9½ km (6 mi) northeast of San Sebastián outside the village of Oiartzun, Hilario Arbelaitz has long been one of San Sebastián's most celebrated chefs due to his original yet simple management of prime raw materials such as tiny spring cuttlefish, baby octopi, or woodcock. The *lenguado con verduritas y chipirones* (sole with baby vegetables and cuttlefish) is another memorable tour de force. The atmosphere is unpretentious: just a few friends sitting down to dine simply—but very, very well. *Plaza Bekosoro 1, Oiartzun 943/491228 AE, DC, MC, V Closed Sun., Wed., Dec. 1–15, Apr. 21–May 5, and Oct. 15–30.*

WHERE TO STAY

$$–$$$ **Europa.** A block inland from the beach and an easy 15-minute walk around La Concha from the booming Parte Vieja, this small midtown San Sebastián hotel is staffed by an ample team of savvy professionals eager to help you make the most of your time in town. The rooms are undistinguished and on the small side but comfortably furnished and equipped with essential items such as hair dryers and computer hookups. **Pros:** well positioned in the middle of town, good value. **Cons:** cluttered rooms, tight spaces. *San Martín 52, Centro 943/470880*

943/471730 68 rooms In-room: Wi-Fi. In-hotel: restaurant, bar, parking (fee) AE, DC, MC, V.

$$$$ ★ **Hotel María Cristina.** The graceful beauty of the Belle Epoque is embodied here, in San Sebastián's most luxurious hotel, which sits on the elegant west bank of the Urumea River. The grandeur continues in salons filled with Oriental rugs, potted palms, and Carrara marble columns, and in bedrooms to match—with gold fixtures and wood wardrobes. Marble bathrooms add still more style. A piano player pounds out an eclectic medley of tunes nightly at the bar. **Pros:** polished service, supreme elegance, the place to stay. **Cons:** certain staffers are occasionally stiff, hotel restaurant disappointing. *Okendo 1, Centro 943/437600 www.westin.com 108 rooms, 28 suites In-room: safe, Wi-Fi. In-hotel: restaurant, room service, bar, laundry service, parking (fee), no-smoking rooms AE, DC, MC, V.*

$–$$$ **Hotel Parma.** Overlooking the Kursaal concert hall and the Zurriola beach at the mouth of the Urumea River, this small but bright new hotel is also at the edge of the Parte Vieja, San Sebastián's prime grazing area for tapas and vinos. Some of the cheerfully decorated rooms (though not all) have views northeast across the Urumea River and out to sea. **Pros:** location, views, the crashing of the waves. **Cons:** rooms are a bit cramped and cluttered, room decor is efficient but drab. *Paseo de Salamanca 10, Parte Vieja 943/428893 www.hotelparma.com 27 rooms In-room: Wi-Fi. In-hotel: bar AE, DC, MC, V.*

$$$–$$$$ **Londres y de Inglaterra.** On the main beachfront promenade overlooking La Concha, this stately hotel has an old-world feel and aesthetic that starts in the bright, formal lobby and continues throughout the hotel. The bar and restaurant face the bay, and the guest rooms with views west out to sea are some of the best in town. **Pros:** sunsets from rooms on the Concha side are stunning, great location over the beach. **Cons:** some rooms in disrepair and in need of updating, street side can be noisy on weekends. *Zubieta 2, La Concha 943/440770 www.hlondres.com 139 rooms, 9 suites In-room: Wi-Fi. In-hotel: restaurant, bar, parking (fee) AE, DC, MC, V.*

NIGHTLIFE

Akerbeltz (*Mari Kalea 10, Parte Vieja 943/460934*), at the corner over the port to the left of Santa María del Coro and the Gaztelubide eating society, is a cozy late-night refuge for music and drinks. San Sebastián's top disco is **Bataplan** (*Paseo de la Concha s/n, Centro 943/460439*), near the western end of La Concha. Filled with couples and night owls, **Bideluze** (*Pl. de Guipúzcoa 14, Centro 943/460219*) is always alive. **Discóbolo** (*Blvd. Zumardía 27, Centro 943/217678*), near the Parte Vieja, is a hot spot. **Kabutzia** (*Paseo del Muelle s/n, Centro 943/429725*), above the Club Nautico seaward from the Casino, is a busy night haunt. **Ku** (*Ctra. Monte Igueldo s/n, Igueldo 943/212050*), up on the hill, has been going strong for three decades. **La Rotonda** (*Paseo de la Concha 6, Centro 943/429095*), across the street from Bataplan, below Miraconcha, is a top nightspot.

SHOPPING

San Sebastián is nonpareil for stylish home furnishings and clothing. Wander Calle San Martín and the surrounding pedestrian-only streets to see what's in the windows. **Bilintx** (⊠ *C. Fermín Calbetón 21, Parte Vieja* ☎ *943/420080*) is one of the city's best bookstores. Stop into **Maitiena** (⊠ *Av. Libertad 32, Centro* ☎ *943/424721*) for a fabulous selection of chocolates. **Ponsol** (⊠ *C. Narrica 4, Parte Vieja* ☎ *943/420876*) is the best place to buy Basque berets; the Leclerq family has been hatting (and clothing) the locals for three generations.

PASAJES DE SAN JUAN

10 km (6 mi) east of San Sebastián.

★ Generally marked as Pasaia Donibane, in Euskera, there are actually three towns around the commercial port of Rentería: **Pasajes Ancho,** an industrial port; **Pasajes de San Pedro,** a large fishing harbor; and historic **Pasajes de San Juan,** a colorful cluster of 18th- and 19th-century buildings along the channel to the sea. Best reached by driving into Pasajes de San Pedro, on the San Sebastián side of the strait, and catching a launch across the mouth of the harbor (about €0.75, depending on the time of day)—this is too sweet a side trip to pass up.

5

In 1777, at the age of 20, General Lafayette set out from Pasajes de San Juan to aid the American Revolution. Victor Hugo spent the summer of 1843 here writing his *Voyage aux Pyrénées.* The **Victor Hugo House** is the home of the tourist office and has an exhibit of traditional village dress. **Ontziola,** a research center for traditional wooden boat design, is directed by Xavier Agote, who taught boat-building in Rockland, Maine. Pasajes de San Juan can be reached via Pasajes de San Pedro from San Sebastián by cab or bus. Or, if you prefer to go on foot, follow the red-and-white-blazed GR trail that begins at the east end of the Zurriola beach—you're in for a spectacular three-hour hike along the rocky coast. By car, take N1 for France and, after passing Juan Mari Arzak's landmark restaurant, Arzak, at Alto de Miracruz, look for a marked left turn into Pasaia or Pasajes de San Pedro.

WHERE TO EAT

$$–$$$ SPANISH Fodor'sChoice ★

✕ **Txulotxo.** Cozy and friendly, this picturesque and unusual restaurant sits like a matchbox on stilts at the edge of the Rentería shipping passage, in the shadow of the occasional freighter passing only a few dozen yards away. The *sopa de pescado* (fish soup), thick and piping hot, is among the best available on the Basque Coast, and the fresh grilled sole and monkfish, not to mention the pimiento (red pepper)-wrapped *bacalao* (codfish) are equally superb. Make sure you leave some time to stroll around town. ⊠ *Pasajes de San Juan* ☎ *943/523952* *Reservations essential* ▭ *AE, DC, MC, V* ⊗ *Closed Tues. and Dec. 23–Jan. 15. No dinner Sun.*

HONDARRIBIA

12 km (7 mi) east of Pasajes.

Hondarribia (Fuenterrabía, in Spanish) is the last fishing port before the French border. Lined with fishermen's homes and small fishing boats, the harbor is a beautiful but touristy spot. If you have a taste for history, follow signs up the hill to the medieval bastion and onetime castle of Carlos V, now a parador.

> **WORD OF MOUTH**
>
> "Just back from a weekend at Hondarribia, an underrated town for no reason at all. Every time I go there I find another new reason to love it . . . Basque mediaeval streets, dozens of cozy corners, a parador in a fortress, great *pintxos* and great food, friendly atmosphere everywhere. . . . A must."
>
> —mikelg

ESSENTIALS

Visitor Information Hondarribia (✉ *Javier Ugarte 6* ☎ *943/645458*).

WHERE TO EAT AND STAY

$$$$ SEAFOOD ✕ **Alameda.** Hot young Hondarribia star chefs Gorka and Kepa Txapartegi opened this restaurant in 1997 after working with, among others, Lasarte's master chef Martín Berasategui. The elegantly restored house in upper Hondarribia is a delight, as are the seasonally rotated combinations of carefully chosen ingredients, from duck to foie gras to vegetables. Both surf and turf selections are well served here, from ibérico ham to fresh tuna just in from the Atlantic. The terrace is the place to be on balmy summer evenings. ✉ *Minasoroeta 1* ☎ *943/642789* ▭ *AE, DC, MC, V* ⊗ *Closed Mon., Dec. 24–Jan. 6, June 12–18, and Oct. 16–22. No dinner Sun.*

$$–$$$ SEAFOOD ★ ✕ **La Hermandad de Pescadores.** This central and clean-lined restaurant with wooden tables and a handsome mahogany bar is owned by the local fishermen's guild and serves simple, hearty fare at better than reasonable prices. Try the *sopa de pescado* (fish soup), the *mejillones* (mussels), or the *almejas a la marinera* (clams in a thick, garlicky sauce). If you are careful to come one side or the other of peak hours (2–4 and 9–11), you'll be able to find space at the long, communal, and fraternal boards. ✉ *C. Zuloaga s/n* ☎ *943/642738* ▭ *AE, DC, MC, V* ⊗ *Closed Wed. No dinner Tues.*

¢ **Caserío "Artzu".** This family barn and house, with its classic low, wide roofline, has been here in one form or another for some 800 years. Just west of the hermitage of Nuestra Señora de Guadalupe, 5 km (3 mi) above Hondarribia, Artzu offers modernized accommodations in an ancient *caserío* overlooking the junction of the Bidasoa estuary and the Atlantic. Better hosts than this warm, friendly clan are hard to find. **Pros:** good value, friendly family. **Cons:** beds only moderately comfortable, bathrooms small. ✉ *Barrio Montaña* ☎ *943/640530* ⊕ *www.euskalnet.net/casartzu* ⇆ *6 rooms, 1 with bath* ♿ *In-room: no a/c, no TV, Wi-Fi. In-hotel: restaurant, bar, no elevator* ▭ *No credit cards.*

$$$–$$$$ **Parador de Hondarribia.** Also known as Parador El Emperador, this medieval bastion dates from the 10th century and housed imperial Spain's founding Emperor Carlos V in the 16th century. Replete with suits of armor and other chivalric bric-a-brac, the place feels like a movie set (and has occasionally been used as one). Many rooms have

views of the Bidasoa estuary. Reserve ahead and ask for one of the three "special" rooms, with canopy beds and baronial appointments, well worth the moderate extra expense. **Pros:** great views, impeccably comfortable. **Cons:** slightly chilly (typical parador) service, no restaurant. ✉*Pl. de Armas 14* ☎*943/645500* 🌐*www.parador.es* *36 rooms* *In-room: Wi-Fi. In-hotel: restaurant, bar, parking (fee)* *AE, DC, MC, V.*

EN ROUTE

The fastest route from San Sebastián to Pamplona is the A15 Autovía de Navarra, which cuts through the Leizarán Valley and gets you there in about 45 minutes. Somewhat more scenic, if slower (2 hrs) and more tortuous, is the 134-km (83-mi) drive on C133, which starts near Hondarribia and follows the Bidasoa River (the border with France) up through Vera de Bidasoa. When C133 meets N121, you can turn left up into the lovely Baztán Valley or right to continue through the Velate pass to Pamplona.

NAVARRA AND PAMPLONA

Bordering the French Pyrenees and populated largely by Basques, Navarra grows progressively less Basque toward its southern and eastern edges. Pamplona, the ancient Navarran capital, draws crowds with its annual feast of San Fermín, but medieval Vitoria, in the Basque province of Alava, is largely undiscovered by tourists. Olite, south of Pamplona, has a storybook castle, and the towns of Puente la Reina and Estella are visually indelible stops on the Camino de Santiago.

PAMPLONA

79 km (47 mi) southeast of San Sebastián.

Pamplona (Iruña, in Euskera) is known worldwide for its running of the bulls, made famous by Ernest Hemingway in his 1926 novel *The Sun Also Rises*. The occasion is the festival of San Fermín, July 6 to 14, when Pamplona's population triples (along with hotel rates), so reserve rooms months in advance. Every morning at 8 sharp a skyrocket is shot off, and the bulls kept overnight in the corrals at the edge of town are run through a series of closed-off streets leading to the bullring, a 902-yard dash. Running before them are Spaniards and foreigners feeling festive enough to risk a goring. The degree of peril in the *encierro* is difficult to gauge. Serious injuries occur nearly every day during the festival; deaths are rare but always a possibility. What's certain is the sense of danger, the mob hysteria, and the exhilaration. Tickets to the bullfights (*corridas*), as opposed to the running (*encierro,* meaning "enclosing"), to which access is free, can be difficult to get.

Founded by the Roman emperor Pompey as Pompaelo, or Pampeiopolis, Pamplona was successively taken by the Franks, the Goths, and the Moors. In 750, the Pamplonians put themselves under the protection of Charlemagne and managed to expel the Arabs temporarily. But the foreign commander took advantage of this trust to destroy the city walls, so that when he was driven out once more by the Moors, the Navarrese took their revenge, ambushing and slaughtering the retreating Frankish

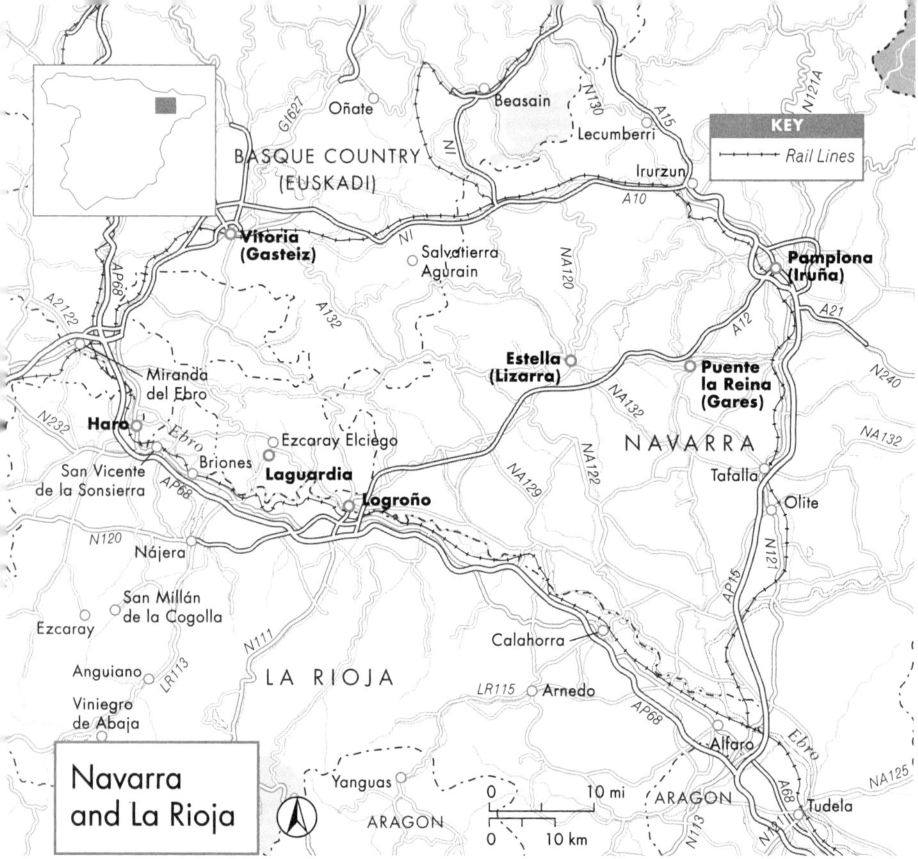

army as it fled over the Pyrenees through the mountain pass of Roncesvalles in 778. This is the episode depicted in the 11th-century *Song of Roland*, although the French (anonymous) author chose to cast the aggressors as Moors. For centuries after that, Pamplona remained three argumentative towns until they were forcibly incorporated into one city by Carlos III (the Noble, 1387–1425) of Navarra.

ESSENTIALS

Bus Station Pamplona (✉ *C. Conde Oliveto 8* ☎ *948/223854*).

Car Rentals Europcar (✉ *Av. Pio XII 43, Pamplona* ☎ *948/172523* ✉ *Aeropuerto de Pamplona* ☎ *948/312798*).

Train Information Pamplona (✉ *Estación de Pamplona, Ctra. de San Sebastián* ☎ *948/130202*).

Visitor Information Pamplona (✉ *Eslava 1* ☎ *848/420420*).

EXPLORING

Pamplona's most remarkable civil building is the ornate **ayuntamiento** *(town hall)* on the Plaza Consistorial, with its rich ocher facade setting off brightly gilded balconies. The interior is a lavish wood and marble display of wealth reminding visitors that Navarra was always a wealthy

CLOSE UP

Running with the Bulls

In *The Sun Also Rises,* Hemingway describes the Pamplona *encierro* (bull running, or, literally, "enclosing") in anything but romantic terms. Jake Barnes hears the rocket, steps out on his balcony, and watches the crowd run by: men in white with red sashes and neckerchiefs, those behind running faster then the bulls. "One man fell, rolled to the gutter, and lay quiet." It's a textbook move, and first-rate observation and reporting: An experienced runner who falls remains motionless (bulls respond to movement). In the next *encierro* in the novel, a man is gored through and through and dies. The waiter at the Iruña café mutters, "You hear? Muerto. Dead. He's dead. With a horn through him. All for morning fun...."

Despite this, generations of young Americans and other internationals have turned this barnyard bull-management maneuver into one of the Western world's most famous rites of passage. The idea is simple: six fighting bulls are guided through the streets by 8 to 10 *cabestros,* or steers (also known as *mansos,* meaning "tame"), to the holding pens at the bullring, from which they will emerge to be fought that afternoon. The course covers 924 yards. The Cuesta de Santo Domingo down to the corrals is the most dangerous part of the run, high in terror and low in elapsed time. The walls are sheer, and the bulls pass quickly. The fear here is of a bull, for some external reason or idiosyncrasy, hooking along the wall of the Military Hospital on his way up the hill, forcing runners out in front of the speeding pack in a classic hammer and anvil movement. Mercaderes is next, cutting left for about 100 yards by the town hall, then right up Calle Estafeta. The outside of each turn and the centrifugal force of 10,000 kilos (22,000 pounds) of bulls and steers are to be avoided here. Calle Estafeta is the bread and butter of the run, the longest (about 400 yards), straightest, and least complicated part of the course.

The classic run, a perfect blend of form and function, is to remain ahead of the horns for as long as possible, fading to the side when overtaken. The long gallop up Calle Estafeta is the place to try to do it. The trickiest part of running with the bulls is splitting your vision so that with one eye you keep track of the bulls behind you and with the other you keep from falling over runners ahead of you.

At the end of Estafeta the course descends left through the *callejón,* the narrow tunnel, into the bullring. The bulls move more slowly here, uncertain of their weak forelegs, allowing runners to stay close and even to touch them as they glide down into the tunnel. The only uncertainty is whether there will be a pileup in the tunnel. The most dramatic photographs of the *encierro* have been taken here, as the galloping pack slams through what occasionally turns into a solid wall of humanity. If all goes well—no bulls separated from the pack, no mayhem—the bulls will have arrived in the ring in less than three minutes.

The cardinal crime, punishable by a $1,000 fine, is to attempt to attract the bull, thus removing him from the pack and creating a deadly danger. After 14 years without a fatality, a young man was gored to death in July of 2009.

kingdom of its own. Originally a 15th-century courthouse, the present building was erected between 1753 and 1759.

Pamplona's **cathedral,** set near the portion of the ancient walls rebuilt in the 17th century, is one of the most important religious buildings in northern Spain, thanks to the fragile grace and gabled Gothic arches of its cloister. Inside are the tombs of Carlos III and his wife, marked by an alabaster sculpture. The **Museo Catedralicio Diocesano** (Diocesan Museum) houses religious art from the Middle Ages and the Renaissance. Call in advance for guided tours in English. ✉*C. Dormitaleria 3–5* ☎*948/212594* *€4.50* ⏲*Museum weekdays 10–1:30 and 4–7, Sat. 10–1:30.*

The central **Ciudadela,** an ancient fortress, is a parkland of promenades and pools. Walk through in late afternoon, the time of the *paseo* (traditional stroll), for a taste of everyday life here.

Archivo Real y General de Navarra. This Rafael Moneo–designed archive of glass and stone ingeniously contained within a Romanesque palace is Pamplona's architectural treasure. Containing papers and parchments going back to the 9th century, the archive holds 23,000 lineal meters of documents and has room for 17,000 meters more. The library and reading rooms are lined with cherry wood and covered with a gilded ceiling. ✉*Dos de Mayo s/n* ☎*848/424609* 🌐*www.cfnavarra.es.*

Edificio Baluarte. The Palacio de Congresos y Auditorio de Navarra, built in 2003 by local architectural star Patxi Mangado, is a sleek assemblage of black Zimbabwean granite with a concert hall of exquisite acoustical perfection made of beechwood from upper Navarra's famed Irati *haya* (beech) forest. Performances and concerts from opera to ballet are held in this modern venue built on the remains of one of the five bastions of Pamplona's 16th-century Ciudadela. ✉*Plaza del Baluarte* ☎*948/066060* 🌐*www.baluarte.com.*

On Calle Santo Domingo, in a 16th-century building once used as a hospital for pilgrims on their way to Santiago de Compostela, is the **Museo de Navarra,** with a collection of regional archaeological artifacts and historical costumes. ✉*C. Santo Domingo 47* ☎*848/426492* 🌐*www.cfnavarra.es* *€2.50* ⏲*Tues.–Sat. 9–2 and 5–7, Sun. 9–2.*

One of Pamplona's greatest charms is the warren of small streets near the **Plaza del Castillo** (especially Calle San Nicolás), which are filled with restaurants, taverns, and bars. Pamplonicas are hardy, rough-and-tumble sorts, well known for their eagerness and capacity to eat and drink.

NEED A BREAK?

Pamplona's gentry has been flocking to the ornate, French-style Café Iruña (✉*Pl. del Castillo 44* ☎*948/222064* 🌐*www.cafeiruna.com*) since 1888, but Ernest Hemingway made it part of world literary lore in *The Sun Also Rises* in 1927. You can still have a drink with a bronze version of the author at his favorite perch at the far end of the bar.

OFF THE BEATEN PATH

Fundación–Museo Jorge Oteiza. Just 8 km (5 mi) east of Pamplona on the road toward France, this museum dedicated to the father of modern Basque art is a must-visit. Jorge Oteiza (1908–2003), in his seminal treatise *Quosque Tandem,* called for Basque artists to find an aesthetic of their own instead of attempting to become part of the Spanish canon. Rejecting ornamentation in favor of essential form and a noninvasive use of space, Oteiza created a school of artists—of which Eduardo Chillida (1924–2002) was the most famous sculptor. The building itself, Oteiza's home for more than two decades, is a large cube of red, earth-color concrete designed by Oteiza's longtime friend, Pamplona architect Francisco Javier Sáenz de Oiza. ✉ *Alzuza, Ctra. N150, Km 8, from Pamplona* ☎ *948/332074* 🌐 *www.museooteiza.org* 🎫 *€4* ⏲ *Tues.–Fri. 10–3, weekends 11–7.*

WHERE TO EAT AND STAY

$–$$$ SPANISH ✕ **Erburu.** In the heart of the nightlife district, this dark restaurant is a true find, frequented by Pamplona locals in the know. Come for a full sit-down meal or just to sample tapas at the bar. Standouts are the Basque classic *merluza con salsa verde* (hake in green sauce) and any of the dishes made with *alcachofas* (artichokes), for which Navarra is justly famous. *Caracoles en salsa de ajos* (snails in garlic sauce) and *rabo de buey* (braised oxtail) also rank near the top of this traditional Pamplona dining enclave's specialties. ✉ *San Lorenzo 19–21* ☎ *948/225169* 💳 *AE, DC, MC, V* ⏲ *Closed Mon. and last 2 wks in July.*

$$$$ SPANISH ✕ **Hartza.** Just a few steps from the bullring and the Paseo de Hemingway, this is a favorite among veteran Pamplonians. Archaic and elegant, this rustic place—somewhat surprisingly, given the decor—serves some of the most creative cuisine in Pamplona. The bustling kitchen is run by three sisters and is known for traditional Navarran cuisine with a contemporary flair. Try the *oca con jugo de trufa y manzana* (goose with apple and truffle sauce). ✉ *Juan de Labrit 19* ☎ *948/224568* 💳 *AE, DC, MC, V* ⏲ *Closed Mon., late July–late Aug., and late Dec.–early Jan. No dinner Sun.*

$$$–$$$$ SPANISH ✕ **Josetxo.** This warm, family-run restaurant in a stately mansion with classically elegant decorations is one of Pamplona's finest addresses for refined cuisine. Traditional, international, Navarran, and contemporary culinary techniques and tastes all find a place on the menu. House favorites range from *hojaldre de marisco* (shellfish pastry) to an *ensalada de langosta* (lobster salad) appetizer or a *muslo de pichón relleno de trufa y foie* (pigeon drumstick stuffed with truffles and foie gras). ✉ *Plaza Príncipe de Viana 1* ☎ *948/222097* 💳 *AE, DC, MC, V* ⏲ *Closed Sun. except during San Fermín, and Aug.*

¢–$$ SPANISH ✕ **Gaucho.** A legendary address for *tapeo* (tapas grazing) and *txikiteo* (wine tippling), this small tavern serves some of the best tapas in Pamplona. Just off Plaza del Castillo, in the eye of the hurricane during *sanfermines*, there is a surprising sense of peace and quiet here, even as the fiesta spins out of control outside. Tapas range from the classical *chistorra* (spicy sausage) to contemporary creations such as the deconstructed *vieira* (scallop), apt metaphor for Pamplona's blend of old and new. ✉ *Espoz y Mina 4* ☎ *948/225073* 💳 *AE, DC, MC, V* ⏲ *Closed July 15–30.*

$–$$$ 🏨 **Europa.** A modest, family-run hotel a block and half from the bullring and within shouting distance of party-central Plaza del Castillo, this is a handy alternative to the grand hotels of Pamplona. The bathrooms have cool marble floors, and the hotel restaurant on the ground floor is a gourmet haven and one of the best in Navarra. **Pros:** central location, good value, excellent cooking. **Cons:** noisy during the fiesta unless you score an interior room, rooms on the small side. ✉*C. Espoz y Mina 11* ☎*948/221800* 🌐*www.heuropa.com* *25 rooms* *In-room: Wi-Fi. In-hotel: restaurant, bar* *AE, DC, MC, V.*

$$$$ **Gran Hotel La Perla.** La Perla is the oldest hotel in Pamplona and, after several years of refurbishing, has reinvented itself as a luxury lodging option. Rooms have been modernized and redecorated in plush pastels and sleek contemporary lines. Several have retained their early 20th-century decor, among them Hemingway's (No. 201, from which he watched the running of the bulls in 1924). The hotel founder's son, Lalo Moreno, was a bullfighter, and the mounted heads of two of his taurine adversaries preside over the restaurant. Prices triple during San Fermín. **Pros:** read your page-worn copy of *The Sun Also Rises* in the place where the book was first conceived, impeccable comfort. **Cons:** round-the-clock mayhem during San Fermín. ✉*Pl. del Castillo 1* ☎*948/223000* 🌐*www.granhotellaperla.com* *44 rooms* *In-room: refrigerator, Wi-Fi. In-hotel: restaurant, bar, parking (fee)* *AE, DC, MC, V.*

$$$$ **Los Tres Reyes.** Named for the three kings of Navarra, Aragón, and Castile—who, it was said, could meet at La Mesa de los Tres Reyes, in the Pyrenees, without stepping out of their respective realms—this modern glass-and-stone refuge operates on the same principle: Come to Pamplona without leaving the comforts of home. **Pros:** a refuge from the excitement of San Fermín, with quiet, leafy gardens, a pool, and modernized and elegant comfort. **Cons:** so modern and streamlined it could just as well be a Marriott in Malibu. ✉*C. de la Taconera s/n* ☎*948/226600* 🌐*www.hotel3reyes.com* *152 rooms, 8 suites* *In-room: Wi-Fi. In-hotel: restaurant, bars, pool, gym, parking (fee)* *AE, DC, MC, V.*

NIGHTLIFE

The city has a thumping student life year-round, especially along the length of Calle San Nicolas. For an ultra-up-to-date nightspot, try **Dodo Club** (✉*San Roque 7* ☎*948/198989*), where breakfast, lunch, free Wi-Fi, and DJs keep things lively around the clock. **Marengo** (✉*Av. Bayona 2* ☎ *948/265542* *€10* *11 PM–6 AM*) is a barnlike rager filled until dawn with young singles and couples. Dress up or you might flunk the bouncer inspection.

SHOPPING

Botas are the wineskins from which Basques typically drink at bullfights or during fiestas. The art lies in drinking a stream of wine from a *bota* held at arm's length—without spilling a drop, if you want to maintain your honor (not to mention your shirt). You can buy botas in any Basque town, but Pamplona's **Anel** (✉*C. Comedías 731001*) sells the best brand, Las Tres Zetas—"The Three Zs," written as ZZZ. **Hijas de C. Lozano** (✉*C. Zapatería 1131001*) sells *café y leche* (coffee and milk) toffees that are prized all over Spain. **Salcedo** (✉*C. Estafeta 3731001*), open since 1800, invented and still sells almond-based *mantecadas* (powder cakes), as well as *coronillas* (delightful almond-and-cream concoctions).

OFF THE BEATEN PATH

Olite, 41 km (25 mi) south of Pamplona, offers an unforgettable glimpse into the life of Spain in the Middle Ages, including the 11th-century church of **San Pedro,** revered for its finely worked Romanesque cloisters and portal. It's the town's **castle,** though, restored by Carlos III in the French style and brimming with ramparts, crenellated battlements, and watchtowers, that captures the imagination most. You can walk the ramparts. And should you get tired or hungry, part of the castle has been converted into a parador, making a fine place to catch a bite or a few z's. *www.castillosnet.org €3.10 Daily 10–7.*

PUENTE LA REINA

24 km (15 mi) southwest of Pamplona.

Puente la Reina (Gares, in Euskera) is an important nexus on the Camino de Santiago: the junction of the two pilgrimage routes from northern Europe, one passing through Somport and Jaca and the other through Roncesvalles and Pamplona. A bronze sculpture of a pilgrim marks the spot. The graceful medieval bridge over the river Arga was built for pilgrims by Navarran King Sancho VII el Fuerte (the Strong) in the 11th century, and the streets, particularly Calle Mayor, are lined with tiny, ancient houses. The **church of Santiago** (*St. James C. Mayor*) is known for its gold sculpture of the saint. The **Iglesia del Crucifijo** (*Church of the Crucifix Ctra. de Pamplona s/n*) has a notably expressive wooden sculpture of Christ on a Y-shaped cross, gift of a 14th-century pilgrim. The octagonal church of **Santa María de Eunate** (*5 km [3 mi] east of Puente la Reina*) in Muruzabal was once used as a burial place for pilgrims who didn't make it.

WHERE TO EAT AND STAY

$$$–$$$$ **Hotel El Peregrino.** A time-honored haven for weary pilgrims and modern bon vivants on sound budgets, this handsome stone house north of town is hard to pass up. The rooms are small but charming. Roasts, *menestra de verduras* (Navarran vegetable stew), rack of suckling lamb or pig, and hearty bean-and-sausage-based soups are among the star offerings at the excellent restaurant ($$–$$$$). **Pros:** rooms furnished with handsome antiques; professional service; superior restaurant. **Cons:** close to highway; minuscule spaces in some (not all) rooms. *Ctra. Pamplona–Logroño, Km 23 948/340075 www.hotelelperegrino.com 10 rooms, 3 junior suites In-room: Wi-Fi. In-hotel: restaurant, bar, pool AE, DC, MC, V Restaurant closed Sun. dinner and Mon.*

ESTELLA

19 km (12 mi) west of Puente la Reina, 48 km (30 mi) northeast of Logroño.

Once the seat of the Royal Court of Navarra, Estella (Lizarra, in Euskera) is an inspiring stop on the Camino de Santiago.

ESSENTIALS

Visitor Information Estella (*San Nicolás 4 948/556301*).

The heart of Estella is the arcaded Plaza San Martín and its chief civic monument, the 12th-century **Palacio de los Reyes de Navarra** *(Palace of the Kings of Navarra)*. **San Pedro de la Rúa** (✉ *C. San Nicolás s/n*) has a beautiful cloister and a stunning carved portal.

Across the River Ega from San Pedro, the doorway to the **church of San Miguel** has fantastic relief sculptures of St. Michael the Archangel battling a dragon. The **Iglesia del Santo Sepulcro** (*Church of the Holy Sepulchre* ✉ *C. Curtidores s/n*) has a beautiful fluted portal. **Santa María Jus del Castillo** (✉ *C. Curtidores s/n*), converted from a synagogue in 1145, is the only vestige of Estella's medieval Jewish quarter. The **Monasterio de Irache** (✉ *Ctra. de Logroño, Km 3*) dates from the 10th century but was later converted by Cistercian monks to a pilgrims' hospital; next door is the famous brass faucet that supplies pilgrims with free-flowing holy wine.

VITORIA-GASTEIZ

93 km (56 mi) west of Pamplona, 115 km (71 mi) southwest of San Sebastián, 64 km (40 mi) southeast of Bilbao.

Vitoria's standard of living is currently rated among the highest in Spain, based on such criteria as square meters of green space per inhabitant (14), sports and cultural facilities, and pedestrian-only zones. Capital of the Basque Country, and its second-largest city after Bilbao, Vitoria (Gasteiz, in Euskera) is, nevertheless, in many ways Euskadi's least Basque city. Neither a maritime nor a mountain enclave, Vitoria occupies the steppe-like *meseta de Alava* (Alava plain) and functions as a modern industrial center with a surprisingly medieval *Casco Antiguo* (Old Quarter). Founded by Sancho el Sabio (the Wise) in 1181, the city was built largely of granite rather than sandstone, so Vitoria's oldest streets and squares seem especially dark, weathered, and ancient.

GETTING AROUND

Vitoria is a big city but the area you'll spend your time in is small, only about a kilometer, and easily walkable.

ESSENTIALS

Bus Station Vitoria (✉ *C. de los Herran 27* ☎ *945/258400*).

Car Rentals Alquibilbo (✉ *General Eguía 20, Bilbao* ☎ *94/441–2012*). **A-Rental** (✉ *C. Pérez Galdos 24, Bilbao* ☎ *94/427–0781*).

Visitor Information Vitoria-Gasteiz (✉ *Pl. General Loma* ☎ *945/161598*). **Vitoria** (✉ *Parque de la Florida* ☎ *945/131321*).

EXPLORING

★ **Artium.** Officially titled Centro-Museo Vasco de Arte Contemporáneo, this former bus station was opened in 2002 by King Juan Carlos I, who called it "the third leg of the Basque art triangle, along with the Bilbao Guggenheim and San Sebastián's Chillida Leku." The museum's permanent collection—including 20th- and 21st-century paintings and sculptures by Jorge Oteiza, Eduardo Chillida, Agustín Ibarrola, and Nestor Basterretxea, among many others—makes it one of Spain's finest treasuries of contemporary art. ✉ *Calle de Francia 24* ☎ *945/209020* 🌐 *www.artium.org* 🎫 *€5* ⏲ *Tues.–Sun. 11–8.*

Plaza de la Virgen Blanca, in the southwest corner of old Vitoria, is ringed by noble houses with covered arches and white-trim glass galleries. The monument in the center commemorates the Duke of Wellington's defeat of Napoléon's army here in 1813. For lunch, coffee, or tapas, look to the plaza's top left-hand corner for the Cafeteria de la Virgen Blanca, with its giant wooden floorboards. The **Plaza de España,** across Virgen Blanca past the monument and the handsome El Victoria café, is an arcaded neoclassical square with the austere elegance typical of formal 19th-century squares all over Spain. The **Plaza del Machete,** overlooking Plaza de España, is named for the sword used by medieval nobility to swear allegiance to the local fueros, or special Basque rights and privileges. A jasper niche in the lateral facade of the Gothic church of **San Miguel** (✉ *Plaza del Machete*) contains the Virgen Blanca (White Virgin), Vitoria's patron saint.

5

The **Palacio de los Alava Esquivel** (✉ *C. de la Soledad*), one of Vitoria's oldest and most splendid buildings, erected in 1488 and reformed in 1535 and 1865, is reached from the Plaza de la Virgen Blanca along Calle de Herrería, which follows the egg-shaped outline along the west side of the old city walls. The 15th-century **Torre de Doña Otxanda** (✉ *Calle Siervas de Jesús 24*) houses Vitoria's **Museo de Ciencias Naturales (Museum of Natural Sciences)**, which contains interesting botanical, zoological, and geological collections along with the museum's most prized items: pieces of amber from the nearby archeological site at Peñacerrada-Urizaharra. **El Portalón** (✉ *C. de la Correría 151*), the ancient brick-and-wood house at the corner across from the museum, a hostelry for 500 years, is an excellent restaurant and wine cellar. The **Museo de la Arqueología** (✉ *C. de la Correría*) has paleolithic dolmens, Roman art and artifacts, medieval objects, and the famous *stele del jinete* (stela of the horseback rider), an early Basque tombstone.

The **Torre de los Hurtado de Anda** (✉ *C. Fray Zacarías Martinez s/n*) is across from the exquisitely sculpted Gothic doorway on the western facade of the cathedral. Go into the courtyard on the west side of this square; in the far right corner, you'll find the sculpted head of a fish protruding from the grass in front of an intensely ornate door. Walk through Calle Txikitxoa and up Cantón de Santa María behind the Catedral de Santa María, noting the tiny hanging rooms and alcoves that have been added to the back of the apse over the centuries, clinging across corners and filling odd spaces.

★ The 1525 Palacio de Bendaña is home to one of Vitoria's main attractions, the **Museo Fournier de Naipes** *(Playing-Card Museum).* In 1868 Don Heraclio Fournier founded a playing-card factory, started amassing cards, and eventually found himself with 15,000 sets, the largest and finest such collection in the world. As you survey rooms of hand-painted cards, the distinction between artwork and game piece is quickly scrambled. The oldest sets date from the 12th century, making them older than the building, and the story parallels the history of printing. The most unusual and finely painted sets come from Japan, India (the Indian cards are round), and the international practice of tarot. One German set has musical bars that can be combined to form hundreds of different waltzes. By the time you reach the 20th-century rooms, contemporary designs have been debunked as unoriginal. You'll never look at cards the same way again. ✉ *C. Cuchillería 54* ☎ *945/255555* 🎫 *Free* ⏲ *Tues.–Fri. 10–2 and 4–6:30, Sat. 10–2, Sun. 11–2.*

Parque de la Florida (✉ *South of Plaza de la Virgen Blanca*) is a nice respite during a tour of Vitoria. Just south of the parque is the **Museo Provincial de Armería** (*Provincial Arms Museum*) has prehistoric hatchets, 20th-century pistols, and a sand-table reproduction of the 1813 battle between the Duke of Wellington's troops and the French. ✉ *Paseo Fray Francisco de Vitoria* ☎ *945/181925* 🎫 *Free* ⏲ *Tues.–Fri. 10–2 and 4–6:30, Sat. 10–2, Sun. 11–2.*

The **Museo de Bellas Artes** (*Museum of Fine Arts* ✉ *Paseo Fray Francisco de Vitoria*) has paintings by Ribera, Picasso, and the Basque painter Zuloaga. Next door is the Palacio Ajuria-Enea, seat of the Basque government. ✉ *Paseo Fray Francisco 8* ☎ *945/181918* 🎫 *Free* ⏲ *Tues.–Fri. 10–2 and 4–6:30, Sat. 10–2 and 5–8, Sun. 11–2.*

WHERE TO EAT AND STAY

$$–$$$$ SPANISH ★ ✕ **El Portalón.** Nestled in among dark, creaky wood floors and staircases, bare brick walls, and ancient beams, pillars, and coats of arms, this rough and rustic 15th-century inn turns out classical Castilian and Basque specialties that reflect Vitoria's geography and social history. The wine cellar should not be missed. Try the *lomo de cebón asado en su jugo con puré de manzanas* (filet mignon with apple puree) or any of the *merluza* (hake) preparations. ✉ *C. Correría 151* ☎ *945/142755* 💳 *AE, DC, MC, V* ⏲ *Closed Sun., last 3 wks in Aug., wk before Easter, and Dec. 24–Jan. 4.*

$$$ ★ 🏨 **Parador de Argómaniz.** Some 15 minutes east of Vitoria off N104 toward Pamplona, this 17th-century palace has panoramic views over the Alava plains and retains a powerful sense of mystery and romance, with long stone hallways punctuated by imposing antiques. Rooms have polished wood floors, and some have glass-enclosed sitting areas and/or hot tubs. The wood-beam dining room ($$–$$$$) on the third floor makes each meal feel like a baronial feast. **Pros:** contemporary rooms and comforts; gorgeous details and surroundings. **Cons:** isolated. ✉ *N1, Km 363, Argómaniz* ☎ *945/293200* 🌐 *www.parador.es* 🛏 *53 rooms* 🛎 *In-room: Wi-Fi. In-hotel: restaurant, bar, parking (no fee)* 💳 *AE, DC, MC, V.*

LAGUARDIA

66 km (40 mi) south of Vitoria, 17 km (10 mi) northwest of Logroño.

Founded in 908 to stand guard—as its name suggests—over Navarra's southwestern flank, Laguardia is on a promontory overlooking the Ebro River and the vineyards of the Rioja Alavesa–La Rioja wine country north of the Ebro in the Basque province of Alava. Flanked by the Sierra de Cantabria, the town rises shiplike, its prow headed north, over the sea of surrounding vineyards. Ringed with walls, Laguardia's dense cluster of emblazoned noble facades and stunning patios may have no equal in Spain. Relish the 50 or so houses with coats of arms and medieval or Renaissance masonry.

ESSENTIALS

Visitor Information Laguardia (✉ *Pl. San Juan 1* ☎ *945/600845*).

EXPLORING

Starting from the 15th-century Puerta de Carnicerías, or Puerta Nueva, the central portal off the parking area on the east side of town, the first landmark is the 16th-century **ayuntamiento** (town hall), with its imperial shield of Carlos V. Farther into the square is the current town hall, built in the 19th century. A right down Calle Santa Engracia takes you past impressive facades—the floor inside the portal at No. 25 is a lovely stone mosaic, and a walk behind the triple-emblazoned 17th-century facade of No. 19 reveals a stagecoach, floor mosaics, wood beams, and an inner porch.The Puerta de Santa Engracia, with an image of the saint in an overhead niche, opens out to the right, and on the left, at the entrance to Calle Víctor Tapia, house No. 17 bears a coat of arms with the Latin LAUS TIBI (Praise Be to Thee). Laguardia's crown architectural jewel is Spain's only Gothic polychrome portal, on the church of **Santa María de los Reyes.** Protected by a posterior Renaissance facade, the door centers on a lovely, lifelike effigy of La Virgen de los Reyes (Virgin of the Kings), sculpted in the 14th century and painted in the 17th by Juan Francisco de Ribera.

5

To the north of the ornate castle and hotel El Collado is the monument to the famous Laguardia composer of fables, Felix María Samaniego (1745–1801), heir to the tradition of Aesop and Lafontaine. Walk around the small, grassy park to the Puerta de Páganos and look right—you can see Laguardia's oldest civil structure, the late-14th-century **Casa de la Primicia,** at Calle Páganos 78 (where fresh fruit was sold). If you walk left of the Casa de la Primicia, past several emblazoned houses to Calle Páganos 13, you can see the *bodega* (wine cellar) at the Posada Mayor de Migueloa, which is usually full and busy. Go through the corridor to the Posada's Calle Mayor entryway and walk up to the **Juanjo San Pedro** gallery at Calle Mayor 1, filled with antiques and artwork.

WHERE TO EAT AND STAY

$–$$ ✕ **Marixa.** Aficionados travel great distances to dine in the lovely restaurant, known for its excellent roasts, views, and value, in the Marixa hotel. The heavy, wooden interior is ancient and intimate, and the cuisine is Vasco-Riojano, combining the best of both worlds. Try the *menestra de riojana verduras,* a mixed-vegetable dish, or the *cordero asado a la parrilla,* lamb roasted over coals. There are 10 guest rooms ($$), which are modern and cheery though not particularly charming. ✉ *C. Sancho Abarca 8* ☎ *945/600165* 🌐 *www.hotelmarixa.com* *10 rooms* 💳 *AE, DC, MC, V* ⊗ *Closed mid-Dec.–mid-Jan.*

$$$$ ★ **Hotel Marqués de Riscal.** Frank Gehry's explosion of genius looks as if a colony from outer space had taken up residence (or crashed) in the middle of La Rioja's oldest vineyards (see below), 6 km (4 mi) outside of Laguardia. The jumble of pink and gold titanium sheets and stainless steel curves around rectilinear sandstone surfaces looks like a gift-

wrapped winery. With the winery's visitor center, the historic cellars, and the rolling hills offering activities from horseback riding to golf, visitors here have plenty to do. The spa provides new ways to use grape juice, while La Rioja's star chef Francis Paniego's gourmet restaurant ($$$$) delights the palate. **Pros:** dazzling environment, superb dining. **Cons:** expensive. ✉ *C. Torrea 1, Elciego* ☎ *945/180880* 🌐 *www.luxurycollection.com* *43 rooms, 11 suites* *In-room: Wi-Fi. In-hotel: restaurant, bar, spa, parking (no fee)* *AE, DC, MC, V.*

$$ Fodor's Choice ★ **Posada Mayor de Migueloa.** With a tavern at Calle Páganos 13 and a passageway leading through to Mayor de Migueloa, this 17th-century palace is a beauty. At the tavern ($$–$$$$), try *patatas a la riojana* (potatoes with chorizo) or *pochas con chorizo y costilla* (beans with sausage and lamb chop). Dinner options range from beef with foie gras to *venado con miel y pomelo* (venison with a honey-and-grapefruit sauce). Guest rooms have beautiful, original, rough-hewn ceiling beams. **Pros:** beautiful rooms; gorgeous stone entryway floors. **Cons:** in a pedestrianized area a long way from your car; rooms on the front side exposed to boisterous racket on weekends. ✉ *C. Mayor de Migueloa 20* ☎ *945/621175* 🌐 *www.mayordemigueloa.com* *8 rooms* *In-room: Wi-Fi. In-hotel: restaurant, bar, no elevator* *AE, DC, MC, V* *Closed mid-Dec.–mid-Jan.*

OFF THE BEATEN PATH

Herederos de Marqués de Riscal. The village of Elciego, 6 km (4 mi) southeast of Laguardia is the site of the historic Marqués de Riscal winery. Tours of the vineyards—one of the most legendary in La Rioja—as well as the cellars are conducted in various languages, including English. Advance reservations are required. ✉ *C. Torrea 1, Elciego* ☎ *945/180888* 🌐 *www.marquesderiscal.com* *€10* *Tours Mon.–Sat. 10, noon, and 4.*

LA RIOJA

A natural compendium of highlands, plains, and vineyards drained by the Ebro River, La Rioja (named for the River Oja) has historically produced Spain's finest wines. Most inhabitants live along the Ebro, in the cities of Logroño and Haro, though the mountains and upper river valleys hold many treasures. A mix of Atlantic and Mediterranean climates and cultures with Basque overtones and the meseta's arid influence as well, La Rioja is composed of the Rioja Alta (Upper Rioja), the moist and mountainous western end, and the Rioja Baja (Lower Rioja), the lower, dryer eastern extremity, more Mediterranean in climate. Logroño, the capital, lies between the two.

LOGROÑO

92 km (55 mi) southwest of Pamplona on NIII.

A busy industrial city of 130,000, Logroño's lovely old-quarter is bordered by the Ebro and the medieval walls, with **Breton de los Herreros** and **Muro Francisco de la Mata** the most characteristic streets.

Near Logroño, the Roman bridge and the *mirador* (lookout) at **Viguera** are the main sights in the lower Iregua Valley. Santiago (St. James), according to legend, helped the Christians defeat the Moors at the **Castillo de Clavijo,** another panoramic spot. The **Leza (Cañon) del Río Leza** is La Rioja's most dramatic canyon.

Logroño's dominant landmarks are the finest sacred structures in Rioja.

ESSENTIALS

Bus Station Logroño (✉ *Av. España 1* ☎ *941/235983*).

Visitor Information Logroño (✉ *Príncipe de Vergara* ☎ *941/291260*).

Train Station Logroño (✉ *Estación de Logroño, Plaza de Europa* ☎ *941/240202*).

EXPLORING

The 11th-century church of the **Imperial de Santa María del Palacio** (✉ *C. Ruavieja s/n*) is known as La Aguja (The Needle) for its pyramid-shaped, 45-yard Romanesque-Gothic tower. The church of **Santiago el Real** (*Royal St. James* ✉ *Plaza de Santiago s/n*), reconstructed in the 16th century, is noted for its equestrian statue of the saint (also known as Santiago Matamoros: St. James the Moorslayer), which presides over the main door. **San Bartolomé** (✉ *C. San Bartolomé s/n*) is a 13th- to 14th-century French Gothic church with an 11th-century Mudejar tower and an elaborate 14th-century Gothic doorway. The **Catedral de Santa María de La Redonda** (✉ *Plaza de los Portales s/n*) is noted for its twin baroque towers. Many of Logroño's monuments, such as the elegant **Puente de Piedra** *(Stone Bridge)*, were built as part of the Camino de Santiago pilgrimage route.

WHERE TO EAT AND STAY

For tapas, **Calle Laurel** or *el sendero de los elefantes* (the path of the elephants)—an allusion to *trompas* (trunks), Spanish for a snootful—offers bars with signature specialties: Bar Soriano for "*champis*" (champiñones), Blanco y Negro for *sepia* (cuttlefish), Casa Lucio for *migas de pastor* (sausage with garlic and bread crumbs), and La Travesía for potato omelet. If you're ordering wine, a *crianza* brings out the crystal. A young *cosechero* comes in small glasses, and *reserva* (selected grapes aged three years in oak and bottle) elicits snifters for proper swirling, smelling, and tasting.

$$–$$$$ SPANISH

✕ **Asador Emilio.** The Castilian rustic decor here includes a coffered wood ceiling, which merits a long look. Roast lamb cooked over wood coals is the specialty, but *alubias* (kidney beans) and *migas de pastor* (literally, "shepherd's bread crumbs," cooked with garlic and sausage) are hard to resist. The wine list, not surprisingly, is stocked with most of La Rioja's top finds from Roda I to Barón de Chirel Reserva. ✉ *República Argentina 8* ☎ *941/233141* ▭ *AE, DC, MC, V* ⊗ *Closed Sun. June–Apr. and Aug.*

$–$$$ SPANISH

✕ **El Cachetero.** Local fare based on roast lamb, goat, and vegetables is the rule at this family-run favorite in the middle of Logroño's main food and wine preserve. Coming in from Calle del Laurel is something like stepping through the looking glass: from street pandemonium to the peaceful hush of this culinary sanctuary. Though the dining room is classical and elegant, with antique furnishings and a serious look, the cuisine is homespun, based on seasonally changing raw materials. *Patatas a la riojana* (potatoes stewed with chorizo) is a classic dish here. ✉ *C. Laurel 3* ☎ *941/228463* ▭ *AE, DC, MC, V* ⊗ *Closed Sun. and last wk in Aug. No dinner Wed.*

$–$$$$ SPANISH ★ ✕ **La Rueda.** Cándida Calleja's upstairs perch over the intersection of the Calle and Travesía del Laurel tapas-grazing scene is close enough to the action below but removed enough to be pleasant. Memorable dishes include *jamón ibérico de bellota* (acorn-fed ham) or *revuelto de gambas y puntas de espárragos trigueros* (eggs scrambled with shrimp and wild asparagus). If trout is on the menu, don't hesitate: Cándida knows how to cook them. The downstairs bar serves excellent sepia (cuttlefish) with chilling hits of Rojanda, La Rueda's own fresh young white wine. ✉ *Travesía del Laurel 1* ☎ *941/227986* ▭ *AE, DC, MC, V* ⊗ *Closed Sun. and Aug.*

$$ **Herencia Rioja.** This modern hotel near the old quarter has contemporary and comfortable rooms, first-rate facilities, a well-trained staff, a fine restaurant ($$–$$$$) with a good wine list, a grill for cooking over coals, and a healthy, businesslike buzz about it. The halls and corridors are somewhat somber and over-lavishly draped with fabrics, but the efficiency of the place makes up for its aesthetic shortcomings. **Pros:** top comfort, two steps from Calle del Laurel's tapas bonanza. **Cons:** undistinguished modern building, lugrubrious interiors. ✉ *Marqués de Murrieta 14* ☎ *941/210222* 🌐 *www.nh-hotels.com* *81 rooms, 2 suites* *In-room: refrigerator, Wi-Fi. In-hotel: restaurant, bar, gym* ▭ *AE, DC, MC, V.*

$–$$$$ **Marqués de Vallejo.** Close to—but not overwhelmed by—the food- and wine-tasting frenzy of nearby Calle del Laurel, this small, family-run hotel within view of the cathedral is nearly dead center amid the most important historic sites and best architecture that Logroño has to offer. Rooms are on the small side but cozy. Stash your car in the garage beneath the nearby Plaza del Espolón. **Pros:** central location, traditional Logroño architecture with renovated interior. **Cons:** street-side rooms can be noisy in summer when windows are open. ✉ *Marqués de Vallejo 8* ☎ *941/248333* 🌐 *www.hotelmarquesdevallejo.com* *30 rooms* *In-room: refrigerator, Wi-Fi. In-hotel: restaurant, bar* ▭ *AE, DC, MC, V.*

LA RIOJA ALTA

The Upper Rioja, the most prosperous part of La Rioja's wine country, extends from the Ebro River to the Sierra de la Demanda. La Rioja Alta has the most fertile soil, the best vineyards and agriculture, the most impressive castles and monasteries, a ski resort at Ezcaray, and the historical economic advantage of being on the Camino de Santiago.

From Logroño, drive 12 km (7 mi) west on N120 to **Navarrete** to see its noble houses and 16th-century Santa María de la Asunción church.

Nájera, 15 km (9 mi) west of Navarrete, was the court of the kings of Navarra and capital of Navarra and La Rioja until 1076, when La Rioja became part of Castile and the residence of the Castilian royal family. The monastery of **Santa María la Real** (✉ *Calle de Monasterio* *s/n, Nájera* ☎*941/361083* 🌐*www.arteguias.com/monasterio/santamariarealnajera.htm* 🎫*€3* ⏲*Tues.–Sun. 10:30–1, 4–6*), "pantheon of kings," is distinguished by its 16th-century Claustro de los Caballeros (Cavaliers' Cloister), a flamboyant Gothic structure with 24 lacy plateresque Renaissance arches overlooking a grassy patio. The sculpted 12th-century tomb of Doña Blanca de Navarra is the monastery's best-known sarcophagus, while the 67 Gothic choir stalls dating from 1495 are among Spain's best.

Santo Domingo de la Calzada, 20 km (12 mi) west of Nájera on the N120, has always been a key stop on the Camino. Santo Domingo was an 11th-century saint who built roads and bridges for pilgrims and founded the hospital that is now the town's parador. The cathedral is a Romanesque-Gothic pile containing the saint's tomb, choir murals, and a walnut altarpiece carved by Damià Forment in 1541. The live hen and rooster in a plateresque stone chicken coop commemorate a legendary local miracle in which a pair of roasted fowl came back to life to protest the innocence of a pilgrim hanged for theft. Be sure to stroll through the town's beautifully preserved medieval quarter.

5

Enter the **Sierra de la Demanda** by heading south 14 km (8½ mi) on LO810. Your first stop is the town of **Ezcaray,** with its aristocratic houses emblazoned with family crests, of which the **Palacio del Conde de Torremúzquiz** (Palace of the Count of Torremúzquiz) is the most distinguished. Good excursions from here are the Valdezcaray winter-sports center; the source of the River Oja at Llano de la Casa; La Rioja's highest point, the 7,494-foot Pico de San Lorenzo; and the Romanesque church of Tres Fuentes, at Valgañón. The town of **San Millán de la Cogolla** is southeast of Santo Domingo de la Calzada. Take LO809 southeast through Berceo to the Monasterio de Yuso, where a 10th-century manuscript on St. Augustine's *Glosas Emilianenses* has notes in what is considered the earliest example of the Spanish language, the vernacular Latin dialect known as Roman Paladino. The nearby Visigothic Monasterio de Suso is where Gonzalo de Berceo, recognized as the first Castilian poet, wrote and recited his 13th-century verse in the Castilian tongue, now the language of more than 300 million people.

WHERE TO STAY

$$–$$$ ★ **Hospedería del Monasterio de San Millán.** Declared a World Heritage Site by UNESCO, this magnificent inn occupies a wing of the historic Monasterio de Yuso, famous as the birthplace of the Spanish language Heavy medieval stone walls conceal a surprisingly contemporary and minimalist interior, with an elongated baronial dining room that serves regional dishes from La Rioja. Guest rooms are elegant and may seem austere at first glance, but the converted and restored monastery has all the modern comforts of any first-class hotel. **Pros:** historic site, graceful building. **Cons:** somewhat isolated, monastic decor. ✉*Monasterio de Yuso, San Millán de la Cogolla* ☎*941/373277* 🌐*www.sanmillan.com* *22 rooms, 3 suites* *In-room: refrigerator, Wi-Fi. In-hotel: restaurant, bar* 💳*AE, DC, MC, V.*

$–$$ Fodor'sChoice ★ **Echaurren.** This rambling roadhouse in Ezcaray, 61 km (37 mi) southwest of Logroño, is 7 km (4 mi) below Valdezcaray, La Rioja's best ski resort. Echaurren is famous for fine traditional cuisine ($$–$$$) engineered by Marisa Sanchez and the postmodern creations by her son, Francis Paniego. Marisa's *patatas a la riojana* (potatoes stewed with peppers and chorizo) are a classic, while Francis, a youthful master chef, experiments with wood coals and aromas and also directs the superb Hotel Marqués de Riscal restaurant in Elciego. Rooms are comfortable, and the staff is warm and engaging. **Pros:** traditional building, comfortable beds, family service. **Cons:** the bells from the church across the way. ✉*Padre José García 17, Ezcaray* ☎*941/354047* 🌐*www.echaurren.com* *25 rooms* *In-room: refrigerator, Wi-Fi. In-hotel: restaurant, bar, parking (fee)* 💳*AE, DC, MC, V.*

> **HARO'S WINE WAR**
>
> June 29, the Fiesta de San Pedro, marks the Batalla del Vino in Haro. Begun around 1710 as a jocular commemoration of a territorial dispute between the towns of Haro and Miranda de Ebro in which hundreds of local revelers and visitors throw some 60,000 liters of not very good wine at each other using everything from buckets to vats, hoses, and water pistols. Traditional fiesta attire is white, which quickly becomes a pink-purple. Traditional dances are performed, and later, wild cows are caped in the bullring.

HARO

20 km (12 mi) northwest of Nájera, 49 km (29 mi) west of Logroño.

ESSENTIALS

Visitor Information Haro (✉*Pl. Monseñor Florentino Rodrríguez* ☎*941/303366*).

EXPLORING

Haro is the wine capital of La Rioja. Its **Casco Viejo** (Old Quarter) and best taverns are concentrated along the loop known as La Herradura (the Horseshoe), with the Santo Tomás church at the apex of its curve and its feet leading down Calle San Martín and Calle Santo Tomás to the upper left-hand (northeast) corner of Plaza de la Paz. Up the left side of the horseshoe, Bar La Esquina is the first of many fine tapas bars. Bar Los Caños, behind a stone archway at San Martín 5, is built into the vaults and arches of the former church of San Martín. The bar serves excellent local crianzas and reservas and a memorable *pincho* of quail egg, anchovy, jalapeño-like pepper, and olive.

Haro's century-old **bodegas** *(wineries)* have been headquartered in the *barrio de la estación* (train-station district) ever since the railroad opened in 1863. Guided tours and tastings, some in English, can be arranged at the facilities themselves or through the tourist office.

The architectural highlight of Haro is the church of **Santo Tomás,** a single-naved Renaissance and late Gothic church completed in 1564, with an intricately sculpted plateresque portal on the south side and a gilded baroque organ facade towering over the choir loft.

WHERE TO EAT AND STAY

$$–$$$$ SPANISH ✕**Terete.** A perennial local favorite, this rustic spot has been roasting lamb in wood ovens since 1877 and serves a hearty *menestra de verduras* (vegetables stewed with bits of ham) that is justly revered as a regional institution. With rough hand-hewn benches and heavy wooden

tables distributed around dark, oak-paneled dining rooms, the medieval stagecoach-inn environment matches the traditional roasts. The wine cellar is a virtual museum stocked with some of the Rioja's best *reservas* and *crianzas*. ✉*C. Lucrecia Arana 17* ☎*941/310023* ▭*AE, DC, MC, V* ⏲*Closed Mon., 1st 2 wks in July, and last 2 wks in Oct.*

$$ **Los Agustinos.** Haro's best hotel is built into a 14th-century monastery with a cloister (now a beautiful covered patio) that's considered one of the best in La Rioja. Arches, a great hall, and Renaissance tapestries complete the medieval look. The restaurant serves creditable local fare in two comfortable dining rooms, and the glassed-in wine cellar holds Haro's greatest treasures. **Pros:** gorgeous public rooms, cozy hotel bar, close to town center but in a quiet corner. **Cons:** room decor plain, staff not very helpful. ✉*San Agustín 2* ☎*941/311308* ⊕*www.hotel-losagustinos.com* *60 rooms, 2 suites* *In-room: refrigerator, Wi-Fi. In-hotel: restaurant, bar, parking (fee)* ▭*AE, DC, MC, V.*

5

THE HIGHLANDS

The rivers forming the seven main valleys of the Ebro basin originate in the Sierra de la Demanda, Sierra de Cameros, and Sierra de Alcarama. **Ezcaray** is La Rioja's skiing capital in the **valley of the Rio Oja,** just below Valdezcaray in the Sierra de la Demanda. The upper **Najerilla Valley** is La Rioja's mountain sanctuary, an excellent hunting and fishing preserve. The Najerilla River, a rich chalk stream, is one of Spain's best trout rivers. Look for the Puente de Hiedra (Ivy Bridge), its heavy curtain of ivy falling to the surface of the Najerilla above Anguiano. The **Monasterio de Valvanera,** off C113 near Anguiano, is the sanctuary of La Rioja's patron saint, the Virgen de Valvanera, a 12th-century Romanesque wood carving of the Virgin and child. **Anguiano** is renowned for its Danza de los Zancos (Dance of the Stilts), held July 22, when dancers on wooden stilts plummet down through the steep streets of the town into the arms of the crowd at the bottom. At the valley's highest point are the Mansilla reservoir and the Romanesque Ermita de San Cristóbal (Hermitage of St. Christopher).

The upper **Iregua Valley,** off N111, has the prehistoric Gruta de la Paz caves at Ortigosa. The artisans of **Villoslada del Cameros** make the region's famous patchwork quilts, called *almazuelas*. Climb to **Pico Cebollera** for a superb view of the valley. Work back toward the Ebro along the River Leza, through Laguna de Cameros and San Román de Cameros (known for its basket weavers), to complete a tour of the Sierra del Cameros. The upper **Cidacos Valley** leads to the **Parque Jurásico** (Jurassic Park) at Enciso, famous for its dinosaur tracks. The main village in the upper **Alhama Valley** is **Cervera del Rio Alhama,** a center for handmade *alpargatas* (rope-sole shoes).

WHERE TO EAT AND STAY

$–$$$ SPANISH ✕**La Herradura.** High over the ancient bridge of Anguiano, this is an excellent place to try the local specialty, *caparrones colorados de Anguiano con sus sacramentos* (small, red kidney beans stewed with sausage and fatback) made with the much-prized, extra-tasty hometown bean. Unpretentious and family run, La Herradura ("horseshoe") is a local favorite usually filled with Riojanos and trout fishermen taking a break from the river. The house wine is an acceptable and inexpensive Uruñuela *cosechero* (young wine of the year) from the Najerilla Valley. ✉*Ctra. de Lerma, Km 14, Anguiano* ☎*941/377151* ▭*MC, V.*

¢ **Hospedería Abadía de Valvanera.** A 16th-century monastery atop a 9th-century hermitage, this is an ideal base for hiking, but note that the 12th-century carving of the Virgin of Valvanera receives an overnight harvest pilgrimage from Logroño every October 15, and it's very hard to book then. Patroness of the grape harvest and barren couples, the Virgin is portrayed with a pomegranate (symbolizing fertility) and vines. Her infant is said to have turned away in embarrassment when a hopeful couple performed the procreative act on the altar. Rooms are simple and the restaurant ($–$$) offers local dishes at unbeatable prices. **Pros:** cool air during summer heat, simplicity and silence. **Cons:** spartan accommodations, limited dining choices. ✉*Monasterio de Valvanera s/n, 5 km (3 mi) west of LR113* ☎*941/377044* 🌐*www.abadiavalvanera.com* *28 rooms* *In-room: no a/c, no TV. In-hotel: restaurant, no elevator* ▭*AE, DC, MC, V.*

¢ **Venta de Goyo.** A favorite with anglers and hunters in season, this cheery spot across from the mouth of the Urbión River (where it meets the Najerilla) has wood-trim bedrooms with red-check bedspreads and an excellent restaurant ($$–$$$$) specializing in venison, wild boar, partridge, woodcock, and game of all kinds. Juan Carlos Jiménez and his nephew, chef Juan Carlos Esteban, serve some of the best *caparrones* (pygmy red beans from Anguiano) in La Rioja. **Pros:** excellent game and mountain cooking; charming rustic bar; unforgettable homemade jams. **Cons:** next to road; hot in summer. ✉*Ctra. LR113, Km 24.6, Viniegra de Abajo* ☎*941/378007* *941/378048* *22 rooms* *In-hotel: restaurant, bar, no elevator* ▭*AE, DC, MC, V.*

The Pyrenees

Rock outcroppings in Huesca, Aragón province

WORD OF MOUTH

"Walking through Ordesa National Park was one of our most beautiful days in the Pyrenees. After snoozing through an afternoon rainstorm under cover, we emerged in twilight to find lovely red-brown *isards* (mountain goats), frolicking along the upper trail of the southern rim of the canyon. It was magic!"

—Lucie

WELCOME TO THE PYRENEES

La Cerdanya's breathtaking landscape.

TOP REASONS TO GO

★ **Eagle-eye Views:** Hike up to Prat d'Aguiló (Eagle's Meadow) in the clouds over the Cerdanya for an unforgettable panorama over the sunniest and widest valley in the Pyrenees.

★ **Highland History:** Visit San Juan de Plan and the Gistaín Valley for a look at early-20th-century village life in one of the most remote central Pyrenean enclaves.

★ **Pyrenean Gems:** Stop at Taüll and see the Noguera de Tor Valley's exquisite Romanesque churches and their mural paintings.

★ **Spain's Grand Canyon:** Walk through the Parque Nacional de Ordesa y Monte Perdido for stunning scenery, complete with marmots and mountain goats.

★ **Basque Navarra:** Explore the lush and verdant Basque highlands in the Baztán Valley, and then follow the Bidasoa River down to colorful Hondarribia and the sparkling Bay of Biscay.

1 The Eastern Catalan Pyrenees. Start from Cap de Creus in the Empordà to get the full experience of the Pyrenean cordillera's rise from the sea; then move west through Camprodón, Setcases, the Ter Valley, and Ripoll.

2 La Cerdanya. The widest and sunniest valley in the Pyrenees, La Cerdanya is an east–west expanse that straddles the French border between two forks of the Pyrenean cordillera. The Segre River flows down the center of the valley, while snowcapped peaks rise to the north and south.

3 Western Catalan Pyrenees. West of La Seu d'Urgell and drained by the Noguera Pallaresa and Pallaresa Ribagorçana rivers, the western Catalan Pyrenees include the Vall de Aran, the Parc Nacional d'Aigüestortes i Estany de Sant Maurici, and the Noguera de Tor valley with its Romanesque treasures.

4 Aragón and the Central Pyrenees. Benasque is the jumping off point for Aneto, the highest peak in the Pyrenees. San Juan de Plan, Gistaín, and Bielsa are typical mountain enclaves. Parque Nacional de Ordesa y Monte Perdido is an unforgettable daylong or two-day trek. Jaca and the Hecho, Ansó, and Roncal valleys are Upper Aragón at its purest, while Huesca and Zaragoza are good lowland alternatives in case bad weather blows you out of the mountains.

GETTING ORIENTED

The Pyrenean valleys, isolated from each other and the world below for many centuries, retain a rugged mountain character, mixing distinct traditions with a common highland spirit of magic and mystery. Spain's natural border with France has also been seen as a nexus where medieval people took refuge and exchanged culture and learning. A haven from the 8th-century Moorish invasion, the Pyrenees became an unlikely repository of Romanesque art and architecture, as well as a natural preserve of wildlife and terrain.

Ordesa National Park

Basilica of Nuestra Señora del Pilar in Zaragoza.

5 The Western and Basque Pyrenees. Beginning in the Roncal Valley, the language you hear may be Euskera, the non–Indo-European language of the Basques. The highlands of Navarra, from Roncesvalles and Burguete down through the Baztán Valley to Hondarribia are a magical realm of rolling hillsides and emerald pastures.

6

THE PYRENEES PLANNER

When to Go

If you're a hiker, stick to the summer (June to September, especially July) when the weather is better and there's less chance of a serious snowfall—not to mention blizzards or lightning storms at high altitudes.

October, with comfortable daytime temperatures and fresh evening chills, is ideal for enjoying the still-green Pyrenean meadows and valleys and hillside hunts for wild mushrooms.

November brings colorful leaves, the last mushrooms, and the first frosts.

For skiing, come between December and April. The green springtime thaw, from mid-March to mid-April, is spectacular for skiing on the snowcaps and trout fishing or golfing on the verdant valley floors.

August is the only crowded month, when all of Europe is on summer vacation and the cooler highland air is at its best.

Four Ways to Say Hello in the Pyrenees

In Spanish: "Buenos días"

In Catalan: "Bon dia"

In Euskera (Basque): "Egun on"

In Fabla Aragonesa: "Buen Diya"

Take a Tour

There are wonderful outdoor activities to be experienced in the Pyrenees, and plenty of guides and outfitters to help. The Puigcerdà travel agency Touring Cerdanya can arrange guides, horses, or jeeps for treks to upper lakes, peaks, and meadows.

Well populated with trout, the Pyrenees' cold-water streams provide excellent angling from mid-March to the end of August. Notable places to cast a line are the Segre, Aragón, Gállego, Noguera Pallaresa, Arga, Esera, and Esca rivers. Pyrenean ponds and lakes also tend to be rich in trout. Ramón Cosiallf and Danica can take you fly-fishing anywhere in the world by horse or helicopter, but the Pyrenees is their home turf. For about €150 a day (depending on equipment), you'll be whisked to high Pyrenean lakes and ponds, streams, and rivers and armed with equipment and expertise.

Contact Danica (☎ *659/735376 or 974/553493* 🌐 *www.danicaguias.com*). **Touring Cerdanya** (✉ *Escuelas Pías 19, Puigcerdà* ☎ *972/880602 or 972/881450*).

Hiking the Pyrenees

There are many reasons to visit the Pyrenees: scenery, hiking, skiing, trout streams, art and architecture, or the opportunity to see what remains of a way of life that has endured largely unchanged. Hiking affords an ideal view of the scenery and remains one of the best ways to drink in the stunning landscape. No matter how spectacular they seem from paved roads, the mountainscapes are exponentially more stunning from upper hiking trails and high *pistas forestales* (forest tracks) that are best traveled in four-wheel drive vehicles. Day hikes or overnight two-day treks to mountain *refugios (refugis in Catalan)*, especially in the Ordesa or Aigüestortes national parks, reveal the full natural splendors of the Pyrenees. Local tourist offices can provide maps and recommend day hikes, while specialized bookshops such as Barcelona's Quera (Carrer Petritxol 2) have complete Pyrenean maps as well as books with detailed hiking instructions for the entire mountain range from the Atlantic to the Mediterranean. Hiking the Alberes range between Le Perthus and Cap de Creus on the well-marked GR (Gran Recorrido) 11 is a favorite two-day spring or autumn hike, with an overnight stay at the Refugi de la Tanyareda, just below Puig Neulós, the highest point in the Alberes. Hiking to the highest peak in the Pyrenees, the 11,168-foot Aneto is a one-day round-trip trek starting from the Refugio de la Renclusa above Benasque. Ordesa is another prized walk, with bed and dinner in the base camp town of Torla or a night up at the Refugio de Goriz at the head of the valley.

Hiking in the Pyrenees should always be undertaken carefully: proper footwear, headwear, water supply, and weather-forecast awareness are essential. Even in the middle of summer, a sudden snowstorm can turn a day hike to tragedy. *See the "Hiking in the Pyrenees" box in this chapter for more details.*

WHAT IT COSTS (IN EUROS)

	¢	$	$$	$$$	$$$$
Restaurants	under €8	€8–€12	€13–€17	€18–€22	over €22
Hotels	under €60	€60–€90	€91–€125	€126–€180	over €180

Prices are per person for a main course at dinner, and for two people in a standard double room in high season, excluding tax.

Planning Your Time

You could walk from Atlantic to Mediterranean in 43 days, but not many have that kind of vacation time. With 10 to 14 days you can drive from sea to sea: from a wade in the Mediterranean at Cap de Creus to Hondarribia and the Cabo Higuer lighthouse on the Bay of Biscay. A week is best for a single area—La Cerdanya and the Eastern Catalan Pyrenees; the Western Catalan Pyrenees and Vall d'Aran; Jaca and the central Pyrenees; or the Basque Pyrenees north of Pamplona.

A day's drive up through Figueres and Olot will bring you to **Camprodón. Sant Joan de les Abadesses** and **Ripoll** are important stops, especially for the famous Sant Maria de Ripoll portal. La Cerdanya's **Puigcerdà, Llívia,** and **Bellver de Cerdanya** are must-visits, too. To the west is **La Seu d'Urgell** on the way to **Parc Nacional d'Aigüestortes i Estany de Sant Maurici,** the **Vall d'Aran,** and the winter-sports center Baqueira-Beret. Stop at **Taüll** and the Noguera de Tor Valley's Romanesque churches. Farther west, **Benasque** is the jumping off point for Aneto, the highest peak in the Pyrenees. **San Juan de Plan and the Gistaín Valley** and **Bielsa** lead you to the remote valleys of Upper Aragón; **Parque Nacional de Ordesa y Monte Perdido** is Spain's grandest canyon, and **Jaca** the central Pyrenees' most important town.

GETTING HERE AND AROUND

By Air

Barcelona's international airport, El Prat de Llobregat (⇨ chapter 7), is the largest gateway to the Catalan Pyrenees. Farther west, the airports at Zaragoza, Pamplona, and Hondarribia (Fuenterrabía) serve the Pyrenees of Aragón, Navarra, and the Basque Country.

By Train

There are three small train stations deep in the Pyrenees: Puigcerdà, in the Cerdanya Valley; La Pobla de Segur, in the Noguera Pallaresa Valley; and Canfranc, north of Jaca, below the Candanchú and Astún ski resorts. The larger gateways are Huesca and Lleida. From Madrid, connect through Barcelona for the eastern Pyrenees; Zaragoza and Huesca for the central Pyrenees; and Pamplona or San Sebastián for the western Pyrenees.

By Bus

Bus travel in the Pyrenees is the only way to cross from east to west (or vice versa), other than hiking or driving, and requires some zigzagging up and down. In most cases, four buses daily connect the main pre-Pyrenean cities (Barcelona, Zaragoza, Huesca, and Pamplona) and the main highland distributors (Puigcerdà, La Seu d'Urgell, Vielha, Benasque, and Jaca). The time lost waiting for buses makes this option a last resort.

Bus Lines **Ágreda La Oscense** (✉ *Paseo María Agustín 7, Zaragoza* ☎ *976/229343* ✉ *Estación Intermodal, Ronda de la Estación s/n, Huesca* ☎ *974/210700*). **Alsina Graells** (✉ *Calle Ali Bei 80, Barcelona* ☎ *93/265–6508* ✉ *Av. Garriga i Masó s/n, La Seu d'Urgell* ☎ *972/350020* ✉ *Calle Saracibar s/n, Lleida* ☎ *973/271470*). **La Baztanesa** (✉ *Calle Conde Oliveta 6, Pamplona* ☎ *948/226712*). **La Roncalesa** (✉ *Estación de Autobuses, Calle Conde Oliveta 6, Pamplona* ☎ *948/222079*).

By Car

The most practical way to tour the Pyrenees is by car. The Eje Pirenaico (Pyrenean Axis), or N260, is a carefully engineered, safe, cross-Pyrenean route that connects Cap de Creus, the Iberian Peninsula's easternmost point on the Mediterranean Costa Brava east of Girona and Cadaqués, with Cabo de Higuer, the lighthouse west of Hondarribia at the edge of the Atlantic Bay of Biscay.

The Collada de Toses (Tosses Pass) to Puigcerdà is the most difficult route into the Cerdanya Valley, but it's cost-free, has spectacular scenery, and you get to include Camprodón, Olot, and Ripoll in your itinerary. Safer and faster, but more expensive (tolls total more than €20 from Barcelona to Bellver de Cerdanya), is the E9 through the Tuñel del Cadí. Once you're there, most of the Cerdanya Valley's two-lane roads are wide and well paved. As you go west, roads can be more difficult to navigate, winding dramatically through mountain passes.

By George Semler

The snowcapped Pyrenees that separate the Iberian Peninsula from the rest of the European continent have always been a special realm, a source of legend and superstition. To explore the Pyrenees fully—appreciating the flora and fauna, the local gastronomy, the remote glacial lakes and streams, the Romanesque art in a thousand hermitages—could take a lifetime.

Each Pyrenean mountain system is drained by one or more rivers, forming some three dozen valleys between the Mediterranean and the Atlantic; these valleys were all but completely isolated until around the 10th century. Local languages still abound, with Castilian Spanish and Euskera (Basque) in upper Navarra; Grausín, Belsetán, Chistavino, Ansotano, Cheso, and Patués (Benasqués) in Aragón; Aranés, a dialect of Gascon French, in the Vall d'Aran; and Catalan at the eastern end of the chain from Ribagorça to the Mediterranean.

6

Throughout the centuries, the Pyrenees have remained a strategic barrier and stronghold to be reckoned with. The Romans never completely subdued Los Vascones (as Greek historian Strabo [63–21 BC] called the Basques) in the western Pyrenean highlands. Charlemagne lost Roland and his rear guard at Roncesvalles in 778, and his Frankish heirs lost all of Catalonia in 988. Napoléon never completed his conquest of the peninsula after 1802, largely because of communications and supply problems posed by the Pyrenees, and Hitler, whether for geographical or political reasons, decided not to use post–civil war Spain to launch his African campaign in 1941. A D-Day option to make a landing on the beaches of northern Spain was scrapped because the Pyrenees looked too easily defendable (you can still see the south-facing German bunkers on the southern flanks of the western Pyrenean foothills). Meanwhile, the mountainous barrier provided a path to freedom for downed pilots, Jewish refugees, and POWs fleeing the Nazis, just as it later meant freedom for political refugees running north from the Franco regime.

EXPLORING THE PYRENEES

As the crow flies, the Pyrenees stretch 435 km (270 mi) along Spain's border with France, though the sinuous borderline exceeds 600 km (370 mi). A drive across the N260 trans-Pyrenean axis connecting the destinations in this chapter would exceed 800 km (495 mi) in all. The three groupings across the cordillera are the Catalan Pyrenees from the Mediterranean to the Noguera Ribagorçana River south of Vielha, the central Pyrenees of Aragón extending west to the Roncal Valley, and the Basque Pyrenees falling gradually westward through the Basque Country to the Bay of Biscay and the Atlantic Ocean. The highest peaks are in Aragón—Aneto, in the Maladeta massif; Posets; and Monte Perdido, all of which are about 11,000 feet above sea level. Pica d'Estats

(10,372 feet) is Catalonia's highest peak, and Pic d'Orhi (6,656 feet) is the highest in the Basque Pyrenees.

ABOUT THE RESTAURANTS

Pyrenean cuisine is characterized by thick soups, stews, roasts, and local ingredients prepared differently in every valley, village, and kitchen from the Mediterranean to the Atlantic. The three main culinary schools correspond to the Pyrenees' three main regional and cultural identities—Catalan, Aragonese, and Basque—but within these are further subdivisions such as La Cerdanya, Vall d'Aran, Benasque, Roncal, and Baztán. Game is common throughout. Trout, wild goat, deer, boar, partridge, rabbit, duck, and quail are roasted over coals or cooked in aromatic stews called *civets* in Catalonia and *estofadas* in Aragón and Navarra. Fish and meat are often seared on slabs of slate (*a la llosa* in Catalan, *a la piedra* in Castilian Spanish).

ABOUT THE HOTELS

Most hotels in the Pyrenees are informal and outdoorsy, with a large fireplace in one of the public rooms. They are usually built of wood and slate under a steep roof, blending with the surrounding mountains. Options include friendly family-owned establishments, rooms in Basque *caseríos* (farmhouses), and town houses. (Larger chain-type hotels are almost unheard of here.)

EASTERN CATALAN PYRENEES

Catalonia's easternmost Pyrenean valley, the Vall de Camprodón, is still hard enough to reach that, despite pockets of Barcelona summer colonies, it has retained much of its agricultural culture and mountain wildness. It has several exquisite towns and churches and, above all, mountains, such as the Sierra de Catllar. Vallter 2000 and Núria are ski resorts at the eastern and western ends of the Pyrenees heights on the north side of the valley, but the middle reaches and main body of the valley have remained pasture for sheep, cattle, and horses, and de facto natural parks.

GETTING HERE AND AROUND

To reach the Vall de Camprodón from Barcelona, you can take the N152 through Vic and Ripoll. From the Costa Brava go by way of either Figueres or Girona, Besalú, and the Capsacosta tunnel. From France, drive southwest through the Col (Pass) d'Ares, which enters the head of the valley at an altitude of 5,280 feet from Prats de Molló.

CAMPRODÓN

127 km (80 mi) northwest of Barcelona.

Camprodón, the capital of its *comarca* (county), lies at the junction of the Ter and Ritort rivers—both excellent trout streams. The rivers flow by, through, and under much of the town, giving it a highland waterfront character (as well as a long history of flooding). The town owes much of its opulence to the summer folks from Barcelona who

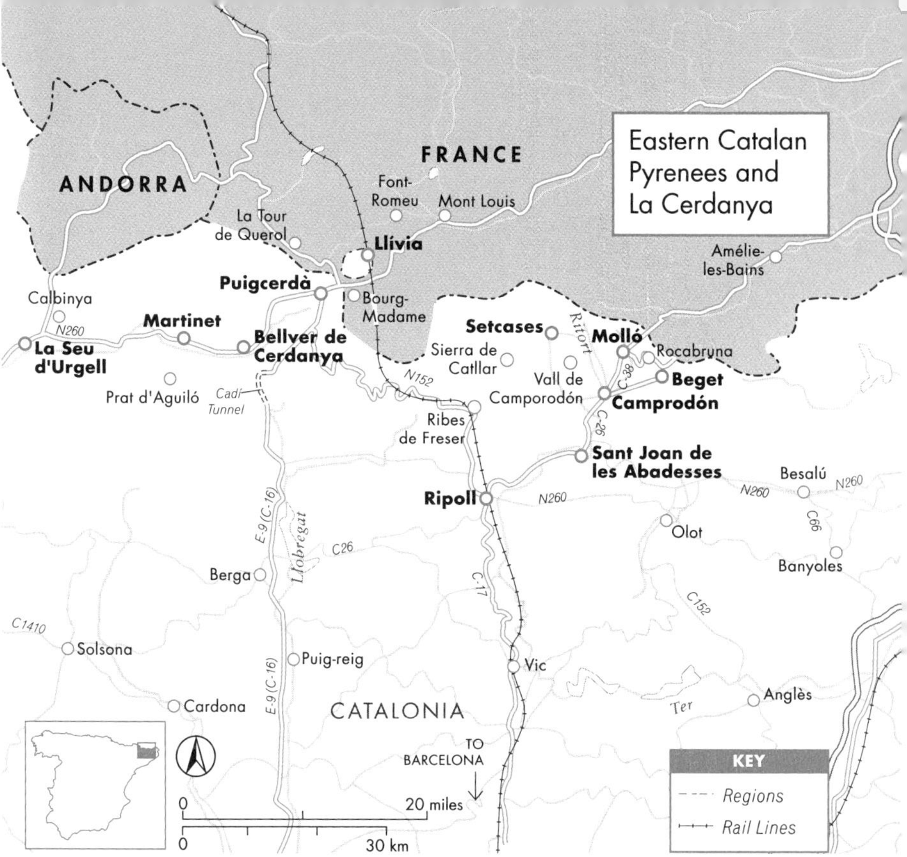

built mansions along the leafy promenade, **Passeig Maristany,** at its northern edge.

ESSENTIALS

Visitor Information Camprodón (✉ *Pl. de Espanya 1* ☎ *972/7400010*).

EXPLORING

Museu Isaac Albéniz. Camprodón's most famous son is composer Isaac Albéniz (1860–1909), whose celebrated classical guitar piece *Asturias* is one of Spain's best-known works. The house and its contents introduce visitors to the life and times of Albéniz, who spent more than 20 years in exile in France, where he became friends with musical luminaries such as Casals, Debussy, and Fauré. ✉ *Carrer Sant Roc 22* ☎ *972/741166* *€3* ⏲ *Wed.–Mon. 11–2 and 4–7.*

Camprodón's best-known symbol is the elegant **12th-century stone bridge** that broadly spans the Ter River in the center of town.

WHERE TO STAY

¢–$ **Fonda Rigà.** A comfortable and renovated highland inn with spectacular views, this mountain perch just 10 km (6 mi) up the Ter Valley from Camprodón is an excellent base camp for hikers, wild-mushroom seekers, equestrian enthusiasts, and anyone interested in Pyrenean flora and fauna. Rooms are simple but tasteful, with bright wood walls and cheerful decor. The restaurant has panoramic views over the valley and specializes in meat cooked over coals. **Pros:** the views and the peace and quiet, newly renovated rooms and facilities. **Cons:** a serious 5 km (3 mi) drive above the valley floor, remote from Camprodón. ✉ *Ctra. de Tregurà de Dalt, Km 4.8* ☎ *972/136000* 🌐 *www.fondariga.com* *16 rooms* *In-room: Wi-Fi, no a/c. In-hotel: bar, no elevator, public Wi-Fi, parking (fee)* 💳 *AE, DC, MC, V.*

$$–$$$ **L'Hotel de Camprodón.** An elegant Moderniste building with rooms over the river on one side and over the bustling Plaça Dr. Robert on the other, this a perfect destination for getting a sense of this stylish little mountain hub. Rooms are furnished with simplicity and taste, and those with terraces look down at the graceful span of Camprodón's emblematic Pont Nou, with mallards splashing alongside brightly speckled (and legally protected) native Pyrenean trout. The Sunday market in the square is an important weekly event with natural food products and crafts. **Pros:** central location, cozy and intimate public rooms. **Cons:** rooms on the square noisy in summer, no Wi-Fi in rooms. ✉ *Pl. Dr. Robert 3* ☎ *972/740013* 🌐 *www.hotelcamprodon.com* *38 rooms* *In-room: no a/c. In-hotel: bar, restaurant, pool, public Wi-Fi, pool, parking (free)* 💳 *AE, DC, MC, V.*

SHOPPING

Cal Xec (✉ *C. Isaac Albéniz 1* ☎ *972/740084*), the legendary sausage and cheese store at the end of the Camprodón Bridge, also sells the much-prized, vanilla-flavored Birbas cookies.

EN ROUTE

From Camprodón, take C38 north toward Molló and the French border at Col d'Ares. After 3 km (1.8 mi) turn east toward **Rocabruna,** a village of crisp, clean Pyrenean stone houses at the source of the clear Beget River. The village is famous as a gastronomical pilgrimage to the excellent Can Po restaurant (⇨ Beget, *below*) on the way to Beget.

BEGET

★ *17 km (11 mi) east of Camprodón.*

The village of Beget, considered Catalonia's *més bufó* (cutest), was completely cut off from motorized vehicles until the mid-1960s, when a *pista forestal* (a jeep track) was laid down; in 1980 Beget was finally fully connected to the rest of the world by an asphalt roadway. Beget's 30 houses are eccentric stone structures with heavy wooden doors and a golden color peculiar to the Camprodón Valley. Graceful stone bridges span the stream in which protected trout feast.

EXPLORING

The 11th-century Romanesque church of **Sant Cristófol** has a diminutive bell tower and a rare 6-foot Majestat—a polychrome wood carving of Christ in a head-to-foot tunic, dating from the 12th or 13th century. The church is usually closed, but townsfolk can direct you to the keeper of the key.

WHERE TO EAT

$$–$$$$ SPANISH ★ **Can Po.** This ancient, ivy-covered, Pyrenean stone-and-mortar farmhouse perched over a deep gully in nearby Rocabruna is a carefully guarded semi-secret gastronomic gem famed for carefully prepared local dishes like *vedella amb crema de ceps* (veal in wild mushroom sauce) and the Catalan classic *anec amb peres* (duck stewed with pears). Try the *civet de porc senglar* (stewed wild boar) in season (winter) or any of the many varieties of wild mushrooms that find their way into the kitchen at this rural and rustic mountain retreat. *Ctra. de Beget s/n, Rocabruna 972/741045 AE, DC, MC, V Closed Mon.–Thurs. mid-Sept.–mid-July, except Dec. 26–Jan. 6 and Easter wk.*

MOLLÓ

25 km (16 mi) northwest of Beget, 24 km (15 mi) south of Prats de Molló.

Molló lies on route C151 on the Ritort stream toward Col d'Ares. The 12th-century Romanesque church of **Santa Cecilia** is a work of exceptional balance and simplicity, with a delicate Romanesque bell tower.

WHERE TO EAT AND STAY

$–$$$ **Calitxó.** Mountain views in all directions are spectacular at this small but comfortable family-run inn. The rooms are cozy and intimate rather than grand, but welcome refuges from the wide-open spaces outside. After breakfast in the lush garden, this is an ideal base for hiking excursions to Beget and elsewhere in the valley. The restaurant serves creative cuisine prepared with originality and fresh mountain ingredients. **Pros:** good mountain base camp, a cozy refuge after a day of hiking. **Cons:** slightly isolated from village life, rooms are a bit small. *Passatge el Serrat 972/740386 www.hotelcalitxo.com 23 rooms, 3 suites In-room: no a/c, Wi-Fi. In-hotel: bar, restaurant, public Wi-Fi AE, DC, MC, V.*

SETCASES

11 km (7 mi) northwest of Camprodón, 15 km (9 mi) west of Molló, 91 km (56 mi) northwest of Girona.

Although Setcases ("seven houses") is somewhat larger than its name would imply, this tiny village nestled at the head of the valley has a distinct mountain spirit.

ESSENTIALS

Visitor Information Setcases (*Carrer del Rec 5 972/136089*).

EXPLORING

On the road back down the valley from Setcases, **Llanars,** just short of Camprodón, has a 12th-century Romanesque church, **San Esteban,** of an exceptionally rich shade of ocher. The wood-and-iron portal depicts the martyrdom of St. Stephen.

6

WHERE TO EAT AND STAY

$–$$$ SPANISH ✕ **Can Tomàs.** On the immediate left coming into town, this funky place, covered with lovingly rendered portraits of wild mushrooms, indeed specializes in aromatic upland fungi used in original ways. The *arròs de bolets* (a paella with wild mushrooms) is the house standard, but the *encenalls de foie i tòfona* (shavings of duck liver with black truffles) and the *magret d'anec amb salsa de gerds* (duck breast with raspberry sauce) give an idea of the creative and international flavor of this little gem. ✉ *Carrer de Jesús 10, Setcases* ☎ *972/136004* ▭ *AE, DC, MC, V* ⊙ *Closed Wed.*

$$–$$$$ **La Coma.** *Coma* is Catalan Pyrenean dialect for "high and fertile meadow"—nothing to do with the English word for profound unconsciousness. The proprietors are kind country folk who know the mountains and can help plan excursions. Rooms are in the modern stone house and done in bright wood trim. The restaurant, with garden seating in summer, specializes in mountain *civets* (stews) and *escudellas* (a typical Catalan thick vegetable, bean, pasta, and pork stew). **Pros:** cozy sense of being as far into the Pyrenees as you can get; good mountain food in rustic dining room. **Cons:** rooms are austere, location at the entrance to town means it can get a bit too busy at times. ✉ *Setcases* ☎ *972/136074* ⊕ *www.hotellacoma.com* *20 rooms* *In-room: no a/c, Wi-Fi. In-hotel: restaurant, pool, gym, no elevator, public Wi-Fi* ▭ *AE, DC, MC, V.*

SPORTS AND THE OUTDOORS

The **Vallter 2000 ski area** (☎ *972/136057* ⊕ *www.vallter2000.com*) above Setcases—built into a glacial cirque reaching a height of 8,216 feet—has a dozen lifts and, on very clear days at the top, views east all the way to the Bay of Roses on the Costa Brava.

SANT JOAN DE LES ABADESSES

21 km (13 mi) southeast of Setcases, 14 km (9 mi) south of Camprodón.

The site of an important church, Sant Joan de les Abadesses is named for the 9th-century abbess Emma and her successors. Emma was the daughter of Guifré el Pilós (Wilfred the Hairy), the founder of the Catalan nation and medieval hero of the Christian Reconquest of Ripoll. The town's arcaded Plaça Major looks and feels plucked from medieval times, and the 12th-century bridge over the Ter is wide and graceful.

ESSENTIALS

Visitor Information Sant Joan de les Abadesses (✉ *Pl. de la Abadía 9* ☎ *972/720599*).

EXPLORING

The altarpiece in the 12th-century Romanesque church of **Sant Joan** (✉ *Plaça de la Abadía s/n* ☎ *972/720013*), a 13th-century polychrome wood sculpture of the Descent from the Cross, is one of the most expressive and human of that epoch.

RIPOLL

10 km (6 mi) southwest of Sant Joan de les Abadesses, 105 km (62 mi) north of Barcelona, 65 km (40 mi) southeast of Puigcerdà.

One of the first Christian strongholds of the Reconquest and a center of religious erudition during the Middle Ages, Ripoll is known as the *bressol* (cradle) of Catalonia's liberation from Moorish domination and the spiritual home of Guifré el Pilós, first count of Barcelona and legendary founder of the Catalan nation in the late 9th century. A dark, mysterious country town built around a **9th-century Benedictine monastery,** the town was a focal point of culture throughout French Catalonia and the Pyrenees, from the monastery's AD 879 founding until the mid-1800s, when Barcelona began to eclipse it.

ESSENTIALS

Visitor Information Ripoll (⊠ *Pl. de l'Abat Oliva* ☎ *972/702351*).

EXPLORING

The 12th-century doorway to the church of **Santa Maria** is one of Catalonia's great works of Romanesque art, crafted as a triumphal arch by stone masons and sculptors of the Roussillon school (that is, the school centered around French Catalonia and the Pyrenees). The sculptures portray the glory of God and of all his creatures from the creation onward. You can pick up a guide to the figures on the portal either in the church or at the information kiosk nearby. *Cloister and door €4, museum €6.50 Tues.–Sun. 10–2 and 3–7.*

Fourteen kilometers (9 mi) north of Ripoll, the **cogwheel train** (☎ *972/732020*) ride from Ribes de Freser up to Núria provides one of Catalonia's most unusual excursions. Known as the *cremallera* (zipper), the line was completed in 1931 to connect Ribes with the Santuari de la Mare de Déu de Núria (Mother of God of Núria) and with mountain hiking and skiing. The ride takes 45 minutes and costs €19.50 round-trip. **Núria,** at an altitude of 6,562 feet at the foot of Puigmal, is a ski area.

The legend of the **Santuari de la Mare de Déu de Núria,** a Marian religious retreat, is based on the story of Sant Gil of Nîmes, who did penance in the Núria Valley during the 7th century. The saint left behind a wooden statue of the Virgin Mary, a bell he used to summon shepherds to prayer, and a cooking pot; 300 years later, a pilgrim found these treasures in this sanctuary. The bell and the pot came to have special importance to barren women, who were believed to be blessed with as many children as they wished by placing their heads in the pot and ringing the bell. ⊠ *Núria* *Free* *Daily except during Mass.*

WHERE TO STAY

¢–$ **Hotel Vall de Núria.** A simple barracks-like hybrid of a mountain refuge and a hotel, this alpine dormitory and the Alberg (100 yards higher up the slope) offer comfortable lodging and dining at an altitude of 2,000 meters above sea level. For a day's outing or as a jumping-off point for a major hike (12 hours) to Ulldeter, above Setcases, or even a weeklong walk to the Mediterranean, this is a handy spot, accessible only by the cogwheel train from Ribes de Freser. **Pros:** perfect location in the heart of the Pyrenees, pristine mountain air, simplicity. **Cons:** a rambling dormitory redolent of boarding school, quasi-monastic austerity. ✉ *Estación de Montaña Vall de Núria, Queralbs* ☎ *972/732030* 🌐 *www.valldenuria.com* *65 rooms* *In-room: Wi-Fi. In-hotel: restaurant, bar, tennis court, no elevator, public Internet* 💳 *AE, MC, V.*

LA CERDANYA

The Pyrenees' widest, sunniest valley is said to be in the shape of the handprint of God. High pastureland bordered north and south by snow-covered peaks, La Cerdanya starts in France, at Col de la Perche (near Mont Louis), and ends in the Spanish province of Lleida, at Martinet. Split into two countries and subdivided into two more provinces on each side, the valley has an identity all its own. Residents on both sides of the border speak Catalan, a Romance language derived from early Provençal French, and regard the valley's political border with undisguised hilarity. Unlike any other valley in the upper Pyrenees, this one runs east–west and thus has a record annual number of sunlight hours.

PUIGCERDÀ

170 km (105 mi) northwest of Barcelona, 65 km (40 mi) northwest of Ripoll.

Puigcerdà is the largest town in the valley—in Catalan, *puig* means "hill"; *cerdà* derives from "Cerdanya". From the promontory upon which it stands, the views down across the meadows of the valley floor and up into the craggy peaks of the surrounding Pyrenees give the town a schizophrenic sense of height and humility. The 12th-century Romanesque bell tower—all that remains of the town church destroyed in 1936 at the outset of the Spanish civil war—and the sunny sidewalk cafés facing it are among Puigcerdà's prettiest spots, as are the Gothic church of Santa Maria and its long square, the **Plaça del Cuartel.** On Sunday, markets sell clothes, cheeses, fruits, vegetables, and wild mushrooms to shoppers from both sides of the border.

ESSENTIALS

Visitor Information Puigcerdà (✉ *Carrer Querol 1* ☎ *972/880542*).

EXPLORING

Plaça Cabrinetty, with its porticoes and covered walks, has a sunny northeastern corner where farmers gather for the Sunday market. The square is protected from the wind and ringed by two- and three-story houses of various pastel colors, some with engraved decorative designs and all with balconies. Visit the Font (spring) d'en Llanas down on Carrer d'en Llanas below the square.

From the balcony next to the **town hall** (✉ *Carrer Querol 1*), there is an ample view of the Cerdanya Valley that stretches all the way past Bellver de Cerdanya down to the sheer granite walls of the Sierra del Cadí, at the end of the valley. A 300-yard walk west from the fountain near Carrer Font d'en Llanas around the edge of town will bring you to the stairs leading up from the train station to the balcony.

Le petit train jaune *(the little yellow train)* leaves daily from Bourg-Madame and from La Tour de Querol, both simple walks into France from Puigcerdà. The border at La Tour, a longer but prettier walk, is marked only by a stone painted with the Spanish and French flags. This *carrilet* (narrow-gauge railway) is the last in the Pyrenees and is used for tours as well as transportation; it winds through the Cerdanya to the walled town of Villefranche de Conflent. The 63-km (39-mi) tour can take most of the day, especially if you stop to browse in Mont Louis or Villefranche. ✉ *Boarding at SNCF stations at Bourg-Madame or La Tour de Querol, France* ☎ *33 (0)4–68–30–85–02* 🌐 *www.le-rail.ch/text/projekt76.htm* 🎫 *€38 La Tour de Querol–Villefranche-de-Conflent round-trip* ⏲ *Schedule at Turismo office in Puigcerdà or at RENFE station below Puigcerdà.*

WHERE TO EAT AND STAY

$$–$$$ SPANISH **Tap de Suró.** Wine store, delicatessen, restaurant, and tapas emporium, this hole-in-the-wall tucked into the western edge of the town ramparts is the perfect place for sunsets, with views down the length of the Cerdanya Valley to the walls of the Sierra del Cadí. Cheeses, duck and goose liver, ibérico hams, caviar, and oysters are the kinds of delicacies best represented on the varied menu here, with a frequently changing selection of wines new and old from all over Spain and southern France as well. ✉ *Carrer Querol 21, Puigcerdà* ☎ *678–655–928* 💳 *AE, DC, MC, V* ⏲ *Closed Mon.*

$$ **Hotel del Lago.** A comfortable old favorite near Puigcerdà's emblematic lake, this hotel is composed of a graceful series of buildings built around a central garden. A two-minute walk from the bell tower or the town market, it feels deceptively bucolic but is actually only a few steps from all the action this bustling little market town can provide. **Pros:** picturesque and central location on the lake at the edge of town, personalized family treatment and service. **Cons:** rooms can be hot on summer days. ✉ *Av. Doctor Piguillem 7* ☎ *972/881000* 🌐 *www.hotellago.com* 🛏 *24 rooms* *In-room: Wi-Fi, no a/c. In-hotel: pool, spa, Wi-Fi, no elevator* 💳 *AE, DC, MC, V.*

$$$$ Fodor'sChoice ★ **La Torre del Remei.** About 3 km (2 mi) west of Puigcerdà is this mansion, built in 1910 and brilliantly restored by José María and Loles Boix of the legendary restaurant Boix in Martinet, 26 km (16 mi) to the west. Everything is superb, from the luxury of the manor house to the tasteful suites, heated bathroom floors, and the bottle of Moët Chandon. The restaurant ($$$$) serves international cuisine with an emphasis on local products. **Pros:** perfect comfort and sublime cuisine surrounded by a hiking, skiing, golfing paradise. **Cons:** the price. ✉ *Camí Reial s/n, Bolvir de Cerdanya* ☎ *972/140182* 🌐 *www.torredelremei.com* 🛏 *5 rooms, 17 suites* *In-hotel: restaurant, golf course, pool* 💳 *AE, DC, MC, V.*

$$$–$$$$ ★ **Villa Paulita.** This stately town-house complex at the edge of Puigcerdà's famous and iconic lake has vaulted to the forefront of the Cerdanya's dining and lodging options since opening in 2008. Along with perfection in peace and comfort, the hotel restaurant, L'Estany Senzone ($$$–$$$$), directed by chef Josep Maria Masó, is one of the best two or three dining establishments in the Pyrenees. **Pros:** near the center of the town's markets, restaurants, and general action but tucked

into a scenic and silent northeast corner. **Cons:** so self-sufficient and peaceful it's easy to forget the many pleasures of exploring the Cerdanya Valley. ✉*Av. Pons i Gasch 15* ☎*972/884622* 🌐*www.hospes.com* *38 rooms* *In-room: refrigerator, Wi-Fi. In-hotel: restaurant, bar, golf course, tennis court, pool, no elevator, public Wi-Fi* 💳*AE, DC, MC, V.*

TIP

If you're planning a long-distance hiking trip, local bus connections will get you to your starting point and retrieve you from the finish line.

NIGHTLIFE

Young Spanish and French night owls fill the town's many clubs until dawn. **Le Clochard** (✉*Carrer Major 54* ☎ *972/881615*) is a thronged pub in the center of town. **Transit**(✉*Casino 3* ☎ *972/881606*) is mid-town Puigcerdà's rock-until-dawn favorite.

SHOPPING

Puigcerdà is one big shopping mall, and long a nexus for contraband clothes, cigarettes, and other items smuggled across the French border. **Carrer Major** is an uninterrupted row of stores selling everything: books, jewelry, fashion, and sports equipment.

The **Sunday market** in Plaça del Cuartel, like those in most Cerdanya towns, is a great place to look for local specialties such as herbs, goat cheese, wild mushrooms, honey, and basketry.

For the best *margaritas* in town (no, not those; these are crunchy-edged madeleines made with almonds), look for the oldest commercial establishment in Catalonia: **Pasteleria Cosp** (✉*Carrer Major 20* ☎*972/880103*), founded in 1806.

Agau Joier (✉*Ramón Cosp 12* ☎*972/880268*), named for the chemical formula for gold, sells superb original jewelry.

LLÍVIA

6 km (4 mi) northeast of Puigcerdà.

A Spanish enclave in French territory, Llívia was marooned by the 1659 Peace of the Pyrenees treaty, which ceded 33 villages to France. Incorporated as a *vila* (town) by royal decree of Carlos V—who spent a night here in 1528 and was impressed by the town's beauty and hospitality—Llívia managed to remain semantically Spanish.

ESSENTIALS

Visitor Information Llívia (✉*Carrer dels Forns 10* ☎*972/896313*).

EXPLORING

At the upper edge of town, the fortified church **Mare de Déu dels Àngels** (✉*Carrer dels Forns 13* ☎*972/896301*) is an acoustic gem; check to see if any choral events are scheduled, especially in August and December, when the Llívia music festival schedules top classical groups.

Across from the church is the ancient pharmacy **Museu de la Farmacia** (✉*Carrer dels Forns 1217527* ☎*972/880103* ⏲*Daily Tues.–Fri. 10–4:20, weekends 10–1:50*), founded in 1415 and thought to be the oldest in Europe. Look for the **mosaic** in the middle of town commemorating Lampègia, *princesa de la pau i de l'amor* (princess of peace and of love), erected in memory of the red-haired daughter of the Duke of Aquitania and lover of Munuza, a Moorish warlord who governed the Cerdanya during the Arab domination.

WHERE TO EAT

$$–$$$$ SPANISH ★ **Can Ventura.** Inside a flower-festooned 17th-century town house made of ancient stones, Jordi Pous's epicurean oasis is a handsome dining space and one of the Cerdanya's best addresses for both fine cuisine and good value. Trout and beef *a la llosa* (seared on slabs of slate) are house specialties, and the wide selection of *entretenimientos* (hors d'oeuvres or tapas) is the perfect way to begin. Ask encyclopedic food and wine savant Jordi's advice on wine selections and game and wild mushrooms in season. *Plaça Major 1 972/896178 Reservations essential AE, DC, MC, V Closed June 20–July 15, Mon. July 16–Oct., and Tues.*

$$$–$$$$ SPANISH Fodor's Choice ★ **La Formatgeria de Llívia.** Conveniently situated on Llívia's eastern edge (en route to Saillagousse, France), this restaurant is in a former cheese factory that still makes fresh mató cheese while you watch; there are tasting tables in the bar for these cheese-sampling sessions. Juanjo Meya and his wife, master chef Marta Pous, have had great success offering fine local cuisine, panoramic views looking south toward Puigmal and across the valley, and general charm and good cheer. The innovative taster's menu adds a creative dimension to the restaurant. *Pla de Rô, Gorguja 972/146279 Reservations essential AE, DC, MC, V Closed June 20–July 12, Tues. and Wed.*

BELLVER DE CERDANYA

★ *31 km (19 mi) southwest of Llívia, 25 km (16 mi) southwest of Puigcerdà.*

Bellver de Cerdanya has preserved its slate-roof and fieldstone Pyrenean architecture more successfully than many of the Cerdanya's larger towns. Perched on a promontory over the **Río Segre,** which winds around much of the town, Bellver is a mountain version of a fishing village—trout fishing, to be exact. The town's Gothic church of **Sant Jaume** and the arcaded **Plaça Major,** in the upper part of town, are lovely examples of traditional Pyrenean mountain-village design.

ESSENTIALS

Visitor Information Bellver de Cerdanya (*Pl. de Sant Roc 9 973/510229*).

WHERE TO EAT AND STAY

$ **Fonda Biayna.** A rustic retreat with woodsy furnishings that seems happily stuck in an early Pyrenean time warp, this hotel has simple and cozy guest rooms. The Catalan fare ($$–$$$) includes such dishes as roast rabbit *allioli* (a sauce of garlic and olive oil), *galtes de porc amb bolets* (pork cheeks with wild mushrooms), and *tiró amb naps i trumfes* (duck with turnips and potatoes). **Pros:** creaky floors and antiques add to the charm, cozy sense of early Pyrenean life. **Cons:** rooms are small, can be hot in summer. ✉ *Carrer Sant Roc 11* ☎ *973/510475* 🌐 *www.fondabiayna.com* 🛏 *16 rooms* 🛎 *In-room: Wi-Fi, no a/c, no phone, no TV. In-hotel: restaurant, Wi-Fi* 💳 *AE, DC, MC, V.*

MARTINET

10 km (6 mi) west of Bellver de Cerdanya.

The town of Martinet hasn't much to offer except a few cozy watering spots that are hard to pass up in the heat of summer. For a course in trout gastronomy, have a close look over the railing along the Río Segre just upstream from its junction with the Llosa River. Martinet's protected trout are famous in these parts: the fish dine from 1 to 4 in the afternoon, when the sun slants in and cooks off hatches of aquatic insects while illuminating every speckle and spot on the feeding trout.

For a spectacular excursion, drive or walk up the valley of the Llosa River into Andorra, or take the short but stunning walk from the village of **Aransa** to Lles: as you pull away from Aransa and onto an alpine meadow, the Cerdanya's palette changes with every twist of the trail. You'll even pass the ruins of a 10th-century hilltop hermitage. (The tourist office in La Seu d'Urgell has simple trail maps.) The village of **Lles** is a famous Nordic-skiing resort with 36 km (22 mi) of cross-country tracks.

WHERE TO EAT AND STAY

$–$$ 🏨 **Cal Rei.** Built into former stables, this graceful and rustic country inn usually has a roaring fire in the common room and offers direct access to one of the Pyrenees' finest cross-country ski areas. There's a common room with a TV. The cuisine is powerful mountain fare ($$–$$$) designed to restore weary trekkers. Views of the Sierra del Cadí are spectacular. **Pros:** high sierra scenery and impeccable comfort, rough and simple enough to remind you that you're in the Pyrenees. **Cons:** rooms are somewhat cramped, paper-thin walls between rooms. ✉ *Cadí 4, Lles de Cerdanya* ☎ *659/063915 mobile* 🌐 *www.lles.net/cal.rei* 🛏 *8 rooms* 🛎 *In-room: no a/c, no phone, Wi-Fi. In-hotel: restaurant, no elevator, public Wi-Fi* 💳 *AE, DC, MC, V.*

OFF THE BEATEN PATH

The majestic **Prat d'Aguiló,** or Eagle's Meadow, 20 km (12 mi) south of Martinet, is one of the highest points in the Cerdanya that you can access without either a four-wheel-drive vehicle or a hike. The winding, bumpy drive up the mountain takes about an hour and a half (start with a full tank) and opens onto some excellent vistas of its own. From the meadow, the roughly three-hour climb to the top of the sheer rock wall of the Sierra del Cadí, directly above, reaches an altitude of nearly 8,000 feet. To get here from Martinet, take a dirt road that is rough but, barring new washouts, navigable by the average car. Follow signs for "Refugio Prat d'Aguiló."

LA SEU D'URGELL

Fodor's Choice ★ *24 km (15 mi) west of Martinet, 20 km (12 mi) south of Andorra la Vella (in Andorra), 50 km (31 mi) west of Puigcerdà.*

La Seu d'Urgell is an ancient town facing the snowy rock wall of the Sierra del Cadí. As the seat (*seu*) of the regional archbishopric since the 6th century, it has a rich legacy of art and architecture. The Pyrenean feel of the streets, with their dark balconies and porticoes, overhanging galleries, and colonnaded porches—particularly **Carrer dels Canonges**—makes Seu mysterious and memorable. Look for the medieval **grain measures** at the corner of Carrer Major and Carrer Capdevila. The tiny food shops on the arcaded Carrer Major are intriguing places to assemble lunch for a hike.

ESSENTIALS

Bus Station La Seu d'Urgell (✉ *Av. Garriga i Masó s/n, La Seu d'Urgell* ☎ *973/350020*).

Visitor Information La Seu d'Urgell (✉ *Av. Valls d'Andorra 33* ☎ *973/351511*).

EXPLORING

★ The 12th-century **Catedral de Santa Maria** is the finest cathedral in the Pyrenees. One of the most moving sights in the Pyrenees is the sunlight casting the rich reds and blues of Santa Maria's southeastern rose window into the deep gloom of the transept. The 13th-century cloister is famous for the individually carved, often whimsical capitals on its 50 columns. (They were crafted by the same Roussillon school of masons who carved the doorway on the church of Santa Maria in Ripoll.) Don't miss either the haunting, 11th-century chapel of **Sant Miquel** or the **Diocesan Museum,** which has a striking collection of medieval murals from various Pyrenean churches and a colorfully illuminated 10th-century Mozarabic manuscript of the monk Beatus de Liébana's commentary on the apocalypse, along with a short film explaining the manuscript. ✉ *Plaça dels Oms* ☎ *973/350981* *Cathedral, cloister, and museum €4* ⏲ *Daily 9–1 and 4–8.*

WHERE TO EAT AND STAY

$$–$$$$ SPANISH **Cal Pacho.** Sample traditional Pyrenean and Mediterranean specialties at very reasonable prices in this dark, rustic spot, built in the typical mountain style with stone and fresh wood beams. A family-run restaurant popular with the local inhabitants, the Río Segre is just a few steps away from this cozy nook in the lower part of town. Count on the filling *escudella* (mountain soup of vegetables, pork or veal, and noodles) in winter, and lamb, sausage, or trout cooked over coals or on slate year-round. ✉ *Carrer La Font 11* ☎ *973/352719* *AE, DC, MC, V.*

¢–$ **Cal Serni.** Ten minutes north of La Seu d'Urgell (off the road to Andorra) in the Pyrenean village of Calbinyà—which has a Museu del Pagès (Farmer's Museum) and a 16th-century farmhouse—is this lovely inn with rustic charm, inexpensive meals, and rooms to spend the night. **Pros:** mountain authenticity just minutes from La Seu, good value. **Cons:** small rooms, no Internet. ✉ *Ctra. de Calbinyà s/n, Valls de Valira* ☎ *973/352809* ⊕ *www.calserni.com* *6 rooms* *In-hotel: restaurant, no elevator, public Wi-Fi* *AE, DC, MC, V.*

$$$$ ★ **El Castell de Ciutat.** Just outside La Seu, this tall wood-and-slate structure is one of the finest places in the Pyrenees. Rooms on the second floor have balconies overlooking the river; those on the third have slanted ceilings and dormer windows. Suites include a salon. The internationally acclaimed restaurant, Tapies ($$$$), specializes in mountain cuisine, such as *civet de jabalí* (wild-boar stew) and *llom de cordet amb trinxat* (lamb cooked over coals and served with puree of potatoes and cabbage). Reserve in advance during summer or Easter week. **Pros:** best restaurant for many miles, supremely comfortable rooms. **Cons:** right next to a busy highway, misses out on the feel of the town of La Seu. ✉ *Ctra. de Lleida (N260), Km 229* ☎ *973/350000* 🌐 *www.hotelelcastell.com* *32 rooms, 6 suites* *In-room: Wi-Fi. In-hotel: restaurant, pools, gym, no elevator, public Wi-Fi* *AE, DC, MC, V.*

$$$ **Parador de la Seu d'Urgell.** These comfortable quarters right in the center of town are built into the 12th-century church and convent of Sant Domènec. The interior patio—the cloister of the former convent—is a lush and tranquil hideaway choked with vegetation. Rooms are spare and simple but warm, and some have views of the mountains. **Pros:** next to the Santa Maria cathedral, handy for wandering through the town. **Cons:** minimalist lines and contemporary interior design clash with the medieval feel of this mountain refuge. ✉ *Carrer Sant Domènec 6* ☎ *973/352000* 🌐 *www.parador.es* *77 rooms, 1 suite* *In-hotel: restaurant, pool, gym* *AE, DC, MC, V.*

WESTERN CATALAN PYRENEES

"The farther from Barcelona, the wilder" is the rule of thumb, and this is true of the rugged countryside and fauna in the western part of Catalonia. Three of the greatest destinations in the Pyrenees are here: the Garonne-drained, Atlantic-oriented Vall d'Aran; the Noguera de Tor Valley (aka Vall de Boí), with its matching set of gemlike Romanesque churches; and Parc Nacional d'Aigüestortes i Estany de Sant Maurici, which has a network of pristine lakes and streams. The main geographical units in this section are the valley of the Noguera Pallaresa River, the Vall d'Aran headwaters of the Atlantic-bound Garonne, and the Noguera Ribagorçana River valley, Catalonia's western limit.

SORT

★ *59 km (37 mi) west of La Seu d'Urgell.*

The capital of the Pallars Sobirà (Upper Pallars Valley) is a center for skiing, fishing, and white-water kayaking. Don't be fooled by the town you see from the main road: one block back, Sort is honeycombed with tiny streets and protected corners built to stave off harsh winter weather.

GETTING HERE

To get here from La Seu d'Urgell, take N260 toward Lleida, head west at Adrall and drive 53 km (33 mi) over the Cantó Pass to Sort.

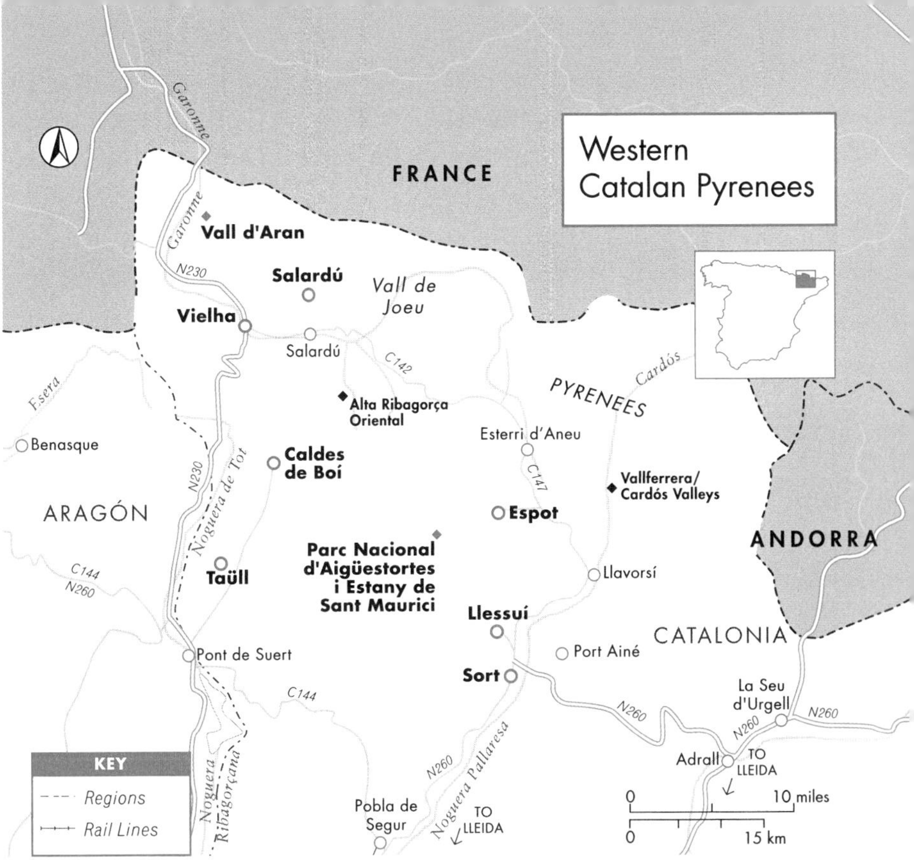

ESSENTIALS

Visitor Information **Pallars Sobirà** (✉ *Camí de la Cabanera* ☎ *973/621002* 🌐 *www.pallarssobira.info*).

WHERE TO EAT

$$–$$$$ SPANISH ★ ✕ **Fogony.** If you hit Sort at lunchtime, Fogony, one of the finest dining establishments in the Pyrenees, is a better than average reason to stop. Come here for contemporary creations such as the *suquet de alcachofas* (stewed artichokes), *colmenillas con salsa de foie de pato macerado con Armagnac y Oporto* (wild mushrooms with sauce of duck liver macerated in Armagnac and Port wine), or the *carré de cordero con falsas migas y espuma de patata* (lamb medallion with false breadcrumbs and foam of potato). ✉ *Av. Generalitat 45* ☎ *973/621225* ▭ *AE, DC, MC, V* ⏲ *Closed 2 wks in Jan. Closed Mon. except Christmas wk, Easter wk, and Aug. No dinner Sun.*

LLESSUÍ

15 km (9 mi) north of Sort.

Llessuí is at the head of the Upper Pallars Valley, under the ski slopes of the now-closed Altars peak.

ESSENTIALS

Visitor Information Pallars Sobirà (✉ *Camí de la Cabanera s/n* ☎ *973/621002* 🌐 *www.pallarssobira.info).*

EXPLORING

The 12th-century Romanesque church of **Sant Pere** is topped with a typical conical Vall d'Aran bell tower resembling a pointed witch's hat. The village is now known for adventure sports such as rafting, mountain biking, hiking, and skiing in nearby Espot or Port Ainé.

WHERE TO EAT AND STAY

$–$$$ SPANISH ✕ **Cal Kiko.** This little restaurant, a rustic Pyrenean enclave also known as El Pigal, is justly famous throughout Catalonia for its simple but peerless Pyrenean cooking and for its "Filiberto," a dessert composed of whipped cream, yogurt, and red currants. The leg of lamb, *el palpis,* another house favorite, is cooked in a deep earthenware *cazuela* with assorted wild mushrooms. For an *escudella* (a stew with beans, pasta, pork, fowl, beef, and abundant vegetables) not soon to be forgotten (or digested), this is the place. ✉ *Ctra. de Llessuí s/n, Llessuí* ☎ *973/621715* ▭ *AE, MC, V* ⊗ *Closed Oct. and Wed. No dinner Tues.*

¢ **Vall d'Àssua.** A cozy refuge, this little family-run and family-oriented place is a sure bet for simple Pyrenean home cooking ($–$$) strong on thick stews and soups such as *escudella* and roasts cooked *a la brasa* (over coals). The *flan casero* (homemade caramel cream) is a delight. Guest rooms are small but comfortable. The family also rents out several rural houses and apartments in country houses in the nearby village of Llagunes. **Pros:** intimate and rustic, pure Pyrenees, simple rural hideaway. **Cons:** spaces are slightly cramped, no Internet. ✉ *Ctra. de Llessuí, Altron* ☎ *973/621738* 🌐 *www.hostalvalldassua.com* *11 rooms* *In-room: no TV. In-hotel: no elevator* ▭ *No credit cards* ⊗ *Closed Nov.*

PARC NACIONAL D'AIGÜESTORTES I ESTANY DE SANT MAURICI

★ *After Escaló, 12 km (7 mi) northwest of Llavorsí, the road to Espot and the park veers west.*

Running water and the abundance of high mountain terrain are the true protagonists in this wild domain in the shadow of the twin peaks of Els Encantats. More than 300 glacial lakes and lagoons drain through flower-filled meadows and woods to the two Noguera River watercourses: the Pallaresa to the east and the Ribagorçana to the west. The ubiquitous water is surrounded by bare rock walls carved out by the glacier that left these jagged peaks and moist pockets. The land ranges from soft lower meadows below 5,000 feet to the highest crags at nearly double that height: the twin Encantats measure more than 9,000 feet, and surrounding peaks Beciberri, Peguera, Montarto, and Amitges hover between 8,700 feet and just under 10,000 feet.

The dozen Aigüestortes mountain refuges are the stars of the Pyrenees, ranging from the 12-bunk Beciberri, the highest bivouac in the Pyrenees at 9,174 feet, to the 80-bunk, 7,326-foot Ventosa i Calvell at the foot of Punta Alta. Between June and September these mountain accommodations fill with tired and hungry hikers sharing trail tips and lore.

The park has strict rules: no camping, no fires, no vehicles beyond certain points, no unleashed pets. Entrance to the park is free. It is accessible from the Noguera Pallares and Ribagorçana valleys, and the Espot and Boí villages. For information and refuge reservations, contact the **park administration offices** (☏*973/694000 Barruera, 973/696189 Boí, 973/624036 Espot* ⊕*www.mma.es/parques/lared.com*).

WHERE TO STAY

There are no hotels in the park, though there are nine refuges, with staff, that provide beds and dinner for hikers from June to October and during shorter periods at Christmas and Easter. When not open and staffed, shelter is available in parts of the refuge. Fireplaces are available for cooking, but food and utensils must be supplied by hikers. The 66-bunk **Refugi d'Amitges** (☏*973/250109*) is near the Amitges lakes, at 7,920 feet. The 24-bunk **Refugi Ernest Mallafré** (☏*973/250118*) is at the foot of Els Encantats, near Lake Sant Maurici. **Refugi Josep Maria Blanc** (☏*973/250108*), at 7,755 feet, offers 40 bunks at the base of a peninsula reaching out into the Tort de Peguera Lake.

ESPOT

15 km (9 mi) northwest of Llavorsí, 166 km (100 mi) north of Lleida.

Espot is at the heart of the valley, along a clear stream, next to the eastern entrance of Aigüestortes–Sant Maurici National Park.

ESSENTIALS

Visitor Information Espot (✉*Pl. Major s/n* ☏*973/624036*).

EXPLORING

Super-Espot is the local ski area. The **Pont de la Capella** *(Chapel Bridge)*, a perfect, mossy arch over the flow, looks as though it might have grown directly from the Pyrenean slate.

VALL D'ARAN AND ENVIRONS

From Esterri d'Aneu, the valley runs 46 km (27 mi) east to Vielha over the Bonaigua Pass.

The Vall d'Aran is at the western edge of the Catalan Pyrenees and the northwestern corner of Catalonia. North of the main Pyrenean axis, it's the Catalan Pyrenees' only Atlantic valley, opening northward into the plains of Aquitania and drained by the Garonne, which flows into the Atlantic Ocean above Bordeaux. The 48-km (30-mi) drive from Bonaigua Pass to the Pont del Rei border with France follows the riverbed.

The valley's Atlantic personality is evidenced by its climate—wet and cold—and its language: the 6,000 inhabitants speak Aranés, a dialect of Gascon French derived from the Occitanian language group. (Spanish and Catalan are also universally spoken.) Originally part of the Aquitanian county of Comminges, the Vall d'Aran maintained feudal ties to

CLOSE UP

Hiking in the Pyrenees

Walking the crest of the Pyrenees' range, with one foot in France and the other in Spain, is an exhilarating experience and within reach of the moderately to extremely fit.

In fall and winter the Alberes Mountains between Cap de Creus, the Iberian Peninsula's easternmost point, and the border with France at Le Perthus are a grassy runway between the Côte Vermeille's curving strand to the north and the moist green patchwork of the Empordá to the south.

The eight-hour walk from Coll de Núria to Ulldeter over the Sierra Catllar, above Setcases, is another grassy corridor in good weather from April to October. The luminous Cerdanya Valley is a hiker's paradise year-round, while the summertime round-Andorra hike is a memorably scenic 360-degree tour of Andorra.

The Parc Nacional d'Aigüestortes i Estany de Sant Mauricio is superb for trekking from spring through fall. The ascent of the 11,168-foot Aneto peak above Benasque is a long full day's round-trip best approached in summer and only by fit and experienced hikers. Much of the hike is over the Maladeta glacier, from the base camp at the Refugio de La Renclusa, where you can rent crampons and ice axes.

In Parque Nacional de Ordesa y Monte Perdido you can take day trips up to the Cola de Caballo waterfall and back around the southern rim of the canyon or, for true mountain goats, longer hikes via the Refugio de Góriz to La Brèche de Roland and Gavarnie or to Monte Perdido, the Parador at La Pineta, and the village of Bielsa.

The Camino de Santiago walk from Saint-Jean-Pied-de-Port to Roncesvalles is a marvelous 8- to 10-hour trek and manageable any time of year, though weather reports should be checked carefully from October to June.

Local *excursionista* (outing) clubs can help you get started; local tourist offices may also have brochures and rudimentary trail maps. Keep in mind that the higher reaches are safely navigable only in summer.

Contacts **Centre Excursionista de Catalunya** (✉ *Carrer Paradís 10, Barcelona* ☎ *93/315–2311*). **Cercle d'Aventura** (☎ *972/881017*). **Giroguies** (☎ *636/490830* 🌐 *www.giroguies.com*). **Guies de Meranges** (☎ *93/825–7104*). **Guies de Muntanya** (☎ *973/626470* 🌐 *www.guiesdemuntanya.com*).

the Pyrenees of Spanish Aragón and became part of Catalonia-Aragón in the 12th century. In 1389 the valley was assigned to Catalonia.

Neither as wide as the Cerdanya nor as oppressively narrow and vertical as Andorra, the Vall d'Aran has a sense of well-being and order, an architectural harmony unique in Catalonia. The clusters of iron-gray slate roofs, the lush vegetation, and dormer windows (a sign of French influence) all make the Vall d'Aran a distinct geographic and cultural pocket that happens to have washed up on the Spanish side of the border.

Hiking and climbing are popular here; guides are available year-round and can be arranged through the **tourist office** (☎ *973/640110*) in Vielha.

VIELHA

79 km (49 mi) northwest of Sort.

Vielha (Viella, in Spanish), capital of the Vall d'Aran, is a lively crossroads vitally involved in the Aranese movement to defend and reconstruct the valley's architectural, institutional, and linguistic heritage.

ESSENTIALS

Visitor Information Vielha (✉ *Carrer Sarriulera 10* ☎ *973/640110*).

EXPLORING

The octagonal, 14th-century bell tower on the Romanesque parish church of **Sant Miquel** is one of the town's trademarks, as is the 15th-century Gothic altar. The partly damaged 12th-century wood carving *Cristo de Mig Aran,* displayed under glass, evokes a sense of mortality and humanity with a power unusual in medieval sculpture.

North of Vielha, the tiny villages over the Garonne River hold intriguing little secrets, such as the sculpted Gallo-Roman heads (funeral stelae, or stone slabs, rehabilitated in the 12th century) carved into the village portal at **Gausac.** The bell tower in **Vilac** has an eccentric charm. **Vilamós**'s church, the oldest in the valley, is known for the three curious carved figures, thought to be Gallo-Roman funeral stelae, on its facade. Beautifully carved capitals on the supporting columns adorn the porticoed square in the border village of **Bossòst.** East of Vielha is the village of **Escunhau,** with steep alley-stairways. **Arties** makes a good stop, with its famous Casa Irene restaurant and historic parador.

6

WHERE TO EAT AND STAY

$$–$$$$ SPANISH ★ **Era Mola.** Also known as Restaurante Gustavo y María José, this rustic former stable with whitewashed walls serves French-inspired Aranese cuisine. The *confit de pato* (duck stewed with apple) and *magret de pato* (breast of duck served with *carradetas,* wild mushrooms from the valley) are favorites, as is the roast kid or lamb. The wine list is particularly strong in Rioja, Ribera de Duero, and Somontano reds, as well as full-bodied whites such as Albariños from Rías Baixas and Ruedas from Valladolid. ✉ *Carrer Marrec 14* ☎ *973/642419* *Reservations essential* *AE, DC, MC, V* *No lunch weekdays Dec.–Apr.*

$$$–$$$$ ★ **Casa Irene.** A rustic haven, this inn 6 km (4 mi) east of Vielha is known for the fine mountain cuisine with a French flair. Three tasting menus ($$$–$$$$) and dishes such as poached foie gras in black truffles and roast wood pigeon in nuts and mint have made Irene a national treasure. The personal style and spacious and elegant rooms make this a highly recommendable address for lodging as well as food. **Pros:** small and personalized, esthetically impeccable. **Cons:** street-side rooms can be noisy on summer nights. ✉ *Carrer Major 3, Arties* ☎ *973/644364* *www.hotelcasairene.com* *22 rooms* *In-room: Wi-Fi. In-hotel: restaurant, public Wi-Fi, parking (fee)* *Reservations essential* *AE, DC, MC, V* *Closed Nov. and May.*

$$$ **Parador de Arties.** Built around the Casa de Don Gaspar de Portolà, once home to the founder of the colony of California, this modern parador has sweeping views of the Pyrenees. Just 7 km (4 mi) from the Baqueira ski slopes and 2½ km (1½ mi) south of Vielha, it's big enough

to be festive but small enough for intimacy. The restaurant ($$–$$$) specializes in Pyrenean soups and stews such as *civet de jabalí* (wild boar stew). **Pros:** marvelous panoramas, quiet and personal for a parador. **Cons:** neither at the foot of the slopes nor in the thick of the Vielha après-ski vibe, requires driving. ✉ *Ctra. Baqueira-Beret s/n, Arties* ☎ *973/640801* 🌐 *www.parador.es* *54 rooms, 3 suites* *In-room: Wi-Fi. In-hotel: restaurant, pools, gym, parking (fee)* *AE, MC, V.*

$$$ **Parador de Vielha.** This modern granite parador has a semicircular salon with huge windows and spectacular views over the Maladeta peaks of the Vall d'Aran. Rooms are furnished with traditional carved-wood furniture and floor-to-ceiling curtains. The restaurant ($$–$$$) serves Catalan and Pyrenean cuisine, ranging from *espinacas a la catalana* (spinach sautéed in olive oil with pine nuts, raisins, and garlic) to *civet d'isard* (wild mountain goat stew). **Pros:** terrific observation post, comfortable and relaxed. **Cons:** somewhat overpopulated when fully booked, overmodern and functional design. ✉ *Ctra. del Túnel s/n* ☎ *973/640100* 🌐 *www.parador.es* *118 rooms* *In-room: Wi-Fi. In-hotel: restaurant, pool, spa, public Wi-Fi, parking (free)* *AE, MC, V.*

NIGHTLIFE

Bar Era Crin (✉ *Carrer Sortaus 2, Escunhau* ☎ *973/642061*) has live performances and pop rock to dance to. **Bar la Lluna** (✉ *Carrer Major 10, Arties* ☎ *973/641115*), a local favorite, occupies a typical Aranese house and has live performances on Wednesday. **Eth Clòt** (✉ *Plaça Sant Orenç, Arties* ☎ *973/642060*) is a hot *bar musicale.* **Glass** (✉ *Centro Comercial Elurra, Betrén* ☎ *973/640332*) is in a commercial complex near Vielha that's filled with a dozen music bars, pubs, and discos.

SALARDÚ

9 km (6 mi) east of Vielha.

Convenient to Tredós, the Montarto peak, the lakes and Circ de Colomers, Aigüestortes National Park, and the villages of Unha and Montgarri, Salardú is a pivotal point in the Vall d'Aran. The town itself, with just over 700 inhabitants, is known for its steep streets and its octagonal fortified bell tower. The 12th-century **Sant Andreu** church's Romanesque wood sculpture of Christ is said to have miraculously floated up the Garonne River.

The tiny village of **Unha** perches on a promontory 3 km (2 mi) above Salardú, with the elegant Ço de Brastet (Brastet House) at its entrance. Unha's 12th-century church of Santa Eulàlia has a curiously bulging 17th-century bell tower. East of Salardú is the village of **Tredós,** home of the Romanesque church of Santa Maria de Cap d'Aran—symbol of the Aranese independence movement and meeting place of the valley's governing body, the Conselh Generau, until 1827.

OFF THE BEATEN PATH

Santa Maria de Montgarri. Partly in ruins, this 11th-century chapel was once an important way station on the route into the Vall d'Aran from France. The beveled, hexagonal bell tower and the rounded stones, which look as if they came from a brook bottom, give the structure a stippled appearance not unlike that of a Pyrenean trout. The Romería de Nuestra Señora de Montgarri (Feast of Our Lady of Montgarri, on July

2, is a country fair with dancing, game playing, and general carrying-on. The sanctuary is 12 km (7 mi) northeast of the town of Bagergue, which is just north of Salardú.

WHERE TO EAT AND STAY

$$–$$$ SPANISH ✕ **Casa Rufus.** Fresh pine on the walls and underfoot, red-and-white checkered curtains, and snowy white tablecloths cozily furnish this restaurant nestled in the tiny, gray-stone village of Gessa, between Vielha and Salardú. Rufus, who also runs the ski school at Baqueira, is especially adept with local country cooking; try the *conejo relleno de ternera* (rabbit stuffed with veal) or one of the *civets* (stews) of mountain goat or wild boar. If venison is on the menu, don't miss it. Open for dinner only during the ski season. ✉ *Sant Jaume 8, Gessa* ☎ *973/645246 or 973/645872* ▭ *MC, V* ⊗ *Closed May–mid-July, Nov., and weekdays in Oct. No dinner Sun. No lunch weekdays mid-Sept.–Apr.*

$$$$ ★ **Meliá Royal Tanau.** This luxurious hotel 7 km (4 mi) east of Salardú is next to the lifts and offers everything from hydrotherapy massage to fine cuisine (with prices to match: $$$–$$$$). Considered one of the top skiing hotels in the Pyrenees, the Royal Tanau will pamper you carefully between assaults on the snowy heights. Top-floor rooms can be snug, but duplex apartments have sleeping lofts with skylights opening directly out into the starry Pyrenean firmament. **Pros:** among the top Pyrenean skiing accommodations, intimate and low-key luxe. **Cons:** some rooms are on the small side, occasional design and layout lapses in certain rooms. ✉ *Ctra. Baqueira-Beret, Km 7* ☎ *973/644446* 🌐 *www.meliaroyaltanau.solmelia.com* *30 rooms, 15 apartments* *In-room: no a/c, Wi-Fi. In-hotel: restaurant, pool, public Wi-Fi* ▭ *AE, MC, V.*

$$$$ **Val de Ruda.** For rustic surroundings light on luxury but long on comfort, and an outdoorsy, alpine feeling, this modern-traditional construction is a good choice. Just a two-minute walk to the lift, the Val de Ruda was one of the first skiing hotels to be built here in the early '80s. This glass, wood, and stone refuge has a friendly staff and pine- and oak-beam warmth for après-ski wining and dining. **Pros:** warm and welcoming after a day in the mountains, friendly family service. **Cons:** some of the dormer rooms are cozy but tiny. ✉ *Ctra. Baqueira-Beret Cota 1500* ☎ *973/645258* 🌐 *www.valderuda-bassibe.com* *34 rooms* *In-room: no a/c, Wi-Fi. In-hotel: restaurant, bar, public Wi-Fi* ▭ *AE, DC, MC, V.*

SPORTS AND THE OUTDOORS

Skiing, white-water rafting, hiking, climbing, horseback riding, and fly-fishing are available throughout the Vall d'Aran. Consult the Vielha **tourist office** (☎ *973/640110*) for information.

DOGSLEDDING **La Pirena** (☎ *974/360098 tourist office in Jaca*), the Pyrenean version of the Iditarod, rages through the Vall d'Aran, from Panticosa, above Jaca, to La Molina, near Puigcerdà, every winter in late January to early or mid-February.

SKIING The **Baqueira-Beret Estación de Esquí** *(Baqueira-Beret Ski Station)* offers Catalonia's most varied and reliable skiing. The station's 87 km (57 mi) of *pistas* (slopes), spread over 53 runs, range from the gentle Beret slopes to the vertical chutes of Baqueira. The Bonaigua area is a mixture of steep and gently undulating trails with some of the longest, most varied runs in the Pyrenees. The internationally FIS-classified super-giant slalom run in Beret is the star attraction, although the Hotel Pirene runs carefully guided helicopter outings to the surrounding peaks of Pincela, Areño, Parros, Mall de Boulard, Pedescals, and Bassibe, among others. A dozen restaurants and four children's areas are scattered about the facilities, and the thermal baths at Tredós are 4 km (2½ mi) away. ✉ *Salardú* ☎ *973/639000* 📠 *973/644488* ✉ *Barcelona office: Av. Diagonal 656, Barcelona* ☎ *93/205–8292* 🌐 *www.baqueira.es.*

OFF THE BEATEN PATH

The **Vall de Joeu** (Joeu Valley), above the town of Les Bordes 9 km (6 mi) northwest of Vielha, was for centuries the unsolved mystery of Vall d'Aran hydraulics. The Joeu River, one of the two main sources of the Garonne, appears to rise at Artiga de Lin, where it then cascades down in the Barrancs Waterfalls. On July 19, 1931, speleologist Norbert Casteret proved, by dumping 132 pounds of colorant into a cavern in neighboring Aragón, that this "spring" was actually glacier runoff from the Maladeta massif in the next valley to the southwest. The glacier melt flows into a huge crater, Els Aïgualluts, and reappears 4 km (3 mi) northeast at the Uelhs deth Joeu (Eyes of Jupiter in Aranés, so named for the Roman deity's association with the heavens, weather, rainfall, and agriculture), where it flows north toward the Garonne, eventually emptying into the Atlantic.

TAÜLL

58 km (36 mi) south of Vielha.

Taüll is a town of narrow streets and tight mountain design—wooden balconies and steep slate roofs. The famous Taüll churches of Sant Climent and Santa Maria are among the best examples of Romanesque architecture in the Pyrenees. Other important churches near Taüll include Sant Feliu, at Barruera; Sant Joan Baptista, at Boí; Santa Maria, at Cardet; Santa Maria, at Col; Santa Eulàlia, at Erill-la-vall; La Nativitat de la Mare de Deu and Sant Quirze, at Durro; Sant Llorenç, at Sarais; and Sant Nicolau, in the Sant Nicolau Valley, at the entrance to Aigüestortes–Sant Maurici National Park.

ESSENTIALS

Visitor Information Taüll (✉ *Av. Valira s/n* ☎ *973/694000*).

EXPLORING

Taüll has a ski resort, **Bohí Taüll,** at the head of the Sant Nicolau Valley.

At the edge of town is the exquisite three-nave Romanesque church of ★ **Sant Climent**, built in 1123. The six-story belfry has exceptionally harmonious proportions, Pyrenean stone that changes hues with the light, and a sense of intimacy that creates notable balance. In 1922 Barcelona's Museu Nacional d'Art de Catalunya became the home of the church's murals, including the famous *Pantocrator,* the work of the "Master of Taüll." The murals presently in the church are reproductions of the original. 🎫 *€3* 🕐 *Daily 10–2 and 4–8.*

CALDES DE BOÍ

6 km (4 mi) north of Taüll.

ESSENTIALS

Visitor Information Vall de Boí (*Pg. Sant Feliu 43 973/694000*).

EXPLORING

The thermal baths in the town of Caldes de Boí include, between hot and cold sources, 40 springs. The caves inside the bath area are a singular natural phenomenon, with thermal steam seeping through the cracks in the rock. Take advantage of the baths' therapeutic qualities at either Hotel Caldes or Hotel Manantial—services range from a bath, at €8 to €12, to an underwater body massage for €19. People with arthritis are frequent takers. *Hotel Caldes 973/696220 Hotel Manantial 973/696210 www.caldesdeboi.com Hotels and baths closed Oct.–May.*

WHERE TO EAT AND STAY

¢ SPANISH **Fondevila.** Wooden trim and simple country furnishings warm the interior of this stone structure 3 km (2 mi) north of Taüll. The rooms are generously proportioned, handsomely furnished, and cozy. The country cuisine ($–$$) includes game in season and various Catalan specialties, from hearty stews such as *escudella* and *civet de porc senglar* (wild boar stew) to venison and *anec amb peres* (duck stewed with pears). **Pros:** friendly and intimate service, simple mountain lodging, top value. **Cons:** sparse room decor may seem stark. *Carrer Única, Boí 973/696011 46 rooms In-room: no a/c, Wi-Fi AE, DC, MC, V Closed Nov. 10–Dec. 26 and Jan. 7–Feb. 1.*

6

ARAGÓN AND CENTRAL PYRENEES

The highest, wildest, and most spectacular range of the Pyrenees is the middle section, farthest from sea level. From Benasque on Aragón's eastern side to Jaca at the western edge are the great heights and most dramatic landscapes of Alto Aragón (Upper Aragón), including the Maladeta (11,165 feet), Posets (11,070 feet), and Monte Perdido (11,004 feet) peaks, the three highest points in the Pyrenean chain.

Communications between the high valleys of the Pyrenees were all but nonexistent until the 19th century: four-fifths of the region had never seen a motor vehicle of any kind until well into the 20th century, and the 150-km (93-mi) border with France between Portalet de Aneu and Vall d'Aran had never had an international crossing. This combination of high peaks, deep defiles, and isolation has produced some of the Iberian Peninsula's best-preserved towns and valleys. Today, numerous ethnological museums bear witness to a way of life that has nearly disappeared since the 1950s. Residents of Upper Aragón speak neither Basque nor Catalan, but local dialects, such as Grausín, Chistavino, Belsetá, and Benasqués (collectively known as *fabla*), and have more in common with each other and with Occitanian or Langue d'Oc (the southwestern French language descended from Provençal) than with modern Spanish and French. Furthermore, each valley has its own variations on everything from the typical Aragonese folk dance, the *jota,* to cuisine and traditional costume.

The largely undiscovered cities of Huesca and Zaragoza are both useful Pyrenean gateways and destinations in themselves; Zaragoza is an unavoidable link between Barcelona and Bilbao. Both cities retain an authentic provincial character that is refreshing in today's cosmopolitan Spain. Huesca's lovely old quarter and Zaragoza's ancient Casco Viejo clustered around its immense basilica, La Pilarica, are memorable places to explore.

HUESCA

75 km (46 mi) southwest of Aínsa, 72 km (45 mi) northeast of Zaragoza, 123 km (74 mi) northwest of Lleida.

Capital of Aragón until the royal court moved to Zaragoza in 1118, Huesca was founded by the Romans a millennium earlier. The city became an independent state with a senate and an excellent school system organized by the Roman general Sertorius in 77 BC. Much later, after centuries of Moorish rule, Pedro I of Aragón liberated Huesca in 1096. The town's university was founded in 1354 and now specializes in Aragonese studies.

ESSENTIALS

Bus Station Huesca (✉ *Ronda de la Estación s/n, Huesca* ☎ *974/210700).*

Visitor Information Huesca (✉ *Pl. López Allué s/n* ☎ *974/292170).*

EXPLORING

An intricately carved gallery tops the eroded facade of Huesca's 13th-century Gothic **cathedral.** Damián Forment, a disciple of the 15th-century Italian master sculptor Donatello, created the alabaster altarpiece with scenes from the Crucifixion. ✉ *Pl. de la Catedral s/n* ☎ *974/292172* *Free* *Mon.–Sat. 8–1 and 4–6:30.*

Twice daily, the Huesca tourist office (in the former market at Plaza Luis Lopez Allué s/n) accompanies visitors into the Renaissance **ayuntamiento** *(town hall)* to see the 19th-century painting of the 12th-century beheading of a group of uncooperative nobles, ordered by Ramiro II. King Ramiro, having called a meeting for the purported pouring of a giant bell that would be audible throughout Aragón, proceeded to massacre the leading troublemakers; the expression *como la campana de Huesca* ("like the bell of Huesca") is still sometimes used to describe an event of surprising resonance. ✉ *Pl. de la Catedral 1* ☎ *974/292170* *Free* *Mon.–Sat. at noon and 6.*

The **Museo Arqueológico Provincial** is an octagonal patio ringed by eight chambers, including the **Sala de la Campana** (Hall of the Bell), where the beheadings of 12th-century nobles took place. The museum is in parts of what was once the royal palace of the kings of Aragón and holds paintings by Aragonese primitives, including *La Virgen del Rosario* by Miguel Jiménez, and several works by the 16th-century Maestro de Sigena. ✉ *Pl. de la Universidad* ☎ *974/220586* *Free* *Tues.–Sat. 10–2 and 5–8, Sun. 10–2.*

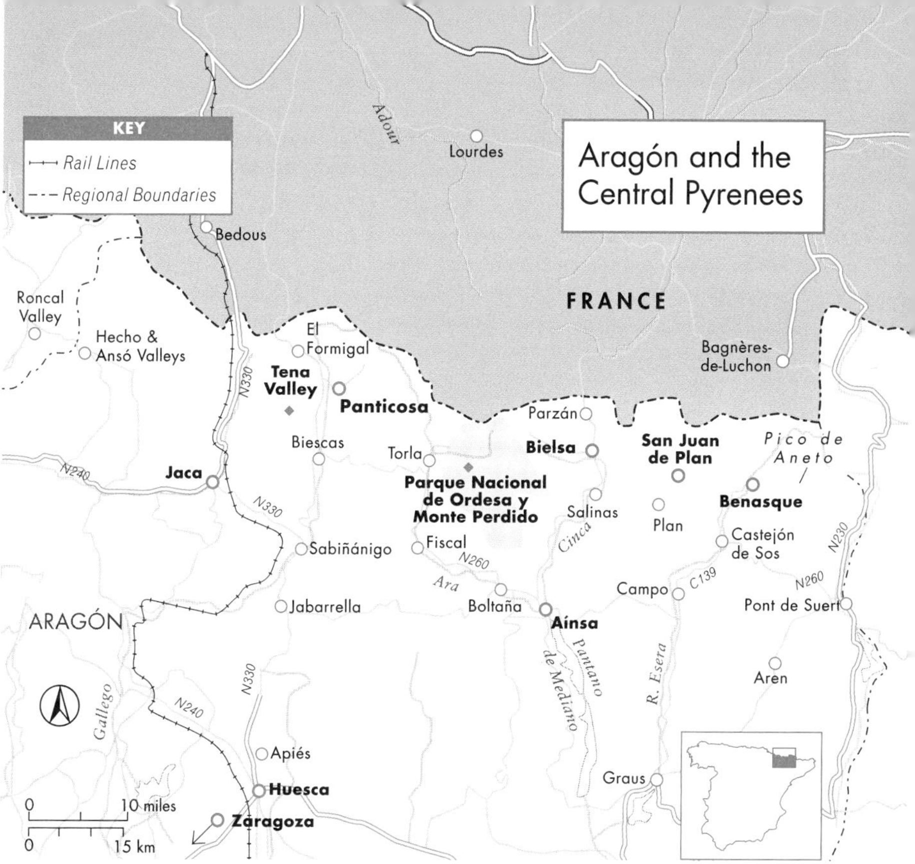

The church of **San Pedro el Viejo** has an 11th-century cloister. Ramiro II and his father, Alfonso I—the only Aragonese kings not entombed at San Juan de la Peña—rest in a side chapel. ✉ *Pl. de San Pedro s/n* ☎ *974/292164* 🎫 *Free* ⏲ *Mon.–Sat. 10–2 and 6–8.*

OFF THE BEATEN PATH

Castillo de Loarre. This massively walled 11th-century monastery, 36 km (22 mi) west of Huesca off Route A132 on A1206, is nearly indistinguishable from the rock outcroppings that surround it. Inside the walls are a church, a tower, a dungeon, and even a medieval toilet with views of the almond and olive orchards in the Ebro basin.

WHERE TO EAT AND STAY

$$–$$$$ SPANISH

✕ **Las Torres.** Huesca's top dining establishment makes inventive use of first-rate local Pyrenean ingredients ranging from wild mushrooms to wild boar, venison, and lamb. The glass-walled kitchen is as original as the cooking that emerges from it, and the wine list is strong in Somontanos, Huesca's own Denomination of Origin. Look for *lomo de ternasco cocinado a baja temperatura con embutidos de Graos* (veal cooked at low temperature with Graos sausage) or the *paticas de cordero deshuesados* (boned lamb's trotters) for a taste of pure upper Aragón. ✉ *María Auxiliadora 3* ☎ *974/228213* 💳 *AE, DC, MC, V* ⏲ *Closed 2 wks at Easter, Aug. 16–31, and Sun.*

$$–$$$ **Pedro I de Aragón.** This modern structure over the leafy Parque Miguel Servet is lush with mirrors and marble in the lobby and furnished with fresh and fragrant pine in the rooms. Comfort is the objective here, and the accommodations and service are the best in Huesca, although the decor is somewhat stuck in a generic '60s time warp. **Pros:** efficient and modern. **Cons:** exterior rooms noisy on summer weekends, no style though very comfortable. ✉*Parque 34* ☎*974/220300* *www.gargallo-hotels.com* *125 rooms, 4 suites* *In-room: no a/c, Wi-Fi. In-hotel: restaurant, bar, pool* *AE, DC, MC, V.*

¢ **San Marcos.** This elegant building dates from the late 19th century, and the public spaces, though updated for comfort, remain tastefully decorated with traditional touches. A family-run enterprise with a personal touch, rooms are small and simply but recently decorated with fresh pine furniture and impeccable bathroom facilities. Centrally located just outside the 1st-century Roman walls, the hotel is a five-minute walk from Huesca's cathedral. **Pros:** convenient central location, historic and elegant building, good value. **Cons:** rooms can seem cluttered and somewhat cramped. ✉*San Orencio 10* ☎*974/222931* *29 rooms* *In-room: no a/c, Wi-Fi. In-hotel: restaurant, bar, pool* *AE, DC, MC, V.*

A PAMPLONA ALTERNATIVE

For an unspoiled Pamplona-like fiesta in another pre-Pyrenean capital, with bullfights, *encierros* (running of the bulls through the streets), and all-night revelry, try Huesca's San Lorenzo celebration August 9–15. Spain's top bullfighters are the main attraction, along with concerts, street dances, and liberal tastings of the excellent Somontano wines of upper Huesca. *Albahaca* (basil) is the official symbol of Huesca and the ubiquitous green sashes and bandannas will remind you that this is Huesca, not Pamplona (where red is the trimming).

ZARAGOZA

72 km (43 mi) southwest of Huesca, 138 km (86 mi) west of Lleida, 307 km (184 mi) northwest of Barcelona, 164 km (98 mi) southeast of Pamplona, 322 km (193 mi) northeast of Madrid.

In high spirits two years after its 2008 Universal Exposition (based on the theme of water and its own mighty Ebro River), Zaragoza is now about as exciting as it's ever been. This traditionally provincial city is experiencing its greatest boom since the Romans established a thriving river port here in 25 BC. Rated one of Spain's most desirable places to live because of its air quality, low cost of living, low population density, and other factors, Zaragoza seems full of self-contained well-being. Despite its hefty size (pop. 660,895), this sprawling provincial capital midway between Barcelona, Madrid, Bilbao, and Valencia is a detour from the tourist track connected by the AVE, Spain's high-speed railroad—both Madrid and Barcelona only 90 minutes away.

ESSENTIALS

Bus Station Zaragoza (✉*Paseo María Agustín 7* ☎*976/229343*).

Visitor Information Zaragoza (central square) (✉ *Pl. de Nuestra Señora del Pilar* ☎ *9o2/201212*). **Zaragoza** (✉ *Calle Torreon de la Zuda, Glorieta de Pío XII* ☎ *902/201212*). **Zaragoza (train station)** (✉ *Rioja 33, Estación Zaragoza-Delicias* ☎ *902/201212*).

EXPLORING

Straddling Spain's greatest river, the Ebro, 2,000-year-old Zaragoza was originally named Caesaraugusta, for Roman emperor Augustus. Its legacy contains everything from Roman ruins and Jewish baths to Arab, Romanesque, Gothic-Mudejar, Renaissance, baroque, neoclassical, and Art Nouveau architecture. Parts of the **Roman walls** are visible near the city's landmark, Basílica de Nuestra Señora del Pilar. Nearby, the medieval **Puente de Piedra** (Stone Bridge) spans the Ebro. Checking out the **Lonja** (Stock Exchange), the Moorish **Aljafería** (Fortified Palace and Jewel Treasury), the **Mercado de Lanuza** (Produce Market), and the many **churches** in the old town is a good way to navigate Zaragoza's jumble of backstreets.

Hulking on the banks of the Ebro, the **Basílica de Nuestra Señora del Pilar** *(Basilica of Our Lady of the Pillar)*, affectionately known as "La Pilarica," is Zaragoza's symbol and pride. An immense baroque structure with no fewer than 11 tile cupolas, La Pilarica is the home of the Virgen del Pilar, the patron saint not only of peninsular Spain but of the entire Hispanic world. The fiestas honoring this most Spanish of saints, held the week of October 12, are events of extraordinary pride and Spanish fervor, with processions, street concerts, bullfights, and traditional *jota* dancing. The cathedral was built in the 18th century to commemorate the appearance of the Virgin on a pillar (*pilar*), or pedestal, to St. James, Spain's other patron saint, during his legendary incarnation as Santiago Matamoros (St. James the Moorslayer) in the 9th century. La Pilarica herself resides in a side chapel that dates from 1754. The frescoes in the cupolas, some of which are attributed to the young Goya, are among the basilica's treasures. The **Museo Pilarista** holds drawings and some of the Virgin's jewelry. The bombs displayed to the right of the altar of La Pilarica chapel fell through the roof of the church in 1936 and miraculously failed to explode. You can still see one of the holes overhead to the left. Behind La Pilarica's altar is the tiny opening where the devout line up to kiss the rough marble pillar where La Pilarica was allegedly discovered ✉ *Pl. del Pilar s/n* 🎫 *Basilica free, museum €2* ⏲ *Basilica daily 5:45 AM–9:30 PM, museum daily 9–2 and 4–6.*

Zaragoza's cathedral, **La Seo** *(Catedral de San Salvador)*, at the eastern end of the Plaza del Pilar, is the city's bishopric, or diocesan *seo* (seat). An amalgam of architectural styles ranging from the Mudejar brick-and-tile exterior to the Gothic altarpiece to exuberant Churrigueresque doorways, the Seo nonetheless has an 18th-century baroque facade that seems to echo those of La Pilarica. The **Museo de Tapices** within contains medieval tapestries. The nearby medieval **Casa y Arco del Deán** form one of the city's favorite corners. ✉ *Pl. del Pilar* 🎫 *Cathedral €2.50, museum €2* ⏲ *Cathedral Mon.–Sat. 10–2 and 4–8, Sun. 5–8; museum Tues.–Sat. 10–2 and 4–6, Sun. 10–2.*

The **Iglesia de la Magdalena,** next to the remains of the Roman forum, has an ancient brick Mudejar bell tower. The church is usually open in the mornings. ✉*Pl. de la Magdalena s/n* ☎*976/299598.*

The **Museo del Foro** displays remains of the Roman forum and the Roman sewage system, though the presentation is in Spanish only. Two more Roman sites, the **thermal baths** at Calle de San Juan y San Pedro and the **river port** at Plaza San Bruno, are also open to the public. ✉*Pl. de la Seo s/n* ☎*976/399752* 🎫*€2.50* ⏲*Tues.–Sat. 10–2 and 5–8, Sun. 10–2.*

The **Museo Camón Aznar** has a fine collection of Goya's works, particularly engravings. ✉*Carrer Espoz y Mina 23* ☎*976/397328* 🎫*Free* ⏲*Tues.–Fri. 9–2 and 6–9, Sat. 10–2 and 6–9, Sun. 11–2.*

The **Museo del Centro de Historia** exhibits a wide range of memorabilia from Zaragoza's 2,000-year history, including audiovisual studies of different facets. The section on the Ebro River and the Roman exploitation of the port of Zaragoza are especially interesting. ✉*Pl. San Agustín 2* ☎*976/205640* 🎫*Free* ⏲*Tues.–Sat. 10–7:15, Sun. 10–1:15.*

The **Museo Provincial de Bellas Artes** contains a rich treasury of Zaragoza's emblematic painter Francisco José Goya y Lucientes, including his portraits of Fernando VII, and his best graphic works: *Desastres de la guerra, Caprichos, and La tauromaquia.* ✉*Pl. de los Sitios 5* ☎*976/222181* 🎫*Free* ⏲*Tues.–Sat. 10–2 and 5–8, Sun. 10–2.*

The **Museo Pablo Gargallo** is one of Zaragoza's most treasured and admired gems, both for the palace as well as for the collection—Gargallo, born near Zaragoza in 1881, was one of Spain's greatest modern sculptors. ✉*Pl. de San Felipe 3* ☎*976/392058* 🎫*Free* ⏲*Tues.–Sat. 9–2 and 5–9, Sun. 9–2.*

The **Museo del Teatro Romano** showcases a restored Roman amphitheater as well as the objects recovered during the excavation process, including theatrical masks, platters, and even Roman hairpins. ✉*Calle San Jorge 12* ☎*976/205088* 🎫*€3.50* ⏲*Tues.–Sat. 10–9, Sun. 10–2.*

The **Palacio de La Aljafería** completes the trio of Spain's great Moorish palaces. If Córdoba's Mezquita shows the energy of the 10th-century Caliphate and Granada's Alhambra is the crowning 14th-century glory of Al-Andalus (the 789-year Moorish empire on the Iberian Peninsula), then the late 11th-century Aljafería can be seen as the intermediate step. Originally a fortress and royal residence, and later a seat of the Spanish Inquisition, the Aljafería is now the home of the Cortes (Parliament) de Aragón. The 9th-century Torre del Trovador (Tower of the Troubadour) appears in Giuseppe Verdi's opera *Il Trovatore.* ✉*Diputados s/n* ☎*976/289683* 🎫*€3* ⏲*Mon.–Wed. and weekends 10–2 and 4–7, Fri. 4–7.*

OFF THE BEATEN PATH

Monasterio de Piedra. An hour's drive south of Zaragoza brings you to the Cistercian Monasterio de Piedra, a lush oasis on the arid Aragonese *meseta* (plain). Founded in 1195 by Alfonso II of Aragón and named for the nearby Río Piedra (Stone River, so-named for the calcified limestone deposits along its banks), the monastery has a 16th-century Renaissance section that is now a moderately priced private hotel (rooms range in price from €130 to €150). The 12th-century cloister, wine museum, and caves, waterfalls, and walkways suspended over the riverbed are spectacular. If you can't stay overnight, you can wander the park for €14. **Pros:** peaceful getaway with top comfort and splendid views, sound of falling water. **Cons:** rooms somewhat monastic and austere. ✉*Rte. C202 south of Calatayud, just beyond Nuévalos* ☎*976/849011* 🌐*www.monasteriopiedra.com* *63 rooms* *In-hotel: restaurant, bar, meeting rooms, park, parking* *AE, DC, MC, V.*

WHERE TO EAT AND STAY

$–$$$ SPANISH **Casa Emilio.** One of the city's most popular restaurants among artists, journalists, and writers, this relaxed and easygoing haven of straightforward cooking and conversation near the Aljafería and the train station offers excellent value and a friendly environment. Specialties include *verduras de temporada* (vegetables in season), *revuelto de bacalao al ajoarriero* (cod and scrambled eggs), *ventresca de bonito marinada* (marinated tuna belly), and *ternasco al horno de leña* (young lamb roasted in a wood oven). The house wines, usually from Somontano, are of good value and quality. ✉*Av. Madrid 3–5* ☎*976/435839* *AE, DC, MC, V.*

$$$–$$$$ SPANISH **La Bastilla.** In what was once the granary of the Santo Sepulcro convent, with heavy stone battlements from the Roman walls showing here and there around the dining room, this is one of Zaragoza's most polished and gastronomically respected dining establishments. The tasting menu based on black truffle recipes served in winter offers a succession of truffle-studded dishes from foie gras to onion soup to scallop risotto to veal with *moixardinas* (wild mushrooms). The wine list has some interesting Somontano, Ribera de Duero, and Rioja selections. ✉*Coso 177* ☎*976/298449* *Reservations essential* *AE, DC, MC, V.*

$–$$ SPANISH ★ **Los Victorinos.** This rustic tavern heavily adorned with bullfight-related paraphernalia—Victorinos are a much-feared and respected breed of fighting bulls—offers an elaborate and inventive selection of *pinchos* (morsels impaled on toothpicks) and original tapas of all kinds. *Jamón ibérico de bellota* (acorn-fed Iberian pork), Spain's caviar, is always a natural choice for nutty aromas and exquisite taste, but also look for quail eggs and the classic *gilda*—olives, green peppers, and anchovies on a toothpick. Tucked in behind the Seo, this local secret opens at 7:30 every evening. ✉*Calle José de la Hera 6* ☎*976/394213* *AE, DC, MC, V* *No lunch.*

$$–$$$ **Goya.** This slightly threadbare hotel provides a balanced combination of comfort and proximity to the historic sights. No more than a five- to ten-minute walk from the Basílica del Pilar and the Ebro River, the location allows guests to feel they're part of the life of the city. Rooms are modern but neither spacious nor luxurious. **Pros:** central location, good value, relaxed vibe. **Cons:** the facilities and bathrooms are little more than adequate. ✉*Cinco de Marzo 5* ☎*976/229331* 🌐*www.palafoxhoteles.com* *148 rooms* *In-room: refrigerator, Wi-Fi. In-hotel: restaurant, bar, public Wi-Fi, parking (fee)* *AE, DC, MC, V.*

$–$$ **Las Torres.** The rooms are small, but the scenery is hard to beat: you may even be able to admire the domes of La Pilarica from your pillow. If you're a light sleeper, you may need earplugs to muffle the bonging of the bells—they ring every 15 minutes all through the night; interior rooms are much quieter. **Pros:** excellent location on central square of old town, top value in town. **Cons:** rooms on the Pilarica side over the square can be noisy in summer. ✉*Pl. del Pilar 11* ☎*976/394250* 🌐*www.hotellastorres.com* *54 rooms* *In-hotel: parking (fee)* *AE, DC, MC, V.*

$$$–$$$$ **Palafox.** One of Zaragoza's top accommodations, the Palafox combines contemporary design-chic with traditional urban service and elegance. Rooms are equipped with state-of-the-art gadgets, including flat-screen TVs and Jacuzzis. The bathrooms are almost private spas. The restaurant, Aragonia Paradís, holds its own with any place in town, with an excellent wine list and the best Havana cigar collection in Aragón. **Pros:** top comfort and service, bright reception area. **Cons:** modern and somewhat antiseptic. ✉*Marqués Casa Jiménez s/n* ☎*976/237700* 🌐*www.palafoxhoteles.com* *160 rooms* *In-room: refrigerator, Wi-Fi. In-hotel: restaurant, bar, gym, pool, parking (fee)* *AE, DC, MC, V.*

SHOPPING

El Tubo (✉*Cinegio 10* ☎*976/391177*) is Zaragoza's best store for handmade leather boots from all over Spain.

BENASQUE

Fodor's Choice ★

79 km (49 mi) southwest of Vielha.

Benasque, Aragón's easternmost town, has always been an important link between Catalonia and Aragón. This elegant mountain hub of a little more than 1,500 people harbors a number of notable buildings, including the 13th-century Romanesque church of **Santa Maria Mayor** and the ancient, dignified manor houses of the town's old families, such as the **palace of the counts of Ribagorça,** on Calle Mayor, and the **Torre Juste.** Take a walk around and peer into the entryways and patios of these palatial facades, left open just for this purpose.

ESSENTIALS

Visitor Information Benasque (✉*Pl. Mayor 5* ☎*974/551289*).

EXPLORING

Anciles, 2 km (1 mi) south of Benasque, is one of Spain's best-preserved and best-restored medieval villages, a collection of farmhouses and *palacetes* (town houses). The summer classical music series is a superb collision of music and architecture, and the village restaurant, Ansils, combines modern and medieval motifs in both cuisine and design.

OFF THE BEATEN PATH

Pico De Aneto. Benasque is the traditional base camp for excursions to Aneto, which, at 11,168 feet, is the highest peak in the Pyrenees. You can rent crampons and a *piolet* (ice ax) for the two- to three-hour crossing of the Aneto glacier at any sports store in town or at the Refugio de la Renclusa—a way station for mountaineers—an hour's walk above the parking area, which is 17 km (11 mi) north of Benasque, off A139. The trek to the summit and back is not difficult, just long—some 20 km (12 mi) round-trip, with a 1,500-yard vertical ascent. Allow a full 12 hours.

WHERE TO EAT AND STAY

$$–$$$$ SPANISH **Asador Ixarso.** Roast goat or lamb cooked over a raised fireplace in the corner of the dining room is why this place is a fine refuge in chilly weather. The *revuelto de setas* (eggs scrambled with wild mushrooms) is a classic highland specialty, while the salads are varied and refreshing, especially after a morning or afternoon of skiing, hiking, or climbing. The mixed grill is a house favorite, and the opportunity to try whatever game—venison, wild boar, or partridge—on the menu should not be missed. *Calle San Pedro 9 974/552057 AE, DC, MC, V Closed weekdays mid-Sept.–1st wk in Dec. and Easter–June.*

$$–$$$$ SPANISH **Restaurante Ansils.** This rustic spot near Anciles on the Benasque-Anciles road is ingeniously designed in glass, wood, and stone, and specializes in local benasqués and Aragonese dishes, such as *civet de jabalí* (wild-boar stew) and *recau* (a thick vegetable broth). *Estofada de perdiz* (partridge stew) is a perennial house favorite. Sometimes closed on unexpected weekdays and out of season, check before you go. Memorable and multitudinous holiday meals are served on Christmas and Easter; reserve well in advance. *Calle Gral. Ferraz 13, Anciles 974/551150 AE, DC, MC, V Closed weekdays Oct.–June.*

$–$$ **Gran Hotel Benasque.** This spacious, modern hotel within walking distance from Benasque is bracketed by the highest crests in the Pyrenees (Aneto and Posets) and serves as an impeccably comfortable base for exploring them. The restaurant's mountain fare ($$–$$$) includes *sopa Benasquesa* (a thick highland stew) and *crepas Aneto* (crepes with ham, wild mushroom, and béchamel sauce). **Pros:** bucolic setting just outside of town, easy access to lovely village of Ansils. **Cons:** modern building with more efficiency than charm, characterless room decor. *Ctra. de Anciles s/n 974/551011 www.hoteles-valero.com 69 rooms In-room: refrigerator, Wi-Fi. In-hotel: restaurant, bar, pools, gym AE, MC, V Closed Nov.*

$–$$ **Hospital de Benasque.** About 13 km (8 mi) north of Benasque off the A139 road, this mountain retreat is an ideal base camp for hiking and cross-country skiing. Constructed and furnished in stone and wood, rooms are simple, with clean lines. The restaurant ($$–$$$) serves classical Pyrenean fare in a glassed-in dining room flooded with natural light. **Pros:** lovely location in a wide meadow surrounded by peaks, literally a breath of fresh air. **Cons:** rooms are spartan, can get hot on summer days. *Camino Real de Francia s/n 974/552012 www.llanosdelhospital.com 57 rooms In-room: no a/c, Wi-Fi. In-hotel: restaurant, bar, parking (no fee) AE, DC, MC, V.*

SPORTS AND THE OUTDOORS

The **Cerler ski area** (*974/551012 www.cerler.com*), 6 km (4 mi) east of Benasque on the Cerler road, covers the slopes of the Cogulla peak. Built on a shelf over the valley at an altitude of 5,051 feet, Cerler has 26 ski runs, three lifts, and a guided helicopter service to drop you at the highest peaks. The outfitter **Danica Guías de Pesca** (*974/553493 or 659/735376 www.danicaguias.com*) can show you the top spots and techniques for Pyrenean fly-fishing.

AÍNSA

66 km (41 mi) southwest of Benasque.

Aínsa's arcaded Plaza Mayor and old town are classic examples of medieval village design, with heavy stone archways and tiny windows.

ESSENTIALS

Visitor Information Aínsa (✉ *Av. Pirenaica 1* ☎ *974/500767*).

EXPLORING

The 12th-century Romanesque church of **Santa María** has a quadruple-vaulted door. ✉ *Old Quarter* *Free* *Daily 9–2 and 4–8.*

WHERE TO EAT AND STAY

$$–$$$$ SPANISH ✕ **Bodegas del Sobrarbe.** Lamb and suckling pig or kid roasted in a wood oven are among the specialties at this excellent restaurant built into an 11th-century wine cellar. The setting is medieval, with vaulted ceilings made of heavy wood and stone. After the welcoming bar at the entrance, a succession of small dining rooms under arches gives a sense of privacy. The tables are decorated with hand-crafted ceramic tiles from Teruel, and the reigning ambience is ancient and mountain rustic. ✉ *Pl. Mayor 2* ☎ *974/500237* *AE, DC, MC, V* *Closed Jan. and Feb.*

¢–$ **Casa Cambra.** A once-abandoned village between Barbastro and Aínsa is home to this little inn, a perfect base for hiking and mountain sports of all kinds. The restored 18th-century town house of stone and timber has rooms for two to four people and is part of a tourist complex that includes a restaurant and a variety of lodging arrangements. **Pros:** rural tourism in a pretty setting, family-run intimate accommodation. **Cons:** close quarters and thin walls in some rooms can be detrimental to privacy. ✉ *Ctra. Barbastro–Aínsa, A138, Km 41.8, Morillo de Tou* ☎ *974/500793* *www.morillodetou.com* *17 rooms* *In-room: no a/c, no TV* *MC, V.*

SAN JUAN DE PLAN AND THE GISTAÍN VALLEY

14 km (8 mi) east of Salinas.

This detour begins with a well-marked road heading east of Salinas, 25 km (15 mi) north of Aínsa. The Cinqueta River drains the Gistaín Valley, flowing by or through the mountain villages of Sin, Señes, Saravillo, Serveta, and Salinas. The town of San Juan de Plan presides at the head of the valley, where an ethnographic museum, a water-powered sawmill, and an early-music and dance ensemble are the pride of the region. The mid-February carnival is among the most distinct and traditional celebrations in the Pyrenees.

ESSENTIALS

Visitor Information Plan (✉ *Calle Capilleta* ☎ *974/506400*).

EXPLORING

The **Museo Etnográfico** is a fascinating glimpse into a traditional way of life (dress, kitchen utensils, bedclothes, field tools) that endured largely intact until about 1975. ✉ *Pl. Mayor s/n* ☎ *974/506052* *€3.50* *Daily 9–2 and 4–8.*

WHERE TO STAY

¢–$ ★ **Casa la Plaza.** Josefina Loste's pleasant country inn has rustic, cozy rooms with antique furniture and sloping ceilings—each is tucked into and under the eaves in a different way. The restaurant ($–$$$) serves excellent local dishes using fresh mountain products prepared lovingly, using traditional recipes in inventive ways. **Pros:** charming decor and sense of authentic Pyrenean village life, excellent fare at the hotel restaurant. **Cons:** rooms are not very spacious and can feel slightly cluttered. ✉ *Pl. Mayor s/n* ☎ *974/506052* *13 rooms* *In-room: no a/c* ▭ *AE, DC, MC, V* ⊙ *Closed sporadically Oct.–May; call to confirm.*

BIELSA

34 km (21 mi) northeast of Aínsa.

Bielsa, at the confluence of the Cinca and Barrosa rivers, is a busy summer resort with some lovely mountain architecture and an ancient, porticoed town hall. Northwest of Bielsa the **Monte Perdido glacier** and the icy **Marboré Lake** drain into the **Pineta Valley** and the Pineta Reservoir. You can take three- or four-hour walks from the parador up to Larri, Munia, or Marboré Lake among remote peaks.

6

ESSENTIALS

Visitor Information Bielsa (✉ *Pl. Mayor s/n* ☎ *974/501127*).

WHERE TO EAT AND STAY

¢–$ ★ **Hotel Valle de Pineta.** This corner castle overlooking the river junction is the most spectacular nest and refuge in town. The restaurant ($$–$$$), offering classic Aragonese and Pyrenean fare, is excellent and the views superb. Try for the top corner room, which perches above and looks across both the Pineta and Cinca valleys. **Pros:** central location in the village center, family service. **Cons:** upper rooms are cozy but tiny, it gets hot if the wind dies down during the hottest part of summer. ✉ *Calle Baja s/n* ☎ *974/501010* ⊕ *www.hotelvalledepineta.com* *26 rooms* *In-room: no a/c, Wi-Fi. In-hotel: restaurant, bar, pool* ▭ *AE, DC, MC, V* ⊙ *Closed Nov., Jan., and Feb.*

$$–$$$ **Parador de Bielsa.** Glass, steel, and stone define this modern structure overlooking the national park, the peak of Monte Perdido, and the source of the Cinca River. Rooms are done in bright wood, but the best part is the proximity to the park and the views. The restaurant ($$–$$$) specializes in Aragonese mountain dishes, such as *pucherete de Parzán* (a stew with beans, sausage, and vegetables). **Pros:** surrounded by nature in complete comfort, views of the highest peaks in the Pyrenees, country cooking. **Cons:** parador service as usual, a little chilly literally due to the thin air at 4,455 feet above sea level. ✉ *Ctra. Valle de Pineta s/n* ☎ *974/501011* ⊕ *www.parador.es* *39 rooms* *In-room: no a/c, Wi-Fi. In-hotel: restaurant, bar* ▭ *AE, DC, MC, V.*

EN ROUTE

You can explore the **Valle del Cinca** from the river's source at the head of the valley above Bielsa. From Bielsa, drive back down to Aínsa and turn west on N260 (alternately marked C138) for Broto.

PARQUE NACIONAL DE ORDESA Y MONTE PERDIDO

Fodor'sChoice ★ *108 km (67 mi) west of Bielsa; from Aínsa, turn west on N260 for the 53-km (33-mi) drive to Torla (park entrance).*

ESSENTIALS

Visitor Information Torla (✉ *C. Fatás s/n* ☎ *974/486378*).

EXPLORING

Ordesa and Monte Perdido National Park is one of Spain's great but often overlooked wonders; some consider it a junior version of North America's Grand Canyon. The entrance lies under the vertical walls of Monte Mondarruego, source of the Ara River and its tributary, the Arazas, which forms the famous Ordesa Valley. The park was founded by royal decree in 1918 to protect the natural integrity of the Central Pyrenees, and it has expanded from 4,940 to 56,810 acres as provincial and national authorities have added the Monte Perdido massif, the head of the Pineta Valley, and the Escuain and Añisclo canyons. Defined by the Ara and Arazas rivers, the Ordesa Valley is endowed with pine, fir, larch, beech, and poplar forests; lakes, waterfalls, and high mountain meadows; and protected wildlife, including trout, boar, chamois, and the *Capra pyrenaica* mountain goat.

Well-marked and well-maintained mountain trails lead to waterfalls, caves, and spectacular observation points. The standard tour, a full day's hike (eight hours), runs from the parking area in the Pradera de Ordesa, 8 km (5 mi) northeast of Torla, up the Arazas River, past the *gradas de Soaso* (Soaso risers; a natural stairway of waterfalls) to the *cola de caballo* (horse's tail), a lovely fan of falling water at the head of the Cirque de Cotatuero, a sort of natural amphitheater. A return walk on the south side of the valley, past the Refugio de los Cazadores (hunters' hut), offers a breathtaking view followed by a two-hour descent back to the parking area. A few spots, although not technically difficult, may seem precarious. Information and guidebooks are available at the booth on your way into the park at Pradera de Ordesa. The best time to come is May to mid-November, but check conditions with regional tourist offices before driving into a blizzard in May or missing out on *el veranillo de San Martín* ("Indian summer") in fall. ☎ *974/243361 Pradera de Ordesa information office* 🌐 *www.mma.es* 🎫 *Free.*

EN ROUTE

Broto is a prototypical Aragonese mountain town with an excellent 16th-century Gothic church. Nearby villages, such as **Oto,** have stately manor houses with classic local features: baronial entryways, conical chimneys, and wooden galleries. **Torla** is the park's entry point and a popular base camp for hikers.

WHERE TO EAT AND STAY

$–$$ SPANISH ✕ **El Rebeco.** In this graceful, rustic building in the upper part of town, the dining rooms are lined with historic photographs of Torla during the 19th and 20th centuries. The black marble-and-stone floor and the *cadiera*—a traditional open fireplace room with an overhead smoke vent—are extraordinary original elements of Pyrenean architecture. In late fall and winter, *civets* (stews) of deer, boar, and mountain goat are the order of the day. In summer, lighter fare and hearty mountain soups restore hikers between treks. ✉ *Calle Lafuente 55, Torla* ☎ *974/486068* ▭ *AE, DC, MC, V* ⊗ *Closed Dec.–Easter.*

$ **Villa de Torla.** This classic mountain refuge has rooms of various shapes and sizes, all with typical Pyrenean details dominated by fresh wood paneling and trim and stone floors. Sun decks, terraces, and a private dining room make it easy to forget that "Spain's Grand Canyon" is just a few minutes up the valley. **Pros:** in the middle of a postcard-perfect Pyrenean village, helpful staff. **Cons:** rooms on the street side can be noisy on weekends and summer nights. ✉ *Pl. Aragón 1* ☎ *974/486156* ⊕ *www.hotelvilladetorla.com* *38 rooms* *In-room: Wi-Fi. In-hotel: restaurant, bar, pool, parking* ▭ *AE, DC, MC, V.*

EN ROUTE

Follow N260 (sometimes marked C140) west over the Cotefablo Pass from Torla to Biescas. This route winds interminably through the pine forest leading up to and down from the pass; expect it to take five times longer than it looks like it should on a map.

PANTICOSA AND THE TENA VALLEY

6

40 km (25 mi) northwest of Ordesa.

The Valle de Tena, a north–south hexagon of 400 square km (154 square mi), is formed by the Gállego River and its tributaries, principally the Aguaslimpias and the Caldares. A glacial valley surrounded by peaks rising to more than 10,000 feet (such as the 10,900-foot Vignemale), Tena is a busy hiking and winter-sports center.

ESSENTIALS

Visitor Information Panticosa (✉ *C. San Miguel 37* ☎ *974/487318*).

EXPLORING

Sallent de Gállego, at the head of the valley, has long been a jumping-off point for excursions to **Aguaslimpias, Piedrafita,** and the meadows of the Gállego headwaters at **El Formigal** (a major ski area) and **Portalet.** The lovely Pyrenean *ibon* (glacial lake) of **Respumoso** is accessible by a 2½-hour walk above the old road from Sallent to Formigal. The villages lining the valley are each unique, with Tramacastilla, Escarrilla, and Piedrafita especially representative of ancient Pyrenean village architecture. **Lanuza,** a ghost town since the reservoir built in 1975 flooded half the village, comes alive every July when a floating stage hosts performers in the Pirineos Sur music festival.

WHERE TO EAT AND STAY

$–$$ SPANISH **Mesón Sampietro.** This cozy tavern and restaurant, a family spot not far from Panticosa's quirky and lovely church, bustles and booms after the skiing or hiking day comes to a close. The house specialty, potatoes in olive oil, garlic, parsley, and vinegar, is an Aragonese favorite not to be missed. Take a seat at one of the traditional *susulia* benches—they have little fold-down tables between the two seats, making them perfect for warm winter dinners for two in front of a roaring fire. ✉ *C. La Parra 5* ☎ *974/487244* ▭ *AE, DC, MC, V.*

$$$$ **Gran Hotel.** The most complete comfort available in Panticosa, this modern hotel with a palatial facade in the former thermal spa zone above town is a perfect base camp for hiking and skiing. Oak floors,

along with marble paving in the bathrooms, set the tone for this lovingly restored mountain resort complex that ranks as one of the best in the Pyrenees. **Pros:** impeccable service and infrastructure, spectacular views into the mountains. **Cons:** not really part of the Panticosa ski scene, far from restaurants and town nightlife. ✉*Balneario de Panticosa, Panticosa* ☎*974/487616* 🌐*www.panticosa.com* *38 rooms, 4 suites* *In-room: Wi-Fi. In-hotel: restaurant, spa* 💳*AE, DC, MC, V.*

¢–$ **Hotel Vicente.** Rooms here are simple but clean and comfortable, and look south over the town to Panticosa's ski area and the jagged peaks of the Sierra de Tendeñera mountains beyond. The lower access to the hotel spills directly down into town, a five-minute walk from the gondola station up to the ski area. **Pros:** good value, pretty views over the old part of town, two minutes from the Mesón Sampietro and Panticosa's restaurants and taverns. **Cons:** room decor is somewhat stark, facilities are minimal. ✉*Ctra. del Balneario 12, Panticosa* ☎*974/487022* 🌐*www.hotelvicente.com* *16 rooms* *In-room: no a/c, no TV, Wi-Fi. In-hotel: restaurant* 💳*AE, DC, MC, V.*

JACA

24 km (15 mi) southwest of Biescas; down the Tena Valley through Biescas, a westward turn at Sabiñánigo onto N330 leaves a 14-km (9-mi) drive to Jaca.

Jaca, the most important municipal center in Alto Aragón (with a population of more than 12,000), is anything but sleepy. Bursting with ambition and blessed with the natural resources and first-rate facilities to express their relentless drive, Jacetanos are determined to make their city the site of a Winter Olympics someday. Founded in 1035 as the kingdom of Jacetania, Jaca was an important stronghold during the Christian Reconquest of the Iberian Peninsula and proudly claims never to have bowed to the Moorish invaders. Indeed, the town still commemorates, on the first Friday of May, the decisive battle in which the appearance of a battalion of women, their hair and jewelry flashing in the sun, so intimidated the Moorish cavalry that they beat a headlong retreat.

ESSENTIALS

Visitor Information Jaca (✉*Pl. San Pedro 11–13* ☎*974/360098*).

EXPLORING

An important stop on the pilgrimage to Santiago de Compostela, Jaca has the 11th-century **Catedral de Santa María,** one of the oldest in Spain. The **Museo Diocesano,** near the cloisters, is filled with excellent Romanesque and Gothic murals and artifacts. ☎*974/356378 Museo* *€5* *June–Sept., Tues.–Sun. 10–2 and 4–8; Oct.–May, Tues.–Sun. 11–1:30 and 4–7.*

The door to Jaca's **ayuntamiento** *(town hall)* (✉*Calle Mayor 24* ☎*974/355758*) has a notable Renaissance design. The massive **Ciudadella** *(Citadel)* is a good example of 17th-century military architecture. It has a display of thousands of military miniatures. ✉*Av.*

Primer Viernes de Mayo s/n ☎974/363018 €5 Daily 11–noon and 4–6.

NEED A BREAK?

One of Jaca's most emblematic restaurants is La Campanilla (✉ *Escuelas Pías 822700*), behind the *ayuntamiento*. The baked potatoes with garlic and olive oil are an institution, unchanged for as long as anyone can remember.

In summer a free guided tour departs from the local RENFE station, covering the valley and the mammoth belle epoque railroad station at **Canfranc,** surely the largest and most ornate building in the Pyrenees, soon to open as a new luxury hotel. The train ticket costs €3.50; ask the tourist office for schedules.

WHERE TO EAT AND STAY

¢–$$ SPANISH ★ **El Fau.** Tucked in next to the cathedral, El Fau overlooks Jaca's finest carved capitals and serves excellent *cazuelitas,* small earthenware casseroles containing anything from piping-hot garlic shrimp to wild mushrooms to small portions of *civet de jabalí* (wild boar stew). In summer the cold beer here is the stuff of legends, and the terrace fills with locals and travelers replenishing forces after hiking and climbing excursions. A pre-dinner, pre-nightlife stop ideal for connecting with old friends or making new ones, this is the town clearinghouse for party recruitment. ✉ *Pl. de la Catedral* ☎ *974/361719* *AE, DC, MC, V* *Closed Mon.*

$$–$$$$ SPANISH **La Cocina Aragonesa.** This Jaca mainstay in the Hotel Conde Aznar is an elegant, rustic space decorated with local farming and mountaineering objects and centered around a mammoth fireplace. The Aragonese-Basque cuisine here is justly famous around town and beyond for constantly changing, fresh and innovative creations, especially game in season: venison, wild boar, partridge, and duck. Try the *perdiz roja estofada con foie* (redleg partridge stuffed with foie gras) or the *cebollitas glaseadas y trufa negra* (glazed baby onions with black truffles). ✉ *Cervantes 5* ☎ *974/361050* *AE, DC, MC, V* *Closed Nov. 15–30 and Wed. June–Sept.*

$–$$$ SPANISH **La Tasca de Ana.** Ana's *tasca* (tavern) is one of Jaca's simplest and best for lamb or beef cooked over coals and a hefty repertoire of satisfying highland cooking. Nearly anyone in town will send you here for superb tapas of every kind. Invent your own meal by starting with a round of olives and working through, say, cured *jamón ibérico de bellota* (acorn-fed Iberian ham), *sepia* (cuttlefish), *albóndigas* (meatballs), and *civet de jabalí* (wild-boar stew), concluding with the famous sheep cheese from the neighboring Roncal Valley. ✉ *Pl. Ramiro I 3* ☎ *974/363621* *AE, DC, MC, V* *Closed Mon.*

$–$$ **Gran Hotel.** This rambling hotel, Jaca's traditional official clubhouse, is central to life, sports, and tourism in this Pyrenean hub. A mid-20th-century structure made of wood, stone, and glass, the complex includes a garden and a separate dining wing with a restaurant serving creditable Aragonese cuisine. The streamlined and comfortable rooms have rich colors and practical wood furniture. **Pros:** quiet location just west of the town center, professional and polished service. **Cons:** modern and functional construction with no special charm or Pyrenean ambience, neo-motel-room decor. ✉ *Paseo de la Constitución 1* ☎ *974/360900* *www.inturmark.es* *165 rooms* *In-room: Wi-Fi. In-hotel: restaurant, pool* *AE, DC, MC, V.*

¢–$ **Hotel Mur.** A simple but sound lodging option in the middle of Jaca, this hotel offers traditional highland decor, a helpful staff, and a central location from which to cruise the après-ski scene. The restaurant serves Pyrenean and Aragonese cooking at excellent prices, especially on weekdays when the *menu del peregrino* (pilgrims' menu) offers *boliches de Embún* (particularly prized white beans from the mountain town of Embún) stewed in sausage, or the classic Aragonese *migas de pastor* (shepherd's breadcrumbs). **Pros:** great location, friendly family management. **Cons:** tight quarters in some of the smaller rooms, street noise in exterior rooms on weekends. *Santa Orosia 1* *974/360100* *www.hotelmur.com* *72 rooms* *In-room: no a/c, Wi-Fi. In-hotel: restaurant* *AE, DC, MC, V.*

NIGHTLIFE

Discos such as Santa Locura and La Trampa throng with skiers and hockey players in season (October–April), but the main nocturnal attractions are Jaca's so-called *bares musicales* (music bars), usually less loud and smoky than the discos. Most of these are in the old town, in Calle Ramiro I and along Calle Gil Bergés and Calle Bellido.

SPORTS AND THE OUTDOORS

The **ski areas** of Candanchú and Astún are 32 km (20 mi) north of Jaca, on the road to Somport and the French border.

THE WESTERN AND BASQUE PYRENEES

The Aragüés, Hecho, and Ansó valleys, drained by the Estarrún, Osia, Veral, and Aragón Subordán rivers, are the westernmost valleys in Aragón and rank among the most pristine parts of the Pyrenees. Today these sleepy hollows are struggling to generate an economy that will save this endangered species of Pyrenean life. With cross-country (Nordic) skiing only, they are less frequented by tourists. As you move west into the Roncal Valley and the Basque Country, you will note smoother hills and softer meadows as the rocky central Pyrenees of Aragón begin to descend toward the Bay of Biscay. These wet and fertile uplands and verdant beech forests seem reflected in the wide lines and flat profiles of the Basque *caseríos* (farmhouses) hulking firmly into the landscape. The Basque highlands of Navarra from Roncal through the Irati Forest to Roncesvalles, and along the Bidasoa River leading down to the Bay of Biscay all seem like some Arcadian paradise with as the jagged Pyrenean peaks give way to sheep-filled pasturelands.

GETTING HERE

To get to the westernmost Pyrenean valleys in Aragón from Jaca, head west on N240 for 20 km (12 mi), take a hard right at Puente de la Reina (after turning right to cross the bridge), and continue north along the Aragón-Subordán River. The first right after 15 km (9 mi) leads into the Aragüés Valley along the Osia River to Aisa and then Jasa.

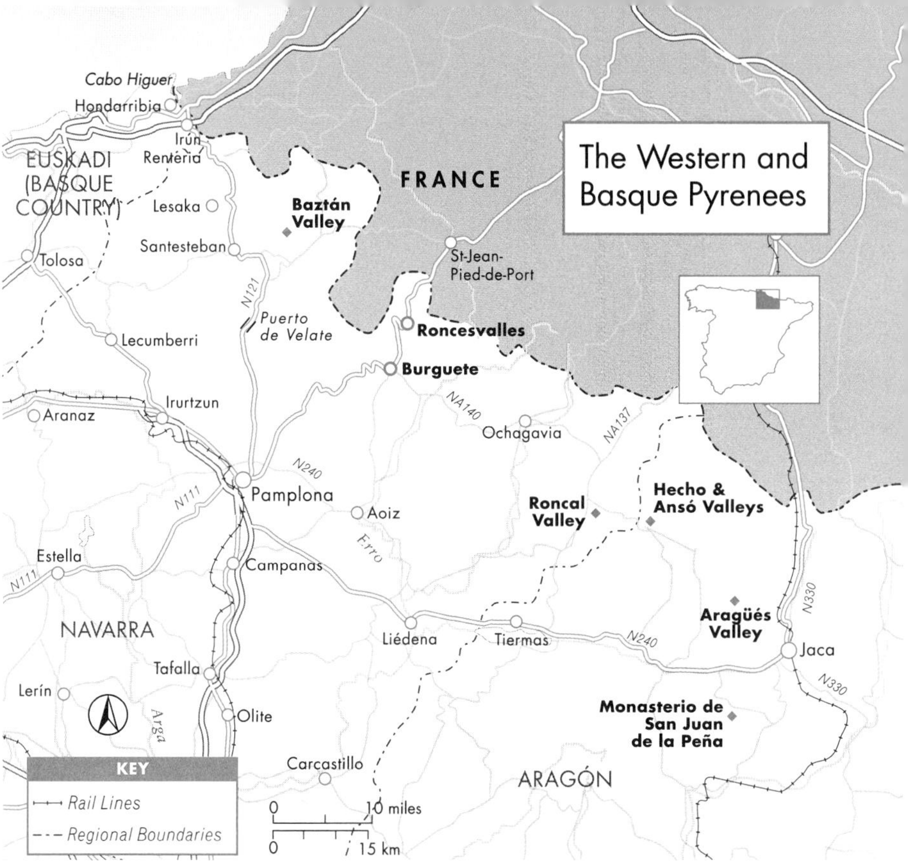

MONASTERIO DE SAN JUAN DE LA PEÑA

★ *22 km (14 mi) southwest of Jaca.*

South of the Aragonese valleys of Hecho and Ansó is the Monastery of San Juan de la Peña, a site connected to the legend of the Holy Grail and another "cradle" of Christian resistance during the 700-year Moorish occupation of Spain. Its origins can be traced to the 9th century, when a hermit monk named Juan settled here on the *peña* (cliff). A monastery was founded on the spot in 920, and in 1071 Sancho Ramirez, son of King Ramiro I, made use of this structure, which was built into the mountain's rock wall, to found the Benedictine Monasterio de San Juan de la Peña. The **cloister,** tucked under the cliff, dates from the 12th century and contains intricately carved capitals depicting biblical scenes. From Jaca, drive 11 km (7 mi) west on N240 toward Pamplona to a left turn clearly signposted for San Juan de la Peña. From there it's another 11 km (7 mi) to the monastery. ✉ *Off N240* ☎ *974/355119* 🌐 *www.monasteriosanjuan.com* 🎫 *€12* ⏲ *Oct.–mid-Mar., Tues.–Sun. 11–1:30 and 4–5:30; mid-Mar.–May, Tues.–Sun. 10–1:30 and 4–7; June–Sept., daily 10–noon and 4–8.*

ARAGÜÉS VALLEY

Aragüés del Puerto is 2 km (1 mi) from Jasa.

ESSENTIALS

Visitor Information Ayuntamiento: Aragüés del Puerto (✉ *Pl. Mayor 1* ☎ *974/371447*).

EXPLORING

Aragüés del Puerto is a tidy mountain village with stone houses and lovely little corners, doorways, and porticoes. The distinctive folk dance in Aragüés is the *palotiau,* a variation of the *jota* performed only in this village. The **Museo Etnográfico** *(Ethnographic Museum)*, in an ancient chapel in Aragüés del Puerto (ask for the caretaker at the town hall), offers a look into the past, from the document witnessing the 878 election of Iñigo Arista as king of Pamplona to the quirky manual wheat grinder. At the source of the River Osia, the Lizara **cross-country ski area** is in a flat expanse between the Aragüés and Jasa valleys. Look for 3,000-year-old megalithic dolmens sprinkled across the flat.

HECHO AND ANSÓ VALLEYS

Hecho Valley is 49 km (30 mi) northwest of Jaca; Ansó Valley is 25 km (15 mi) west of Hecho.

GETTING HERE AND AROUND

You can reach the Valle de Hecho from the Aragüés Valley by returning to the valley of the Aragón-Subordan and turning north again on the A176.

ESSENTIALS

Visitor Information Hecho (✉ *Pallar d'Agustín* ☎ *974/375505*).

EXPLORING

The **Monasterio de San Pedro de Siresa,** above the town of Hecho, is the area's most important monument, a 9th-century retreat of which only the 11th-century church remains. *Cheso,* a medieval Aragonese dialect descended from the Latin spoken by the Siresa monks, is thought to be the closest to Latin of all Romance languages and dialects. Cheso has been kept alive in the Hecho Valley, especially in the works of the poet Veremundo Mendez Coarasa. ✉ *Calle San Pedro, Siresa* 🎫 *Free* ⏲ *July and Aug., daily 11–1 and 5–8; other months, call the Ayuntamiento de Siresa (☎ 974/375002) for key.*

The **Selva de Oza** *(Oza Forest)*, at the head of the Hecho Valley, is above the **Boca del Infierno** (Mouth of Hell), a tight draw where road and river barely squeeze through. Beyond the Oza Forest is a **Roman road** used before the 4th century to reach France through the Puerto del Palo—one of the oldest routes across the border on the pilgrimage to Santiago de Compostela.

The **Valle de Ansó** is Aragón's western limit. Rich in fauna (mountain goats, wild boar, and even a bear or two), the Ansó Valley follows the Veral River up to Zuriza. The three **cross-country ski areas** above Zuriza are known as the Pistas de Linza. Near Fago is the sanctuary of the **Virgen de Puyeta,** patron saint of the valley. Towering over the head of the valley is Navarra's highest point, the 7,989-foot **Mesa de los Tres Reyes** *(Plateau of the Three Kings)*, named not for the Magi but for the kings of Aragón, Navarra, and Castile, whose 11th-century kingdoms all came to a corner here—allowing them to meet without leaving their respective realms. Try to be in the town of **Ansó** on the last Sunday in August, when residents dress in their traditional medieval costumes and perform ancestral dances of great grace and dignity.

WHERE TO EAT AND STAY

¢ **Gaby-Casa Blasquico.** This cozy inn, famed as Hecho's top restaurant ($$–$$$), is known for its Aragonese mountain cuisine. Especially strong on game recipes, the menu also has superb Pyrenean lamb and vegetable dishes. Make sure you call ahead to reserve: Gaby often opens for anyone who reserves in advance, even if the place is theoretically closed. **Pros:** cozy mountain chalet with flowered balconies, the two cute dormered rooms, fine mountain cuisine. **Cons:** rooms lack space, public rooms cluttered with memorabilia. ✉ *Pl. Palacio 1, Hecho* ☎ *974/375007* 🌐 *www.casablasquico.com* *Reservations essential* *6 rooms* *In-room: Wi-Fi, no a/c. In-hotel: restaurant, Wi-Fi, public Internet* *MC, V* *Closed 1st 2 wks in Sept.; restaurant closed weekdays Sept.–Holy Week.*

$ **Usón.** For a base camp for exploring the upper Hecho Valley or the Oza Forest, look no further. The staff at this friendly little Pyrenean inn will tell you where to rent a bike, get you a trout-fishing permit, or send you off in the right direction for a climb or hike. Rooms are simple and airy, decorated with colorful fabrics and quilts. The hotel, equipped with solar panels, generates its own energy. **Pros:** friendly service, great value, stunning views into the mountains. **Cons:** no elevator, remote setting. ✉ *Ctra. Selva de Oza, HU2131, Km 7, Usón* ☎ *974/375358* 🌐 *www.hoteluson.com* *14 rooms* *In-room: Wi-Fi, no a/c. In-hotel: restaurant, public Internet, no elevator* *MC, V* *Closed Nov. 2–Mar. 15.*

EN ROUTE

From Ansó, head west to Roncal on the narrow and winding but panoramic 17½-km (11-mi) road through the Sierra de San Miguel. To enjoy this route fully, count on taking a good 45 minutes to reach the Esca River and the Valle de Roncal.

RONCAL VALLEY

17 km (11 mi) west of Ansó Valley.

The Roncal Valley, the eastern edge of the Basque Pyrenees, is famous for its sheep's-milk cheese, Roncal, and as the birthplace of Julián Gayarre (1844–90), the leading tenor of his time. The 34-km (21-mi) drive through the towns of **Burgui** and **Roncal** to **Isaba** winds through green hillsides and Basque *caseríos*, classical Basque farmhouses covered by long, sloping roofs designed to house animals on the ground floor and the family up above, in order to take advantage of the body heat of the livestock. Burgui's red-tile roofs backed by rolling pastures contrast with the vertical rock and steep slate roofs of the Aragonese and Catalan Pyrenees; Isaba's wide-arched bridge across the Esca is a graceful reminder of Roman aesthetics and engineering techniques.

GETTING HERE

To get to the valley from Jaca, take N240 west along the Aragón River; a right turn north on NA137 follows the Esca River from the head of the Yesa Reservoir up the Roncal Valley.

ESSENTIALS

Visitor Information **Roncal** (✉ *C. Iriartea s/n* ☎ *948/475256*).

EXPLORING

Try to be in the Roncal Valley for **El Tributo de las Tres Vacas** *(the Tribute of the Three Cows)*, which has been celebrated every July 13 since 1375. The mayors of the valley's villages, dressed in traditional gowns, gather near the summit of San Martín to receive the symbolic payment of three cows from their French counterparts, in memory of the settlement of ancient border disputes. Feasting and celebrating follow.

The road west (NA140) to **Ochagavia** through the Puerto de Lazar (Lazar Pass) has views of the Anie and Orhi peaks, towering over the French border. Two kilometers (1 mi) south of Ochagavia, at Escároz, a small secondary roadway winds 22 km (14 mi) over the Abaurrea heights to **Aribe,** known for its triple-arched medieval bridge and ancient *horreo* (granary). A 15-km (9-mi) detour north through the town of Orbaiceta up to the headwaters of the Irati River, at the Irabia Reservoir, gets you a good look at the **Selva de Irati** *(Irati Forest)*, one of Europe's major beech forests and the source of much of the timber for the fleet Spain commanded during her 15th-century golden age.

RONCESVALLES (ORREAGA)

★ *2½ km (1½ mi) north of Burguete, 48 km (30 mi) north of Pamplona, 64 km (40 mi) northwest of Isaba in the Roncal Valley.*

Roncesvalles (often listed as Orreaga, in Euskera) is the site of the Colegiata, cloister, hospital, and 12th-century **chapel of Santiago,** the first Navarran church on the Santiago pilgrimage route.

ESSENTIALS

Visitor Information **Orreaga-Roncesvalles** (✉ *C. Única s/n* ☎ *948/760301*).

EXPLORING

The **Colegiata** (*Collegiate Church* ✉ *Ctra. Pamplona–Francia [N135], KM 48* 🌐 *www.roncesvalles.es*), built at the orders of King Sancho VII el Fuerte (the Strong), houses the king's tomb, which measures more than 7 feet long. The 3,468-foot **Ibañeta Pass,** above Roncesvalles, is a gorgeous route into France. A **menhir** (monolith) marks the traditional site of the legendary battle in *The Song of Roland* in which Roland fell after calling for help on his ivory battle horn. The well-marked eight-hour walk to or from St-Jean-Pied-de-Port (which does *not* follow the road) is one of the most beautiful and dramatic sections of the pilgrimage.

BURGUETE (AURITZ)

2 km (1 mi) south of Roncesvalles, 120 km (75 mi) northwest of Jaca.

Burguete (Auritz in Euskera) lies between two mountain streams forming the headwaters of the Urobi River. The town was immortalized in Ernest Hemingway's *The Sun Also Rises,* with its evocative description of trout fishing in an ice-cold stream above a Navarran village.

ESSENTIALS

Visitor Information Ochagavia (*C. Labaria 25 948/890641*).

WHERE TO EAT AND STAY

$ **Hostal Burguete.** In his 1926 novel *The Sun Also Rises*, Hemingway's character Jake Barnes spends time here clearing his head before plunging back into the psychodrama of the San Fermín Festival and his impossible passion for Lady Brett Ashley. The inn still works for this sort of thing, though there don't seem to be as many trout around these days. Good value and simple Navarran cooking ($–$$$) make this stalwart Basque town house a good stop. You might even be able to sleep in Hemingway's bed, his room is kept exactly as it was when the novelist bunked here in 1924. **Pros:** sense of excitement for Hemingway fans, good value. **Cons:** room decor is stark, beds may actually be from the 1920s. *Calle Única 51 948/760005 948/790488 22 rooms In-room: no a/c. In-hotel: restaurant, no elevator AE, DC, MC, V Closed Feb. and Mar.*

6

EN ROUTE

To skip Pamplona and stay on the trans-Pyrenean route, continue 21 km (13 mi) southwest of Burguete on NA135 until you reach NA138, just before Zubiri. A right turn takes you to Urtasun, where the small NA252 leads left to the town of Iragui and over the pass at Col d'Egozkue (from which there are superb views over the Arga and Ultzana River valleys) to Olagüe, where it connects with NA121 some 20 km (12 mi) north of Pamplona. Turn right onto N121A and climb over the Puerto de Velate (Velate Pass)—or, in bad weather or a hurry, through the tunnel—to the turn for Elizondo and the Baztán Valley, N121B. (Take a good map if you're setting off into the hills.)

BAZTÁN VALLEY

80 km (50 mi) north of Pamplona.

Tucked neatly over the headwaters of the Bidasoa River, under the peak of the 3,545-foot Garramendi Mountain, which looms over the border with France, the rounded green hills of the Valle de Baztán make an ideal halfway stop between the central Pyrenees and the Atlantic. Each village in this enchanted Basque valley seems smaller and simpler than the next: tiny clusters of whitewashed, stone-and-mortar houses with red-tile roofs group around a central *frontón* (handball court).

ESSENTIALS

Visitor Information Elizondo (*Palacio de Arizkunenea 948/581279*).

WHERE TO EAT AND STAY

$–$$ SPANISH ★ **Galarza.** The kitchen in this small but stalwart stone town house overlooking the trout-infested Baztán River turns out excellent Basque fare, with a Navarran emphasis on vegetables. Try the *txuritabel* (roast lamb with a special stuffing of egg and vegetables), which is best in the spring (though available year-round), or *txuleta de ternera* (grass-fed veal raised in the valley), good any time of year. *Rape con hongos* (monkfish with wild mushrooms) is another favorite here; the desserts feature delicious homemade *cuajada* (custard). *Calle Santiago 1, Elizondo 948/580101 MC, V Closed late Sept.–early Oct.*

¢ ★ **Fonda Etxeberria.** In an old farmhouse with creaky floorboards and ancient oak doors, this tiny *caserío* (Basque farmhouse) inn has small, handsome rooms. The palatial bathrooms are shared by guests (usually one bathroom per two to three rooms). The restaurant ($–$$) prepares simple country dishes such as *alubias de Navarra estofadas* (Navarran white beans stewed with chorizo), *trucha a la Navarra* (sautéed and stuffed with ham), and roast lamb. **Pros:** an authentic Basque farmhouse in a remote Pyrenean village, friendly family service. **Cons:** rooms have squeaky beds and floorboards, shared baths. *Kalea Antxitonea Trinketea (next to frontón court) s/n Arizkun 948/453013 948/453433 16 rooms without bath In-room: no a/c, no TV. In-hotel: restaurant, no elevator MC, V.*

Barcelona

The mid-19th century arcaded square Plaça Reial

WORD OF MOUTH

"I think I fell in love with Barcelona at first sight. It's cosmopolitan, urban, quaint, vibrant, full of hidden corners and sights…something new and exciting behind each corner . . . the architectural mix of modern, modernisme, and old. And there is this Mediterranean feeling . . . the beaches, ferries pulling in and out of the port, sigh. It's simply one of the most beautiful and exciting cities of this planet."

—Cowboy1968

www.fodors.com/community

WELCOME TO BARCELONA

TOP REASONS TO GO

★ **La Boqueria:** Barcelona's produce market is the most exciting midcity cornucopia in the world.

★ **Santa Maria del Mar:** The church is peerless in its Mediterranean Gothic style; hearing Renaissance choral music here is one of the ultimate sensory experiences.

★ **La Sagrada Família:** Gaudí's stalagmites, stalactites, and cylindrical towers add up to the city's most surprising architectural marvel.

★ **El Palau de la Música Catalana:** Cavalry erupts from the wings and a stained-glass chandelier plummets from above: this Art Nouveau tour de force is alive with music before the first note sounds.

★ **Fashion and Design:** How could a city famous for its architecture fail to offer a fleet of innovative clothing designers and chic shops?

★ **Castellers and Sardanas:** Human castles and Catalonia's national dance are two of the beloved symbols of this nation-within-a-nation.

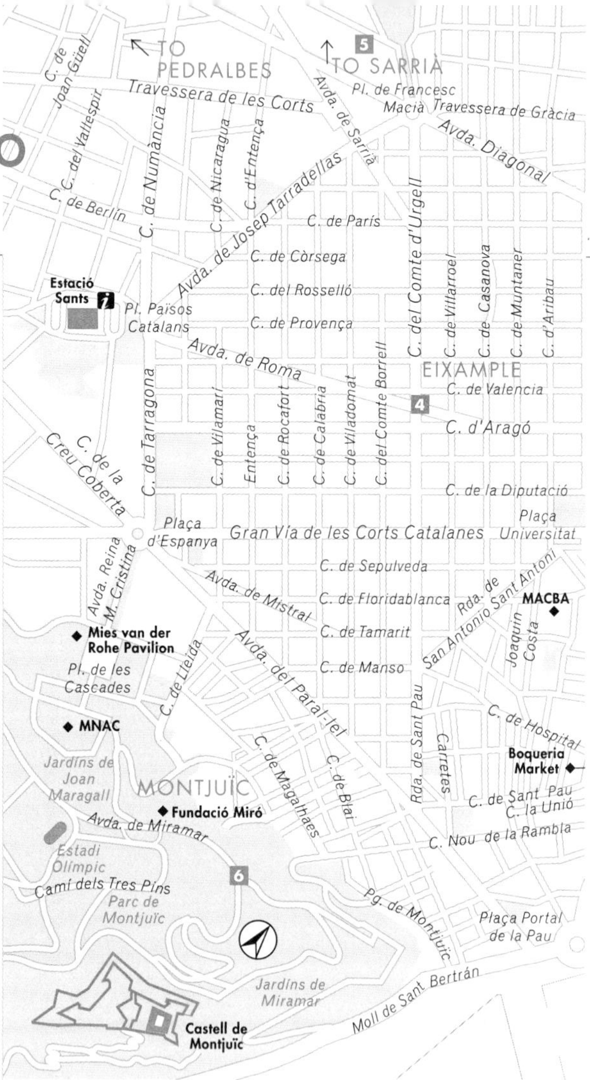

1 La Rambla and El Raval. Ciutat Vella (the Old City) is bisected by the Rambla, the city's all-purpose runway and home of the Boqueria market, the city's heart and soul. The wild Raval, once (and to some extent still) a slum, is a multicultural brawl, spread out around the MACBA contemporary art museum and the medieval Hospital de la Santa Creu.

2 Barri Gòtic and Born-Ribera. Northeast of the Rambla, Ciutat Vella's Gothic Quarter surrounds the cathedral and a jumble of ancient (mostly pedestrianized) streets filled with shops, cafés, and 14th-century Gothic architecture. Born-Ribera is across Via Laietana, around Santa Maria del Mar.

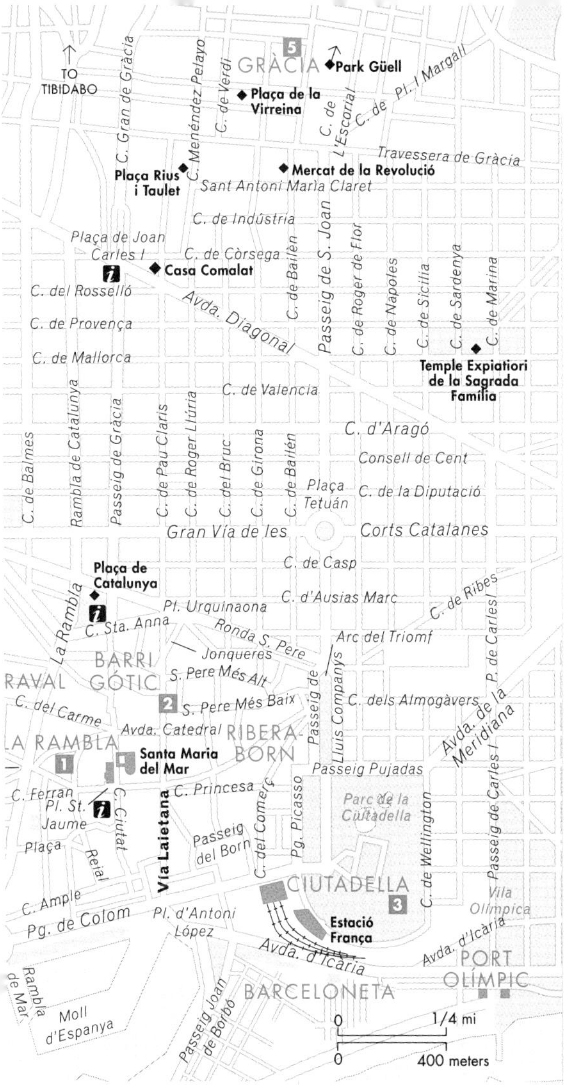

GETTING ORIENTED

Ciutat Vella (Old City) is the heart of Barcelona and a sensory feast, from the Rambla's human parade and the Boqueria's fish, fruit, and vegetables to the steamy corners of the Born. The checkerboard grid expanse north of Ciutat Vella is the post-1860 Eixample (Expansion), rich in Moderniste architecture. Gaudí will take you into the outlying villages of Gràcia and Sarrià, paintings will lead you to the Montjuïc promontory, and music will bring you into the city's finest architecture.

3 Barceloneta, Ciutadella, and Port Olímpic. Barceloneta is a Naples-like fisherman's village, filled with seafood restaurants and lined with sandy beaches. Port Olímpic, built for the 1992 Olympic Games, is a massive succession of restaurants and discos. Ciutadella, just inland, was originally a fortress but is now a park with the city zoo.

4 The Eixample. The post-1860 Eixample spreads out above Plaça de Catalunya and contains most of the city's Art Nouveau (in Spanish, Modernista; in Catalan, Moderniste) architecture, including Gaudí's iconic Sagrada Família church, along with hundreds of shops and places to eat.

5 Upper Barcelona. The village of Gràcia nestles above the Diagonal, with Gaudí's Park Güell at its upper edge. Sarrià and Pedralbes spread out farther west, with two Gaudí buildings, a stunning monastery and cloister, and a rustic village trapped by urban encroachment. Above is Tibidabo, of interest mainly for its views over the city.

6 Montjuïc. The promontory over the south side has artistic treasure not to be missed: Miró, the MNAC, Mies van der Rohe, and CaixaForum.

BARCELONA PLANNER

Festivals and When to Go

Summer can be very hot in Barcelona, and many of the best restaurants and musical venues are closed in August. On the other hand, **El Grec** (*www.barcelonafestival.com*), the summer music festival in June and July, is a delight, and the August **Gràcia Festa Major** is a major block party.

October through June is the time to come to Barcelona, with mid-November–early April pleasantly cool and the rest of the time ideally warm. The **International Music Festival** is in September, and there's an **international jazz festival** in November. Late February's **Carnaval** and *calçot* (long-stemmed onion) season are spectacular and delicious. April and May are best of all: the **Sant Jordi** lovers' day on April 23 and the **Sant Ponç** celebration of natural produce on May 11 are among the most magical moments of the year.

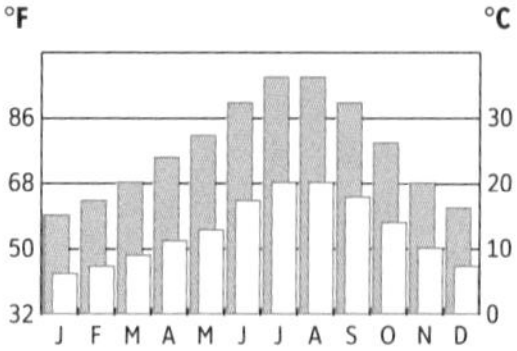

Tours

Bike Tours: Fat Tire Bike Tours and Un Cotxe Menys—"One Car Less," in Catalan—both organize popular guided outings in English.

Boat Tours: Golondrina harbor boats make trips around the harbor from the Portal de la Pau, near the Columbus Monument. The fare is €7.50 for a 40-minute tour. They also have 90-minute (€14) rides in glass-bottom catamarans that parallel the coast up past Barcelona's Olympic Port to the Fòrum complex at the northeastern end of the Diagonal.

Bus Tours: From mid-June to mid-October, the Bus Turistic (9:30–7:30 every 30 minutes) runs a circuit past all the important sights. A day's ticket, which you buy on the bus, costs €9 (€6 half day) and covers the fare for the Tramvía Blau, funicular, and Montjuïc cable car, too. The ride starts at the Plaça de Catalunya. Julià Tours and Pullmantur also run day and half-day excursions outside the city. Popular trips are those to Montserrat and the Costa Brava resorts, the latter including a cruise to the Medes Isles.

Walking Tours: The **Barcelona Tourist Office** (**Turisme de Barcelona**) has daily English-language walking tours of the Gothic Quarter at 10 AM for €12. **Ruta Picasso** tours Barcelona's Picasso sites in English Tuesday, Thursday, and Saturday at 4 PM for €18, including tickets to the Picasso Museum. The **Ruta Moderniste** tours cover the city's best Art Nouveau architecture in English on Friday at 4 PM (6 PM June–Sept.). **Ruta Gourmet** tours take walkers through emblematic points of the city's gastronomic life, with tastings, for €18. **Urbancultours** has English-language walking tours covering the medieval Jewish quarter and other sights.

Contacts Bus Turistic (*93/285–3834* *www.tmb.net*). **Consorci El Far de Barcelona** (*93/217–7457* *www.elfar.diba.es*). **Fat Tire** (*93/342–9275* *www.fattirebiketours.com/barcelona.com*). **Golondrina** (*93/442–3106* *www.lasgolondrinas.com*). **Julià Tours** (*93/317–6454*). **Pullmantur** (*93/318–5195*). **Ruta Gourmet** (*93/285–3832* *www.atrapalo.com*). **Turisme de Barcelona** (*93/285–3832* *www.barcelonaturisme.com*). **Un Cotxe Menys** (*93/268–2105* *www.bicicletabarcelona.com*).

Epicurean Barcelona

"Barcelona, as nowhere else, has always understood that culture was not the butter on the bread of life . . . but the bread itself!" —Robert Hughes

For music lovers: Musical events in Barcelona are worth advance planning. Check schedules for the Liceu opera house, the Palau de la Música Catalana, the Auditori, or the many churches (especially Santa Maria del Mar) that hold concerts. Performances of Handel's *Messiah* at Christmas and Mozart's *Requiem* at Easter, are annual highlights. The **Festival de Música Antiga** (Early Music Festival) in late April to early May brings classical music into some of the Gothic Quarter's prettiest squares and patios.

For Foodies: Reserve well in advance for Barcelona's top gourmet restaurants, including ÀBaC, Comerç 24, Neichel, Drolma, Alkimia, and, especially, Santi Santamariá's El Racó de Can Fabes outside of town in Sant Celoni and Carmen Ruscalleda's Sant Pau in Sant Pol de Mar. Ferran Adrià's world-famous El Bulli, at Cala Montjoi near Roses, is almost impossible to book, and open only from mid-June to mid-December.

Event Listings

El Pais and *La Vanguardia* have daily listings for art openings and concerts (including many free ones), under their Agenda headings. Keeping an eye on these listings can guide you to some of Barcelona's best events, often with tapas and *cava* included. Performances of Castellers, the human tower squads unique to Catalonia, are announced in the weekend agenda section. *La Guia del Ocio* comes out every Thursday and lists the top musical and cultural events for the week; many hotels hand out this guide gratis.

WHAT IT COSTS (IN EUROS)

	¢	$	$$	$$$	$$$$
Restaurants	under €10	€10–€15	€16–€22	€23–€29	over €29
Hotels	under €75	€75–€124	€125–€174	€175–€225	over €225

Prices are per person for a main course at dinner, and for two people in a standard double room in high season, excluding tax.

Planning Your Time

The Rambla is the icebreaker for most trips to Barcelona, starting in Plaça de Catalunya and moving down toward the port past the Boqueria market with all its colors and aromas. Other must-sees on the Rambla are the Liceu opera house, Plaça Reial, and Gaudí's Palau Güell. Main Gaudí masterworks around town include the Sagrada Família church, Park Güell, Casa Batlló, Casa Milà (La Pedrera), and Casa Vicens.

The Gothic Quarter is a warren of Roman and medieval alleys. Once the Roman Forum, Plaça Sant Jaume opens up between the municipal and Catalonian government palaces. Across Via Laietana, the Born-Ribera neighborhood is centered on the exquisite Mediterranean Gothic Santa Maria del Mar basilica, a step away from the Picasso Museum. A 15-minute walk east from Santa Maria del Mar is Barceloneta, the traditional fishermen's quarter, with a dozen good seafood restaurants.

El Raval, home of the medieval hospital, one of the city's finest Gothic spaces, is a good morning's hike. Gràcia and Sarrià are both interesting half-day explorations, while Montjuïc has the Museu Nacional d'Art de Catalunya, the Miró Fundació, and the Mies van der Rohe Pavilion.

GETTING HERE AND AROUND

By Air

Barcelona's main airport is El Prat de Llobregat, 14 km (9 mi) south of Barcelona. A few international and domestic flights (Madrid, Majorca, etc.) land in Girona, an hour north of the city.

The Aerobus leaves El Prat for Plaça de Catalunya every 15 minutes (6 AM–11 PM) on weekdays and every 30 minutes (6:30 AM–10:30 PM) on weekends. From Plaça de Catalunya, it leaves for the airport every 15 minutes (5:30 AM–10 PM) on weekdays and every 30 minutes (6:30 AM–10:30 PM) on weekends. The fare is €5 (round-trip €9).

Cab fare from the airport into town is about €30.

The RENFE airport train is inexpensive and efficient, but trains run only every 20 to 30 min. From the airport, the RENFE station is a 10- to 15-minute walk (with moving walkway) from the gates. Trains run between 6 AM and 12 midnight, stopping at the Estació de Sants, then Passeig de Gràcia, and end at Estació de França. Trains to the airport leave Estació de Sants every 20 minutes from 5:25 AM to midnight. The one-way fare is €2.90. The 10-ride T-10 metro ticket (see By Bus) includes service to the airport station for the price of a single ride.

By Bus

Barcelona's main bus station is Estació del Nord, east of the Arc de Triomf. Buses also depart from the Estació de Sants and from the depots of Barcelona's various private bus companies. You're best off reserving online or through a travel agent, who can quickly book you the best bus passage to your destination (see the Travel Smart chapter for contacts).

By Train

Almost all long-distance trains arrive and depart from Estació de Sants. En route to or from Sants, some trains stop at another station on Passeig de Gràcia at Carrer Aragó; this can be a good way to avoid the long lines that form at Sants during holidays, though even better is dealing directly with ⊕ *www.renfe.es*. The Estació de França, near the port, now handles only a few long-distance trains within Spain. The air shuttle (or a scheduled flight) between Madrid and Barcelona can, if all goes well, get you door to door in less than three hours for only about €40 more than the cost of a train. The AVE, the high-speed RENFE train, now connects Barcelona and Madrid in 2 hours, 38 minutes, for €120.40. Booking two weeks in advance can cut the ticket cost to €48.

The FCG (Ferrocarril de la Generalitat) train from Plaça de Catalunya through the center of town to Sarrià and outlying cities is a commuter train that gets you to within walking distance of nearly everything in Barcelona. Transfers to the regular city metro are free.

By Foot

Modern Barcelona, above the Plaça de Catalunya, is built on a grid system. The old town, however, from the Plaça de Catalunya to the port, is a labyrinth of narrow streets, so you'll need a good street map. Most sightseeing can be done on foot—you won't have any choice in the Barri Gòtic—but you'll have to use the metro, buses, or taxis to link sightseeing areas.

By Bus, Subway, and Tram

City buses run daily 5:30 AM–11:30 PM. Route maps are displayed at bus stops. Schedules are available at bus and metro stations or at *www.bcn.es/guia/welcomea.htm*.

Barcelona's new tramway system is divided into two subsectors: Trambaix serves the western end of the Diagonal; Trambesòs serves the eastern end of the Diagonal.

The subway is the fastest, cheapest, and easiest way to get around Barcelona. Metro lines are color coded, and the FGC trains are marked with a reclining S-like blue-and-white icon. Lines 2, 3, and 5 run weekdays 5 AM–midnight. Lines 1 and 4 close at 1 AM. On Friday, Saturday, and holiday evenings all trains run until 2 AM. The FGC Generalitat trains run until 12:30 on weekdays and 2:15 AM on weekends and eves of holidays. Sunday trains run on weekday schedules. *See the inside back cover for a map of the Barcelona metro.*

The Montjuïc Funicular runs from the junction of Avinguda del Paral.lel and Nou de la Rambla to the Miramar station on Montjuïc (Paral.lel). It operates daily 11 AM–9:30 PM in summer, weekends, and holidays, and 11 AM–8 PM in winter; the fare is €1.40.

Bus, subway, and tram fares are a flat fee of €1.40 no matter how far you travel (with free transfers for up to an hour and 15 minutes), but it's more economical to buy a Targeta T-10 (valid for bus or metro FGC Generalitat trains, the Tramvía Blau blue tram, and the Montjuïc Funicular; 10 rides for €7.70). The Dia T-1 pass is valid for one day of unlimited travel on all subway, bus, and FGC (Ferrocarriles de la Generalitat de Catalunya), part of the city underground system—but the Targeta T-10 is generally better than the Día T-1.

Contact Tram BCN (*902/193–275 www.trambcn.com*). **Transports Metropolitans de Barcelona (TMB)** (*93/298–7000 www.tmb.net*).

Visitor Information

Turisme de Barcelona (*93/368–9700 www.barcelonaturisme.com*).

Discounts and Deals

The moderately worthwhile **Barcelona Card** comes in two-, three-, four-, and five-day versions: for €23.40, €28.35, €32.40, and €37.80 (2009 prices). You get unlimited travel on public transport and discounts at 27 museums, 10 restaurants, 14 leisure sights, and 20 stores. Caveat: the restaurants and shops covered are generally mediocre and the only important museum savings is 20% at the expensive Casa Batlló. You can get the card in Turisme de Barcelona offices in Plaça de Catalunya and Plaça Sant Jaume, and in the Sants train station, the El Prat airport, the El Corte Inglés department store, and the Barcelona Aquarium, among other sites.

By Taxi

Taxis are black and yellow and show a green rooftop light when available for hire. The meter starts at €1.80 (€1.90 at night and on weekends and holidays). There are supplements for luggage, night travel, Sunday and holidays, rides from a station or to the airport, and for trips to or from the bullring or a soccer *(fútbol)* match. On Friday and Saturday nights between midnight and 6 AM there is an automatic supplement of €4. There are cab stands all over town, and you can also hail cabs on the street.

By George Semler

Capital of Catalonia, 2,000-year-old Barcelona commanded a vast Mediterranean empire when Madrid was still a dusty Moorish outpost on the Spanish steppe. Relegated to second-city status only after Madrid became the seat of the royal court in 1561, Barcelona, one of Europe's most visually stunning cities, has long rivaled and often surpassed Madrid's economic and political might.

Barcelona balances the medieval intimacy of its Gothic Quarter with the grace and distinction of the wide boulevards in the Moderniste Eixample—just as the Mediterranean Gothic elegance of the church of Santa Maria del Mar provides a perfect counterpoint to Gaudí's riotous Sagrada Família. Mies van der Rohe's pavilion seems even more minimalist after a look at the Art Nouveau Palau de la Música Catalana, while such exciting contemporary creations as Bofill's neoclassical Parthenon-under-glass Teatre Nacional de Catalunya, Frank Gehry's waterfront goldfish, Norman Foster's Torre de Collserola, and Jean Nouvel's Torre Agbar all add spice to Barcelona's visual soup. Meanwhile, Barcelona's fashion industry is pulling even with those of Paris and Milan, and FC (Futbol Club) is Barcelona's perennial contender for European Championships and the world's most glamorous soccer club.

Barcelona has long had a frenetically active cultural life. It was the home of architect Antoni Gaudí, whose buildings are the most startling statements of Modernisme. Other leading Moderniste architects of the city include Lluís Domènech i Montaner and Josep Puig i Cadafalch, and the painters Joan Miró, Salvador Dalí, and Antoni Tàpies are also strongly identified with Catalonia. Pablo Picasso spent his formative years in Barcelona, and one of the city's treasures is a museum devoted to his works. Barcelona's opera house, the Liceu, is the finest in Spain, and the city claims such native Catalan musicians as cellist Pablo (Pau, in Catalan) Casals, opera singers Montserrat Caballé and José (Josep) Carreras, and early music viola da gamba master Jordi Savall.

In 133 BC the Roman Empire annexed Barcino; Visigoths roared down from the north in the 5th-century; the Moors invaded in the 8th; and in the 9th, Franks under Charlemagne captured Catalonia and made it their buffer zone at the edge of the Moors' Iberian empire. By 988, the autonomous Catalonian counties had gained independence from the Franks, but in 1137 Catalonia was, through marriage, united with the House of Aragón. Another marriage, that of Ferdinand II of Aragón and Isabella of Castile (and queen of León) in 1474, brought Aragón and Catalonia into a united Spain. As the economic capital of Aragón's Mediterranean empire, Barcelona grew powerful between the 12th and 14th centuries and began to falter only when maritime emphasis shifted to the Atlantic after 1492. Despite Madrid's power as seat of Spain's Royal Court, Catalonia enjoyed autonomous rights and privileges until 1714, when, in reprisal for having backed the Austrian Hapsburg pretender to the Spanish throne, all institutions and expressions of Catalan identity were suppressed by Felipe V of the French Bourbon dynasty. Not until the mid-19th century would Barcelona's industrial growth bring about a renaissance of nationalism and a cultural flowering that recalled Catalonia's former opulence.

Catalan nationalism continued to strengthen in the 20th century. After the abdication of Alfonso XIII and the establishment of the Second Spanish Republic in 1931, Catalonia enjoyed renewed autonomy and cultural freedom. Once again backing a losing cause, Barcelona was a Republican stronghold and hotbed of anti-fascist sentiment during the 1936–39 civil war, with the result that Catalan language and identity were suppressed under the 1939–75 Francisco Franco regime by such means as book burning, the renaming of streets and towns, and the banning of the Catalan language in schools and the media. This repression had little lasting effect; Catalans jealously guard their language and culture and generally think of themselves as Catalans first, Spaniards second.

Catalonian home rule was granted after Franco's death in 1975, and Catalonia's governing body, the ancient Generalitat, was reinstated in 1980. Catalan is now Barcelona's co-official language, along with Castilian Spanish, and is eagerly promoted through free classes funded by the Generalitat. Street names are signposted in Catalan, and newspapers, radio stations, and a TV channel publish and broadcast in Catalan.

EXPLORING BARCELONA

Barcelona has several main areas to explore. Between Plaça de Catalunya and the port lies the Old City, or Ciutat Vella including El Barri Gòtic (the Gothic Quarter); the shop-, bar-, and tapas-rich La Ribera (the waterfront, also known as Born-Ribera); the populous central promenade of the Rambla; and El Raval, the former slums or outskirts southwest of the Rambla. Above Plaça de Catalunya is the grid-pattern expansion known as the Eixample (literally, the "Expansion") built after the city's third series of defensive walls were torn down in 1860; this area contains most of Barcelona's Moderniste architecture. Farther north and west, Upper Barcelona includes the former outlying towns of Gràcia and Sarrià, Pedralbes, and, rising up behind the city, Tibidabo and the green hills of the Collserola nature preserve.

Though built in the mid-18th century, Barceloneta is generally considered part of Ciutat Vella. The Port Olímpic, a series of vast terrace restaurants and discos, is just beyond the Frank Gehry goldfish and the Hotel Arts. The Ciutadella park, once a fortress built not to protect but to dominate Barcelona, is just inland.

A final area, less important from a visitor's standpoint, is Diagonal Mar, from Torre Agbar and Plaça de les Glòries, east to the mouth of the River Besòs. This is the new Barcelona built for the 2004 Fòrum de les Cultures.

Numbers in the text correspond to numbers in the margins and on chapter maps.

CIUTAT VELLA: THE RAMBLA AND EL RAVAL

Barcelona's best-known promenade is a constant and colorful flood of humanity that flows past flower stalls, bird vendors, mimes, musicians, newspaper kiosks, and outdoor cafés; traffic plays second fiddle to the endless *paseo* (stroll) of locals and travelers alike. Federico García Lorca called this street the only one in the world that he wished would never end. The whole avenue is referred to as Las Ramblas (Les Rambles, in Catalan) or La Rambla, but each section has its own name: Rambla Santa Monica is at the southeastern, or port, end; Rambla de les Flors in the middle; and Rambla dels Estudis is at the top, near Plaça de Catalunya. El Raval is the area to the west of the Rambla, originally a slum outside Barcelona's second set of walls. Alas, Rambla-happy tourists are tempting prey for thieves and scam artists. Do *not* play the shell game (Barcelona's local three-card monte), keep maps and guidebooks hidden so you are not so obviously a tourist, conceal cameras, and leave wallets and passports in your hotel safe.

A GOOD WALK

Start on the Rambla opposite the Plaça Reial and wander down toward the sea to the **Monument a Colom** ❶ and the Rambla de Mar boardwalk. From here you might make a brief probe into the unprepossessing modern **Port** ❷. As you move back to the Columbus Monument, investigate the **Museu Marítim** ❸ and its medieval Drassanes Reials shipyards. Gaudí's **Palau Güell** ❹, on Carrer Nou de la Rambla, is the next stop before the **Gran Teatre del Liceu** ❺. For a little detour, head over to **Sant Pau del Camp** ❼ and take a peek at Barcelona's red-light district, the **Barri Xinès** ❻, on the way. Back on the Rambla, you can take in the facade and perhaps some savories at **Antigua Casa Figueres** ❽, stroll through the **Boqueria** ❾ food market and the **Palau de la Virreina** ❿ exhibition center next door, and then cut around to the courtyards of the medieval **Antic Hospital de la Santa Creu** ⓫. Next, visit the **Museu d'Art Contemporani de Barcelona** (MACBA) ⓬ and the **Centre de Cultura Contemporànea de Barcelona** (CCCB) ⓭, on Carrer Montalegre, before returning to the Rambla along Carrer Tallers, ending up in **Plaça de Catalunya** ⓮.

TIMING This walk covers 3 km (2 mi). With brief stops, allow three hours; add another hour or two for the MACBA.

TOP ATTRACTIONS

⓫ **Antic Hospital de la Santa Creu.** The 15th-century medieval hospital, now housing the Biblioteca de Catalunya (the "Library of Catalunya") cultural institutions and the Escola Massana art school, is one of the four finest Gothic spaces in Barcelona (along with Drassanes, Santa Maria del Mar, and La Llotja). Approach it from the back door of the Boqueria, starting at the Carrer del Carme end where, across from the **Reial Acadèmia de Cirurgia i Medecina (Royal Academy of Surgery and Medicine)**, the courtyard of the Casa de Convalescència leads in past scenes from the life of St. Paul portrayed in lovely blue-and-yellow ceramic

Fodor's Choice ★

The Rambla and the Raval

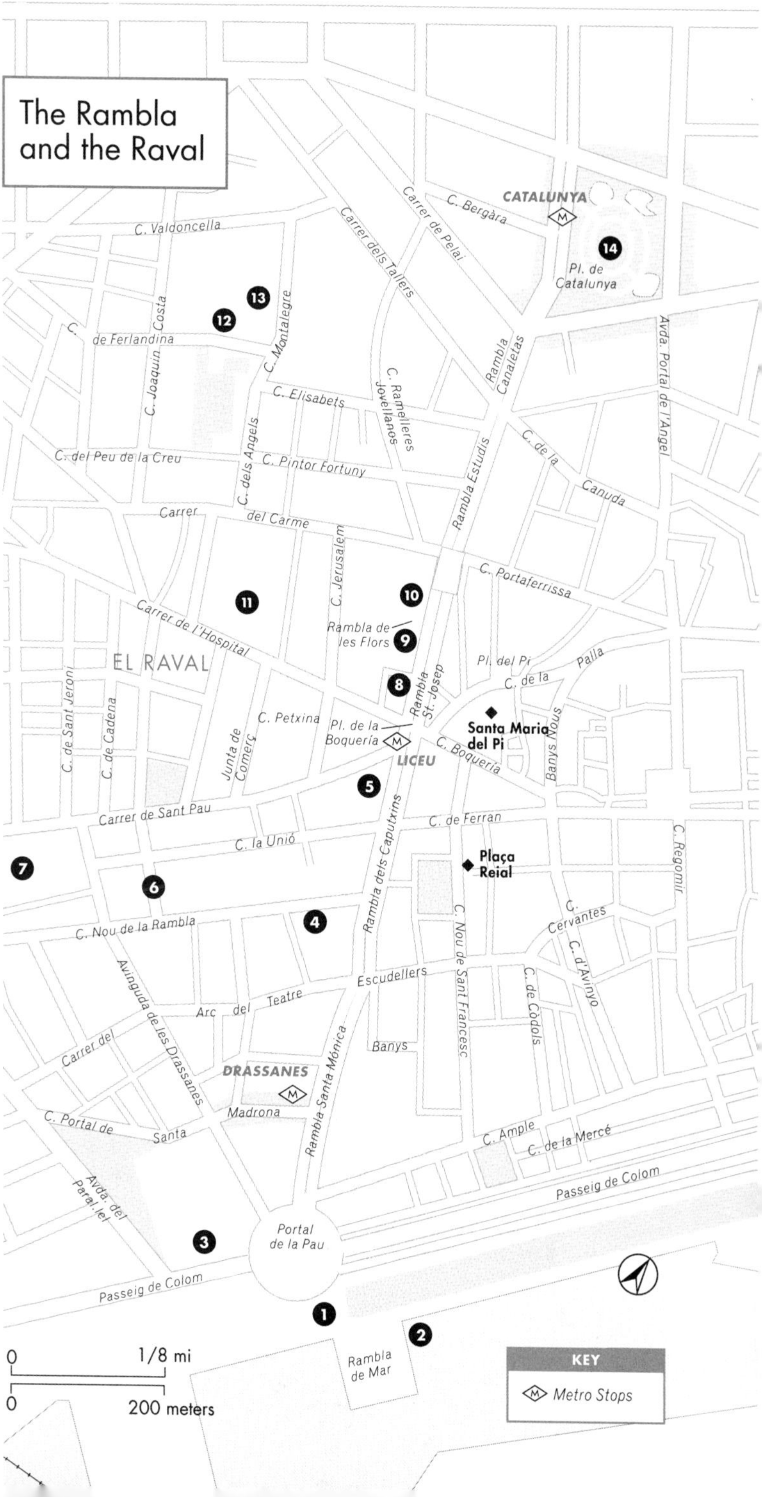

tiles hand-painted by master craftsman Llorenç Passolas in 1680–81. The green-and-white-tiled patio houses the **Institut d'Estudis Catalans.** The second-floor garden behind the clock is dedicated to Catalan novelist Mercé Rodoreda. Turn right as you leave the entryway, take a look into the beautifully vaulted reading rooms on either side down the stairs, and continue through the orange grove in the hospital patio to the stairs leading up to the right for a look at the wide Gothic arches inside the Biblioteca de Catalunya. Out on Carrer Hospital to the left is **La Capella,** once the hospital chapel and now a gallery with contemporary art. ✉ *Carrer del Carme 45, or Carrer Hospital 56, Raval* Ⓜ *Catalunya, Liceu.*

6 **Barri Xinès.** As you walk from Plaça Reial toward the sea, Barcelona's red-light district, the Barri Xinès (traditionally called the Barrio Chino in Castilian Spanish) is on your right. Though literally translatable as Chinatown, China had nothing to do with the area—the name is a generic reference to foreigners of all kinds. The area is ill-famed for prostitutes, drug pushers, and street thieves, but it's not as dangerous as it looks; the reinforced police presence here may make it safer than other parts of the Gothic Quarter.

9 **Boqueria.** Barcelona's most spectacular food market, also known as the Mercat de Sant Josep, is an explosion of life and color sprinkled with delicious little bar-restaurants. **Pinotxo** has long been a sanctuary for food lovers and **Quim de la Boqueria** is hot on its heels. **El Kiosco Universal,** on the northeast corner, has great atmosphere but only average fare. Don't miss mushroom expert and author Petràs and his Fruits del Bosc (Fruits of the Forest), a mad display of wild mushrooms, herbs, nuts, and berries at the very back. ✉ *La Rambla 91, Rambla* 🌐 *www.boqueria.info* ⏲ *Mon.–Sat. 8–8* Ⓜ *Liceu.*

Fodor's Choice ★

12 **Museu d'Art Contemporani de Barcelona** *(Barcelona Museum of Contemporary Art, MACBA).* Designed in 1992 by American architect Richard Meier, this gleaming explosion of glass and planes of white contains 20th-century masters including Calder, Rauschenberg, Oteiza, Chillida, and Tàpies. The optional guided tour takes visitors through the philosophy behind abstract art. ✉ *Pl. dels Àngels 1, Raval* ☎ *93/412–0810* 🌐 *www.macba.es* 🎟 *€7.50, Wed. €3.50* ⏲ *Mon. and Wed.–Fri. 11–7:30, Sat. 10–8, Sun. 10–3; free guided tours daily at 6, Sun. at noon* Ⓜ *Catalunya.*

3 **Museu Marítim.** The superb Maritime Museum is in the 13th-century **Drassanes Reials** (Royal Shipyards), to the east at the foot of the Rambla. The vast medieval space, one of Barcelona's finest Gothic structures, seems more like a cathedral than a boatyard and is filled with ships, including a life-size reconstructed galley, figureheads, and early navigational charts. The Acoustiguide, free with your ticket, is excellent. ✉ *Av. de les Drassanes s/n, Rambla* ☎ *93/342–9920* 🌐 *www.museumaritimbarcelona.org* 🎟 *€6.50; free 1st Sat. of month after 3* ⏲ *Daily 10–7* Ⓜ *Drassanes.*

4 **Palau Güell.** Antoni Gaudí built this mansion during the years 1886–89 for his patron, textile baron Count Eusebi de Güell, and soon found himself in the international limelight. The dark facade is a dramatic

foil for the treasure house inside, where spear-shaped Art Nouveau columns frame the windows and prop up a series of intricately coffered wood ceilings. Gaudí is most himself on the roof, where his playful, polychrome ceramic chimneys fit right in with his later works like Park Güell and La Pedrera. The palace is only partially open (and has free entry) during restorations, which will extend at least through 2009. Check the Web site for updates. ✉ *Carrer Nou de la Rambla 3–5, Rambla* ☎ *93/317–3974* 🌐 *www.palauguell.cat* ⏲ *Tues.–Sat. 10–2:30.* Ⓜ *Drassanes, Liceu.*

OFF THE BEATEN PATH

7 Fodor's Choice ★ **Sant Pau del Camp.** Barcelona's oldest church was originally outside the city walls (*del camp* means "in the fields") and was a Roman cemetery as far back as the 2nd century, according to archaeological evidence. What you see now was built in 1127 and is the earliest Romanesque structure in Barcelona, redolent of the pre-Romanesque Asturian churches or the pre-Romanesque Sant Michel de Cuxà in Prades, Catalunya Nord (Catalonia North, aka southern France). Elements of the church (the classical marble capitals atop the columns in the main entry) are thought to be from the 6th and 7th centuries. The hulking mastodonic shape of the church is a reflection of the defensive mentality of Barcelona's early Christians, for whom the bulwark of the church served as a spiritual, if not physical, refuge during an era of Moorish sackings and invasions. Check for musical performances here because the church is an acoustical gem. Note the tiny stained-glass window high on the facade facing Carrer Sant Pau: if Santa Maria del Pi's rose window is Europe's largest, this is quite probably the smallest. The tiny cloister, the only way in during afternoon opening hours, is Sant Pau del Camp's best feature, one of Barcelona's semisecret treasures. From inside the church, the right side of the altar leads out into this patio surrounded by porches or arcades. Sculpted Corinthian capitals portraying biblical scenes support triple Mudejar arches. ✉ *Sant Pau 101, Raval* ☎ *93/441–0001* ⏲ *Cloister weekdays 4:30–7:30. Sun. mass at 10:30, 12:30, and 8* PM Ⓜ *Catalunya, Liceu, Paral.lel.*

WORTH NOTING

8 **Antigua Casa Figueres.** This Moderniste café, grocery, and pastry store on the corner of Carrer Petxina has a splendid mosaic facade and exquisite Art Nouveau fittings. The best way to get a close look at them is to sit down for a hot chocolate, tea, or coffee. The fluffy (and very sweet) *ensaimadas*, a spiraling Mallorcan pastry sprinkled with confectioner's sugar, are hard to resist. ✉ *La Rambla 83, Rambla* ☎ *93/301–6027* 🌐 *www.escriba.es* Ⓜ *Catalunya, Liceu* ⏲ *Daily 8:30* AM*–9* PM.

13 **Centre de Cultura Contemporànea de Barcelona** *(CCCB)*. Formerly a medieval convent and hospital, the renovated Casa de la Caritat holds the CCCB, a combination museum, exhibition space, and lecture/concert hall. Check out the reflecting wall, which allows you to see over the rooftops to Montjuïc and beyond. ✉ *Carrer Montalegre 5, Raval* ☎ *93/306–4100* 🌐 *www.cccb.org* 🎫 *€5; entry to patio and bookstore free* ⏲ *Tues.–Sun. 11–8* Ⓜ *Catalunya.*

5 **Gran Teatre del Liceu.** Along with Milan's La Scala, Barcelona's opera house has long been considered one of the most beautiful in Europe.

First built in 1848, it burned down in 1861, was bombed in 1893, and was again gutted by a blaze of mysterious origins in early 1994—Barcelona's soprano Montserrat Caballé stood on the Rambla in tears as her beloved venue was consumed. Five years later, a restored and renewed Liceu, equipped for modern productions, opened anew. Even if you don't see an opera, don't miss the tour: regular tours are 70 minutes; express tours are 20. Under the opera house, with entrances on Carrer Sant Pau and the Rambla, Espai Liceu has a cafeteria; a shop specializing in opera-related gifts, books, and recordings; an intimate 50-person-capacity circular concert hall; and a Mediateca with recordings and films of past opera productions. ✉ *La Rambla 51–59, Rambla* ☎ *93/485–9900* 🌐 *www.liceubarcelona.com* 🎫 *Guided tours €8.50, 20-min self-guided express tour €4* ⏲ *Tours daily at 10* AM *in Spanish and English, self-guided express tours daily at 11:30, noon, 12:30, and 1. The backstage tour at 9:30* AM *(€10) must be arranged by reservation (☎ 93/485–9900 ✉ visites@liceubarcelona.com)* Ⓜ *Liceu.*

❶ **Monument a Colom** *(Columbus Monument).* This 60-meter-tall (200-foot-tall) monument at the foot of the Rambla marks the spot where Christopher Columbus stepped back onto Spanish soil in 1493 after discovering America. A viewing platform at the top (reached by elevator; entrance is on the harbor side) gives a bird's-eye view of the city. ✉ *Portal de la Pau s/n, Rambla* ☎ *93/302–5224* 🎫 *€3* ⏲ *Daily 9–8:30* Ⓜ *Drassanes.*

❿ **Palau de la Virreina.** The neoclassical Virreina Palace, built by a viceroy to Peru in 1778, is now an exhibition center for paintings, photography, and historical items usually dedicated to social and environmental issues honoring Catalonia's struggle of "internal exile." The building also houses a bookstore and a tourist office. ✉ *La Rambla 99, Rambla* ☎ *93/316–1000* 🌐 *www.bcn.es/virreinaexposicions* 🎫 *Free; €3 charge for some exhibits* ⏲ *Mon.–Sat. 11–8, Sun. 11–3* Ⓜ *Liceu.*

⓮ **Plaça de Catalunya.** Barcelona's main transport hub, the Plaça de Catalunya, is the frontier between the old city and the post-1860 Eixample. Café Zurich, at the head of the Rambla and the mouth of the metro, is a classic rendezvous point.

❷ **Port.** Beyond the Monument a Colom—behind the Duana, or former customs building (now site of the Barcelona Port Authority)—is the **Rambla de Mar,** a boardwalk with a drawbridge. The Rambla de Mar extends out to the **Moll d'Espanya,** with its Maremagnum shopping center, IMAX theater, and aquarium. Next to the Duana, you can board a Golondrina boat for a tour of the port, to go up the coast to the Olympic Port, or to go to the Fòrum complex at Diagonal Mar. From the Moll de Barcelona's Torre de Jaume I, just to the southeast, you can catch a cable car to Montjuïc or Barceloneta.

CIUTAT VELLA: EL BARRI GÒTIC AND BORN-RIBERA

The Gothic Quarter winds through the church and Plaça of the church of Santa Maria del Pi, the Roman Barcelona around the cathedral, the Plaçà del Rei, past the city's administrative centers at Plaça Sant Jaume with the Jewish Quarter tucked in beside it, and through the Sant Just neighborhood northeast of Plaça Sant Jaume. Across Via Laietana is the Barri de la Ribera, or Born-Ribera, once the waterfront district around the basilica of Santa Maria del Mar. Born-Ribera includes the Museu Picasso and Carrer Montcada, Barcelona's most aristocratic street in the 14th and 15th centuries. Much of the Barri de la Ribera was torn down in 1714 by the victorious Spanish and French army of Felipe V to create a *glacis*, an open no-man's land outside the walls of the occupying stronghold, the La Ciutadella fortress.

On the northeastern edge of this area, Barcelona's old textile neighborhood, around the church of Sant Pere de les Puelles, includes the flagship of the city's Moderniste architecture: the Palau de la Música Catalana, and the Mercat de Santa Caterina, a produce market with several dining options.

LEAVE WITH EVERYTHING YOU BROUGHT—OR BOUGHT

While muggings are practically unheard of in Barcelona, petty thievery is common. Handbags, backpacks, camera cases, and wallets are favorite targets, so tuck those away. Handbags hooked over chairs, on the floor or sidewalk under your feet, or dangling from hooks under bars are easy prey. Even a loosely carried bag is tempting for bag-snatchers. Should you carry a purse, use one with a short strap that tucks tightly under your arm without room for fleet hands to unzip. A plastic shopping bag for your items will attract even less attention.

7

TOP ATTRACTIONS

17 **The Centre d'Interpretació del Call** *(Center for the Interpretation of the Jewish Quarter)*. This 14th-century building in the heart of the *call* is one of the few buildings in the area with its original stones and features still intact. On display are 13th- and 14th-century objects found in the *call* during archaeological excavations, including dishes with Hebrew letters and a facsimile of an illustrated manuscript (the Sarajevo Haggadah), depicting 15th-century scenes. There are also two tombstones with Hebrew inscriptions. The center runs walking tours and discussions about medieval Barcelona and its Jewish community, lectures by experts on Hebrew history and culture, tastings of Catalan-Jewish cuisine, Jewish storytelling sessions, and summer school activities. ✉ *Placeta de Manuel Ribé, Barri Gòtic* ☎ *93/256–2122* 🌐 *www.calldebarcelona.org* 🕓 *Wed.–Fri. 10–2, Sat. 11–6, Sun. 11–3* Ⓜ *Jaume I.*

25 **El Born.** Once the site of medieval jousts, the Passeig del Born is at the end of Carrer Montcada behind the church of Santa Maria del Mar. The numbered cannonballs under the benches are in memory of the 1714 siege of Barcelona that concluded the 14-year War of the Spanish Succession. The Bourbon forces obliged local residents to tear down more than 900 of their own houses, about a fifth of the city at that time, to create an open no-man's land for the fortress built for the occupying army of the great villain of Barcelona history: Felipe V, grandson of Louis XIV. Walk down to the Born itself—a great iron hangar designed by Josep Fontseré in 1876. It was modeled after Les Halles, which used to be Paris's beloved midcity produce market. Renovations of El Born uncovered the perfectly preserved lost city of 1714, complete with blackened fireplaces, taverns, wells, and the canal that brought water

Catedral de la Seu **19**
Centre d'Interpretació del Call **17**
El Born **25**
Fossar de les Moreres **24**
Museu d'Història de la Ciutat **22**
Museu Frederic Marès **20**
Museu Picasso **26**
Palau de la Música Catalana **28**
Plaça del Rei **21**
Plaça Reial **16**
Plaça Sant Jaume **18**
Santa Maria del Mar **23**
Santa Maria del Pi **15**
Sant Pere de les Puelles . **27**

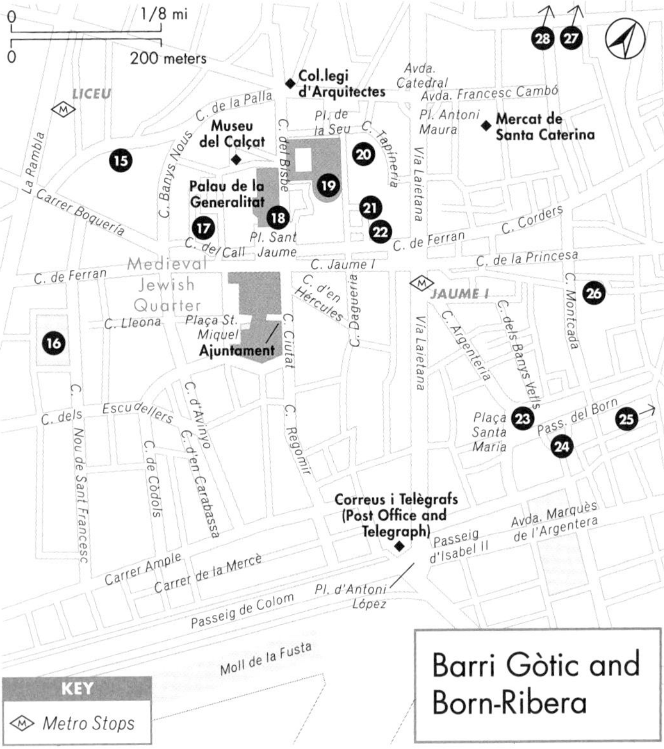

into the city. Sand dunes visible in the cellars attest to La Ribera's early position on the Barcelona waterfront before landfill created Barceloneta and the present harbor. Pending development of a history walk through the streets and houses, the Museu d' Història de la Ciutat (see below) offers free visits overlooking the ruins of the 14th- to 18th-century Barri de la Ribera, weekends 10–3. ✉*Born-Ribera* ☎*93/315–1111 Museu de Història de la Ciutat* Ⓜ*Jaume I.*

24 **Fossar de les Moreres** *(Cemetery of the Mulberry Trees)*. The cemetery on the eastern side of the church of Santa Maria del Mar has been turned into a public plaza where there is a low marble monument inscribed EN EL FOSSAR DE LES MORERES NO S'HI ENTERRA CAP TRAIDOR, or "In the cemetery of the mulberry trees no traitor lies." It refers to the story of the graveyard keeper who refused to bury those who had fought on the invading side during War of the Spanish Succession, in 1714, even when one of them turned out to be his son. The torch-sculpture over the monument, often referred to as a *pebetero* (Bunsen burner), was erected in 2002. ✉ *Fossar de les Moreres, La Ribera* Ⓜ*Jaume I.*

NEED A BREAK?

Mercat de Santa Caterina. This marketplace, a splendid carnival of colors and roller-coaster rooftops, was restored by the late Enric Miralles (though the project was finished in 2005 by his widow, architect Benedetta

Tagliabue). Inside, there are undulating wood and colored ceramic mosaics recalling both Gaudí and Miró, and there is an archaeological display explaining over 2,000 years of the site's history. The spacious Cuines Santa Caterina restaurant has a unique crossword-style menu, listing food products across the top and world cuisines such as Asian, Mediterranean, and Vegetarian down the left margin. ✉ ***Av. Francesc Cambo 16, Born-Ribera*** ☎ ***93/268-9918*** 🌐 ***www.mercatsbcn.com*** Ⓜ ***Jaume I, Catalunya.***

22 **Museu d'Història de la Ciutat** *(City History Museum)*. This fascinating museum traces the evolution of Barcelona from its first Iberian settlement to its alleged founding by the Carthaginian Hamilcar Barca in about 230 BC, to Roman and Visigothic times and beyond. Antiquity is the focus here: Romans took the city during the Punic Wars, and the striking underground remains of their Colonia Favencia Julia Augusta Paterna Barcino, through which you can roam on metal walkways, are the museum's main treasure. Archaeological finds include parts of walls, fluted columns, and recovered busts and vases. Above ground, off the Plaça del Rei, the **Palau Reial Major,** the splendid **Saló del Tinell,** the chapel of **Santa Àgata,** and the **Torre del Rei Martí,** a lookout tower with views over the Barri Gòtic, complete the self-guided tour. ✉ *Plaça del Rei s/n, Barri Gòtic* ☎ *93/256–2100* 🌐 *www.museuhistoria.bcn.cat* 🎫 *€5.50 (includes admission to Monestir de Pedralbes, Centre d'Interpretació del Park Güell, Centre d'Interpretació del Call, Centre d'Interpretació Històrica, Refugi 307, and Museu-Casa Verdaguer)* 🕒 *Oct.–May, Tues.–Sat. 10–2 and 4–7; June–Sept., Tues.–Sat. 10–7; Sun. 10–3* Ⓜ *Catalunya, Liceu, Jaume I.*

7

26 **Museu Picasso.** Picasso spent key formative years (1895–1904) in Barcelona, when he was a young Bohemian, and never forgot these good times. A collection of his work can be found in Carrer Montcada, known for Barcelona's most elegant medieval and Renaissance palaces, five of which are occupied by the Picasso Museum. Picasso's longtime crony and personal secretary, Jaume Sabartés, donated his private collection to this museum in 1960, and Picasso himself donated another 1,700 works in 1970. Though the 3,600-work permanent collection is strong on his early production, don't expect to find many of the artist's most famous works. Displays include childhood and adolescent sketches, works from Picasso's Blue and Rose periods, and the famous 44 cubist studies based on Velázquez's *Las Meninas*. The sketches, oils, schoolboy caricatures, and drawings from Picasso's early years in La Coruña and, later, in Barcelona are perhaps the most fascinating part of the museum, showing the facility the artist possessed from an early age. His *La Primera Communión (First Communion)*, painted at the age of 15, for which he was given a short review in the local press, was an important achievement for the young Picasso, and the Las Meninas studies and the bright *Pichones (Pigeons)* series provide a final explosion of color and light. *Suite 156*, a series of erotic and playful drawings on display when temporary exhibits allow space, may be the best of all. ✉ *Carrer Montcada 15–23, Born-Ribera* ☎ *93/319–6310* 🌐 *www.*

Fodor's Choice ★

CLOSE UP

Picasso's Barcelona

Barcelona's claim to Pablo Picasso (1881–1973) has been contested by Málaga, the painter's birthplace; by Madrid, where *Guernica* hangs; and even by the town of Gernika itself, victim of the 1937 Luftwaffe saturation bombing that inspired the famous canvas. Picasso, a staunch anti-Franco opponent after the war, refused to return to Franco's Spain. In turn, the Franco regime allowed no public display of Picasso's work until 1961, when the artist's *Sardana* frieze at Barcelona's Architects' Guild was unveiled. Picasso did not set foot on Spanish soil for the last 39 years of his life.

The artist did spend a sporadic but formative period of his youth in Barcelona, however (between 1895 and 1904), after which he moved to Paris to join its fertile art scene. Picasso's father had been appointed art professor at the Reial Acadèmia de les Belles Arts in La Llotja, and Picasso, a precocious draftsman, began advanced classes in the academy at the age of 15. A few years later, working in different studios between academic stints in Madrid, the young artist first exhibited at Els Quatre Gats, a tavern still thriving on Carrer Montsió. Much intrigued with the Bohemian life of Barcelona's popular neighborhoods, Picasso's early cubist painting *Les Demoiselles d'Avignon* was inspired not by the French town but by the Barcelona street Carrer d'Avinyó, then known for its brothel. After his move to Paris, Picasso returned occasionally to Barcelona until his last visit in summer of 1934.

Considering Picasso's off-and-on tenure in Barcelona, followed by his 39-year self-imposed exile, it's remarkable that Barcelona and Picasso should be so intertwined in the world's perception of the city. The Picasso Museum, although an excellent visit, is only the fourth-most important art venue on any art connoisseur's list of Barcelona galleries. The museum was the brainchild of the artist's longtime friend Jaume Sabartés, who believed that his vast private collection of Picasso works should be made public. After much wrangling with the Franco regime, who were loath to publicly recognize such a prominent anti-Franco figure and the author of a work titled *The Dream and the Lie of Franco* (1937), the Picasso Museum finally opened in 1963. **Iconoserveis Culturals** (✉ *C. Muntaner 185, Eixample* ☎ *93/410–1405* 🌐 *www.iconoserveis.com*) gives walking tours through the key spots in Picasso's Barcelona life, covering studios, galleries, taverns, the Picasso family apartments, and the painter's favorite haunts and hangouts.

museupicasso.bcn.cat 🎫 *€9.50; free 1st Sun. of month* ⏲ *Tues.–Sun. 10–8* Ⓜ *Catalunya, Liceu, Jaume I.*

28 Fodor's Choice ★ **Palau de la Música Catalana.** A riot of color and form, Barcelona's Music Palace is the flagship of the city's Moderniste architecture. Designed by Lluís Domènech i Montaner in 1908, it was originally conceived by the Orfeó Català musical society as a vindication of the importance of music at a popular level—as opposed to the Liceu opera house's identification with the Catalan (often Castilian-speaking monarchist) aristocracy. The Palau's exterior is remarkable in itself, albeit hard to

see because there's no room to back up and behold it. Above the main entrance are busts of Palestrina, Bach, Beethoven, and (around the corner on Carrer Amadeu Vives) Wagner. Look for the colorful mosaic pillars on the second upper level, a preview of what's inside. The Miquel Blay sculptural group at the corner of Sant Pere Més Alt and Amadeu Vives depicts everyone from St. George the dragon slayer (at the top) to fishermen with oars over their shoulders.

The interior is an uproar. Wagnerian cavalry erupts from the right side of the stage over a heavy-browed bust of Beethoven, and Catalonia's popular music is represented by the flowing maidens of Lluís Millet's song "Flors de Maig" ("Flowers of May") on the left. Overhead, an inverted stained-glass cupola seems to offer the divine manna of music; painted rosettes and giant peacock feathers explode from the tops of the walls. Even the stage is populated with muselike Art Nouveau musicians, each half bust and half mosaic. The visuals alone make music sound different in here, and at any important concert the excitement is palpably thick; if you can't attend one, take a tour of the hall. *Ticket office* ✉ *Carrer Palau de la Música 4–6, just off Via Laietana, around corner from hall, Sant Pere* ☎ *902/442882* 🌐 *www.palaumusica.org* 🎫 *Tour €10* ⏲ *Sept.–June, tours daily 10–3:30, July and Aug., tours daily 10–7* Ⓜ *Catalunya.*

21 **Plaça del Rei.** As chronicled in legend, song, and painting, this austere medieval square has long been believed to be the scene of Columbus's triumphal return from his first voyage to the New World, with Ferdinand and Isabella receiving "the discoverer" on the stairs—though it turns out, the king and queen were actually at a summer palace outside of town. The **Palau Reial Major** was the Catholic Monarchs' official residence in Barcelona. Its main room is the **Saló del Tinell**, a banquet hall built in 1362. Also around the square, as you face the stairway, are the dark 15th-century **Torre Mirador del Rei Martí** (King Martin's Watchtower) above the Saló del Tinell; to the left is the 16th-century **Palau del Lloctinent** (Lieutenant's Palace) and archive of the Corona d'Aragó with its gorgeous patio, a coffered ceiling in the shape of an inverted boat over the stairway, a Josep Maria Subirachs sculpted bronze door, and a display on the life of Jaume I, founder of the Catalan nation. The 14th-century **Capilla Reial de Santa Àgueda** (Royal Chapel of Saint Agatha) is to the right of the stairway; and, moving back out Carrer Veguer, the **Palau Clariana-Padellàs** (Clariana-Padellàs Palace), moved here stone by stone from Carrer Mercaders in the early 20th century, is at the entrance to the Museu d'Història de la Ciutat. The hulking bronze sculpture, *Topos* (Greek for "Place") by Basque sculptor Eduardo Chillida (1924–2002), is a nod to modernity, blending gracefully with the historic setting and the resonating notes from the classical guitarist usually performing in the square. Ⓜ *Catalunya, Liceu, Jaume I.*

16 **Plaça Reial.** Pungent and seedy around the edges but elegant and neoclassical in design, this symmetrical mid-19th-century arcaded square is bordered by ocher facades with balconies overlooking the **Fountain of the Three Graces** and lampposts designed by Gaudí. Restaurants and cafés, sadly identifiable as tourist traps by the photo-menus (the

CLOSE UP

Barcelona's Medieval Jewish quarter

For a tour of Barcelona's *call* (from the Hebrew word for small or dead-end street), the medieval Jewish quarter, leave Plaça Sant Jaume on Carrer del Call, turn right on Sant Domènech del Call, and proceed to the next corner. Early Barcelona's Sinagoga Major (Main Synagogue), the most important surviving landmark of the Jewish community that prospered here until decimated by a 1391 pogrom, opens into Carrer Marlet. The main facade of the synagogue faces southeast, toward Jerusalem. At the next corner is a stone with Hebrew inscriptions (with Spanish and English translations on the nearby plaque). Around the corner to the right through Arc de Sant Ramón del Call in Plaça Manuel Ribé is the **Centre d'Interpretació del Call**.

only good one is Taxidermista, see the listing below), line the square. On Sunday morning, crowds gather to sell and trade stamps and coins. After dark the square is a nightlife hot spot, starring Jamboree for jazz and disco, Los Tarantos for flamenco, and Glaciar for young beer-drinking internationals. Ⓜ *Catalunya, Liceu.*

18 **Plaça Sant Jaume.** Two thousand years ago, this formal square was the center of the Roman forum, which seems fitting for the modern-day site of both Catalonia's and Barcelona's government seats. The Plaça was cleared in the 1840s, but the two imposing buildings facing each other across it are much older, the original Gothic facades on their respective north sides facing Carrer del Bisbat and Carrer Ciutat. The 15th-century *ajuntament* (City Hall) contains impressive black-and-burnished-gold murals (1928) by Josep Maria Sert, and the historic Saló de Cent, where the Council of One Hundred, Europe's earliest proto-democratic body founded in 1372, governed until Felipe V abolished Catalonia's autonomous institutions in 1715. Filled with art, the *ajuntament* is open to the public on Sunday morning (10–1) and on special holidays. During the week, check listings for free concerts or events here. The **Palau de la Generalitat,** seat of the Catalan government, is a majestic 15th-century palace—through the front windows you can see the gilded ceiling of the Saló de Sant Jordi (Hall of St. George), named for Catalonia's dragon-slaying patron saint. Normally you can visit the Generalitat only on certain holidays, such as the Día de Sant Jordi (St. George's Day), April 23; check with the *protocolo* (protocol office). The Generalitat hosts carillon concerts, open to the public, on occasional Sundays at noon. ✉ *Pl. Sant Jaume 1, Barri Gòtic* ☎ *93/402–7000* 🌐 *www.bcn.es* ⏲ *Sun. 10–1* Ⓜ *Catalunya, Liceu, Jaume I.*

23 **Santa Maria del Mar.** The most breathtakingly symmetrical and graceful of all Barcelona's churches is on the Carrer Montcada end of Passeig del Born. It's an early Gothic basilica with Romanesque echoes and overtones; simple and spacious, this pure, classical space enclosed by soaring columns is something of an oddity in ornate and complex Moderniste Barcelona. Santa Maria del Mar (Saint Mary of the Sea)

Fodor's Choice ★

was built from 1329 to 1383, an extraordinarily prompt construction time in that era, in fulfillment of a vow made a century earlier by Jaume I to build a church to watch over all Catalan seafarers. The architect in charge of the construction, a mere stonemason named Montagut de Berenguer, designed a bare-bones basilica (an oblong Roman royal hall used for public meetings and later adapted for early Christian or medieval churches) that's now considered the finest existing example of Catalan (or Mediterranean) Gothic architecture. The number eight (or multiples thereof)—the medieval numerological symbol for the Virgin Mary—runs through every element of the basilica's construction: 16 octagonal pillars rise 16 meters before arching out another 16 meters to the painted keystones at the apex of the arches 32 meters overhead. The sum of the lateral aisles, 8 meters each, equals the width of the center aisle, and the difference in height between the central and lateral naves, 8 meters, equals their width. The result of all this proportional balance is a tonic sense of peace and enlightenment, an almost mystical poise enhanced by a lovely rose window whose circular mass in blues and crimsons perfectly offsets the golden sandstone verticality of the columns. Any excuse to spend time in Santa Maria del Mar, from eavesdropping on a wedding to hearing a concert to using it merely as a shortcut through to the Passeig de Born, is valid. The haunting "Cant de la Sibil.la" ("Song of the Sibyl"), performed on Christmas Eve before the midnight Mass, is a concert not to miss, and Handel's *Messiah* at Christmas and Haydn's *Creation* at Easter are also noteworthy annual events. Any chance to hear Renaissance choral music here—performances of the works of such composers as Tomás Luís de Victoria, Guerrero, Tallis, and Byrd—especially if performed by the Sixteen or the Tallis Scholars, is a special treat. ✉*Pl. de Santa Maria, Born-Ribera* ☎*93/310–2390* ⏲*Daily 9–1:30 and 4:30–8* Ⓜ*Catalunya, Jaume I.*

7

WORTH NOTING

19 **Catedral de la Seu.** On Saturday afternoons, Sunday mornings, and occasional evenings, Barcelona folk gather in the Plaça de la Seu to dance the *sardana,* a somewhat demure circle dance and a great symbol of Catalan identity. The Gothic cathedral was built between 1298 and 1450, with the spire and neo-Gothic facade added in 1892. Architects of Catalan Gothic churches strove to make the high altar visible to the entire congregation, hence the unusually wide central nave and slender side columns. The first thing you see upon entering the Catedral de la Seu are the high relief sculptures on the choir stalls, telling the story of **Santa Eulàlia** (Barcelona's co-patron along with La Mercé, Our Lady of Mercy). The first scene, on the left, shows St. Eulàlia in front of Roman Consul Decius with her left hand on her heart and her right hand pointing at a cross in the distance. In the next scene, Eulàlia is tied to a column and flagellated by Decius's thugs. To the right of the choir entrance, the senseless Eulàlia is hauled away, and in the final scene she is lashed to the X-shaped cross upon which she was crucified in the year 303.To the right of this high relief is a sculpture of St. Eulàlia with her cross, resurrected as a living saint. Other highlights are the beautifully carved choir stalls, St. Eulàlia's tomb in the crypt, and the battle-scarred crucifix in the Lepanto Chapel to the right of the main entrance. The

tall cloisters surround a tropical garden, and outside, at the building's front right corner, is the intimate Santa Llúcia chapel. The cathedral is floodlit in striking yellows at night, and the stained-glass windows are backlit. During the so-called Special Visits, from 1 to 5 PM, visitors can see the entire cathedral, museum, bell tower, and rooftop. ✉ *Pl. de la Seu, Barri Gòtic* ☎ *93/342–8260* 🌐 *www.catedralbcn.org* 🎫 *1–5 PM Special Visit: €5.50; the rest of the time free* 🕒 *Daily 7:45 AM–7:45 PM* Ⓜ *Catalunya, Liceu, Jaume I.*

OFF THE BEATEN PATH

Museu del Calçat. A pair of shoes worn by cello player Pablo Casals and a pair of early clown's shoes are among the amusing curios found in the tiny Shoe Museum between the cathedral and Carrer Banys Nous. The intimate square, originally a graveyard, is just as interesting as the museum, with its shrapnel-pocked walls and quiet fountain. ✉ *Pl. Sant Felip Neri, Barri Gòtic* ☎ *93/301–4533* 🎫 *€4* 🕒 *Tues.–Sun. 11–2* Ⓜ *Catalunya, Liceu, Jaume I.*

20 **Museu Frederic Marès** *(Frederic Marès Museum).* You can browse for hours amid the miscellany assembled by the early-20th-century sculptor-collector Frederic Marès in this trove of art and odds and ends. Everything from paintings and polychrome woodcarvings, such as Juan de Juní's 1537 masterpiece *Pietà* and the Master of Cabestany's late-12th-century *Apparition of Christ to His Disciples at Sea,* to Marès's collection of pipes and walking sticks is stuffed into this rich potpourri. ✉ *Pl. Sant Iu 5, Barri Gòtic* ☎ *93/310–5800* 🌐 *www.museumares.bcn.es* 🎫 *€4.50; free 1st Sun. of month and Wed. afternoon* 🕒 *Tues.– Sat. 10–7, Sun. 10–3* Ⓜ *Catalunya, Liceu, Jaume I.*

27 **Sant Pere de les Puelles** *(St. Peter of the Novices).* One of the oldest medieval churches in Barcelona, this one has been destroyed and restored so many times that there's little left to see except the beautiful stained-glass window, which illuminates the stark interior. *Puelles* comes from the Latin *puella* (girl)—the convent here was known for the beauty and nobility of its young women. ✉ *Lluís El Piadós 1, Sant Pere* ☎ *93/268–0742* 🕒 *Open for mass only* Ⓜ *Catalunya, Jaume I.*

15 **Santa Maria del Pi** *(St. Mary of the Pine).* Like Santa Maria del Mar, the church of Santa Maria del Pi is an example of Mediterranean Gothic architecture, though its bulky, somber interior makes its soaring and elegant sister ship seem even more astounding by comparison. The gigantic rose window is best seen from inside in the late afternoon. The adjoining squares, **Plaça del Pi** and **Plaça de Sant Josep Oriol,** are two of the liveliest, most appealing spaces in the Gothic Quarter. ✉ *Pl. del Pi s/n, Barri Gòtic* ☎ *93/318–4743* 🕒 *Daily 9–1:30 and 4:30–8* Ⓜ *Liceu.*

BARCELONETA, LA CIUTADELLA, AND PORT OLÍMPIC

Barceloneta, once the open sea, was silted in and became a salt marsh until 1753, when French military engineer Prosper de Verboom designed a housing project for families who had lost their homes in La Ribera. Today, Port Olímpic, along the sport marina northeast of the Hotel Arts, is mainly taken up with tourist-filled terrace restaurants and high-decibel discos—it's probably best avoided if this isn't your taste. The Ciutadella, once the fortress that kept watch over Barcelona, is now a leafy park with the city zoo, the Catalan parliament, and pools and waterfalls.

TOP ATTRACTIONS

36 **Barceloneta.** Once Barcelona's pungent fishing port, Barceloneta retains much of its salty maritime flavor. It's an exciting and colorful place to walk through, with narrow streets with lines of laundry snapping in the breeze. Stop in Plaça de la Barceloneta to see the baroque church of **Sant Miquel del Port,** with its oversize sculpture of the winged archangel himself. Look for the splendidly remodeled Barceloneta market and its upstairs and downstairs restaurants, Lluçanès and Els Fogons de la Barceloneta. The original two-story houses and the restaurant Can Solé on Carrer Sant Carles are historic landmarks. Barceloneta's surprisingly clean and sandy **beach,** though overcrowded in midsummer, offers swimming, surfing, and a lively social scene from late May through September.

NEED A BREAK?

Friendly **Can Manel la Puda** (✉ *Passeig de Joan de Borbó 60–61* ☎ *93/221–5013*), in Barceloneta, is always good for an inexpensive feast. Serving lunch until 4 and starting dinner at 7, it's a popular place for *suquets* (fish stew), paella, and *arròs a banda* (rice with shelled seafood). It's closed Monday. On Monday or if Can Manel is booked solid, La Mar Salada next door is just as good.

7

WORTH NOTING

29 **Arc del Triomf.** This imposing, exposed-redbrick arch on Passeig de Sant Joan was built by Josep Vilaseca as the grand entrance for the Universal Exposition of 1888. Similar in size and sense to the triumphal arches of ancient Rome, this one refers to Jaume I El Conqueridor's 1229 conquest of the Moors in Mallorca—the bats, on either side of the arch, are always part of Jaume I's coat of arms.

30 **Castell dels Tres Dragons** *(Castle of the Three Dragons)*. Built by Domènech i Montaner as a restaurant for the Universal Exposition of 1888, this arresting structure was named in honor of a popular mid-19th-century comedy by the father of the Catalan theater, Serafí Pitarra. Greeting you on the right as you enter the Ciutadella from Passeig Lluí Companys, the building has exposed brickwork and visible iron supports, both radical innovations of their time. Moderniste architects later met here to exchange ideas and experiment with traditional crafts. The castle now holds Barcelona's **Museum of Zoology.** ✉ *Passeig Picasso 5, La Ciutadella* ☎ *93/319–6912* 🌐 *www.bcn.es/medciencies* 🎟 *€4.50* ⏲ *Tues., Wed., Fri.–Sun. 10–2:30, Thurs. 10–6:30* Ⓜ *Arc de Triomf.*

37 **El Transbordador Aeri del Port** *(cable car)*. The creaky looking but recently refurbished (2006) cable car leaving from the tower at the end of Passeig Joan de Borbó connects the Torre de San Sebastián on the Moll de Barceloneta, the tower of Jaume I in the boat terminal, and the Torre de Miramar on Montjuïc. The Torre de Altamar restaurant in the tower at the Barceloneta end serves excellent food and wine and has nonpareil views. ✉ *Passeig Joan de Borbó s/n, Barceloneta* ☎ *93/225–2718* 🎟 *€12.50 round-trip, €9 one-way* ⏲ *Daily 10:45–7* Ⓜ *Barceloneta.*

Arc de Triomf .. **29**
Barceloneta ... **36**
Castell dels Tres Dragons ... **30**
Estació de França **40**
La Cascada **32**
Museu d'Història de Catalunya .. **38**
Museu de la Geologia **31**
Parc de la Ciutadella **33**
Port Olimpic ... **35**
Port Vell **39**
El Transbordador Aeri del Port ... **37**
Zoo **34**

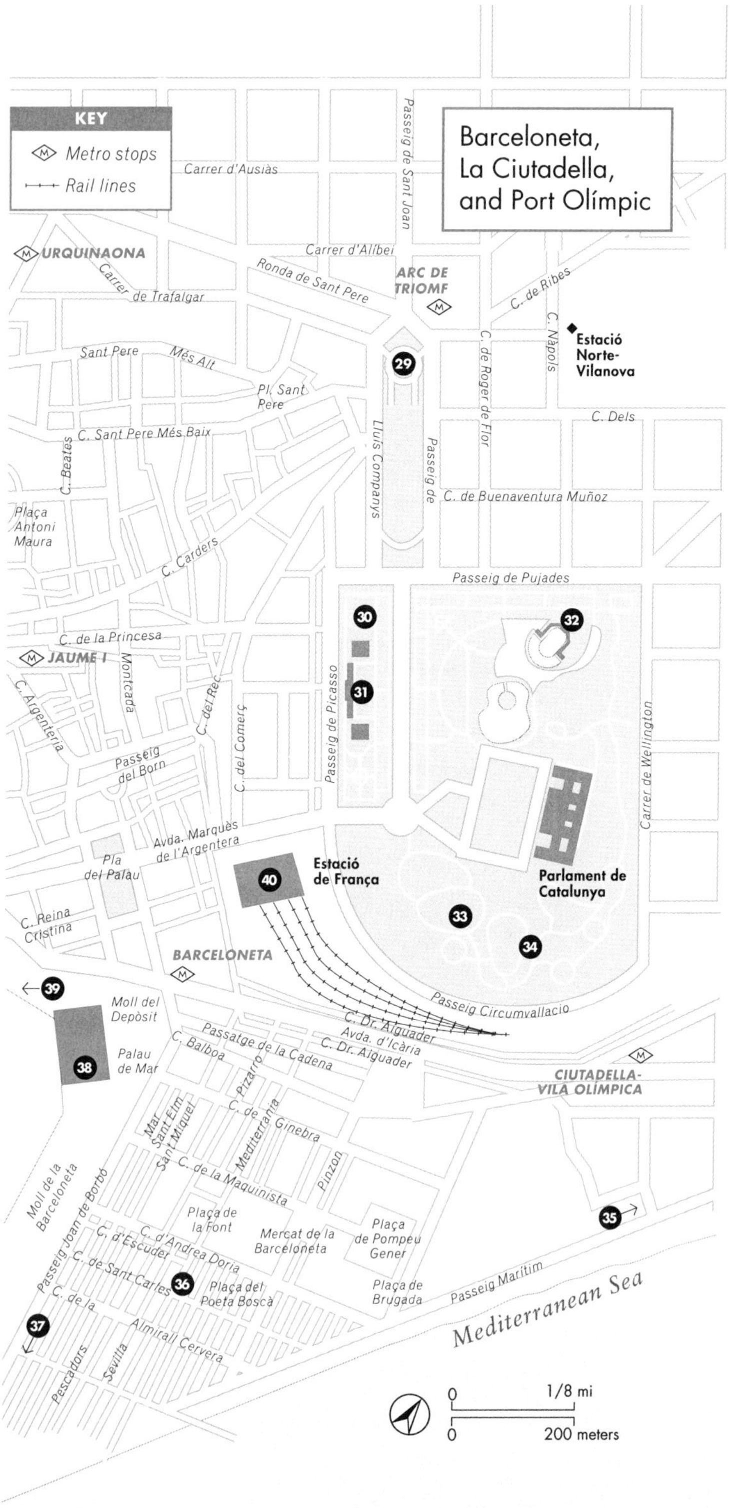

40 **Estació de França.** Outside the west gate of the Ciutadella, the gracefully restored Estació de França was once Barcelona's main train station. Wander in for a rush of European railroad nostalgia. ✉ *Marquès de l'Argentera s/n, Born-Ribera* Ⓜ *Barceloneta.*

32 **La Cascada.** Take a break by the Ciutadella's lake; behind it, you'll find the monumental *Cascada* (Falls), by Josep Fontseré, designed for the Universal Exposition of 1888. The waterfall's rocks were the work of a young architecture student named Antoni Gaudí—his first public work, appropriately natural and organic, a hint of things to come. ✉ *La Ciutadella* Ⓜ *Arc de Triomf, Ciutadella.*

31 **Museu de la Geologia.** The Museum of Geology is next to the Castell dels Tres Dragons and the Umbracle, a shaded place, the black slats of which help create jungle lighting for their collection of tropical plants that grow in penumbral light. Barcelona's first public museum, it has rocks, minerals, and fossils from Catalonia and the rest of Spain. ✉ *Off Passeig de Picasso, La Ciutadella* ☎ *93/319–6895* 🌐 *www.bcn.es/museuciencies* 🎫 *€5.50; free 1st Sun. of month* ⏲ *Tues., Wed., Fri.–Sun. 10–2, Thurs. 10–6:30* Ⓜ *Arc de Triomf, Ciutadella.*

38 **Museu d'Història de Catalunya.** Built into what used to be a port warehouse, this state-of-the-art museum is interactive (visitors can try on armor or ride a mechanical horse along with activating computerized displays), making you part of Catalonian history. Beginning with prehistoric times, the emergence of the language and identity of Catalonia is traced through more than 3,000 years into the contemporary democratic era. Explanations of the exhibits appear in Catalan, Castilian, and English. Guided tours are available on Sunday at noon and 1 PM. The rooftop cafeteria, open to the general public, has excellent views over the harbor. ✉ *Pl. Pau Vila 3, Barceloneta* ☎ *93/225–4700* 🌐 *www.mhcat.net* 🎫 *€4.50; free 1st Sun. of month* ⏲ *Tues. and Thurs.–Sat. 10–7, Wed. 10–8, Sun. 10–2:30* Ⓜ *Barceloneta.*

33 **Parc de la Ciutadella** *(Citadel Park).* Once a fortress designed to consolidate Madrid's military occupation of Barcelona, the Ciutadella is now the city's main downtown park. The clearing dates from shortly after the War of the Spanish Succession, when Felipe V demolished some 2,000 houses in what was then the Barri de la Ribera (Waterfront Neighborhood) to build a fortress and barracks for his soldiers and fields of fire for his artillery. The fortress walls were pulled down in 1868 and replaced by gardens laid out by Josep Fontserè. Within the park are a cluster of museums, the Catalan parliament, and the city zoo. ✉ *Bounded by Passeig Picasso, Passeig Pujades, Carrer de Wellington, and Born-Ribera* Ⓜ *Barceloneta.*

35 **Port Olímpic.** Choked with yachts, restaurants, and tapas bars of all kinds, the Olympic Port is 2 km (1 mi) up the beach, marked by the mammoth Frank Gehry goldfish sculpture in front of Barcelona's first real skyscraper, the Hotel Arts. The port rages on Friday and Saturday nights, especially in summer, with hundreds of young people circling and grazing until daybreak. ✉ *Carrer de la Marina/Passeig Marítim, Born-Ribera* Ⓜ *Ciutadella, Vila Olímpica.*

39 **Port Vell** *(Old Port)*. Barcelona's marina stretches the length of Passeig de Joan de Borbó and encompasses the large pedestrian wharves (*molls*). Just beyond the Lichtenstein sculpture *Barcelona Head,* the modern Port Vell complex stretches up the grassy hill to the wood-panel *Ictineo II* reproduction of the submarine created by Narcis Monturiol (1819–85). The submarine was the world's first, launched in the Barcelona port in 1862. Beyond are the IMAX theater, the aquarium, and the Maremagnum shopping mall along the Moll d'Espanya. The Moll de Barceloneta, with its five (rather pricey and impersonal) terrace restaurants, stretches along the marina across the way. ✉ *Passeig d'Ítaca s/n, Barceloneta-Port Vell* Ⓜ *Barceloneta.*

34 **Zoo.** Barcelona's zoo occupies the bottom part of the Parc de la Ciutadella. A complete cast of all the usual African animals reside in this colony squeezed in between the Catalan Parliament and the Universidad Pompeu Fabra. Look for the statue of *La Senyoreta del Paraigua* (*Lady with Umbrella*) near the dolphins. ✉ *La Ciutadella* ☎ *93/225–6780* 🌐 *www.zoobarcelona.com* *€16.50 (under 12 €9.80)* ⏲ *Daily 10–7* Ⓜ *Arc de Triomf, Ciutadella.*

THE EIXAMPLE

North of Plaça de Catalunya is the checkerboard known as the Eixample. With the dismantling of the city walls in 1860, Barcelona embarked upon an expansion scheme fueled by the return of rich colonials, the influx of provincial aristocrats who had sold their country estates after the debilitating second Carlist War (1847–49), and the city's growing industrial power. The street grid was the work of urban planner Ildefons Cerdà and much of the building here was done at the height of Modernisme. The Eixample's principal thoroughfares are Rambla de Catalunya and Passeig de Gràcia, where the city's most elegant shops vie for space among its best Art Nouveau buildings.

A GOOD TOUR

Starting in the Plaça de Catalunya, walk up Passeig de Gràcia until you reach the corner of Consell de Cent, where you'll enter the vortex of Moderniste architecture, the **Manzana de la Discòrdia** 41. The **Casa Montaner i Simó–Fundació Tàpies** 42 is around the corner on Carrer Aragó. Gaudí's **Casa Milà** 43, known as La Pedrera, is three blocks farther up Passeig de Gràcia; after touring the interior and rooftop, walk up Passeig de Gràcia to the **Vinçon,** one of Barcelona's top design stores, with views into the back of Casa Milà. Just around the corner, at Diagonal 373, is Puig i Cadafalch's intricately sculpted **Palau Baró de Quadras** 44, now housing the Casa Asia cultural center. Two minutes farther east is his Nordic castlelike **Casa de les Punxes** 45 at No. 416–420. From here it's a 10-minute walk to yet another Puig i Cadafalch masterpiece, **Casa Macaia** 46. Finally, walk another 15 minutes along Carrer Provença to Gaudí's emblematic **Temple Expiatori de la Sagrada Família** 47. If you've still got energy and curiosity to burn, stroll over to Domènech i Montaner's **Hospital de Sant Pau** 48.

TIMING Depending on how many taxis you take, this is a four- to five-hour tour, so plan your exploring around a good lunch. Add an hour to

The Eixample

Casa Àsia—Palau Baró de Quadras **44**

Casa Macaia **46**

Casa Milà **43**

Casa Montaner i Simó—Fundació Tàpies ... **42**

Casa de les Punxes **45**

Hospital de Sant Pau **48**

Manzana de la Discòrdia (Casa Lleó Morera, Casa Amatller, Casa Batlló) **41**

Temple Expiatori de la Sagrada Família .... **47** two hours each to visit Casa Battló, Casa Milà, and the Sagrada Família, or plan to return later.

CATALAN FOR BEGINNERS

Catalan is derived from Latin and Provençal French, whereas Spanish is heavy on Arabic vocabulary and phonetics. For language exchange *(intercambios),* check the bulletin board at the central university Philosophy and Letters Faculty on Gran Via or any English bookstore for free half-hour exchanges of English for Catalan (or Spanish), a great way to get free private lessons and meet locals. Who knows? With the right chemistry, intercambios can lead to cross-cultural friendships and even romance. Who said the language of love is French?

TOP ATTRACTIONS

43 ★ **Casa Milà.** Gaudí's Casa Milà, usually referred to as **La Pedrera** (The Stone Quarry), has a curving stone facade that bobs around the corner of the block. When the building was unveiled, in 1910, residents weren't enthusiastic about the cave-like balconies on their most fashionable street. Don't miss Gaudí's rooftop chimney park, especially in late afternoon, when the sunlight slants over the city into the Mediterranean. The handsome **Espai Gaudí** (Gaudí Space) in the attic has excellent critical displays of Gaudí's works, theories, and techniques, including an upside-down model of the Sagrada Família made of hanging beads. The **Pis de la Pedrera,** a restored apartment, gives an interesting glimpse into the life of its resident family in the early 20th century. Guided tours are offered weekdays at 6 PM and weekends at 11 AM. ✉ *Carrer Provença 261–265, Eixample* ☎ *902/400973* 🎫 *€8.50* ⏲ *Daily 9–6:30; guided tours weekdays at 6* PM, *weekends at 11* AM. *Espai Gaudí roof terrace open for drinks evenings June–Sept.* Ⓜ *Diagonal, Provença.*

41 Fodor's Choice ★ **Manzana de la Discòrdia.** A pun on the Spanish word *manzana,* meaning both city block and apple, the reference is to the classical myth of the Apple of Discord, in which Eris, goddess of strife, drops a golden apple with the inscription "to the fairest." Hera, Athena, and Aphrodite all claim the apple; Paris is chosen to settle the dispute and awards the apple to Aphrodite, who promises him Helen, the most beautiful of women, triggering the Trojan War. On this city block you can find the architectural counterpoint, where the three main Moderniste architects go hand to hand, drawing steady crowds of architecture buffs. Of the three, Casa Batlló is clearly the star.

Casa Lleó Morera (No. 35) was extensively rebuilt (1902–06) by Palau de la Música Catalana architect Domènech i Montaner and is a treasure chest of Modernisme. The facade is covered with ornamentation and sculptures of female figures using the modern inventions of the age: the telephone, the telegraph, the photographic camera, and the Victrola. The inside is closed to the public, but a quick glimpse into the entryway on the corner gives an idea of what's upstairs.

The pseudo-Flemish **Casa Amatller** (No. 41) was built by Josep Puig i Cadafalch in 1900 as a residence for the chocolatier Antoni Amattler. Puig i Cadafalch's architectural historicism sought to recover Catalonia's proud past, in combination with eclectic elements from Flemish and Netherlandish architectural motifs. The Eusebi Arnau sculptures range from St. George and the dragon to the figures of a handless drummer with his dancing bear. The flowing-haired "Princesa" is thought to be Amatller's daughter, and the animals up above are pouring chocolate, a reference to the source of the Amatller family fortune. Casa Amatller is closed to the public (call or ask about any change in this), but an office on-site dispenses tickets for the Ruta del Modernisme tour *(see the Moderniste Barcelona box for details).*

At No. 43, the colorful and bizarre **Casa Batlló**—Gaudí at his most spectacular—with its mottled facade resembling anything from an abstract pointillist painting to rainbow sprinkles on an ice-cream cone, is usually easily identifiable by the crowd of tourists snapping photographs on the sidewalk. Nationalist symbolism is hard at work here: the scaly roofline represents the Dragon of Evil impaled on St. George's cross, and the skulls and bones on the balconies are the dragon's victims. These motifs are allusions to Catalonia's Middle Ages, with its codes of chivalry and religious fervor. The interior design follows a gently swirling maritime motif in stark contrast to the terrestrial strife represented on the facade. ✉ *Passeig de Gràcia 43, between Carrer Consell de Cent and Carrer Aragó, Eixample* ☎ *93/216–0306* 🌐 *www.casabatllo.es* 🎫 *€17* 🕗 *Daily 9–8* Ⓜ *Passeig de Gràcia.*

47 Fodor's Choice ★ **Temple Expiatori de la Sagrada Família.** Looming over Barcelona like a magical midcity massif of needles and peaks left by eons of wind erosion and fungal exuberance, Barcelona's most unforgettable landmark, Antoni Gaudí's Sagrada Família, was conceived as nothing short of a Bible in stone. This landmark is one of the most important architectural creations of the 19th to 21st centuries, though it's still under construction.

Start at the **Nativity facade,** where Gaudí addresses the fundamental mystery of Christianity: why does God the Creator become, through Jesus Christ, a creature? Gaudí's answer-in-stone is that God wanted to free man from the slavery of selfishness, symbolized here by the iron fence around the serpent at the base of the central column. The column depicts the genealogy of Christ. Overhead are the constellations in the Christmas sky at Bethlehem. Higher up is the Crowning of the Virgin under an overhang, atop which is a pelican feeding its young with its blood, a symbol of the eucharistic sacrifice. Below, two angels adore the initials of Christ (JHS) under the symbols of the cross, the Alpha and Omega. The cypress at the top is the evergreen symbol of eternity pointing to heaven; the white doves, souls seeking eternity.

To the right, the Portal of Faith, above Palestinian flora and fauna, shows scenes from the youth of Jesus, including his preaching at the age of 13. Higher up are grapes and wheat, symbols of the eucharist, and a sculpture of a hand and eye, symbols of divine providence. The left-hand Portal of Hope begins at the bottom with flora and fauna from the Nile; the Slaughter of the Innocents; the flight of the Holy Family into Egypt; Joseph, surrounded by his carpenter's tools, contemplating his son; and the marriage of Joseph and Mary. Above this is a sculpted boat

Continued on page 414

7

GAUDÍ

ARCHITECTURE THROUGH THE LOOKING GLASS

(left) The rooftop of Park Güell's gatehouse. (top) Construction continues on la Sagrada Família.

Shortly before his 75th birthday in 1926, Antonio Gaudí was hit by a trolley car while on his way to mass. The great architect–initially unidentified–was taken to the medieval Hospital de la Santa Creu in Barcelona's Raval and left in a pauper's ward, where he died two days later without regaining consciousness. It was a dramatic and tragic end for a man whose entire life seemed to court the extraordinary and the exceptional.

Gaudí's singularity made him hard to define. Indeed, eulogists at the time, and decades later, wondered how history would treat him. Was he a religious mystic, a rebel, a bohemian artist, a Moderniste genius? Was he, perhaps, all of these? He certainly had a rebellious streak, as his architecture stridently broke with tradition. Yet the same sensibility that created the avant-garde benchmarks Park Güell and La Pedrera also created one of Spain's greatest shrines to Catholicism, the *Temple Expiatori de la Sagrada Família* (Expiatory Temple of the Holy Family), which architects agree is one of the world's most enigmatic structures (work on the cathedral continues to this day). And while most of Gaudí's works suggest a futurist aesthetic, he also reveled in the use of ornamentation, which 20th century architecture largely eschewed.

What is no longer in doubt is Gaudí's place among the great architects in history. Eyed with suspicion by traditionalists in the 1920s and 30s, vilified during the Franco regime, and ultimately redeemed as a Barcelona icon after Spain's democratic transition in the late 70s, Gaudí's work has finally gained universal admiration.

THE MAKING OF A GENIUS

Gaudí was born in 1852 the son of a boilermaker and coppersmith in Reus, an hour south of Barcelona. As a child, he helped his father forge boilers and cauldrons in the family foundry, which is where Gaudí's fascination with three-dimensional and organic forms began. Afflicted from an early age with rheumatic fever, the young architect devoted his energies to studying and drawing flora and fauna in the natural world. In school he was erratic: brilliant in the subjects that interested him, absent and disinterested in the others. As a seventeen-year-old architecture student in Barcelona, his academic results were mediocre. Still, his mentors agreed that he was brilliant.

Unfortunately being brilliant didn't mean instant success. By the late 1870s, when Gaudí was well into his twenties, he'd only completed a handful of projects, including the Plaça Reial lampposts, a flower stall, and the factory and part of a planned workers' community in Mataró. Gaudí's career got the boost it needed when, in 1878, he met Eusebi Güell, heir to a textiles fortune and a man who, like Gaudí, had a refined sensibility. (The two bonded over a mutual admiration for the visionary Catalan poet Jacint Verdaguer.) In 1883 Gaudí became Güell's architect and for the next three decades, until Güell's death in 1918, the two collaborated on Gaudí's most important architectural achievements, from high-profile endeavors like Palau Güell, Park Güell, and Pabellones Güell to smaller projects for the Güell family.

(top) Interior of Casa Batlló. (bottom) Chimneys on rooftop of Casa Milà recall helmeted warriors or veiled women.

GAUDÍ TIMELINE

1883–1884

Gaudí builds a summer palace, *El Capricho* in Comillas, Santander for the brother-in-law of his benefactor, Eusebi Güell. Another gig comes his way during this same period when Barcelona ceramics tile mogul Manuel Vicens hires him to build his town house, *Casa Vicens*, in the Gràcia neighborhood.

El Capricho

1884–1900

Gaudí whips up the Güell Pabellones, Palau Güell, the Palacio Episcopal of Astorga, Barcelona's Teresianas school, the Casa de los Botines in León, Casa Calvet, and Bellesguard. These have his classic look of this time, featuring interpretation of Mudéjar (Moorish motifs), Gothic, and Baroque styles.

Palacio Episcopal

BREAKING OUT OF THE T-SQUARE PRISON

If Eusebi Güell had not believed in Gaudí's unusual approach to Modernisme, his creations may not have seen the light of day. Güell recognized that Gaudí was imbued with a vision that separated him from the crowd. That vision was his fascination with the organic. Gaudí had observed early in his career that buildings were being composed of shapes that could only be drawn by the compass and the T-square: circles, triangles, squares, and rectangles—shapes that in three dimensions became prisms, pyramids, cylinders and spheres. He saw that in nature these shapes are unknown. Admiring the structural efficiency of trees, mammals, and the human form, Gaudí noted ". . . neither are trees prismatic, nor bones cylindrical, nor leaves triangular." The study of natural forms revealed that bones, branches, muscles, and tendons are all supported by internal fibers. Thus, though a surface curves, it is supported from within by a fibrous network that Gaudí translated into what he called "ruled geometry," a system of inner reinforcement he used to make hyperboloids, conoids, helicoids, or parabolic hyperboloids.

These tongue-tying words are simple forms and familiar shapes: the femur is hyperboloid; the way shoots grow off a branch is helicoidal; the web between your fingers is a hyperbolic paraboloid. To varying degrees, these ideas find expression in all of Gaudí's work, but nowhere are they more clearly stated than in the two masterpieces La Pedrera and Park Güell.

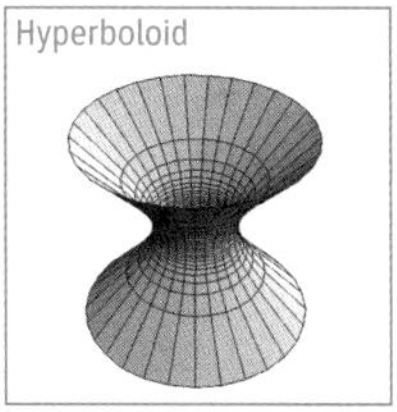

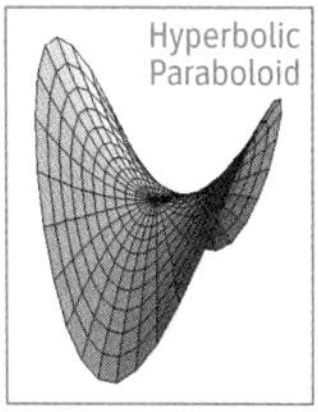

Casa Batlló's scaly dragon-back roof atop a structure composed of tibias, femurs, and skulls show Gaudí's interest in anatomy and organic forms.

1900–1917

Gaudí's Golden Years—his most creative, personal, and innovative period. Topping each success with another, he tackles Park Güell, the reform of Casa Batlló, the Güell Colony church, Casa Milà (AKA La Pedrera), and the Sagrada Família school.

Casa Batlló's complex chimneys

1918–1926

A crushing blow: Gaudí suffers the death of his assistant, Francesc Berenguer. Grieving and rudderless, he devotes himself fully to his great unfinished opus, la Sagrada Família—to the point of obsession. On June 10th, 1926, he's hit by a trolley car. He dies two days later.

La Sagrada Família

HOW TO SEE GAUDÍ IN BARCELONA

(top) The serpentine ceramic bench at Park Güell, designed by Gaudí collaborator Josep Maria Jujol, curves sinuously around the edge of the open square. (bottom) Sculptures byJosep María Subirachs grace the temple of the Sagrada Família.

Few architects have left their stamp on a major city as thoroughly as Gaudí did in Barcelona. Paris may have the Eiffel Tower, but Barcelona has Gaudí's still unfinished masterpiece, the Temple Expiatori de la Sagrada Família, the city's most emblematic structure. Dozens of other buildings, parks, gateways and even paving stones around town bear Gaudí's personal Art Nouveau signature, but the continuing progress on his last and most ambitious project makes his creative energy an ongoing part of everyday Barcelona life in a unique and almost spectral fashion.

In Barcelona, nearly all of Gaudí's work can be visited on foot or, at most, with a couple of metro or taxi rides. A walk from Palau Güell near the Mediterranean end of the Rambla, up past Casa Calvet just above Plaça Catalunya, and on to Casa Batlló and Casa Milà is an hour's stroll, which, of course, could take a full day with thorough visits to the sites. Casa Vicens is a half hour's walk up into Gràcia from Casa Milà. Park Güell is another thirty- to forty-minute walk up from that. La Sagrada Família, on the other hand, is a good hour's hike from the next nearest Gaudí point and is best reached by taxi or metro. The Teresianas school, the Bellesguard Tower, and Pabellones Güell are within an hour's walk of each other, but to get out to Sarrià you will need to take the comfortable Generalitat (FGC) train.

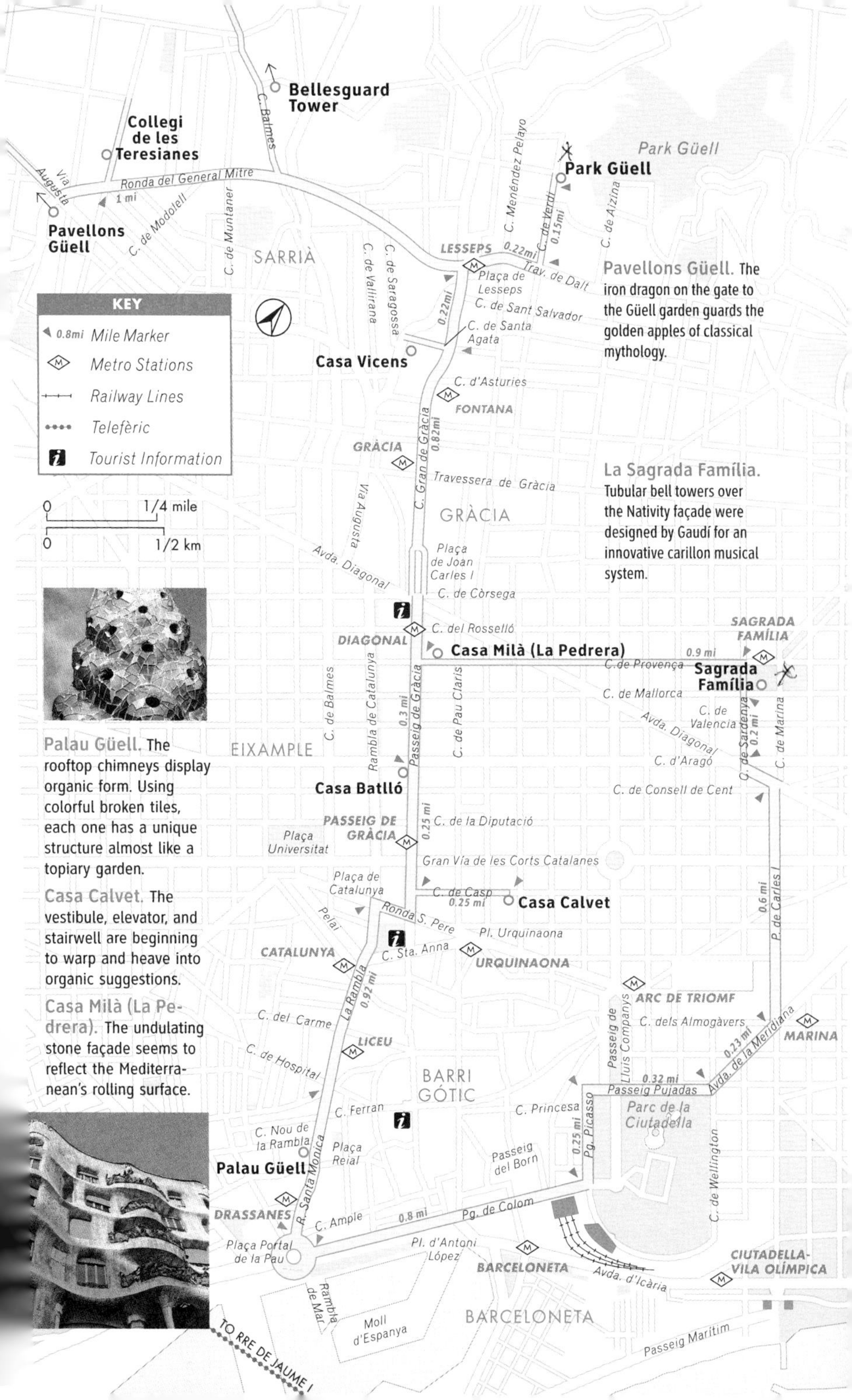

Pavellons Güell. The iron dragon on the gate to the Güell garden guards the golden apples of classical mythology.

La Sagrada Família. Tubular bell towers over the Nativity façade were designed by Gaudí for an innovative carillon musical system.

Palau Güell. The rooftop chimneys display organic form. Using colorful broken tiles, each one has a unique structure almost like a topiary garden.

Casa Calvet. The vestibule, elevator, and stairwell are beginning to warp and heave into organic suggestions.

Casa Milà (La Pedrera). The undulating stone façade seems to reflect the Mediterranean's rolling surface.

CLOSE UP

Moderniste Barcelona

Characterized by intense ornamentation and natural or organic lines and forms, Modernisme (Art Nouveau) swept Europe between 1880 and 1914, proliferating wildly in Barcelona. Beginning with the city's Universal Exposition of 1888, the playful Catalan artistic impulse (evidenced in the works of Gaudí, Miró, and Dalí) and Barcelona's late-19th-century industrial prosperity teamed up with a surge in Catalonian nationalism to run rampant in the Eixample neighborhood, where bourgeois families competed with each other by decorating their opulent mansions.

A cultural movement that went beyond architecture, Modernisme affected everything from clothes to hairstyles to tombstones. Painters, sculptors,, stained-glass artisans, ceramicists, acid engravers, and wood-carvers all contributed to the artistic explosion. The curved line replaced the straight; natural elements such as flowers and fruit were sculpted into facades; and the classical and pragmatic gave way to decorative ebullience.

Barcelona's Palau de la Música Catalana by Lluís Domènech i Montaner is a stunning compendium of Art Nouveau techniques, including acid-engraved and stained glass, polychrome ceramics, carved wooden arches, and sculpture. Josep Puig i Cadafalch's Casa Amatller and his Casa de les Punxes are examples of Modernisme's eclectic, historical tendency. Josep Graner i Prat's Casa de la Papallona, Joan Rubió Bellver's Casa Golferichs, Antoni Gaudí's Casa Batlló, and Salvador Valeri i Pupurull's Casa Comalat converted Barcelona's Eixample into a living Moderniste museum.

The **Ruta del Modernisme** is an itinerary through the Barcelona of Gaudì, Domènech i Montaner, and Puig i Cadafalch, just some of the architects who made Barcelona the world capital of Modernisme in the late 19th and early 20th centuries: palaces, private houses, the temple that has become a symbol of the city, and a huge hospital join pharmacies, lampposts, and benches—115 works in all—tracing Art Nouveau's explosion in Barcelona.

There are three Modernisme Centers—Centre d'Informació de Turisme de Barcelona (Plaça de Catalunya 17, Soterrani); Hospital de la Santa Creu i Sant Pau (Pavelló de Santa Apol. lònia, Carrer Sant Antoni Claret 167); and Pavellons Güell (Av. de Pedralbes 7)—that sell items related to the route, including a **guide book**, which has discount vouchers good for up to 50% on all Moderniste monuments in the city and in another 13 towns. For more details call ☎ *902/076621* or check out *www.rutadelmodernisme.com.*

with anchor (representing the church), piloted by St. Joseph assisted by the Holy Spirit. Overhead is a typical spire from the Montserrat massif. Gaudí intended these towers to house a system of bells capable of playing more complex music than standard bell systems. The towers' peaks represent the apostles' successors in the form of miters, the official headdress of bishops of the Western church.

RECOMMENDED MODERNISTE MONUMENTS	
■ Casa Amatller	■ CosmoCaixa, Museu de la Ciència
■ Casa Batlló	■ Hidroelèctrica
■ Casa Calvet	■ Hospital de la Santa Creu i Sant Pau
■ Casa Comalat	■ Museu Nacional d'Art de Catalunya (MNAC)
■ Casa de les Punxes (Casa Terrades)	■ Museu de Zoologia
■ Casa Fuster	■ Observatori Fabra
■ Casa Lleó Morera	■ Palau de la Música Catalana
■ Casa Macaya	■ Palau del Baró de Quuadras
■ Casa Milà (La Pedrera)	■ Palau Montaner
■ Casa Planells	■ Pavellons Güell
■ Casa Thomas	■ Temple Expiatori de la Sagrada Família
■ Casa Vicens	■ Torre Bellesguard
■ Conservatori Municipal de Música	

The **Passion facade** on the southwestern side, at the entrance to the grounds, is a dramatic contrast to the Nativity facade. Josep Maria Subirachs, the sculptor chosen in 1986 to execute Gaudí's plans—initially an atheist, and author of statements such as "God is one of man's greatest creations"—now confesses to a respectful agnosticism. Known for his distinctly angular, geometrical interpretations of the human form, Subirachs boasted that his work "has nothing to do with Gaudí." When in 1990 artists, architects, and religious leaders called for his resignation after he sculpted an anatomically complete naked Christ on the cross, Subirachs defended the piece as part of the realism of the scene. Despite his staunch ideological and esthetic independence from the master, Subirachs pays double homage to Gaudí in the Passion facade: over the left side of the main entry is the blocky figure of Gaudí making notes or drawings, and the Roman soldiers are modeled on Gaudí's helmeted chimneys on the roof of La Pedrera.

Framed by leaning tibialike columns representing the bones of the dead, the scenes begin at the left with the Last Supper. The faces of the disciples are contorted in confusion and dismay, especially that of Judas, who clutches a bag of money behind his back over the figure of a reclining hound (a symbol of fidelity contrasting with the treachery of Judas). The next sculptural group represents the prayer in the Garden of Gethsemane and Peter awakening, followed by the kiss of Judas.

In the center, Jesus is lashed to a pillar during his flagellation, a tear track carved into his expressive countenance. The column's top stone is off-kilter, a reminder of the stone to be removed from Christ's sepulchre. The knot and broken reed at the base of the pillar symbolize

Jesus's physical and psychological suffering. To the right of the door is a rooster, with Peter lamenting his third denial of Christ "before the cock crows." Farther to the right are Pilate and Jesus with a crown of thorns, and just above, back on the left, is Simon of Cyrene helping Jesus with the cross after his first fall. Over the center, where Jesus consoles the women of Jerusalem ("Don't cry for me; cry for your children"), is a faceless Veronica—faceless because her story is considered apocryphal, holding the veil with which she wiped Christ's face, only to find his likeness miraculously imprinted upon it. To the left is a sculpture of Gaudí making notes, the evangelist in stone, and farther left the equestrian figure of a centurion piercing the side of the church with his spear, the church representing the body of Christ. Above are the soldiers rolling dice for Christ's clothing and the naked, crucified Christ. The moon to the right of the cross refers to the darkness at the moment of Christ's death and to the full moon of Easter; to the right are Peter and Mary at the sepulchre, the egg above Mary symbolizing the Resurrection. At Christ's feet is a figure with a furrowed brow, perhaps suggesting the agnostic's anguished search for certainty, thought to be a self-portrait of Subirachs characterized by the sculptor's giant hand and an "S" on his right arm. High above is a gold figure of the resurrected Christ.

Future of the project. The 125th anniversary of the laying of the first stone was celebrated on March 19, 2007. Plans for the building have been scaled back since it was first conceived by Gaudi but intentions for the completion are still impressive. Towers still to be completed over the apse include those dedicated to the four evangelists (Matthew, Mark, Luke, and John), the Virgin Mary, and the highest of all, dedicated to Christ. The main facade will face east across Carrer Mallorca and a wide esplanade that will be created by the demolition of an entire city block of apartment houses built during the 1960s. Predictions on the completion of a covered apse and the construction of the east-facing main facade range from 20 to 30 years, depending on donations and advances in construction technology. ✉ *Mallorca 401, Eixample* ☎ *93/207–3031* 🌐 *www.sagradafamilia.org* 🎫 *€11, bell tower elevator €2.50* ⏲ *Oct.–Mar., daily 9–6; Apr.–Sept., daily 9–8* Ⓜ *Sagrada Família.*

WORTH NOTING

44 **Casa Àsia–Palau Baró de Quadras.** The neo-Gothic and plateresque (intricately carved in silversmithlike detail) house built by Puig i Cadafalch in 1904 for Baron Quadras displays, on its facade, some of the most spectacular Eusebi Arnau sculptures in town. Look for St. George slaying the dragon, and don't miss the alpine chaletlike windows across the top floor. Casa Àsia, with an excellent library for Asia-related cultural and business research, offers free visits to its main floors and art gallery. ✉ *Av. Diagonal 373, Eixample* ☎ *93/238–7337* 🌐 *www.casaasia.es* 🎫 *Free* ⏲ *Tues.–Sat. 10–8, Sun. 10–2* Ⓜ *Diagonal.*

45 **Casa de les Punxes** *(House of the Spikes).* Also known as Casa Terrades, for the family that commissioned it, this cluster of six conical towers ending in impossibly sharp needles is one of several Puig i Cadafalch inspirations rooted in the Gothic architecture of northern Europe, an ur-Bavarian or Danish castle in downtown Barcelona. It's one of the

few freestanding Eixample buildings visible from 360 degrees. ✉ *Av. Diagonal 416–420, Eixample* Ⓜ *Diagonal.*

46 **Casa Macaia.** Built in 1901, this graceful Puig i Cadafalch building was until recently the seat of the Centre Cultural Fundació "La Caixa," a far-reaching cultural entity funded by the Caixa Catalana (Catalan Savings Bank). The Eusebi Arnau sculptures over the door depict, somewhat cryptically, a man mounted on a donkey and another on a bicycle, reminiscent of the similar Arnau sculptures on the facade of Puig i Cadafalch's Casa Amatller on Passeig de Gràcia. ✉ *Passeig de Sant Joan 108, Eixample* Ⓜ *Verdaguer.*

42 **Casa Montaner i Simó–Fundació Tàpies.** This modern, airy building showcases the work of contemporary Catalan painter Antoni Tàpies, as well as temporary exhibits. ✉ *Carrer Aragó 255, Eixample* ☎ *93/487–0315* 🎫 *€5* ⏲ *Tues.–Sun. 10–8.*

48 **Hospital de Sant Pau.** Certainly one of the most beautiful hospital complexes in the world, a 10-minute walk down Avinguda Gaudí from the Sagrada Família, the Hospital de Sant Pau is notable for its Mudejar motifs and sylvan plantings. The hospital wards are set among gardens under exposed brick facades intensely decorated with mosaics and polychrome ceramic tile. Begun in 1900, this monumental production won Lluís Domènech i Montaner his third Barcelona "Best Building" award, in 1912. (His previous two prizes were for the Palau de la Música Catalana and Casa Lleó Morera.) The Moderniste enthusiasm for nature is apparent here; the architect believed patients are more apt to recover if they are surrounded by trees and flowers rather than ensconced in sterile hospital wards. Domènech i Montaner also believed in the therapeutic properties of form and color and decorated the hospital with Pau Gargallo sculptures and colorful mosaics. ✉ *Carrer Sant Antoni Maria Claret 167, Eixample* ☎ *93/291–9000* 🌐 *www.santpau.es* 🎫 *Free; tour €5* ⏲ *Daily 9–8; tours weekends 10–2, weekdays by advance arrangement* Ⓜ *Hospital de Sant Pau.*

7

UPPER BARCELONA, WITH PARK GÜELL

Barcelona's upper reaches begin with Pedralbes, a neighborhood of graceful mansions grouped around a stunning Gothic monastery. Park Güell is Gaudí's Art Nouveau urban garden. Gràcia and Sarrià were outlying villages swallowed up by the expanding metropolis. Note that the Monestir de Pedralbes closes at 2, so it's a good place to start. Tibidabo, with its amusement park and Norman Foster's Torre de Collserola should be considered only on an (increasingly unusual) unsmoggy day, though there are also some excellent dining options if you make the trip.

A GOOD TOUR

You're best off dividing these sites into several days or choosing among them.

You could spend a full day, with visits and lunch, starting from the **Monestir de Pedralbes** 49. A 20-minute walk gets you to the main square of **Sarrià** 50. After exploring Sarrià, another short walk downhill through the Jardins de la Villa Amèlia leads past Gaudí's Finca Güell gate and gatehouse (now the Cátedra Gaudí research center) to the **Palau Reial de Pedralbes** 51, which, in turn, is a short walk downhill from the FC Barcelona soccer stadium.

Or you could start a morning at **Tibidabo** 52, which has wonderful vistas on clear days, and stop at La Venta (or ÀBaC or the Asador de Aranda) for lunch. A truly fantastic photo op awaits at **Torre de Collserola** 53. Free transportation is provided to the tower from Plaza Tibidabo. Then spend the afternoon at Gaudí's **Park Güell** 54, most easily reached by taxi. While there, don't miss the **Casa-Museu Gaudí** 55. After the park, walk down through **Gràcia** 56 to **Casa Vicens** 57.

TIP→ Park Güell and Tibidabo are best seen in mid- to late afternoon, when the sun backs around to the west and illuminates the Mediterranean.

TOP ATTRACTIONS

57 **Casa Vicens.** Gaudí's first important commission as a young architect was built between 1883 and 1885, at which time he had not yet thrown away his architect's tools, particularly the T-square. The historical eclecticism of the early Art Nouveau movement is evident in the Orientalist themes and Mudejar details lavished on the facade. The house was commissioned by a ceramics merchant, which may explain the eye-catching colored ceramic tiles that render most of the facade a striking checkerboard—Barcelona's first example of this now-omnipresent technique. The palm leaves on the gate and surrounding fence have been attributed to Gaudí assistant, Francesc Berenguer, and the comic iron lizards and bats oozing off the facade are Gaudí's playful nod to the Gothic gargoyle. ✉ *Carrer de les Carolines 24–26, Gràcia.*

56 **Gràcia.** Gràcia isn't just a neighborhood, it's a state of mind: a virtual village republic that has periodically risen in rebellion against city, state, and country. The street names (Llibertat, Fraternitat, Progrès, Venus) reveal the ideological history of this nucleus of working-class sentiment. Barcelona's first collectivized manufacturing operations (i.e., factories) were clustered here—a dangerous precedent, as workers organized into radical groups ranging from anarchists to feminists to esperantists. Once an outlying town, Gràcia joined Barcelona only under duress and attempted to secede from the Spanish state in 1856, 1870, 1873, and 1909. Lying above the Diagonal from Carrer de Córsega up to Park Güell, this jumble of streets is filled with appealing bars and restaurants, movie theaters, and outdoor cafés, usually thronged by hip couples. The August Festa Major fills the streets with the rank-and-file residents of this lively yet intimate little pocket of resistance to Organized Life.

49 Fodor's Choice ★ **Monestir de Pedralbes.** One of Barcelona's hidden treasures, this monastery (in fact, a convent) was founded by Reina Elisenda, widow of Catalonia's Sovereign Count Jaume II, for Clarist nuns in 1326. The Gothic cloister is the finest in Barcelona. The abess's day cell, the Capella de Sant Miquel, has murals painted in 1346 by Ferrer Bassa, a Catalan master much influenced by the Italian Renaissance. Scratched into the painting, on the right side between Saints Francis and Clare, you can make out what is widely considered Barcelona's earliest graffito: *Joan no m'oblides* (John, don't forget me), proof that not all of the novitiates were there by their own choice. You can also visit the medieval living quarters and

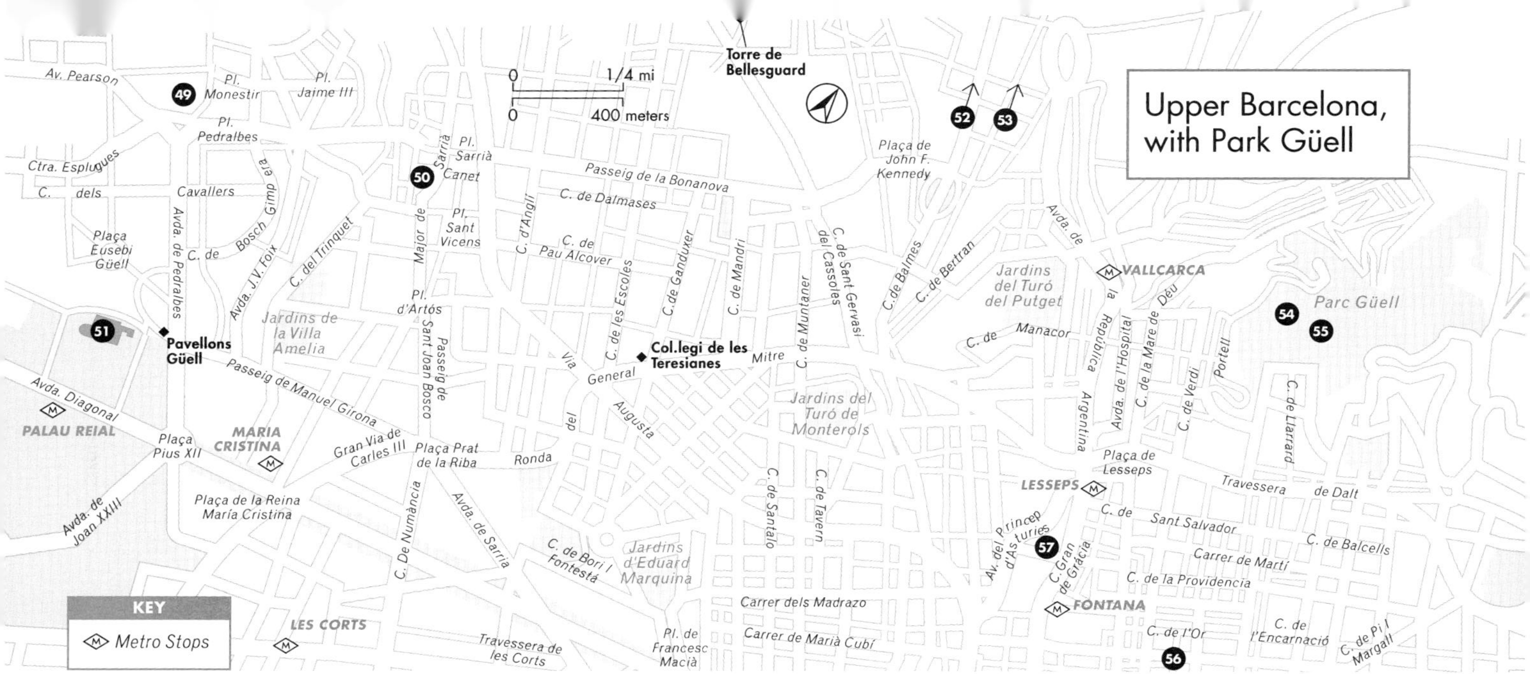

- Casa Vicens **57**
- Casa-Museu Gaudí **55**
- Gràcia **56**
- Monestir de Pedralbes **49**
- Palau Reial de Pedralbes **51**
- Park Güell **54**
- Sarrià **50**
- Tibidabo **52**
- Torre de Collserola **53**

CLOSE UP

A Walk in Gràcia

From Park Güell, dig out your city map and follow Carrer Larrard across Travessera de Dalt and down Carrer Torrent de les Flors through upper Gràcia to **Plaça Rovira i Trias,** where a bronze effigy of architect Antoni Rovira i Trias sits on a bench. Continue downhill and west to **Plaça de la Virreina** to see the work of Francesc Berenguer at Carrer de l'Or 44. (If Barcelona was Gaudí's sandbox, Gràcia was Berenguer's—nearly every major building in this neighborhood is his creation.) Cut over to **Plaça del Diamant** to see, in bronze, the heroine of Mercé Rodoreda's famous 1962 novel *La Plaça del Diamant,* literally: *The Square of the Diamond*—Gràcia had a 19th-century mayor who was a jeweler, thus Ruby Street, Diamond Square, etc. Moving northwest, through Plaça Trilla, cross Gran de Gràcia to Carrer de les Carolines to see Gaudí's very first house, **Casa Vicens.** Make your next stop the produce market **Mercat de la Libertat,** an uptown Boqueria, then cut east along Cisne, cross Gran de Gràcia, and pass another Berenguer creation on Ros de Olano, the Mudejar-style **Centre Moral Instructiu de Gràcia. Plaça del Sol,** one of Gràcia's most popular squares, is down the hill. From here, continue east to Gràcia's other market, the **Mercat de la Revolució.** Walk three blocks back over to Grácia's main square, **Plaça de la Vila de Gràcia,** with its emblematic clock tower. From Plaça de la Vila de Gràcia, cut out to **Gran de Gràcia** for a look at some more Art Nouveau buildings by Berenguer (Nos. 15, 23, 35, 49, 51, 61, and 77). For lunch, consider Galician seafood at Botafumeiro or light and creative cuisine at nearby Folquer.

kitchen. Look for the ruts broken into the arcaded walkways by Napoleonic cannon during the 1809 French occupation. The museum shows religious paintings and artifacts collected over the centuries. ✉ *Baixada Monestir 9, Pedralbes* ☎ *93/203–9282* 🌐 *www.museuhistoria.bcn.es* 🎫 *€5.50; free 1st Sun. of month. Ticket also includes admission to Museu Històrica de la Ciutat, Centre d'Interpretació del Park Güell, Centre d'Interpretació del Call, Centre d'Interpretació Històrica, Refugi 307, and Museu-Casa Verdaguer* ⏲ *Oct.–May, Tues.–Sun. 10–2; June–Sept., Tues.–Sun. 10–5* Ⓜ *Reina Elisenda.*

54 Fodor's Choice ★ **Park Güell.** Güell Park is one of Gaudí's, and Barcelona's, most pleasant and visually stimulating places to spend a few hours; it's light and playful, alternately shady, green, floral, and sunny. Named for and commissioned by Gaudí's main patron, Count Eusebio Güell, the park was intended as a hillside garden suburb on the English model. Barcelona's bourgeoisie seemed happier living closer to "town," however, so only two of the houses were built, and the Güell family eventually turned the land over to the city as a public park. Gaudí highlights here include an Art Nouveau extravaganza with gingerbread gatehouses topped with a hallucinogenic red-and-white fly ammanite wild mushroom (rumored to have been a Gaudí favorite) on the right and a *phallus impudicus* mushroom (no translation necessary) on the left. The gatehouse on the right holds the **Center for the Interpretation and Welcome to Park Güell,** with

plans, scale models, photos, and suggested routes analyzing the park in detail. Other highlights include the **Gaudí Casa–Museu** (the house where Gaudí lived with his niece for 20 years), the Room of a Hundred Columns—a covered market supported by tilted Doric-style columns and mosaic-encrusted buttresses, and guarded by a patchwork lizard—and the fabulous serpentine, polychrome bench that snakes along the main square. ✉ *Carrer d'Olot s/n; take Metro to Lesseps; then walk 10 min uphill or catch Bus 24 to park entrance, Gràcia* ⏲ *Oct.–Mar., daily 10–6; Apr.–June, daily 10–7; July–Sept., daily 10–9* Ⓜ *Lesseps.*

WORTH NOTING

55 The **Casa-Museu Gaudí,** within Park Güell, is a pink, Alice in Wonderland house designed by Gaudí's assistant and right hand, Francesc Berenguer (1866–1914); this is where Gaudí lived with his niece from 1906 to 1926. Exhibits include Gaudí-designed furniture, decorations, drawings, and portraits. ✉ *Park Güell, up hill to right of main entrance, Gràcia* ☎ *93/219–3811* 🎟 *€4* ⏲ *May–Sept., daily 10–8; Oct.–Feb., daily 10–6; Mar. and Apr., daily 10–7.*

OFF THE BEATEN PATH

CosmoCaixa–Museu de la Ciència Fundació "La Caixa." Young scientific minds work overtime in this ever-more-interactive science museum, just below Tibidabo. Among the many displays designed for children 7 and up are the Geological Wall, a history of rocks and rock formations studied through a transversal cutaway section, and the Underwater Forest, showcasing the climate and species of an Amazonian rain forest in a large greenhouse. Expositions of sustainable exploitation techniques, such as "The Red Line: How to Make Wood Without Damaging the Forest," are accompanied by explanations of environmental problems and how to correct them. ✉ *Teodor Roviralta 55, Sant Gervasi* ☎ *93/212–6050* 🌐 *www.cosmocaixa.com* 🎟 *€3.50 (€2 per interactive activity inside)* ⏲ *Tues.–Sun. 10–8* Ⓜ *Avinguda de Tibidabo and Tramvía Blau halfway.*

51 **Palau Reial de Pedralbes** *(Royal Palace of Pedralbes).* Built in the 1920s for King Alfonso XII, this palace now houses the **Museu Tèxtil i d'Indumentària** (which also maintains its Carrer Montcada site for temporary exhibits), the **Museu de Ceràmica,** and the **Disseny Hub** (Design Hub), previously known as the **Museu de les Arts Decoratives.** The textile museum displays the history of clothing fashions as aesthetic canons evolved from medieval times to the present. The ceramics museum covers Spanish ceramic art from its Iberian and Moorish beginnings up through medieval work from Manises and Paterna to Talavera de la Reina and Puente del Arzobispo. Catalan tile work, porcelain from Alcora, and Picasso and Miró creations complete the exhibit. The Disseny Hub or **Museu de les Arts Decoratives** exhibits household and design objects from medieval times through the Industrial Revolution and Spanish civil war up to contemporary design. ✉ *Av. Diagonal 686, Pedralbes* ☎ *93/280–5024 decorative arts museum, 93/280–1621 ceramic museum* 🌐 *www.museuceramica.bcn.es* 🎟 *€4.50 includes both museums; free 1st Sun. of month* ⏲ *Tues.–Sat. 10–6, Sun. 10–3* Ⓜ *Palau Reial.*

50 **Sarrià.** This intimate, bite-size, 1,000-year-old village was once a cluster of farms and country houses overlooking Barcelona from the hills. A

good place to start exploring is the main square, Plaça Sarrià, which holds an antiques market on Tuesday morning, a book market on Friday, occasional *sardana* dances on Sunday morning, and Christmas fairs in season. The Romanesque church tower looms overhead. Across Passeig Reina Elisenda from the church are a brick-and-steel **produce market** and the tiny **Plaça Sant Gaietà** behind it. From in front of the church, you can cut through the Placeta del Roser to the left of the main door to get to the elegant **town hall** in the Plaça de la Vila; note the buxom bronze sculpture of Pomona, goddess of fruit and the harvest, by famed Sarrià sculptor Josep Clarà (1878–1958). After a peek at the massive ceiling beams (and tempting prix-fixe lunch menu) in the restaurant Vell Sarrià, at the corner of Major de Sarrià, go back to the Pomona bronze and turn left toward Carrer dels Paletes (with its tiny Sant Antoni, patron saint of workers, or *paletes,* overhead to the right). Back on Major de Sarrià, continue down this pedestrian-only street and turn left onto **Carrer Canet,** with its cottagelike artisans' quarters, formerly factory workers' housing provided by a nearby 19th-century textile mill. The house at No. 15 is an original two-story village house. No. 21 has unusual floral ornamentation on the facade, and No. 23 is a rustic village dwelling painted a characteristic earthy Mediterranean orange.

Turn right on Carrer Cornet i Mas and walk two blocks down to Carrer Jaume Piquet. A quick probe to the left will take you to No. 30, Barcelona's perfect small-format **Moderniste house,** complete with faux-medieval upper windows, wrought-iron grillwork, floral and fruit ornamentation, and organically curved and carved wooden doors. Don't miss the restored wooden door at No. 9, or the Falangist-style eagle over the entrance of what was until 1976 the local telegraph office. The tiny, two-story pink house at No. 36 is an original Sarrià village house, one of the very few still standing. Across the intersection on the left is Casa Orlandai, a cultural center and café with a gorgeous Moderniste mosaic stairwell and stained-glass windows in the café. Back on Carrer Cornet i Mas, the next opening down is Sarrià's most picturesque square, **Plaça Sant Vicenç,** a leafy space ringed by early village houses and centered on a statue of Sarrià's patron saint. Note the other renditions of the saint over the square's upper right corner. The café Can Pau is the local hangout, once a haven for such authors as Gabriel García Marquez and Mario Vargas Llosa, who lived in Sarrià in the early 1970s, on the cusp of their fame. It's worth a stop at the **Gouthier** oyster-, salmon-, *foie-* (duck or goose liver), caviar-, and wine-tasting bar on the lower corner of the square. To get to the Monestir de Pedralbes from Plaça Sant Vicenç, walk back up Mayor de Sarrià and through the market to the corner of Sagrat Cor and Ramon Miquel Planas; then turn left and walk straight west for 15 minutes, past the splendid upper-city mansions of Pedralbes. ✉ *Pl. Sarrià, Sarrià; take Bus 22 from bottom of Av. de Tibidabo, or U-6 train on FFCC subway to Reina Elisenda.*

NEED A BREAK?

Bar Tomás (✉ *Major de Sarrià 49, Sarrià* ☎ *93/203–1077* Ⓜ *Sarrià*), home of the finest potatoes in town and a Barcelona institution, is on the corner of Jaume Piquet. Order the *doble mixta* of potatoes with *allioli* (garlic and olive oil) and a splash of fiery hot sauce.

52 **Tibidabo.** On clear days, the views from this hill are legendary, particularly from the 850-foot communications tower, Torre de Collserola. There's not much to see here, though, except the vista, and breezy, smog-free days are few and far between in 21st-century Barcelona, but if (and only if) you hit one, this excursion is worth considering. The restaurant **La Venta,** at the base of the funicular, is excellent, a fine place to sit in the sun in cool weather (don't fret over sunburn; the establishment provides straw sun hats). The bar **Mirablau** is a popular hangout for evening drinks if you make it up here, a lovely place to watch the lights of the city come on in the evening. ✉ *Plaça del Doctor Andreu s/n; take Tibidabo train (U-7) from Pl. de Catalunya or buses 24 and 22 to Pl. Kennedy. At Av. Tibidabo, catch Tramvía Blau (Blue Trolley), which connects with funicular to summit* Ⓜ *Tibidabo.*

53 **Torre de Collserola.** Created by Norman Foster, the Collserola Tower was erected for the 1992 Olympics amid controversy over defacement of the traditional mountain skyline. An immense communications mast with a cylindrical midsection housing an observation deck, it's now considered the best piece of contemporary architecture in the city's upper reaches. ✉ *Av. de Vallvidrera, Tibidabo* ✣ *Take the funicular up to Tibidabo; from Pl. Tibidabo there is free transport to the tower* ☎ *93/211–7942* 🌐 *www.torredecollserola.com* 🎟 *€5.50* ⏲ *Wed.–Fri. 11–2:30 and 3:30–6, weekends 11–6* Ⓜ *Tibidabo.*

7

MONTJUÏC

This far-flung, leafy park on a hill to the south of town requires some hiking between sights and lacks the intensity and color of Barcelona street life, but the art is world class. Named for the Roman god Jove, or Jupiter, Montjuïc is best reached by taxi, by Bus 61, on foot from Plaça Espanya, or by the funicular that operates from the Parallel. The cross-harbor cable car from Barceloneta or from the Jaume I midstation in the port is another, spectacular, approach (acrophobes, be warned).

Walking from sight to sight on Montjuïc is possible but not recommended. You'll want fresh feet to see the sights here, especially the vast art displays in the Palau Nacional and the Miró Foundation. Ⓜ *Paral.lel.*

TOP ATTRACTIONS

59 ★ **Fundació Miró.** The Miró Foundation was a gift from the artist Joan Miró to his native city and is one of Barcelona's most exciting showcases of contemporary art. The airy, white building was designed by Josep Lluís Sert and opened in 1975; an extension was added by Sert's pupil Jaume Freixa in 1988. Miró's unmistakably playful and colorful style, filled with Mediterranean light and humor, seems a perfect contrast for its minimalist surroundings. Exhibits and retrospectives here tend to be progressive and provocative. Look for Alexander Calder's mercury fountain. Miró himself rests in the cemetery on Montjuïc's southern slopes. During the Franco regime, which he strongly opposed, Miró

CaixaForum (Casaramona) **63**
Castell de Montjuïc **58**
Estadi Olímpic **60**
Fundació Miró **59**
Mies van der Rohe Pavilion **62**
Museu d'Arqueologia de Catalunya **66**
Museu Nacional d'Art de Catalunya **61**
Plaça d'Espanya **65**
Poble Espanyol **64**

first lived in self-imposed exile in Paris then moved to Majorca in 1956. When he died in 1983, the Catalans gave him a send-off amounting to a state funeral. ✉ *Av. Miramar 71, Montjuïc* ☎ *93/443–9470* 🌐 *www.bcn.fjmiro.es* 🎟 *€8.50* ⏲ *Tues., Wed., Fri., and Sat. 10–7, Thurs. 10–9:30, Sun. 10–2:30.*

62 **Mies van der Rohe Pavilion.** The reconstructed Mies van der Rohe Pavilion (the German contribution to the International Exposition of 1929) is a "less is more" study in interlocking planes of white marble, green onyx, and glass: the aesthetic opposite of the Moderniste Palau de la Música. ✉ *Av. Marquès de Comillas s/n, Montjuïc* ☎ *93/423–4016* 🌐 *www.miesbcn.com* 🎟 *€4.50* ⏲ *Daily 10–8.*

61 **Museu Nacional d'Art de Catalunya** *(MNAC, Catalonian National Museum of Art).* Housed in the imposingly domed, towered, frescoed, and columned **Palau Nacional,** built in 1929 as the centerpiece of the World's Fair, this superb museum was renovated in 1995 by Gae Aulenti, architect of the Musée d'Orsay in Paris. In 2004 the museum's three collections—Romanesque, Gothic, and the Cambó Collection, an eclectic trove—were joined by the 19th- and 20th-century collection of Catalan impressionist and Moderniste painters. Also now on display is the Thyssen-Bornemisza collection of early masters, with works by Zurbarán, Rubens, Tintoretto, Velázquez, and others. With this influx of artistic treasure, the MNAC became Catalonia's grand central museum. Pride of place goes to the Romanesque exhibition: the world's finest collection of Romanesque frescoes, altarpieces, and wood carvings, most of them rescued from chapels in the Pyrenees during the 1920s to save them from deterioration, theft, and art dealers. Many, such as the famous *Cristo de Taüll* fresco (from the church of Sant Climent de Taüll in Taüll), have been reproduced and replaced in their original settings. ✉ *Mirador del Palau 6, Montjuïc* ☎ *93/622–0376* 🌐 *www.mnac.es* 🎟 *€9* (valid for day of purchase and one other day in the same month) ⏲ *Tues.–Sat. 10–7, Sun. 10–2:30.*

Fodor's Choice ★

WORTH NOTING

63 **CaixaForum** *(Casaramona).* Built by architect Josep Puig i Cadafalch in 1911 to house a textile factory, this redbrick Art Nouveau fortress is now a center for cultural events, with top art exhibits and concerts. The contemporary entryway was designed by Arata Isozaki, architect of the nearby Palau Sant Jordi. ✉ *Av. Marquès de Comillas 6–8, Montjuïc* ☎ *93/476–8600* 🌐 *www.fundacio.lacaixa.es* 🎟 *Free; charge for evening concerts* ⏲ *Tues.–Sun. 10–8; later for concerts.*

58 **Castell de Montjuïc.** Built in 1640 by rebels against Felipe IV, the pentagonal structure has been stormed several times, most famously in 1705 by Lord Peterborough for Archduke Carlos of Austria. In 1808, during the Peninsular War, it was seized by the French under General Dufresne. During an 1842 civil disturbance, Barcelona was bombed from its heights by a Spanish artillery battery. During the 1939–75 Franco regime, the castle was notorious as a dungeon for political prisoners, and executions were carried out in the gardens with frequency. Catalonian President Lluís Companys was shot by firing squad here in 1940. The moat has lush green gardens, with one side given over

7

to an archery range, while the terraces have sweeping views over the city and the Mediterranean. The fortress houses, for the moment, the Museu Militar. Plans are in the works to convert the castle, which the Spanish government has formally returned to Catalunya, into a museum dedicated to peace. ✉ *Ctra. de Montjuïc 66, Montjuïc* ☎ *93/329–8613* 🎫 *€3.50* ⏲ *Tues.–Sun. 9:30–8.*

60 **Estadi Olímpic.** The Olympic Stadium was originally built for the International Exposition of 1929, with the idea that Barcelona would then be the site of the 1936 Olympics (ultimately staged in Hitler's Berlin). After failing twice, Barcelona celebrated the attainment of its long-cherished goal by renovating the semiderelict stadium in time for 1992, providing seating for 70,000. The **Galeria Olímpica,** a museum about the Olympic movement in Barcelona, displays objects and shows audiovisual replays from the 1992 games. An information center traces the history of the modern Olympics from Athens in 1896 to the present. Next door and just downhill stands the futuristic **Palau Sant Jordi Sports Palace,** designed by noted Japanese architect Arata Isozaki. The Isozaki structure has no pillars or beams to obstruct the view. The roof was built first, then hydraulically lifted into place. ✉ *Passeig Olímpic 17–19, Montjuïc* ☎ *93/426–0660* 🌐 *www.fundaciobarcelonaolimpica.es* 🎫 *Gallery €4.50* ⏲ *Tues.–Sat. 10–2 and 4–7.*

66 **Museu d'Arqueologia de Catalunya.** Just downhill to the right of the Palau Nacional, the Museum of Archaeology holds important finds from the Greek ruins at Empúries, on the Costa Brava. These are shown alongside fascinating objects from, and explanations of, Megalithic Spain. ✉ *Passeig Santa Madrona 39–41, Montjuïc* ☎ *93/424–6577* 🌐 *www.mac.es* 🎫 *€3.50* ⏲ *Tues.–Sat. 9:30–7, Sun. 10–2:30.*

65 **Plaça d'Espanya.** This busy circle is a good place to avoid, but sooner or later you'll probably need to cross it to go to the convention center or to the Palau Nacional. It's dominated by the so-called Venetian Towers (they're actually Tuscan) built in 1927 as the grand entrance to the 1929 International Exposition. The fountain in the center is the work of Josep Maria Jujol, the Gaudí collaborator who designed the curvy and colorful benches in Park Güell. The sculptures are by Miquel Blay, one of the master artists and craftsmen who put together the Palau de la Música. The neo-Mudejar bullring, Les Arenes, is now used for theater and political rallies.

64 **Poble Espanyol.** The Spanish Village was created for the International Exposition of 1929. A sort of artificial Spain-in-a-bottle, with reproductions of Spain's architectural styles, it takes you from the walls of Ávila to the wine cellars of Jerez de la Frontera with shops, houses, and crafts workshops en route. The liveliest time to come is at night, and a reservation at one of the half-dozen restaurants gets you in free, as does the purchase of a ticket for the two discos or the Tablao del Carmen flamenco club. ✉ *Av. Marquès de Comillas s/n* ☎ *93/508–6300* 🌐 *www.poble-espanyol.com* 🎫 *€8* ⏲ *Mon. 9 AM–8 PM, Tues.–Thurs. 9 AM–2 AM, Fri. 9 AM–4 AM, Sat. 9 AM–5 AM, Sun. 9 AM–midnight.*

BEACHES

Ever since Barcelona revamped its beaches for the 1992 Olympics, the summer beach scene has been multitudinous. Five kilometers (3 mi) of beaches now run from the Platja (Beach) de Sant Sebastià, a nudist enclave, northward through the Barceloneta, Port Olímpic, Nova Icària, Bogatell, Mar Bella, Nova Mar Bella, and Novíssima Mar Bella beaches to the Fòrum complex and the rocky Illa Pangea swimming area. Next to the mouth of the Besòs River is Platja Nova. Topless bathing is common. The beaches immediately north of Barcelona include Montgat, Ocata, Vilasar de Mar, Arenys de Mar, Canet, and Sant Pol de Mar, all accessible by train from the RENFE station in Plaça de Catalunya. Especially worthy is **Sant Pol** (✉ *Passeig Maritim 59* ☎ *93/665–1347*), with clean sand, in Sant Pol de Mar. Also in this handsome old part of town is Carme Ruscalleda's famous **Sant Pau,** one of the top three restaurants in Catalonia. The farther north you go, toward the Costa Brava, the better the beaches. Ten kilometers (6 mi) south is **Castelldefels,** with a long, sandy beach and a series of bars and restaurants. A 15-minute train ride from Passeig de Gràcia's (or Plaça de Catalunya's) RENFE station to Gavà or Castelldefels deposits you on the 10-km-long (6-mi-long) beach for a (usually) windy walk in the sand. From October to March the sun sets into the Mediterranean here, thanks to the westward slant of the coastline. There are several good places for lamb chops, *calçots* (spring onions), and paella; the best, **Can Patricio,** serves lunch until 4:30. **Sitges Beach,** another 25 minutes south, has better sand and clearer water than Castelldefels.

BARS AND CAFÉS

Use the coordinate (⊕B2) at the end of each listing to locate a site on the corresponding map.

Barcelona may have more bars and cafés per capita than any other place in the world, from colorful tapas spots to sunny outdoor cafés, tearooms, chocolaterias, *coctelerías* (cocktail bars), *whiskerias* (often singles bars filled with professional escorts), *xampanyerias* (serving champagne and cava), and beer halls. Most cafés are open long hours, roughly 9 AM to 2 AM; bars from about noon to 2 AM.

CAFÉS

BARRI GÒTIC **Els Quatre Gats.** Picasso staged his first exhibition here, in 1899, and Gaudí and the Catalan impressionist painters Ramón Casas and Santiago Russinyol held meetings of their Centre Artistic de Sant Lluc here in the early 20th century. The restaurant is undistinguished, but the café is a good place to read and people-watch. ✉ *Carrer Montsió 3, Barri Gòtic* ☎ *93/302–4140* Ⓜ *Catalunya* ⊕ *D4.*

Schilling. Near Plaça Reial, the hip Schilling is always packed. Have coffee by day, drinks and tapas by night. ✉ *Carrer Ferran 23, Barri Gòtic* ☎ *93/317–6787* Ⓜ *Catalunya, Liceu* ⊕ *D5.*

Travel Bar. With entrances on Carrer de la Boqueria and Placeta del Pi, and tables in the shady square behind Sant Maria del Pi, this hot spot for young travelers offers everything from Internet access to walking tours. ✉ *Carrer de la Boqueria 27, Barri Gòtic* ☎ *93/342–5252* Ⓜ *Catalunya, Liceu* ✣ *D6.*

BORN-RIBERA **Espai Barroc.** Filled with baroque embellishments and music, this unusual *espai* (space) is on Carrer Montcada's most beautiful patio, the 15th-century Palau Dalmases. The stairway, with a bas-relief of the rape of Europa, leads up to the Omnium Cultural, a center for the study and diffusion of Catalan history and culture. ✉ *Carrer Montcada 20, La Ribera* ☎ *93/310–0673* ⏲ *Closed Sun., Mon.* Ⓜ *Jaume I* ✣ *E5.*

EIXAMPLE **Café Paris.** This is a lively place where everyone from Prince Felipe, heir to the Spanish throne, to poet/pundit James Townsend Pi Sunyer has been spotted. The tapas are excellent and the beer is cold. ✉ *Carrer Aribau 184, at Carrer Paris, Eixample* ☎ *93/209–8530* Ⓜ *Provença* ✣ *C1.*

La Bodegueta. If you can locate this dive (it's two steps down from the sidewalk), you'll find a dozen small tables, a few places at the marble counter, and happy couples having coffee or beer—and maybe some ham or *tortilla española de patatas.* ✉ *La Rambla de Catalunya 100, Eixample* ☎ *93/215–4894* Ⓜ *Provença* ✣ *D2.*

RAMBLA **Café de l'Opera.** Opposite the opera house, this high-ceiling Art Nouveau space has welcomed opera-goers and performers grabbing a cup of tea or coffee for more than 100 years. For locals, it's a central point on the Rambla traffic pattern. ✉ *La Rambla 74, Rambla* ☎ *93/317–7585* Ⓜ *Liceu* ✣ *D5.*

Café Viena. It's always packed with travelers in a party mood, and the pianist upstairs lends a cabaret touch. Draft beer and an ibérico ham *flauta* (thin sandwich) hit the spot. ✉ *La Rambla dels Estudis 115, Rambla* ☎ *93/349–9800* Ⓜ *Catalunya* ✣ *D4.*

Café Zurich. Ever of key importance to Barcelona society, this classic spot at the top of the Rambla is the city's prime meeting place. The outdoor tables offer peerless people-watching; the elegant interior has a high ceiling. ✉ *Pl. de Catalunya 1, Rambla* ☎ *93/317–9153* Ⓜ *Catalunya* ✣ *D4.*

COCTELERÍAS

BARRI GÒTIC **El Paraigua.** Behind the *ajuntament* (city hall), this pricey but stylish bar serves cocktails and plays classical-music recordings in an elegant Art Nouveau space. ✉ *Pas de l'Ensenyança 2, Barri Gòtic* ☎ *93/302–1131* Ⓜ *Jaume I, Liceu* ✣ *D5.*

BORN-RIBERA **El Born.** This former codfish emporium is now a charming and intimate haven for drinks and fondue. The marble cod basins in the entry and the spiral staircase to the second floor are quirky details. ✉ *Passeig del Born 26, La Ribera* ☎ *93/319–5333* Ⓜ *Jaume I* ✣ *E5.*

El Copetín. Right on Barcelona's best-known cocktail avenue, this bar has good drinks and Irish coffee. Dimly lit, it has a romantic South Seas motif. ✉ *Passeig del Born 19, La Ribera* ☎ *93/319–4496* Ⓜ *Jaume I* ✣ *E5.*

Miramelindo. The bar has a range of herbal liquors, fruit cocktails, mojitos, and Brazilian specialties such as *caipirinhas* (crushed lime and sugar with *cachaça,* a sugar-cane liquor), served in a Caribbean wood and wicker setting. The recorded music is usually jazz, bossa nova, or quiet salsa. ✉ *Passeig del Born 15, La Ribera* ☎ *93/310–3727* Ⓜ *Jaume I.*

EIXAMPLE **Dry Martini Bar.** The eponymous specialty is the best bet at this spot, which exudes a kind of genteel wickedness. This seems to be a popular hangout for mature romantics, husbands, and wives (not necessarily each other's). The speakeasy restaurant through the kitchen is excellent, too. ✉ *Carrer Aribau 162, Eixample* ☎ *93/217–5072* Ⓜ *Provença* ✢ *C1.*

RAMBLA **Boadas.** A small, rather formal saloon near the top of the Rambla, Boadas is emblematic of the Barcelona *coctelería* concept, which usually entails a mixture of decorum and expensive mixed drinks amid wood and leather. ✉ *Carrer Tallers 1, Rambla* ☎ *93/318–9592* Ⓜ *Catalunya* ✢ *D4.*

RAVAL **Almirall.** This Moderniste bar in the Raval is quiet, dimly lit, and dominated by the Art Nouveau mirror and frame behind the marble bar. It's an evocative spot, romantic and mischievous. ✉ *Carrer Joaquín Costa 33, Raval* ☎ *93/302–4126* Ⓜ *Catalunya, Liceu, Sant Antoni* ✢ *C3.*

TAPAS BARS

Because of Catalonia's distinct social mores, tapas were not, historically, an important part of Barcelona life. Today, however, astute Catalans and Basque chefs are busy transforming the city into an emerging tapas capital (until now, San Sebastian, Sevilla, Cadiz, or perhaps Madrid led the tapas charge). Especially around Santa Maria del Mar and the Passeig del Born area, nomadic wine tippling and tapa tasting are proliferating. For the most part, beware of tapas bars along Passeig de Gràcia, though: the tapas here are usually microwaved and far from Barcelona's best. Many tapas bars are open from early in the morning until late at night.

BARCELONETA **El Vaso de Oro.** At the uptown edge of Barceloneta, this bar has become more and more popular with young, polished professionals. If you can catch it when it's not crammed with customers, you're in for some of the best beer and tapas in town. ✉ *Carrer Balboa 6, Barceloneta* ☎ *93/319–3098* Ⓜ *Barceloneta* ✢ *E6.*

BARRI GÒTIC **El Irati.** Between Plaça del Pi and the Rambla, this roaring brawl of a Basque bar has only one drawback: it's hard to squeeze into. If there's space, take it; if not, move on. Try coming around 1 PM or 7:30 PM. The standard beverage here is *txakolí,* a Basque white wine. The restaurant in back is excellent. ✉ *Carrer Cardenal Casañas 17, Barri Gòtic* ☎ *93/302–3084* ⏲ *Closed Mon.* ✢ *D4.*

Taller de Tapas. Next to Plaça del Pi, facing the eastern lateral facade of Santa Maria del Pi, this fine tapas specialist has it all: cheery young staff, traditional Catalan dishes in bite-size format, and service from midday to midnight. The other Taller de Tapas on Carrer Argenteria 51 near Santa Maria del Mar is equally excellent. ✉ *Pl. de Sant Josep Oriol 9, Barri Gòtic* ☎ *93/302–6243* Ⓜ *Liceu* ✢ *D5, E5.*

7

BORN-RIBERA **Euskal Etxea.** The tapas and canapés speak for themselves at this Basque cultural enclave (Euskal Etxea means "Basque House") just down from the Picasso Museum. ✉ *Placeta Montcada 13, Born-Ribera* ☎ *93/310–2185* ⊙ *Closed Sun. at 4:30* PM Ⓜ *Jaume I* ⊕ *E5.*

Sagardi. This attractive, wood-and-stone cider house comes close to re-creating its Basque prototype, with cider shooting from mammoth (fake) barrels and piping-hot tapas out front; *txuletas de buey* (beefsteaks) are prepared over coals in the restaurant in back. ✉ *Carrer Argenteria 62, La Ribera* ☎ *93/319–9993* Ⓜ *Jaume I* ⊕ *E55.*

Fodor's Choice ★ **Cal Pep.** A two-minute walk east from Santa Maria del Mar toward the Estació de França, Pep has some of Barcelona's best and freshest selections of tapas, cooked and served piping hot in a boisterous space. ✉ *Pl. de les Olles 8, Born-Ribera* ☎ *93/310–7961* ⊙ *Closed Sun.* Ⓜ *Jaume I* ⊕ *E5.*

EIXAMPLE **Bar Mut.** The *pijo* element, Barcelona's young, beautiful, and affluent, are nearly as mouthwatering as the fare at this Eixample favorite. The risottos, whether cheese or wild mushroom, are excellent, and the various foie gras dishes are so good they should be illegal. The house suggestions are invariably on the money. ✉ *Pau Claris 192, Eixample* ☎ *93/217–4338* ⊙ *Sun. closes at 5* PM Ⓜ *Passeig de Gràcia* ⊕ *D1.*

Casa Lucio. With original dishes flowing from the kitchen, this handsome (though pricey) little gem just two blocks south of the Mercat de Sant Antoni is well worth tracking down. Lucio's wife, Maribel, is relentlessly inventive. Try the *tastum albarole* (cured sheep cheese from Umbria) or the *pochas negras con morcilla* (black beans with black sausage). ✉ *Carrer Viladomat 59, Eixample* ☎ *93/424–4401* ⊙ *Closed Sun.* Ⓜ *Sant Antoni* ⊕ *B4.*

Cata 1.81. Small delicacies such as truffle omelets and foie gras make this a taste treat as well as a wine-tasting *(cata)* sanctuary. The wine selections are thoughtfully and carefully worked out, and the industrial steel tables with center bottle wells are contemporary and chic. ✉ *Carrer Valencia 181, Eixample* ☎ *93/323–6818* ⊙ *Closed Sun.* Ⓜ *Provença* ⊕ *C2.*

Cerveseria la Catalana. This booming bar is filled for a reason: excellent food at fair prices. Try the small *solomillo* (filet mignon)—a mini-morsel that will take the edge off your carnivorous instincts without undue damage to your wallet. ✉ *Mallorca 236, Eixample* ☎ *93/216–0368* Ⓜ *Provença* ⊕ *D2.*

Ciudad Condal. This hot-spot restaurant and grazing ground serves fine tapas to a well-heeled crowd in a classic wooden tavern. ✉ *La Rambla de Catalunya 18, Eixample* ☎ *93/318–1997* Ⓜ *Passeig de Gràcia* ⊕ *D3.*

★ **Inòpia Clàssic Bar.** Albert Adrià, younger brother and culinary researcher for his famous brother, Ferran Adrià, of El Bulli fame, has opened his own tapas bar just a few blocks west of the Mercat de Sant Antoni. Products and preparations are uniformly interesting and excellent. ✉ *Carrer Tamarit 104, Eixample* ☎ *93/424–5231* ⊙ *Closed Mon.* Ⓜ *Rocafort, Poble Sec* ⊕ *A4.*

La Vinacoteca Torres. Miguel Torres of the Torres wine dynasty has finally given Passeig Gràcia a respectable address for tapas and wine with more than 50 selections from Torres wineries around the world. The menu runs from selected Spanish olives to Ramón Peña canned seafood from the Rías de Galicia to stick-to-your-ribs *lentejas estofadas* (stewed lentils) or diced chunks of Galician beef with peppers from Gernika. ✉ *Pg. de Gràcia 78, Eixample* ☎ *93/272–6625* Ⓜ *Passeig de Gràcia* ✥ *D3.*

Mantequeria Can Ravell. Lovers of exquisite wine, ham, cheese, cigars, caviar, and any other delicacy you can think of—this is your spot. The backroom table, where strangers share tastes, is open from about 10 AM to 8 PM. ✉ *Carrer Aragó 313, Eixample* ☎ *93/457–5114* ⏲ *Closed Sun., Mon.* Ⓜ *Passeig de Gràcia* ✥ *E2.*

Tapaç 24. Carles Abellán has done it again. His irrepressibly creative Comerç 24 has been a hit since the day it opened, and his new tapas emporium is headed in the same direction. Here, Abellán shows us how much he admires traditional Catalan and Spanish bar food, from patatas bravas (potatoes in hot sauce) to *croquetas de jamon ibérico* (croquettes of ibérico ham). ✉ *Diputació 269, Eixample* ☎ *93/488–0977* ⏲ *Closed Sun.* Ⓜ *Passeig de Gràcia* ✥ *D3.*

RAVAL **Mam i Teca.** Possibly Barcelona's best bet on Sundays when nearly all else is closed, this six-table foodie pilgrimage spot showcases some of the finest ingredients the Iberian Peninsula has to offer, from acorn-fed Joselito ham from Salamanca to air-dried *mojama* tuna from Barbate in Andalusia to anchovies from the Costa Brava. The goat, sheep, and cow cheese selections are peerless. ✉ *Lluna 4, Raval* ☎ *93/441–3335* Ⓜ *Catalunya* ✥ *C4.*

7

XAMPANYERIAS AND WINE BARS

BORN-RIBERA **El Xampanyet.** Hanging *botas* (wineskins) mark this lively saloon, just down Carrer Montcada from the Picasso Museum. Caveat: the sparkling wine served here is not cava but a sweet brew of indeterminate origin. Stick with beer or one of their excellent wines. ✉ *Carrer Montcada 22, La Ribera* ☎ *93/319–7003* ⏲ *Closed Mon.* ✥ *E5.*

La Vinya del Senyor. Ambitiously named "The Lord's Vineyard," this excellent wine bar across from the entrance to Santa Maria del Mar changes its savvy by-the-glass wine selections every fortnight. ✉ *Pl. de Santa Maria 5, La Ribera* ☎ *93/310–3379* ⏲ *Closed Mon.* ✥ *E5.*

EIXAMPLE **Monvínic.** The name of this sleek designer space is Catalan for "Wineworld," and there is a truly large selection: 3,500 wines ranging in price from €10 to €500. Tapas like eggs with black truffles and creative riffs on classical Catalan cuisine complement the wines. ✉ *Diputació 249, Eixample*08007 ☎ *93/272–6187* ⏲ *Closed Mon.* Ⓜ *Passeig de Gràcia* ✥ *D3.*

SANT PERE **El Bitxo.** An original wine list and ever-changing choices of interesting cava selections accompany creative tapas and small dishes from *foie* (duck or goose liver) to ibérico (native Iberian pigs fattened on acorns) hams and cheeses, all in a rustic wooden setting 50 yards from the Palau de la Música. ✉ *Verdaguer i Callis 9, Sant Pere* ☎ *93/268–1708.*

La Taverna del Palau. Behind a glass facade facing the Palau de la Música, this sleek little tavern is perfect for a hit of cava during intermission or a beer and a *flauta* (thin, flutelike sandwich) of cured ham. ✉ *Carrer Sant Pere Més Alt 8, Sant Pere* ☎ *93/268–8481* ✥ *C5.*

WHERE TO EAT

Use the coordinate (⊕B2) at the end of each listing to locate a site on the corresponding map.

Barcelona's restaurant scene is an ongoing surprise. What with the cutting-edge of avant-garde culinary experimentation and the cosmopolitan and rustic dishes of traditional Catalan fare, there's a fleet of inventive chefs producing some of Europe's finest Mediterranean cuisine.

THE CUISINE

Catalans are legendary lovers of fish, vegetables, rabbit, duck, lamb, and game, as well as natural ingredients from the Pyrenees and the Mediterranean. The *mar i muntanya* (sea and mountain—that is, surf and turf), recipes combining seafood with upland products, are standard: rabbit and prawns, cuttlefish and meatballs, chickpeas and clams are just a few examples. Combining salty and sweet tastes—a Moorish legacy—is another common theme, as in duck with pears, rabbit with figs, or lamb with olives.

The Mediterranean diet, which is based on olive oil, seafood, fibrous vegetables, onions, garlic, and red wine, is at home in Barcelona, and food tends to be seasoned with Catalonia's four basic sauces—*allioli* (garlic and olive oil), *romescu* (almonds, hazelnuts, tomato, garlic, and olive oil), *sofregit* (fried onion, tomato, and herbs), and *samfaina* (a ratatouillelike vegetable mixture). Typical entrées include *habas a la catalana* (a spicy broad-bean stew), *bullabesa* (fish soup-stew similar to French bouillabaisse), and *espinacas a la catalana* (spinach cooked with oil, garlic, pine nuts, raisins, and bits of bacon). Bread is often doused with olive oil and spread with tomato to make *pa amb tomaquet*.

MEAL TIMES

Lunch is served from 1 to 4, dinner 9 to 11. Some restaurants serve continuously from 1 PM to 1 AM.

DEALS AND DISCOUNTS

Menús del día (menus of the day), served only at lunchtime, are good values. In general, beware the advice of hotel concierges and taxi drivers, who have been known to warn that the place you are going is either closed or no good anymore and to recommend places where they get kickbacks.

TO DRINK

Catalan wines from the nearby Penedès region, especially the local *méthode champenoise* (sparkling white wine known in Catalonia as cava), brilliantly accompany regional cuisine. Meanwhile, local winemakers from the Priorat, Montsant, Empordà, and Costers del Segre regions are producing some of Spain's most exciting new wines.

CIUTAT VELLA (OLD CITY): THE RAMBLA, EL RAVAL, EL BARRI GÒTIC, AND BORN-RIBERA

Chic new restaurants and cafés seem to open daily in the old city.

$–$$ CATALAN ✕**Agut.** This is a classic, homey Catalan bistro offering good value and traditional fare. Agut was founded in 1924, and its popularity has

BEST BETS FOR BARCELONA DINING

Need a cheat sheet for Barcelona's thousands of restaurants? Fodor's writers have selected some of their favorites by price, cuisine, and experience in the lists shown here. You can also search by neighborhood or find specific details about a restaurant in our full reviews. ¡Bon profit! (Catalan for Good Eating!)

Fodor'sChoice★

ÀBaC, $$$$, p. 447
Ca l'Isidre, $$$$, p. 434
Cal Pep*, $$, p. 430
Casa Leopoldo, $$$, p. 434
Comerç 24, $$$$, p. 435
Cinc Sentits, $$$-$$$$, p. 441
Drolma, $$$$, p. 442
El Racó de Can Fabes, $$$$, p. 448

By Price

$

Agut, Barri p. 432
Ca l'Estevet, p. 434
Can Manel la Puda, p. 439
Folquer, p. 445

$$

Café de l'Acadèmia, p. 434
Cometacinc, p. 435
El Mató de Pedralbes, p. 446
Silvestre, p. 447
Taxidermista, p. 438

$$$

Can Majó, p. 439
Cinc Sentits, p. 441
Manairó, p. 443
Suquet de l'Almirall, p. 440
Tram-Tram, p. 447
Vivanda, p. 447

$$$$

ÀBaC, p. 447
Ca l'Isidre, p. 434
Can Gaig, p. 441
Comerç 24, p. 435
Drolma, p. 442
El Racó de Can Fabes, p. 448

By Cuisine

TRADITIONAL SPANISH

El Asador de Aranda, $$$-$$$$, p. 448

TRADITIONAL CATALAN

Antiga Casa Solé, $$$-$$$$, p. 438
Ca l'Isidre, $$$$, p. 434
Can Gaig, $$$$, p. 441
Casa Leopoldo, $$$, p. 434
Drolma, $$$$, p. 442
Neichel, $$$$, p. 446
Tram-Tram, $$$-$$$$, p. 447

CONTEMPORARY CATALAN

ÀBaC, $$-$$$$, p. 447
Andaira, $$$$, p. 438
L'Olivé, $$$-$$$$, p. 443
Sant Pau, $$$$, p. 449

EXPERIMENTAL

Cinc Sentits, $$$-$$$$, p. 441
Comerç 24, $$$$, p. 435
Manairó, $$$-$$$$, p. 443

TAPAS

Cal Pep*, $$, p. 430
Casa Lucio*, $$$, p. 430
El Vaso de Oro*, $$, p. 429
Inòpia Clàssic Bar*, $$, p. 430
Mantequeria Can Ravell*, $$, p. 431
Sagardi*, $$, p. 430

STEAK HOUSE

El Asador de Aranda, $$$-$$$$, p. 448
Gorría, $$-$$$$, p. 443

PAELLA

Can Majó, $$-$$$$, p. 439
Suquet de l'Almirall, $$$, p. 440

SEAFOOD

Antiga Casa Solé, $$-$$$$, p. 438
Botafumeiro, $$$-$$$$, p. 445

Tapas bars are marked with *, see previous section of chapter.

never waned, despite the enormous changes in Barcelona's frenetic dining scene. Wood paneling and oil paintings provide the backdrop for the mostly local clientele in the lower reaches of the Gothic Quarter. In season (October through January), try the *pato silvestre agridulce* (sweet-and-sour wild duck). There's a good selection of wines here, but no after-dinner dawdling over coffee or liqueur. ✉ *Gignàs 16, Barri Gòtic* ☎ *93/315–1709* ▭ *AE, MC, V* ⊙ *Closed Mon. and July. No dinner Sun.* Ⓜ *Jaume I* ✥ *D5.*

$–$$$ CATALAN

✕ **Ca l'Estevet.** Estevet and his large extended family are in charge of everything here, from the kitchen to the front door, and the carefully elaborated Catalan cuisine sparkles in this candlelit penumbra, especially at the surprisingly moderate prices that are maintained year after year. Facing the journalism school, this romantic little slot near the MACBA (Contemporary Art Museum) has long been popular with journalists, students, and artists. Try the asparagus cooked over coals, the *chopitos gaditanos* (deep-fried baby octopus), or the *magret de pato* (duck breast). The house wine is inexpensive and perfectly drinkable. ✉ *Valdonzella 46, Raval* ☎ *93/302–4186* ▭ *AE, DC, MC, V* ⊙ *Closed Sun.* Ⓜ *Catalunya* ✥ *C3.*

$$$$ MEDITERRANEAN Fodor's Choice ★

✕ **Ca l'Isidre.** Many epicureans recognize Ca l'Isidre as the finest restaurant in Barcelona. Just off Avinguda del Paral.lel in the Raval, this is a favorite with Barcelona's art crowd, and paintings and engravings by Miró, Dalí, Joan Pere Viladecans, and other stars line the walls. The traditional yet contemporary Catalan cooking draws on fresh produce from the Boqueria and has a slight French accent. Isidre's wines are invariably novelties from all over the Iberian Peninsula; ask for his advice and you'll get a great wine as well as an oenology, geography, and history course delivered with charm, brevity, and wit. ✉ *Carrer de les Flors 12, Raval* ☎ *93/441–1139* ✍ *Reservations essential* ▭ *AE, MC, V* ⊙ *Closed Sun., Easter wk, and mid-July–mid-Aug.* Ⓜ *Paral.lel* ✥ *B5.*

$$–$$$ MEDITERRANEAN

✕ **Café de l'Acadèmia.** With wicker chairs, stone walls, and classical music, this spot is sophisticated yet rustic, and the light and streamlined Mediterranean and Catalan fare makes it much more than a mere café. Just up the alley from the Reial Acadèmia de Bones Lletres (Royal Academy of Arts and Letters) for which it's named, the dining room is frequented by politicians and functionaries from the nearby municipal town hall and the autonomous government of Catalunya, the Generalitat. Reservations are a must, especially at lunchtime. ✉ *Lledó 1, Barri Gòtic* ☎ *93/319–8253* ▭ *AE, DC, MC, V* Ⓜ *Jaume I* ✥ *D5.*

$$$–$$$$ MEDITERRANEAN Fodor's Choice ★

✕ **Casa Leopoldo.** Rosa Gil and her family receive guests warmly at this superb seafood and Catalan restaurant in the Raval, west of the Rambla. To get here, approach along Carrer Hospital, take a left on the wide new Rambla del Raval, go down to Carrer Sant Rafael, and take another left 50 feet to the front door of this clean, well-lit, ceramic-tiled gem. Try the *revuelto de ajos tiernos y gambas* (eggs scrambled with young garlic and shrimp) or the famous Catalan classic *cap-i-pota* (stewed head and hoof of pork). ✉ *Sant Rafael 24, Raval* ☎ *93/441–3014* ▭ *AE, DC, MC, V* ⊙ *Closed Mon. No dinner Sun.* Ⓜ *Liceu* ✥ *C4.*

$$$$ LA NUEVA COCINA

Comerç 24. Artist, aesthete, and chef, Carles Abellan playfully reinterprets traditional Catalan favorites at this sleek, designer dining spot. Try the deconstructed *tortilla de patatas* (potato omelet) or the *huevo kinder* (an egg with surprises—truffled potato purée—inside, based on a popular children's toy). For dessert, prepare for a postmodern version of the traditional Catalan after-school snack of chocolate, olive oil, salt, and bread. Abellán's cuisine is always original and, though sometimes flirting with the border between fine dining and playing with your food, unfailingly delicious. ✉ *Carrer Comerç 24, Born-Ribera* ☎ *93/319–2102* *Reservations essential* ▭ *AE, DC, MC, V* *Closed Sun.* Ⓜ *Jaume I* ✣ *F5.*

$$–$$$ CATALAN

Cometacinc. This stylish spot in the Barri de Sant Just, an increasingly chic neighborhood in which new shops and restaurants open daily, is a fine example of Barcelona's flair for contemporary taste and technology with new-over-old architecture and interior design. The floor-to-ceiling wooden doors and shutters and the giant glass windows are a visual feast, but the carefully prepared interpretations of old standards, lightened up for 21st-century diners, such as the *carpaccio de toro de lidia* (carpaccio of fighting bull) with basil sauce and pine nuts, are equally brilliant. ✉ *Carrer Cometa 5, Barri Gòtic* ☎ *93/310–1558* ▭ *AE, DC, MC, V* *Closed Tues.* Ⓜ *Jaume I* ✣ *D5.*

$$–$$$ ECLECTIC

El Foro. This glassed-in corner café and Argentine bistro in the always-bustling Born-Ribera neighborhood is generally filled to the rafters with lively young and young-at-heart couples in the preliminary stages of night-long revelries. Regularly changing painting and photographic exhibits line the walls, while the light and varied market menu is dominated by pizzas, salads, and Argentine beef cooked over coals. Flamenco and jazz performances downstairs are a good after-dinner option. The midday fixed-price menu (€12) is a bargain only outdone by the half-menu at €8.50. ✉ *Princesa 53, Born-Ribera* ☎ *93/310–1020* ▭ *AE, DC, MC, V* *Closed Mon.* Ⓜ *Jaume I* ✣ *E5.*

$–$$ SPANISH

Mundial Bar. This in one of the few traditional Barcelona bars left, serving delicious tapas and small portions of traditional morsels. The kitchen turns out consistently tasty fare such as *pimientos de Padrón* (green peppers from Padrón, Galicia), *xipirones* (baby squid), thin-sliced aubergines with goat cheese, or the *solomillo con salteado de setas y reducción de Módena y trufa* (filet mignon with sautéed wild mushrooms, reduction of Módena, and truffles). ✉ *Plaça Sant Agustí Vell 1, Born-Ribera* ☎ *93/319–9056* ▭ *AE, DC, MC, V* *Closed Mon.* Ⓜ *Jaume I* ✣ *E4.*

$$–$$$$ MEDITERRANEAN/ ECLECTIC

Nonell. Dishes range from classical Mediterranean to Castilian roast suckling pig at this graceful, eclectic space tucked away on a quiet square behind the block facing the cathedral. In summer, tables on the terrace offer cool alfresco dining, while the glassed-in dining room makes you feel like part of the Gothic Quarter year-round. The wine list features bottles and vineyards you may never have heard of but will be glad to get to know; the service is impeccable and delivered with panache and wit—and more often than not in perfect English. ✉ *Pl. Isidre Nonell, Barri Gòtic* ☎ *93/301–1378* ▭ *AE, DC, MC, V* Ⓜ *Catalunya, Liceu* ✣ *D4.*

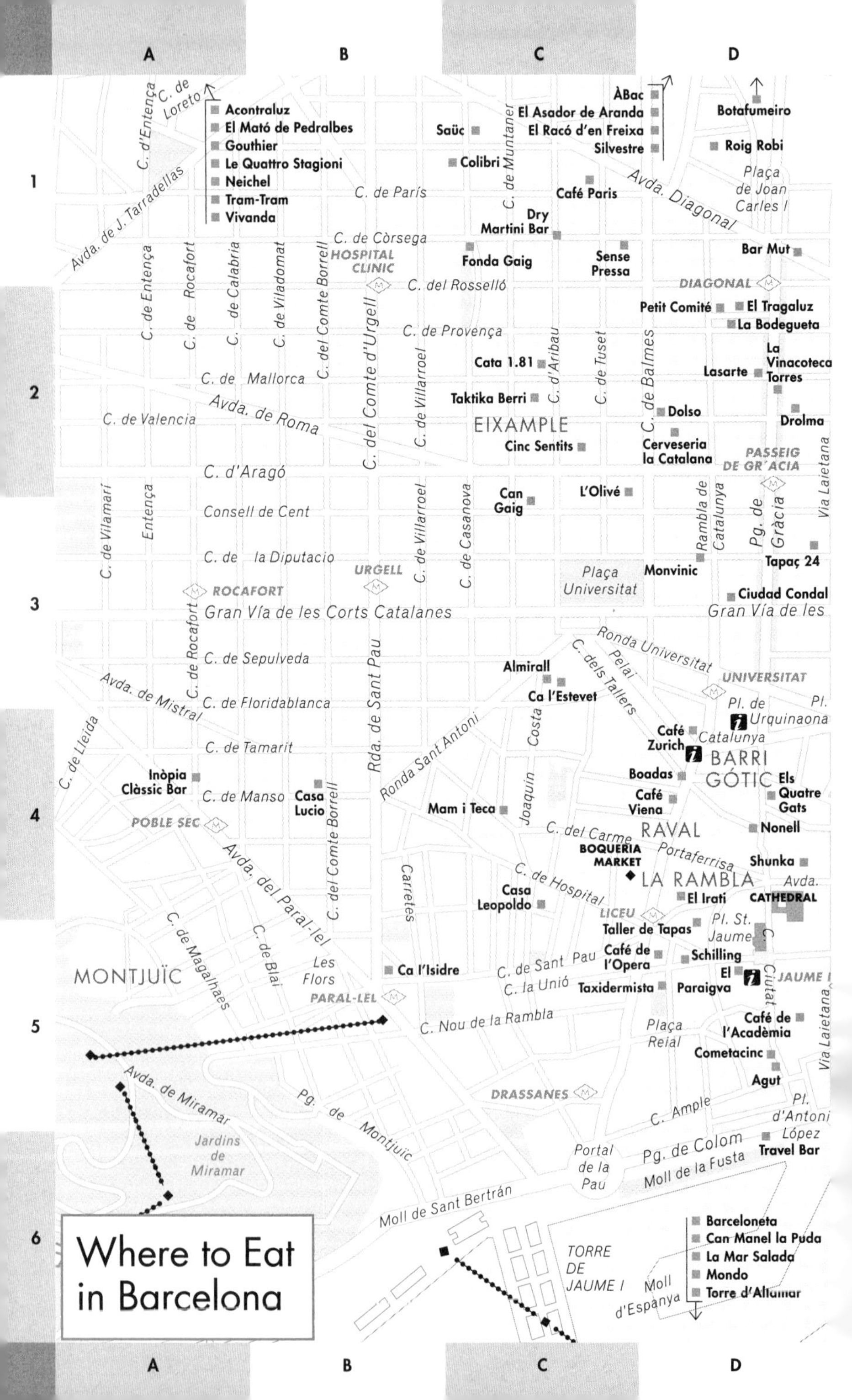
Where to Eat in Barcelona
A
B
C
D
1
2
3
4
5
6
Acontraluz
El Mató de Pedralbes
Gouthier
Le Quattro Stagioni
Neichel
Tram-Tram
Vivanda
Saüc
Colibri
ÀBac
El Asador de Aranda
El Racó d'en Freixa
Silvestre
Botafumeiro
Roig Robi
Café Paris
Dry Martini Bar
Fonda Gaig
Sense Pressa
Bar Mut
Petit Comité
El Tragaluz
La Bodegueta
Cata 1.81
Taktika Berri
Lasarte
La Vinacoteca Torres
Dolso
Drolma
Cinc Sentits
Cerveseria la Catalana
L'Olivé
Can Gaig
Monvinic
Tapaç 24
Ciudad Condal
Almirall
Ca l'Estevet
Café Zurich
Boadas
Café Viena
Els Quatre Gats
Nonell
Shunka
Inòpia Clàssic Bar
Casa Lucio
Mam i Teca
Casa Leopoldo
El Irati
Taller de Tapas
Café de l'Opera
Schilling
Ca l'Isidre
Taxidermista
El Paraigva
Café de l'Acadèmia
Cometacinc
Agut
Travel Bar
Barceloneta
Can Manel la Puda
La Mar Salada
Mondo
Torre d'Altamar
C. de Loreto
C. d'Entença
Avda. de J. Tarradellas
C. de París
C. de Còrsega
C. de Muntaner
Avda. Diagonal
Plaça de Joan Carles I
HOSPITAL CLINIC
C. del Rosselló
DIAGONAL
C. de Entença
C. de Rocafort
C. de Calabria
C. de Viladomat
C. del Comte Borrell
C. del Comte d'Urgell
C. de Provença
C. de Villarroel
C. d'Aribau
C. de Tuset
C. de Balmes
C. de Mallorca
Avda. de Roma
C. de Valencia
EIXAMPLE
PASSEIG DE GR'ACIA
C. d'Aragó
Consell de Cent
C. de la Diputacio
C. de Vilamarí
Entença
C. de Casanova
Rambla de Catalunya
Pg. de Gràcia
Via Laietana
URGELL
Plaça Universitat
ROCAFORT
Gran Vía de les Corts Catalanes
Gran Vía de les
Ronda Universitat
Pelai
C. dels Tallers
UNIVERSITAT
C. de Sepulveda
Avda. de Mistral
C. de Floridablanca
Rda. de Sant Pau
Ronda Sant Antoni
Costa
Joaquin
Pl. de Catalunya
Pl. Urquinaona
BARRI GÓTIC
C. de Lleida
C. de Tamarit
C. de Manso
POBLE SEC
C. del Carme
RAVAL
BOQUERIA MARKET
Portaferrisa
LA RAMBLA
Avda.
CATHEDRAL
Avda. del Paral-lel
C. de Hospital
Carretes
LICEU
Pl. St. Jaume
C. Ciutat
JAUME I
C. de Magalhaes
C. de Blai
Les Flors
C. de Sant Pau
C. la Unió
MONTJUÏC
PARAL-LEL
C. Nou de la Rambla
Plaça Reial
Avda. de Miramar
Pg. de Montjuïc
DRASSANES
C. Ample
Pl. d'Antoni López
Jardins de Miramar
Portal de la Pau
Pg. de Colom
Moll de la Fusta
Moll de Sant Bertrán
TORRE DE JAUME I
Moll d'Espanya

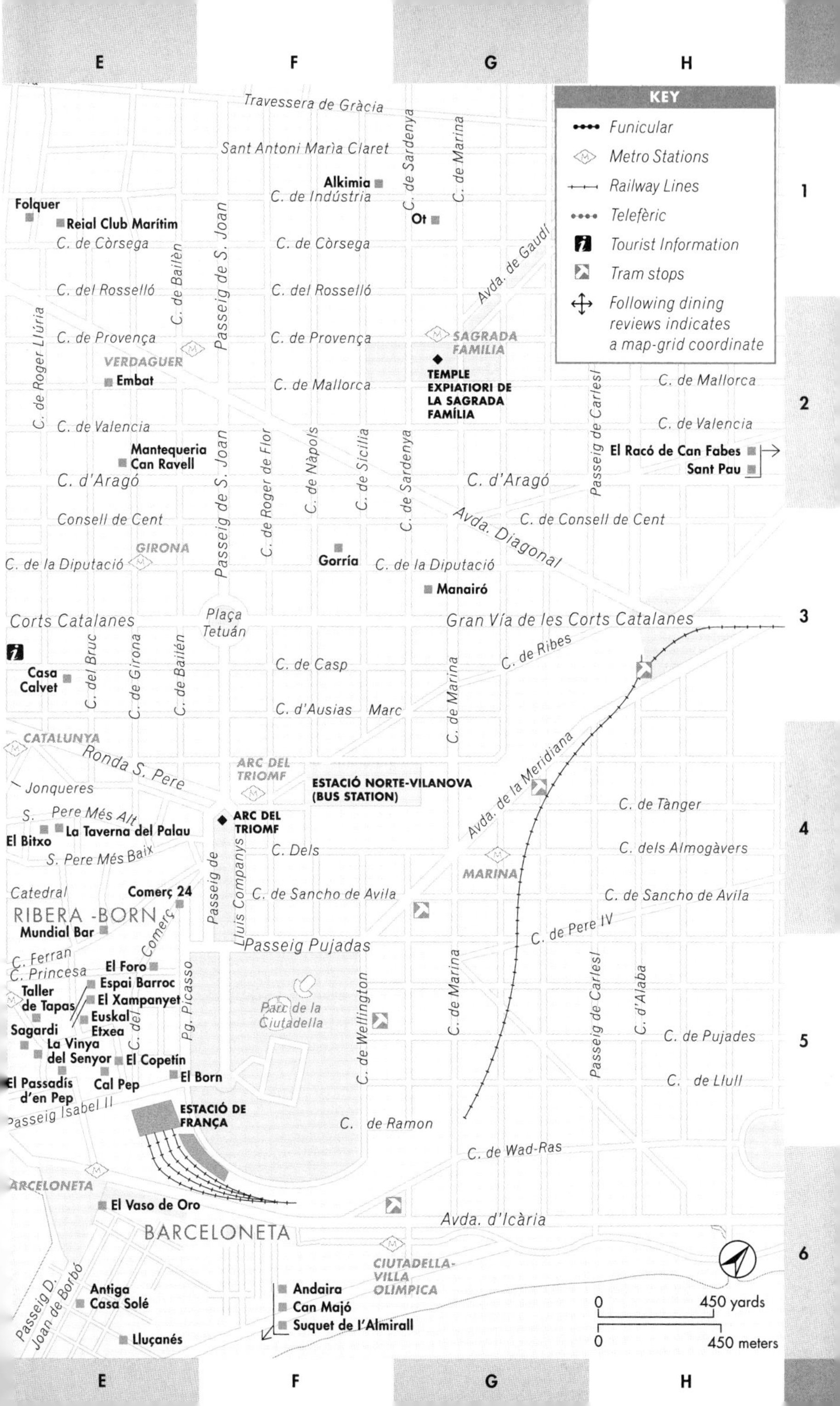

E
F
G
H
1
2
3
4
5
6
KEY
Funicular
Metro Stations
Railway Lines
Telefèric
Tourist Information
Tram stops
Following dining reviews indicates a map-grid coordinate
Travessera de Gràcia
Sant Antoni Marìa Claret
Alkimia
C. de Indústria
C. de Sardenya
C. de Marina
Ot
Folquer
Reial Club Marítim
C. de Còrsega
C. de Bailèn
Passeig de S. Joan
Avda. de Gaudí
C. del Rosselló
C. de Roger Llúria
C. de Provença
VERDAGUER
SAGRADA FAMILIA
TEMPLE EXPIATIORI DE LA SAGRADA FAMÍLIA
Embat
C. de Mallorca
Passeig de Carlesi
C. de Valencia
Mantequeria Can Ravell
C. de Roger de Flor
C. de Nàpols
C. de Sicilia
El Racó de Can Fabes
Sant Pau
C. d'Aragó
Consell de Cent
Avda. Diagonal
C. de Consell de Cent
GIRONA
Gorría
C. de la Diputació
Manairó
Corts Catalanes
Plaça Tetuán
Gran Vía de les Corts Catalanes
C. del Bruc
C. de Girona
C. de Bailén
C. de Casp
C. de Ribes
Casa Calvet
C. d'Ausias Marc
CATALUNYA
Ronda S. Pere
ARC DEL TRIOMF
ESTACIÓ NORTE-VILANOVA (BUS STATION)
Avda. de la Meridiana
Jonqueres
C. de Tànger
S. Pere Més Alt
La Taverna del Palau
El Bitxo
S. Pere Més Baix
Passeig de Lluis Companys
C. Dels
C. dels Almogàvers
MARINA
Catedral
Comerç 24
C. de Sancho de Avila
RIBERA -BORN
C. de Pere IV
Mundial Bar
C. Comerç
Passeig Pujadas
C. Ferran
C. Princesa
El Foro
Espai Barroc
Taller de Tapas
El Xampanyet
Euskal Etxea
Sagardi
C. del
Pg. Picasso
Parc de la Ciutadella
C. de Wellington
C. de Marina
Passeig de Carlesi
C. d'Alaba
C. de Pujades
La Vinya del Senyor
El Copetín
El Born
C. de Llull
El Passadís d'en Pep
Cal Pep
Passeig Isabel II
ESTACIÓ DE FRANÇA
C. de Ramon
C. de Wad-Ras
ARCELONETA
El Vaso de Oro
Avda. d'Icària
BARCELONETA
CIUTADELLA-VILLA OLIMPICA
Passeig D. Joan de Borbó
Antiga Casa Solé
Andaira
Can Majó
Suquet de l'Almirall
Llucanés
0
450 yards
0
450 meters

$$–$$$ JAPANESE ✕**Shunka.** Widely regarded as Barcelona's finest Japanese restaurant, this cozy and popular hideaway near the Catedral de la Seu, behind the Hotel Colón, is at its best straight across the horseshoe-shaped counter from the burners, so try to reserve a place at the bar. Mediterranean and Japanese cuisines have traditionally had much in common and have recently embraced each other fervently with exchanges and symposiums starring everyone from Spain's own Ferran Adrià to internationally acclaimed Japanese chef Seiji Yamamoto. Even the sushi and *esqueixada* (raw cod dressed with tomato, olives, and peppers) traditions speak eloquently to each other. ✉*Sagristans 5, Barri Gòtic* ☎*93/412–4991* ▭*AE, DC, MC, V* Ⓜ*Liceu* ✣*D4.*

WORD OF MOUTH

"The food in Barcelona is great, the culture is quite offbeat, and there is a general air of revelry and youth all over town."
—nessundorma

$$–$$$ MEDITERRANEAN ✕**Taxidermista.** Don't worry, road kill isn't on the menu. Once a natural-science museum and taxidermy shop (from which Salvador Dalí once purchased 200,000 ants and a stuffed rhinoceros), this handsome terrace and dining room in the far northwest corner of sunny Plaça Reial is the only recommendable restaurant in the square. Interior decorator Beth Galí designed the space around the original beams and steel columns. Delicacies such as *bonito con escalivada y queso de cabra* (white tuna with braised eggplant, peppers, and goat cheese) are served at outside tables at their best in the winter sun. ✉*Pl. Reial 8, Rambla* ☎*93/412–4536* ▭*AE, DC, MC, V* ⊙*Closed Mon.* Ⓜ*Liceu* ✣*D5.*

BARCELONETA AND THE PORT OLÍMPIC

Barceloneta and the Port Olímpic (Olympic Port) have little in common beyond their seaside location: the former is a traditional fishermen's quarter; the latter is a crazed disco strip with thousand-seat restaurants.

$$–$$$$ CONTEMPORARY MEDITERRANEAN ✕**Andaira.** New flavors and innovative, contemporary cooking distinguish this young couple's contribution to the Barceloneta dining panorama. It's not that Andaira doesn't do the traditional waterfront rice and fish dishes, but that it does them with a sleek, modern flair, all within sight of the Mediterranean from a contemporary, streamlined second-floor dining room surrounded by picture windows. ✉*Vila Joiosa 52–54, Barceloneta* ☎*93/221–1616* ▭*AE, DC, MC, V* Ⓜ*Barceloneta* ✣*F6.*

$$$–$$$$ SEAFOOD ✕**Antiga Casa Solé.** The sounds, sights, aromas, and warmth of the open kitchen form a natural part of the dining area and enhance the fine fish and rice dishes served in this longtime locally favorite dining spot. This traditional midday-Sunday pilgrimage site is two blocks from the seaside of Plaça de Sant Miquel, Barceloneta's prettiest square, and the restaurant itself occupies an original fisherman's house. Not surprisingly, the seafood is fresh and well-prepared, and whether it's *lenguado a la plancha* (grilled sole) or the exquisite *arroç negre amb sepia en su tinta* (black rice with squid in its ink), everything is loaded with flavor. ✉*Sant Carles*

4, Barceloneta ☎93/221–5012 ▭AE, DC, MC, V ⏲Closed Mon. and last 2 wks of Aug. No dinner Sun. Ⓜ Barceloneta ✥E6.

$$–$$$$ SEAFOOD ✕**Barceloneta.** This rollicking, riverboat of a dining room at the end of the yacht marina in Barceloneta doesn't provide the ideal intimate space for a romantic dinner à deux, but the food is delicious, the service impeccable, and the dozens of fellow diners in full feeding frenzy make the place feel like a raging New Year's Eve celebration. All in all, you're pretty much guaranteed a good time. Rice and fish dishes are the specialty, the salads are excellent, and Albariño white wine flows freely. *✉L'Escar 22, Barceloneta ☎93/221–2111 ▭AE, MC, V Ⓜ Barceloneta ✥D6.*

$$–$$$$ SEAFOOD ★ ✕**Can Majó.** One of Barcelona's premier seafood restaurants, Can Majó combines fine cooking and a cosmopolitan vibe. House specialties include *caldero de bogavante* (a cross between paella and bouillabaisse, with lobster) and *suquet* (fish stewed in its own juices), but whatever you choose will be fresh-caught and prepared with care. From May to October, the parasol-shaded terrace overlooking the Barceloneta beach and the Mediterranean is the closest you can get to dining on the sand. *✉Almirall Aixada 23, Barceloneta ☎93/221–5455 ▭AE, DC, MC, V ⏲Closed Mon. No dinner Sun. Ⓜ Barceloneta ✥F6.*

$–$$ SEAFOOD ✕**Can Manel la Puda.** The first choice for a non-wallet-knocking paella in the sun, year-round, Can Manel is near the end of the main avenue leading out to the Barceloneta beach. Anytime before 4 PM is early enough for an *arròs*; the restaurant then reopens at 7. *Arròs a banda* (rice with peeled shellfish), paella marinera (seafood and rice), or *fideuá* (with noodles instead of rice) are all well prepared here, as are the fresh fish selections. *Xipirones* (baby octopi) make a good shared starter, while *ensalada verde* (the simplest green salad) goes well with the seafood and rice. *✉Passeig Joan de Borbó 60, Barceloneta ☎93/221–5013 ▭AE, DC, MC, V ⏲Closed Mon. Ⓜ Barceloneta ✥D6.*

$–$$ SEAFOOD ✕**La Mar Salada.** Next door to the sometimes-crowded Can Manel la Puda, this terrace restaurant serving seafood and rice offers creditable paella, black rice, *fideuá* (noodle paella), and fresh fish. The house white wine is an acceptable Penedès, though an Albariño from Galicia's Rías Baixas is better. Paella or *arròs negre* (black rice) for two with a mixed salad is about the best you can do for value and quality in Barceloneta. Fish choices include *lubina* (sea bass), *dorada* (sea bream), or *lenguado* (sole), cooked *a la plancha* (grilled), *a la sal* (in a thick coating of salt), or *a suquet* (stewed). *✉Passeig Joan de Borbó 58, Barceloneta ☎93/221–2127 ▭AE, MC, V ⏲Closed Tues. ✥D6.*

$$–$$$$ CATALAN ✕**Lluçanès.** The Barceloneta market was fertile ground for chefs Àngel Pascual and Francesc Miralles when they moved their legendary restaurant from the country town of Prat de Lluçanès to the big city. Upstairs is the grand gourmet option, Lluçanès: it's contemporary and creative, serving such refined interpretations as scallop tartare with white summer truffles. The downstairs **Els Fogons de la Barceloneta** serves typical Barceloneta tapas and seafood; think *bombas* (potato croqettes) and the standard *calamares a la plancha* (grilled cuttlefish), impeccably prepared. *✉Plaça de la Font 1, Barceloneta ☎93/224–2525 ▭AE, DC, MC, V ⏲Closed Mon. No dinner Sun. Ⓜ Barceloneta ✥E6.*

$$$–$$$$ SEAFOOD

✕**Mondo.** Just off the south end of the Rambla, across the Rambla de Mar in the Maremagnum complex, Mondo has gained prestige for its quality seafood preparations in a contemporary design setting overlooking Barcelona's yacht marina. Not coincidentally, the afternoon fish auction is held daily on the Moll dels Pescadors just across the port. Original creations such as *foie con albaricoque y pétalos de tomate seco* (duck liver with apricot and julienned sun-dried tomatoes) join classics like *caldoso de bogavante* (lobster bouillabaisse) on the menu. Around midnight, Mondo morphs into a fashionable dance club and disco. ✉*Moll d'Espanya s/n (IMAX building), Maremagnum, Barceloneta* ☎*93/221–3911* ▭*AE, DC, MC, V* Ⓜ*Drassanes, Barceloneta* ✥*D6.*

$$–$$$$ SEAFOOD

✕**Reial Club Marítim.** For sunset or harbor views, excellent maritime fare, and a sense of escape from the city, however slight, try Barcelona's yacht club, just around the harbor on the Moll d'Espanya. The dining room has a comfortable, old-world, clubby feel and the waitstaff never fails to make guests feel like members of the club. Highlights are the paella *marinera* (seafood paella) and fish specialties such as *rodaballo* (turbot), *lubina* (sea bass), and *dorado* (sea bream). Ask for the freshest fish they have and you won't be disappointed. ✉*Moll d'Espanya, Barceloneta* ☎*93/221–7143* ▭*AE, DC, MC, V* ⏲*No dinner Sun.* Ⓜ*Barceloneta* ✥*E1.*

$$–$$$$ SEAFOOD

✕**Suquet de l'Almirall.** Specialists in rice dishes and *caldoso de bogavante,* a brothy rice with lobster, this is one of Barceloneta's finest seafood havens. With an outdoor terrace for alfresco dining in summer, "The Admiral's Fish Stew," as the name translates, in a setting complete with fishing nets and buoys, indeed serves fare fit for the admiralty. *Lubina a la sal* (sea bass cooked in sea salt) and *suquets* (stews) of monkfish, hake, and cod are favorites at this sidewalk dining room overlooking the marina. ✉*Passeig Joan de Borbó 65, Barceloneta* ☎*93/221–6233* ▭*AE, DC, MC, V* ⏲*Closed Mon. No dinner Sun.* Ⓜ*Barceloneta* ✥*F6.*

$$$$ MEDITERRANEAN

✕**Torre d'Altamar.** Seafood of every stripe, spot, fin, and carapace issue abundantly forth from the kitchen here, but the filet mignon, under a slab of *foie* (duck or goose liver), is a tour de force, too. Acrophobes need not apply: the "Tower of the High Seas," as it translates, is perched atop a steel constructor-set cable-car tower over the far side of the port at a height of 225 feet and has spectacular views of Barcelona as well as far out to the Mediterranean. ✉*Passeig Joan de Borbó 88–Torre de San Sebastián, Barceloneta* ☎*93/221–0007* ▭*AE, DC, MC, V* ⏲*Closed Sun. No lunch Mon.* Ⓜ*Barceloneta* ✥*D6.*

EIXAMPLE

Eixample dining, invariably upscale and elegant, ranges from traditional cuisine to designer fare in sleek minimalist spaces.

$$$–$$$$ LA NUEVA COCINA ★

✕**Alkimia.** Chef Jordi Vilà makes news with his inventive creations and tasting menus at €32, €54, and €68 that pass for bargains in top end Barcelona culinary culture. It's usually packed, but the alcoves are intimate. Vilà's deconstructed *pa amb tomaquet* (in classical usage, toasted bread with olive oil and squeezed tomato) in a shot glass gives a witty culinary wink before things get serious with raw tuna strips, baby squid, or turbot. A dark-meat course (venison or beef) brings the taste progression to a close before dessert provides more comic relief. Alkimia, as its name suggests, is magic. ✉ *Indústria 79, Eixample* ☎ *93/207–6115* ▭ *AE, DC, MC, V* ⏲ *Closed Sat. lunch, Sun., Easter wk, and Aug. 1–21* Ⓜ *Sagrada Família* ✥ *F1.*

$$$$ CATALAN ★ ✕ **Can Gaig.** Market-fresh ingredients and original food pairings such as *mar i muntanya* (literally, sea and mountain, as in surf and turf) are often at the root of traditional recipes in Catalan home cooking, and the menu here balances seafood, bovine, ovine, and poultry options with game and homegrown products from all over Catalonia and the Iberian Peninsula. This longtime Barcelona favorite is famous for mingling its superb contemporary dining space with carefully prepared cuisine. Try the *perdiz asada con jamón ibérico* (roast partridge with Iberian ham) or, if it's available, *becada* (woodcock), one of Carles Gaig's signature dishes. ✉ *Carrer Aragó 214, Eixample* ☎ *93/429–1017* ✍ *Reservations essential* ▭ *AE, DC, MC, V* ⏲ *Closed Mon., Easter wk and Aug.* Ⓜ *Passeig de Gràcia* ✥ *C3.*

$$$–$$$$ MEDITERRANEAN ✕ **Casa Calvet.** This Art Nouveau space in an adjoining wing of Antoni Gaudí's 1898–1900 Casa Calvet, just a block from the Hotel Palace (the former Ritz), is an opportunity to break bread in one of the great Moderniste master's creations. The dining room is a graceful and spectacular display featuring signature Gaudíesque ornamentation such as looping parabolic door handles, polychrome stained glass, and wood carved in floral and organic motifs. The menu offers a creative interpretation of Mediterranean cooking, with an emphasis on light, contemporary fare. ✉ *Casp 48, Eixample* ☎ *93/412–4012* ▭ *AE, DC, MC, V* ⏲ *Closed Sun. and last 2 wks of Aug.* Ⓜ *Urquinaona* ✥ *E3.*

$$$–$$$$ LA NUEVA COCINA Fodor's Choice ★ ✕ **Cinc Sentits.** The engaging Artal family—maître d' and owner Rosa; her son, chef Jordi; and Jordi's wife, the server and eloquent food narrator, Amy—is a Catalan family that has clocked a couple of decades in Canada and the United States. Their restaurant offers a unique Barcelona experience: cutting-edge, creative cuisine explained in perfect English, all in a minimalist, contemporary setting. Three tasting menus—light, tasting, and *omakase* (a "trust the chef" menu, including wine pairings of the chef's choice)—provide a wide range of tastes and textures. ✉ *Aribau 58, Eixample* ☎ *93/323–9490* ▭ *AE, DC, MC, V* ⏲ *Closed Sun. No dinner Mon.* Ⓜ *Provença* ✥ *C2.*

$$–$$$$ MEDITERRANEAN ✕ **Colibrí.** Known for fresh market cuisine prepared in innovative, though never radical or self-conscious ways, Colibrí ("hummingbird" in Catalan) has managed to hum happily along, largely under the international radar. Proving that culinary originality can be successfully elaborated without losing the sense and sensibility of an ingredient's nature, the Colibrí kitchen offers everything from artichoke hearts stuffed with duck liver in French onion and tarragon sauce to sea bream with eggplant and chestnuts. The soothing, minimalist decor in creams and beiges nicely offsets the tastes and textures of the food. The wine list contains exciting surprises such as the gentle but authoritative Taberner Syrah from Cádiz. ✉ *Casanova 212, Eixample* ☎ *93/443–2306* ✍ *Res-*

ervations essential ▭ *AE, DC, MC, V* ⊙ *Closed Mon. No dinner Sun.* Ⓜ *Diagonal, Provença* ✣ *C1.*

$–$$ MEDITERRANEAN ✕ **Dolso.** Known primarily for inventive sweets and desserts such its famous *gintonic*, a clear jelly that tastes uncannily like the drink for which it is named, this creative pudding-café just off Rambla Catalunya also serves excellent fish and meat dishes as well as superb salads. The €12 lunch menu is one of the best bargains in Barcelona. ✉ *València 227, Eixample* ☎ *93/487–5964* ▭ *AE, DC, MC, V* ⊙ *Closed Sun. No dinner Mon.* Ⓜ *Passeig de Gràcia, Provença* ✣ *D2.*

$$$$ MEDITERRANEAN Fodor's Choice ★ ✕ **Drolma.** Chef Fermin Puig's blend of tradition, innovation, and inspiration produces classical Mediterranean excellence based on peerless products and painstakingly perfect execution. Named (in Sanskrit) for Buddha's female side, this intimate refuge has been a success since the doors first opened. The *menú de degustaciòn* (tasting menu) might have pheasant cannelloni in foie gras sauce with fresh black truffles or giant prawn tails with *trompettes de la mort* (black wild mushrooms) and *sot-l'y-laisse* (literally "fool leaves it there"; in fact, chicken morsels). Fermin's foie gras *a la ceniza con ceps* (cooked over wood coals with wild mushrooms) is a typical example of a childhood favorite reinvented in the big city. ✉ *Majestic Hotel, Passeig de Gràcia 70, Eixample* ☎ *93/496–7710* ✍ *Reservations essential* ▭ *AE, DC, MC, V* ⊙ *Closed Sun. and Aug.* Ⓜ *Provença, Passeig de Gràcia* ✣ *D2.*

$$$–$$$$ MEDITERRANEAN ✕ **El Tragaluz.** *Tragaluz* means skylight—literally, "light-swallower"—and this is an interesting environment if you're still on a design high from Gaudí's nearby Pedrera or the famous Vinçon design store just across Passeig de Gràcia. The sliding roof opens to the stars in good weather, and the chairs, lamps, plates, and fittings by Javier Mariscal (creator of the 1992 Olympic mascot Cobi) reflect Barcelona's passion for whimsy and playful design. The Mediterranean cuisine is light and innovative, and the €24 lunch menu offers top value. ✉ *Passatge de la Concepció 5, Eixample* ☎ *93/487–0196* ▭ *AE, DC, MC, V* ⊙ *Closed Jan. 5. No lunch Mon.* Ⓜ *Diagonal* ✣ *D2.*

$$–$$$ CATALAN ✕ **Embat.** An *embat* is a puff of wind in Catalan (and also a crashing wave), and this restaurant is indeed a breath of fresh air in the swashbuckling and hypercommercial Eixample. The market cuisine of partner chefs Santi Rebés and Fidel Puig is always impeccably fresh and freshly conceived, starring thoughtful combinations such as the *cazuelita de alcachofas con huevo poché y papada* (casserole of artichokes and poached egg with pork) or the *pichón con bizcocho de cacao y cebolla confitada* (pigeon with cacao biscuit and onion confit). ✉ *Mallorca 304, Eixample* ☎ *93/458–0885* ▭ *AE, DC, MC, V* ⊙ *Closed Sun., Mon. No dinner Tues., Wed.* Ⓜ *Diagonal* ✣ *E2.*

$–$$ CATALAN ✕ **Fonda Gaig.** A rustic interpretation of the traditional cuisine that has made the Gaig family synonymous with top Barcelona dining since 1869, this new enterprise is making a place for itself in Barcelona's relentlessly evolving culinary world. With some of the steam leaking out of the radically innovative and experimental cookery movement led by Ferran Adrià and El Bulli, Carles Gaig and a growing number of top chefs are going back to simpler and more affordable food. Look for standards such as *botifarra amb mongetes de ganxet* (sausage with white beans) or *canelons de l'Avia* (Grandmother's cannelloni) or *pollastre de gratapallers a la casssola* (stewed free-range chicken). ✉ *Còrsega 200, Eixample* ☎ *93/453–2020* ▭ *AE, DC, MC, V* ⊙ *Closed Sun., Mon. No dinner Sun.* Ⓜ *Hospital Clínic, Provença* ✥ *C1.*

$$–$$$$ BASQUE ✕ **Gorría.** One of the two best Basque restaurants in Barcelona (the other is Taktika Berri, which is nearly impossible to get into except for tapas), this establishment serves everything from stewed *pochas* (white beans) to the classic *chuletón* (steak), which is as fragrant and pristine as the Navarran Pyrenees. The *pimientos de piquillo* (sweet red bell peppers) are legendary. A Chivite Colección 125 Tinto Reserva from Navarra, a deep fruity red wine, provides perfect Bacchic accompaniment at this delicious pocket of Basque Country cooking in the Catalan capital. ✉ *Diputació 421, Eixample* ☎ *93/245–1164* ▭ *AE, DC, MC, V* ⊙ *Closed Sun.* Ⓜ *Monumental* ✥ *F3.*

$$$$ BASQUE ✕ **Lasarte.** Antonio Saez is the chief cook in at this restaurant owned by the famed Basque chef Martín Berasategui—it's named for his home town outside of San Sebastián. The menu features an eclectic selection of Basque, Mediterranean, market, and personal interpretations and creations. Expect whimsical and playful appetizers deepening to surprising combinations such as *foie* and smoked eel or simple wood pigeon cooked to perfection. Traditional Basque classics such as *kokotxas de bacalao al pil-pil* (stewed cod) occasionally find a place on the menu here, but be alert for flights of fancy ranging from frozen cockle scales to turbot with sour apples. ✉ *Mallorca 259, Eixample* ☎ *93/445–0000* ▭ *AE, DC, MC, V* ⊙ *Closed Mon., No dinner Sun.* Ⓜ *Provença* ✥ *D2.*

$$$–$$$$ CATALAN ✕ **L'Olivé.** Urban minimalist design and streamlined cooking make a perfect match in this Barcelona favorite. L'Olivé specializes in contemporary interpretations of traditional Catalan home cooking, and the results draw steady streams of discerning diners to this mid-Eixample dining room. The sleek space—decorated in soothing, clean-lined tans and mauves—is always filled with ravenous-looking young professionals having a great time, and you'll soon see why: excellent fare, smart service, and some of the best *pa amb tomaquet* (toasted bread with olive oil and squeezed tomato) in town. ✉ *Carrer Balmes 47, Eixample* ☎ *93/452–1990* ▭ *AE, DC, MC, V* ⊙ *No dinner Sun.* Ⓜ *Provença* ✥ *C3.*

$$$–$$$$ LA NUEVA COCINA ★ ✕ **Manairó.** A *manairó* is a mysterious Pyrenean elf who helps make things happen, and Jordi Herrera may be one. A demon for everything from blowtorch-fried eggs to meat cooked *al clavo ardiente* (à la burning nail—fillets warmed from within using red-hot spikes, producing meat both rare and warm and never undercooked), Jordi also cooks cod under a lightbulb at 220 degrees (*bacalao iluminado*—"illuminated codfish") and serves a palate-cleansing gin and tonic with liquid nitrogen, gin, and lime. The intimate though postmodern-edgy design of the dining room is a perfect reflection of the cuisine. ✉ *Diputació 424, Eixample* ☎ *93/231–0057* ✍ *Reservations essential* ▭ *AE, DC, MC, V* ⊙ *Closed Sun., Mon., and last 3 wks of Aug.* Ⓜ *Monumental* ✥ *G3.*

$$–$$$$ CATALAN ✕ **Petit Comité.** Fermin Puig of the famous Drolma restaurant at the Hotel Majestic created Petit Comité as a more rustic country cousin of his sleek high-end dining room a few blocks away on Passeig de Gràcia.

Traditional Catalan cooking is the theme in this contemporary design space, which has a square counter in the middle for bar fare. Serving around the clock from midday until after midnight (1 PM–1 AM) makes reservations essential only at peak hours. Traditional favorites include *trinxat* (chopped cabbage with potato and bacon) or *caneloni amb béchamel de tòfona* (cannelloni with truffled béchamel) and the dessert *mel i mató* (fresh cheese and honey). ✉ *Passatge de la Concepció 13, Eixample* ☎ *93/550–0620* ✍ *Reservations essential* ▭ *AE, DC, MC, V* ⏲ *Open daily 1 PM–1 AM* Ⓜ *Diagonal* ✢ *D2.*

$$–$$$$ CATALAN ✕ **Ot.** Streamlined and original contemporary recipes make Ot (Otto, in Catalan), just two blocks up from Gaudí's Sagrada Família, a good choice for hungry and foot-weary diners seeking new experiences. An eight-course tasting menu (€57 at press time) composed of two appetizers, two starters, fish, meat, and two desserts is the standard Ot formula. The abbreviated tasting menu isn't much less expensive, but you get a lot less to eat (one of everything and a choice of fish or meat). The menu changes frequently and includes zingers such as cauliflower soup with herring eggs. ✉ *Carrer Còrsega 537, Eixample* ☎ *93/435–8048* ▭ *AE, DC, MC, V* ⏲ *No lunch Mon.* Ⓜ *Sagrada Família* ✢ *G1.*

$$–$$$$ MEDITERRANEAN ✕ **Sense Pressa.** *Sense pressa* means "without hurry" or "no rush" in Catalan, and if you can score one of the coveted half dozen tables here at the corner of Carrer Còrsega, you are thereby encouraged to take all the time you need to enjoy this minuscule gem of a restaurant. *Risotto de ceps* (wild mushroom risotto), *garbanzos con espardenyas y huevos fritos* (chickpeas with sea cucumbers and fried eggs), or filet mignon of grass-fed Girona beef cooked to perfection are all good choices in this usually packed and intimate bistro. ✉ *Enric Granados 96, Eixample* ☎ *93/218–1544* ✍ *Reservations essential* ▭ *AE, DC, MC, V* ⏲ *Closed Sun. No dinner Mon.* Ⓜ *Provença* ✢ *C1.*

$$$–$$$$ LA NUEVA COCINA ✕ **Saüc.** Named for the curative elderberry plant, Saüc's avant-garde decor is the first hint that the fare here is far from standard. This postmodern *cuina d'autor* (creative contemporary recipes) restaurant, run by an enterprising young couple, Xavi Franco and Anna Donate, combines fine ingredients in flavorful and original (yet artifice-free) surprises, such as scallops with cod tripe and black sausage or monkfish with snails. The taster's menu is a series of unusual combinations of standard meat, fish, and vegetable products, none of which fail to please. Try the *coulant de chocolate y maracuyá* (chocolate pudding with passion fruit) for dessert. ✉ *Pje. Lluis Pellicer 12 baixos, Eixample* ☎ *93/321–0189* ▭ *AE, DC, MC, V* ⏲ *Closed Sun. and Mon., Jan. 1–8, and Aug. 1–15* Ⓜ *Provença* ✢ *C1.*

$$$$ BASQUE ★ ✕ **Taktika Berri.** At this Basque restaurant specializing in San Sebastián favorites such as *tronco de merluza* (hake), *besugo al horno* (roast sea bream), and *txuleta de buey* (ox steak), the only drawback is that a table is hard to come by unless you call weeks (yes, weeks) in advance. The tapas served over the bar, however, are of such high quality that you can barely do better *à table,* and at the little stand-up tables inside the front door you can order anything on the menu. The *morcilla* (black sausage) and the *croquetas de jamón* (ham croquettes) here are arguably the best in Barcelona, and the charming family that owns and runs this little known nugget will take good care of you. ✉ *Valencia 169,*

Eixample ☎*93/453–4759* ✍*Reservations essential* ▭*AE, DC, MC, V* ⊙*No dinner Sat. Closed Sun.* Ⓜ*Provença* ⊕*C2.*

GRÀCIA

This exciting yet intimate neighborhood has everything from the most sophisticated cuisine in town to lively Basque taverns.

$$$$ SPANISH ✕ **Botafumeiro.** Fleets of waiters in white outfits flash by at the speed of light in Barcelona's best Galician restaurant, which specializes in seafood medleys from shellfish to finfish to cuttlefish to caviar. An assortment of non-bank-breaking *media ración* (half-ration) selections is available at the bar, where *pop a feira* (squid on potato) and *jamón ibérico de bellota de Guijuelo* (acorn-fed ham from Guijuelo, Salamanca) make a peerless late-night combination. People-watching is tops here, and the barmen are all talented stand-up comics as well as savvy mixologists. ✉*Carrer Gran de Gràcia 81, Gràcia* ☎*93/218–4230* ▭*AE, DC, MC, V* Ⓜ*Gràcia* ⊕*D1.*

$–$$$ CATALAN ✕ **Folquer.** With one of the best-value taster's menus in Barcelona, this artsy little hideaway at the bottom of Gràcia serves creatively prepared traditional Catalan specialties. Chef Juanjo Carrillo, who has worked with Andoni Aduriz at the famous Mugaritz near San Sebastián, manages to produce surprising combinations such as *tartin de poma amb escalope de foie y salsa lima* (apple tart with breaded duck liver in a lime sauce) or *bacallà amb mongetas vermellas i pil-pil de pernil* (codfish cooked at low temperature with red beans and ham in cod gelatin). The two tasting menu options (€13 and €17) are among Barcelona's top values. ✉*Torrent de l'Olla 3, Gràcia* ☎*93/217–4395* ▭*AE, DC, MC, V* ⊙*Closed Sun. and last 2 wks of Aug. No lunch Sat.* Ⓜ*Diagonal* ⊕*E1.*

$$$–$$$$ CATALAN ✕ **Roig Robí.** Rattan chairs and a garden terrace characterize this simple yet polished dining spot in the bottom corner of Gràcia, just above the Diagonal (near Via Augusta). Rustic and relaxed, Roig Robí ("ruby red" in Catalan, as in the color of certain wines) has maintained a consistently high level of culinary excellence for the past 25 years, serving market cuisine based on the finest ingredients carefully selected from Catalonia, the Iberian Peninsula, and Europe, with original personal touches directed by chef Mercé Navarro. Try the *arròs amb espardenyes i carxofes* (rice with sea cucumbers and artichokes) or the *mandonguilles amb llenegues* (meatballs with wild mushrooms). ✉*Sèneca 20, Gràcia* ☎*93/218–9222* ✍*Reservations essential* ▭*AE, DC, MC, V* ⊙*Closed Sat. lunch, Sun., 3 wks in Aug.* Ⓜ*Gràcia, Diagonal* ⊕*D1.*

SARRIÀ, PEDRALBES, AND SANT GERVASI

An excursion to the upper reaches of town offers an excellent selection of restaurants, little-known Gaudí sites, shops, cool evening breezes, and a sense of village life in Sarrià.

$$–$$$$ ECLECTIC ✕ **Acontraluz.** This stylish covered terrace in the leafy upper-Barcelona neighborhood of Tres Torres has a constantly changing market- and season-based menu ranging from game, such as *rable de liebre* (stewed hare) with chutney, to the more stick-to-your-ribs northern favorites like *pochas con almejas* (beans with clams). The *sopa de setas con crujiente de castañas* (wild mushroom soup with chestnuts) and the *cordero diez aromas* (lamb cooked in ten spices) are representative creations from a cosmopolitan kitchen that draws freely upon French, Italian, and Asian culinary canons. The €20 lunch menu is a bargain. ✉ *Milanesat 19, Tres Torres* ☎ *93/203–0658* 💳 *AE, DC, MC, V* Ⓜ *Tres Torres* ✣ *A1.*

$–$$ MEDITERRANEAN ✕ **El Mató de Pedralbes.** Named for the *mató* (fresh cheese) traditionally prepared by the Clarist nuns who lived across the street in the Monestir de Pedralbes, this is a perfect place to stop for lunch after touring the gorgeous 14th-century monastery, which closes at 2. The restaurant has one of the most typically Catalan and best-value menus in upper Barcelona. Look for rustic favorites such as *civet de porc senglar* (wild boar stew), *sopa de ceba gratinée* (onion soup), *trinxat* (chopped cabbage with bacon bits), and *truite de patata i ceba* (potato-and-onion omelet). ✉ *Bisbe Català 10, Pedralbes* ☎ *93/204–7962* 💳 *AE, DC, MC, V* ⏲ *Closed Sun.* Ⓜ *Reina Elisenda* ✣ *A1.*

$–$$$ CATALAN ✕ **Gouthier.** Thierry Airaud's always bustling minimalist dining room and terrace at the bottom of Plaça Sant Vicenç de Sarrià specializes in oysters, caviar, and *foie* (duck and goose livers), as well as select *cavas* and champagnes. A local favorite on sunny January days when the combination of chilly air and warm sun provides a sensory rush to accompany the morsels and wine, you might even spot Penelope Cruz here, basking in the sweet Mediterranean winter. The half raciones and tasting portions are a golden opportunity to indulge your food fantasies without undue financial damage. ✉ *Carrer Mañé i Flaquer 8, Sarrià* ☎ *93/205–9969* ✍ *Reservations essential* 💳 *AE, DC, MC, V* ⏲ *Closed Sun. and Mon.* Ⓜ *Sarrià* ✣ *A1.*

$$$–$$$$ ITALIAN ✕ **Le Quattro Stagioni.** For first-rate, elegant, and contemporary Italian cuisine with a hint or two of postmodern Catalan culinary originality thrown in, this graceful dining room and terrace in the Tres Torres neighborhood, just down from the Bonanova metro stop on the Sarrià line, is a good choice for lunch or dinner after a visit to upper Barcelona. The classically decorated space is always filled with savvy-looking epicureans, about evenly balanced between hip locals and cosmopolitan visitors from all over Europe. The garden is a cool and fragrant refuge on hot summer nights. ✉ *Dr. Roux 37, Sant Gervasi* ☎ *93/205–2279* 💳 *AE, DC, MC, V* Ⓜ *Tres Torres* ✣ *A1.*

$$$$ FRENCH ★ ✕ **Neichel.** Alsatian chef Jean-Louis Neichel, the first to put Ferran Adrià's now legendary El Bulli on the culinary map of Europe (El Bulli existed long before Adrià came along, and Neichel was the one to win El Bulli's first Michelin stars), masterfully manages a wide variety of exquisite ingredients such as *foie*, truffles, wild mushrooms, herbs, and the best seasonal vegetables. His flawless Mediterranean delicacies include *ensalada de gambas de Palamós al sésamo con puerros* (shrimp from Palamós with sesame-seed and leeks) and *espardenyes amb salicornia* (sea cucumber and sea asparagus) on sun-dried-tomato paste. The formal dining room may seem a trifle overcarpeted and staid, but the hush allows the other senses to kick in with authority. ✉ *Carrer Bertran i Rózpide 1, off Av. Pedralbes, Pedralbes* ☎ *93/203–8408*

Reservations essential *AE, DC, MC, V* *Closed Sun., Mon., and Aug.* *Maria Cristina* *A1.*

$$–$$$$ MEDITERRANEAN ★ **Silvestre.** Modern cuisine at extraordinary value has made a roaring success of this attractive dining spot in upper Barcelona. Just below Via Augusta, 50 yards from the Muntaner train stop on the FGC line, a series of intimate dining rooms and cozy corners are carefully tended by chef Guillermo (Willy) Casañé and Marta Cabot, his charming (and perfect-English-speaking) partner and maître d'. Treading the fine line between creative and traditional cooking, and between quality and value, is Silvestre's forte: look for fresh market produce lovingly prepared and dishes such as tuna tartare or noodles and shrimp. *Santaló 101, Sant Gervasi* *93/241–4031* *AE, DC, MC, V* *Closed Sun., 2 wks in Aug., and Easter wk. No lunch Sat.* *Muntaner* *D1.*

$$$–$$$$ MEDITERRANEAN ★ **Tram-Tram.** Isidre Soler and his wife, Reyes, have put together one of Barcelona's finest culinary offerings at what was once the end of the old tram line above the village of Sarrià. Try the *menú de degustaciò* and you might score marinated tuna salad, cod medallions, and venison filets mignon. Perfect portions and a streamlined reinterpretation of space within this traditional Sarrià house—especially in or near the garden out back—make this a memorable dining experience. The €25 price-fixed lunch menu is a good opportunity to sample Tram-Tram fare at a reasonable price. *Major de Sarrià 121, Sarrià* *93/204–8518* *AE, DC, MC, V* *Closed Sun. and late Dec.–early Jan. No lunch Sat.* *Reina Elisenda* *A1.*

$$–$$$ MEDITERRANEAN **Vivanda.** This leafy garden, a block above Plaça de Sarrià, is especially wonderful between May and October, when outside dining is a delight. (The side entrance on Carrer Graus leads directly into the garden.) The menu specializes in inventive combinations of seafood, upland, and inland products such as the *mar y muntanya de rape y cordero con alcachofas* (surf and turf of monkfish and lamb with artichokes) or *foie fresco de pato a la sarten con salteado de de manzanas al perfume de cardamomo* (pan-fried fresh duck liver with sauteed apples with cardamom). The lunch menu of €14 is a bargain. *Major de Sarrià 134, Sarrià* *93/203–1918* *AE, DC, MC, V* *Closed Sun.* *Reina Elisenda* *A1.*

TIBIDABO

$$$$ LA NUEVA COCINA Fodor's Choice ★ **ÀBaC.** Upper Barcelona's former Andreu mansion, redesigned for this boutique hotel and restaurant, is outfitted with the finest of everything, from Versace plates to Poltrona Frau chairs. Master chef Xavier Pellicer leaves no detail to chance, preparing carefully selected ingredients in innovative recipes. The taster's menu is the best option: trust Xavi to show you his best—any attempt at economy here is analogous to quibbling about deck chairs on the *Titanic*. Look for *tartar de champiñones, aguacate, y buey de mar* (mushroom tartare, avocado, and crab) and surf and turf combos like *perrechicos* (wild mushrooms) with sole. *Avenida del Tibidabo 1–7, Tibidabo* *93/319–6600* *Reservations essential* *AE, DC, MC, V* *Closed Sun. and Aug. No lunch Mon.* *Tibidabo* *D1.*

$$$–$$$$ SPANISH

✕ **El Asador de Aranda.** This immense Art Nouveau mansion a few minutes' walk above the Avenida Tibidabo metro station is a bit of a hike—but worth it if you're in upper Barcelona to see the nearby CosmoCaixa science museum. The kitchen specializes in Castilian cooking, with *cochinillo asado* (roast suckling pig), *cordero lechal* (roast suckling lamb), *morcilla* (black sausage), and *pimientos de piquillo* (sweet red peppers) as star players. The dining room has a terra-cotta floor and a full complement of Art Nouveau ornamentation from carved wood trim to stained-glass partitions, acid-engraved glass, and Moorish archways. ✉ *Av. del Tibidabo 31, Tibidabo* ☎ *93/417–0115* ▭ *AE, DC, MC, V* ⊗ *Closed Easter wk and Sun. in Aug. No dinner Sun.* Ⓜ *Tibidabo* ✥ *D1.*

OUTSKIRTS OF BARCELONA

With the many fine in-town dining options available in Barcelona, any out-of-town recommendations should rank somewhere in the uppermost stratosphere of excellence; these, among the top five or six establishments below the Pyrenees, undoubtedly do.

$$$$ SPANISH

✕ **El Bulli.** Visionary chef Ferran Adrià lays on the planet's most surprising culinary variety show at this famous seaside hideaway on the Costa Brava. Open from mid-June to mid-December, and with an annual two million applications to dine at his science-based gastronomy icon, scoring a reservation is nearly impossible El Bulli's originality is extraordinary. Diners rattle through three dozen or so courses in a set-menu tour de force, ranging in the past (there's no way to guess what Adrià will come up with for 2010) from deconstructed "spherical" olives that explode on the palate to abalone, sea anemone, and melt-on-the-tongue beetroot meringue. Gorgonzola "moshi" balls, suckling pig tails, rabbit ears, veal tendons, green walnuts with endives, and black garlic ravioli are the kinds of things to be prepared for. Plan on spending at least 200 euros a head (the set menu is the only option), and the night nearby if you actually get a dinner reservation—the Almadraba Park Hotel ($$$–$$$$ 🌐 *www.almadrabapark.com*), in Roses, 7 km (4½ mi) away, is a good option. El Bulli is now open for lunch, but reservations are just as hard to get, if you actually achieve a dinner reservation. ✉ *Cala Montjoi, Roses, Girona* ☎ *972/150457* 🌐 *www.elbulli.com* ✍ *Reservations essential* ▭ *AE, DC, MC, V* ⊗ *Closed mid-Dec.–mid June.*

$$$$ MEDITERRANEAN Fodor's Choice ★

✕ **El Racó de Can Fabes.** Santi Santamaria's masterful Mediterranean cuisine merits the 45-minute train ride (or 30-minute drive) north of Barcelona to Sant Celoni. One of the top restaurants in Spain, this is a must for anyone interested in fine dining. Every detail, from the freshly baked bread to the cheese selection, is superb. The taster's menu is the wisest solution. The RENFE stations are at Passeig de Gràcia or Sants—the last train back is at 10:24 PM—but El Racó has five sleek rooms ($$$–$$$$), so you can book a bed just a few steps from the dinner table. ✉ *Sant Joan 6, Sant Celoni* ☎ *93/867–2851* ▭ *AE, DC, MC, V* ⊗ *Closed Mon., 1st 2 wks of Feb., and late June–early July. No dinner Sun.* ✥ *H2.*

$$$$ MEDITERRANEAN ★ **Sant Pau.** Carme Ruscalleda's nonpareil restaurant in Sant Pol de Mar is a delight, from *amuse-bouches* to petits fours. Spain's top-ranked female chef is a pixie-ish powerhouse and her menu changes often, but star dishes may include *vieiras* (scallops) with crisped artichoke flakes on roast potato or *lubina* (sea bass) on baby leeks and chard in *garnatxa* (sweet Catalan wine) sauce. Sant Pol de Mar is a scenic 40-minute train ride along the beach from Plaça de Catalunya's RENFE station: the Calella train stops at the door. (The last evening train is too early for dinner, so attempt this only for lunch.) ✉ *Nou 10, Sant Pol de Mar* ☎ *93/760–0662* ▭ *AE, DC, MC, V* ⊙ *Closed Mon., 2 wks in Mar., and 2 wks in Nov. No dinner Sun.* ✥ *H2.*

WHERE TO STAY

Use the coordinate (✥ B2) at the end of each listing to locate a site on the corresponding map.

Barcelona's hotels offer clear distinctions. Hotels in the Ciutat Vella (Old City)—the Gothic Quarter and along the Rambla—are charming and convenient for sightseeing, though sometimes short on peace and quiet. Relative newcomers to the Barcelona hotel fleet, such as the Neri, the Duquesa de Cardona, and the Casa Camper Barcelona, are contemporary design standouts inhabiting medieval architecture, a combination at which Barcelona architects and decorators are peerless. Eixample hotels (including most of the city's best) are late-19th- or early-20th-century town houses restored and converted into exciting modern environments.

Mid-Eixample hotels, including the Hotel Palace (former Ritz), the Claris, the Majestic, the Condes de Barcelona, and the Hotel Omm, combine style and luxury with a sense of place; the peripheral palaces (like the Hotel Arts) are less about Barcelona and more about generic comfort and luxury. Sarrià and Sant Gervasi upper-city hotels get you up out of the urban crush, and Olympic Port and Diagonal Mar hotels are in high-rise towers (requiring transport to and from the real Barcelona). Smaller budget hotels are less than half as expensive as some of the luxury addresses and more a part of city life.

7

CIUTAT VELLA (OLD CITY)

$$$ **Casa Camper Barcelona.** This revolutionary hotel between the Rambla and the MACBA (Museum of Contemporary Art) is the co-brainchild of the Camper footwear empire and Barcelona's Vinçon design store. No smoking, no tips, a free 24-hour snack facility to which you can invite your friends, ecologically recycled residual waters, and a different, more at-home hotel concept add up to a dazzling new address in the formerly seedy Raval. **Pros:** pivotal location a minute from Rambla and in the middle of the tumultuous Raval, sleek new concept in service, feels like a private club. **Cons:** tight quarters in and around the hotel, snacks superfluous. ✉ *C. Elisabets 11, Raval* ☎ *93/342–6280* 🌐 *www.casacamper.com* *20 rooms, 5 suites* *In-room: refrigerator, Wi-Fi. In-hotel: parking (fee)* ▭ *AE, DC, MC, V* *BP* Ⓜ *Catalunya* ✥ *D2.*

WHERE TO STAY IN BARCELONA

	Neighborhood Vibe	Pros	Cons
Rambla	A solid stream of humanity around the clock, the Rambla is always alive and moving. With a promenade that is chock-full of every type of street life, this is where you can feel the city's pulse.	The Rambla is the city's most iconic runway and always exciting. The Boqueria market, the flower stalls, the opera house and Plaça Reial—all here—are quintessential Barcelona.	The incessant crush of humanity can be overwhelming, especially if FC Barcelona wins a championship and the entire city descends upon the Rambla.
Gothic Quarter and Born-Ribera	The 19th-century gaslight-type lamps glowing in the Roman and Gothic areas, lend romance to this part of town. The Picasso Museum and Santa Maria del Mar basilica are nearby.	The architecture of the Gothic Quarter is tangible evidence of the city's past. Plaça Sant Jaume, the cathedral, Plaça del Rei, and the Born-Ribera district are the main reasons to visit the city.	Echoes reverberate around here and, while there is little serious noise, what there is goes a long way.
Raval	The Raval has always been a rough-and-tumble part of town, but the nightlife is exciting, and the diversity of the neighborhood is exemplary. Bonus: it's right behind the Boqueria market.	For the closest thing to Marrakesh in Barcelona, the Raval has a buzz all its own. A contemporary art museum, the medieval hospital, and the Mercat de Sant Antoni offer plenty to explore.	The Raval can seem dangerous, and in some corners you can find the seamier of Barcelona's elements, but it's still quite safe.
Eixample	Some of Gaudí's best buildings line the sidewalks and many of the city's finest hotels and restaurants are right around the corner. And then there's the shopping....	Eixample remains the world's only Art Nouveau neighborhood, constantly rewarding to the eye. Gaudí's unfinished masterpiece La Sagrada Família is within walking distance.	A bewildering grid without numbers or alphabetization, the Eixample can seem hard-edged compared to the older, quirkier, parts of Barcelona.
Barceloneta and Olympic Port	The onetime fishermen's quarter, Barceloneta retains its informal, working-class ambience, with laundry flapping over the streets and sidewalk restaurants lining Passeig Joan de Borbó.	Staying near the beach generally means absorbing the laid-back feel of this neighborhood. The Olympic Port is a world apart, but Barceloneta has the best seafood dining spots in town.	Barceloneta offers few hotel opportunities, and the Olympic Port offers only one: the monolithic Hotel Arts, which, for all its quality, can seem like a tourist colony away from the rest of town.
Pedralbes, Sarrià and Upper Barcelona	Upper Barcelona is leafy and residential, and the air is always a few degrees cooler. Pedralbes holds Barcelona's finest mansions; Sarrià is a rustic village suspended in the urban sprawl.	Getting above the madding fray into better air has distinct advantages, and the upper reaches of Barcelona offers them. A 15-minute train ride connects Sarrià with the Rambla.	The only drawback to staying in upper Barcelona is the 15-minute commute to the most important monuments and attractions. After midnight on weeknights this will require a taxi.

BEST BETS FOR BARCELONA LODGING

Having trouble deciding where to stay in Barcelona? Fodor's offers a selective listing of high-quality lodging experiences at every price range, from the city's best budget options to its most sophisticated. Here we've compiled our top recommendations by price and experience; full details are in the reviews that follow. The very best properties—those that provide a particularly remarkable experience—are designated with a Fodor's Choice symbol. Sleep tight!

Fodor's Choice ★

Claris, $$$$, p. 458
Condes de Barcelona, $$$–$$$$, p. 458
H1898, $$$$, p. 454
Hostal Gat Raval, $–$$, p. 455
Hotel Colón, $$–$$$$, p. 455
Hotel Granados 83, $$$–$$$$, p. 460
Majestic, $$$$, p. 460
Turó de Vilana, $$–$$$, p. 461

By Price

$

Hostal Chic and Basic Tallers, p. 454
Hostal Gat Raval, p. 455

$$

Hotel Market, p. 456
Jardi, p. 456

$$$

Casa Camper Barcelona, p. 449
Continental Palacete, p. 458

$$$$

Claris, p. 458
Condes de Barcelona, p. 458
Duquesa de Cardona, p. 454
Hotel Arts, p. 457
Hotel Casanova, p. 459
Hotel Neri, p. 456

By Experience

MOST CHARMING

Hotel Neri, $$$$, p. 456
Hotel Casanova, $$$, p. 459
Turó de Vilana, $$–$$$, p. 461

MOST HISTORIC

Duquesa de Cardona, $$$$, p. 454
Hotel Colón, $$–$$$$, p. 455
H1898, $$$–$$$$, p. 454

BEST DESIGN

Claris, $$$$, p. 458
Hotel Chic and Basic Born, $$–$$$$, p. 455
Hotel Granados 83, $$$–$$$$, p. 460
Hotel Omm, $$$–$$$$, p. 460

MOST CENTRAL

Grand Hotel Central, $$$$, p. 454
Hotel Colón, $$–$$$$, p. 455
Hotel Neri, $$$$, p. 456
H1898, $$$–$$$$, p. 454

MOST ROMANTIC

Hotel Chic and Basic Born, $$$–$$$$, p. 455
Claris, $$$$, p. 458
Hotel Arts, $$$$, p. 457

MOST KID-FRIENDLY

Citadines, $$–$$$, p. 454
Hotel Arts, $$$$, p. 457
Hotel Casanova, $$$, p. 459

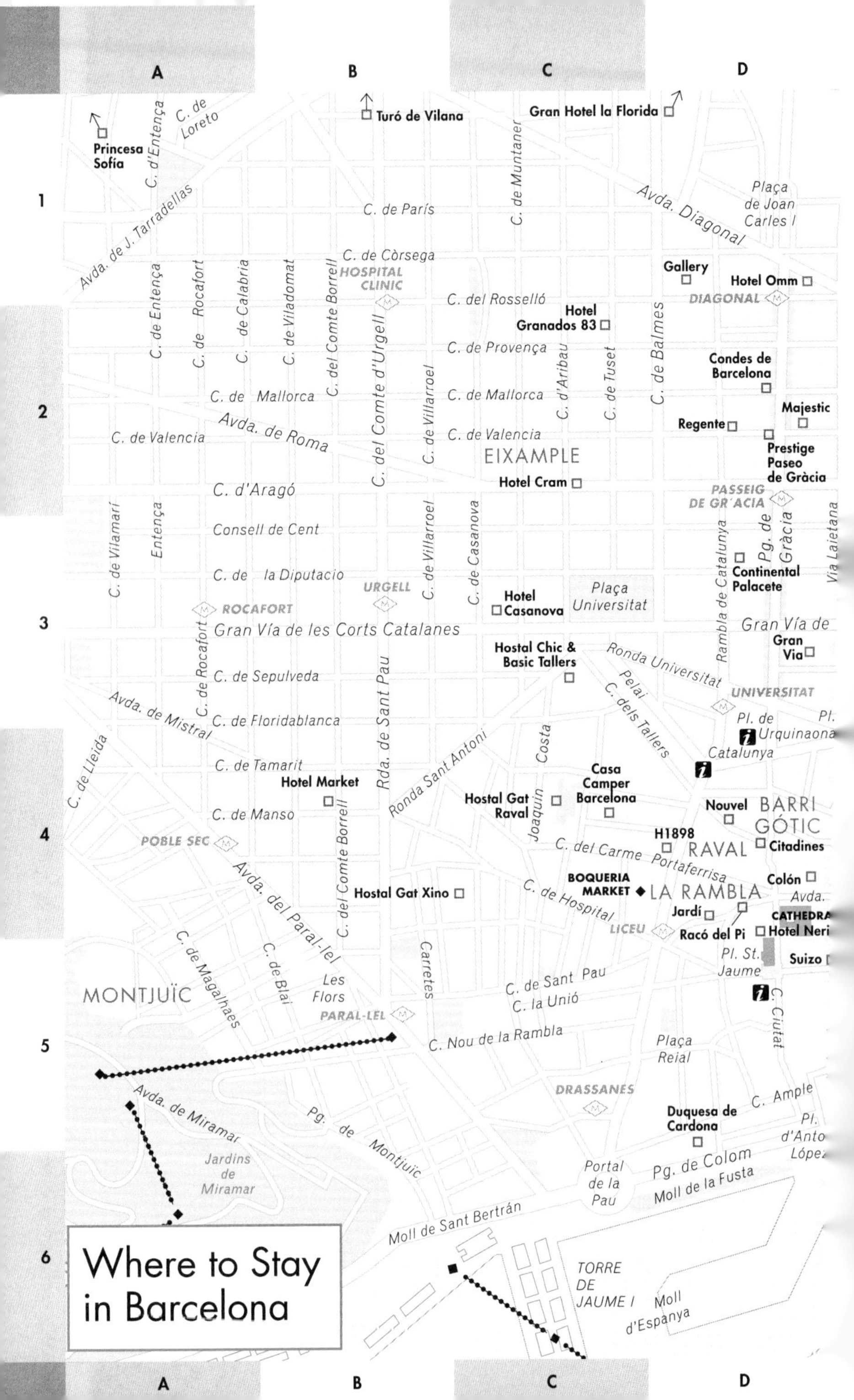

Where to Stay in Barcelona

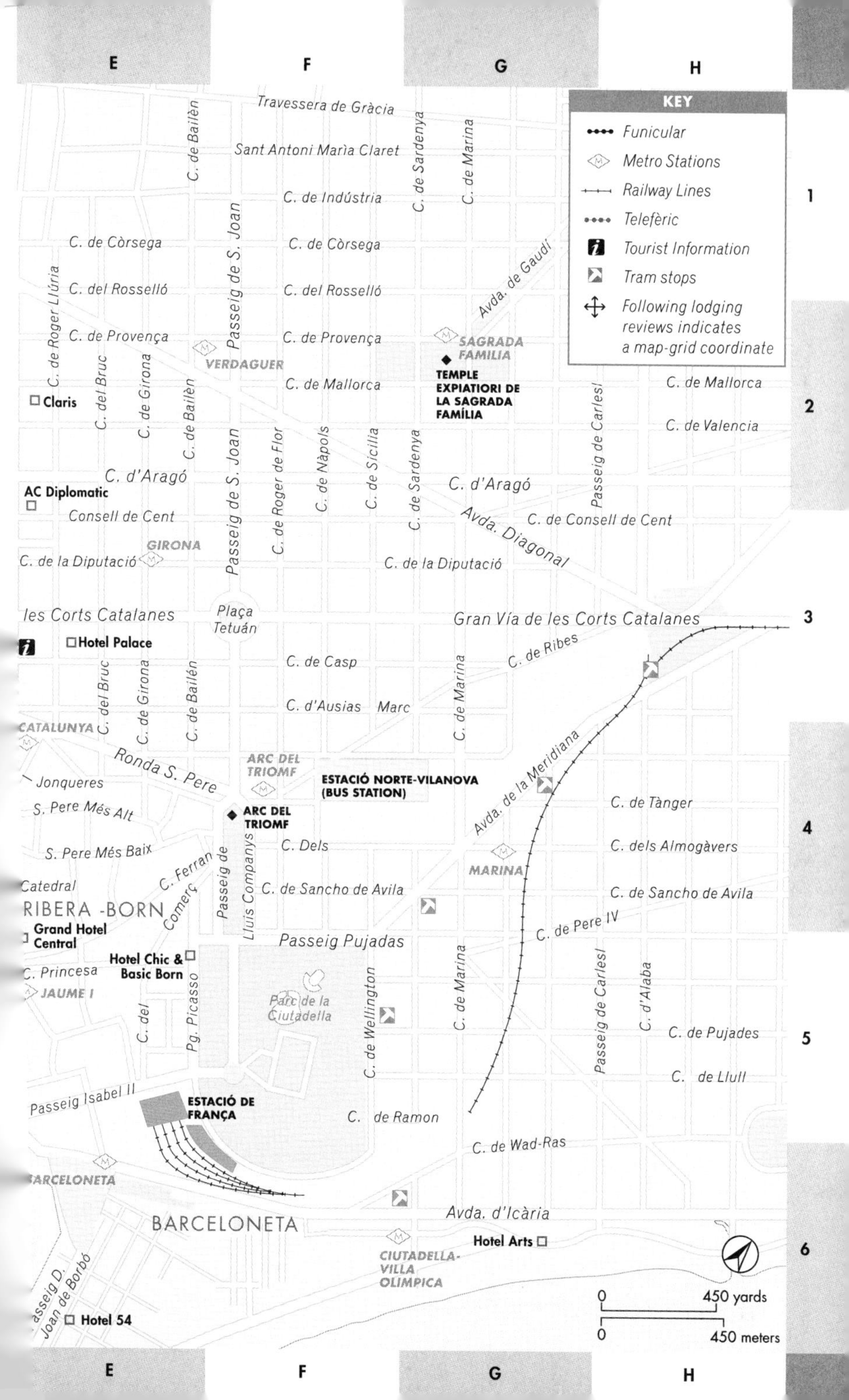
E
F
G
H
KEY
Funicular
Metro Stations
Railway Lines
Telefèric
Tourist Information
Tram stops
Following lodging reviews indicates a map-grid coordinate
1
2
3
4
5
6
Travessera de Gràcia
Sant Antoni Marìa Claret
C. de Indústria
C. de Còrsega
C. del Rosselló
C. de Provença
C. de Mallorca
C. de Valencia
C. d'Aragó
Consell de Cent
C. de Consell de Cent
C. de la Diputació
les Corts Catalanes
Gran Vía de les Corts Catalanes
C. de Bailèn
C. de Sardenya
C. de Marina
Passeig de S. Joan
Avda. de Gaudí
C. de Roger Llúria
C. del Bruc
C. de Girona
C. de Roger de Flor
C. de Nàpols
C. de Sicilia
Passeig de Carlesi
Avda. Diagonal
VERDAGUER
SAGRADA FAMILIA
TEMPLE EXPIATIORI DE LA SAGRADA FAMÍLIA
Claris
AC Diplomatic
GIRONA
Plaça Tetuán
Hotel Palace
C. de Casp
C. d'Ausias Marc
C. de Ribes
CATALUNYA
Ronda S. Pere
Jonqueres
S. Pere Més Alt
S. Pere Més Baix
ARC DEL TRIOMF
ESTACIÓ NORTE-VILANOVA (BUS STATION)
Avda. de la Meridiana
C. de Tànger
C. dels Almogàvers
C. de Sancho de Avila
C. Dels
MARINA
Catedral
C. Ferran
Comerç
Passeig de Lluís Companys
RIBERA -BORN
Grand Hotel Central
Hotel Chic & Basic Born
C. Princesa
JAUME I
Passeig Pujadas
C. de Pere IV
Parc de la Ciutadella
C. de Wellington
C. d'Alaba
C. de Pujades
C. de Llull
C. del
Pg. Picasso
Passeig Isabel II
ESTACIÓ DE FRANÇA
C. de Ramon
C. de Wad-Ras
BARCELONETA
Avda. d'Icària
Hotel Arts
CIUTADELLA-VILLA OLIMPICA
Passeig D. Joan de Borbó
Hotel 54
0
450 yards
0
450 meters

$$–$$$ **Citadines.** This Rambla *aparthotel* (a hotel that rents apartments with kitchens) is good value with a prime location. Impeccably bright and modern, soundproof, and generally well equipped, rooms have small dining areas to go with the kitchenettes—especially convenient for families. The rooftop solarium with views over the Mediterranean and the Rambla may be the hotel's best feature, though rooms over leafy Plaça Villa de Madrid on the back side are quieter. **Pros:** central location, excellent facilities and technology. **Cons:** noisy Rambla hubbub, apartments are small and motel-like. ✉ *La Rambla 122, Rambla* ☎ *93/270–1111* 🌐 *www.citadines.com* *115 studios, 16 apartments* *In-room: kitchen, Wi-Fi. In-hotel: bar* ▭ *AE, DC, MC, V* Ⓜ *Catalunya* ✣ *D4.*

$$$$ **Duquesa de Cardona.** This refurbished 16th-century town house overlooking the port has contemporary facilities with designer touches. Exterior rooms, though small, have views of the harbor. The hotel is a 10-minute walk from everything in the Gothic Quarter or Barceloneta, and no more than a 30-minute walk from the main Eixample attractions. The miniature rooftop pool, more for a plunge than a real swim, provides relief in summer. **Pros:** at a key spot over the port, contemporary technology in a traditional palace. **Cons:** rooms on the small side, roof terrace is tiny, views over port blocked by Maremagnum complex. ✉ *Passeig de Colom 12, Rambla* ☎ *93/268–9090* 🌐 *www.hduquesadecardona.com* *44 rooms* *In-room: Wi-Fi. In-hotel: restaurant, pool* ▭ *AE, DC, MC, V* Ⓜ *Drassanes* ✣ *D5.*

$$$$ **Grand Hotel Central.** In the famous Cambó house on the edge of the Gothic Quarter very near the Barcelona cathedral, this hot midtown hideaway is a magnet for the hip and swashbuckling from around Europe and beyond. Rooms are flawlessly furnished with state-of-the-art technology and design features. The restaurant, Actual, is bound for glory, and the top-floor pool offers a unique perch over the city's 2,000-year-old Roman and Gothic center. **Pros:** excellent location between the Gothic Quarter and the Born, attentive service, high-tech amenities. **Cons:** Via Laietana is noisy, so go by the rule: the higher, the better. ✉ *Via Laietana 30, Barri Gòtic* ☎ *93/295–7900* 🌐 *www.grandhotelcentral.com* *147 rooms* *In-room: Wi-Fi. In-hotel: restaurant, bar, pool, gym, parking (fee)* ▭ *AE, DC, MC, V* Ⓜ *Catalunya* ✣ *E5.*

$$$–$$$$ Fodor's Choice ★ **H1898.** This elegant hotel overlooking the Rambla occupies a building with an illustrious history as the headquarters of the Compañia de Tabacos de Filipinas, a prestigious Barcelona business concern for nearly 100 years. Named for the fateful year when Spain was stripped of its final colonial possessions, the Philippines among them, the hotel's elegance is an homage to bygone glories as well as a sign of the city's present opulence. **Pros:** unbeatable central location on the Rambla, state-of-the-art design and technology (such as flat-screen plasma TVs). **Cons:** noisy Rambla thronging at the threshold, Starbucks just off the lobby. ✉ *La Rambla 109, Rambla* ☎ *93/552–9552* 🌐 *www.nnhotels.es* *166 rooms, 3 suites* *In-room: Wi-Fi. In-hotel: restaurant, bar, pool, gym, parking (fee)* ▭ *AE, DC, MC, V* Ⓜ *Catalunya* ✣ *D4.*

$–$$ **Hostal Chic and Basic Tallers.** Another sleek, contemporary budget choice in the upper Raval, this even more economical version of the

Hotel Chic and Basic over in the Born has a living room called Chill and Basic, with Wi-Fi access and free snacks. Other surprising perks include in-room music speakers that let you to listen to the hotel music director's mix or plug in your own iPod. **Pros:** perfectly designed and situated for an exciting, low-cost Barcelona experience; young and friendly staff. **Cons:** the streets in the Raval can reverberate noisily at night, small rooms. ✉ *Carrer Tallers 82, Raval* ☎ *93/302–5183* 🌐 *www.chicandbasic.com* *14 rooms* *In-room: refrigerator, Wi-Fi. In-hotel: restaurant, bar, public Internet* *AE, DC, MC, V* Ⓜ *Catalunya, Universitat* ✣ *D4.*

$–$$ **Hostal Gat Raval.** This hip little hole-in-the-wall opens into a surprisingly bright and sleekly designed modern space with rooms that come in different shapes, styles, and number of beds, all cheerily appointed and impeccably maintained. Just around the corner from the MACBA, the Gat Raval seems to have been influenced by Richard Meier's shining contemporary structure, though you'd never guess it from the street. Rooms are small and far from luxurious, but the value is among Barcelona's best. **Pros:** central location in the deepest Raval, hip atmosphere. **Cons:** noisy street outside, somewhat cramped rooms and public spaces, few amenities. ✉ *Carrer Joaquín Costa 44, Raval* ☎ *93/481–6670* 🌐 *www.gataccommodation.com* *26 rooms* *In-room: Wi-Fi* *AE, DC, MC, V* Ⓜ *Universitat* ✣ *C4.*

Fodor's Choice ★

$–$$ **Hostal Gat Xino.** A cheery space in one of the Raval's darker corners, hip Hostal Gat Raval's sister ship puts the adventurous traveler in a modern design oasis. Gat Xino is named for the nearby Barrio Chino, one of Barcelona's most historic and tumultuous neighborhoods. Rooms, though tiny, are decorated in bright colors, and the value is unbeatable. There's a roof terrace for chilling out, as well as a breakfast patio. **Pros:** central location, smart and sassy design, up-to-date technology, hostel-like friendly clients and staff. **Cons:** busy and noisy section of the Raval, small rooms and public spaces. ✉ *Carrer Hospital 155, Raval* ☎ *93/324–8833* 🌐 *www.gataccommodation.com* *35 rooms* *In-room: Wi-Fi* *AE, DC, MC, V* Ⓜ *Sant Antoni* ✣ *C4.*

$$–$$$ **Hotel Chic and Basic Born.** A revolutionary concept best exemplified by the middle-of-the-room glass shower stalls, this sleek and impeccably designed hotel is a hit with hipsters looking for a Barcelona experience that combines design, surprise, and originality. It's also perfectly situated to make the most of Barcelona's hot Born-Ribera scene, though the in-house restaurant—called the White Bar for its completely albino decor—will tempt you to stay in at night with its excellent Mediterranean cooking. **Pros:** cool destination and location. **Cons:** noisy nightlife around the hotel requires closed windows on weekends, rooms and spaces are small. ✉ *Carrer Princesa 50, Born-Ribera* ☎ *93/295–4652* 🌐 *www.chicandbasic.com* *31 rooms* *In-room: Wi-Fi. In-hotel: restaurant, bar, public Internet* *AE, DC, MC, V* Ⓜ *Jaume I* ✣ *E5.*

$$–$$$$ **Hotel Colón.** Surprisingly charming and intimate for such a sizable hotel, this slightly ramshackle Barcelona standby is directly across the plaza from the cathedral, so it overlooks weekend *sardana* dancing, the Thursday antiques markets, and the cathedral itself. Rooms are comfortable and tasteful; try to get one with a view of the church.

Fodor's Choice ★

Considering its combination of comfort, style, and location, the Colón may be the best place to stay in Barcelona, though it's far from the most luxurious; it was a favorite of Catalan painter Joan Miró. **Pros:** walking distance from all of central Barcelona, friendly staff. **Cons:** low tech. ✉ *Av. Catedral 7, Barri Gòtic* ☎ *93/301–1404* 🌐 *www.hotelcolon.es* *140 rooms, 5 suites* *In-room: Wi-Fi. In-hotel: restaurant, bar* *AE, DC, MC, V* Ⓜ *Catalunya* ✥ *D4.*

$$ **Hotel Market.** A wallet-friendly boutique hotel and design triumph, the Hotel Market is named for the Mercat de Sant Antoni, the first city market built outside the medieval walls after they were torn down in 1860. On a small alleyway a block from the market and within walking distance of all of the Raval and Gothic Quarter attractions, this high-tech, minimalist lodging is one of Barcelona's best bargains. The hotel restaurant offers excellent value, too. **Pros:** well equipped and designed for a low-cost Barcelona visit; young and friendly staff. **Cons:** rooms are a bit cramped, the Mercat de Sant Antoni itself is presently under reconstruction until 2011. ✉ *Carrer Comte Borrell 68 (side entrance on Passatge Sant Antoni Abat 10), Raval* ☎ *93/325–1205* 🌐 *www.markethotel.com.es* *37 rooms* *In-room: refrigerator, Wi-Fi. In-hotel: restaurant, bar, public Internet* *AE, DC, MC, V* Ⓜ *Sant Antoni* ✥ *B4.*

$$$$ **Hotel Neri.** Owner Bruno Figueras and designer Cristina Gabà have created a unique oasis of taste in the heart of the Gothic Quarter. Built into a 17th-century palace over one of the Gothic Quarter's smallest and most charming squares, Plaça Sant Felip Neri, the Neri is a counterpoint of ancient and avant-garde design. The rooms are medievalesque yet clean lined, hard edged, and equipped with great facilities. **Pros:** central location, roof terrace for cocktails and breakfast. **Cons:** noise from the echo-chamber square can be a problem on summer nights (and winter-morning school days), impractical design details such as the hanging bed lights. ✉ *Carrer Sant Sever 5, Barri Gòtic* ☎ *93/304–0655* 🌐 *www.hotelneri.com* *22 rooms* *In-room: refrigerator, Wi-Fi. In-hotel: restaurant, bar* *AE, DC, MC, V* Ⓜ *Liceu, Catalunya* ✥ *E5.*

$$ **Jardí.** Perched over the traffic-free and charming Plaça del Pi and Plaça Sant Josep Oriol, this budget hotel has some rooms with views of the Gothic church of Santa Maria del Pi; all have pine furniture and small bathrooms. The in-house breakfast is excellent, and the alfresco tables at the Bar del Pi, downstairs, are ideal in summer. There are five floors and an elevator, but this is not the Ritz—it's still a great value, though. **Pros:** central location, good value, impeccable (but small) bathrooms. **Cons:** lightweight beds and furnishings, no amenities, the square can get noisy in summer. ✉ *Pl. Sant Josep Oriol 1, Barri Gòtic* ☎ *93/301–5900* 🌐 *www.hoteljardi-barcelona.com* *40 rooms* *AE, DC, MC, V* Ⓜ *Liceu, Catalunya* ✥ *D4.*

$$$ **Nouvel.** Centrally located on the first side street off the Rambla just below Plaça de Catalunya, this surprisingly lovely little hideaway blends white marble, etched glass, elaborate plasterwork, and dark, carved woodwork in its handsome Art Nouveau interior. Rooms have bright and gleaming marble floors, firm beds, and high-tech bathrooms. The narrow street is pedestrian-only and therefore quiet, but views are nonexistent. **Pros:** central but quiet location, charming Moderniste details,

good value. **Cons:** rooms on the small side, no views, no automobile access. ✉ *Carrer Santa Anna 18–2, Rambla* ☎ *93/301–8274* 🌐 *www.hotelnouvel.com* *71 rooms* *In-room: safe, Wi-Fi. In-hotel: restaurant, bar* *AE, DC, MC, V* Ⓜ *Catalunya* ✥ *E5.*

$$$ **Racó del Pi.** This sleek, modern space on a bustling Gothic Quarter street near the Santa Maria del Pi offers first-rate service and flawless and efficient, if somewhat characterless, accommodations. About equidistant from the cathedral, the Rambla, the Boqueria market, Plaça de Catalunya, and the Palau de la Música Catalana, this cozy *racó* (corner) built over an original 18th-century town house is as practical as it is spotless. **Pros:** convenient to major sights, modern and comfortable. **Cons:** some small and viewless rooms, noisy hallways, light and rather flimsy furnishings. ✉ *Carrer del Pi 7, Rambla* ☎ *93/342–6190* 🌐 *www.h10.es* *37 rooms* *In-room: refrigerator, Wi-Fi. In-hotel: bar* *AE, DC, MC, V* Ⓜ *Catalunya, Liceu* ✥ *D4.*

$$ **Suizo.** Location and value are the main reasons this undistinguished but functional and comfortable hotel has faithfully served Barcelona for the better part of a century. The public rooms have elegant, modern seating and good views over the bustling Via Laietana and the Jaume I subway stop at the front door. The guest rooms, though cramped, have bright walls, wood or tile floors, and minuscule but up-to-date bathrooms. **Pros:** central location right by a subway stop, bright new rooms, friendly staff. **Cons:** a maelstrom of tourists and pedestrians pass the door, short on amenities, no room service. ✉ *Pl. del Àngel 12, Barri Gòtic* ☎ *93/310–6108* 🌐 *www.gargallo-hotels.com* *59 rooms* *In-room: safe, refrigerator, Wi-Fi. In-hotel: bar, laundry service* *AE, DC, MC, V* Ⓜ *Jaume I* ✥ *D5.*

7

BARCELONETA AND THE PORT OLÍMPIC

$$–$$$ **Hotel 54.** Just a few minutes' walk from the beach and with rooms overlooking the Barceloneta port, this modern, minimalist lodging offers much for travelers seeking location, comfort, and economy. The sleek lines and space-age stark facade announce a property with a brash and sassy edge, and the interior lives up to the minimalist outside. **Pros:** near the Born-Ribera neighborhood, has latest technology and equipment. **Cons:** buses roar around the clock on Passeig Joan de Borbó, rooms are minimalist almost to a fault, atmosphere a little chilly. ✉ *Passeig Joan de Borbó 54, Barceloneta* ☎ *93/225–0054* 🌐 *www.hotel54barceloneta.com* *28 rooms* *In-room: refrigerator, Wi-Fi. In-hotel: restaurant, bar, public Internet* *AE, DC, MC, V* Ⓜ *Barceloneta* ✥ *E6.*

$$$$ ★ **Hotel Arts.** This Ritz-Carlton monolith overlooks Barcelona from the Olympic Port, with views of the Mediterranean, the city, and the mountains behind. The hotel is a world of its own, a short taxi ride from vintage Barcelona. True to its name, original art—from Chillida drawings to Susana Solano sculptures—is everywhere. There are three restaurants; Sergi Arola, one of them, is a famous culinary playground. **Pros:** excellent views over Barcelona, fine restaurants and general comfort and technology. **Cons:** a 15-minute hike from Barri de la Ribera, a colony of (mostly American) tourists, not very Spanish (it could be anywhere). ✉ *Calle de la Marina 19, Port Olímpic* ☎ *93/221–1000* 🌐 *www.harts.*

es 397 *rooms, 59 suites, 27 apartments* *In-room: refrigerator, Wi-Fi. In-hotel: 3 restaurants, room service, bar, pool, beachfront, parking (fee)* *AE, DC, MC, V* Ⓜ *Ciutadella–Vila Olímpica* ✣*G6.*

EIXAMPLE

$$$–$$$$ **AC Diplomatic.** Well placed in the midst of the Eixample, within walking distance of nearly everything in town, this newly outfitted, high-tech hotel offers much more value than many of its more expensive neighbors. From flat-screen TVs to free minibars, everything in the building, even the service, seems a notch above, especially if you can negotiate a weekend, low-season bargain. Spare, wood-paneled rooms, the outside pool, and the Mediterranean market-driven cuisine at Nichte, the hotel's restaurant, can make this refuge hard to leave. **Pros:** bright contemporary lobby, friendly staff, high-tech equipment, well soundproofed. **Cons:** somewhat antiseptic, airport-waiting-room design. ✉ *Carrer Pau Claris 122, Eixample* ☎ *93/272–3810* 🌐 *www.ac-hotels.com* *211 rooms* *In-room: Wi-Fi. In-hotel: restaurant, bar, pool, gym, parking (fee)* *AE, DC, MC, V* Ⓜ *Diagonal* ✣*E3.*

$$$$ Fodor's Choice ★ **Claris.** Considered by many cognoscenti to be Barcelona's premier lodging establishment, this midtown refuge is a fascinating mélange of design and tradition. The rooms come in 60 modern layouts, some with restored 18th-century English furniture, some with contemporary furnishings from Barcelona's endless legion of playful lamp and chair designers. Lavishly endowed with wood and marble, the hotel also has a Japanese water garden and a stellar restaurant, East 47. **Pros:** elegant service and furnishings, central location for shopping and Moderniste architecture. **Cons:** street side can be noisy, Internet sometimes unavailable in rooms. ✉ *Carrer Pau Claris 150, Eixample* ☎ *93/487–6262* 🌐 *www.derbyhotels.es* *80 rooms, 40 suites* *In-room: refrigerator, Wi-Fi. In-hotel: 2 restaurants, bar, pool, gym, laundry service, parking (fee)* *AE, DC, MC, V* Ⓜ *Passeig de Gràcia* ✣*E2.*

$$$–$$$$ Fodor's Choice ★ **Condes de Barcelona.** Reserve well in advance because this is one of Barcelona's most popular hotels. The pentagonal lobby has a marble floor and the original columns and courtyard from the 1891 building, while the newest rooms have hot tubs and terraces overlooking interior gardens. An affiliated fitness club nearby has golf, squash, and swimming. The hotel's two restaurants, Lasarte and the less formal bistrolike Loidi, serve excellent Basque-influenced cuisine. **Pros:** elegant Moderniste building with chic contemporary furnishings, prime spot in the middle of the Eixample. **Cons:** too large to have much of a personal touch, the staff sometimes seem overextended. ✉ *Passeig de Gràcia 75, Eixample* ☎ *93/445–0000* 🌐 *www.condesdebarcelona.com* *181 rooms, 2 suites* *In-room: safe, refrigerator, Wi-Fi. In-hotel: restaurant, bar, pools, gym, parking (fee)* *AE, DC, MC, V* Ⓜ *Passeig de Gràcia* ✣*D2.*

$$$ **Continental Palacete.** This former in-town mansion, or *palacete,* has a splendid drawing room at the hub of Barcelona's main attractions. The views over the tree-lined Rambla Catalunya provide people-watching, while the 24-hour free buffet is handy but unnecessary in food-obsessed Barcelona. Ask for one of the exterior rooms, for the views and for

the distance from the elevator shaft. For a splurge, the two elegant suites are swathed in lush carpets, velvet curtains, and tapestries. **Pros:** elegant town house with abundant ornamentation, attentive owners and staff. **Cons:** rooms a little cramped and overtextiled, rooms on the elevator shaft can be noisy. ✉ *La Rambla de Catalunya 30, Eixample* ☎ *93/445–7657* 🌐 *www.hotelcontinental.com* *17 rooms, 2 suites* *In-room: refrigerator, Wi-Fi* ▭ *AE, DC, MC, V* Ⓜ *Passeig de Gràcia* ✣ *D3.*

$$$$ **Gallery.** In the upper part of the Eixample, just below the Diagonal, this modern hotel offers impeccable comfort and service and a central location for middle and upper Barcelona. (In the other direction, you're only a half-hour walk from the waterfront.) It's named for its proximity to the city's prime art-gallery district, a few blocks away on Rambla de Catalunya and Consell de Cent. Rooms are small and charmless but comfortable and efficient. **Pros:** well located for Eixample shopping and Moderniste architecture. **Cons:** slightly cold and high-tech ambience. ✉ *Carrer Rosselló 249, Eixample* ☎ *93/415–9911* 🌐 *www.galleryhotel.com* *108 rooms, 5 suites* *In-room: Wi-Fi. In-hotel: restaurant, bar, gym, parking (fee)* ▭ *AE, DC, MC, V* Ⓜ *Provença* ✣ *D1.*

$$–$$$ **Gran Via.** A Moderniste enclave with an original chapel, a hall-of-mirrors breakfast room, and a sweeping staircase, this slightly down-at-the-heels 19th-century townhouse has an antique charm that compensates for largely missing contemporary technology and extra creature comforts such as flat-screen TVs. Guest rooms have plain walls with alcoves for desks and dressers, bottle-green carpets, and Regency-style furniture; those overlooking Gran Via itself have better views but are noisy. **Pros:** a chance to sleep inside Moderniste architecture. **Cons:** somewhat antiquated, service a little brusque and tourist-weary. ✉ *Gran Via 642, Eixample* ☎ *93/318–1900* 🌐 *www.nnhotels.com* *53 rooms* *In-room: refrigerator, Wi-Fi. In-hotel: public Internet, parking (fee)* ▭ *AE, DC, MC, V* Ⓜ *Passeig de Gràcia* ✣ *D3.*

$$$ **Hotel Casanova.** A sleek part of Barcelona's top-end lodging options, this carefully produced operation is nearly perfect, just a 15-minute walk from the top of the Rambla. Fine Mediterranean-Mexican fusion cuisine is served in the restaurant, Mexiterranée. Spa treatments are available at the Stone Spa therapy center, and the mint or strawberry water at the reception desk is just icing on the cake. The bar at street level, thoroughly soundproofed, offers bustling street life– and people-watching while you sip your tequila. **Pros:** maximum comfort in a hip and happening environment, good location. **Cons:** this is 21st-century, postcontemporary Barcelona: forget about classical Europe. ✉ *Gran Via de les Corts 559, Eixample* ☎ *93/396–4800* 🌐 *www.casanovabcnhotel.com* *124 rooms* *In-room: Wi-Fi. In-hotel: restaurant, bar, spa, pool, gym, parking (fee)* ▭ *AE, DC, MC, V* Ⓜ *Universitat* ✣ *D4.*

$$$–$$$$ **Hotel Cram.** Just a block behind the leafy, orange tree–filled patio of the University of Barcelona's philology and letters school and a short walk from central Eixample and the Rambla, this design hotel is a good place for impeccable and semieconomical accommodations in midtown Barcelona. It's also the home of Carles Gaig's famous restaurant, Can Gaig (entry around the corner). **Pros:** dazzlingly designed, well positioned for the Eixample and Rambla, smart and friendly staff. **Cons:** Carrer Aribau is a major uptown artery and traffic careens through at all hours, rooms are not spacious. ✉ *Carrer Aribau 54, Eixample* ☎ *93/216–7700* 🌐 *www.hotelcram.com* ⇨ *67 rooms* ☝ *In-room: refrigerator, Wi-Fi. In-hotel: restaurant, bar, public Internet* ▭ *AE, DC, MC, V* Ⓜ *Universitat* ✥ *C2.*

$$$–$$$$ Fodor's Choice ★ **Hotel Granados 83.** Constructed of industrial brick, steel, and glass with Buddhist and Hindu art supplying a sense of calm, this is one of Barcelona's best design hotels. A few steps below the Diagonal and well situated for exploring the Eixample and the rest of the city, the hotel, named for Barcelona's famous composer Enric Granados (1867–1916), is an interesting compendium of materials and taste. The first-rate Mediterranean dining options and the rooftop pool and solarium make the hotel a semiautonomous destination. **Pros:** quiet semipedestrian street, elegant building with chic design, polished service. **Cons:** room prices vary wildly according to availability and season. ✉ *Carrer Enric Granados 83, Eixample* ☎ *93/492–9670* 🌐 *www.derbyhotels.es* ⇨ *70 rooms, 7 suites* ☝ *In-room: safe, refrigerator, Wi-Fi. In-hotel: restaurant, bar, pools, spa, gym, parking (fee)* ▭ *AE, DC, MC, V* Ⓜ *Provenca* ✥ *C2.*

$$$–$$$$ **Hotel Omm.** This postmodern architectural marvel seeks a playful sense of peace consistent with its eponymous mantra. The rooms (some upper ones overlook Gaudí's Casa Milá), reception area, and pool all contribute to this aura. The restaurant, Moo, is an oasis of modern cuisine orchestrated by the Roca brothers—Joan, Josep, and Jordi—who have achieved international prestige with their Celler de Can Roca near Girona. **Pros:** perfect location for the upper Eixample, a design triumph at the epicenter of style, hot nightlife scene around the bar on weekends. **Cons:** slightly pretentious, restaurant pricey and precious. ✉ *Carrer Rosselló 265, Eixample* ☎ *93/445–4000* 🌐 *www.hotelomm.es* ⇨ *58 rooms, 1 suite* ☝ *In-room: refrigerator, Wi-Fi. In-hotel: restaurant, bar, pool, parking (fee)* ▭ *AE, DC, MC, V* Ⓜ *Diagonal, Provença* ✥ *D4.*

$$$$ **Hotel Palace.** Founded in 1919 by Caesar Ritz, this grande dame of Barcelona hotels has been restored to the splendor of its earlier years, albeit under another name. The imperial lobby is at once rambling and elegant, while the guest rooms contain Regency furniture, and some have Romanesque baths and mosaics. The restaurant, Caelis, serves superb French and Catalan cuisine. **Pros:** equidistant from Gothic Quarter and central Eixample, elegant and polished service, consummate old-world luxury in rooms. **Cons:** a little stuffy, excessively expensive, on the noisy Gran Via. ✉ *Gran Via de les Corts Catalanes 668, Eixample* ☎ *93/510–1130* 🌐 *www.hotelpalacebarcelona.com* ⇨ *122 rooms* ☝ *In-room: refrigerator, Wi-Fi. In-hotel: restaurant, bar, gym* ▭ *AE, DC, MC, V* Ⓜ *Passeig de Gràcia* ✥ *E3.*

$$$$ Fodor's Choice ★ **Majestic.** This near-perfect place to stay is on Barcelona's most stylish boulevard. The building is part Eixample townhouse and part modern extension. Pastels and Mediterranean hues warm each room, and the furnishings are all state-of-the-art contemporary. The superb restaurant, Fermin Puig's internationally acclaimed Drolma, is a destination in itself. **Pros:** ideally situated in the center of the Eixample, good balance between technology and charm, one of Barcelona's most famous restaurants. **Cons:** faces one of the city's widest, brightest, noisiest,

and most commercial thoroughfares. ✉ *Passeig de Gràcia 68, Eixample* ☎ *93/488–1717* 🌐 *www.hotelmajestic.es* *273 rooms, 30 suites* *In-room: Wi-Fi. In-hotel: 2 restaurants, bar, pool, gym, parking (fee)* *AE, DC, MC, V* Ⓜ *Passeig de Gràcia* ✣ *D2.*

$$$–$$$$ **Prestige Paseo de Gràcia.** A design triumph built around a (mostly original) 1930s staircase, purity of line and minimalist sleekness are the reigning esthetic principles in play here, especially in the guest rooms but also in the lobby. The roof terrace is a tour de force, with the different sections divided by contrasting colors and textures. **Pros:** ideally positioned in the middle of the Eixample, superbly balanced minimalist design, elegant service. **Cons:** opens onto Barcelona's main shopping street, which is wide, bustling, and loud. ✉ *Passeig de Gracià 62, Eixample* ☎ *93/272–4180* 🌐 *www.prestigehotels.com* *45 rooms* *In-room: Ethernet, Wi-Fi. In-hotel: 2 restaurants, bar, pool, gym, public internet, parking (fee), minibar* *AE, DC, MC, V* Ⓜ *Passeig de Gracià* ✣ *D2.*

$$$–$$$$ **Regente.** The Moderniste facade and furnishings and the lovely stained-glass windows in the bar lend style and charm to this smallish hotel. Public rooms are carpeted in a mix of patterns; guest rooms, fortunately, are more restrained. The verdant roof terrace with a small swimming pool helps seal a positive verdict on this central Eixample hotel. **Pros:** intimate hotel with traditional furnishings, leafy Rambla Catalunya is a quiet but always lively promenade, good value. **Cons:** small (though elegant) public rooms. ✉ *La Rambla de Catalunya 76, Eixample* ☎ *93/487–5989* 🌐 *www.hcchotels.com* *79 rooms* *In-room: safe, refrigerator, Wi-Fi. In-hotel: restaurant, bar, pool* *AE, DC, MC, V* Ⓜ *Passeig de Gràcia* ✣ *D2.*

SARRIÀ-PEDRALBES AND SANT GERVASI

$$$$ **Princesa Sofía.** This somewhat aseptic modern high-rise has numerous business facilities and meeting rooms, everything from beauty salons to shops, and three restaurants. The staff is highly professional and efficient, catering primarily to business travelers and convention guests, and the rooms, decorated in soft colors, are ultracomfortable. **Pros:** luxurious, comfortable, and completely equipped for all your needs; near the Barcelona soccer stadium and only a 20-minute walk from Sarrià. **Cons:** far from the Gothic Quarter and the Eixample, facing the wide and high-speed Avinguda Diagonal. ✉ *Pl. Pius XII 4, Diagonal* ☎ *93/508–1000* 🌐 *www.expogrupo.com* *475 rooms, 25 suites* *In-room: refrigerator, Wi-Fi. In-hotel: 3 restaurants, bar, pools, gym, parking (fee)* *AE, DC, MC, V* Ⓜ *Maria Cristina* ✣ *A1.*

$$–$$$ Fodor's Choice ★ **Turó de Vilana.** Surrounded by bougainvillea-festooned villas above Barcelona's Passeig de la Bonanova, this bright, modern hotel has a hot tub in every room, immaculate public areas of stone, steel, and glass, and a pleasant staff. Rooms are luminous. In summer, upper Barcelona is noticeably cooler, and quieter, than the rest of the city. The Turó de Vilana is a 10-minute walk from the Sarrià train that connects you with the city center in 15 minutes. **Pros:** new furnishings and latest technology in rooms, bright and cheery service and design, refreshing surroundings. **Cons:** somewhat removed (10-minute walk plus 15-minute

7

subway) from main exploring neighborhoods. ✉ *Carrer Vilana 7, Sant Gervasi* ☎ *93/434–0363* 🌐 *www.turodevilana.com* ⇨ *20 rooms* ☝ *In-room: refrigerator, Wi-Fi. In-hotel: restaurant, room service* ▭ *AE, DC, MC, V* Ⓜ *Sarrià* ✣ *B1.*

NIGHTLIFE AND THE ARTS

Barcelona's art and nightlife scenes start early and never quite stop. To find out what's on, look in newspapers or the weekly *Guía Del Ocio,* which has a section in English and is available at newsstands all over town. *Activitats,* available at the Palau de la Virreina (La Rambla 99) or the Centre Santa Monica (La Rambla 7) lists cultural events.

THE ARTS

CASTELLERS AND SARDANAS

The Sunday-morning papers carry announcements for local neighborhood celebrations, flea markets and produce fairs, puppet shows, storytelling sessions for children, sardana dancing, bell-ringing concerts, and, best of all, *castellers—* 🌐 *www.bcn.es* has listings in English. The castellers, complex human pyramids sometimes reaching as high as 10 stories, are a quintessentially Catalan phenomenon that originated in the 17th century, in the Penedés region west of Barcelona. Castellers perform regularly at neighborhood fiestas and key holidays. Sardanas usually begin at 1 PM, Castellers start between 11 AM and noon. Most Sunday-morning events are over by 2, when lunchtime officially reigns supreme.

Sardanas are performed in front of the cathedral at 1 PM every Saturday and Sunday and at different points such as Plaça Sant Jaume during the Festes de la Mercé and other festes.

CLASSICAL MUSIC

The basilica of Santa Maria del Mar, the church of Santa Maria del Pi, the Monestir de Pedralbes, Drassanes Reials, and the Saló del Tinell, among other ancient and intimate spaces, hold concerts.

Barcelona's most famous concert hall is the Moderniste **Palau de la Música Catalana** (✉ *Carrer Palau de la Música 4–6, Sant Pere* ☎ *93/295–7200*), with performances September–June. Tickets range from €6 to €100 and are best purchased well in advance, though a last-minute *palco sin vistas* (box seat with no sight of the stage) is a good way to get into the building for a concert. The contemporary **Auditori de Barcelona** (✉ *Carrer Lepant 150, near Plaça de les Glòries, Eixample* ☎ *93/247–9300*) has classical music, with occasional jazz and pop thrown in. Barcelona's **Gran Teatre del Liceu** (✉ *La Rambla 51–59 [box office: La Rambla de Capuchinos 63], Rambla* ☎ *93/485–9900 box office*) stages operas and recitals.

DANCE

L'Espai de Dansa i Música de la Generalitat de Catalunya (✉ *Travessera de Gràcia 63, Eixample* ☎ *93/414–3133*)—generally listed as L'Espai, or "The Space"—is the prime venue for ballet and modern dance, as well as some musical offerings. **El Mercat de les Flors** (✉ *Carrer Lleida 59, Eixample* ☎ *93/426–1875*), near Plaça d'Espanya, is a traditional venue for modern dance and theater.

FILM

Though many foreign films are dubbed, Barcelona has a full complement of original-language cinema; look for listings marked "v.o." (*versión original*).

Verdi (✉ *Carrer Verdi 32, Gràcia*) screens current releases with original-version soundtracks in a fun neighborhood for pre- and postmovie eating and drinking. The **Icaria Yelmo** (✉ *Salvador Espriu 61, Port Olímpic*) complex in the Olympic Port has the city's largest selection of English-language films. **Renoir Les Corts** (✉ *Eugeni d'Ors 12, behind Diagonal's El Corte Inglés, Diagonal*) is a good choice for recently released English-language features of all kinds. **Casablanca** (✉ *Passeig de Gràcia 115, Eixample*) plays original-language movies, generally art flicks.

FLAMENCO

In Catalunya, flamenco, like bullfighting, is regarded as an import from Andalusia. However, unlike bullfighting, there is a strong interest in and market for flamenco in Barcelona. Tour groups in search of flamenco gravitate to **El Cordobés** (✉ *La Rambla 35, Rambla* ☎ *93/317–6653*). **El Patio Andaluz** (✉ *Aribau 242, Eixample* ☎ *93/209–3378*) has rather touristy flamenco shows twice nightly (10 and midnight) and a karaoke section upstairs. **El Tablao de Carmen** (✉ *Poble Espanyol, Av. Marquès de Comillas s/n Montjuïc* ☎ *93/325–6895*) hosts touring flamenco troupes up on Montjuïc. On the Plaça Reial, **Los Tarantos** (✉ *Pl. Reial 17, Barri Gòtic* ☎ *93/318–3067*) spotlights Andalusia's best flamenco. **Palacio del Flamenco** (✉ *Balmes 139, Eixample* ☎ *93/218–7237* 🌐 *www.palaciodelflamenco.com*) showcases some of Barcelona's best flamenco. Prices start at €*30* for a drink and the show, and go up to €40–€60 for dinner and a show.

7

NIGHTLIFE

CABARET

Bcn Seven Dreams (✉ *Plaza Mayor 9, Poble Espanyol, Avda. Marquès de Comillas s/n, Montjuïc* ☎ *93/325–4604*) in Montjuïc's Poble Espanyol, is Barcelona's last true cabaret show, featuring a chorus line, song and dance, and light erotic innuendo. Near the bottom of the Rambla, the minuscule **Bar Pastis** (✉ *Carrer Santa Mònica 4, Rambla* ☎ *93/318–7980*) has live performances and LPs of every Edith Piaf song ever recorded. **Star Class** (✉ *Av. Sarrià 44, Eixample* ☎ *93/430–9156*) has a combination cabaret and disco program. **Joy's** (✉ *Carrer Rocafort 231, Eixample* ☎ *93/430–9156*) hosts a floor show, cabaret, and dancing.

CASINO

The **Gran Casino de Barcelona** (✉ *Carrer de la Marina, Port Olímpic* ☎ *93/225–7878*), under the Hotel Arts, is open daily 1 PM–5 AM.

JAZZ, BLUES, AND LIVE MUSIC VENUES

BARRI GÒTIC The Gothic Quarter's **Harlem Jazz Club** (✉ *Carrer Comtessa Sobradiel 8, Barri Gòtic* ☎ *93/310–0755*) is small but atmospheric, with good jazz and country bands.

BORN-RIBERA **Nao Colón/Club Bamboo** (✉ *Av. Marques de l'Argentera 19, Born-Ribera* ☎ *93/268–7633*) combines the sounds and the cuisine of the Mediterranean followed by jazz, blues, flamenco, fusion, hard rock, and house after midnight.

EIXAMPLE **Luz de Gas** (✉ *Carrer Muntaner 246, Eixample* ☎ *93/209–7711*) hosts every genre from Irish fusion to Cuban sounds. The bustling **Zacarías** (✉ *Av. Diagonal 477, Eixample* ☎ *93/207–5643*) stages live music from a variety of musical genres, including jazz, rock, folk, and blues.

PORT OLÍMPIC **Luna Mora** (✉ *Port Olímpic, next to Hotel Arts, Port Olímpic* ☎ *93/221–6161*) stages the gamut, from country blues to salsa and soul.

RAMBLA **Jamboree-Jazz and Dance-Club** (✉ *Pl. Reial 17, Rambla* ☎ *93/301–7564*) is a center for jazz, rock, and flamenco.

LATE-NIGHT BARS

Bar musical is Spanish for any bar with music loud enough to drown out conversation. **Port Olímpic** and the Port Vell's **Maremagnum** are wildly active but, compared to other options, better to avoid. Especially in summer and on weekends, these are far from Barcelona's best nightlife options.

EIXAMPLE Two blocks from Velodrom is the intriguing *barmuseo* (bar-cum-museum) **La Fira** (✉ *Carrer Provença 171, Eixample* ☎ *93/323–7271*). **George and Dragon** (✉ *Carrer Diputació 269, Eixample* ☎ *93/488–1765*), named for Barcelona's ubiquitous symbols of good and evil, is a rollicking English pub just off Passeig de Gràcia.

Over by the Sagrada Família, the **Michael Collins Irish Pub** (✉ *Pl. Sagrada Família 4, Eixample* ☎ *93/459–1964*) has a strong Anglo following. **Nick Havanna** (✉ *Carrer Rosselló 208, Eixample* ☎ *93/215–6591*) has, along with a consistently hot program of live music, Barcelona's most entertaining urinals. Café-restaurant-bar **Salero** (✉ *Carrer del Rec 60, Eixample* ☎ *93/488–1765*) is always packed with young miscreants. Above Via Augusta in upper Barcelona, the **Sherlock Holmes** (✉ *Carrer Copernic 42–44, Eixample* ☎ *93/414–2184*) is an ongoing Brit-fest with live musical performances and dark intimate corners. **Universal** (✉ *Carrer Marià Cubí 182–184, Eixample* ☎ *93/200–7470*) has been the hottest bar in town for 30 years, and it's still going strong. For a more laid-back scene, with high ceilings, billiards, and tapas, visit the new Carles Abellan-catered **Velodrom** (✉ *Carrer Muntaner 211–213, Eixample* ☎ *93/230–6022*), below the Diagonal.

RAMBLA **Glaciar** (✉ *Pl. Reial 13, Rambla* ☎ *93/302–1163*) is *the* spot for young out-of-towners.

RAVAL **Bar Almirall** (✉ *Carrer Joaquin Costa 33, Raval* ☎ *93/412–1535*) has an Art Nouveau chicness. **Bar Muy Buenas** (✉ *Carrer del Carme 63, Raval* ☎ *93/442–5053*) is an Art Nouveau gem.

Downtown, deep in the Barrio Chino, try the **London Bar**(✉ *Carrer Nou de la Rambla 34, Raval* ☎ *93/302–3102*), an Art Nouveau circus haunt with a trapeze suspended above the bar. **L'Ovella Negra** (✉ *Carrer de les Sitges 5, Raval* ☎ *93/317–1087*) is the top student tavern.

UPPER BARCELONA Above Via Augusta, **Opiniao** (✉ *Carrer Ciutat de Balaguer 67, below Bonanova, La Bonanova* ☎ *93/418–3399*) is another upper-Barcelona dive, aka a hot local club.

NIGHTCLUBS AND DISCOS

Most clubs have a discretionary cover charge and like to inflict it on foreigners, so dress up and be prepared to talk your way past the bouncer. Any story can work; for example, you own a chain of nightclubs and are on a world tour. But don't expect much to happen until 1:30 or 2.

BORN-RIBERA **Luz de Luna** (✉ *Carrer Comerç 21, La Ribera* ☎ *93/310–7542*) lays down wall-to-wall salsa.

EIXAMPLE **Agua de Luna** (✉ *Carrer Viladomat 211, Eixample* ☎ *93/410–0440*) is a torrid salsa scene in the western Eixample. Salsa sizzles at the exuberantly Caribbean **Antilla BCN Latin Club** (✉ *Carrer Aragó 141, Eixample* ☎ *93/451–4564*). A line forms at **Bikini** (✉ *Carrer Deu i Mata 105, at Entença, Eixample* ☎ *93/322–0005*) on festive Saturday nights. **Búcaro** (✉ *Carrer Aribau 195, Eixample* ☎ *93/209–6562*) rocks until dawn, albeit largely for the extremely young. **Buda Barcelona** (✉ *Carrer Pau Claris 92, Eixample* ☎ *93/318–4252*) is the hottest nightspot in the Eixample, with celebrities and glamour galore. **Costa Breve** (✉ *Carrer Aribau 230, Eixample* ☎ *93/200–7346*) accepts postgraduates with open arms. **El Otro** (✉ *Carrer Valencia 166, Eixample* ☎ *93/323–6759*) is kind to aging (over-30) miscreants. Still popular, though not to the heights it once was, is the prisonesque nightclub **Otto Zutz** (✉ *Carrer Lincoln 15, Eixample* ☎ *93/238–0722*), off Via Augusta. **Row Club** (✉ *Carrer Rosselló 208, Eixample* ☎ *93/237–5405*) is big on techno. **Sala Cibeles** (✉ *Carrer de Córsega 363, Eixample* ☎ *93/272–0910*) has a large sound system and singing DJs. The nearly classic **Up and Down** (✉ *Carrer Numancia 179, Eixample* ☎ *93/280–2922*), pronounced "Pen-*dow,*" is a good choice for elegant carousers.

MONTJUÏC **Torres de Avila** (✉ *Av. Marquès de Comillas 25, Montjuïc* ☎ *93/424–9309*), in Pueblo Espanyol, is wild and woolly until broad daylight on weekends.

PEDRALBES **Pachá** (✉ *Carrer Dr. Marañon 17, Pedralbes-Les Corts* ☎ *93/204–0412*) offers two raging discos and a restaurant.

POBLE NOU (EAST BARCELONA) The **Loft** (✉ *Carrer Pamplona 88, Poble Nou* ☎ *93/272–0910*), an offshoot of Sala Razzmatazz, is dedicated to electronic music.

Sala Razzmatazz (✉ *Carrer Almogavers 122, Poble Nou* ☎ *93/320–8200*) offers Friday and Saturday disco madness until dawn. Weeknight concerts have international stars like Ani DiFranco and Enya.

PORT OLÍMPIC The beachfront **CDLC** (✉ *Passeig Maritim 32, Port Olímpic* ☎ *93/224–0470*) has compartmentalized *sofa-camas* (sofa beds of a sort) for prime canoodling. **Shôko** (✉ *Passeig Marítim 36, Port Olímpic* ☎ *93/225–9200*) is an excellent Asian-fusion restaurant until midnight, when it morphs into the beachfront's wildest dance and lounge club.

7

RAVAL **DosTrece** (✉ *Carrer del Carme 40, Raval* ☎ *93/443–0341*) packs in young internationals for dancing and carousing. **It Café** (✉ *Carrer Joaquin Costa 4, Raval* ☎ *93/443–0341*) is a design oasis not far from the MACBA in the Raval. For big-band tango in an old-fashioned *sala de baile* (dance hall), head to **La Paloma** (✉ *Carrer Tigre 27, Raval* ☎ *93/301–6897*), with kitschy 1950s furnishings.

TIBIDABO **Danzatoria** (✉ *Av. Tibidabo 61, Tibidabo* ☎ *93/211–6261*), a fusion of Salsitas and Partycular (two former clubs), is a "multispace" with five venues (disco, hall, dance, chill-out, garden) and fills with models and hopeful guys.

SPORTS AND THE OUTDOORS

HIKING

The **Collserola** hills behind the city offer well-marked trails, fresh air, and lovely views. Take the San Cugat, Sabadell, or Terrassa FFCC train from Plaça de Catalunya and get off at Baixador de Vallvidrera; the information center, 10 minutes uphill next to **Vil.la Joana** (now the Jacint Verdaguer Museum), has maps of this mountain woodland 20 minutes from downtown. The walk back into town can take from two to five hours, depending on your speed and the trails you pick. **Club Excursionista de Catalunya** (✉ *Carrer Paradís 10, Barri Gòtic* ☎ *93/315–2311*) has information on hiking in Barcelona and throughout Catalunya.

SOCCER

If you're in Barcelona between September and June, go see the celebrated FC Barcelona play soccer (preferably against Real Madrid, if you can score a ticket) at Barcelona's gigantic stadium, **Camp Nou** (✉ *Carrer Arístides Maillol, Les Corts* ☎ *93/496–3608* 🌐 *www.fcbarcelona.com* 🎫 *Museum €6, combined ticket including tour of museum, field, and sports complex €10* ⏲ *Museum Mon.–Sat. 10–6:30, Sun. 10–2* Ⓜ *Collblanc, Palau Reial*). A worthwhile alternative to seeing a game is the guided tour of the FC Barcelona museum and facilities. The museum has a five video screens showing the club's most memorable goals, along with player biographies and displays chronicling the history of one of Europe's most colorful soccer clubs.

SHOPPING

Between the surging fashion scene, a host of young clothing designers, clever home furnishings, rare and delicious foodstuffs, and art and antiques, Barcelona might just be the best place in Spain to unload extra ballast from your wallet. It's true, bargains are few, outside saffron and rope-sole shoes, but quality and selection are excellent. Most stores are open Monday–Saturday 9–1:30 and 5–8. Virtually all are closed on Sunday.

SHOPPING DISTRICTS

Barcelona's prime shopping districts are the Passeig de Gràcia, Rambla de Catalunya, Plaça de Catalunya, Porta de l'Àngel, and Avinguda Diagonal up to Carrer Ganduxer.

For high fashion, browse along **Passeig de Gràcia** and the **Diagonal** between Plaça Joan Carles I and Plaça Francesc Macià. There are two dozen antiques shops in the Gothic Quarter, many off the Passeig de Gràcia on Bulevard dels Antiquaris, and still more in Gràcia and Sarrià. **Bulevard Rosa** is a fashion and shopping mall off Passeig de Gràcia. For old-fashioned Spanish shops, prowl the Gothic Quarter, especially **Carrer Ferran.** The area surrounding **Plaça del Pi,** from the Boqueria to Carrer Portaferrissa and Carrer de la Canuda, is thick with boutiques, jewelry, and design shops. The **Barri de la Ribera,** around Santa Maria del Mar, especially El Born area, has a cluster of design, fashion, and food shops. Design, jewelry, and knickknack shops cluster on Carrer Banys Vells and Carrer Flassaders, near Carrer Montcada. The shopping colossus **L'Illa,** on the Diagonal beyond Carrer Ganduxer, includes the department store FNAC, Custo, and myriad temptations. **Carrer Tuset,** north of the Diagonal, has lots of small boutiques. The **Maremagnum** mall, in Port Vell, is convenient to downtown. **Diagonal Mar,** at the eastern end of the diagonal, along with the **Fòrum** complex offer many shopping options in a mega-shopping-mall environment.

SPECIALTY STORES

ANTIQUES

The headquarters of antiques shopping is the Gothic Quarter, where **Carrer de la Palla** and **Carrer Banys Nous** are lined with shops full of prints, maps, books, paintings, and furniture. An antiques market is held in front of the Catedral de la Seu every Thursday from 10 to 8. There are also about 70 shops off Passeig de Gràcia on Bulevard dels Antiquaris. In upper Barcelona, the entire village of **Sarrià** is becoming an antiquer's destination, with shops along Cornet i Mas, Pedró de la Creu, and Major de Sarrià.

EIXAMPLE **Alcanto** (✉ *Passeig de Gràcia 55–57, Eixample*) is a clearinghouse for buying and selling. **Antiguedades J. Pla** (✉ *Carrer Aragó 517, Eixample*) buys and sells antiques.

The Eixample's **Centre d'Antiquaris** (✉ *Passeig de Gràcia 55, Eixample*) contains 75 antiques stores. Moderniste aficionados should check out **Gothsland** (✉ *Carrer Consell de Cent 331, Eixample*). **Novecento** (✉ *Passeig de Gràcia 75, Eixample*) has antique art and jewelry.

ART

There's a cluster of art galleries on Carrer Consell de Cent between Passeig de Gràcia and Carrer Balmes and around the corner on Rambla de Catalunya. The Born–Santa Maria del Mar quarter is another art destination, along Carrer Montcada and the parallel Carrer Banys Vells.

BARRI GÒTIC Carrer Petritxol, which leads down into Plaça del Pi, is lined with galleries, notably **Sala Parès** (✉ *Carrer Petritxol 5, Barri Gòtic*).

BORN-RIBERA The always ticking **Metrònom** (✉*Carrer Fussina 4, La Ribera*) at the north end of the Born has a weakness for performance art and edgy erotic installations and photography.

EIXAMPLE **Eude** (✉*Carrer Consell de Cent 278, Eixample*) showcases young artists.

Fundació La Caixa ✉*Passeig de Gràcia, Eixample*) has regular exhibits at its Casa Milà gallery on Passeig de Gràcia.

Galeria Joan Prats (✉*La Rambla de Catalunya 54, Eixample*) is a veteran, known for the quality of its artists' works. The **Joan Gaspar** (✉*Pl. Letamendi 1, Eixample*) started with Picasso and Miró. **Sala Dalmau** (✉*Carrer Consell de Cent 347, Eixample*) is an established art outlet. **Sala Rovira** (✉*La Rambla de Catalunya 62, Eixample*) has shown top artists Tom Carr and Blanca Vernis.

SHOPPING BEST BETS

Best Antiques shopping street: Carrer de la Palla

Best Bling: Majoral

Best Bookstore: La Central

Best Boutique: Custo Barcelona

Best Ceramics Studio: Art Escudellers

Best Cobbler: La Manual Alpargatera

Best Gourmet Food Market: Mantequeria Can Ravell

Best Music Store: Discos Castelló

Best Spice Shop: Casa Gispert

Best Stationery Boutique: Papirum

RAMBLA The **Espai Xavier Miserachs** (✉*La Rambla 99, Rambla*) in the Palau de la Virreina has eclectic temporary exhibits of painting, photography, design, and illustration.

RAVAL **La Capella de l'Antic Hospital de la Santa Creu** (✉*Carrer Hospital 56, Raval*) exhibits installations and new art.

BOOKS

BARRI GÒTIC **El Corte Inglés** (✉*Porta de l'Àngel 19–21, Barri Gòtic*), especially the branch in Porta del Àngel, sells English guidebooks and novels.

EIXAMPLE **Altair** (✉*Gran Via de les Corts Catalanes 616, Eixample*) is Barcelona's premier travel and adventure bookstore, with many titles in English. **BCN Books** (✉*Carrer Roger de Llúria 118, Eixample*) is a top store for books in English. **Casa del Llibre** (✉*Passeig de Gràcia 62, Eixample*) is a book feast, with English titles.

Fodor's Choice ★ **La Central** (✉*Carrer Mallorca 237, Eixample*) is Barcelona's best bookstore. **La Central del Raval** (✉*Carrer Elisabets 6, Eixample*), in the former chapel of the Casa de la Misericòrdia, sells books on architecture. **Laie** (✉*Carrer Pau Claris 85, Eixample*) is a book lover's sanctuary, with cultural events as well as stacks.

RAMBLA The bookstore in the **Palau de la Virreina** (✉*La Rambla 99, Rambla*) has books on art, design, and Barcelona in general.

CLOTHING BOUTIQUES AND JEWELRY

BARRI GÒTIC **El Ingenio** (✉*Carrer Rauric 6, Barri Gòtic*) has one of the prettiest antique storefronts in town; inside are costumes, puppets, carnival masks, and gadgets for all ages. **May Day** (✉*C. Portaferrissa 16, Barri Gòtic*) carries cutting-edge clothing, footwear, and accessories.

BORN-RIBERA **Custo Barcelona** (✉ *Plaça de les Olles 7, Born-Ribera*) is becoming a city icon and *the* place for colorful, whimsical, tops that you can immediately wear out at the feeding frenzy going on next door at the Cal Pep tapas bar. **Majoral** (✉ *Carrer Argenteria 66, Born-Ribera*) makes and sells organic, almost edible-looking rings, earrings, brooches, pins, and assorted bling.

Otman (✉ *Carrer Cirera 4, La Ribera*) has light and racy frocks, belts, blouses, and skirts.

EIXAMPLE **Adolfo Domínguez** (✉ *Passeig de Gràcia 35, Av. Diagonal 570, Eixample*) is one of Spain's leading designers. **David Valls** (✉ *C. Valencia 235, Eixample*) represents new, young Barcelona fashion design. **El Bulevard Rosa** (✉ *Passeig de Gràcia 53–55, Eixample*) is a collection of boutiques with the latest outfits.

BOOKS & ROSES

Barcelona's April 23, Sant Jordi (Saint George) celebration is a Valentine's Day, Catalan-style, when ladies are given roses and men receive books. On that day, Barcelona becomes one huge rose-scented bookstore, with kiosks full of books next to flower sellers lining the Rambla. The rose tradition began with Barcelona's medieval rose festival, and international book day was appended later, to celebrate the April 23, 1616, deaths of both Miguel de Cervantes and William Shakespeare, thus the tradition of books and roses was born.

The two locations of Toni Miró's **Groc** (✉ *C. Muntaner 382, Eixample* ✉ *La Rambla de Catalunya 100, Eixample*) have the latest looks for men, women, and children. **Janina** (✉ *Rambla Catalunya 94, Eixample*) sells trendy and stylish lingerie by La Perla, Eres, Dolce and Gabbana, and others. **Joaquim Berao** (✉ *C. Rosselló 277, Eixample*) is a top jewelry designer. **No Té Nom** (✉ *Carrer Pau Claris 159, Eixample*) means "it has no name" in Catalan; it sells new fabrics and design accessories. **On Land** (✉ *Valencia 273, Eixample*) is all street fashion, designed by the hottest young designers in town.

SANT PERE **Galeria Meko**(✉ *Sant Pere Més Baix 11, Sant Pere* ☎ *93/268–0222*) is a gorgeously restored 17th-century space showcasing Carmen Pintor's *joieria d'autor* (original jewelry).

CERAMICS

Although perusing smaller establishments is always worthwhile, one of Barcelona's big department stores, **El Corte Inglés,** at Plaça de Catalunya or Avinguda Diagonal (for addresses, look under "Department Stores"), is also a good bet for ceramics.

BARRI GÒTIC **Art Escudellers** (✉ *Carrer Escudellers 23–25, Barri Gòtic*) displays ceramics from more than 200 artisans from all over Spain; Catalonia's famous La Bisbal, Agentona, and La Galera ceramics are well represented with their characteristic cobalt, mustard, and deep green glazed, unglazed, and partially glazed works. **Ítaca** (✉ *Carrer Ferrán 26, Barri Gòtic*) has ceramic plates, bowls, and pottery from Talavera de la Reina and La Bisbal. For Lladró, try **Pla de l'Os** (✉ *Carrer de la Boqueria 3, Barri Gòtic*), off the Rambla.

CLOSE UP

Move Over, Milan

Sure, Barcelona's ladies have always effortlessly adorned themselves for the most important runway of all: the street. But now the fashion scene itself is receiving overdue props, rivaling other European capitals as the home of high fashion. With a legacy in textile creation, avant-garde architecture, and playful design, Barcelona is clearly ready to don the haute couture mantle.

Ever since the 1992 Olympic Games blew the lid off any lingering doubts about Barcelona's contemporary creative potential, new clothing designers and boutiques have been proliferating. The late September Barcelona Fashion Week has taken its place as one of Europe's most important fashion meets, alongside those of Paris, London, and Milan. Largely stripped of public financing, it's forged a path of its own, relying largely on young local designers as well as traditional heavyweights such as Antonio Miró, Armand Basi, Gonzalo Comellas, and Adolfo Domínguez. Even top-name Madrid designers such as Victorio and Lucchino, Miriam Ocáriz, and Soul Aguilar, citing the Catalan capital's innovative, younger image, prefer to show in Barcelona instead of at Madrid's Cibeles fashion event.

And the shops! From local clothing stars Zara and Custo to whimsical design objects at BD (Barcelona Design) or Vinçon to old crafts standbys such as La Manual Alpargatera or S'Avarca de Menorca, Barcelona is becoming as famous for shopping as for architecture and design. El Born, the old waterfront district tucked behind Santa Maria del Mar in the Barri de la Ribera teems with young artisans and designers; the Eixample, the midtown grid labyrinth of Art Nouveau architecture, is rife with innovatively designed shops selling equally original items of all kinds; and the outlying villages of Gràcia and Sarrià are becoming bite-sized boutique havens with much more to admire than quiet streets and leafy palms.

DEPARTMENT STORES

Spain's ubiquitous **El Corte Inglés** (✉Plaça de Catalunya 14, *Eixample* ✉*Porta de l'Angel 19–21, Barri Gòtic* ✉*Plaça Francesc Macià 58, Sant Gervasi* ✉*Avinguda Diagonal 617, Les Corts*) has four locations in Barcelona. On Plaça de Catalunya you can also find the international book and music store **FNAC** and the furniture and household design goods store **Habitat,** also on Carrer Tuset at the Diagonal.

INTERIOR DESIGN AND HOME FURNISHINGS

The area around the church of Santa Maria del Mar, an artisans' quarter since medieval times, is full of cheerful design stores and art galleries.

BARRI GÒTIC

Cutlery flourishes at the stately **Ganiveteria Roca** (✉*Pl. del Pi 3, Barri Gòtic*), opposite the giant rose window of the Santa Maria del Pi church. **Gotham** (✉*Cervantes 7, Barri Gòtic*), behind Town Hall, restores furniture from the '50s and '60s. It's a perennial set for Almodóvar movies. Amid mouthwatering interior design, **La Comercial** (✉ *Carrer del Rec 52 and 73, La Ribera*), off Passeig del Born, has clothes by international designers.

Sita Murt (✉*Carrer d'Avinyó 18, Barri Gòtic*) is a stunning subterranean space with a clever play of mirrors and international collections that include Esteve Sita Murt.

BORN-RIBERA

Estudi Pam2 (✉*Sabateret 1–3, La Ribera*), behind Carrer Montcada, sells ingenious design items. **Papers Coma** (✉*Carrer Montcada 20, La Ribera*) has inventive knickknacks. **Suspect** (✉*Carrer Comerç 29, La Ribera*), north of the Born, specializes in clothes and furniture made by Spastor, a group of Barcelona designers. **Vientos del Sur** (✉*Carrer Argenteria 78, La Ribera*), part of the Natura chain, has a good selection of textile and wood-carved crafts, as well as clothing and gift items.

7

EIXAMPLE

bd (short for *Barcelona Design* ✉*Carrer Mallorca 291–293, Eixample*) is a spare, cutting-edge home-furnishing store in another Moderniste gem, Domènech i Montaner's Casa Thomas. Upscale **Gimeno** (✉*Passeig de Gràcia 102, Eixample*) has everything from clever suitcases to the latest in furniture design. **Vinçon** (✉*Passeig de Gràcia 96, Eixample*) occupies a rambling Moderniste house and carries everything from Filofaxes to handsome kitchenware.

FINE FOODS

BARRI GÒTIC

Caelum (✉*C. de la Palla 8, Barri Gòtic*) sells crafts and such foods as honey and preserves, made in convents and monasteries all over Spain. **La Casa del Bacalao** (✉*Comtall 8, off Portal del Angel, Barri Gòtic*) specializes in salt cod and books of codfish recipes. **OroLíquido** (✉*C. de la Palla 8, Barri Gòtic*) sells the finest olive oils from Spain and the world at large.

BORN-RIBERA

Behind the Picasso Museum, **Born Cooking** (✉*Corretger 9, La Ribera*) is a work of art in itself, serving delicious cakes, quiches, and all manner of sweets and savories.

Casa Gispert (✉*Carrer Sombrerers 23, La Ribera*), on the inland side of Santa Maria del Mar, is one of the most aromatic and esthetically perfect shops in Barcelona, bursting with spices, saffron, chocolates, and nuts. **El Magnífico** (✉*Carrer Argenteria 64, La Ribera*) is famous for its coffees. **Jobal** (✉ *C. Princesa 38, La Ribera*) is a charming and fragrant saffron and spice shop. **La Barcelonesa** (✉ *Carrer Comerç 27, La Ribera*) specializes in dry goods, spices, tea, and saffron. **La Botifarreria de Santa Maria** (✉ *Carrer Santa Maria 4, La Ribera*), next to the church of Santa Maria, has excellent cheeses, hams, pâtés, and homemade *sobrassadas* (pork pâté with paprika). **Tot Formatge** (✉ *Passeig del Born 13, La Ribera*) has cheeses from all over Spain and the world. **Vila Viniteca** (✉ *C. Agullers 7, La Ribera*), near Santa Maria del Mar, is one of the best wine shops in Barcelona; the produce store across the way sells some of the best cheeses around.

EIXAMPLE **La Palmera** (✉ *C. Enric Granados 57, Eixample*) has a superb collection of wines, hams, cheeses, and olive oils.

★ **Mantequeria Can Ravell** (✉ *Carrer Aragó 313, Eixample*), a restaurant and delicatessen, is Barcelona's number one all-around wine, cheese, ham, and fine foods specialist.

SANT GERVASI **Vilaplana** (✉ *C. Francesc Perez-Cabrero, Sant Gervasi*) is famous for its pastries, cheeses, hams, pâtés, caviars, and fine deli items. **Tutusaus** (✉ *C. Francesc Perez-Cabrero 5, Sant Gervasi*) specializes in fine ibérico hams and superb cheeses from all over Europe.

SARRIÀ **La Cave** (✉ *Av. J. V. Foix 80, Sarrià*) is a wine cellar with flair; bottles are arranged by grape varietals, price, and taste.

FOOD AND FLEA MARKETS

Barcelona's spectacular food markets include the Mercat de la Llibertat, near Plaça Gal.la Placidia, and Mercat de la Revolució, on Travessera de Gràcia, both in Gràcia. On Thursday, a natural-produce market (honey, cheese) fills Plaça del Pi with interesting tastes and aromas. On Sunday morning, a stamp and coin market fills Plaça Reial; also on Sunday, the Plaça Sant Josep Oriol holds a painter's market, and there is a general crafts and flea market near the Columbus Monument at the port end of the Rambla.

BARRI GÒTIC The **Mercat Gòtic** (✉ *Pl. de la Seu, Barri Gòtic*) fills the area in front of the Catedral de la Seu on Thursday.

Fodor'sChoice ★ The **Boqueria** (✉ *La Rambla 91, Rambla*) is Barcelona's most colorful food market and the oldest of its kind in Europe. Open Monday to Saturday, 8 to 8, it's most active before 3 PM.

EIXAMPLE Barcelona's largest flea market, **Els Encants** (✉ *Dos de Maig, on Plaça de les Glòries, Eixample* Ⓜ *Glòries*) is held Monday, Wednesday, Friday, and Saturday, from 8 to 7.

The **Mercat de Sant Antoni** (✉ *Ronda Sant Antoni, Eixample*) is an old-fashioned food, clothing, and used-book (many in English) market that's best on Sunday. It's currently closed for restoration until 2011.

GIFTS AND MISCELLANY

BARRI GÒTIC **La Manual Alpargatera** (✉ *Carrer d'Avinyó 7, Barri Gòtic*), off Carrer Ferran, specializes in handmade rope-sole sandals and espadrilles. **La Lionesa** (✉ *C. Ample 21, Barri Gòtic*) is an old-time grocery store. Stationery lovers will want to linger in the Gothic Quarter's **Papirum** (✉ *Baixada de la Llibreteria 2, Barri Gòtic*), a tiny, medievalesque shop with exquisite hand-printed papers and writing implements. **Solé** (✉ C.

Ample 7, Barri Gòtic) makes shoes by hand and sells others from all over the world.

RAVAL **Baclava** (⌧*C. Notariat 10, Raval*) sells artisanal textile products. Barcelona's best music store is **Discos Castelló** (⌧*Carrer Tallers 3, Raval*). For textiles, try **Teranyina** (⌧*C. Notariat 10, Raval*), which shares an address with Baclava.

SANT PERE **Les Muses del Palau** (⌧*Sant Pere Més Alt 1, Sant Pere* , next to the Palau de la Música Catalana, shows and sells Palau de la Música–themed gifts from neckties to pencils, posters, models, jigsaw puzzles, and teacups.

SIDE TRIPS FROM BARCELONA

MONTSERRAT

50 km (30 mi) west of Barcelona.

GETTING HERE AND AROUND

If you're driving, follow the A2/A7 *autopista* on the upper ring road (Ronda de Dalt), or from the western end of the Diagonal as far as Salida (Exit) 25 to Martorell. Bypass this industrial center and follow signs to Montserrat. Alternatively, you can take a train from the Plaça d'Espanya metro station (hourly 8:36–6:36, connecting with the funicular leaving every 15 minutes) or go on a guided tour with Pullmantur or Julià (⇨*Tour Options in Barcelona Planner)*.

7

EXPLORING

A favorite side trip from Barcelona is a visit to the shrine of La Moreneta (the Black Virgin of Montserrat), Catalonia's patron saint, in a Benedictine monastery high in the Serra de Montserrat, west of town. These dramatic, sawtooth peaks have given rise to countless legends: here St. Peter left a statue of the Virgin Mary, carved by St. Luke; Parsifal found the Holy Grail; and Wagner sought inspiration for his opera. Montserrat is as memorable for its strange, pink hills as it is for its religious treasures, so be sure to explore the area. The monastic complex is dwarfed by the grandeur of the jagged peaks, and the crests above are bristling with chapels and hermitages. The hermitage of **Sant Joan** can be reached by funicular. The views over the mountains to the Mediterranean and, on a clear day, to the Pyrenees are breathtaking; the rugged, boulder-strewn terrain makes for dramatic walks and hikes.

Although a monastery has stood on the same site in Montserrat since the early Middle Ages, the present 19th-century building replaced the rubble left by Napoléon's troops in 1812. The shrine is world-famous, and one of Catalonia's spiritual sanctuaries—honeymooning couples flock here by the thousands seeking La Moreneta's blessing on their marriages, and twice a year, on April 27 and September 8, the diminutive statue of Montserrat's Black Virgin becomes the object of one of Spain's greatest pilgrimages.

Only the basilica and museum are regularly open to the public. The **basilica** is dark and ornate, its blackness pierced by the glow of hundreds of votive lamps. Above the high altar stands the famous polychrome statue

of the Virgin and Child, to which the faithful can pay their respects by way of a separate door. ☎93/877–7777 ⏲*Daily 6 AM–10:30 AM and noon–6:30 PM.*

The monastery's **museum** has two sections: the Secció Antiga has old masters, among them works by El Greco, Correggio, and Caravaggio, and the amassed gifts to the Virgin; the Secció Moderna concentrates on recent modern Catalan painters. ☎*93/877–7766 abbey and museum* ⏲*Secció Antiga Tues.–Sat. 10:30–2, Secció Moderna Tues.–Sat. 3–6.*

SITGES, SANTES CREUS, AND SANTA MARIA DE POBLET

This trio of attractions south and west of Barcelona can be seen in a day. Sitges is the prettiest and most popular resort in Barcelona's immediate environs, with an excellent beach and a whitewashed and flowery old quarter. It's also one of Europe's premier gay resorts. The Cistercian monasteries west of here, at Santes Creus and Poblet, are characterized by monolithic Romanesque architecture and beautiful cloisters.

GETTING HERE AND AROUND

By car, head southwest along Gran Via or Passeig Colom to the freeway that passes the airport on its way to Castelldefels. From here, the freeway and tunnels will get you to Sitges in 20 to 30 minutes. From

Sitges, drive inland toward Vilafranca del Penedès and the A7 freeway. The A2 (Lleida) leads to the monasteries. Regular trains leave Sants and Passeig de Gràcia for Sitges; the ride takes a half hour. To get to Santes Creus or Poblet from Sitges, take a Lleida-line train to L'Espluga de Francolí, 4 km (2½ mi) from Poblet. For Poblet, you can also stay with the train to Tarragona and catch a bus to the monastery (Autotransports Perelada ☎*973/202058*).

SITGES

43 km (27 mi) southwest of Barcelona.

The Sitges beach has fine sand that is carefully maintained in pristine condition, and the human flora and fauna usually found sun-worshipping on it lend the display of sea, sand, and celebrants a nearly catwalk-like intensity. The eastern end of the strand is dominated by an alabaster statue of the 16th-century painter El Greco, usually more at home in Toledo, where he spent most of his professional career. The artist Santiago Rusiñol is to blame for this surprise, as he was such an El Greco fan that he not only installed two El Greco paintings in his Museu Cau Ferrat but also had this sculpture planted on the beach.

The most interesting museum here is the **Cau Ferrat,** founded by Santiago Rusiñol (1861–1931) and containing some of his own paintings together with two El Grecos. Connoisseurs of wrought iron will love the beautiful collection of *cruces terminales,* crosses that once marked town boundaries. Next door is the **Museu Maricel de Mar,** with more artistic treasures; **Casa Llopis,** a romantic villa offering a tour of the house and tasting of local wine is a short walk across town. ✉*Fonollar s/n* ☎*93/894–0364* 🌐*www.diba.es* 🎫*€3.50 (€6.50 ticket valid for all three museums), free 1st Wed. of month* ⏲*June 14–Sept. 30, Tues.–Sat. 9:30–2 and 4–7, Sun. 10–2; Oct. 1–June 13, Tues.–Sat. 9:30–2 and 3:30–6:30, Sun. 10–2.*

NEED A BREAK?

Linger over excellent Mediterranean products and cooking with a nonpareil sea view at Vivero (✉*Passeig Balmins* ☎*93/894–2149*). The restaurant is closed Monday all year, and there is no dinner served from January 1 to May 31.

EN ROUTE

After leaving Sitges, make straight for the A2 *autopista* by way of Vilafranca del Penedès. Wine buffs may want to stop here to taste some excellent Penedès wines; you can tour and sip at the **Bodega Miguel Torres** (✉*Carrer Comerç 22* ☎*93/890–0100*). There's an interesting wine museum **Vinseum** (Museu de les Cultures del Vi de Catalunya) (✉*Plaça Jaume I, 1* ☎*93/890–0582*) *(Wine Museum)* in the Royal Palace, with descriptions of wine-making history. Admission is €5; open Tues.–Sun., 10–2 and 4–7.

SANTES CREUS

95 km (59 mi) west of Barcelona.

Founded in 1157, Santes Creus is the first of the monasteries you'll come upon as A2 branches west toward Lleida. Three austere aisles and an unusual 14th-century apse combine with the newly restored cloisters and the courtyard of the royal palace. ✉*Off A2* ☎*977/638329* 🎫*€4*

7

⏲ *Mid-Mar.–mid-Sept., Tues.–Sun. 10–1:30 and 3–7; mid-Sept.–mid-Jan., Tues.–Sun. 10–1:30 and 3–5:30; mid-Jan.–mid-Mar., Tues.–Sun. 10–1:30 and 3–6.*

Montblanc is off A2 at Salida (Exit) 9, its ancient gates too narrow for cars. A walk through its tiny streets reveals Gothic churches with stained-glass windows, a 16th-century hospital, and medieval mansions.

SANTA MARIA DE POBLET

8 km (5 mi) west of Santes Creus.

This splendid Cistercian foundation at the foot of the Prades Mountains is one of the great masterpieces of Spanish monastic architecture. The cloister is a stunning combination of lightness and size, and on sunny days the shadows on the yellow sandstone are extraordinary. Founded in 1150 by Ramón Berenguer IV in gratitude for the Christian Reconquest, the monastery first housed a dozen Cistercians from Narbonne. Later, the Crown of Aragón used Santa Maria de Poblet for religious retreats and burials. The building was damaged in an 1836 anticlerical revolt, and monks of the reformed Cistercian Order have managed the difficult task of restoration since 1940. Today, monks and novices again pray before the splendid retable over the tombs of Aragonese rulers, restored to their former glory by sculptor Frederic Marès; they also sleep in the cold, barren dormitory and eat frugal meals in the stark refectory. ✉ *Off A2* ☎ *977/870254* 🎟 *€6* 🌐 *www.poblet.cat* ⏲ *Guided tours by reservation Apr.–Sept., daily 10–12:30 and 3–6; Oct.–Mar., daily 10–12:30 and 3–5:30.*

OFF THE BEATEN PATH

Valls. The town of Valls, famous for its early spring *calçotada* (long-stem onion roast) held on the last Sunday of January, is 10 km (6 mi) from Santes Creus and 15 km (9 mi) from Poblet. Even if you miss the big day, *calçots* are served from November to April at rustic and rambling farmhouses such as **Cal Ganxo** (☎ *977/605960*) in nearby Masmolets, and the Xiquets de Valls, Catalonia's most famous *castellers* (human castlers), might be putting up a human skyscraper.

Catalonia and Valencia

Valencia's Ciutat de les Arts i les Ciències

WORD OF MOUTH

"Cadaques is wonderful for walking through narrow streets, with sights around every corner. The beach, though pebbly, is very romantic, with colorful fishing boats, ropes, and old seamen mending their nets. . . . Cadaques' main attraction is Salvador Dalí's private house in Port Lligat, a small village, a few kilometres from Cadaques."

—traveller1959

www.fodors.com/community

WELCOME TO CATALONIA AND VALENCIA

Woman in traditional dress during the Fallas festival in Valencia.

TOP REASONS TO GO

★ **Vist the Place Where We All Got Along:** In the old city of Girona, monuments of Christian, Jewish, and Islamic culture are only steps apart.

★ **Valencia:** The past 20 years has seen a transformation of the River Turia into a treasure-trove of museums and concert halls, lovely parks, and architectural wonders.

★ **Catalan Nouveau:** Serious foodies argue that the fountainhead of creative gastronomy has moved from France to Spain—and in particular to the great restaurants of the Ampurdà and Costa Brava.

★ **Hello Dalí:** Surreal doesn't begin to describe the Dalí Museum in Figueres, or the wild coast of the artist's home at Cap de Creus.

★ **Burning Passions:** Las Fallas, in mid-March, a week of fireworks and solemn processions and a finale of spectacular bonfires, is the odds-on favorite for the best festival in Europe.

1 Northern Catalonia. Inland and westward from the towns of Girona and Figueres is perhaps the most dramatic and beautiful part of old Catalonia, in the *comarques* (historical regions) of the Ampurdà, Cerdanya, Garrotxa, and Girones: a land of medieval villages and hilltop monasteries, volcanic landscapes, and lush green valleys.

The Salvador Dali Museum at Figueres with its humorous enlarged eggs.

2 Costa Brava. Native son Salvador Dalí put his mark on the northeastern-most corner of Catalonia, where the Costa Brava begins, especially in the fishing village of Cadaqués and the rugged coast of Cap De Creus. From here, south and west toward Barcelona, lie the beaches, historical settlements, and picturesque towns like Sant Feliu de Guixols that draw millions of summer visitors to the region.

3 Southern Catalonia. Under the Roman Empire, Tarragona, the principal city of this area, was the most important settlement in Spain; between Barcelona and the Ebro River delta, which marks the border of Catalonia, are two of the country's major wine-producing regions, the Penedes and El Priorat.

4 Costa del Azahar. The Valencian Autonomous Community has some 518 km (310 mi) of exquisite coastline; the towns along the so-called "Orange Blossom Coast" in the province of Castellón, between Catalonia and Valencia itself, are popular summer resorts.

5 Valencia and Environs. Spain's third-largest city, with a rich historical and cultural tradition, is now a focus of attention for its cutting-edge modern art and architecture. The Albufera Nature Park, just to the south, is one of the country's most important wildlife sanctuaries.

GETTING ORIENTED

Year-round, Catalonia is the most visited of Spain's autonomous communities. The Pyrenees that separate it from France provide some of the country's best skiing, while the rugged Costa Brava in the north and the Costa Dorada to the south are havens for sun worshippers. The interior is full of surprises, too: an expanding rural tourism industry and the region's growing international reputation for food and wine give Catalonia a broad-based appeal. Excellent rail, air, and highway connections link Catalonia to the beach resorts and vibrant cities of Valencia, its neighbor to the south.

Ciutat de les Arts i les Ciències, Valencia.

CATALONIA AND VALENCIA PLANNER

When to Go

Come for the beaches in the hot summer months, but expect crowds and oppressive heat—up to 40°C (104°F). The Mediterranean coast is more comfortable in May and September.

February and March are the peak months for skiing in the Pyrenees. Winter traveling in the region has other advantages: Valencia still has plenty of sunshine, and if you're visiting villages and wineries in the countryside you might find you've got the run of the place! A word of warning: many restaurants outside the major towns may close on weekdays in winter, so call ahead. Museums and centers of interest tend to have shorter winter hours, many closing at 6 PM.

Tour Options

Bus and boat tours from Barcelona to Girona and Figueres are run by Julià Travel. Buses leave Barcelona at 9 and return at 6. The price for Girona and Figueres is €66 per person. Pullmantur runs tours to several points on the Costa Brava.

Contacts Julià Travel (☎ *93/317–6454* 🌐 *www.juliatravel.com*). **Pullmantur** (☎ *93/317–4708*).

Festivals and Fiestas

In Valencia, **Las Fallas** fill an entire week in March, reaching their climax on March 19, El Día de San José (St. Joseph's Day), also known as the Spanish Father's Day. Las Fallas grew from the fact that St. Joseph is the patron saint of carpenters; in medieval times, carpenters' guilds celebrated by making huge bonfires with wood shavings. These days it's a weeklong celebration of fireworks, flower-strewn floats, carnival processions, and bullfights. On March 19, huge effigies of popular and not-so-popular figures are ceremoniously burned. Tarragona's most important fiestas are **St. Magí** (August 19) and **St. Tecla** (September 23).

If You Like Beaches

The beaches here range from stretches of fine white sand to rocky coves and inlets. On the Costa Brava, summer vacationers flock to San Pol, Roses, and Palafrugell; in all but the busiest weeks of July and August, the tucked-away coves of Cap de Creus national park are oases of peace and privacy. South of Tarragona, Salou has the best beaches, with a lively, palm-lined promenade. More tranquil are the beaches of the Delta de l'Ebre (Ebro Delta), reached by a scenic road from Amposta via Montells. There are views of the wetlands and, as you approach the beach, of the sea. Peñíscola's beach seems to go on forever and the old city rises out of the sea at one end. Benicàssim's long, crescent-shape beach is dramatic, with mountains rising steeply in the background. Valencia has a long beach that's wonderful for sunning and a promenade lined with paella restaurants; for quieter surroundings, head farther south to El Saler.

Rural Tourism: Getting in Touch with the Land

The beaches of the Costa Brava and the attractions of the cities draw the lion's share of visitors to Valencia and Catalonia, but the more relaxed appeal of rural tourism is fast becoming an important part of the hospitality industry.

Depending on your tastes, you can opt for a luxuriously remodeled *masía* (farmhouse) where the owner's family will pamper and indulge you. Or you might decide to rent a farm cottage and cook for yourself and your family. Many agro-tourism accommodations have swimming pools for the hot summer months. On the working farms, the kids can milk the cows, ride the horses, or rent bicycles to go off the beaten track. The adults can visit local villages (most of the masía owners are happy to provide a family member to act as a guide), try the local produce, visit nearby wineries, or just chill out.

Two areas with many rural retreats are La Garrotxa and Cerdanya. La Garrotxa affords easy access to the Parc Natural de la Zona Volcánica, where you can take walks or book hot-air-balloon rides over the lovely little towns of Santa Pau and Valle En Bas.

The Cerdanya region boasts some of the most scenic villages in all of Catalonia. The countryside here is another universe—snow-capped mountains contrast with deep valleys in the center of the region's biggest skiing area (which is surprisingly cheap).

The following tourist office Web sites have excellent English-language information: *www.turismerural.com* *www.turismegarrotxa.com* *www.costabrava.org*

WHAT IT COSTS (IN EUROS)

	¢	$	$$	$$$	$$$$
Restaurants	under €8	€8–€12	€13–€17	€18–€22	over €22
Hotels	under €60	€60–€90	€91–€125	€126–€180	over €180

Prices are per person for a main course at dinner, and for two people in a standard double room in high season, excluding tax.

Planning Your Time

Not far from Barcelona, the beautiful towns of Vic, Ripoll, Girona, and Cadaqués are easily reachable from the city by bus or train in a couple of hours. Figueres is a must if you want to see the Dalí museum.

Girona makes an excellent base from which to explore La Garrotxa; for that, you'll need to rent a car. Tarragona and its environs are definitely worth a few days; the city's Romanic wonders are best seen on foot at a leisurely pace, broken up with a meal at any of its fine seafood restaurants in the Serallo fishing quarter. Tarragona is easily reached via the RENFE train; allow an hour and a half to drive here from Barcelona, especially on weekends and in summer. If you are driving, a visit to the wineries in the Penedes region en route is well worth the detour. Most of Spain's *cava* comes from here.

From Tarragona it's a comfortable one-hour train ride or drive to Valencia. A car will allow you to stop off at the coastal towns of Peñíscola and Benicàssim. Valencia and its old town, great markets, the Santiago Calatrava–designed City of Arts and Sciences, and historical buildings can be covered in a few days; to sample the city's food and get a sense of local life, though, you might want to spend more time in the Barrio del Carmen.

A day trip to the nature reserve at Delta de l'Ebre is also highly recommended.

GETTING HERE AND AROUND

By Air

El Prat de Llobregat in Barcelona, 62 mi north of Tarragona, is the main international airport. Otherwise, Girona is the closest airport to the northern end of this area and a good option if you're flying to Spain via the United Kingdom. Valencia has an international airport with direct flights to London, Paris, Brussels, Lisbon, Zurich, and Milan.

By Boat and Ferry

Ferries leave both Barcelona and Valencia for Majorca and Ibiza Monday through Sunday.

Contacts Acciona Trasmediterránea (*www.trasmediterranea.es*).

By Car

A car is extremely useful if you want to explore inland, where much of the driving is smooth, uncrowded, and scenic. Catalonia and Valencia have excellent roads: if you're in the driver's seat the only drawback is the high toll fees on the *autopistas* (highways), but the coastal N340 can get clogged, so you're often better off paying.

By Bus

Sarfa operates buses from Barcelona to Blanes, Lloret, Sant Feliu de Guixols, Platja d'Aro, Palamos, Begur, Roses, and Cadaqués.

The trip from Barcelona to Tarragona is easy; eight to 10 buses leave Barcelona's Estación Vilanova-Norte every day. Connections between Tarragona and Valencia are frequent, and from Valencia buses continue down the coast and on to Madrid. Valencia's bus station is across the river from the old town; take Bus 8 from the Plaza del Ayuntamiento. Transport inland to Morella and Alcañiz can be arranged from Vinaròs, and Castellón and Sagunto have bus lines that head west to Teruel. Within Valencia, buses are the main mode of public transport; central lines begin at the Plaza del Ayuntamiento. Buses to the beaches and suburbs leave from the Plaza Puerta del Mar. The tourist office has more details.

If you want to go to Vic, contact **Segalés** (☎ *93/889–2577*). For Ripoll, call **Teisa** (✉ *Pau Claris 118* ☎ *93/215–3566*).

By Train

Barcelona's RENFE train system is an efficient and cheap way of discovering both inland and coastal Catalonia. From Plaça Catalunya and Sants Station, RENFE accesses all the major towns like Vic and even skiing towns like Puigcerdà in the lower Pyrenees. North and south along the Mediterranean, RENFE trains stop at all the major beach resorts of the Costa Brava and Costa Dorada—some at stations almost literally on the sand. From Valencia, you can take the RENFE to Madrid (via Cuenca) or Alicante (via Játiva).

The high-speed AVE train from Madrid to Barcelona stops in Zaragoza and Lleida. The trip to Zaragoza is around one and a half hours and starts at €53 each way; to Lleida, the trip is just over two hours and starts at €73 each way. From Lleida, there are numerous train connections to the rest of Catalonia, especially north to the Pyrenees.

The long curve of the Mediterranean from the French border to Costa de Valencia River encompasses the two autonomous communities of Catalonia and Valencia, with the country's second- and third-largest cities (Barcelona and Valencia, respectively). Rivals in many respects, the two communities share a language, history, and culture that set them clearly apart from the rest of Spain.

Girona is the gateway to Northern Catalonia and its attractions—the Pyrenees, the volcanic region of La Garrotxa, and of course the pristine beaches of the upper Costa Brava. Northern Catalonia is memorable for the soft, green hills of the Ampurdà farm country, the Alberes mountain range at the eastern end of the Pyrenees, and the rugged Costa Brava. Sprinkled across the landscape are *masías* (farmhouses) with austere, staggered-stone roofs and square towers that make them look like fortresses. Even the tiniest village has its church, arcaded square, and *rambla,* where villagers take their evening *paseo.*

The province of Valencia was incorporated into the Kingdom of Aragón, Catalonia's medieval Mediterranean empire, when it was conquered by Jaume I in the 13th century. Along with Catalonia, Valencia became part of the united Spanish state in the 15th century, but defenders of its separate cultural and linguistic identity still resent the centuries of Catalan domination. The Catalan language prevails in Tarragona, a city and province of Catalonia, but Valenciano—a dialect of Catalan—is spoken and used on street signs in the Valencian provinces.

The *huerta* (a fertile, irrigated coastal plain) is devoted mainly to citrus and vegetable farming, which lends color to the landscape and fragrance to the air. Arid mountains form a stark backdrop to the lush coast. Over the years these shores have entertained Phoenician, Greek, Carthaginian, and Roman visitors—the Romans stayed several centuries and left archaeological reminders all the way down the coast, particularly in Tarragona, the capital of Rome's Spanish empire by 218 BC. Rome's dominion did not go uncontested, however; the most serious challenge came from the Carthaginians of North Africa. The three Punic Wars, fought over this territory between 264 BC and 146 BC, established the reputation of the Carthaginian general Hannibal.

The coastal farmland and beaches that attracted the ancients now call to modern-day tourists, though a chain of ugly developments has marred much of the shore. Inland, however, local culture has survived intact. The rugged and beautiful territory is dotted with small fortified towns, several of which bear the name of Spain's 11th-century national hero, El Cid, as proof of the battles he fought here against the Moors 900 years ago.

EXPLORING THE COSTA BRAVA TO VALENCIA

Named for its wild and rugged coastline, the Costa Brava is where Salvador Dalí got his inspiration. His birthplace, Figueres, is home to his wacky museum, and the whitewashed fishing village of Cadaqués is where he built his even wackier residence.

Visitors are drawn to Tarragona region for its extensive Roman remains, including its amphitheater and aqueduct. Southwest of Tarragona are the wetlands of the Ebro Delta, rich in birdlife. Inland lie the rugged Sierra de Beceite mountains and the walled town of Morella. The Ebro River snakes its way through the interior, passing through the historical town of Tortosa. The interior is best explored by car, as the bus routes are limited. South of Tortosa, lively resort towns—including Benicarló, Peñíscola, and Benicàssim—dot the Costa del Azahar. The region's crown jewel is artistic Valencia.

ABOUT THE RESTAURANTS

The region of Alt Ampurdà, in the province of Girona, taking in the Costa Brava and its surrounding inland areas, has a justifiably renowned reputation as home to some of the country's premier restaurants. The seafood in this region is excellent, and the anchovies of the Alt Ampurdà are the best in Spain. In and around Valencia, indeed all along the Mediterranean coast, you're in the homeland of *paella valenciana*—a hearty rice dish flavored with saffron and embellished with seafood, poultry, meat, peas, and peppers. Prepared to order in a *caldero* (shallow pan), paella takes a full 20 minutes to cook, so it's not for when you're in a hurry. Good paella is fabulous, but it's often overpriced because of tourist demand, and it's usually best not to choose paella from a *menú del día*—it'll probably be bland and disappointing. ■ TIP→ **No native Valenciano would have paella for dinner: it's strictly a dish for lunch, and even the restaurants that specialize in it will only make it for two people or more.** A variant of paella is *arroz a la banda*, in which the fish and rice are cooked separately; the fish is fried in garlic, onion, and tomato, and the rice is boiled in the resulting stock.

Romesco, a spicy blend of almonds, peppers, and olive oil, is used as a fish and seafood sauce in Tarragona, especially during the *calçotada* (spring onion) feasts of February. If you're here for September's Santa Tecla festival, look for *espineta amb cargolins* (tuna with snails), perhaps accompanied by some excellent wine from one of the nearby Penedés or Priorat vineyards. The Ebro Delta is renowned for its fresh fish and eels, as well as specialties such as *rossejat* (fried rice in a fish broth, dressed with garlic sauce). *Jamones* (hams), *cecinas* (smoked meats), and *carnes a la brasa* (meats cooked over coals) are all staples of cooking in the interior, along with good *trucha* (trout), *conejo* (rabbit), and local *trufas* (truffles).

ABOUT THE HOTELS

Accommodations in beach resorts on the Costa Brava are significantly more expensive in the summer months. A good alternative if you're planning on driving around and exploring inland Northern Catalonia is to seek out *masías*, remodeled farmhouses that are often more kid-friendly and located in less touristy areas. Just north and south of Valencia, the towns of Puzol and El Saler have some famous luxury properties; the city itself offers a reasonable mix of hotels. Book months in advance if you plan to be in Valencia during Las Fallas, the annual festival when effigies of local politicians are set alight in the streets (mid-March).

NORTHERN CATALONIA

Northern Catalonia is for many *the* reason to visit Spain—particularly now that its principal city, Girona, serves as a point of entry to the region for many travelers arriving from the United Kingdom on cheap flights. Girona is a labyrinth of climbing cobblestone streets and staircases, with remarkable Gothic and Romanesque buildings at every turn; the *Call*—the Jewish Quarter here—is one of the best preserved in Europe. Streets in the modern part of the city are lined with smart shops and boutiques, and the overall quality-of-life in Girona is considered among the best in Spain.

The nearby towns of Besalu and Figueres couldn't be more different from each other. Figueres is an unexceptional town made exceptional by the Dalí Musuem. Besalu is a poster-perfect Romanic village perched on a bluff overlooking the River Fluvia, with several of the most prestigious restaurants in Catalonia. You'll eat well, if not cheaply. Less well known are the medieval towns in and around La Garrotxa: Ripoll, Rupit, and Olot all hold wonderful surprises and probably boast the best produce in the region.

GIRONA

8

97 km (60 mi) northeast of Barcelona.

Walk along the river to Plaça de la Independencia and admire Girona's best-known view: the pastel yellow, pink, and orange facades of the houses built right to the edge of the River Onyar reflected in the water. (If you drive here, park in the free lot next to the river, under the train trestle.) Cross the bridge from under the arcades in the corner of the Plaça and find your way to the tourist office, to the right at La Rambla Llibertat 1. Then work your way up through the labyrinth of steep streets, using the cathedral's huge baroque facade as a guide.

GETTING HERE AND AROUND

There are more than 20 daily trains from Barcelona to Girona (continuing on to the French border). Girona airport is also a destination for flights from London via the no frills airways, Ryan Air. Getting around the city is easiest by foot or by taxi; several bridges connect the historic old quarter with the more modern town across the river.

ESSENTIALS

Visitor Information Girona (✉ *Rambla de la Libertat 1* ☎ *972/226575* 🌐 *www.ajuntament.gi*).

EXPLORING

Girona's **cathedral** is known for its immense Gothic nave, which, at 75 feet, is the widest in the world and the epitome of the spatial ideal of Catalan Gothic architects. The **museum** houses the famous *Tapis de*

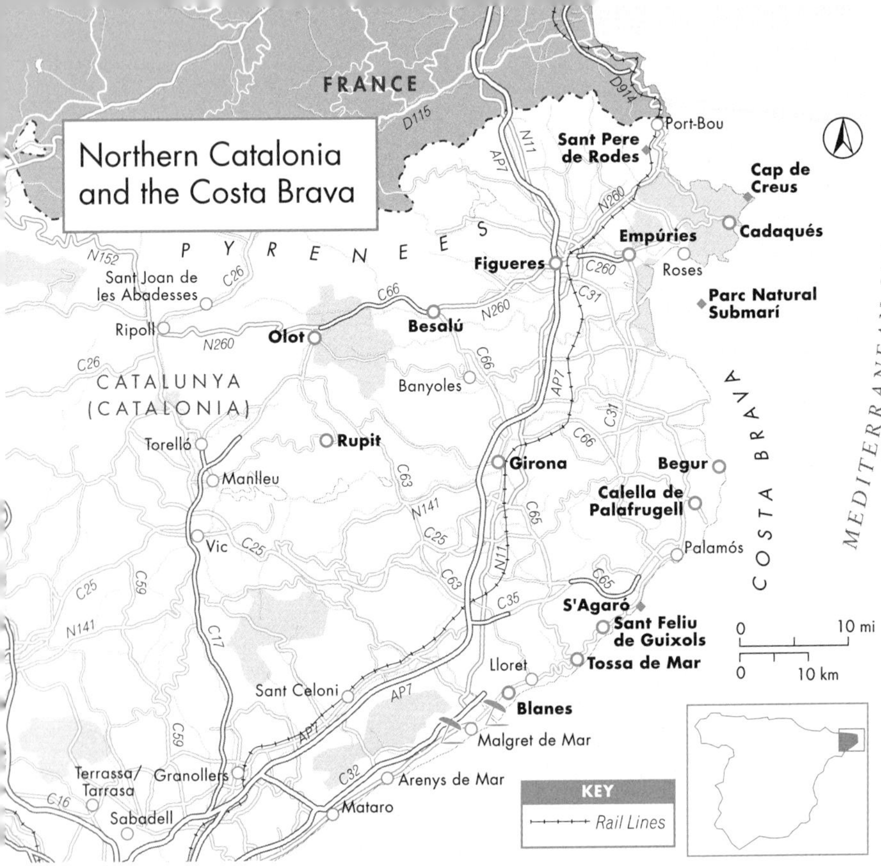

la Creació (*Tapestry of the Creation*) and a 10th-century copy of Beatus's manuscript *Commentary on the Apocalypse*. The stepped Passeig Arqueològic runs below the walls of the Old City; climb through the Jardins de la Francesa to the ramparts for a view of the 11th-century Romanesque **Torre de Carlemany** (Charlemagne Tower), the oldest part of the cathedral. *Museum and cloister €5 Apr.–Oct., daily 10–8, Nov.–Mar., daily 10–7.*

Next door to Girona's cathedral is the 11th-century **Palau Episcopal** (Bishop's Palace), housing the **Museu d'Art**, a good collection of Romanesque, Catalan Gothic, and modern painting and sculpture. Many of the pieces—like the stunning *Pieta* from the Chapel of Santa Caterina in Torroella de Montgri—were rescued from derelict churches and monasteries in the region. ✉ *Pujada de la Catedral 12* ☎ *972/203834* *www.museuart.com* *€2* *Mar.–Oct., Tues.–Sat. 10–7, Sun. 10–1; Nov.–Feb., Tues.–Sat. 10–6, Sun. 10–1.*

From the base of the Girona cathedral's 90 steps, go through the Sobreportes gate to the left and turn right to find the **Banys Àrabs**, or Arab Baths. Built by Morisco craftsmen in the late 12th century, long after Girona's Islamic occupation (795–1015) had ended, the baths are both Romanesque and Moorish in design. *www.banysarabs.org* *€2* *Apr–Sept., Mon.–Sat. 10–7, Sun. 10–2; Oct.–Mar., daily 10–2.*

A five-minute walk from the cathedral leads to the **Torre de Gironella,** the highest point in the Jewish quarter. It was here that Girona's Jewish community took refuge in August 1391 from rioters bent on its destruction, emerging 17 weeks later to find their houses in ruins. Decades of research and restoration have reclaimed much of the city's medieval Jewish past, when Girona was perhaps the most important center of Kabbalistic studies in the world. On December 20, 1998, the first Hanukkah celebration in 607 years was held in the gardens of the tower, with representatives of the Jewish communities of Spain, France, Portugal, Germany, and the United States present and Jerusalem's chief Sephardic rabbi, Rishon Letzion, presiding.

What was once the communal center of the 13th-century *Call,* or Jewish Quarter, is the site of the **Centre Bonastruc ça Porta,** hub of the reclamation of Girona's Jewish heritage. Its **Museu de Història dels Jueus** (Museum of Jewish History) has an extensive collection of medieval Jewish funerary tablets. ✉*Carrer de la Força 8* ☎*972/216761* 🌐*www.ajgirona.org/call/eng/index.php* 🎫*€2* 🕒*Nov.–Apr., Mon.–Sat. 10–6, Sun. 10–3; May–Oct., Mon.–Sat. 10–8, Sun. 10–3.*

The **Museu d'Història de la Ciutat**, in a former Capuchin monastery, is filled with memorabilia from Girona's long, embattled past, from Neolithic and Roman objects to paintings and drawings from the notorious siege by Napoléon's troops to the city's early modernization and the dark days of the Civil War. ✉*Carrer de la Força 27* ☎*972/222229* 🌐*www.ajuntament.gi/museu_ciutat* 🎫*€3* 🕒*Tues.–Sat. 10–2 and 5–7, Sun. 10–2.*

The interactive **Museu del Cinema** has movie-related paraphernalia going all the way back to Chinese shadows, the first rudimentary moving pictures. Look for the Cine Nic toy filmmaking machines, originally developed in 1931 by the Nicolau brothers of Barcelona and now being relaunched commercially. ✉*Carrer Sèquia 1* ☎*972/412777* 🌐*www.museudelcinema.org* 🎫*€4* 🕒*May–Sept., Tues.–Sun. 10–8; Oct.–Apr., Tues.–Fri. 10–6, Sat. 10–8, Sun. 11–3.*

Across the Galligants River is the church of **Sant Pere** *(Holy Father)*, finished in 1131 and notable for its octagonal belfry and the detailed capitals atop the cloister columns. Next door is the **Museu Arqueològic,** which documents the region's archaeological history since Paleolithic times. ✉*Pl. Santa Llucia 8* ☎*972/202632* 🌐*www.mac.es* 🎫*€5* 🕒*Museum June–Sept., Tues.–Sun. 10:30–1:30 and 4–7; Oct.–May, Tues.–Sun. 10–2 and 4–6.*

WHERE TO EAT

$$–$$$$ SPANISH ★ **Cal Ros.** Tucked under the arcades just behind the north end of Plaça de la Llibertat, this perennial favorite combines ancient stone arches with a crisp, contemporary interior and cheerful lighting. The cuisine is pungent and delicious: hot goat-cheese salad with pine nuts and *garum* (black-olive-and-anchovy paste dating back to Roman times), roast duck with olives, sturgeon from the Vall d'Aran, and a chocolate risotto with orange and strawberries not to miss. There is a reasonable *menu del día* for just €18. ✉*C. Cort Reial 9* ☎*972/219176* 💳*AE, DC, MC, V* 🕒*Closed Mon. No dinner Sun.*

$ FRENCH ✕ **Creperie Bretonne.** Located in a great spot for postdining nightlife, this little corner of France serves up delicious authentic French crepes, both savory and sweet, with a delicious range of fillings. The decor is pure '50s retro and the atmosphere young, buzzy, and convivial. ✉ *Cort Reial 14* ☎ *972/218120* 💳 *MC, V* ⏲ *Closed Mon.*

$$$$ SPANISH Fodor's Choice ★ ✕ **El Celler de Can Roca.** Girona's best restaurant boasts two Michelin stars; it's an unusual, spacious, and elegantly simple spot west of town that might serve anything from steak tartare with mustard ice cream to simple *vieiras* (scallops) with peas or a surf and turf of *pies de porc amb espardenyes* (trotters with sea slugs). If this sounds a mite indigestible, you can opt for something gentler, like clams in orange sorbet and Campari. ✉ *Carrer Can Sunyer 48, 2 km (1½ mi) west of Girona, Sant Gregori first roundabout to Taialà* ☎ *972/222157* 🌐 *www.cellercanroca.com* 💳 *AE, DC, MC, V* ⏲ *Closed Sun. and Mon., Dec. 23–Jan. 15, last wk of Aug.*

WHERE TO STAY

$ **Bellmirall.** This lovely pension in the Jewish quarter dates back to the 14th century and offers top value in the heart of Girona's historic section. Rooms are minimal, but there is a comfortable lounge and a delightful flower-filled patio where guests can take breakfast in summer. Ask for a room with a balcony view of the old quarter. **Pros:** friendly staff, ideal location, good for families. **Cons:** two rooms without private bathrooms en suite, no elevator, cathedral bells on the hour all night. ✉ *Carrer Bellmirall 3* ☎ *972/204009* *7 rooms* *In-room: no a/c, no phone, no TV. In-hotel: no elevator* 💳 *No credit cards* ⏲ *Closed Jan. and Feb.*

$$$ **Cuitat de Girona.** Rooms here have tile floors and gray furniture accented with red throw pillows: a bit of a Japanese touch, minimalist but soothing—along with an electric kettle for enjoying complimentary hot drinks in your room. A few steps from the Pont de les Peixateries Velles, Gustave Eiffel's 1877 bridge across the Onyar into the old city, the Cuitat has a good grasp of the details of hospitality—like big umbrellas for guests to borrow when it rains. **Pros:** friendly, English-speaking staff; good location; buffet breakfast included. **Cons:** no views. ✉ *Carrer Nord 2* ☎ *972/483038* 🌐 *www.hotel-ciutatdegirona.com* *44 rooms* *In-room: safe, refrigerator, Ethernet. In-hotel: restaurant, bar, laundry service, public Internet, public Wi-Fi, parking (fee), no-smoking rooms* 💳 *AE, DC, MC, V.*

$$ ★ **Hotel Històric y Apartaments Històric Girona.** This boutique hotel—the only one in the old quarter—is in a 9th-century house and offers rooms, suites, or apartments, with interesting historical architectural features: parts of a 3rd-century Roman wall and a Roman aqueduct can be seen on the ground floor and in one of the apartments. One dining room even contains a wall made in the pre-Romanesque *opus spicatum* herringbone pattern. The suite has views of the cathedral and Gothic vaulting overhead. The apartments, just steps from the Cathedral, are good value and available for any period from a day to a month. **Pros:** friendly, family-run, unbeatable location. **Cons:** cathedral bells on the hour all night. ✉ *Carrer Bellmirall 4A* ☎ *972/223583* 🌐 *www.hotelhistoric.com* *8 rooms, 7 apartments, 1 suite* *In-room: safe, refrigerator, kitchen (some). In-hotel: room service, laundry service, public Internet, parking (no fee), no smoking rooms* 💳 *AE, DC, MC, V.*

CLOSE UP

Catalonia's National Dance

The *sardana*, Catalonia's national dance, is often perceived as a solemn and dainty affair usually danced by senior citizens in front of the Barcelona Cathedral at midday on weekends. Look for an athletic young *colla* (troupe), though, and you'll see the grace and fluidity the *sardana* can create. The mathematical precision of the dance, consisting of 76 steps in sets of four, each dancer needing to know exactly where he or she is at all times, demands intense concentration. Said to be a representation of the passing of time, a choreography of the orbits and revolutions of the moon and stars, the circular *sardana* is recorded in Greek chronicles dating back 2,000 years. Performed in circles of all sizes and of dancers of all ages, the *sardana* is accompanied by the *cobla* (*sardana* combo), five wind instruments, five brass, and the director, who plays a three-holed flute called the *flabiol* and a small drum, the *tabal*, which he wears attached to his flute arm, normally the right.

FIGUERES

37 km (23 mi) north of Girona on the A7.

This bustling country town is the capital of the Alt Ampurdà; it's best know for the Dalí museum. Take a walk along the Figueres Rambla, scene of the *passeig* (*paseo* in Castilian; the constitutional midday or evening stroll), and have a coffee at one of the traditional cafés.

GETTING HERE AND AROUND

Figueres is one of the stops on the regular train service from Barcelona to the French border. Local buses are also frequent, especially from nearby Cadaqués, with more than eight services daily. The town is sufficiently small to explore on foot.

ESSENTIALS

Visitor Information Figueres (✉ *Pl. del Sol* ☎ *972/503155*).

EXPLORING

The **Teatre-Museu Dalí** pays spectacular homage to the unique artist. The museum is installed in a former theater next to the bizarre, ocher-color Torre Galatea, where the artist lived until his death in 1989. The remarkable Dalí collection includes a vintage Cadillac with ivy-cloaked passengers. In August, there are night visits from 10 PM to 1 AM (€12). Dalí is entombed beneath the museum. ✉ *Pl. Gala-Salvador Dalí 5* ☎ *972/677500* 🌐 *www.salvador-dali.org* *€11* ⏲ *Nov.–Feb., Tues.–Sun. 10:30–6; Mar.–May, Tues.–Sun. 9:30–6; June, daily 9:30–6, July–Sept., daily 9–8, Oct., Tues.–Sun. 9:30–6.*

SALVADOR DALI SITES

Artist Salvador Dalí is entombed beneath the Teatre-Museu Dalí, in Figueres. His former home, a castle in Pubol, is where his wife, Gala, is buried. His summer home in Port Lligat Bay, north of Cadaqués, is now a museum focused on the surrealist's life and work.

8

WHERE TO EAT AND STAY

$$$–$$$$ SPANISH ✕ **Hotel Duràn.** Once a stagecoach relay station, the Duràn is now a restaurant and hotel. Dalí had his own private dining room here, and you can take a meal amid pictures of the great surrealist. Try the *mandonguilles amb sepia al estil Anna* (meatballs and cuttlefish), a *mar i muntanya* (surf and turf) specialty of the house. Rooms ($$) are pretty standard. ✉ *C. Lasauca 5* ☎ *972/501250* 🌐 *www.hotelduran.com* ▭ *AE, DC, MC, V.*

$$ Fodor's Choice ★ **Hotel Empordà.** A mile north of town, this hotel and elegant restaurant is hailed as the birthplace of modern Catalan cuisine and has become a pilgrimage destination for foodies seeking superb French, Catalan, and Spanish cooking ($$$–$$$$). Try the *terrina calenta de lluerna a l'oli de cacauet* (hot pot of gurnard fish in peanut oil) or, if it's winter, *llebre a la Royal* (boned hare cooked in red wine). Guest rooms have a cutting-edge, Philippe Starck look. Staying here means you don't have to travel far for dinner, and you can sit in the sun and have a drink on the terrace. **Pros:** helpful, professional staff. **Cons:** sits on a major, noisy road. ✉ *Avda. Salvador Dalí 170* ☎ *972/500562* 🌐 *www.hotelemporda.com* *42 rooms* *In-room: safe, refrigerator, Wi-Fi* *In-hotel: restaurant, room service, bar, laundry service, public Wi-Fi, parking (fee), some pets allowed, no-smoking rooms* ▭ *AE, DC, MC, V.*

$ **Hotel Santa Ana Rural.** The village of Darnius, about a 20-minute drive north from Figueres toward the French border, would be worth a detour if only for the lovely rolling countryside of the Alt Ampurdà and the view of the Pyrenees—but even more so for this charming, quirky hotel. In disuse for many years, it reopened in 2006—with every room painted by Catalan artist Santial from floor to high ceiling in a different style. The Dalí, Monet, and Kandinski rooms have to be seen to be believed. The village itself is a pristine little gem, kept that way by the many well-to-do city dwellers who have bought second homes here. **Pros:** friendly personal service, intimate terrace for summer dining, horseback riding and kayaking nearby. **Cons:** less than ideal for families with children, in-room amenities minimal. ✉ *C. Major 5* ☎ *972/535623* 🌐 *www.santanarural.com* *11 rooms* *In-room: no phone, no TV (some), Wi-Fi. In-hotel: restaurant, room service, bar, laundry service, public Wi-Fi, pets allowed* ▭ *AE, MC, V.*

BESALÚ

34 km (21 mi) north of Girona; 25 km (15 mi) west of Figueres.

The town of Besalú saw the height of its importance in the early Middle Ages.

GETTING HERE AND AROUND

With a population of just over 2,000, the village is certainly small enough to stroll, with all the restaurants and sights within easy distance of each other. There is bus service to Besalú from Figueres and the surrounding Costa Brava resorts.

ESSENTIALS

Visitor Information Besalú (✉ *Pl. de la Libertat 1* ☎ *972/591240*).

EXPLORING

This ancient town's most emblematic sight is its **fortified bridge,** complete with crenellated battlements. **Sant Vicenç** (✉*Carrer de Sant Vicenç s/n*) is Besalú's best Romanesque church. The church of **Sant Pere** (✉*Pl. de Sant Pere s/n*) is all that remains of the 10th-century Benedictine monastery torn down in 1835. The ruins of the convent of **Santa Maria** on the hill above town are a panoramic vantage point over Besalú. The **tourist office** (☎*972/591240*) in the arcaded Plaça de la Llibertat can organize tours of Sant Pere as well as to the *miqwe,* the rare **Jewish baths** discovered in the 1960s. The tours cost €1.50 and should be reserved a day or so in advance. The extraordinary town of **Castellfollit de la Roca** perches on its prowlike basalt cliff over the Fluvià River 16 km (10 mi) west of Besalú.

WHERE TO EAT

$$$$ SPANISH ★ ✕**Els Fogons de Can Llaudes.** A faithfully restored 11th-century Romanesque chapel holds proprietor Jaume Soler's outstanding restaurant, one of Catalonia's best. Typical main dishes on the €55 *menú de degustación,* the set tasting menu (there's no à la carte), include *confitat de bou amb patates al morter i raïm glacejat* (beef confit with glacé grapes, served with mashed potatoes with nutmeg). ✉*Prat de Sant Pere 6* ☎*972/590858 or 629/782388* *Reservations essential, at least a day in advance* ▭*MC, V* ⊙*Closed Tues. Sept. 15–July 14, 2nd and 3rd wks of Nov.*

OLOT

21 km (13 mi) west of Besalú, 55 km (34 mi) northwest of Girona, 130 km (78 mi).

8

Capital of the Garrotxa area, Olot is famous for its 19th-century school of landscape painters and has several excellent Art Nouveau buildings, including one with a facade by Moderniste master Lluís Domènech i Montaner. The **Museu Comarcal de la Garrotxa** *(County Museum of La Garrotxa)* has an assemblage of Moderniste art and sculptures by Miquel Blai, creator of the long-tressed maidens who support the balconies on Olot's main boulevard. ✉*Carrer Hospici 8* ☎*972/279130* *€3* ⊙*July–Sept., Tues.–Sat. 11–2 and 4–7, Sun. 11–2; Oct.–June, Tues.–Fri. 11–1 and 3–6, Sat. 11–2 and 4–7, Sun. 11–2.*

WHERE TO EAT AND STAY

$$–$$$ SPANISH ✕**Restaurante Ramón.** Ramón's eponymous restaurant is the opposite of rustic: sleek, modern, and refined. The accent here is on seasonal fresh market cuisine, with occasional *cuina de la terra* (regional specialties) like *patata de Olot* (potato stuffed with veal) and *cassoleta de judias amb xoriç* (white haricot with sausage). ✉*Carrer Bolós 22* ☎*972/261001* *Reservations essential* ▭*V* ⊙*Closed Thurs.*

$$–$$$ Fodor's Choice ★ **Mas les Comellas.** This 15th-century farmhouse and agro-lodging is in the rolling green plains of La Vall d'en Bas outside of Olot, and, from the moment you arrive, owner Maria Angeles and the Casals family go out of their way to ensure you have a five-star experience. The five double rooms are superbly decorated—the common areas by the open fire, in the lounge room, and by the pool are cleverly thought out—and

the food is five-star in quality but at more accessible prices. There's horseback riding, cow milking, trekking, and hot-air ballooning nearby. **Pros:** family-friendly. **Cons:** off the beaten track. ✉ *Joanetes s/n, Vall d'en Bas, La Garrotxa, Girona* ☎ *628/617759* 🌐 *www.maslescomelles.com* *5 rooms* *In-room: no phone, DVD, Wi-Fi. In-hotel: restaurant, room service, bar, pool, bicycles, no elevator, laundry service, airport shuttle, parking (fee), pets allowed, no-smoking rooms* 💳 *AE, DC, MC, V.*

RUPIT

33 km (20 mi) south of Olot, 97 km (60 mi) north of Barcelona.

Rupit is a spectacular stop for its medieval houses and its food, the highlight of which is beef-stuffed potatoes. Built into a rocky promontory over a stream in the rugged Collsacabra region (about halfway from Olot to Vic), the town has some of the most aesthetically perfect **stone houses** in Catalonia, some of which were reproduced for Barcelona's architectural theme park, Poble Espanyol, for the 1929 International Exposition.

GETTING HERE AND AROUND

There is one daily bus from Barcelona (leaving at 6 PM) and the journey takes about two hours. Rupit is delightful to explore on foot, as well as making a good base for hiking in the surrounding mountainous countryside.

WHERE TO EAT AND STAY

$–$$ SPANISH ★ ✕ **El Repòs.** Hanging over the river that runs through Rupit, this restaurant ($–$$$) serves the best meat-stuffed potatoes around. Ordering a meal is easy: just learn the word *patata.* Other specialties include duck and lamb. The 11 rooms (¢) are rustic but cozy. ✉ *C. Barbacana 1* ☎ *93/852–2100* 💳 *DC, MC, V* ⊙ *Closed weekdays Oct.–Easter. Will open by arrangement.*

THE COSTA BRAVA

The Costa Brava (Wild Coast) is a rocky stretch of shoreline that begins at Blanes and continues north through 135 km (84 mi) of coves and beaches to the French border at Port Bou. Although the area does have it spots of real-estate building excess, there are many pockets—like Tossa, Cap de Begur, and Cadaqués—where the rocky terrain has discouraged overbuilding. On a good day here, the luminous blue of the sea still contrasts with red-brown headlands and cliffs; the distant lights of fishing boats reflect on wine-color waters at dusk. Umbrella pines escort you to the fringes of secluded *calas* (coves) and sandy white beaches.

COSTA BRAVA BEACHES AND SITES

The beaches closest to Barcelona are at **Blanes** (✉ *Crucetours* ☎ *972/314969*), where small boats can take you to Cala de Sant Francesc or the double beach at Santa Cristina between May and October.

The next stop north from Blanes on the coast road is **Tossa de Mar,** christened "Blue Paradise" by painter Marc Chagall, who summered here in 1934. The only Chagall painting in Spain, *Celestial Violinist,* is in the **Museu Municipal** (✉ *Pl. Roig i Soler 1* ☎ *972/340709* 🎫 €3 ⏲ *Oct.–May, Tues.–Sat. 10–2 and 4–8, Sun. 10–2; June–Sept., Tues.–Sat. 10–8, Sun.–Mon. 10–2 and 4–8*). Tossa's walled **medieval town** and pristine beaches are among Catalonia's best.

Sant Feliu de Guixols is 23 km (15 mi) north of Tossa de Mar, around hairpin curves, by hidden inlets. Tiny turnouts or parking spots on this route nearly always lead to intimate coves with stone stairways winding down from the road. Visit Sant Feliu's two fine beaches, the Romanesque Benedictine monastery (which now houses the City History Museum), Sunday market, and lovely **Passeig del Mar.**

S'Agaró, one of the Costa Brava's best clusters of seaside mansions, is 3 km (2 mi) north of Sant Feliu. The 30-minute walk along the **sea wall** from Hostal de La Gavina to Sa Conca Beach is a delight. Likewise, the one-hour hike from Sant Pol Beach over to Sant Feliu de Guixols for lunch and back is a superb look at the Costa Brava at its best.

Up the coast from S'Agaró, a road leads east to **Llafranc,** a small port with quiet waterfront hotels and restaurants, and forks right to **Calella de Palafrugell,** a pretty fishing village known for its July Habaneras festival. (*Habaneras* are Catalan-Cuban sea chants inspired by the Spanish-American War.) Just south is the panoramic promontory **Cap Roig,** with views of the barren Formigues (Ants) Isles and a botanical garden that you can tour with a guide daily (April–September 9–8 and October–December 9–6; weekends only January–February, 9–6) for €4. The left fork drops to **Tamariu,** one of the Costa's prettiest inlet towns. A climb over the bluff leads down to the parador at **Aiguablava,** a modern eyesore overlooking magnificent cliffs and crags.

From **Begur,** north of Aiguablava, you can go east through the *calas* or take the inland route past the rose-color stone houses and ramparts of the restored medieval town of **Pals.** Nearby **Peratallada** is another medieval town with fortress, castle, tower, palace, and well-preserved walls. North of Pals there are signs for **Ullastret,** an Iberian village dating from the 5th century BC.

L'Estartit is the jumping-off point for the spectacular **Parc Natural Submarí** *(Underwater Natural Park)* by the Medes Isles, famous for diving and for underwater photography.

The Greco-Roman ruins at **Empúries** are Catalonia's most important archaeological site. This port is one of the most monumental ancient engineering feats on the Iberian Peninsula. As the Greeks' original point of arrival in Spain, Empúries was also where the Olympic Flame entered Spain for Barcelona's 1992 Olympic Games.

Cadaqués, Spain's easternmost town, still has the whitewashed charm that made this fishing village into an international artists' haunt in the early 20th century. The Marítim bar is the central hangout both day and night; after dark, you might also enjoy the Jardí, across the square. Salvador Dalí's house, now a museum, still stands at Port Lligat, a 30-minute walk north of town.

The **Casa Museu Salvador Dalí** was Dalí's summerhouse and a site long associated with the artist's notorious frolics with everyone from poets such as Federico García Lorca and Paul Eluard (whose wife, Gala, became Dalí's muse and spouse) to filmmaker Luis Buñuel. Filled with bits of the surrealist's daily life, it's an important point in the "Dalí triangle," completed by the castle at Pubol and the Museu Dalí in Figueres. ✉ *3-km (2-mi) walk north from Cadaqués town center, along beach, Port Lligat* ☎ *972/251015* 🌐 *www.salvador-dali.org* 🎫 *€10* ⏲ *Mar. 15–June 14 and Sept. 16–Jan. 6, Tues.–Sun. 10:30–6; June 15–Sept. 15, daily 9:30–9.*

The **Castillo Pubol,** Dalí's former castle-home, is now the resting place of Gala, his perennial model and mate. It's a chance to wander through yet more Dalíesque landscape: lush gardens, fountains decorated with masks of Wagner (the couple's favorite composer), and distinctive elephants with giraffe's legs and claw feet. Two lions and a giraffe stand guard near Gala's tomb. ✉ *Pl. Gala Dalí s/n, Púbol-la Pera (Rte. 255 toward La Bisbal, 15 km [9 mi] east of A7)* ☎ *972/488655* 🎫 *€7* ⏲ *Mar. 14–June 14 and Sept. 16–Nov. 2, Tues.–Sun. 10–6; June 15–Sept. 15, daily 10–8; Nov.–Dec., daily 10–5.*

Roses, south of Cadaqués, is a detour for those who are persistent enough to get a reservation at the legendary restaurant El Bulli, famous for its molecular gastronomy (⇨ see the restaurant review in the Barcelona chapter).

Cap de Creus, north of Cadaqués, Spain's easternmost point, is a fundamental pilgrimage, if only for the symbolic geographical rush. The hike out to the lighthouse—through rosemary, thyme, and the salt air of the Mediterranean—is unforgettable. The Pyrenees officially end (or rise) here. New Year's Day finds mobs of revelers awaiting the first emergence of the "new" sun from the Mediterranean.

The monastery of **Sant Pere de Rodes,** 7 km (4½ mi) by car (plus a 20-minute walk) above the pretty fishing village El Port de la Selva, is one of the most spectacular sites on the Costa Brava. Built in the 10th and early 11th centuries by Benedictine monks—and sacked and plundered repeatedly since—this Romanesque monolith, now being restored, commands a breathtaking panorama of the Pyrenees, the Empordà plain, the sweeping curve of the Bay of Roses, and Cap de Creus. (Topping off the grand trek across the Pyrenees, Cap de Creus is a spectacular six-hour walk from here on the well-marked GR-11 trail.)

WHERE TO EAT

$–$$$$ ECLECTIC ✕ **Bar Cap de Creus.** Right next to the Cap de Creus lighthouse, this excellent Indian/Catalan restaurant has spectacular views. Don't miss the fish soup, with squid rings, shrimp, and cockles. There are occasional musical evenings with foot-tapping jazz or bossa nova. The owner, Chris Little, can also direct you to the very good Moroccan restaurant in Cadaqués itself, called Can Shelabi, which he part owns. ✉ *Cap de Creus, Carretera Cap De Creus, Cadaqués* ☎ *972/199005* 💳 *MC, V* ⏲ *Closed Nov.*

$–$$$ SEAFOOD ✕ **Can Pelayo.** This tiny, no-frills, family-run restaurant serves the best fresh fish and seafood in Cadaqués. It's hidden behind Plaça Port Alguer,

Continued on page 500

El Bulli's Letter Soup

SPAIN'S FOOD REVOLUTION

If milkshake waterfalls, bite-sized soup squares, and smoking cocktails sound like mouthwatering menu items, you may be ready to pull up a chair at the adventurous table of *la nueva cocina*. You won't be sitting alone: Foodies worldwide are lining up for reservations at Spain's hottest restaurants.

The movement, variously termed "*la nueva cocina*" (the new kitchen), "molecular gastronomy," or "avant-garde cooking," is characterized by the exploration of new techniques, resulting in dishes that defy convention. By playing with the properties of food, chefs can turn solids into liquid, and liquid into air. Olive oil "caviar," hot ice cream, and carrot-juice noodles are just a few of the alchemic manifestations of taste, texture, and temperature that have emerged.

Ferran Adrià of El Bulli in Roses is widely credited as the creative force behind Spain's new culinary movement, but chefs throughout the country have followed his lead. Beyond Spain, the movement is already having a seismic impact on the international culinary scene. Chefs from other European countries and the Americas have shifted their focus, looking beyond France—long esteemed as the world's culinary vanguard—to Spain for new techniques and inspiration. —*Erica Duecy*

FERRAN ADRIÀ—*LA NUEVA COCINA'S* VISIONARY

(clockwise from top left): Adrià's spiral of black sesame-seed crunch with coconut ice cream; razor-clam sushi with ginger spray; curry-glazed kaffir lime leaves; beet chips with vinegar powder; the El Bulli kitchen; Adrià in his Barcelona workshop.

Adrià has often been called the world's top chef, but his rise to fame didn't happen overnight. Adrià was an emerging talent in 1987 when he attended a cooking demonstration by legendary French chef Jacques Maximin who spoke about his belief that "creativity means not copying." By Adrià's account, that statement transformed his approach to cooking.

The changeover to conceptual cuisine—where techniques and concepts became the driving force for Adrià's creativity—occurred in 1994, when he developed a technique for producing dense foam from various liquids. A handful of new techniques emerged in those early years, but "nowadays, that process is accelerated," he says. "Within one year, I am working with several types of techniques."

Some of Adrià's most famous dishes include puffed rice paella, Parmesan marshmallows, a cocktail of frozen gin and hot lemon fizz, mini cuttlefish ravioli with bursting pockets of coconut and ginger, and almond ice cream swirled with garlic oil and balsamic vinegar. These creative concoctions are served at El Bulli in meals of 25 to 30 courses, with each course no more than a few bites.

GETTING THERE

Reservations are booked a year in advance for Ferran Adrià's El Bulli restaurant in Roses, located about 175 km north of Barcelona, set on an isolated beach. The El Bulli Web site features a comprehensive photo catalog of Ferran Adrià's creations from 1985 to present: 🌐www.elbulli.com ✉El Bulli, Cala Montjoi. Ap. 30 17480. Girona. ☎972/150457.

TRICKS OF THE TRADE

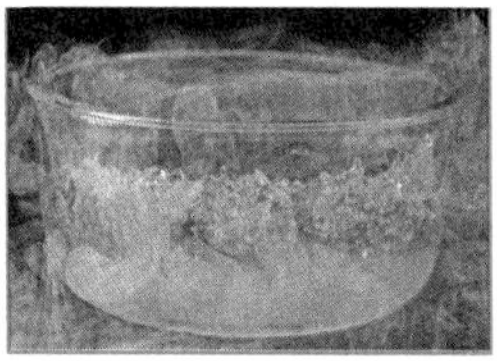

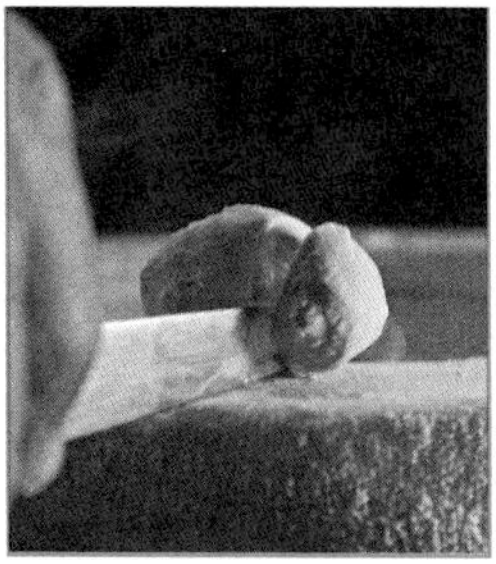

(clockwise from top left): Dry ice changes from a solid directly to a gas without becoming liquid; liquid nitrogen boils in a glass container at room temperature; a nitro-cooled pistachio truffle; a nitro-cooled caipirinha with tarragon essence.

Many techniques of *la nueva cocina* are borrowed from the food processing industry, including the use of liquid nitrogen, dry ice, and gellifying agents. This technological approach to cooking may seem like a departure from Spain's ingredient-driven cuisine, but avant-garde chefs say their creations are no less rooted in Spanish culture than traditional fare like paella.

One leading chef, Juan Mari Arzak, describes his approach as "not traditional Basque cooking, but rather culturally influenced cooking from the region, using the products of the region," he says. "We are doing things that haven't been done before." Using *lyophilization*, a freeze-drying technique, Arzak makes powders from peanuts and licorice. "You use the powder to add flavor to things," he says. "If you dust tuna with peanut powder and salt, it concentrates the underlying flavors to make the tuna taste like a more intense version of tuna."

Additionally, an unprecedented spirit of collaboration has defined the movement. "It is true that in other culinary movements chefs have been reluctant to share their knowledge," Adrià says. "Some people ask us, why do you share everything? Why do you share your secrets? The answer is that that's the way we understand cooking—that it's meant to be shared."

HOW DO THEY DO IT?

Daniel Garcia at El Calima using liquid nitrogen.

Liquid nitrogen: Just a small amount of this cryogenic fluid can be used to make instant ice cream from any liquid, including olive oil. Because liquid nitrogen can cause frostbite if it touches exposed skin, excess amounts of the substance must be allowed to evaporate before the food is served.

Dry ice: Bubbling sauces and cascading milk shakes can be made by adding dry ice to a liquid so it bubbles over the rim of its container.

Gellifiers: Fruit and vegetable juices can be used to make noodles with this technique. When juice is mixed with methylcellulose, a thickening compound derived from cellulose, it solidifies and can be extruded through a thin tube to form noodles.

Freeze-drying: The technique behind freeze-dried ice cream and soups is used to create concentrated powders from items like ham and berries. First, the substance is frozen in a controlled environment. Then, the pressure is lowered while applying heat so the frozen water in the substance becomes a gas.

THE SPANISH ARMADA

Among the most recognized contributors to *la nueva cocina* are Juan Mari Arzak, Martín Berasategui, Alberto Chicote, Quique Dacosta, Daniel García, Joan Roca, and Paco Roncero.

Chef Juan Mari Arzak and his daughter Elena.

Juan Mari Arzak is recognized for modernizing and reinvigorating Basque cuisine at Restaurante Arzak in San Sebastián, which he now operates with his daughter Elena, who represents the fourth generation of Arzak restaurateurs. Despite his deep culinary roots and decades-long career, Arzak says he works to maintain a fresh perspective. "It's important to look at the world through a cook's eyes, but to think like a little kid," he says. "Because when you are a boy, you have the capacity to be amazed and surprised." Restaurante Arzak, ✉Avda. Alcalde Jose Elosegui, 273 / 20015 Donostia / San Sebastian. ☎943/278465. 🌐www.arzak.info.

At his eponymous fine-dining restaurant in Lasarte, **Martín Berasategui** is known for his dedication to local products and fresh flavors. Notable dishes have included foie gras, smoked eel, apple terrine, and *percebes,* goose barnacles served with fresh peas in vegetable broth. Martín Berasategui, ✉Calle Loidi, 4 / E-20160 Lasarte-Oria. ☎943/366471. 🌐www.martin-berasategui.com.

The cuisine at **Alberto Chicote's** Nodo fuses Spanish and Japanese ingredients and techniques. His version of tuna tataki, for example, features seared tuna, which is macerated in soy sauce and rice vinegar then chopped and served with chilled garlic cream, and garnished with drops of olive oil and black olive powder. Nodo, ✉Calle Velázquez 150, Retiro/Salamanca, Madrid. ☎915/644044.

Quique Dacosta is the inventive self-taught chef at the helm of El Poblet in Dénia, a coastal town in the Alicante region. The restaurant specializes in contemporary seafood but can veer also into highly conceptual fare like his "Guggenheim Bilbao oysters," a dish of shimmering oysters in barnacle stock, glazed with a sauce made from aloe vera, agar agar (a seaweed-based gellifier), and powdered silver. El Poblet, ✉Ctra Les Marines, km. 3, Dénia. ☎965.784179. 🌐www.elpoblet.com.

IT'S AN ADVENTURE

Puffed-rice paella may not be a dish that appeals to every diner. But try to view the experience as an exploration of the palate, and a teaser for the mind. Practitioners of *la nueva cocina* typically serve their creative concoctions in small servings over several courses, a presentation style meant to stimulate a thoughtful, conscious eating experience. Sure, customers may not like everything they put into their mouths, but still they come to be dazzled by the bold flavors and unexpected textures. Don't be surprised to see diners exclaim in delight and awe as they dive into these new sensory experiences.

In his early 30s, **Daniel García** is one of the younger practitioners of *la nueva cocina*, as well as head chef at El Calima, the restaurant in the Hotel Don Pepe in Marbella. "My cultural inspiration comes from the area where I work, in Andalusia, the south of Spain," he says. Acclaimed dishes include gazpacho with anchovies and *queso fresco* snow, and a passion fruit flan with herb broth and eucalyptus-thyme essence. Hotel Gran Meliá Don Pepe, ✉Ave. José Meliá, Marbella. ☎952/764252.

Joan Roca is chef at El Celler de Can Roca in Girona, which he runs with his two brothers, Josep and Jordi. Roca is known for his work exploring the intersection between aroma and flavor, with dishes such as his "Adaptation of the Perfume *Angel* by Thierry Mugler," featuring cream of toffee, chocolate, gelée of violet and bergamot, and red fruits ice cream with vanilla. Savories include smoked lemon prawn with green peas and liquorice, and white and green asparagus with cardamom oil and truffles. El Celler de Can Roca, ✉Carretera de Taialá. ☎972/222157. 🌐www.cellercanroca.com.

Chefs in action, demonstrating their creativity in the kitchen: (top) Alberto Chicote with his assistants; (bottom) Martín Berasategui.

Paco Roncero is chef at La Terraza del Casino in Madrid, one of the city's most acclaimed establishments. He is considered one of Ferran Adrià's most outstanding students. "When I started working with Ferran (in 1998), my whole concept of cuisine changed," he says. "I started researching and trying to do new things. Now my cuisine is modern, *vanguardia*, without losing sight of tradition."

a few minutes' walk south of the town center. Try the *llobarro a la planxa* (grilled sea perch) if it's available. ✉ *Carrer Pruna 11, Cadaqués* ☎ *972/258356* ▭ *MC, V* ⊗ *Closed weekdays Oct.–Feb.*

$$$ SPANISH ★ ✕ **Eldorado Rambla.** Lluis Cruañes, one of the best-known and most respected restaurateurs on the Costa Brava, presides over this restaurant his father opened in 1940. Many transformations later, Eldorado is sleek and modern, and the menu features Mediterranean cuisine with a Catalan accent. Try the crayfish with almond sauce, or the rape (monkfish) with potato purée—and don't miss the chocolate mousse with olive oil and crystal salt. Dinner is à la carte, but the prix-fixe lunch at €16.95 offers a great choice of Eldorado's signature dishes; a second menu, for €10, provides a smaller choice of daily specials. ✉ *Rambla Vidal 19, Sant Feliu de Guixols* ☎ *972/821414* ▭ *MC, V* ⊗ *Closed Tues. Sept.–June.*

$–$$$ SPANISH ✕ **La Xicra.** Somewhat of an institution, this rustic, almost kitschy restaurant provides local fare that includes, in winter, *es niu,* a powerful combination of game fowl, fish tripe, pork meatballs, and cuttlefish, all stewed in a rich sauce. In summer the cuisine is lighter, with options that include fresh grilled fish served with a crisp green salad. ✉ *C. Sant Antoni 17, Palafrugell* ☎ *972/305630* ▭ *DC, MC, V* ⊗ *Closed Wed. and Nov. No dinner Tues.*

$–$$ SPANISH ✕ **Tragamar.** This seafood restaurant is a step above the rest with a menu that leans toward imaginative twists on traditional fish dishes, like crayfish prepared in a pastry cheese crust. More traditional *tapas* are also available, such as *jamón ibérico, gambas al ajillo* (garlic-spiked prawns), and *berberechos* (cockles), prepared with garlic and a dousing of *fino* (sherry). The restaurant is on the beach and has a large terrace overlooking the waves. ✉ *Platja del Canadell s/n, Calella de Palafrugell, Palafrugell* ☎ *972/615189* ▭ *MC, V.*

WHERE TO STAY

$$$$ ★ **El Hostal de la Gavina.** La Gavina has been the symbol of elegance on the Costa Brava since it opened in 1932, and the rooms and public spaces are graced with marble fireplaces, Catalan art and ceramics, and ebony furniture inlaid with ivory. The hotel has two full-time craftsmen on staff just to restore and care for the museum-quality appointments. Guests over the years have included Orson Welles, Frank Sinatra, Ava Gardner, and Sean Connery. **Pros:** huge (saltwater) pool with terrace and cabanas, family-friendly. **Cons:** no beachfront, restaurant is not great. ✉ *Pl. de la Rosaleda s/n, S'Agaró* ☎ *972/321100* 🌐 *www.lagavina.com* *58 rooms, 16 suites* *In-room: Wi-Fi.* *In-hotel: 3 restaurants, room service, bar, tennis courts, pools, gym, spa, water sports, bicycles, laundry services, concierge, public Internet, airport shuttle, parking (no fee), some pets allowed, no-smoking rooms* ▭ *AE, DC, MC, V.*

$ **La Riera.** Built into a medieval house, this rustic hotel and restaurant ($–$$$) is a quiet hideaway in lovely Peratallada, near Begur. The rooms have terra-cotta tiles and dark wood furniture; several have magnificent carved bed headboards. The hotel's dining room is in the former wine cellar, and menu options include such local specialties as *peu de porc amb cargols* (pig's feet with snails). Breakfast is a reasonable €5 extra.

Pros: location a lovely medieval village, good value, close to Costa Brava beaches. **Cons:** Peratallada is jammed in summer, dead in winter. ✉*Pl. de les Voltes 3, Peratallada* ☎*972/634142* 🌐*www.lariera.es* *8 rooms* *In-hotel: restaurant, room service, parking (no fee)* *AE, DC, MC, V.*

$$$–$$$$ **Playa Sol.** Open for more than 40 years, this hotel has the experience that comes with longevity. Rooms are done tastefully in red and ocher, and some overlook the sea. The Playa Sol is in the cove of Es Pianc on the left side of the bay of Cadaqués as you face the sea, a five-minute walk from the village center. All types of boats tie up here, thanks to Catalan writer Josep Pla, who spread its fame as the best place to drop anchor in Cadaqués. **Pros:** great ocean view, helpful English-speaking staff, good value. **Cons:** showers a bit primitive, extra charges for Internet and parking. ✉*Platja Pianc 3, Cadaqués, Girona* ☎*972/258100* 🌐*www.playasol.com* *49 rooms* *In-room: safe, dial-up, Wi-Fi. In-hotel: restaurant, room service, bar, tennis court, pool, beachfront, water sports, bicycles, public Internet, parking (fee), no-smoking rooms* *AE, DC, MC, V* *BP* *Closed mid-Dec.–mid-Feb.*

SOUTHERN CATALONIA

South of Barcelona, the coast and interior of the region offer a variety of things to see and do. Public transportation puts some of that—like the ancient city of Tarragona—in easy reach, but much of Southern Catalonia requires a car. The picture-postcard villages of Montsant and the Priorat wine country, the wetlands of the Ebre Delta, the natural beauty of the sierras west of Gandesa and Tortosa—wandering the network of country roads that connect these destinations is serenity at its best. Inland Valencia province beckons with hilltop fortress towns and dramatic villages like Morella and Ares del Maestre. Relatively few summer visitors to Valencia and the Levante get that far inland, though, as the long sweep of the Costa del Azahar from Benicarló to the Costa de Valencia and the Turia river delta has some of Spain's finest white-sand beaches and sailing waters, seaport villages steeped in history, thousands of acres of natural park, and the great city of Valencia itself.

8

TARRAGONA

98 km (60 mi) southwest of Barcelona, 251 km (155 mi) northeast of Valencia.

Just over an hour from Barcelona, Tarragona was the most important transalpine city of the Roman Empire for some 400 years. The Empire's Iberian provinces were ruled from Tarraco, as it was called and the emperor Augustus briefly governed Rome itself from here. By the 1st century BC its wine was already famous, and its people were the first in Spain to become Roman citizens. The apostle Paul preached here in AD 58, and Tarragona became the seat of the Christian church in Spain until it was superseded by Toledo in the 11th century. With its vast Roman remains, walls, and fortifications, and its medieval Christian monuments, Tarragona was selected by UNESCO in 2000 as a World Heritage Site. The city today is a vibrant center of culture and arts, a busy fishing and shipping port, and a natural jumping-off point for the towns and pristine beaches of the Costa Daurada, 216 km (134 mi) of coastline north of the Costa del Azahar around Tarragona.

GETTING HERE AND AROUND

Tarragona is well connected by train: there are hourly trains from Barcelona and regular train service from other major cities, including Madrid. There are bus connections with the main Andalusian cities, plus Alicante, Madrid, and Valencia.

The €14 Tarragona Card, valid for 24 hours (€19 for 48 hours), gives free entry to all the city's museums and historical sites, free passes on municipal buses, and discounts at more than 100 shops, restaurants, and bars. It's sold at the main tourist office and at most hotels.

Tarragona is divided clearly into old and new by the Rambla Vella. Tours of the cathedral and archaeological sites are conducted by the tourist office.

ESSENTIALS

Visitor Information Tarragona (✉ *Carrer Major 39 [just below the cathedral]* ☎ *977/245203*).

EXPLORING

Approaching from Barcelona, your first encounter with Roman Tarraco, 20 km (12 mi) from Tarragona on Rte. N340 (the Via Augusta), is the **triumphal arch of Berà,** dating from the 3rd century BC. From the Lleida (Lérida) road, or *autopista,* you can see the 1st-century **Roman aqueduct** that helped carry fresh water 32 km (19 mi) from the Gayo River.

★ Start your tour of Tarragona at the acacia-lined Rambla Nova, at the end of which is a balcony overlooking the sea, the Balcó del Mediterràni. Walking uphill along Passeig de les Palmeres, you'll arrive at the well-preserved remains of Tarragona's **amphitheater**. You can wander through the access tunnels and along the seating rows. In the center of the theater are the remains of two superimposed churches, the earlier of which was a Visigothic basilica built to mark the martyrdom of St. Fructuosus and his deacons in AD 259 (they were burned alive). ✉ *Parc de Miracle* ☎ *977/242579* 🎫 *€3* ⏲ *Wk after Easter–Sept., Tues.–Sat. 9–9, Sun. 9–3; Oct.– Easter wk, Tues.–Sat. 9–5, Sun. 9–3.*

The plans just inside the gate of the excavated vaults of the 1st-century Roman **Circus Maximus**, across the Rambla Vella from the amphitheater, show that these formed only a small corner of a vast arena (350 yards long), where as many as 23,000 spectators gathered to watch chariot races. Excavations reveal that the circus was one of the largest and best preserved in the Roman world. ☎ *977/241952* 🎫 *€3 joint entry with the Praetorium* ⏲ *Wk after Easter–Sept., Tues.–Sat. 9–9, Sun. 9–3; Oct.–Easter wk, Tues.–Sat. 9–7, Sun. 9–3.*

The former **Praetorium** served as Augustus's town house and is said to be the birthplace of Pontius Pilate. Its Gothic appearance is the result of extensive alterations during the Middle Ages, when it housed the kings of Catalonia and Aragón during their visits to Tarragona. The

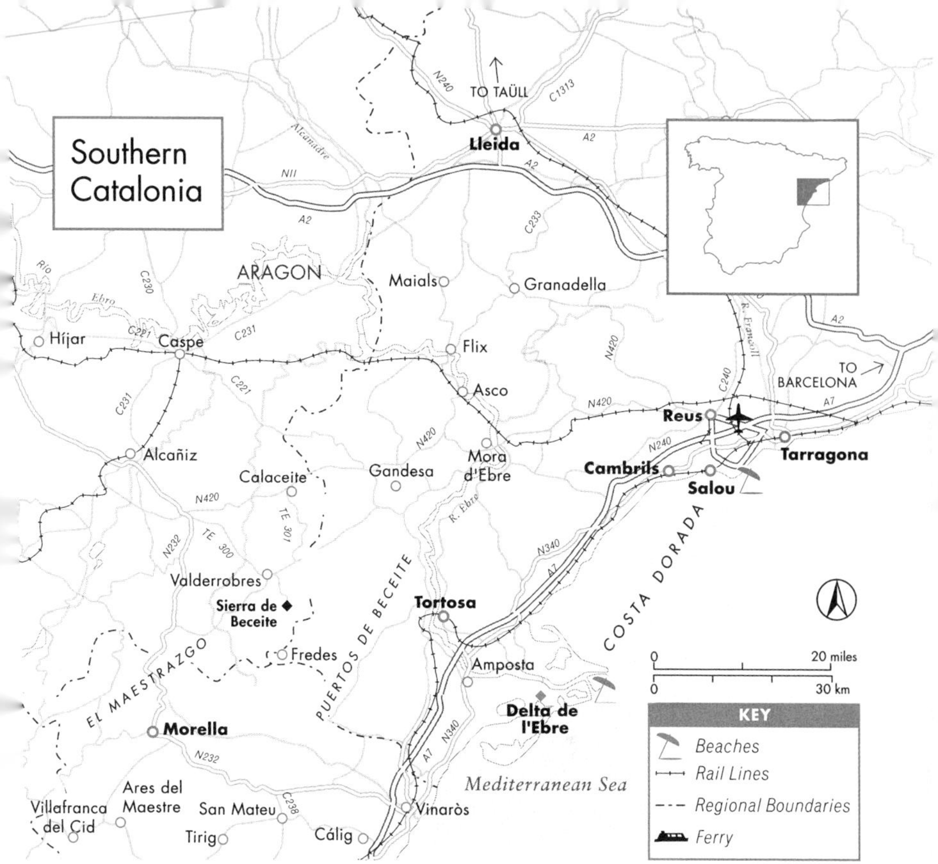

Praetorium now has a **Museu d'Història** (History Museum), with plans showing the evolution of the city; the highlight is the **Hippolytus sarcophagus,** which has a bas-relief depicting the legend of Hippolytus and Fraeda. The Praetorium is around the corner from the Circus Maximus. ✉*Pl. del Rei s/n* ☎*977/221736* *€3, joint entry with Circus Maximus* ⏲*Wk after Easter–Sept., Tues.–Sat. 9–9, Sun. 9–3; Oct.–Easter wk, Tues.–Sat. 9–7, Sun. 9–3.*

★ Next door to the Praetorium, in a 1960s neoclassical building, is the **Museu Nacional Arqueològic.** It includes Roman statuary, keys, bells, and belt buckles, and a Head of Medusa, with its piercing stare. There's an excellent video on Tarragona's history. ✉*Pl. del Rei 5* ☎*977/251515* *www.mnat.cat* *€2.40, free Tues.* ⏲*June–Sept., Tues.–Sat. 9:30–8:30, Sun. 10–2; Oct.–May, Tues.–Sat. 10–1:30 and 4–7, Sun. 10–3.*

Under the arcade on the Carrer de la Merceria is a stairway leading to Tarragona's **cathedral.** If no mass is in progress, enter through the 13th-century cloister—adorned with some of the finest Romanesque sculpture in Catalonia. The main attraction is the **altarpiece** of St. Tecla, a detailed depiction of the life of Tarragona's patron saint. The **Diocesan Museum,** next to the cloister, has a fine collection of medieval and modern religious sculpture, painting, and metalwork. ✉*Pl. de la Seu*

☎977/211080 🎫€3.50 ⏲June–mid-Oct., Mon.–Sat. 10–7; mid-Oct.–mid-Nov., Mon.–Sat. 10–5; mid-Nov.–mid-Mar., Mon.–Sat. 10–2; mid-Mar.–May, Mon.–Sat. 10–1 and 4–7.

Built by Tarragona nobility in the 18th century, **Casa Castellarnau,** a Gothic *palacete,* or town house, is now a museum with furnishings from the 18th and 19th centuries. The last member of the Castellarnau family vacated the house in 1954. *✉Carrer Cavallers 14 ☎977/242220 🎫€3 ⏲June–Sept., Tues.–Sat. 9–9, Sun. 9–3; Oct.–May, Tues.–Sat. 9–7, Sun. 9–3.*

Les Voltes (*✉End of Carrer Cavallers at Plaça Pallol*) is a Roman forum with a Gothic upper story and also one of the prettiest corners in Tarragona. The **Passeig Arqueològic** (*✉Through Portal del Rose*) is a path that skirts the 3rd-century BC Ibero-Roman ramparts and is built on even earlier walls of giant rocks. The glacis was added by English military engineers in 1707, during the War of the Spanish Succession. Look for the rusted bronze of Romulus and Remus.

At the **Serallo** fishing quarter, boats unload their catch at the quayside. Peek inside the market, where fish are auctioned to fishmongers and restaurateurs. Take Bus 2 here from the Portal del Rose. Near the fish market is the **Necròpolis i Museu Paleocristià** *(Paleochristian Necropolis Museum). ✉Av. Ramón y Cajal 80 ☎977/211175 🎫€2.40 combination ticket with Museu Arqueològic, free Tues. ⏲Mar.–May and Oct., Tues.-Sat. 9:30–1:30 and 3–6, Sun. 10–2; June–Sept., Tues.–Sat. 10–1:30 and 4–8, Sun. 10–2.*

WHERE TO EAT

$ SPANISH — ✕**El Tiberi.** Just steps off the Rambla Nova sits this bustling, rustic restaurant famous for its buffet (there's no à la carte) of Catalan dishes, from *butifarra* (Catalan sausage) to *pa amb tomaquet* (toasted bread with tomato and drizzled in olive oil). Finish off with *crema catalana,* Catalonia's answer to crème brûlée. The value is excellent at just €10 (lunch) or €11.25 (dinner and weekends), excluding drinks. *✉Carrer Martí d'Ardenya 5 ☎977/235403 ▭MC, V ⏲Closed Mon.*

$$$–$$$$ SEAFOOD — ✕**La Puda.** The prime quayside location guarantees fresh seafood, and a good option is the mixed platter of hake, sole, and monkfish with spicy *salsa Romesco.* But the daily lunch menu is generous and well-priced at €18.50. Locals love this place, even though the menu is tourist-accessible and written in several languages. The restaurant is simply decorated with a tile floor and white tablecloths. *✉Muelle Pescadores 25 ☎977/211511 ▭AE, DC, MC, V ⏲No dinner Sun. Oct.–May.*

$$$$ SPANISH ★ — ✕**Les Coques.** If you have time for only one meal in Tarragona, eat it at this elegant little restaurant in the heart of the old town. Both mountain and Mediterranean food are served, from hearty *cordero* (lamb) to *calamarsets* (baby calamari sautéed in olive oil, garlic, and secret seasonings) to *lubina* (sea bass). Wild *zetas* (mushrooms) are another specialty, prepared several tasty ways. The year 2009 marked the 25th anniversary of the restaurant. *✉Carrer San Lorenzo 15 ☎977/228300 ✍Reservations essential ▭AE, DC, MC, V ⏲Closed Sun. Closed 1st 2 wks in Feb. and late July–mid-Aug. No dinner Wed.*

$$–$$$ SPANISH ✕ **Les Voltes.** Built into the vaults of the 2,000-year-old Roman Circus Maximus, this vast dining room seating some 250 people could be a spectacular sight, but falls just short: with such a great setting, why put refrigerator cases out in plain view? The menu of fish and international fare includes the specialty of the house, *rap al all cremat* (monkfish in fried garlic); the Tuesday–Friday prix-fixe lunch—three courses with wine for €9.50—is a bargain. The bar is a popular late-night spot. ✉ *Carrer Trinquet Vell 12* ☎ *977/230651* ▭ *MC, V* ⊙ *Closed Mon. No dinner Sun.*

WHERE TO STAY

$ **Hotel Lauria.** An elegant-looking hotel on one of the classiest boulevards in the city, the Lauria has a homey, slightly old-fashioned feel. Guest rooms are basic, but the parquet floors and solid wood armoires with drawers make them agreeable. The hotel's terraces overlook the pool and patio area, the Rambla Nova, or—on the third floor only—the sea. This is the most pleasant place to stay downtown. **Pros:** good location, 24-hour room service. **Cons:** tiny TVs, bathrooms a bit cramped. ✉ *Rambla Nova 20* ☎ *977/236712* ⊕ *www.hlauria.es* *72 rooms* *In-room: safe. In-hotel: room service, bar, pool, laundry service, concierge, public Internet, public Wi-Fi, parking (fee), pets allowed, no-smoking rooms* ▭ *AE, DC, MC, V* *CP.*

$$ **Imperial Tarraco.** Overlooking the Mediterranean, this large hotel on the esplanade has comfortable guest rooms, and each has a private balcony—ask for a sea view. The large public rooms have cool marble floors and black leather furniture. The hotel caters to business travelers and conferences during the week, so off-season weekend accommodations can be a bargain. There is a small casino. **Pros:** spacious bathrooms. **Cons:** service a bit impersonal, building design is an eyesore. ✉ *Passeig Palmeres s/n* ☎ *977/233040* ⊕ *www.husa.es* *170 rooms* *In-room: safe, refrigerator, Wi-Fi. In-hotel: restaurant, room service, bar, tennis court, pool, laundry service, concierge, executive floor, public Wi-Fi, parking (no fee), no-smoking rooms* ▭ *AE, DC, MC, V* *BP.*

NIGHTLIFE AND THE ARTS

The **Teatro Metropol** (✉ *Rambla Nova 46* ☎ *977/244795*) is Tarragona's center for music, dance, theater, and cultural events, including *castellers* (human-castle formations), usually performed in August and September. Castellers is a centuries-old Catalan tradition in which participants in typical Catalan dress climb atop one another to create a towering human castle. On Rambla Nova, near Plaça Imperial Tarraco, is a life-size paean to Tarragona's gravity-defying castellers. At the top of the sculpture is a child with his hand in the air, the official gesture signaling the dismantling of the human tower.

Nightlife in Tarragona takes two forms: older and quieter in and around the Casco Viejo, and younger and more raucous in the southern, newer part of town, south of Rambla Nova. There's a row of restaurants and dance spots in the Puerto Deportivo, a pleasure-boat harbor separate from the working port.

For a dose of culture to go with your cocktail, try **Antiquari** (✉*Santa Anna 3* ☎*977/241843*), a bar with film screenings (usually Wednesday at 10 PM) and live music on Thursday, Friday, and Saturday nights. It's closed Sunday and Monday. For quiet talking, tippling, and tapas tasting, **El Càndil** (✉*Pl. del Forum* ☎*977/230916*) is a serene spot. In the shadow (literally) of Tarragona's cathedral is the casual café-bar **Plaça La Seu** (✉*Plaça de la Seu 5* ☎*977/230407*).

SHOPPING

Carrer Major has some good antiques stores; expect to haggle for bargains, and rummage thoroughly, as the gems are often hidden away. Also try the shops in front of the cathedral. **Poblet** (✉*Carrer Major 27–2943005* ☎*977/23492*) has antique furniture, lamps, fans, watches, porcelain, and bronze busts. **Mercat d'Antiguitats** *(antiques market)* fills the Plaça de la Seu, Carrer Merceria, and Plaça Forum on Sunday 9–3.

LLEIDA

150 km (90 mi) south of Taüll, 150 km (90 mi) east of Zaragoza.

The pleasant provincial capital of Lleida (Lérida in Castilian) borders the banks of the River Segre in the heart of Catalonia's farm country. The Romans settled here around 200 BC; the Arabs took control of the city in the 8th century.

GETTING HERE AND AROUND

There are up to 14 daily buses to and from Barcelona and around 22 trains. Both the train and bus stations are an easy 15-minute walk to the newly renovated Plaça de Sant Joan. The city is similarly well connected to the surrounding cities and towns, including Zaragoza and Tarragona. The historic part of town and the old cathedral can be reached by escalator from Plaça de Sant Joan (see Exploring below).

ESSENTIALS

Bus Station (✉*Calle Saricíbar*).

Train Station (✉*Pl. del Erminta s/n*).

Visitor Information Lleida (✉*Pl. de Ramon Berenguer IV* ☎*973/248840*).

EXPLORING

The landmark **La Seu Vella,** the old cathedral, was built between the 13th and 15th centuries in a transitional Romanesque-Gothic style and was converted to a military barracks after the 1707 siege of Felipe V, which makes it seem like a fortress. It's especially panoramic in late afternoon, when the low light spotlights the city, the Segre River, and the countryside beyond. Open daily 10–1:30 and 4–7:30, it can be reached by escalator and elevator (€0.40) from Plaça Sant Joan or on foot via Carrer Cavallers. The medieval chapel of **Sant Jaume Peu de Rome** is on the Catalan route of the Camino de Santiago pilgrimage. Lleida's sculptor Jaume Gort fashioned the sculpture of Saint James, and local artist Miquel Roig Nadal painted a work hung in the altar.

One block inside the old town, the most vital pedestrian artery, **Carrer Major,** runs parallel to the river. After 8 PM the newer area around Plaça Ricard Viñas is the hub of café, terrace, and restaurant life. Two key architectural sights here are **La Paeria,** a 13th-century Gothic mansion distinguished by massive stone archways, and the immense arched entrance to the **Antic Hospital de Santa Maria,** now housing a permanent archaeological display, the Sala d' Arqueologia, which includes Roman and Iberian finds from the region. ☎ *973/271500* *Free* ⊙ *June–Sept., Tues.–Fri. 10–2 and 6–9, Sat. 11–2 and 6–9, Sun. 11–2; Oct.–May, Tues.–Fri. 10–1 and 5:30–8:30, Sat. 12–2 and 5:30–8:30, Sun. 12–2.*

Worth checking out while you're here is the **Arc del Pont,** opposite the Pont Vell (Old Bridge), the bridge leading across the Segre just upstream from La Paeria. This arch was the ancient gateway into the walled city; the bronze figures depict the two fallen heroes of the local Ilergetes tribe, Indíbil and Mandoni. The 14th-century church of **Sant Llorenç** has a slender bell tower and porticoed doorway.

REUS

13 km (8 mi) northwest of Tarragona.

No city matches Barcelona, of course, for the sheer density of its Modernisme, but it all began here: Antoni Gaudí was born in Reus, and his contemporary, Lluís Domènech i Montaner—lesser known but in some ways the more important architect—lived and worked here for much of his earlier career. The oldest part of the city, defined by a ring of streets called "Ravals" where the medieval walls once stood, has narrow streets and promenades with many of Reus's smartest shops, boutiques, and coffee houses. Inside the ring, and along the nearby Carrer de Sant Joan, are some 20 of the stately homes by Domènech, Pere Caselles, and Joan Rubió that make Reus a must for fans of the Moderniste movement.

GETTING HERE AND AROUND

A new express bus service operates 23 daily buses between Tarragona (main bus station) and Reus (Plaça de les Oques); the trip takes less than 25 minutes (each way). There are four daily buses between Barcelona and Reus. There is also a regular train service connecting Reus with Tarragona and main Catalonian and Andalusian cities and destinations.

ESSENTIALS

Bus Station (✉ *Avinguda de Jaume s/n*).

Train Station (✉ *Sants Carrer de Viriat s/n*).

Visitor Information Reus (✉ *Pl. del Mercadal 3* ☎ *902/360200* 🌐 *turisme.reus.net*).

EXPLORING

The **Gaudí Centre,** a small museum that opened in 2007, showcases the life and work of the city's most illustrious son. There are copies of the models Gaudí made for his major works, a replica of his studio, and his original notebook filled with his thoughts on structure and ornamentation, complaints about clients, and calculations of cost-and-return on his projects—with English translations. A pleasant café on the third floor overlooks the main square of the old city and the bell tower of the

Church of Sant Pere. The Centre also houses the **Tourist Office**; come early and book a guided tour that includes the museum (11 AM) and two of Domènech's most important buildings: the Casa Navàs (1 PM) and the Institut Pere Mata (4:30 PM). The guided visits to Domènech's works are given October–June only, two Saturdays a month, depending on demand, and only in Catalan; July–September the tours are offered daily (except Sunday) and available in English. ✉ *Pl. del Mercadal 3* ☎ *977/010670* 🌐 *www.gaudicentrereus.com* 🎫 *Museum €6, combination ticket for tour and admission to other city museums €14* ⏲ *Oct.–June, Mon.–Sat. 10–2 and 4–8, Sun. 10–2; July–Sept., Mon.–Sat. 10–8, Sun. 10–2.*

Domènech's **Casa Navàs** (1901) is in the Plaça del Mercadal, in the center of the old city, opposite the *ajuntament* (town hall). The rich interior decoration includes mosaics, stained glass, tiles with characteristic Moderniste floral motifs, and oddly shaped leather chairs. The building is a private home; visits must be arranged with the Tourist Office, normally for groups of five people or more.

Institut Pere Mata. A five-minute drive from the center of Reus, Domènech's 1897 psychiatric hospital, still in service, is one of the masterpieces of the Catalan Moderniste period. Domènech had the revolutionary notion that what hospital patients really needed to get well is a healing environment, and he designed the Pere Mata as a complex of richly ornamented pavilions in a park. Building #6, the so-called Wing of the Distinguished, was originally a men's pavilion for patients from wealthy families; it's an astonishing fantasy of stained-glass windows, wrought-iron chandeliers, and decorative elements of ceramic tile, with a billiards room and a balcony above the dining hall for a chamber orchestra. No longer in use, it is open to visitors on guided tours, by arrangement through the Tourist Office in the Plaça del Mercadal. ✉ *Ctra. de l'Institut Pere Mata 1* 🎫 *€14 combination ticket for guided tour of the hospital, Casa Navàs, Gaudí Center, and all city museums* ⏲ *Oct.–June, 2 Sat. a month (advance booking required); July–Sept., Mon.–Sat. at 4:30.*

SALOU

11 km (7 mi) south of Reus.

If you're starting to crave a sunny afternoon on the beach, stop in Salou, a modern resort with a long esplanade of young palms. The town itself is long on glitz but short on charm. History buffs might appreciate that the conquerors of Majorca set out from the old port here in 1229 to retake the island from the Moors.

CAMBRILS

7 km (4½ mi) west of Salou, 18 km (11 mi) southwest of Tarragona.

Food lovers come to Cambrils to dine in the Joan Gatell restaurant. Refreshingly less developed than Salou, Cambrils has a marina and a bustling fishing port. The fine-sand beaches draw Spanish families, who stroll the town's cobbled streets.

GETTING HERE AND AROUND

There is regular bus service from Tarragona to Cambrils; it's a 15-minute journey, and you can ask to be dropped at the harbor front. The train station is a 15-minute walk from the center of town. The tourist office can advise on public transport schedules.

ESSENTIALS

Bus Station (✉ *Calle Vicente*).

Train Station (✉ *Carrer d'Andalusia*).

Visitor Information Cambrils (✉ *Pl. del Mercadal 3* ☎ *902/360200* 🌐 *turisme.reus.net*).

WHERE TO EAT

$$$$ SPANISH Fodor'sChoice ★ **Joan Gatell.** Since 1970, Joan Pedrell Font—assisted by wife Fanni and now son Jordi, too—has been preparing exquisite imaginative dishes starring the freshest fish and seafood. Try the baby eels, *fideos negros amb sepionets* (paella in baby-squid ink), or the superb *suquet*, a traditional Catalan fish stew. Increasingly popular with international visitors, Joan Gatell is a total eating experience—the modern fittings and clean lines inside the beautiful restored stone building make it welcoming, the service is attentive, and the loving cooking brings out the best in the local seafood. Clear some room on your credit cards! ✉ *Miramar 26* ☎ *977/360057* 💳 *AE, DC, MC, V* ⊗ *Closed Mon., mid-Dec.–mid-Jan., and 1st 2 wks of May. No dinner Sun.*

DELTA DE L'EBRE

77 km (48 mi) southwest of Tarragona, 60 km (37 mi) south of Cambrils.

GETTING HERE AND AROUND

As most of the delta is a protected area, there is very little public transportation here, though you can find buses to and from the nearest towns of Sant Carles de la Ràpita, Deltebre, and Amposta, from where you can rent boats to get to the mouth of the river. To get to the park from the AP7 toll road, take Exit 41 for highway N230 and follow signs to Amposta; then take TV3454 to Deltebre (Rumar).

ESSENTIALS

Visitor Information Amposta (✉ *Sant Jaume 1* ☎ *977/703453*).

EXPLORING

The estuary of the Ebro River, where it flows into the Mediterranean, embraces the largest wetland park in Catalonia, the 20,000-acre **Parc Natural del Delta de l'Ebre**—a vast region of salt marshes, sand dunes, reed beds, lagoons, small islands, and rice paddies. The waters teem with fish (largemouth bass, pike, black bullheads), while frogs, toads, and spiny-footed lizards populate the marshlands and beaches. The park is a major migration terminus and breeding ground for more than 200,000 birds of more than 300 species—an impressive 60% of Europe's bird species can be seen here during the year. A large variety of waterbirds (shoveler ducks, mallards, coots) descend by the thousands in October and November, when the rice has been harvested but the fields are still full of water. Morning and early evening in autumn and winter yield the best bird-watching. Unfortunately, the delta's most widespread critter is the mosquito, so you'll need a strong repellent to explore the wetlands. The **Park Information Office**, just off the roundabout at the edge of town (✉ *Carrer Doctor Martí Buera 22* ☎ *977/489679* 🌐 *www.deltebre.net*) has excellent itinerary maps and suggestions for a whole range of ways to visit the reserve: walking and cycling tours, blinds and towers for bird-watching, boat cruises, and places to rent kayaks. Outside are informative displays about fishing and rice growing, and upstairs is a small display about the ecology of the delta. There is also a small duck pond that the children will enjoy; it's open Monday–Saturday 10–2 and 3–6 and Sunday 10–2 and costs just €1.20.

WHERE TO EAT

$–$$ SPANISH ✕ **L' Estany.** At this restaurant (also known as Casa de la Fusta) smack in the middle of wetlands and rice paddies, chef-owner Luis García is committed to serving the best fish and game, caught just off the doorstep, and to honoring the cultural heritage of the area. Dishes include an abundance of tasty seafood-and-rice options. In a separate building, groups of 20 or more can arrange for a meal of regional fare served by a waitstaff in traditional dress. ✉ *Partida La Encanyissada s/n, en route from Amposta to Sant Jaume* ☎ *977/261026* 💳 *MC, V* ⏲ *Closed Mon. Nov.–Feb. No dinner Mon.–Thurs. Oct.–June.*

TORTOSA

80 km (50 mi) southwest of Tarragona.

Tortosa, straddling the Ebro River 10 km (6 mi) inland, was successively Roman, Visigothic, Moorish, and Christian, and was also the scene of one of the Spanish civil war's bloodiest battles. The Republicans, loyal to the democratically elected government and already in control of Catalonia, crossed the Ebro in July 1936 to attack the rebel Nationalists' rear guard. They got no farther than Tortosa, and were pinned down in trenches until they were forced to retreat, having lost 150,000 lives. You can see the city's sights in a few hours.

GETTING HERE AND AROUND

There are regular trains and buses from Barcelona, Lleida, and Tarragona. You can also catch a bus from here to the Delta de l'Ebre.

ESSENTIALS

Visitor Information Tortosa (✉ *Pl. España* ☎ *977/449648*).

EXPLORING

Tortosa's local parador, in the ruined hilltop **Castillo de la Zuda,** is worth visiting even if you don't stay the night. The castle (and town) passed into the hands of the Moors around the year 713, where it remained until its reconquest in 1153 by Ramón Berenguer IV, count of Barcelona. Moors, Christians, and Jews then lived peacefully together in the town for more than 300 years. From the castle walls are views across the fertile Ebro Valley to the Sierra de Beceite. ✉ *Parador Castillo de la Zuda* ☎ *977/444450.*

The Renaissance **Reales Colegios** comprise two former schools and a convent; Colegio Jaimé has a stunning arcaded patio, embellished with a frieze depicting the kings of Aragón. It houses an impressive archival collection, including a population map of Tortosa dated 1149 and signed by Ramón Berenguer IV. The 13th-century *El Llibre de les Costums de Tortosa* is the first judicial text written in Catalan. ✉*Sant Domènec s/n.*

Tortosa's **cathedral** looks baroque, but if you enter through the cloister you can see that the building itself is purely Gothic. It was common in 18th-century Spain to tack these exuberant stuccos on to Gothic structures; the style is called Churrigueresque, after its first practitioner, José Churriguera. ✉*Croera s/n* ⏲*Cloister daily, cathedral for mass only.*

WHERE TO EAT AND STAY

$–$$ SEAFOOD ✕**Rosa Pinyol.** Following in his mother's illustrious footsteps, chef and owner Joan Pinyol concocts regional dishes based on the Ebro Delta's teeming underwater population, from sea bass to sole, and fresh seasonal vegetables. Try the *rape asado con calcots* (grilled monkfish with calcots, a springtime green onion native to this region). The restaurant is just west of the old town, across the Pont de l'Estat (Estat Bridge). ✉*Hernan Cortés 17* ☎*977/502001* ▭*AE, DC, MC, V* ⏲*Closed Sun. No dinner Mon.*

$$$–$$$$ ★ **Parador de Tortosa.** Few sights around Tortosa can equal the superb view from the old Arab Castillo de la Zuda across the Ebro Valley to the Sierra de Beceite. Guest rooms have heavy wood furniture and terra-cotta floors. Rooms in the west wing have the best views of the old city and the Ebro River. The restaurant serves Catalan fare, including *bacalao con espinacas y allioli* (cod with spinach and garlic mayonnaise) and *pato del Delta con mandarinas* (duck with mandarins). **Pros:** tranquil, family-friendly, historical setting. **Cons:** no deck furniture on balconies, impersonal service, avoid the four rooms without views. ✉*Castillo de la Zuda s/n, Tortosa* ☎*977/444450* 🌐*www.parador.es* *62 double rooms, 10 suites* *In-room: safe, refrigerator. In-hotel: restaurant, room service, bar, pool, laundry service, public Wi-Fi, parking (no fee), no-smoking rooms* ▭*AE, DC, MC, V.*

MORELLA

★ *136 km (82 mi) south and west of Gandesa, 64 km (40 mi) northwest of Benicarló.*

The walled town of Morella stands on a towering crag in Castellón, the northernmost Valencian province. It's not immediately evident if you approach from the north, but from the south and east the land drops away sharply, creating a natural fortress—the scene of numerous bloody battles from the 11th through the 19th centuries.

GETTING HERE AND AROUND

Morella can be frustrating to reach via public transport, although there is a daily service from both Vinaròs and Castellón.

8

ESSENTIALS

Visitor Information Morella (✉ *Pl. San Miguel* ☎ *964/173032* 🌐 *www.morella.net*).

EXPLORING

Morella's main thoroughfare is the arcaded **Calle Don Blasco de Alagón.** Morella's **castle** is accessible through the gate on the Plaza de San Francisco, on the uppermost of the town's contoured streets. Just inside the gate is the ruined cloister and small church of an old Franciscan monastery; inside the church vault are several polychrome reliefs of Saint Francis. In 1088 El Cid scaled these walls and wreaked havoc on the occupying Moors. During the Carlist Wars of the 16th century, the castle became a stronghold for General Cabrera, who captured Morella in 1838 for Don Carlos, pretender to the Spanish throne. The walk up to the castle takes a good 15 minutes. ☎ *964/173128* 🌐 *www.morella.net* *€2* *Oct.–Mar., daily 10:30–6:30; Apr.–Sept., daily 9–9.*

The blue-tile dome on the church of **Santa María la Mayor** lends an exotic note to this otherwise Gothic structure. The larger of the church's two doorways, depicting the Apostles, dates from the 14th century. A spiral marble staircase leads to the raised, flat-vaulted choir. The sanctuary got the full baroque treatment, as did the high altar. The **museum** has a painting by Francisco Ribalta and some 15th-century Gothic panels. The church is near Morella's castle on Calle Hospital. *€1.50* *July–Sept., Tues.–Sun. 11–2 and 4–7; Oct.–June, daily 11–2 and 4–6.*

WHERE TO EAT AND STAY

$–$$ SPANISH **Restaurante El Mesón del Pastor.** In a restored 14th-century stone mansion on a steeply stepped street off Calle Don Blasco de Alagón, chef José Ferrer specializes in Maestrazgan fare (food from the Ares del Maestre region) such as *conejo relleno trufado* (rabbit stuffed with truffles), *conejo con caracoles* (rabbit with snails), and dishes with wild and farmed mushrooms. Desserts include *buñuelos con miel* (fried dumplings with honey), *tarta de almendras* (almond tart), and homemade *cuajada,* a firm curd yogurt. ✉ *Cuesta Jovaní 5–7* ☎ *964/160249* *DC, MC, V* *Closed Wed. No dinner Sun.–Fri. (except Aug.).*

$ Fodor's Choice ★ **Cardenal Ram.** As the name suggests, this is a hotel rich in history—the ancestral home of the important 15th-century Spanish prelate of that name. Its stone walls and ubiquitous coats of arms set the tone. The lobby mural depicts the 1414 visit to the town by the Antipope Benedict XIII. Rooms have pine floors, bare white walls, and high ceilings. The restaurant ($$) serves a succulent *solomillo* (sirloin) and fragrant *perdiz* (partridge). **Pros:** good value. **Cons:** no elevator, no parking nearby. ✉ *Cuesta Suñer 1* ☎ *964/173085* 🌐 *www.cardenalram.com* *19 rooms* *In-room: refrigerator. In-hotel: restaurant, Wi-Fi, no-smoking rooms* *MC, V.*

THE COSTA DEL AZAHAR

Named for the orange blossom and its all-pervading fragrance along this sweet coastal plain, the Costa del Azahar was transformed by the tourist-inspired building boom of the 1960s and '70s. Benicarló and

Peñíscola are, with Vinaròs, the northernmost towns on the Costa del Azahar (in Castellón de la Plana province), and Sagunto marks the start of the Costa de Valencia.

BENICARLÓ

77 km (48 mi) south of Tarragona, 46 km (29 mi) north of Benicàssim.

Benicarló has become a major tourist center. The harbor is a lively confusion of fishing and pleasure craft, and the beaches are jammed with locals and northern European sunseekers most of the year.

GETTING HERE AND AROUND

Benicarló is accessible via bus from other coastal resorts; there is increased service during the summer months. By car the A7 highway and the N340 are the main access roads into town.

ESSENTIALS

Visitor Information Benicarló (✉ *Ferreres Bretó 10* ☎ *964/475908*).

WHERE TO EAT AND STAY

$$$–$$$$ SEAFOOD ✕ **Casa Pocho.** Literally translated as "The Tubby One's House"—owner Paco Puchal is affectionately known as El Pocho (tubby)—this maritime-theme restaurant is famous for turning out good seafood. *Langostinos* (prawns) are a good choice, as are the *almejas* (clams), *lubina* (sea bass), and fillet of sole. The atmosphere is warm and convivial, with large Spanish families filling up the tables in summer. ✉ *San Gregorio 49, Vinaròs* ☎ *964/451095* ▭ *MC, V* ⊙ *Closed Mon. No dinner Sun.*

$$$ **Parador de Benicarló.** The main attraction here is the large, semiformal garden, which runs down to the sea—a perfect place to rest away from the crowded beaches. Public rooms are huge and bright, with wicker armchairs and white walls. Guest rooms have tile floors and functional furniture; ask for a seaside view. The restaurant ($$$) is well known for its fish and seafood dishes. **Pros:** gated access to the beach, playground for kids. **Cons:** boxy modern building, service can be perfunctory and bureaucratic. ✉ *Av. Papa Luna 5* ☎ *964/470100* ⊕ *www.parador.es* *108 rooms* *In-room: safe, refrigerator, Ethernet, Wi-Fi. In-hotel: restaurant, room service, tennis court, pool, beachfront, bicycles, laundry service, public Internet, public Wi-Fi, parking, no-smoking rooms* ▭ *AE, DC, MC, V.*

PEÑÍSCOLA

7 km (4½ mi) south of Benicarló, 60 km (37 mi) northeast of Benicàssim.

Peñíscola owes its foundation to the Phoenicians, though it later became the bridgehead by which the Carthaginian Hamilcar (father of Hannibal) imported his elephants and munitions to wage the first of the three Punic Wars. Carthaginian influence in Iberia reached its zenith some 20 years later, in 230 BC, but was eventually eroded by that of Rome.

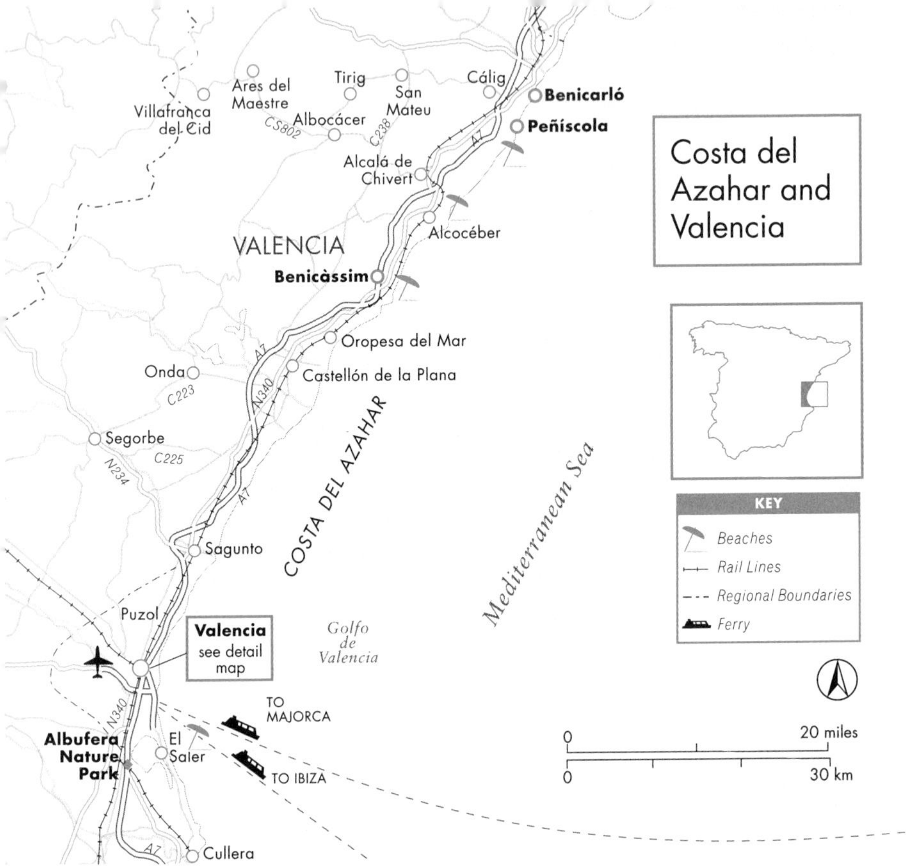

GETTING HERE AND AROUND

There is good bus service among Benicarló, Vinaròs, and Peñíscola, with greater frequency in summer. Trains run daily to Valencia and Barcelona.

ESSENTIALS

Visitor Information **Peñíscola** (✉ *Paseo Marítimo* ☎ *964/480208*).

EXPLORING

Fodor'sChoice ★ Peñíscola's **old town** is a cluster of white houses and tiny narrow streets on a steep promontory, with an impregnable-looking 14th-century fortress (used for part of the filming of Charlton Heston's *El Cid*) at the top. The beach here is one of the best in the area.

You can drive up to the **fortress**, but in summer the traffic makes it smarter to leave your car by the town walls and walk. Of chief interest are the chapel and study of the Antipope Benedict XIII, born Pedro Martínez de Luna and known affectionately in Spain as Papa Luna. Elected by a council of cardinals at Avignon in France, Benedict was eventually excommunicated by Rome as a schismatic in 1417; by this time accepted as the true Pope only by the Kingdom of Aragon, he fled to the castle at Peñíscola, where he lived until his death in 1423. From the upper courtyard, a flight of stone steps leads down to what were once the conclave hall and dungeons, now a small museum of the history of the Knights Templar, who built the fortress when the town was recaptured from the Moors. *964/480021 €3.50 Mar. 15–Oct. 15, daily 9:30–9:30; Oct. 16–Mar. 14, daily 9:30–5:30.*

WHERE TO EAT AND STAY

$ **Hostería del Mar.** Most guest rooms have balconies; some overlook the old town and others the beach. Inside, they have white walls, tile floors, and Castilian-style dark wood and leather furniture. The rustic public rooms surround a leafy pool terrace. Los Ficus restaurant serves fish in season, including *rape* (monkfish) and *merluza* (hake), and tasty *chuletas* (pork chops). Note that in July and August the all-meals-included or breakfast-and-dinner plan is required. **Pros:** good value, family-friendly. **Cons:** beachfront promenade can get raucous on summer nights. *Av. Papa Luna 18 902/480600 www.hosteriadelmar.net 86 rooms In-room; safe, refrigerator. In-hotel: restaurant, bar, tennis court, pool, Wi-Fi, some pets allowed (fee) AE, DC, MC, V.*

BENICÀSSIM

60 km (37 mi) southwest of Peñíscola, 13 km (8 mi) northeast of Castellón de la Plana.

Geographically blessed, the coastal town of Benicàssim is backed by the dramatic shapes of the Desierto de las Palmas mountain range, and the Mediterranean laps the town's long, sandy swimming beaches. Early vacationers—mostly wealthy Valencians—were suitably charmed, and the first vacation villa was built here in 1887. By 1900, Benicàssim was a genteel getaway, prompting its nickname: the Biarritz of the Costa de Azahar. This all changed during Spain's tourist boom in the early 1960s, when package tours arrived en masse along the coast, resorts replaced rusticity, and the local flavor of many coastal towns faded in the face of high-rise concrete jungles and quadrilingual menus. Although Benicàssim has its share of characterless apartment blocks, it was spared the worst resort-style excesses. Pleasant pedestrian promenades run alongside its clean, sandy beaches, and today most summer visitors are vacationing Spanish families. The well-preserved 16th-century **Torre de San Vicente,** a watchtower (not open to the public), once guarded against marauding pirates and looms over a popular beach of the same name.

8

GETTING HERE AND AROUND

There is frequent bus service to Castellón, which has a major train station with links to cities and towns throughout the country.

ESSENTIALS

Visitor Information **Benicàssim** (*Santo Tomas 74 964/300102 www.benicassim.org*).

EXPLORING

Seven kilometers (4 mi) inland from Benicàssim against the backdrop of silent mountain peaks is the **Monasterio del Desierto de las Palmas,** a Carmelite monastery founded in 1694. The small museum houses Carmelite religious figurines and clothing from centuries past. *Ctra. Desierto de las Palmas s/n 964/300950 Museum €2 Monastery daily 10:30–1 and 4–6, museum (by reservation) Sun. 1–2.*

WHERE TO EAT AND STAY

$$–$$$ Fodor'sChoice ★ **Voramar.** On the beach at the north end of town, this jewel box of a hotel was built in 1930 and renovated in 2000. Rooms facing the sea have large balconies with hammocks and gorgeous vistas of the Mediterranean. Prices dip considerably for mountain-facing rooms, and more so for rooms with no balcony. Rooms are plain and functional, with tile floors, white walls, and blonde-wood furniture. The lovely glassed-in dining room, overlooking the sea, is worth a trip in itself; try the *lubina* (sea bass) with julienne of fresh vegetables. **Pros:** family-friendly, eager-to-please staff, outstanding value. **Cons:** bathtubs a bit small, rooms opposite the beach face a busy main street. ✉ *Paseo Pilar Coloma 1* ☎ *964/300150* 🌐 *www.voramar.net* *58 rooms* *In-room: no a/c (some), DVD (some), Wi-Fi. In-hotel: restaurant, room service, tennis court, beachfront, water sports, bicycles, laundry service, public Wi-Fi, parking (fee), pets allowed, no-smoking rooms* *AE, DC, MC, V* *CP.*

NIGHTLIFE AND THE ARTS

Since 1995 Benicàssim has made a name for itself on the indie-music circuit, and thousands descend for the annual **Festival Internacional de Benicàssim** (🌐 *www.fiberfib.com*) in August. Past headlining artists include Nick Cave, Mouse on Mars, and Björk. On a more traditional note, late July brings the **Festival de Habaneras,** featuring sorrowful sailor songs on the guitar, often with Cuban rhythms. In summer, Benicàssim pulsates with the liveliest *marcha* (night "scene") on the Costa de Azahar. The city center is the nocturnal hot spot, and **Plaza de los Dolores** and **Calle Santo Tomás** are packed with pubs and clubs. Enjoy the Mediterranean's balmy nights on Benicàssim's seaside promenade, **Paseo del Pilar Coloma,** where graceful 19th-century villas have been converted into classy terrace bars and restaurants. A classic drinking spot is the elegant **Villa María** (✉ *Bernat Artola 36* ☎ *964/300662*). The outdoor terrace, surrounded by well-tended gardens, draws couples and groups of coworkers out for an evening cocktail. At the north end of the promenade is the **Voramar Hotel** (✉ *Paseo Pilar Coloma 1* ☎ *964/300150*) with a lovely beachfront terrace bar. A lively mix of tourists and locals enjoy the breezes off the sea in the early evening; the summer beverage of choice is a *clara* (beer mixed with lemon soda). Groove to rock and pop at **K'asim** (✉ *Av. Gimeno Tomás*), a happening nightclub that swarms with locals and foreigners in the summer.

VALENCIA AND ENVIRONS

Spain's third-largest city and the capital of the region and province of Valencia, Valencia is nearly equidistant from Barcelona and Seville. If you have time for a day trip (or you decide to stay in the coastal town of El Saler), make your way to the Albufera, a scenic coastal wetland teeming with native wildlife, especially migratory birds. Tourist buses leave from Plaza de la Reina daily.

VALENCIA

362 km (224 mi) south of Barcelona, 351 km (218 mi) southeast of Madrid.

Valencia is a defiantly proud city. It was the last holdout in Spain to stand with the Republicans against General Franco before the country fell to 40 years of dictatorship. Today it represents the essence of contemporary Spain—daring design and cutting-edge cuisine—but still deeply conservative and proud of its historical traditions. Despite its proximity to the Mediterranean, Valencia's history and geography have been defined most significantly by the River Turia and the fertile floodplain (*huerta*) that surrounds it.

The city has been fiercely contested ever since it was founded by the Greeks. El Cid captured Valencia from the Moors in 1094 and won his strangest victory here in 1099: he died in the battle, but his corpse was strapped to his saddle and so frightened the waiting Moors that it caused their complete defeat. In 1102, his widow, Jimena, was forced to return the city to Moorish rule; Jaume I finally drove them out in 1238. Modern Valencia was best known for its flooding disasters until the River Turia was diverted to the south in the late 1950s. Since then the city has been on a steady course of urban beautification. The lovely *puentes* (bridges) that once spanned the Turia look equally graceful spanning a wandering municipal park, and the spectacular futuristic Ciutat de les Arts i les Ciències (Ciudad de las Artes y de las Ciencias, or City of Arts and Sciences), designed by Valencian-born architect Santiago Calatrava, has at long last created an exciting architectural link between this river town and the Mediterranean. If you're in Valencia, an excursion to Albufera Nature Park is a worthwhile day trip.

GETTING HERE AND AROUND

Valencia is well connected by bus and train, with regular service to/from cities throughout the country, including 10 daily express trains to Madrid and around the same number to Barcelona.

Once you're here, the city has an efficient network of buses, trams, and metro. For timetables and more information, stop by the local tourist office.

The double-decker Valencia Bus Turistic (daily 10:30–7:30, until 9 in summer; departing every hour) travels through the city passing the main sights: a 24-hour ticket (€14) lets you get on and off at four main boarding points: Plaza de la Reina, Institut Valencià d'Art Modern (IVAM), Museo de Bellas Artes, and Ciutat de les Arts i les Ciències. The same company also offers a two-hour guided trip (€14) to and around Albufera Nature Park, departing from the Plaza de la Reina in Valencia. In summer (and during the rest of the year, depending on demand) Valencia's regional tourist office also organizes tours of Albufera: you tour the port area before continuing south to the lagoon itself, where you can visit a traditional *barraca* (thatch farmhouse) and end up in the Devesa Gardens, a nature park around the lake, and you can hire a boat to explore the rice paddies.

ESSENTIALS

Bus Station Valencia (✉ *Av. Menendez Pidal 13* ☎ *963/497222*).

Tour Info Valencia Bus Turistic (☎ *96/341–4400* 🌐 *www.valenciabusturistic.com*).

Train Station Valencia–Estación del Norte (✉ *Pl. de Toros, Valencia* ☎ *902/240202*).

Visitor Information Valencia (✉ *Pl. de la Reina 19* ☎ *963/153931* 🌐 *www.turisvalencia.es*).

EXPLORING

2 **Casa Museo José Benlliure.** The modern Valencian painter-sculptor José Benlliure is known for his portraits and large-scale historical and religious paintings, many of which hang in Valencia's Museo de Bellas Artes (Museum of Fine Arts). Here in his elegant house and studio are 50 of his works, including paintings, ceramics, sculptures, and drawings. On display are also works by his son, Pepino, who painted in the small, flower-filled garden in the back of the house, and iconographic sculptures by Benlliure's brother, the well-known sculptor Mariano Benlliure. To get here, cross the Puente de Serranos, turn right down Calle Blanquerías, and stop at No. 23. ☎ *963/919103* *€2; free weekends and holidays* ⏲ *Tues.–Sat. 10–2 and 4:30–8:30, Sun. 10–3.*

6 **Cathedral.** Valencia's 13th- to 15th-century cathedral is the heart of the city. The building has three portals—Romanesque, Gothic, and rococo. Inside, Renaissance and baroque marble were removed in a successful restoration of the original Gothic style, as is now the trend in Spanish churches. The Capilla del Santo Cáliz (Chapel of the Holy Chalice) displays a purple agate vessel once said to be the Holy Grail (Christ's cup at the Last Supper) and thought to have been brought to Spain in the 4th century. Behind the altar you can see the left arm of **St. Vincent,** who was martyred in Valencia in 304. Stars of the cathedral **museum** are Goya's two famous paintings of St. Francis de Borja, Duke of Gandia. To the left of the cathedral entrance is the octagonal tower **El Miguelete,** which you can climb: the roofs of the old town create a kaleidoscope of orange and brown terra-cotta, and the sea appears in the background. It's said that you can see 300 belfries from here, including bright-blue cupolas made of ceramic tiles from nearby Manises. The tower was built in 1381, and the final spire added in 1736. ✉ *Pl. de la Reina* ☎ *963/918127* *Cathedral and museum €3, tower €1.20* ⏲ *Cathedral Mon.–Sat. 7:30–1 and 4:30–8:30, Sun. 7:30–1 and 5–8:30. Museum and chapel Dec.–Feb., Mon.–Sat. 10–1; Mar.–May, Oct., and Nov., Mon.–Sat. 10–1 and 4:30–6; June–Sept., Mon.–Sat. 10–1 and 4:30–7. Tower weekdays 10–12:30 and 4:30–6:30, weekends 10–1:30 and 5–6:30.*

14 Fodor's Choice ★ **Ciutat de les Arts i les Ciències.** Designed by native son Santiago Calatrava, this sprawling futuristic complex is the home of Valencia's **Museu de les Ciències Príncipe Felipe** (Prince Philip Science Museum), **L'Hemisfèric** (Hemispheric Planetarium), **L'Oceanogràfic** (Oceanographic Park), and **Palau de les Arts** (Palace of the Arts). With resplendent buildings resembling combs and crustaceans, the Ciutat is a favorite of architecture

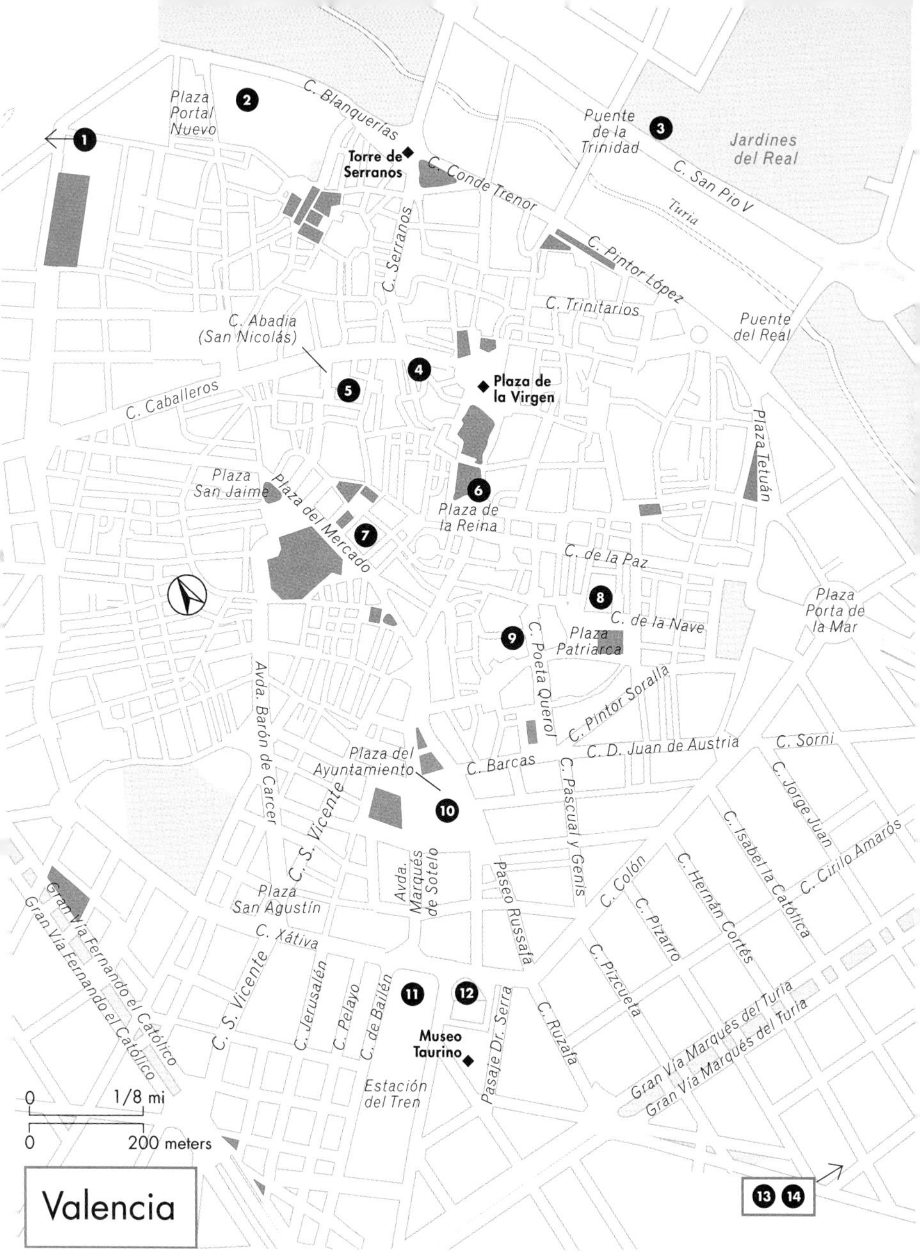

Casa Museo José Benlliure 2
Cathedral 6
Ciutat de les Arts i les Ciències 14
Estación del Tren 11
Institut Valencià d'Art Modern (IVAM) 1
Lonja de la Seda 7
Museo de Bellas Artes 3
Palacio del Marqués de Dos Aguas (Ceramics Museum) 9
Palau de la Generalitat 4
Palau de la Música 13
Plaza del Ayuntamiento 10
Plaza de Toros 12
Real Colegio del Patriarca 8
San Nicolás 5

CLOSE UP

A Good Walk

A good place to begin your stroll through Valencia's historic center is at the **cathedral** ❻ in the Plaza de la Reina (climb the Miguelete Tower for good city views). Cross the Plaza de la Virgen and before you to the left stands the Gothic **Palau de la Generalitat** ❹. Continuing down Calle Caballeros, you pass Valencia's oldest church, **San Nicolás** ❺. After spending time inside, walk to the Plaza del Mercado and the 15th-century **Lonja de la Seda** ❼. Opposite are the Iglesia de los Santos Juanes, whose interior was destroyed during the civil war, and the Mercado Central. Walk down Avenida María Cristina to the **Plaza del Ayuntamiento** ❿, one of the city's liveliest areas. A five-minute walk down Avenida Marqués de Sotelo then takes you to the Moderniste **Estación del Tren (Train Station)** ⓫. Next to it is the **Plaza de Toros** ⓬. Head back to the city center via the bustling Plaza del Ayuntamiento and then walk along Calle Poeta Querol to the wedding-cake facade of the **Palacio del Marqués de Dos Aguas** ❾. Cross the Calle Poeta Querol to Plaza Patriarca and enter the **Real Colegio del Patriarca** ❽. Wander old town's streets on your way north toward the Turia River—cross by Puente de la Trinidad to see the **Museo de Bellas Artes** ❸, adjoined by the Jardines del Real (Royal Gardens). Walk up Calle San Pio V to the Puente de Serranos and cross back to the 14th-century Torre de Serranos, which once guarded the city's entrance. Turn right for the **Casa Museo José Benlliure** ❷, and continue west to the **Institut Valencià d'Art Modern (IVAM)** ❶. On a separate outing, cross the Turia and stroll south to the **Palau de la Música** ⓭ and **Ciutat de les Arts i les Ciències** ⓮.

TIMING

Allow a day to tour the old quarter, the Museo de Bellas Artes, and the IVAM. Tack on a few hours the next day for the Palau de la Música and Ciutat de les Arts i les Ciències.

buffs and curious kids. The Science Museum has soaring platforms filled with lasers, holograms, simulators, and hands-on lab experiments. The eye-shaped planetarium projects 3-D virtual voyages on its huge IMAX screen. At the Oceanographic Park you can take a submarine ride through a coastal marine habitat. New additions include an amphitheater, an indoor theater, and a chamber-music hall. ✉*Av. Autovía del Saler 7* ☎*902/100031* 🌐*www.cac.es* 🎫*Museu de les Ciències €7.50, L'Hemisfèric €7.50, €11.20 for admission to both, L'Oceanogràfic €23.90* ⏲*Museum mid-Sept.–June, Sun.–Fri. 10–8, Sat. 10–9; July–mid-Sept., daily 10–9. L'Oceanogràfic mid-Sept.–June, Sun.–Fri. 10–6, Sat. 10–8; July–mid-Sept. 10* AM*–midnight. L'Hemisfèric daily shows generally every hr on the hr 11–8; Fri. and Sat., additional show at 9.*

⓫ **Estación del Tren.** Designed by Demetrio Ribes Mano in 1917, the train station is a splendid Moderniste structure replete with citrus motifs. ✉*C. Játiva s/n* ☎*963/106253*

❶ **Institut Valencià d'Art Modern (IVAM).** Dedicated to modern and contemporary pieces, the art institute has a permanent collection of 20th-century avant-garde works, European Informalism (including the Spanish artists Saura, Tàpies, and Chillida), pop art, and photography. The museum is out near the Turia riverbed's elbow. ✉*Guillem de Castro 118* ☎*963/863000* 🌐*www.ivam.es* 🎫*€2, free Sun.* ⏲*July–Aug., Tues.–Sun. 10–10; Sept.–June, Tues.–Sun. 10–8.*

7 **Lonja de la Seda** *(Silk Exchange).* Downhill from San Nicolás, on the Plaza del Mercado, is the 15th-century Lonja. It's a product of Valencia's golden age, when the arts came under the patronage of Ferdinand I. Widely regarded as one of Spain's finest Gothic buildings, its Gothic facade is decorated with ghoulish gargoyles, complemented inside by high vaulting and twisted columns. Opposite the Lonja stands the **Iglesia de los Santos Juanes** (Church of the St. Johns), whose interior was destroyed during the civil war, and, next door, the Moderniste **Mercado Central** (Central Market), built entirely of iron and glass. The bustling food market is open Monday–Saturday 8-2, with stalls full of fruit, vegetables, meat, fish, and nuts. ✉*Pl. del Marcado s/n* 🎫*Free* ⏲*Tues.–Sat. 10–2 and 4:30–8:30, Sun. 10–3.*

3 ★ **Museo de Bellas Artes** *(Museum of Fine Arts).* Valencia was a thriving center of artistic activity in the 15th century, and the city's Museum of Fine Arts is one of the best in Spain. To get here, walk behind the cathedral and cross the Puente de la Trinidad (Trinity Bridge) to the river's north bank; the museum is at the edge of the **Jardines del Real** (Royal Gardens), with fountains, rose gardens, tree-lined avenues, and a small zoo. The Royal Gardens are open daily 8–dusk. Many of the best paintings by Jacomart and Juan Reixach, two of several artists known as the Valencian Primitives, are here, as is work by Hieronymus Bosch—or El Bosco, as they call him here. The ground floor has the murky, 17th-century Tenebrist masterpieces of Francisco Ribalta and his pupil José Ribera, together with a Velázquez self-portrait and a room devoted to Goya. Upstairs, look for Joaquín Sorolla (Gallery 66), the luminous Valencian painter of everyday Spanish life in the 19th century. ✉*C. San Pío V s/n* ☎*963/870300* 🌐*www.cult.gva.es/mbav* 🎫*Free* ⏲*Tues.–Sun. 10–8.*

8

9 ★ **Palacio del Marqués de Dos Aguas** *(Ceramics Museum).* This building, near the Plaza Patriarca and across Calle Poeta Querol, has a fascinating baroque alabaster facade. Embellished with fruits and vegetables, it centers on the figures of the *Dos Aguas* (*Two Waters*), carved by Ignacio Vergara in the 18th century. The palace contains the recently reopened **Museo Nacional de Cerámica,** with a magnificent collection of mostly local ceramics. Look for the Valencian kitchen on the second floor. ✉*C. Poeta Querol 2* ☎*963/516392* 🎫*Palace and museum €3, free Sat. afternoon and Sun. morning* ⏲*Tues.–Sat. 10–2 and 4–8, Sun. 10–2.*

4 **Palau de la Generalitat.** On the left side of the Plaza de la Virgen, fronted by orange trees and box hedges, is the elegant eastern facade of what was once the Gothic home of the Valencia Cortés (Parliament), until it was suppressed by Felipe V for supporting the wrong (losing) side during the War of the Spanish Succession in the 18th century. The two *salones* (reception rooms) in the older of the two towers have superb woodwork on the ceilings. Don't miss the *Salon de los Reyes,* a long

corridor lined with portraits of Valencia's kings through the ages. Call in advance for permission to enter. ✉*C. Caballeros 2* ☎*963/863461* ⏲*Weekdays 9–2.*

13 **Palau de la Música** *(Concert Hall)*. On one of the nicest stretches of the Turia riverbed is this huge glass vault: Valencia's Palace of Music. Supported by 10 porticoed pillars, the dome gives the illusion of a greenhouse, both from the street and from within its sun-filled, tree-landscaped interior. Home of the Orquesta de Valencia, the main hall also hosts performers on tour from around the world, including chamber and youth orchestras, opera, and an excellent concert series featuring early, baroque, and classical music. For concert schedules, pick up a *Turia* guide or one of the local *periódicos* (newspapers) at any newsstand. To see the building without concert tickets, pop into the **art gallery,** which hosts free changing exhibits. ✉*Paseo de la Alameda 30* ☎*963/375020* ⏲*Gallery daily 10:30–1:30 and 5:30–9.*

10 **Plaza del Ayuntamiento.** Down Avenida María Cristina from the market, this plaza is the hub of city life, with the massive baroque facades of the *ayuntamiento* (City Hall) and the central Post Office facing each other across the park. City Hall itself houses the municipal tourist office and a museum of paleontology. ⏲*Ayuntamiento weekdays 8:30–2:30.*

12 **Plaza de Toros.** Adjacent to the train station is the bullring, one of the oldest in Spain. The best bullfighters are featured during Las Fallas in March, particularly March 18 and 19. Just beyond, down Pasaje Dr. Serra, the **Museo Taurino** *(Bullfighting Museum)* has bullfighting memorabilia, including bulls' heads and matadors' swords. ✉*Pasafe Doctor Serra 10* ☎*963/883738* 🎫*Free* ⏲*Bullring and museum Mon. 10–2, Tues.–Sun. 10–8.*

8 **Real Colegio del Patriarca** *(Royal College of the Patriarch)*. The colegio stands on the far side of Plaza Patriarca, toward the center of town. Founded by San Juan de Ribera in the 16th century, it has a lovely Renaissance patio and an ornate church, and its museum holds works by Juan de Juanes, Francisco Ribalta, and El Greco. ✉*C. de la Nave 1* 🎫*€1.20* ⏲*Daily 11–1:30.*

5 **San Nicolás.** A small plaza contains Valencia's oldest church, once the parish of the Borgia Pope Calixtus III. The first portal you come to, with a tacked-on, rococo bas-relief of the Virgin Mary with cherubs, hints well at what's inside: every inch of the originally Gothic church is covered with Churrigueresque embellishments. ✉*C. Caballeros 35* 🎫*Free* ⏲*Open for mass daily 8–9* AM *and 7–8* PM*; Sat. 6:30–8:30* PM*; Sun. various masses 8–1:15.*

WHERE TO EAT

$$–$$$$ SEAFOOD

✕**El Timonel.** Decorated like the inside of a yacht, this central restaurant (two blocks east of the bullring) serves outstanding shellfish. The cooking is simple but makes use of the freshest ingredients; try the *pescado de roca* (rockfish), grilled *lenguado* (sole), or *lubina* (sea bass). Also top notch are the eight different kinds of *arrozes*, including paella with lobster and peeled *mariscos* (shellfish). For a sweet finale, delve into the house special *naranjas a la reina,* oranges spiced with rum and topped with *salsa de fresa* (strawberry sauce). Lunch attracts businesspeople, and dinner brings in a crowd of locals and foreigners. ✉ *Félix Pizcueta 13* ☎ *963/526300* ▭ *AE, DC, MC, V* ⊙ *Closed Mon.*

$ MEDITERRANEAN ✕ **Fresc Co.** Don't be put off by the fact that this restaurant is one of a chain: it's still a great value restaurant and ideal for those who are desperate for something you rarely find in Spain: a salad bar! The buffet has excellent cold and hot (generally pizza or pasta) options, there is a choice of homemade desserts. The decor is warm and inviting with exposed brick walls and light wood furnishings. ✉ *Calle Felix Pizcueta 6* ☎ *963/106388* ▭ *MC, V.*

$$–$$$ SPANISH ✕ **La Pepica.** Locals regard this bustling informal restaurant, on the promenade at the El Cabanyal beach, as the best in town for seafood paella. Founded in 1898, the walls of the establishment are covered with signed pictures of appreciative visitors, from Hemingway and Manolete (Valencia is, after all, a bullfight city) to King Juan Carlos and the royal family. Try the *arroz marinero* (seafood paella) topped with shrimp and mussels or hearty platters of *calamare* (squid) and *langostinos* (prawns). Save room for the delectable tarts made with fruit in season. ✉ *Paseo Neptuno 6* ☎ *963/710366* ▭ *AE, DC, MC, V* ⊙ *Closed last 2 wks of Nov. No dinner Mon.–Thurs. Sept.–May.*

$$–$$$ SPANISH ✕ **La Riuà.** A favorite with Valencia's well connected and well-to-do since 1982, this family-run restaurant a few steps from the Plaza de la Reina specializes in seafood dishes like *anguilas* (eels) prepared with *all i pebre* (garlic and pepper), *pulpitos guisados* (stewed baby octopus), and traditional paellas. Lunch begins at 2 and not a moment before. The walls are covered with decorative ceramics and the gastronomic awards the restaurant has won over the years. ✉ *C. del Mar 27* ☎ *963/914571* ✍ *Reservations essential.* ▭ *AE, DC, MC, V* ⊙ *Closed Sun., Easter wk, and Aug. No dinner Mon.*

$$$$ MEDITERRANEAN ✕ **La Sucursal.** La Sucursal is solid proof that Valencia can match the cutting-edge contemporary cuisine of its big brother Barcelona. The thoroughly modern but cozy spot within the IVAM (Institut Valencia d'Art Modern) is simply a taste sensation. You won't leave with a full wallet, but it's unlikely you'll sample deer carpaccio anywhere else or partake of an *arroz caldoso de bogavante* (rice soup with lobster) as good. At times the food veers toward the indescribable, but there's barely a weakness. Best to let the attentive staff make suggestions and go with it. ✉ *Guillem de Castro 188* ☎ *963/746665* ✍ *Reservations essential* ▭ *AE, DC, MC, V* ⊙ *Closed Sun. No lunch Sat.*

WHERE TO STAY

$$$–$$$$ ★ **Ad Hoc.** This 19th-century town house, restored in 1994, is on a quiet street at the edge of the old city, a minute's walk from the Plaza Almoina and the Cathedral in one direction, and steps from the Turia gardens in the other. Owner Luis García Alarcón is an antiquarian, and the hotel reflects his eye for classic design and architectural elegance: original decorative brickwork, geometric tile floors, and curved ceiling beams. A buffet breakfast is included. The restaurant ($$$–$$$$) is excellent, too; try the unusual paella with quail and seasonal mushrooms, or the suckling lamb, and top it off with a divine passion-fruit sorbet. **Pros:** ideal location—close to sights but quiet, a courteous, helpful staff, great value. **Cons:** navigating by car and parking can be a nightmare. ✉ *Boix*

4 ☎963/919140 🌐www.adhochoteles.com ⇨28 rooms ☝In-room: safe, Ethernet, Wi-Fi. In-hotel: restaurant, room service, laundry service, public Internet, public Wi-Fi, pets allowed, no-smoking rooms ▭AE, DC, MC, V.

$$ **Catalonia Excelsior.** For its price category, this hotel in a 1930s building offers the best value. From the Art Deco restaurant-cum-bar, a spiral marble staircase leads to a dark wood-panel salon with a terrace. Rooms have parquet wood floors, modern furnishings, and soothing pastel-colored walls. The general vibe is very friendly, and the hotel is central, just steps from the Plaza del Ayuntamiento. **Pros:** good location, good value. **Cons:** nothing special but fine for a short stay. ✉*Barcelonina 5 ☎963/514612 🌐www.hoteles-catalonia.es ⇨81 rooms ☝In-hotel: restaurant, bar, Wi-Fi ▭AE, DC, MC, V.*

$$–$$$$ **Neptuno.** This beachfront hotel is a slick modern newcomer to the city's accommodation options. Giant colorful abstracts decorate the public spaces, and the rooms are stylish and minimalist with excellent facilities, including hydromassage tubs, that appeal to business travelers and families. A spacious sun terrace overlooks the tempting swath of beach, while the gourmet restaurant has fast made its mark on the local culinary scene. **Pros:** superb restaurant, great location for families. **Cons:** a 15-minute walk to the historic center, gets booked up early in the summer. ✉*Paseo de Neptuno 2 ☎963/567777 🌐www.hotelneptunovalencia.com ⇨58 rooms, 2 suites ☝In-room: Wi-Fi. In-hotel: restaurant, pool, gym, spa, Wi-Fi ▭AE, MC, V 🍽 EP.*

$$$–$$$$ **Palau de la Mar.** In a restored 19th-century palace, this self-proclaimed boutique hotel looks out at the Porta de La Mar, which marked the entry to the old walled quarter of Valencia. White marble and frosted glass provide a sense of light and quiet elegance, and the spa is truly luxurious. Ask for a room facing the interior courtyard. The Senzone ($$$$) restaurant serves gourmet cuisine like rock octopus in a citrus sauce. **Pros:** big bathrooms with double sinks, great location. **Cons:** rooms on the top floor have low, slanted ceilings. ✉*Av. Navarro Reventer 14 ☎963/162884 🌐www.fuenso.com ⇨66 rooms ☝In-room: safe, DVD (some), Ethernet, Wi-Fi. In-hotel: restaurant, room service, pool, gym, spa, laundry service, concierge, public Internet, public Wi-Fi, airport shuttle, parking (fee), some pets allowed, no-smoking rooms ▭AE, DC, MC, V.*

$$$$ ★ **Reina Victoria.** Valencia's grande dame is an excellent choice if you want timeworn charm and a good location next to the Plaza del Ayuntamiento. The spacious reception rooms have cool marble floors (with rugs to take the chill off), as does the smart, classy restaurant. The smallish guest rooms are clothed in green or burgundy chintz and deep-pile carpets. A buffet breakfast is included in the rate. **Pros:** large rooms, walking distance to both central railway station and major sights of the old city. **Cons:** room soundproofing not up to par, service can be perfunctory. ✉*Barcas 4 ☎963/520487 🌐www.husa.es ⇨97 rooms ☝In-room: safe, refrigerator, Wi-Fi. In-hotel: restaurant, room service, bar, laundry service, Wi-Fi, no-smoking rooms ▭AE, DC, MC, V.*

$$$$ **Sidi Saler.** The stretch of coastline just south of Valencia suffers from ongoing construction, but this hotel, surrounded by the El Saler Nature

Park, is an oasis of luxury. All the brightly furnished guest rooms have balconies with views of the sea or gardens, and breakfast is included in the price—fill up on a buffet of *revueltos* (scrambled eggs), breads, and fresh fruit. **Pros:** family-friendly, free shuttle bus to/from Valencia, good golfing nearby. **Cons:** rooms a bit overfurnished. ✉ *Gola del Puchol s/n, Playa El Saler* ☎ *961/610411* 🌐 *www.hotelessidi.es* *276 rooms* *In-room: safe, Ethernet, Wi-Fi. In-hotel: restaurant, room service, 2 bars, tennis court, 2 pools, gym, spa, beachfront, bicycles, laundry service, public Internet, public Wi-Fi, parking (no fee), some pets allowed (fee), no-smoking rooms* 💳 *AE, DC, MC, V* *BP.*

NIGHTLIFE AND THE ARTS

Sleep is usually anathema here, and you can experience Valencia's nocturnal way of life at any time except summer, when locals disappear on vacation and the international set moves to the beach. Nightlife in the old town centers around Barrio del Carmen, a lively web of streets that unfolds north of Plaza del Mercado. A string of very popular bars and pubs dots Calle Caballeros, leading off Plaza de la Virgen; the Plaza del Tossal also has some popular cafés, as does Calle Alta, leading off Plaza San Jaime. Some of the funkier, newer places are to be found in and around Plaza del Carmen. Across the river in the new town, look for appealing hangouts along Avenida Blasco Ibáñez and on Plaza de Cánovas del Castillo and Plaza Zuquer. Out by the sea, Paseo Neptuno and Calle de Eugenia Viñes are lined with loud clubs and bars. Castellón and Valencia jointly publish *Que y Donde,* the major listings magazine; *Turia* focuses on Valencia.

Fodor'sChoice ★ If you want nonstop nightlife at its frenzied best, come during **Las Fallas** (🌐 *www.fallas.com*) in March, when revelers throng the streets and last call at many of the bars and clubs isn't until the wee hours of morning, if at all. The **Feria de Julio** is July's month-long festival of theater, film, dance, and music.

The airy, perennially popular, bar-club-performance-space **Radio City** (✉ *Santa Teresa 19* ☎ *963/914151*) offers an eclectic nightly showcase from flamenco (on Tuesday at 11 PM) and Afro-jazz fusion to theater. For quiet after-dinner drinks, try the jazzy, lighthearted bar **Café de la Seu** (✉ *Santo Cáliz 7* ☎ *963/915715*), with contemporary art and animal-print chairs. For a taste of *el ambiente andaluz* (Andalusian atmosphere) tuck into tapas and cocktails at **El Albero** (✉ *Ciscar 12* ☎ *963/356273*). At 11 PM Thursday through Saturday, there's Andalusian singing. Locals out for a cocktail before hitting the clubs start their evening at **Xuquer Palace** (✉ *Pl. Xuquer 8* ☎ *963/615811*), with Barcelona-style Modernisté furnishings. **Casablanca** (✉ *Eugenia Viñes 152* ☎ *963/713366*) has an elegant postwar look; it's open Thursday through Sunday and has everything from waltz to swing music. Valencia has a lively gay nightlife, with a string of bars and clubs on Calle Quart and around the Plaza del Mercado. Follow the trendsters to the hopping **Venial** (✉ *Quart 26* ☎ *963/917356*), where you can enjoy a tipple or two, groove on the packed dance floor, or just take in the *gran espectáculos* of sequined and/or muscled performers strutting their stuff on stage.

SHOPPING

A flea market is held every Sunday morning by the cathedral. Another crafts and flea market takes place on Sunday morning in Plaza Luis Casanova, near the *campo de fútbol* (soccer stadium). If it's great local designer wear you're after, then head straight to the Barrio Carmen.

ALBUFERA NATURE PARK

11 km (7 mi) south of Valencia.

This beautiful freshwater lagoon was named by Moorish poets—*albufera* means "the sun's mirror." Dappled with rice paddies, the Parque Natural de la Albufera is a nesting site for more than 250 bird species, including herons, terns, egrets, ducks, and gulls. Admission is free, and there are miles of lovely walking and cycling trails.

From Valencia, buses depart from the corner of Sueca and Gran Vía de Germanías on the hour (every half hour in summer) daily 7 AM to 9 PM. ☎*961/627345.*

WHERE TO EAT

$$–$$$$ ★ SPANISH

✕ **La Matandeta.** With its white garden walls and rustic interior, this restaurant is an oasis in the rice paddies for Valencian families who come to the Albufera on Sundays, when many of the city's better restaurants are closed. From May through September, genial host-owners Maria Dolores Baixauli and Rafael Galvez preside over evening meals on the terrace: fish fresh off the boats are grilled over an open fire, and the traditional main dish here is the *paella de pato, pollo, y conejo* (paella with duck, chicken, and rabbit). Choose from among 50 types of olive oil on the sideboard for your bread or salad. ✉*Ctra. Alfafar/El Saler, Km 4* ☎*962/112184* ▭*MC, V* ⏲*Closed Mon.*

The Balearic Islands

The cobblestoned streets of Ibiza Town (Eivissa)

WORD OF MOUTH

"We liked Port de Sóller, once a small fishing village, now a reasonable sized resort. Boat trips from the harbour along the very picturesque coast line, buses to Deià, Valldemossa etc. Palma is well worth a day trip: magnificent cathedral and Arab baths."

—Diz01

WELCOME TO THE BALEARIC ISLANDS

TOP REASONS TO GO

★ **Stop Me Before I Pamper Myself Again:** Luxurious boutique hotels on restored and redesigned rural estates are *the* hip accommodations in the Balearics. Many have their own holistic spas: restore and redesign yourself at one of them.

★ **Spines and All:** Seafood specialties like Minorca's *caldereta de langosta* (spiny lobster stew) come straight from the boat to portside restaurants all over the islands.

★ **Hard Day's Night:** Ibiza's summer club scene is the biggest, wildest, glitziest in the world.

★ **On the Rocks:** The *miradores* (lookouts) of Majorca's Tramuntana, along the road from Valldemossa to Sóller, highlight the most spectacular seacoast in the Mediterranean.

★ **In the Swim:** The islands abound with small sandy coves called *calas,* like Cala'n Turqueta, on Minorca's south coast—many so isolated you can reach them only by boat.

1 Majorca. Palma, the island's capital, is a trove of art and architectural gems. The Tramuntana, in the northwest, is a region of forested peaks and steep sea cliffs that few landscapes in the world can match.

Woman wearing a traditional outfit in Ibiza.

2 Minorca. Mahón, the capital city, commands the largest and deepest harbor in the Mediterranean. Many of the houses above the port date to the 18th-century occupation by the Imperial British Navy.

3 Ibiza (Eivissa). Sleepy from November to May, the island is Party Central in midsummer for retro hippies and nonstop clubbers. Dalt Vila, the medieval quarter of Eivissa, on the hill overlooking the town, is a UNESCO World Heritage site.

Hiking the Tramuntana.

GETTING ORIENTED

The Balearic islands lie 50 to 190 mi off the Spanish mainland, roughly between Valencia and Barcelona. In the center, Majorca, with its rolling eastern plains and mountainous northwest, is the largest of the group. Minorca, its closest neighbor, is virtually flat—but like Ibiza and tiny Formentera to the west, it's blessed with a rugged coastline of small inlets and sandy beaches.

4 **Formentera.** Partygoers from Ibiza make day trips to chill out at this (comparatively) quiet little island with long stretches of protected beach.

Eivissa in full swing.

THE BALEARIC ISLANDS PLANNER

When to Go

July and August are peak season in the Balearics; it's hot, and even the most secluded beaches are crowded. Weatherwise, May and October are ideal, with June and September just behind. Winter is quiet; it's too cold for the beach but fine for hiking, golfing, and exploring. The clubbing season on Ibiza begins in June, but you can beat the crowds with a visit in mid-May for the Medieval Festival in Dalt Vila. Late February is a good time to be on Majorca because of *Sa Rua*, the carnival season in the year-round city of Palma in the week before Lent (beach resorts and tourist-oriented places might be closed, but Palma is a substantial, year-round city). Plan to be on Minorca the last weekend of June for the spectacular displays of horsemanship at the Festival of Sant Joan in Ciutadella. Note: Between November and February many hotels and restaurants are closed for their own holidays or seasonal repairs.

Tour Options

Most Majorca hotels and resorts offer guided tours. Typical itineraries are the Caves of Artà or Drac, on the east coast, including the nearby Auto Safari Park and an artificial-pearl factory in Manacor; the Chopin museum in the old monastery at Valldemossa, returning through the writers' and artists' village of Deià; the port of Sóller and the Arab gardens at Alfàbia; the Thursday market and leather factories in Inca; Port de Pollença; Cape Formentor; and northern beaches.

The resorts also run excursions to neighboring beaches and coves—many inaccessible by road—and to the islands of Cabrera and Dragonera. Visitors to Cabrera can take a self-guided tour of the island's underwater ecosystem—using a mask and snorkel with a sound system incorporated; the recording explains the main points of interest as you swim. Contact Excursions a Cabrera or the National Park Office in Palma.

On Minorca, sightseeing trips leave Mahón's harbor from the quayside near the Xoriguer gin factory; several boats have glass bottoms. Fares average around €10. Departure times vary; check with the Tourist Information office on the Moll de Ponent, at the foot of the winding stairs from the old city to the harbor.

Ibiza resorts run trips to neighboring beaches and to smaller islands. Trips from Ibiza to Formentera include an escorted bus tour. In Sant Antoni, which has little to offer in the way of beaches, there are a flotilla of tour organizers to choose from.

Contacts Mahón (✉ *Moll de Llevant 2* ☎ *971/355952*). **Excursions a Cabrera** (☎ *971/649034*). **National Park Office** (✉ *Plaza de España 8* ☎ *971/725–010*).

Eat Well Locally

One thing you should be able to count on, from any self-respecting Mediterranean island, is great seafood—and the Balearics deliver. Majorcans revel in their *sopas i panades de peix* (fish soups and pies). On Minorca, the harbor restaurants of Mahón, Ciutadella, and Fornells are famous for their *llagosta* (spiny lobster), grilled or served in a *caldereta*—a stew with peppers, onion, tomato, and garlic; another Minorcan specialty is the ugly but succulent *cap roig* (scorpion fish). From Ibiza's little coves and inlets, fishermen venture out for sea bass, bream, grouper, and *dorada* (John Dory); they sell the catch directly to beach shacks and family restaurants celebrated for *bullit* (fish casserole), *guisat de peix* (a kind of hot-pot dish that can also include varieties of shellfish), and *burrida de ratjada* (ray poached with almonds).

The Balearic farms and forests yield another sort of bounty: traditional dishes like *sofrit pagès* (country-style sausage with potatoes and red peppers stewed in olive oil and garlic), *rostit* (oven-roasted pork with liver, eggs, bread, and apples), and *tumbet* (fried zucchini, potatoes, eggplant, and bell peppers baked in tomato sauce). Restaurants in the Ibizan countryside serve wonderful lamb and goat chops *a la brasa* (on a wood-fired outdoor grill); Minorcan free-range beef is lean and tender; any Majorcan chef worth his or her salt has a recipe for rabbit; and no meal should begin without *sopas mallorquinas,* a rich vegetable soup in meat stock. Delicatessen specialties are also traditional, like *sobrasada,* the pork-and-red-pepper Majorcan sausage paste. Even the fluffy, sweet *ensaimada*—a powdery spiral pastry—is based on *saim* (pork fat).

Meat, fish, and noodle dishes are usually served with a helping of garlic mayonnaise called *allioli.* Minorca also has one of the 12 *denominación de origen,* officially designated cheese-producing regions in Spain. The *curado* (fully cured) cheese is the best.

WHAT IT COSTS (IN EUROS)

	¢	$	$$	$$$	$$$$
Restaurants	under €6	€6–€10	€10–€15	€15–€20	over €20
Hotels	under €40	€40–€60	€60–€100	€100–€180	over €180

Prices are per person for a main course at dinner. Prices are for two people in a standard double room in high season, excluding tax.

Planning Your Time

Most European visitors to the Balearics pick an island and stick with it, but you could see all three. Start in Majorca with **Palma.** Begin early at the Cathedral and explore the Llotja, the Almudaina Palace, the Plaça Major. The churches of Santa Eulalia and Sant Francesc, and the Arab Baths are a must. Staying overnight in Palma means you can sample the nightlife and have time to visit the museums.

Take the old train to **Sóller** and rent a car for a trip over the Sierra de Tramuntana to **Deià, Son Marroig,** and **Valldemossa.** The roads are twisty so give yourself a full day. Spend the night in Sóller and you can drive from there in less than an hour, via **Lluc** and **Pollença** to the Roman and Arab remains at **Alcúdia.**

By hydrofoil it's just over three hours from Port d'Alcúdia to **Ciutadella,** on Minorca; the port, the **Cathedral,** and the narrow streets of the old city can be explored in half a day. Make your way across the island to **Mahón,** and devote an afternoon to the highlights there. From Mahón, you can take a 30-minute interisland flight to **Eivissa.** On Ibiza, plan a full day for the World Heritage site of **Dalt Vila** and the shops of **Sa Penya,** and the better part of another for **Santa Gertrudis** and the north coast. But if you've come to Ibiza to party, of course, time has no meaning.

GETTING HERE AND AROUND

By Air

Each of the islands is served by an international airport, all of them within 15 or 20 minutes by car or bus from the capital city. There are daily domestic connections to each from Barcelona (40 min), Madrid, and Valencia: no-frills and charter operators fly to Palma, Mahón, and Eivissa from many European cities, especially during the summer. There are also interisland flights. In high season, book early.

Airports **Aeropuerto de Ibiza (IBZ)** (☎ *902/404704*). **Aeropuerto de Minorca (MAH)** (☎ *902/404704*). **Aeropuerto de Palma de Majorca (PMI)** (☎ *902/404704*).

By Bike

The Balearic Islands—especially Formentera and Ibiza—are ideal for exploration by bicycle. Parts of Majorca are quite mountainous, with challenging climbs through spectacular scenery; along some country roads, there are designated bicycle lanes. Bicycles are easy to rent, and tourist offices have details on recommended routes. Minorca is relatively flat, with lots of roads that wander through pastureland and olive groves to small coves and inlets. Ibiza, too, is relatively flat and easy to negotiate, though side roads can be in poor repair. Formentera is level, with bicycle lanes on all connecting roads.

By Bus

There is bus service on all of the islands, although it's not extensive, especially on Formentera. Check each island's Getting Here and Around information for details.

By Car

A car is essential if you want to beach-hop on Majorca or Minorca. Ibiza is best explored by car or motor scooter: many of the beaches lie at the end of rough, unpaved roads. Tiny Formentera can almost be covered on foot, but renting a car at La Sabina is an obvious time-saver.

By Boat and Ferry

From Barcelona: The most romantic way to get to the Balearic Islands is by overnight ferry from Barcelona. Depending on the line and the season, the Trasmediterránea, Balearia, and Iscomar car ferries to Palma, Majorca, sail between 11 and 11:30 PM; you can watch the lights of Barcelona sinking into the horizon for hours—and when you arrive in Palma, around 6 AM, see the spires of the cathedral bathed in the morning sun. All three lines serve Minorca and Ibiza as well. Overnight ferries have lounges and private cabins. Round-trip fares vary with the line, the season, and points of departure and destination, but are around €140 for lounges or €280–€360 for a double cabin.

Fast ferries and catamarans, also operated by Trasmediterránea and Balearia, with passenger lounges only, speed from Barcelona to Palma and Alcúdia (Majorca), to Ciutadella (Minorca), and to Eivissa (Ibiza). Depending on the destination, the trip takes between three and five hours.

From Valencia: Trasmediterránea ferries leave Valencia in midmorning for Palma, arriving early evening. There are also ferries from Valencia to Ibiza and Minorca: departure days and times vary with the season; service is more frequent in summer.

From Denia: Balearia runs a daily two-hour Super Fast Ferry service for passengers and cars between Denia and Eivissa, and a similar three-hour service between Denia and Palma on weekends. Iscomar runs a slower car-and-truck ferry service between Denia and Sant Antoni, Ibiza.

Inter island: Daily ferries connect Alcúdia (Majorca) and Ciutadella (Minorca) in three to four hours, depending on the weather; a hydrofoil makes the journey in about an hour. From May to October, daily hydrofoil service connects Palma and Ibiza; fares range from €15 to €40 one-way There are frequent car and fast ferry services between Ibiza and Formentera.

Boat and Ferry Information Balearia (🌐 *www.balearia.com*). **Formentera port information** (☎ *971/323082*). **Iscomar** (🌐 *www.iscomar.com*). **Mediterránea Pitiusa** (☎ *971/322443*). **Trasmapi** (🌐 *www.trasmapi.com*). **Trasmediterránea** (🌐 *www.trasmediterranea.es*).

By Taxi

Taxis in Palma are metered. For trips beyond the city, charges are posted at the taxi stands. On Minorca, you can pick up a taxi at the airport or in Mahón or Ciutadella; on Ibiza, taxis are available at the airport and in Eivissa, Figueretas, Santa Eulalia, and Sant Antoni. On Formentera, there are taxis in La Sabina and Es Pujols. Most taxis in Minorca, Ibiza, and Formentera are not metered.

By Train

The public *Ferrocarriles de Mallorca* railway line connects Palma and Inca, with stops at about half a dozen villages en route. A journey on the privately owned Palma–Sóller railway is a must: completed in 1912, it still uses the carriages of that era. The line trundles across the plain to Bunyola, then winds through tremendous mountain scenery to emerge high above Sóller. An ancient tram connects the Sóller terminus to Port de Sóller, leaving every hour on the hour, 9 to 6; the Palma terminal is near the corner of the Plaça d'Espanya, on Calle Eusebio Estada next to the Inca rail station.

Updated by Hannah Semmler

Could anything go wrong in a destination that gets, on average, 300 days of sunshine a year? True, the water is only warm enough for a dip from May through October—but the climate does seem to give the residents of the Balearics a year-round sunny disposition. They are a remarkably *hospitable* people, not merely because tourism accounts for such a large chunk of their economy, but because history and geography have combined to put them in the crossroads of so much Mediterranean trade and traffic.

The Balearic Islands were outposts, successively, of the Phoenician, Carthaginian, and Roman empires before the Moors invaded in 902 and took possession for some 300 years. In 1235, the Moors were ousted by Jaume I of Aragón, and the islands became part of the independent kingdom of Majorca until 1343, when they returned to the Crown of Aragón under Pedro IV. Upon the marriage of Isabella of Castile to Ferdinand of Aragón in 1469, the Balearics were joined to a united Spain. Great Britain occupied Minorca in 1704, during the War of the Spanish Succession, to secure the superb natural harbor of Mahón as a naval base. Under the Treaty of Amiens, Britain finally returned Minorca to Spain in 1802.

During the Spanish Civil War, Minorca remained loyal to Spain's democratically elected Republican government, while Majorca and Ibiza sided with Franco's insurgents. Majorca became a home base for the Italian fleet supporting the fascist cause. This topic is still broached delicately on the islands; they remain fiercely independent of one another in many ways. Even Mahón and Ciutadella, at opposite ends of Minorca—all of 44 km (27 mi) apart—remain estranged over differences dating from the war.

The tourist boom, which began during Francisco Franco's regime (1939–75), turned great stretches of Majorca's and Ibiza's coastlines into strips of high-rise hotels, fast-food restaurants, and discos.

EXPLORING THE BALEARIC ISLANDS

Majorca and Ibiza are the most heavily developed of the islands, in terms of resorts and tourist infrastructure, and draw most of the foreign visitors, especially from Germany and Great Britain. The north coasts of both have spectacular rocky coastlines, undeveloped areas, and clear waters. Minorca is the preferred destination of Spanish and Catalan families on holiday, and much of it is still farms and pastures, checkerboarded with low stone walls, and nature reserves. Formentera has virtually no tourism outside the summer months.

ABOUT THE BEACHES

MAJORCA

The closer a beach is to Palma, the more crowded it's likely to be. West of the city is Palma Nova; behind the lovely, narrow beach rises one of the most densely developed resorts on the island. Paguera, with several small beaches, is the only sizable local resort not overshadowed by high-rises. Camp de Mar, with a good, white sand beach, is small and relatively undeveloped but is sometimes overrun with day-trippers from other resorts. Sant Elm, at the end of this coast, has a pretty bay. East of Palma, a 5-km (3-mi) stretch of fine white sand runs along the coastal road from C'an Pastilla to Arenal, known collectively as Playa de Palma.

On the northwest coast, there's a popular beach at Port de Sóller. Farther north, the quiet cove at Sa Calobra Beach draws lots of day visitors in the summer. Moderately developed Cala St. Vicenç has fine sand in two narrow bays. From Port de Pollença, on the north coast, there's frequent water-taxi service to Formentor, one of the best beaches on Majorca. The north coast also has the island's longest beach; it stretches 8 km (5 mi) from Port de Alcúdia to beyond C'an Picafort. Ses Casetes, near Port des Pins, is the best stretch.

Majorca's east coast has numerous beaches and coves, though few are easily reachable by car. Canyamel, near the Caves of Artà, is a large, undeveloped strand. Farther south, Costa d'es Pins is an extensive development, with a good sandy stretch backed by a line of pines. Tourist buses run from here to Cala Millor, where the beach is accessible only on foot. Farther south, Cala d'Or is a pleasant resort, and Cala Gran, a short walk away, is even more attractive. Cala Mondrajó is a tiny, sandy bay with little development; it's most easily reached by boat from Portopetre or Cala Figuera. On the south coast, the dune-backed beach at Es Trenc, near Colònia de Sant Jordi, is a quiet seaside patch. The 10-km (6-mi) walk along the beach from Colònia de Sant Jordi to the Cap Salines lighthouse is one of Majorca's treasures.

MINORCA

Cala Sa Mesquida, north of Mahón, is a popular beach with limited access by road. Farther north, Es Grau, a sandy stretch with dunes behind it, lies at the edge of the S'Albufera nature reserve. Before the lighthouse at the end of Cap Favaritx are the nudist beaches Cala Presili and Playa Tortuga. Arenal d'en Castell, a sheltered circular bay, and Arenal de Son Saura (Son Parc) are the north's biggest sandy beaches. At the junction of the Mahón–Fornells and Mercadal–Fornells roads, take the small lane leading west and follow signs to Binimellà, an excellent sandy beach. It's often deserted, and the caves in the tiny coves to the west provide welcome shade in the summer.

The only accessible beach north of Ciutadella is Cala Morell. Minorcans claim that the inlets and beaches at Cala Algaiarens are the nicest. Son Saura, Cala en Turqueta, Macarella, and Cala Galdana at the west end of the south coast are all reached by driving southeast from Ciutadella toward Son Saura. All three are classic Minorcan beaches with trees down to the water's edge, horseshoe coves, and white sand. To the east, Cala Mitjana, Cala Trebaluger, Cala Fustam, and Cala Escorxada are accessible by land only on foot, but you can rent boats with outboard engines to reach them or Son Saura. You can get to the long, straight, sandy stretches of Binigaus, Sant Adeodato, and Sant Tomas from Mercadal, and to Son Bou, the island's longest beach (with a nudist section), from Alaior. Cala'n Porter is a British enclave sheltered by cliffs. On the southeastern tip of the island is the windswept, white-sand beach at Punta Prima.

IBIZA South of Ibiza Town (aka Eivissa) is a long, sandy beach, the nearly 3-km (2-mi) Playa d'en Bossa. Farther on, a left turn at Sant Jordi on the way to the airport leads across the salt pans to Cavallet and Ses Salines, two of the best beaches on the island. Year-round Ibizans also like Cala de Comte, on the west coast, and Cala Llenya and Cala Mastella, in the northeast. Also in the northeast is the curved cove of Cala Sant Vicent, popular with families. Santa Eulària des Riu, the largest resort town on the east coast, has a long, narrow beach sloping down from a promenade—one that gets a lot less crazy in the summer than Sant Antoni. Topless bathing is accepted all over Ibiza.

FORMENTERA Wild and lonely beaches are the rule on Formentera. Playa de Mitjorn stretches for 7 km (4 mi) along the south of the island. Trucadors, a long, thin spit at the north, has 2 km (1 mi) of sand on each side, and in summer you can wade to Es Palmador, where you can find more sandy beaches and a preponderance of nude bathers.

ABOUT THE HOTELS

Many hotels on the islands include a Continental or full buffet breakfast in the room rate.

MAJORCA Majorca's large-scale resorts—more than 1,500 of them—are concentrated mainly on the southern coast, and primarily serve the package-tour industry. Perhaps the best accommodations on the island are the number of grand old country estates and town houses that have been converted into boutique hotels, ranging from simple and relatively inexpensive *agroturismos* to stunning outposts of luxury.

MINORCA Apart from a few hotels and hostels in Mahón and Ciutadella, almost all of Minorca's tourist lodgings are in beach resorts. As on the other islands, many of these are fully reserved by travel operators in the high season and often require a week's minimum stay, so it's generally most economical to book a package that combines airfare and accommodations. Alternatively, inquire at the tourist office about boutique and country hotels, especially in and around Sant Lluis.

IBIZA Ibiza's hotels are mainly in coastal Sant Antoni and Playa d'en Bossa. Many of these are excellent, but unless you're eager to be part of a mob, Sant Antoni has little to recommend it. Playa d'en Bossa, close to Eivissa, is prettier, but it lies under the flight path to the airport. To get off the beaten track and into the island's largely pristine interior, look for *agroturismo* lodgings in Els Amunts (The Uplands) and in villages such as Santa Gertrudis or Sant Miquel de Balanzat.

FORMENTERA If July and August are the only months you can visit, reserve well in advance. To get the true feel of Formentera, look for the most out-of-the-way *calas* and fishing villages, especially on the south Platja de Mitjorn coast.

CELEBRATIONS FROM ISLAND TO ISLAND

MAJORCA FIESTAS

Sant Joan Pelós is celebrated June 23–24 in Felanitx; a man dressed in sheepskins represents John the Baptist. The **Romería de Sant Marçal** (Pilgrimage of St. Mark), a procession of townspeople in costume to the church of their patron saint to draw water from a consecrated cistern—thought to give health and strength of heart—is held June 30 in Sa Cabaneta.

MINORCA FIESTAS

Ciutadella's feast of **Sant Joan** (June 23–24) has townspeople dancing on horseback, trying to keep the horses up on their hind legs while the crowd gathers beneath. **Sant Lluís,** at the end of August, spotlights equestrian activities. Mahón's **Fiestas de Gràcia** (September 7–9) are the season's final celebrations.

IBIZA FIESTAS

Ibiza's patron saint, **Mare de Déu de les Neus** (Our Lady of the Snows), is honored on August 8 in memory of the conquest of Ibiza. **Sant Antoni d'Abat** (January 17) has processions of pets, livestock, and cavalry. On February 12 the **Festes de Santa Eulalia** is a boisterous winter carnival with folk dancing and live music. **Sant Josep** (March 19) is known for folk dancing, which you can also see in Sant Joan every Thursday evening. On June 23 and 24, witness the islandwide **Festa Major de Sant Joan** (Feast of St. John the Baptist). The **Festa del Mar,** honoring the Mare de Déu del Carme (Our Lady of Carmen), is held July 16 in Eivissa, Santa Eulalia, Sant Antoni, and Sant Josep, and on Formentera.

FORMENTERA FIESTAS

On July 16 islanders honor the **Virgen del Carmen,** patron saint of sailors, with processions of boats and anything else that floats. On July 25, Sant Francesc dances in honor of **Sant Jaume** (St. James), Spain's male patron saint.

9

MAJORCA

Saddle-shaped Majorca is more than five times the size of either Minorca or Ibiza. The Sierra de Tramuntana, a dramatic mountain range soaring to nearly 5,000 feet, runs the length of its northwest coast, and a ridge of hills borders the southeast shores; between the two lies a flat plain that in early spring becomes a sea of almond blossoms, "the snow of Majorca." The island draws more than 10 million visitors a year—Palma's international airport is bigger than Barcelona's—many of them bound for summer vacation packages in the coastal resorts. The beaches are beautiful, but save time for the charms of the northwest and the interior: caves, bird sanctuaries, monasteries and medieval cities, local museums, outdoor cafés, and village markets.

GETTING HERE AND AROUND

From Barcelona, Palma de Majorca is a 40-minute flight, an eight-hour overnight ferry, or a 4½-hour catamaran journey from Barcelona.

If you're traveling by car, Majorca's main highways are well surfaced, and a fast, 25-km (15-mi) motorway penetrates deep into the island between Palma and Inca. Palma is ringed by an efficient beltway, the Vía Cintura. For destinations in the north and west, follow the ANDRATX and

OESTE signs on the beltway; for the south and east, follow the ESTE signs. Driving in the mountains that parallel the northwest coast and descend to a cliff-side corniche is a different matter; you'll be slowed not only by winding roads but by tremendous views and tourist traffic.

ESSENTIALS

Visitor Information Oficina de Turismo de Majorca (✉ *Aeropuerto de Palma* ☎ 971/789556).

PALMA DE MAJORCA

If you look north of the cathedral (La Seu, or the "seat" of the Bishopric, to Majorcans) on a map of the city of Palma, you can see around the Plaça Santa Eulalia a jumble of tiny streets that made up the earliest settlement. Farther out, a ring of wide boulevards, known as the Avenues, follows a path made from walls built by the Moors to defend the larger city that emerged by the 12th century. The zigzags mark the bastions that jutted out at regular intervals. By the end of the 19th century most of the walls had been demolished; the only place where you can still see the massive defenses is at Ses Voltes, along the seafront west of the cathedral.

A streambed (*torrent*) used to run through the middle of the old city, dry for most of the year but often a raging flood in the rainy season. In the 17th century it was diverted to the east, along the moat that ran outside the city walls. The stream's natural course is now followed by La Rambla and the Passeig d'es Born, two of Palma's main arteries. The traditional evening *paseo* (promenade) takes place on the Born.

If you come to Palma by car, park in the garage beneath the Parc de la Mar (the ramp is just off the highway from the airport, as you reach the cathedral) and stroll along the park. Beside it run the huge bastions guarding the Almudaina Palace; the cathedral, golden and massive, rises beyond. Where you exit the garage, there's a **ceramic mural** by the late Catalan artist and Majorca resident Joan Miró, facing the cathedral across the pool that runs the length of the park.

If you begin early enough, a walk along the ramparts at Ses Voltes from the *mirador* beside the cathedral is spectacular. The first rays of the sun turn the upper pinnacles of La Seu bright gold and begin to work their way down the sandstone walls. From the Parc de la Mar, follow Avinguda Antoni Maura past the steps to the palace. Just below the Plaça de la Reina, where the **Passeig d'es Born** begins, turn left on Carrer de la Boteria into the Plaça de la Llotja (don't miss a chance to visit the Llotja itself, the Mediterranean's finest civic Gothic building, if it's open), and stroll from there through the Plaça Drassana to the **Museu d'Es Baluard,** at the end of Carrer Sant Pere. Retrace your steps to Avinguda Antoni Maura. Walk up the Passeig d'es Born to Plaça Joan Carles I, then left on Avenida de La Unió and up Carrer de Sant Joan.

GETTING HERE AND AROUND

Palma's Empresa Municipal de Transportes runs 34 bus lines and a tourist train in and around the Majorcan capital. Most buses leave from the city station, next to the Inca railway terminus on the Plaça d'Espanya; a few terminate at other points in Palma. The tourist office on the Plaça d'Espanya has schedules. Bus No. 1 connects the airport with the city center and the port. The new No. 21 line connects S'Arenal with the airport. Bus No. 2 circumnavigates the historic city center. Bus No. 20 connects the city center with Porto Pi and the Fundació Pilar i Joan Miró. Fare for a single ride is 1.25.

For sightseeing in Palma, take the open-top City Sightseeing bus that departs from stops throughout the town, including Plaça de la Reina, and travels along the Passeig Marítim and up to the Castell de Bellver. Tickets (€13) are valid for 24 hours, and you can get on and off as many times as you wish. All Palma tourist offices have information and details. Also in Palma, you can hire a horse-drawn carriage with driver at the bottom of the Born; on Avinguda Antonio Maura; in the nearby cathedral square; and on the Plaça d'Espanya, at the side farthest from the railway station. A tour of the city costs about €25.

Boats from Palma, Majorca, to neighboring beach resorts leave from the jetty opposite the Auditorium, on the Passeig Marítim. The tourist office has a schedule.

ESSENTIALS

Bike Rentals Bimont (✉ *Camí de Jesús 62, Palma* ☎ *971/731866*). **Mallorca Rent Bikes** (✉ Bartolomé Riutort 27, *Palma* ☎ *971/864336*).

Bus Information Empresa Municipal de Transports (🌐 *www.emtpalma.es*).

Bus Station Palma de Majorca (✉ *Estación Central* ☎ *971/752224*).

Taxi Information Associación Fono-Taxi (✉ *Palma* ☎ *971/728081*). **Radio-Taxi** (✉ *Palma* ☎ *971/755440*). **Taxis-Palma-Radio** (✉ *Palma* ☎ *971/401414*).

Tour Bus Information City Sightseeing (☎ *902/101081*).

Train Station Palma Train Station (✉ *Ferrocarriles de Mallorca, Pl. d'Espanya, Palma* ☎ *971/752245*)

Visitor Information Palma (✉ *Pl. de la Reina 2* ☎ *971/173990* ✉ *Passeig d'es Born 27* ☎ *902/102365* ✉ *Parc de Ses Estacions, across from train station and near Pl. España* ☎ *902/102365*).

EXPLORING

About 110 yards west of the Plaça Joan Carles I, on the Plaça del Mercat, is **San Nicolau** (✉ *Pl. del Mercat*), a 14th-century church with a hexagonal bell tower. The ornate facades of the **Casas Casasayas** (✉ *Pl. del Mercat 13–14*), on opposite corners of Carrer Santa Cilia, were designed by Moderniste architect Francesc Roca Simó in 1908. Although brilliant examples of the Moderniste style, the Casas Casasayas are outshone by the **Gran Hotel** (✉ *Pl. Weyler 3*), across the square, built between 1901 and 1903 by Luis Domènech i Montaner, author of Barcelona's Palau de la Música Catalana. The alabaster facade is sculpted like a wedding cake, with floral motifs, angelic heads, and coats of arms; the original interiors, alas, have been "refurbished." No longer a hotel, the building is owned by the Fundació "La Caixa," a cultural and social organization funded by the region's largest bank. Don't miss the permanent exhibit of Majorcan impressionist Anglada Camarassa.

Take time to appreciate the neoclassical symmetry of the **Teatre Principal** (☎*971/725548*), at the top of the Plaça Weyler, Palma's chief venue for opera and classical music. Near the steps leading up to the right of the Teatre Principal is the **Forn des Teatre** (✉*Pl. Weyler 12*), a bakery known for its *ensaimadas* (a typically Spanish fluffy pastry) and *cocas* (meat pies). From the Forn des Teatre, climb the steps to the **Plaça Major.** A crafts market fills this elegant neoclassical square on Monday, Friday, and Saturday between 10 and 2. A flight of steps on the east side of the Plaça Major leads down to **Las Ramblas,** a pleasant promenade lined with flower stalls.

★ A few steps from the north archway of the Plaça Major is the **Museu d'Art Espanyol Contemporani.** This fine little museum was established by the Joan March Foundation to display what had been a private collection of modern Spanish art; the building itself was a sumptuous private home dating to the 18th century. The second and third floors were redesigned to accommodate a series of small galleries, with one or two works at most—by Picasso, Miró, Juan Gris, Dalí, Antoni Tàpies, Miquel Barceló, among others—on each wall. ✉*Carrer Sant Miguel 11* ☎*971/713515* 🌐*www.march.es/museupalma* 🎫*Free* 🕒*Weekdays 10–6:30, Sat. 10:30–2.*

South of the Plaça Major on Carrer Colom, above the Cacao Sampaka chocolate shop in the next small square is the **Can Forteza Rei** (✉*Pl. Marqués Palmer 1*), an Art Nouveau delight designed by the original owner, Luis Forteza Rei, in 1909. The building has twisted wrought-iron railings and surfaces inlaid with bits of polychrome tile, signature touches of Gaudí and his contemporaries. A wonderful carved stone face, in a painful grimace, flanked by dragons ironically frames the stained-glass windows of a third-floor dental clinic.

Along Carrer Colom is the 17th-century **Ajuntament** (*Town Hall* ✉*Pl. Cort*); stop in to see the collection of *gigantes*—the huge painted and costumed mannequins paraded through the streets at festivals—on display in the lobby. The olive tree on the right side of the square is one of Majorca's so-called *olivos milenarios*—purported to be 1,000 years old—and may be even older.

Turn right at the olive tree for a brief detour to the end of the Plaça Cort. On the left at the corner of Carrer de Jaume II is yet another gem of Palma's early Moderniste architecture: the **Can Corbella** (✉*Pl. Cort 3*), designed in the 1890s by Nicolás Lliteras.

A few steps along the Carrer de la Cadena bring you to the imposing Gothic church of **Santa Eulalia.** In 1435, 200 Jews were converted to Christianity in this church after their rabbis were threatened with being burned at the stake. ✉*Pl. Santa Eulalia, Barrio Antiguo.*

From the Plaça de Sant Eulalia, take the Carrer del Convent de Sant Francesc to the beautiful 13th-century monastery church of **Sant Francesc,** established by Jaume II when his eldest son took monastic orders and gave up rights to the throne. Fra Junípero Serra, the missionary who founded San Francisco, California, was later educated here; his statue stands to the left of the main entrance. The basilica houses the tomb of the eminent 13th-century scholar Ramón Llull. ✉*Pl. Sant Francesc 7, Barrio Antiguo* 🎫*€1* ⏲*Mon.–Sat. 9:30–1 and 3–6, Sun. 9:30–1.*

9

NEED A BREAK?

The café Ca'n Joan de S'aigo (✉*C. de Ca'n Sanç 10, Barrio Antiguo* ☎*971/710759* ⏲*Mon. and Wed.–Sat. 8 AM–9 PM*), on a side street behind the church of Sant Francesc, is one of Palma's venerable institutions, in business since 1700. Drop in for coffee or hot chocolate, with an *ensaimada* (spiral-shaped Majorcan treat) or a sinfully rich cream cheese pastry. With its green-glass chandeliers, cane-back chairs, and marble tabletops, the setting is a treat in itself.

From the Plaça Sant Francesc, take Carrer Pere Nadal south toward the bay; the street changes names as it descends, crossing Carrer del Call (in many Spanish cities and towns, the term *call* indicates the site of the medieval Jewish quarter) to become Carrer Santa Clara, then Carrer de Can Pont i Vic. On the left as it turns to Carrer de la Portella is the **Museu de Majorca.** Housed in the 18th-century ducal palace of the Condes de Ayamans, the museum exhibits the findings of all the major archaeological research on Majorca, from prehistory to the Roman, Vandal, and Moorish occupations. ✉*Carrer de la Portella 5, Barrio Antiguo* ☎*971/717540* 🎫*€2.40* ⏲*Tues.–Sat. 10–7, Sun. 10–2.*

From the Museu de Majorca, walk down Carrer de la Portella and turn left before the archway at the bottom of the street; follow the signs to one of Palma's oldest monuments, the 10th-century **Banys Arabs** *(Arab Baths)*, in a wonderful walled garden of palms and lemon trees. In its day, it was not merely a public bathhouse but a social institution where you could soak, relax, and gossip with your neighbors. ✉ *Serra 7, Barrio Antiguo* ☎ *971/721549* 🎫 *€2* ⏲ *Dec.–Mar., daily 9–7; Apr.–Nov., daily 9–7:30.*

Fodor's Choice ★ Palma's **cathedral** is an architectural wonder that took almost 400 years to build (1230–1601). The wide expanse of the nave is supported on 14 slender 70-foot-tall columns, which fan out at the top like palm trees. The nave is dominated by an immense rose window, 40 feet in diameter, from 1370. Over the main altar (consecrated in 1346) is the almost surrealistic **baldoquí** by Antoni Gaudí, completed in 1912: an enormous canopy, lamps suspended from it like elements of a mobile, rising to a Crucifixion scene at the top. To the right of it, in the Chapel of the Santísimo, is an equally remarkable work, by the modern sculptor Miquel Barceló: a painted ceramic tableau that covers the walls of the chapel like a skin. Unveiled in 2007, the tableau is based on the New Testament account of the miracle of the loaves and fishes; Barceló renders this story in a bizarre composition of rolling waves, gaping cracks, protruding fish heads, and human skulls. The **bell tower** above the cathedral's Plaça Almoina door holds nine bells, the largest of which is known as N'Eloi, meaning "Praise." N'Eloi was cast in 1389, weighs 5½ tons, needs six men to ring it, and has shattered stained-glass windows with its sound. ✉ *Pl. Almoina s/n, Barrio Antiguo* ☎ *971/723130* 🌐 *www.catedraldemallorca.org* 🎫 *€4* ⏲ *Apr.–May, weekdays 10–5:15; June–Sept., weekdays 10–6:15; Nov.–Mar., weekdays 10–3:15; year-round, Sat 10–2:15, Sun. for worship only, 8:30–1:45, 6:30–7:45.*

Opposite Palma's cathedral is the **Palau de l'Almudaina** *(Almudaina Palace)*, residence of the ruling house during the Middle Ages and originally an Arab citadel. It's now a military headquarters, and the king's official residence when he is in Majorca. Guided tours generally depart hourly during open hours. ✉ *Carrer Palau Reial s/n, Barrio Antiguo* ☎ *971/214134* 🎫 *€3.20; €4 with a guided tour; audioguide €2* ⏲ *Oct.–Mar., weekdays 10–1:15 and 4–5:15, Sat. 10–1:15; Apr.–Sept., weekdays 10–5:45, Sat. 10–1:15.*

The **Llotja** *(Exchange)*, on the seafront west of the Plaça de la Reina, was built in the 15th century and is connected by an interior courtyard to the **Consolat de Mar** (Maritime Consulate). With its decorative turrets, battlements, fluted pillars, and Gothic stained-glass windows—part fortress, part church—it attests to the wealth Majorca achieved in its heyday as a Mediterranean trading power. The interior can be visited only when there are special exhibitions in the Merchants Chamber. ✉ *Pl. de la Llotja 5, La Llotja* ☎ *971/711705* ⏲ *During exhibits, Tues.–Sat. 11–2 and 5–9, Sun. 11–2.*

★ Inaugurated in January 2004, the **Museu d'Es Baluard** *(Museum of Modern and Contemporary Art of Palma)* rises on a long-neglected archaeological site at the western end of the city, parts of which date back to the

12th century. The building itself is an outstanding convergence of old and new: the exhibition space uses and merges into the surviving 16th-century perimeter walls of the fortified city, with a stone courtyard facing the sea and a promenade along the ramparts. There are three floors of galleries; the collection includes work by Miró, Picasso, Magritte, Tapiès, Calder, and other major artists. The café-terrace Restaurant del Museu (Tuesday–Sunday 1–4 and 8–11), in the courtyard, affords a fine view of the marina. ✉ *Pl. Porta de Santa Catalina 10, Puig Sant Pere* ☎ *971/908200* 🌐 *www.esbaluard.org* 🎟 *€6* ⏲ *Oct.–June 15, Tues.–Sun. 10–8; June 16–Sept., Tues.–Sun. 10* AM*–10* PM.

The **Castell de Bellver** *(Bellver Castle)* overlooks the city and the bay from a hillside. It was built at the beginning of the 14th century, in Gothic style but with a circular design—the only one of its kind in Spain. An archaeological **museum** of the history of Majorca and a small collection of classical sculpture sit inside. ✉ *Camilo José Cela s/n* ☎ *971/730657* 🎟 *€2.10, free Sun.* ⏲ *Castle and museum Oct.–Mar., Mon.–Sat. 8–7; Apr.–Sept., Mon.–Sat. 8–9. Castle only Sun. 10–4:30.*

The permanent collection in the **Museu Fundació Pilar y Joan Miró** *(Pilar and Joan Miró Foundation Museum)* includes a great many drawings and studies by the Catalan artist, who spent his last years on Majorca, but shows far fewer finished paintings and sculptures than the Fundació Miró in Barcelona. Don't miss the adjacent studio, built for Miró by his friend the architect Josep Lluis Sert. The artist did most of his work here from 1957 on. ✉ *Carrer Joan de Saridakis 29, Cala Major, Marivent* ☎ *971/701420* 🌐 *miro.palmademallorca.es/english/index.htm* 🎟 *€6* ⏲ *Sept. 16–May 15, Tues.–Sat. 10–6, Sun. 10–3; May 16–Sept. 15, Tues.–Sat. 10–7, Sun. 10–3.*

OFF THE BEATEN PATH

ILLA DE CABRERA. Off the south coast of Majorca lies one of the last unspoiled verdant slivers in the Mediterranean—the Illa de Cabrera, largest of the 19 islands and islets that make up the Cabrera archipelago. Determined to protect it, local environmental activists succeeded in 1991 in having the archipelago, with its dramatic landscape, wildlife, and lush vegetation, declared a national park. Throughout its history, Cabrera has had its share of visitors, from the Romans to the Arabs. Today, the only intact historical remains are those of a 14th-century castle overlooking the harbor. Tour boats called *golondrinas* make day trips to the island (mainly April–October); contact Excursiones a Cabrera (☎ *971/649034* 🌐 *www.excursionsacabrera.com*). Boats generally depart from Colònia de Sant Jordi, 47 km (29 mi) southeast of Palma, around 9:30 AM, returning at 6 PM; tickets are €29, with lunch provided for an additional cost. The trip takes about 30 minutes. Departure times vary, so inquire at any of the Palma tourist offices for current information.

WHERE TO EAT AND STAY

$–$$ SPANISH

✕ **Café la Lonja.** A great spot for hot chocolate or one of their unique teas and coffees, this classic establishment in the old fishermen's neighborhood has a young vibe that goes well with the decor. Both the sunny terrace in front of the Llotja—a privileged dining spot—and the restaurant inside are excellent places for drinks, tapas, baguettes, sandwiches, and salads. The seasonal menu might include a salad of tomato, avocado, and manchego cheese; fluffy quiche; and tapas of squid or mushrooms. It's a good rendezvous point and watering hole. ✉ *Carrer Lonja del Mar 2, La Llotja* ☎ *971/722799* ▭ *AE, MC, V* ⊙ *Closed Sun.*

> **WORD OF MOUTH**
>
> "Palma and the little towns in the north have lots of foreign residents, but they're still very Spanish. The weather is great, and the people are very friendly." —Fiona

$$$–$$$$ SPANISH ★ **Koldo Royo.** Crowded with modern art, this chic yellow dining room overlooks the marina. Having grown up in San Sebastián, chef-owner Koldo Royo conjures up Basque specialties such as lamprey eel, salt cod, tripe, and stuffed quail; try one of the two seven-course tasting menus (€40 and €60) for an introduction to this unique cuisine. As the chef says, "My creations follow simple cooking, and use fresh Spanish produce, in order to always keep the maternal tastes alive." ✉ *Av. Gabriel Roca 3, Paseo Marítimo* ☎ *971/732435* ▭ *AE, MC, V* ⊙ *Closed Sun. and Mon.*

$$ SPANISH **La Bóveda.** Within hailing distance of the Llotja, this popular restaurant serves tapas and inexpensive platters such as chicken or ham croquettes, grilled cod, garlic shrimp, and *revuelto con setas y jamón* (scrambled eggs with mushrooms and ham). The tables in the back are always at a premium (they're nice and cool on summer days, if you don't mind the smoking), but there's additional seating at the counter or on stools around upended wine barrels. The ample portions of traditional tapas are nothing fancy but very good. ✉ *Carrer de la Botería 3, La Llotja* ☎ *971/714863* ▭ *AE, MC, V* ⊙ *Closed Sun.*

$$ **Born.** Romanesque arches and a giant palm tree spectacularly cover the central courtyard and reception area of this hotel, which occupies the former mansion of a noble Majorcan family. Guest rooms are modest, though some have the original coffered and painted ceilings, and the rates are more than reasonable. A buffet breakfast is included in the price. **Pros:** convenient for sightseeing, romantic courtyard floodlit at night, fine value for price. **Cons:** small rooms on the street side, poor soundproofing, no elevator. ✉ *Carrer Sant Jaume 3, Centro* ☎ *971/712942* ⊕ *www.hotelborn.com* *29 rooms* *In-hotel: bar, no elevator, laundry service, public Wi-Fi, airport shuttle, no-smoking rooms* ▭ *AE, DC, MC, V* *BP.*

$$$–$$$$ **Dalt Murada.** Dating back to the 15th century, this town house in the old part of Palma was the Sancha Moragues family home until 2001, when the family opened it as a hotel. Most of the furniture, paintings, and decor were the family's own, handed down for generations, but with modernization came enormous Jacuzzi tubs in the tile bathrooms. Weather permitting, a basic breakfast is served in the lovely interior garden, overgrown with bougainvillea, orange, and lemon trees. The location, a minute's walk to the cathedral, is ideal. **Pros:** location, helpful service, homey feel. **Cons:** thin walls, a bit pricey for what you get. ✉ *Carrer Almudaina 6A, Barrio Antiguo* ☎ *971/425300* ⊕ *www.daltmurada.org* *8 rooms* *In-room: safe, refrigerator, DVD. In-hotel: cafeteria, laundry service, public Internet* ▭ *AE, MC, V* *BP.*

$$$$ **Gran Hotel Son Net.** This restored estate house—parts of which date back to 1672—is one of Majorca's most luxurious hotels. Poplars and

palms shade the terrace above the 30-meter pool, with the village of Puigpunyent and the countryside below. Room decors can be a bit over the top—a lot of red and rose pink—but the bathrooms are truly palatial. The hotel's showcase restaurant, Oleum, set in an ancient olive press, is an ideal showcase for the creations of chef Christian Rullan, trained at Le Nôtre in Paris but fiercely proud of his Majorcan roots; try his lamb in rosemary sauce. **Pros:** attentive staff, family-friendly, convenient to Palma. **Cons:** pricey breakfast. ✉ *Carrer Castillo de Son Net, Puigpunyent* ☎ *971/147000* 🌐 *www.sonnet.es* *20 rooms, 11 suites* *In-room: safe, refrigerator, DVD, Wi-Fi. In-hotel: 2 restaurants, room service, 2 bars, pool, gym, spa, bicycles, laundry service, concierge, public Internet, airport shuttle, parking (no fee), no-smoking rooms* *AE, DC, MC, V.*

$$$$ ★ **Palau Sa Font.** Warm Mediterranean tones and crisp, clean lines give this boutique hotel in the center of Palma's shopping district an atmosphere very different from anything else in the city. A 16th-century Episcopal palace, restored as a hotel in 2000, it has ample rooms with linen curtains and plump comforters. From the terrace in the tower, you have 360-degree views of Palma's old quarter. **Pros:** buffet breakfast until 11, helpful English-speaking staff, chic design. **Cons:** pool is small, surroundings can be a bit noisy in midsummer. ✉ *Carrer Apuntadores 38, Barrio Antiguo* ☎ *971/712277* 🌐 *www.palausafont.com* *19 rooms* *In-room: refrigerator, Ethernet. In-hotel: bar, pool, elevator, some pets allowed* *AE, MC, V* *BP.*

$$$$ Fodor's Choice ★ **Reads Hotel and Spa.** A 15-minute drive from Palma, this peaceful retreat centers on a restored 18th-century estate house, with its own vineyard. Detached suites have private gardens. Each room is furnished in a different, fanciful style, from Moorish-exotic to traditional and modern; lobby and lounge areas are filled with antiques from the owner's collection. The spa has an indoor pool and rooms for esthetic and deep-relaxation treatments. Chef-Director Marc Fosh has won top honors for his superb Bacchus restaurant ($$$$); serious eaters will book the "chef's table" in the evening—an alcove in the kitchen itself, with seating for six. **Pros:** huge estate good for long walks, indoor/outdoor pools, spa. **Cons:** no minibars, room decor a bit too busy to allow for pure relaxation. ✉ *Ctra. Santa María–Alaró s/n* ☎ *971/140261* 🌐 *www.readshotel.com* *8 rooms, 15 suites* *In-room: safe, DVD, Wi-Fi. In-hotel: 2 restaurants, room service, bar, tennis court, 2 pools, gym, spa, bicycles, no elevator, laundry service, concierge, public Internet, airport shuttle, parking (no fee), no children under 12, no-smoking rooms* *AE, DC, MC, V* *BP.*

NIGHTLIFE

Majorca's nightlife is never hard to find. Many of the hot spots are concentrated 6 km (4 mi) west of Palma at **Punta Portals**, in Portals Nous, where King Juan Carlos I often moors his yacht when he's in Majorca in early August for the Copa del Rey international regatta. In Palma, the section of the Passeig Marítim known as **Avinguda Gabriel Roca** is a nucleus of taverns, pubs, and clubs. **Abraxas** (✉ *Paseo Maritimo 42* ☎ *971/455908* 🌐 *www.abraxasmallorca.com*) thumps to house music until the wee hours. Once a week (usually Sunday) they host a gay night with an infectious anything-goes vibe; the cover charge can be pricey (€10–€20). Outdoor elevators transport you from Avinguda Gabriel Roca to the dance floor at the sleek and futuristic **Tito's** (☎ *971/730017*).

★ The **Plaça de la Llotja** and surrounding streets are where to go for *copas* (drinking, tapas sampling, and general carousing). Elegant **Abaco** (✉ *Carrer de Sant Joan 1, La Llotja* ☎ *971/714939*) offers baroque music amid fragrant flowers and fruit.

Carrer Apuntadores, a street on the Born's west side in the old town, is lined with casual bars that appeal especially to night owls in their twenties and thirties. On the weekends, you can often come across impromptu live rock and pop acts performed on small back stages. Some of Palma's best jazz acts play the small, smoky jazz club **Barcelona** (✉ *Carrer Apuntadores 5, La Llotja* ☎ *971/713557*) on weekends.

Join the after-work crowd basking in the Palma of yesteryear at **Cappuccino Grand Café** (✉ *Carrer Sant Miquel 53, La Llotja* ☎ *971/719764*), a fun evening venue (not to be confused with the restaurant and coffee shop with the same name in the Barrio Antiguo commercial area. **Bluesville** (✉ *Carrer Mas del Morro 3, Barrio Antiguo* ☎ *No phone*) is a laid-back bar popular with both locals and foreigners. You can listen to rock and blues on Saturday nights. In summer (June–September), head to the nearby suburb of Magalluf and dance the night away at the gargantuan disco **BCM Planet Dance** (✉ *Av. S'Olivera s/n, Magalluf* ☎ *971/132715*).

Palma's **Gran Casino de Majorca** is a short distance from the harbor. There's an admission charge of €4, and you'll need your passport to enter; dress is informal, but T-shirts, shorts, and sandals are considered inappropriate. ✉ *Urb. Sol de Majorca s/n, Calvià* ☎ *971/130000* ⏲ *Daily 5 PM–5 AM*.

SPORTS AND THE OUTDOORS

BALLOONING For spectacular views of the island, float up with **Majorca Balloons** (✉ *Ca'n Melis 22, Cala Rajada* ☎ *971/818182, 639/818109 in winter*).

BICYCLING With long flat stretches and heart-pounding climbs, Majorca's 675 km (400 mi) of rural roads adapted for cycling make this the most popular sport on the island; many European professional teams do preseason training here. Tourist board offices have excellent leaflets on bike routes with maps, details about the terrain, sights, and distances.

BIRD-WATCHING Majorca has two notable nature reserves, ideal for bird-watchers. **S'Albufera de Majorca** (✉ *Ctra. Port d'Alcúdia–Ca'n Picafort, Hotel Parc Natural* ☎ *971/892250* 🌐 *www.mallorcaweb.net/salbufera* ⏲ *Apr.–Sept., daily 9–7; Oct.–Mar., daily 9–5*) is the largest wetlands zone in Majorca, with binoculars for rent. **Sa Dragonera** (✉ *Llista de Correus E-07458 Can Picafort, Majorca* ☎ *971/180632* ⏲ *Apr.–Sept., daily 9–5; Oct.–Mar., daily 9–4*) has a large colony of sea falcons and is accessible by boat from Sant Elm, the western tip of Majorca. **Cruceros Margarita** (☎ *639/617545*) excursion boats to Sa Dragonera leave from the port of Sant Elm, at the western tip of the island, and from Port d'Andratx, Monday–Saturday (except December and January) at 10:15, 11:15, 12:15, and 1:15. The fare is €10.

GOLF Majorca has more than a score of 18-hole golf courses, among them PGA championship venues of fiendish difficulty. For more information, contact the **Federación Balear de Golf** (*Balearic Golf Federation* ✉ *Av. Jaime III 17, Palma* ☎ *971/722753* 🌐 *www.fbgolf.com*).

HANG GLIDING For memorable views of the island, glide above it on an ultralight. Arrange a trip at **Escuela de Ultraligeros "El Cruce"** (✉ *Ctra. Palma–Manacor, Km 42, Vilafranca de Bonany* ☎ *629/392776*). For hang gliding, contact **Parapente Alfàbia** (☎ *622/600900* 🌐 *www.parapentealfabia.com*). **Club Vol Lliure Majorca** (☎ *655/766443* 🌐 *www.cvlmallorca.com*) conducts weekend and intensive hang-gliding courses.

HIKING Majorca is excellent for hiking. In the Sierra de Tramuntana, you can easily arrange to trek one way and take a boat, bus, or train back. Ask the tourist office for the free booklet *20 Hiking Excursions on the Island of Majorca,* with detailed maps and itineraries. For more hiking information, contact the **Grup Excursionista de Majorca** (*Majorcan Hiking Association* ✉ *Carrer del Horts 1 baixos, Palma* ☎ *971/718823* 🌐 *www.gemweb.org*). A useful travel agency that organizes trekking is **Explorador** (☎ *600/557770* 🌐 *www.islavision.com*).

SAILING For information on sailing, call the **Federación Balear de Vela** (*Balearic Sailing Federation* ✉ *Carrer Joan Miró s/n [San Agustin], Palma* ☎ *971/402412* 🌐 *www.federacionbalearvela.org*). The **Escuela Nacional de Vela de Calanova** (*National Sailing School* ✉ *Av. Joan Miró 327, San Agustí* ☎ *971/402512*) can clue you in about sailing in the Balearics. The **Club de Mar** (✉ *Muelle de Pelaires, south end of Passeig Marítim, Palma* ☎ *971/403611* 🌐 *www.clubdemar-mallorca.com*) is famous among yachties. It has its own hotel, bar, disco, and restaurant. Charter a yacht at **Cruesa Majorca Yacht Charter** (✉ *Carrer Contramuelle Mollet 12, Palma* ☎ *971/282821* 🌐 *www.cruesa.com*).

SCUBA DIVING Ask about scuba diving at **Escuba Palma** (✉ *Av. Rey Jaume I 84, Santa Ponsa* ☎ *971/694968*). **Big Blue** (🌐 *www.bigblediving.net* ☎ *971/681686*) is a source for all things scuba related.

WATER SPORTS You can rent windsurfers and dinghies at most beach resorts; both skin and scuba diving are excellent; and the island has some 30 yacht marinas. On the northwest coast at Port de Sóller, canoes, windsurfers, dinghies, motor launches, and waterskiing gear are available for rent from Easter to October at **Escola d'Esports Nàutics** (✉ *Calle Marina s/n, Port de Sóller* ☎ *609/354132* 🌐 *www.nauticsoller.com*).

SHOPPING

Majorca's specialties are shoes and leather clothing, porcelain, utensils carved from olive wood, handblown glass, and artificial pearls. Look for designer fashions on the **Passeig des Born,** and for antiques on **Costa de la Pols,** a narrow little street near the Plaça Riera. The **Plaça Major** has a modest crafts market Monday, Thursday, Friday, and Saturday 10–2. In summer the market is open daily 10–2; January and February, it's open weekends only. Another crafts market is held May 15–October 15, 8 PM–midnight in **Plaça de les Meravelles.**

Many of Palma's best shoe shops are on Avda. Rei Jaime III, between the Plaça Juan Carles I and the Passeig Mallorca. **Barrats** (✉ *Av. Jaime III 5, Centro* ☎ *971/213024*) specializes in leather coats and shoes for

9

women.**Camper** (✉ *Av. Jaime III 16, Centro* ☎*971/714635*) has an internationally popular line of sport shoes. **Carmina** (✉*Avda. de la Unió 4, Centro* ☎*971/229047*) is the place for top-quality handcrafted men's dress shoes. **Farrutx** (✉*Passeig des Born 16, Centro* ☎*971/715308*) gets top prices for its elegant line of women's shoes and bags. **Jaime Mascaró** (✉*Av. Jaime III 10, Centro* ☎*971/729842*) is known for its original high-fashion designer shoes for women. Majorca's most popular footwear is its simple, comfortable slip-on espadrilles (usually with a leather front over the first half of the foot and a strap across the back of the ankle). Look for a pair at **Alpargatería La Concepción** (✉*Concepción 17, Barrio Antiguo* ☎*971/710709*).

Mediterráneo (✉*Av. Jaume III 11, Centro* ☎*971/712159*) sells high-quality artificial pearls in its elegant sit-down showroom. **Las Columnas** (✉*C. Sant Domingo 8, Barrio Antiguo* ☎*971/712221*) has ceramics from all over the Balearic Islands. Visit **Gordiola** (✉*Carrer Jaume II 14, Barrio Antiguo* ☎*971/715518*), glassmakers since 1719, for a variety of original bowls, bottles, plates, and decorative objects. The company's factory is in Alguida, on the Palma–Manacor road, where you can watch the glass being blown and even try your hand at making a piece. Just down the street from Gordiola is **Lafiore** (✉*Carrer Jaume II 6, Barrio Antiguo* ☎*971/716517*), the island's other venerable glassmaker, which has its factory showroom in S'Esgleieta, on the road from Palma to Valldemossa. The **Colmado Santo Domingo** (✉*Carrer Santo Domingo 1* ☎*971/714887* 🌐*www.colmadosantodomingo.com* ⏲*Mon.–Sat. 10–8*) is a wonderful little shop for the *artisanal* food specialties of Majorca: *sobresada* (soft salami) of black pork, sausages of all sorts, cheeses, jams, and honeys and preserves.

JARDINS D'ALFÀBIA

17 km (10½ mi) north of Palma.

Here's a sound you don't often hear in the Majorcan interior: the sound of falling water. The Moorish viceroy of the island developed the springs and hidden irrigation systems here sometime in the 12th century, to create this remarkable oasis on the road to Sóller, with its 40-odd varieties of trees, climbers, and flowering shrubs. The 17th-century manor house, furnished with antiques and painted panels, has a collection of original documents that chronicle the history of the estate. ✉*Ctra. Palma–Sóller, Km. 17* ☎*971/613123* 🎟*€4.50* ⏲*Nov.–Mar., weekdays 9–5:30, Sat. 9–1; Apr.–Oct., Mon.–Sat. 9–6:30.*

SÓLLER

★ *13 km (8 ½ mi) north of Jardins d'Alfàbia, 30 km (19 mi) north of Palma.*

All but the briefest visits to Majorca should include at least an overnight stay in Sóller, one of the most beautiful towns on the island, notable for the palatial homes built in the 19th and early 20th centuries by the landowners and merchants who thrived on the export of the region's oranges, lemons, and almonds. Many of the buildings here, like the

Church of Sant Bartomeu and the **Bank of Sóller,** on the Plaça Constitució, and the nearby **Can Prunera,** are gems of the Moderniste style, designed by contemporaries of Antoni Gaudí. The tourist information office in the **Town Hall,** next to Sant Bartomeu, has a walking tour map of the important sites.

GETTING HERE AND AROUND

TIP→ If you're driving to Sóller from Palma, take the tunnel (€4.10) at Alfàbia, rather than the road over the mountains. The latter is spectacular—lemon and olive trees on stone-walled terraces, farmhouses perched on the edges of forested cliffs—but demanding. Save your strength for even better mountain roads ahead. You can travel in retro style to Sóller from Palma on one of the seven daily trains (round-trip €17) from Plaça d'Espanya—a string of wooden coaches with leather-covered seats dating from 1912.

In Sóller, a charming old trolley car (€4) threads its way from the train station down through town to Port de Sóller.

ESSENTIALS

Trolley Contact Sóller trolley (✉ *Eusebi Estada 1, Palma de Mallorca* ☎ *902/364711* ✉ **Sóller** *Plaça d'Espanya 6* ☎ *902/364711* 🌐 *www.trendesoller.com*).

Visitor Information Port de Sóller (✉ *Canonge Oliver 10* ☎ *971/633042* ✉ **Sóller** *Plaça d'Espanya 1* ☎ *971/638008*).

EXPLORING

Sóller's **Station Building Galleries** (✉ *Pl. Espanya 6* ☎ *971/630301* *Free* ⏲ *Daily 10:30–6:30*) have two small collections, one of engravings by Joan Miró, the other of ceramics by Picasso.

WHERE TO STAY

$$ **El Guía.** Built in 1880, El Guía (The Guide) is furnished in a comfortable mix of rustic and Moderniste styles, with nothing fancy in the way of services or amenities. A few steps from the railroad station, it has a pretty courtyard with wrought-iron gates, rooms with a view of the mountains, and a restaurant ($) popular for Majorcan specialties. **Pros:** good value for price, friendly-family service, location. **Cons:** just the basics, neighborhood can be a bit noisy. ✉ *Carrer Castanyer 2* ☎ *971/630227* 🌐 *www.sollernet.com/elguia* *18 rooms* *In-room: no phone, no TV. In-hotel: restaurant, room service, no elevator, laundry service* *MC, V* ⏲ *Closed Nov.–Mar.* *BP.*

$$–$$$ **La Vila.** Owner Toni Oliver opened this lovingly restored town house on Sóller's central square in 2006. Rooms (four on the square, four facing the interior garden) are plainly furnished, but the public spaces keep much of the original lush Moderniste detail: coffered ceilings, alabaster walls cut in floral patterns, arches in carved and painted plaster, a three-story central staircase with a cupola. Book well in advance, on La Vila's Web site. **Pros:** friendly service, good location, palm-shaded garden terrace restaurant. **Cons:** rooms on the square can be noisy, no elevator. ✉ *Pl. Constitució 14* ☎ *971/634641* 🌐 *www.lavilahotel.com* *8 rooms* *In-room: safe, refrigerator, Wi-Fi. In-hotel: restaurant, room service, bar, laundry service, no-smoking rooms* *MC, V.*

9

$$$$ **L'Avenida.** This boutique hotel was a stately private home, built in 1910 by Joan Rubio, a disciple of Gaudí, for a wealthy local merchant. The transformation retains some of the original Moderniste features—frescoed ceilings, a marble staircase with wrought-iron railing—but from there it goes ultramodern, with white rugs and black furniture, animal-print fabrics, designer lamps, and jet chandeliers. The house blends its own herbal toiletries. **Pros:** peaceful poolside terrace, quiet surroundings. **Cons:** lounge decor is over the top, not especially family-friendly. *⊠Gran Via 9 ☎971/634075 ⊕www.avenida-hotel.com 4 doubles, 4 suites In-room: safe, refrigerator, DVD, Wi-Fi. In-hotel: restaurant, room service, bar, pool, no elevator, laundry service, concierge, airport shuttle, no children under 14, no-smoking rooms ▭MC, V.*

DEIÀ

★ *9 km (5½ mi) southwest of Sóller.*

Deià is perhaps best known as the adopted home of the English poet and writer Robert Graves, who lived here off and on from 1929 until his death in 1985. The village is still a favorite haunt of writers and artists, including Graves's son Tomás, author of *Pa amb Oli (Bread and Olive Oil)*, a guide to Majorcan cooking, and British painter David Templeton. Ava Gardner lived here for a time; so, briefly, did Picasso. The setting is unbeatable; all around Deià rise the steep cliffs of the Sierra de Tramuntana. There's live jazz on summer evenings. On warm afternoons, literati gather at the beach bar in the rocky cove at Cala de Deià, 2 km (1 mi) downhill from the village. Walk up the narrow street to the village church; the small **cemetery** behind it affords views of mountains terraced with olive trees and of the coves below. It's a fitting spot for Graves's final resting place, in a quiet corner.

GETTING HERE AND AROUND

The Palma-Port de Sóller bus passes through Deià five times daily in each direction.

EXPLORING

In 2007, the Fundació Robert Graves opened a museum dedicated to Deià's most famous resident, in **Ca N'Alluny,** the house he built in 1932, overlooking the sea. It's something of a shrine: Graves' furniture and books, personal effects, and the press he used to print many of his works are all preserved. *⊠Ctra. Deià-Sóller s/n ☎971/636185 ⊕www.fundaciorobertgraves.org €5 Tues.–Fri. 9–5, Sat. 9–2, Sun. 10–3.*

WHERE TO STAY

$$$$ ★ **Es Molí.** A converted 17th-century manor house in the hills above the valley of Deià, the Es Molí is a haven of peace and relaxation, of an older sort of luxury (as a hotel it dates to 1965) without the over-the-top pretensions. There are acres of gardens and secluded corners, with deck chairs under the orange trees; as well as bamboo groves and ancient olive trees, and everywhere the sound of water tumbling from a mountain spring. Rooms are spacious and classically furnished; most have private balconies with stone balustrades and stunning views. A shuttle bus runs five times a day to the hotel's private cove at Sa Muleta, with

a cliffside solarium and lounge deck. **Pros:** attentive service, open-air chamber music concerts twice a week at dinner, great value for price. **Cons:** steep climb to rooms in the annex, short season. ✉ *Ctra. Valldemossa—Deià s/n* ☎ *971/639000* 🌐 *www.esmoli.com* *84 rooms, 3 suites* *In-room: safe, refrigerator, Wi-Fi. In-hotel: 2 restaurants, room service, 2 bars, tennis court, pool, gym, elevator, laundry service, concierge, public Wi-Fi, airport shuttle* *AE, DC, MC, V* *Closed Nov.–Mar.*

$$$$ **La Residencia.** Fodor's Choice ★ Two 16th- to 17th-century manor houses have been artfully combined to make this exceptional hotel on a hill facing the village of Deià. It is superbly furnished with Majorcan antiques, modern canvases, and canopied four-poster beds. Herbs, olives, fruit, and flowers come straight to the kitchen and guest rooms from the hotel's lush landscaped gardens. The new annex (eight rooms on two levels, four with private heated plunge pools) combines the latest in luxury with the best views of the mountains. El Olivo, the restaurant ($$$–$$$$), offers an inventive continental menu that includes eclectic but delicious zingers such as lobster with ibérico ham. The hotel has its own shuttle to the sea at Lluc Alcari. **Pros:** impeccable service, view from the terrace. **Cons:** only gnomes can negotiate the stairs to the Tower Suite. ✉ *Son Canals s/n* ☎ *971/639011* 🌐 *www.hotellaresidencia.com* *75 rooms* *In-room: safe, refrigerator, DVD, Ethernet, Wi-Fi. In-hotel: 3 restaurants, room service, 2 bars, 2 tennis courts, 3 pools, gym, spa, bicycles, children's programs, laundry service, concierge, public Internet, airport shuttle, parking (no fee), no kids under 10, no-smoking rooms* *AE, DC, MC, V* *BP.*

$$$ **s'Hotel D'Es Puig.** This family-run "hotel on the hill" has a back terrace with a lemon tree garden and a wonderful view of the mountains; the simply furnished balcony doubles, with exposed beams, share the view. D'Es Puig gets a lot of repeat business from British visitors, so book early. **Pros:** peaceful setting, friendly service. **Cons:** pool is small, beds could be more comfortable, parking difficult. ✉ *Es Puig 4* ☎ *971/639409 or 637/820805* 🌐 *www.hoteldespuig.com* *8 rooms* *In-room: safe, refrigerator, Wi-Fi. In-hotel: cafeteria, bar, pool, bicycles, no elevator, laundry service, public Wi-Fi, parking (no fee), no-smoking rooms* *AE, DC, MC, V* *Closed Dec. and Jan.* *BP.*

9

SON MARROIG

4 km (2½ mi) west of Deià.

West of Deià is Son Marroig, one of the estates of Austrian archduke Luis Salvador (1847–1915), who arrived in Majorca as a young man and fell in love with the place. The archduke acquired huge tracts of land along the northwest coast, where he built *miradores* at the most spectacular points but otherwise left the pristine beauty of the land intact. Below the *mirador* at Son Marroig itself you can see **Sa Foradada,** a rock peninsula pierced by a huge archway, where the archduke moored his yacht. Now a museum, the estate house contains the archduke's collections of Mediterranean pottery and ceramics, old Majorcan furniture, and paintings. From April through early October, the Deià International Festival holds classical concerts here. ✉ *Ctra. Deià–Valldemossa s/n* ☎ *971/639158* 🎫 *€3* ⏲ *Apr.–Sept., Mon.–Sat. 9:30–7:30; Oct.–Mar., Mon.–Sat. 9:30–5:30.*

On the road south from Deià to Valldemossa is the **Monestir de Miramar,** founded in 1276 by Ramón Llull, who established a school of Asian languages here. It was bought in 1872 by the Archduke Luis Salvador and restored as a *mirador*. Explore the garden and the tiny cloister, then walk below through the olive groves to a spectacular lookout. ✉ *Ctra. Deià–Valldemossa s/n* ☎ *971/616073* 🎫 *€3* ⏲ *Apr.–Oct., Mon.–Sat. 10–7; Nov.–Mar., Mon.–Sat. 9:30–7.*

VALLDEMOSSA

18 km (11 mi) north of Palma.

Visitor Information Valldemossa (✉ *Av. de Palma 7* ☎ *971/612019*).

EXPLORING

The **Reial Cartuja** *(Royal Carthusian Monastery)* was founded in 1339, but when the monks were expelled in 1835, it was privatized, and the cells became apartments for travelers. The most famous lodgers were Frédéric Chopin and his lover, the Baroness Amandine Dupin—a French novelist who used the pseudonym George Sand. The two spent three difficult months here in the cold, damp winter of 1838–39. The tourist office, in the plaza next to the church, sells a ticket good for all of the monastery's attractions.

In the **church,** note the frescoes above the nave—the monk who painted them was Goya's brother-in-law. The **pharmacy,** in the cloisters, was made by the monks in 1723 and is almost completely preserved; from here, a long corridor leads to the apartments occupied by Chopin and Sand, furnished in period style. The piano is original. Nearby, another set of apartments houses the local **museum,** with mementos of Archduke Luis Salvador and a collection of old printing blocks. From here you return to the ornately furnished **King Sancho's palace,** a group of rooms originally built by King Jaume II for his son Sancho. ✉ *Pl. de la Cartuja 11* ☎ *971/612106* 🌐 *www.valldemossa.com* 🎫 *€8* ⏲ *Dec. and Jan., Mon.–Sat. 9:30–5; Feb. and Nov., Mon.–Sat. 9:30–5, Sun. 10–1; Mar. –Oct., Mon.–Sat. 9:30–5:30, Sun. 10–1.*

WHERE TO EAT AND STAY

$$$$ ★ **Valldemossa Hotel.** The breathtaking vistas alone are worth a stay. Once part of the Valldemossa Carthusian monastery, this beautifully restored Majorcan stone house–turned–luxury hotel sits on a hill amid acres of olive trees and has sweeping views of the Tramuntana mountains, the town, and the monastery. Modern rooms have snowy white curtains and comforters, and antique bedsteads. You can relax on rattan chairs shaded by palms in the sunny patio and then ease into the evening at the elegant restaurant ($$$$), which serves Mediterranean and international dishes. **Pros:** private, with peaceful surroundings. **Cons:** restaurant needs more variety, service can be spotty. ✉ *Ctra. Valldemossa s/n* ☎ *971/612626* 🌐 *www.valldemossahotel.com* *3 double rooms, 9 junior suites* *In-room: safe, refrigerator, DVD, Ethernet, Wi-Fi.*

In-hotel: restaurant, room service, bar, pools, spa, bicycles, no elevator, laundry service, public Internet, public Wi-Fi, airport shuttle, parking (no fee), no-smoking rooms ▭*AE, MC, V* 🍴*BP.*

BANYALBUFAR

23 km (14 mi) northwest of Palma.

Originally terraced by the Romans, this tiny town overlooks its tiny harbor from high on a cliff. A 1½-km (1-mi) walk southwest leads to the **Mirador Ses Animes** observation point.

WHERE TO STAY

$$$ ★ **Mar i Vent.** This small hotel has been run by the same family since 1931. At the north end of Banyalbufar, the property faces the ocean and has mountains at its back. Paths lead down to two small, rocky coves for sea swimming. All guest rooms have balconies with sea or mountain views and are furnished in traditional style with simple blond wood furniture and red-brown tile floors. **Pros:** base camp for great excursions, friendly service. **Cons:** minimal amenities, not much to do in town. ✉*Carrer Major 49, Banyalbufar* ☎*971/618000* 🌐*www.hotelmarivent.com* *29 rooms* *In-room: no a/c (some), safe, Ethernet. In-hotel: restaurant, room service, bar, tennis court, pool, bicycles, laundry service, public Internet, public Wi-Fi, airport shuttle, parking (no fee), no-smoking rooms* ▭*MC, V* ⏲*Closed Dec. and Jan.* 🍴*BP.*

BINISSALEM

25 km (15 mi) northeast of Palma.

Visitor Information Binissalem (✉*Carrer de la Concepció 7* ☎*971/511043*).

EXPLORING

Binissalem is the center of one of the island's two D.O. (Denominación de Orígen) registered wine regions and has a riotous harvest festival in mid-September, when surplus grapes are dumped by the truckload for participants to fling at each other. The town is a good base, not just for visits to the local **bodegas** *(wineries)*, but for forays around the island: Palma remains a half hour away by car.

WHERE TO STAY

$$$–$$$$ **Scott's.** American George Scott and Brit Judy Brabner converted this 18th-century Majorcan mansion into a guesthouse for people looking for peace and quiet. A lovely interior garden leads back to rooms and suites facing the courtyard, done in a range of decors from traditional—with canopied beds—to modern. A Spanish breakfast is included in the room price. The couple also run a sister hotel, equally soothing, in an artists' colony above the village of Galilea, northwest of Palma. Ask about a package combining stays at both hotels for a discount. ✉*Pl. Iglesia 12* ☎*971/870100* 🌐*www.scottshotel.com* *13 rooms, 4 suites* *In-room: no TV. In-hotel: bar, pool, no elevator, laundry service, parking (no fee), no kids under 12, no-smoking rooms* ▭*MC, V* 🍴*BP.*

EN ROUTE

In and around Binissalem are some of Majorca's best wineries, most of them open for tastings and tours. One of the largest is **Bodegas José Ferrer** (✉ *Conquistador 103* ☎ *971/511050*). A hard winery to find, but worth a detour, since it exports none of its production, is Antonio Nadal's **Finca Son Roig** (✉ *Camino de Son Roig s/n* ☎ *971/451146*).

INCA

29 km (17 mi) northeast of Palma.

Inca and environs is shoe heaven: major firms like **Camper** (✉ *Poligon Industrial s/n* ☎ *902/364598*), **Barrats** (✉ *Avda. General Luque 480* ☎ *971/213024*), and **Munper** (✉ *Carrer Jocs 170* ☎ *971/881000*) have their factory showrooms here, and there are dozens of smaller craft ateliers all over town specializing in different kinds of footwear and leather apparel. The Thursday market is the largest on Majorca.

WHERE TO EAT

$$ SPANISH ✕ **Celler C'an Amer.** A *celler* is a uniquely Majorcan combination of wine cellar and restaurant, and Inca has no fewer than six. C'an Amer is the best, with heavy oak beams and huge wine vats lining the walls behind the tables and banquettes. Antonia, the dynamic chef-owner, serves some of the best *lechona* (suckling pig) and *tumbet* (vegetables baked in layers) on the island. Portions here are heroic. Winter specialties include a superb oxtail soup prepared with red wine and seasonal mushrooms. After lunch, take your coffee around the corner in the pleasant little church square of Plaça de Santa Maria la Major. ✉ *Carrer Pau 39* ☎ *971/501261* ▭ *AE, MC, V* ⊗ *Closed weekends, Mar.–Sept.*

MANACOR

50 km (30 mi) east of Palma.

Majorca's second-largest town, Manacor is known primarily for its Majórica artificial-pearl industry; from here, it's only a few minutes' drive to any of the beaches on the island's eastern coast. Prehistoric settlement sites abound in this area; later, the Romans moved in, followed by the Moors, who built a mosque where the Gothic parish church of **Nostra Senyora de les Dolores** (Our Lady of Sorrows) now stands.

ESSENTIALS

Visitor Information Manacor (✉ *Carre Mola s/n* ☎ *971/834144*).

ALCÚDIA

54 km (34 mi) northeast of Palma.

The first city on the site of Alcúdia was a Roman settlement, in 123 BC. The Moors reestablished a town here, and after the Reconquest it became a feudal possession of the Knights Templars; the first ring of city walls dates to the early 14th century. Begin your visit at the **Church of Sant Jaume,** and walk through the maze of narrow streets inside to the **Porta de Xara,** with its twin crenellated towers.

ESSENTIALS

Visitor Information Alcúdia (✉ *Passeig Marítim s/n* ☎ *971/847241*).

EXPLORING

The **Museu Monogràfic de Pollentia** has a good collection of Roman items. ✉ *Carrer Sant Jaume 30* ☎ *971/547004* *€2* ⏲ *Tues.–Fri. 10–3:30, weekends 10:30–1.*

Just outside Alcúdia, off the port road, a signposted lane leads to the small, 1st-century BC **Teatre Romà** *(Roman Amphitheater).*

POLLENÇA

5 km (3 mi) inland of the port.

The history of this pretty little town goes back at least as far as the Roman occupation of the island; the only trace of that period is a small **stone bridge** at the edge of town. In the 13th century Pollença and much of the land around it was owned by the Knights Templars—who built the imposing **Church of Nuestra Senyora de Los Ángeles,** on the west side of the present-day Plaça Major. The church looks east to the 330-meter peak of the Puig de Maria, with the 15-century **Sanctuary** at the top. The **Calvari** of Pollença is a flight of 365 stone steps to a tiny **chapel,** and a panoramic view as far as Cap de Formentor. There's a colorful weekly **market** here on Sunday mornings.

ESSENTIALS

Visitor Information Pollença (✉ *Carrer Sant Domingo 2* ☎ *971/535077*).

EXPLORING

OFF THE BEATEN PATH

Cap de Formentor. The winding road north from Port de Pollença to the tip of the island is spectacular. Stop at the **Mirador de la Cruete**: here, the rocks crest into the sea to form deep narrow inlets of multishaded blue; off to the right, a winding road leads to a stone tower called the **Talaia d'Albercuix,** at the highest point on the peninsula.

WHERE TO STAY

$$$ **Hotel Juma.** This little hotel on Pollença's main square marked its 100th birthday in 2007. Rooms are small and simply but comfortably furnished with traditional Majorcan pieces and hand-embroidered drapes. It's a good choice for a weekend stay becayse of the Sunday market in the square. The owners have another seven-room property, L'Hostal, around the corner (✉ *Carrer Mercat 18* ☎ *971/535282* *www.hostalpollensa.com*) in an old stable that's been converted to a modern boutique hotel. **Pros:** great location, good breakfast in the bar downstairs, good value for price. **Cons:** parking can be a problem. ✉ *Pl. Major 9 (L'Hostal)* ☎ *971/535002* *www.hoteljuma.com* *7 rooms* *In-room: safe, Ethernet, Wi-Fi (some). In-hotel: bar, no elevator, laundry service, public Wi-Fi, no-smoking rooms* *AE, MC, V* *BP.*

THE ARTS

★ Pollença hosts an acclaimed international **music festival** in July and August. Founded in 1961, it has brought in such performers as Mstislav Rostropovic, Jessye Norman, the St. Petersburg Philharmonic, the Camerata Köln and the Alban Berg Quartet. Concerts are held in the

9

cloister of the **Convent of Sant Domingo.** Contact the **Festival ticket office** (☎*971/535077 or 971/534012* 🌐*www.festivalpollenca.org*).

LLUC

20 km (12 mi) southwest of Pollença.

The **Santuari** in the remote mountain village of Lluc is widely considered Majorca's spiritual heart. La Moreneta, also known as La Virgen Negra de Lluc (the Black Virgin of Lluc), is here in the 17th-century **church.** The **museum** has an eclectic collection of ceramics, paintings, clothing, folk costumes, and religious items. A boys' choir sings psalms in the chapel August–May, weekdays at 11:15 AM and around 4:45 PM, and 11 AM for Sunday mass; hours change during holidays and the summer. The Christmas Eve performance of Cant de la Sibila (Song of the Sybil) is an annual choral highlight. ☎*971/871525* *Museum €3; admission to the monastery free* *Daily 8–8.*

WHERE TO STAY

¢ **Santuari de Lluc.** The Lluc monastery offers simple, clean, and cheap accommodation, mostly in cells once occupied by priests. All have bathrooms and sleep between two and six people. Although the vast building has one bar and three Majorcan restaurants ($–$$), nightlife is restricted, and guests are asked to be silent after 11 PM. ✉*Santuari de Lluc, Pl. Pelegrins s/n* ☎*971/871525* 🌐 *www.lluc.net/eng/ahostatg.html* *136 rooms* *In-room: no a/c, kitchenettes (some), no TV. In-hotel: 3 restaurants, bar* *V.*

MINORCA

Minorca, the northernmost Balearic island, is a knobby, cliff-bound plateau with a single central hill—El Toro—from whose 1,100-foot summit you can see the whole island. Prehistoric monuments—*taulas* (huge stone T-shapes), *talayots* (spiral stone cones), and *navetes* (stone structures shaped like overturned boats)—left by the first Neolithic settlers are everywhere on the island.

Tourism came late to Minorca, as it was traditionally more prosperous than its neighbors, and Franco punished the island—which aligned with the Republic in the Civil War—by restricting development here. Having sat out the early Balearic boom, Minorca has avoided many of the other islands' industrialization troubles: there are no high-rise hotels, and the herringbone road system, with a single central highway, means that each resort is small and separate. There's less to see and do on Minorca, and more unspoiled countryside, than on the other Balearics; it's where Spaniards and Catalans tend to take their families on holiday.

GETTING HERE AND AROUND

To get to Minorca from Barcelona take the overnight ferry, fast hydrofoil (about three hours), or a 40-minute flight. It's a six-hour ferry from Palma.

Several buses a day run the length of Minorca between Mahón and Ciutadella, stopping at Alaior, Mercadal, and Ferreries en route. From smaller towns there are daily buses to Mahón and connections, though often indirect, to Ciutadella. Regular bus service from the west end of Ciutadella's Plaça Explanada shuttles beachgoers between town and the resorts to the south and west.

For bus travel around Minorca, the bus line Autos Fornells serves the northeast. Transportes Minorca connects Mahón with Ciutadella and with the major beaches and calas around the island.

If you want to beach hop in Minorca, it's best to have your own transportation, but most of the island's historic sights are in Mahón or Ciutadella, both of which have reasonable bus service from other parts of the island, and once you're in town, everything is within walking distance. You can see the island's archaeological remains in a day's drive, so you may want to rent a car for just part of your visit.

MAHÓN (MAÓ)

Established as the island's capital in 1722, when the British began their nearly 80-year occupation, Mahón stills bears the stamp of its former rulers. The streets nearest the port are lined with four-story Georgian town houses in various states of repair; the Mahónese drink gin and still nurse a craving for Chippendale furniture; English is widely spoken. Mahón is quiet for much of the year, but between June and September the waterfront pubs and restaurants swell with foreigners.

GETTING HERE AND AROUND

For bus travel around Minorca, the bus line Autos Fornells serves the northeast. Transportes Minorca connects Mahón with Ciutadella and with the major beaches and *calas* around the island. Buses depart from Av. J.A. Clavé next to Plaça de s'Esplanada.

Within Mahón, Torres Alles Autocares (*www.e-torres.net*) has three bus lines around the city and to the airport.

In summer, excursions to Minorca's remotest beaches leave daily from the jetty next to the Nuevo Muelle Comercial, in Mahón's harbor.

9

ESSENTIALS

Bike Rentals **Velo Rent Bike** (*S'Arraval 97, Mahón 971/353798*).

Bus Contacts **Autos Fornells** (*www.autosfornells.com*). **Transportes Minorca** (*www.tmsa.es*).**Torres Alles Autocares** (*www.e-torres.net*).

Bus Station **Estació Autobuses** (*Carrer Josep Anselm Clavé 2 971/360457*).

Taxi Contact **Minorca Radio-Taxi** (*Mahón 971/367111*).

Visitor Information **Aeropuerto de Minorca** (*Ctra. de San Clemente s/n 971/157115*). **Mahón** (*Moll de Llevant 2 971/355952*).

EXPLORING

Stop in at No. 25 on the Carrer de Sa Rovellada de Dalt, the **Ateneo,** a cultural and literary society with wildlife, seashells, minerals, and stuffed birds. Side rooms include paintings and mementos of Minorcan writers, poets, and musicians. *Carrer Rovellada de Dalt 25 971/360553 Free Weekdays 10–2 and 4–10, Sat. 10–1:30.*

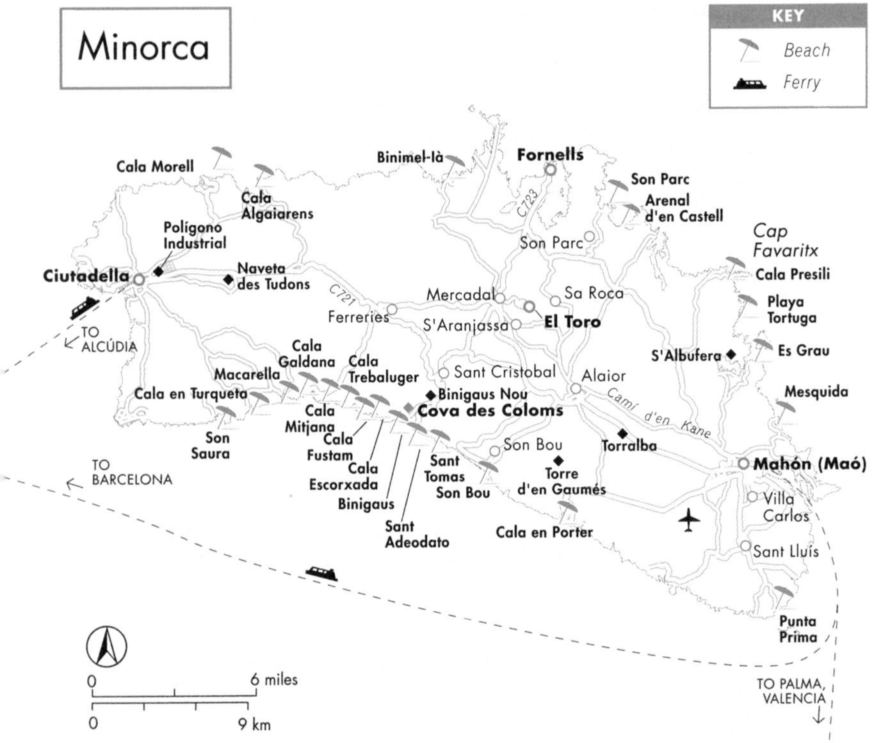

From Sa Rovellada de Dalt, turn left on Carrer de ses Moreres, then right on Carrer Bastió to where it becomes Carrer Costa Deià, and—if it's open—have a look at the **Teatre Principal** (☒*Carrer Costa Deiàa 40* ☎*971/355776* 🌐*www.teatromao.com*). The theater was built in 1824 as an opera house, with five tiers of boxes, red plush seats, and gilded woodwork—a La Scala in miniature. Fully restored in 2005, the Principal still hosts a brief opera season; if you're visiting in the first week of December or June, get tickets at all costs.

Carrer Costa Deià descends to the Plaça Reial (a bit grandiosely named, for an unimposing little rectangle), where it becomes the Carrer sa Ravaleta. Ahead is the church of **La Verge del Carme** (☒*Pl. del Carme* ☎*971/362402*), which has a fine painted and gilded altarpiece. Adjoining the church are the cloisters, now used as a **public market,** with stalls selling fresh produce and a variety of local specialties such as cheeses and sausages.

A few steps north from the Cloister del Carme bring you to the church of **Santa María** (☒*Pl. de la Constitució* ☎*971/363949*), which dates from the 13th century but was rebuilt during the British occupation and restored after being sacked during the civil war. The church's pride is its 3,200-pipe baroque organ, imported from Austria in 1810. There are concerts (€3) here weekdays 11:30–12:30.

Behind the church of Santa María is the **Plaça de la Conquesta,** with a statue of Alfons III of Aragón, who wrested the island from the Moors in 1287. From the Plaça de la Conquesta, walk up Carrer Alfons III and turn right at the **Ajuntament** (✉ *Pl. de la Constitució 1* ☎ *971/369800*) to Carrer Isabel II, a street lined with many Georgian homes. Turn west from Carrer Isabel II on Carrer Rector Mort, and at the far end of the street is the massive gate of **Puerta de San Roque,** the only surviving portion of the 14th-century city walls, rebuilt in 1587 to protect Mahón from the pirate Barbarossa (Redbeard).

WHERE TO EAT AND STAY

$$–$$$ SPANISH

✕ **Antigua Casa Pilar.** On a side street a few steps from the Plaça de l'Esplinada, in the center of Mahón, this pleasant little restaurant (just eight tables) has simple decor of white walls and beams and antique sideboards. Under owners Jesús Saavedra and Fanny Mateu it offers a range of traditional Spanish dishes—including a hearty *sopa de ajo* (garlic soup) with cured ham, chorizo (spicy sausage), and whole cooked cloves of garlic. ✉ *Carrer des Forn 61* ☎ *971/366817* ▭ *AE, DC, MC, V* ⊙ *Closed Sun. and Jan. 1–15. No dinner Mon.–Thurs.*

$$$–$$$$ SEAFOOD

✕ **El Jàgaro.** Named for a mussel-like bilvalve that has a tail used for propelling itself across the ocean floor, this simple waterfront restaurant is a local favorite. The eager lunchtime crowd comes for the platter of lightly fried mixed fish with potatoes, while in the evening you can enjoy grilled *pescado de roca* (rockfish), *sepia* (cuttlefish), or *bacalao* (salt cod). The menu takes a quantum leap in price for the €72 spiny lobster, a delicacy in its various forms. The ortigues (sea anemones) are a house specialty not to be missed. ✉ *Moll de Llevant 334–35* ☎ *971/362390* ▭ *AE, MC, V* ⊙ *Closed Mon. No dinner Sun.*

$$$$ SPANISH Fodor'sChoice ★

✕ **Es Moli de Foc.** Originally a flour mill—de foc means "of fire," signifying that the mill was operated by internal combustion rather than wind—this is the oldest building in the village of Sant Climent, about 3 km (2 mi) from the airport. Es Moli may not look like much, but the food is exceptional. Don't miss the prawns carpaccio with cured Mahón cheese and artichoke oil, or the black paella with monkfish and squid. Order off the menu for the *carrilleras de ternera* (boiled beef cheeks) with potato purée. End with ice cream of Minorcan cheese and figs. In summer, book a table on the terrace. ✉ *Carrer Sant Llorenç 65, Sant Climent* ☎ *971/153222* ▭ *MC, V* ⊙ *Closed Jan. and Mon. Oct.–May. No dinner Sun.*

$$$–$$$$ ECLECTIC

✕ **Itake.** Itake is an amiable clutter of 12 tables, a chalkboard listing specials of the day, paper place mats, and frosted-glass lamps. This is arguably the best place in Mahón for an inexpensive, informal meal with a different touch. Where neighboring eateries pride themselves on fresh fish, Itake serves warm goat cheese, burgers, kangaroo steaks in mushroom sauce, and ostrich breast with strawberry coulis. That said, nothing here is made with any real elaboration: orders come out of the kitchen at nearly the rate of fast food. ✉ *Moll de Llevant 317* ☎ *971/354570* ▭ *AE, DC, MC, V* ⊙ *Closed Mon. No dinner Sun. Sept.–June.*

$$$–$$$$ SPANISH ★

✕ **Marivent.** Mahónese generally agree this is the best kitchen in town, with a seasonal menu that always features fresh fish and Minorcan free-range beef. The sea bream with black-rice risotto and Mahón cheese is wonderful. There is a second-floor patio for dining alfresco; the third-floor main room, with a harbor view, is done in understated elegance. The staff is attentive, and the wine list has some 200 Spanish and French labels. August is the busiest month. ✉ *Moll de Llevant 314* ☎ *971/369801 or 699/062117* *Reservations essential* ▭ *AE, MC, V* ⊙ *Closed Tues. and Christmas–3rd wk of Jan. No dinner Feb.–May, Mon., Wed., and Sun.*

$$$–$$$$ **Biniarroca Country House Hotel.** Floral print duvets, shelves with knick-knacks, comfy chairs: this is an English vision of a secluded rural retreat. The real glory of Biniarroca, though, is the garden of irises, lavender, and flowering trees. The hotel's fine restaurant combines rustic decor with eclectic international cooking. **Pros:** restaurant gets rave reviews, poolside suites have private terraces. **Cons:** bit of a drive to the nearest good beach. ✉ *Cami Vell 57, Sant Lluis* ☎ *971/150059 or 619/460942* ⊕ *www.biniarroca.com* *17 rooms, 2 suites* *In-room: safe, refrigerator (some), DVD (some), Ethernet, Wi-Fi. In-hotel: 2 restaurants, room service, bars, pools, bicycles, no elevator, laundry service, concierge, public Internet, parking (no fee), some pets allowed, no children under 16, no-smoking rooms* ▭ *MC, V* ⊙ *Closed Nov.–Mar.*

Fodor's Choice ★

$$$ **Casa Albertí.** The most centrally of the Mahón hotels, the Casa Alberti was built in 1740 as a private home, during the British occupation, and is registered as a *patrimonio historico-cultural.* The house had been empty some 15 years when Dani Crespo and his partners bought it and turned it into a friendly, comfortable boutique hotel in 2004. The house has 15-foot ceilings, the original marble staircases, and tile floors; the rooms are furnished in rustic style from local and Barcelona antiques shops. Rates include breakfast. **Pros:** good-natured, anything-to-help hospitality, just-right location for exploring Mahón. **Cons:** a bit pricey for the dearth of amenities. ✉ *Carrer Isabel II 9* ☎ *971/354210 or 686/393569* ⊕ *www.casalberti.com* *4 rooms, 2 suites* *In-room: no phone, safe, refrigerator, Ethernet. In-hotel: room service, no elevator, public Internet, no-smoking rooms* ▭ *MC, V.*

$$–$$$ **Catalonia Mirador des Port.** Just a five-minute walk down to the harbor, this hotel is in a quiet residential district at the edge of the old city. The rooms, with cream-and-beige decor and marble floors, range from basic to excellent; the best doubles, above the terrace, have a great view by night of the Romanesque church of Sant Francesc and the whole extent of the harbor. The restaurant ($$–$$$$) specializes in fish and Mediterranean cuisine and serves only lunch in the summers. **Pros:** good location, value for price. **Cons:** reception service can be a bit perfunctory. ✉ *Dalt Vilanova 1* ☎ *971/360016* ⊕ *www.hoteles-catalonia.com* *69 rooms* *In-room: safe, refrigerator, Wi-Fi. In-hotel: restaurant, coffee shop, room service, bar, pool, gym, laundry facilities, public Wi-Fi, no-smoking rooms* ▭ *AE, DC, MC, V.*

$$$$ **Sant Joan de Binissaida.** Approach this lovely restored farmhouse, some 15 km (9 mi) from Mahón, on an avenue lined with chinaberry and fig trees. There's an excellent restaurant, with meals on the deck in good weather; a row of adjoining stables has been converted to additional guest accommodations, with individual terraces. All the rooms at Sant Joan are named for composers; the first-floor "Rossini" is fully

wheelchair accessible. The decor is antique, including a wonderful common room with deep leather chairs, a baize-topped card table—and an oratory. **Pros:** vistas clear to the port of Mahón, huge pool. **Cons:** bit pricey for the lack of amenities, rooms in the annex lack privacy. ✉ *Camí de Binissaida 108, Es Castell* ☎ *971/355598 or 618/874381* 🌐 *www.binissaida.com* *10 rooms, 2 suites* *In-room: safe, refrigerator (some), DVD, Wi-Fi. In-hotel: restaurant, room service, bar, pool, no elevator, laundry service, public Internet, public Wi-Fi, parking (fee), no-smoking rooms* 💳 *MC, V* *Closed Jan.–Mar.*

NIGHTLIFE

Akelarre (✉ *Anden de Poniente 43* ☎ *971/368520*) is a smart drinking venue near the port with live concerts (jazz and blues) on Thursday and Friday nights. Catch live jazz Tuesday (May–September) at the **Casino** (✉ *Sant Jaume 4, Sant Climent* ☎ *971/153418* *€10*) bar and restaurant. It's closed Wednesday. Sant Climent is 4 km (2½ mi) southwest of Mahón. The hottest spot in relatively staid Minorca is the **Cova d'en Xoroi** (✉ *C. Cova s/n* ☎ *971/377236* *€6*), in the beach resort of Cala en Porter, about a 20-minute drive from Mahón. The setting is a series of caves in a cliff high above the sea that, according to local legend, was once the refuge of a castaway Moorish pirate. By day (11–7) it's a tourist attraction, with bars and café terraces; by night, it's a dance-until-dawn disco. In Mahón itself, the bars opposite the ferry terminal fill with locals and visitors. The longtime favorite **Mambo** (✉ *Moll de Llevant 209* ☎ *971/356782*) has rustic stone walls and tasty cocktails.

SPORTS AND THE OUTDOORS

DIVING The clear Mediterranean waters here are ideal for diving. Equipment and lessons are available at Cala En Bosc, Son Parc, Fornells, and Cala Tirant. For scuba diving, compressed air is available at **Club Marítimo** (✉ *Moll de Llevant 287, Mahón* ☎ *971/365022*). For exploring the waters off the western end of the island, equipment and services are available at **Club Náutico** (✉ *Camí del Baix s/n, Ciutadella* ☎ *971/383918* 🌐 *www.cnciutadella.com*).

GOLF Minorca's sole golf course is **Golf Son Parc** (✉ *Urb. Son Parc s/n* ☎ *971/188875* 🌐 *www.golfsonparc.com*), 9 km (6 mi) east of Mercadal.

WALKING In the south, each cove is approached by a *barranca* (ravine or gully), often from several miles inland. The head of **Barranca Algendar** is down a small, unmarked road immediately on the right of the Ferreries–Cala Galdana Road; the barranca ends at the local beach resort, and from there you have a lovely walk north along the sea to an unspoiled half moon of sand at **Cala Macarella.** Extend your walk north, if time allows, through the forest along the riding trail to **Cala Turqueta,** where you find some of the island's most impressive sea grottoes.

WINDSURFING AND SAILING Charter a yacht from **Nautica Tecnimar** (✉ *Ctra. de Cal'n Blanes s/n, Ciutadella* ☎ *971/384469* 🌐 *www.nauticatecnimar.com*) Monday–Saturday. For charters and trips around the island, contact **Blue Mediterraneum** (✉ *Moll de Llevant s/n, Mahón* ☎ *609/305314, 971/354482* 🌐 *www.chartermenorca.com*) Tuesday–Sunday.

SHOPPING

Minorca is known for shoes and leather wear, as well as cheese, gin, and, recently, wine. In Mahón, buy leather goods at **Marks** (✉ *Sa Ravaleta 18* ☎ *971/362660*). Inland, the showroom of **Pons Quintana** (✉ *Calle San Antonio 120, Alaior* ☎ *971/371050*) has a full-length window overlooking the factory where they make their ultrachic women's shoes. It's closed weekends. The company also has a shop in Mahón, at Sa Ravaleta 21, that stays open on Saturday. The showroom of **Jaime Mascaro** (✉ *Poligon Industrial s/n, Ferreries* ☎ *971/373837*), on the main highway from Alaior to Cuitadella, features not only shoes and bags but fine leather coats and belts for men and women. Mascaro also has a shop in Mahón, at Carrer ses Moreres.

A good place to buy the tangy, Parmesan-like Mahón cheese is **Hort de Sant Patrici** (✉ *Camí Ruma-Sant Patrici s/n, Ferreries* ☎ *971/373702* 🌐 *www.santpatrici.com*). You can't visit the dairy itself, but Sant Patrici has a shop, beautiful grounds with a small vineyard and botanical garden, and a display of traditional cheese-making techniques and tools.

In the 18th century, wine was an important part of the Minorcan economy: the British, who knew a good place to grow wine when they saw one, planted the island thick with vines. Viticulture was simply abandoned when Minorca returned to the embrace of Spain, and it has emerged again only in the past few years. The most promising of the small handful of new Minorcan wineries is **Bodegas Binifadet** (✉ *Ses Barraques s/n, Sant Lluis* ☎ *971/150715* 🌐 *www.binifadet.com*); the robust young Binifada wines are on the shelves all over Minorca. The winery is open for tastings May–October, Monday–Saturday 10–1 and 4–8, and well worth a visit.

The other gastronomic legacy of the British occupation was gin. Visit the **Xoriguer distillery** (✉ *Anden de Poniente 91* ☎ *971/362197*), on Mahón's quayside near the ferry terminal, and take a guided tour, sample various types of gin, and buy some to take home.

SIDE TRIP TO TORRALBA

Puzzle over Minorca's prehistoric past at **Torralba.** Driving west from Mahón, you turn south at Alaior on the road to Cala en Porter. Torralba, a megalithic site with a number of stone constructions, is 2 km (1 mi) ahead at a bend in the road, marked by an information kiosk on the left. The massive ***taula*** ("table," a T-shaped stone monument) is through an opening to the right. Behind it, from the top of a stone wall, you can see, in a nearby field, the monolith **Fus de Sa Geganta.**

SIDE TRIP TO TORRE D'EN GAUMÉS

Torre d'en Gaumés, 16 km (9½ mi) west of Mahón, is a far more complex set of stone constructions than Torralba. Fortifications, monuments, deep pits of ruined dwellings, huge vertical slabs, and taulas mark the site. Turn south toward Son Bou on the west side of Alaior. After about 1 km (½ mi), the first fork left will lead you to the ruins.

CIUTADELLA

44 km (27 mi) west of Mahón.

Ciutadella was Minorca's capital before the British settled in Mahón, and its history is richer. As you arrive via the ME1, the main artery across the island from Mahón, turn left at the second roundabout and follow the ring road to the Passeig Marítim; at the end, near the **Castell de Sant Nicolau** watchtower (June–October, daily 10–1 and 5–10) is a **monument to David Glasgow Farragut,** the first admiral of the U.S. Navy, whose father emigrated from Ciutadella to the United States. From here, take Passeig de Sant Nicolau to the **Plaça de s'Esplanada,** and park near the Plaça d'es Born.

GETTING HERE AND AROUND

Autocares Torres has a single bus line serving Ciutadella and the beaches and calas near the city.

ESSENTIALS

Bike Rentals Bike Minorca (✉*Av. Fransesc Femenias 4, Ciutadella* ☎*971/487827*).

Bus Contact Torres Alles Autocares (🌐*www.e-torres.net*).

Bus Station Ciutadella (✉*Pl. de S'Esplanada, across from tourist office*).

Taxi Contact Minorca Parada de Taxis de Ciutadella (☎*971/381197*).

Visitor Information Ciutadella (✉*Pl. de la Catedral 5* ☎*971/382693*).

EXPLORING

From a passage on the left side of Ciutadella's columned and crenellated **Ajuntament** (✉*Pl. d'es Born*), on the west side of the Born, steps lead up to the **Mirador d'es Port,** a lookout from which you can survey the harbor. The local **Museu Municipal** houses artifacts of Minorca's prehistoric, Roman, and medieval past, including records of land grants made by Alfons III to the local nobility after defeating the Moors. It's in an ancient defense tower, the Bastió de Sa Font (Bastion of the Fountain), at the east end of the harbor. ☎*971/380297* 🌐*www.ciutadella.org/museu* *€2.25, free Wed.* *Oct.–Apr., Tues.–Sat. 10–2; May–Sept., Tues–Sat. 10–2 and 6–9.*

The monument in Plaça d'es Born commemorates the citizens' resistance of a Turkish invasion in 1588. South from the plaza along the east side of the Born is the block-long 19th-century **Palau Torresaura** (✉*Carrer Major del Born 8*), built by the Baron of Torresaura, one of the noble families from Aragón and Catalonia that repopulated Minorca after it was captured from the Moors in the 13th century. The interesting facade faces the plaza, though the entrance is on the side street (it is not open to the public). The **Palau Salort,** on the opposite side of the Carrer Major, is the only noble home regularly open to the public. The coats of arms on the ceiling are those of the families Salort (a salt pit and a garden: *sal* and *ort,* or *huerta*) and Martorell (a marten). ✉*Carrer Major des Born* *€2* *May–Oct., Mon.–Sat. 10–2.*

The Carrer Major leads to the Gothic **Cathedral** (✉*Pl. de la Catedral at Pl. Píus XII*), which has some beautifully carved choir stalls. The side

9

chapel has round Moorish arches, remnants of the mosque that once stood on this site; the bell tower is a converted minaret.

Follow the arcade of Carrer de Quadrado north from the cathedral and turn right on Carrer del Seminari, lined on the west side with some of the city's most impressive historic buildings. Among them is the **Seminari of the 17th-century Convent and Eglésia del Socors** (✉ *Carrer del Seminari at Carrer Obispo Vila*), which hosts Ciutadella's summer festival of classical music.

Ciutadella's **port** is accessible from steps that lead down from Carrer Sant Sebastià. The waterfront here is lined with seafood restaurants, some of which burrow into caverns far under the Born.

WHERE TO EAT AND STAY

$$$–$$$$ SEAFOOD **Cafe Balear.** Seafood doesn't get much fresher than here, since the owners' boat docks nearby every day—except Sunday—and the restaurant fish tank is seldom empty. The relaxed atmosphere here welcomes either a quick bite or a full dining experience. The house special, *arroz caldoso de langosta* (lobster and rice stew), is a masterpiece, as are *pulpo a la gallega* (octopus in paprika and olive oil), *cigalas* (crayfish), lobster with onion, and grilled *navajas* (razor clams). ✉ *Paseo San Juan 15* ☎ *971/380005* ▭ *AE, DC, MC, V* ⊙ *Closed Mon. Oct.–June. No dinner Sun. July–Sept. Closed Nov.*

$$–$$$ SPANISH **Cas Cònsol.** On the north side of the Plaça D'Es Born, this informal little restaurant is the place to take a lunch break while exploring the old city. The decor is minimal, with plank floors and unfinished wood/rattan chairs, but the patio upstairs has an unrivalled view of the port. Fresh seafood tapas, as well as the *mar i muntanya* (sea and mountain) option of *pollastre amb gambes* (chicken and prawns) or their famous *croquetas de sepia* (cuttlefish croquettes), can be a light alternative to their main courses. The specialty here is oven-roasted cod on a bed of cumin potatoes topped with thin sliced tomatoes and served with a pear allioli. ✉ *Pl. D'Es Born 17, Ciutadella* ☎ *971/484654* ▭ *AE, DC, MC, V* ⊙ *Closed Jan. 20–Mar. 1. Open Wed.–Sun., Mar.–June. Open daily July–Aug. Closed Sun., Sept.–Jan.*

$$–$$$$ SPANISH **Casa Manolo.** On the east side of Ciutadella's narrow yacht and fishing port, this well-established paella and seafood restaurant has a cool summer terrace over the harbor, and the dining room's whitewashed walls and exposed wood beams extend back into the rock face of the steep cliffs rising above the port. Look for *caldereta de langosta* (stewed sea crawfish) or the *parrillada de pescado al estilo menorquín* (Minorcan mixed seafood grill), as well as an ample variety of fresh fish. ✉ *Marina 117–121* ☎ *971/380003* ▭ *AE, DC, MC, V* ⊙ *Closed Dec.–Feb.*

$$$–$$$$ ★ **Hotel Rural Sant Ignasi.** Ciutadella is not especially well endowed with hotels, but 10 minutes by car from the central square, in the countryside, is this comfortable and relatively reasonably priced delight. The main building is a manor house dating to 1777; the original barn now accommodates five large suites. Rooms have stone arches, cupboard closets, and English and Minorcan antiques. Ask for a ground-floor double with a private garden. Es Loc, the hotel's excellent restaurant, specializes in Minorcan seafood; in summer, meals are served on the tree-shaded poolside terrace. The Sant Ignasi is a favorite with young

Spanish families. **Pros:** great value for price, friendly staff. **Cons:** kids in the pool all day. ✉ *Ctra. Cala Morell s/n, Ciutadella* ☎ *971/385575* 🌐 *www.santignasi.com* *17 doubles, 9 suites* *In-room: safe, refrigerator, Ethernet (some). In-hotel: restaurant, room service, bar, pool, bicycles, no elevator, laundry service, public Internet, parking (no fee), some pets allowed, no-smoking rooms* 💳 *MC, V.*

SHOPPING

Gin, shoes, leather, costume jewelry, and cheese are the items to shop for here; try the Ses Voltes area, the Es Rodol zone near Plaça Artrutx and Ses Voltes, and along the Camí de Maó between Plaça Palmeras and Plaça d'es Born. **Nadia Rabosio** (✉ *Carrer Santissim 4* ☎ *971/384080*) is an inventive designer with an original selection of jewelry and hand-painted silks. **Maria Juanico** (✉ *Carrer Seminari 38* ☎ *971/480879* ⏲ *Weekdays 10:30–2 and 5:30–8, Sat. 10:30–2*) has an atelier in the back of the shop, where she makes her interesting plated and anodized silver jewelry and accessories.The industrial complex *(polígono industrial)* on the right as you enter Ciutadella has shoe factories, each with shops. Prices may be the same as in stores, but the selection is greater. In Plaça d'es Born, a market is held on Friday and Saturday. Visit **ARTEME** (*Artesanos de Minorca* ✉ *Carrer Comerciants 9* ☎ *971/381550*) for the town's only *alferería* (pottery maker).

EL TORO

24 km (15 mi) northwest of Mahón.

Follow signs in Es Mercadal (the crossroads at the island's center) to the peak of El Toro, Minorca's highest point, at all of 1,555 feet. From the monastery on top you can see the whole island and across the sea to Majorca.

WHERE TO EAT

$$ SPANISH ✕ **Molí d'es Reco.** A great place to stop for lunch, this restaurant is in an old windmill just off the highway, at the west end of Es Mercadal; it has fortress-thick whitewashed stone walls and low vaulted ceilings, and a constant air of cheerful bustle. On warm summer days there are tables on the terrace. Minorcan specialties here include squid stuffed with anglerfish and shrimps, and chicken with *centollo* (spider crab). The thick vegetable soup, called *sopas menorquinas,* is excellent. ✉ *Carrer Major 53, Mercadal* ☎ *971/375392* 💳 *AE, DC, MC, V.*

FORNELLS

35 km (21 mi) northwest of Mahón.

The first fortifications built here to defend the Bay of Fornells from pirates date to 1625. A little village (full-time population: 500) of whitewashed houses with red tile roofs, Fornells comes alive in the summer high season, when Spanish and Catalan families arrive in droves to open their holiday chalets at the edge of town and in the nearby beach resorts. The bay—Minorca's second largest and deepest—offers ideal conditions for windsurfing, sailing, and scuba diving.

WHERE TO EAT

$$$–$$$$ SEAFOOD **✕ Es Pla.** The modest wooden exterior of this waterside restaurant in Fornells' harbor, on the north coast, is misleading. King Juan Carlos is said to make regular detours here during Balearic jaunts to indulge in the *Es Pla caldereta de langosta* (lobster stew)—which, at market price/weight, skews an otherwise reasonably priced menu. Excellent fish dishes include scallops "Gallega" style, anglerfish with *maresco* (seafood) sauce, and grilled scorpion fish—a local specialty. ✉ *Pasaje Es Pla, Puerto de Fornells* ☎ *971/376655* ▭ *AE, DC, MC, V.*

WINDSURFING AND SAILING

Several miles long and a mile wide but with a narrow entrance to the sea and virtually no waves, the Bay of Fornells gives the beginner a feeling of security and the expert plenty of excitement.

Wind Fornells (✉ *Ctra. Mercaval Fornells s/n, Es Mercadal* ☎ *971/188150 or 659/577760* 🌐 *www.windfornells.com*) rents boards, dinghies, and catamarans, and gives lessons; they're open May–October.

COVA DES COLOMS

40 km (24 mi) west of Mahón.

The massive Cova Des Coloms (Cave of Pigeons), also known as the Cathedral, is the most spectacular cave on Minorca. Eerie rock formations rise up to a 77-foot-tall ceiling. To reach the cave, take the Ferreries road at San Cristóbal and turn up to the primary school; beyond the school the paved road continues for about 3 km (2 mi) toward Binigaus Nou. Leave the car in the designated parking area, climb over the stile, and take the path that follows the right-hand side of the barranca (ravine or gully) toward the sea; you'll come to a well-trodden path bearing down into the bottom of the barranca and up the other side. The entrance to the cave is around an elbow, camouflaged by a tree. A flashlight helps.

IBIZA

Settled by the Carthaginians in the 5th century BC, Ibiza has seen successive waves of invasion and occupation—the latest of which began in the 1960s, when it became a tourist destination. With a full-time population of barely 140,000, it now gets some 2 million visitors a year. Blessed with beaches—50 of them, by one count—it also has the world's largest disco, Privilege, with a capacity of 10,000. About 25% of the people who live on Ibiza year-round are foreigners.

From October to April, the pace of life here is decidedly slow, and many of the island's hotels and restaurants are closed. In the 1960s and early '70s Ibiza was discovered by sun-seeking hippies, eventually emerging as an icon of counterculture chic. Ibizans were—and still are—friendly and tolerant of their eccentric visitors. In the late 1980s and 1990s, club culture took over. Young ravers flocked here from all over the world to dance all night and pack the sands of built-up beach resorts like Sant Antoni. That party-hardy Ibiza is still alive and well, but a new wave of luxury rural hotels, offering oases of peace and privacy, with spas and gourmet restaurants, marks the most recent transformation of the island into a venue for "quality tourism."

GETTING HERE AND AROUND

Ibiza is a 40-minute flight or a nine-hour ferry ride from Barcelona.

Eivissabus serves the island. Buses run every half hour from Eivissa (Av. Isidoro Macabich, until the new CETIS Intermodal Transportation Services Center in Carrer Canarias opens) to Sant Antoni and Playa d'en Bossa, roughly hourly to Santa Eulalia. Buses from Ibiza to other parts of the island are less frequent, as is the cross-island bus between Sant Antoni and Santa Eulalia. The schedule is published in newspapers.

On Ibiza, a six-lane divided highway connects the capital with the airport and Sant Antoni. Roundabouts and one-way streets make it a bit confusing to get in and out of Eivissa, but out in the countryside driving is easy and remains the only feasible way of getting to some of the island's smaller coves and beaches.

ESSENTIALS

Bus Contact **Eivissabus** (🌐 *www.eivissabus.info*).

Taxi Contacts **Radio-Taxi** (✉ *Eivissa* ☎ *971/398483*). **Cooperativa Limitada de Taxis de Sant Antoni** (✉ *Sant Antoni* ☎ *971/340074 or 971/346026*).

Visitor Information **Aeropuerto de Ibiza** (✉ *Ctra. Sa Caleta s/n, Sant Josep* ☎ *971/809118*).

IBIZA TOWN (EIVISSA)

★ Hedonistic and historical, Eivissa (Ibiza, in Castilian), is a city jam-packed with cafés, nightspots, and trendy shops; looming over it are the massive stone walls of **Dalt Vila**—the medieval city declared a UNESCO World Heritage site in 1999—and its Gothic cathedral. Squeezed between the north walls of the old city and the harbor is **Sa Penya,** a long labyrinth of stone-paved streets that offer some of the city's best off-beat shopping, snacking, and exploring.

ESSENTIALS

Visitor Information **Eivissa** (✉ *Paseo Vara de Rey 1* ☎ *971/301900*).

EXPLORING

Enter Sa Penya from the west end of Passeig Vara de Rey. Across from the Hotel Montesol, take **Carrer Rimbau** and turn on Carrer Guillem Montgri to the **Plaça de la Constitució**; the little Hellenic-looking building in the square is the town's open-air produce market. Beyond it, a ramp leads up to the **Portal de Ses Taules,** the main gate of **Dalt Vila,** the walled upper town.

Inside Dalt Vila, the ramp continues to the right between the outer and inner walls and opens into Sa Carroza, a long, narrow plaza lined with boutiques and sidewalk cafés. A little way up, a sign on the left points left toward the **Museu d'Art Contemporani,** above the gateway arch. ✉ *Ronda Pintor Narcis Putget s/n* ☎ *971/302723* 🎟 *€2, Sun. free* ⏲ *Oct.–Apr., Tues.–Fri. 10–1:30 and 4–6, weekends 10–1:30; May–Sept., Tues.–Fri. 10–1:30 and 5–8, weekends 10–1:30.*

9

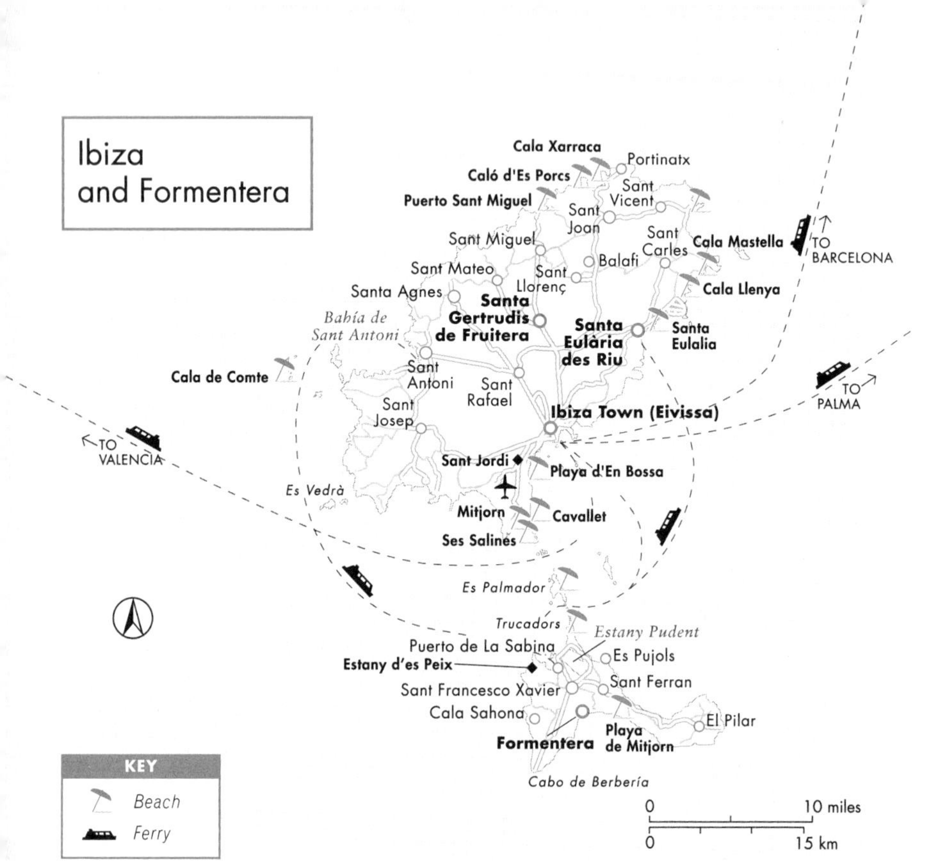

Uphill from the museum, on the left, the wide **Bastió de Santa Llúcia** *(Bastion of Ste. Lucia)* has a panoramic view.

Wind your way up past the 16th-century church of **Sant Domingo** (✉ *Carrer de Balanzat*), its roof an irregular landscape of tile domes, and turn right in front of the ajuntament housed in the church's former monastery. From the church of Sant Domingo, follow any of the streets or steps leading uphill to Carrer Obispo Torres (Carrer Major). (Don't worry about losing your way: aim uphill for the cathedral, downhill for the gate.) The **cathedral** is on the site of religious structures from each of the cultures that have ruled Ibiza since the Phoenicians. Built in the 13th and 14th centuries and renovated in the 18th century, it has a Gothic tower and a baroque nave. ✉ *Carrer Major* ☎ *971/312774* ⏲ *Weekdays 10–1, Sun. 10:30–noon.*

Behind the cathedral, from the **Bastió de Sant Bernat** *(Bastion of St. Bernard),* a promenade with sea views runs west to the bastions of Sant Jordi and Sant Jaume, past the **Castell**—a fortress formerly used as an army barracks, turned over to the city of Ibiza in 1973. In 2007 work began to transform it into a 70-room luxury parador. The promenade ends at the steps to the **Portal Nou** (New Gate).

WHERE TO EAT AND STAY

$$$–$$$$ FRENCH ✕ **El Portalón.** Just inside and left of the main gate into Dalt Vila, this intimate French restaurant has two dining rooms; one medieval, with heavy beams, antiques, oils, and coats of arms; another, modern, with dark-orange walls and sleek black furniture—the two spaces are perfect metaphors for the traditional cuisine with contemporary touches served here. Excellent offerings include *pato con salsa de moras* (duck with blueberry sauce), *solomillo* (sirloin) and grilled *lubina* (sea bass), and *dorada* (sea bream). ✉ *Pl. Desamparados 1–2, Dalt Vila* ☎ *971/300852* ▭ *AE, DC, MC, V* ⊙ *Closed Sun. Nov.–mid-Apr. No lunch Nov.–mid-Apr. No dinner Sun. mid-Apr.–Oct.*

$$$–$$$$ SPANISH ✕ **S'Oficina.** Some of the best Basque cuisine on Ibiza is served at this restaurant just 2 km (1 mi) outside town, in Sant Jordi. Marine prints hang on the white walls and ships' lanterns from the ceiling; the bar is adorned with ships' wheels. *Lomo de merluza con almejas* (hake with clams) and *kokotxas* (cod cheeks) are among the specialties. From Ibiza Town, take Carretera toward the airport and turn off for Playa d'en Bossa. ✉ *C. Begonias 17, Playa d'en Bossa* ☎ *971/390081* ▭ *AE, DC, MC, V* ⊙ *Closed weekends Oct.–Mar. and Mon.*

$$$ **Hotel Montesol.** Location, location, location. The Montesol opened in 1934 (it was the island's first hotel) and still hasn't done anything—despite an overhaul in 2000—to lift itself from the category of a one-star accommodation. But it's clean and comfortable, and it sits smack on the northwest corner of the Vara de Rey, the promenade in the center of Eivissa, where everyone comes to see and be seen—steps from the port, at the foot of the Dalt Vila. Rooms are simple and spare, with bare, white tile floors and flower-print bedspreads mismatched to plaid drapes. Only four rooms have double beds: the rest are twins and singles. Fashion photographers love the balconies facing the promenade. **Pros:** value for price, convenient, good for meeting people. **Cons:** noisy, small rooms, bare minimal amenities. ✉ *Paseo Vara de Rey 2* ☎ *971/310161* 🌐 *www.hotelmontesol.com* *55 rooms* *In-room: safe. In-hotel: restaurant* ▭ *MC, V* *BP.*

$$$ **La Ventana.** Inside the medieval walls, this intimate hillside hotel is within a 10-minute stroll of the port. Rooms are painted in soothing pastel blues and yellows; all have beds draped in white canopies. The little roof terrace offers a chill-out space with Moroccan-style sofas; rooms on the third floor have fine views of the old town and the harbor. **Pros:** historic setting is charming, good value. **Cons:** rooms are small, lots of stairs to climb, surroundings can be noisy until the wee hours. ✉ *Sa Carrossa 13* ☎ *971/390857* 🌐 *www.laventanaibiza.com* *2 suites, 12 rooms* *In-room: safe, refrigerator, Wi-Fi. In-hotel: restaurant, room service, no elevator, laundry service, public Internet, public Wi-Fi, some pets allowed* ▭ *AE, MC, V.*

$$$$ **Mirador de Dalt Vila.** Originally the palatial home of the Fajarnés family, this recent addition to the hotels in the historic old city—it opened in 2007—is filled with the owner's museum-quality furniture, Oriental rugs, and works of art. The style is classical, with ultramodern touches like Jacuzzis and onyx or white marble walls in the baths—and in-room music systems with iPod docking stations. The elegant little

restaurant ($$$$) offers nouvelle creations like monkfish with pear compote and curry foam, and sirloin of beef with foie gras and porcini mushrooms in ginger and coffee sauce. **Pros:** polished and professional service, small business center, private cabin cruiser for charters. **Cons:** tiny pool, not geared to families. ✉*Pl. de España 4, Dal Vila* ☎*971/303045 or 971/398519* 🌐*www.hotelmiradoribiza.com* *6 rooms, 7 suites* *In-room: safe, refrigerator, Ethernet, Wi-Fi. In-hotel: restaurant, room service, bar, pool, laundry service, concierge, public Internet, public Wi-Fi, airport shuttle, parking (no fee), no-smoking rooms* *AE, DC, MC, V.*

NIGHTLIFE

Fodor's Choice ★ **Ibiza's discos** are famous throughout Europe. Keep your eyes open during the day for free invitations handed out on the street—these can save you expensive entry fees. Also note that a handy, all-night "Discobus" service (☎*971/192456*) runs from June through September between Eivissa, Sant Antoni, Santa Eulalia, and the major party venues (midnight–7; €2.10 one way). As a rule, the clubs open in mid-June and close in late September, though some will have special parties on New Year's Eve.

Down in the town, the trendy place to start the evening is **Keeper** (✉*Paseo Marítimo, Ibiza Nueva* ☎*971/310509*), where you can sip your drink sitting on a carousel horse. A lively, very young scene rocks **El Divino Café** (✉*Carrer Lluís Turi Palau 10* ☎*971/311016*). In summer, boats depart between 1 AM and 4 AM from in front of El Divino Café for the marina and **El Divino Disco** (✉*Puerto Deportivo, Ibiza Nueva* ☎*971/318338* 🌐*www.eldivino-ibiza.com*), which is a typical Ibiza disco with throbbing dance music (and spectacular views of Ibiza Town). The "in" place for older nighthawks is the stylish bar in the foyer of the former **Teatre Pereira** (✉*Carrer Roselló 3* ☎*971/191468*). A young, international crowd dances to techno at **Pacha** (✉*Av. 8 de Agosto s/n* ☎*971/313612* 🌐*www.pacha.com*). The popular **Amnesia San Rafael** (✉*Ctra. Sant Antoni, opposite Km 5 marker* ☎*971/198041*) has several ample dance floors that throb to house and funk. **Privilege** (✉*Ctra. Ibiza–Sant Antoni, Km 7, San Rafael* ☎*971/198086*) is the grande dame of Ibiza's nightlife, with a giant dance floor, a swimming pool, and more than a dozen bars. **Space** (✉*Playa d'en Bossa* ☎*971/396793* 🌐*www.space-ibiza.es*) is where the serious clubbers come to dance "after hours."

The **Casino de Ibiza** is a small gaming club with roulette tables, blackjack, and slots. You need your passport to enter. ✉*Ctra. Sant Antoní, junto a Rotonda Juan XXIII s/n* ☎*971/313312* 🌐*www.casinoibiza.com* *€5 1st visit, free subsequent visits* *Weekdays 6 PM–5 AM, weekends 6 PM–6 AM.*

Gay nightlife converges on **Carrer de la Verge,** in **Sa Penya.** The popular gay bar **Dome** (✉*Carrer Alfonso XII* ☎*971/317456*) has a leafy terrace that overflows with revelers in summer.

SPORTS AND THE OUTDOORS

For information on sports on Ibiza and Formentera, obtain a free copy of the magazine **Touribisport** (🌐*www.touribisport.com*), available locally.

BOATING Explore Ibiza by sea with **Coral Yachting** (✉*Marina Botafoc, Eivissa* ☎*971/303569* 🌐*www.coralyachting.com*). **Ibiza Azul** (✉ *Ctra. Sant Joan, Km 8* ☎*971/325264* 🌐*www.ibizazul.com*) has motorboats and Jet Skis for rent, as well as a 12-meter live-aboard sailboat for weekend or week-long excursion charters.

GOLF Ibiza's only 18-hole course is **Golf de Ibiza** (✉*Ctra. Jesús–Cala Llonga, Km 6, Santa Eulària* ☎*971/196118* 🌐*www.golfibiza.com*). Greens fees are €90 a day.

HORSEBACK RIDING **Can Mayans** (✉*Ctra. Santa Gertrudis a Sant Lorenç, Km 3* ☎*971/187388*) has horses for hire for rides along the coast and inland.

SCUBA DIVING Year-round a team with a decompression chamber is on standby at the **Policlínica de Nuestra Señora del Rosario** (✉*Via Romana s/n* ☎*971/301916*).

Go scuba diving in Sant Antoní with **Centro de Buceo Sirena** (✉*Balanzat 21 bajo, Sant Antoní* ☎*971/342966*). Dive in Sant Joan with **Centro Subfari** (✉*Cala Portinatx, San Joan* ☎*689/253001*). **Diving Center San Miguel** (✉*Puerto de San Miguel* ☎*971/334539* 🌐*www.divingcenter-sanmiguel.com*) also offers diving. **Active Generation** (✉*Edifici Faro II, Local 10, Pasea Marítimo, San Antoní* ☎*971/341344* 🌐*www.active-generation.com*) offers instruction and guided dives, as well as kayaking, parasailing, and boat rentals. Rent scuba gear in Eivissa at **Vellmari** (✉*Marina Botafoc, Local 101–102* ☎*971/192884* 🌐*www.vellmari.com*).

TENNIS **Ibiza Club de Campo** (✉*Ctra. Sant Josep, Km 2.5* ☎*971/300088* 🌐*www.ibizaclubdecampo.org*), with six clay and two composition courts, is the largest tennis club on the island. Nonmembers can play here for €6.40 per hour. There are public tennis courts at **Port Sant Miquel**.

WALKING **Ecoibiza** (✉*Avda. de Juan Carlos I, Edificio Transat, Local 10, Ibiza Ciutat* ☎*971/302347* 🌐*www.ecoibiza.com*) has lots of ecologically friendly countryside hikes and can also arrange horseback riding, sailing, and sea fishing.

SHOPPING

Although the Sa Penya area of Eivissa still has a few designer boutiques, much of the area is now home to the so-called Hippie Market, with stalls selling clothing and craftwork of all sorts May to October from 5 PM to well past midnight. For trendy casual gear, sandals, belts, and bags, try **Ibiza Republic** (✉*Carrer Antoni Mar 15* ☎*971/314175*). For wines and spirits, visit **Enotecum** (✉*Av. d'Isidoro Macabich 43* ☎*971/399167*).

9

SANTA EULÀRIA DES RIU

15 km (9 mi) northeast of Ibiza.

At the edge of this town on the island's eastern coast, to the right below the road, a Roman bridge crosses what is claimed to be the only permanent river in the Balearics (hence "des Riu," or "of the River"). The town itself follows the curve of a long sandy beach, a few blocks deep with restaurants, shops, and holiday apartments. From here it's a 10-minute drive to Sant Carles and the open-air hippie market held there every Saturday morning.

ESSENTIALS

Bike Rentals Kandani (✉ *Ctra. Es Canar 109, Santa Eulària des Riu* ☎ *971/339264*).

WHERE TO EAT AND STAY

$$ ✕ **Mezzanotte.** Opened in 2006, this charming little portside restaurant is a branch of the popular Mezzanotte in Eivissa. There are just 12 tables inside, softly lighted with candles and track lights; in summer, seating expands to an interior patio and tables on the sidewalk. The kitchen prides itself on hard-to-find fresh ingredients flown in from Italy. The linguine with jumbo shrimp, saffron, and zucchini—or with *bottarga* (dried and salted mullet roe from Sardinia)—is wonderful. Value for price here is excellent; the €19.50 prix-fixe menu, served at dinner in summer and lunch in winter, is an absolute bargain. ✉ *Paseo de s'Alamera 22, Santa Eulària* ☎ *971/319498* ▭ *AE, MC, V* ⊗ *Closed Jan.–Feb. and Mon.; no lunch June–Aug.*

$$$$ Fodor's Choice ★ **Can Curreu.** The traditional Ibizan architecture here feels a lot like a Greek-island village: a cluster of low buildings with thick whitewashed walls, the edges and corners gently rounded off. Each accommodation at Can Curreu has one of these buildings to itself, with a private patio, artfully separated from its neighbors. Rooms have comfortable, deep sofas, upholstered in orange-red and yellow, built-in pine cupboard closets, red-brown tile floors: the overall effect is supremely soothing. Suites have fireplaces and Jacuzzi tubs. The hotel has its own stables and orange and lemon groves. The Can Curreu restaurant (closed Monday in winter) serves an excellent five-course tasting menu. Mick Jagger and his family stayed here. No satisfaction? Hard to believe. **Pros:** superbly designed for privacy; friendly, efficient staff; horses. **Cons:** restaurant is pricey. ✉ *Ctra. de Sant Carles, Km 12, Santa Eulària* ☎ *971/335280* 🌐 *www.cancurreu.com* *10 rooms, 7 suites* *In-room: safe, refrigerator, kitchen (some), Wi-Fi. In-hotel: restaurant, bar, room service, pool, health spa, gym, bicycles, no elevator, public Wi-Fi, parking (no fee), some pets allowed* ▭ *AE, MC, V* *BP.*

$$$$ ★ **Can Gall.** In 2001 owner Santi Marí Ferrer remodeled his family *finca* (farmhouse)—with its massive stone walls and native *savina* wood beams—into one of the friendliest and most comfortable *agroturisme* country inns on the island. Rooms are huge; original stone arches separate sleeping from bathing areas. Oranges, lemons, and olives, fresh produce, meat and eggs all come from the family farm. The 25-meter pool has an access ramp for guests with disabilities. Relax in the pergola at sunset, with a view of the mountains, and nurse a glass of

Santi's homemade five-year-old *ierbas* (herb liqueur). A spa is set to open in 2009. **Pros:** family-friendly, espresso maker in the room, big, fluffy terry-cloth robes. **Cons:** 15-minute drive to nearest good beaches. ✉*Crta. Sant Joan Km 17.2, Sant Lorenç* ☎*971/337031 or 670/876054* 🌐*www.agrocangall.com* *17 rooms* *In-room: safe, refrigerator, DVD, Ethernet, Wi-Fi. In-hotel: room service, bar, pool, bicycles, no elevator, laundry service, public Internet, public Wi-Fi, airport shuttle, parking (no fee)* ▭*DC, MC, V* *BP.*

SANTA GERTRUDIS DE FRUITERA

15 km (9 mi) north of Eivissa.

Blink and you miss it: that's true of most of the small towns in the island's interior—and especially so of Santa Gertrudis, not much more than a bend in the road. But don't blink: Santa Gertrudis is strategic, and it's cute. The town square was renovated in 2008, paved with brick and closed to vehicle traffic—perfect for the sidewalk cafés. From here, you are only a few minutes' drive from some of the island's flat-out best resort hotels and spas, and the most beautiful secluded north coves and beaches: **S'Illa des Bosc, Benirrás** (where they have drum circles to salute the setting sun), **S'Illot des Renclí, Portinatx, Caló d'En Serra.** Artists and expats like it here: they've given the town an appeal that now makes for listings of half a million dollars or more for a modest two-bedroom chalet.

WHERE TO EAT AND STAY

$$$ ✕ **Can Caus.** Ibiza might pride itself on its seafood, but there comes a time for meat and potatoes. When it does, take the 20-minute drive to the outskirts of Santa Gertrudis, to this informal, family-style roadside restaurant and feast on skewers of barbecued *sobrasada* (soft pork sausage), goat chops, lamb kebabs, or grilled sweetbreads with red peppers, onions, and eggplant. Most people eat at the long wooden tables on the terrace. ✉*Ctra. Sant Miquel, Km 3.5, Santa Gertrudis* ☎*971/197516* ▭*AE, MC, V* *Closed Mon. Sept.–June.*

$$$$ ★ **Cas Gasí.** With splendid views of Ibiza's one and only mountain, the 1,567-foot Sa Talaiassa, this lovely late-19th-century manor house is surrounded by hills of olive trees, redolent of Tuscany. Privacy—the sort that draws people like Richard Gere and Claudia Schiffer—is the key here: there's a monitored gate at the driveway; the restaurant and spa are exclusively for guests. Airy, rustic rooms with wood-beam ceilings are gracefully furnished; bathrooms have Moroccan-style tiling. One hitch: a minimum five-night stay is required in July and August. **Pros:** attentive personal service, peace and quiet, sailing charters arranged. **Cons:** 15-minute drive to the nearest good beaches, not particularly geared to families. ✉*Cami Vell a Sant Mateu s/n, Santa Gertrudis* ☎*971/197700* 🌐*www.casgasi.com* *10 double rooms, 2 suites* *In-room: safe, kitchenettes (some), refrigerator, DVD, Ethernet, Wi-Fi. In-hotel: restaurant, room service, bar, 2 pools, gym, spa, bicycles, no elevator, laundry service, public Internet, public Wi-Fi, airport shuttle, parking (no fee), some pets allowed* ▭*AE, DC, MC, V* *BP.*

NEED A BREAK?

Bar Costa (✉ *Pl. de la Iglesia s/n, Santa Gertrudis* ☎ *971/197021*) is just the right place to sit out under the awning with a coffee and croissant or a *bocadillo* (sandwich) and contemplate your next move. Inclement weather? The back room has a fireplace, and the walls are covered with funny, irreverent modern art from the owner's collection.

SHOPPING

te Cuero (✉ *Pl. de la Iglesia s/n, Santa Gertrudis* ☎ *971/197100* ⏲ *Mon.–Sat. 11–1:30 and 5–8*) specializes in hand-tooled leather bags and belts with great designer buckles.

FORMENTERA

Much of Formentera is strictly protected from the rampant development that plagues the other islands, so it's a calm respite from Ibiza's dance-'til-you-drop madness. Though it does get crowded in the summer, the island's long white-sand beaches are among the finest in the Mediterranean; inland, you can explore quiet country roads by bicycle in relative solitude.

From the port at La Sabina, it's only 3 km (2 mi) to Formentera's capital, **Sant Françesc Xavier,** a few yards off the main road. There's an active hippie market in the small plaza in front of the church. At the main road, turn right toward Sant Ferran, 2 km (1 mi) away. Beyond Sant Ferran the road travels for 7 km (4 mi) along a narrow isthmus, keeping slightly closer to the rougher northern side, where the waves and rocks keep yachts—and thus much of the tourist trade—away.

The plateau on the island's east side ends at the lighthouse **Faro de la Mola.** Nearby is a **monument to Jules Verne,** who set part of his novel *Journey Through the Solar System* in Formentera. The rocks around the lighthouse are carpeted with purple thyme and sea holly in spring and fall.

Back on the main road, turn right at Sant Ferran toward Es Pujols. The few hotels here are the closest Formentera comes to beach resorts, even if the beach is not the best. Beyond Es Pujols the road skirts **Estany Pudent,** one of two lagoons that almost enclose La Sabina. Salt was once extracted from Pudent, hence its name, which means "stinking pond," although the pond now smells fine. At the northern tip of Pudent, a road to the right leads to a footpath that runs the length of **Trucadors,** a narrow sand spit. The long, windswept beaches here are excellent.

GETTING HERE AND AROUND

Formentera is a one-hour ferry ride from Ibiza, or 25 minutes on the jet ferry. Both Balearia and Iscomar operate ferry services to Formentera from Ibiza and Denia, the nearest landfall on the Spanish mainland.

On Ibiza, Santa Eulalia and Sant Antoni also run ferries to Formentera's La Sabina (one hour, €23) as well as numerous ferries to the coves and *calas* on the east and west coasts of Ibiza. Day-trippers can go to Formentera for lunch and a few hours in the sun before heading back to Ibiza to plug into the nightlife. If you plan to picnic, buy supplies in Ibiza. La Sabina has several car-, bicycle-, and moped-rental agencies.

A very limited bus service connects Formentera's villages, shrinking to one bus each way between San Francisco and Pilar on Saturday and disappearing altogether on Sunday and holidays.

ESSENTIALS

Bike Rentals Extra Rent (✉ *Av. Santa Eulalia 25–27/ Estación Marítimo* ☎ *971/190408*).

Ferry Contacts Balearia (🌐 *www.balearia.com*). **Iscomar** (🌐 *www.iscomar.com*).

Taxi Information Parada de Taxis La Sabina (✉ *La Sabina* ☎ *971/322002* ✉ *Es Pujols* ☎ *971/332016*).

Visitor Information Formentera (✉ *Carrer Calpe s/n, Port de La Sabina* ☎ *971/322057*). **Santa Eulalia** (✉ *Carrer Mariano Riquer Wallis 4* ☎ *971/330728*). **Sant Antoni** (✉ *Passeig de Ses Fonts s/n* ☎ *971/343363*). **Sant Joan** (✉ *Carrer de l'Ajuntament 4* ☎ *971/333003*).

WHERE TO EAT AND STAY

$$–$$$ FRENCH ★ ✕ **Le Cyrano.** This family-run restaurant on the Es Pujols waterfront is one of the best on Formentera. Foie gras and snails are favorites, but the star players are the simple and straightforward preparations (usually baked or cooked over coals) of fresh fish, ranging from *llobarro* (sea bass) to *llenguado* (sole) or whatever the fishing fleet brought in that day. Rice dishes and bouillabaisse-like fish soups with *allioli* are also good at this no-nonsense, roll-up-your-sleeves-and-dig-in establishment. ✉ *Passeig Marítim, Es Pujols* ☎ *971/328386* ▭ *AE, DC, MC, V* ⊙ *Closed mid-Nov.–Mar.*

$$–$$$ SEAFOOD ✕ **Sa Palmera.** On the beachfront in Es Pujols, Sa Palmera is known for its rice dishes and the extremely fresh fish served in the garden or on the terrace overlooking the beach. Specialties include the grilled *dorada* (gilthead bream) and lubina (sea bass), while the *frito de sepia* (fried cuttlefish) is a house favorite, as is the *parrillada,* a mixed grill of three types of fish cooked over coals (depending on the catch of the day) served with potatoes and a salad. ✉ *Calle Aguadulce 15–31, Es Pujols* ☎ *971/328356* ▭ *MC, V* ⊙ *Closed Mon. and last Fri. of Oct.–1st Fri. of Mar.*

$$–$$$ **Cala Saona.** On a charming fisherman's cove and a sleepy little beach, backed by a pine grove, this gleaming white complex could be a beached ocean liner at first glance. Rooms are simple, comfortable, and breezy, and the restaurant ($$–$$$)—serving dinner only—prepares the daily catch with skill and care. **Pros:** panoramas of windswept, peaceful expanses of beach and sea. **Cons:** remote location, some rooms have better views than others. ✉ *Apdo. de Correos 88, San Francisco* ☎ *971/322030* 🌐 *www.guiaformentera.com/calasaona* *116 rooms* *In-hotel: restaurant, bar, tennis court, pool, no elevator* ▭ *AE, DC, MC, V* ⊙ *Closed mid-Oct.–Apr.*

$$–$$$ ★ **Hostal Rafalet.** This simple inn is a few steps from the water at the tiny fishing cove of Es Caló; stay here and one of the fishing boats drawn up on the rocky strand is likely to have come in that morning with your lunch. Paellas are the specialties here; don't miss the rice with *bogavante*

9

(lobster). The lack of a sandy beach has saved Es Caló from rampant development, but the setting is lovely: the brilliant blue-green of the water is bounded on the east by a long, dramatic line of cliffs. The hotel is 12 km (7 mi) from La Sabina. **Pros:** peace and quiet. **Cons:** middle of nowhere. ✉ *Ctra. La Mola, Km 12 Apdo. de Correos 225, Es Caló de Sant Agustí, Sant Francesc Xavier* ☎ 📠 *971/327016* 🌐 *www.hostal-rafalet.com* *15 rooms* *In-room: no phone, refrigerator (some) no TV. In-hotel: restaurant, bar, beachfront, no elevator, parking (no fee)* 💳 *MC, V* ⏲ *Closed Nov.–Mar.*

SHOPPING

El Pilar is the chief crafts village here. Stores and workshops sell handmade items, including bags, ceramics, jewelry, and leather goods. El Pilar's crafts market draws shoppers on Sunday afternoon, May–September. From June through August, the market is also on Wednesday afternoon. From May through September, crafts are sold in the morning at the San Françesc Xavier market and in the evening in Es Pujols.

SPORTS AND THE OUTDOORS

You can rent bikes and motorcycles in La Sabina at **Moto Rent Mitjorn** (✉ *Playa de Migjorn* ☎ *971/322306 or 696/014292*).

DIVING You can take diving courses at **Vell Marí** (✉ *Puerto Deportivo Marina de Formentera, Local 14–16, La Sabina* ☎ *971/322105*).

The Southeast

Balconies in Cartagena, Murcia region

10

WORD OF MOUTH

"If you decide Costa Blanca, I recommend small towns like Calpe, Javea, or Denia. These are the most charming towns in Marina Alta, which is my favorite part of Costa Blanca."

—walksntalks

www.fodors.com/community

WELCOME TO THE SOUTHEAST

TOP REASONS TO GO

★ **Castillo de Santa Barbara, Alicante:** This grande dame of a castle dates from the 16th century and is the city's must-see main attraction. The best approach is via a lift cut deep into the mountainside.

★ **Cartagena, Murcia:** Roam Hannibal's namesake city (after Carthage in North Africa); the historic center is a wonderful tangle of medieval streets.

★ **Guadalest, Alicante:** This town is pure dramatic panoramic views. Dating from the 16th century, the Moorish influence is reflected in buildings seemingly carved out of the rock face.

★ **Altea:** This historic hilltop village is picturesque and unspoiled; the narrow cobbled lanes are delightful for strolling.

★ **La Manga, Murcia:** The place to come to if you feel like a dip in the warm therapeutic waters of the Mar Menor, followed by a round of golf at the magnificently landscaped La Manga Resort.

1 South of Valencia to the Costa Blanca. Lush coastal plains with orchards of citrus trees that scent the air and produce an impressionist painting of orange blossoms and ripe fruit. The rice paddies stretching south provide Valencia's iconic *paella.*

2 The Costa Blanca. This is *the* place to come for sandcastles, sea breezes, and fun in the sun. Fishing villages still reflect their seafaring heritage with superb fish restaurants, while Alicante's historic center and vibrant night-owl scene occupy the hub of a rich agricultural area punctuated by towns like Elche, a World Heritage site.

Esplanada de Espana, Alicante City.

3 Inland from the Costa Blanca. The road to towns such as Guadalest tour through a wide variety of terrain, from the miniature canyons of the lowlands to the lush and spectacular mountain passes above.

4 The Murcia Coast. La Manga del Mar Menor, a long "sleeve" of sandy beach enclosing a giant lagoon of still salt water, is a famous therapeutic getaway teeming with estuary life and seafood.

5 Murcia and Lorca. The inland city of Murcia is a university town with a stunning cathedral and a cuisine known for vegetable dishes. Lorca, rich in Baroque architecture, is the market center of Murcia's arid southwest corner.

GETTING ORIENTED

Culturally and geographically diverse, the region's most populated coastal resorts stretch north from the provincial capital of Alicante. Benidorm has the unenviable reputation of being the largest resort in the world, yet has magnificent sweeping beaches and a something-for-everyone nightlife scene. South of here are such traditional working cities as Murcia and Alicante, while, heading inland, the scenery is dramatically diverse with flat scrubland, olive and citrus groves interspersed with craggy mountain ranges, nature reserves, and stuck-in-a-time-warp villages where you still need to speak Spanish to order a beer.

The church square of Nuestra Señora del Consuelo in Altea.

THE SOUTHEAST PLANNER

When to Go

Try to visit this region between late September and November or between April and June.

Summer is crowded, oppressively hot, and more expensive, with accommodations at a premium. In contrast, springtime is mild and an excellent time to tour the region, particularly the rural areas where blossoms infuse the air with pleasant fragrances and wild flowers dazzle the landscape.

Easter week (Semana Santa) is a lively time to visit, with parades and traditional ceremonies throughout the province.

The early fall is still warm enough for a dip in the sea, but pack your umbrella as there may be rain.

Winter can be chilly with central heating still a rarity, but with many clear, sunny days, it's an ideal season for outdoor activities, such as hiking.

If you like beaches

The southeastern coastline varies from the long stretches of sand dunes north of Dénia and south of Alicante to the coves and crescents of the Costa Blanca. The benign climate permits lounging on the beach almost year-round.

Altea, popular with families, is busy and pebbly, but the old town has retained a traditional *pueblo* feel with narrow cobbled streets and attractive squares. **Benidorm's** two white, crescent-shape beaches, packed in summer, extend for more than 5 km (3 mi) and are widely considered the best in Spain. **Calblanque** is on the road between Los Belones and Cabo de Palos, which takes you down a longish, rough track to a succession of nearly deserted sands frequented mainly by young Murcians. **Calpe's** beaches have the scenic advantage of the sheer outcrop Peñón de Ifach (Cliff of Ifach), which stands guard over stretches of sand to either side. **Dénia** and **Jávea** both have family beaches where children paddle in relatively safe waters. **Gandía's** sandy beach is well kept, its promenade lined with bars and restaurants.

Fiestas and Festivals

Dénia throws a **mini Fallas** March 16–19; you'll find dancing, traditional costumes, and *cremàs* (bonfires), but without the mondo crowds of Valencia. Alcoy's spectacular **Moros y Cristianos** (Moors and Christians) festival, held April 21–24, includes a reenactment of clashes from the Christian Reconquest, the long battle to dislodge the Moors between the 8th and the 15th centuries. Murcia's **Semana Santa** (Holy Week) processions are among the most illustrious in Spain; those in Lorca are known for the opulent costumes of both Christian and Roman participants and for the penitents' solemn robes. Alicante's main festival is **Hogueras de San Juan** (St. John's Day Bonfires), June 2–24. **El Misteri** (the Mystery Play) is performed in Elche in two parts, August 14–15, preceded by a public dress rehearsal. During Dénia's **Bous a la Mar**, the first week of July, local youths display their bravado by luring bulls over the edge of a sea wall into the sea.

Outdoor Activities

Although many visitors to the Costa Blanca seek nothing more energetic than lying on the beach while reading a book, others may prefer something mildly more bracing. For visitors in the cooler months, for example, the region offers some excellent walking and hiking opportunities, particularly around the Sierra Mariola and Sierra Aitana regions, both easily accessible from the Costa Blanca resorts. There are many companies that offer "walking vacations," most based in the United Kingdom. Check the following Web sites for information: *www.waymarkholidays.com*, *www.fell-walker.co.uk/costablanca.htm*, and *www.mountainwalks.com*. This area is also suitably mountainous for climbers. The most obvious rock is Peñon de Ifach in Calpes, although this is a perilous peak and only recommended for advanced climbers. The best-known area is northwest of Valencia in the Turia Valley.

There are several riding schools, which provide classes as well as trekking opportunities. Pick up brochures at the local tourist offices. Water sports are also widely available, and you can learn to sail in most of the major resorts. Benidorm has a multilingual cable-ski and water-sports center; check *www.surf.to/cableski* for more details. Kite-surfing is becoming increasingly popular; the necessary gear is available for rent direct from several beaches, including Santa Pola, Benidorm, and Cullera; the same applies to windsurfing. Scuba diving is also a favorite and in the smaller coastal towns it's possible to go into reserve waters if you book ahead. A list of schools can be found at *www.idealspain.com/pages/sports/divingcostablanca.htm*. If pedal power is more your thing, several companies offer a range of cycling holidays. Check *www.realholidays.com* and *www.ciclocostablanca.com*.

This region is a bird-watcher's paradise. The main coastal plain is a migratory highway for thousands of birds winging their way between Europe and Africa. The salt pans of Santa Pola and Albufera Lake are particular hot spots.

WHAT IT COSTS (IN EUROS)

	¢	$	$$	$$$	$$$$
Restaurants	under €8	€8–€12	€13–€17	€18–€22	over €22
Hotels	under €60	€60–€90	€91–€125	€126–€180	over €180

Prices are per person for a main course at dinner, and for two people in a standard double room in high season, excluding tax.

Planning Your Time

There are many different sorts of trips to choose from in southeast Spain: there are the beaches of the Costa Blanca and the less populated Mojácar; inland are the steppes around Albacete and the mountains near Murcia; and there are three major cities (Alicante, Albacete, and Murcia). For a taste of the area in just a few days, start at the lakeside village of El Palmar for perfect paella, then head down through La Albufera. Continue south through the elegant coastal town of Dénia to the curved bay at Cabo de la Nao. Check out the small stylish village of Altea, then head to Alicante before moving inland through Elche. Stop in Murcia to see its superb cathedral, then Cartagena. If you have more time, there is no shortage of additional places to see, including the playground of La Manga del Mar Menor or a boat trip to Tabarca Island.

Alicante's town hall and travel agencies arrange tours of the city and bus and train tours to Guadalest, the Algar waterfalls, Benidorm, the Peñón de Ifach (Calpe), and Elche. There are also tours to Jijona, where you can visit one of the *turrón* (nougat) factories before ogling the stalactites and stalagmites at the Cueva de Canalobre (Cave of Canalobre).

GETTING HERE AND AROUND

By Air

Iberia has the most flights to this part of Spain. However, if you are arriving from the United States, it may be more economical for you to fly to London and then catch one of the no-frills flights on airlines like easyJet and Ryanair, which have frequent flights to Alicante. There are three airports serving the region: Valencia, Alicante, and San Javier (for Mar Menor and Murcia).

By Boat or Ferry

The shortest ferry connections to the Balearic Islands (100 km to Ibiza) originate in Dénia. Balearia sails to Ibiza, Formentera, and Mallorca; Iscomar sails to Ibiza and then onward to Palma de Mallorca.

By Train

Arriving by train lands you in Alicante, which has two train stations: the main Estación de Madrid and the local Estación de la Marina, from where the local FGV line (not affiliated with RENFE) runs along the Costa Blanca from Alicante to Dénia. The Estación de la Marina is at the far end of Playa Postiguet and can be reached by buses C1 and C2 from downtown.

Bus

Bus travel is generally inexpensive and comfortable. Private companies run buses down the coast and from Madrid to Valencia, Benidorm, and Alicante. Alsa is the main bus line in this region; check the Web site for timetables and bus stations, or contact the respective local tourist office.

Bus Lines Alsa (☎ *902/422242* 🌐 *www.alsa.es*).

By Car

The *autopista* (toll highway) AP7 runs from the French border at La Jonquera through Barcelona, Valencia, and Alicante as far as Murcia. Just south of Elche, AP7 veers southeast and continues down the coast to Cartagena, while the toll-free A7/E15 forks southwest to Murcia. The Autovia del Mediterráneo or A7 is an alternate toll-free divided highway that, when completed, will run 1,300 km (780 mi) from the French border at La Jonquera all the way to Algeciras, making it the longest motorway of its kind in Europe. At present, the A7 begins just north of Valencia at Benicassim and continues south through Murcia, Almería, and Málaga to Algeciras. The other main links with the region are the A3 from Madrid to Valencia and the AP36/A30/A31 from Madrid to Murcia via Albacete. There are several car rental agencies at Alicante airport, as well as in the larger towns. Hotels also have car-hire information and can book you a car with advance notice.

By Taxi

Taxi Companies Cooperativa de Taxis (☎ *96/578–6565 in Dénia*). **Radio Taxi** (☎ *96/525–2511 in Benidorm*).

Visitor Information

Regional Tourist Offices Alicante (✉ *Rambla de Mendez Nuñez 23* ☎ *96/520–0000* 🌐 *www.comunitatvalenciana.com*). **Murcia** (✉ *Pl. Julian Romea 4* ☎ *902/101070* 🌐 *www.murciaturistica.com*).

By George Semler

Spain's southeastern corner is a holiday-brochure cliché of contrasts, best known for its sand and sunshine—and planes full of tourists—but the region's varied terrain ranges from the coastal plains of the far north to the peaceful soft sands and still waters of La Manga del Mar Menor. Despite the large number of foreign residents and the annual swell of summer visitors, locals have remained fiercely protective of their regional culture. The traditional fiestas here are wonderfully colorful and exuberant, as are the distinctive local cuisine and crafts.

Literary buffs can contemplate the inland province of Albacete, historically part of Murcia, and the scene of Don Quijote's exploits in the Castilian expanse of La Mancha. The windmills (Los Molinos) in the foothills of the Parque Natural del Montgó in Jávea are from the 14th century and remind one of those Quixotic giants. Fertile river valleys wiggle their way between the mountains here like a silk cord, while the villages are simple and traditional; you'll probably need Spanish to order a beer or ask for directions, though in the coastal towns you'll find English-language bookstores thanks to a lively British population.

There's a heady sense of history throughout the region, especially in the southeastern towns where the architecture reflects the area's long Moorish occupation. Alicante was in Moorish hands from 718 to 1249; Murcia, from 825 to 1243. Post–civil war reconstruction has transformed small fishing villages like Benidorm into leading tourist resorts in less than a generation. Agriculture and industry have also continued to grow, and Alicante is now the fourth-wealthiest province in Spain.

EXPLORING THE SOUTHEAST

From Valencia's Albufera region to the beginning of the Costa Blanca, down the coast through Alicante and on through the Murcia coastline, this part of Spain is rich in beaches, salt lagoons, steppes, mountain villages, and Mediterranean port cities.

ABOUT THE RESTAURANTS

Rice grows better in the Valencian provinces than anywhere else in Spain, which explains why paella was born here. Don't order it from a *menú del día* (menu of the day) unless you can be sure it's fresh—it's best served straight out of the pan as the carmelized rice at the bottom of the paella pan is a delicacy to be savored. Another rice dish to try is *arroz a la banda* (rice and vegetables with meat or fish, cooked over a wood fire). Alicante and Jijona are known for their *turrón,* nougat made with almonds and flavored with honey. In Elche you can savor fresh dates. Murcian cooking uses products of the *huerta* (floodplain) and the sea, with a marked Arab influence in preparation. *Caldero de Mar Menor,* a traditional fisherman's rice dish, is cooked in huge iron pots, has a distinctly oily consistency, and is flavored by fish cooked in its own juices. Delicious as tapas or entrees are *muchirones* (broad beans in a spicy sauce, similar to the Catalan *habas a la catalana*) and *cocas* (meat pies akin to empanadas). Dénia, in particular, is a city of culinary riches, where you can find everything from family recipes to traditional cuisine, prepared creatively.

ABOUT THE HOTELS

Many hotels on this coast are modern high-rises, but there are also some very tasteful independent hotels offering warm Mediterranean hospitality. Some coastal hotels close for the winter.

SOUTH OF VALENCIA TO THE COSTA BLANCA

Traveling around this area takes you through the Albufera wetlands and into the northern end of the Costa Blanca, known as La Marina Alta (the High Shore). Compared with the sunbathers' strip south of Dénia, these lonely marshlands and deserted duned beaches are wonderfully undiscovered.

LA ALBUFERA

16 km (10 mi) south of Valencia.

One of the largest bodies of freshwater in Spain, the **Parque Natural de La Albufera** supports four main environments: a sandbar, a marsh, the Albufera lagoon, and (to a lesser extent) hills and woodlands. More than 250 species of birds have been identified here—90 species breed here regularly. Bird-watching companies offer boat rides all along the Albufera. ✉*Centre d'Informació Raco del'Olla, El Palmar* ☎*96/162–7345* 🌐*www.albufera.com* ⏲*Mon., Wed., and Fri. 9–2, Tues., Thurs., and weekends 9–2 and 3:30–5:30.*

El Palmar, the major village in the area, has numerous restaurants specializing in paella Valenciana: the most traditional kind is made with rabbit or game birds, though seafood is also popular in this region because it's so fresh.

WHERE TO EAT AND STAY

$$–$$$ Fodor'sChoice ★ ✕ **La Casota.** Hidden from the main drag, this family-run restaurant in the village of El Palmar is frequented by local families. To start, try the *chipirones de playa con habitas* (squid with baby broadbeans) and a few *croquetas de bacalao a la crema de ajo* (salt cod croquettes in a garlic-cream sauce), then move on to *paella valenciana*, with rabbit, chicken, and green and lima beans or the classic *anguilas all i pebre* (eels cooked with garlic and green peppers). The presentation of an entire lobster in the *arroz con bogavante* is both photogenic and delicious. All ingredients are grown or caught in and around the rich Albufera lagoon. ✉*Calle Vizconde de Valdesoto 12* ☎*96/162–0168* 💳*DC, MC, V* ⏲*Closed Mon.*

$$$–$$$$ **Hotel Sidi Saler.** On the edge of La Albufera, and just 15 minutes south of Valencia via the hotel's free shuttle bus, this slick but airy hotel with comfortable, carpeted rooms is a Frisbee-throw away from miles of unspoiled beaches. Though the hotel is large, the staff is personal and organizes extensive programs for children from May to August and during holidays. **Pros:** good for families, on the beach yet near the city. **Cons:** not an intimate hotel, having a car is recommended. ✉ *Playa el Saler, Valencia* ☎ *96/161–0411* 🌐 *www.sidi-saler.com* *276 rooms, 16 suites* *In-hotel: 2 restaurants, bar, tennis courts, pools, gym, spa, beachfront, children's programs (ages 6–12), public Internet, public Wi-Fi, airport shuttle, parking (no fee), some pets allowed* 💳 *AE, DC, MC, V.*

GANDÍA

30 km (19 mi) northwest of Dénia.

Gandía is a prosperous commercial town with a lively nightlife, enjoyed particularly by visiting madrileños on the weekends. The town also has a coastal resort, Playa de Gandía, with a long sandy beach recognized as being one of the best on the Costa Blanca. The old town is 4 km (2½ mi) inland and is best known for its sumptuous former palace of the Borja dynasty. Gandía became the Borgia fief after King Ferdinand granted the duchy to the family in 1485. The canny Borgia pope Alexander VI was one of the most notorious of all Renaissance prelates, but the family's reputation was later redeemed by the local Jesuit St. Francis Borgia (1510–72), who was canonized in 1671.

GETTING HERE AND AROUND

Autobuses La Marina run shuttle services along the Paseo Marítimo between the port and the beaches.

ESSENTIALS

Bus Contacts **Autobuses La Marina** (☎ *96/287–1465*).

Visitor Information **Gandía** (✉ *Marqués del Campo* ☎ *96/287–7788* 🌐 *www.gandiaturistica.com*).

EXPLORING

The **Palau Ducal dels Borja** *(Ducal Palace)*, signposted from the city center, was founded by St. Francis in 1546 and serves as a Jesuit college. Elaborate ceilings and bright-color *azulejos* (glazed tiles) adorn the 17th-century state rooms. ☎ *96/287–1465* 🌐 *www.palauducal.com* *€6* *Guided tours June–Aug., Tues.–Sat. hourly 10–2 and 3–7, Sun. 10–2; Sept.–May, Tues.–Sat. hourly 10–2 and 4–8, Sun. 10–2.*

WHERE TO EAT

$$–$$$ SPANISH **Gamba Marisquería.** Justifiably famous in these parts, this restaurant is a family-run affair and a local favorite. The food is attractively presented, and only the freshest ingredients are used. The menu varies, but try the *fideuà de mariscos* (seafood paella made with noodles instead of rice), or the standard *arreglo Gamba* (Gamba medley), which offers a wide range of seasonally changing specialties from *berenjena gamba* (Gamba eggplant) to *cigala y langostino hervido* (boiled prawns and crawfish), to *ostras* (oysters), *calamares* (cuttlefish), or *navajas* (razor clams). ✉ *Carretera Nazaret-Oliva s/n* ☎ *96/284–1310* *Reservations essential* *AE, DC, MC, V* *Closed Mon. No dinner Oct.–June.*

$ SPANISH **Mesón Gallego.** This Galician restaurant dishes up hearty typical dishes like *pulpo a la gallega* (octopus) cooked over coals and dressed with oil and paprika, and plenty of meat and game. The surroundings are unpretentious and rustic, with tables spilling out onto the bustling port area. Ask for Galician *culcas,* shallow ceramic bowls for drinking the young Ribeiro wines. ✉ *C. Rioja 1 (near Casino de la Playa)* ☎ *96/284–1892* *AE, MC, V* *Closed Wed. No dinner Tues.*

$$$ **La Falconera.** A charming French couple, Thérèse and Yves, are the owners and managers of this elegant mansion in the village of Marxuquera, 7 km (4 mi) inland from Gandía. The lush garden is filled with palms, eucalyptus, orange trees, and towering pines, while the ample rooms overlooking this peaceful scene are furnished with antiques and traditional furniture, and equipped with high-tech renovated bathrooms. **Pros:** all the comforts and pleasures of visiting old friends in the country. **Cons:** somewhat isolated from the beach scene, nightlife, and the life of the village. ✉ *Camí Pinet 32, Marxuquera* ☎ *96/286–8315* 🌐 *www.lafalconera.com* *4 rooms* *In-hotel: bar, pool, terrace, garden Wi-Fi, parking (no fee), no-smoking rooms* *AE, DC, MC, V.*

THE COSTA BLANCA

The stretch of coastline known as the Costa Blanca (White Coast) begins between Gandía and Dénia and ends near Murcia's border, just north of the Mar Menor. It's best known for its magic vacation combo of sand, sea, and sun, and there are some excellent, albeit crowded, beaches here, as well as more secluded coves and stretches of sand. Alicante is the largest city and still largely overlooked by visitors, who typically head for the better-known coastal resorts such as Benidorm.

DÉNIA

Fodor'sChoice ★ *100 km (62 mi) south of Valencia, 8 km (5 mi) north of Jávea and east of Ondara.*

Widely known as the gastronomic capital of the Costa Blanca, Dénia is a good place to sample Mediterranean seafood—try *picaetes* (tapas in the Valencian dialect) *de sépia y calamar* (squid and cuttlefish), *suquet de rape* (stewed monkfish), or *gambas rojas de Dénia* —a special breed of shrimp found in the waters around Dénia that are served simply boiled or grilled and are nearly as coveted as truffles.

The northernmost beach resort on the Costa Blanca, Dénia is also a busy tourist town known for its fishing boats and fiestas, which culminate in the midsummer Hogueras de San Juan (June 23, St. John's Day eve bonfires). Backed by the Montgó massif, rising to more than 2,100 feet to the west, Dénia's beaches to the north—Les Marines, Les Bovetes, and Les Deveses—are smooth and sandy, whereas the coast to the south is rocky, forming *calas* (tiny secluded inlets that recall the Costa Brava, north of Barcelona).

ESSENTIALS

Visitor Information **Dénia** (*✉ Plaza Oculista Buigues 9 ☎ 96/642–2367 🌐 www.denia.net*)

EXPLORING

Dénia's most interesting architectural attraction is the **Palau del Governador,** the Governor's Palace, within a Moorish-era castle. Overlooking the town, the castle has an interesting archaeological museum as well as a Renaissance bastion and a Moorish portal with a lovely horseshoe arch. *✉ C. San Francisco s/n ☎ 96/642–0656 €3 ⏲ Daily 10–1:30 and Jan.–Mar. and Nov.–Dec. 3–6, Apr.–May 4:30–7, June 4–7:30, Jul.–Aug. 5–8:30, Sept. 4–8, and Oct. 3–6:30).*

★ Inland from Dénia, the **Cueva de las Calaveras** *(Cave of the Skulls)* (*✉ Ctra. Benidoleig-Pedreguera, km 1.5, Benidoleig ☎ 96/640–4235 🌐 www.cuevasturisticas.com €3.50 ⏲ June–Sept., daily 10–8:30; Oct.–May, daily 10–6*), named for the 12 Moorish skulls found there when the cave was discovered in 1768, was inhabited by Paleolithic humans some 50,000 years ago. More than 400 yards long, the cave of stalactites and stalagmites has a dome rising to more than 60 feet and leads to an underground lake.

WHERE TO EAT AND STAY

$\$\$–\$\$\$\$$ SEAFOOD **Drassanes.** Built into Dénia's original medieval shipyards (for which it's named—*drassanes* is Catalan for shipyards), this time-honored dining spot is well-known for fresh local seafood and rice dishes of every kind. Informal and spread out over two rambling levels of dining rooms, the food here is authentic and delicious. *Arròs a banda* (rice with peeled seafood) is the house specialty, but the *paella marinera* (seafood paella) is a close second, while the *gamba roja de Dénia* (local red prawn) is de rigueur when available. *C. Puerto 15* *96/578–1118* *AE, MC, V* *Closed Mon. and Nov. No dinner Sun.*

$$$$ SEAFOOD Fodor's Choice ★ **El Poblet.** Quique Dacosta's exquisite cooking has been making headlines up and down the Costa Blanca and beyond for a decade, and diners get to choose between contemporary rustic dining rooms with views into the kitchen, alfresco tables on the terrace, or the glassed-in pavilion. The cuisine is based on first-rate local produce from the sea and the garden. Dacosta's repertoire is in constant flux, so the tasting menu is the surest way to experience his latest burst of creativity. *Urb. Poblet (3 km northwest of Dénia)* *96/578–4179* *MC, V* *Closed Monday. No dinner Sun.*

$–$$ SEAFOOD **El Port.** In the old fishermen's and seafarers' quarter just across from the port, this is a classic Dénia dining spot, featuring all kinds of fish fresh off the boats, along with shellfish dishes and the full range of rice specialties, from *arros negre* (black rice) to a classic *paella marinera* (seafood paella). In addition, the tapas here are ample and excellent, while a creditable selection of mouthwatering desserts awaits anyone still hungry enough to consider trying them. *Esplanada Bellavista 12* *96/578–4973* *AE, MC, V* *Closed Mon.*

$$$–$$$$ SEAFOOD **La Seu.** Chef Miquel Ruiz has been called a "chef-poet" because of his innovative melding of international, Mediterranean, and traditional cuisine at this distinguished restaurant in the center of town. Standout dishes include Mediterranean sushi with orange vinaigrette or a rice dish with shellfish and shrimp. Diners can choose from a warmly lit stone cave (for groups), a glass-ceiling modern art space, or a classic dining room. To get the full measure of chef Ruiz's repertoire, the *menu de degustación* is pricey but, in the end, good value. *C. Loreto 59* *96/642–4478* *AE, MC, V* *Closed Mon. No dinner Sun.*

$$$ **Dénia Marriott La Sella Golf Resort and Spa.** This large hotel, about 15 minutes west of Dénia and 1½ km (1 mi) past the small town of La Xara, is ideal if you want to combine sporting facilities and a fine spa with sightseeing and the beaches of the coast. Rooms are larger than what you usually find in the area, and the hotel is child-friendly, with on-site babysitting and a seasonal Kids' Club. **Pros:** many amenities and activities, good for families. **Cons:** large hotel with a chain atmosphere. *Alqueria Ferrando s/n, Jesus Pobre* *96/645–4054* *www.marriott.com* *178 rooms, 8 suites* *In-hotel: 2 restaurants, bar, golf course, tennis court, pool, gym, children's programs (ages 4–12), laundry facilities, laundry service, public Wi-Fi, parking (no fee), no-smoking rooms, some pets allowed* *AE, DC, MC, V.*

$ **Hotel Chamarel.** Named after a region in Mauritania where seven different cultures are found, this hotel aims to show that different styles can coexist in harmony. Art Deco furniture, bold mix-and-match color themes, high-tech facilities, and a tranquil patio surrounded by lush greenery all work in harmony to create an oasis. There are two standards of rooms; the superior rooms have four-poster beds, beamed ceilings, spacious bathrooms, and original tiles. A suite in back is perfect for a family. The staff arranges museum visits and water activities at the port. **Pros:** friendly staff, individual attention. **Cons:** no pool, close to town but not on the beach. ✉ *Calle Cavallers 13* ☎ *96/643–5007* 🌐 *www.hotelchamarel.com* *9 rooms, 5 suites* *In-room: Wi-Fi. In-hotel: restaurant, bar, no elevator, parking (fee)* *AE, DC, MC, V.*

$$$ **La Posada del Mar.** Directly under Dénia castle, and a few steps across from the harbor, this hotel is in the former 13th-century customs post and has been renovated with a slightly nautical theme, most evident in the portal windows and sailor's-knot ironwork along the staircase. The original Tuscan stone arch has been preserved in the lobby, along with antique vases, giving an ancient but clean Mediterranean feel. Most rooms have generous balconies, and all have views of the harbor and sea. La Posada's rooftop terrace is particularly inviting. **Pros:** serene environment, across from harbor, close to center of town. **Cons:** no pool. ✉ *Pl. de les Drassanes 2* ☎ *96/643–2966* 🌐 *www.laposadadelmar.com* *20 rooms, 5 suites* *In-room: safe, Ethernet. In-hotel: bar, gym, laundry facilities, public Internet, public Wi-Fi, parking (no fee)* *AE, DC, MC, V.*

EN ROUTE

The Playa del Arenal, a tiny bay cut into the larger one, is worth a visit in the summer. You can reach it via the coastal road, CV736, between Dénia and Jávea.

JÁVEA (XÀBIA)

108 km (67 mi) southeast of Valencia, 92 km (57 mi) northeast of Alicante, 8 km (5 mi) south of Dénia.

On more than 25 km of coast, Jávea is a labyrinth of tiny streets and houses with arched portals and Gothic windows, with an antique aspect contrasted only (and ironically) by its modern church, **Santa María de Loreto.** The church-fortress of **San Bartolomé** is the town's architectural gem with gothic vaulted ceilings inside. Restaurants around the port's **Aduanas del Mar** area serve an excellent variety of versions of the local classic, *arroz a la marinera* (seafood paella).

10

ESSENTIALS

Visitor Information Jávea (✉ *Pl. Almirante Bastarreche 11* ☎ *96/579–0736* 🌐 *www.xabia.org*).

EXPLORING

The **Soler Blasco,** an ethnological and archaeological museum, has a superb set of Iberian gold jewelry discovered in 1904 during building excavation works. ✉ *Calle Primicies s/n* ☎ *96/579–1098* *Free* *Mar.–Oct., Tues.–Fri. 10–1 and 6–8, weekends 10–1; Nov.–Feb., Tues.–Sun. 10–1.*

Following the bay south from the town, the beach transforms itself into strange, small rock formations with numerous rock pools. After a mile or so, you reach the small, sandy bay-within-a-bay, the **Playa del Arenal.** This is a nice little resort in its own right, with numerous bars, restaurants, lounges, and shops around the beach.

WHERE TO EAT AND STAY

$$–$$$$ SEAFOOD ✕**Balcón del Puerto.** On the first floor of a delightful building between the beach and the harbor, this restaurant has a terrace in back, though it has no view of the water. The cuisine is typically *levantina* (from the Levante, Spain's east coast), and specialties include paellas, *zarzuela de mariscos* (a shellfish and crustacean medley), and rice dishes. The *cazuela de rape* (stewed monkfish) is a favorite, as is the *arroz de bogavante* (soupy rice with lobster). The special lunchtime *menú del día* for two offers top value for under €16. ✉*Aduanas del Mar* ☎*96/579–1064* 💳*AE, DC, MC, V.*

$–$$$ SPANISH ✕**Bar El Clavo.** Traditional tapas in this no-frills bar in the port, across the street from the beach, attract a savvy local crowd. The *patatas bravas* (potatoes with hot sauce) are legendary here, universally recognized as the best in Jávea, and ideally accompanied by a cold *caña* (draft beer). Try the artichokes and fried fish or the *pulpo gallego* (slices of Galician octopus served with paprika on potato wafers). Reserve in advance if you want to ensure a table, or take your chances on bar space. ✉*Almirante Bastarreche 15* ☎*96/579–1014* 💳*AE, MC, V.*

$$–$$$$ **El Rodat.** This chic hotel is a comfortable option with lots of extras, including an extensive health and beauty center, two restaurants (Restaurante El Rodat has more adventurous food than Rodat Terraza), and the option of renting your own villa with private garden. The terraced, red stucco buildings have plush, if conservative interiors, with a gold, gray, and cream color scheme. The grounds are home to lofty palms, pine trees, and brilliantly colored mimosa and bougainvillea. The restaurant terrace has panoramic views of the adjacent Montgó nature park. The hotel often organizes local wine tours. **Pros:** community feel, many amenities. **Cons:** removed from town and beaches. ✉*Calle de la Murciana 9, Ctra. al Cabo de la Nao s/n* ☎*96/647–0710* 🌐*www.elrodat.com* *34 suites, 8 rooms, 12 villas* *In-hotel: 2 restaurants, bar, pool, spa, tennis court, public Internet, public Wi-Fi, parking (no fee)* 💳*AE, DC, MC, V.*

$ **Hotel Miramar.** This small, unpretentious hotel may lack luxuries, but it more than makes up for it with its cheerful service, impeccable rooms, and the location right on the promenade along the bay in the center of town. Rooms with sea views—albeit out of diminutive windows—cost slightly more than interior rooms. **Pros:** fabulous location, top value, friendly staff. **Cons:** not much in the way of decor, a bit musty, no pool or terraces. ✉*Plaza Almirante Bastareche 12* ☎*96/579–0100* 📠*96/579–0102* *26 rooms* *In-hotel: bar, restaurant, no elevator* 💳*MC, V.*

$$$$ **Parador de Jávea.** Ensconced in a lush palm grove with terrific views of the bay and the expanse of white-sand beach below, this modern parador is four stories high and far more tasteful than many of the high-rise hotels elsewhere on the Costa Blanca. The oak-trim, ceramic-tile guest rooms are airy and pleasant with wicker furniture. The parador restaurant is known for its carefully prepared local Costa Blanca

specialties, most of them from the Mediterranean. **Pros:** beautiful views, modern but cozy, many activities possible. **Cons:** modern building lacks charm. ✉ *Av. del Mediterráneo 7* ☎ *96/579–0200* 🌐 *www.parador.es* *70 rooms* *In-room: Wi-Fi. In-hotel: restaurant, bar, pool, gym* *AE, DC, MC, V.*

CABO DE LA NAO (CAP DE LA NAU)

10 km (6 mi) southeast of Jávea.

Essentially part of the beach resorts of Jávea, Cabo de la Nao (Cape Nao) is a great spur of land jutting into the Mediterranean toward Ibiza, which is barely 100 km (62 mi) away. As you round the point, you turn from a coast that looks toward Italy to one that faces Africa. The main strip of beach is white pebbles, and quite lively. Make your way to Cala de la Granadella beach if you're looking to get away from the mass tourism resort world.

CALPE (CALP)

★ *15 km (9 mi) southwest of Jávea, 8 km (5 mi) north of Altea.*

The road from Cabo de la Nao to Calpe is very scenic, winding through the cliffs and hills covered in villas and passing small, rocky, and pebbly bays. Calpe has an ancient history, and its strategic location has attracted Phoenicians, Greeks, Romans, and Moors dedicated to trading, agriculture, and fishing. After the Reconquest by Jaume I in 1240, the Christians and Moors lived together peacefully, but between the 14th and 17th centuries they were under almost constant threat from the Barbary Pirates. This led to the construction of numerous fortifications such as the Torreó de la Peça (Tower of the Piece), a defense tower named after an artillery piece used to defend the city. (Two of these cannons can be seen next to the Torreó.) Today the Old Town, full of striking small streets and squares, is a delightful place to wander.

ESSENTIALS

Visitor Information Calpe (✉ *Av. Ejércitos Españoles 44* ☎ *96/583–6920* 🌐 *www.calpe.es*).

EXPLORING

Calpe has always been dominated by the **Peñón d'Ifach,** a huge calcareous rock more than 1,100 yards long, 1,090 feet high, and joined to the mainland by a narrow isthmus. The area is rich in flora and fauna, with more than 300 species of plant life and 80 species of land and marine birds identified here. A visit to the top is not for the fainthearted; wear shoes with traction for the hike, which includes a trip through a tunnel to the summit. The views are spectacular, reaching to the island of Ibiza on a clear day.

The fishing industry is still very important in Calpe, and every evening the fishing boats return to port with their catch. The subsequent auction at the **Fish Market** can be watched from the walkway of La Lonja de Calpe. ✉ *Port* *Weekdays 5–7.*

The **Mundo Marino** company offers a complete range of sailing trips, including cruises between the towns up and down the coast. Some of the vessels have glass bottoms, so you can keep an eye on the abundant marine life. ✉*Port* 🌐*www.mundomarino.es.*

CASTLES GALORE

There are close to 100 castles in the Costa Blanca region; most originate from the days of the Moors and were built between the 8th and 13th centuries. Built as a defense against such predictable threats as pirates and other outside invaders, they also protected the city against tax collectors.

WHERE TO EAT AND STAY

$$–$$$$ SPANISH ✕ **Playa.** Quite simply, this ample terrace and its adjacent sister restaurant La Lonja are a seafood and shellfish lovers' paradise, offering a wide selection of fish, rice, and marine dishes at competitive prices. Just opposite the fishing port, the terrace and rambling series of dining rooms can provide everything from a few oysters for a handful of euros up to family-style combination plates for as much as a €100 a throw. The "menu" consists of tables covered with living examples of each dish currently available, so diners know exactly what they're getting. ✉*Explanada del Puerto* ☎*96/583–0032* ▭*MC, V.*

$$–$$$ **Hotel Bahía.** The slick, modern Bahía provides all the creature comforts, with the added attractions of stylish decor and exceptional service. Rooms are classy in an understated way, with splashes of bright color complementing the neutral color scheme and design. Bedroom terraces overlook the Playa Arenal, but the hotel is equally well located for sidewalk cafés and a stroll around town. The spa has a wide range of treatments for those seeking a spot of self-pampering in between plunges at the pool. **Pros:** beachfront, city-center location. **Cons:** very large hotel, modern architecture. ✉*Av. de Valencia 24* ☎*96/583–9702* 🌐*www.bahiacalpe-hotel.com* *284* rooms *In-hotel: restaurant, room service, bar, pool, gym, spa, beachfront, public Wi-Fi, parking (fee)* ▭*MC, V* *BP.*

¢ **Pensión el Hidalgo.** This pleasant family-run *pensión* near a small *cala* (inlet) and the beach has small but cozy rooms that are decorated with a friendly, easy-going, spare-room feel. Several of the rooms have small private balconies overlooking the Mediterranean. A major perk is the intimate breakfast terrace with a sea view for which you would normally have to pay a premium. **Pros:** beachfront location, very reasonable prices. **Cons:** simple rooms, you must book far ahead in summer, especially in August. ✉*Av. Rosa de los Vientos 19, edificio Santa Maria* ☎*96/583–9317* 🌐*www.pensionelhidalgo.com* *9 rooms* ▭*MC, V* *BP.*

ALTEA

10 km (6 mi) south of Calpe, 11 km (7 mi) north of Benidorm.

Altea is an old fishing village with white houses and a striking church with a blue ceramic-tile dome. One of the best-conserved towns on the Costa Blanca, it serves as a foil to the skyscraping tourist towers of

Benidorm. The beach is pebbly. North of town, the Altea Hills area is more built up, with pretty villas lining the hills and cliffs.

ESSENTIALS

Visitor Information Altea (*San Pedro 9* *96/584–4114* *www.altea.es*).

WHERE TO EAT AND STAY

$$–$$$ FRENCH **La Costera.** This popular restaurant and bistro, once a goat corral, mixes excellent French cooking with bizarre furnishings and a nightly show—anything from complicated harmonies and percussion on bottles behind the bar to singing. Specialties include *ensalada périgourdine con jamón de pato casero* (Périgourd-style salad with homemade duck ham), *fondue bourgignon* (Burgundy fondue), a range of fresh fish from roast *lubina* (sea bass) to *suquet de cola de rape* (stewed monkfish) to a variety of game in season, including venison and partridge. *Costera del Mestre la Música 8* *96/584–0230* *www.lacosteradealtea.com* *Reservations essential* *MC, V* *Closed Mon. and Nov.–Feb. No lunch Tues.–Fri.*

$$$–$$$$ FRENCH **Oustau de Altea.** In one of the prettiest corners of the old part of Altea, this sleek and rustic 200-year-old space, formerly a cloister and a schoolhouse, combines contemporary design details gracefully juxtaposed over a rustic background. Named for the Provençal word for inn or hostelry, Oustau serves polished international cuisine with a French flair, inside and on a terrace. Dishes are named for classic films, such as "Love Story" (beef and strawberry coulis). Contemporary artists display work here, so the art changes regularly. *Mayor 5* *96/584–2078* *www.oustau.com* *Reservations essential* *MC, V* *Closed Feb. and Mon. Oct–June. No lunch.*

Hostal Fornet. Rooms at this pleasant, small hotel at the highest point of Altea's historic center are modest but squeaky clean, with white walls and pine furnishings. The friendly owners are multilingual, but the real *pièce de résistance* is the roof terrace with its stunning view of the church's distinctive blue tiled cupola and surrounding tangle of streets with a Mediterranean backdrop. **Pros:** the views, the staff, the location, top value. **Cons:** no pool or beach, not easy to reach by car. *C. Beniardá 1* *96/584–3005* *www.albir21-hostalfornet.com* *35 rooms* *In-hotel: restaurant, bar, no elevator* *MC, V* *Closed Jan.* *EP.*

BENIDORM

11 km (7 mi) south of Altea, 42 km (26 mi) northeast of Alicante.

Benidorm is an overdeveloped resort with tens of thousands of hotel beds and a seemingly bottomless capacity for tourists. Hundreds of thousands still flock to the twin, white crescent-shaped beaches annually. The resultant glut of karaoke clubs and British-run pubs offering all-day breakfasts and satellite soccer games give Benidorm a decidedly un-Spanish feel—and it's certainly not the place for those seeking a quiet vacation by the Mediterranean. Those with children, though, may appreciate the nearby famous Terra Mítica theme park, the animal and water parks, and the available boat trips. For a fantastic view, follow signs to Club Sierra Dorada at the eastern edge of town and climb up to the **Rincón de Loix** (Loix Corner).

GETTING HERE AND AROUND

Benidorm Tour Bus offers comprehensive tours of Benidorm with multilingual audio guides. Check with tourist office or hotel concierge for hourly departure points.

ESSENTIALS

Tour Bus Contact Benidorm Tour Bus (*Av. Martínez Alejos 16 96/528–0592*).

Visitor Information Benidorm (*Av. Martínez Alejos 16 96/585–1311 www.benidorm.org*).

EXPLORING

Excursiones Marítimas Benidorm. Of the many boat trips offered by this company, the excursion to the Isla de Benidorm is one of the best: you can swim and look at the local birdlife. Boats depart every hour, 10–5; the fare is €13 for adults. If you want to see more of the beautiful coastline, opt for the one-hour cruise up to Calpe for €20 after which you can do some sightseeing before returning; these trips depart Monday–Saturday at 12, with a return sail to Calpe at 4:30. *96/585–0052 www.excursionesmaritimasbenidorm.com.*

Terra Mítica. Owned by Paramount, this is one of Europe's largest theme parks. In addition to many rides, there are shows that include pirate battles, chariot races, and fighting gladiators. *Just outside Benidorm, Carretera de Benidorm a Finestrat, da de Moralet s/n 902/020220 www.terramiticapark.com €35 Daily 10–8, some nights/weekends longer hours (call to confirm).*

WHERE TO EAT AND STAY

$$$–$$$$ ITALIAN **Kataria.** This clean, well-lit dining spot in the Hotel Belroy, an all-white, geometrically dazzling design tour de force, is Benidorm's premier culinary haven. Dishes range from traditional offerings like *suquet de rape con punto de ñora* (stewed monkfish with red pepper) to the postmodern *bacalao skrei sobre judías al dente y puré de zanahoria* (cod on tender white beans with carrot purée). A seasonally changing menu and a daring wine list featuring new local wines as well as traditional selections make for interesting dining. *Av. del Mediterráneo 13 96/683–1372 www.katariagastronomica.com AE, DC, MC, V Closed Sun. Nov.–May*

$ **Hotel Colón.** Positioned on the front line of the Platja de Ponent (Benidorm's westernmost beach), at the edge of the old town, this family hotel has lots to offer, in addition to the very reasonable rates. Rooms are decorated in classic Mediterranean blue with sparkling white tiled bathrooms, and the hotel restaurant serves creditable fare (a breakfast-and-dinner rate is available for a minimal extra cost). **Pros:** reasonably priced for waterfront location and ample sea views, impeccably clean, friendly service. **Cons:** no pool, closed for five months a year. *Paseo Colón 3 96/585–0412 www.hotelcolon.net 37 rooms In-hotel: restaurant, bar, Wi-Fi, beachfront, some pets allowed MC, V Closed Nov.–Mar. BP.*

$$$$ **Montíboli.** A few miles south of Benidorm, in the town of Villajoyosa (Vila Joiosa), this hotel sits on a cliff overlooking a beautiful bay. Surrounded by luxuriant vegetation, the swimming pool has the blue Mediterranean waters as background. This is, undoubtedly, the hotel of choice for many miles around. The rooms are luxurious, as are the public rooms and the two gourmet restaurants, Emperador and Minarete (lunch only). **Pros:** beautiful scenery and location. **Cons:** most activities except water sports are off premises. ✉*Partida Montiboli s/n, Villajoyosa* ☎*96/589–0250* 🌐*www.hotelelmontiboli.com* *85 rooms* *In-hotel: restaurant, bar, pools, gym, spa, beachfront, laundry service, public Wi-Fi, parking (no fee)* *MC, V.*

NIGHTLIFE

Countless bars and discos with names such as Jockey's and Harrods (reflecting Benidorm's popularity with Brits and Germans) line Avenida de Europa and the Ensanche de la Playa de Levante. The **Benidorm Palace** (✉*Av. Severo Ochoa* ☎*96/585–1661* 🌐*www.benidorm-palace.com*) offers a cabaret Tuesday–Saturday, with Spanish dance, international musical shows, and sometimes even operas. Dinner starts at 8:30; the show at 10. Since its opening in 1977, the Palace, with capacity for 1,500, has been one of the major tourist attractions for the region. Admission for dinner and show is €44 (with a €53 menu also available); for the show only, it's €27.

ALICANTE (ALACANT)

82 km (51 mi) northeast of Murcia, 183 km (113 mi) south of Valencia by coast road, 42 km (26 mi) south of Benidorm.

The Greeks called it Akra Leuka (White Summit), and the Romans named it Lucentum (City of Light), since as a crossroads for inland and coastal routes, Alicante has always been known for its luminous skies. The city is dominated by the Castillo de Santa Bárbara, but also memorable is its grand **Explanada,** lined with date palms. Directly under the castle is the city beach, the Playa del Postiguet, but the city's pride is the long, curved Playa de San Juan, which runs north from the Cap de l'Horta to El Campello.

GETTING HERE AND AROUND

The small TRAM train goes from the city center on the beach to El Campello. From the same open-air station in Alicante the FGV train departs to Dénia, with stops in El Campello, Benidorm, Altea, Calpe, and elsewhere.

ESSENTIALS

Tram Contact TRAM (🌐*www.tram-alicante.com*).

Visitor Information Alicante (✉*Rambla Mendez Nuñez 23* ☎*96/520–0000* 🌐*www.costablanca.org*).

OLD TOWN

Concatedral of San Nicolás de Bari. Built between 1616 and 1662 on the site of a former mosque, this church (denominated *con*catedral because it shares the seat of the regional bishopric with the Concatedral de

Orihuela) has an austere facade that was designed by Agustín Bernardino, a disciple of the great Spanish architect Juan de Herrera (1530–97), architect of El Escorial. Inside, it's dominated by a dome nearly 150 feet high, a pretty cloister, and a lavish baroque side chapel. Its name comes from the day that Alicante was reconquered, December 6, 1248—the feast day of St. Nicolás. ☒*Pl. del Abad Penalva 2* ☎*96/521–2662* ⏲*Daily 7:30–12:30 and 5:30–8:30.*

Iglesia de Santa María. Constructed in a Gothic style over the city's main mosque between the 14th and 16th centuries, this is Alicante's oldest church. The main door is flanked by beautiful baroque stonework by Juan Bautista Borja while the interior highlights are the golden rococo high altar, a Gothic image in stone of St. Mary, and a sculpture of the Sants Juanes by Rodrigo de Osona. ☒*Pl. de Santa María* ☎*96/521–6026* ⏲*Tues.–Sun. 4–8:30.*

Museo de Belenes *(Nativity Scene Museum)*. It is believed that St. Francis of Assisi sponsored the first nativity scene in Greccio, Italy, in 1223, and the first staged in Spain was in the cathedral at Barcelona in 1300. The Spanish exported the concept to the Americas, and these days at Christmastime in Spain the tradition of creating nativity scenes in churches, public places, and private homes remains very strong. This museum, in a typical early-19th-century house complete with an original well, has a collection of nativity scenes by some of the finest Spanish artists and others from around the globe. ☒*San Agustín 3* ☎*96/520–2232* *Free* ⏲*Apr.–Oct., weekdays 10–2 and 5–8, Sat. 10–2; Nov.–Mar., Tues.–Fri. 10–2 and 4:30–7:30, Sat. 10–2.*

Museo de Bellas Artes Gravina. Inside the beautiful 18th-century Palacio del Conde de Lumiares, MUBAG, as it's known, has some 500 works of art ranging from the 16th to the early 20th century. ☒*Gravina 13–15* ☎*96/514–6780* *www.mubag.org* *Free* ⏲*May–Oct., Tues.–Sat. 10–2 and 5–9; Nov.–Apr., Tues.–Sat. 10–2 and 4–8.*

Ayuntamiento. Constructed between 1696 and 1780, the town hall is a beautiful example of baroque civic architecture. Inside, a gold sculpture by Salvador Dalí, of San Juan Bautista holding the famous cross and shell, rises to the second floor in the stairwell. Ask gate officials for permission to explore the ornate halls and rococo chapel on the first floor. ☒*Pl. de Ayuntamiento* ☎*96/514–9100.*

OUTSIDE OLD TOWN

Castillo de Santa Bárbara (*Santa Bárbara Castle*). Benacantil Mountain, rising to a height of 545 feet, forms a strategic position overlooking not just the city but the sea and the whole Alicante plain for many miles. Remains from civilizations dating from the Bronze Age onward have been found here, and the oldest parts, at the highest level, are from the 9th to 13th centuries. This is one of the largest existing medieval fortresses in Europe. It is most easily reached by first walking through a 200-yard tunnel entered from Av. Jovellanos 1, along Postiguet Beach by the pedestrian bridge, then taking the elevator up 472 feet to the entrance. ☒*Near Postiguet Beach* ☎*96/516–2128* *Free, elevator €2.40* ⏲*Elevator and castle daily 10–7:30; last elevator up at 7.*

Capa Collection. Professor Eduardo Capa, of Madrid's Academía Real de Bellas Artes de San Fernando, donated this collection of contemporary Spanish sculpture, the largest such collection in the world. Some 250 of the total of 700 works are permanently displayed here, including pieces by Benlliure, Pérez Comendador, and Alberto Sánchez. ✉ *Castillo de Santa Bárbara* ☎ *96/515–2969* *Free* *Tues.–Sat. 10:30–2:30 and 4–6:30, Sun. and holidays 10:30–2:30.*

Museo Arqueológico Provincial (*MARQ*). Inside the old hospital of San Juan de Dios, this museum has a collection of artifacts from the Alicante region dating from the Palaeolithic era to modern times, with a particular emphasis on Iberian art. In 2004, the Marq, as it is known, won recognition as the European Museum Forum's European Museum of the Year. ✉ *Plaza Dr. Gómez Ulla s/n* ☎ *96/514–9000* *www.marqalicante.com* *€3* *Tues.–Sat. 10–7, Sun. and holidays 10–2.*

Museo Taurino. In the Plaza de Toros, the Bullfighting Museum is a must for taurine aficionados. There are fine examples of costumes (the "suits of lights"), bulls' heads, posters, capes, and sculptures. ✉ *Pl. de España s/n* ☎ *96/521–9930* *Free* *Tues.–Fri. 10:30–1:30 and 5–8, Sat. 10:30–1:30.*

Museo de Fogueres. Bonfire festivities are popular in this part of Spain, and the effigies can be elaborate and funny, including satirized political figures and entertainment stars. Every year the best *ninots* (effigies) are saved from the flames and placed in this museum, which also has an audiovisual presentation of the festivities, scale models, photos, and costumes. ✉ *Av. Rambla de Méndez Núñez 29* ☎ *96/514–6828* *Free* *May–Oct., Tues.–Sun. 10–2 and 5–8; June–Sept., Tues.–Sun. 10–2 and 6–9, Sun. and holidays 10–2.*

WHERE TO EAT AND STAY

$ SPANISH **Nou Manolín.** This inviting exposed-brick and wood-lined space is generally packed with locals, here for the excellent-value daily menu. It's a superb place to tuck into an authentic paella or one of many other regional rice concoctions. Market cuisine dedicated to quality produce is the trademark here, and everything from fresh fish to *foie* is selected and prepared with utmost care. If you can't find a bench, head for the tapas bar, which serves generous *raciones*, ideally accompanied by a glass of ice-cold *fino* (dry sherry). ✉ *C. Villegas 3* ☎ *96/520–0368* *MC, V.*

$$$ **Amérigo.** This former Dominican convent is right in the historic center of Alicante. The building has been tastefully refurbished to blend its historic tendencies with the best of modern design and technology, and is one of the newest and best luxury hotels in the city center. It also incorporates a fashionable tapas bar, a rooftop terrace and pool, as well as on-site private parking—a real luxury in Alicante. It's a short walk from here to nearby places of interest, including Postiguet Beach. **Pros:** near all museums, the port, and the beach. **Cons:** city center can be hot and busy in summer. ✉ *Rafael Altamira 7* ☎ *96/514–6570* *www.hospes.es* *81 rooms* *In-hotel: restaurant, bars, pool, gym, public Wi-Fi, parking (fee)* *MC, V.*

10

$–$$$$ **Hotel Mediterránea Plaza.** You'll find this elegant hotel tucked back under the arches in the central Plaza del Ayuntamiento, dominated by the colossal and magnificent baroque town hall. The lobby sets the tone for the hotel, with its acres of glossy marble and refined decor. The rooms have parquet floors and a soothing blue-and-white Mediterranean seafaring color scheme with luxurious marble-clad bathrooms with tubs. The roof terrace has stunning views over the city and seascape. **Pros:** opulent common spaces and bedrooms. **Cons:** large chain hotel, no pool. ✉ *Pl. del Ayuntamiento 6* ☎ *965/210188* 🌐 *www.hotelmediterraneaplaza.com* *50 rooms* *In-hotel: bar, gym, spa, public Wi-Fi* *MC, V* *EP.*

¢ **Les Monges Palace.** In a restored 1912 building, this family-run hostal is behind the *Ayuntamiento* in Alicante's central old quarter. Exposed stone walls, ceramic tile floors, and the original building materials were lovingly preserved during the restoration. Rooms are furnished with eccentric artwork and quirky charm. The Japanese Suite ($$) is equipped with furniture from Japan, a hot tub, and a sauna. **Pros:** small, with personalized service, location is ideal, decor has character. **Cons:** all services cost extra, must book well in advance. ✉ *C. San Agustín 4* ☎ *96/521–5046* 🌐 *www.lesmonges.net* *22 rooms, 2 suites* *In-room: dial-up. In-hotel: parking (fee), public Internet, public Wi-Fi* *MC, V.*

Fodor'sChoice ★

NIGHTLIFE

El Barrio, the old quarter west of Rambla de Méndez Núñez, is the prime nightlife area of Alicante, with music bars and discotheques every couple of steps. In summer, or after 3 AM, the liveliest places are along the water, on the Ruta del Puerto and Ruta de la Madera. It's an Alicante tradition to start the night with overflowing mojitos at **El Coscorrón** (✉ *C. Tarifa 303002*). **Astrónomo** (✉ *C. Virgen de Belén 22* ☎ *647/654298*) has a great patio with tiki torches and traditional dancing. In summer, or after 3 AM, the liveliest places are along the water, on the Ruta del Puerto and Ruta de la Madera. Among the slicker pubs and discos is **Z-Club** (✉ *Calle San Fernando s/n* ☎ *96/521–0646*), where Alicante twentysomethings groove to house and techno. Thirtysomething couples gather at **Byblos Disco** (✉ *C. San Francisco s/n* ☎ *647/654298*).

SHOPPING

Local **crafts** include basketwork, embroidery, leatherwork, and weaving, each specific to a single town or village. The most satisfying places to shop are often neighborhood markets, so inquire about market days. For **ceramics**, travel to the town of Agost, 20 km (12 mi) inland from Alicante. Potters here make jugs and pitchers from the local white clay, with porosity that is ideal for keeping liquids cool.

SANTA POLA

19 km (12 mi) south of Alicante.

This fishing town, which has nearly 15 km (10 mi) of mainly fine-sand and safe beaches with shallow, clear water, is an ideal location for families with children. The closest mainland city to Tabarca Island, Santa Pola has the port for several boats that make regular trips here.

There are records showing that people have lived in this area since the 4th century BC, when a fortified city was built to protect the settlers who fished and traded with other Mediterranean societies. Many of the fortifications seen today, including the town's castle, date from the 16th century and were built to defend the town from raids by the Barbary Pirates, who had taken over nearby Tabarca Island.

ESSENTIALS

Visitor Information Santa Pola (*Pl. Diputación 6 96/669–2276 www.santapola.com*).

EXPLORING

Exhibits at **Museo del Mar** detail Santa Pola's history and its close relationship with the sea, from prehistoric times through the fortification of the coast. *Santa Pola Castle 96/669–1532 €1.60 (also valid for Museo de la Pesca) May–Sept., Tues.–Sat. 11–1 and 6–10, Sun. 11–1:30; Oct.–Apr., Tues.–Sat. 11–1 and 4–7, Sun. 11–1:30.*

The eight rooms of **Museo de la Pesca** detail the life of fishermen in Santa Pola. There are models of boats, historic documents, and even the reconstruction of a fisherman's house. *Santa Pola Castle 96/541–3351 €1.60 Tues.–Sat. 11–1 and 6–10 (4–7 in off-season, Oct.–May), Sun. 11–1:30.*

Inside an old salt mill within the natural park, **Museo de la Sal** tells the story of salt production, including all aspects of the actual extraction, as well as the salt's uses and characteristics. There are bird-watching observatories, too. *Av. Zaragoza 45 96/669–3546 Free Fri.–Mon. and Wed. 9–2:30, Tues. and Thurs. 9–2:30 and 4–6.*

Acuario. This aquarium has nine large tanks with creatures native to the local Mediterranean environment—including *musolas* (a type of shark), crossbow fish, conger eels, octopi, and morays. *Pl. Fernández Ordoñez s/n 96/541–6916 €2.50 Apr.–Oct., daily 11–1 and 6–10; Nov.–Mar., Tues.–Sat. 10–1 and 5–7, Sun. 10–1.*

Parque Natural de Les Salines de Santa Pola. This natural park of 6,103 acres overlaps with an early-18th-century hunting and fishing reserve. It wasn't until a salt factory was opened in 1890 that the area was transformed, and by making the seawater flow through a circuit of ponds to precipitate out the salt, the area has developed its own ecosystem. The park supports about 8,000 flamingos, one of the few places on the Iberian Peninsula with a permanent flock, as well as many other species, including sandpipers, osprey, and herons. *South of Santa Pola, on either side of N332 Rd.*

Rio Safari Elche. Surrounded by more than 4,000 palm trees, you can take a small train to view large animals; visit smaller ones, such as crocodiles, reptiles, and birds; take in the animal shows; and even take a dip in the pool. *Ctra. Santa Pola-Elche 96/663–8288 www.riosafari.com €20 May–Oct., daily 10:30–8, with shows throughout the day from 12–6; Nov.–Apr., daily 10:30–6, with shows at 1 and 6.*

ISLA DE TABARCA

4½ km (3 mi) east of Santa Pola.

Fans of *Pirates of the Caribbean* and treasure map tales might enjoy the pirate connection of this small island off the Alicante coast that became a base for the Barbary Pirates in the Middle Ages. A little more than a mile long, 437 yards wide, and car-free, the small fortified enclosure was listed as a National Historic Artistic Complex in 1964. The few restaurants specialize in seafood; the secluded beaches are great for snorkeling or sunbathing.

Cruceros Baeza-Parodi (☎ *608/330422 or 639/893920*) and **Transtabarca** (☎ *689/123623* 🌐 *www.islatabarca.com*) operate glass-bottom catamarans between the Puerto de Santa Pola and Tabarca. Crossings with Transtabarca, which take around 25 minutes, cost €14 and run October–April at 10, 11:30, 1, and 4, and May–September 10 –7:30 (every half hour).

INLAND FROM THE COSTA BLANCA

GUADALEST

24 km (15 mi) north of Benidorm.

The ancient town of Guadalest, originally Moorish, perches impossibly atop a crag within the walls of a castle ruined in a 1644 earthquake. Because of the steep terrain, the tiny streets are stepped. To the north are splendid views over a large reservoir. The population is only 200, but this small perch is one of the most visited villages in Spain. People are drawn here for the seven museums in town and the one just outside it. The diminutive old town contains more than 14 micro-museums, with more opening each year. Guadalest is a world unto itself.

ESSENTIALS

Visitor Information **Guadalest** (✉ *Av. de Alicante s/n* ☎ *96/588–5298* 🌐 *www.guadalest.es*).

EXPLORING

Built after the earthquake of 1644 by a family of nobility, the **Museo Municipal Casa Orduña** was plundered during the War of the Spanish Succession in 1708. All the furnishings on display belong to the family and show how the affluent lived in the 19th century. The museum also serves as the entrance to the castle. ✉ *Iglesia 2* ☎ *96/588–5393* 🎟 *€4* 🕑 *May–Oct., daily 10:15–1:45 and 3:15–8; Nov.–Apr., daily 10:15–1:45 and 3:15–6.*

Attached to a natural rock, the **Antonio Marco Museum** contains miniature models of churches and homes made by tanner and miniaturist Antonio Marco (1940–). On the top floor is a huge nativity scene, weighing 12 tons. ✉ *Calle de la Virgen 2* ☎ *96/588–5323* 🎟 *€3* 🕑 *May–Oct., daily 10–9; Nov.–Apr., daily 10–6.*

The name says it all. At the **Museo de Tortura Medieval** you can see torture and capital punishment methods used from the Spanish Inquisition through the 20th century here. All kinds of instruments are displayed on the four floors, including finger screws and whips. History buffs, horror fans, and older kids seem to get a kick out of the gory details. ✉ *Honda 2* ☎ *61/005–1001* 🎫 *€4* ⏲ *May–Oct., daily 10:30–9; Nov.–Apr., daily 10:30–6.*

The **Museo Ribera Girona** exhibits contemporary art from numerous artists, including those of the founder, sculptor Manuel Ribera Girona (1931–). Many of the works here have been displayed in famous museums around the world. ✉ *Peña 1* ☎ *96/588–5062* 🎫 *€4* ⏲ *May–Oct., daily 10–8; Nov.–Apr., daily 10–6.*

The **Museo Etnológico** is a typical 18th-century rural house displaying tools, artifacts, and everyday items including clothing and a scale model cereal mill. ✉ *Iglesia 1* ☎ *661/152774* 🎫 *€4* ⏲ *May–Oct., daily 10–8; Nov.–Apr., daily 10–6.*

WHERE TO EAT

$ SPANISH ★ ✕ **El Tossal.** Just outside the pedestrian-only area of the old town, El Tossal is a rustic country tavern with a wood-beamed ceiling over the dining room, and outside terraces clinging to the hillside. Traditional local dishes include *olleta de blat* (stewed vegetables, beans, wheat, and pork), *cordero asado* (roast lamb), and *conejo allioli* (rabbit with allioli). On weekdays there's a set lunch menu with a selection of tapas, main course, dessert, wine, and bread—all for €9.90. Open for lunch only. ✉ *Aitana* ☎ *96/588–5352* 💳 *MC, V.*

OFF THE BEATEN PATH

Just 10 km (6 mi) northwest of Altea, the hilltop town of **Polop** has two interesting features: a castle and the Plaza Fuente de la Provincia, which holds a collection of 221 taps for water, each donated by a different town in the province. Villagers armed with jugs can obtain free, constant mountain water from this square.

JIJONA (XIXONA)

24 km (15 mi) north of Alicante.

Jijona is the home of *turrón*, an almond-and-honey-based nougat of Moorish origin, famous as a Christmas treat, still produced by more than 25 family-run businesses.

10

ESSENTIALS

Visitor Information Jijona (✉ *Av. de la Constitución 6* ☎ *96/561–0300* 🌐 *www.valencians.com*).

EXPLORING

Museo del Turrón. This museum is in the old Turrones El Lobo carpentry works, in a business park, on the outskirts of Jijona on the road to Busot. Guided tours (in Spanish, with brochures in English) of this three-floored museum explain the production of *turrón*, marzipan, and other confections that have been the economic foundation of this town since the early 20th century. ✉ *Poligon industrial "Ciutat del Turrón," sector 10, Ctra. Xixona-Busot 2, Km 1* ☎ *96/561–0225* 🌐 *www.museodelturron.com* 🎫 *€2* ⏲ *Hourly guided tours weekdays 10–7, weekends 10–1.*

EN ROUTE

Cuevas de Canelobre (Candelabra Caves) is one of the most spacious caves in Spain, with a length of 50 feet and a high ceiling. The stalactites hanging from above have created candlelike shapes (thus the name), while the cave's acoustic properties are often put to use for musical events. At an elevation of 2,300 feet on the slopes of the Cabezón de Oro (Golden Head) mountain, the location offers impressive views across the Mediterranean and the plain of Alicante. ✉*3 km (2 mi) north of Busot* ☎*96/569–9250* *€5* *July–Sept., daily 10:30–7:50; Oct.–June, daily 11–5:50.*

ELCHE (ELX)

24 km (15 mi) southwest of Alicante, 34 km (21 mi) northeast of Orihuela, 58 km (36 mi) northeast of Murcia.

If Alicante is torrid in summer, Elche (Elx in Valencian) is even hotter. The largest palm forest in Europe surrounds Elche, however, granting some escape from the worst of the heat. The Moors first planted the palms for dates, Europe's most reliable crop, and the trees still produce these as well as yellow fronds. (Throughout Spain the fronds are blessed on Palm Sunday and hung on balconies to ward off evil during the coming year.) Colonized by ancient Rome, Elche was later ruled by the Moors for 500 years. The remarkable stone bust known as *La Dama de Elche,* one of the earliest examples of Iberian sculpture (now in Madrid's Museum of Archaeology), was discovered here in 1897.

ESSENTIALS

Visitor Information Elche (✉*Plaça del Parc 3* ☎*96/665–8196* *www.turismedelx.com*).

EXPLORING

Elche's history dates back to the Neolithic period, when it was a mile south of the present town—it was at this site, L'Alcúdia, that La Dama de Elche was discovered. The site includes the **Museo Arqueológico,** with exhibits from the Copper and Bronze ages, as well as pieces from the Iberian and Roman eras. ✉*Ctra. Dolores, Km 2* ☎*96/661–1506* *€3* *Apr.–Sept., Tues.–Sat. 10–2 and 4–8, Sun. 10–2; Oct.–Mar., Tues.–Sat. 10–5, Sun. 10–2.*

Fodor's Choice ★ **El Palmeral** (Elche Palm Grove). The Moors originally irrigated the land and started planting palm trees here, and today there are more than 200,000 palm trees growing within the city. Many of the plantations have been turned into public parks, and efforts are being made to bring back traditional crafts. The blanched palm leaves are used in Elche's two most important cultural events—the Palm Sunday procession and the Mystery Play of Elche. The latter, dating from the Middle Ages and performed every year, represents the last days of Mary's life, her death, assumption, and coronation. ✉*Porta de la Morera* ☎*96/545–1936* *www.huertodelcura.com* *€5* *Apr.–Sept., daily 9–8:30; Oct.–Mar., daily 9–6.*

In the cellar of the 16th-century **Arab Baths Convent of Our Lady of Mercy** is an intriguing complex of Arab baths, with tiled walls and ceilings. ✉*Passeig de les Eres de Santa Llúcia 13* ☎*96/545–2887* *Free* ⊙*Tues.–Sat. 10–1:30 and 4:30–8, Sun. 10:30–1:30.*

WHERE TO EAT AND STAY

$$$–$$$$ SPANISH ✕ **Els Capellans.** This restaurant in the Huerto del Cura hotel is an exceptional culinary sanctuary, where creative cooking is combined with polished service. Surrounded by Europe's greatest palm grove, chef Jesús Gomez Bedoya serves Mediterranean specialties from *gazpacho de melón y bogavante* (melon and lobster gazpacho) to *arroz con costar* (paella caramelized around the edges). Cold appetizers might include spider crab and avocado cake with green apples or creamed asparagus with salmon croquettes. For a main dish you might find lamb kebab on a bed of eggplant or grilled fillets of sole with razor clams in an artichoke cream sauce. ✉*Porta de la Morera 14* ☎*96/661–0011* ▭*AE, DC, MC, V.*

$$–$$$ ★ **Huerto del Cura.** A subtropical location and a large, private garden in Elche's palm grove make this modern hotel a perfect refuge for rest and relaxation. The bedrooms, in bungalow huts, may seem a bit gloomy because of the shade provided by the palm forest, but the tasteful decoration and the lower temperatures in summer more than make up for the lack of light. **Pros:** excellent restaurant and many sports on premises. **Cons:** can be very hot in summer, despite the palm forest; too far from beach. ✉*Porta de la Morera 14* ⊕*www.huertodelcura.com* *71 rooms, 10 suites* *In-hotel: restaurant, bar, tennis court, pool, gym, public Wi-Fi* ▭*AE, DC, MC, V.*

THE MURCIA COAST

The Murcia Coast is markedly different from the coastline to the north: here you're met by the curious Mar Menor, an inland sea hemmed in by La Manga, the narrow strip of land that has beaches on either side. These days, La Manga is famous for its numerous hotels, particularly the huge La Manga complex on the mainland, just before the Cabo de Palos. The main town along the coast is Cartagena, which has a long and glorious history and is well worth a visit. Águilas, almost at the border with Andalusia, is a pleasant surprise, with a mild climate and fine beaches

LA MANGA DEL MAR MENOR

45 km (28 mi) southeast of Murcia.

The advance of rocks and sand from two headlands into the Mediterranean Sea transformed what was once a bay into the Mar Menor (Smaller Sea), a famously calm expanse of water about 20 feet deep. The Mar Menor is Europe's largest saltwater lake (170 square km [105 square mi]), and, because of its high salt and iodine content, it's used as a therapeutic health resort for rheumatism patients. The Manga ("sleeve") is the 21-km (13-mi) spit of sand averaging some 990 feet wide that separates it from the Mediterranean. Four canals, called *golas*, connect the Mar Menor with the Mediterranean. The Manga has 42 km (26 mi) of immense, sandy beaches on both the Mediterranean

and the Mar Menor sides, allowing swimmers to choose more or less exposed locations and warmer or colder water according to season and weather.

ESSENTIALS

Visitor Information La Manga del Mar Menor (✉ *Gran Vía de la Manga s/n* ☎ *96/814–6136* 🌐 *www.marmenor.net*).

EXPLORING

Museo de Carruajes y Motocicletas Zamar. Just before the exit to the Hyatt Regency La Manga, this museum has an interesting collection of carriages from the 17th century to the present, as well as one of the largest collections of motorcycles in Spain. ✉ *Ctra. La Unión, Km 2, El Algar* ☎ *96/813–6656* 🌐 *www.museodecarruajeszamar.com* ⏲ *Tues.–Sun. 10–2 and 4–9.*

WHERE TO EAT AND STAY

$$–$$$$ SPANISH ✕ **Club Naútico Dos Mares.** The yacht club restaurant, which accepts landlubbers and nonmembers gleefully, is a good place to order *dorada a la sal* (gilthead bream cooked in a carapace of salt) or *caldero de mujol* (soupy rice made with rock fish broth), which you can eat overlooking the placid surface of the Mar Menor. The wine list is an interesting amalgam of options from Murcia and beyond; a bracing Jumilla red

drunk with meat cooked over coals is a nice change from fish, if you're in the mood. ✉*Camino Varadero s/n* ☎*96/833–7005* ▭*MC, V.*

$$$$ **Hyatt Regency La Manga.** Golf pervades this superbly situated luxury clubhouse-hotel, just above the Mar Menor. For nongolfers, the resort has no fewer than 22 tennis courts and a regulation cricket pitch, the latter of which may account for the surfeit of British-registered Range Rovers in the parking lot. You can also rent apartments or villas. **Pros:** on-property golf, tennis, and cricket. **Cons:** removed from beach and town. ✉*Los Belones, Murcia* ☎*96/833–1234* 🌐*www.lamanga.hyatt.com* *192 rooms* *In-hotel: restaurant, bars, golf, tennis courts, pool, public Wi-Fi* ▭*AE, DC, MC, V.*

SPORTS AND THE OUTDOORS

Notable for its absence of waves of any kind, the Mar Menor is a serious sailing destination. Various schools offer windsurfing, waterskiing, catamaran sailing, and other marine diversions.

Socaire Watersports School. In Santiago de la Ribera, to the north on the mainland side of the Mar Menor, this school offers sailing and windsurfing courses using a variety of vessels, and rents out equipment to qualified adults who wish to sail around the lake. ✉*Playa del Castillico* ☎*606/111813* 🌐*www.socaire.com.*

CARTAGENA

48 km (29 mi) south of Murcia.

Founded in the 3rd century BC by the Carthaginians, Cartagena is Spain's principal naval base. From here there is easy access to the resort La Manga del Mar Menor and the twisty, scenic 100-km (62-mi) drive along N332 to the start of the Costa de Almería.

It was from here that Hannibal set out in 218 BC with a mighty army and his elephants, crossing the Pyrenees and the Alps before narrowly failing to destroy the Roman Republic. The Romans had their revenge in 209 BC, when they conquered Cartagena during the Second Punic War. This began a period of splendor under Roman rule that lasted until the beginning of the 2nd century AD. In 44 BC Cartagena was honored with the title of Colony—Colonia Urbs lulia Nova Carthago—and it prospered because of its mines and its easily defended natural harbor and the inland sea, Mar Menor, then known as El Almarjal, directly to the north.

In the early 16th century, castles and the huge city walls—both still visible today—were constructed, but they couldn't stop Sir Francis Drake from sacking Cartagena in 1585. The city was named capital of the Mediterranean Maritime Department in 1728, resulting in a large population growth to support the construction of arsenals, barracks, and castles. Mining was economically important at this time and remained so until the end of the 1920s. During the Spanish civil war, Cartagena remained steadfastly loyal to the Republican government, and was one of the last cities in Spain to surrender to Generalísimo Francisco Franco's troops.

GETTING HERE AND AROUND

A tour bus departs from outside the tourist office, directly across from the Punic Wall. With commentary about the city's attractions, the tour is a good introduction to Cartagena.

There is an "Abono," or "city card," that gets you in to all of Cartagena's sites for €20. It's available at the tourist office at Puerto de Culturas (🌐 *www.puertodeculturas.com*).

ESSENTIALS

Tour Bus Contact (✉ *Tourist Office* 🎫 *€4*).

Visitor Information Cartagena (✉ *Pl. Almirante Bastarreche* ☎ *968/506483* 🌐 *www.cartagena.es*).

EXPLORING

Most of what can be seen of the **Castillo de la Concepción** today was built by Enrique III in the 14th century, using the remains of nearby Roman ruins. The views from here are astounding, reaching out over the town, harbor, and the Mediterranean. A **panoramic lift** (elevator) on Calle Gisbert rises nearly 150 feet to a gangway that leads to the Concepción Castle. Besides saving a strenuous walk, the gangway offers great views on the way up. The lift costs €1. ✉ *Colina de la Concepción 1* ☎ *96/852–5326* 🎫 *€3* ⏲ *Mid-June–mid-Sept., daily 10:30–8:30.*

Cartagena suffered through much aerial bombardment during the Spanish civil war, because it was the base for most of the Republican fleet. At the **Refugio Museo de la Guerra Civil,** visitors can see the conditions people had to endure during those harrowing days. ✉ *Gisbert 10* ☎ *96/850–0093* 🎫 *€3.50* ⏲ *Mon.–Sat. 10–2:30 and 4–6:30.*

The **Pabellón de Autopsias,** near the panoramic lift, was a part of the naval hospital when it was built in 1768. Exhibits cover the anatomy sessions of the late 18th century, when constant epidemics swept Cartagena. Across the road, and under Plaza de Toros, are some remains of the Roman Amphitheatre. Dating from the 1st century BC, it's one of the oldest of its kind on the Iberian Peninsula. ✉ *Calle Gisbert* ☎ *96/852–9582* 🎫 *€1.50* ⏲ *Tues.–Sun. 10–2:30 and 4–6:30.*

Across from the tourist office on the San José hill, the **Muralla Púnica** *(Punic Wall)* dates from 227 BC. The walls enclosed and helped defend the Punic city that became the capital of the Carthaginians on the Iberian Peninsula. ✉ *San Diego 25* ☎ *96/852–5477* 🎫 *€3.50* ⏲ *Tues.–Sun. 10–2:30 and 4–6:30.*

A block from the House of Fortune, the **Augusteum** remains were once two important public Roman buildings dating from the 1st century BC. It's thought that they were used as a place where the priests of the cult of the Emperor Augustus met to spread the imperial ideology during his reign. ✉ *Caballero 2* ☎ *96/852–9582* 🎫 *€2.50.*

On display at the **Decumano Calzada Romana** is a section of the Roman road known as the Decumano Máximo, which joined the harbor to the Forum. ✉ *Plaza de los Tres Reyes s/n* 🎫 *€3* ⏲ *July–Sept., Tues.–Sun. 4–6; Oct.–June, Tues.–Sun. 12:30–2:30.*

Discovered in 1987, the **Teatro Romano** dates from the late 1st century BC. It was built into the northern slopes of the Colina de la Concepción hill. ✉ *Plaza Condesa Peralta s/n.*

A little distance outside the old town, and built over the 4th-century Roman necropolis of San Antón, the **Museo Arqueológico** is the headquarters for all archaeological study in this area. ✉ *Ramón y Cajal 45* ☎ *96/853–9027* *Free* *Tues.–Fri. 10–2 and 5–8, weekends 11–2.*

With all of Cartagena's maritime influences, it's appropriate to take to the water and find out more about this natural harbor. Guides on the **Barco Turístico** (*Tourist Catamaran*) talk about the harbor's system of fortifications, as well as intriguing legends and stories about Cartagena's trading and military role. ✉ *Muelle Alfonso XII* *€5.50.*

WHERE TO EAT

$$–$$$$ SPANISH ✕ **Mare Nostrum.** "Our Sea" in Latin, this restaurant reflects Spain's long naval history in the Mediterranean, with portraits and paintings that allude to the famous 1571 naval battle of Lepanto. On the ground floor is a welcoming bar for drinks and tapas, while upstairs is a more formal dining room offering a staggering variety of seafood, shellfish, and meat entrées, accompanied by such rice dishes as *arroz caldero* (fish and rice stew) and *arroz con bogavante* (rice with lobster). The *solomillo* (filet mignon) *Mare Nostrum* is the top meat choice. ✉ *Paseo Alfonso XII s/n, at the Puerto Deportivo* ☎ *968/522131* *AE, DC, MC, V.*

$–$$$$ **NH Cartagena.** Inside a harmoniously designed square building, the NH Cartagena is close to all the monuments and museums and around the corner from the harbor. It's designed in a very modern style. **Pros:** excellent location in old city center. **Cons:** no pool; small rooms. ✉ *Real 2, Plaza Héroes de Cavite* ☎ *96/812–0908* *www.nh-hotels.com* *96 rooms, 4 suites* *In-hotel: restaurant, bar, laundry service, Wi-Fi, public Internet, parking (fee)* *AE, DC, MC, V.*

ÁGUILAS

96 km (60 mi) southwest of Cartagena.

Águilas, the last town of any size in Murcia, sits in a privileged position between two fine beaches and under the 16th-century Castillo de San Juan, which dominates a 280-foot-tall promontory in the center of town. The crystal-clear waters along the coastline hold fascinating, colorful underwater life.

Visitor Information Águilas (✉ *Pl. Antonio Cortijo s/n* ☎ *968/493285* *www.aguilas.org*).

Centro de Buceo–Águilas leads dives between Águilas and Cabo Cope, rents all necessary equipment, and runs diving courses. ✉ *Isaac Peral 13* ☎ *968/493215* *www.buceoaguilas.com.*

WHERE TO EAT AND STAY

$$–$$$ SPANISH ✕ **Delicias del Mar.** This large restaurant decorated with lush vegetation has a spacious terrace with delightful views across the bay over the marina to the commanding castle. The menu features a wide range of typical local specialties with an emphasis on rice dishes and seafood of

all kinds, as the name of the place would suggest. *Lubina al papillon* (roast sea bass) is a stellar fish option, while the meat department features *solomillo de cerdo ibérico* (filet mignon of ibérico pig). ✉*Aire 145* ☎*968/410015* ▭*MC, V* ⊙*Closed Mon.–Tues. No dinner Wed.*

$ **Calypso.** A few miles south of Águilas, in the first small community over the border, into Almería province, this hotel is a good value. On the corner of a charming beach, Calypso has bright, simply furnished rooms with balconies overlooking the Mediterranean. **Pros:** small, charming building with great location, reasonably priced. **Cons:** rooms and beds very basic, no pool. ✉*Playa de San Juan de los Terreros* ☎*950/466032* ⊕*www.calypsoalmeria.com* *28 rooms* *In-hotel: restaurant, gym, spa, watersports, laundry facilities, parking (no fee)* ▭ *MC, V.*

$–$$$ **Don Juan Spa and Resort.** Enjoying an ace position at the edge of the beach at Playa del Poniente, this hotel is widely considered the best and most luxurious place to stay in town. The rooms are large and modern with plush furnishings in beige tones and unparalleled views of the Mediterranean and the beach. The resort is also the home of the Mondariz Spa and Beauty center. **Pros:** good for families, romantic setting, horizon pool. **Cons:** large hotel lacking intimate character, service slightly frosty. ✉*Playa Poniente, Av. del Puerto Deportivo 1* ☎*968/493493* ⊕*www.hoteldonjuan.es* *128 rooms* *In-room: Ethernet. In-hotel: restaurant, bar, Wi-Fi, pools, gym, spa, public Internet* ▭*AE, DC, MC, V.*

INLAND FROM THE MURCIA COAST

There are really only two towns inland that are worth venturing away from the coast to explore: the capital, Murcia, which these days is a busy, modern city; and Lorca, a considerably smaller community to the southwest.

MURCIA

82 km (51 mi) southwest of Alicante, 146 km (91 mi) southeast of Albacete, 219 km.

A provincial capital and university town of more than 300,000, Murcia was first settled by Romans. Later, in the 8th century, the conquering Moors used Roman bricks to build the city proper. The result was reconquered and annexed to the crown of Castile in 1243. Murcia retains much of its Moorish heritage in its architecture and in the Arabic words still present in the Murcian Spanish dialect.

GETTING HERE AND AROUND

Murcia's Latbus bus lines serve the city limits and beyond. Line No. 2, beginning and ending just one block from the cathedral at Glorieta de España, is the most useful. Buhobus (*buho* is Spanish for owl) is a night bus that runs until 5:30 AM on Fridays, Saturdays and nights preceding holidays.

ESSENTIALS

Bus Info Latbus (⊕*www.latbus.com*).

Visitor Information Murcia (✉ *Pl. Cardenal Belluga* ☎ *96/835–8749* 🌐 *www.murciaciudad.com*).

EXPLORING

★ Murcia's **cathedral** is a masterpiece of eclectic architecture. Begun in the 14th century, the cathedral received its magnificent facade—considered one of Spain's fullest expressions of the Churrigueresque style—as late as 1737. The 15th century brought the Gothic **Door of the Apostles** and, inside, the splendid chapel of **Los Vélez,** with a beautiful, star-shape stone vault. Carvings by the 18th-century Murcian sculptor Francisco Salzillo were added later. The **bell tower,** built between 1521 and 1792, offers splendid views over the city. ✉ *Pl. Cardenal Belluga s/n* ☎ *96/822–1371* 🎫 *€2* ⏲ *June–Sept., daily 10–1 and 5–8; Oct.–May, daily 10–1 and 4–7.*

Wander north on the pedestrian shopping street Calle de la Trapería and you soon reach the 19th-century **Casino,** which retains the aura of a British gentleman's club. Despite the name, this has never been a gambling center—Murcians come to read the newspaper and play billiards. ✉ *C. de la Trapería.*

The **Museo Salzillo,** by the bus station, has the main collection of Francisco Salzillo's disturbingly realistic polychrome *pasos* (carvings of scenes from the passion of Christ), carried in Easter processions. ✉ *Pl. San Agustín 1* ☎ *96/829–1893* 🌐 *www.museosalzillo.es* 🎫 *€3* ⏲ *Tues.–Sat. 9:30–2 and 5–8, Sun. 11–2.*

WHERE TO EAT AND STAY

$$–$$$ SPANISH ★ ✕ **Hispano.** For a typically Spanish brand of rusticity, look no further than this establishment run by a well-known Murcian family of restaurateurs-hoteliers named Abellán, who opened the Hispano in 1979. It's popular for Murcian and Mediterranean cuisine with nouvelle touches and traditional fare such as paella, *solomillo* (beef filet mignon), or the simple but delicious *plancha de verdura* (grilled vegetables). The tapas section of the restaurant is lively and has a wide selection of products from the sea as well as from upland Murcia. ✉ *Arquitecto Cerdá 7* ☎ *96/821–6152* 💳 *AE, DC, MC, V* ⏲ *Closed Sun. in July and Aug.*

$–$$$ ★ 🏨 **Rincón de Pepe.** In the center of the old town, this comfortable hotel is 50 yards from the cathedral. The guest rooms, lobby, and reception areas are bright and modern and have pink Portugese marble floors. The restaurant ($$–$$$) serves a good selection of *tapeo murciano,* samples of favorite Murcian dishes using produce grown on the hotel's own organic farm, plus fish from the nearby Mar Menor, and lamb from Segura. Highlights on the extensive menu include *cordero segureño asado a la murciana* (local lamb roasted Murcian-style). There is also an in-house casino. **Pros:** beautiful design, central location. **Cons:** no sports or spa facilities. ✉ *Pl. Apóstoles 34* ☎ *96/821–2239* 🌐 *www.nh-hoteles.com* *148 rooms* *In-room: Wi-Fi. In-hotel: restaurant, parking (fee)* 💳 *AE, DC, MC, V* ⏲ *No dinner Sun.*

NIGHTLIFE

Bars come and go, but you can always find action near the university, especially **Calle Doctor Fleming.** West of campus, a well-dressed young set gathers on the streets in front of the Teatro Romea; **Los Claveles** (✉ *C.*

Alfaro 10 ☎*No phone*) is the center of action in this zone. It's closed Sunday through Tuesday. When the university bars close, there's always the main disco in the city center, **DNC Dance Club** (✉*Centrofama, C. Puerta Nueva s/n* ☎*No phone* 🌐*www.dncdanceclub.com*).

LORCA

62 km (39 mi) southwest of Murcia, 37 km (23 mi) inland from Mediterranean at Águilas.

Leave the highway for a glimpse of Lorca, an old market town and the scene of some of Spain's most colorful Holy Week celebrations. The Casa de los Guevara, on Lope Gisbert, houses the tourist office; from here head down Alamo to the elegant **Plaza de España,** ringed by rich baroque buildings, including the *ayuntamiento*, law courts, and Colegiata (collegiate church). Follow signs from the plaza up to the **castle.**

ESSENTIALS

Visitor Information Lorca (✉*Lope Gisbert* ☎*96/844–1914* 🌐*www.ayuntalorca.es*).

WHERE TO EAT

$$ SPANISH ★ **Casa Cándido.** A happy mix of Lorcans and travelers partake of the locally inspired food here; try the classic *trigo con conejo y caracoles* (bulgar wheat with rabbit and snails). With a location just outside the town center, this rustic, relaxed, old-fashioned restaurant has been going strong on home cooking for more than half a century. *Lubina a la espalda* (sea bass cooked sunny side up with a sauce of spicy peppers and vegetables) and *quisquilla de Águilas* (a local red shrimp) are house favorites. ✉*Santo Domingo 13* ☎*96/846–6907* 💳*MC, V* ⏲*No dinner Sun.*

Andalusia

The Mosque of Cordoba

WORD OF MOUTH

"While you are in Granada, seeing the Alhambra at night is an incomparable experience. It is worth visiting the Alhambra twice—once during the day to see the gardens and once at night to tour the interiors, when few tourists go, the cats come out, and it becomes incredibly atmospheric."

—zeppole

www.fodors.com/community

WELCOME TO ANDALUSIA

Córdoba's Great Mosque.

TOP REASONS TO GO

★ **Arabian Romance:** Soak in the history and drama of Granada's exquisite Alhambra.

★ **Enchanted Dancing:** Olé deep into the night at a full-throated, heel-clicking flamenco performance in Jerez de la Frontera, the "cradle of flamenco."

★ **Priceless Paintings:** Bask in the golden age of Spanish art at Seville's Museo de Bellas Artes.

★ **Exquisite Architecture:** Marvel at the marble, granite, and onyx of Córdoba's Mezquita.

★ **Tempting Tapas:** Try a little bit of everything on an evening tapas crawl.

★ **Tumultuous Fiestas:** Celebrate Semana Santa (Holy Week) with rich festivities in Granada, Cordóba, or Seville.

★ **Matador Movements:** Witness a bullfight in the historic bullrings of Seville or Ronda.

★ **Ancient Glory:** Explore Cádiz, believed to be the oldest port in Europe, resplendent with its sumptuous architecture and a magnificent cathedral.

1 Seville. Long Spain's chief riverine port, the captivating town of Seville sits astride the Guadalquivir River, which launched Columbus to the New World and Magellan around the globe. South of the capital is fertile farmland; in the north are highland villages.

2 Huelva. Famed as live oak–forested grazing grounds for the treasured *cerdo ibérico* (Iberian pig), Huelva's Sierra de Aracena is a fresh and leafy mountain getaway on the border of Portugal. The province's Doñana National Park is one of Spain's greatest national treasures.

Holy Week procession in Granada.

GETTING ORIENTED

Andalusia is infinitely varied and diverse within its apparent unity. Seville and Granada are like feuding sisters, one vivaciously flirting, the other darkly brooding; Córdoba and Cádiz are estranged cousins, one landlocked, the other virtually under sail; Huelva is a verdant Atlantic Arcadia; and Jaén is an upland country bumpkin—albeit with its Renaissance palaces—compared with the steamy cosmopolitan seaport of Málaga, all of which, along with the southern Andalusian cities and towns of Marbella, and Ronda, are covered in the Costas chapter.

3 Cádiz Province and Jerez de la Frontera. Almost completely surrounded by water, the city of Cádiz is Western Europe's oldest continually inhabited city, a dazzling bastion at the edge of the Atlantic. Jerez de la Frontera is known for sherries, flamenco, and equestrian culture.

4 Córdoba. A center of world science and philosophy in the 9th and 10th centuries, Córdoba is a living monument to its past glory. Its prized building is the Mezquita (Mosque). In the countryside, acorns and olives thrive.

5 Jaén. Andalusia's northwesternmost province is a striking contrast of olive groves, pristine wilderness, and Renaissance towns with elegant palaces and churches.

6 Granada. Christian and Moorish cultures are dramatically counterposed in Granada, especially in the graceful enclave of the Alhambra.

ANDALUSIA PLANNER

When to Go

The best months to go to Andalusia are October and November and April and May. It's blisteringly hot in the summer so if this is only chance to come, plan time in the Sierra de Aracena in Huelva, the Pedroches of northern Córdoba province, Granada's Sierra Nevada and Alpujarra highlands, or the Sierra de Cazorla in Jaén to beat the heat. Autumn catches the cities going about their business, the temperatures are moderate, and you will rarely see a line form.

December through March tend to be cool, uncrowded, and quiet, but come spring, it's fiesta time, with Seville's Semana Santa (Holy Week, between Palm Sunday and Easter), the most moving and multitudinous. April showcases whitewashed Andalusia at its floral best, every patio and facade covered with everything from bougainvillea to honeysuckle.

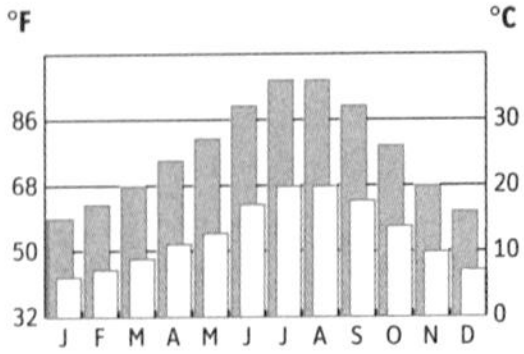

Sports Tours

Rustic Blue organizes walking and riding excursions in Andalusia, and is a good resouce for villa rentals in the area. **Rustic Blue** (⊠ *Barrio de la Ermita, Bubión* ☎ *958/763381* ⊕ *www.rusticblue.com*)

Based in the Alpujarras, **Nevadensis** (⊠ *Pl. de la Libertad, Pampaneira* ☎ *958/763127* ⊕ *www.nevadensis.com*) leads guided tours of the Alpujarra region on bike, foot, and horseback.

In Granada, **Sólo Aventura** (⊠ *Pl. de la Romanilla 1, Centro, Granada* ☎ *958/804937* ⊕ *www.soloaventura.com*) offers one- to seven-day outdoor sports—trekking, mountaineering, climbing, mountain biking, and other activities—around the Alpujarras, Sierra Nevada, and the rest of the province.

Kayak Sur (⊠ *Calle Arabial, Urbanizació Parque del Genil, Edificio Topacio, Sur, Granada* ☎ *958/523118* ⊕ *www.kayaksur.com*) organizes kayaking and canoeing trips to the Alpujarra's River Guadalfeo. **Granada Romántica/Grupo Al Andalus** (⊠ *Calle Santa Ana 16, Granada* ☎ *958/805481* ⊕ *www.grupoalandalus.com*) takes up to five people in balloon trips above the city of Granada and its surroundings.

Excursiones Bujarkay (☎ *953/721111* ⊕ *www.guiasnativos.com*) leads guided hikes as well as horseback and four-wheel-drive tours in the Sierra de Cazorla.

In Zuheros, the **Alúa** (⊠ *Calle Horno 3, Zuheros* ☎ *957/694527* ⊕ *www.aluactiva.com*) can help you with planning and getting the equipment for hiking, rock climbing, mountain biking, caving, and other active sports. **Cabalgar Rutas Alternativas** (⊠ *Calle Bubión, Bubión, Alpujarras* ☎ *958/763135* ⊕ *www.ridingandalucia.com*) is an established Alpujarras equestrian agency. **Dallas Love** (⊠ *Ctra. de la Sierra, Bubión, Alpujarras* ☎ *958/763038* ⊕ *www.spain-horse-riding.com*) offers trail rides for up to 10 days in the Alpujarras. The price includes overnight stays and most meals.

Fiesta Fun

February is Cádiz's famous Carnival.

Seville throws the most spectacular fiesta in all of Spain during **Semana Santa** (Holy Week), between Palm Sunday and Easter, followed by the decidedly more secular **Feria de Abril**, starring horses and bullfights.

May is Córdoba's **Cruces de Mayo** (Festival of Crosses) and its floral patio competition.

Early June in Huelva means the gypsy favorite, the **Romería del Rocío** festival: a pilgrimage on horseback and carriage to the hermitage of la Virgen del Rocío, Our Lady of the Dew.

From mid-June to mid-July is Granada's **Festival Internacional de Música y Danza de Granada** (🌐 *www.granadafestival.org*), with some events in the Alhambra itself.

Early August showcases horse races on the beaches of Sanlúcar de Barrameda.

Jaén celebrates the olive harvest in the second week of October.

November is the time for Granada's **Festival Internacional de Jazz de Granada** (🌐 *www.jazzgranada.net*).

The annual Early December means Granada's **Encuentro Flamenco** festival, which attracts some of the country's best performers.

WHAT IT COSTS (IN EUROS)

	¢	$	$$	$$$	$$$$
Restaurants	under €8	€8–€12	€13–€17	€18–€22	over €22
Hotels	under €60	€60–€90	€91–€125	€126–€180	over €180

Prices are per person for a main course at dinner, and for two people in a standard double room in high season, excluding tax.

Planning Your Time

A week in Andalusia should include visits to Córdoba, Seville, and Granada to see, respectively, the Mezquita, the Cathedral and its Giralda minaret, and the Alhambra. Two days in each city nearly fills the week, though the extra day would be best spent in Seville, Andalusia's most vibrant concentration of art, architecture, culture, and excitement.

Indeed, a week or more in Seville alone would be ideal, especially during the Semana Santa celebration when the city becomes a giant street party. With more time on your hands, Cádiz, Jerez de la Frontera, and Sanlúcar de Barrameda form a three- or four-day jaunt through flamenco, sherry, Andalusian equestrian culture, and tapas emporiums.

A three-day trip through the Sierra de Aracena will introduce you to a lovely Atlantic upland, filled with Mediterranean black pigs deliciously fattened on acorns, while the Alpujarra Mountains east of Granada offer anywhere from three days to a week of hiking and trekking opportunities in some of Iberia's highest and wildest reaches. For nature enthusiasts, the highland Cazorla National Park and the wetland Doñana National Park are Andalusia's highest and lowest outdoor treasures.

GETTING HERE AND AROUND

By Air

Andalusia's regional airports can be reached via Spain's domestic flights or from major European hubs. Málaga Airport (⇨ *see the Costa del Sol and Costa de Almería chapter*) is one of Spain's major hubs and a good access point for exploring this part of Andalusia.

The region's second-largest airport, after Málaga, is in Seville. There's also the smaller Aeropuerto de Jerez is 7 km (4 mi) northeast of Jerez on the road to Seville; there's no public transport into Jerez so you have to take a taxi (approximately €22).

By Bus

Once you're in Andalusia, the best way to get around, if you're not driving, is by bus. Buses serve most small towns and villages and are faster and more frequent than trains. Alsina Gräells is the major regional bus company, but there are also others.

Bus Lines **Alsa** (☎ *902/422242* 🌐 *www.alsa.es*). **Alsina Gräells** (☎ *950/238197 in Almería, 957/278100 in Córdoba, 958/185480 in Granada, 953/255014 in Jaén, 95/234–1738 in Málaga, 95/441–8811 in Seville* 🌐 *www.alsinagraells.es*). **Aucorsa** (☎ *957/764676* 🌐 *www.aucorsa.net*). **Autocares Bonal** (☎ *958/273100*). **Comes** (✉ *Pl. Hispanidad, Cádiz* ☎ *956/224271*). **La Valenciana** (✉ *Bus station, Pl. Madre de Dios, Jerez de la Frontera* ☎ *956/341063*). **Los Amarillos** (✉ *Calle Diego Fernández Herreras 34, Cádiz* ☎ *956/285852, 956/329347 Jerez*). **Rober** (☎ *958/813750 or 900/710900* 🌐 *www.transportesrober.com*).

By Boat and Ferry

From Cádiz, Trasmediterránea operates ferry services to the Canary Islands with stops at Las Palmas de Gran Canaria (39 hours) and connecting ferries on to La Palma (8 hours) and Santa Cruz de Tenerife (6.5 hours). There are no direct ferries from Seville.

Contacts **Trasmediterránea** (✉ *Estación Marítima* ☎ *956/227421 or 902/454645* 🌐 *www.trasmediterranea.es*).

By Car

If you're planning to go outside Seville, Granada, and Córdoba, a car makes travel convenient.

The main road south from Madrid is the A4/E5.The main road from Madrid is the A4/E5 through Córdoba to Seville, a four-lane *autovía* (highway). From Granada or Málaga, head for Antequera, then take A92 *autovía* by way of Osuna to Seville. Road trips from Seville to Córdoba, Granada, and the Costa del Sol (by way of Ronda) are slow but scenic. Driving in Western Andalusia is easy—the terrain is mostly flat land or slightly hilly, and the roads are straight. From Seville to Jerez and Cádiz, the A4/E5 toll road gets you to Cádiz in under an hour. The only way to access Doñana National Park by road is to take the A49/E1 Seville–Huelva highway, exit for Almonte/Bollullos par del Condado, then follow the signs for El Rocío and Matalascañas. The A49/E1 west of Seville will also lead you to the freeway to Portugal and the Algarve.

With the exception of parts of La Alpujarra, most roads in this region are smooth, and touring by car is one of the most enjoyable ways to see the countryside. Local tourist offices can advise about scenic drives. One good route heads northwest from Seville on the N433 passing through stunning scenery; turn northeast on the N435 to Santa Olalla de Cala to the village of Zufre, dramatically set at the edge of a gorge. Backtrack and continue on to Aracena. Return via the Minas de Riotinto (signposted from Aracena), which will bring you back to the N433 heading east to Seville.

Local Rental Agencies Autopro (✉ *Málaga* ☎ *952/176030* 🌐 *www.autopro.es*). **Crown Car Hire** (☎ *952/176486* 🌐 *www.crowncarhire.com*). **Niza Cars** (☎ *952/236179* 🌐 *www.nizacars.com*).

By Taxi

Taxis are plentiful throughout Andalusia and may be hailed on the street or from specified taxi stands. Fares are reasonable, and meters are strictly used; the minimum fare is about €4. You are not required to tip taxi drivers, although rounding off the amount is appreciated.

In Seville or Granada, expect to pay around €20 for the cab fare from the airport to the city center.

By Train

From Madrid, the best approach to Andalusia is via the high-speed railroad connection, the AVE. In less than three hours, the spectacular ride winds from Madrid's Atocha Station through the olive groves and rolling fields of the Castilian countryside to Córdoba and on to Seville.

Seville, Córdoba, Jerez, and Cádiz all lie on the main rail line from Madrid to southern Spain. Trains leave Madrid for Seville (via Córdoba) almost hourly, most of them high-speed ones that reach Seville in 2½ hours. Two of the non-AVE trains continue on to Jerez and Cádiz; travel time from Seville to Cádiz is 1½ to 2 hours. Trains also depart regularly for Barcelona (3 daily, 11 hours), Cáceres (1 daily, 6 hours), and Huelva (4 daily, 1½ hours). From Granada, Málaga, Ronda, and Algeciras, trains go to Seville via Bobadilla.

Gypsies, flamenco, horses, bulls—Andalusia is the Spain of story and song. Andalusia is, moreover, at once the least and most surprising part of Spain: least surprising because it lives up to the hype and stereotype that long confused all of Spain with the Andalusian version, and most surprising because it is, at the same time, so much more.

To begin with, five of the eight Andalusian provinces are maritime, with colorful fishing fleets and a wealth of seafood usually associated with the north. Secondly, there are snowcapped mountains and ski resorts in Andalusia, the kind of high sierra resources long thought most readily available in the Alps, or even the Pyrenees, yet the Sierra Nevada, with Granada at the foothills, is within sight of North Africa. Thirdly, there are wildlife-filled wetlands and highland pine and oak forests rich with game and trout streams, not to mention free-range Iberian pigs. And lastly, there are cities like Seville that somehow manage to combine all of this natural plenty with the creativity and cosmopolitanism of London or Barcelona.

Andalusia—for 781 years (711–1492) a Moorish empire and named for Al-Andalus (Arabic for "Land of the West")—is where the authentic history and character of the Iberian Peninsula and Spanish culture are most palpably, visibly, audibly, and aromatically apparent.

Though church- and Franco regime–influenced historians endeavor to sell a sanitized, Christians-versus-infidels portrayal of Spanish history, what most distinctively imprinted and defined Spanish culture—and most singularly marked the art, architecture, language, thought, and even the cooking and dining customs of most of the Iberian Peninsula—was the almost eight-century reign of the Arabic-speaking peoples who have become known collectively as the Moors.

An exploration of Andalusia must begin with the cities of Seville, Córdoba, and Granada as the fundamental triangle of interest and identity. All the romantic images of Andalusia, and Spain in general, spring vividly to life in Seville: Spain's fourth-largest city is a cliché of matadors, flamenco, tapas bars, gypsies, geraniums, and strolling guitarists. But there's so much more than these urban treasures. A more thorough Andalusian experience includes such unforgettable natural settings as Huelva's Sierra de Aracena and Doñana wetlands, Jaén's Parque Natural de Cazorla, Cádiz's *pueblos blancos* (white villages), and Granada's Alpujarras mountains. The smaller cities of Cádiz—the Western world's oldest metropolis, founded by Phoenicians more than 3,000 years ago—and Jerez, with its sherry cellars and purebred horses, have much to recommend themselves as well. And in between the urban and rural attractions is another entire chapter of Andalusian life: the noble towns of the countryside, ranging from Carmona—Alfonso X's "Lucero de España" (Morning Star of Spain)—to Jaén's Renaissance gems of Úbeda, Baeza, Málaga's Ronda *(see chapter 12)*, and Cádiz's Arcos de la Frontera.

EXPLORING ANDALUSIA

ABOUT THE RESTAURANTS

Spaniards drive for miles to sample the succulent seafood of Puerto de Santa María and Sanlúcar de Barrameda and to enjoy *fino* (a dry and light sherry from Jerez) and Manzanilla (a dry and delicate Sanlúcar sherry with a hint of saltiness). Others come to feast on tapas in Seville or Cádiz. Look for Spain's top dining delicacy *jamon ibérico de bellota* (Iberian acorn-fed ham) on menus—the village of Jabugo in Huelva is famous for its cured ham from the free-ranging Iberian pig. Córdoba's specialties are *salmorejo* (a thick version of gazpacho topped with hard-boiled egg) and *rabo de toro* (bull's-tail or oxtail stew). A glass of *fino de Moriles,* a dry, sherrylike wine from the Montilla-Moriles district, makes a good aperitif.

Moorish dishes such as *bstella* (from the Moorish *bastilla,* a salty-sweet puff pastry with pigeon or other meat, pine nuts, and almonds) and spicy *crema de almendras* (almond cream soup) are not uncommon on Granada menus. *Habas con jamón de Trevélez* (broad beans with ham from the Alpujarran village of Trevélez) is Granada's most famous regional dish, with *tortilla al Sacromonte* (an omelet made of calf's brains, sweetbreads, diced ham, potatoes, and peas) just behind. *Sopa sevillana* (tasty fish and seafood soup made with mayonnaise), surprisingly named for Granada's most direct rival city, is another staple, and *choto albaicinero* (braised kid with garlic, also known as *choto al ajillo*) is also a specialty.

Many restaurants are closed Sunday night; some close for all of August.

ABOUT THE HOTELS

Seville has grand old hotels, such as the Alfonso XIII, and a number of former palaces converted into sumptuous hostelries. The Parador de Granada, next to the Alhambra, is a magnificent way to enjoy Granada. Hotels on the Alhambra hill, especially the parador, must be reserved long in advance. Lodging establishments in Granada's city center, around the Puerta Real and Acera del Darro, can be unbelievably noisy, so if you're staying there, ask for a room toward the back. Though Granada has plenty of hotels, it can be difficult to find lodging during peak tourist season—Easter to late October. In Córdoba, several pleasant hotels occupy houses in the old quarter, close to the mosque. Other than during Holy Week and the May Patio Festival, it's easy to find a room in Córdoba, even if you haven't reserved one.

SEVILLE

550 km (340 mi) southwest of Madrid.

Seville's whitewashed houses bright with bougainvillea, its ocher-colored palaces, and its baroque facades have long enchanted both Sevillanos and travelers. Lord Byron's well-known line, "Seville is a pleasant city famous for oranges and women," may be true, but is far too tame a comment: yes, the orange trees are pretty enough, but the fruit is too bitter to eat except as Scottish-made marmalade. And as for the women, stroll down the swankier pedestrian shopping streets and you can't fail to notice just how good-looking everyone is. Aside from being blessed with even features and flashing dark eyes, Sevillanos exude a cool sophistication that seems more Catalan than Andalusian.

This bustling city of more than 700,000 does have some downsides: traffic-choked streets, high unemployment, a notorious petty-crime rate, and at times the kind of impersonal treatment you won't find in the smaller cities of Granada and Córdoba.

GETTING HERE AND AROUND

Seville's airport is about 7 km (4.3 mi) east of the city. There's a bus from the airport to the center of town every half hour on weekdays (6:30 AM–8 PM; €2.10 one-way), and every hour on weekends and holidays. Taxi fare from the airport to the city center is about €24. There are also a number of private companies, including J. González, who operate private airport shuttle services.

Seville has two intercity bus stations: Estación del Prado de San Sebastián, serving the west and northwest, and the Estación Plaza de Armas, which serves central and eastern Spain.

Seville's urban bus service is efficient and covers the greater city area. Buses C1, C2, C3, and C4 run circular routes linking the main transportation terminals with the city center. The C1 goes east in a clockwise direction, from the Santa Justa train station via Avenida de Carlos V, Avenida de María Luisa, Triana, the Isla de la Cartuja, and Calle de Resolana. The C2 follows the same route in reverse. The C3 runs from the Avenida Menéndez Pelayo to the Puerta de Jerez, Triana, Plaza de Armas, and Calle de Recaredo. The C4 does that route counterclockwise. Buses do not run within the Barrio de Santa Cruz because the streets are too narrow, though convenient access points around the periphery of this popular tourist area are amply served.

City buses operate limited night service between midnight and 2 AM, with no service between 2 and 4 AM. Single rides cost €1.10, but it is more economical to buy a ticket for 10 rides, which costs €5.70, for use on any bus. Special tourist passes (Tarjeta Turística) valid for one or three days of unlimited bus travel cost (respectively) €3.25 and €7.50. Tickets are sold at newspaper kiosks and at the main bus station, Prado de San Sebastián.

A three-line metro system is scheduled to open in Seville in late 2010. It will cover a distance of 19 km (13 mi) and run from Mairena de Aljarafe to Montequinto with 23 stations, including Puerta de Jerez and Plaza de Cuba.

There is a surface tramway line originating in Plaza Nueva and running through Avenida de la Constitución and Puerta de Jerez to Prado de San Sebastián.

Seville is perfect for bike travel, and there are several bike rental companies within the city, including those listed below. Seville also operates a free bike rental service with pickup and drop-off points throughout the city. For further details, contact the tourist office.

Train connections with Seville are generally good and include the high-speed AVE service from Madrid with a journey time that takes less than 2½ hours.

In Seville, the **Asociación Provincial de Informadores Turísticos (APIT), Guidetour,** and **ITA** can hook you up with a qualified English-speaking guide. **Sevilla Walking Tours** offers a choice of three walking tours in English, leaving Plaza Nueva (Statue of San Fernando) at 10:30 AM, Monday–Saturday; the fee is €6 (the Alcázar or Cathedral Tour), €12 (city walking tour) and €22 (city walking tour, plus Alcázar and Cathedral). The tourist office (⇨Visitor Information) has information on open-bus city tours run by Servirama, Hispalense de Tranvias, and others; buses leave every half hour from the Torre del Oro, with stops at Parque María Luisa and the Isla Mágica theme park. You can hop on and off at any stop; the complete tour lasts about 90 minutes.

Getting in and out of Seville by car isn't difficult, thanks to the SE30 ring road, but getting around in the city by car is problematic. We advise leaving your car at your hotel or in a lot while you're here.

ESSENTIALS

Airport Contacts **Airport Tranfers J. González** (☎ *958/490164*).

Bike Contacts **Rent and Tours** (✉ *Calle General Castaños 33, Seville* ☎ *954/229883* 🌐 *www.bici4city.com*). **Cyclotour/Telebike** (✉ *Residencial Virgen de Rocío 3, 4th fl., A, Mairena del Aljarafe, Seville* ☎ *605/252-8312* 🌐 *www.cyclotouristic.com*).

Bus Stations **Seville–Estación Plaza de Armas** (✉ *Calle Cristo de la Expiración*). **Seville–Estación del Prado de San Sebastián** (✉ *Prado de San Sebastián s/n*).

Taxi Contacts **Radio Teléfono Giralda** (✉ *Seville* ☎ *95/467-5555*).

Tour Contacts **Sevilla Walking Tours** (☎ *902/158226 or 616/501100* 🌐 *www.sevillawalkingtours.com*). **Sevirama** (✉ *Paseo de las Delicias, 2nd fl. on right, Edifico Cristina, Arenal, Seville* ☎ *95/456-0693*). **SevillaTour** (✉ *Calle Jaén 2* ☎ *95/450-2099* 🌐 *www.citysightseeing-spain.com*). **Sevilla Visión** (✉ *Pl. Cristo de Burgos 9, Santa Catalina, Seville* ☎ *95/422-4641*).

Train Stations **Seville–Estación Santa Justa** (✉ *Av. Kansas City*).

Visitor Information **Seville** (✉ *Av. de la Constitución 21, Arenal* ☎ *95/422-1404* 🌐 *www.sevilla.org* ✉ *Costurero de la Reina, Paseo de las Delicias 9, Arenal* ☎ *95/423-4465*). **Seville** (provincial tourist office) (✉ *Pl. de Triunfo 1-3, by cathedral, Santa Cruz* ☎ *95/421-0005* 🌐 *www.turismosevilla.org*).

EXPLORING

The layout of the historic center of Seville makes exploring easy. The central zone—**Centro**—around the cathedral, the Alcázar, Calle Sierpes, and Plaza Nueva is splendid and monumental, but it's not where you'll find Seville's greatest charm. **El Arenal,** home of the Maestranza bullring, the Teatro de la Maestranza concert hall, and a concentration of picturesque taverns, still buzzes the way it must have when stevedores (ship loaders) loaded and unloaded ships from the New World. Just southeast of Centro, the medieval Jewish quarter, **Barrio de Santa**

Cruz, is a lovely, whitewashed tangle of alleys. The **Barrio de la Macarena** to the northeast is rich in sights and authentic Seville atmosphere. The fifth and final neighborhood to explore, on the far side of the river Guadalquivir, is in many ways the best of all—**Triana,** the traditional habitat for sailors, Gypsies, bullfighters, and flamenco artists, as well as the main workshop for Seville's renowned ceramics artisans.

CENTRO

3 Fodor'sChoice ★ **Alcázar.** The Plaza Triunfo forms the entrance to the Mudejar palace built by Pedro I (1350–69) on the site of Seville's former Moorish *alcázar* (fortress). Don't mistake the Alcázar for a genuine Moorish palace, like Granada's Alhambra, though—it may look like one, and it was designed and built by Moorish workers brought in from Granada, but it was commissioned and paid for by a Christian king more than 100 years after the reconquest of Seville. In its construction, Pedro the Cruel incorporated stones and capitals he pillaged from Valencia, from Córdoba's Medina Azahara, and from Seville itself. The palace is the official Seville residence of the king and queen when they're in town.

Entering the Alcázar through the Puerta del León (Lion's Gate) and the high, fortified walls, you'll first find yourself in a garden courtyard, the **Patio del León** (Courtyard of the Lion). Off to the left are the oldest parts of the building, the 14th-century **Sala de Justicia** (Hall of Justice) and, next to it, the intimate **Patio del Yeso** (Courtyard of Plaster), the only part of the original 12th-century Almohad Alcázar. Cross the **Patio de la Montería** (Courtyard of the Hunt) to Pedro's Mudejar palace, arranged around the beautiful **Patio de las Doncellas** (Court of the Damsels), resplendent with delicately carved stucco. Opening off this patio, the **Salón de Embajadores** (Hall of the Ambassadors), with its cedar cupola of green, red, and gold, is the most sumptuous hall in the palace. It was here that Carlos V married Isabel of Portugal in 1526.

Other royal rooms include the three baths of Pedro's powerful and influential mistress, María de Padilla. María's hold over her royal lover—and his courtiers, too—was so great that legend says they all lined up to drink her bathwater. The **Patio de las Muñecas** (Court of the Dolls) takes its name from two tiny faces carved on the inside of one of its arches, no doubt as a joke on the part of its Moorish creators. Here Pedro reputedly had his half brother, Don Fadrique, slain in 1358; and here, too, he murdered guest Abu Said of Granada for his jewels—one of which is now among England's crown jewels. (The huge ruby came to England by way of the Black Prince—Edward, Prince of Wales [1330–76], eldest son of Edward III. Pedro gave the ruby to him for helping during the revolt of his illegitimate brother in 1367.)

The Renaissance **Palacio de Carlos V** (Palace of Charles V) is endowed with a rich collection of Flemish tapestries depicting Carlos's victories at Tunis. Look for the map of Spain: it shows the Iberian Peninsula upside down, as was the custom in Arab mapmaking. There are more goodies—rare clocks, antique furniture, paintings, and tapestries—on the upper floor, in the **Estancias Reales** (Royal Chambers).

In the **gardens,** inhale jasmine and myrtle, wander among terraces and baths, and peer into the well-stocked goldfish pond. From the gardens, a passageway leads to the **Patio de las Banderas** (Court of the Flags), which has a classic view of the Giralda.

Tours depart in the morning only, every half hour in summer and every hour in winter. ✉*Pl. del Triunfo, Santa Cruz* ☎*95/450–2323* 🌐*www.patronato-alcazarsevilla.es* 🎫*€7.50* 🕒*Tues.–Sun. 9:30–7.*

A CRAZY CHURCH?

In building Seville's cathedral, the clergy renounced their incomes for the cause, and a member of the chapter is said to have proclaimed, "Let us build a church so large that we shall be held to be insane."

19 **Ayuntamiento** (City Hall). This Diego de Riaño original, built between 1527 and 1564, is in the heart of Seville's commercial center. A 19th-century plateresque facade overlooks the Plaza Nueva. The other side, on the Plaza de San Francisco, is Riaño's work. ✉*Pl. Nueva 1, Centro* ☎*95/459–0101* 🎫*Free* 🕒*Tours Tues.–Thurs. at 5:30.*

20 **Calle Sierpes.** This is Seville's classy main shopping street. Near the southern end, at No. 85, a plaque marks the spot where the Cárcel Real (Royal Prison) once stood (now a bank). Miguel de Cervantes began writing *Don Quijote* in one of its cells.

1 ★ **Cathedral.** Seville's cathedral can be described only in superlatives: it's the largest and highest cathedral in Spain, the largest Gothic building in the world, and the world's third-largest church, after St. Peter's in Rome and St. Paul's in London. After Ferdinand III captured Seville from the Moors in 1248, the great mosque begun by Yusuf II in 1171 was reconsecrated to the Virgin Mary and used as a Christian cathedral. But in 1401 the people of Seville decided to erect a new cathedral, one that would equal the glory of their great city. They pulled down the old mosque, leaving only its minaret and outer court, and built the existing building in just over a century—a remarkable feat for the time.

When visiting, head first for the **Patio de los Naranjos** (Courtyard of Orange Trees), on the northern side and part of the original mosque. The fountain in the center was used for ablutions before people entered the mosque. Near the Puerta del Lagarto (Lizard's Gate), in the corner near the Giralda, try to find the wooden crocodile—thought to have been a gift from the emir of Egypt in 1260 as he sought the hand of the daughter of Alfonso the Wise—and the elephant tusk, found in the ruins of Itálica. The cathedral's exterior, with its rose windows and flying buttresses, is a monument to Gothic beauty. The dimly illuminated interior, aside from the well-lighted high altar, can be disappointing: Gothic purity has been largely submerged in ornate baroque decoration. In the central nave rises the **Capilla Mayor** (Main Chapel) and its intricately carved altarpiece, begun by a Flemish carver in 1482. This magnificent *retablo* (altarpiece) is the largest in Christendom (65 feet by 43 feet). It depicts some 36 scenes from the life of Christ, with pillars carved with more than 200 figures.The whole work is lavishly adorned with gold leaf.

On the south side of the cathedral is the **monument to Christopher Columbus:** his coffin is borne aloft by the four kings representing the medieval kingdoms of Spain: Castile, León, Aragón, and Navarra. Columbus's

A GOOD WALK: SEVILLE

Allow at least a day to tour Seville.

Start with the **cathedral** ❶ and a climb up the Giralda, the earlier Moorish mosque's minaret. Down Avenida de la Constitución is the **Archivo de las Indias** ❷, with the walled **Alcázar** ❸ fortress and palace behind.

From the Giralda, plunge into the Barrio de Santa Cruz, a tangle of narrow streets and squares that was Seville's medieval Jewish Quarter, near the **Plaza de los Refinadores** ❹. Don't miss the baroque **Hospital de los Venerables** ❺, a hospice with a leafy patio and several notable paintings. On Calle Santa Teresa is the **Jardines de Murillo** ❻, and at the far end of the gardens is the **University of Seville** ❼, once the tobacco factory where Bizet's Carmen rolled stogies.

Across the Glorieta de San Diego is the **Parque de María Luisa** ❽, with **Plaza de España** ❾ at its northwest end and **Plaza de América** ❿ on its southeast flank, site of the **Museo Arqueológico** ⓫, displaying Roman sculpture and mosaics. Opposite is the **Museo de Artes y Costumbres Populares** ⓬.

Back toward the center along the Paseo de las Delicias on Avenida de Roma is the baroque **Palacio de San Telmo** ⓭, seat of Andalusia's autonomous government, with the neo-Mudejar **Hotel Alfonso XIII** ⓮ behind it.

South along Calle Almirante Lobo stands the riverside **Torre de Oro** ⓯, opposite the **Teatro de la Maestranza** ⓰. Behind the theater is the **Hospital de la Caridad** ⓱, exhibiting Seville's leading painters. Downriver is the **Plaza de Toros de la Real Maestranza** ⓲. Finally, head away from the river toward the Plaza Nueva, in the heart of Seville to see the **Ayuntamiento** ⓳.

North of the town hall is **Calle Sierpes** ⓴, Seville's famous shopping street. Backtrack down Calle Cuna, parallel to Sierpes, to No. 8 to see the **Palacio de la Condesa de Lebrija** ㉑. Continue down Calle Cuna to Plaza del Salvador and the **Iglesia del Salvador** ㉒, a former mosque. Walk up Alcaicería to Plaza de la Alfalfa and along Sales y Ferrer toward Plaza Cristo del Burgos, and from there follow Descalzos and Caballerizas to the **Casa de Pilatos** ㉓, modeled on Pontius Pilate's house in Jerusalem. Nearby is the excellent **Museo del Baile Flamenco** ㉔, well worth a short visit.

Several Seville visits may require separate trips: if you're an art lover, set aside half a day for the **Museo de Bellas Artes** ㉕. Across the Pasarela de la Cartuja bridge is the **Isla de La Cartuja** ㉖, a Carthusian monastery now the Andalusian Center of Contemporary Art. To visit the **Basílica de la Macarena** ㉗, home of the beloved Virgen de la Macarena, either walk an hour or taxi from the center.

Other key sites in the Macarena area are the Gothic **Convento de Santa Paula** ㉘ and the church of **San Lorenzo y Jesús del Gran Poder** ㉙, where Holy Week floats are on display.

son Hernando Colón (1488–1539) is also interred here; his tombstone is inscribed with the words A CASTILLA Y A LEÓN, MUNDO NUEVO DIO COLÓN (To Castile and León, Columbus gave a new world).

> **WHERE'S COLUMBUS?**
>
> Christopher Columbus knew both triumph and disgrace, yet he found no repose—he died, bitterly disillusioned, in Valladolid in 1506. No one knows for certain where he's buried; he was reportedly laid to rest for the first time in the Dominican Republic and then moved over the years to other locations. His remains are thought to be in Seville's Cathedral.

Between the elder Columbus's tomb and the Capilla Real, at the eastern end of the central nave, the cathedral's treasures include gold and silver, relics, and other works of art. In the **Sacristía de los Cálices** (Sacristy of the Chalices) look for Martínez Montañés's wood carving *Crucifixion, Merciful Christ*; Valdés Leal's *St. Peter Freed by an Angel*; Zurbarán's *Virgin and Child*; and Goya's *St. Justa and St. Rufina*. The **Sacristía Mayor** (Main Sacristy) holds the keys to the city, which Seville's Moors and Jews presented to their conqueror, Ferdinand III. Finally, in the dome of the **Sala Capitular** (Chapter House), in the cathedral's southeastern corner, is Murillo's *Immaculate Conception,* painted in 1668.

One of the cathedral's highlights, the **Capilla Real** (Royal Chapel), is reserved for prayer and concealed behind a ponderous curtain, but you can duck in if you're quick, quiet, and properly dressed (no shorts or sleeveless tops): enter from the Puerta de los Palos, on Plaza Virgen de los Reyes (signposted ENTRADA PARA CULTO—entrance for worship). Along the sides of the chapel are the tombs of the wife of 13th century's Ferdinand III, Beatrix of Swabia, and his son Alfonso X, called the Wise; in a silver urn before the high altar rest the relics of Ferdinand III himself, Seville's liberator. Canonized in 1671, he was said to have died from excessive fasting. In the (rarely open) vault below lie the tombs of Ferdinand's descendant Pedro the Cruel and Pedro's mistress, María de Padilla.

You can climb to the top of the **Giralda,** the minaret that dominates Seville's skyline. Once the minaret of Seville's great mosque, from which the faithful were summoned to prayer, it was built between 1184 and 1196, just 50 years before the reconquest of Seville. The Christians could not bring themselves to destroy the tower when they tore down the mosque, so they incorporated it into their new cathedral. In 1565–68 they added a lantern and belfry to the old minaret and installed 24 bells, one for each of Seville's 24 parishes and the 24 Christian knights who fought with Ferdinand III in the reconquest. They also added the bronze statue of Faith, which turned as a weather vane—*el giraldillo,* or "something that turns," thus the name Giralda. To give it a rest after 400 years of wear and tear, the original statue was replaced with a copy in 1997. With its baroque additions, the slender Giralda rises 322 feet. Inside, instead of steps, 35 sloping ramps—wide enough for two horsemen to pass abreast—climb to a viewing platform 230 feet up. It is said that Ferdinand III rode his horse to the top to admire the city he had conquered. If you follow his route, you'll be rewarded with a view of tile roofs and the Guadalquivir shimmering beneath palm-lined banks. ✉*Pl. Virgen de los Reyes, Centro* ☎*95/421–4971* 🎫*Cathedral and Giralda €8* ⏲*Cathedral May–Sept., Mon.–Sat. 9.30–4, Sun. 2:30–6; Oct.–Apr., Mon.–Sat. 11–5, Sun. 2:30–6 and for mass (8:30, 9, 10, noon, 5).*

22 **Iglesia del Salvador.** Built between 1671 and 1712, the Church of the Savior stands on the site of Seville's first great mosque, and remains can be seen in the Courtyard of the Orange Trees. Also of note are the sculptures of *Jesús de la Pasión* and St. Christopher by Martínez Montañés. In 2003 archaeologists discovered an 18th-century burial site here; walkways have been installed to facilitate visits. ✉*Pl. del Salvador, Centro* ☎*95/421–1679* 🎫*€2 with guide* ⏲*Mon.–Sat. 8:45–10 and 6:30–9, Sun. 10:30–2 and 7–8:45.*

21 **Palacio de la Condesa de Lebrija.** This lovely palace has three ornate patios, including a spectacular courtyard graced by a Roman mosaic taken from the ruins in Itálica, surrounded by Moorish arches and fine azulejos. The side rooms house a collection of archaeological items. ✉*Calle Cuna 8, Centro* ☎*95/422–7802* 🎫*€8, €4 for ground floor only* ⏲*May–Sept., Mon.–Fri. 10:30–1:30 and 5–7:30, Sat. 10:30–1; Oct.–Apr., Mon.–Sat. 10:30–1:30 and 4:30–7:30, Sat. 10–1.*

BARRIO DE SANTA CRUZ

2 **Archivo de las Indias** (Archives of the Indies). Opened in 1785 in the former Lonja (Merchants' Exchange), this dignified Renaissance buildingstores archives of more than 40,000 documents, including drawings, trade documents, plans of South American towns, and even the autographs of Columbus, Magellan, and Cortés. ✉*Av. de la Constitución, Santa Cruz* ☎*95/421–1234* 🎫*Free* ⏲*Mon.–Sat. 10–4, Sun. 10–2.*

★ The twisting alleyways and traditional whitewashed houses add to the tourist charm of this barrio, the old **Jewish Quarter.** On some streets, bars alternate with antiques stores and souvenir shops, but most of the quarter is quiet and residential. On the Plaza Alianza, pause to enjoy the antiques shops and outdoor cafés. In the Plaza de Doña Elvira, with its fountain and *azulejo* (painted tile) benches, young Sevillanos gather to play guitars. Just around the corner from the hospital, at Callejón del Agua and Jope de Rueda, Rossini's Figaro serenaded Rosina on her Plaza Alfaro balcony. Adjoining the Plaza Alfaro, in the Plaza Santa Cruz, flowers and orange trees surround a 17th-century filigree iron cross, which marks the site of the erstwhile church of Santa Cruz, destroyed by Napoléon's General Soult.

23 ★ **Casa de Pilatos.** This palace was built in the first half of the 16th century by the dukes of Tarifa, ancestors of the present owner, the Duke of Medinaceli. It's known as Pilate's House because Don Fadrique, first marquis of Tarifa, allegedly modeled it on Pontius Pilate's house in Jerusalem, where he had gone on a pilgrimage in 1518. With its fine patio and superb azulejo decorations, the palace is a beautiful blend of Spanish Mudejar and Renaissance architecture. The upstairs apartments, which you can see on a guided tour, have frescoes, paintings, and antique furniture. ✉*Pl. Pilatos 1, Santa Cruz* ☎*95/422–5298* 🎫*€8, €5 for ground floor only* ⏲*May–Sept., daily 9–7; Oct.–Apr., daily 9–6.*

Seville

Alcázar 3
Archivo de las Indias 2
Ayuntamiento . 19
Basílica de la Macarena 27
Calle Sierpes .. 20
Casa de Pilatos 23
Cathedral 1
Convento de Santa Paula 28
Hospital de la Caridad 17
Hospital de los Venerables 5
Hotel Alfonso XIII 14
Iglesia del Salvador 22
Isla de La Cartuja 26
Jardines de Murillo 6
Museo Arqueológico .. 11
Museo de Artes y Costumbres Populares 12
Museo de Bellas Artes 25
Museo del Baile Flamenco 24
Palacio de la Condesa de Lebrija 21
Palacio de San Telmo 13
Parque de María Luisa 8
Plaza de América 10
Plaza de España 9
Plaza de los Refinadores 4
Plaza de Toros Real Maestranza 18
San Lorenzo y Jesús del Gran Poder 29
Teatro de la Maestranza 16
Torre de Oro ... 15
University of Seville 7

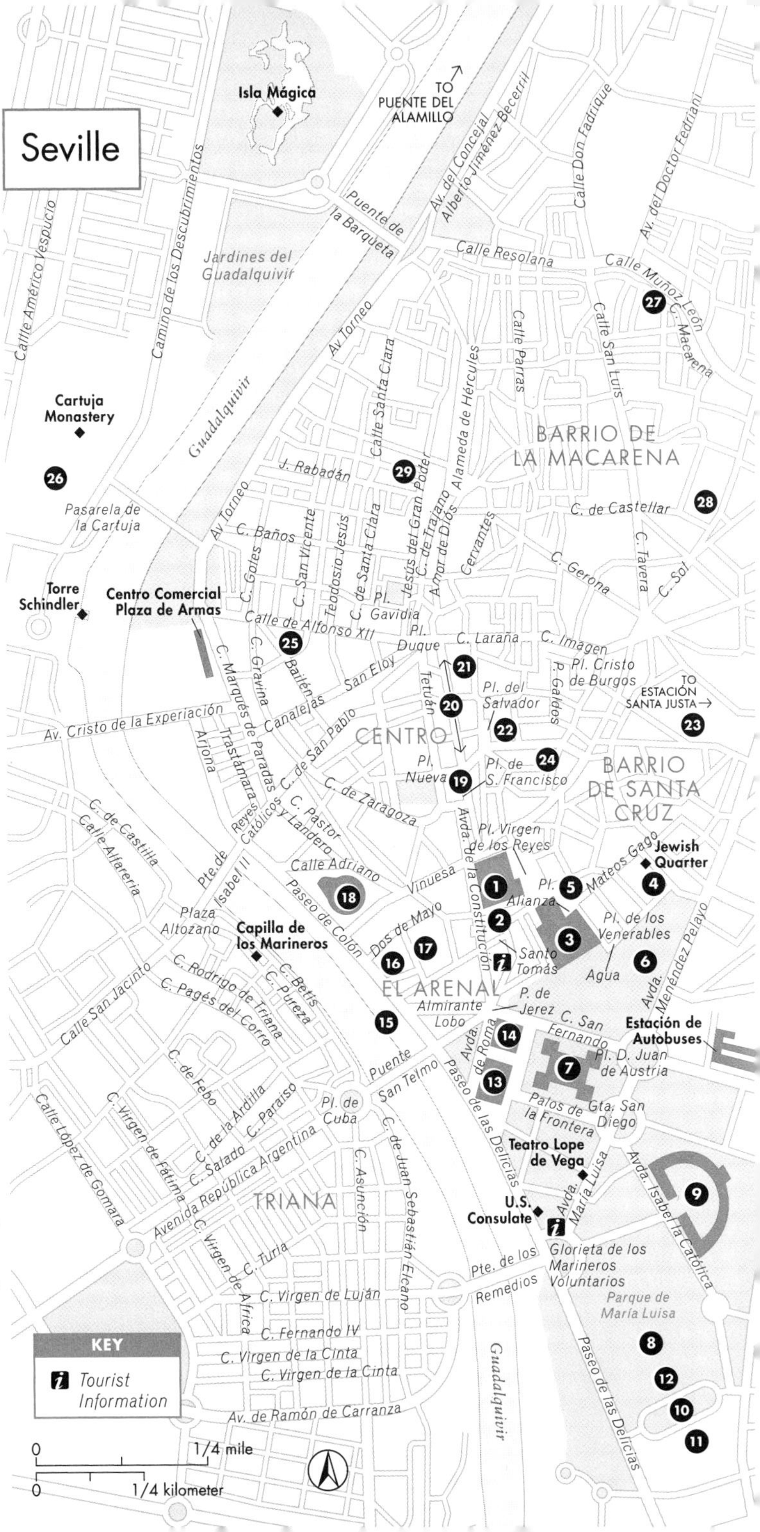

5 **Hospital de los Venerables.** Once a retirement home for priests, this baroque building now has a cultural foundation that organizes on-site art exhibitions. The tour takes in a splendid *azulejo* patio with an interesting sunken fountain (designed to cope with low water pressure) and upstairs gallery, but the hospital's highlight is its chapel, featuring frescoes by Juan Valdés Leal and sculptures by Pedro Roldán. ✉ *Pl. de los Venerables 8, Santa Cruz* ☎ *95/456–2696* 🎫 *€4.75 with audio guide* ⏲ *Daily 10–2 and 4–8.*

6 **Jardines de Murillo** (Murillo Gardens). From the Plaza Santa Cruz you can stroll through these shady gardens, where you'll find a statue of Christopher Columbus. ✉ *Pl. Santa Cruz, Santa Cruz.*

4 **Plaza de los Refinadores.** This shady square filled with palms and orange trees is separated from the Murillo gardens by an iron grillwork and ringed with stately glass balconies. At its center is a monument to Don Juan Tenorio, the famous Don Juan known for his amorous conquests. ✉ *Santa Cruz.*

24 **Museo del Baile Flamenco.** This superb museum in the heart of Santa Cruz (follow the signs) was opened in 2007 by the legendary flamenco dancer Cristina Hoyos and includes audiovisual and multimedia displays explaining the history, culture, and soul of Spanish flamenco. There are also regular classes and shows. ✉ *C. Manuel Rojas Marcos 3, Santa Cruz* ☎ *95/424–0311* 🌐 *www.museoflamenco.com* 🎫 *€10* ⏲ *Mon.–Sun. 9–6.*

Fodor's Choice ★

EL ARENAL AND PARQUE MARIA LUISA

Parque María Luisa is part shady midcity forestland and part monumental esplanade. El Arenal, named for its sandy riverbank soil, was originally a neighborhood of shipbuilders, stevedores, and warehouses. The heart of Arenal lies between the Puente de San Telmo just upstream from the Torre de Oro and the Puente de Isabel II (Puente de Triana). El Arenal extends as far north as Avenida Alfonso XII to include the Museo de Bellas Artes. Between the park and Arenal is the university.

17 **Hospital de la Caridad.** Behind the Maestranza Theater is this almshouse for the sick and elderly, where six paintings by Murillo (1617–82) and two gruesome works by Valdés Leal (1622–90), depicting the Triumph of Death, are displayed. The baroque hospital was founded in 1674 by Seville's original Don Juan, Miguel de Mañara (1626–79). A nobleman of licentious character, Mañara was returning one night from a riotous orgy when he had a vision of a funeral procession in which the partly decomposed corpse in the coffin was his own. Accepting the apparition as a sign from God, Mañara renounced his worldly goods and joined the Brotherhood of Charity, whose unsavory task was to collect the bodies of executed criminals and bury them. He devoted his fortune to building this hospital and is buried before the high altar in the chapel. Admission includes an audio guide (available in English). ✉ *C. Temprado 3, El Arenal* ☎ *95/422–3232* 🎫 *€5* ⏲ *Mon.–Sat. 9–1:30 and 3:30–7:30, Sun. 9–1.*

14 **Hotel Alfonso XIII.** Seville's most emblematic hotel, this grand, Mudejar-style building next to the university was built—and named—for the king's visit to the 1929 fair. Nonguests are welcome to admire the

Fodor's Choice ★

DON JUAN: LOVER OF LEGENDS

Originally brought to literary life by the Spanish Golden Age playwright Fray Gabriel Téllez (better known as Tirso de Molina) in 1630, the figure of Don Juan has been portrayed in countless variations through the years, usually changing to reflect the moral climate of the times. As interpreted by such notables as Molière, Mozart, Goldoni, Byron, and Bernard Shaw, Don Juan has ranged from voluptuous hedonist to helpless victim and from fiery lover to cold-hearted snake.

The plaques around his effigy in Plaza de los Refinadores translate as: "Here is Don Juan Tenorio, and no man is his equal. From haughty princess to a humble fisherwoman, there is no female he doesn't desire, nor affair of gold or riches he will not pursue. Seek him ye rivals; surround him players all; may whoever values himself attempt to stop him or be his better at gambling, combat, or love."

gracious Moorish-style courtyard, best appreciated while sipping an ice-cold *fino* (dry sherry) from the adjacent bar. ✉ *Calle San Fernando 2, El Arenal* ☎ *95/491–7000.*

⓫ **Museo Arqueológico** (Museum of Archaeology). This fine Renaissance-style building has artifacts from Phoenician, Tartessian, Greek, Carthaginian, Iberian, Roman, and medieval times. Displays include marble statues and mosaics from the Roman excavations at Itálica and a faithful replica of the fabulous Carambolo treasure found on a hillside outside Seville in 1958: 21 pieces of jewelry, all 24-karat gold, dating from the 7th and 6th centuries BC. ✉ *Pl. de América, El Arenal/Porvenir* ☎ *95/423–2401* 🎫 *€1.50* ⏲ *Tues. 2:30–8:30, Wed.–Sat. 9–8:30, Sun. 9–2:30.*

⓬ **Museo de Artes y Costumbres Populares** (Museum of Folklore). The Mudejar pavilion opposite the Museum of Archaeology is the site of this museum of mainly 19th- and 20th-century Spanish folklore. The first floor has re-creations of a forge, a bakery, a wine press, a tanner's shop, and a pottery studio. Upstairs, exhibits include 18th- and 19th-century court dress, stunning regional folk costumes, carriages, and musical instruments. ✉ *Pl. de América 3, El Arenal/Porvenir* ☎ *95/423–2576* 🎫 *€2* ⏲ *Tues. 3–8, Wed.–Sat. 9–8, Sun. 9–2.*

㉕ Fodor's Choice ★ **Museo de Bellas Artes** (Museum of Fine Arts). This museum is second only to Madrid's Prado for Spanish art. It's in the former convent of La Merced Calzada, most of which dates from the 17th century. The collection includes works by Murillo and the 17th-century Seville school, as well as by Zurbarán, Velázquez, Alonso Cano, Valdés Leal, and El Greco; outstanding examples of Seville Gothic art; and baroque religious sculptures in wood (a quintessentially Andalusian art form). In the rooms dedicated to Sevillian art of the 19th and 20th centuries, look for Gonzalo Bilbao's *Las Cigarreras,* a group portrait of Seville's famous cigar makers. ✉ *Pl. del Museo 9, El Arenal/Porvenir* ☎ *95/478–6482* 🌐 *www.museosdeandalucia.es* 🎫 *€1.50* ⏲ *Tues. 2:30–8:15, Wed.–Sat. 9–8:15, Sun. 9–2:15.*

13 **Palacio de San Telmo.** This splendid baroque palace is largely the work of architect Leonardo de Figueroa. Built between 1682 and 1796, it was first a naval academy and then the residence of the Bourbon dukes of Montpensier, during which time it outshone Madrid's royal court for sheer brilliance. The palace gardens are now the Parque de María Luisa, and the building itself is the seat of the Andalusian government. The main portal, vintage 1734, is a superb example of the fanciful Churrigueresque style. ■ TIP→ **Call in advance if you want to arrange a visit.** ✉ *Av. de Roma, El Arenal* ☎ *95/503–5500.*

8 **Parque de María Luisa.** Formerly the garden of the Palacio de San Telmo, this park is a blend of formal design and wild vegetation. In the burst of development that gripped Seville in the 1920s, it was redesigned for the 1929 Exhibition, and the impressive villas you see now are the fair's remaining pavilions, many of them consulates or schools. Note the **statue of El Cid** by Rodrigo Díaz de Vivar (1043–99), who fought both for and against the Muslim rulers during the Reconquest. ✉ *Main entrance: Glorieta San Diego, El Arenal.*

Fodor's Choice ★

10 **Plaza de América.** Walk to the south end of the Parque de María Luisa, past the Isla de los Patos (Island of Ducks), to find this plaza designed by Aníbal González and typically carpeted with a congregation of white doves (children can buy grain from a kiosk here to feed them). It's a blaze of color, with flowers, shrubs, ornamental stairways, and fountains tiled in yellow, blue, and ocher. The three impressive buildings surrounding the square—in neo-Mudejar, Gothic, and Renaissance styles—were built by González for the 1929 fair. Two of them now house Seville's museums of archaeology and folklore.

9 **Plaza de España.** This grandiose half-moon of buildings on the eastern edge of the Parque de María Luisa was Spain's centerpiece pavilion at the 1929 Exhibition. The brightly colored azulejo pictures represent the 50 provinces of Spain, while the four bridges symbolize the medieval kingdoms of the Iberian Peninsula. In summer you can rent small boats for rowing along the arc-shaped canal.

18 **Plaza de Toros Real Maestranza** (Royal Maestranza Bullring). Sevillanos have spent many a thrilling Sunday afternoon in this bullring, built between 1760 and 1763. Painted a deep ocher, the stadium is the one of the oldest and loveliest *plazas de toros* in Spain. The 20-minute tour takes in the empty arena, a museum with elaborate costumes and prints, and the chapel where matadors pray before the fight. ✉ *Paseo de Colón 12, El Arenal* ☎ *95/422–4577* *Plaza and bullfighting museum €6 with English-speaking guide* ⊙ *May–Oct., daily 9:30–8; Nov.–Apr., daily 9:30–7 (bullfighting days 9:30–3).*

16 **Teatro de la Maestranza** (Maestranza Theater). Seville's opera house is opposite the Torre de Oro. One of Europe's leading halls, the Maestranza presents opera, zarzuela (Spanish light opera), classical music, and jazz. ✉ *Paseo de Colón 22, El Arenal* ☎ *95/422–6573 or 95/422–3344* 🌐 *www.teatromaestranza.com.*

15 **Torre de Oro** (Tower of Gold). Built by the Moors in 1220 to complete the city's ramparts, this 12-sided tower on the banks of the Guadalquivir served to close off the harbor when a chain was stretched across

CLOSE UP

Seville's Long and Noble History

Conquered in 205 BC by the Romans, Seville gave the world two great emperors, Trajan and Hadrian. The Moors held Seville for more than 500 years and left it one of their greatest works of architecture—the iconic Giralda tower that served as the minaret over the main city mosque. Saint King Ferdinand (Fernando III) lies enshrined in the glorious cathedral, and his rather less saintly descendant, Pedro the Cruel, builder of the Alcázar, is buried here as well.

Seville is justly proud of its literary and artistic associations. The painters Diego Rodríguez de Silva Velázquez (1599–1660) and Bartolomé Estéban Murillo (1617–82) were sons of Seville, as were the poets Gustavo Adolfo Bécquer (1836–70), Antonio Machado (1875–1939), and Nobel Prize–winner Vicente Aleixandre (1898–1984). The tale of the ingenious knight of La Mancha was begun in a Seville debtors' prison, where Don Quixote's creator, Miguel de Cervantes, once languished. Tirso de Molina's Don Juan seduced his lovers in Seville's mansions; Rossini's barber, Figaro, was married in the Barrio de Santa Cruz; and Bizet's sultry Carmen first met Don José in the former tobacco factory that now houses the university.

the river from its base to another tower on the opposite bank. In 1248, Admiral Ramón de Bonifaz broke through the barrier, and Ferdinand III captured Seville. The tower houses a small naval museum. ✉ *Paseo Alcalde Marqués de Contadero s/n, El Arenal* ☎ *95/422–2419* 💶 *€2* ⏲ *Tues.–Fri. 10–2, Sat.–Sun. 11–2.*

7 **University of Seville.** At the far end of the Jardines de Murillo, opposite Calle San Fernando, stands what used to be the **Real Fábrica de Tabacos** (Royal Tobacco Factory). Built in the mid-1700s, the factory employed some 3,000 *cigarreras* (female cigar makers) less than a century later, including Bizet's opera heroine Carmen, who reputedly rolled her cigars on her thighs. ✉ *C. San Fernando s/n, Parque María Luisa* ☎ *95/455–1000* 💶 *Free* ⏲ *Weekdays 9–8:30.*

BARRIO DE LA MACARENA

This immense neighborhood covers the entire northern half of historic Seville and deserves to be walked not once but many times. Most of the best churches, convents, markets, and squares are concentrated around the center of this barrio in an area delimited by the Arab ramparts to the north, the Alameda de Hercules to the west, the Santa Catalina church to the south, and the Convento de Santa Paulato the east. The area between the Alameda de Hercules and the Guadalquivir is known to locals as the Barrio de San Lorenzo, a Barrio de la Macarena subdivision that's ideal for an evening of tapas grazing.

27 **Basílica de la Macarena.** This church holds Seville's most revered image, the Virgin of Hope—better known as La Macarena. Bedecked with candles and carnations, her cheeks streaming with glass tears, the Macarena steals the show at the procession on Holy Thursday, the highlight of Seville's Holy Week pageant. She's the patron of gypsies and the protector of the matador. So great are her charms that young Sevillian

bullfighter Joselito spent half his personal fortune buying her emeralds. When he was killed in the ring in 1920, the Macarena was dressed in widow's weeds for a month. There's a small adjacent museum devoted to her costumes and jewels, but it's closed for refurbishment until late 2010; check at the tourist office for an update. ✉ *C. Bécquer 1, La Macarena* ☎ *95/490–1800* 🎫 *Free* ⏲ *Basilica daily 9:30–2 and 5–9.*

> **FIESTA TIME!**
>
> Seville's color and vivacity are most intense during Semana Santa, when lacerated Christs and bejeweled, weeping Mary statues are paraded through town on floats borne by often barefooted penitents. A week later, Sevillanos throw April Fair, featuring midday horse parades with men in broad-brim hats and Andalusian riding gear astride prancing steeds, and women in ruffled dresses riding sidesaddle behind them. Bullfights, fireworks, and all-night singing and dancing complete the spectacle.

28 Fodor's Choice ★ **Convento de Santa Paula.** This 15th-century Gothic convent has a fine facade and portico, with ceramic decoration by Nicolaso Pisano. The chapel has some beautiful azulejos and sculptures by Martínez Montañés. There's a small museum and shop selling delicious cakes and jams made by the nuns. ✉ *C. Santa Paula 11, La Macarena* ☎ *95/453–6330* 🎫 *€3* ⏲ *Tues.–Sun. 10–1.*

29 **San Lorenzo y Jesús del Gran Poder.** This 17th-century church has many fine works by such artists as Montañés and Pacheco, but its outstanding piece is Juan de Mesa's *Jesús del Gran Poder* (*Christ Omnipotent*). ✉ *C. Jesús del Gran Poder, La Macarena* ☎ *95/438–4558* 🎫 *Free* ⏲ *Daily 8–1:30 and 6–9.*

TRIANA

Across the Guadalquivir from central Seville, Triana used to be the gypsy quarter. Today it has a tranquil, neighborly feel by day, while its atmospheric clubs and flamenco bars throb at night. Enter Triana by the **Puente Isabel II** (better known as the Puente de Triana), built in 1852, the first bridge to connect the city's two sections. Walk across Plaza Altozano up Calle Jacinto and turn right at **Calle Alfarería** (Pottery Street) to see a slew of pottery shops. Return to Plaza Altozano and walk down Calle Pureza as far as the small **Capilla de los Marineros** (Seamen's Chapel), home to a venerated statue of Mary called the Esperanza de Triana. Head back toward the river and **Calle Betis** for some of the city's most colorful bars, clubs, and restaurants.

26 **Isla de La Cartuja.** Named after its 14th-century Carthusian monastery, this island in the Guadalquivir river across from northern Seville was the site of the decennial Universal Exposition (Expo) in 1992. The island has the Teatro Central, used for concerts and plays; Parque del Alamillo, Seville's largest and least-known park; and the Estadio Olímpico, a 60,000-seat covered stadium. The best way to get to La Cartuja is by walking across one or both (one each way) of the superb Santiago Calatrava bridges spanning the Guadalquivir. The Puente de la Barqueta crosses to La Cartuja, while downstream the Puente del Alamillo connects la Isla Mágica with Seville. Buses C1 and C2 also serve La Cartuja. ✉ *Av. Americo Vespucci 2, La Cartuja.*

The eastern shore holds the **Isla Mágica** (☎ *902/161716* 🌐 *www.islamagica.es* 🎫 *Apr. and May €25, June–Oct. €28* ⏲ *Apr. and May, weekends 11 AM–midnight; June–Oct., daily 11 AM–midnight*) with 14 attractions, including the hair-raising Jaguar roller coaster. The 14th-century **Monasterio de Santa María de las Cuevas** (Monasterio de La Cartuja ✉ *Isla de la Cartuja* ☎ *95/503–7070* 🎫 *€3, free Tues. for EU citizens* ⏲ *Tues.–Fri. 10–7:30, Sat. 11–8, Sun. 10–2:30*) was regularly visited by Christopher Columbus, who was buried here for a few years. Part of the building houses the Centro Andaluz de Arte Contemporáneo, which has an absorbing collection of contemporary art.

WHERE TO EAT AND STAY

Use the coordinate (✥ B2) at the end of each listing to locate a site on the corresponding map.

TAPAS BARS

Bar Estrella. This prizewinning tapas emporium does excellent renditions of everything from *paté de espárragos trigueros* (wild asparagus pâté) to *fabas con pringá* (stewed broad beans). ✉ *C. Estrella 3, Santa Cruz* ☎ *95/422–7535* ✥ *C3.*

Bar Giralda. This old Moorish bathhouse across from the Giralda has been a tapas bar since 1934. The outdoor seating area has cathedral views. One specialty is *patatas a la importancia* (fried potatoes stuffed with ham and cheese). ✉ *Calle Mateos Gago 1, Santa Cruz* ☎ *95/422–7435* ✥ *C3.*

Bar Gran Tino. Named for the giant wooden wine cask that once dominated the bar, this busy spot with outside seating on the funky Plaza Alfalfa serves an array of tapas, including *calamares fritos* (fried squid) and wedges of crumbly Manchego cheese. ✉ *Pl. Alfalfa 2, Centro* ☎ *95/421–0883* ✥ *C2.*

★ **Bar Rincón San Eloy.** This place is always heaving with a happy mix of shoppers and students. You can buy stacked mini-sandwiches, as well as tapas and sherry from the barrel. If no tables are left, grab a pew on the tiled steps. ✉ *Calle San Eloy 2, Centro* ☎ *95/421–8079* ✥ *B2.*

El Rinconcillo. Founded in 1670, this lovely spot serves a classic selection of dishes, such as the *caldereta de venado* (venison stew), a superb *salmorejo* (thick gazpacho-style soup), and *espinacas con garbanzos* (creamed spinach with chickpeas). The views of the Iglesia de Santa Catalina out the front window are unbeatable. Your bill is chalked up on the wooden counters. ✉ *C. Gerona 40, La Macarena* ☎ *95/422–3183* ⏲ *Closed Wed* ✥ *C2.*

WHERE TO EAT

$$$–$$$$ LA NUEVA COCINA ★ ✕ **Abades Triana.** With panoramic views across the Guadalquivir River to the Torre de Oro and the Maestranza bullring, Willy Moya's slick modern restaurant offers the best of several worlds: a large space for brasserie fare and a smaller gastronomical enclave for more sophisticated dining. Chef Moya trained in Paris and blends local Andalusian and cosmopolitan cuisine in creations such as the *salmorejo encapotado* (thick, garlic-laden gazpacho topped with diced egg and ham) or the *besugo con gambitas* (sea bream with shrimp). Desserts include a

Moorish-derived riff on French toast, with slivered almonds and cinnamon ice cream, and the head-swimmingly different *sorbete de gin tonic.* ✉ *C. Betis 69, Triana* ☎ *95/428–6459* 💳 *AE, DC, MC, V* ⊙ *Closed Sun. No dinner Mon.* ✥ *B4.*

$$–$$$ SPANISH ✕ **Becerrita.** The affable Jesús Becerra runs this cozy—verging on cramped—establishment decorated with traditional columns, tiles, and wallpaper. Diligent service and tasty modern treatments of such classic Spanish dishes as *lomo de cordero a la miel* (loin of lamb in a honey sauce) and *rape con salsa de manzana* (monk fish with applesauce) have won the favor of Sevillanos, as has the signature dish: oxtail croquettes. Smaller appetites can try such tasty tapas as stuffed calamari and garlic-spiked prawns. ✉ *Calle Recaredo 9, Santa Cruz/Santa Catalina* ☎ *95/441–2057* 🌐 *www.becerrita.com* ✍ *Reservations essential* 💳 *AE, MC, V* ⊙ *No dinner Sun. and Aug.* ✥ *D2.*

¢–$ MEDITERRANEAN Fodor's Choice ★ ✕ **Borear.** Near Plaza de Armas, in a disarmingly bland-looking building (from the outside), this restaurant hits the mark for innovative cuisine. Dishes are often culinary works of art, and there are vegetarian options like *mosaico de verduras atemperadas con caramelo de vino do jerez* (lightly grilled vegetables in a caramelized sherry sauce) and *espárragos con berenjenas al pesto* (asparagus and eggplant in a pesto sauce). Other choices include a *wok de pollo* (chicken)—a stir fry is pretty unusual around here—and *verduras* (vegetables). The interior is decorated in slick black and white. ✉ *Plaza Puerta Real 6, El Arenal* ☎ *954/916334/* 💳 *MC, V* ✥ *A2.*

$$$$ SPANISH ★ ✕ **Egaña-Oriza.** Owner José Mari Egaña is Basque, but he's considered one of the fathers of modern Andalusian cooking. His restaurant, on the edge of the Murillo Gardens opposite the university, has spare contemporary decor with high ceilings and wall-to-wall windows; in warm weather, you can eat on the terrace under the orange trees. The menu might include *lomos de lubina con salsa de erizos de mar* (sea bass with sea urchin sauce) or *solomillo con foie natural y salsa de ciruelas* (fillet steak with foie gras and plum sauce). On the downside, the service can be slow. You can always drop into the adjoining Bar España for tapas such as stuffed mussels with béchamel sauce. ✉ *San Fernando 41, Santa Cruz Jardines de Murillo* ☎ *95/422–7211* 💳 *AE, DC, MC, V* ⊙ *Closed Sun. and Aug. No lunch Sat.* ✥ *C4.*

$–$$$ SPANISH ✕ **El Corral del Agua.** Abutting the outer walls of the Alcázar on a narrow pedestrian street in the Santa Cruz neighborhood, this restored 18th-century palace has a patio filled with geraniums and a central fountain. Andalusian specialties, such as *cola de toro al estilo de Sevilla* (Seville-style bull's tail), *caldereta* (lamb stew), and fresh salads are prepared with contemporary flair. Round off your meal with one of the Arab-inspired desserts before strolling around the corner to one of the prettiest squares in Santa Cruz: Plaza Doña Elvira, flanked by orange trees behind traditionally tiled seating. ✉ *Callejón del Agua 6, Santa Cruz* ☎ *95/422–4841* 💳 *AE, DC, MC, V* ⊙ *Closed Sun. and Jan. and Feb.* ✥ *C3.*

$$$ SPANISH Fodor's Choice ★ ✕ **Enrique Becerra.** Excellent tapas and a lively bar await at this restaurant run by the fifth generation of a family of celebrated restaurateurs (Enrique's brother Jesús owns Becerrita). The menu focuses on traditional, home-cooked Andalusian dishes, such as *pez espada al amontillado*

(swordfish cooked in dark sherry) and *cordero a la miel con espinacas* (honey-glazed lamb stuffed with spinach and pine nuts). Don't miss the cumin seed–laced *espinacas con garbanzos* (spinach with chickpeas). The wine list is excellent. ✉ *Calle Gamazo 2, El Arenal* ☎ *95/421–3049* 💳 *AE, DC, MC, V* ⊗ *Closed Sun. and last 2 wks of July* ✥ *B3.*

$$$–$$$$ SPANISH Fodor's Choice ★

✕ **La Albahaca.** Overlooking one of Seville's prettiest small plazas in the Barrio de Santa Cruz, this wonderful old manor house was built by the celebrated architect Juan Talavera for his own family. Inside, four dining rooms are decorated with tiles, oil paintings, and plants. There's a Basque twist to many dishes—consider the *lubina al horno con berenjenas y yogur al cardamomo* (baked sea bass with eggplant in a yogurt-and-cardamom sauce) or *foie de oca salteado* (lightly sautéed goose liver) followed by the delicious fig mousse. There's an excellent €28 daily menu. ✉ *Pl. Santa Cruz 12, Santa Cruz* ☎ *95/422–0714* ✍ *Reservations essential* 💳 *AE, DC, MC, V* ⊗ *Closed Sun.* ✥ *C3.*

$–$$$ SPANISH

✕ **Mesón Don Raimundo.** Tucked into an alleyway off Calle Argote de Molina near the cathedral, this former 17th-century convent with its dark wood furniture and eclectic decor of religious artifacts tends to attract the tour buses. Still, it's worth the trip for the generous portions of traditional fare, including Mozarab-style wild duck (braised in sherry), solomillo *a la castellana* (Castilian-style steak), and the refreshingly straightforward fillet of seabass with pine nuts and prawns. Start with the crisp *tortillitas de camarones* (batter-fried shrimp pancakes) or stuffed peppers. The wine list is excellent, as is the house wine, which is well-priced for the quality. ✉ *Argote de Molina 26, Santa Cruz* ☎ *95/422–3355* 💳 *AE, DC, MC, V* ✥ *C3.*

$–$$ SPANISH

✕ **Modesto.** Downstairs is a lively, crowded tapas bar; upstairs is the dining room, which has stucco walls decorated with blue-and-white tiles. The house specialty is a crisp *fritura Modesto* (a selection of small fish fried in top-quality olive oil); another excellent choice is the *cazuela al Tío Diego* (Uncle Diego's casserole—ham, mushrooms, and shrimp simmering in an earthenware dish). You can dine cheaply here, but beware: *mariscos* (shellfish) take the bill to another level. ✉ *Calle Cano y Cueto 5, Santa Cruz* ☎ *95/441–6811* 💳 *AE, DC, MC, V* ✥ *D3.*

$$–$$$ ITALIAN ★

✕ **San Marco.** In a 17th-century palace on one of the most charming pedestrian streets in the shopping district, this elegant restaurant has original frescoes, stately columns, and a gracious patio flanked by cascading ivy, and the menu combines Italian, French, and Andalusian cuisine. Pasta dishes, such as ravioli stuffed with shrimp and pesto sauce, are notable. The restaurant has two satellites, including one in the heart of the Santa Cruz district in a similarly historic building—an original Arab bathhouse. This one has the edge, however, as far as culinary skill in the kitchen is concerned. ✉ *Calle Cuna 6, Centro* ☎ *95/421–2440* ✍ *Reservations essential* 💳 *AE, DC, MC, V* ✥ *B2.*

WHERE TO STAY

Use the coordinate (✥ B2) at the end of each listing to locate a site on the corresponding map.

$$$$ Fodor's Choice ★

🏨 **Casa Numero 7.** Dating from 1847, the interior of this converted town house retains a homey, lived-in feel with family-owned antiques, original oil paintings, and plush furnishings throughout. The owner is

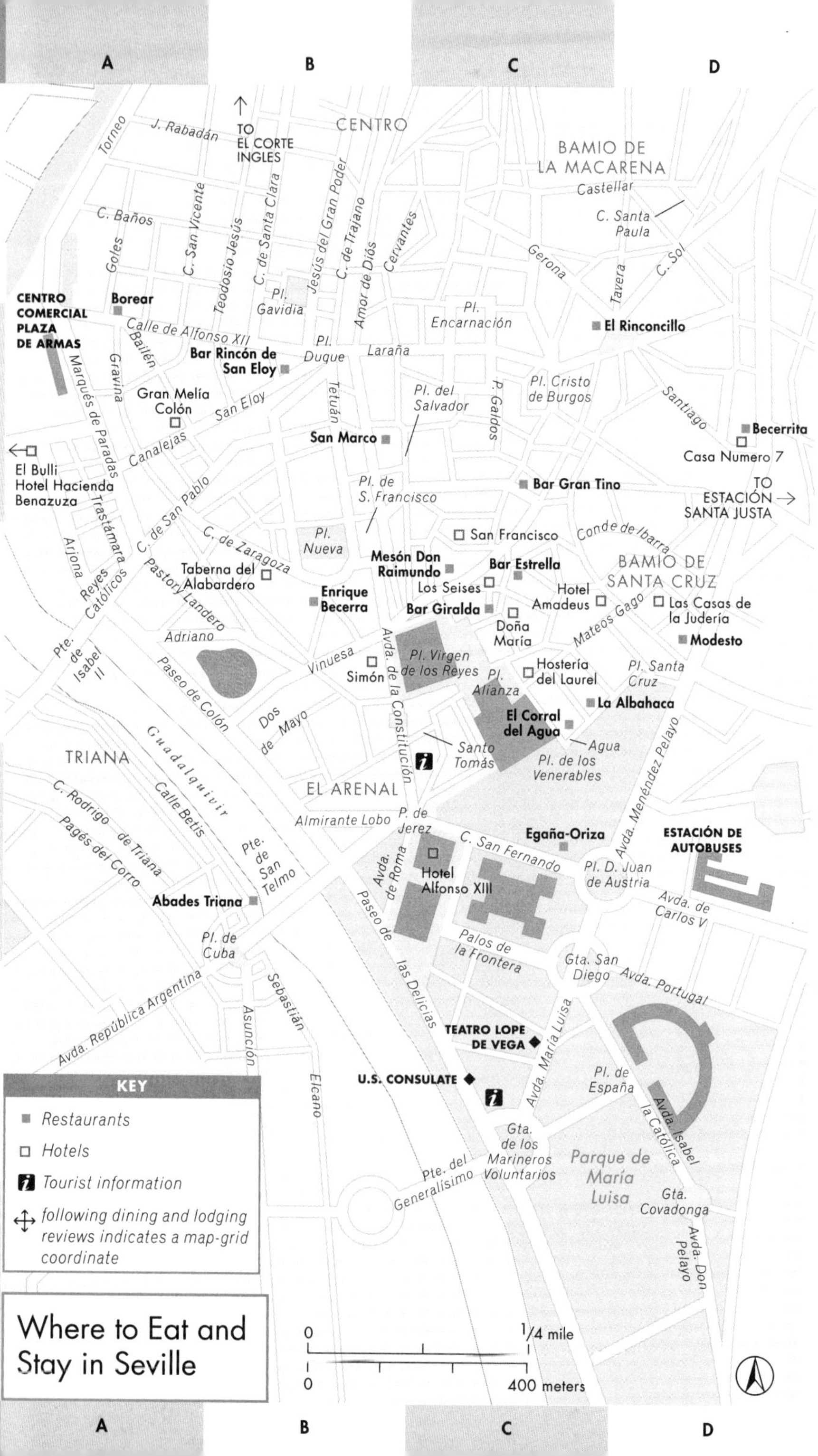

Where to Eat and Stay in Seville

a director of González Byass, a major sherry producer, who apparently spent three years restoring the house, the result being that each room is individually designed and stylish with tasteful artwork and antiques. There is also an elegant salon with a fireplace and comfy chairs. The roof terrace has Giralda views, and breakfast is excellent, with fluffy scrambled eggs an agreeable option. **Pros:** the personal touch of a B&B, delightfully different. **Cons:** some rooms on interior patios have no natural light. ✉ *C. Virgenes 7, Santa Cruz* ☎ *95/422–1581* 🌐 *www.casanumero7.com* *6 rooms* *In-hotel: bar* *AE, V* *BP* ✢ *D2.*

$$ **Doña María.** In a 14th-century former mansion near the cathedral, this is one of Seville's most charmingly old-fashioned hotels. Some rooms have been refurbished in minimalist chic, but most are more ornate and furnished with antiques and floral fabrics—perhaps a bit too feminine for some guests. Bathrooms are spacious and well equipped. There's also a rooftop pool with a terrace and bar boasting fabulous, sweeping views of the Giralda. Check the Internet for substantial discounts, particularly out of season. **Pros:** traditional old Seville hotel, elegant service, perfect location. **Cons:** hard to find, old-fashioned decor overall, erratic air-conditioning. ✉ *Calle Don Remondo 19, Santa Cruz* ☎ *95/422–4990* 🌐 *www.hdmaria.com* *65 rooms* *In-room: Wi-Fi. In-hotel: bar, pool* *AE, DC, MC, V* ✢ *C3.*

$$$$ Fodor's Choice ★ **El Bulli Hotel Hacienda Benazuza.** This luxury hotel is in a rambling 10th-century country palace near Sanlúcar la Mayor, 15 km (9 mi) outside Seville. Surrounded by olive and orange trees and in a courtyard with towering palms, the building incorporates an 18th-century church. The interior has clay-tile floors and ocher walls. The acclaimed Michelin star restaurant, La Alquería ($$$$), serves Spanish and international dishes, creative variations on the recipes of superstar Catalan chef (and hotel owner) Ferran Adrià. **Pros:** nonpareil beauty and taste, polished service. **Cons:** too far from Seville, budget unfriendly. ✉ *C. Virgen de las Nieves, Sanlúcar la Mayor* ☎ *95/570–3344* 🌐 *www.elbullihotel.com* *26 rooms, 18 suites* *In-room: Wi-Fi. In-hotel: 2 restaurants, bar, tennis court, pool, public Internet, parking (no fee), some pets allowed* *AE, DC, MC, V* *Closed Jan.* ✢ *A2.*

$$$$ **Gran Meliá Colón.** This hotel has recently benefited from a total refurbishment although, thankfully, some of the original decor highlights remain, including a marble staircase leading up to the central lobby, which is crowned by a magnificent stained-glass dome and crystal candelabra. Originally built for the 1929 Expo, each floor celebrates a different Spanish artist, with reproduction paintings set against an artful combination of Belle Epoque and contemporary design. Downstairs is the El Burladero bar and restaurant, with a bullfight theme and packed midday with local businessmen. The new spa on the seventh floor offers massages and a range of treatments. **Pros:** good central location not far from the river, excellent restaurant, some rooms have great views. **Cons:** some rooms have views of airshaft only, busy and noisy street. ✉ *Calle Canalejas 1, El Arenal/San Vicente* ☎ *95/450–5599* 🌐 *www.granmeliacolon.com* *162 rooms, 25 suites* *In-room: Wi-Fi. In-hotel: restaurant, bar, spa, Wi-Fi, public Internet* *AE, DC, MC, V* *BP* ✢ *A2.*

$$–$$$ ★ **Hostería del Laurel.** A small tree-lined square in the heart of the Barrio de Santa Cruz makes an unbeatable setting for this hotel. It's known for its bodega, which is mentioned in Zorilla's popular 19th-century play *Don Juan Tenorio,* and for the hostería's adjoining restaurant, which specializes in traditional local cuisine such as *pollo a la Sevillana* (chicken in a rich gravy), *espinacas con garbonzos* (spinach with chick-peas), and squid in garlic. The rooms are a relatively recent addition and are spotlessly clean and simply furnished. **Pros:** exciting location in the thick of the Jewish Quarter, pretty square and rooms, reasonably priced. **Cons:** rooms small, street side rooms noisy, some interior rooms airless. ✉ *Pl. de los Venerables 5, Santa Cruz* ☎ *95/422–0295* 🌐 *www.hosteriadellaurel.com* *21 rooms* *In-hotel: restaurant, bar, public Internet* ▭ *MC, V* 🍽 *BP* ✣ *C3.*

$$$$ ★ **Hotel Alfonso XIII.** Inaugurated by King Alfonso XIII in 1929, this grand hotel is a splendid, historical Mudejar-style palace, built around a central patio and surrounded by ornate brick arches. Public rooms have marble floors, wood-panel ceilings, heavy Moorish lamps, stained glass, and ceramic tiles in typical Seville colors. There are a Spanish and a Japanese restaurant and an elegant bar. If you can't afford a room, you can still enjoy the sumptuous surroundings: sip a glass of *fino* (sherry) overlooking the fabulous central courtyard while looking appropriately superior (and rich). **Pros:** both stately and hip, impeccable service. **Cons:** a tourist colony, colossally expensive. ✉ *San Fernando 2, El Arenal* ☎ *95/491–7000* 🌐 *www.westin.com/hotelalfonso* *127 rooms, 19 suites* *In-room: Wi-Fi. In-hotel: 2 restaurants, bar, pool, parking (fee)* ▭ *AE, DC, MC, V* ✣ *C4.*

$$ Fodor's Choice ★ **Hotel Amadeus.** With pianos in some of the soundproof rooms and a music room off the central patio, and classical concerts regularly held on the patio, this acoustic oasis is ideal for touring professional musicians and music fans in general. Rooms are all designed after a different composer, and the 18th-century manor house has been equipped with such modern amenities as Wi-Fi and a small glass-wall elevator that moves quietly up and down a corner of the central patio. You can enjoy breakfast (an extra €8) on the roof terrace overlooking the Judería and Giralda. **Pros:** small but charming rooms, some in-room pianos, roof terrace. **Cons:** certain rooms are noisy, staff not always that helpful. ✉ *Calle Farnesio 6, Santa Cruz* ☎ *95/450–1443* 🌐 *www.hotelamadeussevilla.com* *14 rooms* *In-room: Wi-Fi. In-hotel: restaurant, parking (fee)* ▭ *AE, DC, MC, V* ✣ *C3.*

$$$ **Las Casas de la Judería.** This labyrinthine hotel tucked into a passageway off the Plaza Santa María occupies three of the barrio's old palaces, each arranged around inner courtyards, complete with fountains, traditional tile work, and plenty of greenery. The spacious guest rooms are painted in subdued pastels and decorated with prints of Seville; most have four-poster beds. **Pros:** lovely buildings, at the end of a quiet alley, charming rooms. **Cons:** slightly dark and damp, some rooms get almost no natural light, rooms vary. ✉ *Callejón de Dos Hermanas 7, Santa Cruz* ☎ *95/441–5150* 🌐 *www.casasypalacios.com* *103 rooms, 3 suites* *In-room: Wi-Fi. In-hotel: restaurant, bar, parking (fee)* ▭ *AE, DC, MC, V* ✣ *D3.*

$$$$ ★ **Los Seises.** This hotel is in a section of Seville's 16th-century Palacio Episcopal (Bishop's Palace), and the combination of modern and Renaissance architecture is striking: Room 219, for instance, is divided by a 16th-century brick archway, and breakfast (for an extra €18) is served in the old chapel. A pit in the center of the basement restaurant reveals the building's foundations and some archaeological finds, including a Roman mosaic. The rooftop pool and summer restaurant are in full view of the Giralda. The hotel is now part of the prestigious Spanish Husa hotel chain, and you can usually save a substantial sum by booking on the Internet. **Pros:** midtown location, interesting design and decor, rooftop pool, helpful staff. **Cons:** noisy streets, sometimes careless maintenance and management. ✉ *Calle Segovias 6, Santa Cruz* ☎ *95/422–9495* 🌐 *www.hotellosseises.com* *42 rooms, 2 suites* *In-room: refrigerator. In-hotel: restaurant, pool, public Wi-Fi, parking (fee)* *AE, DC, MC, V* *BP* ✥ *C3.*

$ **San Francisco.** An 18th-century town house near the cathedral and the main shopping area houses this modest hotel. A central patio enlivens the entrance, and the simple rooms have traditional dark wood furniture, tiled floors, and small en suite marble bathrooms. The upstairs terrace is a major perk, with its five-star cathedral views, and the several rooms leading off from this terrace are the best, if you can get one. The friendly owner speaks some English. **Pros:** patient and attentive management, excellent value, fine location. **Cons:** festive and resonant area, rooms small and drab. ✉ *Calle Álvarez Quintero 38, Santa Cruz* ☎ *95/450–1541* 🌐 *www.sanfranciscoh.com* *17 rooms* *In-room: Wi-Fi. In-hotel: bar, parking (fee)* *AE, DC, MC, V* ✥ *C3.*

$–$$ **Simón.** A rambling turn-of-the-19th-century town house, this hotel is a good choice for inexpensive, comfortable accommodations near the cathedral. The spacious, fern-filled, azulejo-tile patio makes a fine initial impression, and the marble stairway and high-ceilinged dining room are cool, stately spaces. The rooms are less grand, particularly those on the top floor (the former servants' quarters), but the mansion's style permeates the house. **Pros:** ideal location, breezy Andalusian decor. **Cons:** rooms plain, service pleasant but lackadaisical. ✉ *Calle García de Vinuesa 19, El Arenal* ☎ *95/422–6660* 🌐 *www.hotelsimonsevilla.com* *29 rooms* *In-room: Wi-Fi. In-hotel: restaurant, some pets allowed* *AE, DC, MC, V* ✥ *B3.*

$$–$$$ **Taberna del Alabardero.** Near the Plaza Nueva, this highly regarded hotel and restaurant is a superb mid-Seville retreat in a traditional setting. Rooms are decorated with great style and elegance, and all have a Jacuzzi. A central courtyard with a bar and festooned with greenery precedes the dining area, which is decorated in Sevillian tiles. The restaurant ($$$–$$$$) serves modern dishes such as *bacalao a la parrilla trija de hongos sobre pil-pil y aceite de jamón* (grilled cod with mushrooms in a spicy chili-and-ham sauce). **Pros:** gorgeous house, intimate and romantic. **Cons:** air-conditioning not up to battling the summer heat, rooms get booked up quickly in the summer months. ✉ *Calle Zaragoza 20, El Arenal* ☎ *95/456–0637* 🌐 *www.tabernadelalabardero.com* *7 rooms* *In-hotel: bar, public Wi-Fi, public Internet, parking (fee)* *AE, DC, MC, V* *Closed Aug* ✥ *B3.*

NIGHTLIFE AND THE ARTS

Seville has lively nightlife and plenty of cultural activity. The free monthly magazine *El Giraldillo* (🌐*www.elgiraldillo.es*) lists classical and jazz concerts, plays, dance performances, art exhibits, and films in Seville and all major Andalusian cities. (For American films in English, look for the designation *v.o.*, for *versión original.*)

NIGHTLIFE

FLAMENCO CLUBS

Seville has a handful of commercial *tablaos* (flamenco clubs), patronized more by tourists than locals. They generally offer somewhat mechanical flamenco at high prices, with mediocre cuisine. Check local listings and ask at your hotel for performances by top artists. Spontaneous flamenco is often found for free in *peñas flamencas* (flamenco clubs) and flamenco bars in Triana.

Casa Anselma is a semisecret (unmarked) bar on the corner of Antillano Campos where Anselma and her friends sing and dance for the pure joy and catharsis that are at the heart of flamenco. ✉*Calle Pagés del Corro 49, Triana* ☎*No phone* 🎫*Free* ⏲*Shows nightly after 11.*

★ **Casa de la Memoria de Al-Andaluz,** in an 18th-century palace, has a nightly show plus classes for the intrepid. ✉*Calle Ximenez de Enciso 28, Santa Cruz* ☎*95/456–0670* 🌐*www.casadelamemoria.es* 🎫*€15* ⏲*Shows nightly at 9.*

Casa del Carmen is a relative newcomer to the Seville flamenco scene, but the flamenco here is generally as passionate and raw as it needs to be to retain credibility. ✉*Calle Marqués de Paradas 30, El Arenal* ☎*95/421–2889* 🎫*€16* ⏲*Shows nightly at 8:30 and 10.*

El Tamboril is a late-night bar in the heart of the Barrio de Santa Cruz, noted for its great glass case in which the Virgin of Rocío sits in splendor. At 11 each night, locals pack in to sing the *Salve Rociera,* an emotive prayer to her. Afterward, everything from flamenco to salsa continues until the early hours. ✉*Pl. Santa Cruz, Santa Cruz* 🎫*Free.*

★ **La Carbonería,** a rambling former coal yard, is usually packed on Thursdays when the flamenco is spontaneous. There's no entry charge, and it's open the rest of the week, too, except Sunday. ✉*C. Levíes 18, Santa Cruz* ☎*95/421–4460* ⏲*First show at 11* PM, *the second at 1* AM.

La Madrugá collects Triana fans and flamenco faithful hoping to catch a spontaneous outburst of dance. ✉*Calle Salado, at Calle Virgen de las Huertas, Triana* ☎*No phone* 🎫*Free* ⏲*Shows nightly after 11.*

Los Gallos is an intimate club in the heart of the Barrio de Santa Cruz. Performances are good and reasonably authentic. ✉*Pl. Santa Cruz 11, Santa Cruz* ☎*95/421–6981* 🌐*www.tablaolosgallos.com* 🎫*€30 with 1 drink* ⏲*Shows nightly at 8 and 10:30. Closed Jan.*

THE ARTS

Long prominent in the opera world, Seville is proud of its opera house, the **Teatro de la Maestranza** (✉*Paseo de Colón 22, El Arenal* ☎*95/422–3344* 🌐*www.teatromaestranza.com*). Classical music and ballet are performed at the **Teatro Lope de Vega** (✉*Av. María Luisa s/n, Parque de María Luisa* ☎*95/459–0853*). The modern **Teatro Central** (✉*José de Gálvez s/n, Isla de la Cartuja* ☎*95/503–7200* 🌐*www.teatrocentral.com*) stages theater, dance, and classical and contemporary music.

BULLFIGHTING Bullfighting season is Easter through Columbus Day; most *corridas* (bullfights) are held on Sunday. The highlight is the April Fair, with Spain's leading toreros; other key dates are Corpus Christi (date varies; about seven weeks after Easter), Assumption (August 15), and the last weekend in September. Bullfights take place at the **Maestranza Bullring** (✉*Paseo de Colón 12, Arenal* ☎*95/422–4577*). Bullfight tickets are expensive; buy them in advance from the official **despacho de entradas** (*ticket office* ✉*Calle Adriano 37, El Arenal* ☎*95/450–1382*), alongside the bullring. Other despachos sell tickets on Calle Sierpes, but these are unofficial and charge a 20% commission.

SHOPPING

Seville is the region's main shopping area and the place for archetypal Andalusian souvenirs, most of which are sold in the Barrio de Santa Cruz and around the cathedral and Giralda, especially on Calle Alemanes. The shopping street for locals is Calle Sierpes, along with neighboring Cuna, Tetuan, Velázquez, Plaza Magdalena, and Plaza Duque—boutiques abound here. **El Postigo** is a permanent arts-and-crafts market, open every day except Sunday, near the cathedral (✉*Calle Arfe s/n, El Arenal* ☎*95/456–0013*). Near the Puente del Cachorro bridge, the old Estación de Córdoba train station has been converted into a stylish shopping center, the **Centro Comercial Plaza de Armas** (✉*Enter on Pl. de la Legión, El Arenal*), with boutiques, bars, fast-food joints, a nightclub, and a cinema complex. The main branch of the pan-Spanish department store **El Corte Inglés** (✉*Pl. Duque 8, Centro* ☎*95/422–0931*) does not close for siesta.

ANTIQUES

For antiques, try Mateos Gago, opposite the Giralda, and in the Barrio de Santa Cruz on Jamerdana and Rodrigo Caro, off Plaza Alianza.

BOOKS

A large assortment of books in English, Spanish, French, and Italian is sold at the American-owned **Librería Vértice** (✉*San Fernando 33–35, Santa Cruz* ☎*95/421–1654*), near the cathedral.

CERAMICS

In the Barrio de Santa Cruz, browse along Mateos Gago; on Romero Murube, between Plaza Triunfo and Plaza Alianza, on the edge of the barrio; and between Plaza Doña Elvira and Plaza de los Venerables. Look for traditional azulejo tiles and other ceramics in the Triana **potters' district,** on Calle Alfarería and Calle Antillano Campos. **Cerámica Montalván** (✉*Calle Alfarería 23, El Zurraque* ☎*95/434–4608*) is the only ceramics store in Triana that doubles as a workshop. If you ask nicely, you may be able to watch the craftsmen at work. In central Seville, **Martian Ceramics** (✉*Calle Sierpes 74, Centro* ☎*95/421–3413*) has high-quality dishes, especially the finely painted flowers-on-white patterns native to Seville.

FANS

Casa Rubio (✉*Sierpes 56, Centro* ☎*95/422–6872*) is Seville's premier fan store—no mean distinction.

Continued on page 648

FLAMENCO

THE HEARTBEAT OF SPAIN

Palmas, the staccato clapping of flamenco.

Rule one about flamenco: You don't see it. You feel it. There's no soap opera emoting here. The pain and yearning on the dancers' faces and the eerie voices—typically communicating grief over a lost love or family member—are real. If the dancers manage to summon the supernatural *duende* and allow this inner demon to overcome them, then they have done their jobs well.

DUENDE HEAD TO TOE

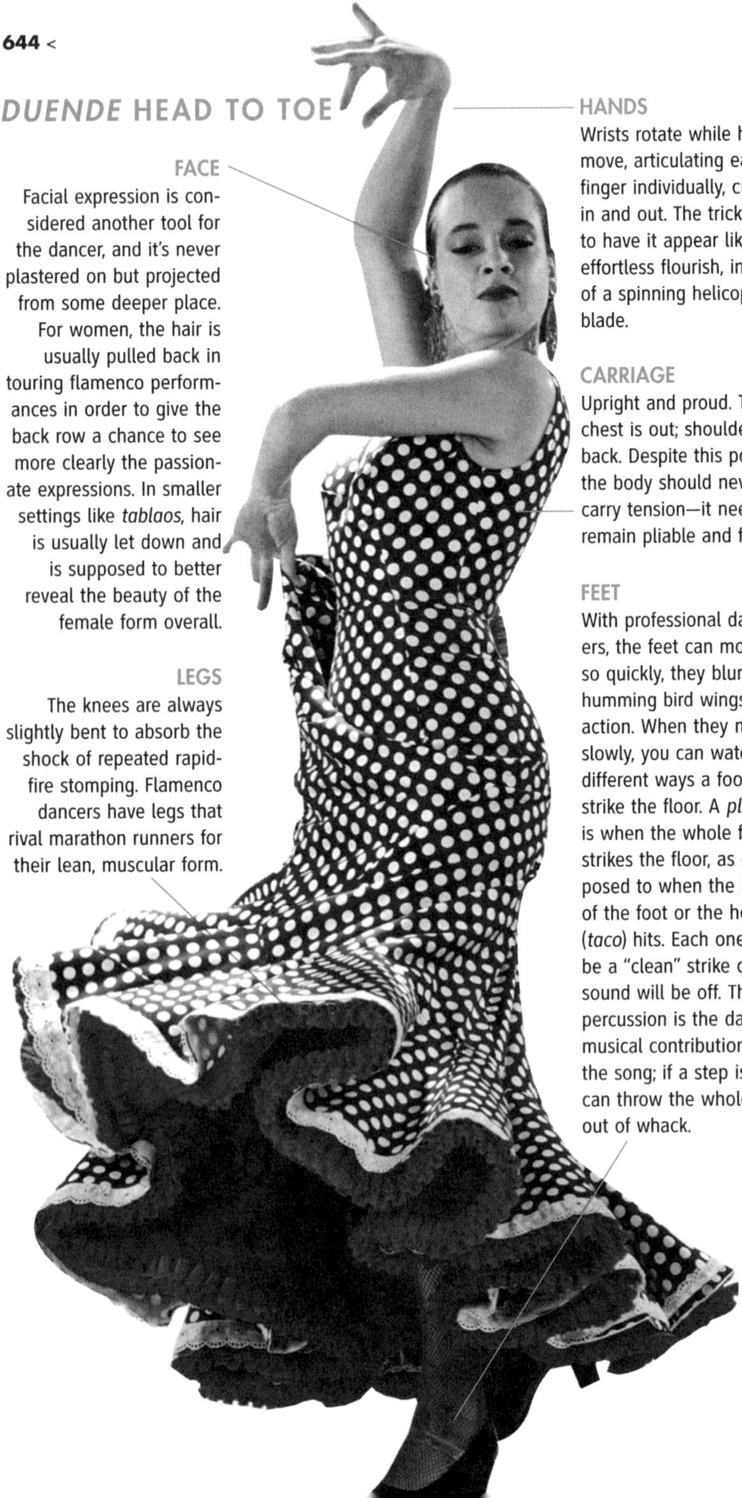

FACE

Facial expression is considered another tool for the dancer, and it's never plastered on but projected from some deeper place. For women, the hair is usually pulled back in touring flamenco performances in order to give the back row a chance to see more clearly the passionate expressions. In smaller settings like *tablaos*, hair is usually let down and is supposed to better reveal the beauty of the female form overall.

LEGS

The knees are always slightly bent to absorb the shock of repeated rapid-fire stomping. Flamenco dancers have legs that rival marathon runners for their lean, muscular form.

HANDS

Wrists rotate while hands move, articulating each finger individually, curling in and out. The trick is to have it appear like an effortless flourish, instead of a spinning helicopter blade.

CARRIAGE

Upright and proud. The chest is out; shoulders back. Despite this position, the body should never carry tension—it needs to remain pliable and fluid.

FEET

With professional dancers, the feet can move so quickly, they blur like humming bird wings in action. When they move slowly, you can watch the different ways a foot can strike the floor. A *planta* is when the whole foot strikes the floor, as opposed to when the ball of the foot or the heel (*taco*) hits. Each one must be a "clean" strike or the sound will be off. This percussion is the dancers' musical contribution to the song; if a step is off, it can throw the whole song out of whack.

FLAMENCO 101

All the elements of flamenco working in harmony.

ORIGINS

The music is largely Arabic in its beginnings, but you'll detect echoes of Greek dirges and Jewish chants, with healthy doses of Flemish and traditional Castillian thrown in. Hindu sways, Roman mimes, and other movement informs the dance, but we may never know the specific origins of flamenco.

The dance, along with the nomadic Gypsies, spread throughout Andalusia and within a few centuries had developed into many variations and styles, some of them named after the city where they were born (such as Malagueñas, Sevillanas) and others taking on the names after people, emotions, or bands. In all, there are over 50 different styles (or *palos*) of flamenco, four of which are the stylistic pillars others branch off from—differing mainly in rhythm and mood: *Toná*, *Soleá*, *Fandango,* and *Seguiriya*.

CLAPPING AND CASTANETS

The sum of its parts are awe-inspiring, but if you boil it down, flamenco is a combination of music, singing, and dance. Staccato hand-clapping almost sneaks in as a fourth part—the sounds made from all the participants' palms, or *palmas* is part of the *duende*—but this element remains more of a

continued on following page

THE FLAMENCO HOOK-UP

When *duende* leads to love.

That cheek-to-cheek chemistry that exists between dance partners isn't missing in flamenco—it's simply repositioned between the dancer and the musicians. In fact, when you watch flamenco, you may feel what seems like an electric wire connecting the dancer to the musicians. In each *palo* (style) of music there are certain *letras* (lyrics) inherent within the song that tip off dancers and spark a change in rhythm. If the cues are off, the dancer may falter or simply come off flat. At its best, the dancer and the guitarist are like an old married couple that can musically finish each other's sentences. This interconnectedness has been known to lead into the bedroom, and it's not unusual for dancers and musicians to hook up offstage. Two famous couples include dancer Eva La Yerbabuena with guitarist Paco Jarano and dancer Manuela Carrasco with guitarist Joaquín Amador.

connector that all in the performance take part in when their hands are free.

Hand-clapping was likely flamenco's original key instrument before the guitar, *cajón* (wooden box used for percussion), and other instruments arrived on the scene. Perhaps the simplest way to augment the clapping is to add a uniquely designed six-string guitar, in which case you've got yourself a *tablao*, or people seated around a singer and clapping. Dance undoubtedly augments the experience, but isn't necessary for a *tablao*. These exist all throughout Andalusia and are usually private affairs with people who love flamenco. One needn't be a Gypsy in order to take part in it. But it doesn't hurt.

Castanets (or *palillos*) were absorbed by the Phoenician culture and adopted by the Spanish, now part of their own folklore. They accompany other traditional folk dances in Spain and are used pervasively throughout flamenco (though not always present in some forms of dance). Castanets can be secured in any number of ways. The most important thing is that they are securely fastened to the hand (by thumb or any combination of fingers) so that the wrist can snap it quickly and make the sound.

FLAMENCO NOW

Flamenco's enormous international resurgence has been building for the past few decades. Much of this revival can be attributed to pioneers like legendary singer Camarón de la Isla, guitarist Paco de Lucía, or even outsiders like Miles Davis fusing flamenco with other genres like jazz and rock. This melding brought forth flamenco pop—which flourished in the 80s and continues today—as well as disparate fusions with almost every genre imaginable, including heavy metal and hip-hop. Today the most popular flamenco fusion artists include Ojos de Brujo and Chambao—all of which have found an audience outside of Spain.

IT'S A MAN'S WORLD

Joaquín Cortés

In the U.S., our image of a flamenco dancer is usually a woman in a red dress. So you may be surprised to learn that male dancers dominate flamenco and always have. In its beginnings, men did all the footwork and only since the 40s and 50s have women started to match men step-for-step and star in performances. And in the tabloids, men usually get the sex symbol status more than women (as seen through Farruquito and Cortés). Suits are the traditional garb for male dancers, and recent trends have seen female dancers wearing them as well—presumably rebelling against the staid gender roles that continue to rule Spain. Today, male dancers tend to wear a simple pair of black trousers and a white button-down shirt. The sex appeal comes from unbuttoning the shirt to flash a little chest and having the pants tailor-made to a tightness that can't be found in any store. In traditional *tablaos*, male dancers perform without accessories, but in touring performances—upping the razzle dazzle—anything goes: canes, hats, tuxedos, or even shirtless (much to the delight of female fans).

DANCING WITH THE STARS

SEX, MANSLAUGHTER, EVEN MONOGAMY

EVA LA YERBABUENA, The Pro

Farruquito was born into a flamenco dynasty. He started dancing when he was 8 years old and rose very high in the flamenco and celebrity world (*People* magazine named him one of the 50 most beautiful people in the world) until September 2003 when he ran two lights in an unlicensed, uninsured BMW, hitting and killing a pedestrian.

FARRUQUITO, The Wild Child

This young dancer from Granada has won numerous prizes, including the coveted Flamenco Hoy's Best Dancer award in 2000. In 2006, she took her tour around Asia and New Zealand. She tends to stay away from the tabloids because she doesn't run red lights and enjoys a stable relationship with flamenco guitarist Paco Jarano.

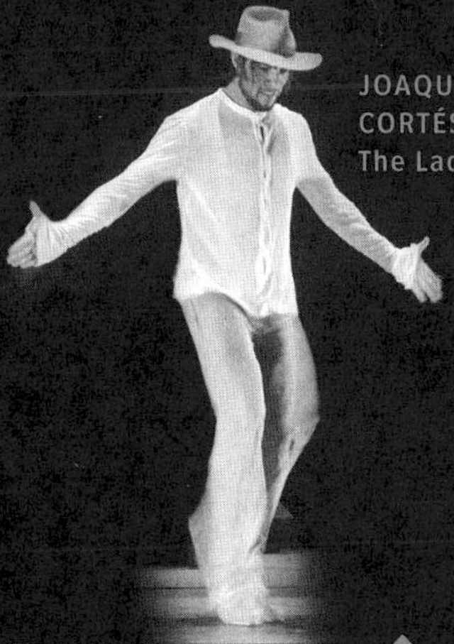

JOAQUÍN CORTÉS, The Lady's Man

Stateside, we're still swooning over her Oscar-nominated sister, Penélope, but in Spain, Mónica also captures the spotlight. With the same dark hair and pillowy lips as her sibling, Mónica works as a flamenco dancer and actress. Most recently she stared in a soap opera in Spain called *Paso Adelante*, a Spanish version of *Fame*.

MÓNICA CRUZ, The Bombshell

He's considered a visionary dancer, easily the most famous worldwide for the past 15 years. Despite this, he's often in the press for the hotties he's dated rather than his talent; former flames include Oscar-winner Mira Sorvino and supermodel Naomi Campbell. Even *Sports Illustrated* cover girl Elle MacPherson labeled him "pure sex."

FLAMENCO WEAR

Flamenco wear can be expensive; local women will gladly spend a month's grocery money, or more, on their frills, with dresses ranging from €100 to €400 and up. Try recommended shops **Lola Azahare** (✉ *Calle Cuna 31, Centro* ☎ *95/422–6287*) and **Molina** (✉ *Sierpes 11, Centro* ☎ *95/422–9254*), which also sells the traditional foot-tapping shoes. For privately fitted and custom-made flamenco dresses, try **Taller de Diseño** (✉ *Calle Luchana 6, Centro* ☎ *95/422–7186*).

PASTRIES

Seville's most celebrated pastry outlet is **La Campana** (✉ *Sierpes 1, Centro* ☎ *95/422–3570*), founded in 1885. Andalusia's convents are known for their homemade pastries, and you can sample sweets from several convents at **El Torno** (✉ *Pl. del Cabildo s/n, Santa Cruz* ☎ *95/421–9190*).

PORCELAIN

La Cartuja china, originally crafted at La Cartuja Monastery but now made outside Seville, is sold at **La Alacena** (✉ *Calle Alfonso XII 25, San Vicente* ☎ *95/422–8021*). **El Corte Inglés** department stores are also good places to shop.

STREET MARKETS

A few blocks north of Plaza Nueva, **Plaza del Duque** has a crafts market on Friday and Saturday. The flea market **El Jueves** is held on Calle Feria in the Barrio de la Macarena on Thursday morning.

TEXTILES

You can find blankets, shawls, and embroidered tablecloths woven by local artisans at the three shops of **Artesanía Textil** (✉ *Calle García de Vinuesa 33, El Arenal* ☎ *95/456–2840* ✉ *Sierpes 70, Centro* ☎ *95/422–0125* ✉ *Pl. de Doña Elvira 4, Santa Cruz* ☎ *95/421–4748*).

SIDE TRIPS FROM SEVILLE

CARMONA

32 km (20 mi) east of Seville off NIV.

Claiming to be one of the oldest inhabited places in Spain (both Phoenicians and Carthaginians had settlements here), Carmona, on a steep, fortified hill, became an important town under the Romans and the Moors. As you wander its ancient, narrow streets, you can see many Mudejar and Renaissance churches, medieval gateways, and simple whitewashed houses of clear Moorish influence, punctuated here and there by a baroque palace. Local fiestas are held in mid-September.

ESSENTIALS

Visitor Information Carmona (✉ *Arco de la Puerta de Sevilla* ☎ *95/419–0955* 🌐 *www.turismo.carmona.org*).

EXPLORING

Park your car near the Puerta de Sevilla in the imposing **Alcázar de Abajo** (Lower Fortress), a Moorish fortification built on Roman foundations. Maps are available at the tourist office, in the tower beside the gate.

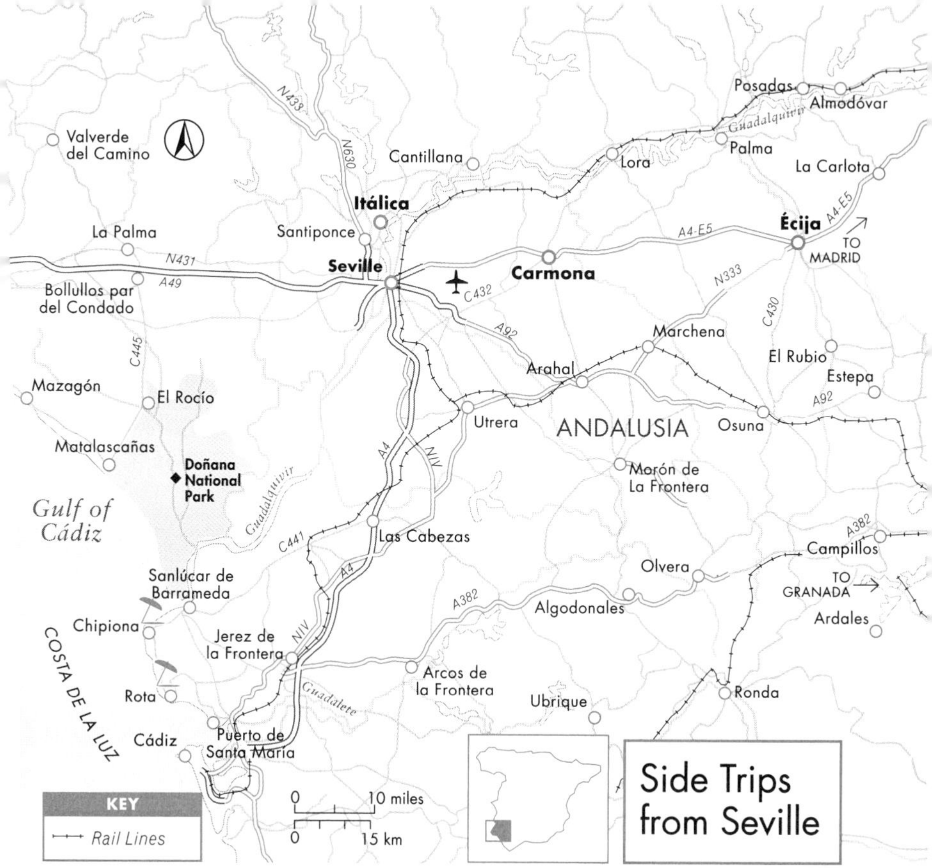

On the edge of the "new town," across the road from the Alcázar de Abajo, is the church of **San Pedro** (✉ *Calle San Pedro*), begun in 1466. Its interior is an unbroken mass of sculptures and gilded surfaces, and its baroque tower, erected in 1704, is an unabashed imitation of Seville's Giralda. Up Calle Prim is the **Plaza San Fernando,** in the heart of the old town; its 17th-century houses have Moorish overtones.

The Gothic church of **Santa María** (✉ *Calle Martín*) was built between 1424 and 1518 on the site of Carmona's former Great Mosque and retains its beautiful Moorish courtyard, studded with orange trees. It's open Monday–Saturday, and entrance is €3. Behind Santa María is the **Museo de la Ciudad,** with exhibits on Carmona's history. There's plenty for children, and the interactive exhibits are labeled in English and Spanish. ✉ *Calle San Ildefonso 1* ☎ *954/140128* €2 ⏲ *Mon. 11–2, Tues.–Sun. 11–7.*

Stroll down to the **Puerta de Córdoba** (Córdoba Gate) on the eastern edge of town. This old gateway was first built by the Romans around AD 175, then altered by Moorish and Renaissance additions. The Moorish **Alcázar de Arriba** (Upper Fortress) was built on Roman foundations and later converted by King Pedro the Cruel into a Mudejar palace. Pedro's summer residence was destroyed by a 1504 earthquake, but the parador amid its ruins has a breathtaking view.

★ The **Roman necropolis** lies at the western edge of town in underground chambers where 900 tombs were placed between the 2nd and 4th centuries BC. The walls, decorated with leaf and bird motifs, have niches for burial urns and tombs such as the **Elephant Vault** and the **Servilia Tomb**, a complete Roman villa with colonnaded arches and vaulted side galleries. ✉ *C. Enmedio* ☎ *95/562–4615* 🎫 *2€* ⏲ *Mid-Sept.–mid-June, Tues.–Fri. 9–4:45, weekends 10–1:45; mid-June–mid-Sept., Tues.–Fri. 8:30–1:45, Sat. 10–2.*

WHERE TO EAT AND STAY

$$–$$$ SPANISH ✕ **San Fernando.** You enter from a side street, but this second-floor restaurant in an 18th-century palace looks out onto the Plaza de San Fernando. The beige dining room is quietly elegant in its simplicity, and the kitchen serves Spanish dishes with flair—as in cream of green apple soup or lightly fried potato slivers shaped like a bird's nest. Game, including partridge, is a perennial favorite. Larger appetites can opt for the special menu with five tasting dishes—a steal at under €30. ✉ *Calle Sacramento 3* ☎ *95/414–3556* 💳 *AE, DC, MC, V* ⏲ *Closed Mon. and Aug. No dinner Sun.*

$$$ Fodor'sChoice ★ **Parador Alcázar del Rey Don Pedro.** The Parador de Carmona has superb views from its hilltop position among the ruins of Pedro the Cruel's summer palace. The public rooms surround a central, Moorish-style patio, and the vaulted dining hall and adjacent bar open onto an outdoor terrace overlooking the sloping garden. The spacious guest rooms have rugs and dark furniture. All but six, which face onto the front courtyard, look south over the valley; the best rooms are on the top floor. **Pros:** unbeatable views over the fields, great sense of history. **Cons:** feels slightly lifeless after Seville. ✉ *Calle del Alcázar s/n* ☎ *95/414–1010* 🌐 *www.parador.es* *63 rooms* *In-room: Wi-Fi. In-hotel: restaurant, bar, pool, public Internet* 💳 *AE, DC, MC, V.*

ÉCIJA

48 km (30 mi) northeast of Carmona.

Écija is dubbed the "the frying pan," "furnace," or "oven" of Andalusia because its midsummer temperatures often reach 100°F/37°C. On a more positive note, it has more ceramic-tiled baroque church towers per capita (11) than any other town in Spain.

EXPLORING

Écija's most famous ornamented church is the **Iglesia de Santa María** in the palm tree–shaded Plaza de España, an important meeting point on infernally hot summer evenings. The **Iglesia de San Juan** has an intricate and harmoniously crafted Mudejar bell tower. The **Iglesia de Santiago** assembles Mudejar windows from an earlier structure with an 18th-century patio and 17th-century nave and side aisles.

Important civil structures in Écija begin with the baroque **Palacio de Peñaflor** (✉ *Calle Emilio Castelar 26* ☎ *95/483–0273* 🎫 *Free* ⏲ *Patio only: weekdays 10–1 and 4:30–7:30, weekends 11–1*) with its concave facade and its *trampantojo* (trompe l'oeil) faux-relief paintings. Note the presentation of the stable windows below the false wrought-iron balcony, which is the noblest feature in the facade. The Renaissance **Valdehermoso Palace** (✉ *Calle Emilio Castelar 37*) near the Iglesia de San Juan is an elegant and aristocratic structure. The **Palacio de Benamejí** (✉ *Plaza de la Consitución s/n*) with its two watchtowers is another of Écija's finest houses. The **Palacio del Conde de Aguilar** (✉ *Calle Sor Angela Cruz s/n*) has a lovely baroque portal and a wrought-iron gallery.

WHERE TO EAT

$ ✕ **Platería.** This modern hideaway in Écija's old silversmiths' quarter has a good restaurant ($$–$$$) serving regional and national dishes, as well as 18 breezy guest rooms. ✉ *C. Platería 4* ☎ *95/590–2754* 🌐 *www.hotelplateria.net* 💳 *AE, DC, MC, V.*

ITÁLICA

12 km (7 mi) north of Seville, 1 km (½ mi) beyond Santiponce.

Fodor's Choice ★

One of Roman Iberia's most important cities in the 2nd century, with a population of more than 10,000, Itálica today is a monument of Roman ruins, complete with admission charge. Founded by Scipio Africanus in 205 BC as a home for veteran soldiers, Itálica gave the Roman world two great emperors: Trajan (52–117) and Hadrian (76–138). You can find traces of city streets, cisterns, and the floor plans of several villas, some with mosaic floors, though all the best mosaics and statues have been removed to Seville's Museum of Archaeology. Itálica was abandoned and plundered as a quarry by the Visigoths, who preferred Seville. It fell into decay around AD 700. The remains you can see include the huge, elliptical **amphitheater**, which held 40,000 spectators, a **Roman theater**, and **Roman baths.** ☎ *95/599–7376 or 95/599–6583* 🎫 *€1.50* ⏲ *Tues.–Sat. 9–5:30, Sun. 10–4.*

WESTERN ANDALUSIA'S GREAT OUTDOORS: PROVINCE OF HUELVA

When you've had enough of Seville's urban bustle, nature awaits in Huelva. From the Parque Nacional de Doñana to the oak forests of the Sierra de Aracena, nothing is much more than an hour's drive from Seville. If you prefer history, hop on the miners' train at Riotinto or visit Aracena's spectacular caves. Columbus's voyage to the New World was sparked near here, at the monastery of La Rábida and in Palos de la Frontera. The visitor center at La Rocina has Doñana information.

Once a thriving Roman port, the city of Huelva itself, an hour east of Faro, Portugal, was largely destroyed by the 1755 Lisbon earthquake. As a result, Huelva claims the dubious honor of being the least distinguished city in Andalusia. If you do end up here, **Taberna el Condado** is the place to go for tapas and beer.

ESSENTIALS

Bus Station Huelva (✉ *Av. Doctor Rubio s/n* ☎ *959/256900*).

Taxi Contacts Tele Taxi (☎ *959/250022*).

Train Station Huelva (✉ *Av. de Italia* ☎ *959/246666*).

DOÑANA NATIONAL PARK

100 km (62 mi) southwest of Seville.

Fodor's Choice ★

One of Europe's most important swaths of unspoiled wilderness, these wetlands spread out along the west side of the Guadalquivir estuary. The site was named for Doña Ana, wife of a 16th-century duke, who, prone to bouts of depression, one day crossed the river and wandered into the wetlands, never to be seen alive again. The 188,000-acre park sits on the migratory route from Africa to Europe and is the winter home and breeding ground for as many as 150 species of rare birds. Habitats range from beaches and shifting sand dunes to marshes, dense brushwood, and sandy hillsides of pine and cork oak. Two of Europe's most endangered species, the imperial eagle and the lynx, make their homes here, and kestrels, kites, buzzards, egrets, storks, and spoonbills breed among the cork oaks. A good base of exploration is the hamlet of **El Rocío,** on the park's northern fringe. In spring, during the Romería del Rocío pilgrimage (40 days after Easter Sunday), up to a million people converge on the local *santuario* (shrine) to worship the Virgen del Rocío. The rest of the year, many of El Rocío's pilgrim-brotherhood houses are empty. Most of the streets are unpaved to make them more comfortable for horses, as many of the yearly pilgrimage events are on horseback or involve horse-drawn carts. At the Doñana **La Rocina visitor center** (☎ *959/442340*), less than 2 km (1 mi) from El Rocío, you can peer at the park's many bird species from a 3½-km (2-mi) footpath. It's open daily 9–7. Five kilometers (3 mi) away, an exhibit at the **Palacio de Acebrón** (✉ *Ctra. de la Rocina s/n* ☎ *959/448–711*) explains the park's ecosystems. It's open daily 9–6:30; last entrance is one hour before closing.

DOÑANA TOURS

Jeep tours of Doñana National Park depart twice daily at 8 and 3 (from May to September there is a 5 PM tour as well) from the park's Acebuche reception center, 2 km (1 mi) from Matalascañas. Tours take four hours, cost €25 and cover a 70-km (43-mi) route through beaches, sand dunes, marshes, and scrub. Jeep tours should be booked well in advance. Passengers can arrange to be picked up from hotels in Matalascañas. Contact **Parque Nacional de Doñana** (✉ *Av. Canaliega s/n, El Rocio-Huelva* ☎ *959/442474* 🌐 *www.donanareservas.com*).

Two kilometers (1 mi) before Matalascañas is **Acebuche** (✉ *El Acebuche s/n* ☎ *959/448640* 🌐 *www.parquenacionaldonana.com*), the park's main interpretation center and the departure point for jeep tours. The center is open June–September, daily 8 AM–9 PM, and October–May, daily 9–7. There's also a visitor center for the park in Cádiz, at Sanlúcar de Barrameda (*see below*).

WHERE TO STAY

$$–$$$ **El Cortijo de Los Mimbrales.** On the Rocío–Matalascañas road, this convivial, one-story Andalusian farm-hacienda is perched on the park's edge, a mere 1 km (½ mi) from the visitor center at La Rocina. It's a lovely place to spend a relaxed evening with fellow nature lovers in comfy chairs by the fireplace in the large common lounge. Pick a

colorfully decorated room or a bungalow that sleeps two to four with a kitchenette and small private garden. Some rooms and bungalows have fireplaces. There are stables on the premises, and the hotel can arrange horseback rides on the fringes of the park. **Pros:** ne plus ultra observation point over Doñana, rustic retreat. **Cons:** mosquitoes, gnats, sand fleas, heat in midsummer. ✉ *Ctra. del Rocío a Matalascañas (A483), Km 30* ☎ *959/442237* 🌐 *www.cortijomimbrales.com* *24 rooms, 2 suites, 5 bungalows* *In-room: no a/c. In-hotel: restaurant, bar, pool, public Wi-Fi, some pets allowed* *AE, DC, MC, V* *BP.*

MAZAGÓN

22 km (14 mi) northwest of Matalascañas.

There isn't much to see or do in this coastal town, but its parador makes a good base for touring La Rábida, Palos de la Frontera, and Moguer. Mazagón's sweeping sandy beach, sheltered by steep cliffs, is among the region's nicest.

ESSENTIALS

Visitor Information Mazagón (✉ *Av. de los Conquistadores s/n* ☎ *959/376300*).

WHERE TO STAY

$$$ **Parador de Mazagón.** This peaceful modern parador stands on a cliff surrounded by pine groves, overlooking a sandy beach 3 km (2 mi) southeast of Mazagón. Most of the spacious and comfortable rooms have balconies overlooking the garden, and the restaurant serves Andalusian dishes and local seafood specialties, such as stuffed baby squid and hake medallions. **Pros:** good base for bird-watching, views, and biking through the wetlands. **Cons:** mediocre dining, functional but drab rooms. ✉ *Playa de Mazagón* ☎ *959/536300* 🌐 *www.parador.es* *63 rooms* *In-room: Wi-Fi. In-hotel: restaurant, bar, tennis courts, pools, bicycles, parking (no fee)* 💳 *AE, DC, MC, V.*

LA RÁBIDA

8 km (5 mi) northwest of Mazagón.

ESSENTIALS

Visitor Information La Rábida (✉ *Paraje de la Rábida s/n* ☎ *959/531137*).

The monastery of **Santa María de La Rábida** is nicknamed "the birthplace of America": in 1485 Columbus came from Portugal with his son Diego to stay in this Mudejar-style Franciscan monastery, and here he discussed his theories with friars Antonio de Marchena and Juan Pérez, who interceded on his behalf with Queen Isabella. The early-15th-century church holds a much-venerated 14th-century statue of the **Virgen de los Milagros** (Virgin of Miracles). The **frescoes** in the gatehouse were painted by Daniel Vázquez Díaz in 1930. ✉ *Camino del Monasterio, Ctra. de Huelva21070* ☎ *959/350411* *€3.50 with audio guide, €3 without* ⏲ *Tues.–Sun. 10–1 and 4–7.*

Two kilometers (1 mi) from the monastery, on the seashore, is the **Muelle de las Carabelas** (Caravels' Wharf), a reproduction of a 15th-century port. The star exhibits here are the full-size models of Columbus's flotilla, the *Niña, Pinta,* and *Santa María,* built using the same techniques as in Columbus's day. You can go aboard each and learn more about the discovery of the New World in the adjoining museum. ✉ *Paraje de la Rábida* ☎ *959/530597 or 959/530312* *€3.50* ⏲ *Tues.–Sun. 9–7.*

PALOS DE LA FRONTERA

4 km (2½ mi) northwest of La Rábida, 12 km (7 mi) northeast of Mazagón.

On August 2, 1492, the *Niña,* the *Pinta,* and the *Santa María* set sail from Palos de la Frontera. At the door of the church of **San Jorge** (1473), the royal letter ordering the levy of the ships' crew and equipment was read aloud, and the voyagers took their water supplies from the fountain known as La Fontanilla (fountain) at the town's entrance.

RIOTINTO

74 km (46 mi) northeast of Huelva.

Heading north from Palos and Huelva on the N435, you'll reach the turnoff to Minas de Riotinto, the mining town near the source of the

Riotinto (literally, "Red River"). The waters are the color of blood because of the minerals leached from the surrounding mountains; this area has some of the richest copper deposits in the world, as well as gold and silver. In 1873 the mines were taken over by the British Rio Tinto Company Ltd., which started to dig an open-pit mine and build a 64-km (40-mi) railway to the port of Huelva to transport mineral ore. The British left in 1954, but mining activity continues today, albeit on a smaller scale.

Riotinto's landscape, scarred by centuries of intensive mining, can be viewed as part of a **tour** conducted by the Fundación Riotinto. The tour's first stop, the **Museo Minero** (Museum of Mining), has archaeological finds and a collection of historical steam engines and rail coaches. Next comes the **Corta Atalaya,** one of the largest open-pit mines in the world (4,000 feet across and 1,100 feet deep), and **Bellavista,** the elegant English quarter where the British mine managers lived. The tour ends with an optional ride on the **Tren Minero** (Miners' Train), which follows the course of the Riotinto along more than 12 restored km (7.4 mi) of the old mining railway. Opt for the full tour as described (offered the first Sunday of each month, October–May), or just visit individual sights. *959/590025 Fundación Riotinto www.parquemineroderiotinto.com Full tour €17 Museum daily 10:30–3 and 4–8. Miners' Train mid-Apr.–mid-May and mid-Sept.–mid-Oct., weekends at 5 PM; mid-May–mid-July and mid-Oct.–mid-Apr., weekends at 4 PM; mid-July–mid-Sept., daily at 1:30 PM.*

ARACENA

105 km (65 mi) northeast of Huelva, 100 km (62 mi) northwest of Seville.

Stretching north of the Riotinto mines is the 460,000-acre Sierra de Aracena nature park, an expanse of hills cloaked in cork and holm oak. This region is known for its cured Ibérico hams, which come from the prized free-ranging Iberian pigs that gorge on acorns in the autumn months before slaughter; the hams are buried in salt and then hung in cellars to dry-cure for at least two years. The best Ibérico hams have traditionally come from the village of **Jabugo.**

ESSENTIALS

Visitor Information Aracena (*Pl. de San Pedro s/n 959/128825*).

The capital of the region is Aracena, whose main attraction is the spectacular cave known as the **Gruta de las Maravillas** (Cave of Marvels). Its 12 caverns contain long corridors, stalactites and stalagmites arranged in wonderful patterns, as well as stunning underground lagoons. *Pl. Pozo de Nieves, Pozo de Nieves 959/128355 €9 Guided tours, if sufficient numbers, weekdays hourly 10:30–3 and 4–6; weekends hourly 10:30–1:30 and 3–6.*

WHERE TO EAT AND STAY

$–$$ SPANISH **Casas.** There's not much wall space left in the intimate beamed dining room of this typical Sierra Morena restaurant: plates, pots, pans, mirrors, and religious pictures cover every inch. Specializing in the region's famous ham and pork, the honest, home-style cooking is at its best with dishes prepared according to what is in season, including snails. The owner is an expert on sierra cuisine, but vegetarians may go hungry as there is little that is not meat-oriented. ✉*Calle Colmenetas 41* ☎*959/128044* ▭*MC, V* ⏲*No dinner.*

$–$$$ Fodor's Choice ★ **Finca Buenvino.** This lovely country house inn, nestled in 150 acres of woods, is run by a charming British couple, Sam and Jeannie Chesterton. The room price includes a big breakfast; dinner with tapas is available for a moderate extra sum. Jeannie also conducts Spanish cookery and tapas courses for groups of up to six people. Three woodland self-catering cottages are available, each with its own pool. The house is 6 km (4 mi) from Aracena. Note that there are price reductions for longer stays. **Pros:** intimate and personal, friendly hosts. **Cons:** somewhat removed from village life. ✉*N433, Km 95, Los Marines* ☎*959/124034* 🌐*www.fincabuenvino.com* *5 rooms, 3 cottages* *In-room: no a/c, no phone, kitchen (some), no TV, Wi-Fi. In-hotel: restaurant, bar, pools* ▭*MC, V* ⏲*Closed mid-July–mid-Sept.* *MAP.*

$$ ★ **Finca de la Silladilla.** In a wild Iberian pig–infested oak forest, this ranch offers a chance to see Spain's most prized products priming themselves for your palate. The rooms and small stone houses are impeccably decorated in heavy slabs of beautifully finished wood, and the bathrooms have unusual ceramic-and-copper washbasins. Communal areas combine warm tones with whites, ochers, and terra-cottas. The staff can organize tours of the Sierra de Aracena, equestrian outings, and visits to nearby Jabugo, famed for its *jamón ibérico de bellota* (acorn-fed Ibérico ham). **Pros:** rustic chic, semiwild Ibérico pig sightings. **Cons:** far from nearest village, no restaurant. ✉*Ctra. Los Romeros, Los Romeros, Jabugo* ☎*959/501350* 🖷*959/501184* *2 rooms, 2 suites, 3 houses for 4, 1 house for 6* *In-room: kitchen. In-hotel: pool, no elevator, some pets allowed* ▭*AE, DC, MC, V* *BP.*

THE LAND OF SHERRY: CÁDIZ PROVINCE AND JEREZ DE LA FRONTERA

A trip through Cádiz is a trip back in time. Winding roads take you through scenes ranging from flat and barren plains to seemingly endless vineyards, and the rolling countryside is carpeted with blindingly white soil known as *albariza*—unique to this area and the secret to the grapes used in sherry. Throughout the province, *los pueblos blancos* (the white villages) provide striking contrasts with the terrain, especially at Arcos de la Frontera, where the village sits dramatically on a crag overlooking the gorge of the Guadalete River. In Jerez de La Frontera, you can savor the town's internationally known sherry or delight in the skills and forms of purebred Carthusian horses. Finally, in the city of Cádiz, absorb about 3,000 years of history in what is generally considered the oldest continuously inhabited city in the Western world.

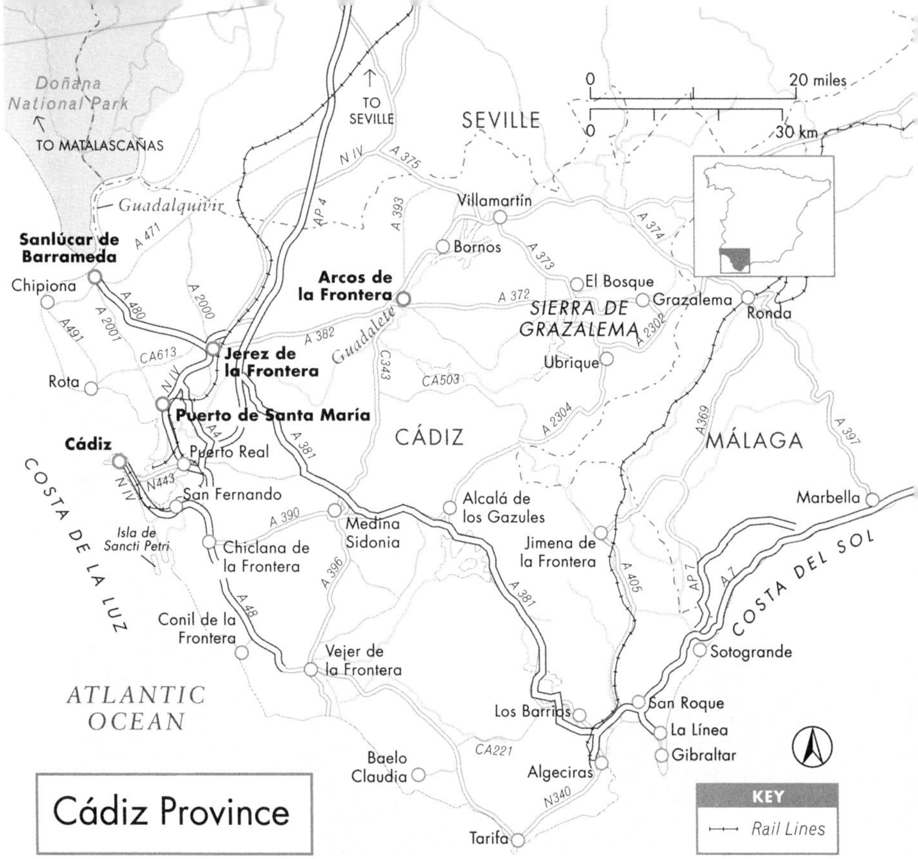

JEREZ DE LA FRONTERA

★ *97 km (60 mi) south of Seville.*

Jerez, world headquarters for sherry, is surrounded by vineyards of chalky soil, whose Palomino grapes have funded a host of churches and noble mansions. Names such as González Byass, Domecq, Harvey, and Sandeman are inextricably linked with Jerez. The word "sherry," first used in Great Britain in 1608, is an English corruption of the town's old Moorish name, Xeres. Both sherry and horses are the domain of Jerez's Anglo-Spanish aristocracy, whose Catholic ancestors came here from England centuries ago. At any given time, more than half a million barrels of sherry are maturing in Jerez's vast aboveground cellars.

ESSENTIALS

Bus Station Jerez de la Frontera (✉ *Calle de la Cartuja* ☎ *956/345207*).

Taxi Contacts Tele Taxi (✉ *Jerez de la Frontera* ☎ *956/344860*).

Train Station Jerez de la Frontera (✉ *Pl. de la Estación s/n, off Calle Diego Fernández Herrera* ☎ *956/342319*).

Visitor Information Jerez de la Frontera (✉ *Calle Larga 39* ☎ *956/350129* 🌐 *www.turismojerez.com*).

EXPLORING

The 12th-century **Alcázar** was once the residence of the caliph of Seville, and its small, octagonal **mosque** and **baths** were built for the Moorish governor's private use. The baths have three sections: the *sala fria* (cold room), the larger *sala templada* (warm room), and the *sala caliente* (hot room) for steam baths. In the midst of it all is the 17th-century **Palacio de Villavicencio**, built on the site of the original Moorish palace. A camera obscura, a lens-and-mirrors device that projects the outdoors onto a large indoor screen, offers a 360-degree view of Jerez. ✉*Alameda Vieja* ☎*956/350129* *€3, €5.40 including camera obscura* ⏲*Mid-Sept.–Apr., daily 10–6; May–mid-Sept., daily 10–8.*

Across from the Alcázar and around the corner from the González Byass winery, the **cathedral** (✉*Pl. de la Encarnación* ⏲*Weekdays 11–1 and 6–8, Sat. 11–2 and 6–8, Sun. 11–2*) has an octagonal cupola and a separate bell tower, as well as Zurbarán's canvas *La Virgen Niña* (the Virgin as a young girl).

On the **Plaza de la Asunción,** one of Jerez's most intimate squares, you can find the Mudejar church of **San Dionisio** and the ornate **cabildo municipal** (city hall), whose lovely plateresque facade dates from 1575.

Diving into the maze of streets that form the scruffy San Mateo neighborhood east of the town center, you come to the **Museo Arqueológico,** one of Andalusia's best archaeological museums. The collection is strongest on the pre-Roman period and the star item, found near Jerez, is a Greek helmet dating from the 7th century BC. ✉*Pl. del Mercado s/n* ☎*956/341350* *€3.50* ⏲*Sept.–mid-June, Tues.–Fri. 10–2 and 4–7, Sat. 10–2:30; mid-June–Aug., Tues.–Sun. 10–2:30.*

NEED A BREAK?

Bar Juanito (✉*Pescadería Vieja 8 and 10* ☎*956/334838*) has a flowery patio and is a past winner of the national Best Tapas Bar in Spain award. Jolly Faustino Rodríguez and his family serve 50 different tapas and larger-portion *raciones*.

Just west of the town center, the **Parque Zoológico (Zoo Botánico)** is set in lush botanical gardens where you can usually spy up to 33 storks' nests. Primarily a place for the rehabilitation of injured or endangered animals native to Spain, the zoo also houses white tigers, elephants, and a giant red panda. ✉*C. Taxdirt* ☎*956/153164* 🌐*www.zoobotanicojerez.com* *€9* ⏲*June–Sept, Tues.–Sun. 10–8, Oct.–May, Tues.–Sun. 10–6.*

Fodor's Choice ★

The **Real Escuela Andaluza del Arte Ecuestre** *(Royal Andalusian School of Equestrian Art)* operates on the grounds of the Recreo de las Cadenas, a 19th-century palace. This prestigious school was masterminded by Alvaro Domecq in the 1970s, and every Thursday (and at various other times throughout the year) the Cartujana horses—a cross between the native Andalusian workhorse and the Arabian—and skilled riders in 18th-century riding costume demonstrate intricate dressage techniques and jumping in the spectacular show "Cómo Bailan los Caballos Andaluces" (roughly, "The Dancing Horses of Andalusia"). Reservations are essential. Admission price depends on how close to the arena you sit; the first two rows are the priciest. The rest of the week, you can visit the stables and tack room, watch the horses being schooled, and

A TOAST TO JEREZ: WINERY TOURS

On a **bodega** (winery) visit, you'll learn about the *solera* method of blending old wine with new, and the importance of the *flor* (yeast that forms on the wine as it ages) in determining the kind of sherry.

Most bodegas welcome visitors, but it's advisable to phone ahead for an appointment, if only to make sure you join a group that speaks your language. Cellars usually charge an admission fee of €10 (€15 with wine and tapas tasting). Tours, about an hour, go through the aging cellars, with their endless rows of casks. (You won't see the actual fermenting and bottling, which take place in more modern, less romantic plants outside town.) Finally, you'll be invited to sample generous amounts of pale, dry *fino*; nutty *amontillado*; or rich, deep *oloroso*, and, of course, to purchase a few robustly priced bottles in the winery shop.

If you have time for only one bodega, tour the **González Byass** (✉ *Calle Manuel María González* ☎ *956/357000* 🌐 *www.gonzalezbyass.com*), home of the famous Tío Pepe. This tour is well organized and includes La Concha, an open-air aging cellar designed by Gustave Eiffel. Jerez's oldest bodega is **Domecq** (✉ *Calle San Ildefonso 3* ☎ *956/151500* 🌐 *www.bodegasfundadorpedrodomecq.com*), founded in 1730. Aside from sherry, Domecq makes the world's best-selling brandy, Fundador. **Harveys** (✉ *Calle Pintor Muñoz Cebrián s/n* ☎ *956/319650* 🌐 *www.harveys-usa.com*) is the source of Harveys Bristol Cream. **Sandeman** (✉ *Calle Pizarro 10* ☎ *956/301100* 🌐 *www.sandeman.com*) is known for its man-in-a-cape logo.

see rehearsals. ✉ *Av. Duque de Abrantes s/n* ☎ *956/319635* 🌐 *www.realescuela.org* 🎫 *€18–€25, €10 for rehearsals* 🕓 *Shows Mar.–Dec. 14, Tues. and Thurs. at noon (also Fri. at noon in Aug.); Dec. 15–Feb., Thurs. at noon. Check locally for additional late-Apr. Feria de Caballo exhibitions, museum visits, and the rehearsal schedule.*

Jerez's **bullring** is on Calle Circo, northeast of the city center. Tickets are sold at the official ticket office on Calle Porvera, though only about five bullfights are held each year, in May and October. Six blocks from the bullring is the **Museo Taurino,** a bullfighting museum where admission includes a drink. ✉ *Calle Pozo del Olivar 6* ☎ *956/319000* 🎫 *€5* 🕓 *Daily 9.30–2.*

WHERE TO EAT AND STAY

$–$$$ SPANISH ✕ **El Bosque.** In a modern villa with contemporary paintings of bullfighting themes, this is one of the most stylish dining spots in town. The smaller of the two dining rooms has picture windows overlooking a park, and the food is contemporary Spanish. *Sopa de galeras* (shrimp soup) is a rich appetizer; follow up with *confit de pato de laguna* (leg of wild duck) or *perdiz estofado con castañas* (partridge stewed with chestnuts). Desserts are less exciting and include the ubiquitous flan (caramel custard) which is, notwithstanding, creamy and delicious. ✉ *Av. Alcalde*

Alvaro Domecq 26 ☎ *956/307030* ▭ *AE, DC, MC, V* ⊙ *Closed Mon. No dinner Aug.*

$–$$$ SPANISH ✕ **Gaitán.** Within walking distance of the riding school, this restaurant has brick arches and white walls decorated with colorful ceramic plates and photos of famous guests. It's crowded with businesspeople at lunchtime. The menu is Andalusian, with a few Basque dishes thrown in. *Setas* (seasonal wild mushrooms) make a delicious starter; follow with *cordero asado* (roast lamb) in a sauce of honey and locally produced brandy. Finish with a slice of the delicious almond tart specialty. ✉ *Calle Gaitán 3* ☎ *956/168021* ▭ *AE, DC, MC, V* ⊙ *No dinner Sun.*

SPRING IN JEREZ

May and September are the most exciting times to visit Jerez, as spectacular fiestas transform the town. For the Feria del Caballo (Horse Fair), in early May, carriages and riders fill the streets, and purebreds from the School of Equestrian Art compete in races and dressage displays. September brings the Fiesta de Otoño (Autumn Festival), when the first of the grape harvest is blessed on the steps of the cathedral.

$ VEGETARIAN ★ ✕ **La Alternativa.** This may not be the most atmospheric place in town (bright lights and steel chairs), but the food makes a welcome change from the carnivorous norm in these parts, and the location in the historic center is convenient. Starters include dishes like *polenta gratinada con rúcula y parmesano* (polenta with Parmesan and arugula), and you can follow with such international choices as *moussaka con ensalada verde y pan de ajo* (vegetable moussaka with a green salad and garlic bread). The restaurant is not too pious to offer calorific desserts like traditional English trifle and a banana and toffee cake. ✉ *San Pablo 7* ☎ *956/343961* ▭ *MC, V.*

$$–$$$ SPANISH ✕ **La Carboná.** This cavernous restaurant in a former bodega has a rustic atmosphere with arches, original beams, and a fireplace for winter nights. In summer you can often enjoy live music, and sometimes flamenco, while you dine. The chef has worked at several top restaurants, and his menu provides an innovative twist to classic dishes, such as *pechuguitas de cordorniz rellenas de pétalos de rosa y foié* (quail stuffed with rose petals and liver pâté) and, for dessert, cinnamon cake with licorice ice cream. There's an excellent tapas menu and wine list. ✉ *C. San Francisco de Paula 2* ☎ *956/347475* ▭ *AE, DC, MC, V* ⊙ *Closed Tues.*

$–$$ SPANISH ★ ✕ **La Mesa Redonda.** Owner José Antonio Valdespino spent years researching the classic recipes once served in aristocratic Jerez homes, and now his son, José, presents them in this small, friendly restaurant off Avenida Alcalde Alvaro Domecq, around the corner from the Hotel Avenida Jerez. Don't be put off by the bland exterior—within, the eight tables are surrounded by watercolors and shelves lined with cookbooks; the round table at the end of the room gave the restaurant its name. The menu typically includes wild game dishes like boar and rabbit. ✉ *Calle Manuel de la Quintana 3* ☎ *956/340069* ▭ *AE, DC, MC, V* ⊙ *Closed Sun. and mid-July–mid-Aug.*

$–$$ SEAFOOD **Venta Antonio.** Crowds come to this roadside inn for superb, fresh seafood cooked in top-quality olive oil. You enter through the busy bar, where lobsters await their fate in a tank. Try the specialties of the Bay of Cádiz, such as *sopa de mariscos* (shellfish soup) followed by succulent *bogavantes de Sanlúcar* (local lobster). Be prepared for large, noisy Spanish families dining here on the weekends, particularly during the winter months. *Ctra. de Jerez–Sanlúcar, Km 5* *956/140535* *AE, DC, MC, V* *No dinner Sun.*

$ **El Ancla.** With yellow-and-white paint, wrought-iron balconies, and wooden shutters, El Ancla's architecture is classic Jerez. The hotel doubles as a popular bar, which is good for atmosphere—and it's where breakfast is served—but it also means you may need ear plugs on Saturday nights. Rooms are plainly furnished but comfortable, and the bathrooms are modern, if on the small side. The underground parking lot across the street is a bonus. **Pros:** attractive traditional architecture, budget friendly. **Cons:** noisy nocturnal activities, rooms small and drab. *Pl. del Mamelón* *956/321297* *956/325005* *20 rooms* *In-room: Wi-Fi. In-hotel: bar, parking (fee)* *MC, V.*

$$$–$$$$ Fodor's Choice ★ **Hotel Palacio Garvey.** Dating from 1850, this luxurious hotel was the home of the prestigious local Garvey family. The original neoclassical architecture and decor has been exquisitely restored, and parts of the ancient city wall are visible from the gardens. Tastefully minimalist rooms have shiny parquet floors and simple Zen-style furniture. The artwork throughout the hotel is edgy and modern while the restaurant's red lacquered chairs provide a suitably innovative impact to match the modern Mediterranean cuisine. **Pros:** well located near the main center, fashionable and contemporary feel. **Cons:** small pool. *Calle Tornería 24* *956/326700* *www.sferahoteles.net* *16 rooms* *In-room: DVD, Internet, Wi-Fi. In-hotel: restaurant, room service, pool laundry service, Wi-Fi, parking (no fee)* *AE, D, DC, MC, V.* *BP.*

¢ **Hotel San Andrés.** This charming low-rise hotel has an inviting traditional entrance patio and rooms set around a courtyard filled with plants, local tile work, and arches. The rooms are modestly decorated with pine furniture set against dazzling white walls. There is also a less expensive *hostal* within the same building, with similar quality rooms but shared bathrooms. **Pros:** charming owners, easy on-street parking. **Cons:** small rooms, no frills. *Calle Morenos 12* *956/341983* *www.hotelsanandres.es* *38 hotel, 18 hostal* *In-room: no TV (hostal only)* *MC, V.*

$$$–$$$$ **Hotel Villa Jerez.** This hacienda-style, tastefully furnished hotel offers luxury on the outskirts of town. The gardens surround a traditional courtyard and are lushly landscaped with palm trees and a dazzle of colorful plants and flowers. Facilities include an elegant restaurant with terrace, a saltwater swimming pool, and a gym. The bedrooms are individually decorated, plush, and well equipped, and the staff is friendly and efficient. **Pros:** elegant surroundings, noble architecture. **Cons:** outside of town, small pool. *Av. de la Cruz Roja 7* *956/153100* *www.villajerez.com* *14 rooms, 4 suites* *In-room: Wi-Fi. In-hotel: restaurant, bar, pool* *AE, DC, MC, V.*

SPORTS

Formula One Grand Prix races—including the Spanish motorcycle Gran Prix on the first weekend in May—are held at Jerez's racetrack, the **Circuito Permanente de Velocidad** (✉*Ctra. Arcos, Km 10* ☎*956/151100* 🌐*www.circuitodejerez.com*).

SHOPPING

Calle Corredera and **Calle Bodegas** are the places to go if you want to browse for wicker and ceramics. **Duarte** (✉*Calle Lancería 15* ☎*956/342751*) is the best-known saddle shop in town. It sends its beautifully wrought leather all over the world, including to the British royal family.

ARCOS DE LA FRONTERA

★ *31 km (19 mi) east of Jerez.*

Its narrow and steep cobblestone streets, whitewashed houses, and finely crafted wrought-iron window grilles make Arcos the quintessential Andalusian *pueblo blanco* (white village). Make your way to the main square, the Plaza de España, the highest point in the village; one side of the square is open, and a balcony at the edge of the cliff offers views of the Guadalete Valley. On the opposite end is the church of **Santa María de la Asunción**, a fascinating blend of architectural styles: Romanesque, Gothic, and Mudejar, with a plateresque doorway, a Renaissance retablo, and a 17th-century baroque choir. The *ayuntamiento* (town hall) stands at the foot of the old castle walls on the northern side of the square; across from here is the Casa del Corregidor, onetime residence of the governor and now a parador. Arcos is the most western of the 19 pueblos blancos dotted around the Sierra de Cádiz.

ESSENTIALS

Visitor Information **Arcos de la Frontera** (✉*Pl. del Cabildo s/n* ☎*956/702264*).

WHERE TO EAT AND STAY

$$–$$$ SPANISH ★ **El Convento.** With tables set around a graceful Andalusian patio in a former 17th-century palace, this rustic-style restaurant (owned by but separate from the hotel on Calle Maldonado) is known for its fine regional cooking. The *sopa de tagarninas* (wild asparagus soup) is one of the town treasures, as are the *garbanzos con tomillo* (chickpeas with thyme) and the *abajado* (wild rabbit or lamb stew). Among the traditional desserts, the *tocino del cielo* (a meringue-topped cake) is particularly recommended. Service is fast and efficient, and some English is spoken. ✉*Calle Marqués de Torresoto 7* ☎*956/703222* 💳*AE, DC, MC, V* ⊗*Closed Jan.*

$ Fodor's Choice ★ **El Convento.** Perched atop the cliff behind the town parador, this tiny hotel in a former 17th-century convent shares the same amazing view, though the rooms are much smaller—and cheaper—than their swish neighbor. Some rooms have private terraces, and all are furnished tastefully with period artwork and sculptures. In addition guests have the use of a large rooftop terrace on the edge of the cliff. **Pros:** location, intimacy. **Cons:** small spaces. ✉*Calle Maldonado 2* ☎*956/702333* *www.webdearcos.com/elconvento 11 rooms In-room: Wi-Fi. In-hotel: restaurant AE, DC, MC, V Closed Jan.*

$–$$ ★ **La Casa Grande.** Built in 1729, this extraordinary 18th-century mansion encircles a lushly vegetated central patio and is perched on the edge of the 400-foot cliff to which Arcos de la Frontera clings. Catalan owners Elena Posa and Ferran Grau have restored each room, and the artwork, the casually elegant design of the living quarters, and inventive bathrooms are all a delight. The breakfast terrace allows you to look down on falcons circling hundreds of feet above the riverbed below. The rooftop rooms El Palomar (The Pigeon Roost) and El Soberao (The Attic) are the best. **Pros:** attentive owners, impeccable aesthetics. **Cons:** inconvenient parking and, as a result, some baggage hauling; long climb to the top floor. *C. Maldonado 10 956/703930 www.lacasagrande.net 8 rooms In-room: Wi-Fi. In-hotel: no elevator AE, DC, MC, V BP.*

$$$ ★ **Parador Casa del Corregidor.** Expect a spectacular view from the terrace, since the parador clings to the cliff side, overlooking the rolling valley of the Guadalete River. Public rooms include a popular bar and restaurant that opens onto the terrace and an enclosed patio. Spacious guest rooms are furnished with dark Castilian furniture, *esparto* (reed) rugs, and abundant tiles. The best are rooms 15–18, which overlook the valley. At the restaurant, try a local dish such as *berenjenas arcenses* (spicy eggplant with ham and chorizo) or sample 10 regional specialties with the *menú degustacíon* (tasting menu). **Pros:** gorgeous views from certain rooms, elegant decor. **Cons:** blindingly bright, populous public rooms. *Pl. del Cabildo 956/700500 www.parador.es 24 rooms In-room: dial-up, Wi-Fi. In-hotel: restaurant, bar, public Internet AE, DC, MC, V.*

SANLÚCAR DE BARRAMEDA

24 km (15 mi) northwest of Jerez.

Columbus sailed from this harbor on his third voyage to the Americas, in 1498, and 20 years later Magellan began his circumnavigation of the globe from here. Today this fishing town has a crumbling charm and is best known for its *langostinos* (jumbo shrimp) and Manzanilla, an exceptionally dry sherry. The most popular restaurants are in the **Bajo de Guía** neighborhood, on the banks of the Guadalquivir. Here, too, is a visitor center for Doñana National Park.

Boat trips can take you up the river, stopping at various points in the park; the **Real Fernando**, with bar and café, does a four-hour cruise up the Guadalquivir to the Coto de Doñana. *Bajo de Guía, Sanlúcar de Barrameda 956/363813 www.visitasdonana.com €17 Cruises Apr., May, and Oct., daily at 10 AM and 4 PM; Nov.–Mar., daily at 10 AM; June–Sept., daily at 10 AM and 5 PM.*

WHERE TO EAT AND STAY

$–$$$ SEAFOOD **Casa Bigote.** Colorful and informal, this spot near the beach is known for its fried *acedias* (a type of small sole) and langostinos, which come from these very waters. The seafood paella is also catch-of-the-day fresh. To get here head down the Bajo de Guía; the restaurant is toward the end. Reservations are essential in summer as the place gets packed with holidaymakers and locals. ✉ *Bajo de Guía* ☎ *956/362696* ▭ *AE, DC, MC, V* ⊙ *Closed Sun. and Nov.*

$–$$ SEAFOOD **Mirador de Doñana.** This Bajo de Guía landmark overlooking the water serves delicious *chocos* (crayfish), shrimp, and the signature dish *mi barca mirador* (white fish in a tomato sauce). You can also find the delicious *langostinos de Sanlúcar* (local lobster) here, which is particularly recommended when washed down with a glass of locally produced *manzanilla* sherry. The dining area overlooks the large, busy tapas bar. ✉ *Bajo de Guía* ☎ *956/364205* ▭ *MC, V* ⊙ *Closed Jan.*

$ ★ **Los Helechos.** Named for the ferns *(los helechos)* that dominate the public spaces, this former private mansion has rooms set around two delightful courtyards, with traditional stone fountains and leafy plants and palms. The spacious rooms are painted in cool pastels and have cozy drapes and wooden floors. There is a lovely rooftop terrace that has the distinct advantage of being out of earshot but within stumbling distance of the Plaza del Cabildo. **Pros:** ideal location, top value. **Cons:** not easy to find, rooms spartan. ✉ *Pl. Madre de Dios 9* ☎ *956/361349* 🌐 *www.hotelloshelechos.com* *56 rooms* *In-room: Wi-Fi. In-hotel: restaurant, bar, parking (fee)* ▭ *AE, DC, MC, V.*

PUERTO DE SANTA MARÍA

12 km (7 mi) southwest of Jerez, 17 km (11 mi) north of Cádiz.

This attractive, if somewhat dilapidated, little fishing port on the northern shores of the Bay of Cádiz, with lovely beaches nearby, has white houses with peeling facades and vast green grilles covering the doors and windows. The town is dominated by the Terry and Osborne sherry and brandy bodegas. Columbus once lived in a house on the square that bears his name (Cristóbal Colón), and Washington Irving spent the autumn of 1828 at Calle Palacios 57. The marisco bars along the Ribera del Marisco (Seafood Way) are Puerto de Santa María's current claim to fame. Casa Luis, Romerijo, La Guachi, and Paco Ceballos are among the most popular, along with Er Beti, at Misericordia 7. The tourist office has a list of six tapas routes that take in 39 tapas bars.

ESSENTIALS

Visitor Information Puerto de Santa María (✉ *Calle Luna 22* ☎ *956/542413* 🌐 *www.elpuertosm.es*).

EXPLORING

The **Castillo de San Marcos** was built in the 13th century on the site of a mosque. Created by Alfonso X, it was later home to the Duke of Medinaceli. Among the guests were Christopher Columbus—who tried unsuccessfully to persuade the duke to finance his voyage west—and Juan de la Cosa, who, within these walls, drew up the first map ever to include the Americas. The red lettering on the walls is a 19th-century addition. ✉ *Pl. del Castillo* ☎ *965/851751* *€5.50, free Tues.* ⊙ *Tues.–Sat. 10–2.*

This stunning neo-Mudejar **Plaza de Toros** was built in 1880 thanks to a donation from the winemaker Thomas Osborne. It originally had seating for exactly 12,816 people, the population of Puerto at that time. ✉ *Los Moros* 🎫 *Free* ⊙ *Apr.–Oct., Thurs.–Tues. 11–1:30 and 6–7:30; Nov.–Mar., Thurs.–Tues. 11–1:30 and 5:30–7. Closed bullfight days plus 1 day before and after each bullfight.*

WHERE TO EAT AND STAY

$–$$$ SPANISH ✕ **El Faro del Puerto.** In a villa outside town, the "Lighthouse in the Port" is run by the same family that established the classic El Faro in Cádiz. Like its predecessor, it serves excellent fish, as well as delicacies such as veal rolls filled with foie gras in a sweet sherry sauce and several vegetarian options, including *canalones de puerros rellenos de calabaza con jugo de setas* (pasta with leeks and zucchini in an oyster mushroom sauce). Finish with the heavenly chocolate soufflé. ✉ *Ctra. Fuentebravia–Rota, Km 0.5* ☎ *956/858003 or 956/870952* ⊕ *www.elfarodelpuerto.com* ▭ *AE, DC, MC, V* ⊙ *No dinner Sun. Sept.–July.*

$–$$$ SEAFOOD ★ ✕ **Los Portales.** A Ribera del Marisco favorite, this elegant dining room has walls washed in dark ocher, glittering tile work, and tasteful original artwork. Come here hungry and select from one of the two delicious *menús gastronómicos.* Smaller appetites can join the locals at the popular bar and sample *ortiguillas* (fried sea anemones), a traditional favorite, plus more standard seafood, grilled or fried. ✉ *Calle Ribera del Río 13* ☎ *956/541812* ▭ *AE, DC, MC, V.*

$$$–$$$$ Fodor's Choice ★ **Monasterio San Miguel.** Dating from 1733, this monastery is a few blocks from the harbor. There's nothing spartan about the former cells; they're now plush air-conditioned rooms with all the trappings. The restaurant is in a large, vaulted hall (formerly the nuns' laundry), the baroque church is now a concert hall, and the cloister's gardens provide a peaceful refuge. Beam ceilings, polished marble floors, and huge brass lamps enhance the 18th-century feel. If you're traveling out of season, check the Web site for discounts. **Pros:** supremely elegant, efficient service. **Cons:** air-conditioning erratic, authoritarian hotel staff. ✉ *C. Virgen de los Milagros 27* ☎ *956/540440* ⊕ *www.jale.com* *139 rooms, 11 suites* *In-room: Wi-Fi. In-hotel: restaurant, bar, pool, public Internet, parking (fee)* ▭ *AE, DC, MC, V.*

CÁDIZ

★ *32 km (20 mi) southwest of Jerez, 149 km (93 mi) southwest of Seville.*

Surrounded by the Atlantic Ocean on three sides, Cádiz was founded as Gadir by Phoenician traders in 1100 BC and claims to be the oldest continuously inhabited city in the Western world. Hannibal lived in Cádiz for a time, Julius Caesar first held public office here, and Columbus set out from here on his second voyage, after which the city became the home base of the Spanish fleet. In the 18th century, when the Guadalquivir silted up, Cádiz monopolized New World trade and became the wealthiest port in Western Europe. Most of its buildings—including the cathedral, built in part with gold and silver from the New World—date from this period. The old city is African in appearance and immensely intriguing—a cluster of narrow streets opening onto charming small squares. The golden cupola of the cathedral looms above low white houses, and the whole place has a slightly dilapidated air. Spaniards flock here in February to revel in the carnival celebrations, but in general it's not very touristy.

GETTING HERE AND AROUND

Cadíz is easy to get to and navigate by car; the old city is easily explored by foot.

The city has two bus stations: Comes, which serves most destinations in Andalusia, and Los Amarillos, which serves Jerez, Seville, Córdoba, Puerto de Santa María, Sanlúcar de Barrameda, and Chipiona.

Every day, a dozen or more local trains connect Cádiz with Seville, Puerto de Santa María, and Jerez, though there are no trains to Doñana National Park, Sanlúcar de Barrameda, or Arcos de la Frontera, or between Cádiz and the Costa del Sol.

ESSENTIALS

Bus Stations **Cádiz–Estación de Autobuses Comes** (☒ *Pl. de la Hispanidad 1* ☎ *956/342174*).

Taxi Contacts **Unitaxi** (☒ *Cádiz* ☎ *956/212121*).

Train Station **Cádiz** (☒ *Pl. de Sevilla s/n* ☎ *956/251010*).

Visitor Information **Regional Tourist Office** (☒ *Av. Ramón de Carranza s/n* ☎ *956/258646*). **Provincial Tourist Office** (☒ *Pl. de San Antonio 3, 2nd fl.* ☎ *956/807061*). **Local Tourist Office** (☒ *Pl. San Juan de Dios 11* ☎ *956/241001* ⊕ *www.cadizturismo.com*)

EXPLORING

Begin your explorations in the Plaza de Mina, a large, leafy square with palm trees and plenty of benches. The tourist office is in the northwestern corner.

On the east side of the Plaza de Mina, is the **Museo de Cádiz** (Provincial Museum). Notable pieces include works by Murillo and Alonso Cano as well as the *Four Evangelists* and set of saints by Zurbarán, which have much in common with his masterpieces at Guadalupe, in Extremadura. The archaeological section contains Phoenician sarcophagi from the time of this ancient city's birth. ☒ *Pl. de Mina* ☎ *956/212281* €2 *Tues. 2:30–8, Wed.–Sat. 9–8, Sun. 9–2.*

A few blocks east of the Plaza de Mina, next door to the Iglesia del Rosario, is the **Oratorio de la Santa Cueva,** an oval 18th-century chapel with three frescoes by Goya. ☒ *C. Rosario 10* ☎ *956/222262* €3 *Tues.–Fri. 10–1 and 4:30–7:30, weekends 10–1.*

Farther up Calle San José from the Plaza de la Mina is the **Oratorio de San Felipe Neri.** Spain's first liberal constitution was declared at this church in 1812, and the Cortes (Parliament) of Cádiz met here when the rest of Spain was subjected to the rule of Napoléon's brother, Joseph Bonaparte (more popularly known as Pepe Botella, for his love of the bottle). On the main altar is an *Immaculate Conception* by Murillo, the great Sevillian artist who in 1682 fell to his death from a scaffold while working on his *Mystic Marriage of St. Catherine* in Cádiz's Chapel of Santa Catalina. ✉*Calle Santa Inés 38* ☎*956/211612* 🎫*€3* ⏲*Mon.–Sat. 10–1:30.*

Next door to the Oratorio de San Felipe Neri, the small but pleasant **Museo de las Cortes** has a 19th-century mural depicting the establishment of the Constitution of 1812. Its real showpiece, however, is a 1779 ivory-and-mahogany model of Cádiz, with all of the city's streets and buildings in minute detail, looking much as they do now. ✉*Santa Inés 9* ☎*956/221788* 🎫*Free* ⏲*Oct.–May, Tues.–Fri. 9–1 and 4–7, weekends 9–1; June–Sept., Tues.–Fri. 9–1 and 5–8, weekends 9–1.*

Four blocks west of Santa Inés is the Plaza Manuel de Falla, overlooked by an amazing neo-Mudejar redbrick building, the **Gran Teatro Manuel de Falla.** The classic interior is impressive as well; try to attend a performance. ✉*Pl. Manuel de Falla* ☎*956/220828.*

Fodor's Choice ★ Backtrack along Calle Sacramento toward the city center to get to **Torre Tavira.** At 150 feet, this tower, attached to an 18th-century palace that's now a conservatory of music, is the highest point in the old city. More than a hundred such watchtowers were used by Cádiz ship owners to spot their arriving fleets. A camera obscura gives a good overview of the city and its monuments; the last show is a half hour before closing time. ✉*Calle Marqués del Real Tesoro 10* ☎*956/212910* 🎫*€4* ⏲*Mid-June–mid-Sept., daily 10–8; mid-Sept.–mid-June, daily 10–6.*

Five blocks southeast of the Torre Tavira are the gold dome and baroque facade of Cádiz's **cathedral,** begun in 1722, when the city was at the height of its power. The Cádiz-born composer Manuel de Falla, who died in 1946 at the age of 70, is buried in the **crypt.** The cathedral **museum,** on Calle Acero, displays gold, silver, and jewels from the New World, as well as Enrique de Arfe's processional cross, which is carried in the annual Corpus Christi parades. The cathedral is known as the New Cathedral because it supplanted the original 13th-century structure next door, which was destroyed by the British in 1592, rebuilt, and renamed the church of **Santa Cruz** when the New Cathedral came along. The entrance price includes the crypt, museum, and church of Santa Cruz. ✉*Pl. Catedral* ☎*956/259812* 🎫*€5* ⏲*Mass Sun. at noon; museum Tues.–Fri. 10–2 and 4:30–7:30, Sat. 10–1.*

Next door to the church of Santa Cruz are the remains of a 1st-century BC **Roman theater** (✉*Campo del Sur s/n, Barrio del Pópulo* 🎫*Free* ⏲*Daily 10–2*); it's still under excavation.

The impressive **ayuntamiento** *(city hall)* (✉*Pl. de San Juan de Dios s/n*) overlooks the Plaza San Juan de Diós, one of Cádiz's liveliest hubs. The building is attractively illuminated at night. The **Plaza San Francisco,** near the *ayuntamiento*, is a pretty square surrounded by white-and-yellow houses and filled with orange trees and elegant street lamps. It's especially lively during the evening *paseo* (promenade).

WHERE TO EAT AND STAY

$–$$$ SPANISH Fodor's Choice ★ **Casa Manteca.** Cádiz's most quintessentially Andalusian tavern is just down the street from El Faro restaurant and a little deeper into the La Viña barrio (named for the vineyard that once grew here). *Chacina* (Iberian ham or sausage) served on waxed paper and Manzanilla (sherry from Sanlúcar de Barrameda) are standard fare at this low wooden counter that has served bullfighters and flamenco singers, as well as dignitaries from around the world, since 1953. The walls are covered with colorful posters and other memorabilia from the annual carnival, flamenco shows, and ferias. ✉ *Corralón de los Carros 66* ☎ *956/213603* 💳 *AE, DC, MC, V* ⊗ *Closed Mon. No lunch Sun.*

$$–$$$$ SPANISH Fodor'sChoice ★ ✕ **El Faro.** This famous fishing-quarter restaurant near Playa de la Caleta is deservedly known as the best in the province. From the outside, it's one of many low-rise, white houses with bright-blue flowerpots; inside it's warm and inviting, with half-tile walls, glass lanterns, oil paintings, and photos of old Cádiz. Fish dishes dominate the menu, but alternatives include *cebón al queso de cabrales* (venison in blue-cheese sauce). If you don't want to go for the full splurge (either gastronomically or financially), there's an excellent tapas bar as well. ✉ *Calle San Felix 15* ☎ *956/211068* 💳 *AE, DC, MC, V.*

$–$$$ SPANISH ✕ **El Ventorrillo del Chato.** Standing on its own on the sandy isthmus connecting Cádiz to the mainland, this former inn was founded in 1780 by a man ironically nicknamed "El Chato" (small-nosed) for his prominent proboscis. Run by a scion of El Faro's Gonzalo Córdoba, the restaurant serves tasty regional specialties in charming Andalusian surroundings. Seafood is a favorite, but meat, stews, and rice dishes are also well represented on the menu, and the wine list is very good. ✉ *Vía Augusta Julia s/n* ☎ *956/250025* 💳 *AE, DC, MC, V* ⊗ *Closed Sun.*

$ ★ **Bahía.** Just off the bustling Plaza de San Juan de Dios, on a tree-lined pedestrian street, this is a budget winner. Rooms are modern and bright with firm beds, and most have small balconies. The lack of a dining room is compensated for by the variety and proximity of bars and restaurants. **Pros:** good value, pivotal location. **Cons:** busy street corner on weekends, rooms over Calle Plocia can be noisy. ✉ *Calle Plocia 5* ☎ *956/259061* 📠 *956/254208* *21 rooms* 💳 *MC, V.*

$$$ **Parador de Cádiz.** Cádiz's modern Parador Atlántico has a privileged position on the headland overlooking the bay and is the only hotel in its class in the old part of Cádiz. The spacious public rooms have marble floors, and tables and chairs surround a fountain on the small patio. The cheerful, bright-green bar, decorated with ceramic tiles and bullfighting posters, is a popular meeting place for Cádiz society. Most rooms have small balconies facing the sea. The pool also has ocean views and is surrounded by a lush green lawn. **Pros:** panoramic and central location, bright and cheerful. **Cons:** large, characterless modern building. ✉ *Av. Duque de Nájera 9* ☎ *956/226905* 🌐 *www.parador.es* *143 rooms, 6 suites* *In-room: dial-up, Wi-Fi. In-hotel: restaurant, bar, pool, gym, parking (no fee), some pets allowed* 💳 *AE, DC, MC, V* *BP.*

CÓRDOBA

166 km (103 mi) northwest of Granada, 407 km (250 mi) southwest of Madrid, 239 km (143 mi) northeast of Cádiz, 143 km (86 mi) northeast of Seville.

Once a medieval city famed for the peaceful and prosperous coexistence of its three religious cultures—Islamic, Jewish, and Christian—Córdoba is a perfect analogue for the cultural history of the Iberian Peninsula. Strategically located on the north bank of the Guadalquivir River, Córdoba was the Roman and Moorish capital of Spain, and its old quarter, clustered around its famous mosque (Mezquita), remains one of the country's grandest and yet most intimate examples of its Moorish heritage.

The Romans invaded in 206 BC, later making it the capital of Rome's section of Spain. Nearly 800 years later, the Visigoth king Leovigildus took control. The tribe was soon supplanted by the Moors, whose emirs and caliphs held court here from the 8th century to the early 11th century. At that point Córdoba was one of the greatest centers of art, culture, and learning in the Western world; one of its libraries had a staggering 400,000 volumes. Moors, Christians, and Jews lived together in harmony within Córdoba's walls. In that era, it was considered second in importance only to Constantinople. However, in 1009 Prince Muhammad II and Omeyan led a rebellion that broke up the Caliphate, leading to power flowing to separate Moorish kingdoms.

Córdoba remained in Moorish hands until it was conquered by King Ferdinand in 1236 and repopulated with people from the north of Spain. Later, the Catholic Monarchs used the city as a base from which to plan the conquest of Granada. In Columbus's time, the Guadalquivir was navigable as far upstream as Córdoba, and great galleons sailed its waters. Today, the river's muddy water and marshy banks evoke little of Córdoba's glorious past, but an old Arab waterfall and the city's bridge—of Roman origin, though much restored by the Arabs and successive generations—recall a far grander era.

Córdoba today, with its modest population of just over 300,000, offers a cultural depth and intensity—a direct legacy from the great emirs, caliphs, philosophers, physicians, poets, and engineers of the days of the caliphate—that far outstrips the city's current commercial and political power. The city's artistic and historical treasures begin with the *mezquita-catedral* (mosque-cathedral), as it is ever-more-frequently called, and continue through the winding, whitewashed streets of the Judería (the medieval Jewish quarter); the jasmine-, geranium-, and orange blossom–filled patios; the Renaissance palaces; and the two dozen churches, convents, and hermitages, built by Moorish artisans directly over former mosques.

GETTING HERE AND AROUND

Córdoba is easily accessible by bus, train, or car. If you opt for the latter, however, note that the city's one-way system can be something of a nightmare to navigate.

Córdoba has an extensive public bus network with frequent service. Buses usually start running at 6:30 or 7 AM and stop around midnight. You can buy 10-trip passes at newsstands and the bus office in Plaza de Colón. A single-trip fare is €1.10.

The city's modern train station is the hub for a comprehensive network of regional trains, with regular services to Seville, Málaga, Madrid, and Barcelona. Trains for Granada change at Bobadilla.

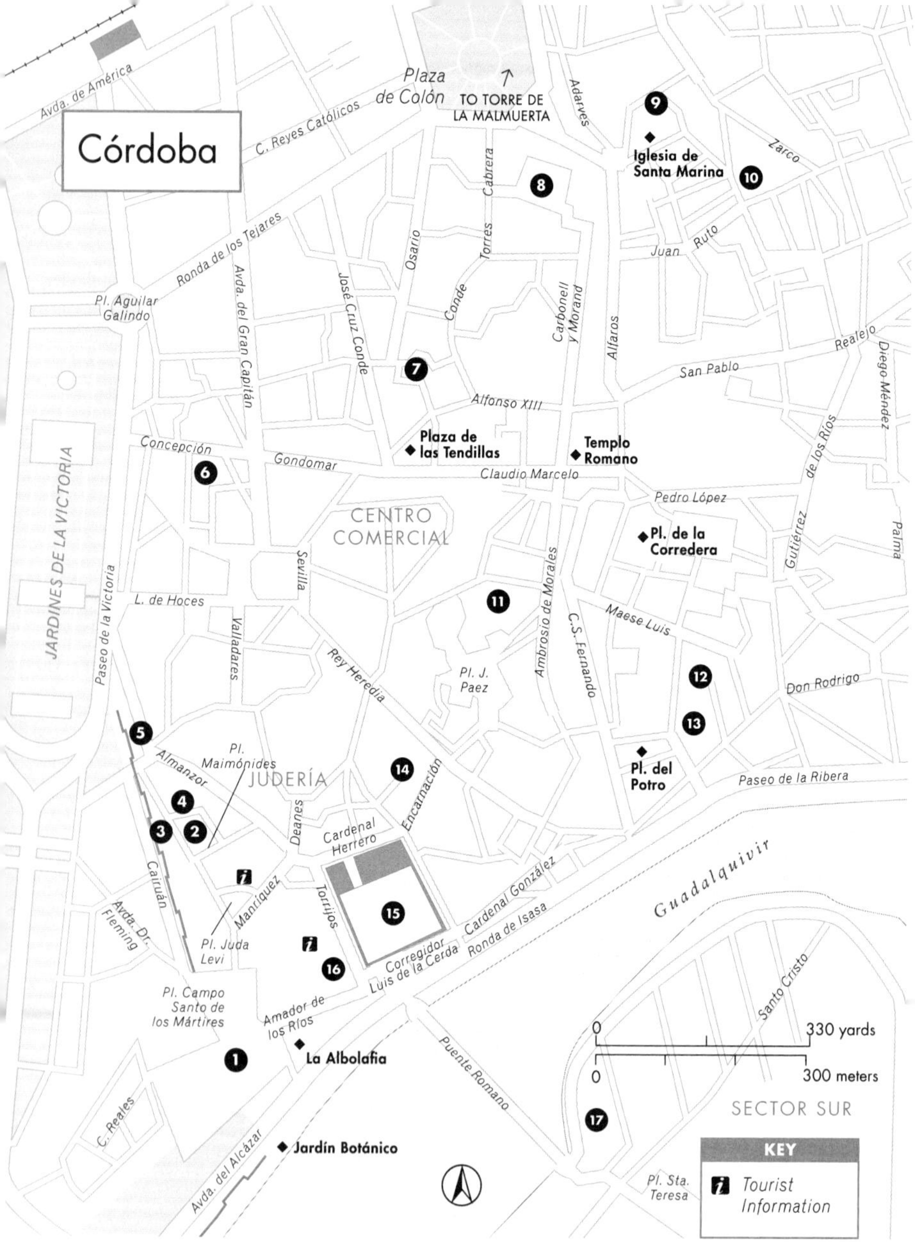

Alcázar de los Reyes Cristianos **1**
Calleja de las Flores **15**
Iglesia de San Miguel **7**
Mezquita **16**
Museo Arqueológico **12**
Museo de Bellas Artes **13**
Museo Diocesano **17**
Museo Julio Romero de Torres **14**
Museo Taurino **2**
Palacio de Viana **10**
Plaza de los Dolores **8**
Plaza Santa Marina **9**
Puerta de Almodóvar **5**
San Nicolás de Villa **6**
Synagogue **3**
Torre de la Calahorra **18**
Zoco **4**

Córdoba has a number of organized open-top bus tours of the city that can be booked via the tourist office or contacting the company directly.

ESSENTIALS

Bus Station Córdoba (✉ *Glorieta de las Tres Culturas, Córdoba* ☎ *957/404040*).

Taxi Contacts Radio Taxi (✉ *Córdoba* ☎ *957/764444*).

Train contacts Train Station (✉ *Glorieta de las Tres Culturas s/n* ☎ *957/403480*).

Tour contacts Córdoba Visión (✉ *Av. de Doctor Fleming, Centro, Córdoba* ☎ *957/760241*). **GranaVisión** (✉ *Calle Reyes Católicos 47–49, Centro, Córdoba* ☎ *958/535875*

Visitor Information Provincial Tourist Office (✉ *Palacio de Exposiciones, Calle Torrijos 10, opposite mosque, Judería* ☎ *957/471235*). **Local Tourist Office** (✉ *Pl. Juda Levi, Judería* ☎ *957/200522* 📠 *957/200277*).

EXPLORING

Córdoba is an easily navigable city, with twisting alleyways that hold surprises around every corner. The main city subdivisions used in this book are the **Judería** (which includes the Mezquita); **Sector Sur,** around the **Torre de la Calahorra** across the river; the area around the **Plaza de la Corredera,** a historic gathering place for everything from horse races to bullfights, and the **Centro Comercial,** from the area around Plaza de las Tendillas to the Iglesia de Santa Marina and the Torre de la Malmuerta. Incidentally, this Centro Comerical is much more than a succession of shops and stores. The town's real life, the everyday hustle and bustle, takes place here, and the general ambience is very different from that of the tourist center around the Mezquita, with its plethora of souvenir shops. Some of the city's finest Mudejar churches and best taverns, as well as the Palacio de los Marqueses de Viana, are in this pivotal part of town well back from the Guadalquivir waterfront.

Some of the most characteristic and rewarding places to explore in Córdoba are the parish churches and the taverns that inevitably accompany them, where you can taste *finos de Moriles*, a dry, sherrylike wine from the Montilla-Moriles district, and *tentempies* (tapas—literally, "keep you on your feet"). The *iglesias fernandinas* (so-called for their construction after Saint-King Fernando III's conquest of Córdoba) are nearly always built over mosques with stunning horseshoe arch doorways and Mudejar towers. The taverns tended to spring up around these populous hubs of city life. Examples are the Taberna de San Miguel (aka Casa el Pisto) next to the church of the same name, and the Bar Santa Marina (aka Casa Obispo) next to the Santa Marina Church.

TIP→ Córdoba's council authorities and private institutions frequently change the hours of the city's sights; before visiting an attraction, confirm hours with the tourist office or the sight itself.

❶ **Alcázar de los Reyes Cristianos** *(Fortress of the Christian Monarchs)*. Built by Alfonso XI in 1328, the Alcázar is a Mudejar-style palace with splendid gardens. (The original Moorish Alcázar stood beside the

Mezquita, on the site of the present Bishop's Palace.) This is where, in the 15th century, the Catholic Monarchs held court and launched their conquest of Granada. Boabdil was imprisoned here in 1483, and for nearly 300 years the Alcázar served as the Inquisition's base. The most important sights here are the Hall of the Mosaics and a Roman stone sarcophagus from the 2nd or 3rd century. ✉ *Pl. Campo Santo de los Mártires, Judería* ☎ *957/420151* 🎟 *Free Fri.* ⏲ *May–Sept., Tues.–Sat. 10–2 and 6–8, Sun. 9:30–3; Oct.–Apr., Tues.–Sat. 10–2 and 4:30–6:30, Sun. 9:30–2:30.*

CÓRDOBA ON TWO WHEELS

Never designed to support modern motor traffic, Córdoba's medieval layout is ideal for bicycles. **Todo Bici** (✉ *Calle Sereria 5* ☎ *957/485766* 🌐 *www.todobici.net*) rents bikes at reasonable rates (€2 per hour/€20 per day). Or, if this sounds like too much pedal power, opt for a Segway from **Blobject** (✉ *Avenida Dr Fleming s/n* ☎ *957/760-033* 🌐 *www.blobject.es*), where the rental cost includes a training session. Prices range from €15–€40 (30 minutes to two hours).

OFF THE BEATEN PATH

Jardín Botánico *(Botanical Garden)*. By the river, near the Alcázar de los Reyes Cristianos and across from Córdoba's modest zoo is the city's modern botanical garden, with outdoor spaces—including a section devoted to aromatic herbs—as well as greenhouses full of plants from South America and the Canary Islands. The **Museo de Etnobotánica** explores the way in which humans interact with the plant world. ✉ *Av. de Linneo s/n, Parque Zoológico* ☎ *957/200018* 🎟 *€2* ⏲ *Apr.–Oct., Tues.–Sun. 10–2:30 and 5:30–7:30; Nov.–Mar., Tues.–Sat. 10:30–2:30 and 4:30–6:30, Sun. 10:30–6:30.*

15 **Calleja de las Flores.** You'd be hard pressed to find prettier patios than those along this tiny street, a few yards off the northeastern corner of the Mezquita. Patios, many with ceramics, foliage, and iron grilles, are key to Córdoba's architecture, at least in the old quarter, where life is lived behind sturdy white walls—a legacy of the Moors, who honored both the sanctity of the home and the need to shut out the fierce summer sun. Between the second and the third week of May, right after the early May **Cruces de Mayo** (Crosses of May) competition, when neighborhoods compete at setting up elaborate crosses decorated with flowers and plants, Córdoba throws a **Patio Festival,** during which private patios are filled with flowers, opened to the public, and judged in a municipal competition. Córdoba's council publishes a map with an itinerary of the best patios in town—note that most are open only in the late afternoon during the week but all day on weekends.

16 **Mezquita** *(Mosque)*. Built between the 8th and 10th centuries, Córdoba's mosque is one of the earliest and most transportingly beautiful examples of Spanish Muslim architecture. The plain, crenellated walls of the outside do little to prepare you for the sublime beauty of the interior. As you enter through the **Puerta de las Palmas** (Door of the Palms), some 850 columns rise before you in a forest of jasper, marble, granite, and onyx. The pillars are topped by ornate capitals taken from the Visigothic church that was razed to make way for the mosque. Crowning these, red-and-white-stripe arches curve away into the dimness, and the

Fodor's Choice ★

ceiling is carved of delicately tinted cedar. The Mezquita has served as a cathedral since 1236, but its origins as a mosque are clear. Built in four stages, it was founded in 785 by Abd ar-Rahman I (756–88) on a site he bought from the Visigoth Christians. He pulled down their church and replaced it with a mosque, one-third the size of the present one, into which he incorporated marble pillars from earlier Roman and Visigothic shrines. Under Abd ar-Rahman II (822–52), the Mezquita held an original copy of the Koran and a bone from the arm of the prophet Mohammed and became a Muslim pilgrimage site second only to Mecca in importance.

Al Hakam II (961–76) built the beautiful **Mihrab** (prayer niche), the Mezquita's greatest jewel. Make your way over to the **Qiblah,** the south-facing wall in which this sacred prayer niche was hollowed out. (Muslim law decrees that a Mihrab face east, toward Mecca, and that worshippers do likewise when they pray. Because of an error in calculation, the Mihrab here faces more south than east. Al Hakam II spent hours agonizing over a means of correcting such a serious mistake, but he was persuaded by architects to let it be.) In front of the Mihrab is the **Maksoureh,** a kind of anteroom for the caliph and his court; its mosaics and plasterwork make it a masterpiece of Islamic art. A last addition to the mosque as such, the Maksoureh was completed around 987 by Al Mansur, who more than doubled its size.

After the Reconquest, the Christians left the Mezquita largely undisturbed, dedicating it to the Virgin Mary and using it as a place of Christian worship. The clerics did erect a wall closing off the mosque from its courtyard, which helped dim the interior and thus separate the house of worship from the world outside. In the 13th century, Christians had the **Capilla de Villaviciosa** built by Moorish craftsmen, its Mudejar architecture blending with the lines of the mosque. Not so the heavy, incongruous baroque structure of the **cathedral,** sanctioned in the very heart of the mosque by Charles V in the 1520s. To the emperor's credit, he was supposedly horrified when he came to inspect the new construction, exclaiming to the architects, "To build something ordinary, you have destroyed something that was unique in the world" (not that this sentiment stopped him from tampering with the Alhambra to build his Palacio Carlos V). Rest up and reflect in the **Patio de los Naranjos** (Orange Court), perfumed in springtime by orange blossoms. The **Puerta del Perdón** (Gate of Forgiveness), so named because debtors were forgiven here on feast days, is on the north wall of the Orange Court. It's the formal entrance to the mosque. The **Virgen de los Faroles** (Virgin of the Lanterns), a small statue in a niche on the outside wall of the mosque along the north side on Cardenal Herrero, is behind a lantern-hung grille, rather like a lady awaiting a serenade. The **Torre del Alminar,** the minaret once used to summon Moorish faithful to prayer, has a baroque belfry. ✉*C. de Torrijos s/n, Judería* ☎*957/470512* 🎫*€8* ⏲*Mon.–Sat. 10–6, Sun. 9–10:45 and 1:30–6:30.*

NEED A BREAK?

The lively Plaza Juda Levi, surrounded by a maze of narrow streets and squares, lies at the heart of the Judería and makes a great spot for indulg-

ing in a little people-watching. Sit outside here with a drink or, better still, an ice cream from Helados Juda Levi.

⓬ **Museo Arqueológico.** In the heart of the old quarter, the Museum of Archaeology has finds from Córdoba's varied cultural past. The ground floor has ancient Iberian statues and Roman statues, mosaics, and artifacts; the upper floor is devoted to Moorish art. By chance, the ruins of a Roman theater were discovered right next to the museum in 2000—have a look from the window just inside the entrance. The alleys and steps along Altos de Santa Ana make for great wandering. ✉ *Pl. Jerónimo Paez, Judería* ☎ *957/474011* 🎫 *€1.50* 🕓 *Tues. 2:30–8:30, Wed.–Sat. 9–8:30.*

⓱ **Museo Diocesano.** Housed in the former Bishop's Palace, facing the mosque, the Diocesan Museum is devoted to religious art, with illustrated prayer books, tapestries, paintings (including some Julio Romero de Torres canvases), and sculpture, although it was closed for restoration at the time of publication—check before you go. The medieval wood sculptures are the museum's finest treasures. ✉ *Calle Torrijos 12, Judería* ☎ *957/496085* 🎫 *€3, free with ticket for Mezquita* 🕓 *Apr–Sept., weekdays 9:30–3, Sat. 9:30–1:30; Oct.–Mar., weekdays 9:30–1:30 and 3:30–5:30, Sat. 9:30–1:30.*

❷ **Museo Taurino** (Museum of Bullfighting). Two adjoining mansions on the Plaza Maimónides (or Plaza de las Bulas) house this museum, and it's worth a visit, as much for the chance to see a restored mansion as for the posters, Art Nouveau paintings, bull's heads, suits of lights (bullfighter outfits), and memorabilia of famous Córdoban bullfighters, including the most famous of all, Manolete. To the surprise of the nation, Manolete, who was considered immortal, was killed by a bull in the ring at Linares in 1947. It's closed for renovations until Fall 2010 at the earliest. ✉ *Pl. Maimónides, Judería* ☎ *957/201056.*

❺ **Puerta de Almodóvar.** Outside this old Moorish gate at the northern entrance of the Judería is a statue of **Seneca,** the Córdoban-born philosopher who rose to prominence in Nero's court in Rome and was forced to commit suicide at his emperor's command. The gate stands at the top of the narrow and colorful Calle San Felipe.

❸ **Synagogue.** The only Jewish temple in Andalusia to survive the expulsion and inquisition of the Jews in 1492, Córdoba's synagogue is also one of only three ancient synagogues left in all of Spain (the other two are in Toledo). Though it no longer functions as a place of worship, it's a treasured symbol for Spain's modern Jewish communities. The outside is plain, but the inside, measuring 23 feet by 21 feet, contains some exquisite Mudejar stucco tracery. Look for the fine plant motifs and the Hebrew inscription saying that the synagogue was built in 1315. The women's gallery, not open for visits, still stands, and in the east wall is the ark where the sacred scrolls of the Torah were kept. ✉ *C. Judíos, Judería* ☎ *957/202928* 🎫 *€1* 🕓 *Tues.–Sat. 9:30–2 and 3:30–5:30, Sun. 9:30–1:30.*

⓲ **Torre de la Calahorra.** The tower on the far side of the Puente Romano (Roman Bridge) was built in 1369 to guard the entrance to Córdoba. It now houses the **Museo Vivo de Al-Andalus** (Museum of Al-Andalus, which is Arabic for "Land of the West"), with films and audiovisual guides (in English) on Córdoba's history. Climb the narrow staircase to the top of the tower for the view of the Roman bridge and city on the other side of the Guadalquivir. ✉ *Av. de la Confederación, Sector Sur* ☎ *957/293929* 🌐 *www.torrecalahorra.com* 🎫 *€4.50 including audio guide, €1.20 extra for slide show* ⏲ *Daily 10–6.*

4 **Zoco.** *Zoco* is the Spanish word for the Arab souk, the onetime function of this courtyard near the synagogue. It's now the site of a daily crafts market, where you can see artisans at work, and evening flamenco in summer. ✉ *Calle Judíos 5, Judería* ☎ *957/204033* 🎫 *Free.*

NEED A BREAK?

Wander over to the Plaza de las Tendillas, which is halfway between the Mezquita and Plaza Colón. The terraces of Café Boston and Café Siena are both enjoyable places to relax with a coffee when the weather is warm.

13 **Museo de Bellas Artes.** Hard to miss because of its deep-pink facade, Córdoba's Museum of Fine Arts, in a courtyard just off the Plaza del Potro, belongs to a former Hospital de la Caridad (Charity Hospice). It was founded by Ferdinand and Isabella, who twice received Columbus here. The collection includes paintings by Murillo, Valdés Leal, Zurbarán, Goya, and Sorolla. ✉ *Pl. del Potro 1, San Francisco* ☎ *957/473345* 🌐 *www.juntadeandalucia.es/cultura/museos/MBACO* 🎫 *€1.50* ⏲ *Tues. 2:30–8:30, Wed.–Sat. 9–8:30, Sun. 9–2:30.*

Fodor's Choice ★

14 ★ **Museo Julio Romero de Torres.** Across the courtyard from the Museum of Fine Arts, this museum is devoted to the early-20th-century Córdoban artist Julio Romero de Torres (1874–1930), who specialized in mildly erotic portraits of demure, partially dressed Andalusian temptresses. Romero de Torres, who was also a flamenco *cantador* (singer), died at the age of 56 and is one of Córdoba's greatest folk heroes. ✉ *Pl. del Potro 1, San Francisco* ☎ *957/491909* 🌐 *www.museojulioromero.com* 🎫 *€4, free Fri.* ⏲ *Tues.–Sat. 10–2 and 4:30–6:30, Sun. 9:30–2:30.*

7 ★ **Iglesia de San Miguel.** Complete with Romanesque doors built around Mudejar horseshoe arches, the San Miguel Church, the square and café terraces around it, and its excellent tavern, Taberna San Miguel-Casa El Pisto, form one of the city's finest combinations of art, history, and gastronomy. ✉ *Pl. San Miguel, Centro.*

10 **Palacio de Viana.** This 17th-century palace is one of Córdoba's most splendid aristocratic homes. Also known as the **Museo de los Patios,** it contains 12 interior patios, each one different; the patios and gardens are planted with cypresses, orange trees, and myrtles. Inside the building are a carriage museum, a library, embossed leather wall hangings, filigree silver, and grand galleries and staircases. As you enter, note that the corner column of the first patio has been removed to allow the entrance of horse-drawn carriages. ✉ *Pl. Don Gomé, Centro* ☎ *957/496741* 🎫 *Patios only €3.50, patios and interior €6* ⏲ *May–Sept., Mon.–Sat. 9–2; Oct.–Apr., Mon.–Sat. 10–1 and 4–6.*

8 **Plaza de los Dolores.** The 17th-century Convento de Capuchinos surrounds this small square north of Plaza San Miguel. The square is where you feel most deeply the city's languid pace. In its center, a statue of

Cristo de los Faroles (Christ of the Lanterns) stands amid eight lanterns hanging from twisted wrought-iron brackets. ✉ *Centro 14002.*

9 **Plaza Santa Marina.** At the edge of the **Barrio de los Toreros,** a quarter where many of Córdoba's famous bullfighters were born and raised, stands a statue of the famous bullfighter Manolete (1917–47) opposite the lovely *fernandina* church of Santa Marina de Aguas Santas (St. Marina of Holy Waters). Not far from here, on the Plaza de la Lagunilla, is a Manolete bust. ✉ *Pl. Conde Priego, Centro.*

6 **San Nicolás de Villa.** This classically dark Spanish church displays the Mudejar style of Islamic decoration and art forms. Córdoba's well-kept city park, the **Jardínes de la Victoria,** with tile benches and manicured bushes, is a block west of here. ✉ *C. San Felipe, Centro.*

WHERE TO EAT

¢ SPANISH Fodor's Choice ★ **Bar Santos.** This very small, quintessentially Spanish bar, with no seats and numerous photos of matadors and flamenco dancers, seems out of place surrounded by the tourist shops and overshadowed by the Mezquita but its appearance—and its prices—are part of its charm. Tapas such as *morcillo ibérico* (Iberian blood sausage) and *bocadillos* (sandwiches; literally "little mouthfuls") are excellent in quality and value, while the Santos *tortilla de patata* (potato omelet) is renowned and celebrated both for its taste and heroic thickness. ✉ *Calle Magistral González Francés 3, Judería* ☎ *957/479360* 💳 *MC, V.*

$$–$$$ SPANISH Fodor's Choice ★ **Bodegas Campos.** A block east of the Plaza del Potro, this restaurant in a traditional old wine cellar is the epitome of all that's great about Andalusian cuisine and service. The dining rooms are in barrel-heavy rustic rooms and leafy traditional patios (take a look at some of the signed barrels—you may recognize a name or two, such as the former U.K. prime minister, Tony Blair. Regional dishes include *ensalada de bacalao y naranja* (salad of salt cod and orange with olive oil) and *solomillo con salsa de setas* (sirloin with a wild mushroom sauce). The *menu degustacíon* (taster's menu) costs €49. There's also an excellent tapas bar. ✉ *Calle Los Lineros 32, San Pedro* ☎ *957/497643* 💳 *AE, MC, V* ⊗ *No dinner Sun.*

$$–$$$ SPANISH **Casa Pepe de la Judería.** Antiques and some wonderful old oil paintings fill this three-floor labyrinth of rooms just around the corner from the mosque, near the Judería, and the restaurant is always packed, noisy, and fun. May through October, the rooftop opens for barbecues, and there is live Spanish guitar music most nights. A full selection of tapas and house specialties includes *presa de paletilla ibérica con salsa de trufa* (pork shoulder fillet with a truffle sauce) and the solidly traditional *rabo de toro* (oxtail stew). ✉ *Calle Romero 1, off Deanes, Judería* ☎ *957/200744* 💳 *AE, DC, MC, V.*

¢–$$ MOROCCAN **Comedor Árabe Andalussí.** This tiny restaurant is warm and cozy, with Oriental carpets and ornate drapes and cushions. All the Moroccan favorites are here, including tabbouleh, falafel, and couscous, which make it especially good for vegetarians. The *tagines* (earthenware vessels with conical tops used for stewing meat and vegetables in Morocco) for two are excellent and will easily feed four. Note that no wine is

CÓRDOBA FIESTAS

Córdoba parties hard during **Carnival**, on the days leading up to Ash Wednesday. **Semana Santa** (Holy Week, between Palm Sunday and Easter) is always intensely celebrated with dramatic religious processions.

May brings **Las Cruces de Mayo** (The Crosses of May) during the first week of the month and the **Festival de los Patios** (Patio Festival) during the second; the **Concurso Nacional de Flamenco** (National Flamenco competition) is also during the second week of May, but only every third year. Córdoba's annual **Feria de Mayo** is the city's main street party, held during the last week of May.

The **International Guitar Festival** brings major artists to Córdoba in early July. **Nuestra Señora de Fuensanta**, one of the many saints days celebrated in Spain, is the last Sunday in September, and the **Romería de San Miguel** (Procession of St. Michael) is on September 29.

served here, in accordance with Islamic religious law, but if you ask nicely the management may allow you to bring in your own wine—try this phrase: *¿Por favor, podemos traer una botella de vino para acompañar nuestra comida?* (May we please bring in a bottle of wine to accompany our meal?) ✉*Pl. Abades 4, Judería* ☎*957/475162* ▭*No credit cards.*

$$–$$$ SPANISH ✕**El Blasón.** In an old inn one block west of Avenida Gran Capitán, El Blasón has a Moorish-style entrance bar leading onto a patio enclosed by ivy-covered walls. Downstairs there is a lounge with a red tile ceiling and old polished clay plates on the walls. Upstairs are two elegant dining rooms where blue walls, white silk curtains, and candelabras evoke early-19th-century luxury. The menu includes *salmón fresco al cava* (fresh salmon in cava, Spanish sparkling wine) and *muslos de pato al vino dulce* (leg of duck in sweet wine sauce). ✉*José Zorrilla 11, Centro* ☎*957/480625* ▭*AE, DC, MC, V.*

$–$$$ SPANISH ✕**El Burlaero.** A block from the front of the Mezquita, El Burlaero—so named for a bullring's wooden barrier—dates from the 16th century and has wood-beamed ceilings and an antique, traditional charm. The seven different rooms, all decorated with bullfight memorabilia and hunting trophies, can serve as many as 200 diners. There's also a terrace for outdoor dining. Typical dishes include grilled swordfish, meat-and-vegetable brochette, Iberian pork, and partridge with onions. ✉*Calleja de la Hoguera 5, Judería* ☎*957/472719* ▭*MC, V.*

$$$–$$$$ SPANISH Fodor'sChoice ★ ✕**El Caballo Rojo.** This is one of the most famous traditional restaurants in Andalusia, frequented by royalty and society folk. The interior resembles a cool, leafy Andalusian patio, and the dining room is furnished with stained glass, dark wood, and gleaming marble; the upstairs terrace overlooks the Mezquita. The menu mixes traditional specialties, such as *rabo de toro* (oxtail stew) and *salmorejo* (a thick version of gazpacho), with dishes inspired by Córdoba's Moorish and Jewish heritage, such as *alboronia* (a cold salad of stewed vegetables flavored with honey, saffron, and aniseed), *cordero a la miel* (lamb roasted with honey), and *rape mozárabe* (grilled monkfish with Moorish spices).

✉Calle Cardenal Herrero 28, Judería ☎957/475375 🌐www.elcaballorojo.com 💳AE, DC, MC, V.

$$–$$$$ SPANISH ★ ✕**El Churrasco.** The name suggests grilled meat, but this restaurant in the heart of the Judería serves much more than that. Try tapas such as the *berenjenas crujientes con salmorejo* (crispy fried eggplant slices with thick gazpacho) in the colorful bar. In the restaurant, the grilled fish is supremely fresh, and the steak is the best in town, particularly the namesake *churrasco* (grilled meat in a spicy tomato-based sauce). On the inner patio, there's alfresco dining when it's warm outside, when it's also the season to try another Churrasco specialty: *gazpacho blanco de piñones* (a white gazpacho based on pine nuts). ✉*Calle Romero 16, Judería* ☎*957/290819* 💳*AE, DC, MC, V* ⏲*Closed Aug.*

TOP 3 TAPAS BARS IN CÓRDOBA

You can find delicious tapas at most of the restaurants we list, but if you're just looking for a tapas destination before you embark on dinner, try one of these spots.

Plateros de San Francisco, *Calle San Francisco 6*
Taberna Plateros, *Calle Maria Auxilliadora 25*
Taberna San Miguel, *Plaza San Miguel 1*

$–$$ SPANISH ✕**El Tablón.** Opened in 1890 as a bodega, El Tablón became a restaurant with simple decor in 1985. From inside or on the pleasing columned patio, you can select from a typical Córdoba-style menu that includes a good choice of two courses plus a drink and dessert for just €9.80 (there is a slightly more sophisticated choice for €12). Pizzas, tapas, and sandwiches are also available. The small bar, with no seats and a marble counter, retains a 19th-century feel. ✉*Calle Cardenal González 69, Judería* ☎*957/476061* 💳*MC, V.*

$$–$$$$ MEDITERRANEAN ★ ✕**Los Marqueses.** Los Marqueses is in the heart of the Judería area, in a delightful 17th-century palace. The atmosphere is sophisticated and elegant, and diners are greeted with a complimentary taste of gazpacho. The restaurant specializes in Mediterranean and Andalusian cuisine and the menu might include such options as fried eggplant with honey, wild mushroom risotto with prawns, and turbot fillets with potato and mascarpone sauce. The lunch menu, served Monday–Saturday, is a bargain at €19.90 and showcases typical Córdoba dishes, such as oxtail stew and *salmorejo* (a thick version of gazpacho). ✉*Calle Tomás Conde 8, Judería* ☎*957/202094* 💳*AE, DC, MC, V* ⏲*Closed Mon. and 15 days in Sept.*

¢–$ MIDDLE EASTERN ★ ✕**Medina Califal.** Above Córdoba's Arab hammam baths, the cuisine here includes vegetarian and vegan choices, like the *ensalada de sultan* starter with pine nuts, raisins, and dried fruits in an orange-and-almond dressing. Traditional *moutabal* and hummus are tempting dips served with freshly made, warm pita bread, and you can follow with a choice of couscous, including meat or vegetables, or more conventional mains, like roasted lamb in a honey-based sauce. Adjourn to the *tetería* (tea shop) after dinner for an herb tea or a *batido* (fruit smoothie)—the yogurt-date-banana version is delicious. There are packages available that combine a visit to the baths (including massage) with a meal in the restaurant. ✉ *Calle Corregidor Luís de la Cerda 5, Judería* ☎ *957/484746* ▭ *MC, V.*

$ MEDITERRANEAN **✕Pizarro.** Owner Luis Pizarro offers a diverse menu of traditional and international dishes at his bright modern restaurant with peach-colored walls, exposed brick, and pine furniture. Starters include eggplant crepes with prawns and salmon and *madrileño*-style garlic soup topped with a poached egg. Meaty mains include duck magret and roasted lamb with rosemary and garlic, while fish lovers can opt for a seafood menu that includes cod *pil-pil* (cod baked in a spicy chili-based sauce) or grilled prawns. There is a €25 set menu at dinner. ✉ *Calle Deanes 10, Judería* ☎ *957/422047* ▭ *MC, V* ⊙ *No dinner Sun.*

$–$$$ SPANISH **✕Taberna Salinas.** This has been an established favorite in Córdoba since 1879: the tiles, paintings, wooden furniture, glassed-in patio, bodega with barrels, and small bar all reflect the bygone era, and the cuisine is typical of the Córdobese mountains: goat cheese, meatballs, blood sausage, and lamb chops are usual choices. Kick-start your appetite with a tapas of fried and breaded eggplant slices drizzled with local honey. ✉ *Calle Tundidores 3, Plaza de la Corredera* ☎ *957/480135* ▭ *AE, DC, MC, V* ⊙ *Closed Sun.*

$$–$$$ SPANISH Fodor's Choice ★ **✕Taberna de San Miguel-Casa El Pisto.** This central and atmospheric Córdoba hot spot behind Plaza de las Tendillas is always booming with happy diners, most of them Córdobans, enjoying a wide range of typical *pinchos* and *raciones* accompanied by chilled glasses of Montilla-Moriles, the excellent local dry sherrylike wine. The heavy wooden bar is as good a spot as any, but the tables in the back rooms crackle with conviviality. ✉ *Pl. de San Miguel 1, Centro* ☎ *957/470166* ▭ *AE, DC, MC, V* ⊙ *Closed Sun.*

¢–$$ SPANISH **✕Taberna Plateros.** On a narrow side street opposite the Maestre hotel, this delightful spot dates from the 17th century. A large patio restaurant leads to more rooms and the traditional marble bar, where blue-collar types and businessmen meet. Photographs of iconic local bullfighter Manolete line the walls, and the patio is decorated with giddily patterned tiles and bricks. The food is solid home-style cooking and choices include fried green peppers, Spanish potato omelet, and lamb chops; the starters are meals in themselves. ✉ *San Francisco 6, Plaza de la Corredera* ☎ *957/470042* ▭ *MC, V* ⊙ *Closed Sun. and Mon.*

WHERE TO STAY

$$$–$$$$ ★ **Amistad Córdoba.** Two 18th-century mansions that look out on the Plaza de Maimónides in the heart of the Judería are now a stylish hotel. (You can also enter through the old Moorish walls on Calle Cairuán.) There's a cobblestone Mudejar courtyard, carved-wood ceilings, and a plush lounge area; the newer wing across the street is done in blues and grays and Norwegian wood. Guest rooms are large and comfortable. **Pros:** perfect design and comfort, pleasant and efficient service. **Cons:** parking near the hotel difficult. ✉ *Pl. de Maimónides 3, Judería* ☎ *957/420335* ⊕ *www.nh-hoteles.com* *84 rooms* *In-room: Wi-Fi. In-hotel: restaurant, room service, bar, laundry service, parking (fee)* ▭ *AE, DC, MC, V.*

$$–$$$ **Casa de los Azulejos.** Although renovated in 1934, this 17th-century house still has its underground rooms with vaulted ceilings. Decorated with colorful tiles, it mixes Andalusian and Latin American influences. All rooms are painted in warm, pastel colors, filled with antique furnishings, and open onto the central patio with banana trees, lofty palms, and ferns. The floors in the rooms are tiled with stunning original azulejos (hence the name). There's an excellent Mexican cantina, La Guadalupana, on the premises, and a generous breakfast buffet. **Pros:** interesting and unusual environment, friendly staff and clientele. **Cons:** hyper-busy decor, limited privacy. *Calle Fernando Colón 5, Centro 957/470000 www.casadelosazulejos.com 7 rooms, 1 suite In-room: Wi-Fi. In-hotel: restaurant, no elevator, public Internet MC, V.*

Fodor's Choice ★

$$$ **Conquistador.** Ceramic tiles and inlaid marquetry adorn the bar and public rooms at this contemporary, Andalusian Moorish–style hotel next to the Mezquita, and the reception area overlooks a colonnaded patio, fountain, and small enclosed garden. Rooms are comfortable and classically Andalusian, with marble floors and elegant fabrics; those at the front have small balconies overlooking the mosque, which is floodlit at night. Note that there are excellent deals if you book over the Internet. **Pros:** views into Mezquita, central location. **Cons:** bells, busy street at the door. *Magistral González Francés 17, Judería 957/481102 or 957/481411 www.hotelconquistadorcordoba.com 99 rooms, 3 suites In-room: Wi-Fi. In-hotel: room service, bar, laundry service, parking (fee) AE, DC, MC, V.*

$$$ **Eurostars Maimónides.** Named after the Arab mathematician and philosopher, this hotel, a new member of the prestigious Eurostars hotel chain, is well priced given the position and quality. The lobby has a colonnaded hall with tile floors and a remarkable *mocárabe* (ornamental carved wood) ceiling, while outside there's a small patio with wrought-iron tables and chairs. Rooms and bathrooms have marble floors and are decorated in light tones with striped fabrics and writing desks. Some rooms feel almost close enough to the Mezquita that you can touch it. **Pros:** central location, elegant decor. **Cons:** in the busiest part of town, street side rooms can be noisy on weekends and holiday eves. *Torrijos 4, Judería 957/471500 www.hotelmaimonides.com 82 rooms In-room: dial-up, Wi-Fi. In-hotel: restaurant, public Internet, parking (fee) MC, V.*

$ ★ **Gonzalez.** A few minutes from the Mezquita, the Gonzalez was originally built as a 16th-century palace for the son of the famous local artist Julio Romero de Torres. The building has been since been converted into an aesthetically pleasing small hotel with an elegant marble entrance, sumptuous decor, and a typical Córdoban flower-filled patio, and many of the single, double, twin, and triple rooms overlook this colorful central courtyard. **Pros:** top value, central location. **Cons:** minimal amenities, exterior rooms noisy. *Calle Manrique 3, Judería 957/479819 957/486187 17 rooms AE, DC, MC, V.*

$$$$ **Hospes Palacio del Bailío.** This beautiful 17th-century mansion built over the ruins of a Roman house in the historic center jumped to the top of the city's lodging options as soon as it opened. The company

Fodor's Choice ★

in charge specializes in tastefully renovating impressive and historic buildings to the highest of expected modern standards, and this hotel is exemplary of its work. Archaeological remains are combined with contemporary features, as in Roman ruins visible beneath the glass floor of one of the patios. Clever lighting and a relaxing spa complete the contemporary-antiquity mélange. **Pros:** dazzling lines and decor, impeccable comforts. **Cons:** not easy to reach by car. ✉*Calle Ramírez de las Casas Deza 10–12, Plaza de La Corredera* ☎*957/498993* 🌐*www.hospes.es* *53 rooms* *In-room: Ethernet, Wi-Fi. In-hotel: restaurant, bar, pools, spa, bicycles, laundry facilities, public Internet* 💳*MC, V.*

$$$–$$$$ **La Hospedería de El Churrasco.** As should be expected from a place associated with the nearby restaurant of the same name, this small hotel is a lovely, tasteful place to stay. Each room is individually furnished with fine antiques, luxurious wallpaper, and fine old oil paintings but also comes with such modern facilities as plasma TVs and Wi-Fi connection. The terrace-solarium has fine views of the Mezquita. **Pros:** excellent combination of traditional design and contemporary comfort, intimate and personal service. **Cons:** lengthy baggage haul from car, tumultuous street on weekends. ✉*Calle Romero 38, Judería* ☎*957/294808* 🌐*www.elchurrasco.com* *9 rooms* *In-room: Wi-Fi. In-hotel: parking (fee)* 💳*AE, DC, MC, V* *BP.*

$$–$$$ **Lola.** Lola, the owner, has decorated the rooms (each is named after an Arab princess) in this former 19th-century palace with decorative flair and attention to detail. There are original beams, woven rugs, antique wardrobes, and Art Deco accents throughout, and the bathrooms are airy, modern, and marbled. Tucked down a side street, Lola is far enough away from the tour groups but within walking distance of all the big-city sights. Breakfast is served on the roof terrace, from where there are Mezquita tower views. There's parking on nearby Plaza Vallinas. **Pros:** good value for the money, lively decor. **Cons:** difficult to book a room in high season, some might consider the decor excessive. ✉*Calle Romero 3, Judería* ☎*957/200305* 🌐*www.hotelconencantolola.com* *8 rooms* 💳*AE, MC, V* *CP.*

$$$ **Parador de Córdoba.** A peaceful garden surrounds this modern parador on the slopes of the Sierra de Córdoba, 5 km (3 mi) north of town on the site of Abd ar-Rahman's summer palace—he was the one who first founded the Mezquita, as a mosque, in 785. Rooms are sunny, with wood or wicker furnishings, and the pricier ones have balconies overlooking the lush green garden or facing Córdoba. **Pros:** wonderful views from south-facing rooms, sleek decor. The restaurant serves quality traditional cuisine. **Cons:** characterless modern building, far from city's main sights. ✉*Av. de la Arruzafa, El Brillante* ☎*957/275900* 🌐*www.parador.es* *89 rooms, 5 suites* *In-room: dial-up, Wi-Fi. In-hotel: restaurant, room service, tennis court, pool, parking (no fee)* 💳*AE, DC, MC, V.*

NIGHTLIFE AND THE ARTS

NIGHTLIFE

Córdoba locals hang out mostly in the areas of Ciudad Jardín (the old university area), Plaza de las Tendillas, and the Avenida Gran Capitán.

Café Málaga (✉ *Calle Málaga 3, Centro*), a block from Plaza de las Tendillas, is a laid-back hangout. **Salón de Té** (✉ *Calle del Buen Pastor 13, Judería*), a few blocks from the Mezquita, is a beautiful place for tea, with a courtyard, side rooms filled with cushions, and a shop selling Moroccan clothing. It closes at midnight. **Sojo** (✉ *Calle Benito Pérez Galdós 3, off Av. Gran Capitán, Centro* ☎ *957/487211* ✉ *José Martorell 12, Judería*) has a trendy crowd. The branch in the Judería has DJs on weekends. **O'Donoghue's** (✉ *Av. Gran Capitán 38, Centro* ☎ *957/481678*) is an Irish pub favored by locals. For some of the best views of Córdoba, drop by **Hotel Hesperia** (✉ *Av. de la Confederación 1, Sector Sur* ☎ *957/421042* 🌐 *www.hesperia-cordoba.com*), across the Guadalquivir. The hotel has a rooftop bar in summer.

FLAMENCO Córdoba's most popular flamenco club, the year-round **Tablao Cardenal** (✉ *Calle Torrijos 10, Judería* ☎ *957/483320* 🌐 *www.tablaocardenal.com*) is worth the trip just to see the courtyard of the 16th-century building, which was Córdoba's first hospital. Admission is €20.

SHOPPING

Córdoba's main shopping district is around Avenida Gran Capitán, Ronda de los Tejares, and the streets leading away from Plaza Tendillas. **Artesanía Andaluza** (✉ *Calle Tomás Conde 3, Judería* ☎ *957/203781*), near the Museo Taurino, sells Córdoban crafts, including fine embossed leather (a legacy of the Moors) and jewelry made of filigree silver from the mines of the Sierra Morena. Córdoba's artisans sell their crafts in the **Zoco** (✉ *C. Judíos, opposite synagogue, Judería* ☎ *957/204033*), though many stalls are open May–September only. **Meryan** (✉ *Calleja de las Flores 2 and Encarnación 12* ☎ *957/475902* 🌐 *www.meryancor.com*) is one of Córdoba's best workshops for embossed leather.

EN ROUTE

Medina Azahara (sometimes written in Arabic as Madinat Al-Zahra) was built in the foothills of the Sierra Morena—about 8 km (5 mi) west of Córdoba on C431—by Abd ar-Rahman III for his favorite concubine, az-Zahra (the Flower). Construction on this once-splendid summer pleasure palace began in 936; historians say it took 10,000 men, 2,600 mules, and 400 camels 25 years to erect this fantasy of 4,300 columns in dazzling pink, green, and white marble and jasper brought from Carthage. On three terraces stood a palace, a mosque, luxurious baths, fragrant gardens, fish ponds, an aviary, and a zoo. In 1013 the place was sacked and destroyed by Berber mercenaries. In 1944 the Royal Apartments were rediscovered, and the Throne Room carefully reconstructed. The outline of the mosque has also been excavated. The only covered part of the site is the Salon de Abd ar-Rahman III; the rest is a sprawl of foundations and arches that hint at the splendor of the original city-palace. There is no public transport to here, but there

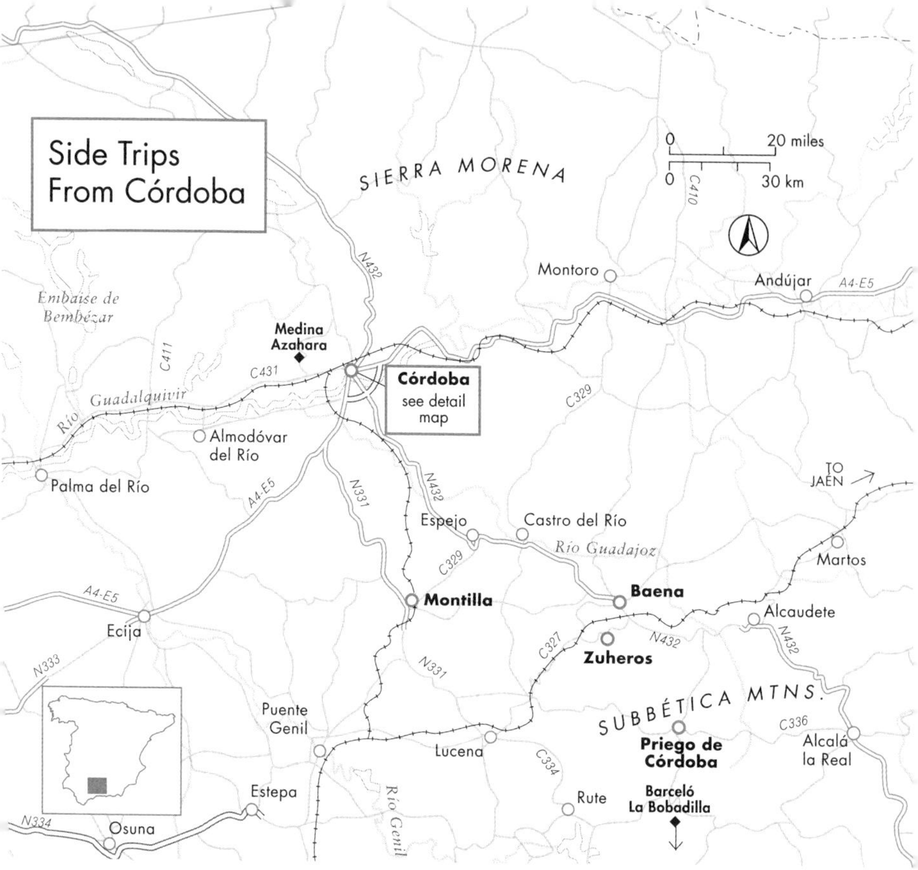

is a daily tourist bus; check with the tourist office. ✉ *Off C431; follow signs en route to Almodóvar del Río* ☎ *957/355506* 🎫 *€3* ⏲ *Tues.–Sat. 10–8:30, Sun. 10–2.*

SIDE TRIPS FROM CÓRDOBA

If you have time to go beyond Córdoba and have already seen the Medina Azahara palace ruins, head south to the wine country around Montilla, olive oil–rich Baena, and the Subbética mountain range, a cluster of small towns virtually unknown to travelers.

The enitre Subbética region is protected as a natural park, and the mountains, canyons, and wooded valleys are stunning. You'll need a car to explore, though, and in some parts, the roads are rather rough. To reach these meriting-a-visit towns in *la campiña* (the countryside), take the low road (N331) through Montilla, cutting north to Baena via Zuheros, or take the high road (N432) through Espejo and Baena, cutting south through Cabra. For park information or hiking advice, contact the **Mancomunidad de la Subbética** (✉ *Ctra. Carcabuey–Zagrilla, Km 5.75, Carcabuey* ☎ *957/704106* 🌐 *www.subbetica.org*). You can also pick up information, including a pack of maps titled *Rutas Send-*

eristas de la Subbética, from any local tourist office. The handy cards detail 10 walks with sketched maps.

Southern Córdoba is also the province's main olive-producing region, with the town of **Lucena** at its center. If you follow the Ruta del Aceite (olive oil route), you'll pass some of the province's most picturesque villages. In Lucena is the Torre del Moral, where Granada's last Nasrid ruler, Boabdil, was imprisoned in 1483 after launching an unsuccessful attack on the Christians; and the Parroquia de San Mateo, a small but remarkable Renaissance–Gothic cathedral. The town makes furniture and brass and copper pots. Southeast of Lucena, C334 crosses the **Embalse de Iznájar** (Iznájar Reservoir) amid spectacular scenery. On C334 halfway between Lucena and the reservoir, in **Rute,** you can sample the potent *anís* (anise) liqueur for which this small, whitewashed town is famous.

MONTILLA

46 km (28 mi) south of Córdoba.

Heading south from Córdoba toward Malaga, you'll pass through hills ablaze with sunflowers in early summer before you reach the Montilla-Morilés vineyards. Every fall, 47,000 acres' worth of Pedro Ximénez grapes are crushed here to produce the region's rich Montilla wines, which are similar to sherry. Recently, Montilla has started developing a young white wine similar to Portugal's Vinho Verde.

ESSENTIALS

Visitor Information Montilla (✉ *Capitán Alonso de Vargas 3* ☎ *957/652462* 🌐 *www.turismomontilla.com*).

EXPLORING

Bodegas Alvear. Founded in 1729, this bodega in the center of town is Montilla's oldest. Besides being informative, the fun tour and wine tasting gives you the chance to buy a bottle or two of Alvear's tasty version of the sweet Pedro Ximenez aged sherry. Tours must be booked in advance, and there must be a minimum of seven people. ✉ *Calle María Auxiliadora 1* ☎ *957/652939* 🌐 *www.alvear.es* *Tour €3, with wine tasting €4–€5.50* *Guided tour and wine tasting Mon.–Fri. 12:30; shop Mon. 4:30–6:30, Tues.–Fri. 10–2 and 4:30–6:30, Sat. 11–1:30.*

WHERE TO EAT AND STAY

$–$$$ SPANISH ★ **Las Camachas.** The best-known restaurant in southern Córdoba Province is in an Andalusian-style hacienda outside Montilla—near the main road toward Málaga. Start with tapas in the attractive bar, then move on to one of the six dining rooms. Regional specialties include *alcachofas al Montilla* (artichokes braised in Montilla wine), *salmorejo* (a thick garlicky gazpacho), *perdiz campiña* (country-style partridge), and *cordero a la miel* (lamb with honey). You can also try local wines here. ✉ *Av. Europa 3* ☎ *957/650004* *AE, DC, MC, V.*

$ **Don Gonzalo.** Just 3 km (2 mi) southwest of Montilla is one of Andalusia's better roadside hotels. The wood-beam-covered common areas have a mixture of decorative elements: note the elephant tusks flanking the TV in the lounge. The clay-tile rooms are large and comfortable;

some look onto the road, others onto the garden and pool. Ask to see the wine cellar; it's a beauty. The hotel also has a highly regarded and elegant restaurant. **Pros:** easy to get to, refreshing swimming pool. **Cons:** outside of town, heavy trucking traffic on nearby highway. ✉*Ctra. Córdoba–Málaga, Km 47* ☎*957/650658* 🌐*www.hoteldongonzalo.com* *35 rooms, 1 suite* *In-room: Wi-Fi. In-hotel: restaurant, bar, tennis court, pool, spa* 💳*AE, DC, MC, V.*

SWEET WINE

Montilla's grapes contain so much sugar (transformed into alcohol during fermentation) that they are not fortified with the addition of extra alcohol. For this reason, the locals claim that Montilla wines do not give you a hangover.

SHOPPING

On the outskirts of town, coopers' shops produce barrels of various sizes, some small enough to serve as creative souvenirs. On Montilla's main road, **Tonelería J. L. Rodríguez** (✉*Ctra. Córdoba–Málaga, Km 43.3* ☎*957/650563* 🌐*www.toneleriajlrodriguez.com*) is worth a stop not just to see the barrels and other things for sale—such as local wines—but also to pop in the back and see them being made.

BAENA

66 km (43 mi) southeast of Córdoba, 42 km (26 mi) east of Montilla.

Outside the boundaries of Subbética and surrounded by chalk fields producing top-quality olives, Baena is an old town of narrow streets, whitewashed houses, ancient mansions, and churches clustered beneath Moorish battlements.

The **Museo del Olivar y el Aceite** is housed in the old olive mill owned and operated by Don José Alcalá Santaella until 1959. The machinery on display dates from the middle of the 19th century, when the mill was capable of processing up to 3 tons a day. The museum aims to demonstrate the most important aspects of olive cultivation, olive oil production, and the way of life of workers in this important industry. You can taste, and buy, olive oil at the shop. ✉*Calle Cañada 7* ☎*957/691641* 🌐*www.museoaceite.com* *€2* *May–Sept., Tues.–Sat. 11–2 and 6–8, Sun. 11–2; Oct.–Apr., Tues.–Fri. 11–2 and 4–6, Sun. 11–2.*

WHERE TO STAY

$–$$ **Fuente las Piedras.** This stylish hotel is on the edge of the Parque Natural Sierra Subbética, 25 km (15 mi) northeast of Baena in the town of Cabra on the A316 road to Jaén. The rooms are elegantly modern and generous in size, and a large pool is surrounded by gardens. **Pros:** good stop midway between Córdoba and Granada, Subbética natural park access. **Cons:** too far from Córdoba and Granada to comfortably use as a base for visiting the cities, hulking facade. ✉*Av. Fuente de las Piedras s/n, Cabra* ☎*957/529740* 🌐 *www.mshoteles.com* *61 rooms* *In-room: Wi-Fi. In-hotel: restaurant, bar, pool, laundry facilities, laundry service, parking (no fee)* 💳*MC, V.*

$$–$$$ ★ **La Casa Grande.** In the center of town just a few steps from the famous Nuñez de Prado olive oil mill, this is the top hotel in Baena, and for miles around. The reception hall is high-ceilinged and elegant, the restaurant is a good reason for stopping in for a meal, and the professional and friendly staff are always helpful. The public rooms throughout the hotel are sumptuous to an almost over-the-top degree with antiques, chandeliers, suits of armor, and old-fashioned paintings, and the rooms are only slightly more muted, so if you like modern minimalist, this hotel is probably not for you. **Pros:** classical elegance, walking distance from everything in town. **Cons:** monumental, more formal than relaxed. ✉*Av. De Cervantes 35* ☎*957/671905* 🌐*www.lacasagrande.es* *38 rooms* *In-room: Wi-Fi. In-hotel: restaurant, bar, pool, laundry facilities, laundry service, parking (no fee)* 💳*AE, DC, MC, V.*

ZUHEROS

80 km (50 mi) southeast of Córdoba, 10 km (6 mi) south of Baena.

At the northern edge of the Subbética mountain range and at an altitude of 2,040 feet, Zuheros is one of the most attractive villages in the province of Córdoba. From the road up, it's hidden behind a dominating rock face topped off by the dramatic ruins of a castle built by the Moors over a Roman castle. The view from here back over the valley is expansive. Next to the castle is the Iglesia de Santa María, built over a mosque. The base of the minaret is the foundation for the bell tower.

WHAT TO SEE

The **Museo Histórico-Arqueológico Municipal** displays archaeological remains found in local caves and elsewhere; some date back to the Middle Palaeolithic period some 35,000 years ago. You can also visit the remains of the Renaissance rooms in the castle, across the road. Call ahead for tour times. ✉*Pl. de la Paz 2* ☎*957/694545* *€2* ⏲*Apr.–Sept., Tues.–Fri. 10–2 and 5–7; weekends 10–7; Oct.–Mar., Tues.–Fri. 10–2 and 4–6; weekends 10–6.*

Housed in an impressive square mansion from 1912, the **Museo de Costumbres y Artes Populares Juan Fernandez Cruz** is at the edge of the village. Exhibits detail local customs and traditions. ✉*Calle Santo s/n* ☎*957/694690* *€2* ⏲*Tues.–Sun. 11–2 and 4–7.*

Found some 4 km (2½ mi) above Zuheros along a windy, twisty road, the **Cueva de los Murciélagos** *(Cave of the Bats)* runs for about 2 km (1¼ mi), although only about half of that expanse is open to the public. The main attractions are the wall paintings dating from the Neolithic Age (6000–3000 BC) and Chalcolithic Age (3000–2000 BC), but excavations have indicated that the cave was inhabited as far back as 35,000 years ago. Items from the Copper and Bronze ages as well as from the Roman period and the Middle Ages have also been found here. Note that due to ongoing restoration work, visits are limited to 20 people. ✉*Information and reservations: Calle Nueva 1* ☎*957/694545 weekdays 10–2 and 5–7* 🌐*www.cuevadelosmurcielagos.com* *€5* ⏲*By appointment only: weekdays 10–2 and 4–6.*

WHERE TO EAT AND STAY

$–$$$ SPANISH **Los Palancos.** Literally built into the cliff face of the towering mountain that Zuheros is built on, this small restaurant and tavern has a fair bit of charm. Expect local mountain-style cuisine featuring roast young goat, rabbit, partridge, and acorn-fed suckling pig, and choose from many items of local produce to take home with you. Vegetarians can opt for the restaurant's renowned goat cheese salad. Apparently, famous soccer player David Beckham likes the food here, and there's a photo on the wall to prove it. *Calle Llana 43 957/694538 MC, V.*

$–$$$ Fodor's Choice ★ **Hacienda Minerva.** This stylish hotel was created out of a country estate dating from the late 19th century. The original features, including the historic oil mill, have been aesthetically preserved, while the rooms are typical Andalusian farmhouse style. The living room has a large fireplace flanked by panoramic windows framing a gorgeous landscape. The restaurant serves creative dishes such as wild boar in a red-current sauce and cannelloni stuffed with partridge. **Pros:** tranquil surroundings, superb gastronomic restaurant. **Cons:** outside the town of Zuheros, no pool. *Carretera Zuheros, Doña Mencia 957/090951 www.haciendaminerva.com 10 rooms In-room: Wi-Fi. In-hotel: restaurant AE, MC, V BP.*

¢ **Zuhayra.** On a narrow street in Zuheros, this small hotel has comfortable large rooms painted a sunny yellow with views over the village rooftops to the valley below. There's a cozy bar and dining room with original beams and an open fireplace. During the summer months diners can sit outside on the attractive cobbled patio. Groups of artists on organized trips often stay here. **Pros:** excellent base camp for exploring the Subbética mountains, cozy public spaces, stunning vistas. **Cons:** a bit far from the center of town, austere decor. *C. Mirador 10 957/694693 www.zercahoteles.com 18 rooms In-room: Wi-Fi. In-hotel: restaurant, bar AE, DC, MC, V.*

PRIEGO DE CÓRDOBA

★ *103 km (64 mi) southeast of Córdoba, 25 km (15 mi) southeast of Zuheros, and 37 km (23 mi) east of Lucena via A339.*

The jewel of Córdoba's countryside is **Priego de Córdoba,** a town of 14,000 inhabitants at the foot of Mt. Tinosa. Wander down Calle del Río, opposite the town hall, to see 18th-century mansions, once the homes of silk merchants. At the end of the street is the Fuente del Rey (King's Fountain), with some 130 water jets, built in 1803. Don't miss the lavish baroque churches of La Asunción and La Aurora or the Barrio de la Villa, an old Moorish quarter with a maze of narrow streets of white-walled buildings.

WHERE TO STAY

$$$$ ★ **Barceló La Bobadilla.** On its own 1,000-acre estate amid olive and oak trees, this complex 42 km (24 mi) west of Priego de Córdoba resembles a Moorish village, or a rambling *cortijo* (ranch). The buildings have white walls, tile roofs, and patios, and there are fountains and an artificial lake on the property. Guest buildings center around a 16th-century-style chapel that houses a 1,595-pipe organ. Each room has a balcony,

a terrace, or a garden. One restaurant serves creative international cuisine, the other is more down-to-earth. The hotel is just south of the La Subbética region, technically in Granada Province, and offers some of the best accommodations in the area. ✉ *Finca La Bobadilla, Apdo 144 E, Loja* ☎ *958/321861* 🌐 *www.barcelolabobadilla.com* *52 rooms, 10 suites* *In-hotel: 3 restaurants, 2 bars, tennis courts, pools, gym, public Wi-Fi* 💳 *AE, DC, MC, V.*

$ **Villa Turística de Priego.** Clustered to form an Andalusian pueblo, the semidetached units of this gleaming-white complex sleep from two to six people each and are surrounded by attractive gardens and a patio. Some have a terrace or balcony. The property is in the heart of the Subbética nature park—near Zagrilla, 6 km (4 mi) from Priego de Córdoba, and the hotel management can arrange activities including horseriding and guided walks. **Pros:** good family base camp, quiet retreat. **Cons:** separated from town life, artificial community. ✉ *Aldea de Zagrilla* ☎ *957/703503* 🌐 *www.villadepriego.com* *47 apartments/villas, 5 rooms* *In-hotel: restaurant, bar, pool, no elevator, public Internet, public Wi-Fi* 💳 *AE, DC, MC, V* ⏲ *Closed Jan.*

LAND OF OLIVES: JAÉN PROVINCE

Jaén is dominated by its *alcázar* (fortress). To the northeast are the olive-producing towns of Baeza and Úbeda. Cazorla, the gateway to the Parque Natural Sierra de Cazorla Segura y Las Villas, lies beyond.

JAÉN

107 km (64 mi) southeast of Córdoba, 93 km (58 mi) north of Granada.

Nestled in the foothills of the Sierra de Jabalcuz, Jaén is surrounded by towering peaks and olive-clad hills. The Arabs called it Geen (Route of the Caravans) because it formed a crossroad between Castile and Andalusia. Captured from the Moors by Saint King Ferdinand III in 1246, Jaén became a frontier province, the site of many a skirmish and battle over the next 200 years between the Moors of Granada and Christians from the north and west. Today the province earns a living from its lead and silver mines and endless olive groves.

ESSENTIALS

Visitor Information **Jaén** (✉ *C. Maestra, 13-Bajo* ☎ *953/242624*).

★ The **Castillo de Santa Catalina,** perched on a rocky crag 400 yards above the center of town, is Jaén's star monument. The castle may have originated as a tower built by Hannibal, but whatever its start, the site was fortified continuously over the centuries. The Nasrid king Alhamar, builder of Granada's Alhambra, constructed an *alcázar* here, but King Ferdinand III captured it from him in 1246 on the feast day of Santa Catalina (St. Catherine). Catalina consequently became Jaén's patron saint, so when the Christians built a castle and chapel here, they dedicated both to her. ✉ *Ctra. del Castillo de Santa Catalina* ☎ *953/120733* 🌐 *www.castillosnet.org* *€3* ⏲ *June–Sept., Thurs.–Tues. 10–2 and 4:30–7; Oct.–May, Thurs.–Tues. 10–2 and 3:30–6.*

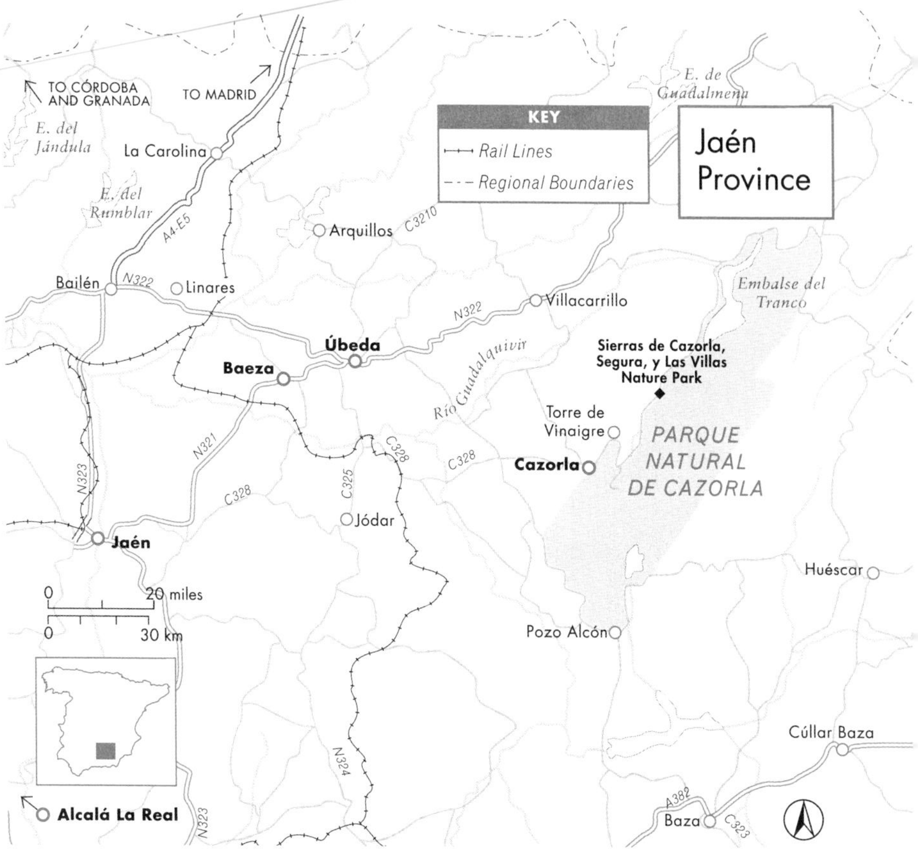

Jaén's **cathedral** is a hulk that looms above the modest buildings around it. Begun in 1492 on the site of a former mosque, it took almost 300 years to build. Its chief architect was Andrés de Vandelvira (1509–75)—many more of his buildings can be seen in Úbeda and Baeza. The ornate facade was sculpted by Pedro Roldán, and the figures on top of the columns include San Fernando (King Ferdinand III) surrounded by the four evangelists. The cathedral's most treasured relic is the **Santo Rostro** (Holy Face), the cloth with which, according to tradition, St. Veronica cleansed Christ's face on the way to Calvary, leaving his image imprinted on the fabric. The *rostro* (face) is displayed every Friday. In the underground **museum,** look for *San Lorenzo,* by Martínez Montañés; the *Immaculate Conception,* by Alonso Cano; and a Calvary scene by Jácobo Florentino. ✉ *Pl. Santa María* ☎ *953/234233* 🎟 *Cathedral free, museum €3* ⏲ *Cathedral Mon.–Sat. 8:30–1 and 5–8, Sun. 9–1 and 6–8; museum Tues.–Sat. 10–1 and 5–8.*

Explore the narrow alleys of old Jaén as you walk from the cathedral to the **Baños Árabes** (Arab Baths), which once belonged to Ali, a Moorish king of Jaén, and probably date from the 11th century. Four hundred years later, in 1592, Fernando de Torres y Portugal, a viceroy of Peru, built himself a mansion, the **Palacio de Villardompardo,** right over the baths, so it took years of painstaking excavation to restore them to their original form. The palace contains a fascinating, albeit small, museum of folk crafts and a larger museum devoted to native art. There are guided tours of the baths, one of the largest and best conserved in Spain, every 30 minutes. ✉ *Palacio de Villardompardo, Pl. Luisa de Marillac* ☎ *953/248068* 🎟 *€1.50* ⏲ *Tues.–Fri. 9–8, weekends 9:30–2:30.*

★ Jaén's **Museo Provincial** has one of the best collections of Iberian (pre-Roman) artifacts in Spain. The newest wing has 20 life-size Iberian sculptures discovered by chance near the village of Porcuna in 1975. The museum proper is in a 1547 mansion and has a patio with the facade of the erstwhile Church of San Miguel. The fine-arts section has a roomful of Goya lithographs. ✉ *Paseo de la Estación 29* ☎ *953/313339* 🎟 *Free* ⏲ *Tues. 3–8, Wed. and Thurs.–Sat. 9–8:30, Sun. 9–2:30.*

WHERE TO EAT AND STAY

$$–$$$$ SPANISH ✕ **Casa Antonio.** Exquisite Andalusian food with a contemporary twist is served at this somber yet elegant restaurant with three small dining rooms, all with cherrywood-panel walls and dramatic contemporary artwork. Try the *foie y queso en milhojas de manzana verde caramelizada en aceite de pistacho* (goose or duck liver and cheese with julienned green apples caramelized in pistachio oil) or *salmonetes de roca en caldo tibio de molusco y aceite de vainilla* (red mullet in a warm mollusk broth and vanilla oil). ✉ *Calle Fermín Palma 3* ☎ *953/270262* 💳 *AE, DC, MC, V* ⏲ *Closed Aug. and Mon. No dinner Sun.*

$$–$$$$ SPANISH ✕ **Casa Vicente.** Locals typically pack this family-run restaurant around the corner from the cathedral. You can have drinks and tapas in the colorful tavern, then move to the cozy dining room or outside patio (depending on the time of year). The traditional local dishes—*pastel de carne de caza* (game pie), *espinacas jienenses* (Jaén-style spinach, cooked with garlic, red peppers, and laurel), and *cordero Mozárabe* (Mozarab-style roast lamb with a sweet-and-sour sauce)—are especially good. ✉ *Calle Francisco Martín Mora 1* ☎ *953/232816* 💳 *AE, MC, V* ⏲ *Closed Aug. and Wed. No dinner Sun.*

$$–$$$ Fodor'sChoice ★ 🏨 **Parador de Jaén.** Built amid the mountaintop towers of the Castillo de Santa Catalina, this 13th-century castle is one of the showpieces of the Parador chain and a reason in itself to visit Jaén. The parador's grandiose exterior echoes the Santa Catalina fortress next door, as do the massive vaulted halls, tapestries, baronial shields, and suits of armor inside. Comfortable bedrooms, with lofty ceilings, Islamic tilework, and canopy beds, have balconies overlooking fields stretching toward a dramatic mountain backdrop. **Pros:** unparalleled architectural grandeur, panoramic views. **Cons:** driving distance (3 mi) from Jaén. ✉ *Calle Castillo de Santa Catalina* ☎ *953/230000* 🌐 *www.parador.es* 🛏 *45 rooms* 👍 *In-room: Wi-Fi. In-hotel: restaurant, pool, Wi-Fi* 💳 *AE, DC, MC, V.*

ALCALÁ LA REAL

75 km (46.5 mi) south of Jaén on N432 and A316.

This ancient city, known to the Iberians and Romans, grew to prominence under the Moors who ruled here for more than 600 years. It was they who gave it the first part of its name, Alcalá, which originated from a word meaning "fortified settlement."

The **Fortaleza de la Mota,** or the "Hilltop Fortress," as it's known today, was installed by the Moors in 727 and sits imperiously at an elevation of 3,389 feet, dominating not only the town but the whole area for miles around. Spectacular views of the peaks of the Sierra Nevada are visible on the southern horizon. During the 12th century the city changed hands frequently as the Moors fought to maintain control of the area. Finally, in 1341, Alfonso XI conquered the town for good, adding Real (Royal) to its name. It remained of strategic importance until the Catholic Monarchs took Granada in 1492—indeed, it was from here that they rode out to accept the keys of the city and the surrender. Hundreds of years later, French forces left the town in ruins after their retreat in the early 19th century. The town itself was gradually rebuilt, but the fortress, consisting of the *alcazaba* (citadel) and the abbey church that Alfonso XI built, were more or less ignored. Up until the late 1990s, it was possible just to drive up and look around—exposed skeletons were visible in some open tombs on the floor of the church. Today visitors can wander around the ruins and visit the small archeological museum. *€1.50 June–Sept., daily 10:30–1:30 and 5–8; Oct.–May, daily 10:30–1:30 and 3:30–6:30.*

WHERE TO STAY

¢ **Hospedería Zacatín.** This smallish hideaway in the center of town is an inexpensive and cozy way station for visitors to Alcalá la Real. Rooms are simply furnished with pine furniture but well equipped with contemporary facilities, including Wi-Fi. The more expensive rooms are slightly larger, with wrought-iron bedsteads and warm peach-colored paint. The restaurant is rustic and comfortable. **Pros:** roof terrace for barbecues and cool evening breezes, typical Andalusian cooking. **Cons:** no frills, street-side rooms can be noisy on weekends. *Calle Pradillo 2 953/580568 www.hospederiazacatin.com 15 rooms In-room: Wi-Fi. In-hotel: restaurant, bar, parking (no fee) AE, DC, MC, V.*

BAEZA

Fodor's Choice ★ *48 km (30 mi) northeast of Jaén on N321.*

The historic town of Baeza is nestled between hills and olive groves. Founded by the Romans, it later housed the Visigoths and became the capital of a Moorish *taifa,* one of some two dozen mini-kingdoms formed after the Ummayad Caliphate was subdivided in 1031. Saint King Ferdinand III captured Baeza in 1227, and for the next 200 years it stood on the frontier of the Moorish kingdom of Granada. In the 16th and 17th centuries, local nobles gave the city a wealth of Renaissance palaces.

ESSENTIALS

Visitor Information Baeza (*Pl. del Pópulo 953/740444*).

EXPLORING

The **Casa del Pópulo,** in the central paseo—where the Plaza del Pópulo (or Plaza de los Leones) and Plaza de la Constitución (or Plaza del Mercado Viejo) merge to form a cobblestone square—is a graceful town house built around 1530. The first Mass of the Reconquest was supposedly celebrated on its curved balcony; it now houses Baeza's tourist office.

In the center of the town square is an ancient Iberian-Roman statue thought to depict Imilce, wife of Hannibal; at the foot of her column is the **Fuente de los Leones** *(Fountain of the Lions).*

Baeza's **cathedral** was originally begun by Ferdinand III on the site of a former mosque. The structure was largely rebuilt by Andrés de Vandelvira, architect of Jaén's cathedral, between 1570 and 1593, though the west front has architectural influences from an earlier period. A fine 14th-century rose window crowns the 13th-century Puerta de la Luna (Moon Door). Don't miss the baroque silver monstrance (a vessel in which the consecrated Host is exposed for the adoration of the faithful), which is carried in Baeza's Corpus Christi processions—the piece is kept in a concealed niche behind a painting, but you can see it in all its splendor by putting a coin in a slot to reveal the hiding place. Next to the monstrance is the entrance to the clock tower, where a small donation and a narrow spiral staircase take you to one of the best views of Baeza. The remains of the original mosque are in the cathedral's Gothic cloisters. ✉ *Pl. de Santa María* ☎ *953/744157* 🎫 *Cathedral free, cloister and small museum €2* ⏲ *May–Sept., daily 10–1 and 5–7; Oct.–Apr., daily 10:30–1 and 4–6.*

Plaza de Santa María. The main square of the medieval city is surrounded by not just the cathedral but also other palaces. The highlight is the fountain, built in 1564 and resembling a triumphal arch.

Iglesia de Santa Cruz. This rather small and plain church dates from the early 13th century. One of the first built here after the Reconquest, it's also one of the earliest Christian churches in all of Andalusia. It has two Romanesque portals and a curved stone altar. ✉ *Pl. de Santa Cruz s/n* 🎫 *Free* ⏲ *Mon.–Sat. 11–1 and 4–5:30, Sun. noon–2.*

Casa Museo de Vera Cruz. Immediately behind the Santa Cruz church, and housed in a building dating from 1540, this museum has religious artifacts from the 16th, 17th, 18th, and 19th centuries. There's also a small shop selling souvenirs, such as local honey, and Virgin Mary key rings. ✉ *Pl. de Santa Cruz s/n* 🎫 *Free* ⏲ *Daily 11–1 and 4–6.*

Palacio de Jabalquinto. Built between the 15th and 16th centuries by Juan Alfonso de Benavides as a palatial home, this palace has a flamboyant Gothic facade and a charming marble colonnaded Renaissance patio. It's a perfect example of how the old can be retained and incorporated into the new. It now encompasses the International University of Andalucía, but you can still wander in and view the patio for free. ✉ *Pl. de Santa Cruz s/n* ⏲ *Weekdays 9–2 and 4–6.*

The ancient student custom of inscribing names and graduation dates in bull's blood (as in Salamanca) is still evident on the walls of the seminary of **San Felipe Neri** (✉ *Cuesta de San Felipe*), built in 1660. It's opposite Baeza's cathedral.

Baeza's ***ayuntamiento*** (town hall) (✉*Pl. Cardenal Benavides, just north of Pl. del Pópulo*) was designed by cathedral master Andrés de Vandelvira. The facade is ornately plateresque; look between the balconies for the coats of arms of Felipe II, the city of Baeza, and the magistrate Juan de Borja. Arrange for a visit to the *salón de plenos,* a major meeting hall with painted, carved woodwork. A few blocks west of the *ayuntamiento,* the 16th-century **Convento de San Francisco** (✉*C. de San Francisco*) is one of Vandelvira's architectural religious masterpieces. You can see its restored remains—the building was spoiled by the French army and partially destroyed by a light earthquake in the early 1800s.

WHERE TO EAT AND STAY

$$–$$$$ SPANISH

Vandelvira. How often do you get the chance to eat in a 16th-century convent? This restaurant, in two galleries on the first floor of the Convento de San Francisco, has lots of character and magnificent antiques, and for food, specialties include the *pâté de perdiz con aceite de oliva virgen* (partridge pâté with olive oil), *solomillo al carbon* (char-grilled steak), and the *manitas de cerdo rellenas de perdiz y espinacas* (pig's knuckles filled with partridge and spinach). There is a summer terrace that doubles as a tavern. ✉*C. de San Francisco 14* ☎*953/748172* *AE, DC, MC, V* *Closed Mon. No dinner Sun.*

¢ ★

Juanito. Rooms in this small, unpretentious hotel are simple and comfortable. The proprietor is a champion of Andalusian food, and the chef has revived such regional specialties in the restaurant ($$) as *alcachofas Luisa* (braised artichokes), *ensalada de perdiz* (partridge salad), and *cordero con habas* (lamb and broad beans); desserts are based on old Moorish recipes. The hotel is next to a gas station on the edge of town, toward Úbeda. **Pros:** fine in-house dining, friendly family staff. **Cons:** on the main road into town, undistinguished modern building. ✉*Paseo Arca del Agua* ☎*953/740040* *www.juanitobaeza.com* *36 rooms, 1 suite* *In-hotel: restaurant, tennis court, pool* *AE, DC, MC, V* *No dinner Sun. and Mon.*

ÚBEDA

Fodor'sChoice ★

9 km (5½ mi) northeast of Baeza on N321.

Úbeda's *casco antiguo* (old town) is one of the most outstanding enclaves of 16th-century architecture in Spain. It's a stunning surprise in the heart of Jaén's olive groves, set in the shadow of the wild Sierra de Cazorla mountain range. For crafts enthusiasts, this is Andalusia's capital for everything from ceramics to leather. Follow signs to the *Zona Monumental* (Monumental Zone), where there are countless Renaissance palaces and stately mansions, though most are closed to the public.

ESSENTIALS

Visitor Information Úbeda (✉*Palacio Marqués del Contadero, C. Baja del Marqués 4* ☎*953/750897*).

EXPLORING

The Plaza del Ayuntamiento is crowned by the privately owned **Palacio de Vela de los Cobos.** It was designed by Andrés de Vandelvira (1505–75), a key figure in the Spanish Renaissance era, for Úbeda's magistrate,

Francisco de Vela de los Cobos. The corner balcony has a central white marble column that's echoed in the gallery above.

Vandelvira's 16th-century Palacio Juan Vázquez de Molina is better known by its nickname, the **Palacio de las Cadenas** (House of Chains), because decorative iron chains were once affixed to the columns of its main doorway. It's now the town hall and has entrances on both Plaza Vázquez de Molina and Plaza Ayuntamiento. Molina was a nephew of Francisco de los Cobos, and both served as secretaries to Emperor Carlos V and King Felipe II.

The Plaza Vázquez de Molina, in the heart of the old town, is the site of the **Sacra Capilla de El Salvador.** This building is photographed so often that it's become the city's unofficial symbol. Sacra Capilla was built by Vandelvira, but he based his design on some 1536 plans by Diego de Siloé, architect of Granada's cathedral. Considered one of the masterpieces of Spanish Renaissance religious art, the chapel was sacked in the frenzy of church burnings at the outbreak of the civil war. However, it retains its ornate western facade and altarpiece, which has a rare Berruguete sculpture. ⊠*Pl. Vázquez de Molina* ☎*953/758150* *€3* *Mon.–Sat. 10–2 and 4:30–7, Sun. 10:45–2 and 4:30–7.*

The **Ayuntamiento Antiguo** (Old Town Hall), begun in the early 16th century but restored as a beautiful arcaded baroque palace in 1680, is now a conservatory of music. From the hall's upper balcony, the town council watched celebrations and *autos-da-fé* ("acts of faith"—executions of heretics sentenced by the Inquisition) in the square below. You can't enter the town hall, but on the north side you can visit the 13th-century church of San Pablo, with an Isabelline south portal. ⊠*Pl. Primero de Mayo, off C. María de Molina Free* *1-hr tour at 7* PM.

The **Hospital de Santiago,** sometimes jokingly called the Escorial of Andalusia (in allusion to Felipe II's monolithic palace and monastery outside Madrid), is a huge, angular building in the modern section of town, and yet another one of Andrés de Vandelvira's masterpieces in Úbeda. The plain facade is adorned with ceramic medallions, and over the main entrance is a carving of Santiago Matamoros (St. James the Moorslayer) in his traditional horseback pose. Inside are an arcaded patio and a grand staircase. Now a cultural center, it holds some of the events at the International Spring Dance and Music Festival. ⊠*Av. Cristo Rey* ☎*953/750842* *Free* *Daily 8–3 and 4–10.*

Casa Museo Arte Andalusi. The town's latest museum is in an attractive building with a traditional patio. The exhibits are a former private collection of period antiques including Moorish, Mudejar, and Mozarabic pieces. ⊠*Calle Narvaez 11* ☎*619/076132* *Free* *Daily 10:30–2:30 and 4–8:30.*

WHERE TO EAT AND STAY

$–$$ SPANISH ✕**La Posada de Úbeda.** This inn and restaurant on a back street doubles as a modest little agricultural museum and is one of Úbeda's most characteristic concentrations of charm, folklore, and authentic no-fuss regional cuisine. The *migas* (bread crumbs, sausage, bacon, and garlic) is a typical dish, as is the *andrajos* (a stew of fish, pasta, and vegetables). You can gaze at the various agricultural artifacts while you dine. ✉ *Calle de San Cristóbal 17* ☎ *953/790473* ▭ *AE, DC, MC, V.*

$–$$ SPANISH ✕ **Mesón Gabino.** A stalwart and respected defender of Úbeda's culinary traditions, with the standard *andrajos de Úbeda* (fish, pasta, and vegetable stew) and *migas* on the menu, this cavelike restaurant on the edge of the Renaissance town near the Puerta del Losal is well worth the walk out from Plaza 1 de Mayo. Beef, lamb, and fish cooked over coals are always delicious here, while the wine list offers an ample range of Rioja and Ribera de Duero selections. Lighter appetites can opt for tapas at the bar. ✉ *Calle Fuente Seca s/n* ☎ *953/757553* ▭ *AE, DC, MC, V* ⊗ *Closed Sun.*

$$–$$$ **Palacio de la Rambla.** In old Úbeda, this beautiful 16th-century mansion has been in the same family since it was built, and part of it still hosts the regal Marquesa de la Rambla when she's in town. Eight of the rooms are open to overnighters; each is unique, but all are large and furnished with original antiques, tapestries, and works of art, and some have chandeliers and four-poster beds. The palace is arranged on two levels, around a cool, ivy-covered patio. **Pros:** central location, elegant decor. **Cons:** public space limited, parking problematic (property accommodates only four compact cars). ✉ *Pl. del Marqués 1* ☎ *953/750196* 🌐 *www.palaciodelarambla.com* *6 rooms, 2 suites* *In-hotel: no elevator, parking (fee)* ▭ *AE, DC, MC, V.*

$$$ Fodor's Choice ★ **Parador de Úbeda.** This splendid parador is in a 16th-century ducal palace in a prime location on the Plaza Vázquez de Molina, next to the Capilla del Salvador. A grand stairway decked with tapestries and suits of armor leads up to the guest rooms, which have tile floors, lofty ceilings, dark Castilian-style furniture, four-poster beds, and large bathtubs. The dining room ($$$), specializing in regional dishes, serves some of the best food in Úbeda; try the typical local favorite *perdiz* (partridge) with *habas* (broad beans). There's a bar in the vaulted basement. **Pros:** elegant Renaissance surroundings, perfect location. **Cons:** parking is difficult, El Salvador's bells begin early in the morning. ✉ *Pl. Vázquez de Molina s/n* ☎ *953/750345* 🌐 *www.parador.es* *35 rooms, 1 suite* *In-room: Wi-Fi. In-hotel: restaurant, bar* ▭ *AE, DC, MC, V.*

$–$$ **Rosaleda de Don Pedro.** This beautiful 16th-century mansion, in the city's *Zona Monumental*, blends the best of the old with many of the comforts a modern traveler would want, including king-size beds. Rooms and public areas are spacious and the pool offers relief from the summer heat. The restaurant serves good traditional cuisine. **Pros:** easy parking, good food. **Cons:** hard to find, less than effusive reception. ✉ *Calle Obispo Toral 2* ☎ *953/795147* 🌐 *www.rosaledadedonpedro.com* *45 rooms* *In-room: Wi-Fi. In-hotel: restaurant, bar, pool, public Internet, parking (fee)* ▭ *AE, DC, MC, V.*

SHOPPING

Little Úbeda is the crafts capital of Andalusia, with workshops devoted to carpentry, basket weaving, stone carving, wrought iron, stained glass, and, above all, the city's distinctive green-glaze pottery. Calle Valencia is the traditional potters' row, running from the bottom of town to Úbeda's general crafts center, northwest of the old quarter (follow signs to Calle Valencia or Barrio de Alfareros). Úbeda's most famous potter was Pablo Tito, whose craft is carried on at three different workshops run by two of Tito's sons, Paco and Juan, and a son-in-law, Melchor, each of whom claims to be the sole true heir to the art.

All kinds of ceramics are sold at **Alfarería Góngora** (✉ *Calle Cuesta de la Merced 32* ☎ *953/754605*). **Antonio Almazara** (✉ *Calle Valencia 34* ☎ *953/753692* ✉ *Calle Fuenteseca 17* ☎ *953/753365*) is one of several shops specializing in Úbeda's green-glaze pottery. The extrovert **Juan Tito** (✉ *Pl. del Ayuntamiento 12* ☎ *953/751302*) can often be found at the potter's wheel in his rambling shop, which is packed with ceramics of every size and shape. **Melchor Tito** (✉ *Calle Valencia 44* ☎ *953/753365*) focuses on classic green-glaze items. **Paco Tito** (✉ *Calle Valencia 22* ☎ *953/751496*) devotes himself to clay sculptures of characters from *Don Quixote,* which he fires in an old Moorish-style kiln. His shop has a small museum as well as a studio.

CAZORLA

48 km (35 mi) southeast of Úbeda.

Unspoiled and remote, the village of Cazorla is at the east end of Jaén province. The pine-clad slopes and towering peaks of the Cazorla and Segura sierras rise above the village, and below it stretch endless miles of olive groves. In spring, purple jacaranda trees blossom in the plazas.

EXPLORING

For a break from human-made sights, drink in the scenery or watch for wildlife in the **Parque Natural Sierra de Cazorla, Segura y Las Villas** *(Cazorla, Segura and Las Villas Nature Park).* Deer, wild boar, and mountain goats roam the slopes of this carefully protected patch of mountain wilderness 80 km (50 mi) long and 30 km (19 mi) wide, and hawks, eagles, and vultures soar over the 6,000-foot peaks. Within the park, at **Cañada de las Fuentes** (Fountains' Ravine), is the source of Andalusia's great river, the Guadalquivir. The road through the park follows the river to the shores of **Lago Tranco de Beas.** Alpine meadows, pine forests, springs, waterfalls, and gorges make Cazorla a perfect place to hike. Past Lago Tranco and the village of Hornos, a road goes to the **Sierra de Segura** mountain range, the park's least crowded area. At 3,600 feet, the spectacular village of **Segura de la Sierra,** on top of the mountain, is crowned by an almost perfect castle with impressive defense walls, a Moorish bath, and a nearly rectangular bullring.

A short film shown in the **Centro de Interpretación Torre del Vinagre** (✉ *Ctra. del Tranco, Km 37.8* ☎ *953/713040* ⏲ *Daily 11–2 and 4–6*), in Torre de Vinagre, introduces the park's main sights. Displays explain the park's plants and geology, and the staff can advise you on camping, fishing, and hiking trails. There's also a **hunting museum,** with random attractions such as the interlocked antlers of bucks who clashed in autumn rutting season, became helplessly trapped, and died of starvation. Nearby are a **botanical garden** and a **game reserve.**

Early spring is the ideal time to visit; try to avoid the summer and late spring months, when the park teems with tourists and locals. It's often difficult, though by no means impossible, to find accommodations in fall, especially on weekends during hunting season (between September and February). Between June and October the park maintains seven well-equipped campsites. For information on hiking, camping, canoeing, horseback riding, or guided excursions, contact the **Agencia de Medio Ambiente** (✉*Tejares Altos, Cazorla* ☎*953/720125* ✉*Fuente de Serbo 3, Jaén* ☎*953/012400*), or the park visitor center. For hunting or fishing permits, apply to the Jaén office well in advance.

Déjate Guiar-Excursiones organizes four-wheel-drive trips into restricted areas of the park to observe the flora and fauna and photograph the larger animals. ✉*Paseo del Santo Cristo 17, Bajo, Edificio Parque* ☎*953/721351* 🌐*www.turisnat.org.*

EN ROUTE

Leave Cazorla Nature Park by an alternative route—drive along the spectacular **gorge** carved by the Guadalquivir River: it's a rushing torrent beloved by kayak enthusiasts. At the El Tranco Dam, follow signs to Villanueva del Arzobispo, where N322 takes you back to Úbeda, Baeza, and Jaén.

WHERE TO STAY

$ Fodor's Choice ★ **Casa Rural La Calerilla.** Tucked into the mountainside on the road leading down to Cazorla, and almost hidden from the road itself, is this charming stone *casa rural* (rural house), which has been exquisitely transformed into a sophisticated small hotel. The rooms are tastefully decorated with terra-cotta tiles, brass bed heads, and white linens, and have superb countryside views. The garden and pool area is a great place to wind down. The management can organize activities like horseriding, guided walks, and rock climbing. **Pros:** personal touch, proximity to natural park, equestrian and other sports options. **Cons:** remote location, scant Internet. ✉*Ctra. del Tranco, Km 24.5, Burunchel* ☎*953/727326* 🌐*www.casaruralcalerilla.com* *11 rooms* *In-hotel: restaurant, bar, pool, no elevator, public Internet, parking (no fee)* *MC, V.*

$ **Coto del Valle.** This delightful hotel in Cazorla's foothills is easily recognized by the huge fountain outside. Surrounded by pine trees, the modern hotel has been built using a traditional highland stone architectural style, with wooden beams and terra-cotta tiles. The rooms have a simple rustic decor, and there is a large restaurant with a fireplace and mounted game ranging from mountain goats to red leg partridges. **Pros:** nature lover's paradise, perfect hiker's base camp. **Cons:** undistinguished restaurant, 10-minute drive from nearest town. ✉*Ctra. del Tranco, Km 34.3* ☎*953/124067* 🌐*www.hotelcotodelvalle.com* *59 rooms* *In-hotel: restaurant, bar, pool, public Wi-Fi, parking (no fee)* *AE, DC, MC, V* *Closed Dec.*

$$–$$$ **Parador de Cazorla.** You'll find this modern, white parador with its red-tile roof isolated in a valley at the edge of the nature reserve, 26 km (16 mi) above Cazorla village. Despite the disappointing exterior, the setting is bucolic, amid a pine forest on a hillside. It's a quiet place, popular with hunters and anglers. The restaurant ($$–$$$$) serves regional dishes such as *pipirrana* (a salad of finely diced peppers, onions, and tomatoes) and, in season, game. **Pros:** lovely views from the pool, mountain cooking. **Cons:** only nine rooms have views, slow going in bad weather. ✉*Calle Sierra de Cazorla* ☎*953/727075* 🌐*www.parador.es*

34 rooms In-room: Wi-Fi. In-hotel: restaurant, pool, parking (no fee) AE, DC, MC, V Closed Dec. 19–Feb. 6.

$ **Villa Turística de Cazorla.** On a hill with superb views of the village of Cazorla, this leisure complex rents semidetached apartments that sleep four to six guests. Each has a balcony or terrace as well as a kitchenette—some have a full kitchen—and fireplace. The restaurant ($–$$$), done in welcoming warm ocher tones, specializes in trout, lamb, and, in particular, game, with dishes like wild boar in a honey-based sauce on the menu. **Pros:** self-catering option. **Cons:** popular with noisy families, decor functional but plain. *Ladera de San Isicio s/n 953/710100 www.villacazorla.com 32 apartments In-room: kitchen. In-hotel: restaurant, bar, pool MC, V.*

GRANADA

430 km (265 mi) south of Madrid, 261 km (162 mi) east of Seville, and 160 km (100 mi) southeast of Córdoba.

The Alhambra and the tomb of the Catholic Monarchs are the pride of Granada. The city rises majestically from a plain onto three hills, dwarfed—on a clear day—by the Sierra Nevada. Atop one of these hills perches the reddish-gold Alhambra palace. The stunning view from the palace promontory takes in the sprawling medieval Moorish quarter, the caves of the Sacromonte, and, in the distance, the fertile *vega* (plain), rich in orchards, tobacco fields, and poplar groves.

Split by internal squabbles, Granada's Moorish Nasrid dynasty gave Ferdinand of Aragón an opportunity in 1491; spurred by Isabella's religious fanaticism, he laid siege to the city for seven months, and on January 2, 1492, Boabdil, the "Rey Chico" (Boy King), was forced to surrender the keys of the city to the Catholic Monarchs. As Boabdil fled the Alhambra via the Puerta de los Siete Suelos (Gate of the Seven Floors), he asked that the gate be sealed forever.

GETTING HERE AND AROUND

In Granada, **J. González** buses (€3) run between the center of town and the airport, leaving every 30 minutes from the Palacio de Congresos, and making a few other stops along the way to the airport. Times are listed at the bus stop; service is reduced in winter. **Line 14**, a municipal bus service (€1), also operates between the airport and the city center, with buses every 30 minutes.

Granada's main bus station is at Carretera de Jaén, 3 km northwest of the center of town beyond the end of Avenida de Madrid. Most buses operate from here, except for buses to nearby destinations such as Fuentevaqueros, Viznar, and some buses to Sierra Nevada, which leave from the city center's Plaza del Triunfo near the Renfe station. Luggage lockers (*la consigna*), at the main bus station, cost €2.

Autocares Bonal operates buses between Granada and the Sierra Nevada. **Alsina Gräells** buses run to Las Alpujarras, Córdoba (8 times daily), Seville (10 times daily), Málaga (14 times daily), and Jaén, Baeza, Úbeda, Cazorla, Almeria, Almuñécar, and Nerja several times daily.

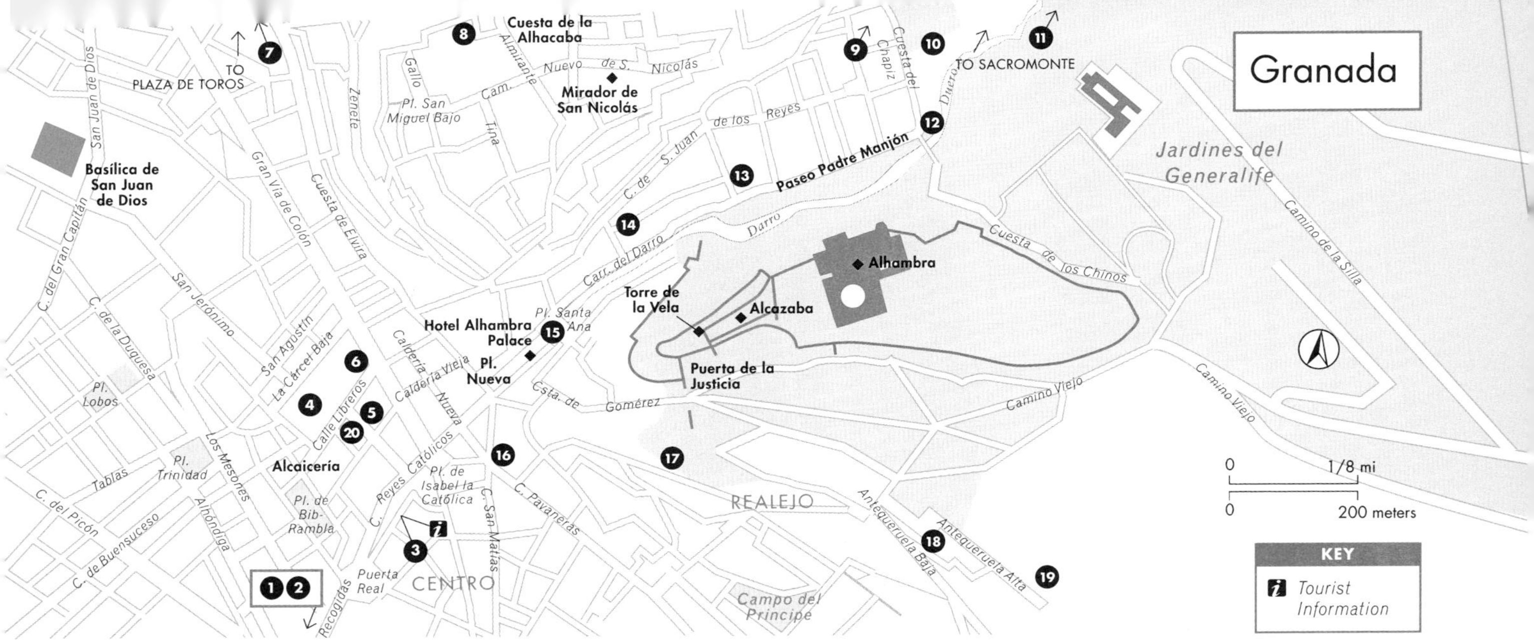

Abadia de Sacromonte ... **11**
Capilla Real **6**
Carmen de los Mártires **19**
Casa de Castril **13**
Casa de los Pisa **15**
Casa del Chapíz **10**
Casa-Museo de Manuel de Falla **18**
Casa-Museo Federico García Lorca **2**
Cathedral **4**
Centro de Interpretación del Sacromonte **9**
Centro José Guerrero **20**
Corral del Carbón **3**
Dar al-Horra **8**
El Bañuelo **14**
Fundación Rodríguez-Acosta/ Instituto Gómez Moreno .. **17**
Monasterio de La Cartuja **7**
Museo de Artes y Costumbres Populares— Casa de los Tiros **16**
Palacio de los Córdova ... **12**
Palacio Madraza **5**
Parque de las Ciencias **1**

There are regular trains to Seville and Almeria, but service to Málaga and Córdoba are less convenient, necessitating a change at Bobadilla. A new fast track is currently under construction, however, which will reduce these journey times considerably. There are a couple of daily trains to Madrid, Valencia, and Barcelona from Granada

Granada has an extensive public bus network within the city. You can buy 6- and 21-trip discount passes on the buses and 10-trip passes at newsstands. The single-trip fare is €1.10.

In Granada, **CitySightseeing Granada** bus tours include informative commentary on major sights. Tickets, which cost €10 and are valid for 24 hours (€18 for 48 hours), allow you to hop on and off both the large open-topped bus that takes in the sights in the lower city and the minibus that winds up to the Alhambra and through the narrow streets of Albaicín.

ESSENTIALS

Airport Contacts Aeropuerto de Granada (Aeropuerto Federico García Lorca) (☎ *958/245200*).

Bus Station Granada (✉ *Ctra. Jaén, Granada* ☎ *958/185480*).

Taxi Contacts Asociació de RadioTaxi (✉ *Granada* ☎ *958/132323*).**Tele Radio Taxi** (✉ *Granada* ☎ *958/280654*).

Tour Contacts CitySightseeing Granada (✉ *Gran Vía de Colón s/n, Granada* ☎ *902/101081*).

Train Contacts Station (✉ *Av. de los Andaluces s/n* ☎ *958/271272*).

Visitor Information Provincial Tourist Office (✉ *Pl. Mariana Pineda 10, Centro* ☎ *958/247146* 🌐 *www.turismodegranada.org*).

EXPLORING

Granada can be characterized by its major neighborhoods: East of the Darro River and up the hill is **La Alhambra.** South of it and around a square and a popular hangout area, Campo del Príncipe, is **Realejo.** To the west of the Darro and going from north to south are the two popular neighborhoods, **Sacromonte** and **Albayzín** (also spelled Albaicín) The latter is the young and trendy part of Granada, full of color, flavor, and charming old architecture and narrow, hilly streets. On either side of Gran Vía de Colón and the streets that border the cathedral (Reyes Católicos and Recogidas—the major shopping areas) is the area generally referred to as **Centro,** the city center. These days much of the Alhambra and Albayzín areas are closed to cars, but starting from the Plaza Nueva there are now minibuses—numbers 30, 31, 32, and 34—that run frequently to these areas.

LA ALHAMBRA

Fodor'sChoice ★ **Alhambra.** With more than 2 million visitors a year, the Alhambra is Spain's most popular attraction. The complex has three main parts: the Alcazaba, the Palacios Nazaríes (Nasrid Royal Palace), and the Generalife, the ancient summer palace. The Museo de la Alhambra is in the Alhambra building, too. *See the Alhambra In-Focus feature for more details.*

19 **Carmen de los Mártires.** Up the hill from the Hotel Alhambra Palace, this turn-of-the-20th-century Granada *carmen* (private villa), and its gardens—the only area open to tourists—are like a Generalife in miniature. ✉ *Paseo de los Mártires, Alhambra* ☎ *958/227953* 🎫 *Free* ⏲ *Apr.–Oct., weekdays 10–2 and 5–7, weekends 10–7; Nov.–Mar., weekdays 10–2 and 4–6, weekends 10–6.*

18 **Casa-Museo de Manuel de Falla.** The composer Manuel de Falla (1876–1946) lived and worked for many years in this rustic house tucked into a charming hillside lane with lovely views of the Alpujarra Mountains. In 1986 Granada paid homage to Spain's classical-music composer by naming its new concert hall (down the street from the Carmen de los Mártires) the Auditorio Manuel de Falla—and from this institution, fittingly, you have a view of his little white house. Note the bust in the small garden: it's placed where the composer once sat to enjoy the sweeping view. ✉ *C. Antequeruela Alta 11, Alhambra* ☎ *958/228318* 🌐 *www.museomanueldefalla.com* 🎫 *€2* ⏲ *Sept.–June, Tues.–Sun. 10–1:30; July and Aug., Thurs.–Sun. 10–1:30.*

REALEJO

17 **Fundación Rodríguez-Acosta/Instituto Gómez Moreno.** A few yards from the impressive Alhambra Hotel, this nonprofit organization was founded at the bequeath of the painter José Marí Rodríguez-Acosta. Inside a typical Granadino *carmen* (private villa), it houses works of art, archaeological findings, and a library collected by the Granada-born scholar Manuel Gómez-Moreno Martínez. Other exhibits include valuable and unique objects from Asian cultures and the prehistoric and classical eras. ✉ *Callejón Niños del Rollo 8, Realejo* ☎ *958/227497* 🌐 *www.fundacionrodriguezacosta.com* 🎫 *€4* ⏲ *Wed.–Sun. 10–2; last entrance 30 min before closing.*

15 **Museo de Artes y Costumbres Populares–Casa de los Tiros.** This 16th-century palace, adorned with the coat of arms of the Grana Venegas family who owned it, was named House of the Shots for the musket barrels that protrude from its facade. The stairs to the upper-floor displays are flanked by portraits of miserable-looking Spanish royals, from Ferdinand and Isabella to Philip IV. The highlight is the carved wooden ceiling in the Cuadra Dorada (Hall of Gold), adorned with gilded lettering and portraits of royals and knights. Old lithographs, engravings, and photographs show life in Granada in the 19th and early 20th centuries. ✉ *Calle Pavaneras s/n, Realejo* ☎ *958/221072* 🌐 *www.juntadeandalucia.es/cultura/museocasadelostiros* 🎫 *€3* ⏲ *Tues. 2:30–8:30, Wed.–Sat. 9–8:30, Sun. 9–2:30.*

SACROMONTE

The third of Granada's three hills, the Sacromonte rises behind the Albayzín. The hill is covered with prickly pear cacti and riddled with caverns. The Sacromonte has long been notorious as a domain of Granada's gypsies and thus a den of thieves and scam artists, but its reputation is largely undeserved. The quarter is more like a quiet Andalusian *pueblo* (village) than a rough neighborhood. Many of the quarter's colorful *cuevas* (caves) have been restored as middle-class homes, and some of the old spirit lives on in a handful of *zambras*—flamenco performances

A GOOD WALK: GRANADA

Save a full day for the Alhambra and the Alhambra hill sights: the **Alcazaba, Generalife, Alhambra Museum, Fundación Rodríguez Acosta/Instituto Gomez Moreno** ⓱, **Casa-Museo de Manuel de Falla** ⓲, and **Carmen de los Mártires** ⓳. This walk covers the other major Granada sights.

Begin at Plaza Isabel la Católica (corner of Gran Vía and Calle Reyes Católicos), with its statue of Columbus presenting the Queen with his New World maps. Walk south on Calle Reyes Católicos and turn left into the **Corral del Carbón** ❸—the oldest building in Granada.

Cross back over Calle Reyes Católicos to the **Alcaicería,** once the Moorish silk market and now a maze of alleys with souvenir shops and restaurants. Behind the Alcaicería is Plaza Bib-Rambla, with its flower stalls and historic Gran Café Bib-Rambla, famous for hot chocolate and *churros.* Calle Oficios leads to **Palacio Madraza** ❺, the old Moorish University, and the **Capilla Real** ❻, next to the **cathedral** ❹.

Off the cathedral's west side is the 16th-century Escuela de las Niñas Nobles, with its plateresque facade. Next to the cathedral, just off Calle Libreros, are the Curia Eclesiástica, an Imperial College until 1769; the Palacio del Arzobispo; and the 18th-century Iglesia del Sagrario. Behind the cathedral is the Gran Vía de Colón. Detour to the **Museo de Artes Y Costumbres Populares-Casa de los Tiros** ⓰ (on Calle Pavaneras) before heading to Plaza Isabel la Católica. Follow Reyes Católicos to Plaza Nueva and the ornate 16th-century Real Cancillería (Royal Chancery), now the Tribunal Superior de Justicia (High Court). Just north is Plaza Santa Ana and the church of Santa Ana.

Walk through Plaza Santa Ana to Carrera del Darro—which flanks the river and is lined with shops, hotels, bars, and restaurants—and you come to the 11th-century Arab bathhouse, **El Bañuelo** ⓮, and the 16th-century **Casa de Castril** ⓭, site of Granada's Archaeological Museum.

Follow the river along the Paseo del Padre Manjón (Paseo de los Tristes)—to the **Palacio de los Córdoba** ⓬. Climb Cuesta del Chapíz to the Morisco **Casa del Chapíz** ❿. To the east are the caves of Sacromonte and the **Centro de Interpretación del Sacromonte (Cuevas)** ❾. Turn west into the streets of the Albayzín, with the **Casa de los Pisa** ⓯ and **Dar al-Horra** ❽ nearby. Best reached by taxi are the 16th-century **Monasterio de La Cartuja** ❼, the interactive science museum **Parque de las Ciencias** ❶, and **Casa-Museo Federico García Lorca** ❷.

in caves garishly decorated with brass plates and cooking utensils. These shows differ from formal flamenco shows in that the performers mingle with you, usually dragging one or two onlookers onto the floor for an improvised dance lesson. Ask your hotel to book you a spot on a cueva tour, which usually includes a walk through the neighboring Albayzín and a drink at a tapas bar in addition to the *zambra.*

⓫ The caverns on Sacromonte are thought to have sheltered early Christians; 15th-century treasure hunters found bones inside and assumed

Continued on page 711

ALHAMBRA

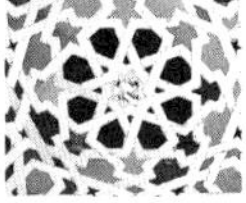

Floating mirage-like on its promontory overlooking Granada, the mighty and mysterious Alhambra shimmers vermilion in the clear mountain air, with the white peaks of the Sierra Nevada rising behind it. This sprawling palace-fortress, named from the Arabic for "red citadel" *(al-Qal'ah al-Hamra)*, was the last bastion of the 800-year Moorish presence on the Iberian Peninsula. Composed of royal residential quarters, court chambers, baths, and gardens, surrounded by defense towers and massive walls, the Alhambra is an architectual gem where Moorish kings worked and played—and even murdered their enemies.

LOOK UP

Among the stylistic elements you can see in the Alhambra are **Arabesque** geometrical designs, and elaborate **Mocárabe** arches.

Built of perishable materials, the Alhambra was meant to be forever replenished and replaced by succeeding generations. Currently, it is the Patio de los Leones's (above) season for restoration.

INSIDE THE FORTRESS

More than 2 million annual visitors come to the Alhambra today, making it Spain's top attraction. Vistors revel in the palace's architectural wonders, most of which had to be restored after the alterations made after the Christian reconquest of southern Spain in 1492 and the damage from an 1821 earthquake. Incidentally, Napoléon's troops commandeered the site in 1812 with intent to level it; their attempts were foiled.

The courtyards, patios, and halls offer an ethereal maze of Moorish arches, columns, and domes containing intricate stucco carvings and patterned ceramic tiling. The intimate arcades, fountains, and light-reflecting pools throughout are identified in the ornamental inscriptions as physical renderings of paradise taken from the Koran and Islamic poetry. The contemporary visitor to this dreamlike space feels the fleeting embrace of a culture that brought its light to a world emerging from medieval darkness.

ARCHITECTURAL TERMS

Arabesque: An ornament or decorative style that employs flower, foliage, or fruit, and sometimes geometrical, animal, and figural outlines to produce an intricate pattern of interlaced lines.

Mocárabe: A decorative element of carved wood or plaster based on juxtaposed and hanging prisms resembling stalactites. Sometimes called *muquarna* (honeycomb vaulting), the impression is similar to a beehive and the honey has been described as light.

Mozárabe: Sometimes confused with Mocárabe, the term Mozárabe refers to Christians living in Moorish Spain. Thus, Christian artistic styles or recourses in Moorish architecture (such as the paintings in the Sala de los Reyes) also are identified as *mozárabe*, or, in English, mozarabic.

Mudéjar: This word refers to Moors living in Christian Spain. Moorish artistic elements in Christian architecture, such as horseshoe arches in a church, also are referred to as Mudéjar.

ALHAMBRA'S ARCHITECTURAL HIGHLIGHTS

The **columns** used in the construction of the Alhambra are unique, with extraordinarily slender cylindrical shafts, concave base moldings, and carved rings decorating the upper extremities. The capitals have simple cylindrical bases under prism-shaped heads decorated in a variety of vegetal motifs. Nearly all of these columns support false arches constructed purely for decorative purposes. The 124 columns surrounding the Patio de los Leones (Court of the Lions) are the best examples.

Cursive epigraphy is used to quote the Koran and Arabic poems. Considered the finest example of this are the Ibn-Zamrak verses that decorate the walls of the Sala de las Dos Hermanas.

Glazed ceramic tiles covered with geometrical patterns in primary colors cover the walls of the Alhambra with a profusion of styles and shapes. Red, blue, and yellow are the colors of magic in Sufi tradition, while green is the life-giving color of Islam.

The **horseshoe arch**, widening before rounding off with lower ends extending around the circle until they begin to converge, was the quintessential Moorish architectural innovation, used not only for aesthetic and decorative purposes but because it allowed greater height than the classical, semicircular arch inherited from the Greeks and Romans. The horseshoe arch also had a mystical significance in recalling the shape of the *mihrab*, the prayer niche in the *qibla* wall of a mosque indicating the direction of prayer and suggesting a door to Mecca or to paradise. Horseshoe arches and arcades are found throughout the Alhambra.

The Koran describes paradise as "gardens underneath which rivers flow," and **water** is used as a practical and ornamental architectural element throughout the Alhambra. Whether used musically, as in the canals in the Patio de los Leones or visually, as in the reflecting pool of the Patio de los Arrayanes, water is used to enhance light, enlarge spaces, or provide musical background for a desert culture in love with the beauty and oasis-like properties of hydraulics in all its forms.

Court of the Lions

Cursive epigraphy

Ceramic tiles

Gate of Justice

Alhambra fountains

The Alcazaba was built chiefly by Nasrid kings in the 1300s.

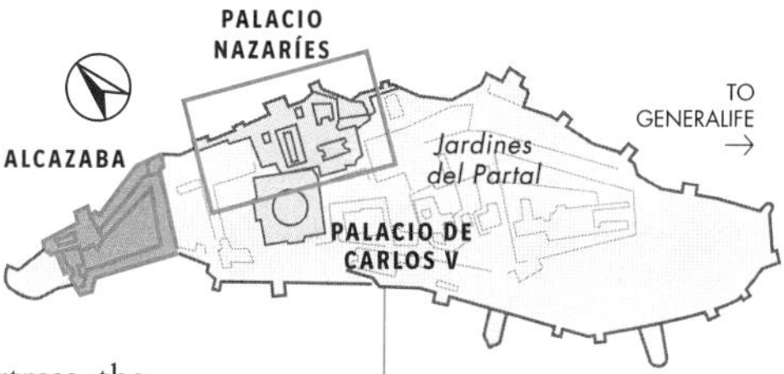

LAY OF THE LAND

The complex has three main parts: the Alcazaba, the Palacio Nazaríes (Nasrid Royal Palace), and the Generalife. Across from the main entrance is the original fortress, the **Alcazaba**. Here, the watchtower's great bell was once used to announce the opening and closing of the irrigation system on Granada's great plain.

A wisteria-covered walkway leads to the heart of the Alhambra, the **Palacios Nazaríes**. Here, delicate apartments, lazy fountains, and tranquil pools contrast vividly with the hulking fortifications outside. It is divided into three sections: the *mexuar,* where business, government, and palace administration were headquartered; the *serrallo,* a series of state rooms where the sultans held court and entertained their ambassadors; and the harem, which in its time was entered only by the sultan, his family, and their most trusted servants, most of them eunuchs. Nearby is the Renaissance Palacio de Carlos V (Palace of Charles V), featuring a perfectly square exterior but a circular interior courtyard. Designed by Pedro Machuca, a pupil of Michelangelo, it is where the sultan's private apartments once stood. Part of the building houses the free **Museo de la Alhambra**, devoted to Islamic art. Upstairs is the more modest **Museo de Bellas Artes.**

Over on Cerro del Sol (Hill of the Sun) is **Generalife**, ancient summer palace of the Nasrid kings.

TIMELINE

1238 First Nasrid king, Ibn el-Ahmar, begins Alhambra.

1391 Nasrid Palaces is completed.

1492 Boabdil surrenders Granada to Ferdinand and Isabella, parents of King Henry VIII's first wife, Catherine of Aragon.

1524 Carlos V begins Renaissance Palace.

1812 Napoléonic troops arrive with plans to destroy Alhambra.

1814 The Duke of Wellington sojourns here to escape the pressures of the Peninsular War.

1829 Washington Irving lives on the premises and writes *Tales of the Alhambra,* reviving interest in the crumbling palace.

1862 Granada municipality begins Alhambra restoration that continues to this day.

2006 The Patio de los Leones undergoes a multiyear restoration.

ALHAMBRA'S PASSAGES OF TIME

From Columbus's commissioning to a bloody murder, historic events as well as everyday affairs happened between these walls.

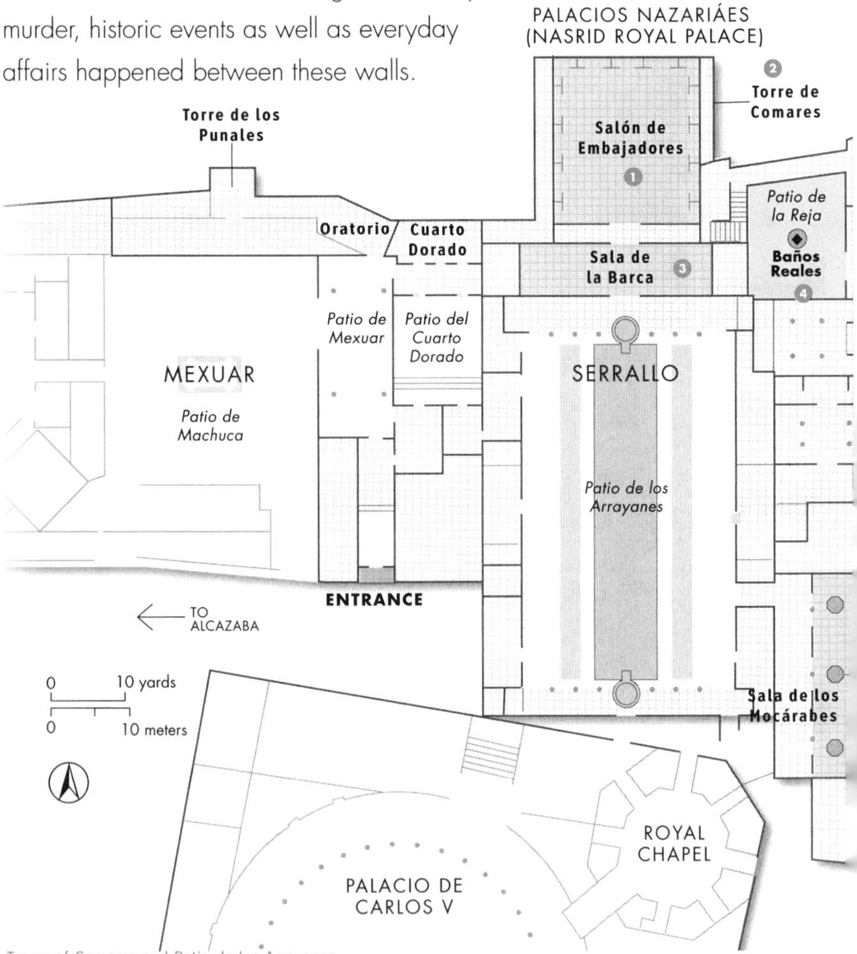

Tower of Comares and Patio de los Arrayanes

❶ In **El Salón de Embajadores**, Boabdil drew up his terms of surrender, and Christopher Columbus secured royal support for his historic voyage in 1492. The carved wooden ceiling is a portrayal of the seven Islamic heavens, with six rows of stars topped by a seventh-heaven cupulino or micro-cupola.

❷ **Torre de Comares**, a lookout in the corner of this hall is where Carlos V uttered his famous line, "Ill-fated the man who lost all this."

❸ Mistakenly named from the Arabic word *baraka* (divine blessing), **Sala de la Barca** has a carved wooden ceiling often described as an inverted boat.

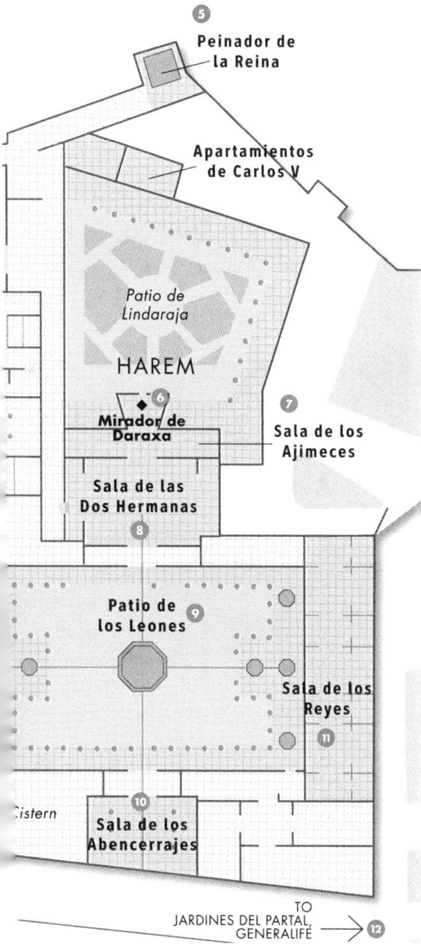

Sala de los Reyes

4 The **Baños Reales** is where the sultan's favorites luxuriated in brightly tiled pools beneath star-shape pinpoints of light from the ceiling above. It is open to visitors on certain days. An up-to-date timetable can be obtained from the tourist office.

5 **El Peinador de la Reina**, a nine-foot-square room atop a small tower was the Sultana's boudoir. The perforated marble slab was used to infiltrate perfumes while the queen performed her toilette. Washington Irving wrote his *Tales of the Alhambra* in this romantic tree house-like perch.

6 Sultana Zoraya often found refuge in this charming little balcony (**Mirador de Daraxa**) overlooking the Lindaraja garden.

7 Shhh, don't tell a secret here. In the **Sala de los Ajimeces**, a whisper in one corner can be clearly heard from the opposite corner.

8 In the **Sala de las Dos Hermanas**, twin slabs of marble embedded in the floor are the "sisters," though Washington Irving preferred the story of a pair of captive Moorish beauties.

9 In the **Patio de Los Leones** (Court of the Lions), a dozen crudely crafted lions support the fountain at the center of this elegant courtyard, representing the signs of the zodiac sending water to the four corners. (The lions are currently not on display while the court undergoes restoration through 2008.)

10 In the **Sala de los Abencerrajes**, Muley Hacen (father of Boabdil) murders the male members of the Abencerraje family in revenge for their chief's seduction of his daughter Zoraya. The rusty stains in the fountain are said to be bloodstains left by the pile of Abencerraje heads.

The star-shaped cupola, reflected in the pool, is considered the Alhambra's most beautiful example of stalactite or honeycomb vaulting.

The octagonal dome over the room is best viewed at sunset when the 16 small windows atop the dome admit sharp, low sunlight that refracts kaleidoscopically through the beehive-like prisms.

11 In the **Sala de los Reyes**, the ceiling painting depicts the first 10 Nasrid rulers. It was painted by a Christian artist since Islamic artists were not allowed to usurp divine power by creating human or animal figures.

The overhead painting of the knight rescuing his lady from a savage man portrays chivalry, a concept introduced to Europe by Arabic poets.

12 The terraces of **Generalife** grant incomparable views of the city.

Generalife gardens

PLANNING YOUR VISIT

The acoustics in the Palace of Charles V are ideal for the summer symphony concerts at the Alhambra.

GETTING THERE & AROUND

The best approach to the Alhambra is straight up the Cuesta de Gomérez from Plaza Nueva to the Puerta de la Justicia. From hotels up the river Darro in the Albayzín, the walk around the back walls of the palace along the Cuesta de los Chinos is a good hike. Buses 30 and 32 run from Plaza Nueva to the Alhambra. If you're driving, don't park on the street (it leaves your car vulnerable to a break-in). Instead, use the Alhambra parking lot or park underground on Calle San Agustín, just north of the cathedral, and take a taxi or the minibus from Plaza Nueva.

The entrance to the Nasrid Royal Palace is behind Carlos V's Renaissance Palace and leads into the *mexuar*, the chambers of state. The best route through the Alhambra traces an s-shaped path through the *mexuar*, the *serrallo*, and the harem, starting with the Patio de los Leones and ending with the Peinador de la Reina.

Wheelchairs are available on request; inquire at the Entrance Pavilion.

WHEN TO GO

Winter's low, slanting sunlight is best for seeing the Alhambra, and the temperatures are ideal for walking. Spring brings lush floral colors to the gardens. Fall is also sharp, cooler, and clear. July and August are crowded and hot.

The **Festival Internacional de Música y Danza de Granada** (☎34 958/276241 🌐www.granadafestival.org) held annually from mid-June to mid-July offers visitors an opportunity to hear a concert in the Alhambra or watch a ballet in the Generalife amphitheater.

GETTING TICKETS

Entrance to the Alhambra complex of the Alcazaba, Nasrid Palaces, Mosque Baths, and Generalife is strictly controlled by quotas. There are three types of timed tickets: morning, afternoon, and evening; note that the evening ticket is valid only for the Nasrid Palaces.

Tickets for the Alhambra complex and the Nasrid Palaces cost €12. Tickets can be obtained online at 🌐www.alhambratickets.com, by phone at ☎902/224460 in Spain or ☎34 91/537–9178 outside Spain, or at any BBVA (Banco Bilbao Vizcaya Argentaria) branch.

You can visit the Palace of Charles V and its two museums (Museo de la Alhambra and Museo de Bellos Artes) independently of the Alhambra. They're open Tues.–Sat. 9–2:30

HOURS OF OPERATION

The Alhambra is open every day except December 25 and January 1.

November through February, morning visits are daily from 8:30 to 2, with a maximum capacity of 3,300; afternoon visits are daily from 2 to 6, with a maximum capacity of 2,100; and evening visits are Friday and Saturday from 8 to 9:30, with a maximum capacity of 400.

March to October, morning visits are daily from 8:30 to 2, with a maximum capacity of 3,300; afternoon visits are daily from 2 to 8, with a maximum capacity of 3,300; and evening visits are Tuesday through Saturday from 10 to 11:30, with a maximum capacity of 400.

Visits to the main gardens are allowed daily, from 8:30 to 6 year-round; from March through October access is until 8.

CONTACT INFORMATION

Patronato de la Alhambra ☎34 958/027900 ✉informacion.alhambra.pag@juntadeandalucia.es 🌐www.alhambra-patronato.es.

they belonged to San Cecilio, the city's patron saint. Thus the hill was sanctified—*sacro monte* (holy mountain)—and an abbey built on its summit, the **Abadía de Sacromonte** (✉ *C. del Sacromonte, Sacromonte* ☎ *958/221445* 🎫 *€3* ⏲ *Tues.–Sat. 11–1 and 4–6, Sun. 4–6; guided tours every ½ hr*).

BICYCLING IN GRANADA

At the foot of the Iberian Peninsula's tallest mountain—the 11,427-foot Mulhacén peak—Granada offers challenging mountain-biking opportunities, and spinning through the hairpin turns of the Alpujarra mountain range east of Granada is both scenic and hair-raising. For more information about cycling tours around Granada (and Andalusia), contact **Cycling Country** (✉ *C. Salmerones 18, Alhama de Granada* ☎ *958/360655* 🌐 *www.cycling-country.com*), run by husband-and-wife team Geoff Norris and Maggi Jones in a town about 55 km (33 mi) away.

9 **Centro de Interpretación del Sacromonte.** A word of warning: even if you take the number 34 minibus (from Plaza Nueva) or the city sightseeing bus to get here, you will still be left with a steep, 200-meter (219-yard) walk to reach the center. The Museo Etnográfico shows how people lived here, and other areas show the flora and fauna of the area as well as cultural activities. There are live flamenco concerts here during the summer months. ✉ *Calle Barranco de los Negros s/n* ☎ *958/215120* 🌐 *www.sacromontegranada.com* 🎫 *€5 museum, €1 for other areas* ⏲ *Apr.–Oct., Tues.–Fri. 10–2 and 5–9; Nov.–Mar., Tues.–Fri. 10–2 and 4–7, weekends 11–7.*

ALBAYZÍN

Fodor's Choice ★ Covering a hill of its own, across the Darro ravine from the Alhambra, this ancient Moorish neighborhood is a mix of dilapidated white houses and immaculate *carmenes* (private villas in gardens enclosed by high walls). It was founded in 1228 by Moors who fled Baeza after Saint King Ferdinand III captured the city. Full of cobblestone alleyways and secret corners, the Albayzín guards its old Moorish roots jealously, though its 30 mosques were converted to baroque churches long ago. A stretch of the Moors' original city wall runs beside the ridge called the **Cuesta de la Alhacaba**. If you're walking—the best way to explore—you can enter the Albayzín from either the Cuesta de Elvira or the Plaza Nueva. Alternatively, on foot or by taxi (parking is impossible), begin in the Plaza Santa Ana and follow the Carrera del Darro, Paseo Padre Manjón, and Cuesta del Chapíz. One of the highest points in the quarter, the plaza in front of the church of San Nicolás—called the **Mirador de San Nicolás**—has one of the finest views in all of Granada: on the hill opposite, the turrets and towers of the Alhambra form a dramatic silhouette against the snowy peaks of the Sierra Nevada. The sight is most magical at dawn, dusk, and on nights when the Alhambra is floodlighted. Take note of Granada's brand new mosque just behind the church. Interestingly, given the area's Moorish history, the two sloping, narrow streets of Calderería Nueva and Calderería Vieja that meet at the top by the Iglesia San Gregorio have developed into something of a North African bazaar, full of shops and stalls selling clothes, bags, crafts, and trinkets. The numerous little teahouses and restaurants here have a decidedly Moroccan flavor. Be warned that there have been some thefts in the Albayzín area, so keep your money and valuables out of sight.

15 **Casa de los Pisa.** Originally built in 1494 for the Pisa family, this house's claim to fame is its relationship to San Juan de Dios, who came to Granada in 1538 and founded a charity hospital to take care of the poor and abandoned. Befriended by the Pisa family, he was taken into the Pisa home when he fell ill in February 1550. A month later, he died there, at the age of 55. Since that time, devotees of the saint have traveled from around the world to this house with a stone Gothic facade, now run by the Hospital Order of St. John. Inside are numerous pieces of jewelry, furniture, priceless religious works of art, and an extensive collection of paintings and sculptures depicting St. John. ✉ *Calle Convalecencia 1, Albayzín* ☎ *958/222144* 🎫 *€3* ⏲ *Mon.–Sat. 10–1.*

13 **Casa de Castril.** Bernardo Zafra, secretary to Queen Isabella, once owned this richly decorated 16th-century palace. Before you enter, notice the exquisite portal and the facade carvings depicting scallop shells and a phoenix. Inside is the **Museo Arqueológico** (Archaeological Museum), where you can find artifacts from provincial caves and from Moorish times, Phoenician burial urns from the coastal town of Almuñécar, and a copy of the *Dama de Baza* (Lady of Baza), a large Iberian sculpture discovered in northern Granada Province in 1971 (the original is in Madrid). ✉ *Carrera del Darro 41, Albayzín* ☎ *958/225640* 🎫 *€1.50* ⏲ *Tues. 2:30–8, Wed.–Sat. 9–8:30, Sun. 9–2:30.*

10 **Casa del Chapíz.** There's a delightful garden in this fine 16th-century Morisco house (built by Moorish craftsmen under Christian rule). It houses the School of Arabic Studies and is not generally open to the public, but if you knock the caretaker might show you around. ✉ *C. Cuesta del Chapíz at C. del Sacromonte, Albayzín.*

8 **Dar al-Horra.** Hidden in the back of the upper Albayzín, this semisecret gem was built in the 15th century for the mother of Boabdil, last Nasrid ruler of Granada. After the 1492 conquest of Granada, Dar al-Horra—House of the Honest Woman—was ceded to royal secretary Don Hernando de Zafra. Isabel la Católica later founded the Convent of Santa Isabel la Real here, which continued until the 20th century. Typical of Nasrid art, the interior resembles that of the Alhambra. The north side is the most interesting, with two floors and a tower. The bottom floor is covered with an exquisite flat wooden ceiling decorated with geometric figures. ✉ *Callejón de las Monjas s/n, Albayzín* ☎ *958/027800* 🎫 *Free* ⏲ *Weekdays 10–2.*

14 **El Bañuelo** *(Little Bath House).* These 11th-century Arab steam baths might be a little dark and dank now, but try to imagine them some 900 years ago, filled with Moorish beauties. Back then, the dull brick walls were backed by bright ceramic tiles, tapestries, and rugs. Light comes in through star-shaped vents in the ceiling, à la the bathhouse in the Alhambra. ✉ *Carrera del Darro 31, Albayzín* ☎ *958/027800* 🎫 *Free* ⏲ *Tues.–Sat. 10–2.*

NEED A BREAK?

The cafés and bars of Paseo Padre Manjón (along the Darro River), also known as the Paseo de los Tristes (Promenade of the Sad) because funeral processions once passed this way, are a good place for a coffee break. The park on the paseo, dappled with fountains and stone walkways, has a stunning view of the Alhambra's northern side.

⓬ **Palacio de los Córdova.** At the end of the Paseo Padre Manjón, this 17th-century noble house today holds Granada's municipal archives and is used for municipal functions and art exhibits. You're free to wander about the large garden. ✉ *Cuesta del Chapiz 4, Albayzín.*

CENTRO

❻ **Capilla Real** *(Royal Chapel).* Catholic Monarchs Isabella of Castile and Ferdinand of Aragón are buried at this shrine. The couple originally planned to be buried in Toledo's San Juan de los Reyes, but Isabella changed her mind when the pair conquered Granada in 1492. When she died in 1504, her body was first laid to rest in the Convent of San Francisco (now a parador), on the Alhambra hill. The architect Enrique Egas began work on the Royal Chapel in 1506 and completed it 15 years later, creating a masterpiece of the ornate Gothic style now known in Spain as Isabelline. In 1521 Isabella's body was transferred to a simple lead coffin in the Royal Chapel crypt, where it was joined by that of her husband, Ferdinand, and later her unfortunate daughter, Juana la Loca (Joanna the Mad), and son-in-law, Felipe el Hermoso (Philip the Handsome). Felipe died young, and Juana had his casket borne about the peninsula with her for years, opening the lid each night to kiss her embalmed spouse good night. A small coffin to the right contains the remains of Prince Felipe of Asturias, a grandson of the Catholic Monarchs and nephew of Juana la Loca who died in his infancy. The **crypt** containing the five lead coffins is quite simple, but it's topped by elaborate marble **tombs** showing Ferdinand and Isabella lying side by side (commissioned by their grandson Charles V and sculpted by Domenico Fancelli). The **altarpiece,** by Felipe Vigarini (1522), comprises 34 carved panels depicting religious and historical scenes; the bottom row shows Boabdil surrendering the keys of the city to its conquerors and the forced baptism of the defeated Moors. The **sacristy** holds Ferdinand's sword, Isabella's crown and scepter, and a fine collection of Flemish paintings once owned by Isabella. ✉ *Calle Oficios, Centro* ☎ *958/229239* 🌐 *www.capillarealgranada.com* 🎫 *€3.50* ⏲ *Apr.–Oct., Mon.–Sat. 10:30–1 and 4–7, Sun. 11–1 and 4–7; Nov.–Mar., Mon.–Sat. 10:30–1 and 3:30–5:30, Sun. 11–1 and 3:30–6:30.*

❹ **Cathedral.** Granada's cathedral was commissioned in 1521 by Charles V, who considered the Royal Chapel "too small for so much glory" and wanted to house his illustrious late grandparents someplace more worthy. Charles undoubtedly had great intentions, as the cathedral was created by some of the finest architects of its time: Enrique Egas, Diego de Siloé, Alonso Cano, and sculptor Juan de Mena. Alas, his ambitions came to little, for the cathedral is a grand and gloomy monument, not completed until 1714, and never used as the crypt for his grandparents (or parents). You enter through a small door at the back, off the Gran Vía. Old hymnals are displayed throughout, and there's a museum, which includes a 14th-century gold-and-silver monstrance (used for communion) given to the city by Queen Isabella. Audio guides are available for an extra €3. ✉ *Gran Vía s/n, Centro* ☎ *958/222959* 🎟 *€3.50* ⏲ *Apr.–Oct., Mon.–Sat. 10:30–1:30 and 4–8, Sun. 4–8; Nov.–Mar., Mon.–Sat. 10:45–1:30 and 4–7, Sun. 4–7.*

3 **Corral del Carbón** *(Coal House).* This building was used to store coal in the 19th century, but its history goes further back. Dating from the 14th century, it was used by Moorish merchants as a lodging house, and then later by Christians as a theater. It's one of the oldest Moorish buildings in the city and the only Arab structure of its kind in Spain. ✉ *Pl. Mariana Pineda s/n, Centro* ☎ *958/221118* 🎟 *Free* ⏲ *Weekdays 10–1:30 and 5–8, weekends 10:30–2.*

5 **Palacio Madraza.** This building conceals the old Islamic seminary built in 1349 by Yusuf I. The intriguing baroque facade is elaborate; inside, across from the entrance, an octagonal room is crowned by a Moorish dome. There are occasional free art and cultural exhibitions. ✉ *C. Zacatín s/n, Centro* ☎ *958/223447.*

OUTSKIRTS OF TOWN

2 **Casa-Museo Federico García Lorca.** Granada's most famous native son, the poet Federico García Lorca, gets his due here, in the middle of a park devoted to him on the southern fringe of the city. Lorca's onetime summer home, **La Huerta de San Vicente,** is now a museum—run by his niece Laura García Lorca—with such artifacts as his beloved piano and changing exhibits on specific aspects of his life. ✉ *Parque García Lorca, Virgen Blanca s/n, Arabial* ☎ *958/258466* 🌐 *www.huertadesanvicente.com* 🎟 *€3, free Wed.* ⏲ *July and Aug., Tues.–Sun. 10–3; Apr., May, June, and Sept., Tues.–Sun. 10–1 and 5–8; Oct.–Mar., Tues.–Sun. 10–1 and 4–7. Guided tours every 45 min until 30 min before closing.*

20 **Centro José Guerrero.** Just across a lane from the Cathedral and Capilla Real, this houses some very colorful and modern paintings by José Guerrero. Born in Granada in 1914, Guerrero traveled throughout Europe and lived in New York for a time in the '50s before returning to Spain. The center also runs excellent temporary contemporary art shows. ✉ *Oficios 8, Centro* ☎ *958/225185* 🌐 *www.centroguerrero.org* 🎟 *Free* ⏲ *Tues.–Sat. 11–2 and 5–9, Sun. 11–2.*

7 **Monasterio de La Cartuja.** This Carthusian monastery in northern Granada (2 km [1 mi]) from the center of town and reached by the number 8 bus) was begun in 1506 and moved to its present site in 1516, though construction continued for the next 300 years. The exterior is sober and monolithic, but inside are twisted, multicolor marble columns; a profusion of gold, silver, tortoiseshell, and ivory; intricate stucco; and the extravagant sacristy—it's easy to see why Cartuja has been called the Christian answer to the Alhambra. Among the wonders of the Cartuja are the trompe l'oeil spikes, shadows and all, in the Sanchez Cotan cross over the Last Supper painting at the west end of the refectory. If you're lucky you may see small birds attempting to land on these faux perches. ✉ *C. de Alfacar, Cartuja* ☎ *958/161932* 🎟 *€4* ⏲ *Apr.–Oct., Mon.–Sat. 10–1 and 4–8, Sun. 10–noon and 4–8; Nov.–Mar., daily 10–1 and 3:30–6.*

Parque de las Ciencias *(Science Park)*. Across from Granada's convention center, and easily reached on either a number 1 or 5 bus, this museum has a planetarium and interactive demonstrations of scientific experiments. The 165-foot observation tower has views to the south and west. This is the most-visited museum in Andalusia. ✉ *Av. del Mediterráneo, Zaidín* ☎ *958/131900* 🌐 *www.parqueciencias.com* *Park €5.50, planetarium €2.50* ⏲ *Tues.–Sat. 10–7, Sun. and holidays 10–3. Closed Sept. 15–30.*

WHERE TO EAT AND STAY

TAPAS BARS

Poke around the streets between the Carrera del Darro and the Mirador de San Nicolás, particularly around the bustling Plaza San Miguel Bajo, for Granada's most colorful twilight hangouts. Also try the bars and restaurants in the arches underneath the Plaza de Toros (Bullfighting Ring), on the west side of the city, a bit farther from the city center. For a change, check out some Moroccan-style tea shops, known as *teterías*—these first emerged in Granada and are now also popular in Seville and Málaga, particularly among students. Tea at such places can be expensive, so be sure to check the price of your brew before you order. The highest concentration of *teterías* is in the Albayzín, particularly around Calle Caldereria Nueva where, within a few doors from each other, you find Kasbah Tetería, Tetería Oriental, and El Jardín de los Sueños.

La Trastienda (✉ *Calle Cuchilleros 11, Centro* ☎ *958/226985*) is named "The Backroom" because after you get your tapas and drink, you take them to the dining area in back. **La Brujidera** (✉ *Monjas del Carmen 2, Centro* ☎ *958/222595*) has innovative tapas like marinated pork loin and attracts a buzzy student crowd.

Taberna Salínas (✉ *Elvira 13, Centro* ☎ *958/221411*) has brick-and-beam decor and great wine to accompany its delicious tapas. There's another branch at 5 Calle Almireceros near Plaza Nueva. More filling fare is also available. Off Calle Navas in Plaza Campillo is **Chikito** (✉ *Pl. del Campillo 9, Puerta Real* ☎ *958/223364*), best known for its tasty sit-down meals, but the bar is an excellent place for tapas. It's usually packed, so additional tables are set up on the square in summer. Moroccan-run **Al-Andalus** (✉ *Elvira 12, Centro*) serves tasty tapas, including bite-size falafel and other vegetarian options. **La Taberna de Baco** (✉ *Campo del Príncipe 22, Realejo* ☎ *958/226732*) fuses Ecuadoran and Andalusian flavors. **El Pilar del Toro** (✉ *C. Hospital de Santa Ana 12, Albayzín* ☎ *958/225470*) is a bar and restaurant with a beautiful patio. The popular **Bodegas Castañeda** (✉ *Elvira 6, Centro* ☎ *958/226362*) serves classic tapas, as well as baked potatoes with a choice of fillings. **Bodega Peso La Harina** (✉ *Placeta del Peso de la Harina, Sacromonte*), on a square right at the entrance of Camino de Sacromonte, prepares reliably good tapas. Southeast of Granada's cathedral, **Café Botánico** (✉ *Calle Málaga 3, Centro* ☎ *958/271598*) is a modern hot spot with a diverse menu that serves twists on traditional cuisine for a young, trendy crowd.

WHERE TO EAT

$–$$ SPANISH ✕ **Antigua Bodega Castañeda.** This traditional bodega close to Plaza Nueva is the ideal place to pop into for a snack and a quick drink. The menu is appealingly diverse and should suit the fussiest of families with salads, sandwiches, smoked fish, cheeses, pâtés, stews, tapas, stuffed baked potatoes, and desserts, as well as an interesting range of wines. ✉ *Calle Elvira 5, Centro* ☎ *958/226362* 💳 *MC, V.*

$–$$$$ LA NUEVA COCINA ✕ **Azafrán.** A charming surprise nestled at the foot of the Albayzín by the Darro River, this sleek contemporary space in the shadow of the Alhambra offers a selection of specialties. The menu is interesting and diverse and includes dishes like spinach crepes with shrimp, raisins, and pine nuts; lamb couscous; and several salads including mango and goat cheese salad with fresh spinach leaves, basil, and sweet raspberry vinegar. Steel furniture and black and red decor contribute to the air of sophistication. ✉ *Paseo de los Tristes 1, Albayzín* ☎ *958/226882* 💳 *AE, DC, MC, V.*

$–$$$ SPANISH ★ ✕ **Bodegas Castañeda.** A block from the Cathedral across Gran Vía, this is a delightfully typical Granadino bodega with low ceilings and dark wood furniture. In addition to the wines, specialties here are *jamón ibérico de bellota* (acorn-fed Ibérico ham) and *embutidos* (sausages). The extensive list of tapas includes *queso viejo en aceite* (cured cheese in olive oil), bacon with Roquefort cheese, and *jamón de Trevélez* (ham from the Alpujarran village of Trevélez). If you like garlic, don't miss the Spanish tortilla tapa served with creamy *alioli* (garlic-spiked mayonnaise). ✉ *Calle Almireceros 1–3, Centro* ☎ *958/223222* 💳 *MC, V.*

$–$$$ SPANISH ✕ **Carmen Verde Luna.** This intriguingly named restaurant, Carmen (Arabic for "summer cottage") Green Moon, a reference to Federico García Lorca's famous poem "Romance Somnámbulo" (Sleepwalking Ballad), has a terrace with views across to the Alhambra and Sierra Nevada. Run by a dynamic young team, the menu changes regularly according to what's fresh in the market. Regional dishes might include toasted and stuffed eggplant with pâté, stuffed sea bass and vegetables, hake with prawns, and, for vegetarians, an unusual and delicious vegetable mousse based on fresh artichokes (when in season). ✉ *Calle Nuevo de San Nicolás 16, Albayzín* ☎ *958/291794* 💳 *MC, V.*

$$–$$$ SPANISH ★ ✕ **Cunini.** Around the corner from the cathedral is, arguably, Granada's best fish restaurant. Catch of the day fish and seafood, fresh from the boats at Motril, are displayed in the window at the front of the tapas bar, adjacent to the cozy wood-paneled dining room. Both the *pescaditos fritos* (fried) and the *parrillada* (grilled) fish are good choices, and if it's chilly, you can warm up with *caldereta de arroz, pescado y marisco* (rice, fish, and seafood stew). There are tables outdoors overlooking a pretty plaza in warm weather. ✉ *Calle Pescadería 14, Centro* ☎ *958/250777* 💳 *AE, DC, MC, V* ⊗ *Closed Mon. No dinner Sun.*

$–$$ MOROCCAN ✕ **Kasbah Tetería.** On a sloping pedestrian street lined with Moroccan *teterías* (teashops), Moroccan bakeries, Moroccan souvenir shops, and Moroccan restaurants, stepping out here is, well, just like being in Morocco. Kasbah Tetería is primarily a teashop but also has a short menu of dishes that include couscous with chicken, lamb, and vegetables, as well as tasty *pasteles árabes* (cakes), exotic teas, and milkshakes like honey and date or almond pistachio. ✉ *Calle Caldrería Nueva 4, Centro* ☎ *958/227936* ▭ *MC, V.*

$$–$$$$ SPANISH ✕ **La Ermita en la Plaza de Toros.** Whether for tapas or a meal, this terrace and restaurant, built in under the vaults supporting the Granada bullring, is a carnivore's delight: its specialties are meats ranging from *solomillo de buey sobre salsa de hongos* (filet mignon in a wild mushroom sauce) to *jamón ibérico de bellota* (acorn-fattened Ibérico ham). Fish lovers have a modest choice that includes Galician-style octopus and Biscay-style cod fish. The exposed brick walls are decorated with mounted fighting bulls' heads and bullfight posters. ✉ *Calle Dr. Olóriz 25, Centro* ☎ *958/290257* ▭ *MC, V.*

$–$$$ SPANISH ✕ **La Yedra Real.** This modern restaurant with an ample terrace has a good selection of menu items at reasonable prices. Fish and meat dishes, as well as salads and soups, are well prepared, with touches of Moorish aromas. The *cordero con ciruelas, pases y piñones* (lamb with plums, raisins, and pine nuts) is a favorite, as is the *remojón granadino* (a salad of cod and oranges). Close to the Alhambra's main entrance, this is an ideal stop for visitors to Spain's most iconic monument. ✉ *Paseo de la Sabika 15, Alhambra* ☎ *958/229145* ▭ *MC, V* ⏲ *Closed Mon.*

¢–$ SPANISH ✕ **Los Diamantes.** This hole-in-the-wall is short on elbow space but long on value and taste. The specialty is battered and fried seafood, as well as grilled prawns and other fishy delights. The long bar and tiled walls are invitingly traditional, as are the free tapas you receive with every drink. ✉ *Calle Navas 28, Centro* ☎ *No phone* ▭ *No credit cards.*

$–$$ SPANISH ✕ **Mesón Blas Casa.** In the choicest square in the Albayzín, which is covered with tables and chairs in the summer, this restaurant serves solidly traditional cuisine that includes *rabo de toro* (oxtail), *habas con jamón* (ham with broad beans), and swordfish Mozarab (swordfish grilled with a Moorish-inspired combination of dried fruits, grapes, and nuts). There's a cheap and filling *menú del día* (daily menu), and the fireplace will warmyour toes when there's snow on the Sierras. ✉ *Pl. San Miguel Bajo 15, Albayzín* ☎ *958/273111* ▭ *MC, V* ⏲ *Closed Mon.*

$–$$$$ SPANISH ★ ✕ **Mirador de Morayma.** Buried in the Albayzín, this restaurant is hard to find and might appear to be closed (ring the doorbell). Once inside, you'll have unbeatable views across the gorge to the Alhambra, particularly from the wisteria-laden outdoor terrace. In colder weather you can enjoy the open fireplace and attractive dining space inside. The menu has some surprises, such as smoked *esturión* (sturgeon) from Riofrío, served cold with cured ham and a vegetable dip, and the *ensalada de remojón granadino,* a salad of cod, orange, and olives. Actress Gwyneth Paltrow likes this place—it was one of the few restaurants she selected in Granada for inclusion in her recent *Spain–On the Road Again* television series. ✉ *Calle Pianista García Carrillo 2, Albayzín* ☎ *958/228290* ▭ *AE, MC, V* ⏲ *No dinner Sun.*

$$$–$$$$ ★ SPANISH ✕ **Ruta del Veleta.** It's worth the short drive 5 km (3 mi) out of town to this restaurant, which serves some of the best food in Granada. Menu items are innovative twists on Spanish recipes using seasonal ingredients—the restaurant grows many of its own vegetables. Innovative options include *librito de mango y esturión sobre espejo de picual con huevos de trucha asalmonada* (a layered stack of mango and sturgeon,

topped with salmon trout eggs) and mildly more conventional dishes such as *solomillo de jabalí con frutos de otoño y salsa de vinagre* (wild boar with autumn fruits in a vinegar-and-honey sauce). Dessert might be *natillas ligeras de caramelo con bizcocho de nueces y miel y helado de chirimoya* (light caramel custard with a nut and honey biscuit and custard apple ice cream). ✉ *Ctra. de la Sierra 136, on road to Sierra Nevada, Cenes de la Vega* ☎ *958/486134* ▭ *AE, DC, MC, V* ⏲ *No dinner Sun.*

$–$$$ SPANISH ★ ✕ **San Nicolás.** Near the Mirador San Nicolás, this elegant restaurant has panoramic views of the Alhambra from the upstairs dining room (the Green Room) and outside terrace. New chef Enrique Martín from Córdoba has introduced such attractive dishes as crunchy mango and *foie* ravioli with herb bread and a yogurt sauce and sautéed baby calamari with vegetable risotto and also offers a more traditional menu of oxtail stew, grilled sea bass, and lobster and rice. The second dining room, the Red Room, has traditional black-and-white tiles and warm ocher paintwork. Service is exemplary. ✉ *San Nicolás 3, Albayzín* ☎ *958/804262* ▭ *AE, DC, MC, V* ⏲ *Closed Mon. No dinner Sun.*

$$–$$$ SPANISH ★ ✕ **Sevilla.** Open since 1930, this colorful, central two-story restaurant has fed the likes of composer Manuel de Falla and poet Federico García Lorca. There are four dining rooms and a small but superb tapas bar, all furnished traditionally with lots of dark wood and decorative plates and pictures on the walls. On sunny days opt for the outdoor terrace overlooking the Royal Chapel and Cathedral. The dinner menu includes Granada favorites such as *sopa sevillana* (soup with fish and shellfish), fresh whitebait stuffed with black pudding, and *tortilla al Sacromonte* (with bull's brains and testicles) for braver diners, along with more elaborate dishes. ✉ *Calle Oficios 12, Centro* ☎ *958/221223* ▭ *AE, DC, MC, V* ⏲ *No dinner Sun.*

$ SPANISH ✕ **Tot Taberna Tofe.** Despite the odd name, this is not a restaurant geared toward small children with a sweet tooth. One of an energetic stretch of similarly appealing traditional and contemporary bars and restaurants, it's a good choice for tapas or more substantial fare like roasted chicken. The *surtido de tapas* is a platter of tasty selections that includes *patatas bravas* (fried potatoes in a spicy chili-spiked tomato sauce), grilled mushrooms with garlic, and wedges of tortilla. A jug of sangria makes a good accompaniment. The interior is an attractive well-lit space with pine furniture, plus there is an outside terrace for al fresco dining. ✉ *Campo del Principe 18, Centro* ☎ *958/226207* ▭ *MC, V.*

WHERE TO STAY

Staying in the immediate vicinity of the Alhambra tends to be pricier than the city center. The latter is a good choice if you want to combine your Alhambra visit with enjoying the vibrant commercial center with its excellent shops, restaurants, and magnificent cathedral. The Abayzín is also a good place to stay for sheer atmosphere: this historic Arab quarter still has a tangible Moorish feel with its pint sized plazas and winding pedestrian streets.

$$$ **Carmen.** This hotel has a prized city-center location on a busy shopping street, and is directly across from the El Corte Inglés department store. The rooms are spacious and have a mix of modern and classic

decor; standard ones are carpeted, while the superior have glossy parquet floors. The rooftop terrace and pool have stunning views of the city. For entertainment there's an English-style pub with live music nightly. **Pros:** pivotal downtown location, rooftop pool. **Cons:** hot and airless area of the city from June to October, air-conditioning erratic. ✉*Acera del Darro 62, Centro* ☎*958/258300* 🌐*www.hotelcarmen.com* *270 rooms, 13 suites* *In-room: Wi-Fi. In-hotel: restaurant, bar, pool, parking (fee)* 💳*AE, DC, MC, V.*

$$–$$$ **Carmen de la Alcubilla del Caracol.** In a traditional Granadino *carmen* (small villa) on the slopes of the Alhambra, this is one of Granada's most stylish hotels. The rooms are bright, airy, and furnished with antiques, and they also have views over the city and the Sierra Nevada. The terraced garden, with watering troughs fed by an irrigation system from the Alhambra itself, is a peaceful oasis. Try to book the room in the torre (tower). **Pros:** views, small and personal, impeccable taste. **Cons:** tough climb in hot weather. ✉*Calle Aire Alta 12, Alhambra* ☎*958/215551* 🌐*www.alcubilladelcaracol.com* *7 rooms* *In-room: Wi-Fi. In-hotel: restaurant, bar, parking (no fee)* 💳*AE, DC, MC, V* *Closed Aug.*

$$–$$$ ★ **Casa Morisca.** The architect-owner of this 15th-century building transformed it into a hotel and received the 2001 National Restoration Award for the project. The brick building has many original architectural elements, three floors, and a central courtyard with a small pond and well. The rooms aren't large, but they do have a heady Moorish feel as a result of their wonderful antiques and views of the Alhambra and Albayzín. Even if you don't stay in it, ask for a look at the bridal suite, with its intricately carved and painted wooden ceiling. **Pros:** handy to Albayzín, easy free parking in front of the hotel. **Cons:** breakfast expensive and mediocre, interior rooms are stuffy and airless. ✉*Cuesta de la Victoria 9, Albayzín* ☎*958/221100* 🌐*www.hotelcasamorisca.com* *12 rooms, 2 suites* *In-room: Wi-Fi* 💳*AE, DC, MC, V.*

$–$$ **Guadalupe.** This charming hotel is close to the Alhambra, and some of the attractive rooms have views of it. All the singles, doubles, and triples are traditionally styled with Andalusian tiles and ocher-and-cream paintwork. Several rooms have private balconies, and those on the fourth floor have Jacuzzis. There is a popular bar and a good-quality, elegant restaurant ($–$$$). **Pros:** location next to Alhambra, lovely setting, traditional decor. **Cons:** thin walls, room size varies, a 20-minute hike from bars and nightlife. ✉*Paseo de la Sabica 30, Alhambra* ☎*958/223423* 🌐*www.hotelguadalupe.es* *58 rooms* *In-room: Wi-Fi. In-hotel: bar, restaurant, public Internet* 💳*AE, DC, MC, V.*

$$$ ★ **Palacio de los Navas.** In the center of the city, this palace was built by aristocrat Francisco Navas in the 16th century and later became the Casa de Moneda (the Mint). Original architectural features blend well with modern features. Rooms, set around a traditional columned inner patio, are decorated with understated elegance, and there is an outside terrace where you can enjoy breakfast on warm days. **Pros:** great location, peaceful oasis at the eye of the storm. **Cons:** can be noisy at night on street side, some rooms small and viewless. ✉*Calle Navas 1, Centro* ☎*958/215760* 🌐*www.palaciodelosnavas.com* *19 rooms* *In-room: Wi-Fi. In-hotel: parking (fee)* 💳*AE, DC, MC, V.*

$$$$ ★ **Palacio de los Patos.** This beautifully restored palace is unmissable, as it sits proudly on its own in the middle of one of Granada's busiest shopping streets. While retaining its 19th-century classical architecture, the hotel also includes all the most up-to-date elements of contemporary hostelry including a highly praised restaurant and a luxurious spa. The rooms are spacious and have a zen look, with dazzling white decor and shiny parquet floors. **Pros:** central location, top comforts in historic setting. **Cons:** restaurant service decidedly adagio, noisy street. ✉ *Calle Solarillo de Gracia 1, Centro* ☎ *958/536516* 🌐 *www.hospes.es* *42 rooms* *In-room: Wi-Fi. In-hotel: restaurant, bar, pool, spa, parking* *AE, DC, MC, V.*

$$–$$$ **Palacio de Santa Inés.** It's not often you get to stay in a 16th-century palace, and this one has a stunning location in the heart of the Albayzín. Each room is magnificently decorated with antiques and modern art; some have balconies with Alhambra views, others boast the original carved wooded ceiling. Rooms on the two upper floors are centered around a courtyard with frescoes painted by a disciple of Raphael. **Pros:** perfect location for exploring the Albayzín, gorgeous decor. **Cons:** can't get there by car as it's in a pedestrianized zone, service slow and sloppy. ✉ *Cuesta de Santa Inés 9, Albayzín* ☎ *958/222362* 🌐 *www.palaciosantaines.com* *15 rooms, 20 suites* *In-room: Wi-Fi. In-hotel: restaurant, parking (fee)* *AE, DC, MC, V.*

$$$$ Fodor's Choice ★ **Parador de Granada.** This is Spain's most expensive and popular parador, and it's right in the Alhambra neighborhood. The building, a former Franciscan monastery built in the 15th century by the Catholic Monarchs after they captured Granada, is soul-stirringly gorgeous. Try to get a room in the old section where there are beautiful antiques, woven curtains, and bedspreads. Rooms in the newer wing are also charming but more simply decorated. **Pros:** location, decor, garden restaurant. **Cons:** no views of Granada or the Albayzín, removed from city life. ✉ *Calle Real de la Alhambra s/n, Alhambra* ☎ *958/221440* 🌐 *www.parador.es* *34 rooms, 2 suites* *In-room: dial-up. In-hotel: restaurant, bar, parking (no fee)* *AE, DC, MC, V.*

$$ ★ **Reina Cristina.** In the former family residence of the poet Luis Rosales, where poet Federico García Lorca was arrested after taking refuge when the Spanish civil war broke out, the Reina Cristina is near Plaza de la Trinidad. Plants trail from the windowsills of the reception area and from a patio with a small marble fountain. A marble stairway leads to the simply but cheerfully furnished guest rooms. The restaurant, El Rincón de Lorca ($$–$$$$) is very good. **Pros:** like staying in a private home, quiet street, fine cuisine. **Cons:** not easy to drive to because of one-way streets, air-conditioning unreliable, some rooms have no views at all. ✉ *Calle Tablas 4, Centro* ☎ *958/253211* 🌐 *www.hotelreinacristina.com* *43 rooms* *In-room: Wi-Fi. In-hotel: restaurant, bar, parking (fee)* *AE, DC, MC, V* *BP.*

NIGHTLIFE AND THE ARTS

FLAMENCO

Flamenco can be enjoyed throughout the city, especially in the gypsy *cuevas* (caves) of the Albayzín and Sacromonte, where *zambra* shows—informal performances by gypsies—take place almost daily, all year round. The most popular *cuevas* are along the Camino de Sacromonte, the major street in the neighborhood of the same name. Be warned that this area has become very tourist oriented, and for any Sacromonte show, prepare to part with lots of money (€18–€20 is average). In August free shows are held at the delightful El Corral del Carbón square—home of the tourist office. If you do not want to show up randomly at the flamenco clubs, join a tour through a travel agent or your hotel, or contact **Los Tarantos** (✉ *Calle del Sacromonte 9, Sacromonte* ☎ *958/224525*), which has lively nightly shows with midnight performances on Friday and Saturday. **Sala Alhambra** (✉ *Parque Empresarial Olinda, Edif. 12* ☎ *958/412269 or 958/412287*) runs well-organized, scheduled performances. **La Rocío** (✉ *Calle del Sacromonte 70, Albayzín* ☎ *958/227129*) is a good spot for authentic flamenco shows. **María La Canastera** (✉ *Calle del Sacromonte 89, Sacromonte* ☎ *958/121183*) is another one of the *cuevas* on Camino de Sacromonte with unscheduled *zambra* shows.

NIGHTLIFE

Granada's ample student population makes for a lively bar scene. Some of the trendiest bars are in converted houses in the Albayzín and Sacromonte and in the area between Plaza Nueva and Paseo de los Tristes. Calle Elvira, Calderería Vieja, and Calderería Nueva are crowded with laid-back coffee and pastry shops. In the modern part of town, Pedro Antonio de Alarcón and Martinez de la Rosa have larger but less glamorous offerings. Another nighttime gathering place is the Campo del Príncipe, a large plaza surrounded by typical Andalusian taverns.

El Eshavira (✉ *Calle Postigo de la Cuna 2, Albayzín* ☎ *958/290829*) is a smoky, dimly lit club where you can hear sultry jazz and occasional flamenco. **Planta Baja** (✉ *C. Horno de Abad 11, Centro* ☎ *958/207607*) is a funky late-night club that hosts bands playing everything from exotic pop to garage and soul. **Fondo Reservado** (✉ *Calle Santa Inés 4, Albayzín* ☎ *958/222375*) is a hip hangout mainly for students and has late-night dance music. **Granada 10** (✉ *Calle Carcel Baja 10, Centro* ☎ *958/224001*), with an upscale crowd, is a discotheque in a former theater. **La Industrial Copera** (✉ *Calle de la Paz 7, Ctra. de la Armilla* ☎ *958/258449*) is a popular disco, especially on Friday night. **Zoo** (✉ *C. Mora 2, Puerta Real* ☎ *No phone*) is one of the longest-established and largest discos in town.

SHOPPING

A Moorish aesthetic pervades Granada's ceramics, marquetry (especially the *taraceas,* wooden boxes with inlaid tiles on their lids), woven textiles, and silver-, brass-, and copper-ware. The main shopping streets, centering around the Puerta Real, are the Gran Vía de Colón, Reyes

Católicos, Zacatín, Ángel Ganivet, and Recogidas. Most antiques stores are on Cuesta de Elvira, and Alcaicería—off Reyes Católicos. Cuesta de Gomérez, on the way up to the Alhambra, also has many handicraft shops. **Cerámica Fabre** (⊠*Pl. Pescadería 10, Centro*), near the cathedral, has typical Granada ceramics: blue-and-green patterns on white, with a pomegranate in the center. For wicker baskets and *esparto*-grass mats and rugs, head off the Plaza Pescadería to **Espartería San José** (⊠*C. Jaudenes 22, Centro*).

SIDE TRIPS FROM GRANADA

The fabled province of Granada spans the Sierra Nevada mountains, with the beautifully rugged Alpujarras, and the highest peaks on mainland Spain—Mulhacén at 11,407 feet and Veleta at 11,125 feet. This is where you can find some of the prettiest, most ancient villages, and it's one of the foremost destinations for Andalusia's increasingly popular rural tourism. Granada's *vega* (plain), covered with orchards and tobacco and poplar groves, is blanketed in snow half the year.

EN ROUTE

Eight miles (12 km) south of Granada on N323, the road reaches a spot known as the **Suspiro del Moro** (Moor's Sigh). Pause here a moment and look back at the city, just as Granada's departing "Boy King," Boabdil, did 500 years ago. As he wept over the city he'd surrendered to the Catholic Monarchs, his scornful mother pronounced her now legendary rebuke: "You weep like a boy for the city you could not defend as a man."

SANTA FE

8 km (5 mi) west of Granada just south of N342.

Santa Fe was founded in winter 1491 as a campground for Ferdinand and Isabella's 150,000 troops as they prepared for the siege of Granada. It was here, in April 1492, that Isabella and Columbus signed the agreements that financed his historic voyage, and thus the town has been called the Cradle of America. Santa Fe was originally laid out in the shape of a cross, with a gate at each of its four ends, inscribed with Ferdinand and Isabella's initials. The town has long since transcended those boundaries, but the gates remain—to see them all at once, stand in the square next to the church at the center of the old town.

FUENTEVAQUEROS

10 km (6 mi) northwest of Santa Fe.

Federico García Lorca was born in the village of Fuentevaqueros on June 5, 1898, and lived here until age 6. The **Museo Casa Natal Federico García Lorca,** the poet's childhood home, opened as a museum in 1986, when Spain commemorated the 50th anniversary of the poet's assassination (he was shot without trial by Nationalists at the start of the civil war in August 1936) and celebrated his reinstatement as a national figure after 40 years of nonrecognition during the Francisco Franco regime. The house has been restored with original furnishings, and the

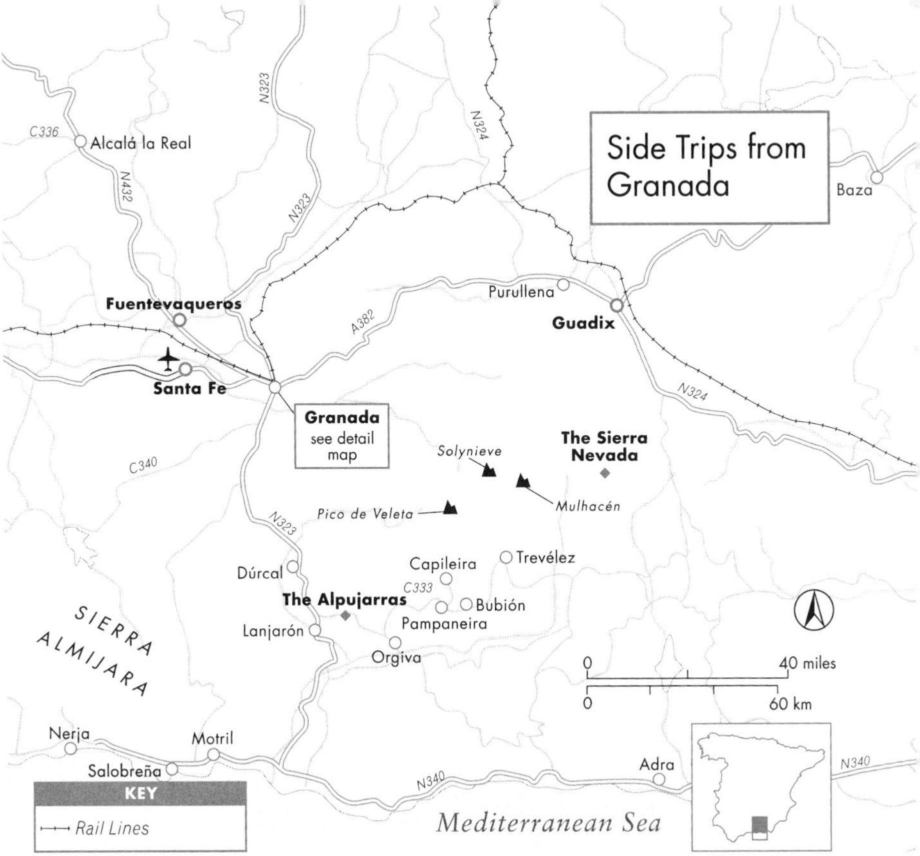

former granary, barn, and stables have been converted into exhibition spaces, with temporary art shows and a permanent display of photographs, clippings, and other memorabilia. A two-minute video shows the only existing footage of Lorca. Tour hours vary; call ahead. ✉ *Calle del Poeta García Lorca 4* ☎ *958/516453* 🌐 *www.museogarcialorca.org* 🎫 *€3* 🕒 *Closed Mon.*

THE SIERRA NEVADA

The drive southeast from Granada to Pradollano along the N420/A395—Europe's highest road, by way of Cenes de la Vega—takes about 45 minutes. It's wise to carry snow chains from mid-November to as late as April or even May. The mountains here make for an easy and worthwhile excursion, especially for those keen on trekking.

The **Pico de Veleta**, peninsular Spain's second-highest mountain, is 11,125 feet high. The view from its summit across the Alpujarra range to the sea at distant Motril is stunning; on a very clear day you can see the coast of North Africa. In July and August you can drive or take a minibus to within hundreds of yards of the summit—a trail takes you to the top. **TIP→ It's cold up here, so bring a warm jacket and scarf, even if Granada is sizzling hot.** To the east, the mighty **Mulhacén**, the highest peak in mainland Spain, soars to 11,427 feet. Legend has it that it came by its name when Boabdil, the last Moorish king of Granada, deposed his father, Muly Abdul Hassan, and had the body buried at the summit of the mountain so that it couldn't be desecrated. For more information on trails to the two summits, call the **Natural Park's Service office** (☎*958/763127* ⊕*www.nevadensis.com*) in Pampaneira.

SKIING

The **Estación de Esquí Sierra Nevada** is Europe's southernmost ski resort and one of its best equipped. At the Pradollano and Borreguiles stations there's good skiing from December through May; each has a special snowboarding circuit, floodlighted night slopes, a children's ski school, and après-ski sun and swimming in the Mediterranean less than an hour (33 km [20 mi]) away. In winter, **buses** (✉*Autocares Bonal* ☎*958/465022*) to Pradollano leave Granada's bus station three times a day on weekdays and four times on weekends and holidays. Tickets are €6 round-trip. As for Borreguiles, you can get there only on skis. There's an **information center** (☎*958/249100*) at Plaza de Andalucía 4 ⊕*www.cetursa.es.*

WHERE TO STAY

$$$$ **El Lodge.** A fantastic slope-side location and friendly, professional service add up to the best hotel in the Sierra Nevada. The lodge is built of Finnish wood—unusual for southern Spain but appropriate in this alpine area. Rooms are luxurious yet cozy and the en suite bathrooms have hydromassage tubs: perfect for the après-ski soak. The lodge also has an excellent restaurant specializing in Basque cuisine. The hotel is geared for families and has a purpose-designed playroom for the tots. **Pros:** perfect location next to ski lift, cozy and comfortable. **Cons:** some rooms are small. ✉*C. Maribel 8* ☎*958/480600* ⊕*www.ellodge.com* *16 rooms, 4 suites* *In-room: Wi-Fi. In-hotel: restaurant, bar, gym* *AE, DC, MC, V* *BP* *Closed May–Oct.*

THE ALPUJARRAS

★ *Village of Lanjarón: 46 km (29 mi) south of Granada.*

A trip to the Alpujarras, on the southern slopes of the Sierra Nevada, takes you to one of Andalusia's highest, most remote, and most scenic areas, home for decades to painters, writers, and a considerable foreign population. The Alpujarras region was originally populated by Moors fleeing the Christian Reconquest (from Seville after its fall in 1248, then from Granada after 1492). It was also the final fiefdom of the unfortunate Boabdil, conceded to him by the Catholic Monarchs after he surrendered Granada. In 1568 rebellious Moors made their last stand against the Christian overlords, a revolt ruthlessly suppressed by Philip II and followed by the forced conversion of all Moors to Christianity and their resettlement farther inland and up Spain's eastern coast. The villages were then repopulated with Christian soldiers from Galicia, who were granted land in return for their service against the Moors. To this day the Galicians' descendants continue the Moorish custom of weaving rugs and blankets in the traditional Alpujarran colors of red, green, black, and white, and they sell their crafts in many of the villages. Be on the lookout for handmade basketry and pottery as well.

Houses here are squat and square; they spill down the southern slopes of the Sierra Nevada, bearing a strong resemblance to the Berber homes in the Rif Mountains, just across the sea in Morocco. If you're driving, the road as far as Lanjarón and Orgiva is smooth sailing; after that come steep, twisting mountain roads with few gas stations. Beyond sightseeing, the area is a haven for outdoor activities such as hiking and horseback riding. Inquire at the **Information Point** at Plaza de la Libertad s/n, at Pampaneira.

EN ROUTE

Lanjarón, the western entrance to the Alpujarras some 46 km (29 mi) from Granada, is a spa town famous for its mineral water collected from the melting snows of the Sierra Nevada and drunk throughout Spain. **Orgiva,** the next and largest town in the Alpujarras, has a 17th-century castle. Here you can leave C348 and follow signs for the villages of the Alpujarra Alta (High Alpujarra), including **Pampaneira, Capileira,** and especially **Trevélez,** which lies on the slopes of the Mulhacén at 4,840 feet above sea level. Reward yourself with a plate of the locally produced *jamón serrano* (cured ham). Trevélez has three levels, the Barrio Alto, Barrio Medio, and Barrio Bajo; the butchers are concentrated in the lowest section (Bajo). The higher levels have narrow cobblestone streets, whitewashed houses, and shops.

WHERE TO STAY

$–$$ Fodor's Choice ★

Alquería de Morayma. Close to the banks of the Guadalfeo River, the buildings in this charming complex have been remodeled in the old Alpujarreño style, including some rooms that are in an old chapel. The setting is quite lovely, surrounded by 40 hectares of organically cultivated vineyards and woodland with almond, fig, olive, and fruit trees, and there's an old bodega and nearby farm that supply the hotel. The two dining rooms, one more formal and the other with an inviting fireplace, serve traditional Spanish food. The management can arrange walking and trekking activities. **Pros:** tranquil, lots of activities. **Cons:** removed from the city so you need a car for shopping and sightseeing, no restaurants nearby except for hotel restaurant. ✉ *Cádiar* ☎ *958/343221* 🌐 *www.alqueriamorayma.com* *13 rooms, 10 apartments* *In-hotel: restaurant, pool, parking (no fee)* *MC, V.*

$ **Taray Botánico.** This hotel has its own farm and is a perfect base for exploring the Alpujarras. Public areas and guest rooms are in a low, typical Alpujarran building. The sunny quarters are decorated with Alpujarran handwoven bedspreads and curtains; three rooms have rooftop terraces, and there's a pleasant common terrace. Most of the restaurant's ($–$$$) food comes from the estate, including trout and lamb; in season, you can even pick your own raspberries or oranges for breakfast. **Pros:** sustainable tourism in perfect comfort, great organic food. **Cons:** somewhat isolated, livestock attract abundant flies. ✉ *Ctra. Tablate–Albuñol, Km 18, Órgiva* ☎ *958/784525* 🌐 *www.hoteltaray.com* *15 private bungalows* *In-room: Wi-Fi. In-hotel: restaurant, pool* *AE, DC, MC, V.*

GUADIX

47 km (30 mi) east of Granada on A92.

Guadix was an important mining town as far back as 2,000 years ago and has its fair share of monuments, including a cathedral (built 1594–1706) and a 9th-century Moorish *alcazaba* (citadel). Today, however, Guadix and the neighboring village of Purullena are best known for their cave communities. Around 2,000 caves were carved out of the soft, sandstone mountains, and most are still inhabited. Far from being troglodytic holes in the wall, they are well furnished and comfortable, with a pleasant year-round temperature; a few serve as hotels. A small cave museum, **Cueva Museo,** is in Guadix's cave district. Toward the town center, the **Cueva la Alcazaba** has a ceramics workshop. A number of private caves have signs welcoming you to inspect the premises, though a tip is expected if you do. Purullena, 6 km (4 mi) from Guadix, is also known for ceramics.

Costa del Sol and Costa de Almería

Nerja, Málaga province

WORD OF MOUTH

"Marbella old town is located just slightly up from the more modern town and is absolutely gorgeous with orange trees, narrow winding streets and quaint restaurants. The modern town is nice too, though, surprisingly untacky for the area with beautiful beaches, nice restaurants & bars . . . Puerto Banus is where the wild nights and seriously monied are and everything is extortionate!! . . . I would much rather stay in the modern side of Marbella than Fuengirola or Benalmádena—but that's just my opinion. Marbella is lovely!"

—carolemg

www.fodors.com/community

WELCOME TO THE COSTA DEL SOL

TOP REASONS TO GO

★ **Sun and Sand:** Relax at any of the plethora of beaches; they're all free, though in summer there is not much towel space on the sand.

★ **Lovely Strolls:** Spend a morning in Marbella's old town, stopping for a drink at Plaza de los Naranjos before the shops shut for the afternoon siesta.

★ **Puerto Banús:** Wine, dine, and celebrity watch at the Costa's most luxurious and attractive port.

★ **Sensational Seafood:** Tuck into a dish of delicious *fritura malagueño* (fried fish, anchovies, and squid) at La Carihuela restaurant in Torremolinos.

★ **Cabo de Gato Nature Reserve:** This natural and protected reserve is one of the wildest and most beautiful stretches of coast in Spain.

★ **Souvenir Shopping:** Check out the weekly market in one of the Costa resorts to pick up bargain-price souvenirs, like ceramics or Spanish music CDs.

1 The Costa de Almería. This Costa region is hot and sunny virtually year-round and is famed for its spectacular beaches, unspoiled countryside, miles of golf courses, and (less appealingly) plastic greenhouse agriculture. Just west of the Murcia Coast, Almería, a handsome, underrated city, boasts a fascinating historic center with narrow pedestrian streets flanked by sun-baked ocher buildings and tapas bars.

2 The Costa Tropical. Less developed than the Costa del Sol, this stretch of coastline is distinctive for its attractive seaside towns, rocky coves, excellent water sports, and mountainous interior.

Horsemen in El Real de la Feria, Fuengirola, Málaga province,

3 Málaga Province. Don't miss the capital of the province: Málaga is an increasingly sophisticated city yet retains a traditional Andalusian feel; better known are the coastal resorts due west with their sweeping beaches and excellent tourist facilities.

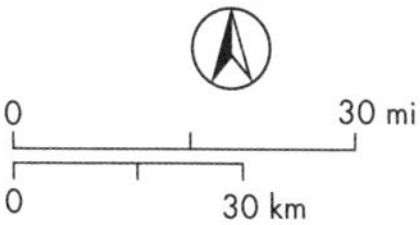

4 Gibraltar. The "Rock" is an extraordinary combination of Spain and Britain, and has a fascinating history. There are also some fine restaurants here, as well as traditional olde English pubs.

GETTING ORIENTED

The towns and resorts along the southeastern Spanish coastline vary considerably according to whether they lie to the east or to the west of Málaga. To the east lie the Costa de Almería and Costa Tropical, less developed stretches of coastline. Towns like Nerja also act as a gateway to the dramatic mountainous region of La Axarquía. West from Málaga along the Costa del Sol proper, the strip between Torremolinos and Marbella is the most densely populated. Seamless though it may appear, as one resort merges into the next, each town has a distinctive character, with its own sights, charms, and activities.

Resort views in Torremolinos.

THE COSTA DEL SOL PLANNER

When to Go

Fall and spring, especially May, June, and September are the best times to visit this coastal area: this is when there's plenty of sunshine but fewer tourists than in the high season of July and August, when it's hot and crowded. Winter can have bright sunny days, but you may feel the chill: many hotels in the lower price bracket have heat for only a few hours a day; you can also expect several days of rain at this time. Holy Week, the week before Easter, is a fun time to visit.

Fairs and Fiestas

Málaga's **Semana Santa** (Holy Week; the week before Easter) processions are dramatic. Nerja and Estepona celebrate **San Isidro** (May 15) with typically Andalusian ferias that have plenty of flamenco and *fino* (sherry). The feast of **San Juan** (June 23 and 24) is marked by midnight bonfires on beaches along the coast. Coastal communities honor the **Virgen del Carmen,** the patron saint of fishermen, on her feast day (July 16). The annual **ferias** (more general and usually lengthier celebrations than fiestas) in Málaga (early August) and Fuengirola (early October) are among the best for sheer exuberance.

Tour Options

Many one- and two-day excursions from Costa del Sol resorts are run by the national company Pullmantur and by smaller firms. All local travel agents and most hotels can book you a tour; excursions leave from Málaga, Torremolinos, Fuengirola, Marbella, and Estepona, with prices varying by departure point. Most tours last half a day, and in most cases you can be picked up at your hotel. Popular tours include Málaga, Gibraltar, the Cuevas de Nerja, Mijas, Marbella, and Puerto Banús; and a countryside tour of Alhaurín de la Torre, Alhaurín el Grande, Coín, Ojén, and Ronda. Night tours include a barbecue evening, a bullfighting evening with dinner, and a night at the Casino Torrequebrada. The varied landscape here is also wonderful for hiking and walking, and several companies offer walking tours. All provide comprehensive information on their Web sites.

Tour Operators Pullmantur (🌐 *www.pullmantur-spain.com*). **Walking Holidays** (🌐 *www.walksinspain.com*). **Bicycling Holidays** (🌐 *www.sierracycling.com*).

Visitor Information

The official Web site of the Andalusian government is 🌐 www.andalucia.org; it has further information on sightseeing and events as well as contact details for the regional and local tourist offices, which are listed under the respective towns and cities. Tourist offices are generally open Monday–Saturday, 10–2 and 5–8.

Golf in the Sun

Nicknamed the Costa del Golf, the Sun Coast has some 40 golf courses within putting distance of the Mediterranean, making it a prime golfing destination. Most of the courses are between Rincón de la Victoria (east of Málaga) and Gibraltar, and the best time for golfing is October to June; greens fees are lower in summer. Check out the comprehensive Web site 🌐 www.spainguides.com/costagolf.html for up-to-date information.

Bird-Watching in Andalusia

A bird-watcher's paradise, Andalusia attracts ornithologists throughout the year, but the variety of birds increases in spring, when you can see many wintering species along with those arriving for the summer months.

The Straits of Gibraltar are a key point of passage for birds migrating between Africa and Europe. Soaring birds, such as raptors and storks, cross here because they rely on thermals and updrafts, which occur only over narrower expanses of water. One of the most impressive sights over the Straits is a crossing of flocks of storks, from August to October—numbers sometimes reach up to 3,000.

Overall, northern migrations take place between mid-February and June, while birds heading south will set off between late July and early November, when there's a westerly wind. Gibraltar itself is generally good for bird-watchers, although when there isn't much wind the Tarifa region on the Atlantic coast can be better.

There are also some 13 resident raptor species in Andalusia, and several that migrate here annually from Africa. The hillier inland parts of the Costa del Sol are the best places to see them circling high in the sky.

WHAT IT COSTS (IN EUROS)

	¢	$	$$	$$$	$$$$
Restaurants	under €8	€8–€12	€13–€17	€18–€22	over €22
Hotels	under €60	€60–€90	€91–€125	€126–€180	over €180

Prices are per person for a main course at dinner, and for two people in a standard double room in high season, excluding tax.

WHAT IT COSTS (IN GIBRALTAR POUNDS)

	¢	$	$$	$$$	$$$$
Restaurants	under £5	£5–£12	£13–£18	£19–£25	over £25
Hotels	under £30	£30–£80	£81–£120	£121–£165	over £165

Prices are per person for a main course at dinner, and for two people in a standard double room in high season, excluding tax.

Planning Your Time

Travelers with their own wheels who want a real taste of the area in just a few days could start by exploring the relatively unspoiled villages of the Costa Tropical: wander around quaint **Salobreña**, then hit the larger coastal resort of **Nerja** and head inland for a look around pretty **Frigiliana.**

Move on to **Málaga** next; it has lots to offer, including museums, excellent restaurants, and some of the best tapas bars in the province. And don't miss stunning, mountaintop **Ronda** (also on a bus route), which has plenty of atmosphere and memorable sights.

Hit the coast at **Marbella,** the Costa del Sol's swankiest resort, then take a leisurely stroll around **Puerto Banús.** Next, head west to **Gibraltar** for a day of shopping and sightseeing before returning to the coast and **Torremolinos** for a night on the town.

If you have more time, explore rural Andalusia: **Setenil de las Bodegas, Olvera,** and **Grazalema.**

GETTING HERE AND AROUND

By Bus

Until the high-speed AVE train line opens in 2010, buses are the best way to reach the Costa del Sol from Granada, and, aside from the train service from Málaga to Fuengirola, the best way to get around once you're here.

During holidays it's wise to reserve your bus seat in advance for long-distance bus travel. On the Costa del Sol, bus service connects Málaga with Cádiz (4 daily), with Córdoba (5 daily), with Granada (18 daily), and with Seville (12 daily). In Fuengirola you can catch buses for Mijas, Marbella, Estepona, and Algeciras. The Portillo bus company serves most of the Costa del Sol. Alsina Gräells serves Granada, Córdoba, Seville, and Nerja. Los Amarillos serves Cádiz, Jerez, Ronda, and Seville. Málaga's tourist office has details on other bus lines.

By Air

Delta Airlines has weekly service from JFK (New York) to Málaga. All other flights from the United States connect in Madrid. Iberia and British Airways fly once daily from London to Málaga, and numerous British budget airlines, such as Easyjet and Monarch, also link London with Málaga. There are direct flights to Málaga from most other major European cities on Iberia or other national airlines. Iberia has up to eight flights daily from Madrid (flying time is 1 hour), three flights a day from Barcelona (1½ hours), and regular flights from other Spanish cities.

Málaga's Pablo Picasso airport is 10 km (6 mi) west of town. Trains from the airport into town run every half hour (6:49 AM–11:49 PM, journey time 12 minutes, €1.45) and from the airport to Fuengirola every half hour (5:34 AM–10:45 PM, journey time 25 minutes, €2), stopping at several resorts en route, including Torremolinos and Benalmádena.

From the airport there's also bus service to Málaga every half hour from 6:30 AM to 11:30 PM (€1). Ten daily buses (more July–September) run between the airport and Marbella (journey time 1 hour, €4). Taxi fares from the airport to Málaga, Torremolinos, and other resorts are posted inside the terminal: from the airport to Marbella is about €45, to Torremolinos €15, and to Fuengirola €28. Many of the better hotels and all tour companies will arrange for pickup at the airport.

By Taxi

Taxis are plentiful throughout the Costa del Sol and may be hailed on the street or from specified taxi ranks marked TAXI. Restaurants are usually obliging and will call you a taxi, if you request it. Fares are reasonable and meters are strictly used. You are not required to tip taxi drivers, though rounding off the amount will be appreciated.

By Car

A car allows you to explore Andalusia's mountain villages. Mountain driving can be hair-raising but it's getting better as highways are improved.

Málaga is 580 km (360 mi) from Madrid, taking the N–IV to Córdoba, then N331 to Antequera and the N321; 182 km (114 mi) from Córdoba via Antequera; 214 km (134 mi) from Seville; and 129 km (81 mi) from Granada by the shortest route of N342 to Loja, then N321 to Málaga.

There are some beautiful scenic drives here about which the respective tourist offices can advise you. The A369 (also known as C341) heading southwest from Ronda to Gaucín passes through stunning whitewashed villages. Another camera-clicking route is the N334 from Churriana to Coín, via Alhaurín de la Torre and Alhaurín el Grande. From here, take the N337 toward Marbella, which travels via the villages of Monda and Ojén, finally ending at the coast just north of Marbella.

To take a car into Gibraltar you need, in theory, an insurance certificate and a logbook (a certificate of vehicle ownership). In practice, all you need is your passport. Head for the well-signposted multistory car park, as street parking on the Rock is scarce.

National Car-Rental Agencies **Autopro** (🌐 *www.autopro.es*).

By Bike

The Costa del Sol is famous for its sun and sand, but many people supplement their beach time with mountain-bike forays into the hilly interior, particularly around Ojén, near Marbella, and also along the mountain roads around Ronda. A popular route, which affords sweeping vistas, is via the mountain road from Ojén west to Istán. The Costa del Sol's temperate climate is ideal for biking, though it's best not to exert yourself on the trails in July and August, when temperatures soar. There are numerous bike-rental shops in the area, particularly in Marbella, Ronda, and Ojén; many shops also arrange bike excursions. The cost to rent a mountain bike for the day ranges between €15 and €20. Guided bike excursions, which include bikes, support staff, and cars, generally start at about €62 a day.

Contacts Spanish Cycling Federation (☎ *91/542–0421* 🌐 *www.rfec.com*).

By Train

Málaga is the main rail terminus in the area, with three high-speed trains a day from Madrid (2½ hours), plus five slower trains (via Córdoba, 4½ hours). In January 2009, a new high-speed train was introduced linking Málaga with Barcelona (3 daily, 5 hours and 40 minutes). Five daily trains also link Seville with Málaga in less than two hours.

From Granada to Málaga (3–3½ hours), you must change at Bobadilla, making buses more efficient from here (a high-speed AVE line is currently under construction from Granada to Málaga, due for completion in the fall of 2010). Málaga's train station is a 15-minute walk from the city center, across the river.

RENFE connects Málaga, Torremolinos, and Fuengirola, stopping at the airport and all resorts along the way. The train leaves Málaga every half hour between 5.19 AM and 10:19 PM and Fuengirola every half hour from 6:35 AM to 11:17 PM. For the city center get off at the last stop: María Zambrano, which is also the main train station, from where it is a 15-minute walk to the city center. A daily train connects Málaga and Ronda via the dramatic Chorro gorge, with a change at Bobadilla. Travel time is about three hours. Three trains a day make the direct two-hour trip between Ronda and Algeciras on a spectacular mountain track. All routes are operated by RENFE.

With an average of 320 days of sunshine a year, the Costa del Sol well deserves its name, "the Sunshine Coast." It's no wonder much of the coast has become built up with resorts and high-rise hotels. Don't despair, though, you can still find some classic Spanish experiences, whether it be the old city of Marbella or one of the smaller villages like Casares. And despite the hubbub during high season, visitors can unwind here, basking or strolling on mile after mile of sandy beach.

Technically, the stretch of Andalusian shore known as the Costa del Sol runs west from the Costa Tropical, near Granada, to the tip of Tarifa, the southernmost tip of Europe, just beyond Gibraltar. For most of the Europeans who have flocked here over the past 40 years, though, the Sunshine Coast has been largely restricted to the 70-km (43-mi) sprawl of hotels, vacation villas, golf courses, marinas, and nightclubs between Torremolinos, just west of Málaga, and Estepona, down toward Gibraltar. Since the late 1950s this area has mushroomed from a group of impoverished fishing villages into an overdeveloped seaside playground and retirement haven. The city of Almería and its coastline, the Costa de Almería, is southwest of Granada's Las Alpujarras region, and due west of the Costa Tropical (around 147 km [93 mi] from Almuñecar.

Choose your base carefully, since the various towns and areas here make for a very different experience. Málaga is a vibrant Spanish city, virtually untainted by tourism, and, despite the tour bus trade, Ronda is also intrinsically Andalusian, with the added perk of a stunning inland setting. On the coast, Torremolinos is a budget destination catering almost exclusively to the mass market; it appeals to young families, the gay community, and to those who come purely for sun-bronzing and the late-night scene. Fuengirola is quieter, with a large, and notably middle-aged, foreign resident population; farther west, the Marbella–San Pedro de Alcántara area is more exclusive and expensive.

EXPLORING THE COSTA DEL SOL

ABOUT THE BEACHES

Beaches range from shingle (small stones, pebbles, shells) in Almuñecar, Nerja, and Málaga to fine, gritty sand (from Torremolinos westward). The best—and most crowded—beaches are El Bajondillo and La Carihuela, in Torremolinos; the stretch between Carvajal (which is just beyond Fuengirola in the direction of Torremolinos), Los Boliches, and Fuengirola; and those around Marbella. You may also find secluded beaches west of Estepona. Shingle beaches are popular with European vacationers. For wide beaches of fine golden sand, head west past Gibraltar, to Tarifa and the Cádiz coast—though the winds are usually quite strong, hence all the sails.

Beaches are free, and packed July through August and on Sundays from May through October. It's acceptable for women to go topless; if you want to take it all off, go to beaches designated *playa naturista*. The most popular nude beaches are in Maro (near Nerja), Benalmádena Costa, and near Tarifa.

ABOUT THE RESTAURANTS

Spain's southern coast is known for fresh fish and seafood, grilled or quickly fried in olive oil. Sardines barbecued on skewers at beachside restaurants are a popular treat. Gazpacho and *ajo blanco* (based on almonds, grapes, and garlic) are typically refreshing cold soups. Málaga is best for traditional Spanish cooking, with a wealth of bars and seafood restaurants serving *fritura malagueña,* the city's famous fried seafood. Torremolinos's Carihuela district is also a good destination for lovers of Spanish seafood. The area resorts serve every conceivable foreign cuisine, from Thai to the Scandinavian smorgasbord.

For delicious cheap eats, try the *chiringuitos*: strung out along the beaches, these rough-and-ready, summer-only restaurants serve seafood fresh off the boats. Because there are so many foreigners, meals on the coast are served earlier than elsewhere in Andalusia; most restaurants open at 1 PM or 1:30 PM for lunch and 7 PM or 8 PM for dinner.

ABOUT THE HOTELS

Most hotels on the developed stretch between Torremolinos and Fuengirola offer large, functional rooms near the sea at competitive rates, but the area's popularity as a budget destination means that most such hotels are booked in high season by package-tour operators. Finding a room at Easter, in July and August, or over holiday weekends can be difficult if you haven't reserved in advance. Málaga is an increasingly attractive base for visitors to this corner of Andalusia and has some good hotels. Marbella, meanwhile, has more than its fair share of grand lodgings, including some of Spain's most expensive accommodations. Rooms in Gibraltar's handful of hotels tend to be more expensive than most comparable lodgings in Spain.

There are also apartments and villas for short- or long-term stays, ranging from traditional Andalusian farmhouses to luxury villas. An excellent source for apartment and villa rentals is *www.andalucia.com*. You can also try **Gilmar** (*952/861341* *www.gilmar.es*) or **Viajes Rural Andalus** (*952/276229* *www.ruralandalus.es*).

THE COSTA DE ALMERÍA

West of Spain's Murcia Coast lie the shores of Andalusia, beginning with the Costa de Almería. Several of the coastal towns here, like Cabo de Gata and Agua Amarga, have a laid-back charm, with miles of sandy beaches and a refreshing lack of high-rise developments. The mineral riches of the surrounding mountains gave rise to Iberia's first true civilization, whose capital can still be glimpsed in the 4,700-year-old ruins of Los Millares, near the village of Santa Fe de Mondújar.

The small towns of Níjar and Sorbas maintain an ages-old tradition of pottery-making and other crafts, and the western coast of Almería has tapped unexpected wealth from a parched land, thanks to modern (if unaesthetic) farming techniques, with produce grown in plastic greenhouses. In contrast to the inhospitable landscape of the mountain-fringed Andarax Valley, the area east of Granada's Las Alpujarras, near Alhama, has a cool climate and gentle landscape, both conducive to making fine wines.

AGUA AMARGA

22 km (14 mi) north of San José and 55 km (30 mi) east of Almería.

Agua Amarga is perhaps the most pleasant village on the Cabo de Gata coast. Like other coastal hamlets, it started out in the 18th century as a tuna-fishing port. Today it attracts more visitors, but remains a fishing village at heart, less developed than San José. One of the coast's best beaches is just to the north: the dramatically named **Playa de los Muertos** (Beach of the Dead), a long stretch of fine sand bookended with volcanic outcrops.

GETTING HERE AND AROUND

If you're driving here from Almería, follow signs to the airport, then continue north on the A7; Agua Amarga is signposted just north of the Parque Natural Cabo de Gato. Once here, the village is small enough to explore on foot.

WHERE TO EAT AND STAY

$$–$$$ CONTEMPORARY ★ ✕**La Chumbera.** This stylish restaurant, in a villa off the coastal road just north of Agua Amarga, is one of the province's finest dining spots. Reservations are required, but phoning a day ahead or even on the same morning should secure you a table. Try to come for sunset and enjoy stunning sea views from the terrace. The menu changes regularly, and an Italian chef means some interesting Mediterranean dishes with a healthy dose of fresh Italian flavors and influence, like risotto with wild *setas* (oyster mushrooms). The presentation and service are superb and the atmosphere one of relaxed elegance. ✉*Los Ventorrillos* ☎*950/168321* ▭*MC, V* ⏲*Closed Dec./Jan.–Apr. No lunch July and Aug.*

$$$–$$$$ **MiKasa.** Set in a resplendent modern villa of typical Almería design, this small, smart hotel has become a byword for tasteful decor and attention to detail. Each room is different, but they all share a distinctly design-conscious look. Some have terraces and some have king-size beds. In keeping with a "peace and silence" policy, cell phone use isn't allowed in public spaces, and the rooms don't have telephones, though you can use the reception phone. **Pros:** heated pool and Jacuzzi, gourmet breakfast. **Cons:** could be too quiet for some, not suitable for young children or late-night party animals! ✉*Ctra. de Carboneras s/n* ☎*950/138073* 🌐*www.mikasasuites.com* *20 rooms* *In-room: no phone. In-hotel: restaurant, tennis court, pools, gym* ▭*AE, MC, V* ⏲*Closed Jan.–Mar.*

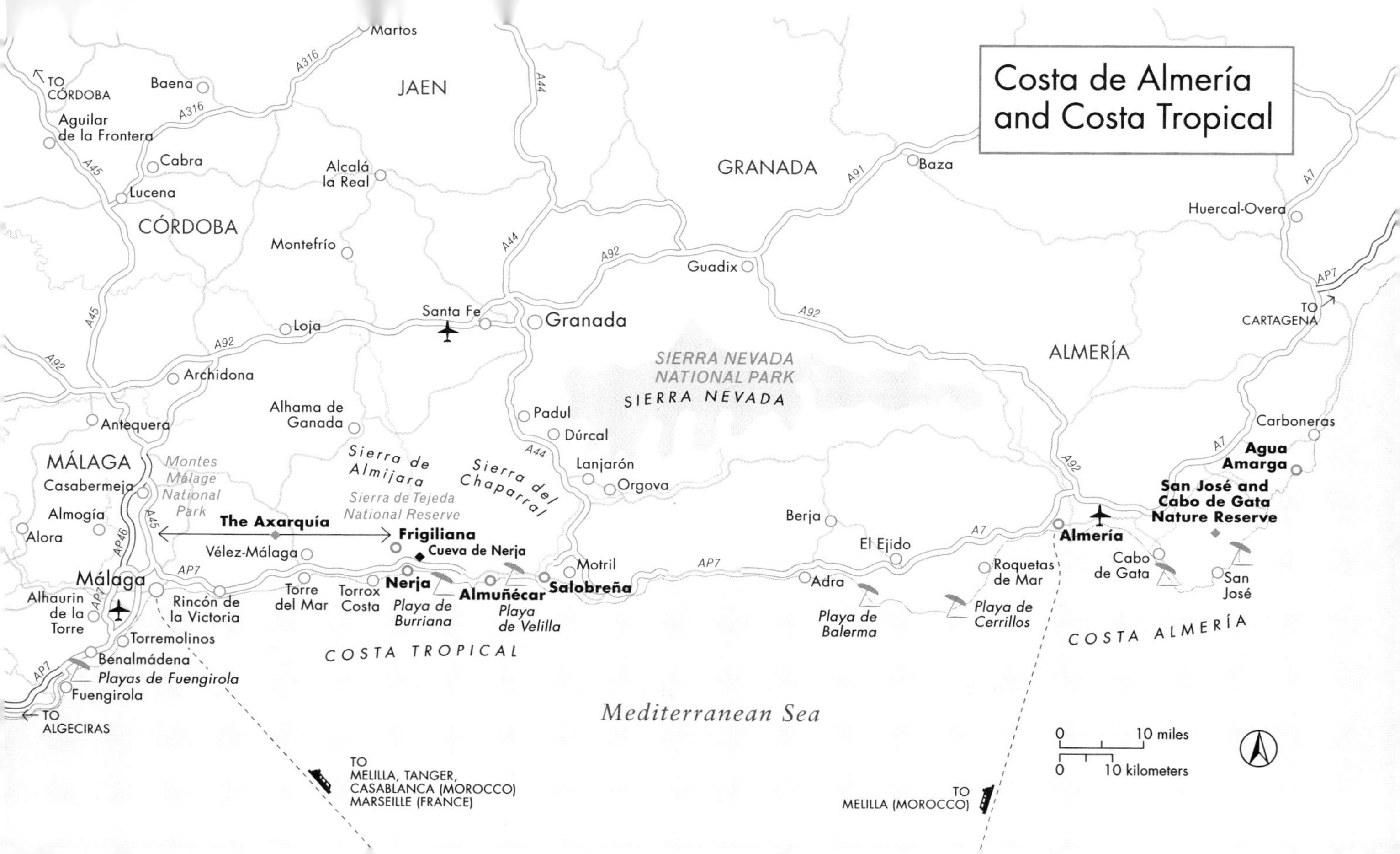

Costa de Almería and Costa Tropical
JAEN
GRANADA
CÓRDOBA
MÁLAGA
ALMERÍA
TO CÓRDOBA
Martos
Baena
Aguilar de la Frontera
Cabra
Lucena
Alcalá la Real
Montefrío
Loja
Santa Fe
Granada
Guadix
Baza
Huercal-Overa
TO CARTAGENA
Archidona
Antequera
Alhama de Ganada
Casabermeja
Almogía
Alora
Montes Málage National Park
Sierra de Almijara
Sierra de Tejeda National Reserve
Sierra del Chaparral
SIERRA NEVADA NATIONAL PARK
SIERRA NEVADA
Padul
Dúrcal
Lanjarón
Orgova
The Axarquía
Frigiliana
Cueva de Nerja
Vélez-Málaga
Málaga
Alhaurin de la Torre
Rincón de la Victoria
Torremolinos
Benalmádena
Playas de Fuengirola
Fuengirola
TO ALGECIRAS
Torre del Mar
Torrox Costa
Nerja
Playa de Burriana
Almuñécar
Playa de Velilla
Salobreña
Motril
Berja
El Ejido
Adra
Playa de Balerma
Roquetas de Mar
Playa de Cerrillos
Almería
Cabo de Gata
San José
Carboneras
Agua Amarga
San José and Cabo de Gata Nature Reserve
COSTA TROPICAL
COSTA ALMERÍA
Mediterranean Sea
TO MELILLA, TANGER, CASABLANCA (MOROCCO) MARSEILLE (FRANCE)
TO MELILLA (MOROCCO)
0 10 miles
0 10 kilometers
A316
A45
A92
A44
A91
A7
AP7
AP46

SAN JOSÉ AND THE CABO DE GATA NATURE RESERVE

40 km (25 mi) east of Almería, 86 km (53 mi) south of Mojácar.

San José is the largest village in the southern part of the Cabo de Gata Nature Reserve and has a pleasant bay, though these days the village has rather outgrown itself and can be quite busy in summer. Those preferring smaller, quieter destinations should look farther north at places such as Agua Amarga and the often-deserted nearby beaches.

GETTING HERE AND AROUND

You really need your own wheels to explore the nature reserve and surrounding villages, including San José.

EXPLORING

Just south of San José is the **Parque Natural Marítimo y Terrestre Cabo de Gata—Níjar** (✉ *Road from Almería to Cabo de Gata, Km* 6). Birds are the main attraction at this nature reserve; it's home to several species native to Africa, including the *camachuelo trompetero* (large beaked bullfinch), which is not found anywhere else outside Africa. Check out the **Centro Las Amuladeras visitors center** (☎950/160435 🌐*www.cabodegata-nijar.com*). It's located at the park entrance and has an exhibit and information on the region.

For beach time, follow signs south to the **Playa Los Genoveses** and **Playa Monsul.** A rough road follows the coast around the spectacular cape, eventually linking up with the N332 to Almería. Alternatively, follow the signs north for the towns of Níjar (approx. 20 km north) and Sorbas (32 km northeast of Níjar); both towns are famed for their distinctive green glazed pottery, which you can buy directly from the workshops.

WHERE TO STAY

$ **La Isleta.** This small hotel with the same name as the village tucked around a charming bay, nestles right up against the blue waters of the Mediterranean. It's nothing fancy, and you're paying for the location, within a stone's throw of the beach, with superb sea views. According to the management, the rooms are gradually receiving a long overdue overhaul, so be sure to request one of those that has been refurbished. The downstairs restaurant is noted for its excellent seafood while, on the downside, readers have complained that the reception service can be offhand. **Pros:** fabulous location. **Cons:** no frills; can be noisy with families in summer; service can be offhand. ✉*La Isleta del Moro* ☎*950/389713* 🖷*950/389764* *10 rooms* *In-hotel: restaurant* *MC, V* *BP.*

ALMERÍA

219 km (136 mi) southwest of Murcia (Murcia is in Chapter 10), 183 km (114 mi) east of Málaga.

Warmed by the sunniest climate in Andalusia, Almería is a youthful Mediterranean city, basking in sweeping views of the sea from its coastal perch. It's also a capital of the grape industry, thanks to its wonderfully mild climate in spring and fall. Rimmed by tree-lined boulevards and some landscaped squares, the city's core is a maze of narrow, winding alleys formed by flat-roof, distinctly Mudejar houses. Though now surrounded by modern apartment blocks, these dazzling-white older homes give Almería an Andalusian flavor.

GETTING HERE AND AROUND

Airport bus, No. 20, runs roughly every half hour from the airport to the center of town (Calle del Doctor Gregorio Marañón).

The city center is compact, and most of the main sights are within easy strolling distance of each other. The beach is roughly 1 km (0.6 mi) away, however, so consider catching a cab.

ESSENTIALS

Visitor Information **Almería** (*✉ Parque Nicolás Salmerón s/n ☎ 960/281501*).

EXPLORING

Dominating the city is its **Alcazaba** *(Fortress)* built by Caliph Abd ar-Rahman I and given a bell tower by Carlos III. From here you have sweeping views of the port and city. Among the ruins of the fortress, damaged by earthquakes in 1522 and 1560, are landscaped gardens of rock flowers and cacti. *✉ C. Almanzor ☎ 950/271617 €1.50; free for EU citizens ⊙ Apr.–Oct., Tues.–Sun. 10–7:30; Nov.–Mar., Tues.–Sun. 9–6:30.*

Below the Alcazaba stands the **cathedral,** whose buttressed towers make it look like a castle. It's Gothic in design, but with some classical touches around the doors. *€3 ⊙ Weekdays 10–2 and 4–6, Sat. 10–2.*

WHERE TO EAT AND STAY

$$ SPANISH ✕ **Valentín.** This popular, central spot serves fine regional specialties, such as *cazuela de rape* (monkfish baked in a sauce of almonds and pine nuts), *arroz negro* (rice flavored with squid ink), and the deliciously simple *pescado en adobe* (dog fish baked in clay with garlic, oregano, and paprika). If you're considering serious credit-card overdrive, go for the lobster. The surroundings are rustic, yet elegant Andalusian: lime-washed white walls, dark wood, and exposed brick work. Come on the early side (around 9) to get a table. The generous *menú del día* is €42. *✉ Tenor Iribarne 7 ☎ 950/264475 ▭ AE, MC, V ⊙ Closed Mon. No dinner Sun.*

$$ SEAFOOD ✕ **Veracruz.** In Almería's beach barrio, El Zapillo, this justly popular seafood restaurant has its own storage tank for oysters, clams, prawns, and lobsters. The specialty is *parillada de pescado,* a mixed grill of everything that swims in the Mediterranean. If this sounds like too large a catch for you, there are simpler dishes, like barbecued sardines and the ultimate in small, but delicious, starters: *boquerónes en vinagre* (fresh anchovies served whole in a tangy vinaigrette dressing). The portions are generous and the service is swift and efficient. Get here early to grab a table, since Veracruz is popular with the locals. *✉ Av. Cabo de Gata 119 ☎ 950/251220 ▭ AE, MC, V ⊙ Closed Mon.*

$ **Hotel Sevilla.** Looking for inexpensive comfort? This is the place. In the labyrinth of old town, the Sevilla has both style and charm. Rooms vary—those on the street side have small terraces; those on the quiet interior look out over the courtyards and rooftops of the old town. **Pros:** friendly and traditional. **Cons:** small rooms, poor TV reception.

✉Granada 25 ☎950/230009 🌐www.hotelsevillaalmeria.es ⇨37 rooms ▭MC, V.

$$$ **NH Ciudad de Almería.** One of the newest hotels in Almería, the NH Ciudad has the appealing mix of traditional and modern style—including avant-garde art—often found in NH hotels, and offers larger rooms than usually found in the region. The decor is comfortably plush with fabrics and furnishings in earth colors accentuated by dark purple or burgundy. A modern yet attractive block with a glass front, the hotel is just to the east of the town center and directly across from the train and bus station. **Pros:** efficient multilingual staff and excellent facilities. **Cons:** can be noisy with late-night travelers (opposite bus and train stations), popular with tour groups. *✉Jardín de Medina s/n ☎950/182500 🌐www.nh-hotels.com ⇨140 rooms In-hotel: restaurant, bar, laundry facilities, Wi-Fi ▭AE, DC, MC, V.*

$$ **Torreluz III.** Value is the overriding attraction of this comfortable yet elegant modern hotel. Guest rooms are slick and bright, with the kind of amenities for which you'd expect to pay more. The restaurant, Torreluz Mediterráneo ($$), is famous among locals for robust portions and brisk lunchtime service; it serves an excellent cross section of southeastern fare—try the *zarzuela de marisco a la marinera* (mixed seafood in a zesty red marinade). The cheaper Torreluz Hotel, with just 24 rooms ($) next door (with the same phone number) is also good value, as are the nearby apartments, which offer more space for the same price as the main hotel. **Pros:** great central location, parking. **Cons:** no pool. *✉Plaza Flores 3 ☎950/234399 🌐www.torreluz.com ⇨94 rooms In-hotel: 2 restaurants, bar, parking ▭AE, DC, MC, V.*

OFF THE BEATEN PATH

The archaeological site of **Los Millares** (*☎677/903404 Free Tues.–Sat. 9:30–4*) is 2.3 km (1½ mi) southwest from the village of Santa Fe de Mondújar and 19 km (12 mi) from Almería. This collection of ruins scattered on a windswept hilltop was the birthplace of civilization in Spain nearly 5,000 years ago. Large, dome-shaped tombs show that the community had an advanced society, and the existence of formidable defense walls indicates they had something to protect. A series of concentric fortifications shows that the settlement increased in size over the generations, eventually holding some 2,000 people. The town was inhabited from 2700 to 1800 BC and came to dominate the entire region. From the reception center at the edge of the site, a guide will take you on a tour of the ruins. Phone in advance for all visits.

NIGHTLIFE

Nocturnal action in Almería centers on **Plaza Flores,** moving down to the beach in summer. In town, try the small **Cajón de Sastre** (*✉Plaza Marques de Heredia 804001*) for typical *copas* (libations) and a mainly Spanish crowd. For foot-stomping live flamenco, check out the excellent **Peña El Taranto** (*✉C. Tenor Iribame 20 ☎950/235057*) with nightly performances.

THE COSTA TROPICAL

East of Málaga and west of Almería lies the Costa Tropical. It's escaped the worst excesses of the property developers, and its tourist onslaught has been mild. A flourishing farming center, the area earns its keep from tropical fruit, including avocados, mangoes, and papaws (also known as custard apples). Housing developments are generally inspired by Andalusian village architecture rather than bland high-rise design. You may find packed beaches and traffic-choked roads at the height of the season, but for most of the year the Costa Tropical is relatively free of tourists, if not also devoid of expatriates.

SALOBREÑA

102 km (63 mi) east of Málaga.

You can reach Salobreña by descending through the mountains from Granada or by continuing west from Almería on N340. Detour from the highway and you'll reach this unspoiled village of near-perpendicular streets and old white houses on a steep hill beneath a Moorish fortress. It's a true Andalusian *pueblo,* separated from the beachfront restaurants and bars in the newer part of town.

ALMUÑÉCAR

85 km (53 mi) east of Málaga.

Almuñécar has been a fishing village since Phoenician times, 3,000 years ago, when it was called Sexi and, later, the Moors built a castle here for the treasures of Granada's kings. Today, Almuñécar is a small-time resort with a shingle beach, popular with Spanish and northern-European vacationers. The road west from Motril and Salobreña passes through what was the empire of the sugar barons, who brought prosperity to Málaga's province in the 19th century: the cane fields now give way to litchis, limes, mangoes, papaws, and olives. The village is actually two, separated by the dramatic rocky headland of Punta de la Mona. To the east is Almuñécar proper, and to the west is **La Herradura,** a quiet fishing community. Between the two is the Marina del Este yacht harbor, which, along with La Herradura, is a popular diving center.

GETTING HERE AND AROUND

The N340 highway runs north of town. There is an efficient bus service to surrounding towns and cities, including Málaga, Granada, Nerja, and, closer afield, La Herradura a few miles west along the coast. Almuñecar's town center is well laid out for strolling, and the local tourist office has information on bicycle and scooter rental.

ESSENTIALS

Visitor Information Almuñécar (✉ *Calle Alta del Mar 8* ☎ *958/634007*).

EXPLORING

Crowning Almuñécar is the **Castillo de San Miguel** *(St. Michael's Castle).* A Roman fortress once stood here, later enlarged by the Moors, but the castle's present aspect owes more to 16th-century additions. The building was bombarded during the Peninsular War in the 19th century and what was left was used as a cemetery until the 1990s. You can wander the ramparts and peer into the dungeon; the skeleton at the bottom is a reproduction of human remains discovered on the spot. €2, *includes admission to Cueva de Siete Palacios* *July and Aug., Tues.–Sat. 10:30–1:30 and 6–9, Sun. 10–2; Sept.–June, Tues.–Sat. 10:30–1:30 and 4–6:30, Sun. 10:30–2.*

Beneath the Castillo de San Miguel is a large, vaulted stone cellar of Roman origin, the **Cueva de Siete Palacios** *(Cave of Seven Palaces)*, now Almuñecar's archaeological museum. The collection is small but interesting, with Phoenician, Roman, and Moorish artifacts. €2, *includes admission to Castillo de San Miguel* *July and Aug., Tues.–Sat. 10:30–1:30 and 6–9, Sun. 10–2; Sept.–June, Tues.–Sat. 10:30–1:30 and 4–6:30, Sun. 10:30–2.*

WHERE TO EAT AND STAY

$$ FRENCH **Jacquy-Cotobro.** One of the finest French restaurants on Spain's southern coast, Jacquy-Cotobro is cozy, with brick walls and green wicker chairs; a beachfront terrace is open in summer. Try the *menú gourmet,* (€36) with four courses plus dessert and wine; it might include fresh pasta topped with oyster mushrooms and prawns, lobster salad with truffle oil or duck in orange sauce, then a calorific delight such as the strawberry mousse with Kirsch. Service is excellent. *Edificio Río, Playa Cotobro* *958/631802* *MC, V* *Closed Mon.*

$$ **Casablanca.** There's something quaint about this family-run hotel with its neo-Moorish facade and arches, and the location is choice, next to the beach (Playa de San Cristóbal) and near the botanical park. The rooms, which are all different, have modern fittings juxtaposed with antiques and the occasional four-poster bed. All have private balconies or large picture windows with superb views. The restaurant ($) specializes in traditional cuisine, such as *migas* (bread crumbs fried with sausage and spices), grilled meats, and paella. **Pros:** family run, atmospheric. **Cons:** rooms vary, with some on the small side. *Pl. San Cristóbal 4* *958/635575* *35 rooms* *In-hotel: restaurant, bar, public Internet, parking* *D, MC, V* *BP.*

$$$ **Sol Los Fenicios.** The Spanish hotel chain, Sol Melia, rarely disappoints, and at Sol Los Fenicios, you'll get superb location near the beach in La Herradura. It's a modern, Andalusian-style hotel with views of the bay and the cliffs of Punta de Mona to the east, and the rocky headland of Cerro Gordo to the west. Rooms are set around a traditional interior patio, complete with a pretty ornamental pond and plenty of greenery; ask for one with a sea view. **Pros:** beach views, private balconies. **Cons:** conservative decor, pricey for the area. *Paseo Andrés Segovia s/n, La Herradura* *958/827900* *www.sollosfenicios.solmelia.com* *42 rooms* *In-room: Wi-Fi. In-hotel: restaurant, pool, parking (fee)* *AE, DC, MC, V* *BP* *Closed late Nov.–early Apr.*

NERJA

52 km (32 mi) east of Málaga, 22 km (14 mi) west of Almuñécar.

Nerja—the name comes from the Moorish word *narixa,* meaning "abundant springs"—has a large foreign resident community living mainly outside town in *urbanizaciones* ("village" developments). The old village is on a headland above small beaches and rocky coves, which offer reasonable swimming despite the gray, gritty sand. In July and August, Nerja is packed with tourists, but the rest of the year it's a pleasure to wander the old town's narrow streets.

GETTING HERE AND AROUND

Nerja is a speedy hour's drive northeast from Málaga on the A7. If you're driving, park in the underground car park just west of the Balcón de Europa (it's signposted) off Calle La Cruz. The town is small enough to explore on foot.

ESSENTIALS

Visitor Information Nerja (⊠ *Puerta del Mar* ☎ *952/521531* 🌐 *www.nerja.org*).

EXPLORING

The highlight of the town is the **Balcón de Europa,** a tree-lined promenade with magnificent views, on a promontory just off the central square.

★ The **Cuevas de Nerja** *(Nerja Caves)* lie between Almuñécar and Nerja on a road surrounded by giant cliffs and dramatic seascapes. Signs point to the cave entrance above the village of Maro, 4 km (2½ mi) east of Nerja. Its spires and turrets created by millennia of dripping water are now floodlit for better views. One suspended pinnacle, 200 feet long, is the world's largest known stalactite. The awesome subterranean chambers create an evocative setting for concerts and ballets during the Nerja Festival of Music and Dance, held annually during the second and third weeks of July. ☎ *952/529520* 🌐 *www.cuevanerja.com* €7 *Oct.–Apr., daily 10–2 and 4–6:30; May–Sept., daily 10–2 and 4–8.*

WHERE TO EAT AND STAY

$$ SPANISH ✕ **Casa Luque.** One of Nerja's most authentic Spanish restaurants, Casa Luque is in an old Andalusian house in a lovely square just off the Balcón de Europa. During the summer a large and picturesque terrace affords sweeping views of the coast. The innovative menu offers an haute culinary twist to traditional dishes from northern Spain, often of Basque or Navarrese origin, with an emphasis on meat and game; vegetarian and seafood options are also available. The restaurant is noted for its excellent and extensive tapas menu, two or three of which can easily equal a relatively inexpensive and filling meal. ⊠ *Pl. Cavana 2* ☎ *952/521004* *AE, DC, MC, V* *Closed Wed. No dinner Sun.*

$–$$ SPANISH ✕ **El Mesón de Julio.** Check the blackboard outside this longstanding and reliably good restaurant for the day's specialties and the long list of tapas. There's comfortable seating outside on the terrace or an attractive pine-clad interior with bare brick columns, wood beams, and an inviting bar with stools at the ready. The menu includes familiar Andalusian meat, like leg of lamb and roast pork, and fish dishes, along with more international options, including baked camembert with strawberry preserves and goat cheese salad. Julio's is popular with the local business community at midday, so get here early if you want a table for lunch. ✉ *Calle Cristo 7* ☎ *952/521190* ▭ *MC, V.*

$$–$$$ ★ **Hotel Carabeo.** Tucked away down a side street near the center of town and the sea, this British-owned boutique hotel has shelves of books, antiques, and cozy overstuffed sofas in the downstairs sitting room. Hung throughout are colorful oil paintings by local artist David Broadhead. In the main building there are seven rooms, five with sea views, and a private terrace overlooking the sea. A newer annex has six more rooms, plus a small gym and games room. **Pros:** friendly owners, great location. **Cons:** rooms in the annex lack character, winter closure. ✉ *C. Hernando de Carabeo 34* ☎ *952/525444* 🌐 *www.hotelcarabeo.com* *20 rooms* *In-hotel: restaurant, bar, pool, gym, public Internet* ▭ *MC, V* *CP* *Closed late Oct.–mid-Mar.*

NIGHTLIFE AND THE ARTS

El Colono (✉ *Granada 6, Nerja* ☎ *952/521826*) is a flamenco club in the town center. Although the show is obviously geared toward tourists, the club has an authentic *olé* atmosphere. The food is good, and local specialties, including paella, are served. Dinner shows begin at 9 PM on Wednesday and Friday from February until the end of October.

FRIGILIANA

58 km (36 mi) east of Málaga.

ESSENTIALS

Visitor Information Frigiliana (✉ *Plaza del Ingenio* ☎ *952/534261*).

The village of Frigiliana, on a mountain ridge overlooking the sea, was the site of one of the last battles between the Christians and the Moors. The short drive from the highway rewards you with spectacular views and an old quarter of narrow, cobbled streets and dazzling white houses decorated with pots of geraniums. (If you don't have a car, you can take a bus here from Nerja.)

THE AXARQUÍA

Vélez-Málaga: 36 km (22 mi) east of Málaga.

The Axarquía region stretches from Nerja to Málaga, and the area's charm lies in its mountainous interior, peppered with pueblos, vineyards, and tiny farms. Its coast consists of narrow, pebbly beaches and drab fishing villages on either side of the high-rise resort town of Torre del Mar.

GETTING HERE AND AROUND

Although the bus routes are fairly comprehensive throughout the Axarquía, reaching the smaller villages may involve long delays; renting a car is convenient and lets you get off the beaten track and experience some of the beautiful unspoiled hinterland in this little known part of Andalusia. The four-lane E15 highway speeds across the region a few miles in from the coast; traffic on the old coastal road (N340) is slower.

ESSENTIALS

Visitor Information Cómpeta (✉ *Avenida de la Constitucion* ☎ *952/553685*).

EXPLORING

Vélez-Málaga is the capital of the Axarquía: it's a pleasant agricultural town of white houses, a center for strawberry fields, and vineyards. Worth quick visits are the **Thursday market,** the ruins of a **Moorish castle,** and the church of **Santa María la Mayor,** built in Mudejar style on the site of a mosque that was destroyed when the town fell to the Christians in 1487.

If you have a car and an up-to-date road map, explore the Axarquía's inland villages: You can follow the **Ruta del Vino** *(Wine Route)* 22 km (14 mi) from the coast, stopping at villages that produce the sweet, earthy local wine, particularly Cómpeta. Alternatively you can take the **Ruta de la Pasa** *(Raisin Route)* through Moclinejo, El Borge, and Comares. Comares perches like an eagle's nest atop one of La Serrazuela's highest mountains and dates back to Moorish times. This area is especially spectacular during the late-summer grape-harvest season or in late autumn, when the leaves of the vines turn gold. A short detour to Macharaviaya (7 km [4 mi] north of Rincón de la Victoria) might lead you to ponder the past glory of this now sleepy village: In 1776 one of its sons, Bernardo de Gálvez, became Spanish governor of Louisiana and later fought in the American Revolution (Galveston, Texas, takes its name from the governor). Macharaviaya prospered under his heirs, and for many years enjoyed a lucrative monopoly on the manufacture of playing cards for South America. Both the Ruta del Vino and the Ruta de la Pasa are signposted locally.

WHERE TO EAT AND STAY

¢–$ ★ **El Molino de los Abuelos.** Under a canopy of jasmine and bougainvillea, this former olive mill in Comares has a cobbled courtyard where you can enjoy a glass of *fino* (sherry) at sundown while ogling the stunning views. The rooms are all different, varying from small and simple with shared bath to a sumptuous suite with a hot tub. The restaurant has fabulous views too, but, unfortunately, while the new Dutch-Columbian owners organize terrific themed entertainment (like tango nights), they have paid little heed to the cuisine, which is decidedly mediocre. Instead go around the corner to the excellent, English-run La Vendimia. **Pros:** full of traditional Andalusian character, fabulous views. **Cons:** rooms are plain, several bathrooms are old-fashioned (including their plumbing), mediocre food. ✉ *Plaza 2, Comares* ☎ *952/509309* 🌐 *www.hotelmolinodelosabuelos.com* *6 rooms* *In-room: no TV (some). In-hotel: restaurant, no elevator* 💳 *AE, MC, V.*

$$$ **Molino de Santillán.** This small country hotel and restaurant is typically Andalusian, with arches, terra-cotta floors, and dark oak furniture. There are superb countryside views from the rooms as well as from the timbered restaurant ($$–$$$), where the cooks use organic ingredients grown at the hotel (try the fresh quince salad with Burgos cheese). At the end of a signposted dirt road north of the main highway, the hotel is a short drive from the Añoreta golf club and 5 km (2½ mi) from the nearest beach. Pottery and woodcarving workshops are regularly

held here. **Pros:** quiet and tranquil, great views. **Cons:** a car is essential for sightseeing or dining farther afield. ✉ *Ctra. de Macharaviaya, Km 3, Rincón de la Victoria* ☎ *952/400949* 🌐 *www.molinodesantillan.es* *22 rooms* *In-hotel: restaurant, tennis, pool, public Wi-Fi, some pets allowed* *AE, DC, MC, V.*

MÁLAGA PROVINCE

The city of Málaga and the provincial towns of the upland hills and valleys to the north create the kind of contrast that makes travel in Spain so tantalizing. The region's Moorish legacy—tiny streets honeycombing the steamy depths of Málaga, the rocky cliffs and gorges, the layout of the farms and the crops themselves, including olives, grapes, oranges, and lemons—is a unifying visual theme. Ronda and the whitewashed villages of the mountains behind the Costa del Sol comprise one of Spain's most scenic and emblematic driving routes.

To the west of Málaga, along the coast, the sprawling outskirts of Torremolinos signal that you're leaving the "real" Spain and entering, well, the "real" Costa del Sol, with its beaches, high-rise hotels, and serious tourist activity. On the far west, you can still discern Estepona's fishing village and Moorish old quarter amid its booming coastal development. Just inland, Casares piles whitewashed houses over the bright-blue Mediterranean below.

MÁLAGA

175 km (109 mi) southeast of Córdoba.

With about 550,000 residents, the city of Málaga is technically the capital of the Costa del Sol, though most travelers head straight for the beaches west of the city. Approaching Málaga from the airport, you'll be greeted by huge 1970s high-rises that march determinedly toward Torremolinos. But don't despair: in its center and eastern suburbs, Málaga is a pleasant port city, with ancient streets and lovely villas amid exotic foliage. Blessed with a subtropical climate, it's covered in lush vegetation and averages some 324 days of sunshine a year.

Málaga has been spruced up with tastefully restored historic buildings and the steady emergence of increasingly sophisticated shops, bars, and restaurants. The opening of the prestigious Museo Carmen Thyssen Bornemisza in late 2009 will doubtless further boost tourism to this Costa capital, although there are still far fewer visitors here than in the other grand-slam Andalusian cities of Seville, Córdoba, and Granada. ☞ *Note that more tourists usually means more pickpockets, so stay alert, particularly around the historic city center.*

Arriving from Nerja, you'll enter Málaga through the suburbs of El Palo and Pedregalejo, once traditional fishing villages. Here you can eat fresh fish in the numerous *chiringuitos* (beachside bars) and stroll Pedregalejos's seafront promenade or the tree-lined streets of El Limonar. At sunset, walk along the **Paseo Marítimo** and watch the lighthouse start its nightly vigil. A few blocks inland from here is Málaga's

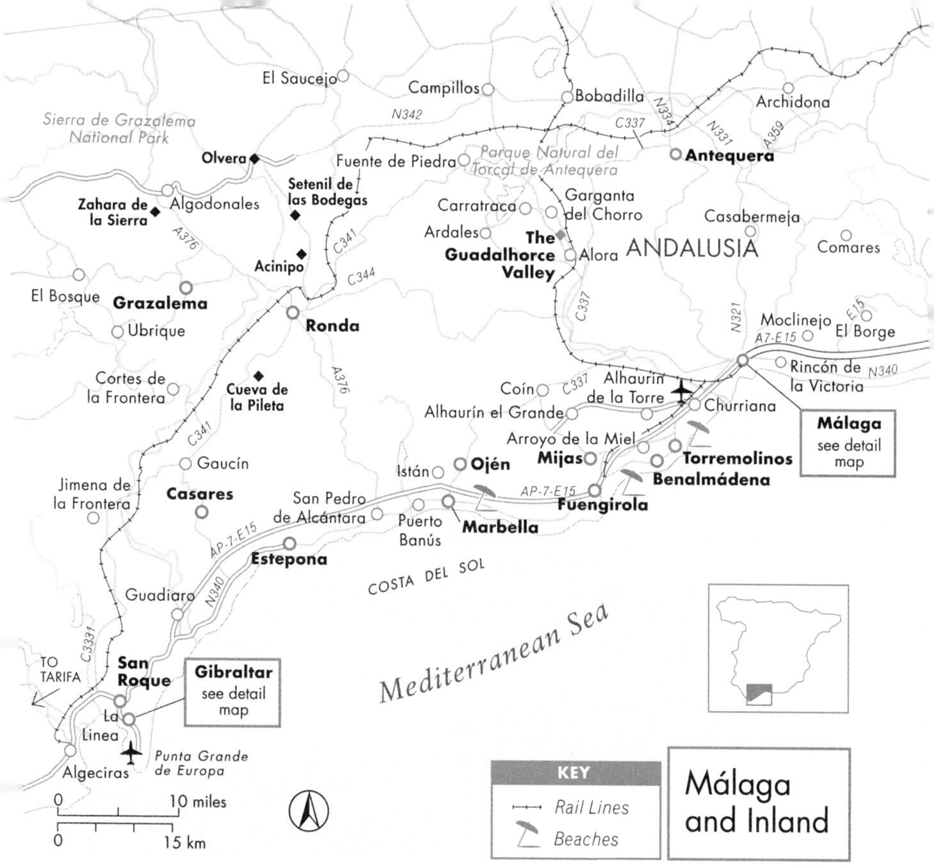

bullring, **La Malagueta**, built in 1874. Continuing west you'll soon reach the city center and the inviting **Plaza de la Marina**; with cafés and an illuminated fountain overlooking the port, it's a pleasant place for a drink. From here, stroll through the shady, palm-lined gardens of the **Paseo del Parque** or browse on **Calle Marqués de Larios**, the elegant pedestrian-only main shopping street.

GETTING HERE AND AROUND

If you're staying at one of the coastal resorts between Málaga and Fuengirola, the easiest way to reach Málaga is via the half-hourly train. Otherwise, there are several new, well-signposted underground car parks, and it's not a daunting place to negotiate by car. The best way to explore Málaga is by foot, but you could also hop on an open-top sightseeing bus or rent a bike. There is a comprehensive bus network, too, and the tourist office can advise on routes and schedules. The city is in the throes of introducing a metro but, given the inevitability of delays caused by archaeological discoveries, the completion date is, as yet, undetermined.

The colorful, open-top Málaga Tour City Sightseeing Bus is a good way to see the city's attractions in a day. The bus stops at all the major sights in town, including the Gibralfaro and the cathedral.

ESSENTIALS

Airport Contact **Aeropuerto de Málaga (AGP)** (*Pablo Picasso Airport ☎ 952/048804 🌐 www.ccoo-agp.com*).

Bike Rental Ccontact **Cyclo Point** (*✉ Av. Juan Sebastian Elcano 50, Málaga ☎ 952/297324 🌐 www.cyclo-point.com*).

Bus Contacts **Málaga bus station** (*✉ Paseo de los Tilos ☎ 952/350061*).

Car Rental Contacts **Crown Car Hire** (*✉ Málaga Airport 🌐 www.crowncarhire.com*). **Niza Cars** (*✉ Málaga Airport 🌐 www.nizacars.com*).

Taxi Companies **Morales Rodriguez–Málaga** (*☎ 952/430077*).

Tour Information **Málaga Tour City Sightseeing Bus** (*🌐 www.citysightseeing-spain.com*).

Train Information **Málaga train station** (*✉ Explanada de la Estación ☎ 952/360202*).

Visitor Information **Málaga** (*✉ Av. Cervantes 1, Paseo del Parque ☎ 952/604410*).

EXPLORING

4 Just beyond the ruins of a Roman theater on Calle Alcazabilla, the Moorish **Alcazaba** is Málaga's greatest monument. This fortress was begun in the 8th century, when Málaga was the principal port of the Moorish kingdom, though most of the present structure dates from the 11th century. The inner palace was built between 1057 and 1063, when the Moorish emirs took up residence; Ferdinand and Isabella lived here for a while after conquering Málaga in 1487. The ruins are dappled with orange trees and bougainvillea and include a small museum; from the highest point you can see over the park and port. *✉ Entrance on Alcazabilla 🎫 €1.95, €3.20 combined entry with Gibralfaro ⏲ Nov.–Mar., Tues.–Sun. 9:30–7; Apr.–Oct., Tues.–Sun. 9:30–8.*

6 Málaga's **cathedral,** built between 1528 and 1782, is a triumph, although a generally unappreciated one, having been left unfinished when funds ran out. Because it lacks one of its two towers, the building is nicknamed *La Manquita* (The One-Armed Lady). The enclosed choir, which miraculously survived the burnings of the civil war, is the work of 17th-century artist Pedro de Mena, who carved the wood wafer-thin in some places to express the fold of a robe or shape of a finger. The choir also has a pair of massive 18th-century pipe organs, one of which is still used for the occasional concert. Adjoining the cathedral is a small museum of religious art and artifacts. A walk around the cathedral on Calle Cister will take you to the magnificent Gothic Puerta del Sagrario. *✉ C. de Molina Larios ☎ 952/215917 🎫 €3.50 ⏲ Weekdays 10–6, Sat 10–5:45.*

12 **Centro de Arte Contemporáneo** *(Contemporary Arts Center)*. This museum includes photographic studies and paintings, some of them immense. With 7,900 square feet of bright exhibition hall, the museum aims to showcase ultramodern artistic trends in four exhibitions—a changing show from the permanent collection, two temporary shows, and one show dedicated to up-and-coming Spanish artists. The gallery attracts world-class modern artists like the UK's Tracy Emin, whose famously

Alcazaba 4
Cathedral 6
Centro de Arte Contemporáneo de Málaga 12
Fundación Picasso 2
Gibralfaro 3
La Concepción ...1
Museo Carmen Thyssen Bornemisza 9
Mercado de Atarazanas 11
Museo de Artes Populares 10
Museo Picasso ...5
Palacio Episcopal 7
Pasaje Chinitas ..8

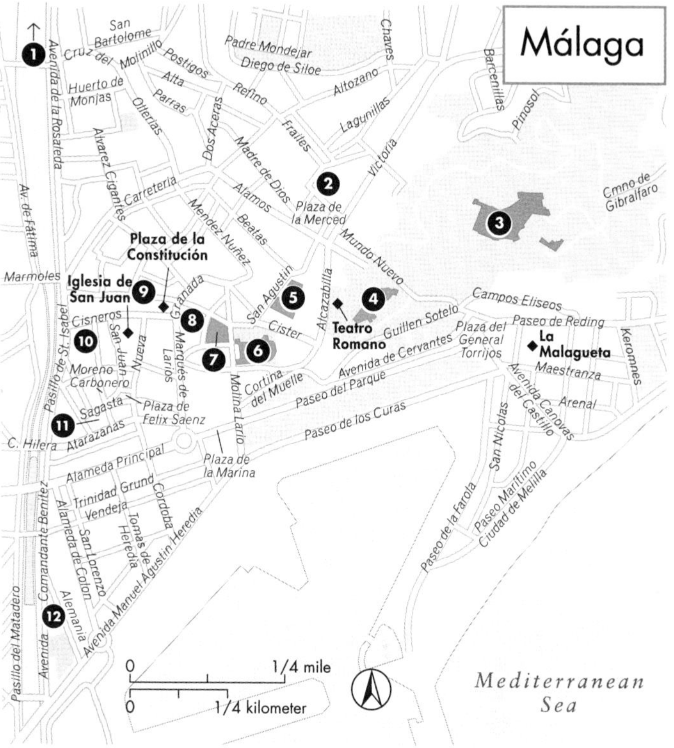

controversial "unmade bed" was included in a two-month exhibition here in early 2009. ✉*Alemania s/n* ☎*952/12055* 🎟*Free* ⏲*Tues.–Sun. 10–8.*

2 The childhood home of Málaga's most famous native son, Pablo Picasso, born here in 1881, is on the Plaza de la Merced. Now the **Fundación Picasso,** the building has been painted and furnished in the style of the era and houses a permanent exhibition of Picasso's early sketches and sculptures, as well as memorabilia, including the artist's christening robe and family photos. ✉*Pl. de la Merced 15* ☎*952/600215* 🎟*€1* ⏲*Mon.–Sat. 10–8, Sun. 10–2.*

3 Magnificent vistas beckon at **Gibralfaro,** which is floodlit at night. The fortifications were built for Yusuf I in the 14th century; the Moors called them Jebelfaro, from the Arab word for "mount" and the Greek word for "lighthouse," after a beacon that stood here to guide ships into the harbor and warn of pirates. The beacon has been succeeded by a small parador *(see Where to Stay)*. You can drive here by way of Calle Victoria or take a minibus that leaves 10 times a day, between 11 and 7, roughly every hour, from the bus stop in the park near the Plaza de la Marina. ✉*Gibralfaro Mountain* ☎*952/220043* 🎟*€1.95, €3.20 combined entry with Alcazaba* ⏲*Nov.–Mar., daily 9–5:45; Apr.–Oct., daily 9–7:45.*

8 A 150-year-old botanical garden, **La Concepción** was created by the daughter of the British consul, who married a Spanish shipping magnate—the captains of the Spaniard's fleet had standing orders to bring back seedlings and cuttings from every "exotic" port of call. The garden is just off the exit road to Granada—too far to walk, but well worth the cab fare from the city center. *Ctra. de las Pedrizas, Km 216 952/252148 €4.20 Tues.–Sun. 9:30* AM*–dusk.*

11 From the Plaza Felix Saenz, at the southern end of Calle Nueva, turn onto Sagasta to reach the **Mercado de Atarazanas**. The typical 19th-century iron structure incorporates the original **Puerta de Atarazanas**, the exquisitely crafted 14th-century Moorish gate that once connected the city with the port. The actual market stalls have been moved to a purpose-built building on the corner of nearby Calle Agujero and Paseo Santa Isabel while the interior is being refurbished. The estimated completion date is early 2010.

NEED A BREAK?

The Antigua Casa de Guardia (*Alameda 18 952/214680*), around the corner from the Mercado de Atarazanas, is Málaga's oldest bar, founded in 1840. Andalusian wines and finos (sherries) flow straight from the barrel, the walls are lined with sepia-photos of old Málaga—including Picasso who was evidently a frequent customer here—and the floor is ankle-deep in discarded shrimp shells.

9 Visitors who've been to Madrid will be familiar with that city's Museo Thyssen Bornemisza—in late 2009 a further 358 works from the private collection of Baroness Thyssen are to go on show at Málaga's very own **Museo Carmen Thyssen Bornemisza**, housed in an aesthetically renovated 16th-century palace. The collection is set to include paintings by some of Spain's greatest artists, like Sorolla, Zurbarán, and Dominguez Bécquer. At this writing, opening hours and admission costs were not set in stone; check with the tourist office (*952/213445*) before visiting. *C. Compañia Unavailable at time of publication €6 Tues.–Sun. 10–7.*

10 In the old Mesón de la Victoria, a 17th-century inn, is the **Museo de Artes Populares** *(Arts and Crafts Museum)*. On display are horse-drawn carriages and carts, old agricultural implements, folk costumes, a forge, a bakery, an ancient grape press, and Malagueño painted clay figures and ceramics. *Pasillo de Santa Isabel 10 952/217137 www.museoartespopulares.com €2 Oct.–May, weekdays 10–1:30 and 4–7, Sat. 10–1:30; June–Sept., weekdays 10–1:30 and 5–8, Sat. 10–1:30.*

5 Fodor's Choice ★ The charm of the **Museo Picasso**, one of the city's most prestigious museums, is that it's such a family affair. These are the works that Pablo Picasso kept for himself or gave to his family and include the heartfelt *Paulo con gorro blanco* (Paulo with a white cap), a portrait of his first-born son painted in the early 1920s, and *Olga Kokhlova con mantilla* (Olga Kokhlova with mantilla), a 1917 portrait of his certifiably insane first wife. The holdings were largely donated by two family members—Christine and Bernard Ruiz-Picasso, the artist's daughter-in-law and her son. The works are displayed in chronological order according to

the periods that marked Picasso's development as an artist, from Blue and Rose to Cubism, and beyond. The museum is housed in a former palace where, during restoration work, Roman and Moorish remains were discovered. These are now on display, together with the permanent collection of Picassos and temporary exhibitions. ✉ *C. de San Agustín* ☎ *952/602731* 🌐 *www.museopicassomalaga.org* 🎫 *Permanent exhibition €6, combined permanent and temporary exhibition €8, last Sun. of every month free* ⏲ *Tues.–Thurs. 10–8, Fri. and Sat. 10–9.*

7 **Palacio Episcopa** *(Bishop's Palace)*, which faces the cathedral's main entrance, has one of the most stunning facades in the city. It's now a venue for temporary art exhibitions. ✉ *Pl. Obispo 6* ☎ *952/602722* 🎫 *Free* ⏲ *Tues.–Sun. 10–2 and 6–9.*

The narrow streets and alleys on each side of Calle Marqués de Larios have charms of their own. Wander the warren of passageways around
8 **Pasaje Chinitas,** off Plaza de la Constitución, and peep into the dark, vaulted bodegas where old men down glasses of *seco añejo* or *Málaga Virgen,* local wines made from Málaga's muscatel grapes. Silversmiths and vendors of religious books and statues ply their trades in shops that have changed little since the early 1900s. Backtrack across Larios, and, in the streets leading to Calle Nueva, you can see shoeshine boys, lottery-ticket vendors, Gypsy guitarists, and tapas bars serving wine from huge barrels.

WHERE TO EAT

$$–$$$ SPANISH

✕ **El Chinitas.** Decorated with traditional mosaic tiles and original paintings by Malagueño artists, this restaurant sits at one end of Pasaje Chinitas, Málaga's most *típico* (typical) street. The tapas bar is popular, especially for its cured ham. Try the *sopa castellana* (soup made with fresh garlic, bread, paprika, and egg), followed by fillet steak in Málaga wine sauce or one of the excellent casseroles like the exemplary rice, cod, and Norwegian lobster. Ask for a menu in English and consider the €38 *menú de degustación,* which is a reasonable option given the quality—and quantity: small appetites should resist. ✉ *Moreno Monroy 4* ☎ *952/210972* 💳 *AE, DC, MC, V.*

$$–$$$ SPANISH

✕ **La Ménsula.** If you're looking to sample traditional Andalusian cuisine in an elegant yet cozy atmosphere, this is the place. The setting is warm and woody, with arches, beams, and a barrel vault ceiling, and the service is appropriately hospitable and efficient. Stone-cooked steak, warm fish salad, and king prawns with *setas* (oyster mushrooms) are just some of the menu options. You can also enjoy a range of tapas at the adjacent bar. The restaurant is on a fairly anonymous side street between the port and the city center. ✉ *C. Trinidad Grund 28* ☎ *952/221314* 💳 *DC, MC, V* ⏲ *Closed Sun.*

¢–$ SPANISH Fodor's Choice ★

✕ **Logueno.** This traditional tapas bar has two dining spaces: the original well-loved bar, shoehorned into a deceptively small space on a side street near Calle Larios, and a more recent expansion across the street. The original is especially appealing, with its L-shaped wooden bar crammed with a choice of more than 75 tantalizing tapas, including many Logueno originals such as grilled oyster mushrooms with garlic, parsley, and goat cheese. There's an excellent selection of Rioja wines, and the service is fast and good, despite the lack of elbow room. ✉ *Marin Garcia s/n* ☎ *No phone* ▭ *No credit cards* ⊙ *Closed Sun.*

$ SPANISH ✕ **Tintero.** Come to this sprawling, noisy restaurant for the experience rather than the food. There's no menu—the waiters circle the restaurant carrying various dishes (tapas and main courses) and you choose whatever looks good. The bill is totaled up according to the number and size of the plates on the table at the end of the meal. On the El Palo seafront, Tintero specializes in catch-of-the-day seafood, such as *boquerones* (fresh anchovies), *sepia* (cuttlefish), and the all-time familiar classic, *gambas* (grilled prawns). Be warned that it's packed on Sundays with the local expat community and boisterous Spanish families; in other words, this is not the place for a romantic lunch for two. ✉ *Playa del Dedo, El Palo* ☎ *952/204464* ▭ *No credit cards* ⊙ *No dinner.*

$–$$$ ECLECTIC ✕ **Vino Mio.** This Dutch-owned restaurant is well placed, just off Plaza de la Merced, and the menu is diverse and interesting, including dishes like *cocodrilo Dundee* (crocodile steaks with red pepper chutney, potatoes, and seasonable vegetables) that have fast made this one of the city's most fashionable see-and-be-seen dining spots. Slightly more conservative dishes include *pollo Indonesia* (chicken prepared in a peanut sauce), *pasta Lili* (rigatoni with oyster mushrooms, walnuts, and zucchini), and seven salad choices including the *Marrakesh* (couscous with vegetables, raisins, and herbs). The atmosphere is contemporary chic with regular art exhibitions and live music nightly, ranging from flamenco to jazz. ✉ *Calle Alamos 11* ☎ *952/609093* ▭ *MC, V.*

WHERE TO STAY

$ **Castilla.** This gracious hotel in a butter-color building is located between the city center and the port. Rooms are excellent value, if small, with attractive fabrics, primrose yellow walls, and curtains to help block out any late-night street revelry. The adjacent cafeteria is handy for a typical *desayuno* (breakfast) of *café con leche* and *tostada con tomate* (toast with fresh tomatoes and olive oil) or an early evening aperitif before going out on the town. The owners are helpful and friendly but speak only Spanish. **Pros:** central location, parking. **Cons:** rooms are small, no Internet access. ✉ *C. Córdoba 7* ☎ *952/218635* *37 rooms* ▭ *MC, V* *EP.*

$$ Fodor's Choice ★ **Humaina.** In this small hotel 16 km (10 mi) north of the city, the rooms are painted a sunny yellow and have terra-cotta tile floors. Balconies overlook a thickly forested park of olive, pine, and oak trees. Solar energy, an organic garden, and serious recycling are part of the eco-friendly package. Horseback riding, bird-watching, and hiking excursions can be arranged. The restaurant dishes up healthful, tasty dishes, and vegetarians are happily accommodated—a rarity in these parts. **Pros:** environmentally friendly, bucolic countryside surroundings. **Cons:** a car is essential for exploring the coast and inland, room views vary. ✉ *Parque Natural Montes de Málaga, Ctra. del Colmenar s/n* ☎ *952/641025* ⊕ *www.hotelhumaina.es* *10 rooms, 4 suites* *In-hotel: restaurant, pool, no elevator* ▭ *MC, V* *BP.*

$$–$$$ **Larios.** On the central Plaza de la Constitución, this lodging is in a 19th-century building that's been elegantly restored. Black-and-white tile floors lend subdued elegance to the second-floor lobby, while the rooms

are luxuriously furnished with carpeting throughout and king-size beds, unusual in Spain. Several have balconies overlooking the sophisticated strut of shops and boutiques along Calle Marqués de Larios. The roof terrace has views of the cathedral, and the restaurant has a sophisticated choice of dishes, including crispy duck. The choice of 11 bottled waters from all over the world makes for entertaining reading. **Pros:** stylish and efficiently run. **Cons:** on busy shopping street that can be noisy in daytime, some rooms on the small side. ✉ *Marqués de Larios 2* ☎ *952/222200* 🌐 *www.hotel-larios.com* *34 rooms, 6 suites* *In-room: Wi-Fi. In-hotel: restaurant, bar* 💳 *AE, DC, MC, V* *BP.*

$$$ Fodor's Choice ★ **Parador de Málaga–Gibralfaro.** Surrounded by pine trees and crowning the Gibralfaro (castle) hill, 3 km (2 mi) above the city, this cozy, gray-stone parador has spectacular views of Málaga and the bay. Rooms are attractive—with blue curtains and bedspreads and woven rugs on bare tile floors—and are some of the best in Málaga, so reserve well in advance. All have terraces with panoramic views. The restaurant ($–$$$) excels at such classic Mediterranean dishes as calamari and fried green peppers. **Pros:** some of the best views on the Costa, excellent service. **Cons:** a bit of a hike into town, books up quickly. ✉ *Monte de Gibralfaro s/n* ☎ *952/221902* 🌐 *www.parador.es* *38 rooms* *In-room: Ethernet. In-hotel: restaurant, bar, pool, parking (no fee)* 💳 *AE, DC, MC, V.*

NIGHTLIFE AND THE ARTS

Málaga's main nightlife districts are Maestranza, between the bullring and the Paseo Marítimo, and the beachfront in the suburb of Pedregalejos. Central Málaga also has a lively bar scene around Plaza Uncibay.

ANTEQUERA

64 km (40 mi) northwest of Málaga, 108 km (67 mi) northeast of Ronda, via Pizarra.

Antequera became a stronghold of the Moors after their defeat at Córdoba and Seville in the 13th century. Its fall to the Christians in 1410 paved the way for the reconquest of Granada—the Moors retreated, leaving a fortress on the town heights.

GETTING HERE AND AROUND

There are several daily buses from Málaga and Ronda to Antequera. Drivers should head for the underground car park on Calle Diego Ponce in the center of town and well signposted.

ESSENTIALS

Visitor Information **Antequera** (✉ *Plaza de San Sebastian 7* ☎ *952/702505* 🌐 *www.antequera.es*).

EXPLORING

Next to the town fortress is the former church of **Santa María la Mayor,** one of 27 churches, convents, and monasteries in Antequera. Built of sandstone in the 16th century, it has a ribbed vault that is now a concert hall. The church of **San Sebastián** has a brick baroque Mudejar tower topped by a winged figure called the Angelote ("big angel"), the symbol of Antequera. The church of **Nuestra Señora del Carmen** (Our

Lady of Carmen) has an extraordinary baroque altarpiece that towers to the ceiling.

Antequera's pride and joy is *Efebo,* a beautiful bronze statue of a boy that dates back to Roman times. Standing almost 5 feet high, it's on display in the **Museo Municipal.** ✉ *Pl. Coso Viejo* ☎ *952/704051* 🎫 *€3* ⏲ *Tues.–Fri. 10–1:30 and 4:30–6:30, Sat. 10–1:30, Sun. 11–1:30.*

The mysterious prehistoric **dolmens** are megalithic burial chambers, built some 4,000 years ago out of massive slabs of stone weighing more than 100 tons each. The best-preserved dolmen is La Menga. They're just outside Antequera. ✉ *Signposted off Málaga exit Rd.* 🎫 *Free* ⏲ *Tues.–Sat. 9–6, Sun. 9:30–2:30.*

Europe's major nesting area for the greater flamingo is **Fuente de Piedra,** a shallow saltwater lagoon. In February and March, these birds arrive from Africa by the thousands to breed, returning to Africa in August when the water dries up. The visitor center has information on wildlife. Don't forget your binoculars. ✉ *10 km (6 mi) northwest of Antequera, off A92 to Seville* ☎ *952/111715* 🎫 *Free* ⏲ *May–Sept., Wed.–Sun. 10–2 and 4–6; Oct.–Apr., Wed.–Sun. 10–2 and 6–8.*

East of Antequera, along N342, is the dramatic silhouette of the **Peña de los Enamorados** *(Lovers' Rock),* an Andalusian landmark. Legend has it that a Moorish princess and a Christian shepherd boy eloped here one night and cast themselves to their deaths from the peak the next morning. The rock's outline is often likened to the profile of the Cordobés bullfighter Manolete.

About 8 km (5 mi) from Antequera's Lovers' Rock, the village of **Archidona** winds its way up a steep mountain slope beneath the ruins of a Moorish castle. This unspoiled village is worth a detour for its **Plaza Ochavada,** a magnificent 17th-century square resplendent with contrasting red and ocher stone. ✉ *8 km (5 mi) beyond Peña de los Enamorados, along N342, Antequera.*

Fodor's Choice ★ Well-marked walking trails (stay on them) guide you at the **Parque Natural del Torcal de Antequera** *(El Torcal Nature Park),* where you can walk among eerie pillars of pink limestone sculpted by eons of wind and rain. Guides can be arranged for longer hikes. The visitor center has a small museum. ✉ *Centro de Visitantes, Ctra. C3310, 10 km (6 mi) south of Antequera* ☎ *649/472688* 🎫 *Free* ⏲ *Daily 10–5.*

WHERE TO EAT AND STAY

$ SPANISH ✕ **Caserío San Benito.** If it weren't for the cell-phone transmission tower looming next to this country restaurant 11 km (7 mi) north of Antequera, you might think you've stumbled into an 18th-century scene. Popular dishes include *porra antequerana* (a thick version of gazpacho topped with diced ham) and *migas* (fried bread crumbs with sausage and spices). It's a popular Sunday lunch spot for hungry *malagueños* in the winter months (in summer they head for the beach). Many of the items found during the renovation of this former farmhouse fronted by a cobbled courtyard are displayed in a small adjacent museum. ✉ *Ctra. Málaga–Córdoba, Km 108* ☎ *952/111103* 💳 *AE, MC, V* ⏲ *Closed Mon. and 1st 2 wks in July. No dinner Tues.–Thurs.*

$–$$ SPANISH **Coso San Francisco.** This delightful restaurant in the hotel of the same name is an evocative 17th-century building complete with low ceilings, uneven floors, ancient beams, and an intimate dining room, which a hefty wood-burning stove makes cozy in winter. The menu uses fresh ingredients and includes some interesting twists on traditional dishes, like the *porrilla de espárragos* (asparagus soup with fried bread and an egg). Egg, meat, and fish dishes are accompanied by crisp wide-cut fries and salads. Most of the vegetables are grown organically by the owner. *Calle Calzada 27–29* *952/840014* *www.cososanfrancisco.com* *MC, V.*

$$ SPANISH Fodor's Choice ★ **El Angelote.** Across the square from the Museo Municipal, El Angelote is one of Antequera's most popular, well-established restaurants. Kick-start your appetite with a glass of *fino* (sherry) at the traditional L-shaped bar, then you can head to one of the two wood-beam dining rooms in back, which fill up fast at lunchtime. The menu is solidly traditional and includes local specialties like *porrilla de setas* (wild mushrooms in an almond-and-wine sauce) or *perdiz hortelana* (stewed partridge). Antequera's typical dessert is *bienmesabe* (literally, "tastes good to me"), a delicious concoction of almonds, chocolate, and apple custard. *Pl. Coso Viejo* *952/703465* *DC, MC, V* *Closed Mon. No dinner Sun.*

$ **Coso San Francisco.** Surrounded by shops, bars, and cafés, this charming hotel and restaurant (*see Where to Eat*) is in a lovely 17th-century building, complete with a first-floor gallery that overlooks the central courtyard dining room. There are just 10 rooms, all appropriately furnished in a rustic manner, with dark wood, and several still have features from the original building, such as niches, low beams, and original timber doors. It's worth the extra cost for breakfast, since the downstairs restaurant is excellent, as testified by the delicious smells that waft up from the dining room. **Pros:** atmospheric historic building, great restaurant. **Cons:** rooms are rather spartan for some, right in town so can be noisy. *C. Calzada 27–29* *952/840014* *www.cososanfrancisco.com* *10 rooms* *In-room: refrigerator. In-hotel: restaurant, bar, parking* *AE, DC, MC, V* *BP.*

$$$–$$$$ **La Posada del Torcal.** Surrounded by the lunar landscape of El Torcal, this small hotel is just the place to chill out and relax after a long day on the trail. There are king-size beds (a rarity in Spain) and a fireplace in each room, as well as a cozy common sitting room with a DVD and book library. In the warmer months guests can cool down in the outside pool with its prime-positioned Jacuzzi and dramatic Torcal views. Skillful copies of paintings by Spanish masters grace the walls throughout the hotel. The Posada's restaurant uses organic, locally produced ingredients in the preparation of Spanish dishes with an innovative twist. **Pros:** friendly British owners, great for walkers and hikers. **Cons:** building exterior looks disarmingly anonymous and modern, coast is a considerable distance away. *Partido de Jeva, Villanueva de la Concepción* *952/031177* *www.laposadadeltorcal.com* *10 rooms* *In-hotel: restaurant, bar, tennis court, pool, gym, Internet terminal* *AE, MC, V* *Closed Dec. and Jan.* *BP.*

THE GUADALHORCE VALLEY

About 5 km (3 mi) from Antequera, via the El Torcal exit and turn right onto A343.

From the village of Alora, follow the small road north to the awe-inspiring **Garganta del Chorro** *(Gorge of the Stream)*, a deep limestone chasm where the Guadalhorce River churns and snakes its way some 600 feet below the road. The railroad track that worms in and out of tunnels in the cleft is, amazingly, the main line heading north from Málaga for Bobadilla junction and, eventually, Madrid. Clinging to the cliff side is the **Caminito del Rey** *(King's Walk)*, a suspended catwalk built for a visit by King Alfonso XIII at the beginning of the 19th century. The catwalk has been closed for construction and renovations since 1992, and there's still no word on completion.

North of the gorge, the Guadalhorce has been dammed to form a series of scenic reservoirs surrounded by piney hills, which constitute the **Parque de Ardales** nature area. Informal, open-air restaurants overlook the lakes and a number of picnic spots. Driving along the southern shore of the lake, you reach Ardales and, turning onto A357, the old spa town of **Carratraca.** Once a favorite watering hole for both Spanish and foreign aristocracy, it has a Moorish-style *ayuntamiento* (town hall) and an unusual **polygonal bullring.** Carratraca's original hotel, the **Hostal del Príncipe,** once sheltered Empress Eugénie, wife of Napoléon III; Lord Byron also came here seeking the cure. Today it has been renovated into a luxury Ritz-Carlton spa hotel. The splendid Roman-style marble-and-tile **bathhouse** has benefited from extensive restoration.

TORREMOLINOS

11 km (7 mi) west of Málaga, 16 km (10 mi) northeast of Fuengirola, 43 km (27 mi) east of Marbella.

Torremolinos is all about fun in the sun. It may be more subdued than it was in the action-packed '60s and '70s, but scantily attired northern Europeans of all ages still jam the streets in season, shopping for bargains on Calle San Miguel, downing sangria in the bars of La Nogalera, and congregating in the karaoke bars and English pubs. By day, the sunseekers flock to the El Bajondillo and La Carihuela beaches, where, in high summer, it's hard to find towel space on the sand.

ESSENTIALS

Bike Rental Contacts Moto Mercado (✉ *Plaza de los Comunidades, Torremolinos* ☎ *952/052671* 🌐 *www.rentabike.org*).

Bus Contacts Bus Station (✉ *Calle Hoyo* ☎ *952/382419*).

Taxi Contacts Radio Taxi Torremolinos (☎ *952/380600*).

Tour Information Pullmantur (✉ *Av. Imperial, Torremolinos* ☎ *952/384400* 🌐 *www.pullmantur.es*).

Visitor Information Torremolinos (✉ *Pl. Blas Infante 1* ☎ *952/379512*).

12

EXPLORING

Torremolinos has two sections. The first, **Central Torremolinos,** is built around the Plaza Costa del Sol; Calle San Miguel, the main shopping street; and the brash Nogalera Plaza, which is full of overpriced bars and restaurants. The Pueblo Blanco area, off Calle Casablanca, is more pleasant; and the Cuesta del Tajo, at the far end of Calle San Miguel, winds down a steep slope to Bajondillo Beach. Here, crumbling walls, bougainvillea-clad patios, and old cottages hint at the quiet fishing village of bygone years. The second, much nicer, section of Torremolinos is **La Carihuela.** (To find it, head west out of town on Avenida Carlota Alessandri and turn left following the signs.) Far more authentically Spanish, the Carihuela still has a few fishermen's cottages and excellent seafood restaurants. The traffic-free esplanade is pleasant for strolling, especially on a summer evening or Sunday at lunchtime, when it's packed with Spanish families.

WHERE TO EAT AND STAY

$$–$$$ SEAFOOD ✕ **Casa Juan.** An institution among *malagueño* families, who flock here on weekends for the legendary fresh seafood, this restaurant has been steadily spreading its girth, and there are now several Casa Juans surrounding an attractive square, one line back from the seafront. Try for a table overlooking the mermaid fountain. This is a good place to indulge in *fritura malagueña* (fried seafood) or *arroz marinera* (seafood with rice), one of 10 different rice dishes prepared here; others include lobster rice, vegetable rice, and black rice flavored with squid ink. ✉ *Plaza San Gines, La Carihuela* ☎ *952/373512* ▭ *MC, V* ⊗ *Closed Mon.*

$$$$ SPANISH ✕ **La Consula.** Just north of Torremolinos (toward Coín), this cooking school is well worth the detour. The main building dates from 1856—in the 1850s it was the residence of an American family, and Ernest Hemingway was a frequent visitor—and is surrounded by tropical gardens. Today, diners can enjoy excellent and innovative cuisine prepared by the students. Typical dishes include cherry gazpacho with strawberries and yogurt, lightly steamed sea bass with a white wine and ginger sauce, and desserts like the irresistible nougat and raspberry bombe glacée. The restaurant is very popular with businessmen from Málaga, so reserve well in advance. ✉ *Finca La Consula, Churriana* ☎ *952/262-2562* ⊕ *www.laconsula.com* ▭ *MC, V* ⊗ *Closed Sat.–Sun., lunch only.*

$$$ MEDITERRANEAN ★ ✕ **Med.** An elevator whisks you up to this elegant restaurant tucked away around the corner from the car-free San Miguel. A blue-and-white nautical setting, seamless Mediterranean views, and impeccable service greet you; the beautifully presented food is from a menu that changes every six months, with dishes such as *solomillo de ternero con setas, patata machacona y tempura de verduras* (braised veal with oyster mushrooms, creamed potatoes, and vegetable tempura) followed by *sorbete de limón o mandarina con cava* (lemon or orange sorbet with champagne). There's also an excellent wine selection. ✉ *Las Mercedes 12* ☎ *952/058830* ✍ *Reservations essential* ▭ *AE, DC, MC, V.*

$ **Cabello.** The rooms at this small hotel have few frills, but most have impressive sea views—it's just a block from the beach in La Carihuela, the attractive former fishing village district of Torremolinos. Near the ground-floor bar is a comfortable sitting area, with overstuffed chairs, a piano, and a pool table. Some of the best seafood restaurants in town are a short stroll away. The owners are friendly and helpful, though they speak only Spanish. **Pros:** close to the beach, excellently priced. **Cons:** across from a primary school so can be noisy, plain rooms. ✉ *Calle Chiriva 28* ☎ *952/384505* *19 rooms* *In-hotel: bar, no elevator* ▭ *No credit cards.*

$$$ **Don Pedro.** Extremely comfortable and well maintained, this three-story, traditional Andalusian-style hotel is part of the reliable Spanish Sol Melia chain. Rooms are spacious and have balconies; sea views get snapped up fast. The bodega-style bar is popular at happy hour, and nightly entertainment here includes flamenco shows. The hearty breakfast buffet should set you up for the day; lunch is more mediocre. **Pros:** across from the beach, good-size balconies. **Cons:** popular with tour groups, pool area gets very crowded and noisy in peak season. ✉ *Av. del Lido* ☎ *952/386844* 🌐 *www.solmelia.com* *524 rooms* *In-hotel: restaurant, pools, beachfront* ▭ *AE, DC, MC, V* *BP.*

$$ **Miami.** Something of a find, this small hotel dates from 1950, when it was designed by Manolo Blascos, Picasso's cousin, for flamenco Gypsy dancer Lola Medina. Rooms are individually furnished, if a little dated, and there's a sitting area with a TV, cozy fireplace, and small library. The inn is surrounded by a shady garden west of the Carihuela, making a stay here like visiting a private Spanish home. Many guests return here year after year. Reserve ahead. **Pros:** plenty of character, close to the beach. **Cons:** rooms could use some updating, inconvenient for public transport. ✉ *Aladino 14, at C. Miami* ☎ *952/385255* 🌐 *www.residencia-miami.com* *26 rooms* *In-room: no TV. In-hotel: bar, pool, some pets allowed* ▭ *No credit cards* *CP.*

$$$ **Tropicana.** On the beach at the far end of the Carihuela, in one of the most pleasant parts of Torremolinos, this low-rise resort hotel has its own beach club. A tropical theme runs throughout, from the purple passion-flower climbers covering the brickwork to the common areas with exotic plants and bamboo furniture, and also to the rooms, with their warm color schemes and dazzling white fabrics. The hotel has a friendly, homey feel that keeps many guests returning year after year. **Pros:** great for families, surrounded by bars and restaurants. **Cons:** can be noisy, a half-hour walk to the center of Torremolinos. ✉ *Trópico 6, La Carihuela* ☎ *952/386600* 🌐 *www.hoteltropicana.es* *84 rooms* *In-room: refrigerator. In-hotel: restaurant, bar, pool, beachfront, public Wi-Fi* ▭ *AE, DC, MC, V* *BP.*

NIGHTLIFE AND THE ARTS

Most nocturnal action is in the center of town. Many of the better hotels stage flamenco shows, but you may also want to check out the **Taberna Flamenca Pepe López** (✉ *Pl. de la Gamba Alegre* ☎ *952/381284*), which has nightly shows at 10 PM from April to October. The rest of the year shows are weekends only.

BENALMÁDENA

9 km (5½ mi) west of Torremolinos, 9 km (5½ mi) east of Mijas.

ESSENTIALS

Visitor Information Benalmádena Costa (✉ *Av. Antonio Machado 14* ☎ *952/379512*).

EXPLORING

★ **Benalmádena-Pueblo,** the village proper, is on the mountainside 7 km (4 mi) from the coast. It's surprisingly unspoiled and offers a glimpse of the old Andalusia. **Benalmádena-Costa,** the beach resort, is practically an extension of Torremolinos; it's run almost exclusively by package-tour operators, although the marina does have shops, restaurants, and bars aimed at a more sophisticated clientele and which may appeal to the independent traveler.

In Benalmádena-Costa's marina, **Sea Life Benalmádena** is an above-average aquarium with fish from local waters, including rays, sharks, and sunfish; there's also a turtle reef where you can watch rare green turtles and learn about various conservation projects. Adjacent is a pirate-theme miniature golf course. ✉ *Puerto Marina Benalmádena* ☎ *952/560150* 🌐 *www.sealife.es* 🎫 *€11.95 mini golf €6* ⏲ *May–Sept., daily 10 AM–midnight; Oct.–Apr., daily 10–6.*

The Costa del Sol's leading amusement park is **Tivoli World,** with rides, Wild West shows, and 40-odd restaurants and snack bars. A 4,000-seat, open-air auditorium showcases international stars alongside cancan, flamenco, and Spanish ballet performances. You can take a cable car to the top of Calamorro Mountain for hiking trails. ✉ *Av. Tivoli s/n, Arroyo de la Miel* ☎ *952/757-7016* 🌐 *www.tivoli.es* 🎫 *€4* ⏲ *May–Sept., daily 1 PM–1 AM; Oct.–Apr., weekends noon–8.*

WHERE TO EAT AND STAY

$–$$ CONTINENTAL ✕ **Casa Fidel.** This Benalmádena-Pueblo restaurant is in a typical Andalusian house complete with arches, terra-cotta tiles, a large fireplace, and a small leafy patio. For a starter, try *crema fría de aguacate con salmón marinado* (cold avocado soup with marinated salmon) or *ensalada templada de setas y gambas* (warm salad with shrimp and wild mushrooms). Main courses include *langostinos con chalotas y puré de garbanzos* (king prawns with shallots and garbanzos) and T-bone steak for two. Parking is near impossible in the surrounding narrow streets, instead head for the car park at the base of the elevator near the Iglesia Santo Domingo church. ✉ *Maestra Ayala 1* ☎ *952/449165* 💳 *AE, DC, MC, V* ⏲ *Closed Tues. and Aug. 1–15. No lunch Wed.*

$–$$ SPANISH ★ ✕ **Ventorillo de la Perra.** If you've been scouring the coast for something typically Spanish, you may find it at this old inn, which dates from 1785. Outside there's a leafy patio; inside is a beamed and cozy dining room and bar with curing hams hanging from the ceiling. Choose between local Malagueño cooking, including *gazpacuelo malagueño* (a warm gazpacho of potatoes, rice, and shrimp), and typical Spanish food, such as *conejo en salsa de almendras* (rabbit in almond sauce). The *ajo blanco* (a cold, garlicky almond-based soup) is particularly good but available only during the summer months. ✉ *Av. Constitución*

115, Km 13, Arroyo de la Miel ☎952/441966 ▭AE, DC, MC, V ⊗Closed Mon. and Nov.

$$$$ **Riu Marina Hotel.** This dazzling white hotel fits in well with the surrounding quasioriental architecture of the Puerto Deportivo. Rooms are spacious and smart, with bold fabrics contrasting with pastel paintwork and arty prints. Most of the balconies have sea views. There is nightly entertainment ranging from flamenco to magic shows, and the breakfast buffet has been applauded by guests for its wide choice of hot and cold choices. The hotel is also ideally placed for La Carihuela's famed seafood restaurants and more the international dining choices to be found in the port. **Pros:** part of the prestigious and quality Riu hotel chain, superb location. **Cons:** can be noisy from nearby late-night clubs and bars, lunch buffet a little bland. ✉*Avenida del Puerto Deportivo, Benalmádena* ☎*952/961–696* 🌐*www.riu.es* *272* *In-room: safe, Wi-Fi. In-hotel: restaurant, room service, bar, pool, gym, bicycles, laundry facilities, laundry service, parking (fee)* ▭*AE, D, DC, MC, V* *BP.*

$$ **La Fonda.** You'll find a true taste of Andalusia at this small hotel on one of the prettiest streets in the pueblo, between the church and the main square. Rooms have white walls, marble floors, and bright floral fabrics: some have peerless views of the coast and the Mediterranean; others look onto the cool interior patio shaded by palms. In the same building, under different management, is an excellent restaurant ($–$$) run by an official hotel school; it's open for lunch on weekdays. **Pros:** superb location, traditional atmosphere. **Cons:** rooms are on the small side, restaurant closed on weekends. ✉*Santo Domingo 7* ☎*952/568324* 🌐*www.fondahotel.com* *26 rooms* *In-hotel: restaurant, bar, pool* ▭*AE, DC, MC, V* *BP.*

NIGHTLIFE

For discos, piano bars, and karaoke, head for the port. The **Fortuna Nightclub** in the **Casino Torrequebrada** (✉*Av. del Sol s/n* ☎*952/446000*) has flamenco and an international dance show with a live orchestra, starting at 10:30 PM. A passport, jacket, and tie are required in the casino, open daily 9 PM–4 AM.

FUENGIROLA

16 km (10 mi) west of Torremolinos, 27 km (17 mi) east of Marbella.

Fuengirola is less frenetic than Torremolinos. Many of its waterfront high-rises are vacation apartments that cater to budget-minded sun-seekers from northern Europe and, in summer, a large contingent from Córdoba and other parts of Spain. The town is also a haven for British retirees (with plenty of English and Irish pubs to serve them) and a shopping and business center for the rest of the Costa del Sol. Its Tuesday market is the largest on the coast, and a major tourist attraction.

GETTING HERE AND AROUND

Fuengirola is the last stop on the train line from Málaga. There are also regular buses that leave from Málaga's main bus station.

ESSENTIALS

Bike Rental Contacts Moto Mercado (✉ *Avda. Niro Padre Jesús Cautivo 27, Los Boliches* ☎ *952/052671* 🌐 *www.rentabike.org*).

Bus Contacts Bus Station (✉ *Av. Alfonso X111* ☎ *952/475066*).

Taxi Contacts Radio Taxi Fuengirola (☎ *952/471000*).

Visitor Information Fuengirola (✉ *Av. Jesús Santos Rein 6* ☎ *952/467625*).

EXPLORING

The most prominent landmark in Fuengirola is **Castillo de Sohail.** The original structure dates from the 12th century, but the castle served as a military fortress until the early 19th century. Just west of town, the castle makes a dramatic performance venue for the annual summer season of music and dance. *€1.30* ⏲ *Tues.–Sun. 10–3.*

The American company Rain Forest operates the cageless **Fuengirola Zoo.** Four different habitats have been created, providing a natural environment for the animals, which include chimpanzees, big cats, and dolphins. The company is heavily involved with worldwide conservation programs. ✉ *Av. José Cela 6* ☎ *952/666301* 🌐 *www.zoofuengirola.com* *€15.50* ⏲ *Daily 10* AM*–dusk.*

WHERE TO EAT AND STAY

$–$$ CONTINENTAL ✕ **Bistro.** A series of pine-clad rooms, this restaurant is in the most charming part of Fuengirola, a neighborhood with low-rise buildings punctuated by the occasional fisherman's cottage. The Bistro has a loyal following of foreign residents who come for the reliably good food and reasonable prices; the cuisine caters to the international palates with such dishes as chicken salad with Philadelphia cheese sauce, crepes stuffed with spinach, and fillet steak with a choice of sauces. Desserts are disappointing, however, with the all-too-predictable flan and commercial ice cream choices. The bow-tied waiters are charming and efficient. ✉ *Calle Palangreros 30* ☎ *952/477701* ▭ *MC, V* ⏲ *Closed Sun.*

$$$ FRENCH ✕ **Le Chardon.** This restaurant is a real class act with impeccable service and delicious nouvelle French-Mediterranean cuisine. Chef and co-owner Patrick Bausier studied the art of contemporary French cuisine in Paris, and it's reflected in such dishes as red partridge terrine with foie gras and caramelized onions, and roast monkfish with French mustard. Agreeable extras include complimentary cava (Spanish sparkling wine) upon arrival and delicious homemade bread and rolls. The decor is elegant and romantic with candles, white tablecloths, and tasteful artwork on the walls. ✉ *Calle Río Grande 1, Las Lagunas, Fuengirola* ☎ *952/463212* ▭ *AE, DC, MC, V* ⏲ *Closed Sun., no lunch.*

$ VEGETARIAN ✕ **Vegetalia.** Finnish owner Katya runs this attractive, long-established restaurant that has a large, pleasant dining space decorated with plants and giant prints of (surprise, surprise) vegetables. It's best known for its excellent, and vast, lunchtime buffet that includes salads and hot dishes like lentil burgers and seitan cutlets, and it's increasingly popular with the local expatriate "ladies who lunch" brigade. The dinner menu includes curries, vegetable kebabs, pasta dishes, and stir-fries. Leave room for the blueberry pie, homemade by Katya's mother. Biodynamic wines are available, as well as the more mainstream Spanish varieties.

⊠C Santa Isabel 8, Los Boliches ☎952/586031 ▭MC, V ⊙Closed Jul.–Aug., Sun. and Mon. year-round.

$ **Hostal Italia.** Right off the main plaza and near the beach, this small, family-run hotel is deservedly popular, and guests come here year after year, particularly during the October *feria*. Rooms are small but full of light and very comfortable, and nearly all have small balconies. There's a larger sun terrace for catching the rays. The hostal is surrounded by restaurants and bars so finding a *desayuno* (breakfast) destination is no problem. If you're here during Easter, the owners display one of the most impressive *belenes* (model nativity scenes) in town. **Pros:** friendly owners, spotless rooms. **Cons:** very little English spoken, rooms are small. *⊠C. de la Cruz 1 ☎952/474193 ⊕www.hostal-italia.com 40 rooms ▭MC, V.*

$$ **Villa de Laredo.** At the quieter end of the promenade, a Frisbee throw from the beach, this hotel has a mildly old-fashioned feel, but it's excellently priced given the location and facilities, which include a rooftop pool. Rooms have small terraces with sea views. The restaurant ($–$$) has an aquarium of catch-of-the-day options to choose from. **Pros:** across from the beach, excellent for families. **Cons:** can be noisy, decor would benefit from an update. *⊠Paseo Marítimo 42, Rey de España ☎952/477689 ⊕www.hotelvilladelaredo.com 50 rooms In-room: dial-up. In-hotel: restaurant, pool, Wi-Fi ▭AE, DC, MC, V.*

NIGHTLIFE AND THE ARTS

Amateur local troupes regularly stage plays and musicals in English at the **Salón de Variétés Theater** (*⊠Emancipación 30 ☎952/474542*). For concerts—from classical to rock to jazz—check out the modern **Palacio de la Paz** (*⊠Recinto Ferial, Av. Jesús Santo Rein ☎952/589349*) between Los Boliches and the town center.

MIJAS

★ *8 km (5 mi) north of Fuengirola, 18 km (11 mi) west of Torremolinos.*

Mijas is in the foothills of the sierra just north of the coast. The pretty whitewashed pueblo (town) was discovered long ago by foreign retirees, and, though the large, touristy square may look like an extension of the Costa, beyond this are hilly residential streets with time-worn homes. Try to visit late in the afternoon, after the tour buses have left.

GETTING HERE AND AROUND

Buses leave Fuengirola every half hour for the 20-minute drive through hills peppered with villas. If you have a car and don't mind a mildly hair-raising drive, take the more dramatic approach from Benalmádena-Pueblo, a winding mountain road with splendid views. You can park in the underground parking garage signposted on the approach to the village.

ESSENTIALS

Visitor Information Mijas (*⊠Pl. Virgen de la Peña ☎958/589034*).

EXPLORING

The **Museo Mijas** occupies the former town hall. Themed rooms, including an old-fashioned bakery and bodega, surround a patio, and regular art exhibitions are mounted in the upstairs gallery. ✉ *Pl. de la Libertad* ☎ *952/590380* 🎟 *Free* ⏲ *Daily 10–2 and 5–8.*

Bullfights take place year-round, usually on Sunday at 4:30 PM, at Mijas's tiny **bullring.** One of the few square bullrings in Spain, it's off the Plaza Constitución—Mijas's old village square—and up the slope beside the Mirlo Blanco restaurant. ✉ *Pl. Constitución* ☎ *952/485248* 🎟 *Museum €3* ⏲ *June–Sept., daily 10–10; Oct.–Feb., daily 9:30–7; Mar., daily 10–7:30; Apr. and May, daily 10–8:30.*

Worth a visit is the delightful village church **Iglesia Parroquial de la Inmaculada Concepción** *(The Immaculate Conception).* It's impeccably decorated, especially at Easter, and the terrace and spacious gardens have a splendid panoramic view. The church is up the hill from the Mijas bullring. ✉ *Pl. Constitución.*

NEED A BREAK?

The Bar Porras on Plaza de la Libertad (at the base of Calle San Sebastián—the most photographed street in the village) attracts a regular crowd of locals with its good-value, tasty tapas.

Mijas extends down to the coast, and the coastal strip between Fuengirola and Marbella is officially called **Mijas-Costa.** This area has several hotels, restaurants, and golf courses.

WHERE TO EAT AND STAY

$$$–$$$$ SPANISH

✕ **El Padrastro.** Perched on a cliff above the Plaza Virgen de la Peña, "The Stepfather" is accessible by elevator from the square or, if you're energetic, by stairs. The dining room is surrounded by large windows, and the view over Fuengirola and the coast is the restaurant's main draw, but the food isn't bad either. Options might include *lubina cocida con ragout de alcachofa y mantequilla al limón* (sea bass with artichokes) or, for vegetarians, a creamy leek tart. When the weather's right, you can dine alfresco on the large terrace. ✉ *Paseo del Compás 22* ☎ *952/485000* 💳 *AE, DC, MC, V.*

$$$ SPANISH

✕ **Mirlo Blanco.** In an old house on the pleasant Plaza de la Constitución, with a terrace for outdoor dining, this restaurant is run by a Basque family that's been in the Costa del Sol restaurant business for decades. The interior is welcoming and intimate, with original noteworthy artwork interspersed among the arches, hanging plants, and traditional white paintwork. Good choices here are Basque specialties such as *txangurro* (spider crab) and *kokotxas de bacalau* (cod cheeks). Don't miss the sensational Grand Marnier soufflé for dessert. There's an outside terrace for alfresco summer dining. ✉ *Pl. de la Constitución 2* ☎ *952/485700* 💳 *AE, MC, V* ⏲ *Closed Jan.*

$$–$$$ CONTINENTAL

✕ **Valparaíso.** Halfway up the road from Fuengirola on the way to Mijas, this sprawling villa stands in its own garden, complete with swimming pool. There's live music nightly, ranging from flamenco to opera and jazz. Valparaíso is a favorite among local (mainly British) expatriates, some of whom come in full evening dress to celebrate birthdays or other events. In winter, logs burn in a cozy fireplace. The *pato a la* *naranja* (duck in orange sauce) is popular, but there's also an emphasis on Italian cuisine with pasta choices that include linguine with seafood, tortellini with smoked salmon and caviar, and penne with tomatoes, porcini mushrooms, and chilies. ✉ *Ctra. de Mijas–Fuengirola, Km 4* ☎ *952/485996* ▭ *AE, DC, MC, V* ⊙ *No dinner Sun. No lunch Oct.–June.*

$$$ **Beach House.** The epitome of cool Mediterranean-inspired decor, the Beach House seems not so much a hotel but a sumptuous villa owned by a hospitable (and wealthy) friend. From the pleasing bougainvillea-draped bar, the pool seems to merge seamlessly with the sea; the interior of the hotel is all clean lines, sparkling marble, and minimalist good taste. There's a stylish lounge with a fireplace for relaxing on cooler evenings. The town and restaurants of Fuengirola are 10 minutes away. **Pros:** exclusive feel; gracious, efficient service. **Cons:** lack of nearby shops or entertainment. ✉ *Urbanización El Chaparral, CN340, Km 203* ☎ *952/494540* ⊕ *www.beachhouse.nu* *10 rooms* *In-room: Ethernet (some). In-hotel: pool* ▭ *MC, V* *CP.*

Fodor's Choice ★

$$$$ **Gran Hotel Guadalpin.** ★ On the edge of Mijas's golf course (closer to Fuengirola than to Mijas), in a huge garden of palms, cypresses, and fountains, this is one of the most exclusive hotels on the Costa del Sol. It's primarily a spa known for its thalassotherapy, a skin treatment using seawater and seaweed, applied in a Roman-like temple of cool, white-and-blue marble tiles. Three outstanding restaurants ($$$–$$$$) serve savory regional and international dishes. You can often get good deals by booking through their Web site. **Pros:** luxurious, large rooms. **Cons:** not much in the way of views, can seem rather sterile. ✉ *Urbanización Mijas-Golf, Mijas-Costa* ☎ *952/473050* ⊕ *www.granhotelguadalpin.com* *109 rooms, 35 suites* *In-room: Ethernet. In-hotel: 3 restaurants, bars, golf courses, tennis courts, pools, gym, spa, public Internet, public Wi-Fi, some pets allowed* ▭ *AE, DC, MC, V* *BP.*

$$$ **TRH Mijas.** It's easy to unwind here, thanks to the poolside restaurant and bar, and the gardens with views of the hillsides stretching down to Fuengirola and the sea. The tasteful decor is marked by marble floors throughout, wrought-iron window grilles, and wooden shutters. The lobby is large and airy, and there's an attractive glass-roof terrace. All rooms are comfortably furnished, with wood fittings and marble floors. TRH Mijas is at the entrance to Mijas village. The management can advise on activities that may be enjoyed in the surrounding countryside, including horse riding and golf. **Pros:** superb panoramic views, traditional Andalusian atmosphere. **Cons:** inconvenient for the beach, touristy village. ✉ *Urbanización Tamisa* ☎ *952/485800* ⊕ *www.hoteltrhmijas.com* *204 rooms, 2 suites* *In-room: dial-up. In-hotel: restaurant, tennis court, pool, gym* ▭ *AE, DC, MC, V.*

MARBELLA

27 km (17 mi) west of Fuengirola, 28 km (17 mi) east of Estepona, 50 km (31 mi) southeast of Ronda.

Playground of the rich and home of movie stars, rock musicians, and dispossessed royal families, Marbella has attained the top rung on Europe's social ladder. Dip into any Spanish gossip magazine and chances are the glittering parties that fill its pages are set in Marbella. Much of this action takes place on the fringes—grand hotels and luxury restaurants line the waterfront for 20 km (12 mi) on each side of the town center. In the town itself, you may well wonder how Marbella became so famous. The main thoroughfare, Avenida Ricardo Soriano, is distinctly charmless, and the Paseo Marítimo, though pleasant, with a mix of seafood restaurants and pizzerias overlooking an ordinary beach, is far from spectacular. About 4 mi west lies **Puerto Banús**, comprising a marina with some of the most expensive yachts you will see this side of Dubai, fringed by restaurants, bars, and designer boutiques.

GETTING HERE AND AROUND

There are regular buses departing from the bus station to the surrounding resorts and towns, including Fuengirola, Estepona, and Málaga.

ESSENTIALS

Bus Contacts Bus Station (☒*Av. Trapiche* ☎*952/764400*).

Visitor Information Marbella (☒*Glorieta de la Fontanilla* ☎*952/822818*) can provide a map of town and monthly calendar of exhibits and events.

EXPLORING

Marbella's appeal lies in the heart of the **old village,** which remains surprisingly intact. Here, a block or two back from the main highway, narrow alleys of whitewashed houses cluster around the central **Plaza de los Naranjos** (Orange Square), where colorful, albeit pricey, restaurants vie for space under the orange trees. Climb onto what remains of the old fortifications and stroll along the Calle Virgen de los Dolores to the Plaza de Santo Cristo.

The **Museo del Grabado Español Contemporáneo,** in a restored 16th-century palace in the heart of the old town, has contemporary Spanish prints and temporary exhibitions. ☒*Hospital Bazán* ☎*952/765741* 🌐*www.museodelgrabado.com* 🎫*€2.50* ⏲*Tues.–Sat. 10–2 and 5:30–8:30.*

In a modern building just east of Marbella's old quarter, the **Museo de Bonsai** has a collection of miniature trees, including a 300-year-old olive tree from China. ☒*Parque Arroyo de la Repesa, Av. Dr. Maiz Viñal* ☎*952/862926* 🎫*€3* ⏲*June–Sept., daily 10:30–1:30 and 5–8:30; Oct.–May, daily 10:30–1:30 and 4–7.*

NEED A BREAK?

Enjoy a glass of wine and a transplanted Basque delight at La Taberna del Pintxo (☒*Av. Miguel Cano 7* ☎*952/829321*). A *pintxo* is a little morsel served on a slice of bread or with a toothpick. There's platter after platter of creative examples, from shellfish to slices of omelet to mushrooms baked in garlic to vegetables in vinaigrette.

Marbella's wealth glitters most brightly along the Golden Mile, a tiara of star-studded clubs, restaurants, and hotels west of town stretching from Marbella to **Puerto Banús.** A mosque, an Arab banks, and the former residence of Saudi Arabia's late King Fahd betray the influence of oil money in this wealthy enclave. About 7 km (4½ mi) west of central Marbella (between Km 175 and Km 174), a sign indicates the turnoff leading down to Puerto Banús. Though now hemmed in by a belt of high-rises, Marbella's plush marina, with 915 berths, is a gem of ostentatious wealth, a Spanish answer to St. Tropez. Huge, flashy yachts, beautiful people, and countless expensive stores and restaurants make up the glittering parade that marches long into the night. The backdrop is an Andalusian pueblo—built in the 1960s to resemble the fishing villages that once lined this coast.

WHERE TO EAT AND STAY

$$ ITALIAN ✕**Amore e Fantasía.** Without knowing better, you could be mistakenly take this for an antique and decor shop rather than a restaurant, what with the Buddha statues, gilt mirrors, Moorish lights, and the Pompeii-themed frieze. One of the first restaurants to open in the port, back in the 1980s, the menu is vast and includes traditional choices like *risotto al funghi porcini* (with porcini mushrooms), more sophisticated dishes including *cannelloni al foie gras,* and the downright unusual, such as *lasagna di pollo al curry* (lasagna with chicken in a curry sauce). The dessert to go for is the superbly moist dark chocolate soufflé served with vanilla ice cream. ✉ *Muelle Benabolá 5–6, Puerto Banús* ☎ *952/813464* ▭ *AE, DC, MC, V.*

$$ SPANISH ✕**El Balcón de la Virgen.** A special treat here is to dine alfresco on the traditional Andalusian patio, which is overlooked by a 300-year-old statue of the Virgin (hence the name) surrounded by a colorful dazzle of plants. The menu includes hearty options like meat and fish dishes, including roasted pork and marinated swordfish, as well as lighter bites like crisp salads, fluffy omelets, and gazpacho. One of the specialties is *calderada de mariscos* (seafood stew with rice and spices). After your meal, you can stroll round the corner for a coffee in lovely Plaza de los Naranjos. ✉ *C. Virgen de los Dolores 2* ☎ *952/776092* ▭ *AE, DC, MC, V* ⏲ *Closed Tues.*

$$–$$$ ECLECTIC ✕**La Comedia.** This Swedish-run restaurant is on one of the old town's most traditional Andalusian plazas and has one of the most imaginative menus among Marbella's 600-plus restaurants. Starters include such delights as blue mussel carpaccio topped with grilled scallops and truffles. Entrées include avocado-and-salmon spring rolls with mango and marie rose sauce (a thousand island–style dressing) and duck breast in fruit compote. For dessert try the unusual deep-fried apple-cinnamon wonton with vanilla and white chocolate mousse or, for lightweights, the pistachio mousse. Reserve a seat on the terrace in summer—there's limited space. ✉ *Pl. de la Victoria* ☎ *952/776478* ✍ *Reservations essential* ▭ *AE, DC, MC, V* ⏲ *Closed Mon. No lunch.*

$$$–$$$$ CONTINENTAL ✕**La Hacienda.** In a large, pleasant villa 12 km (7 mi) east of Marbella, the Hacienda was founded in the early '70s by the late Belgian chef Paul Schiff, who helped transform the Costa del Sol culinary scene with his modern approach and judicious use of local ingredients. His legacy lives on here through his daughter, Cati, who continues to prepare her father's famous signature dishes, such as *pintada con pasas al vino de Málaga* (guinea fowl with raisins in Málaga wine sauce) and *croquetas de langosta* (lobster croquettes). The large terrace with its arches and plants creates a suitably Mediterranean atmosphere on balmy summer evenings. ✉ *Urbanización Las Chapas, N340, Km 193* ☎ *952/831116*

Reservations essential *AE, MC, V* *Closed Mon. and Tues. mid-Nov.–mid-Dec. No lunch July and Aug.*

$$–$$$ MEDITERRANEAN Fodor's Choice ★ **Zozoi.** Tucked into the corner of one of the town's squares, the upbeat, Art Deco Zozoi receives rave reviews. The fashionably Mediterranean menu makes little distinction between starters and main courses, since all the portions are generous, but imaginative use of ingredients is shown in such dishes as grilled fillet of sea bass with saffron fettuccini and green asparagus, and roasted duck breast with black cherries and pepper. For dessert, try the red forest fruits with *mille-feuilles* (puff pastry) or lemon sorbet spiked with vodka. The large courtyard terrace has a cozy traditional feel with its brightly tiled walls and terra-cotta tiled floor. *Plaza Altamirano 1* *952/858868* *Reservations essential* *MC, V* *Closed Sun. No lunch.*

$ **Juan.** On a quiet street in a charming historic neighborhood, this budget hotel offers excellent value. The public areas are traditional and homey, with Andalusian tiles gracing the walls. The rooms are small but very clean, and the TV is a surprising extra given the price. It's a short stroll to both the beach and the historic center. Rooms also have refrigerators, so this is a good choice if you plan on ecomomizing on eating out. **Pros:** great location. **Cons:** plain rooms, fills up quickly. *Calle Luna 18* *952/779475* *4 rooms* *In-room: no a/c, refrigerator. In-hotel: no elevator* *No credit cards.*

$$ **Lima.** This mid-range option is in downtown Marbella, two blocks from the beach. The tastefully decorated rooms are a bit generic, with dark wood furniture, bright floral bedspreads, and balconies; corner rooms are the largest. Towels are provided for the beach so you don't have to sneak the fluffy white ones out from the bathroom! **Pros:** location good for town and beach. **Cons:** room sizes vary considerably. *Av. Antonio Belón 2* *952/770500* *www.hotellimamarbella.com* *64 rooms* *In-hotel: restaurant, bicycles, laundry service, Wi-Fi, parking (paid)* *AE, DC, MC, V.*

$$$$ Fodor's Choice ★ **Marbella Club.** The grande dame of Marbella hotels was a creation of the late Alfonso von Hohenlohe, a Mexican-Austrian aristocrat who helped turn Marbella into a playground for the rich and famous. The exquisite grounds have lofty palm trees, dazzling flower beds, and a beachside tropical pool area. The bungalow-rooms vary in size; some have private pools. The main restaurant ($$$) has a classy, eclectic menu of modern Mediterranean cuisine. If you can't afford to stay here, at least stop by for afternoon tea, served daily in summer from 4 to 6:30. **Pros:** classic hotel, superb service and facilities. **Cons:** a drive from Marbella's restaurants and nightlife, slightly stuffy atmosphere. *Blvd. Principe Alfonso von Hohenlohe at Ctra. de Cádiz, Km 178, 3 km (2 mi) west of Marbella* *952/822211* *www.marbellaclub.com* *84 rooms, 37 suites, 16 bungalows* *In-room: DVD, Wi-Fi. In-hotel: 3 restaurants, golf course, pools, gym, beachfront, public Internet, parking (free)* *AE, DC, MC, V* *BP.*

$$$$ ★ **Puente Romano.** West of Marbella, between the Marbella Club and Puerto Banús, is this palatial hotel designed like an Andalusian pueblo, complete with gardens and fountains. As the name suggests, there's a genuine Roman bridge on the grounds, running down to the beach.

There are four restaurants, including El Puente, and Roberto; the latter serves Italian food in the hotel's beach club, a popular summer nightlife venue. In summer, there's also a beachfront *chiringuito* (seafood restaurant), serving fresh fish. **Pros:** luxurious atmosphere, plenty of restaurants. **Cons:** a car (or taxi) is essential for access to Marbella or Puerto Banús. ✉ *Ctra. Cádiz, Km 177* ☎ *952/820900* 🌐 *www.puenteromano.com* *149 rooms, 77 suites* *In-room: DVD, Wi-Fi. In-hotel: 4 restaurants, golf course, tennis courts, pools, gym, beachfront* 💳 *AE, DC, MC, V* 🍴 *BP.*

$$$ Fodor's Choice ★ **The Town House.** In a choice location in one of old town Marbella's prettiest squares, this former family house has been exquisitely transformed into a boutique hotel. A combination of antiques and modern fittings make for luxurious rooms, accentuated by earthy colors and white linen. The spacious bathrooms are decked out in shiny marble with plenty of complimentary soaps to encourage pampering. There is an attractive bar and plenty of restaurants nearby. Guests are also within easy strolling distance of the Puente Romano Beach Club, where day beds can be rented for €16 a day. **Pros:** upbeat design, great central location. **Cons:** small rooms, street noise on weekends. ✉ *C. Alderete 7, Plaza Tetuan* ☎ *952/901791* 🌐 *www.townhouse.nu* *9 rooms* *In-hotel: bar, no elevator* 💳 *MC, V.*

NIGHTLIFE AND THE ARTS

Art exhibits are held in private galleries and in several of Marbella's leading hotels, notably the Puente Romano.

Much of the nighttime action revolves around the **Puerto Banús,** in such bars as Sinatra's and Joy's Bar. Marbella's most famous nightspot is the Fodor's Choice ★ **Olivia Valére disco** (✉ *Ctra. de Istán, Km 0.8* ☎ *952/828861*), decorated to resemble a Moorish palace; head inland from the town's mosque (it's easy to spot).

The trendy **Dreamers** (✉ *CN 340 km, Puerto Banús* ☎ *952/812080*) attracts a young, streetwise crowd with its live bands, international DJs, and massive dance space. The **Casino Nueva Andalucía** (✉ *Bajos Hotel Andalucía Pl., N340* ☎ *952/814000*), open 8 PM–6 AM May–October (until 5 AM November–April), is a chic gambling spot in the Hotel Andalucía Plaza, just west of Puerto Banús. Jacket and tie are required for men, and passports for all. In the center of Marbella, **Ana María** (✉ *Pl. de Santo Cristo 5* ☎ *952/775646*) is a popular flamenco venue but open only from May to September.

OJÉN

10 km (6 mi) north of Marbella.

For a contrast to the glamour of the coast, drive up to Ojén, in the hills above Marbella. Take note of the beautiful pottery and, if you're here the first week in August, don't miss the **Fiesta de Flamenco,** which attracts some of Spain's most respected flamenco names, including the Juan Peña El Lebrijano, Chiquetete, and El Cabrero. Four kilometers (2½ mi) from Ojén is the **Refugio del Juanar,** a former hunting lodge in the heart of the Sierra Blanca, at the southern edge of the Serranía de Ronda, a mountainous wilderness. A bumpy trail takes you a mile from the Refugio to the **Mirador** (lookout), with a sweeping view of the Costa del Sol and the coast of northern Africa.

GETTING HERE AND AROUND

There are approximately a dozen buses that leave from the Marbella main bus station with the destination of Ojén.

ESSENTIALS

Bike Rental Contacts **Monte Aventura** (*Pl. de Andalucía 1, Ojén 952/881519 www.monteaventura.com*).

WHERE TO EAT AND STAY

$$$ **Castillo de Monda.** Designed to resemble a castle, this hotel incorporates the ruins of Monda's Moorish fortress, some of which date back to the 8th century. The interior is decorated with ceramic tiles, elaborate arches, and extensive use of Moorish-style stucco bas-relief. Guest rooms are sumptuous and fun, with four-poster beds, marble heated bathroom floors, and colorful fabrics. Several have a private Jacuzzi and sauna. The main restaurant ($$–$$$), which resembles a medieval banquet hall, has terrific views of the countryside, while the library with fireplace is wonderfully inviting in cooler months. **Pros:** a theatrical feel, pretty village. **Cons:** inconvenient for the beach, rather formal. *Monda 952/457142 www.mondacastle.com 17 rooms, 6 suites In-room: DVD, Internet. In-hotel: restaurant, bar, pool, Wi-Fi, parking (free) AE, MC, V.*

$$–$$$ **Refugio del Juanar.** Once an aristocratic hunting lodge (King Alfonso XIII came here), this secluded hotel and restaurant was sold to its staff in 1984 for the symbolic sum of 1 peseta. The hunting theme prevails, both in the common areas—where a log fire roars in winter—and on the restaurant menu ($–$$), where game is emphasized. The rooms are simply decorated, and six (including the three suites) have their own fireplace. Good deals can usually be found, out of season, on the Web site. **Pros:** superb for hikers, traditional Andalusian decor. **Cons:** can seem very cut off, a long way from the coast. *Sierra Blanca s/n 952/881000 www.juanar.com 23 rooms, 3 suites In-hotel: restaurant, tennis court, pool, Internet terminal AE, DC, MC, V.*

RONDA

Fodor's Choice ★ *61 km (38 mi) northwest of Marbella, 108 km (67 mi) southwest of Antequera (via Pizarra).*

Ronda, one of the oldest towns in Spain, is known for its spectacular position and views. Secure in its mountain fastness on a rock high over the Río Guadalevín, the town was a stronghold for the legendary Andalusian bandits who held court here from the 18th to early 20th centuries. Ronda's most dramatic element is its ravine (360 feet deep and 210 feet across)—known as **El Tajo**—which divides La Ciudad, the old Moorish town, from El Mercadillo, the "new town," which sprang up after the Christian Reconquest of 1485. Tour buses roll in daily with sightseers from the coast 49 km (30 mi) away, and on weekends affluent Sevillanos flock to their second homes here. Stay overnight midweek to see this noble town's true colors.

The most attractive approach is from the south. The winding but well-maintained A376 from San Pedro de Alcántara travels north up through the mountains of the Serranía de Ronda. Take the first turn-off to Ronda from A376. Entering the lowest part of town, known as El Barrio, you can see parts of the old walls, including the 13th-century Puerta de Almocobar and the 16th-century Puerta de Carlos V gates. The road climbs past the Iglesia del Espíritu Santo (Church of the Holy Spirit) and up into the heart of town.

PICASSO'S CUBES

It's been suggested that Picasso, who was born in Málaga, was inspired to create cubism by the *pueblos blancos* of his youth. The story may or may not be apocryphal, but it's nonetheless easy to imagine—there *is* something wondrous and inspiring about Andalusia's whitewashed villages, with their dwellings that seem to tumble down the mountain slopes like giant dice. Perhaps it's the contrast in color: the bright white against the pine green. Or perhaps the mountaintop isolation: at these altitudes, the morning light breaks silently over the slopes, the only movement a far-off shepherd guiding his flock.

GETTING HERE AND AROUND

There are at least three daily buses that run here from Marbella (via San Pedro de Alcántara), the same number from Antequera, and six daily buses from Málaga (via Grazalema).

ESSENTIALS

Visitor Information Ronda (✉ *Pl. de España 1* ☎ *952/871272*). **Ronda** (✉ *Paseo de Bas Infante s/n* ☎ *952/187119*).

EXPLORING

Begin in El Mercadillo, where the **tourist office** (*see Essentials, above*) in the Plaza de España can supply you with a map.

Immediately south of the Plaza de España is Ronda's most famous bridge, the **Juan Peña El Lebrijano** *(New Bridge)*, an architectural marvel built between 1755 and 1793. The bridge's lantern-lit parapet offers dizzying views of the awesome gorge. Just how many people have met their ends here nobody knows, but the architect of the Puente Nuevo fell to his death while inspecting work on the bridge. During the civil war, hundreds of victims were hurled from it.

Cross the Puente Nuevo into **La Ciudad,** the old Moorish town, and wander the twisting streets of white houses with birdcage balconies.

The so-called House of the Moorish King, **Casa del Rey Moro,** was actually built in 1709 on the site of an earlier Moorish residence. Despite the name and the *azulejo* (painted tile) plaque depicting a Moor on the facade, it's unlikely that Moorish rulers ever lived here. The garden has a great view of the gorge, and from here a stairway of some 365 steps, known as **La Mina,** descends to the river. The house, across the Puente Nuevo on Calle Santo Domingo, is being converted into a luxury hotel but the project has been fraught with delays and, at the time of research, no completion date was available. Check with the tourist office for an update.

The excavated remains of the **Baños Árabes** *(Arab Baths)* date from Ronda's tenure as capital of a Moorish *taifa* (kingdom). The star-shape vents in the roof are an inferior imitation of the ceiling of the beautiful bathhouse in Granada's Alhambra. The baths are beneath the Puente Árabe (Arab Bridge) in a ravine below the Palacio del Marqués de Salvatierra. *€3 Weekdays 10–6, weekends 10–3.*

The collegiate church of **Santa María la Mayor,** which serves as Ronda's cathedral, has roots in Moorish times: originally the Great Mosque of Ronda, the tower and adjacent galleries, built for viewing festivities in the square, retain their Islamic design. After the mosque was destroyed (when the Moors were overthrown), it was rebuilt as a church and dedicated to the Virgen de la Encarnación after the Reconquest. The naves are late Gothic, and the main altar is heavy with baroque gold leaf. The church is around the corner from the remains of a mosque, Minarete Árabe (Moorish Minaret) at the end of the Marqués de Salvatierra. ✉ *Pl. Duquesa de Parcent €3 May–Sept., daily 10–8; Oct.–Apr., daily 10–6.*

A stone palace with twin Mudejar towers, the **Palacio de Mondragón** *(Palace of Mondragón)* was probably the residence of Ronda's Moorish kings. Ferdinand and Isabella appropriated it after their victory in 1485. Today you can wander through the patios, with their brick arches and delicate Mudejar-stucco tracery, and admire the mosaics and *artesonado* (coffered) ceiling. The second floor holds a small museum with archaeological items found near Ronda, plus the reproduction of a dolmen, a prehistoric stone monument. ✉ *Plaza Mondragón* ☎ *952/878450 €3 Apr.–Oct., weekdays 10–6, weekends 10–3; May–Sept., weekdays 10–8, weekends 10–3.*

The main sight in Ronda's commercial center, El Mercadillo, is the **Plaza de Toros.** Pedro Romero (1754–1839), the father of modern bullfighting and Ronda's most famous native son, is said to have killed 5,600 bulls here during his long career. In the museum beneath the plaza you can see posters for Ronda's very first bullfights, held here in 1785. The plaza was once owned by the late bullfighter Antonio Ordóñez, on whose nearby ranch Orson Welles's ashes were scattered (as directed in his will)—indeed, the ring has become a favorite of filmmakers. Every September, the bullring is the scene of Ronda's *corridas goyescas,* named after Francisco Goya, whose bullfight sketches (*tauromaquias*) were inspired by the skill and art of Pedro Romero: the participants and the dignitaries in the audience don the costumes of Goya's time for the occasion. Seats for these fights cost a small fortune and are booked far in advance. Other than that, the plaza is rarely used for fights except during Ronda's May festival. ☎ *952/874132 €5 Oct.–Apr., daily 10–6; May–Sept., daily 10–8*

NEED A BREAK?

Beyond the bullring in El Mercadillo, you can relax in the shady Alameda del Tajo gardens, one of the loveliest spots in Ronda. At the end of the gardens, a balcony protrudes from the face of the cliff, offering a vertigo-inducing view of the valley below. Stroll along the cliff-top walk to the Reina Victoria hotel, built by British settlers from Gibraltar at the turn of

the 20th century as a fashionable rest stop on their Algeciras–Bobadilla railroad line.

WHERE TO EAT AND STAY

$–$$$ SPANISH **Almocábar.** Tucked agreeably away from the main tourist hub, this unpretentious tapas bar and restaurant offers great value and inventive, tasty cuisine. Dishes include unusual fish options, like battered squid rings stuffed with chives and truffle, and several salad choices, including goat cheese on a bed of mixed lettuces. Get here early if you want to sample the tapas, as the narrow bar gets packed with the local crowd on their *tapear* bar crawl. The delicious *patatas alioli* (cooked potatoes in a creamily pungent garlic sauce) are excellent to share. ✉ *Calle Ruedo Alameda 5* ☎ *952/875977* ▭ *No credit cards* ⊙ *Closed Tues.*

$$ SPANISH **Pedro Romero.** Named for the father of modern bullfighting, this restaurant opposite the bullring is packed with bullfight paraphernalia. Mounted bull heads peer down at you as you tuck into *sopa de la casa* (soup with ham and eggs), or *perdiz estofada con salsa de vino blanco y hierbas* (stewed partridge with white-wine-and-herb sauce), and, for dessert, *helado de higos con chocolate* (fig ice cream with chocolate sauce). Vegetarian options include a reasonably adventurous fried-goat-cheese dish served with fresh apple sauce. Previous diners include Ernest Hemingway and Orson Wells, whose photos are displayed. ✉ *Virgen de la Paz 18* ☎ *952/871110* ▭ *AE, DC, MC, V.*

$$$$ ECLECTIC ★ **Tragabuches.** Málagueño chef Benito Goméz is famed for his innovative menu, and the best way to sample it is to choose the *menú de degustación,* a taster's menu of five courses and two desserts: it includes imaginative choices such as a casserole of noodles with octopus sashimi and butter, and white-garlic ice cream with pine nuts (delicious, despite how it sounds). Traditional and modern furnishings blend in the two dining rooms. This Michelin-star restaurant is around the corner from Ronda's parador. You can also purchase a cookbook that contains some of the restaurant's best-loved dishes. Do be wary, though, when ordering bottled water as there have been complaints that unnecessarily expensive imports are presented, which can hike up the price. ✉ *José Aparicio 1* ☎ *952/190291* ▭ *AE, DC, MC, V* ⊙ *Closed Mon. No dinner Sun.*

$$ ★ **Alavera de los Baños.** This small, German-run hotel was used as a backdrop for the film classic *Carmen.* Fittingly, given its location next to the Moorish baths, there's an Arab-influenced theme throughout, with terra-cotta tiles, graceful arches, and pastel-color washes. The two rooms on the first floor have their own terraces, opening up onto the split-level garden—well worth the extra €10 on the bill. The dinner-only restaurant ($) specializes in Moroccan cuisine using predominantly organic foods. Breakfast includes homemade jams and breads, plus local cheeses. **Pros:** very atmospheric and historic, owners speak several languages. **Cons:** rooms vary in size, no lunch available. ✉ *Hoya San Miguel s/n* ☎ *952/879143* 🌐 *www.andalucia.com/alavera* *9 rooms* *In-room: no a/c. In-hotel: restaurant, bar, pool* ▭ *MC, V* *BP.*

$$$ **Ancinipo.** The artistic legacy of its former owners, Ronda artist Téllez Loriguillo and acclaimed Japanese watercolor painter Miki Haruta, is evidenced throughout this boutique hotel. The interior has exposed stone panels, steel-and-glass fittings, and mosaic-tile bathrooms—and

many murals and paintings. The more expensive rooms have small sitting areas and bathrooms with hydromassage tubs. Most rooms have dramatic mountain views. The Atrium restaurant ($$) dishes up such traditional favorites as *migas* (fried bread crumbs with sausage and spices) and oxtail stew, followed by chestnuts with brandy and cream. **Pros:** very central position, cutting-edge design. **Cons:** a few rooms lack panoramic view. ✉*José Aparicio 7* ☎*952/161002* 🌐*www.hotelacinipo.com* *14 rooms* *In-room: Wi-Fi. In-hotel: restaurant, bar, parking* 💳*AE, DC, MC, V.*

$$$ **El Molino del Santo.** In a converted olive mill next to a rushing stream near Benaoján, 10 km (7 mi) from Ronda, this British-run establishment was one of Andalusia's first country hotels. Guest rooms are arranged around a pleasant patio and come in different sizes, some with a terrace. This is a good base for walks in the mountains, and the hotel also rents mountain bikes. They're eco-conscious, too, and use solar panels for hot water and to heat the pool. The restaurant ($–$$) has an excellent reputation and has good vegetarian options. **Pros:** superb for hikers, friendly owners. **Cons:** you won't hear much Spanish spoken (most guests are British), a car is essential if you want to explore further afield. ✉*Estación de Benaoján s/n, Benaoján* ☎*952/167151* 🌐*www.andalucia.com/molino* *18 rooms* *In-hotel: restaurant, pool, bicycles. In-room: no TV* 💳*AE, DC, MC, V* *Closed mid-Nov.–mid-Feb.* *BP.*

$$ **Finca la Guzmana.** This traditional Andalusian *corijo* (cottage) 4 km (2½ mi) east of Ronda has been lovingly restored with bright, fresh decor to complement the original beams, wood-burning stoves, and the sublime setting—the cottage is surrounded by olive trees and grapevines. Walkers, bird-watchers, and painters are frequent guests. The owners also organize trips (guided or unguided) through the villages in a classic sports car. Breakfast is more generous here than many other places, with homemade bread, preserves, and local cheeses. **Pros:** surrounded by beautiful countryside, English-speaking owners. **Cons:** it's a hike to Ronda and the shops, no restaurant. ✉*Aptdo de Correos 408* ☎*600/006305* 🌐*www.laguzmana.com* *5 rooms* *In-room: Wi-Fi. In-hotel: pool* 💳*No credit cards* *CP.*

$$ ★ **San Gabriel.** In the oldest part of Ronda, this hotel is run by a family who converted their 18th-century home into an elegant, informal hotel (the family still lives in part of the building). The common areas, furnished with antiques, are warm and cozy, and include a DVD screening room with autographed photos of actors. (John Lithgow, Isabella Rossellini, and Bob Hoskins, in town to film the 2000 television movie version of *Don Quixote,* were among the first to stay at the hotel.) Some guest rooms have small sitting areas; all are stylishly furnished with antiques. **Pros:** traditional Andalusian house, atmospheric location. **Cons:** some rooms are rather dark, no panoramic views. ✉*Marqués de Moctezuma 19* ☎*952/190392* 🌐*www.hotelsangabriel.com* *15 rooms, 1 suite* *In-hotel: restaurant, Internet terminal, Wi-Fi, parking (free)* 💳*AE, MC, V.*

CLOSE UP

Olive Oil, the Golden Nectar

Inland from the Costa de Sol's clamor and crowds, the landscape is stunning. Far in the distance, tiny villages cling precariously to the mountainside like a tumble of sugar cubes, while in the foreground, brilliant red poppies and a blaze of yellow mimosa are set against a rippling quilt of cool-green olive trees and burnt-ocher soil.

Up close, most of the trees have dark twisted branches and gnarled trunks, which denote a lifetime that can span more than a century. It's believed that many of the olive trees here are born from seeds of the original crop brought to the Mediterranean shores in the 7th century BC by Greek and Phoenician traders. Since that time, the oil produced has been used for innumerable purposes, ranging from monetary to medicinal.

These days, the benefits of olive oil are well known. The locals don't need convincing. Olive oil has long been an integral part of the traditional cuisine and is used lavishly in every meal, including breakfast—when the country bars fill up with old men wearing flat caps, starting their day with coffee, brandy, and black tobacco along with slabs of toasted white bread generously laden with olive oil, garlic, and salt.

Spain's most southerly province produces a copious 653 metric tons of olive oil each year, or 90% of the entire Spanish production. The area currently exports to more than 95 countries, with the main buyers of bulk oil being Italy, France, Germany, Portugal, and the United Kingdom. The type and grade of oil varies according to the destination. Some oils taste sweet and smooth; others have great body and character, and varying intensities of bitterness. North Americans like their oil to be light, with little distinctive taste, while Mexicans prefer olive oil that is dark and strong.

It has been years since medical journals revealed that people living in the southern Mediterranean countries had the lowest case of heart disease in the Western world, which led to increased use of olive oil throughout the West, not only for salad dressing but also as a healthy and tasty substitute for butter and vegetable oil in almost every aspect of cooking—except, that is, as a spread for toast; it may take several decades more before olive oil on toast becomes standard breakfast fare anywhere else but in rural Andalusia!

AROUND RONDA: CAVES, ROMANS, AND PUEBLOS BLANCOS

This area of spectacular gorges, remote mountain villages, and ancient caves is fascinating to explore and a dramatic contrast with the clamor and crowds of the coast.

About 20 km (12 mi) west of Ronda toward Seville is the prehistoric **Cueva de la Pileta** *(Pileta Cave)*. Take the left exit for the village of Benaoján—from here the caves are well signposted. A Spanish guide (who speaks some English) will hand you a paraffin lamp and lead you on a roughly 90-minute walk that reveals prehistoric wall paintings of bison, deer, and horses outlined in black, red, and ocher. One highlight is the Cámara del Pescado (Chamber of the Fish), whose drawing of a huge fish is thought to be 15,000 years old. Tours take place hourly with a maximum of 25 people per group. ☎*952/167343* *€8* *Nov.–Apr., daily 10–1 and 4–6; May–Oct., daily 10–1 and 4–5.*

Ronda la Vieja (Old Ronda), 20 km (12 mi) north of Ronda, is the site of the old Roman settlement of **Acinipo.** A thriving town in the 1st century AD, Acinipo was abandoned for reasons that still baffle historians. Today it's a windswept hillside with piles of stones, the foundations of a few Roman houses, and what remains of a theater. Excavations are often under way at the site, during which times it's closed to the public. Call the tourist office in Setenil to check before visiting. ✉*Take A376 toward Algodonales; turnoff for ruins is 9 km (5 mi) from Ronda on MA449* ☎*956/134261* *www.setenil.com* *Free* *Weekdays 10–2:30 and 5–8, weekends noon–2 and 5–8.*

Setenil de las Bodegas, 8 km (5 mi) north of Acinipo, is in a cleft in the rock cut by the Guadalporcín River. The streets resemble long, narrow caves, and on many houses the roof is formed by a projecting ledge of heavy rock.

In **Olvera,** 13 km (8 mi) north of Setenil, two imposing silhouettes dominate the crest of the hill: the 11th-century castle Vallehermoso, a legacy of the Moors, and the neoclassical church of La Encarnación, reconstructed in the 19th century on the foundations of the old Moorish mosque.

A solitary watchtower dominates a crag above the village of **Zahara de la Sierra,** its outline visible for miles around. The tower is all that remains of a Moorish castle where King Alfonso X once fought the emir of Morocco; the building remained a Moorish stronghold until it fell to the Christians in 1470. Along the streets you can see door knockers fashioned like the hand of Fatima: the fingers represent the five laws of the Koran and are meant to ward off evil. ✉*From Olvera, drive 21 km (13 mi) southwest to village of Algodonales then south on A376 to Zahara de la Sierra 5 km (3 mi).*

SIERRA DE GRAZALEMA

Village of Grazalema: 28 km (17 mi) northwest of Ronda, 23 km (14 mi) northeast of Ubrique.

The Sierra de Grazelema Natural Park encompasses series of mountain ranges known as the Sierra de Grazalema, which straddle the provinces of Málaga and Cádiz. These mountains trap the rain clouds that roll in from the Atlantic and thus the area has the distinction of being the wettest place in Spain, with an average annual rainfall of 88 inches. Because of the park's altitude and prevailing humidity, it's one of the last habitats for the rare fir tree *Abies pinsapo*; it's also home to ibex, vultures, and birds of prey. Parts of the park are restricted, accessible only on foot and accompanied by an official guide. The village of Grazalema itself is quite small.

ESSENTIALS

Visitor Information Grazalema (✉*Plaza de España* ☎*956/132073*).

EXPLORING

Standing dramatically at the entrance to the park, the village of **Grazalema** is the prettiest of the *pueblos blancos*. Its cobblestone streets of houses with pink-and-ocher roofs wind up the hillside, red geraniums splash white walls, and black wrought-iron lanterns and grilles cling to the house fronts.

From Grazalema, the A374 takes you to **Ubrique,** on the slopes of the Saltadero Mountains and known for its leather tanning and embossing industry. Look for the **Convento de los Capuchinos** (Capuchin Convent), the church of **San Pedro,** and, 4 km (2½ mi) away, the ruins of the Moorish castle **El Castillo de Fátima.**

Another excursion from Grazalema takes you through the heart of the protected reserve. Follow the A344 west through dramatic mountain scenery, past Benamahoma, to **El Bosque,** home to a trout stream and information center.

WHERE TO STAY

$ **La Mejorana.** This is the spot to find rural simplicity: though a mere 20 years old, the house has been cleverly designed and built to resemble an old-fashioned village home, complete with beams, tiled floors, and thick whitewashed walls. The rooms have simple wrought-iron beds, but the mountain views are stunning. There is a tranquil flower-filled garden for sunny days, and when temperatures drop, there's a cozy fireplace in the communal sitting room. Those opting for a weeklong stay will be rewarded with one night free of charge. **Pros:** in the center of the village, tastefully furnished. **Cons:** rooms may seem a bit bare to some, no TV. ✉ *C. Santa Clara 6, Grazalema* ☎ *956/132327* 🌐 *www.lamejorana.net* *5 rooms* *In-room: no TV. In-hotel: pool, no elevator* *CP.*

ESTEPONA

17 km (11 mi) west of San Pedro de Alcántara, 22 km (13 mi) west of Marbella.

Estepona is a pleasant and relatively tranquil seaside resort, despite being surrounded by an ever-increasing number of urban developments. The beach, more than 1 km (½ mi) long, has better-quality sand than the Costa norm, and the promenade is lined with well-kept, aromatic flower gardens. The gleaming white **Puerto Deportivo** is lively and packed with bars and restaurants, serving everything from fresh fish to Chinese food. Back from the main Avenida de España, the old quarter of cobbled narrow streets and squares is surprisingly unspoiled.

GETTING HERE AND AROUND

Buses run every half hour from 6:40 AM to 10:40 PM from Marbella to Estepona. The town is compact enough to make most places accessible via foot.

ESSENTIALS

Bus Contacts Bus Station (✉ *Av. de España* ☎ *952/800249*).

Visitor Information Estepona (✉ *Av. San Lorenzo* ☎ *952/802002*).

WHERE TO EAT AND STAY

$$–$$$ SPANISH **Alcaría de Ramos.** José Ramos, a winner of Spain's National Gastronomy Prize, opened this restaurant in the El Paraíso complex, between Estepona and San Pedro de Alcántara, and has watched it garner an enthusiastic following as his two sons followed in his culinary footsteps. Try the ensalada *de lentejas con salmón ahumado* (with lentils and smoked salmon), followed by *el pato asado con pure de manzana* (grilled duck with apple puree)—but leave room for the exemplary crepes Suzette with raspberry sauce or his equally irresistible fried ice cream. *Urbanización El Paraíso, Ctra. N340, Km 167 952/886178 MC, V Closed Sun. No lunch.*

$ SEAFOOD **La Escollera.** This cheerful, family-friendly seafood restaurant is appropriately located at the fishing boat end of the port, next to the shipyard. Expect no-frills decor and paper tablecloths but excellent fresh fish and seafood. This place is a favorite with locals—always a good sign. The menu changes according to the catch of the day, but you can expect delicious fresh *mejillones* (mussels), *chopitos* (baby squid), and, of course, the famous barbecued fresh *sardinas* (sardines) that bear absolutely no relation to their tiny, oily cousins that you find in a tin. *Puerto Pesquero de Estepona 952/806354 No credit cards Closed Mon.*

$$$ ★ **Albero Lodge.** Owner Myriam Perez Torres's love for travel infuses this boutique hotel, where each room is named after a city with decor to match. Exotic Fez has rich fabrics and colors; European rooms, such as Florence and Berlin, are elegantly decorated with antiques; the New York room is dramatically avant-garde with a black-and-white theme. There are private terraces, and a sandy path leads to the beach. Myriam can arrange hiking, horseback riding, and boat trips, as well as therapeutic massages. **Pros:** funky decor, friendly owner. **Cons:** decor in the rooms varies (make your preference known), no bar or restaurant. *Urb. Finca La Cancelada, Calle Támesis 16 952/880700 www.alberolodge.com 9 rooms In-hotel: pool AE, DC, MC, V.*

$$$$ **Kempinski.** This luxury resort between the coastal highway and the beach looks like a cross between a Moroccan casbah and the Hanging Gardens of Babylon: tropical gardens, with a succession of large swimming pools, meander down to the beach. The rooms are spacious, modern, and luxurious, with faux–North African furnishings and balconies overlooking the Mediterranean. Nightly live music can be enjoyed during the summer at the hotel's La Brisa Italian restaurant. **Pros:** great beachside location, excellent facilities. **Cons:** no shops or nightlife within walking distance. *Playa El Padrón, Ctra. N340, Km 159 952/809500 www.kempinski-spain.com 133 rooms, 16 suites In-room: Ethernet, dial-up, Wi-Fi. In-hotel: 4 restaurants, pools, gym, children's programs (ages 5–12), laundry service, parking (free), some pets allowed AE, DC, MC, V BP.*

$$$$ ★ **Las Dunas.** Rising like a multicolor apparition next to the beach, this spectacular hotel is halfway between Estepona and Marbella. Trickling fountains and copious exotic plants help create a sense of the palatial, and the large guest rooms are suitably sumptuous. Sea views command a premium. The El Lido Restaurant ($$$$) serves first-rate international cuisine and has a romantic tropical setting. The health center

offers several spa therapies. **Pros:** atmosphere of utter opulence, near the beach. **Cons:** outside Estepona, so a car or taxi is necessary for shops and nightlife; room views vary. ✉*La Boladilla Baja, Ctra. de Cádiz, Km 163.5* ☎*952/794345* 🌐*www.las-dunas.com* *33 rooms, 39 suites, 33 apartments* *In-room: Ethernet, Wi-Fi. In-hotel: 3 restaurants, pools, gym, spa, children's programs (ages 6–12), parking (free)* *AE, DC, MC, V* *BP.*

CASARES

20 km (12 mi) northwest of Estepona.

The mountain village of Casares lies high above Estepona in the Sierra Bermeja. Streets of ancient white houses piled one on top of the other perch on the slopes beneath a ruined but impressive Moorish castle. The heights afford stunning views over orchards, olive groves, and cork woods to the Mediterranean, sparkling in the distance.

SAN ROQUE

92 km (57 mi) southwest of Ronda, 64 km (40 mi) west of Marbella, 40 km (25 mi) west of Estepona, 14 km (9 mi) east of Gibraltar, and 35 km (22 mi) east of Tarifa.

The town of San Roque was founded within sight of Gibraltar by Spaniards who fled the Rock when the British captured it in 1704. Almost 300 years of British occupation have done little to diminish the ideals of San Roque's inhabitants, who still see themselves as the only genuine Gibraltarians. Fourteen kilometers (10 mi) east of San Roque is the luxury **Sotogrande** complex, a gated community with sprawling millionaires' villas, a yacht marina, and four golf courses, including the legendary Valderrama, which once hosted the Ryder Cup.

WHERE TO EAT AND STAY

$$–$$$ SEAFOOD ✕ **Los Remos.** The dining room in this gracious colonial villa has peach-color walls with quasi-baroque adornments: gilt rococo mirrors, swirling cherubs, friezes of grapes, and crystal lamps. It overlooks a formal, leafy garden full of palms, cedars, and trailing ivy. There's also a terrace for those balmy summer nights. Entrées include *potaje de sepia con garbanzos* (cuttlefish stew with chickpeas), *lubina confitada al aceite de oliva y aroma de jerez* (grilled seabass in an olive oil and sherry dressing), and vermicelli with clams. All the seafood comes from the Bay of Algeciras area, and the wine cellar contains some 20,000 bottles. ✉*Villa Victoria, Campomento de San Roque* ☎*956/698412* *AE, DC, MC, V* *Closed Mon. No dinner Sun.*

$$–$$$ **NH Sotogrande.** The NH chain rarely disappoints for style and comfort, and the Sotogrande is no exception. The sleek modern exterior of this well-situated hotel is also evident inside, with a dramatic minimalist lobby boldly decorated in red, black, and white. The rooms are light and airy with modern furnishings and eye-catching decor; the facilities are excellent and include a sumptuous buffet breakfast guaranteed to set you up for the day. Check the Web site for excellent off-season and weekend deals. **Pros:** top-notch service and facilities, stylish.

Cons: slightly anonymous, corporate feel. ✉*Autovia A-7, Salida 130* ☎*956/695444* 🌐*www.nh-hoteles.com* *106 rooms* *In-room: dial-up, Wi-Fi. In-hotel: 2 restaurants, bar, tennis court, pool, parking (free)* *AE, DC, MC, V* *BP.*

NIGHTLIFE

The **Casino de San Roque** (✉*N340, Km 124* ☎*956/780100* 🌐*www.casinosanroque.com* *Mar.–Sept., daily 8 PM–5 AM; Oct.–Feb., daily 9 PM–5 AM*) has a gaming room with roulette and blackjack tables and a less formal slot-machine area. Passports, and a jacket and tie for men, are required in the casino.

TARIFA

Fodor's Choice ★ *35 km (21 mi) west of San Roque.*

On the Straits of Gibraltar at the southernmost tip of mainland Europe—where the Mediterranean and the Atlantic meet—Tarifa was one of the earliest Moorish settlements in Spain. Strong winds kept Tarifa off the tourist maps for years, but they have ultimately proven a source of wealth; the vast wind farm on the surrounding hills creates electricity, and the wide, white-sand beaches stretching north of the town have become Europe's biggest wind- and kite-surfing center. As a result, the town has continued to grow and prosper. Downtown cafés, which a couple of years ago were filled with men in flat caps playing dominoes and drinking *anís,* now serve croissants with their *café con leche* and make fancier tapas for a more cosmopolitan crowd.

Tarifa's 10th-century **castle** is famous for the siege of 1292, when the defender Guzmán el Bueno refused to surrender even though the attacking Moors threatened to kill his captive son. In defiance, he flung his own dagger down to them, shouting, "Here, use this"—or something to that effect (and they did indeed kill his son afterward). The Spanish military turned the castle over to the town in the mid-1990s, and it now has a **museum** on Guzmán and the sacrifice of his son. *€1.50* *Tues.–Sun. 10–2 and 4–6.*

Ten kilometers (6 mi) north of Tarifa on the Atlantic coast are the Roman ruins of **Baelo Claudia.** This settlement was a thriving production center of *garum,* a salty fish paste appreciated in Rome. ☎*956/688530* *Free* *July–mid-Sept., Tues.–Sat. 10–6, Sun. 10–2; mid-Sept.–June, Tues.–Sat. 10–5, Sun. 10–2.*

WHERE TO STAY

$$ **100% Fun.** This funky hotel across from Tarifa's sandy strip is popular with the wind- and kite-surfing crowd. There's an exotic Amazonian theme here, with thatched roofs, bubbling fountains, and thick, exuberant greenery. In bungalows surrounding the pool, rooms are washed in shades of ocher, complimented by crisp white bedding and terra-cotta tiles. The restaurant ($) serves Tex-Mex, including sizzling prawn fajitas, chili con carne, and several vegetarian options. **Pros:** across from the beach, young vibe. **Cons:** the predominantly young, fun-loving crowd makes peace and quiet hard to find, if that's what you're looking for. ✉*Ctra. Cádiz-Málaga, Km 76* ☎*956/680330* 🌐*www.tarifa.*

net/100fun 22 *rooms* *In-room: no a/c. In-hotel: restaurant, bar, pool* *MC, V* *EP.*

$$ **Convento de San Francisco.** The rooms here are comfortable and attractive, with exposed stone walls and arches, but the main draw is the setting: a restored 17th-century convent in the spectacular village of Vejer, just west of Tarifa, overlooking the coast. The original cloisters are quite lovely, lined with plants and bench seating for those in a reflective mood. Breakfast is served in the former refectory, now a restaurant specializing in traditional Andalusian cuisine. **Pros:** great location in the center of village, friendly owners. **Cons:** rooms rather bare, it's a long way from the beach. *La Plazuela* *956/451001* *www.tugasa.com* 25 *rooms* *In-hotel: restaurant* *MC, V* *EP.*

GIBRALTAR

20 km (12 mi) east of Algeciras, 77 km (48 mi) southwest of Marbella.

The tiny British colony of Gibraltar—nicknamed Gib, or simply the Rock—whose impressive silhouette dominates the strait between Spain and Morocco, was one of the two Pillars of Hercules in ancient times, marking the western limits of the known world. Gibraltar today is a bizarre anomaly of Moorish, Spanish, and British influences in a prime position commanding the narrow pathway between the Mediterranean Sea and the Atlantic Ocean.

The Moors, headed by Tariq ibn Ziyad, seized the peninsula in 711 as a preliminary to the conquest of Spain. After the Moors had ruled for 750 years, the Spaniards recaptured Tariq's Rock in 1462. The English, heading an Anglo-Dutch fleet in the War of the Spanish Succession, gained control in 1704, and, after several years of local skirmishes, Gibraltar was finally ceded to Great Britain in 1713 by the Treaty of Utrecht. Spain has been trying to get it back ever since. In 1779 a combined French and Spanish force laid siege to the Rock for three years to no avail. During the Napoléonic Wars, Gibraltar served as Admiral Horatio Nelson's base for the decisive naval Battle of Trafalgar, and during the two World Wars, it served the Allies well as a naval and air base. In 1967 Franco closed the land border with Spain to strengthen his claims over the colony, and it remained closed until 1985.

The Rock is like Britain with a suntan. There are double-decker buses, policemen in helmets, and red mailboxes. Millions of dollars have been spent in developing its tourist potential, and a steady flow of expat Brits come here from Spain to shop at Morrisons supermarket and High Street shops. Gibraltar's economy is further boosted by its status as an offshore financial center. Britain and Spain have been talking about joint Anglo-Spanish sovereignty, much to the ire of the majority of Gibraltarians, who remain fiercely patriotic to the crown. The relationship between the two traditional foes has relaxed a little with the introduction of flights from the Spanish mainland to Gibraltar in 2006.

GETTING HERE AND AROUND

There are frequent day tours organized from the Costa del Sol resorts, either via your hotel or any reputable travel agency. If you're driving, consider parking at the well-signposted underground lot at La Linea (*see Exploring the Rock, below*).

ESSENTIALS

Visitor Information Gibraltar (✉ *Duke of Kent House, Cathedral Square* ☎ *200/74950*).

There are likely few places in the world that you enter by walking or driving across an airport runway, but that's what happens in Gibraltar. First you show your passport; then you make your way out onto the narrow strip of land linking Spain's La Linea with Britain's Rock. Unless you have a good reason to take your car—such as loading up on cheap gas or duty-free goodies—you're best off leaving it in a guarded parking area in La Linea, the Spanish border town—and don't bother hanging around here; it's a seedy place. In Gibraltar you can hop on buses and taxis that expertly maneuver the narrow, congested streets. The Official Rock Tour—conducted either by minibus or, at a greater cost, taxi—takes about 90 minutes and includes all the major sights, allowing you to choose where to come back and linger, later. When you call Gibraltar from Spain or another country, prefix the seven-digit telephone number with 00–350. If you're calling from within Gibraltar, note that the former five-digit number is now prefixed by 200. Prices in this section are given in British pounds.

EXPLORING

The famous Barbary Apes are a breed of cinnamon-color, tailless monkeys native to Morocco's Atlas Mountains. Legend holds that as long as the apes remain in Gibraltar, the British will keep the Rock; Winston Churchill went so far as to issue an order for their preservation when the apes' numbers began to dwindle during World War II. They are publicly
8 fed twice daily, at 8 and 4, at **Apes' Den**, a rocky area down Old Queens Road and near the Wall of Charles V (this is the famous wall built in 1552 after an attack by Turkish pirates). Among the apes' mischievous talents are grabbing food, purses, and cameras.

★ You can reach St. Michael's Cave—or ride all the way to the top of Gibraltar—on a **cable car.** The car doesn't go high off the ground, but the views of Spain and Africa from the Rock's pinnacle are superb. It leaves from a station at the southern end of Main Street. *Cable car £8 round-trip* ⏲ *Daily 9:30–5:45.*

1 **Casemates Square,** in the northern part of town, is Gibraltar's social hub. It has been pedestrianized, and there are plenty of places to sit out with a drink and watch the world go by. There's a **tourist office** (☎ *200/50762* ⏲ *Weekdays 9–5:30, weekends 10–4*) branch here, as well as the **Gibraltar Crystal** company, where you can watch the glassblowers at work.

4 **Catalan Bay,** a fishing village founded by Genoese settlers, is now a resort on the eastern shores. The massive water catchments once supplied the colony's drinking water. ✉ *From the Rock's eastern side, go left down Devil's Tower Rd. as you enter Gibraltar.*

⓭ From **Europa Point,** have a look across the straits to Morocco, 23 km (14 mi) away. You're now standing on one of the two ancient Pillars of Hercules. In front of you, the lighthouse has dominated the meeting place of the Atlantic and the Mediterranean since 1841; sailors can see its light from a distance of 27 km (17 mi). Construction is under way here for a new commercial complex with restaurants and bars. ✉ *Continue along coast road to the Rock's southern tip.*

❺ The dignified Regency architecture of Great Britain blends well with the shutters, balconies, and patios of southern Spain in colorful, congested **Gibraltar.** Shops, restaurants, and pubs beckon on Main Street; at the Governor's Residence, the ceremonial Changing of the Guard takes place six times a year and the Ceremony of the Keys takes place twice a year. Make sure you see the Law Courts, where the famous case of the sailing ship *Mary Celeste* was heard in 1872; the Anglican Cathedral of the Holy Trinity; and the Catholic Cathedral of St. Mary the Crowned. The **main tourist office** (✉ *Duke of Kent House, Cathedral Sq.* ☎ *200/45000* ⏲ *Weekdays 9–5:30*) is on Cathedral Square.

❻ The **Gibraltar Museum** is often overlooked by visitors heading to the Upper Rock Reserve. It houses a beautiful 14th-century Moorish bathhouse and an 1865 model of the Rock; the displays evoke the Great Siege and the Battle of Trafalgar. There's also a reproduction of the "Gibraltar Woman," the Neanderthal skull discovered here in 1848. ✉ *Bomb House La.* ☎ *200/74289* 🌐 *www.gib.gi/museum* 🎫 *£2* ⏲ *Weekdays 10–6, Sat. 10–2.*

❸ The **Great Siege Tunnels,** formerly known as the Upper Galleries, were carved out during the Great Siege of 1779–82 at the northern end of Old Queen's Road. You can plainly see the openings from where the guns were pointed at the Spanish invaders. These tunnels form part of what is arguably the most impressive defense system anywhere in the world. The nearby and privately managed World War II Tunnels are also open to the public but are less dramatic.

❷ The **Moorish Castle** was built by the descendants of Tariq, who conquered the Rock in 711. The present Tower of Homage dates from 1333, and its besieged walls bear the scars of stones from medieval catapults (and, later, cannonballs). Admiral George Rooke hoisted the British flag from its summit when he captured the Rock in 1704, and it has flown here ever since. The castle is on Willis's Road but may be viewed from outside only.

❼ The 18th-century **Nefusot Yehuda Synagogue,** on Line Wall Road, is one of the oldest synagogues on the Iberian Peninsula, dating back to 1724. There are guided tours twice a day at 12:30 PM and 2:30 PM, accompanied by a short history of the Gibraltar Jewish community. ☎ *200/78804.*

❿ There are fine views to be had if you drive up above **Rosia Bay.** The bay was where Nelson's flagship, HMS *Victory,* was towed after the Battle of Trafalgar in 1805. On board were the dead, who were buried in Trafalgar Cemetery on the southern edge of town—except for Admiral Nelson, whose body was returned to England, preserved in a barrel of

CLOSE UP

A Rocky History

Plenty of places in Spain are culturally a country apart, but Gibraltar is—literally—a country apart. A little piece of Britain at the bottom of Spain, Gibraltar has an amusing mix of tea-and-biscuits culture paired with the baking sun of its Mediterranean surroundings. This strategic spot, a quick skip into Africa and a perfect point of departure around the base of Europe, has inspired a number of turf wars, ultimately placing it in the hands of the British. Today the relationship is amicable, but in the beginning it was anything but.

Although the Romans ruled the area from 500 BC to AD 475, it was left to the Moors to establish the first settlement here in 1160. The Duke of Medina Sidonia then recaptured the Rock for Spain in 1462. In 1501 Isabella the Catholic declared Gibraltar a crown property and the following year it received the Royal Warrant that bestowed on it a coat of arms consisting of a castle and a key. In 1704 an Anglo-Dutch force eventually captured Gibraltar—and this developed into Spain's ceding of Gibraltar to Britain in 1713.

In 1779, combined Spanish and French forces totaling more than 50,000 troops laid the final Great Siege against a mere 5,000 defenders. The attack highlighted all the unusual problems involved in defending Gibraltar: the great north face of the Rock guarded the entrance to Gibraltar, but it seemed impossible to mount guns on it. The answer: tunnels. Of course the solution had one major problem: cannons are designed to fire upward, not down. This problem was circumvented by digging tunnels that sloped downward. Later, in World War II, tunnels were used again to defend Gibraltar. General Eisenhower conducted the Allied invasion of North Africa from one of the tunnels—and all of them remain under military control today.

From 1963 to 1964, Gibraltar's future was debated at the United Nations, but in a referendum on September 10, 1967, which has now become Gibraltar's National Day, 99.9% of Gibraltarians voted to remain part of Britain. In 1969 this resulted in a new constitution granting self-government. These events severely provoked General Franco, and he closed the coastal border that same year. It stayed closed until February 5, 1985. Despite this, Spain occasionally decided to make the crossing more difficult. In 2002, finally, the governments of the U.K. and Spain reached an agreement in principle on joint sovereignty. Another referendum resulted in 99% voting against the idea. Nevertheless, this led to the creation of a tripartite forum, including the Gibraltar government and, in turn, direct flights from Madrid were started in November 2006.

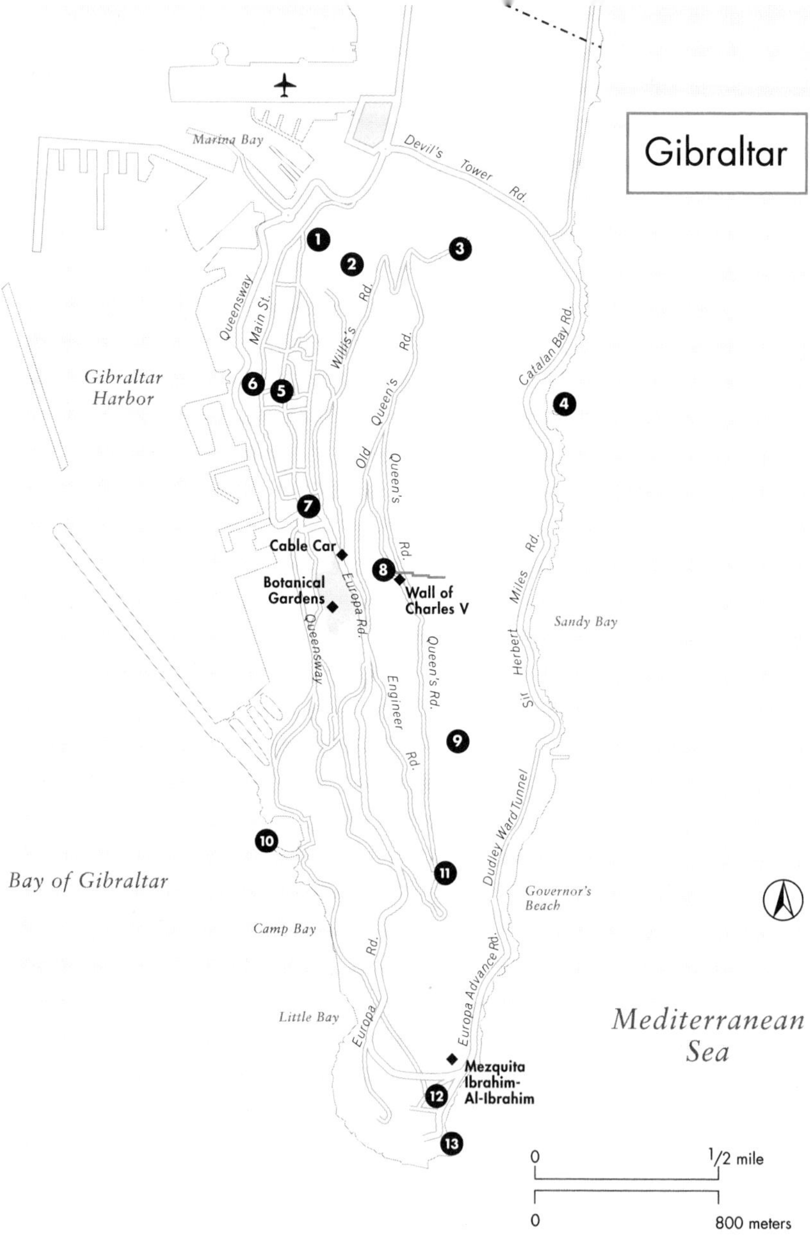

Apes' Den **8**
Casemates Square **1**
Catalan Bay **4**
Europa Point **13**
Gibraltar Museum **6**
Gibraltar Town **5**
Great Siege Tunnels **3**
Moorish Castle **2**
Nefusot Yehuda Synagogue **7**
Rosia Bay **10**
Shrine of Our Lady of Europe **12**
St. Michael's Cave **9**
Upper Rock Nature Reserve **11**

rum. ✉ *From Europa Flats, follow Queensway back along the Rock's western slopes.*

12 To the north of the lighthouse is the **Shrine of Our Lady of Europe,** venerated by seafarers since 1462. Once a mosque, the small Catholic chapel has a small museum with a 1462 statue of the Virgin and some documents. ✉ *Just north of Europa Point and lighthouse, along Rock's southern tip* *Free* *Weekdays 10–7.*

9 **St. Michael's Cave** is the largest of Gibraltar's 150 caves. A series of underground chambers hung with stalactites and stalagmites, it's an ideal performing-arts venue. The skull of a Neanderthal woman (now in the British Museum) was found at nearby Forbes Quarry eight years before the world-famous discovery in Germany's Neander Valley in 1856; nobody paid much attention to it at the time, which is why the prehistoric race is called Neanderthals rather than *Homo calpensis* (literally, "Gibraltar Man"—after the Romans' name for the Rock, *Calpe*). ✉ *Queen's Road.*

MONKEYING AROUND ON THE ROCK

The most privileged—and popular—residents of Gibraltar are the 200 or so tailless Barbary apes, the only nonhuman primates in all of Europe. Treated with great respect, the apes receive health care at the local military hospital as if they were any other patient. They live in the Upper Rock Nature Reserve (although occasionally one is seen wandering into the town), and a popular stop for visitors is the Apes' Den. With their friendly, playful, and inquisitive nature, it's easy to forget they're semiwild creatures, but remember: don't touch them, feed them, or go near the young.

11 The **Upper Rock Nature Preserve,** accessible from Jews' Gate, includes St. Michael's Cave, the Apes' Den, the Great Siege Tunnels, the Moorish Castle, and the Military Heritage Center, which chronicles the British regiments who have served on the Rock. ✉ *From Rosia Bay, drive along Queensway and Europa Rd. as far as Casino, above Alameda Gardens. Make a sharp right here, up Engineer Rd. to Jews' Gate, a lookout over docks and Bay of Gibraltar toward Algeciras.* *£8, includes all attractions, plus £1.50 per vehicle* *Daily 9–6:15.*

WHERE TO EAT AND STAY

$ MEDITERRANEAN ✕ **Gauchos.** Found within the atmospheric 200-year-old casemates, the dining rooms of this restaurant are suitably moody, with low barrel-vault ceilings and dark wood furnishings. As the name suggests, the emphasis here is on Argentinean grills, like rump steak with a choice of mushroom, green peppercorn, béarnaise, or mustard sauce. Options for less carnivorous folk are surprisingly innovative and include baked blue cheese in pastry; salmon with grilled banana, mango, and avocado; and vegetable stuffed mushrooms. ✉ *Waterport Casemates* ☎ *200/59700* *MC, V.*

$ BRITISH ✕ **Sacarello's.** Right off Main Street, this dining spot is as well known for its excellent coffee and cakes as it is for the rest of its food. There's a lavish salad buffet, as well as filled baked potatoes; panfried noodles with broccoli, mussels, and chicken; and rack of lamb with wine and fine herbs. Top your meal off with a specialty coffee with cream and vanilla. The restaurant has several warmly decorated rooms with cozy corners, dark-wood furnishings, and low-beamed ceilings. The whole place has an old-fashioned England feel. ✉ *57 Irish Town* ☎ *70625* ▭ *MC, V* ⏲ *No dinner Sun.*

$$ **Bristol.** This stately, colonial-style hotel in the heart of town has splendid views of the bay and the cathedral. The public spaces are spacious and comfortable, especially the downstairs lounge, which exudes an air of faded elegance with graceful chandeliers and sink-into sofas. The rooms are carpeted throughout, and the overall color scheme is a warm burgundy and cream—which might feel a bit stifling in midsummer; the tropical garden is a cool haven, however. **Pros:** superb location near restaurants, shops, and nightlife; comfortable carpeted rooms. **Cons:** hotel exterior dingy, interior needs updating. ✉ *10 Cathedral Sq.* ☎ *7200/76800* 🌐 *www.bristolhotel.gi* *60 rooms* *In-hotel: bar, pool, parking (no fee)* ▭ *AE, DC, MC, V.*

$$$$ **O'Callaghan Eliott.** If you want to stay at the most slick and modern of the Rock's hotels, try this one right in the center of the town. Ask for a room at the top of the hotel, with a view over the Bay of Gibraltar; failing that, check out the rooftop pool. **Pros:** views of either marina or the Rock, well located for pubs and restaurants. **Cons:** very business-traveler oriented, room decor a little stark. ✉ *2 Governor's Parade* ☎ *200/70500* 🌐 *www.ocallaghanhotels.com* *106 rooms, 8 suites* *In-room: dial-up, Wi-Fi. In-hotel: 2 restaurants, bars, gym, pool, no-smoking rooms* ▭ *AE, DC, MC, V* *BP.*

$$$$ **The Rock.** This hotel overlooking the straits first opened in 1932, and although furnishings in the rooms and restaurants are elegant and colorful, they still preserve something of the English colonial style—bamboo, ceiling fans, and a terrace bar covered with wisteria. There are various whimsical touches, like ducks (plastic!) in the bath and toy-monkey key rings, plus more thoughtful touches, like complimentary tea, coffee, and biscuits. The buffet breakfast is lavish, including the typical English fry up of eggs, bacon, sausages, mushrooms, tomatoes, and baked beans. **Pros:** old-fashioned excellent service, magnificent Gibraltar bay views. **Cons:** inconvenient for High Street shopping, conservative decor. ✉ *3 Europa Rd.* ☎ *200/7300* 🌐 *www.rockhotelgibraltar.com* *101 rooms, 2 suites* *In-room: dial-up, Wi-Fi. In-hotel: restaurant, bar, pool* ▭ *AE, DC, MC, V* *BP.*

NIGHTLIFE

Lord Nelson (✉ *Casemates Square* ☎ *200/50009*), a restaurant during the day but a lively bar at night, has live bands—ranging from jazz and blues to rock—on Friday and Saturday nights, starting at about 10 PM.

SPORTS AND THE OUTDOORS

Bird- and dolphin-watching, diving, and fishing are popular activities on the Rock. For details on tours and outfitters, visit the Gibraltar government Web site's "On Holiday" page (🌐 *www.gibraltar.gov.uk*) or call the local tourist office (☎ 200/745000).

Extremadura

Square and Church of San Mateo and Torre de las Cigüeñas, Caceresw

WORD OF MOUTH

"We just returned from a three week trip to Spain. We visited some popular places (Barcelona, Madrid, Salamanca, Segovia), as well as Zaragoza and Caceres (really loved it). It was a great trip filled with many friendly and helpful people, amazing sights, and beautiful villages."

—Jago

www.fodors.com/community

WELCOME TO EXTREMADURA

A Roman amphitheatre in Mérida.

TOP REASONS TO GO

★ **Visit stuck-in-a-time-warp Cáceres:** The walled old city is wonderfully evocative, particularly at dusk when the skyline takes on an otherworldly air with its ancient spires, towers, and cupolas.

★ **In the pink:** Impress the folks back home with photographs of the beautiful cherry blossoms in upper Extremadura's spectacular Jerte Valley.

★ **A medieval block-buster:** Enjoy a coffee or *cerveza* in Trujillo's Plaza Mayor while admiring a jumble of ancient buildings with nary a modern apartment block in sight.

★ **Heady views:** Splurge on a night at the parador in Guadalupe; the panoramic landscapes will leave you dazzled for weeks.

★ **Get to know *La Dehesa*:** Southwest Iberia's unique oak park ecosystem, home of the acorn-fed black Iberian pig that provides *jamón ibérico de bellota*, Spain's most prized food product.

1 Upper Extremadura. Green valleys and pristine mountain villages along with the monumental cities of Plasencia, Cáceres, and Trujillo provide the main attractions in upper Extremadura. The three valleys of Jerte, La Vera, and Ambroz are stunning natural settings with remote villages that the 20th century seems to have skipped entirely, while the Monfragüe Natural Park offers an anthology of rare animal and plant life from Eurasian vultures to wild olive trees.

2 Lower Extremadura. Southern Extremadura shows the pull of Portugal and Andalusia, while the early Roman capital of Lusitania at Mérida is Iberia's finest compendium of Roman ruins. Badajoz, on the border with Portugal, seems to have a foot on both sides of the border with its large Portuguese population. The *dehesa*, southwestern Spain's rolling oak forest and meadowland, is prime habitat for the semiwild Iberian pig and covers much of southern Extremadura, while Zafra is more Andalusian than Castilian.

Trujillo: Cradle of the Conquistadors.

GETTING ORIENTED

Extremadura, just to the west of Madrid, covers an area of 41,602 square km (16,063 square mi) and consists of two provinces: Cáceres to the north and Badajoz to the south, divided by the Toledo Mountains. To the west, this region borders Portugal, to the south, Andalusia, and to the east, Castilla–La Mancha. Northern Extremadura is typified by stunning mountain scenery with green valleys and unspoiled villages and towns. Southern Extremadura has verdant farmland between Badajoz and Mérida; south of here to Zafra, the area is mainly flat and harsh until you reach the lush Sierra Morena mountain range that borders Andalusia.

Inhabitants of Las Hurdes in Cáceres dress for Carnaval.

EXTREMADURA PLANNER

When to Go

Summer in Extremadura can get brutally hot, particularly in the south. If you have to visit at this time of year, head for the cooler mountains and natural parks in the north.

Spring is the ideal season, especially in the countryside when the valleys and hills are covered with a dazzle of wild flowers. If you can time it right, the stunning spectacle of cherry-blossom season in the Jerte Valley and La Vera takes place around mid-March.

Bird-watchers should try to time visits in late February, after the migrating storks have arrived to nest and before the European cranes have returned to northern Europe.

Fall is also a good time for Extremadura, when the weather cools down considerably and the summer crowds have left. You may have rain starting in late October.

Take a Tour

A great way to really get to know this varied and dramatic province is by bike, and you can cut down on the map-reading by following the Ruta Vía de la Plata: it runs through Extremadura from north to south along A66, dividing it in two, and passes by such villages as Plasencia, Cáceres, Mérida, and Zafra. This route more or less follows the ancient Roman way called Vía de la Plata. Parts of the road are still preserved and bicycleable. Note that the region north of the province of Cáceres, including the Jerte Valley, La Vera, and the area surrounding Guadalupe, is mountainous and uneven. If you attempt it, be prepared for a bumpy and exhausting ride. The regional government has opened a Vía Verde, which goes from Logrosán (a couple of miles southwest of Guadalupe) to Villanueva de la Serena (east of Mérida and near Don Benito). This path is a roughly cleared track, more like a nature trail for hikers and bikers, and closed to motor vehicles.

Other options for bicyclists are the paved areas of the national parks of Monfragüe (near Cáceres). Rural lodgings sometimes provide bikes for their guests, but serious cyclists should plan to bring their own bicycles.

Horseback riding tours are also an option, **Hidden Trails,** based in Vancouver Canada, offers weeklong riding tours of the Gredo Mountains on the border of Cáceres province. **Valle Aventura** organizes hiking, horseback riding, cycling, and kayaking trips in the Jerte Valley.

Extremadura is famous for its birdlife, and several companies offer bird-watching tours. The U.K.–based **Spainbirds** specializes in nature and birding trips throughout Spain. **EuroAdventures Vacations** also organizes specialized tours, including a half-day walking tour of the Cáceres Jewish quarter. With an office in town, Guías Turísticos de Cáceres offers tours around the city and information on accredited guides throughout Extremadura. In addition, several travel agencies can arrange custom-designed tours of the region.

Contacts **EuroAdventures Vacations** (*www.euroadventures.net*). **Hidden Valley** (*604/323–1141* *www.hiddentrails.com*). **Spainbirds** (*www.spainbirds.com*). **Valle Aventura** (*927/472196* *www.valleaventura.com*).

Festivals and Fiestas

The annual WOMAD (World of Music, Arts and Dance, *www.bme.es/womad*) festival is held in Cáceres center every May, attracting some 75,000 spectators.

Extremadura is not typically a land of running bulls, except for the **fiestas de San Juan** in Coria, Cáceres, on the week of June 24, or the **Capeas,** in Segura de León, Badajoz, around September 14, when locals show off their bullfighting skills. Instead, the province of Cáceres has its share of festivals commemorating past saints and sinners. February 3 is the day to toast **San Blas** (St. Blaise), believed to heal sore throats, with hot cakes bearing his name and multiple feasts.

Semana Santa (Holy Week) is celebrated with rituals in cities throughout the region. In early May, Trujillo's Feria del Queso (Cheese Festival) is popular with foodies. At the Cáceres September **Celebración del Cerdo y Vino** (Pig and Wine Celebration), the area's innumerable pork products are prepared in public demonstrations. On December 7, Jarandilla de la Vera fills the city with bonfires to celebrate **Los Escobazos,** when locals play-fight with torches made out of brooms.

In Badajoz the year opens on the 16th and 17th of January with **La Encamisá,** in Navalvillar de Pela. Horsemen re-create a medieval battle of the town's citizens against Arab invaders. During the **Carnival** celebration in Badajoz, parades of thousands wear extravagant costumes. Also colorful are the **Holy Week** celebrations at Oliva de la Frontera. Badajoz says *adios* to winter with the fiestas of **La Primavera** (Spring Festival) and **Los Mayos** (May Days), usually at the end of April and beginning of May.

The highlight of the cultural calendar in Mérida is the annual **Festival de Teatro Clásico,** held in the Roman theater from early July to mid-August. Contact the tourist office in advance for information and tickets.

WHAT IT COSTS (IN EUROS)

	¢	$	$$	$$$	$$$$
Restaurants	under €6	€6–€9	€10–€15	€16–€20	over €20
Hotels	under €40	€40–€59	€60–€100	€101–€180	over €180

Prices are per person for a main course at dinner, and for two people in a standard double room in high season, excluding tax.

Planning Your Time

You can get a lightning impression of Extremadura in a day's drive from Madrid. It's about 2½ hours from Madrid to **Jerte**; from there, you can take the A66 south to **Cáceres,** then head east to **Trujillo** on the N521. Split your time evenly between Cáceres and Trujillo.

If you have a weekend to explore Extremadura, divide your time with a day at the **Parque Natural de Monfragüe,** an evening and morning in **Trujillo,** and lunch and afternoon sightseeing in **Cáceres.** If time allows, spend a third day exploring the Roman monuments in **Mérida.** Those with time for a longer stay should travel west from Mérida on the A5 to the provincial capital of **Badajoz** with a side trip to **Olivenza,** 25 km (15 mi) southwest of Badajoz. Spend at least one night at the sumptuous parador in Jarandilla de la Vera. While there, you can visit the Monasterio de Yuste, where Spain's founding emperor Carlos V died in 1558.

GETTING HERE AND AROUND

By Air

Extremadura's only airport is at Badajoz, which receives domestic flights from Madrid, Barcelona, and Bilbao. The nearest international airports are in Madrid and Seville.

By Train

Trains from Madrid stop at Monfragüe, Plasencia, Cáceres, Mérida, Zafra, and Badajoz, running as often as six times daily. From Seville there are daily trains to Mérida, Cáceres, and Plasencia. The journey from Madrid to Cáceres takes about 5 hours; from Seville to Cáceres, 7½ hours. Within the province there are services from Badajoz to Cáceres (2 daily, 1 hour 55 minutes) and to Mérida (7 daily, 1 hour); from Cáceres to Badajoz (3 daily, 2 hours), to Mérida (5 daily, 1 hour), to Plasencia (2 daily, 1 hour 20 minutes), and to Zafra (2 daily, 2 hours 10 minutes); from Plasencia to Badajoz (1 daily, 3 hours 30 minutes), to Cáceres (3 daily, 1 hour 20 minutes), and to Mérida (3 daily, 2 hours 20 minutes). Note that train stations in Extremadura tend to be some distance from town centers.

By Bus

If you're traveling in Extremadura via public transportation, buses are the way to go. Links between Extremadura and the other Spanish provinces are plentiful, reliable, and inexpensive, serving Extremadura's main cities from Madrid, Seville, Lisbon, Valladolid, Salamanca, and Barcelona. The first bus of the day on lesser routes tends to set off early in the morning, so plan carefully to avoid getting stranded. Some examples of destinations from Madrid are: Cáceras (8 daily); Guadalupe (2 daily); Trujillo (10 daily); and Mérida (8 daily). Bus routes within the vicinity are similarly well serviced; the following routes run frequently from Badajoz: Cáceres (7 daily); Caia, on the Portuguese border (4 daily); Mérida (8 daily); and Zafra (8 daily).

For schedules and prices, check the tourist offices or contact the Auto Res bus line.

Bus Stations Cáceres (✉ *Ctra. Gijón–Sevilla s/n, Cáceres* ☎ *927/232550*).

By Car

If you're heading to Extremadura by car from Madrid, the main gateway, the four-lane NV moves quickly. The N630, or Vía de la Plata, which crosses Extremadura from north to south, is also effective. The fastest approach from Portugal is the A6 from Lisbon to Badajoz. If you're in any kind of a hurry, driving is the most feasible way to get around Extremadura. The main roads are well surfaced and not too congested. Side roads—particularly those that cross the wilder mountainous districts, such as the Sierra de Guadalupe—can be poorly paved and badly marked, but the Sierra de Guadalupe affords some of the most spectacular views in Extremadura. (For some of the best views, head north of Guadalupe on EX118, toward the village of Navalmoral.) The surrounding countryside is rugged and beautiful. For more scenic countryside, continue northwest from here on the EX102 at Cañamero and on to the main Navalmoral–Trujillo road near the Puerto de Miravete, where you can enjoy a fabulous lookout point with sweeping views of Trujillo in the distance.

Updated by George Semler

The very name Extremadura, widely accepted as "the far end of the Duero," as in the Duero river, expresses the wild, remote, isolated, and end-of-the-line character of this haunting region.

With its poor soil and minimal industry, Extremadura never experienced the kind of modern economic development typical of other parts of Spain, although tourism to the region is steadily increasing. All the same, it's hard to believe that, in the distant past, this was one of Spain's most important and wealthy regions: no other place in Spain has as many Roman monuments as Mérida, capital of the vast Roman province of Lusitania, which included most of the western half of the Iberian Peninsula. Mérida guarded the Vía de la Plata, the major Roman highway that crossed Extremadura from north to south, connecting Gijón with Seville. The economy and the arts declined after the Romans left, but the region revived in the 16th century, when explorers and conquerors of the New World—from Francisco Pizarro and Hernán Cortés to Francisco de Orellana, first navigator of the Amazon—returned to their birthplace. These men built the magnificent palaces that now glorify towns such as Cáceres and Trujillo, and they turned the remote monastery of Guadalupe into one of the great artistic repositories of Spain.

EXPLORING EXTREMADURA

Rugged Extremadura is a find for those who like the outdoors. The lush Jerte Valley and the craggy peaks of the Sierra de Gredos mark Upper Extremadura's fertile landscape. South of the Jerte Valley is the historical town of Plasencia and the 15th-century Yuste Monastery. In Extremadura's central interior is the provincial capital of Cáceres and the Monfragüe Nature Park. Lower Extremadura's main towns—Mérida, Badajoz, Olivenza, and Zafra—have long exuded a Portuguese flavor, bolstered by the sizable Portuguese population.

ABOUT THE RESTAURANTS

Extremaduran food reflects the austerity of the landscape: peasant fare, with a strong character. In addition to fresh produce, Extremadurans rely on pigs, of which every part is used, including the *criadillas* (testicles—don't confuse them with *criadillas de la tierra,* which are "earth testicles," also known as truffles). Meats are outstanding, most notably the complex and nutty *jamón ibérico de bellota* (ham from acorn-fed Iberian pigs) such as those from the Sierra de Montánchez north of Cáceres or the Dehesa de Extremadura from the southern oak parks around Zafra. Equally irresistible are the chorizo and *morcilla* (blood pudding), often made here with potatoes. The *caldereta de cordero* (lamb stew) is particularly tasty, as is the beef from the *retinto,* a local breed of longhorn cattle. Game is common, and *perdiz al modo de Alcántara,* partridge cooked with truffles, is a specialty. Extremadurans make a gazpacho based on cucumbers, green peppers, and broth rather than tomatoes and water. A common accompaniment is *migas,* bread crumbs soaked in water and fried in olive oil with garlic, peppers, and sausage.

Local sheep, goat, and cow cheeses are known for strong flavors. If you have a chance, try the *tortas,* the round, semisoft cheeses of Cáceres: Torta de Casar and Torta de La Serena are frequent Best Spanish Cheese prizewinners. Pimentón de la Vera, a smoked paprika from the Vera Valley, has long been a much-valued Extremaduran product. Favorite *extremeño* desserts include the *técula mécula* (an almond-flavor marzipan tart), which combines the flavors of Spain and Portugal.

Marketed under the generic appellation "Ribera del Guadiana," Extremadura's little-known fruity red wines are up and coming on the Spanish wine scene, and a good value. Typical digestifs include liqueurs made from cherries or acorns.

ABOUT THE HOTELS

Extremadura's paradors are remarkable, occupying buildings of great historic or architectural interest in all major tourist areas. The Extremaduran government runs a few *hospederías,* a sort of regional version of the parador chain; some have historic quarters in scenic areas. Most other high-end hotels, with a few exceptions, are modern boxes with little character. Throughout Extremadura's countryside are a number of charming bed-and-breakfast inns (*hoteles rurales*) and 135 guesthouses (*casas rurales*).

UPPER EXTREMADURA

JERTE AND EL VALLE DEL JERTE (JERTE VALLEY)

220 km (137 mi) west of Madrid. For a scenic route, follow N110 southwest from Ávila to Plasencia.

ESSENTIALS

Visitor Information Valle del Jerte (✉ *Paraje Virgen de Peñas Albas s/n* ☎ *927/472558* 🌐 *www.turismovalledeljerte.com*).

EXPLORING

There's no more striking introduction to Extremadura than the **Puerto de Tornavacas** *(Tornavacas Pass)*—literally, the "point where the cows turn back." Part of the N110 road northeast of Plasencia, the pass marks the border between Extremadura and the stark plateau of Castile. At 4,183 feet above sea level, it has a breathtaking view of the valley formed by the fast-flowing Jerte River. The valley's lower slopes are covered with a dense mantle of ash, chestnut, and cherry trees, whose richness contrasts with the granite cliffs of Castile's Sierra de Gredos. Cherries are the principal crop. To catch their brilliant blossoms, visit in spring. Camping is popular in this region, and even the most experienced hikers can find some challenging trails.

Cabezuela del Valle, full of half-timber stone houses, is one of the valley's best-preserved villages. Follow N110 to Plasencia, or, if you have a taste for mountain scenery, detour from the village of Jerte to Hervás, traveling a narrow road that winds 35 km (22 mi) through forests of low-growing oak trees and over the Honduras Pass.

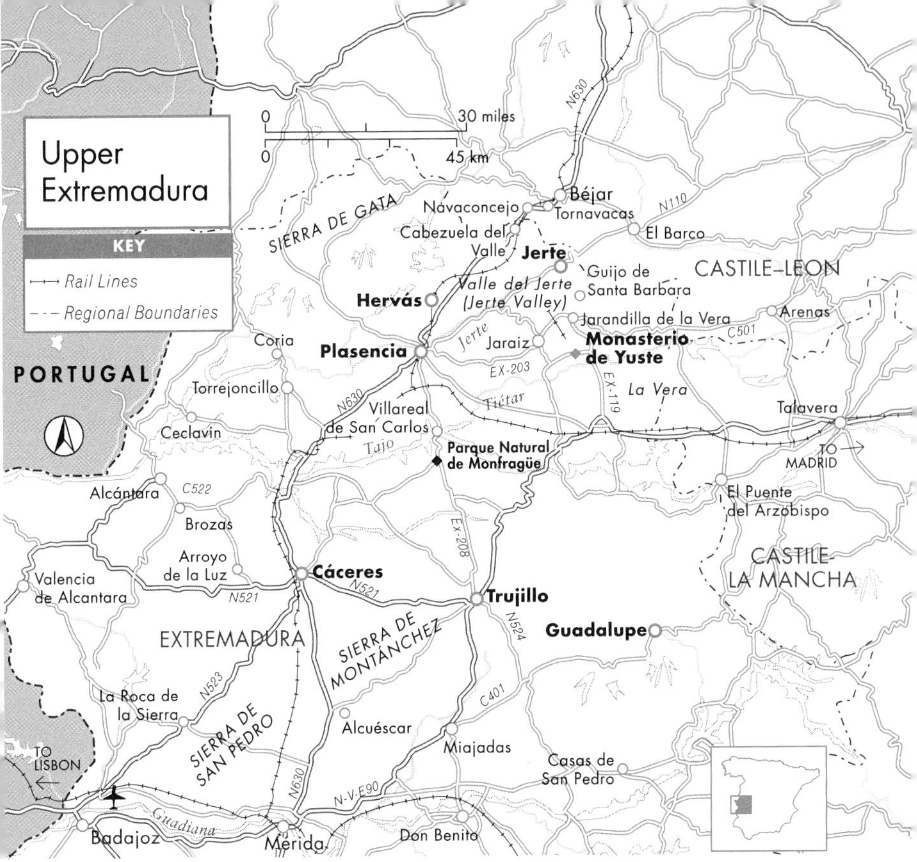

WHERE TO EAT AND STAY

$–$$$ SPANISH ✕**Valle del Jerte.** Service is always cheerful in this family-run restaurant (with five cozy rooms for overnights) just off the N110 in the village of Jerte. House specialties include gazpacho, *cabrito* (suckling goat), and local trout from the Jerte river. The homemade, regional desserts are outstanding, with many featuring the Jerte Valley's famed cherries; ask for the *tarta de cerezas* (cherry tart) or try the *queso fresco de cabra con miel de cerezo* (goat cheese topped with cherry-flavored honey). Ask to see the ancient and wonderful wine cellar. ✉*Gargantilla 16, Jerte* ☎*927/470052* 🌐*www.donbellota.com* ▭*MC, V.*

$–$$ **Hotel Rural Finca El Carpintero.** In two adjacent stone buildings, this hotel has three types of rooms, the best of which has a fireplace, a sitting room (salon), and its own entrance. The simpler rooms are elegant and colorful and have canopy wrought-iron beds; all the bathrooms have hydromassage tubs. The restaurant has wood beams and a cozy rustic feel, as well as a reasonably priced set menu. **Pros:** cozy atmosphere inside, nice grounds outside, good value. **Cons:** suites are much nicer than the rooms. ✉*N110, Km 360.5, Tornavacas* ☎*927/177089 or 659/732–8110* 🌐*www.fincaelcarpintero.com* *4 rooms, 2 suites* *In-hotel: restaurant, pool, Wi-Fi, no elevator* ▭*AE, D, MC, V.*

$–$$ **La Casería.** This rambling home is on a 120-acre working farm, once a 16th-century Franciscan convent. One of Extremadura's first rural guesthouses, this a place for animal lovers, as the household keeps lots of dogs and cats. Aside from the six rooms in the main lodge, there are three cottages. Activities such as horseback riding, mountain biking, and paragliding can be arranged. It's wise to reserve in advance. Caveat: the sign is easy to miss. **Pros:** privacy in the cottages, outdoor activities. **Cons:** main lodge often rented out to groups, a bit isolated. *N110, Km 378.6, Navaconcejo 927/173141 www.lacaseria.net 6 rooms, 3 cottages In-room: no a/c, no TV, Wi-Fi. In-hotel: pool, no elevator MC, V.*

HERVÁS

42 km (26 mi) northeast of Plasencia, 124 km (74 mi) northeast of Cáceres, 20 km (13 mi) northwest of Jerte.

Surrounded by pine and chestnut groves, this charming, hilly village makes an interesting detour from either the Jerte Valley or Plasencia. Hervás was a predominantly Jewish settlement during the Middle Ages, populated by Jews escaping Christian and Muslim persecution in Spain's larger cities. In 1492, when the Jews were expelled from the country altogether, the Jewish quarter was left intact but the possessions of its inhabitants were ceded to the local nobility. Stripped of its wealth, the village lost its commercial reputation and was forgotten. Now fully restored, the **Judería** (Jewish quarter) is among the best-preserved in Spain.

ESSENTIALS

Visitor Information Hervás (*Braulio Navas 6 927/473618*).

EXPLORING

The Judería contains the 17th-century **Convento de los Trinitarios** (*927/474828*), part of which has been turned into a tastefully furnished *hospedería,* El Jardín del Convento. At the top of the quarter there's a 16th- to 17th-century Renaissance church called the **Santa María de Aguas Vivas.**

The **Museo Pérez Comendador-Leroux,** a graceful 18th-century mansion in the center of town, houses a permanent exhibition of sculpture and paintings by local 20th-century artist Enrique Perez Comendar and his French artist wife, Magdalena Leroux. *C. de Asensio Neila 5 927/421843 www.hervasviva.com/Hervas/MuseosdeHervas €3 Tues. 5–8, Wed.–Fri. 11–2 and 5–8, weekends 10:30–2.*

WHERE TO STAY

$$ **El Jardín del Convento.** The prettiest square in the old part of Hervás is the setting for this handsome 19th-century town house lovingly restored down to the last door handle, lock, and ceramic tile. With some bedroom walls in the original exposed stone, a lush garden, and views from the upper rooms out into the mountains, the lines and harmony of the house and garden approach perfection. Rooms are comfortable, elegant, and yet simple enough to respect the history of what was once the Convento de los Trinitarios Descalzos (Monastery of Trinitarian Barefoot Monks). **Pros:** Ideal location in historic center with lovely gardens, spectacular views from higher floors. **Cons:** no elevator or a/c.

⊠Plaza del Convento 22, Hervás ☎927/481161 ⊕www.eljardindelconvento.com 5 rooms, 1 suite In-room: Wi-Fi. In-hotel: restaurant ▭MC, V.

PLASENCIA

255 km (160 mi) west of Madrid, 79 km (49 mi) north of Cáceres, 42 km (26 mi) southwest of Hervás.

Rising dramatically from the banks of the narrow Jerte River and backed by the peaks of the Sierra de Gredos, this community was founded by Alfonso VIII in 1180, just after he captured the entire area from the Moors. The town's motto, *ut placeat Deo et hominibus* ("To give pleasure to God and men"), might well have been a ploy on Alfonso's part to attract settlers to this wild, isolated place on the southern border of the former kingdom of León. Badly damaged during the Peninsular War of 1808, Plasencia retains far less of its medieval quarter than other Extremaduran towns, but it still has extensive remains of its early walls and a smattering of fine old buildings. In addition to being a site for visiting ruins, the city makes a good base for side trips to Hervás and the Jerte Valley, the Monasterio de Yuste and Monfragüe Nature Park, or, farther northwest, the wild Las Hurdes and Sierra de Gata.

ESSENTIALS

Visitor Information Plasencia (*⊠Santa Clara 2 ☎927/423843*).

EXPLORING

Plasencia's **cathedral** was founded in 1189 and rebuilt after 1320 in an austere Gothic style that looks a bit incongruous looming over the town's red-tile roofs. In 1498 the great architect Enrique Egas designed a new structure, intending to complement or even overshadow the original, but despite the later efforts of other notable architects of the time, such as Juan de Alava and Francisco de Colonia, his plans were never fully realized. The entrance to this incomplete, curious, and not wholly satisfactory complex is through a door on the cathedral's ornate but somber north facade. The dark interior of the new cathedral is notable for the beauty of its pilasters, which sprout like trees into the ribs of the vaulting. You enter the old cathedral through the Gothic cloister, which has four enormous lemon trees. Off the cloister stands the building's oldest surviving section, a 13th-century chapter house (now the chapel of **San Pablo**)—a late-Romanesque structure with an idiosyncratic, Moorish-inspired dome. Inside are medieval hymnals and a 13th-century gilded wood sculpture of the Virgen del Perdón. The **museum** in the truncated nave of the old cathedral has ecclesiastical and archaeological objects. *⊠Pl. de la Catedral ☎927/414852 Old cathedral €3.50 ⏲Oct.–Apr., Mon.–Sat. 9–12:30 and 4–5:30, Sun. 9–1; May–Sept., Mon.–Sat. 9–12:30 and 5–6:30, Sun. 9–1.*

The cloister of the elegant **Palacio Episcopal** (*Bishop's Palace ⊠Pl. de la Catedral*) is open weekdays from 9 to 2.

Lined with orange trees, the narrow, carefully preserved **Plaza de San Vicente** is at the northwest end of the old medieval quarter. At one end is the 15th-century church of **San Vicente Ferrer,** with an adjoining convent that's now the Parador Plasencia. The north side of the square is dominated by the Renaissance **Palacio de Mirabel** (*Palace of the Marquis of Mirabel* ☎*927/410701*)—go through the central arch for a back view. The hours can be sporadic, but it's usually open daily 10–2 and 4–6; tip the caretaker.

East of the Plaza de San Vicente, at the other end of the Rúa Zapatería, is the cheerful, arcaded square **Plaza Mayor**. The mechanical figure clinging to the town-hall clock tower depicts the clock maker and is called the **Mayorga** in honor of his Castilian hometown. Also east of the Plaza de San Vicente you can find a large section of the town's **medieval wall**—on the other side of which is a heavily restored Roman aqueduct. Walk southeast from the Plaza de San Vicente to the **Parque de los Pinos**, home to wildlife that includes peacocks, cranes, swans, pheasants, and monkeys.

WHERE TO EAT AND STAY

$$–$$$ SPANISH ✕**Hotel Alfonso VIII.** The hotel may be a few decades past its prime, but the restaurant here has long been regionally renowned for its excellent fare; the *ensalada de perdiz* (partridge salad) makes for a tasty starter. ✉*Alfonso VIII 32* ☎*927/410250* 🌐*www.hotelalfonsoviii.com* 💳*AE, DC, MC, V.*

$$$ **Parador de Plasencia.** In a 15th-century Gothic convent, this parador cultivates a medieval environment. Common areas are majestic and somber; guest rooms are decorated with monastic motifs and heavy wood furniture. Rooms are spacious and comfortable with stylishly modern bathrooms; most have sitting rooms. The high-ceiling, stone-and-wood-beam restaurant—the former convent Refectory—is almost intimidating in its architectural magnificence. Parking adds a hefty €14 nightly. **Pros:** successful fusion of old and new, good restaurant. **Cons:** free (legal) parking a long walk away. ✉*Pl. de San Vicente Ferrer* ☎*927/425870* 🌐*www.parador.es* *64 rooms, 2 suites* *In-room: Wi-Fi. In-hotel: restaurant, bar, pool, parking (fee)* 💳*AE, D, MC, V.*

$–$$ **Rincón Extremeño.** Off the Plaza Mayor in the old quarter, this property is basic and well maintained. There's a popular bar and restaurant ($$), the latter serving regional dishes like *caracoles de tierra* (snails in a spicy sauce). You'll have pleasanter views, though more noise, in a guest room facing the street. **Pros:** in the middle of the action, good value. **Cons:** noisy streets on weekends, busy and booming tavern. ✉*Vidrieras 6* ☎*927/411150* 🌐*www.hotelrincon.com* *13 rooms, 7 with bath* *In-room: Wi-Fi. In-hotel: restaurant, bar* 💳*MC, V.*

SHOPPING

If you're in Plasencia on Tuesday morning, head for the Plaza Mayor and do what the locals have been doing since the 12th century: scout bargains in the weekly market. On the first Tuesday of August the market is larger, with vendors from all over the region. For local art and crafts, try **Bámbara de Artesanía** (✉*Sancho Polo 12* ☎*927/411766*). Near the parador is **Artesanías Canillas** (✉*C. San Vicente Ferrer s/n* ☎*927/411668*), which sells regional costumes, pottery, and handmade straw hats. At **Casa del Jamón** (✉*C. Sol 18, east of Pl. Mayor* ☎*927/419328* ✉*C. Zapatería 17, between Pl. Mayor and parador*

927/419328), you can stock up on local charcuterie and sausages, *jamón ibérico*, cheeses, extremeño wines, and cherry liqueur.

LA VERA AND MONASTERIO DE YUSTE

45 km (28 mi) from Plasencia. Turn left off C501 at Cuacos and follow signs for the monastery (1 km [½ mi]).

ESSENTIALS

Visitor Information Jaraíz de la Vera (*Av. de la Constitución 67* *927/170587*).

13

EXPLORING

In the heart of La Vera, a region of steep ravines (*gargantas*), rushing rivers, and villages (including the town of Jaraíz de la Vera), lies **Monasterio de Yuste** *(Yuste Monastery)*. It was founded by Hieronymite monks in the early 15th century. Badly damaged in the Peninsular War, it was left to decay after the suppression of Spain's monasteries in 1835, but it has since been restored and taken over once more by the Hieronymites. Carlos V (1500–58), founder of Spain's vast 16th-century empire, spent his last two years in the Royal Chambers, enabling the emperor to attend Mass within a short stumble of his bed. The required guided tour also covers the church, the crypt where Carlos V was buried before being moved to El Escorial (near Madrid), and a glimpse of the monastery's cloisters. *927/172197* *€3* *Tues.–Sun. 10–6:30.*

WHERE TO EAT AND STAY

$$ **Camino Real.** In a village in the highest valley of the Vera, this hotel is in a modernized rural mansion. Rooms have exposed stone walls and wood-beam ceilings. There's a sitting room with fireplace, plus an outside hot tub. The room rate includes a lavish buffet breakfast. The owners organize local excursions and can arrange anything from equestrian outings to golf to guided fly-fishing expeditions. **Pros:** views over the valley, rough stone decor. **Cons:** can be windy and cold in midwinter. *C. El Monje 27, Guijo de Santa Bárbara* *927/561119* *www.casaruralcaminoreal.com* *10 rooms* *In-room: Wi-Fi. In-hotel: restaurant, no elevator* *MC, V* *BP.*

$$$ **Parador de Jarandilla de la Vera.** Nestled in the town of Jarandilla de la Vera, this parador (sometimes called Parador Carlos V) was built in the early 16th century as a fortified palace. Carlos V, founder of Spain's 16th-century global empire, stayed here for three months while he waited for his quarters at Yuste to be completed. The halls have medieval furnishings, and the regal dining room—where the restaurant is—is perfect for indulging royal fantasies. In the restaurant ($$–$$$), start with a humble classic, *huevos fritos con migas* (fried eggs with bread crumbs); then savor one of the house specialties, *caldereta de cordero* (lamb stew). **Pros:** medieval decor. **Cons:** rooms in the unrenovated wing are mediocre, town of little interest. *Av. García Prieto 1, 59 km (36 mi) east of Plasencia, 17 km (11 mi) west of Monasterio de Yuste* *927/560117* *www.parador.es* *53 rooms* *In-room: Wi-Fi. In-hotel: restaurant, bar, tennis court, pool* *AE, DC, MC, V.*

EN ROUTE

At the junction of the rivers Tiétar and Tajo, 20 km (12 mi) south of Plasencia on the EX208, is the **Parque Natural de Monfragüe.** This rocky-mountain wilderness is known for its plant and animal life, including lynx, boar, deer, fox, black storks, imperial eagles, and the world's largest colony of black vultures. Bring binoculars and find the lookout point called Salto del Gitano (Gypsy's Leap), on the C524 just south of the Tajo River—this is where the vultures can often be spotted wheeling in the dozens at close range. The park's visitor center and main entrance is in the hamlet of Villareal de San Carlos. ⊠ *Villareal de San Carlos* ☎ *927/199134* ⏲ *Oct.–Apr., daily 9–2:30 and 4–6; May–Sept., daily 9–2:30 and 4:30–7:30; audiovisual show every hr on ½ hr.*

CÁCERES

Fodor's Choice ★

307 km (190 mi) west of Madrid, 79 km (49 mi) south of Plasencia, 125 km (78 mi) southwest of Monasterio de Yuste, 90 km (55 mi) west of Monasterio de Guadalupe.

ESSENTIALS

Visitor Information Cáceres (⊠ *Pl. Mayor* ☎ *927/010834*).

EXPLORING

Cáceres, the provincial capital, is a prosperous agricultural town whose vibrant nightlife draws villagers from the surrounding pueblos every weekend. It's one of Spain's oldest cities. The Roman colony called Norba Caesarina was founded in 35 BC, but when the Moors took over in the 8th century, they named the city Quazris, which eventually morphed into the Spanish Cáceres. It has been prosperous ever since noble families helped Alfonso IX expel the Moors in 1229, and the pristine condition of the city's medieval and Renaissance quarter is the result of the families' continued occupancy of the palaces first erected in the 15th century.

Cáceres Viejo (Old Cáceres), which begins just east of Plaza San Juan, is the best part of town to stay in and explore. On the long, inclined, arcaded **Plaza Mayor,** you can see several outdoor cafés, tourist offices, and, on breezy summer nights, nearly everyone in town. In the middle of the arcade opposite the old quarter is the entrance to the lively Calle General Ezponda, lined with tapas bars, student hangouts, and discos that keep the neighborhood awake and moving until dawn.

On high ground on the eastern side of the Plaza Mayor, a portal beckons through the town's intact wall, which in turn surrounds one of the best-preserved medieval quarters in Spain. Literally packed with treasures, Cáceres's **Ciudad Monumental** (monumental city or old town, is also called the *casco antiguo* or *Cáceres Viejo*) is a marvel: small, but without a single modern building to distract from its aura. The old town is, however, virtually deserted in winter. Once you pass through the gate leading to the old quarter, note the **Palacio de los Golfines de Arriba** (⊠ *C. Adarve de Santa Ana*), dominated by a soaring tower dating from 1515. The ground floor is a now stylish restaurant with same name, though there are better dining options around.

On the Plaza San Mateo is the **San Mateo church** (✉ *C. Ancha*). Built mainly in the 14th century, but with a 16th-century choir, it has an austere interior, the main decorative notes being the baroque high altar and some heraldic crests. The battlement tower of the **Palacio del Capitán Diego de Cáceres** (✉ *Pl. San Mateo*) is also known as the Torre de las Cigüeñas (Tower of the Storks) for obvious reasons. It's now a military residence, but some rooms are occasionally opened up for exhibitions.

STORKS DROPPING BY

Storks are common in the old quarter of Cáceres, and virtually every tower and spire is topped by nests of storks, considered since the Roman era to be sacred birds emblematic of home, the soul, maternity, spring, and well-being.

The **Casa de las Veletas** *(House of the Weather Vanes)* is a 12th-century Moorish mansion that is now the **Museo de Cáceres.** Filled with archaeological finds from the Paleolithic through the Visigothic periods, the art section includes medieval to contemporary painters from El Greco to Tàpies. A highlight is the superb Moorish cistern—the *aljibe*—with horseshoe arches supported by moldy stone pillars. ✉ *1 Pl. de las Veletas* ☎ *927/010877* 🌐 *www.museosextremadura.com/caceres* 🎫 *€1.20, free Sun. and for EU citizens* ⏲ *Oct.–Apr., Tues.–Sat. 9–2:30 and 4–7, Sun. 10–2:30; May–Sept., 9–2:30 and 5–8, Sun. 10–2:30.*

The stony severity of the **Palacio de los Golfines de Abajo** (✉ *Cuesta de la Companía*) seems appropriate when you consider it was once the headquarters of General Franco. However, the exterior is somewhat relieved by elaborate Mudejar and Renaissance decorative motifs.

The Gothic church of **Santa María,** built mainly in the 16th century, is now the town cathedral. The elegantly carved high altar, dating from 1551, is barely visible in the gloom. A small museum displays religious objects. ✉ *Cuesta de la Companía* ☎ *927/215313* 🎫 *€2 for cathedral, tower, and museum* ⏲ *Mon.–Sat. 10–2 and 5–8, Sun. 9:30–2 and 5–7:30.*

Near the cathedral of Santa María is the elegant **Palacio de Carvajal,** the only old palace you can tour besides the Casa de las Veletas (which houses the Museo de Cáceres). It has an imposing granite facade and an arched doorway, and the interior has been restored, with period furnishings and art, to look as it did when the Carvajal family lived here in the 16th century. ✉ *Pl. de Santa María* 🎫 *Free* ⏲ *Weekdays 8* AM*–9* PM*, Sat. 9:30–2 and 5–8, Sun. 10–3.*

From Santa María cathedral, a 110-yard walk down Calle Tiendas takes you to the old city's northern wall. Don't miss the 16th-century **Palacio de los Moctezuma-Toledo** (now a public-records office), built by Juan Cano de Saavedra with the dowry provided by his wife, the Aztec princess Techichpotzin (known as Doña Isabel), daughter of the Aztec leader Montezuma (aka Moctezuma). ✉ *Pl. Conde de Canilleros 1* ☎ *927/249294* 🎫 *Free* ⏲ *Weekdays 8:30–2:30.*

The chief building of interest outside the wall of the old town is the church of **Santiago de los Caballeros** (✉ *C. Villalobos*), rebuilt in the 16th century by Rodrigo Gil de Hontañón, Spain's last great Gothic architect. The easiest way to reach the church is by exiting the old town on the west side, through the Socorro gate.

Just up the hill behind Cáceres's Ciudad Monumental is the **Santuario de la Virgen de la Montaña** *(Sanctuary of the Virgin of the Mountain)*. Inside are a golden baroque altar and a statue of the patroness virgin, which is paraded through town each May. On a clear day the view of old Cáceres from the front of the building is spectacular, well worth the 15-minute drive up the hill. ✉ *Follow C. Cervantes until it becomes Ctra. Miajadas; the sanctuary is just off the town tourist map, which you can pick up from the local tourist office.* ☎ *927/220049* *Donation accepted* ⏲ *Daily 8:30–2 and 4–8.*

WHERE TO EAT AND STAY

$$$$ SPANISH Fodor's Choice ★ ✕ **Atrio.** On a side street off the southern end of the main boulevard of Cáceres, this elegant restaurant is the best in Extremadura, possibly the best in Andalusia. Toño Pérez and his staff specialize in highly refined contemporary cooking and the menu changes often, but you won't be disappointed with any of the selections, especially if they include venison, partridge, wild mushrooms, or truffles. *Vieiras asadas con trufa negra* (roast scallops with truffle) or *pichón asado* (roast wood pigeon) are two of the signature offerings. ✉ *Av. de España 30* ☎ *927/242928* ▭ *AE, DC, MC, V* ⏲ *Closed Sept. 1–15. No dinner Sun.*

$$$$ FRENCH ✕ **Chez Manou.** Enjoying a prime location in the historic old quarter of town, this French restaurant features a traditional menu, starting with quiche lorraine, and followed by the full gamut of duck specialties, starring the inevitable as *à l'orange*. An ideal finish is the chocolate mousse *par excellence*. The dining area was formerly used as the town house horse stables, and the atmosphere is still suitably rustic, with beamed ceiling, antiques, and an eclectic selection of old prints and photos adorning the walls. During the warmer months you can sit at tables outside. ✉ *Plaza de las Veletas 4* ☎ *927/227682* ▭ *MC, V* ⏲ *Closed Sun. dinner and Mon.*

$$$–$$$$ SPANISH ✕ **El Figón de Eustaquio.** A fixture on the quiet and pleasant Plaza San Juan, across from the Melía hotel, Eustaquio is always busy, especially at lunchtime. In its jumble of small, old-fashioned dining rooms with low beamed ceilings, you'll be served mainly regional delicacies, including *venado de montería* (wild venison) or *perdiz estofada* (partridge stew). Fine Spanish wines are also available. ✉ *Pl. San Juan 12* ☎ *927/244362* *Reservations essential* ▭ *AE, MC, V.*

$–$$ ★ **Iberia Plaza Mayor.** At the entrance to the historic part of Cáceres, this 18th-century palace furnished with antiques offers good value, a strategic spot from which to explore the most interesting part of town, and more than adequate comforts. The tastefully refurbished guest rooms have breezy blue-tile bathrooms and attractive dark wood furniture. The location on a pedestrian shopping street just off Plaza Mayor is excellent but likely to be noisy on weekend nights in summer—pack your earplugs. **Pros:** good value, classical furnishings. **Cons:** nearest parking 100 meters away, can get noisy. ✉ *C. Pintores 2* ☎ *927/247634* 🌐 *www.iberiahotel.com* *37 rooms* *In-room: Wi-Fi. In-hotel: some pets allowed, no elevator* ▭ *MC, V.*

$$$ ★ **Meliá Cáceres.** This 16th-century palace built by the Marqueses de Oquendo is just outside the walls of the old town, on the Plaza San Juan. The hotel gracefully blends exposed brick and contemporary designer touches with antique furniture. Rooms have ample bathrooms with ornate fittings, while La Cava del Emperador, a street-level bar and restaurant with a vaulted brick ceiling, is a popular meeting place for the town's well-heeled. **Pros:** elegantly furnished, perfect location. **Cons:** nicotine fragrances in some rooms, rooms functional but plain. ✉ *Pl. San Juan 11–13* ☎ *927/215800* 🌐 *www.solmelia.com* *84 rooms, 2 suites* *In-room: Wi-Fi. In-hotel: restaurant, room service, bar, laundry service, public Wi-Fi, parking (fee)* *AE, DC, MC, V.*

$$$ **Parador de Cáceres.** This 14th-century palace provides a noble setting, decorated in soft cream tones offset by stone walls and heavy wood beams. Rooms are comfortable, and public spaces are antique-filled and elegant. The Torreorgaz restaurant ($$–$$$), with tables on the terrace in summer, offers *solomillo de ibérico a la Torta del Casar* (fillet of ibérico pig with creamy Torta del Casar sheep cheese) or *cabrito asado al romero* (young goat roasted with rosemary). Friday to Sunday the parador's wine cellar, Enoteca Torreorgaz, holds wine tastings. **Pros:** good blend of tradition and comfort, fine cuisine and wines. **Cons:** some rooms are basic, old-town location can be confusing to reach by car. ✉ *Ancha 610003* ☎ *927/211759* 🌐 *www.parador.es* *32 rooms, 1 suite* *In-room: Wi-Fi. In-hotel: restaurant, parking (fee)* *AE, DC, MC, V.*

NIGHTLIFE AND THE ARTS

Bars in Cáceres are lively until the wee hours. Nightlife centers on the **Plaza Mayor,** which fills after dinner with families out for a *paseo* (stroll) as well as students swigging *calimocho,* a mix of red wine and Coca-Cola, or *litronas*, 1-liter bottles of beer. In the adjacent old town, you can take in live music at **El Corral de las Cigueñas** (✉ *Cuesta de Aldana 610003*), which from October to April is open only Thursday to Sunday evenings. **Calle de Pizarro.** south of Plaza San Juan, is lined with cafés and bars.

TRUJILLO

★ *48 km (30 mi) east of Cáceres, 250 km (155 mi) southwest of Madrid.*

Trujillo rises up from the fertile fields around it like a great granite schooner under full sail. Up close, the rooftops and towers seem medieval; down below, Renaissance architecture flourishes in squares such as the Plaza Mayor, with its elegant San Martín church. The storks' nests that top many of the towers in and around the center of the old town have become a symbol of Trujillo. Dating back at least to Roman times, the city was captured from the Moors in 1232 and colonized by a number of leading military families.

GETTING HERE AND AROUND

It is practical to see Trujillo only on foot, as the streets are mostly cobbled or crudely paved with stone. The two main roads into Trujillo leave you at the town's unattractive bottom. Things get progressively older the farther you climb, but even on the lower slopes—where most of the shops are concentrated—you need walk only a few yards to step into what seems like the Middle Ages.

ESSENTIALS

Visitor Information Trujillo (✉ *Pl. Mayor* ☎ *927/659140*).

EXPLORING

Trujillo's large **Plaza Mayor,** one of the finest in Spain, is a superb Renaissance creation and the site of the local tourist office. At the foot of the stepped platform on the plaza's north side stands a large, bronze equestrian statue of conqueror Francisco Pizarro—the work, curiously, of an American sculptor, Charles Rumsey.

The **Palacio de los Duques de San Carlos** *(Palace of the Dukes of San Carlos)* is next to the church of San Martín. The palace's majestically decorated facade dates from around 1600. The building is now a convent of Hieronymite nuns, who can occasionally be glimpsed on the balconies in full habit, hanging laundry or watering their flowers. To visit, ring the bell by pulling the chain in the foyer. The convent also produces and sells typical pastries, including *perrunillas* (almond cookies) and *tocinillos del cielo* (custardlike egg-yolk sweets). ✉ *Pl. Mayor* ☎ *927/320058* *€1* *Mon.–Sat. 10–1 and 4:30–6, Sun. 10–12:30.*

NEED A BREAK?

If the intense summer sun leaves you parched and tired, rehydrate at Bar Pillete Cafeteria (✉ *Pl. Mayor 28* ☎ *927/321449*), where you can buy fresh-squeezed juices, shakes, and other exotic fruit concoctions—a rarity in these remote parts.

The **Palacio del Marqués de la Conquista** (*Palace of the Marquis of the Conquest* ✉ *Pl. Mayor*) is the most dramatic building on the square. Built by Francisco Pizarro's half-brother Hernando, the stone palace is immediately recognizable by its rich covering of early Renaissance plateresque ornamentation. Flanking its corner balcony are imaginative busts of the Pizarro family.

Adjacent to the Palacio de la Conquista is the arcaded former town hall, now a court of law; the alley that runs through its central arch takes you to the **Palacio de Orellana-Pizarro,** which functions as a school and has the most elegant Renaissance courtyard in town. Cervantes, on his way to thank the Virgin of Guadalupe for his release from prison, spent some time writing here. *Free* *Weekdays 10–1 and 4–6, weekends 11–2 and 4–7.*

Trujillo's oldest section, known as **La Villa,** is entirely surrounded by its original, much restored, walls. Follow the wall along Calle Almenas, which runs west from the Palacio de Orellana-Pizarro, beneath the **Alcázar de Los Chaves,** a castle-fortress that was turned into a guest lodge in the 15th century and hosted visiting dignitaries, including Ferdinand and Isabella. The building has seen better days and is now a college. Passing the Alcázar, continue west along the wall to the **Puerta de San Andrés,** one of La Villa's four surviving gates (there were originally seven).

Attached to a Romanesque bell tower, the Gothic **Church of Santa María la Mayor** is occasionally used for masses, but its interior has been virtually untouched since the 16th century. The upper choir has an exquisitely carved balustrade; the coats of arms at each end indicate the seats Ferdinand and Isabella occupied when they attended Mass here. Note the high altar, circa 1480, adorned with great 15th-century Spanish paintings; to see it properly illuminated, place a coin in the box next to the church entrance. Climb up the tower for stunning views of the town and surrounding vast plains stretching toward Cáceres and the Sierra de Gredos. ✉ *Pl. de Santa María* 🎫 *€1* ⏲ *Oct.–Apr., daily 10–2 and 4–7; May–Sept., daily 10–2 and 4–8.*

13

The Pizarro family home has been restored and is now a modest museum, the **Casa Museo de Pizarro,** dedicated to the links between Spain and Latin America. ✉ *Pl. de Santa María* 🎫 *€1* ⏲ *Oct.–Apr., daily 10–2 and 4–6; May–Sept., daily 10–2 and 4–8.*

Near the Puerta de la Coria, housed in a former Franciscan convent, is the **Museo de la Coria.** Its exhibits on Spain and Latin America's connection are similar to those in the Casa Museo de Pizarro (formerly the Pizarro family home) but they're more impressive, with an emphasis on the troops as well as other (non-Pizarro) conquistadors who led missions over the water. ☎ *927/321898* 🎫 *Free* ⏲ *Weekends 11:30–2.*

For spectacular views of the town and its surroundings, climb to the top of the fortress of Trujillo's large **castle,** built by the Moors on Roman foundations. To the south are silos, warehouses, and residential neighborhoods; to the north are only green fields and flowers, partitioned by a maze of nearly leveled Roman stone walls. 🎫 *€1* ⏲ *Oct.–Apr., daily 10–2 and 4–7; May–Sept., daily 10–2 and 5–8:30.*

WHERE TO EAT AND STAY

$–$$$ SPANISH ✕ **Mesón La Troya.** An institution in these parts, this restaurant is fronted by a noisy tapas bar papered with photos of celebrity diners happily posing with the restaurant's late, great owner, Concha. The atmospheric dining room has a barrel-vaulted brick ceiling. If you choose the €22 prix-fixe meal, you're served a starter of *tortilla de patatas* (potato omelet), *chorizo ibérico* (ibérico pork sausage), and a salad. One notable main dish is the *pruebas de cerdo* (ibérico pork casserole with garlic and spices). Arrive ravenous, as the portions are enormous. ✉ *Pl. Mayor 10* ☎ *927/321364* 💳 *MC, V.*

$$–$$$$ SPANISH ★ ✕ **Pizarro.** Traditional Extremaduran home cooking is the draw of this friendly restaurant right on the main plaza in a small but quiet and elegant upstairs dining room. The restaurant is run by two sisters who do nearly everything themselves. A long-revered house specialty is the *gallina trufada* (truffled hen), a sweet-salty recipe with Moorish roots that includes cognac, black truffles, and nutmeg. Once a common Christmas dish in western Spain, the Pizarro sisters are among the few restaurateurs who know how to prepare this recipe today. ✉ *Pl. Mayor 13* ☎ *927/320255* 💳 *MC, V* ⏲ *Closed Tues. and July.*

$$$ ★ 🏨 **Meliá Trujillo.** Once a 16th-century convent, this splendid hotel has a rusty reddish–ocher color scheme on its facade, in its cloisters, and in its courtyard, where there's a swimming pool (much appreciated in the

heat of midsummer) surrounded by wrought-iron furniture. The restaurant in the former refectory serves regional dishes such as wild boar, free-range ibérico pork, and red-leg partridge stewed with broad beans during the October–January hunting season. **Pros:** aesthetically impeccable, friendly and efficient staff. **Cons:** small swimming pool, rooms vary in size. ✉*Pl. del Campillo 1* ☎*927/458900* 🌐*www.solmelia.com* *74 rooms, 3 suites* *In-room: Wi-Fi. In-hotel: restaurant, bar, pool* *AE, DC, MC, V* *BP.*

$$$ ★ **Parador de Trujillo.** Originally the 16th-century Convent of Santa Clara, Trujillo's elegant and cozy parador centers around a harmonious Renaissance courtyard complete with bubbling fountain. The living-in-a-museum quality is reflected in the furniture, paintings, and engravings, though it's still very comfortable. In the restaurant, try the tomato soup spiced with cumin seeds or the *revueltos* (scrambled eggs) with asparagus or mushrooms. Carnivores may prefer one of the game dishes, such as wild boar in an acorn-and-wine sauce. **Pros:** modern bedrooms with historic architecture, gorgeous dining room. **Cons:** rooms are occasionally noisy and some fill with cooking aromas, some rooms are quite small. ✉*C. Santa Beatriz de Silva 1* ☎*927/321350* 🌐*www.parador.es* *48 rooms, 2 suites* *In-room: Wi-Fi. In-hotel: restaurant, bar, pool, public Internet, parking (fee)* *AE, DC, MC, V.*

$$ **Viña Las Torres.** This family-run hotel is in the mountains, 6 mi south of Trujillo. A former private house, the rooms are individually decorated with rustic tiles, rugs, and wrought-iron headboards. A colonnaded terrace overlooks the gardens, tennis court, and pool. This area is renowned for its bird life, thus this quote from a contented guest: "If you want to be serenaded by owls and nightingales outside your window, awake to hoopoe and blue rock thrush on the hotel tower, and view red-rumped swallows nesting in the courtyard, this is the place." **Pros:** views from the tower. **Cons:** isolated from village life, good home cooking but little choice. ✉*EX208, Km 87.6* ☎*927/319350* 🌐*www.vinalastorres.com* *8 rooms* *In-room: Wi-Fi. In-hotel: pool, tennis court, no elevator* *MC, V* *BP.*

SHOPPING

Trujillo sells more folk arts and crafts than almost any other place in Extremadura, among the most attractive of which are multicolor rugs, blankets, and embroideries. **Eduardo Pablos Mateos** (✉*Plazuela de San Judas 12* ☎*927/321066*) specializes in wood carvings, basketwork, and furniture. Several shops on the **Plaza Mayor** have enticing selections; the one just across from the tourist office displays a centuries-old loom along with the work of local craftswoman Maribel Vallar; store hours are erratic.

GUADALUPE

★ *200 km (125 mi) southwest of Madrid, 96 km (60 mi) east of Trujillo.*

ESSENTIALS

Visitor Information Guadalupe (✉*Pl. Santa María de Guadalupe* ☎*927/154128*).

EXPLORING

The **Real Monasterio de Santa María de Guadalupe** *(Royal Monastery of Our Lady of Guadalupe)* is one of the most inspiring sights in Extremadura. Whether you come from Madrid, Trujillo, or Cáceres, the last stage of the ride takes you through wild, astonishingly beautiful mountain scenery. The monastery itself clings to the slopes, forming a profile that echoes the gaunt wall of mountains behind it. Pilgrims have been coming here since the 14th century, but for the past 10 years they have been joined by a growing number of tourists. Even so, the monastery's isolation—it's a good two-hour drive from the nearest town—has saved it from commercial excess. The story of Guadalupe goes back to around 1300, when a local shepherd uncovered a statue of the virgin, supposedly carved by St. Luke. King Alfonso XI, who often hunted here, had a church built to house the statue and later vowed to found a monastery should he defeat the Moors at the battle of Salado in 1340. After his victory, he kept his promise. The greatest period in the monastery's history was between the 15th and 18th centuries, when, under the rule of the Hieronymites, it was turned into a pilgrimage center rivaling Santiago de Compostela in importance. Documents authorizing Columbus's first voyage to the Western Hemisphere were signed here. The Virgin of Guadalupe became the patroness of Latin America, honored by the dedication of thousands of churches and towns in the New World. The monastery's decline coincided with Spain's loss of overseas territories in the 19th century. Abandoned for 70 years and left to decay, it was restored after the civil war.

In the middle of the tiny, irregularly shaped **Plaza Mayor** (also known as the Plaza de Santa María de Guadalupe and transformed during festivals into a bullring) is a 15th-century **fountain,** where Columbus's two American Indian servants were baptized in 1496. Looming in the background is the late-Gothic facade of the **monastery church,** flanked by battlement towers. The entrance to the monastery is to the left of the church. From the large Mudejar cloister, the required guided tour progresses to the **chapter house,** with hymnals, vestments, and paintings, including a series of small panels by Zurbarán. The ornate 17th-century **sacristy** has a series of eight Zurbarán paintings of 1638–47. These austere representations of monks of the Hieronymite order and scenes from the life of St. Jerome are the artist's only significant paintings still in the setting for which they were intended. The tour concludes with the garish, late-baroque **Camarín,** the chapel where the famous Virgen Morena (Black Virgin) is housed. The dark, mysterious wooden figure hides under a heavy veil and mantle of red and gold; painted panels tell the virgin's life story. Each September 8, the virgin is brought down from its altarpiece and a procession walks it around the cloister, with pilgrims following on their knees. Outside, the monastery's gardens have been restored to their original, geometric Moorish style. ✉ *Entrance on Pl. Mayor* ☎ *927/367000* 🌐 *www.monasterioguadalupe.com* 🎫 *€4* 🕒 *Daily 9:30–1 and 3:30–6, guided tours every ½ hr.*

WHERE TO EAT AND STAY

$-$$ SPANISH ✕ **Extremadura.** For authentic flavors and a hearty meal, particularly if you're a fan of Spain's vast assortment of wild mushrooms, try this restaurant just down the road from the monastery. The menu *de la casa* (prix-fixe house menu) includes *migas de pastor* (breadcrumbs cooked with garlic and bits of ham), *sopa de ajo* (garlic soup), *chuletillas de cerdo* (pork chops) with green beans, and *solomillo* (filet mignon) topped with aromatic *setas* (wild mushrooms) of different varieties according to the season. ✉ *Gregorio López 18* ☎ *927/367351.*

$$ Fodor's Choice ★ **Hospedería del Real Monasterio.** An excellent and considerably cheaper alternative to the town parador, this inn was built around the 16th-century Gothic cloister of the monastery itself—the cloister's courtyard is also an outdoor café, open to all, from May to September. The simple, traditional rooms with wood-beam ceilings are handsome and comfortable. Fine local dishes at the restaurant ($–$$) include *caldereta de cabrito* (baby goat stew), *revuelto de cardillos* (scrambled eggs with thistle), and *morcilla de berza* (blood sausage with cabbage). **Pros:** excellent restaurant, helpful staff. **Cons:** bells around the clock. ✉ *Pl. Juan Carlos I s/n* ☎ *927/367000* 🌐 *www.monasterioguadalupe.com* *46 rooms, 1 suite* *In-hotel: restaurant, bar, public Internet* 💳 *MC, V* ⏲ *Closed mid-Jan.–mid-Feb.*

$$$ ★ **Parador de Guadalupe.** The first autopsy in Spain was performed in this building, a 15th-century hospital and then pilgrim's hostel. Despite this prior use, the parador has an unusually luxurious feel, thanks to its Mudejar architecture, Moorish-style rooms, and exotic vegetation. The best rooms look out onto the monastery. The restaurant ($$–$$$) serves simple local dishes, such as *bacalao monacal* ("monastic codfish" with spinach and potatoes) and *frite de cordero* (lamb stew). **Pros:** authentic *extremeño* cooking, stunning architecture. **Cons:** tight parking, long hike from reception to farthest rooms. ✉ *C. Marqués de la Romana 12* ☎ *927/367075* 🌐 *www.parador.es* *41 rooms* *In-room: Wi-Fi. In-hotel: restaurant, bar, tennis court, pool* 💳 *AE, DC, MC, V.*

SHOPPING

On sale everywhere in Guadalupe is the copper-ware that has been crafted here since the 16th century.

LOWER EXTREMADURA

Extremadura's southern half sometimes seems more Andalusian or even Portuguese than classically Spanish, and long stretches of dusty farmland and whitewashed villages make it feel light-years away from Castile. Mérida was established in 25 BC as a settlement for Roman soldiers; it soon became the capital of the Roman province of Lusitania (the western Iberian Peninsula), and its many ruins bear witness to its former splendor. Badajoz has also been a settlement since prehistoric times; Paleolithic remains have been found nearby. Minutes from the Portuguese border, it has long served as a gateway to Portugal and is home to many Portuguese as well as Portuguese descendants. Extremadura's links with Portugal come alive in Olivenza, whereas Zafra, near the southern end of the province, feels more like an Andalusian town.

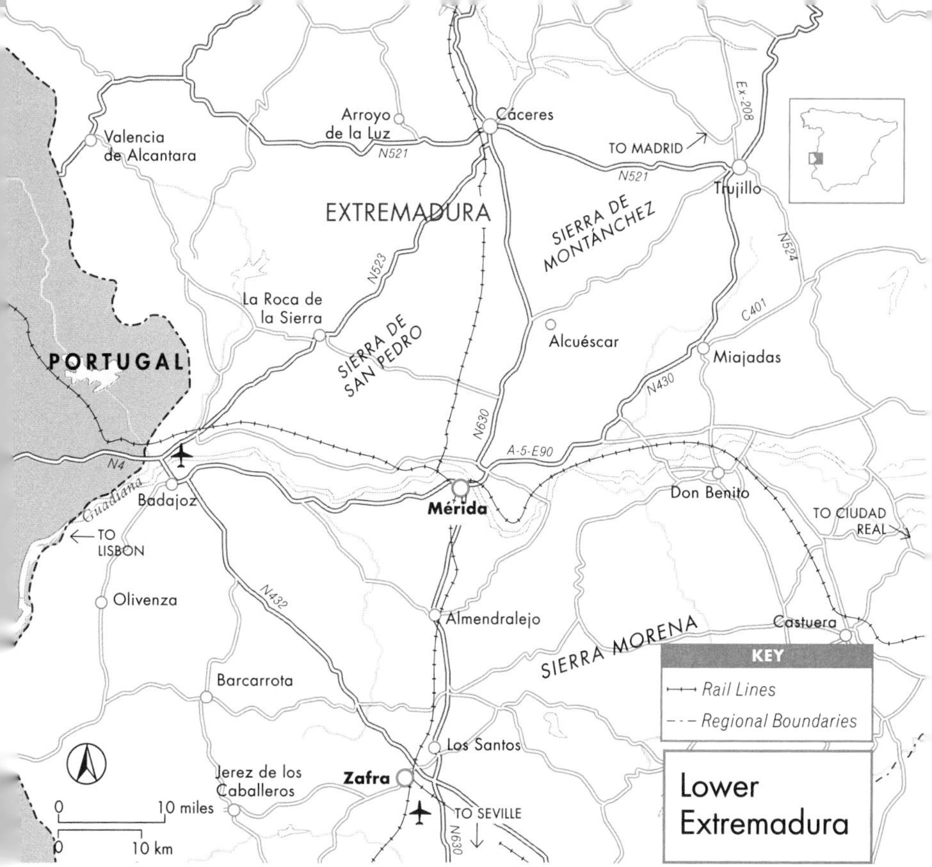

MÉRIDA

70 km (43 mi) south of Cáceres, 250 km (155 mi) north of Seville, 347 km (216 mi) southwest of Madrid.

Mérida is the administrative capital of Extremadura. Strategically situated at the junction of major Roman roads from León to Seville and Toledo to Lisbon, Mérida was founded by the Romans in 25 BC on the banks of the Río Guadiana. Then named Augusta Emerita, it became the capital of the vast Roman province of Lusitania soon after its founding. A bishopric in Visigothic times, Mérida never regained the importance that it had under the Romans, and it's now a rather plain large town—with the exception of its Roman monuments; they pop up all over town, surrounded by thoroughly modern buildings.

The glass-and-steel bus station is in a modern district on the other side of the river from the town center. It commands a good view of the exceptionally long **Roman bridge,** which spans two forks of this sluggish river. On the farther bank is the Alcazaba fortress.

Some other Roman sites require a drive. Across the train tracks in a modern neighborhood is the **circo** (circus), where chariot races were held. Little remains of the grandstands, which seated 30,000, but the outline of the circus is clearly visible and impressive for its size: 1,312

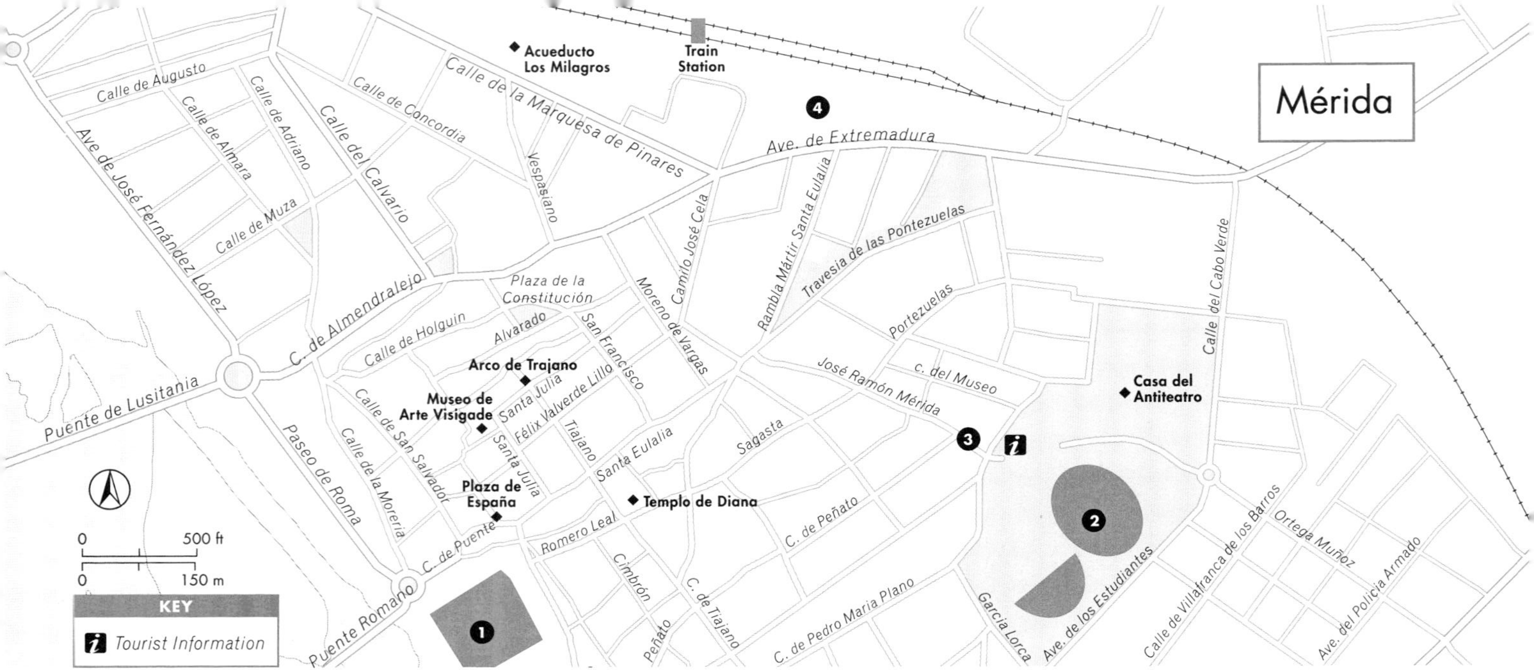

Alcazaba 1

Basilica de Santa Eulalia 4

Museo Nacional de Arte Romano 3

Teatro Romano & Anfiteatro 2

feet long and 377 feet wide. Of the existing aqueduct remains, the most impressive is the **Acueducto de los Milagros** (Aqueduct of Miracles), north of the train station. It carried water from the Roman dam of Proserpina, which still stands, 5 km (3 mi) away.

GETTING HERE AND AROUND

Mérida is definitely walkable, but there is a small tourist train, the Tren Turístico, that does a 35-minute circle past all of the sites for €3, starting from the tourist office.

ESSENTIALS

Tram Contact Tren Turístico (☎ *667/471907*).

Visitor Information Mérida (✉ *C. de Santa Eulalia 64* ☎ *924/330722*).

EXPLORING

2 Fodor's Choice ★ To reach Mérida's best-preserved **Roman monuments**—the **teatro** (theater) and **anfiteatro** (amphitheater)—by car, follow signs to the MUSEO DE ARTE ROMANO. The sites are arranged in a verdant park, and the theater, the best preserved in Spain, is used for a classical drama festival each July; it seats 6,000. The amphitheater, which holds 15,000 spectators, opened in 8 BC for gladiatorial contests. Parking is usually easy to find. Next to the entrance to the Roman ruins is the **main tourist office,** where you can pick up maps and brochures. You can buy a ticket to see only the Roman ruins or, for a slightly higher fee, an *entrada conjunta* (joint admission), which also grants access to the Basílica de Santa Eulalia and the Alcazaba. ✉ *Calle Pedro Maria Plano s/n* ☎ *924/312530* 🎟 *Theater and amphitheater €7; combined admission to Roman sites, basilica, and Alcazaba €10* ⏲ *Oct.–Apr., daily 9:30–1:45 and 4–6:15; May–Sept., 9:30–1:45 and 5–7:15.*

3 ★ Across the street from the entrance to the Roman sites, and connected by an underground passageway, is Mérida's superb, modern **Museo Nacional de Arte Romano** *(National Museum of Roman Art)*, in a monumental building designed by the renowned Spanish architect Rafael Moneo. You walk through a series of passageways to the luminous, cathedral-like main exhibition hall, which is supported by arches the same proportion and size (50 feet) as the Roman arch in the center of Mérida: the Arco de Trajano (Trajan's Arch). The exhibits include mosaics, frescoes, jewelry, statues, pottery, household utensils, and other Roman works. Visit the **crypt** beneath the museum—it houses the remains of several homes and a necropolis that were uncovered while the museum was built, in 1981. ✉ *José Ramón Mélida 2* ☎ *924/311690* 🌐 *www.mnar.es* 🎟 *€3, free Sat. afternoon and Sun.* ⏲ *Oct.–Apr., Tues.–Sat. 10–2 and 4–6, Sun. 10–2; May–Sept., Tues.–Sat. 10–2 and 5–7, Sun. 10–2.*

1 **Alcazaba** *(fortress)*. To get to this sturdy square fortress, built by the Romans and later strengthened by the Visigoths and Moors, continue west from the Museo Nacional de Arte Romano, down Suarez Somontes toward the river and the city center. Turn right at Calle Baños and you can see the towering columns of the **Templo de Diana,** the oldest of Mérida's Roman buildings. To enter the Alzazaba, follow the fortress walls around to the side farthest from the river. Climb up to the battle-

ments for sweeping river views. ☎924/317309 €4 ⏲Oct.–Apr., daily 9:30–1:45 and 4–6; May–Sept., daily 9:30–1:45 and 5–7:15.*

Mérida's main square, the **Plaza de España,** adjoins the northwestern corner of the Alcazaba and is highly animated both day and night. The plaza's oldest building is a 16th-century palace, now a Meliá hotel (there are more atmospheric places to stay). Behind the palace stretches Mérida's most charming area, with Andalusian-style white houses shaded by palms—in the midst of which stands the **Arco de Trajano,** part of a Roman city gate.

4 The **Basílica de Santa Eulalia,** originally a Visigothic structure, marks both the site of a Roman temple and supposedly where the child martyr Eulalia was roasted alive in AD 304 for spitting in the face of a Roman magistrate. In 1990, excavations surrounding the tomb of the famous saint revealed layer upon layer of Paleolithic, Visigothic, Byzantine, and Roman settlements. ✉*Rambla Mártir Santa Eulalia* ☎*924/303407* *€4* ⏲*Oct.–Apr., Mon.–Sat. 10–1:15 and 4–6:15; May–Sept., 10–1:15 and 5–7:15.*

WHERE TO EAT AND STAY

$$$$ SPANISH ✕ **Altair.** Under the same ownership as the renowned Atrio in Cáceres, Altair, on the bank of the Río Guadiana, delivers high-quality regional food with a modern twist. Chef Ramón Caso's specialties include *rollitos crujientes de prueba de ibérico* (crunchy pasta rolls stuffed with pork), *bacalao fresco con manitas de cerdo* (fresh cod with pig's trotters), and *patito asado con miel y higos* (roast duckling baked with honey and figs). Consider going for the six-course tasting menu if you can afford the €60 price tag. A translucent wall facing the river provides a silhouetted view of the Roman Bridge. ✉*Av. José Fernández López s/n* ☎*924/304512* ▭*AE, DC, MC, V* ⏲*Closed Sun.*

$$–$$$ SPANISH ✕ **Casa Benito.** Famous for its tasty tapas and local *pitarra* wine, this atmospheric bar-restaurant founded in 1870 and hidden on a square off Calle Santa Eulalia also has a small, rustic dining area in back with a reasonably priced daily set menu as well as decent à la carte options. The terrace is refreshing in summer, while the bar is popular year-round for its vast selection of morsels of all kinds. The walls are covered with pictures and memorabilia of matadors and bullfights. ✉*C. San Francisco 3* ☎*924/330769* ▭*AE, MC, V* ⏲*Closed Sun.*

¢ SPANISH ✕ **Cervecería 100 Montaditos.** Don't be put off by the fact that this popular local tavern is part of a nationwide chain. It's still an excellent informal restaurant specializing in both classic and creative *montaditos* (canapés or open sandwiches)—at least a hundred of them, topped with anything from torti*lla de patatas* (potato omelette) to *jamón ibérico* to *mousse de pato* (duck pâté), salmon with julienned garlic and parsely, or wild mushrooms. With draught beer or a local wine, these light morsels are tasty and excellent value. ✉*C. Félix Valverde Lillo 3 06800* ☎*924/318105* ▭*AE, MC, V.*

$$–$$$$ SPANISH ✕ **Nicolás.** Mérida's best-known restaurant is in a distinctive house with yellow awnings, near the municipal market. There's a tavern serving tapas downstairs and a dining room upstairs. The regionally inspired food includes *perdiz en escabeche* (marinated partridge), lamb dishes,

and frogs' legs. Desserts might include the traditional *tocino del cielo* made with honey and egg yolks, or a superb and creamy (nearly soupy) sheep cheese from La Serena, usually served with a spoon, called Torta de la Serena. ✉ *Félix Valverde Lillo 13* ☎ *924/319610* 💳 *AE, DC, MC, V* ⊗ *No dinner Sun.*

$$$ ★ **Parador de Mérida.** Built over the remains of a Roman temple that later became a baroque convent and then a prison, this spacious white-washed building exudes an Andalusian cheerfulness, with hints at its Roman and Moorish past. Also called Parador Vía de la Plata, the hotel has bright guest rooms with traditional dark wood furniture. The brilliant-white interior of the convent's former church has been turned into a restful lounge. Try the restaurant's ($$–$$$) *revuelto* (scrambled eggs) prepared in myriad ways, including *con aroma de pimentón* (in paprika sauce) and with *cabrito al ajillo* (baby goat fried with garlic). **Pros:** central location, dazzling light and decor. **Cons:** expensive parking, erratic Wi-Fi signal. ✉ *Pl. Constitución 3* ☎ *924/313800* 🌐 *www.parador.es* *80 rooms, 2 suites* *In-room: Wi-Fi. In-hotel: restaurant, bar, pool, gym, public Wi-Fi, parking (fee)* 💳 *AE, DC, MC, V.*

NIGHTLIFE AND THE ARTS

The many cafés, tapas bars, and restaurants surrounding the Plaza España and in the Plaza de la Constitución fill with boisterous crowds late into the evening. Calle John Lennon, off the northwest corner of the plaza, is your best bet for late-night dance action, especially in summer. As you walk south on Santa Eulalia, the bars get cheaper and the music louder. Locals pack **Rafael II** (✉ *C. Santa Eulalia 13*) for ham, cheese, and sausages; there's also a small, cork-lined dining room in the back.

ZAFRA

62 km (38 mi) south of Mérida, 135 km (84 mi) north of Seville.

ESSENTIALS

Visitor Information Zafra (✉ *Plaza de España 10* ☎ *924/551036*).

EXPLORING

Worth a stop on your way to or from Seville, Zafra is an attractive and lively town with a **Plaza Mayor** that's actually two contiguous squares: the 16th-century Plaza Chica, once a marketplace, and the 18th-century Plaza Grande, ringed by mansions flaunting their coats of arms. Connected by a graceful archway, both plazas make for enjoyable tapas crawls. There are several churches here, too, the finest being **Nuestra Señora de Candelaria** (✉ *Conde de la Corte*) a block west off the Plaza Mayor and a short walk from the parador—its *retablo* (altarpiece) has nine extraordinary panels by Zurbarán.The main reason travelers stop in Zafra, however, is the parador itself, otherwise known as the 15th-century **Alcázar de los Duques de Feria** (✉ *Pl. Corazón de María 7*).

WHERE TO STAY

$$–$$$$ ★ **Casa Palacio Conde de la Corte.** With the theme of bull fighting as the centerpiece at this aristocratic palace built in 1840, the elegant townhouse immerses visitors in the culture of 19th-century Extremadura at its most refined. The central patio surrounded by glass galleries

and covered with a skylight is one of the architectural gems of Spain's southwestern corner, while the rooms speak volumes about the power and grace of Iberia's landed gentry. **Pros:** gorgeous antiques, elegant rooms. **Cons:** in the heart of Zafra, streets are labyrinthical leading in to the square, not easy to find. ✉ *Pl. del Pilar Redondo 2* ☎ *924/563311* 🌐 *www.condedelacorte.com* *15 rooms* *In-room: Wi-Fi. In-hotel: pool, no elevator* ▭ *AE, DC, MC, V.*

$$$ ★ **Parador Hernán Cortés.** This hotel is in the 15th-century castle where Hernán Cortés stayed before his voyage to Mexico. The military exterior conceals a refined and elegant 16th-century courtyard attributed to Juan de Herrera. The suite and the chapel, which together now serve as a conference room, have an elaborate *artesonado* (coffered) ceiling. The rooms surround a Renaissance patio and are spacious and elegant, with high ceilings, antique furniture, and decorative ironwork. At the restaurant ($$), try *pierna de cordero asado* (roasted leg of lamb). **Pros:** elegant Renaissance design, hearty roasts and regional cooking. **Cons:** busy and noisy streets on front side, echoes around patio. ✉ *Pl. Corazón de María 7* ☎ *924/554540* 🌐 *www.parador.es* *51 rooms* *In-room: Wi-Fi. In-hotel: restaurant, pool* ▭ *AE, DC, MC, V.*

$$$$ ★ **Rocamador.** Between Olivenza and Zafra, this peaceful 16th-century hilltop monastery has rooms in the former library, the kitchen, or the monks' cells, with cavernous arches, heavy wooden-beamed ceilings and rustic furniture. The monastery chapel is now a prestigious restaurant ($$$–$$$$) directed by the young Catalan chef Xavier Lahuerta, who combines fresh and seasonal products in an eclectic cuisine based on Extremaduran products, Catalan techniques, and international classics (such as oysters Napoleon with caviar). The two fixed-price tasting menus will more than satisfy your culinary curiosity. Reserve well in advance. **Pros:** flawless rustic-chic decor, gorgeous natural beauty of the surrounding *dehesa* (oak park). **Cons:** isolated, cold in winter. ✉ *Ctra. Nacional Badajoz–Huelva, Km 41.1, Almendral* ☎ *924/489000* 🌐 *www.rocamador.com* *25 rooms, 5 suites* *In-hotel: restaurant, bar, pool, no elevator* ▭ *AE, DC, MC, V* ⏲ *Closed Mon.–Tues., no dinner Sun.*

VOCABULARY

	ENGLISH	SPANISH	PRONUNCIATION
BASICS			
	Hello	Hola	**oh**-la
	Yes/no	Sí/no	see/no
	Please	Por favor	pohr fah-**vohr**
	May I?	¿Me permite?	meh pehr-**mee**-teh
	Thank you (very much)	(Muchas) gracias	(**moo**-chas) **grah**-see-as
	You're welcome	De nada	deh **nah**-dah
	Excuse me	Con permiso/perdón	con pehr-**mee**-so/ pehr-**dohn**
	Pardon me/ what did you say?	¿Perdón?/Mande?	pehr-**dohn/mahn**-deh
	Could you tell me . . . ?	¿Podría decirme . . . ?	po-**dree**-ah deh-**seer**-meh
	I'm sorry	Lo siento	lo see-**en**-to
	Good morning!	¡Buenos días!	**bway**-nohs **dee**-ahs
	Good afternoon!	¡Buenas tardes!	**bway**-nahs **tar**-dess
	Good evening!	¡Buenas noches!	**bway**-nahs **no**-chess
	Goodbye!	¡Adiós!/ ¡Hasta luego!	ah-dee-**ohss/ ah**-stah-**lwe**-go
	Mr./Mrs.	Señor/Señora	sen-**yor**/sen-**yohr**-ah
	Miss	Señorita	sen-yo-**ree**-tah
	Pleased to meet you	Mucho gusto	**moo**-cho **goose**-to
	How are you?	¿Cómo está usted?	**ko**-mo es-**tah** oo-**sted**
	Very well, thank you.	Muy bien, gracias.	**moo**-ee bee-**en, grah**-see-as
	And you?	¿Y usted?	ee oos-**ted**
	Hello (on the phone)	Diga	**dee**-gah
DAYS OF THE WEEK			
	Sunday	domingo	doh-**meen**-goh
	Monday	lunes	**loo**-ness
	Tuesday	martes	**mahr**-tess
	Wednesday	miércoles	me-**air**-koh-less
	Thursday	jueves	hoo-**ev**-ess
	Friday	viernes	vee-**air**-ness

Saturday	sábado	**sah**-bah-doh

NUMBERS

1	un, uno	oon, **oo**-no
2	dos	dohs
3	tres	tress
4	cuatro	**kwah**-tro
5	cinco	**sink**-oh
6	seis	saice
7	siete	see-**et**-eh
8	ocho	**o**-cho
9	nueve	new-**eh**-veh
10	diez	dee-**es**
11	once	**ohn**-seh
12	doce	**doh**-seh
13	trece	**treh**-seh
14	catorce	ka-**tohr**-seh
15	quince	**keen**-seh
16	dieciséis	dee-**es**-ee-**saice**
17	diecisiete	dee-**es**-ee-see-**et**-eh
18	dieciocho	dee-**es**-ee-**o**-cho
19	diecinueve	dee-**es**-ee-new-**ev**-eh
20	veinte	**vain**-teh
21	veinte y uno/ veintiuno	**vain**-te-oo-noh
30	treinta	**train**-tah
32	treinta y dos	train-tay-**dohs**
40	cuarenta	kwah-**ren**-tah
50	cincuenta	seen-**kwen**-tah
60	sesenta	sess-**en**-tah
70	setenta	set-**en**-tah
80	ochenta	oh-**chen**-tah
90	noventa	no-**ven**-tah
100	cien	see-**en**
200	doscientos	doh-see-**en**-tohss
500	quinientos	keen-**yen**-tohss
1,000	mil	meel
2,000	dos mil	dohs meel

USEFUL PHRASES

Do you speak English?	¿Habla usted inglés?	**ah**-blah oos-**ted** in-**glehs**
I don't speak Spanish	No hablo español	no **ah**-bloh es-pahn-**yol**
I don't understand (you)	No entiendo	no en-tee-**en**-doh
I understand (you)	Entiendo	en-tee-**en**-doh
I don't know	No sé	no seh
I am American/ British	Soy americano (americana)/ inglés(a)	soy ah-meh-ree-**kah**-no (ah-meh-ree-**kah**-nah)/in-**glehs**(ah)
My name is . . .	Me llamo . . .	meh **yah**-moh
Yes, please/ No, thank you	Sí, por favor/ No, gracias	**see** pohr fah-**vor**/ no **grah**-see-ahs
Yesterday/today/ tomorrow	Ayer/hoy/mañana	ah-**yehr**/oy/mahn-**yah**-nah
This morning/ afternoon	Esta mañana/tarde	**es**-tah mahn-**yah**-nah/**tar**-deh
Tonight	Esta noche	**es**-tah **no**-cheh
This/Next week	Esta semana/ la semana que entra	**es**-tah seh-**mah**-nah/lah seh-**mah**-nah keh **en**-trah
This/Next month	Este mes/el próximo mes	**es**-teh mehs/el **prok**-see-moh mehs
How?	¿Cómo?	**koh**-mo
When?	¿Cuándo?	**kwahn**-doh
What?	¿Qué?	keh
What is this?	¿Qué es esto?	keh es **es**-toh
Why?	¿Por qué?	por **keh**
Who?	¿Quién?	kee-**yen**
Where is . . . ?	¿Dónde está . . . ?	**dohn**-deh es-**tah**
the train station?	la estación del tren?	la es-tah-see-**on** del **train**
the subway station?	la estación del metro?	la es-ta-see-**on** del **meh**-tro
the bus stop?	la parada del autobus?	la pah-**rah**-dah del oh-toh-**boos**
the bank?	el banco?	el **bahn**-koh
the hotel?	el hotel?	el oh-**tel**
the post office?	la oficina de correos?	la oh-fee-**see**-nah deh-koh-**reh**-os
the museum?	el museo?	el moo-**seh**-oh
the hospital?	el hospital?	el ohss-pee-**tal**
the bathroom?	el baño?	el **bahn**-yoh

Here/there	Aquí/allá	ah-**key**/ah-**yah**
Open/closed	Abierto/cerrado	ah-bee-**er**-toh/ ser-**ah**-doh
Left/right	Izquierda/derecha	iss-key-**er**-dah/ dare-**eh**-chah
Straight ahead	Todo recto	**toh**-doh-**rec**-toh
Is it near/far?	¿Está cerca/lejos?	es-**tah sehr**-kah/ **leh**-hoss
I'd like . . . a room the key a newspaper a stamp	Quisiera . . . una habitación la llave un periódico un sello	kee-see-**ehr**-ah **oo**-nah ah-bee-tah-see-**on** lah **yah**-veh oon pehr-ee-**oh**-dee-koh **say**-oh
How much is this?	¿Cuánto cuesta?	**kwahn**-toh **kwes**-tah
A little/a lot	Un poquito/ mucho	oon poh-**kee**-toh/ **moo**-choh
More/less	Más/menos	mahss/**men**-ohss
I am ill	Estoy enfermo(a)	es-**toy** en-**fehr**-moh(mah)
Please call a doctor	Por favor llame un médico	pohr fah-**vor ya**-meh oon **med**-ee-koh
Help!	¡Ayuda!	ah-**yoo**-dah

ON THE ROAD

Avenue	Avenida	ah-ven-**ee**-dah
Broad, tree-lined boulevard	Paseo	pah-**seh**-oh
Highway	Carretera	car-reh-**ter**-ah
Port; mountain pass	Puerto	poo-**ehr**-toh
Street	Calle	**cah**-yeh
Waterfront promenade	Paseo marítimo	pah-**seh**-oh mahr-**ee**-tee-moh

IN TOWN

Cathedral	Catedral	cah-teh-**dral**
Church	Iglesia	**tem**-plo/ee-**glehs**-see-ah
City hall, town hall	Ayuntamiento	ah-yoon-tah-me-**yen**-toh
Door, gate	Puerta	poo-**ehr**-tah
Main square	Plaza Mayor	plah-thah mah-**yohr**
Market	Mercado	mer-**kah**-doh

Neighborhood	Barrio	**bahr**-ree-o
Tavern, rustic restaurant	Mesón	meh-**sohn**
Traffic circle, roundabout	Glorieta	glor-ee-**eh**-tah
Wine cellar, wine bar, wine shop	Bodega	boh-**deh**-gah

DINING OUT

A bottle of . . .	Una botella de . . .	**oo**-nah bo-**teh**-yah deh
A glass of . . .	Un vaso de . . .	oon **vah**-so deh
Bill/check	La cuenta	lah **kwen**-tah
Breakfast	El desayuno	el deh-sah-**yoon**-oh
Dinner	La cena	lah **seh**-nah
Menu of the day	Menú del día	meh-**noo** del **dee**-ah
Fork	El tenedor	ehl ten-eh-**dor**
Is the tip included?	¿Está incluida la propina?	es-**tah** in-cloo-**ee**-dah lah pro-**pee**-nah
Knife	El cuchillo	el koo-**chee**-yo
Large portion of tapas	Ración	rah-see-**ohn**
Lunch	La comida	lah koh-**mee**-dah
Menu	La carta, el menú	lah **cart**-ah, el meh-**noo**
Napkin	La servilleta	lah sehr-vee-**yet**-ah
Please give me . . .	Por favor déme . . .	pohr fah-**vor** **deh**-meh
Spoon	Una cuchara	**oo**-nah koo-**chah**-rah

MENU GUIDE

STARTERS

aguacate con gambas avocado and prawns
caldo thick soup
champiñones al ajillo mushrooms in garlic
consomé clear soup
gazpacho chilled soup made with tomatoes, onions, peppers, cucumbers, and oil
huevos flamencos eggs with spicy sausage and tomato
judías con tomate/jamón green beans with tomato/ham
sopa soup
sopa de ajo garlic soup
sopa de garbanzos chickpea soup
sopa de lentejas lentil soup
sopa de mariscos shellfish soup
sopa sevillana soup made with mayonnaise, shellfish, asparagus, and peas

OMELETS (TORTILLAS)

tortilla de champiñones mushroom omelet
tortilla de gambas prawn omelet
tortilla de mariscos seafood omelet
tortilla de patatas, tortilla española Spanish potato omelet
tortilla francesa plain omelet
tortilla sacromonte (in Granada) omelet with ham, sausage, and peas

MEATS (CARNES)

beicón bacon
bistec steak
cerdo pork
lomo de cerdo pork tenderloin
cabrito roasted kid
chorizo seasoned sausage
chuleta chop, cutlet
cochinillo suckling pig
cordero lamb
filete steak
jamón ham
jamón de York cooked ham
jamón serrano cured raw ham
morcilla blood sausage
salchicha sausage
salchichón Spanish salami (cured pork sausage)
solomillo de ternera fillet of beef
ternera veal

POULTRY (AVES) AND GAME (CAZA)

conejo rabbit
cordonices quail
faisán pheasant
jabalí wild boar
oca, ganso goose
pato duck
pato salvaje wild duck
pavo turkey
perdiz partridge
pollo chicken

ORGAN MEATS

callos tripe
criadillas bull's testicles (shown on Spanish menus as "unmentionables")
hígado liver
lengua tongue
mollejas sweetbreads
riñones kidneys
sesos brains

FISH (PESCADOS)

ahumados smoked fish (i.e. trout, eel, salmon)
anchoas anchovies
anguila eel
angulas baby eel
atún, bonito tuna
bacalao salt cod
besugo sea bream
boquerones fresh anchovies
lenguado sole
lubina sea bass
merluza hake, whitefish
mero grouper fish
pez espada, emperador swordfish
rape angler fish
raya skate
salmón salmon
salmonete red mullet
sardina sardine
trucha trout

SHELLFISH AND SEAFOOD (MARISCOS)
almeja clam
calamares squid
cangrejo crab
centolla spider crab
chipirones, chopitos small squid
cigalas crayfish
concha scallops
gambas prawns, shrimp
langosta lobster
langostino prawn
mejillones mussels
ostra oyster
percebes barnacles
pulpo octopus
sepia cuttlefish
vieiras scallop (in Galicia)
zarzuela de mariscos shellfish casserole

VEGETABLES (VERDURAS)
aceituna olive
aguacate avocado
ajo garlic
alcachofa artichoke
apio celery
berenjena eggplant
berza green cabbage
brécol/bróculi broccoli
calabacín zucchini
cebollo onion
calabaza pumpkin
champiñon mushroom
col cabbage
coliflor cauliflower
endivia endive
escarola chicory
ensalada salad
ensaladilla rusa potato salad
espárragos asparagus
espinacas spinach
espinacas a la catalana spinach with garlic, rasins, and pine nuts
garbanzos chickpeas
guisantes peas
habas broad beans
judías dried beans
judías verdes green beans
lechuga lettuce
lenteja lentil
palmitos palm hearts
patata potato
pepinillo gherkin
pepino cucumber
pimientos green/red peppers
puerro leek
seta chanterelle
tomate tomato
verduras green vegetables
zanahoria carrot

FRUIT (FRUTAS)
albaricoque apricot
ananás, piña pineapple
cereza cherry
chirimoya custard apple
ciruela plum
frambuesa raspberry
fresa strawberry
fresón large strawberry
grosella negra black currant
limón lemon
manzana apple
melocotón peach
melón melon
naranja orange
pera pear
plátano banana
sandía watermelon
uvas grapes
zarzamora blackberry

DESSERTS (POSTRES)
bizcocho, galleta biscuit
bizocho de chocolate chocolate cake
buñuelos warm, sugared, deep-fried doughnuts, sometimes cream-filled
con nata with cream
cuajada thick yogurt with honey
ensalada de frutas, macedonia fruit salad
flan caramel custard
fresas con nata strawberries and cream
helado de vainilla, fresa, café, chocolate vanilla, strawberry, coffee, chocolate ice cream
melocotón en almibar canned peaches
pastel cake
pera en almibar canned pears
pijama ice cream with fruit and syrup
piña en almibar canned pineapple

postre de músico dessert of dried fruit and nuts
la tarta de queso cheesecake
tarta helada ice-cream cake
la tartaleta de frutas fruit cake
yogur yogurt

MISCELLANEOUS

a la brasa barbequed
a la parrilla grilled
a la plancha grilled
aceite de oliva olive oil
al horno roasted, baked
arroz rice
asado roast
azúcar sugar
carbonade pot roasted
churros: baton-shaped donuts for dipping in hot chocolate, typically eaten at breakfast.
crudo raw
espaguettis spaghetti
fideos noodles
frito fried
guisado stewed
huevo egg
mahonesa mayonnaise
mantequilla butter
mermelada jam
miel honey
mostaza mustard
pan bread
patatas fritas french fries
perejil parsley
poché poached
queso cheese
relleno filled, stuffed
sal salt
salsa sauce
salsa de tomate catsup
vinagre vinegar

DRINKS (BEBIDAS)

agua water
agua con gas carbonated mineral water
agua sin gas still mineral water
blanco y negro cold black coffee with vanilla ice cream
café con leche coffee with cream
café solo black coffee (espresso)
caliente hot
caña small draught beer
cava, champán sparkling wine, champagne
cerveza beer
chocolate hot chocolate
cuba libre rum and coke
fino very dry sherry
frío/fría cold
gaseosa soda
granizado de limón (de café) lemon (or coffee) on crushed ice
hielo ice
horchata cold summer drink made from ground nuts
jerez sherry
jugo fruit juice
leche milk
limonada lemonade
manzanilla very dry sherry or camomile tea
sidra cider
té tea
con limón with lemon
con leche with milk
vaso glass
un vaso de agua a glass of water
vermut vermouth
vino wine
vino añejo vintage wine
vino blanco white wine
vino dulce sweet wine
vino espumoso sparkling wine
vino rosado rosé
vino seco dry wine
vino tinto red wine
zumo de naranja orange juice

Travel Smart Spain

WORD OF MOUTH

"The AVE is a wonderful thing. Both the trip between Seville and Madrid and Toledo and Madrid were flawless and on time. The trains are comfortable and Atocha station is a marvel (I commute out of North Station in Boston, so if you're familiar with that you'll know that I am green with envy over Atocha!)."

—amyb

"I agree with those who recommend you read through the trip reports in this forum [fodors.com]. They were invaluable in helping plan our recent 10 day trip to Spain."

—screen_name_taken

GETTING HERE AND AROUND

BY AIR

Flying time from New York to Madrid is about seven hours; from London, it's just over two hours.

Regular nonstop flights serve Spain from many major cities in the eastern United States; flying from other North American cities usually involves a stop. If you're coming from North America and want to land in a city other than Madrid or Barcelona, consider flying a British or other European carrier.

There are a few solid package flight options for travel to and within Spain. If you buy a round-trip transatlantic ticket on Iberia, you might want to purchase an Iberiabono Spain air pass, which provides access to economy-class travel across Spain (its maximum period of use corresponds to the time for which the international ticket is valid). The pass must be purchased before you arrive in Spain, and all flights must be booked in advance; the cost starts at €60 per ticket, with a minimum purchase of two. On certain days of the week, Iberia also offers *minitarifas* (minifares), which can save you up to 40% on domestic flights. Tickets must be purchased at least two days in advance, and you must stay over Saturday night. Another option is to join the Iberia Plus Internet club, which can offer exceptionally low fares.

The Europe By Air Flight Pass is a unique flat-rate ticket. For $99 or $129 per flight within Europe, and with no minimum purchase, you get access to more than 170 destinations on 20-plus airlines. There are no blackout dates, no charges for reservation charges, and no fare zones.

Air Europa offers a special called "Talonair 20," which allows travelers to choose nonstop flights in coach on any of its domestic routes (except to the Canary Islands, which requires two coupons).

FODORS.COM CONNECTION

Before your trip, be sure to check out what other travelers are saying in the forums on www.fodors.com.

Since 2004, there's been a revolution in cheap flights from the United Kingdom to Spain, with the emergence of scores of new carriers such as Monarch (*www.flymonarch.com*) and bmi (*www.flybmi.com*) providing competition to the market's main players—easyJet (*www.easyjet.com*) and Ryanair (*www.ryanair.com*). All these carriers offer frequent flights, cover small cities as well as large ones, and have very competitive fares. Attitude Travel (*www.attitude travel.com/lowcostairlines*), Skyscanner (*www.skyscanner.net*), and Wegolo (*www.wegolo.com*) are comprehensive search sites for low-cost airlines worldwide.

Contacts Air Europa (*800/238–7672 in the U.S. or 902/401501 in Spain* *www.air-europa.com*). **FlightPass** (*888/321–4737* *www.europebyair.com*). **Iberia** (*800/772–4642* *www.iberia.com*).

Transportation Security Administration (*www.tsa.gov*) has answers for almost every question that might come up.

AIRPORTS

Most flights from the United States and Canada land in, or pass through, Madrid's Barajas (MAD). The other major gateway is Barcelona's El Prat de Llobregat (BCN). From England and elsewhere in Europe, regular flights also land in Málaga (AGP), Alicante (ALC), Palma de Mallorca (PMI), and many other smaller cities, too. Many of the new budget airlines flying from the United Kingdom to Barcelona land at the increasingly busy Girona airport, some 90 minutes north of Barcelona. The bus company Sagalés runs a shuttle service between Girona's airport and Barcelona in conjunction with the departure and arrival times of Ryanair flights.

Airport Information **Madrid-Barajas** (☎ *91/30-58343* 🌐 *www.aena.es*). **Barcelona-El Prat de Llobregat** (☎ *902/404704* 🌐 *www.aena.es*). **Girona-Girona** (☎ *972/186600*). **Sagalés Buses** (☎ *902/361550* 🌐 *www.sagales.com*).

FLIGHTS

From North America, Air Europa and Spanair fly to Madrid; American, Continental, Delta, Iberia, and USAirways fly to Madrid and Barcelona—some of these airlines use shared facilities and do not operate their own flights. Within Spain, Iberia is the main domestic airline, but Air Europa and Spanair fly most domestic routes at lower prices. The budget airline Vueling (now merged with rival lost-cost carrier Clickair) heavily promotes its Internet bookings, which are often the country's cheapest domestic flight prices. The further from your travel date you purchase the ticket, the more bargains you're likely to find. Air Europa and Spanair also travel both within Spain and to the rest of Europe.

Iberia runs a shuttle, the *puente aereo*, offering flights just over an hour long between Madrid and Barcelona, every 15 minutes from around 7 AM to 11 PM. You don't need to reserve ahead; you can buy your tickets at the airport ticket counter upon arriving or book online at Iberia.com. Passengers can also use the newly installed self-service check-in counters to avoid queues. Terminal C in the Barcelona airport is used exclusively by the shuttle; in Madrid, the shuttle departs from Iberia-only Terminal 4.

Airline Contacts **Air Europa** (☎ *888/238-7672 in the U.S.; 902/401501 or 807/505050 in Spain* 🌐 *www.air-europa.com*). **American Airlines** (☎ *800/4337300* 🌐 *www.aa.com*). **Continental Airlines** (☎ *800/523-3273 for U.S. and Mexico reservations, 800/231-0856 for international reservations* 🌐 *www.continental.com*). **Delta Airlines** (☎ *800/221-1212 for U.S. reservations, 800/241-4141 for international reservations* 🌐 *www.delta.com*). **Iberia** (☎ *800/772-4642* 🌐 *www.iberia.com*). **Northwest Airlines** (☎ *800/225-2525* 🌐 *www.nwa.com*). **Spanair** (☎ *888/545-5757* 🌐 *www.spanair.com*). **United Airlines** (☎ *800/864-8331 for U.S. reservations, 800/538-2929 for international reservations* 🌐 *www.united.com*). **USAirways** (☎ *800/428-4322 for U.S. and Canada reservations, 800/622-1015 for international reservations* 🌐 *www.usairways.com*).

Within Spain **Air Europa** (☎ *902/401501 or 807/505050* 🌐 *www.air-europa.com*). **Iberia** (☎ *902/400500 or 807/123456* 🌐 *www.iberia.com*). **Spanair** (☎ *902/131415 or 807/5051052* 🌐 *www.spanair.com*). **Vueling** (☎ *902/333933 or 807/001717* 🌐 *www.vueling.com*).

BY BIKE

Taking bikes on Spanish intercity trains is restricted to overnight trains (on which bikes go under your bunk). Short-range daytime trains normally accept bicycles, though the conductor may decide that the train's too crowded and bump you and your bike. The very expensive alternative is to courier them. Cycling on freeways is against the law. For bike rentals, contact local tourist offices or check with rural hotels; we list some in individual cities.

BY BOAT

Regular car ferries connect the United Kingdom with northern Spain. Brittany Ferries sails from Plymouth and Portsmouth to Santander; P&O European Ferries sails from Portsmouth to Bilbao. Trasmediterránea and Balearia connect mainland Spain to the Balearic and Canary islands. Direct ferries from Spain to Tangier leave daily from Tarifa (on FRS, which also operates from Gibraltar) and from Algeciras (on Trasmediterránea). Otherwise, you can take your car either to Ceuta (via Algeciras, on Balearia) or Melilla (via Malaga, on Trasmediterránea), two Spanish enclaves on the North African coast, and then move on to Morocco.

INFORMATION

U.K. to Spain Brittany Ferries (☎ *0870/907–6103 in U.K., 94/236–0611 in Spain* 🌐 *www.brittany-ferries.com*). **Direct Ferries (booking site)** (🌐 *www.directferries.co.uk*). **P&O European Ferries** (☎ *0871/664–8005 in U.K., 902/020461 in Spain* 🌐 *www.poferries.com*).

In Spain Balearia (☎ *902/160180* 🌐 *www.balearia.com*). **FRS** (☎ *956/681830* 🌐 *www.frs.es*). **Trasmediterránea** (☎ *902/454645* 🌐 *www.trasmediterranea.com*). **Grimaldi** (☎ *902/531333* 🌐 *www.grimaldi-ferries.com*).

BY BUS

Within Spain, a mix of private companies provides bus services that ranges from knee-crunchingly basic to luxurious. Fares are almost always lower than the corresponding train fares, and service is more extensive: if you want to reach a town not served by train, you can be sure a bus goes there. Smaller towns don't usually have a central bus depot, so ask the tourist office where to wait for the bus to your destination. Note that service is less frequent on weekends. Spain's major national long-haul bus line is Alsa-Enatcar.

For longer hauls, you can travel to Spain by bus (Eurolines/National EXpress, for example) from European destinations such as London, Paris, Rome, Frankfurt, Prague, and other major European cities. It's a long journey, but the buses are modern. Although it may once have been the case that international bus travel was significantly cheaper than air travel, new budget airlines have changed the equation. For perhaps a little more money and a large savings of travel hours, flying is increasingly the better option.

Most of Spain's larger bus companies have buses with comfortable seats and adequate legroom; on longer journeys (two hours or longer), a movie is shown on board, and earphones are provided. Except for smaller, regional buses that travel only short hops, all buses have bathrooms on board; most long-haul buses also usually stop at least once every two to three hours for a snack and bathroom break. Smoking is prohibited on board.

Alsa-Enatcar has two luxury classes in addition to its regular seating. Supra Clase includes roomy leather seats and onboard meals; also, you have the option of *asientos individuales*, individual seats (with no other seat on either side) that line one side of the bus. The next class is the Eurobus, with comfortable seats and plenty of legroom. The Supra Clase and Eurobus usually cost, respectively, up to one-third and one-fourth more than the regular seats.

If you plan to return to your initial destination, you can save by buying a round-trip ticket. Also, some of Spain's smaller, regional bus lines offer multitrip passes, which are worthwhile if you plan to move back and forth between two fixed destinations within the region. Generally, these tickets offer a savings of 20% per journey; you can buy them only in the bus station (not on the bus). The general rule for children is that if they occupy a seat, they pay. Check the bus Web sites for deals (*ofertas*); you'll often find discounts for midweek and/or round-trip tickets to specific destinations.

In Spain's larger cities, you can pick up schedule and fare information at the bus station; smaller towns may not have a bus station but just a bus stop. Schedules are usually posted at the bus stop itself; otherwise, call the bus company directly or ask at the tourist office, which can usually supply all schedule and fare information.

At bus station ticket counters, generally all major credit cards (except American Express) are accepted. If you buy your ticket on the bus, it's cash only. Big lines such as Enatcar are now encouraging online purchasing. Once your ticket is booked, there's no need to go to the terminal sales desk—it's simply a matter of showing up at the bus with your ticket number and ID. The smaller regional services are increasingly providing online purchasing, too, but will often require that your ticket be picked up at the terminal sales desk.

During peak travel times (Easter, August, and Christmas), it's a good idea to make a reservation at least a week in advance.

From the U.K. **Eurolines/National Express** (☎ *0871/781-8181* 🌐 *www.eurolines.co.uk*).

In Spain **Alsa-Enatcar** (✉ *Estación Sur de Autobuses, Calle Méndez Álvaro, Madrid* ☎ *902/422242* 🌐 *www.enatcar.com*). **Eurolines Spain** (☎ *902/405040* 🌐 *www.eurolines.es*). **Movelia (booking site)** (☎ *902/335533* 🌐 *www.movelia.es*).

Bus Tours **Marsans** (✉ *Calle Mahonia 2, ed. Pórtico, Madrid* ☎ *902/306090*). **Pullmantur** (✉ *Pl. de Oriente 8, Madrid* ☎ *91/541-1805* 🌐 *www.pullmantur-spain.com*).

BY CAR

RENTAL CARS

Alamo, Avis, Budget, Europcar, Hertz, and National (partnered in Spain with the Spanish agency Atesa) have branches at major Spanish airports and in large cities. Smaller, regional companies and wholesalers offer lower rates. The online outfit Pepe Car has been a big hit with travelers; in general, the earlier you book, the less you pay. All agencies have a range of models, but virtually all cars in Spain have a manual transmission. **TIP→ If you don't want a stick shift, reserve weeks in advance and specify automatic transmission, then call to reconfirm your automatic car before you leave for Spain.** Rates in Madrid begin at the equivalents of U.S.$65 a day and $300 a week for an economy car with air-conditioning, manual transmission, and unlimited mileage. Add to this a 16% tax. Although you should always rent the size car that makes you feel safest, a small car, aside from saving you money, is prudent for the tiny roads and parking spaces in many parts of Spain.

Anyone over 18 with a valid license can drive in Spain, but some rental agencies will not rent cars to drivers under 21.

Major Agencies **Alamo** (☎ *877/222-9075* 🌐 *www.alamo.com*). **Avis** (☎ *800/331-1084, 902/135531 in Spain* 🌐 *www.avis.com*). **Budget** (☎ *800/472-3325, 901/201212 in Spain* 🌐 *www.budget.com*). **Europcar** (☎ *902/105030 in Spain* 🌐 *www.europcar.es*). **Hertz** (☎ *800/654-3001, 902/402405 in Spain* 🌐 *www.hertz.com*). **National Car Rental/Atesa** (☎ *800/227-7368, 902/100101 in Spain* 🌐 *www.atesa.es*). **Pepe Car** (☎ *807/414243 in Spain* 🌐 *www.pepecar.com*).

Your own driver's license is valid in Spain, but U.S. citizens planning to drive here are highly encouraged to obtain an International Driving Permit (IDP) before they come to Spain. The IDP may facilitate car rental and help you avoid traffic fines—it translates your state-issued driver's license into 10 languages so officials can easily interpret the information on it. Permits are available from the American or Canadian Automobile Association (AAA or CAA), or, in the United Kingdom, from the Automobile Association or Royal Automobile Club (AA or RAC). These international permits, valid only in conjunction with your regular driver's license (so have both on hand), are universally recognized. For more information, contact Spanish Traffic Authorities (☎ *900/123505*)

Driving is the best way to see Spain's rural areas. The main cities are connected by a network of excellent four-lane *autovías* (freeways) and *autopistas* (tollways; "toll" is *peaje*), which are designated with the letter A and have speed limits—depending on the area—of between 80 KPH (50 MPH) to 120 KPH (74 MPH). The letter N indicates a *carretera nacional* (basic national route), which may have four or two lanes, but these days they have largely been replaced with an E prefix, denoting the European route number, and an A prefix, denoting the new national route number. Smaller towns and villages are connected by a network of secondary roads maintained by regional, provincial, and local governments. Spain's major routes bear heavy traffic, especially during holidays. Drive with care: the annual death toll on Spain's roads is ghastly—most accidents are speed related. The roads are shared by a potentially perilous mixture of local drivers and non-Spanish vacationers, some of whom are accustomed to driving on the left side of the road. Be prepared, too, for heavy truck traffic on national routes, which, in the case of two-lane roads, can have you creeping along for hours.

GASOLINE

Gas stations are plentiful, and most on major routes and in big cities are open 24 hours. On less-traveled routes, gas stations are usually open 7 AM–11 PM. If a gas station is closed, it's required by law to post the address and directions to the nearest open station—but this is rarely adhered to, so plan your trip carefully. Most stations are self-service, though prices are the same as those at full-service stations. You punch in the amount of gas you want (in euros, not in liters), unhook the nozzle, pump the gas, and then pay. At night, however, you must pay before you fill up. Most pumps offer a choice of gas, including leaded, unleaded, and diesel, so be careful to pick the right one for your car. All newer cars in Spain use *gasolina sin plomo* (unleaded gas), which is available in two grades, 95 and 98 octane. *Super,* regular 97-octane leaded gas, is gradually being phased out. Prices vary little among stations and were at this writing €1 a liter for leaded, 97 octane; €1 a liter for unleaded, 95 octane; and €1.05 a liter for unleaded, 98 octane. A good site to monitor prices is 🌐*www.aaroadwatch.ie/eupetrolprices*. Credit cards are widely accepted.

PARKING

Parking is, almost without exception, a nightmare in Spanish cities and towns. Don't park where the curb is painted yellow or where there is a yellow line painted a few inches from the curb. No-parking signs are also fairly easy to recognize. In most cities, there are street parking spaces marked by blue lines. Look for a nearby machine with a blue and white "P" sign to purchase a parking ticket, which you leave inside your car, on the dashboard, before you lock up. Sometimes an attendant will be nearby to answer questions. Parking time limits, fees, and fines vary. Parking lots are available, often underground, but spaces are at a premium. Another frequent problem is that many cities now have one-way systems, and it can be more than frustrating to drive around and around trying to find an empty space. The rule of thumb is if you don't need to go into a city or town center with your car, then leave it at your hotel and take public transport or a taxi.

ROAD CONDITIONS

Spain's highway system includes some 6,000 km (3,600 mi) of beautifully maintained superhighways. Still, you'll find some stretches of major national highways that are only two lanes wide, where traffic often backs up behind slow, heavy trucks. *Autopista* tolls are steep, but as a result, these highways are often less crowded than the free ones. If you're driving down through Catalonia, be aware that there are more tolls here than anywhere else in Spain. This can result in a quicker journey but at a sizable cost. If you spring for the autopistas, you'll find that many of the rest stops are nicely landscaped and have cafeterias with decent but overpriced food. Skip the platters: a cheese or ham *bocadillo* (baguette-style sandwich) offers a much cheaper and often tastier alternative.

Most Spanish cities have notoriously long morning and evening rush hours. Traffic jams are especially bad in and around Barcelona and Madrid. If possible, avoid the morning rush, which can last until noon, and the evening rush, which lasts from 7 to 9. Also be aware that on the dates corresponding to the beginning, the middle, and the end of July and August, the country suffers its worst traffic jams (delays of six to eight hours are common) as millions of Spaniards embark on, or return from, their annual vacations.

ROADSIDE EMERGENCIES

The rental agencies Hertz and Avis have 24-hour breakdown service. If you belong to an auto club (AAA, CAA, or AA), you can get emergency assistance from the Spanish counterpart, RACE.

Emergency Services RACE (✉ RACE Oficinas centrales Isaac Newton 4, Parque Tecnológico de Madrid ☎ *902/404545 for info, 902/300505 for assistance* 🌐 *www.race.es*).

RULES OF THE ROAD

Spaniards drive on the right; they pass on the left, so stay in the right-hand slow lane when not passing. Horns are banned in cities—a rule Spaniards ferociously ignore when something is holding them up. Children under 12 may not ride in the front seat, and seat belts are compulsory for both front- and backseat riders. Speed limits are 50 KPH (31 MPH) in cities, 100 KPH (62 MPH) on N roads, 120 kph (74 MPH) on the *autopista* or *autovía*, and, unless otherwise signposted, 90 KMPH (56 MPH) on other roads. The use of mobile phones, even on the side of the road, is now illegal, except with completely hands-free devices.

Severe fines are enforced throughout Spain for driving under the influence of alcohol. Spot Breathalyzer checks are often carried out, and you will be cited if the level of alcohol in your bloodstream is found to be 0.05 percent or above.

Spanish highway police are increasingly vigilant about speeding and illegal passing. Due to the high incidence of road accidents, fines for traffic offenses are strictly enforced in Spain and police are empowered to demand payment from non-Spanish drivers on the spot. It is an unfortunate reality that rental-car drivers are disproportionately targeted by police for speeding and illegal passing, so play it safe.

BY CRUISE SHIP

Barcelona is the busiest cruise port in Spain and Europe. Other popular ports of call in the country are Málaga, Alicante, and Palma de Mallorca. Nearby Gibraltar is also a popular stop. Although cruise lines such as Silversea and Costa traditionally offer cruises that take in parts of Spain and other Mediterranean countries such as Italy and Greece, it is becoming increasingly common to find package tours wholly within Spain. Two popular routes consist of island-hopping in the Balaerics or around the Canary Islands. Among the many cruise lines that call on Spain are Royal Caribbean, Holland America Line, Norwegian Cruise Line, and Princess Cruises.

BY TRAIN

International overnight trains run from Madrid to Lisbon (9 hours) and from Barcelona and Madrid to Paris (both around 12½ hours). An overnight train also runs from Barcelona to Geneva (10 hours) and Zurich (14½ hours).

Spain's wonderful high-speed train, the 290-KPH (180-MPH) AVE, travels between Madrid and Seville (with a stop in Córdoba) in 2.5 hours on average; prices start at €70 each way, with discounted fares available for advanced purchase, round-trip purchase, etc. The AVE also travels from Madrid to Lleida (with a stop in Zaragoza), Madrid to Huesca, Madrid to Málaga, and Madrid to Valladolid (with a stop in Segovia). In early 2008, the AVE began serving the Madrid–Barcelona route, cutting travel time to two hours and 38 minutes. The trip to Zaragoza is about 1.5 hours and starts at €42 each way; to Lleida, the trip is just over two hours and starts at €59 each way. The fast Talgo service is also efficient; however, the rest of the state-run rail system—known as RENFE—remains below par by European standards and many long-distance trips are tediously slow. Although some overnight trains have comfortable sleeper cars, first-class fares that include a sleeping compartment are comparable to, or more expensive than, airfares.

For shorter routes with convenient schedules, trains are the most economical way to go. First- and second-class seats are reasonably priced, and you can get a bunk in a compartment with five other people for a supplement of about €32.

Commuter trains and most long-distance trains forbid smoking, though some long-distance trains have smoking cars.

Check for RENFE discounts in Spain. If you purchase a round-trip ticket on AVE or any of RENFE's Grandes Lineas, which are its faster, long-distance trains (including the Talgo) while in Spain, you'll get a 20% discount. You have up to 60 days to use the return portion of your ticket. Passengers with international airline tickets who are traveling on the AVE within 48 hours of their arrival receive a 25% discount on their AVE ticket. On regional trains, you receive a 10% discount on round-trip tickets, and you have up to 15 days to use the return portion. Note that even if you just buy a one-way ticket to your destination, you can still receive the round-trip discount if you present your ticket stub at the train station when buying your return (provided your return is within the allotted time frame, either 15 or 60 days).

Most Spaniards buy train tickets in advance at the train station's *taquilla* (ticket office). The lines can be long, so give yourself plenty of time. For popular train routes, you will need to reserve tickets more than a few days in advance and pick them up at least a day before traveling; call RENFE to inquire. The ticket clerks at the stations rarely speak English, so if you need help or advice in planning a more complex train journey, you may be better off going to a travel agency that displays the blue-and-yellow RENFE sign. A small commission (American Express Viajes charges €3) should be expected. For shorter, regional train trips, you can often buy your tickets directly from machines in the main train stations. Note that if your itinerary is set in stone and has little room for error, you can buy RENFE tickets through Rail Europe before you leave home.

You can buy train tickets with a major credit card (except for American Express) at most city train stations. In the smaller towns and villages, it's cash only. Seat reservations are required on most long-distance and some other trains, particularly high-speed trains, and are wise on any train that might be crowded. You'll also need a reservation if you want a sleeping berth.

The easiest way to make reservations is to use the TIKNET service on the RENFE Web site (🌐*https://w1.renfe.es/vbi/indexu.html*). TIKNET involves registering and providing your credit-card information. When you make the reservation, you'll be given a car and seat assignment and a *localizador* (translated as "localizer" on the English version of the site; it is similar to a confirmation number). Print out the reservations page or write down the car number, seat number, and localizer. When traveling, go to your assigned seat on the train. When the conductor comes around, give him the localizer, and he will issue the ticket on the spot. You'll need your passport and, in most cases, the credit card you used for the reservation (in Spain, credit cards are often used for an additional form of ID). The AVE trains check you in at the gate to the platform, where you provide the localizer. You can review your pending reservations online at any time.

Caveats: the first time you use TIKNET, you must pick up the tickets at a RENFE station (most major airports have a RENFE booth, so you can retrieve your tickets as soon as you get off your plane). A 15% cancellation fee is charged if you cancel more than two hours after making the reservation. You cannot buy tickets online for certain regional lines or for commuter lines (*cercanias*). Station agents cannot alter TIKNET reservations: you must do this yourself online.

If a train is booked, the TIKNET process doesn't reveal this until the final stage of the reservation attempt—then it gives you a cryptic error message in a little box—but if you reserve a few days in advance, it's unlikely you'll encounter this problem except at Easter, Christmas, or during the first week of August.

RAIL PASSES

If you're coming from the United States or Canada and are planning extensive train travel throughout Europe, check Rail Europe for Eurail passes. Whichever of the many available passes you choose, remember that you must buy your pass before you leave for Europe.

Spain is one of 20 European countries in which you can use the Eurail Global Pass, which buys you unlimited first-class rail travel in all participating countries for the duration of the pass. If you plan to rack up the miles, get a standard pass. These are available for 15 days ($689), 21 days ($895), one month ($1,109), two months ($1,569), and three months ($1,935). A more limited option (formerly called the Flexi Pass), buys you either 10 days of rail travel in 2 months at $815 or 15 days in 2 months for $1069.

If Spain is your only destination, check into Rail Europe's Spain passes. Consider a Eurail Spain Pass that allows three days of unlimited train travel in Spain within a two-month period for $259 (first class) and $209 (second class); for 10 days of unlimited travel within two months, the passes are $529 and $425, respectively. The Eurail Spain Rail 'n Drive Pass combines three days of unlimited train travel with two days of car rentals. There are also combination passes for those visiting Spain and Portugal, Spain and France, and Spain and Italy.

Many travelers assume that rail passes guarantee them seats on the trains they wish to ride: not so. Reserve seats in advance even if you're using a rail pass.

Contacts Eurail (*www.eurail.com*). **Rail Europe** (*800/622-8600 in the U.S. or 800/361-7245 in Canada* *www.raileurope.com*). **RENFE** (*902/243402* *www.renfe.es*).

ESSENTIALS

ACCOMMODATIONS

By law, hotel prices in Spain must be posted at the reception desk and should indicate whether or not the value-added tax (I.V.A.; 7%) is included. Note that high-season rates prevail not only in summer but also during Holy Week and local fiestas. In much of Spain, breakfast is normally *not* included.

TIP→ **See each chapter's Planner section for price charts.**

Most hotels and other lodgings require you to give your credit-card details before they will confirm your reservation. If you don't feel comfortable e-mailing this information, ask if you can fax it (some places even prefer faxes). However you book, get confirmation in writing and have a copy when you check in.

Be sure you understand the hotel's cancellation policy. Some places allow you to cancel without any kind of penalty—even if you prepaid to secure a discounted rate—if you cancel at least 24 hours in advance. Others require you to cancel a week in advance or penalize you the cost of one night. Small inns and B&Bs are most likely to require you to cancel far in advance.

TIP→ **Assume that hotels operate on the European Plan (EP, no meals) unless we specify that they use the Breakfast Plan (BP, with full breakfast), Continental Plan (CP, Continental breakfast), Full American Plan (FAP, all meals), or Modified American Plan (MAP, breakfast and dinner).**

APARTMENT AND HOUSE RENTALS

If you are interested in a single-destination vacation, or are staying in one place and using it as a base for exploring the local area, renting an apartment or a house can be a good idea. However, it is not always possible to ensure the quality beforehand, and you may be responsible for supplying your own bed linens, towels, etc.

WORD OF MOUTH

Did the resort look as good in real life as it did in the photos? Did you sleep like a baby, or were the walls paper thin? Did you get your money's worth? Rate hotels and write your own reviews in Travel Ratings, or start a discussion about your favorite places in Travel Talk on www.fodors.com. Your comments might even appear in our books. Yes, you, too, can be a correspondent!

Contacts **Barclay International Group** (☎ *516/364–0064 or 800/845–6636* ⊕ *www.barclayweb.com*). **Homes Away** (☎ *416/920–1873 or 800/374–6637* ⊕ *www.homesaway.com*). **Interhome** (☎ *954/791–8282 or 800/882–6864* ⊕ *www.interhome.us*). **Villas and Apartments Abroad** (☎ *212/213–6435 or 800/433–3020* ⊕ *www.vaanyc.com*). **Villas International** (☎ *415/499–9490 or 800/221–2260* ⊕ *www.villasintl.com*).

HOSTELS

Youth hostels (*albergues juveniles*) in Spain are usually large and impersonal (but clean) with dorm-style beds. Most are geared to students, though many have a few private rooms suitable for families and couples. These rooms fill up quickly, so book at least a month in advance. Other budget options are the university student dorms *(residencia estudiantil)*, some of which offer accommodation in summer, when students are away.

TIP→ **Note that in Spain *hostales* are not the same as the dorm-style youth hostels common elsewhere in Europe—hostales are inexpensive hotels with individual rooms, not communal quarters.**

Information **Hostelling International—USA** (☎ *301/495–1240* ⊕ *www.hiusa.org*).

HOTELS AND BED-AND-BREAKFASTS

The Spanish government classifies hotels with one to five stars, with an additional rating of five-star GL (Gran Luxo) indicating the highest quality. Although quality is a factor, **the rating is technically only an indication of how many facilities the hotel offers.** For example, a three-star hotel may be just as comfortable as a four-star hotel but may lack a swimming pool. Similarly, Fodor's price categories (¢–$$$$) indicate room rates only, so you might find a well-kept $$$ inn more charming than the famous $$$$ property down the street.

All hotel entrances are marked with a blue plaque bearing the letter H and the number of stars. The letter R (standing for *residencia*) after the letter H indicates an establishment with no meal service, with the possible exception of breakfast. The designations *fonda* (F), *pensión* (P), *casa de huéspedes* (CH), and *hostal* (Hs) indicate budget accommodations. In most cases, especially in smaller villages, rooms in such buildings will be basic but clean; in large cities, these rooms can be downright dreary.

All hotels listed have private bath and air-conditioning (*aire acondicionado*) unless otherwise noted. When inquiring in Spanish about whether a hotel has a private bath, ask if it's an *habitación con baño*. Although a single room (*habitación sencilla*) is usually available, singles are often on the small side. Solo travelers might prefer to pay a bit extra for single occupancy of a double room (*habitación doble uso individual*). Make sure you request a double bed (*matrimonial*) if you want one—if you don't ask, you may end up with two singles placed together.

There's a growing trend in Spain toward small country hotels and agrotourism. Estancias de España is an association of more than 40 independently owned hotels in restored palaces, monasteries, mills, and estates, generally in rural Spain; contact them for a free directory. Similar associations serve individual regions, and tourist offices also provide lists of establishments. In Galicia, *pozos* are beautiful, old, often stately homes converted into small luxury hotels; Pozos de Galicia is the main organization for them. In Cantabria, *casonas* are small to large country houses, but as they don't have individual Web sites, it is necessary to check the regional tourist office Web sites.

A number of *casas rurales* (country houses similar to bed-and-breakfasts) offer pastoral lodging either in guest rooms or in self-catering cottages. You may also come across the term *finca,* which is a country estate house. Many *agroturismo* accommodations are *fincas* that people have inherited and converted to upscale B&Bs. Comfort and conveniences vary widely. Ask the local tourist office about *casas rurales* and *fincas* in the area.

A word to the wise: many of the smaller regional associations of country hotels and inns typically upload the pictures and information they get from the individual properties they list but take no particular responsibility for verification or updating. If there's something you really need to be sure about (do they accept pets? is breakfast really included? can I pay by credit card?), make a point of asking the hotel directly when you book.

PARADORS

The Spanish government runs almost 100 *paradors*—upmarket hotels in historic buildings or near significant sites. Rates are reasonable, considering that most paradores have four- or five-star amenities; and the premises are invariably immaculate and tastefully furnished, often with antiques or reproductions. Each parador has a restaurant serving regional specialties, and you can stop in for a meal or a drink without spending the night. Breakfast, however, is often an expensive buffet, so if you just want coffee and a roll, you'll do better to walk down the street to a local café—though note that many paradores are far from town centers. Paradores are popular with foreigners and

Spaniards alike, so make reservations well in advance. (⇨*See the* Paradors: A Night with History *feature, in the Experience chapter, for more details.*)

Contacts **Paradores de España** (🌐 *www.parador.es*).

COMMUNICATIONS

INTERNET

The Internet boom came a bit late to Spain, with few or limited Internet cafés in the big cities at the turn of this century. But all that has changed, and the Internet is now in full swing. Huge increases in migration to the country's bigger cities means demand has skyrocketed for *locutorios* (cheap international phone centers), which double as places to get on the Internet. In addition to the locutorios, where Internet access is not always reliable, there are upmarket cafés and bars that provide Internet service, often at faster speeds. The most you're likely to pay for Internet access is about €3 an hour.

Internet cafés are most common in tourist and student precincts. If you can't find one easily, ask at either the tourist office or a hotel's front desk. There's no perfect guide to the many cybercafés in Spain, but Gonuts4free has a good list.

Internet access within Spanish hotels is not widespread and tends to be offered only in the more expensive hotels. And those that do offer Internet access have varying services: Internet kiosks or rooms, in-room data ports or DSL, and/or Wi-Fi (either free or with a fee; sometimes in-room, sometimes in common areas).

Contacts **Cybercafes** (🌐 *www.cybercafes.com*) lists more than 4,000 Internet cafés worldwide. **Gonuts4free** (🌐 www.gonuts4free.com/yellow/internetcafes/index.htm).

PHONES

The good news is that you can now make a direct-dial telephone call from virtually any point on earth. The bad news? You can't always do so cheaply. Calling from a hotel is almost always the most expensive option; hotels usually add huge surcharges to all calls, particularly international ones. In some countries you can phone from call centers or even the post office. Calling cards usually keep costs to a minimum, but only if you purchase them locally. And then there are mobile phones, which are sometimes more prevalent—particularly in the developing world—than land lines; as expensive as mobile phone calls can be, they are still usually a much cheaper option than calling from your hotel.

Spain's phone system is perfectly efficient but can be expensive. Direct dialing is the norm. Most travelers buy phone cards, which for €5 or €6 allows for about three hours of calls nationally and internationally. Phone cards can be used with any hotel, bar, or public telephone. Although some phone cards from Australia, the United Kingdom, and the United States can be used in Spain, those with the best value are found in Spain itself. There are many cards that work for only certain regions of the country, but the all-encompassing Fantastic card works for anywhere in the world. Phone cards can be bought at any tobacco shop or at most Internet cafés. Such cafés also often provide phone booths that allow you to call at cheaper rates. If you do use coins, be aware that the public phones in the street are cheaper than the green and blue phones found inside most bars and restaurants. Spain's main telephone company is Telefónica.

Note that only cell phones conforming to the European GSM standard will work in Spain. Buying a cell phone without a contract (i.e., paying for your calls by adding money to your phone either via a cell-phone card or at a cell-phone store) is popular in Spain. If you're going to be traveling in Spain for an extended period of time and plan on using a cell phone frequently to call within Spain, then buying a phone will often turn out to be a big money-saver. Using a Spanish cell phone means avoiding the hefty long-distance charges accrued when using your cell phone from home to call within Spain. Prices fluctuate, but offers start at about €40 for a phone with about €30 worth of calls.

The country code for Spain is 34. The country code is 1 for the United States and Canada.

CALLING WITHIN SPAIN

For general information in Spain, dial 1003. International operators, who generally speak English, are at 025.

All area codes begin with a 9. To call within Spain—even locally—dial the area code first. Numbers preceded by a 900 code are toll-free in Spain, however, 90x numbers are not (i.e., 901, 902, etc.). Phone numbers starting with a 6 belong to cellular phones. Note that when calling a cell phone, you do not need to dial the area code first; also, calls to cell phones are significantly more expensive than calls to regular phones.

You'll find pay phones in individual booths, in special telephone offices (*locutorios*), and in many bars and restaurants. Most have a digital readout so you can see your money ticking away. If you're calling with coins, you need at least €0.15 to call locally and €0.45 to call another province. Simply insert the coins and wait for a dial tone. (With older models, you line coins up in a groove on top of the dial and they drop down as needed.) Note that rates are reduced on weekends and after 8 PM during the week.

CALLING OUTSIDE SPAIN

International calls are awkward from coin-operated pay phones because of the many coins needed; and they can be expensive from hotels, as the hotel often adds a hefty surcharge. Your best bet is to use a public phone that accepts phone cards or go to the local telephone office, the *locutorio:* every town has one, and major cities have several. The locutorios near the center of town are generally more expensive; farther from the center, the rates are sometimes as much as one-third less. You converse in a quiet, private booth, and you're charged according to the meter. If the call ends up costing around €4 or more, you can usually pay with Visa or MasterCard.

To make an international call yourself, dial 00, then the country code, then the area code and number.

The country code for the United States is 1.

Madrid's main telephone office is at Gran Vía 28. There's another at the main post office, and a third at Paseo Recoletos 43, just off Plaza Colón. In Barcelona you can phone overseas from the office at Carrer de Fontanella 4, off Plaça de Catalunya.

General Information AT&T (☎ *800/222–0300*). **MCI WorldCom** (☎ *800/444–3333*). **Sprint** (☎ *800/793–1153*).

CALLING CARDS

To use a newer pay phone you need a special phone card (*tarjeta telefónica*), which you can buy at any tobacco shop or newsstand, in various denominations. Some such phones also accept credit cards, but phone cards are more reliable.

MOBILE PHONES

If you have a multiband phone (some countries use different frequencies than what's used in the United States) and your service provider uses the world-standard GSM network (as do T-Mobile, AT&T, and Verizon), you can probably use your phone abroad. Roaming fees can be steep, however: 99¢ a minute is considered reasonable. And overseas you normally pay the toll charges for incoming calls. It's almost always cheaper to send a text message than to make a call, since text messages have a very low set fee (often less than 5¢).

If you just want to make local calls, consider buying a new SIM card (note that your provider may have to unlock your phone for you to use a different SIM card) and a prepaid service plan in the destination. You'll then have a local number and can make local calls at local rates. If your trip is extensive, you could also

LOCAL DO'S AND TABOOS

GREETINGS

When addressing Spaniards with whom you are not well acquainted or who are elderly, use the formal *usted* rather than the familiar *tu*.

DRESS

Some town councils are cracking down on people wearing swimsuits in public spaces. Use your common sense—it's unlikely you'd be allowed entry in a bar or restaurant wearing swimming attire back home, so don't do it when overseas. Be respectful when visiting churches: casual dress is fine if it's not gaudy or unkempt. Spaniards object to men going bare-chested anywhere other than the beach or poolside.

OUT ON THE TOWN

These days, the Spanish are generally very informal, and casual-smart dress is accepted in most places.

DOING BUSINESS

Spanish office hours can be confusing to the uninitiated. Some offices stay open more or less continuously from 9 to 3, with a very short lunch break. Others open in the morning, break up the day with a long lunch break of two to three hours, then reopen at 4 or 5 until 7 or 8. Spaniards enjoy a certain notoriety for their lack of punctuality, but this has changed dramatically in recent years, and you are expected to show up for meetings on time. Smart dress is the norm.

Spaniards in international fields tend to conduct business with foreigners in English. If you speak Spanish, address new colleagues with the formal *usted* and the corresponding verb conjugations, then follow their lead in switching to the familiar *tu* once a working relationship has been established.

LANGUAGE

One of the best ways to avoid being an Ugly American is to learn a little of the local language. You need not strive for fluency; even just mastering a few basic words and terms is bound to make chatting with the locals more rewarding.

Although Spaniards exported their language to all of Central and South America, Spanish is not the principal language in all of Spain. Outside their big cities, the Basques speak Euskera. In Catalonia, you'll hear Catalan throughout the region, just as you'll hear Gallego in Galicia and Valenciano in Valencia (the latter, as with Mallorquín in Majorca and Menorquín in Menorca, are considered Catalan dialects). Although almost everyone in these regions also speaks and understands Spanish, local radio and television stations may broadcast in their respective languages, and road signs may be printed (or spray-painted over) with the preferred regional language. Spanish is referred to as Castellano, or Castilian.

Fortunately, Spanish is fairly easy to pick up, and your efforts to speak it will be graciously received. Learn at least the following basic phrases: *buenos días* (hello—until 2 PM), *buenas tardes* (good afternoon—until 8 PM), *buenas noches* (hello—after dark), *por favor* (please), *gracias* (thank you), *adiós* (goodbye), *sí* (yes), *no* (no), *los servicios* (the toilets), *la cuenta* (bill/check), and *habla inglés?* (do you speak English?), *no comprendo* (I don't understand). If your Spanish breaks down, you should have no trouble finding people who speak English in major cities and coastal resorts, but you won't necessarily be able to count on the bus driver or the passerby on the street. It's much more likely that you'll find an English-language speaker if you approach people under age 30.

simply buy a new cell phone in your destination, as the initial cost will be offset over time.

■ TIP→ **If you travel internationally frequently, save one of your old mobile phones or buy a cheap one on the Internet; ask your cell phone company to unlock it for you, and take it with you as a travel phone, buying a new SIM card with pay-as-you-go service in each destination.**

Contacts **Cellular Abroad** (☎ *800/287-5072* 🌐 *www.cellularabroad.com*) rents and sells GMS phones and sells SIM cards that work in many countries. **Mobal** (☎ *888/888-9162* 🌐 *www.mobalrental.com*) rents mobiles and sells GSM phones (starting at $49) that will operate in 140 countries. Per-call rates vary throughout the world. **Planet Fone** (☎ *888/988-4777* 🌐 *www.planetfone.com*) rents cell phones at $40 a week, but discounts can cut that fee almost in half.

EATING OUT

Sitting around a table eating and talking is a huge part of Spanish culture, defining much of people's daily routines. Sitting in the middle of a typical bustling restaurant here goes a long way toward understanding how fundamental food can be to Spanish lives.

Although Spain has always had an extraordinary range of regional cuisine, in the past decade or so its restaurants have won it international recognition at the highest levels. A new generation of Spanish chefs—led by the revolutionary Ferran Adrià—has transformed classic dishes to suit contemporary tastes, drawing on some of the freshest ingredients in Europe and bringing an astonishing range of new technologies into the kitchen.

One of the major drawbacks of drinking and eating in Spanish bars and restaurants used to be the unbridled smoking in almost all of them. The antismoking laws introduced by the national government at the beginning of 2006 are changing all that. Establishments within shopping malls, theaters, and cinemas are now strictly no smoking. All establishments that measure 100 meters square or more are obliged to provide a no-smoking section. Children may not eat outside this section. However, establishments smaller than this size retain the option for the time being to permit smoking across the board or to ban it altogether. With a few exceptions, the proprietors of these establishments have maintained the status quo, presumably because of the fact that one in three Spaniards smokes, and they are fearful of losing clients. This may change over time as locals become more accustomed to the new regulations forbidding smoking in public places, shops, and places of work. All eating and drinking establishments are obliged to inform clients by posting a sign at the entrance. *Se permite fumar* means you can smoke, *no se permite fumar* means you can't, and *sala habilitada para no fumadores* means a nonsmoking section is available.

MEALS AND MEALTIMES

Most restaurants in Spain do not serve breakfast (*desayuno*); for coffee and carbs, head to a bar or *cafetería*. Outside major hotels, which serve morning buffets, breakfast in Spain is usually limited to coffee and toast or a roll. Lunch (*comida* or *almuerzo*) traditionally consists of an appetizer, a main course, and dessert, followed by coffee and perhaps a liqueur. Between lunch and dinner the best way to snack is to sample some tapas (appetizers) at a bar; normally you can choose from quite a variety. Dinner (*cena*) is somewhat lighter, with perhaps only one course. In addition to an à la carte menu, most restaurants offer a daily fixed-price menu (*menú del día*), consisting of a starter, main plate, drink (wine, beer, water, soda, etc), and usually either coffee or dessert at a very attractive price (usually between €8 and €12). If your waiter does not suggest the menú del día when you're seated, ask for it—"*Hay menú del día, por favor?*" Restaurants in many of the larger tourist areas will have the menú del día posted outside. The menú del día is traditionally offered only at lunch, but increasingly it's also offered at dinner in popular tourist destinations.

Mealtimes in Spain are later than elsewhere in Europe, and later still in Madrid and the southern region of Andalusia. Lunch starts around 2 or 2:30 (closer to 3 in Madrid), and dinner after 9 (as late as 11 or midnight in Madrid). Weekend eating times, especially dinner, can begin upward of about an hour later. In areas with heavy tourist traffic, some restaurants open a bit earlier.

Unless otherwise noted, the restaurants listed in this guide are open daily for lunch and dinner.

PAYING

Credit cards are widely accepted in Spanish restaurants, but be aware that smaller establishments often do not take them. If you pay by credit card and you want to leave a small tip above and beyond the service charge, leave the tip in cash.

For guidelines see Tipping.

RESERVATIONS AND DRESS

Regardless of where you are, it's a good idea to make a reservation if you can. In some places, it's expected. We only mention them specifically when reservations are essential (there's no other way you'll ever get a table) or when they are not accepted. For popular restaurants, book as far ahead as you can (often 30 days), and reconfirm as soon as you arrive. (Large parties should always call ahead to check the reservations policy.) We mention dress only when men are required to wear a jacket or a jacket and tie.

WINES, BEER, AND SPIRITS

Apart from its famous wines, Spain produces many brands of lager, the most popular of which are San Miguel, Moritz, Cruzcampo, Aguila, Voll Damm, Mahou, and Estrella. Jerez de la Frontera is Europe's largest producer of brandy and is a major source of sherry. Catalonia produces most of the world's *cava* (sparkling wine). Spanish law prohibits the sale of alcohol to people under 18.

WORD OF MOUTH

Was the service stellar or not up to snuff? Did the food give you shivers of delight or leave you cold? Did the prices and portions make you happy or sad? Rate restaurants and write your own reviews in Travel Ratings or start a discussion about your favorite places in Travel Talk on www.fodors.com. Your comments might even appear in our books. Yes, you, too, can be a correspondent!

ELECTRICITY

Spain's electrical current is 220–240 volts, 50 cycles alternating current (AC); wall outlets take Continental-type plugs, with two round prongs.

Consider making a small investment in a universal adapter, which has several types of plugs in one lightweight, compact unit. Most laptops and mobile phone chargers are dual voltage (i.e., they operate equally well on 110 and 220 volts), and require only an adapter. These days the same is true of small appliances such as hair dryers. Always check labels and manufacturer instructions to be sure. Don't use 110-volt outlets marked FOR SHAVERS ONLY for high-wattage appliances such as hair dryers.

EMERGENCIES

The pan-European emergency phone number (☎112) is operative in some parts of Spain but not all. If it doesn't work, dial the emergency numbers below for the national police, local police, fire department, or medical services. On the road, there are emergency phones marked SOS at regular intervals on *autovías* (freeways) and *autopistas* (toll highways). If your documents are stolen, contact both the local police and your embassy. If you lose a credit card, phone the issuer immediately.

Foreign Embassies **Canadian Embassy** (*✉ Goya Building, Calle Nuñez de Balboa 35, Madrid, Apt. 1C ☎ 91/422–3250*). **UK Embassy** (*✉ Calle de Fernando el Santo 16, Madrid ☎ 91/319–0200*). **U.S. Embassy** (*✉ Calle Serrano 75, Madrid ☎ 91/587–2200*).

General Emergency Contacts **National police** (*☎ 091*). **Local police** (*☎ 092*). **Fire department** (*☎ 080*). **Medical service** (*☎ 061*).

HEALTH

The most common types of illnesses are caused by contaminated food and water. Make sure food has been thoroughly cooked and is served to you fresh and hot; avoid vegetables and fruits that you haven't washed (in bottled or purified water) or peeled yourself. If you have problems, mild cases of traveler's diarrhea may respond to Imodium (known generically as loperamide) or Pepto-Bismol. Be sure to drink plenty of fluids; if you can't keep fluids down, seek medical help immediately.

Infectious diseases can be airborne or passed via mosquitoes and ticks and through direct or indirect physical contact with animals or people. Some, including Norwalk-like viruses that affect your digestive tract, can be passed along through contaminated food. Condoms can help prevent most sexually transmitted diseases, but they aren't absolutely reliable and their quality varies from country to country. Speak with your physician and/or check the CDC or World Health Organization Web sites for health alerts, particularly if you're pregnant, traveling with children, or have a chronic illness.

SPECIFIC ISSUES IN SPAIN

Medical care is good in Spain, but nursing can be perfunctory, as relatives are expected to stop by and look after patients' needs. In some popular destinations, such as the Costa del Sol, there are volunteer English interpreters on hand at hospitals and clinics.

In the summer, sunburn and sunstroke are real risks in Spain. On the hottest sunny days, even if you're not normally bothered by strong sun, you should cover yourself up, carry sunblock (*protector solar*), drink plenty of fluids, and limit sun time for the first few days. If you require medical attention for any problem, ask your hotel's front desk for assistance or go to the nearest public **Centro de Salud** (day hospital); in serious cases, you'll be referred to the regional hospital.

OVER-THE-COUNTER REMEDIES

Over-the-counter remedies are available at any *farmacia* (pharmacy), recognizable by the large green crosses outside. Some will look familiar, such as *aspirina* (aspirin), and other medications are sold under various brand names. If you get traveler's diarrhea, ask for *un antidiarréico* (the general term for antidiarrheal medicine); Fortasec is a well-known brand. Mild cases may respond to Imodium (known generically as loperamide) or Pepto-Bismol. To keep from getting dehydrated, drink plenty of purified water or herbal tea. In severe cases, rehydrate yourself with a salt-sugar solution—½ teaspoon salt (*sal*) and 4 tablespoons sugar (*azúcar*) per quart of water, or pick up a package of oral rehydration salts at any local farmacia.

If you regularly take a nonprescription medicine, take a sample box or bottle with you, and the Spanish pharmacist will provide you with its local equivalent.

HOURS OF OPERATION

The ritual of a long afternoon siesta is no longer as ubiquitous as it once was. However, the tradition does remain, and many people take a postlunch nap before returning to work or continuing on with their day. The two- to three-hour lunch makes it possible to eat and then snooze. Midday breaks generally begin at 1 or 2 and end between 4 and 5, depending on the city and the sort of business. The midafternoon siesta—often a half-hour power nap in front of the TV—fits naturally into the workday cycle, since Spaniards tend to work until 7 or 8 PM.

Traditionally, Spain's climate created the siesta as a time to preserve energy while afternoon temperatures spiked. After the sun began setting, Spaniards went back to working, shopping, and taking their leisurely *paseo*, or stroll. In the big cities—particularly with the advent of air-conditioning—the heat has less of an effect on the population; in the small towns in the south of Spain, however, many still use a siesta as a way to wait out the weather.

Until a decade or so ago, it was common for many businesses to close for a month in the July/August period. Europeanization, changing trading hours, and a booming consumerism are gradually altering that custom. These days many small businesses are more likely to close down for two weeks only, maybe three. When open, they often run on a summer schedule, which can mean a longer-than-usual siesta (sometimes up to four hours), a shorter working day (until 3 PM only), and no Saturday afternoon trading at all.

Banks are generally open weekdays from 8:30 or 9 until 2 or 2:30. From October to May the major banks open on Saturday from 8:30 or 9 until 2 or 2:30, and savings banks are also open Thursday 4:30 to 8. Currency exchanges at airports, train stations, and in the city center stay open later; you can also cash traveler's checks at El Corte Inglés department stores until 10 PM (some branches close at 9 PM or 9:30 PM). Most government offices are open weekdays 9–2.

Most museums are open from 9:30 to 2 and 4 to 7 or 8 six days a week, every day but Monday. Schedules are subject to change, particularly between the high and low seasons, so confirm opening hours before you make plans. A few large museums, such as Madrid's Prado and Reina Sofía and Barcelona's Picasso Museum, stay open all day, without a siesta.

Pharmacies keep normal business hours (9–1:30 and 5–8), but every midsize town (or city neighborhood) has a duty pharmacy that stays open 24 hours. The location of the duty pharmacy is usually posted on the front door of all pharmacies.

When planning a shopping trip, remember that almost all shops in Spain close from 1 or 2 PM for at least two hours. The only exceptions are large supermarkets and the department-store chain El Corte Inglés. Most shops are closed on Sunday, and in Madrid and several other places they're also closed Saturday afternoon. Larger shops in tourist areas may stay open Sunday in summer and during the Christmas holiday.

HOLIDAYS

Spain's national holidays are New Year's Day on January 1 (Año Nuevo), Three Kings Day on January 6 (Día de los Tres Reyes), Father's Day on March 19 (San José), Good Friday (Viernes Santo), Easter Sunday (Día de Pascua), Labor Day on May 1 (Día del Trabajo), St. John's Day on June 24 (San Juan: the bonfire celebrations are the night before), Corpus Christi (June), St. Peter/St. Paul Day on June 29 (San Pedro y San Pablo), St. James Day on July 25 (Santiago), Assumption on August 15 (Asunción), Columbus Day on October 12 (Día de la Hispanidad), All Saints Day on November 1 (Todos los Santos), Constitution Day on December 6 (Día de la Constitución), Immaculate Conception on December 8 (Immaculada Concepción), and Christmas Day on December 25 (Navidad).

In addition, each region, city, and town has its own holidays honoring political events and patron saints. Madrid holidays are May 2 (Madrid Day), May 15 (St. Isidro), and November 9 (Almudena). Barcelona celebrates Carnival in February, April 23 (St. George), April 27 (Virgin of Montserrat), June 23 (Día de Sant Joan), September 11 (Catalonia Day), and September 24 (Merce).

Many stores close during *Semana Santa* (Holy Week—also sometimes translated as Easter Week); it is the week that precedes Easter.

If a public holiday falls on a Tuesday or Thursday, remember that many businesses also close on the nearest Monday or Friday for a long weekend, called a *puente* (bridge). If a major holiday falls on a Sunday, businesses close on Monday.

MAIL

Spain's postal system, the *correos,* does work, but delivery times vary widely. An airmail letter to the United States may take from four days to two weeks; delivery to other destinations is equally unpredictable. Sending your letters by priority mail (*urgente*) or the cheaper registered mail (*certificado*) ensures speedier and safer arrival.

Airmail letters to the United States and Canada cost €0.78 up to 20 grams. Letters to the United Kingdom and other EU countries cost €0.60 up to 20 grams. Letters within Spain are €0.31. Postcards carry the same rates as letters. You can buy stamps at post offices and at licensed tobacco shops.

Because mail delivery in Spain can often be slow and unreliable, it's best to have your mail held at a Spanish post office; have it addressed to LISTA DE CORREOS (the equivalent of *poste restante*) in a town you'll be visiting. Postal addresses should include the name of the province in parentheses, for example, Marbella (Málaga).

SHIPPING PACKAGES

When time is of the essence, or when you're sending valuable items or documents overseas, you can use a courier (*mensajero*). The major international agencies, such as Federal Express, UPS, and DHL, have representatives in Spain; the biggest Spanish courier service is Seur. MRW is another local courier that provides express delivery worldwide.

Express Services Correos (☎ *902/197197* 🌐 *www.correos.es*). **DHL** (☎ *902/122424 for air, 902/123030 for ground* 🌐 *www.dhl.es*). **Federal Express** (☎ *902/100871* 🌐 *www.fedex.com/es_english*). **MRW** (☎ *900/300400* 🌐 *www.mrw.es/index_en.asp*). **Seur** (☎ *902/101010* 🌐 *www.seur.com*). **UPS** (☎ *902/888820* 🌐 *www.ups.es*).

MONEY

Spain is no longer a budget destination, even less so in the expensive cities of Barcelona, San Sebastián, and Madrid. However, prices still compare slightly favorably with those elsewhere in Europe.

Prices throughout this guide are given for adults. Substantially reduced fees are almost always available for children, students, and senior citizens.

TIP→ **Banks never have every foreign currency on hand, and it may take as long as a week to order. If you're planning to exchange funds before leaving home, don't wait until the last minute.**

ATMS AND BANKS

Your own bank will probably charge a fee for using ATMs abroad; the foreign bank you use may also charge a fee. Nevertheless, you'll usually get a better rate of exchange at an ATM than you will at a currency-exchange office or even when changing money in a bank. And extracting funds as you need them is a safer option than carrying around a large amount of cash.

TIP→ **PINs with more than four digits are not recognized at ATMs in many countries. If yours has five or more, remember to change it before you leave.**

You'll find ATMs in every major city in Spain, as well as in most smaller cities. ATMs will be part of the Cirrus and/or Plus networks and will allow you to withdraw euros with your credit or debit card, provided you have a valid PIN (pronounced *peen*). Make sure your PIN code is four digits, which is required in Spain. Note that at some ATMs the keyboard is reverse from the American keyboard, starting with a 9 in the top left.

Spanish banks tend to maintain an astonishing number of branch offices, especially in the cities and major tourist destinations, and the majority will have an ATM. The largest banks in Spain are Banco Popular (*www.bancopopular.es*), Banesto (*www.banesto.es*), BBVA (Banco Bilbao-Vizcaya Argentara *www.bbva.es*), and BSCH (Banco Santander Central Hispano *www.gruposantander.com*). *See Hours of Operation.*

CREDIT CARDS

Throughout this guide, the following abbreviations are used: **AE**, American Express; **DC**, Diners Club; **MC**, MasterCard; and **V**, Visa.

It's a good idea to inform your credit-card company before you travel, especially if you're going abroad and don't travel internationally very often. Otherwise, the credit-card company might put a hold on your card owing to unusual activity—not a good thing halfway through your trip. Record all your credit-card numbers—as well as the phone numbers to call if your cards are lost or stolen—in a safe place, so you're prepared should something go wrong. Both MasterCard and Visa have general numbers you can call (collect if you're abroad) if your card is lost, but you're better off calling the number of your issuing bank, since MasterCard and Visa usually just transfer you to your bank; your bank's number is usually printed on your card.

If you plan to use your credit card for cash advances, you'll need to apply for a PIN at least two weeks before your trip. Although it's usually cheaper (and safer) to use a credit card abroad for large purchases (so you can cancel payments or be reimbursed if there's a problem), note that some credit-card companies *and* the banks that issue them add substantial percentages to all foreign transactions, whether they're in a foreign currency or not. Check on these fees before leaving home, so there won't be any surprises when you get the bill.

TIP→ Before you charge something, ask the merchant whether he or she plans to do a dynamic currency conversion (DCC). In such a transaction the shop, restaurant, or hotel (not Visa or MasterCard) converts the currency and charges you in dollars. In most cases you'll pay the merchant a 3% fee for this service in addition to any credit-card company and issuing-bank foreign-transaction surcharges.

Dynamic currency conversion programs are becoming increasingly widespread. Merchants who participate in them are supposed to ask whether you want to be charged in dollars or the local currency, but they don't always do so. And even if they do offer you a choice, they may well avoid mentioning the additional surcharges. The good news is that you *do* have a choice. And if this practice really gets your goat, you can avoid it entirely thanks to American Express; with its cards, DCC simply isn't an option.

Reporting Lost Cards **American Express** (*800/528–4800 in the U.S., 336/393–1111 collect from abroad www.americanexpress.com*). **Diners Club** (*800/234–6377 in the U.S., 303/799–1504 collect from abroad www.dinersclub.com*). **MasterCard** (*800/627–8372 in the U.S., 636/722–7111 collect from abroad www.mastercard.com*). **Visa** (*800/847–2911 in the U.S. www.visa.com*).

Use these toll-free numbers in Spain. **American Express** (*917/437000*). **Diners Club** (*901/101011*). **MasterCard** (*900/971231*). **Visa** (*900/991124*).

CURRENCY AND EXCHANGE

Since 2002, Spain has used the European monetary unit, the euro (€). Euro notes come in denominations of 5, 10, 20, 50, 100, 200, and 500; coins are worth 1 cent of a euro, 2 cents, 5 cents, 10 cents, 20 cents, 50 cents, 1 euro, and 2 euros. Forgery is quite commonplace in parts of Spain, especially with 50-euro notes. You can generally tell a forgery by the feel of the paper: counterfeits tend to be smoother than the legal notes, and the metallic line down the middle is darker than those in real bills.

At this writing the euro has yet to regain the strength it lost in 2008 and 2009 against the U.S. dollar and other currencies: it stands at €1.40 to the U.S. dollar and €1.55 to the Canadian dollar.

TIP→ Even if a currency-exchange booth has a sign promising no commission, rest assured that there's some kind of huge, hidden fee. (Oh . . . that's right. The sign didn't say no *fee*.) And as for rates, you're almost always better off getting foreign currency at an ATM or exchanging money at a bank.

PASSPORTS AND VISAS

Visitors from the United States need a passport valid for a minimum of six months to enter Spain.

TIP→ Before your trip, make two copies of your passport's data page (one for someone at home and another for you to carry separately). Or scan the page and e-mail it to someone at home and/or yourself.

VISAS

Visas are not necessary for those with U.S. passports valid for a minimum of six months and who plan to stay in Spain for tourist or business purposes for up to 90 days. Should you need a visa to stay longer than this, contact the Spanish consulate office nearest to you in the U.S. to apply for the appropriate documents.

RESTROOMS

Spain has some public restrooms (*servicios*), including, in larger cities, small coin-operated booths, but they are few and far between. Your best option is to use the facilities in a bar or cafeteria, remembering that at the discretion of the establishment you may have to order something. Gas stations have restrooms (you usually have to request the key to use them), but they are more often than not in terrible condition.

The Bathroom Diaries (🌐*www.thebathroomdiaries.com*) is flush with unsanitized info on restrooms the world over—each one located, reviewed, and rated.

SAFETY

Petty crime is a huge problem in Spain's most popular tourist destinations. The most frequent offenses are pickpocketing (particularly in Madrid and Barcelona) and theft from cars (all over the country). Never leave anything valuable in a parked car, no matter how friendly the area feels, how quickly you'll return, or how invisible the item seems once you lock it in the trunk. Thieves can spot rental cars a mile away, and they work very efficiently. In airports, laptop computers are choice prey. Except when traveling between the airport or train station and your hotel, don't wear a money belt or a waist pack, both of which peg you as a tourist. (If you do use a money belt while traveling, opt for a concealed one and don't reach into it when you're in public.) Distribute your cash and any valuables (including your credit cards and passport) between a deep front pocket or an inside jacket or vest pocket. When walking the streets, particularly in large cities, carry as little cash as possible. Men should carry their wallets in the front pocket; women who need to carry purses should strap them across the front of their bodies. Another alternative is to carry money or important documents in both your front pockets. Leave the rest of your valuables in the safe at your hotel. On the beach, in cafés, and restaurants (particularly in the well-touristed areas), and in Internet centers, always keep your belongings on your lap or tied to your person in some way.

Be cautious of any odd or unnecessary human contact, verbal or physical, whether it's a tap on the shoulder, someone asking you for a light for their cigarette, someone spilling their drink at your table, and so on. Thieves often work in twos, so while one is attracting your attention, the other could be swiping your wallet.

TAXES

Value-added tax, similar to sales tax, is called I.V.A. in Spain (pronounced "*ee*-vah," for *impuesto sobre el valor añadido*). It's levied on both products and services, such as hotel rooms and restaurant meals. When in doubt about whether tax is included, ask, "*Está incluido el I.V.A.?*" The I.V.A. rate for hotels and restaurants is 7%, regardless of their number of stars. A special tax law for the Canary Islands allows hotels and restaurants there to charge 4% I.V.A. Menus will generally say at the bottom whether tax is included (*I.V.A. incluido*) or not (*más 7% I.V.A.*).

Although food, pharmaceuticals, and household items are taxed at the lowest rate, most consumer goods are taxed at 16%. A number of shops participate in Global Refund (formerly Europe Tax-Free Shopping), a V.A.T. refund service that makes getting your money back relatively hassle-free. You cannot get a refund on the V.A.T. for such items as meals or services such as hotel accommodation, or taxi fares. There are also some taxable consumption items for which the refund doesn't apply, such as perfume.

When making a purchase that qualifies for Global Refund, find out whether the merchant gives refunds—not all stores do, nor are they required to—and ask for a V.A.T. refund form. Have the form stamped like any customs form by customs officials when you leave the country or, if you're visiting several European Union countries, when you leave the EU. After you're through passport control, take the form to a refund-service counter for an on-the-spot refund (which is usually the quickest and easiest option), or mail it to the address on the form (or the envelope with it) after you arrive home. You receive the total refund stated on the form, but the processing time can be long, especially if you request a credit-card adjustment.

Global Refund is a Europe-wide service with 225,000 affiliated stores and more than 700 refund counters at major airports and border crossings. The refund form, called a Tax Free Check or Refund Cheque, is the most common across the European continent. The service issues refunds in the form of cash, check, or credit-card adjustment.

V.A.T. Refunds Global Refund (☎ *800/566–9828* 🌐 *www.globalrefund.com*).

TIME

Spain is on central European time, one hour ahead of Greenwich mean time, and six hours ahead of eastern standard time. Like the rest of the European Union, Spain switches to daylight saving time on the last weekend in March and switches back on the last weekend in October.

Time Zones Timeanddate.com (🌐 *www.timeanddate.com/worldclock*) can help you figure out the correct time anywhere.

TIPPING

Service staff expect to be tipped, and you can be sure that your contribution will be appreciated. On the other hand, if you experience bad or surly service, don't feel obligated to leave a tip.

Restaurant checks do not list a service charge on the bill, but consider the tip included. If you want to leave a small tip in addition to the bill, do not tip more than 10% of the bill, and leave less if you eat tapas or sandwiches at a bar—just enough to round out the bill to the nearest €1. Tip cocktail servers €0.30–€0.50 a drink, depending on the bar.

Tip taxi drivers about 10% of the total fare, plus a supplement to help with luggage. Note that rides from airports carry an official surcharge plus a small handling fee for each piece of luggage.

Tip hotel porters €0.50 a bag, and the bearer of room service €0.50. A doorman who calls a taxi for you gets €0.50. If you stay in a hotel for more than two nights, tip the maid about €0.50 per night.

Tour guides should be tipped about €2, ushers in theaters or at bullfights €0.15–€0.20, barbers €0.50 to €1, and women's hairdressers at least €1 for a wash and style. Restroom attendants are tipped €0.15.

TOURS

SPECIAL-INTEREST TOURS

Madrid and Beyond (☎ *91/758–0063* 🌐 *www.madridand beyond.com*) offers an array of customized private luxury tours, focusing on culinary, cultural, and sports-related themes.

ART

In the U.S., **Atlas Cruises and Tours** (☎ *800/942–3301* 🌐 *www.escortedspaintours.com*) offers a range of tours with accents on art, cultural history, and the outdoors.

Ole Spain Tours (☎ *91/551–5294* 🌐 *www.olespaintours.com*) also offers art and historical tours to Spain.

Based in New York, **Heritage Tours** (☎ *800/378–4555 or 212/206–8400 in NYC* 🌐 *www.heritagetoursonline.com*) helps arrange customized cultural tours based on your interests and budget. Guides are drawn from a network of curators, gallery owners, and art critics.

BIRD-WATCHING

In the Coto Doñana National Park in Andalucía, **Discovering Doñana Ltd.** (☎ *959/442466* 🌐 *www.discoveringdonana.com*) offers some of the best guided bird-watching tours and expeditions in Spain.

CULINARY AND WINE

Artisans of Leisure (☎ *800/214–8144* 🌐 *www.artisansofleisure.com*) offers personalized food and wine and cultural tours to Spain. Based in Madrid, **Cellar Tours** (☎ *91/521–3939* 🌐 *www.cellartours.com*) offers a wide array of wine and cooking tours to Spain.

GOLF

The following Spanish-based companies offer golf tours and information. **Golf Spain** (☎ *902/200052* 🌐 *www.golfspain.com*). **Golf in Spain** (☎ *952/474848* 🌐 *www.golfinspain.com*).

HIKING

For a company that offers all kinds of adventure tours check out **Spain Adventures** (☎ *877/717–7246* 🌐 *www.spainadventures.com*).

LANGUAGE PROGRAMS

One of the best resources for language schools in Spain is **Go Abroad** (☎ *720/570–1702* 🌐 *www.goabroad.com*).

VOLUNTEER PROGRAMS

The best resource for volunteering in Spain is **Go Abroad** (☎ *720/570–1702* 🌐 *www.goabroad.com*).

ONLINE TRAVEL TOOLS

ALL ABOUT SPAIN

For more information on Spain, visit the Tourist Office of Spain at 🌐 *www.spain.info* or 🌐 *www.okspain.org*. Also check out the sites 🌐 *www.in-spain.info*, 🌐 *www.red2000.com/spain*, and 🌐 *www.idealspain.com*; the latter focuses more on living, working, or buying property in Spain. A useful craigslist-type site listing everything from vacation rentals to language lessons is 🌐 *www.loquo.com/en_us*. For a virtual brochure on Spain's *paradores*, and online booking, go to 🌐 *www.parador.es*.

INDEX

S

Photo Credits: 5, *Javier Larrea/age fotostock.* **Chapter 1: Experience Spain:** 9, *J.D. Dallet/age fotostock.* 10, *Kolvenbach/Alamy.* 11 (left), *J.D. Dallet/age fotostock.* 11 (right), *Javier Larrea/age fotostock.* 12, *Joe Viesti/viestiphoto.com.* 13 (left), *Corbis.* 13 (right), *Wojtek Buss/age fotostock.* 15, *Factoria Singular/age fotostock.* 16, *Juan Manuel Silva/age fotostock.* 17 (left), *Alex Segre/Alamy.* 17 (right), *Nils-Johan Norenlind/age fotostock.* 18, *Doco Dalfiano/age fotostock.* 19, *Doug Scott/age fotostock.* 20 (left), *Malcolm Case-Green/Alamy.* 20 (top center), *Javier Larrea/age fotostock.* 20 (bottom center), *Fougras G./age fotostock.* 20 (right), *Adriaan Thomas Snaaijer/Shutterstock.* 21 (top left), *Atlantide S.N.C./age fotostock.* 21 (bottom left), *Victor Kotler/age fotostock.* 21 (bottom center), *Paco Gómez García/age fotostock.* 21 (right), *José Fuste Raga/age fotostock.* 22, *Joe Viesti/viestiphoto.com.* 23 (left and right), *J.D. Dallet/age fotostock.* 24, *Felipe Rodriguez/Alamy.* 25, *Alan Copson/age fotostock.* 26, *Atlantide S.N.C./age fotostock.* 27 (left), *Corbis.* 27 (right), *Francesc Guillamet.* 33, *Ezio Bocci/age fotostock.* 34, *Howard/age fotostock.* 35 (left), *Juan Manuel Silva/age fotostock.* 35 (right), *Ken Welsh/age fotostock.* 36, *Pedro Salaverría/age fotostock.* 37 (left), *J.D. Dallet/age fotostock.* 37 (right), *Alberto Paredes/age fotostock.* 40, *Carlos Nieto/age fotostock.* 41, *Javier Larrea/age fotostock.* 42 (top), *The Print Collector/Alamy.* 42 (bottom), *Pictorial Press Ltd./Alamy.* 43 (top), *Paradores de Turismo de España, S.A.* 43 (bottom), *Jean Dominique Dallet/Alamy.* 44, *Fernando Fernández/age fotostock.* **Chapter 2: Madrid:** 45, *David Noton/age fotostock.* 46, *Sergio Pitamitz/age fotostock.* 47, *Scott Warren/Aurora Photos.* 49, *Factoria Singular/age fotostock.*72, *Peter Barritt/Alamy.* 73, *David R. Frazier Photolibrary, Inc./Alamy.* 74 (top), *Factoria Singular/age fotostock.* 74 (bottom), *Susana Vera/Reuters/Newscom.* 76 (top), *Mary Evans Picture Library/Alamy.* 78 (bottom center), *A.H.C./age fotostock.* 78 (bottom), *Tramonto/age fotostock.* 118, *Berchery/age fotostock.* 119, *imagebroker/Alamy.* 120, *G. Haling/age fotostock.* 121 (top left), *sebastiancastella.net.* 121 (bottom left), *Marcelo del Pozo/Reuters.* 121 (center right), *Felipe Rodriguez/Alamy.* 121 (bottom right), *Heino Kalis/Reuters.* 122 (top), *Paco Ayala/age fotostock.* 122 (center), *Charles Sturge/Alamy.* 122 (bottom), *Jean Du Boisberranger/Hemis.fr/Aurora Photos.* **Chapter 3: Castile-León & Castile-La Mancha:** 141, *José Fuste Raga/age fotostock.* 142, *Juan Carlos Muñoz/age fotostock.* 143 (top), *J.D. Dallet/age fotostock.* 143 (bottom), *Juan José Pascual/age fotostock.* 144, *Josep Curto/age fotostock.* 189 (top and bottom), *J.D. Dallet/age fotostock.* 190 (top), *Javier Larrea/age fotostock.* 190 (center), *Mary Evans Picture Library/Alamy.* 190 (bottom), *Robert Harding Picture Library Ltd./Alamy.* 192, *Daniel P. Acevedo/age fotostock.* 194 (top), *Oso Media/Alamy.* 194 (second from top), *Wild Horse Winery (Forrest L. Doud).* 194 (third from top), *Napa Valley Conference Bureau.* 194 (fourth from top), *Panther Creek Cellars (Ron Kaplan).* 194 (fifth from top), *Napa Valley Conference Bureau.* 194 (sixth from top), *Clos du Val (Marvin Collins).* 194 (bottom), *Panther Creek Cellars (Ron Kaplan).* 195 (top left), *Mauro Winery.* 195 (second from top left), *Cephas Picture Library/Alamy.* 195 (third from top left), *Alvaro Palacios Winery.* 205 (top right), *Mas Martinet Winery.* 205 (bottom), *Mike Randolph.* **Chapter 4: Galicia & Asturia:** 209, *Aguililla & Marín/age fotostock.* 210, *Alberto Paredes/age fotostock.* 211, *Alan Copson/age fotostock.* 212, *Aguililla & Marín/age fotostock.* 213, *Alberto Paredes/age fotostock.* 214, *Arco Images/Alamy.* 229, imagebroker/Alamy. 230, Schütze Rodemann/age fotostock. 231 (top), John Warburton-Lee Photography/Alamy. 231 (bottom), Visual Arts Library (London)/Alamy. 232 (top), Javier Larrea/age fotostock. 232 (bottom), R. Matina/age fotostock. 233, J.D. Dallet/age fotostock. 234 (top left), Toño Labra/age fotostock. 234 (bottom center), Anthony Collins/Alamy. 234 (top right), Ian Dagnall/Alamy. 235 (left), Javier Larrea/age fotostock. 235 (right), Miguel Angel Munoz Pellicer/Alamy. **Chapter 5: Bilbao & the Basque Country:** 267, *Tolo Balaguer/age fotostock.* 268 (top), *Javier Larrea/age fotostock.* 268 (bottom), *Juan Carlos Muñoz/age fotostock.* 269 (top and bottom), *Javier Larrea/age fotostock.* 270, *Gonzalo Azumendi/age fotostock.* 283, *Bernager E./age fotostock.* 284 (top left and top right), *Javier Larrea/age fotostock.* 284 (bottom), *Profimedia International s.r.o./Alamy.* 285 (top right), *Robert Fried/Alamy.* 285 (left center), *Le Naviose/age fotostock.* 285 (right center and bottom) and 286, *Mark Baynes/Alamy.* 292 (bottom), *Jon Arnold Images/Alamy.* 292-293, *Alan Copson City Pictures/Alamy.* 294 (top), *Tom Till/Alamy.* 294 (second from top), *mediacolor's/Alamy.* 294 (third from top), *Ramon Grosso Dolarea/Shutterstock.* 294 (bottom), *Peter Cassidy/age fotostock.* 295 (left), *Kathleen Melis/Shutterstock.* 295 (top right), *Mark Baynes/Alamy.* 295 (second from top right), *Alex Segre/Alamy.* 295 (third from top right), *Peter Cassidy/age fotostock.* 295 (bottom right), *Frank Heuer/laif/Aurora Photos.* **Chapter 6: The Pyrenees:** 329, *Martin Siepmann/age fotostock.* 330, *Gonzalo Azumendi/age fotostock.* 331 (left), *Javier Larrea/age fotostock.* 331(right), *Guy Christian/age fotostock.* 334, *Tolo Balaguer/age fotostock.* **Chapter 7: Barcelona:** 379, *Rene Mattes/age fotostock.* 408, *Lagui/Shutterstock.* 409, *Sandra Baker/Alamy.* 410 (second from top), *Zina Seletskaya/Shutterstock.* 410 (third from top), *Kevin Foy/Alamy.* 410 (bottom left), *Gonzalo Azumendi/age fotostock.* 410 (bottom right), *Luis M. Seco/Shutterstock.* 411 (top), *Javier Larrea/age fotostock.* 411 (bottom left), *Matz Sjöberg/age fotostock.* 411 (bottom right), *Steven Newton/Shutterstock.* 412 (top), *SuperStock/age* *fotostock*. 412 (bottom), *Jan van der Hoeven/Shutterstock*. 413 (top), *Vibrant Pictures/Alamy*. 413 (bottom), *rubiphoto/Shutterstock*. **Chapter 8: Catalonia & the Levante:** 477, *Hermes/age fotostock*. 478 (top), *Bjorn Svensson/age fotostock*. 478 (bottom), *Barry Mason/Alamy*. 479, *Rafael Campillo/age fotostock*. 495, *Francesc Guillamet*. 496 (top row and center photo), *Francesc Guillamet*. 496 (bottom), *Patricia Esteve/age fotostock*. 497 (top left), *Peter Arnold, Inc./Alamy*. 497 (bottom left), *Francesc Guillamet*. 497 (top center), *Kari Marttila/Alamy*. 497 (bottom center), *Francesc Guillamet*. 497 (right), *Sol Melia Hotels & Resorts*. 498, *Vittorio Sciosia/age fotostock*. 499 (top and bottom), *Javier Espinosa*. **Chapter 9: The Balearic Islands:** 527, *Stuart Pearce/age fotostock*. 528 (top), *Casteran/age fotostock*. 528 (bottom), *Factoria Singular/age fotostock*. 529 (top), *Martin Siepmann/age fotostock*. 529 (bottom), *Salvador Álvaro Nebot/age fotostock*. 532, *Joan Mercadal/age fotostock*. **Chapter 10: The Southeast:** 577-578, *Alan Copson/age fotostock*. 579 (top), *Juan Carlos Muñoz/age fotostock*. 579 (bottom), *Hidalgo & Lopesino/age fotostock*. 580, *Luis Alberto Aldonza/age fotostock*. **Chapter 11: Andalusia:** 611, *Javier Larrea/age fotostock*. 612, *Sylvain Grandadam/age fotostock*. 613, *Paco Ayala/age fotostock*. 615 , *José Fuste Raga/age fotostock*. 616, *J.D. Dallet/age fotostock*. 642, *Marina Spironetti/Alamy*. 643, *Kimball Hall/Alamy*. 644, *Profimedia International s.r.o./Alamy*. 645(top), *Amjad El-Geoushi/Alamy*. 645 (center), *Redferns Music Picture Library/Alamy*. 645 (bottom), *Felipe Trueba/Alamy*. 646, *Christina Wilson/Alamy*. 647 (top left), *Marco Brindicci/Reuters/Corbis*. 646 (bottom left), *AFP/Getty Images*. 647(top right), *Ted Pink/Alamy*. 647 (bottom right), *Christina Wilson/Alamy*. 703, *JLImages/Alamy*. 704, *Peter Horree/Alamy*. 705, *Jerónimo Alba/age fotostock*. 706(top), *Werner Otto/age fotostock*. 706 (second from top), *Sylvain Grandadam/age fotostock*. 706 (third from top), *Tom Wright/earthscapes/Alamy*. 706 (fourth from top), *Ken Welsh/age fotostock*. 706 (bottom), *Victor Kotler/age fotostock*. 707, *Javier Larrea/age fotostock*. 708, *Hideo Kurihara/Alamy*. 709 (top and bottom), *Javier Larrea/age fotostock*. 710, *Jerónimo Alba/age fotostock*. **Chapter 12: The Costa del Sol:** 727, *Jordi Puig/age fotostock*. 728 (top), *Philippe Renault/age fotostock*. 728 (bottom) and 729 (top), *Jerónimo Alba/age fotostock*. 729 (bottom), *José Francisco Ruiz/age fotostock*. 731, *Taka/age fotostock*. 783, *Ken Welsh/age fotostock*. **Chapter 13: Extremadura:** 787, *José Antonio Moreno/age fotostock*. 788, *José Fuste Raga/age fotostock*. 789 (top), *Carlos Nieto/age fotostock*. 789 (bottom), *Aguililla & Marín/age fotostock*. 790, *José Antonio Moreno/age fotostock*. 791, *Nacho Moro/age fotostock*. **Color Section:** Step into 14th-century Spain at Majorca's Bellver Castle: *Alvaro Leiva/age fotostock*. Wine makers roll barrels of sherry in Cádiz: *Jean-Dominique Dallet/age fotostock*. Asturian house: *Juan Carlos Muñoz/age fotostock*. Gaudí's Casa Battlló: *Jean-Dominique Dallet/age fotostock*. Valencia's City of Arts & Sciences complex: *José Fuste Raga/age fotostock*. Alhambra, Granada: *Javier Larrea/age fotostock*. Viura grapes are harvested for white wine in the Rueda region: *Cephas Picture Library/Alamy*. Candles reflect pilgrims' devotion at Montserrat's monastery: *John Ivern/age fotostock*. Moroccan Barbary Ape sits atop a cannon in Gilbraltar: *Ludke and Sparrow/Alamy*. Guggenheim Museum, Bilbao: *Ken Ross/viestiphoto.com*. Galicia's Celtic roots pop up in its modern port city of A Coruña: *Juan José Pascual/age fotostock*. Tapas entice in Jerez de la Frontera: *San Rostro/age fotostock*. Parador, Olite: *Joe Viesti/viestiphoto.com*. *Guernica* at the Queen Sofía Art Center: *Sergio Pitamitz/age fotostock*. La Endiablada in Cuenca: *Joe Viesti/viestiphoto.com*. Horses carry festive pilgrims in El Rocío to the Virgin of the Dew site: *travelstock44/Alamy*. Yachts in Marina Bay transport vacationers around the Rock of Gibraltar: *Ken Welsh/age fotostock*.

ABOUT OUR WRITERS

Originally from Worcestershire in England, Paul Cannon arrived in Barcelona in 2000. He sold sandwiches on the beach and painted boats before becoming a writer. When he is not commentating on soccer games for TV and writing guidebooks, he likes to get lost in rural Spain—especially the Pyrenees—or camp on a cliff-top along the coast.

Born and raised in Madrid, economist Ignacio Gómez spent three years living and working in New York, then rode the online journalism wave in Madrid, writing about technology, leisure, and travel for various publications. He is now the deputy director of entertainment for the interactive media department of RTVE, the Spanish broadcasting corporation.

Jared Lubarsky is a university teacher and freelance journalist who has been writing for Fodor's since 1997, first on Japan, where he lived for 30 years, and more recently—having relocated to Barcelona—on Spain. His credits include in-flight magazines and general interest magazines, guides, and newspapers.

Writer and journalist George Semler has lived in Spain for the last 30-odd years. During that time he has written on Spain, France, Morocco, Cuba, and the Mediterranean region for *Forbes, Sky, Saveur,* the *International Herald Tribune,* and the *Los Angeles Times* and has published walking guides to Madrid and Barcelona. When not sampling Catalonia's hottest restaurants, this James Beard Journalism Awards Finalist forges ahead on his magnum opus about the Pyrenees.

Hannah Semler grew up in Barcelona in a family dedicated to finding and writing about the most authentic places to visit in Spain. Educated in Catalan, Spanish, French, and English, she has also studied several Mayan languages while researching and writing about the indigenous cultures, traditions, history, and food of Mexico and Guatemala. She has recently returned to Spain, where she continues to explore.